IF FOUND, please notify and arrange return to owner. This text is an important study guide for the owner's career and/or exam preparation.

Name: ____________________

Address: ____________________

City, State, ZIP: ____________________

Telephone: (____) ____________ Email: ____________________

Gleim Publications, Inc., offers five university-level study systems:

Auditing & Systems Exam Questions and Explanations with Test Prep Software
Business Law/Legal Studies Exam Questions and Explanations with Test Prep Software
Federal Tax Exam Questions and Explanations with Test Prep Software
Financial Accounting Exam Questions and Explanations with Test Prep Software
Cost/Managerial Accounting Exam Questions and Explanations with Test Prep Software

The following is a list of Gleim examination review systems:

CIA Review: Part I, Internal Audit's Role in Governance, Risk, and Control
CIA Review: Part II, Conducting the Internal Audit Engagement
CIA Review: Part III, Business Analysis and Information Technology
CIA Review: Part IV, Business Management Skills
CIA Review: A System for Success

CMA Review: Part 1, Financial Planning, Performance, and Control
CMA Review: Part 2, Financial Decision Making
CMA Review: A System for Success

CPA Review: Financial
CPA Review: Auditing
CPA Review: Business
CPA Review: Regulation
CPA Review: A System for Success

EA Review: Part 1, Individuals
EA Review: Part 2, Businesses
EA Review: Part 3, Representation, Practices, and Procedures
EA Review: A System for Success

An order form is provided at the back of this book or contact us at www.gleim.com or (800) 874-5346.

All orders must be prepaid. Shipping and handling charges will be added to all orders. Library and company orders may be purchased on account. Add applicable sales tax to shipments within Florida. All payments must be in U.S. funds and payable on a U.S. bank. Please write or call for prices and availability of all foreign country shipments. Orders will usually be shipped the day your request is received. Allow 10 days for delivery in the United States. Please contact us if you do not receive your shipment within 2 weeks.

Gleim Publications, Inc., guarantees the immediate refund of all resalable texts and unopened and un-downloaded Test Prep Software and unopened and un-downloaded audios purchased directly from Gleim Publications, Inc., if they are returned within 30 days. Shipping and handling charges are nonrefundable. Returns of books purchased from bookstores and other resellers should be made to the respective bookstore or reseller.

Groundwood Paper and Highlighters — All Gleim books are printed on high quality groundwood paper. We recommend you use a non-bleed-through (dry) highlighter (ask for it at your local office supply store) when highlighting items within these books.

Visit www.gleim.com for the latest updates and information on all of our products.

REVIEWERS AND CONTRIBUTORS

Garrett Gleim, B.S., CPA (not in public practice), is a graduate of the Wharton School at the University of Pennsylvania and is one of our vice presidents. Mr. Gleim coordinated the production staff, reviewed the manuscript, and provided production assistance throughout the project.

Grady M. Irwin, J.D., is a graduate of the University of Florida College of Law, and he has taught in the University of Florida College of Business. Mr. Irwin provided substantial editorial assistance throughout the project.

John F. Rebstock, B.S.A., is a graduate of the Fisher School of Accounting at the University of Florida and has passed the CIA and CPA exams. He specializes in ensuring that our answer explanations and Knowledge Transfer Outlines are user-friendly. Mr. Rebstock reviewed portions of the manuscript.

Stewart B. White, B.M., *Cum Laude*, University of Richmond, B.S., Virginia Commonwealth University, has passed the CPA and CISA exams and has worked in the fields of retail management, financial audit, IT audit, COBOL programming, and data warehouse management. Mr. White provided editorial assistance throughout the project.

A PERSONAL THANKS

This manual would not have been possible without the extraordinary effort and dedication of Jacob Brunny, Julie Cutlip, Teresa Soard, Joanne Strong, Candace Van Doren, and Kristin Walls, who typed the entire manuscript and all revisions and drafted and laid out the diagrams and illustrations in this book.

The authors appreciate the proofreading and production assistance of Katie Gallagher, James Harvin, Katherine Larson, Jean Marzullo, Shane Rapp, Katie Wassink, and Martha Willis.

The authors also appreciate the critical reading assistance of Brett Babir, Ellen Buhl, Reed Daines, Holly Johnson, Scott Lawton, and David Tyson.

Finally, we appreciate the encouragement, support, and tolerance of our families throughout this project.

Ninth Edition

BUSINESS LAW/ LEGAL STUDIES

Exam Questions and Explanations

by

Irvin N. Gleim, Ph.D., CPA, CIA, CMA, CFM

with the assistance of

Grady M. Irwin, J.D.

ABOUT THE AUTHOR

Irvin N. Gleim is a Professor Emeritus in the Fisher School of Accounting at the University of Florida and is a member of the American Accounting Association, Academy of Legal Studies in Business, American Institute of Certified Public Accountants, Association of Government Accountants, Florida Institute of Certified Public Accountants, The Institute of Internal Auditors, and the Institute of Management Accountants. He has had articles published in the *Journal of Accountancy*, *The Accounting Review*, and *The American Business Law Journal* and is author/coauthor of numerous accounting and aviation books and CPE courses.

Gleim Publications, Inc.
P.O. Box 12848
University Station
Gainesville, Florida 32604
(800) 87-GLEIM or (800) 874-5346
(352) 375-0772
Fax: (352) 375-6940
Internet: www.gleim.com
Email: admin@gleim.com

ISSN: 1092-4140
ISBN: 978-1-58194-919-3

This is the first printing of the ninth edition of ***Business Law/Legal Studies Exam Questions and Explanations***. Please email update@gleim.com with **LAW EQE 9-1** as the subject or text. You will receive our current update as a reply. Updates are available until the next edition is published.

EXAMPLE:

To:	update@gleim.com
From:	*your email address*
Subject:	**LAW EQE 9-1**

First Printing: August 2011

ACKNOWLEDGMENTS

Material from Uniform Certified Public Accountant Examination questions and unofficial answers, Copyright © 1971-2009 by the American Institute of Certified Public Accountants, Inc., is reprinted and/or adapted with permission.

The authors appreciate and thank The Institute of Internal Auditors, Inc. for permission to use the Institute's Certified Internal Auditor Examination questions, Copyright © 1978-1997, by The Institute of Internal Auditors, Inc.

The authors also appreciate and thank the Institute of Certified Management Accountants for permission to use questions from past CMA examinations, Copyright © 1977-1996 by the Institute of Management Accountants.

The authors also appreciate and thank the National Conference of Bar Examiners for permission to use Multistate Bar Examination questions, Copyright © 1972, 1974, 1978, 1980, and 1981 by the National Conference of Bar Examiners/Educational Testing Service.

NOTE: In accordance with the Bankruptcy Reform Act of 1994, for bankruptcy cases filed on or after April 1 of the year of adjustment, exemption amounts are adjusted to reflect the change in the Consumer Price Index for All Urban Consumers (CPI) published by the U.S. Department of Labor for the 3-year period ending on December 31 preceding the date of adjustment. For this edition of the text, we have used the April 1, 2010, amounts. The next automatic adjustment of these amounts will commence on April 1, 2013.

TABLE OF CONTENTS

PREFACE FOR ACCOUNTING STUDENTS

The purpose of this book is to help you understand business law and concepts dealing with the legal environment of business and their applications. In turn, these skills will enable you to perform better on your undergraduate examinations, as well as look ahead to (and prepare for) professional examinations.

One of the major benefits of this book is comprehensive coverage of business law and legal environment topics. Accordingly, when you use this book to help prepare for your courses and examinations, you are assured of covering virtually all topics that can reasonably be expected to be studied in typical college or university business law and legal environment courses. See Appendix A for a comprehensive list of cross-references.

The question-and-answer format is designed and presented to facilitate effective study. Students should be careful not to misuse this text by referring to the answers, which appear to the immediate right of each question, before independently answering each question. One way to overcome the temptation is to use our *EQE Test Prep* Software Download, which is packed with features and priced with a student's budget in mind.

Many of the questions in this book are from past CMA and CPA examinations. Although a citation for the source of each question is provided, a substantial number of the questions have been modified to accommodate changes in law, to clarify meaning, and/or to emphasize a point of law or its application. In addition, hundreds of publisher-written questions are used to provide comprehensive coverage of the material in current textbooks. Finally, we are pleased to be using some questions submitted by business law and legal studies professors.

Note that this book should not be relied upon to prepare for the professional examinations. You should use review materials specifically developed for each examination. Gleim *CIA Review*, *CMA Review*, *CPA Review*, and *EA Review* are up-to-date and comprehensively cover all material necessary for successful completion of each examination. Further descriptions of these examinations and our review materials are provided in the Introduction. To obtain any of these materials, order online at www.gleim.com, call us at (800) 874-5346, or use the order form provided at the back of this book.

Thank you for your interest in this book. We deeply appreciate the many letters and suggestions received during the past years from students and educators, as well as CIA, CMA, CPA, and EA candidates. Please go to www.gleim.com/feedbackLAW to share your suggestions on how we can improve this edition

Please read the Introduction carefully. It is short but very important.

Good Luck on Your Exams,

Irvin N. Gleim

August 2011

CONTRIBUTING PROFESSORS

The authors appreciate questions contributed by the following individuals: Eliza
Robert L. Cherry, Jr., Diane Costantino, Karen J. Elwell, Louis J. Fischl, John C. Folk…
Daniel A. Levin, Murray S. Levin, Diane B. MacDonald, Debbie L. Mescon, John M. Norwood, Eugene O'Connor, David Paas, Jeffrey Pittman, Elinor Rahm, Shirley M. Rand, Ellen B. Rubert, William Schuster, Ira Schwartz, Scott Sibary, Daphne Sipes, Ralph Welton, Kay Wilburn, Susan Willey, and Dexter Woods. Each question submitted by these individuals can be noted by viewing the question source, which appears in the first line of its answer explanation in the column to the right of the question.

Success stories!

Gleim is the perfect combination of value and thoroughness. As someone who had to complete the CPA program within a budget, I needed to select the company I used for my review carefully. With Gleim, I got everything I needed: excellent support, complete, organized, and easy-to-understand materials! I strongly recommend Gleim to any self-starter preparing for the CPA exam.

- Kevin L. Cohen, CPA, President, KCG Accounting, LLC

Thanks to Gleim I have passed my CIA Exams. I passed all three (Parts 1, 2, and 3) the first time. You have an excellent self-study system, especially the tests on the computer. Thanks.

- Stef Borghouts, CIA

The GLEIM Review System was simply amazing! Complex content was broken down into easily conquered study units, and the GLEIM support team provided encouragement and tactical advice when faced with particularly difficult subject matter. Thanks in large part to GLEIM, I passed all four parts of the CPA Exam on the first try. I strongly recommend the total review system.

- Crystal G., CPA

I have recently passed all 4 sections of the exam. I found your study material to be very effective and will recommend your product to any CPA candidate. I was able to pass all sections on the first attempt with the following scores: AUD 97, BEC 86, REG 89, FAR 91. Thanks again for distributing such a quality product.

- Alan Vanhorn

INTRODUCTION

The format and content of this study manual are innovative in the accounting and business law text market. The purpose is to provide accounting and business law students with a well-organized, comprehensive collection of objective questions covering the topics taught in typical business law and legal environment undergraduate courses.

The Gleim exam question and explanation books and Test Prep Software really work! You can pretest yourself before class to see if you are strong or weak in the assigned area. You can retest after class to see if you really understand the material. The questions in these books cover **all** topics in your related courses, so you will encounter few questions on your exams for which you will not be well prepared.

The titles and organization of Study Units 1 through 40 are based on the current business law and legal environment textbooks listed in Appendix A. Appendix A contains the table of contents of each listed book with cross-references to Gleim study units and subunits. If you are using a textbook that is not included in our list or if you have any suggestions on how we can improve these cross-references to make them more relevant/useful, please submit your request/feedback at www.gleim.com/crossreferences/LAW or email them to LAWcrossreferences@gleim.com.

OUR USE OF SUBUNITS

Each study unit of this book is divided into subunits to assist your study program. Subunits permit broad and perhaps overwhelming topics to be divided into more manageable study components.

Choosing subunits and arranging questions within them was challenging. Thus, topics and questions may overlap somewhat. The number of questions offers comprehensive coverage but does not present an insurmountable task. We define each subunit narrowly enough to cover a single topic but broadly enough to prevent questions from being repetitious.

SOURCES OF OBJECTIVE QUESTIONS

Past CIA, CMA, and CPA examinations and sample questions from the Multistate Bar Examination (MBE) are the primary sources of questions included in this study manual.

Gleim Publications will continue to prepare questions (coded in this text as *Publisher, adapted*) based upon the content of business law/legal environment textbooks listed in Appendix A. These *Publisher* questions review topics not adequately covered by questions from the other sources. Also, professionals and professors from schools around the country have contributed questions. See page vii for a list of their names and affiliations.

If you, your professor, or your classmates wish to submit questions, we will consider using them in future editions. Please email questions you develop, complete with answers and explanations, to accounting@gleim.com. Alternatively, you can mail questions to

Gleim Publications, Inc.
EQE Question Bank
P.O. Box 12848, University Station
Gainesville, FL 32604

Writing and analyzing multiple-choice questions is an excellent way to prepare yourself for your exams. We will make every effort to consider, edit, and use questions you submit. However, we ask that you send us only serious, complete, carefully considered efforts.

IDENTIFICATION OF THE SOURCE OF EACH QUESTION

The source of each question appears in the first line of its answer explanation in the column to the right of the question. Summary of source codes:

CIA	Certified Internal Auditor Examination
CMA	Certified Management Accountant Examination
CPA	Uniform Certified Public Accountant Examination
MBE	Multistate Bar Examination
Publisher	EQE LAW author
Individual's name	Name of professional or professor who contributed the question

UNIQUENESS OF OBJECTIVE QUESTIONS

The major advantage of objective questions is their ability to cover a large number of topics with little time and effort when compared to essay questions and/or computational problems.

A multiple-choice question is actually a series of statements of which all but one are incorrect given the facts of the question. The advantage of multiple-choice questions over true/false questions is that they require more analysis and result in a lower score for those with little or no knowledge. Random guessing on questions with four answer choices results in an expected grade of 25%. Random guessing on a true/false test results in an expected grade of 50%.

Students and professors both like multiple-choice questions. Because they present alternative answers from which only one needs to be selected, students find them relatively easy to answer. Professors like objective questions because they are easy to grade and because much more material can be tested in the same period of time. Most professors will also ask students to complete essay or computational questions.

ANSWER EXPLANATIONS ALONGSIDE THE QUESTIONS

The format of our book presents objective questions and their answer explanations side by side. The answer explanations are to the right of each question. The example below is publisher-developed.

Gudrun owned a 2,000-acre country estate. She signed a written agreement with Johann, selling the house on the property and "a sufficient amount of land surrounding the house to create a park." The price was stated to be $200,000. When Gudrun refused to honor the agreement, Johann brought suit. What will be the result?

A. Gudrun will win because the agreement is not reasonably definite.

B. Johann will win because the quantity of land is implied.

C. Johann will win because the parties intended to make a contract.

D. Gudrun will win because no financing term was included in the agreement.

Answer (A) is correct. *(Publisher, adapted)*

REQUIRED: The result when a contract for the sale of land does not state the quantity.

DISCUSSION: For an agreement between the parties to be enforceable, it must be reasonably definite and certain (not ambiguous). A court must be able to determine with reasonable accuracy what the parties agreed upon. In this case, it is not reasonably clear from the writing what land Gudrun agreed to sell.

Answer (B) is incorrect. Some objective basis must exist for measuring the implied term. The court would have no means of determining how much land is needed for a park. Answer (C) is incorrect. Intent alone does not suffice. The agreement also must be reasonably definite and certain. Answer (D) is incorrect. The quantity term is more significant than the financing term. The price is given and payment in cash (or its equivalent) is implied.

The format of this study manual is designed to facilitate your study of objective questions, their answers, and the answer explanations. The intent is to save you time and effort by eliminating the need to turn pages back and forth from questions to answers.

Be careful, however. Do not misuse this format by consulting the answers before you have answered the questions. Misuse of the readily available answers will give you a false sense of security and result in poor performance on examinations and decreased benefit from your studies. The best way to use this study manual is to cover the answer explanations with a sheet of paper as you read and answer each question. Alternatively, our *EQE Test Prep* Software automates this function as one of its many features. As a crucial part of the learning process, you must honestly commit yourself to an answer before looking at the answer explanation. Whether you are right or wrong, your memory of the correct answer will be reinforced by this process.

STUDY SUGGESTIONS

The emphasis in the next few pages is on developing strategies, approaches, and procedures to help you learn and understand better, in less time.

Using Tests as Study/Learning Devices

Tests, especially quizzes and midterms, provide feedback on your study and test-taking procedures. It is extremely important to diagnose your mistakes on quizzes and tests at the beginning of the term so you can take corrective action on subsequent tests, including your final exam.

When your test is returned, determine how you did relative to the rest of your class and your professor's grading standards. Next, analyze your relative performance between types of questions (essay vs. multiple-choice) and types of subject matter (topics or study units). The objective is to identify the areas where you should take corrective action.

Using Objective Questions to Study

Experts on testing continue to favor multiple-choice questions as a valid means of examining various levels of knowledge. Using objective questions to study for undergraduate examinations is an important tool not only for obtaining good grades, but also for long-range preparation for certification and other examinations. The following suggestions will help you study in conjunction with each Gleim *Exam Questions and Explanations* book and *EQE Test Prep* Software (visit www.gleim.com or see our order form at the back of this book):

1. Locate the study unit that contains questions on the topic you are currently studying. Each *Exam Questions and Explanations* book and *EQE Test Prep* contains cross-references to the tables of contents of most textbooks.
2. Work through a series of questions, selecting the answers you think are correct.
3. **If you are using the Gleim book, do not consult the answer or answer explanations on the right side of the page until after you have chosen and written down an answer.**
   a. It is crucial that you cover the answer explanations and intellectually commit yourself to an answer. This method will help you understand the concept much better, even if you answered the question incorrectly. *EQE Test Prep* Software automates this process for you.

4. Study the explanations to each question you answered incorrectly. In addition to learning and understanding the concept tested, analyze **why** you missed the question.
   - Did you misread the question?
   - Did you make a math error?
   - Did you not know the concept tested?

   Studying the important concepts that we provide in our answer explanations will help you understand the principles to the point that you can answer that question (or any other like it) successfully.
5. Identify your weaknesses in answering multiple-choice questions and take corrective action (before you take a test). Prepare a summary analysis of your work on each subunit (topic). With *EQE Test Prep* Software, simply view your performance analysis information. Some sample column headings could be

Date	Subunit	Time to Complete	Questions Answered	Avg. Time per Question	Questions Correct	Percent Correct

   The analysis will show your weaknesses (areas needing more study) and also your strengths (areas of confidence). You can improve your performance on objective questions both by increasing your percentage of correct answers and by decreasing the time spent per question.

Multiple-Choice Question-Answering Technique

You need a personalized control system **(technique)** for answering multiple-choice questions, essay questions, and computational problems. The objective is to obtain complete, correct, and well-presented answers.

The following series of steps is suggested for answering multiple-choice questions. The important point is that you need to devote attention to and develop **the technique that works for you**. Personalize and practice your multiple-choice question-answering technique on questions in this study manual. Begin now, and develop **your** control system.

1. **Budget your time.**
   a. We make this point with emphasis. Just as you would fill up your gas tank prior to reaching empty, so too should you finish your exam before time expires.
   b. Calculate the time allowed for each multiple-choice question after you have allocated time to the other questions (e.g., essays) on the exam. If 20 multiple-choice questions are allocated 40 minutes on your exam, you should spend a little under 2 minutes per question (always budget extra time for transferring answers to answer sheets, interruptions, etc.).
   c. Before beginning a series of multiple-choice questions, write the starting time on the exam near the first question.
   d. As you work through the questions, check your time. Assuming a time allocation of 120 minutes for 60 questions, you are fine if you worked 5 questions in 9 minutes. If you spent 11 minutes on 5 questions, you need to speed up. Remember that your goal is to answer all questions and achieve the maximum score possible.
2. **Answer the items in consecutive order.**
   a. Do **not** agonize over any one item. Stay within your time budget.
   b. Mark any questions you are unsure of and return to them later as time allows.
   c. Never leave a question unanswered if you will not be penalized for incorrect answers. Make your best guess in the time allowed.

3. **For each multiple-choice question,**
   a. **Try to ignore the answer choices.** Do not allow the answer choices to affect your reading of the question.
      1) If four answer choices are presented, three of them are incorrect. These incorrect choices are called **distractors** for good reason. Often, distractors are written to appear correct at first glance until further analysis.
      2) In computational items, distractors are carefully calculated so they are the result of making common mistakes. Be careful, and double-check your computations if time permits.
   b. **Read the question** carefully to determine the precise requirement.
      1) Focusing on what is required enables you to ignore extraneous information and to proceed directly to determining the correct answer. You may wish to underline or circle key language or data.
         a) Be especially careful to note when the requirement is an **exception**; e.g., "Which of the following accounts is **not** valid acceptance of an offer?"
   c. **Determine the correct answer** before looking at the answer choices.
   d. **Read the answer choices carefully.**
      1) Even if the first answer appears to be the correct choice, do **not** skip the remaining answer choices. Questions often ask for the "best" of the choices provided. Thus, each choice requires your consideration.
      2) Treat each answer choice as a true/false question as you analyze it.
   e. **Select the best answer.**
      1) If you are uncertain, guess intelligently (see "If You Don't Know the Answer" below). Improve on your 25% chance of getting the correct answer with blind guessing.
      2) For many multiple-choice questions, two answer choices can be eliminated with minimal effort, thereby increasing your educated guess to a 50-50 proposition.
4. After you have answered all of the questions, **transfer your answers to the objective answer sheet**, if one is provided.
   a. Make sure you are within your time budget so you will be able to perform this vital step in an unhurried manner.
   b. Do not wait to transfer answers until the very end of the exam session because you may run out of time.
   c. Double-check that you have transferred the answers correctly; e.g., recheck every 5th or 10th answer from your test paper to your answer sheet to ensure that you have not fallen out of sequence.

If You Don't Know the Answer

If the exam you are taking does not penalize incorrect answers, you should guess. Make it an educated guess, which means select the best answer. First, rule out answers that you think are incorrect. Second, speculate on what the examiner is looking for and/or the rationale behind the question. Third, select the best answer or guess between equally appealing answers. Mark the question with a "?" in case you have time to return to it for further analysis.

If you cannot make an educated guess, read the stem and each answer, and pick the best or most intuitive answer. It's just a guess! Do **not** look at the previous answer to try to detect an answer. Answers are usually random, and it is possible to have four or more consecutive questions with the same answer letter, e.g., answer (B).

NOTE: Do not waste time beyond the amount you budgeted for each question. Move forward and stay on or ahead of schedule.

EXAM QUESTIONS AND EXPLANATIONS SERIES IMPROVES GRADES AND INCREASES COMPETITIVENESS

Use the Gleim exam questions and explanations series to ensure your understanding of each topic you study in your accounting and business law courses. Access the largest bank of exam questions (including thousands from past certification exams) that is widely used by professors. Get immediate feedback on your study effort while you take your "practice" tests.

- Each book or Test Prep Software contains over 1,000 multiple-choice questions with correct and incorrect answer explanations and can be used in two or more classes.
- Exhaustive cross-references are presented for all related textbooks so that you can easily determine which group of questions pertains to a given chapter in your textbook.
- You absorb important information more efficiently, more quickly, and more permanently through *"programmed learning."*
- Questions taken directly from professional certification exams demonstrate the standards to which you will be held as a professional accountant and help prepare you for certification exams later.

The Gleim Series works! Each book is a comprehensive source of questions with thorough explanations of each correct and incorrect answer. You learn from our explanations regardless of your answers to the questions. Pretest before class to see if you are strong or weak in the assigned area. Retest after class and before each exam or quiz to be certain you really understand the material. The questions in these books cover virtually all topics in your courses. Rarely will you encounter questions for which you are not well prepared.

After graduation, you will compete with graduates from schools across the country in the accounting job market. Make sure you measure up to standards that are as demanding as the standards of your counterparts at other schools. These standards will be tested on professional certification exams.

AUDITING & SYSTEMS EXAM QUESTIONS AND EXPLANATIONS (Seventeenth Edition)

1. Engagement Responsibilities
2. Professional Responsibilities
3. Risk Assessment
4. Strategic Planning Issues
5. Internal Control Concepts and Information Technology
6. Internal Control – Sales-Receivables-Cash Receipts Cycle
7. Internal Control – Purchases, Payroll, and Other Cycles
8. Responses to Assessed Risks
9. Internal Control Communications and Reports
10. Evidence – Objectives and Nature
11. Evidence – The Sales-Receivables-Cash Cycle
12. Evidence – The Purchases-Payables-Inventory Cycle
13. Evidence – Other Assets, Liabilities, and Equities
14. Evidence – Key Considerations
15. Evidence – Sampling
16. Reports – Opinions and Disclaimers
17. Reports – Other Modifications
18. Review, Compilation, and Special Reports
19. Related Reporting Topics
20. Governmental Audits
21. Internal Auditing
22. Information Systems

COST/MANAGERIAL ACCOUNTING EXAM QUESTIONS AND EXPLANATIONS (Tenth Edition)

1. Overview and Terminology
2. Absorption vs. Variable Costing
3. Job-Order Costing
4. Process Costing
5. Activity-Based Costing
6. Cost Allocation: Support Costs and Joint Costs
7. Standard Costs and Variances
8. Inventory Management: Traditional and Modern Approaches
9. Responsibility Accounting, Performance Measurement, and Transfer Pricing
10. Quality
11. Cost-Volume-Profit Analysis
12. Budgeting
13. Nonroutine Decisions
14. Capital Budgeting
15. Probability and Statistics
16. Regression Analysis
17. Linear Programming
18. Other Quantitative Approaches

FINANCIAL ACCOUNTING EXAM QUESTIONS AND EXPLANATIONS (Sixteenth Edition)

1. The Financial Reporting Environment
2. The Accounting Process
3. Reporting Income
4. The Time Value of Money
5. Current Assets, Cash, Accounts Receivable, and Notes Receivable
6. Inventories
7. Property, Plant, and Equipment
8. Depreciation and Depletion
9. Intangible Assets and Research and Development Costs
10. Investments
11. Current Liabilities, Compensated Absences, and Contingencies
12. Noncurrent Liabilities
13. Pensions and Other Postretirement Benefits
14. Leases
15. Corporate Equity
16. EPS and Share-Based Payment
17. Accounting for Income Taxes
18. Accounting Changes and Error Corrections
19. Statement of Cash Flows
20. Accounting for Changing Prices
21. Financial Statement Disclosures
22. Long-Term Construction-Type Contracts, Installment Sales, and Consignments
23. Financial Statement Analysis Based on Percentage Relationships
24. GAAP Accounting for Partnerships
25. Business Combinations and Consolidated Financial Reporting
26. Interim Financial Reporting
27. Foreign Currency Translation and Transactions
28. State and Local Governments
29. Not-for-Profit Entities

FEDERAL TAX EXAM QUESTIONS AND EXPLANATIONS (Twenty-First Edition)

1. Gross Income
2. Exclusions from Gross Income
3. Business Expenses and Losses
4. Limitations on Losses
5. Other Deductions for Adjusted Gross Income
6. Deductions from AGI
7. Individual Tax Computations
8. Credits
9. Basis
10. Depreciation, Amortization, and Depletion
11. Capital Gains and Losses
12. Sale of Business Property
13. Nontaxable Property Transactions
14. Partnerships: Formation and Operation
15. Partnerships: Distributions, Sales, and Exchanges
16. Corporate Formations and Operations
17. Advanced Corporate Topics
18. Income Taxation of Estates, Trusts, and Tax-Exempt Organizations
19. Accounting Methods
20. Employment Taxes and Withholding
21. Wealth Transfer Taxes
22. Preparer Rules
23. Federal Tax Process and Procedure

BUSINESS LAW/LEGAL STUDIES EXAM QUESTIONS AND EXPLANATIONS (Ninth Edition)

1. The American Legal System
2. The American Court System
3. Civil Litigation and Procedure
4. Constitutional Law and Business
5. Administrative Law
6. Criminal Law and Procedure
7. Tort Law
8. Contracts: The Agreement
9. Contracts: Consideration
10. Contracts: Capacity, Legality, Mutuality, and Statute of Frauds
11. Contracts: Interpretation, Conditions, Discharge, and Remedies
12. Contracts: Third-Party Rights and Duties
13. Sale of Goods: The Sales Contract, Interpretation, and Risk of Loss
14. Sale of Goods: Performance, Remedies, and Warranties
15. Negotiable Instruments: Types, Negotiation, and Holder in Due Course
16. Negotiable Instruments: Liability, Bank Transactions, and Electronic Fund Transfers
17. Documents of Title and Letters of Credit
18. Secured Transactions
19. Suretyship
20. Bankruptcy
21. Personal Property and Bailments
22. Computers and the Law
23. Real Property: Interests and Rights
24. Real Property: Transactions
25. Mortgages
26. Creditor Law and Liens
27. Landlord and Tenant
28. Wills, Estate Administration, and Trusts
29. Agency
30. Partnerships and Other Entities
31. Corporations: Nature, Formation, and Financing
32. Corporations: Operations and Management
33. Federal Securities Regulation
34. Insurance
35. Environmental Law
36. Antitrust
37. Consumer Protection
38. Employment Regulation
39. International Business Law
40. Accountants' Legal Responsibilities

ACCOUNTING CERTIFICATION PROGRAMS--OVERVIEW

The CPA (Certified Public Accountant) exam is the grandparent of all the professional accounting examinations. Its origin was in the 1896 public accounting legislation of New York. In 1917, the American Institute of CPAs (AICPA) began to prepare and grade a uniform CPA exam. It is currently used to measure the technical competence of those applying to be licensed as CPAs in all 50 states, Guam, Puerto Rico, the Virgin Islands, and the District of Columbia.

The CIA (Certified Internal Auditor), CMA (Certified Management Accountant), and EA (IRS Enrolled Agent) examinations are relatively new certification programs compared with the CPA exam. The CMA exam was first administered in 1972 and the first CIA exam in 1974. The EA exam dates back to 1959. Why were these certification programs begun? Generally, the requirements of the CPA designation instituted by the boards of accountancy, especially the necessity for public accounting experience, led to the development of the CIA and CMA programs. The EA certification is available for persons specializing in tax.

ACCOUNTING CERTIFICATION PROGRAMS--PURPOSE

The primary purpose of professional exams is to measure the technical competence of candidates. Competence includes technical knowledge, ability to apply such knowledge with good judgment, comprehension of professional responsibility, and ethical considerations. Additionally, the nature of these exams (low pass rate, broad and rigorous coverage, etc.) has several very important effects:

1. Candidates are forced to learn all of the material that should have been presented and learned in a good accounting educational program.
2. Relatedly, candidates must integrate the topics and concepts that are presented in individual courses in accounting education programs.
3. The content of each exam provides direction to accounting education programs; i.e., what is tested on the exams will be taught to accounting students.

Certification is important to professional accountants because it provides

1. Participation in a recognized professional group
2. An improved professional training program arising out of the certification program
3. Recognition among peers for attaining the professional designation
4. An extra credential for the employment market/career ladder
5. The personal satisfaction of attaining a recognized degree of competency

These reasons hold true in the accounting field due to wide recognition of the CPA designation. Accountants and accounting students are often asked whether they are CPAs when people learn they are accountants. Thus, there is considerable pressure for accountants to become *certified*.

A new development is multiple certifications, which is important for the same reasons as initial certification. Accounting students and recent graduates should look ahead and obtain multiple certifications to broaden their career opportunities.

Examination Content

The content of certification examinations is specified by the respective governing boards with lists of topics to be tested. In the Gleim review manuals – *CIA Review*, *CMA Review*, *CPA Review*, and *EA Review* – the material tested is divided into subtopics we call study units. A study unit is a more manageable undertaking than an overall part of each exam. The listings of study units on pages 10 through 14 provide an overview of the scope and content of these exams.

Examination Summary

	CIA (Certified Internal Auditor)	CMA (Certified Management Accountant) (New 2-Part Exam, effective 05/01/2010)	EA (IRS Enrolled Agent)	CPA (Certified Public Accountant) (New CBT-e version)
Sponsoring Organization	Institute of Internal Auditors	Institute of Management Accountants	Internal Revenue Service	American Institute of Certified Public Accountants
Contact Information	www.theiia.org (407) 937-1100	www.imanet.org (201) 573-9000	www.irs.gov (313) 234-1280	www.aicpa.org (201) 938-3750
Cost for Entire Exam	$675	$1,110	$303	$784.50 plus State Board fee
Student Discount	about 30%	50%	None	None
Exam Parts	I – The Internal Audit Activity's Role in Governance, Risk, and Control (3 hrs.) II – Conducting the Internal Audit Engagement (3 hrs.) III – Business Analysis and Information Technology (3 hrs.) IV – Business Management Skills (3 hrs.)	1 – Financial Planning, Performance, and Control (4 hrs.) 2 – Financial Decision Making (4 hrs.)	1 – Individuals (3.5 hrs.) 2 – Businesses (3.5 hrs.) 3 – Representation, Practice, and Procedures (3.5 hrs.)	Auditing and Attestation (4 hrs.) Business Environment and Concepts (3 hrs.) Financial Accounting and Reporting (4 hrs.) Regulation (3 hrs.)
Exam Format	Parts I, II, III, and IV: 100 multiple-choice questions	Parts 1 and 2: 100 multiple-choice questions 2 essays	Parts 1, 2, and 3: 100 multiple-choice questions	AUD: 90 multiple-choice questions 7 TBS BEC: 72 multiple-choice questions 3 written communications FAR: 90 multiple-choice questions 7 TBS REG: 72 multiple-choice questions 6 TBS
Avg. Pass Rate	I – 51% II – 62% III – 53% IV – 57%	1 – 40% 2 – 36%	1 – 76% 2 – 69% 3 – 80%	No results yet for new program
Testing Windows	On demand throughout the year	January-February May-June September-October	May – February (e.g., 5/01/2010 - 2/28/2011)	January-February April-May July-August October-November

LISTING OF *CIA REVIEW* STUDY UNITS

Part I: Internal Audit's Role in Governance, Risk, and Control

1. Standards and Proficiency
2. Charter, Independence, and Objectivity
3. Internal Audit Roles
4. Control Knowledge Elements
5. Specific Controls
6. Control Aspects of Management
7. Managing the Internal Audit Activity
8. Planning and Supervising the Engagement
9. Internal Audit Ethics
10. Internal Audit Responsibilities for Fraud

Part II: Conducting the Internal Audit Engagement

1. Engagement Information
2. Communicating Results and Monitoring Progress
3. Financial, Consulting, and Control Self-Assessment Engagements
4. Compliance, Quality, and Other Engagements
5. IT Software, Networks, and Planning
6. IT Databases, Roles, and Business Applications
7. Audit Sampling
8. Other Engagement Tools
9. Internal Audit Ethics
10. Internal Audit Responsibilities for Fraud

Part III: Business Analysis and Information Technology

1. Business Processes
2. Managing Business Resources
3. Financial Accounting -- Basic
4. Financial Accounting -- Advanced
5. Finance
6. Managerial Accounting
7. Regulatory, Legal, and Economic Issues
8. IT Controls, Networks, and Business Applications
9. IT Roles, Software, and Application Development
10. IT Contingency Planning, Systems Security, and Databases

Part IV: Business Management Skills*

1. Structural Analysis and Strategies
2. Industry and Market Analysis
3. Industry Environments
4. Strategic Decisions
5. Global Business Issues
6. Motivation and Communications
7. Organizational Structure and Effectiveness
8. Managing Groups
9. Influence and Leadership
10. Time Management, Conflict, and Negotiation

*Persons who have passed the CPA or CMA exams (and many other professional exams) are not required to take Part IV of the CIA exam.

The number of candidates sitting for the CIA exam has seen major growth, which is certainly the result of a combination of factors, including the Sarbanes-Oxley legislation and the Enron/WorldCom scandals.

Management cannot personally observe the functioning of all officers, employees, and specialized functions (finance, marketing, operations, etc.) because each has its own special point of view. Only internal auditing is in a position to take a total company point of view, and firms are increasingly enlisting the ranks of certified professionals.

The CIA exam is computerized to facilitate testing. Each of the four parts consists of 100 multiple-choice questions and lasts about 3 hours (2 hours and 45 minutes for exam, 15 minutes for tutorial and survey).

The first two parts of the CIA exam focus on the theory and practice of internal auditing. The body of knowledge of internal auditing and the auditing skills to be tested consist of

1. The typical undergraduate auditing class (as represented by auditing texts, e.g., Arens, Elder, and Beasley)
2. Internal auditing textbooks (e.g., *Sawyer's Internal Auditing* and Cascarino and van Esch's *Internal Auditing: An Integrated Approach*)
3. Various IIA (Institute of Internal Auditors) pronouncements (e.g., IIA *Code of Ethics*, *International Standards for the Professional Practice of Internal Auditing*, and Statement of Responsibilities of Internal Auditing)
4. Reasoning ability, communications and problem-solving skills, and dealing with auditees in an audit context (i.e., the questions will cover audit topics but test audit skills)

The remaining 50% of the exam, Parts III and IV, ensures that internal auditors are conversant with topics, methodologies, and techniques ranging from individual and organizational behavior to economics and information technology.

LISTING OF *CMA REVIEW* STUDY UNITS

Part 1: Financial Planning, Performance, and Control

1. Budgeting Concepts and Forecasting Techniques
2. Budget Methodologies and Budget Preparation
3. Cost Management Terminology and Concepts
4. Cost Accumulation Systems
5. Cost Allocation Techniques
6. Operational Efficiency and Business Process Performance
7. Cost and Variance Measures
8. Responsibility Accounting and Performance Measures
9. Internal Controls I
10. Internal Controls II and Ethics for Management Accountants

Part 2: Financial Decision Making

1. Basic Financial Statement Analysis
2. Financial Performance Metrics – Financial Ratios
3. Profitability Analysis and Analytical Issues
4. Investment Risk and Portfolio Management
5. Financial Instruments and Cost of Capital
6. Managing Current Assets
7. Raising Capital, Corporate Restructuring, and International Finance
8. Decision Analysis and Risk Management
9. Investment Decisions I
10. Investment Decisions II and Ethical Considerations for the Organization

The CMA exam consists of two parts: (1) Financial Planning, Performance, and Control and (2) Financial Decision Making. Both parts consist of 100 multiple-choice questions and two 30-minute essay questions. Four hours is allowed for the completion of a part (3 hours for the multiple-choice, 1 hour for the essays).

The CMA certification program has four objectives:

- *To establish management accounting as a recognized profession by identifying the role of the management accountant and financial manager, the underlying body of knowledge, and a course of study by which such knowledge is acquired;*
- *To encourage higher educational standards in the management accounting field;*
- *To establish an objective measure of an individual's knowledge and competence in the field of management accounting; and*
- *To encourage continued professional development by management accountants.*

The exam tests the candidates' knowledge and ability with respect to the current state of the field of management accounting.

We have arranged the subject matter tested on the CMA examination into 10 study units for each part. Each part is presented in a separate book. Both of these books contain review outlines; prior CMA exam questions, answers, and answer explanations; and essay questions.

The CMA exam has broader coverage than the CPA exam in several areas. For example,

1. CMA topics like risk management, finance, management, and marketing are covered lightly, if at all, on the CPA exam.
2. The CMA exam focuses very heavily on internal decision making, such as special orders and capital budgeting, whereas the CPA exam is concerned with external reporting.
3. The CMA exam tests business ethics but not business law.

CMA questions are generally more analysis-oriented than CPA questions. On the CPA exam, the typical requirement is the solution of an accounting problem, e.g., consolidated worksheet, funds statement, etc.

LISTING OF *CPA REVIEW* STUDY UNITS

Business Environment and Concepts

1. Corporate Governance
2. Microeconomics
3. Macroeconomics
4. Globalization
5. Financial Risk Management
6. Forecasting Analysis
7. Corporate Capital Structure
8. Working Capital
9. Short-Term Financing and Capital Budgeting I
10. Capital Budgeting II and Corporate Performance
11. IT Roles, Systems, and Processing
12. IT Software and Data Organization
13. IT Networks and Electronic Commerce
14. IT Security
15. Strategic Planning and Budgeting Concepts
16. Budgeting
17. Quality Considerations and Benchmarking
18. Responsibility Accounting and Other Topics
19. Costing Fundamentals
20. Costing Systems and Variances

Financial Accounting and Reporting

1. The Financial Reporting Environment
2. Financial Statements
3. Income Statement Items
4. Financial Statement Disclosure
5. Cash and Investments
6. Receivables
7. Inventories
8. Property, Plant, Equipment, and Depletable Resources
9. Intangible Assets and Other Capitalization Issues
10. Payables and Taxes
11. Employee Benefits
12. Noncurrent Liabilities
13. Leases and Contingencies
14. Equity
15. Business Combinations and Consolidated Financial Reporting
16. Derivatives, Hedging, and Other Topics
17. Governmental Accounting
18. Governmental Reporting
19. Not-for-Profit Concepts
20. Not-for-Profit Accounting and Reporting

Regulation

1. Ethics and Professional Responsibilities
2. CPAs and the Law
3. Agency
4. Contracts
5. Sales and Secured Transactions
6. Negotiable Instruments and Related Topics
7. Debtor-Creditor Relationships
8. Regulation and Certain Business Entities
9. Corporations
10. Federal Tax Legislation, Procedures, and Planning
11. Gross Income
12. Deductions
13. Tax Computations
14. Property Transactions
15. Corporate Taxable Income
16. Corporate Tax Computations
17. Corporate Tax Special Topics
18. S Corporations
19. Partnerships and Exempt Organizations
20. Estates, Trusts, and Wealth Transfer Taxes

Auditing and Attestation

1. Engagement Responsibilities
2. Professional Responsibilities
3. Risk Assessment
4. Strategic Planning Issues
5. Internal Control Concepts and Information Technology
6. Internal Control -- Sales-Receivables-Cash Receipts Cycle
7. Internal Control -- Purchases, Payroll, and Other Cycles
8. Responses to Assessed Risks
9. Internal Control Communications and Reports
10. Evidence -- Objectives and Nature
11. Evidence -- The Sales-Receivables-Cash Cycle
12. Evidence -- The Purchases-Payables-Inventory Cycle
13. Evidence -- Other Assets, Liabilities, and Equities
14. Evidence -- Key Considerations
15. Evidence -- Sampling
16. Reports -- Opinions and Disclaimers
17. Reports -- Other Modifications
18. Review, Compilation, and Special Reports
19. Related Reporting Topics
20. Governmental Audits

The CPA exam is an on-demand test administered the first 2 months of every calendar quarter. As of January 1, 2011, the AICPA has changed the CPA exam from the CBT format to the CBT-e format. This transformation affects each section of the exam on multiple levels, from structure to time allocation to content.

All of the following information reflects the CPA exam as tested beginning January 1, 2011.

1. You must pass all four sections in 18 months or lose credit for any section passed more than 18 months prior to the current date.

2. The exam sections are:

Auditing & Attestation	4.0 hours	Financial Accounting & Reporting	4.0 hours
Regulation	3.0 hours	Business Environment & Concepts	3.0 hours

3. The CPA exam is administered at Prometric testing centers and is composed of a series of testlets. The testlet sequence is predetermined. You will have three multiple-choice testlets followed by one task-based simulation testlet in Auditing, Financial, and Regulation. For Business, you will have three testlets of multiple choice and one testlet with written communication essays.
   a. Multiple-choice testlets: There will be three groups of 30 multiple-choice questions given as testlets on Auditing and Financial. On Business and Regulation, there will be 24 instead of 30 multiple-choice questions.
   b. Task-based simulation testlets: Auditing, Financial, and Regulation will each have six or seven task-based simulations. These simulations will account for 40% of the grade in each exam section.
   c. Written communication testlets: Business will have one written communication testlet with three essay questions (two graded, one pretest). These questions will account for 15% of the total grade on this section.
4. Each testlet will be completed separately. Once you complete a testlet, you cannot return to it. You may take breaks between testlets to stretch or go to the bathroom, but the time remaining in the exam continues to run during breaks.

Steps to Become a CPA

1. Become knowledgeable about the exam, and decide which section you will take first.
2. Purchase the Gleim CPA Review System to thoroughly prepare for the CPA exam. Commit to our systematic preparation for the exam as described in our review materials, including *CPA Review: A System for Success*.
3. Communicate with your Personal Counselor to design a study plan that meets your needs. Call (800) 874-5346 or email CPA@gleim.com.
4. Determine the board of accountancy (i.e., state) to which you will apply to sit for the CPA exam.
5. Obtain, complete, and submit your application form, including transcripts, fees, etc., to your State Board or NASBA. You will receive your Notice to Schedule (NTS) from NASBA in about 8 weeks.
   a. Do not apply for a section of the exam until you are ready to take it. An NTS is valid for a specific period established by the boards of accountancy, and you will forfeit any fees you paid for sections not taken.
6. Schedule your test with Prometric (online, national 800 number, or with your local Prometric testing site). Schedule at least 45 days before the date you plan to set for the exam.
7. Work systematically through each study unit in the Gleim CPA Review System (Auditing, Business, Financial, and Regulation), taking advantage of each instructional element in CPA Gleim Online especially.
8. Use the Gleim *CPA Test Prep* Software: Thousands of CPA questions, all updated to current tax law, the FASB Accounting Standards Codification, etc. Listen to CPA Audio Review as a supplement.
9. Sit for and PASS the CPA exam while you are in control.
10. Enjoy your career and pursue multiple certifications (CIA, CMA, EA, etc.), recommend Gleim to others who are also taking these exams, and stay up-to-date on your CPE with Gleim CPE.

LISTING OF *EA REVIEW* STUDY UNITS

Part 1: Individuals

1. Gross Income
2. Business Deductions
3. Above-the-Line Deductions and Losses
4. Itemized Deductions
5. Filing Requirements
6. Tax Credits
7. Basis
8. Adjustments to Asset Basis and Capital Gains and Losses
9. Business Property, Related Parties, and Installment Sales
10. Nonrecognition Property Transactions
11. Individual Retirement Accounts
12. Estate Tax
13. Gift Tax

Part 2: Businesses

1. Accounting Methods and Periods
2. Income and Property Transactions
3. Business Expenses
4. Other Deductions
5. Basis
6. Depreciation
7. Credits, Losses, and Additional Taxes
8. Contributions to a Partnership
9. Partnership Operations
10. Disposition of a Partner's Interest
11. Corporations
12. Corporate Formation
13. Corporate Income and Losses
14. Corporate Deductions
15. Distributions
16. Corporate Liquidations and Redemptions
17. S Corporations
18. Decedent, Estate, and Trust Income Tax Returns
19. Retirement Plans for Small Businesses
20. Exempt Organizations

Part 3: Representation, Practices, and Procedures

1. Practice before the IRS
2. Tax Preparers and Penalties
3. Representation
4. The Collection Process
5. Examination of Returns and the Appeals Process
6. Tax Authority
7. Record Keeping and Electronic Filing

Enrolled agents are individuals who have demonstrated special competence in tax matters and professional ethics and have been enrolled to practice before the IRS as taxpayers' agents or legal representatives. Practice before the IRS includes all matters connected with presentations to the IRS relating to a client's rights, privileges, and liabilities under laws or regulations administered by the IRS. Such presentations include

1. Preparing and filing documents;
2. Communicating with the IRS; and
3. Representing a client at conferences, hearings, and meetings.

The 10.5-hour (12 hours total seat time to include tutorials and surveys) examination covers federal taxation and tax accounting and the use of tax return forms for individuals, partnerships, corporations, trusts, estates, and gifts. It also covers ethical considerations and procedural requirements.

The exam consists of three parts, with 3.5 hours for each part (4 hours total seat time to include tutorial and survey). The questions on the examination are directed toward the tasks that enrolled agents must perform to complete and file forms and tax returns and to represent taxpayers before the Internal Revenue Service. Each part of the examination consists of approximately 100 multiple-choice questions and covers the following tax topics:

Part 1 - Individuals
Part 2 - Businesses
Part 3 - Representation, Practices, and Procedures

When to Sit for the Certification Exams

Sit for all examinations as soon as you can. While all of the certification programs except the EA have education requirements, candidates are allowed to sit for the exam and then complete the requirements within a certain time period. The CIA program allows full-time students in their senior year to sit for the exam, and the CMA program offers a 7-year window for submission of educational credentials. The CIA and CMA exams are offered at a reduced fee for students. The requirements for the CPA vary by jurisdiction, but many state boards allow candidates to sit for the exam before they have completed the required hours.

It would be difficult if not impossible to complete all four exams in 1 year. But it is a smart move to take full advantage of the knowledge and study habits you are gaining in your classes. Register for and schedule yourself to take the parts of each exam that best match up to the courses you are currently taking. For example, if you are taking a Business Law course and a Federal Tax course this semester, schedule your CPA Regulation date for the week after classes end. And, soon after you finish your Cost and Managerial Accounting class, schedule yourself for and take both parts of the CMA exam on the same day – doing so will save you over $300 in membership and exam fees!

Examination Pass Rates

The pass rates on the CPA, CIA, CMA, and EA exams are presented in the tables below. See also page 9.

Many schools and review courses advertise the quality of their programs by reporting pass rates. Obviously, the best rates are emphasized. Thus, the reported percentage may be that for first-time candidates, all candidates, candidates passing a specific section of the examination, candidates completing the examination, or even candidates successfully completing the exam after a specified number of sittings.

Pass Rates

CPA Exam

	2008	2009	2010
AUD	49.1	49.8	48.9
BEC	47.5	48.3	47.8
FAR	49.2	48.5	46.7
REG	48.7	49.8	50.6

The passing percentages for the CPA exam have been in the high-forties when only one section is taken per exam window. We expect the per-section passing percentages to continue to be 40-50% with the advent of the CBT-e exam. The pass rate on passing all four sections the first time in one exam window is about 7%.

CIA Exam

	2008	2009	2010
Part I	59.5	51.1	50.9
Part II	67.2	58.6	62.2
Part III	55.1	50.2	52.8
Part IV	64.7	58.7	56.6

CMA Exam

	2008*	2009*	2010
Part 1	49	49	40
Part 2	55	50	36
Part 3	56	52	N/A
Part 4	64	57	N/A

EA Exam

	2007-2008	2008-2009	2009-2010
Part 1	38	49	76
Part 2	45	67	69
Part 3	68	79	80

*These pass rates are for the four-part exam.

Reasons for the Low Pass Rates

Although a very high percentage of serious candidates successfully complete each of the examinations, the 40%-60% CPA, CIA, and CMA pass rates warrant an explanation. First, the pass rates are low (relative to bar and medical exams) because these examinations reflect the high standards of the accounting profession, which contribute greatly to the profession's reputation and also attract persons with both competence and aspiration.

Second, the pass rates are low because most accounting educational programs are at the undergraduate rather than graduate level. Undergraduate students are generally less career-oriented than graduate students. Undergraduates may look on their program as a number of individual courses required for graduation rather than as an integrated program to prepare them for professional practice.

Third, the pass rates are low because accounting programs and curricula at most colleges and universities are not given the budgetary priority they deserve. Accounting faculties are often understaffed for the number of accounting majors, the number and nature of accounting courses (problem-oriented vs. descriptive), etc., relative to other faculties. However, you cannot use this as an excuse or reason for not achieving your personal goals. You must do your best to improve your control systems and study resources.

Cost to Maintain Professional Certification

The cost to take the CIA exam for members of The Institute of Internal Auditors (The IIA) is a one-time $75 Exam Application fee plus a $150-per-part Registration fee, which totals $675 (assuming you pass all parts the first time you take them). Full-time students save $45 per part and $25 on the Exam Application fee. Membership in The IIA is not required. Nonmembers pay a $100 Exam Application fee plus a $200-per-part Registration fee. Nonmembers must also include a $100 processing fee when they submit their CPE report every 2 years. Annual membership dues vary from $60 to $225. See The IIA website at www.theiia.org for more information.

The cost to take the new two-part CMA exam is $350 for each part and a $200 Certification Entrance fee plus Institute of Management Accountants (IMA) membership dues, which vary from $39 for students to $195 for regular members. Membership in the IMA is required, and all new members (except Students and Young Professionals) must pay a one-time registration fee of $15. Students may take each part of the examination once at a reduced fee of $175 per part, with a $75 Certification Entrance fee. See the IMA website at www.imanet.org for more information.

The cost of the entire CPA exam is $784.50 plus a varying State Board fee per section. See the NASBA website at www.nasba.org for links to each state board. Most states require an annual fee to maintain the CPA certificate and/or license. See www.cpa-exam.org for more information.

For the EA exam, the $101 testing fee for each of the three parts is due at the time the examination is scheduled. The exam fee is non-transferable and non-refundable. There is no fee for rescheduling at least 30 days prior to the scheduled date. A $35 fee applies if the exam is rescheduled 5 to 29 days before the scheduled date. If an exam is rescheduled less than 5 days before the scheduled date, the full $101 fee must be paid again. (The same applies to absenteeism and late arrivals not allowed to test.) Once you have passed the exam, there is a $30 fee to apply for your enrollment to practice before the IRS. You must renew your enrollment every 3 years. The renewal fee is $125. See the test administrator's website at www.prometric.com/irs/default.html for more information.

OTHER PROFESSIONAL CERTIFICATION PROGRAMS

Chartered Property Casualty Underwriter (CPCU)

The CPCU designation is granted by the American Institute for Chartered Property Casualty Underwriters, located in Malvern, Pennsylvania (outside of Philadelphia). The CPCU designation is granted after successful completion of eight courses (four foundation courses, one elective course, and three courses in either the commercial or personal concentration) in addition to fulfillment of certain ethics and experience requirements. (Note: This is one of the very few certification examinations that does not rely heavily on multiple-choice questions.) The four foundation courses are

- Foundations of Risk Management and Insurance
- Insurance Operations
- Business Law for Insurance Professionals
- Finance and Accounting for Insurance Professionals

The "Business Law for Insurance Professionals" course is based on the typical business law course, but emphasizes tort, contract, and agency law with application to insurance situations. Those interested in the CPCU program should visit their website at www.aicpcu.org.

Chartered Life Underwriter (CLU)

The CLU designation is the professional credential for persons involved in the protection, accumulation, preservation, and distribution of the economic values of human life. Since the first examinations were held in 1927, over 94,000 men and women have met the educational, experience, and ethics mandates needed to earn the CLU designation. The CLU program allows financial planners to prove they have expertise in the specialized subjects of life insurance applications, insurance law and taxation, and applied estate planning. To earn the CLU designation, students must complete eight courses -- five required and three electives. See www.theamericancollege.edu for more information.

State Real Estate Licensure Examinations

All states have real estate licensing examinations, usually a salesperson exam and a broker exam. The sales examination generally tests the laws, rules, etc., of the particular state, including real estate law (which makes up approximately 50% of the exam). The broker examination tests more advanced topics, but also has up to 50% coverage of real estate law. These tests are usually multiple-choice and consist of 30 to 100 questions, depending on the state. The broker exam is usually the longer of the two exams.

Real estate law includes contracts, agency, property, leases, mortgages, etc.

Law School Admission Test (LSAT)

The LSAT is a standard admission test developed and administered by Law School Admission Council (LSAC or Law Services) in Newtown, Pennsylvania. This one-half-day test is given worldwide four times a year: February, June, October, and December. All tests are given on Saturdays, except the June test, which is given on Monday. In October 2011, the test will also be given on a Tuesday, and in December 2011 and February 2012, the test will also be given on a Monday. Law schools generally require that you take the test by December to be considered for admission the following Fall (with a similar lead time for admission other times of the year). The Law Services Information Booklet (includes a sample LSAT exam and an LSAT registration form) can be acquired by visiting their website at www.lsac.org.

The LSAT consists of five 35-minute sections of multiple-choice questions, of which four of the five sections (you do not know which four) contribute to the test taker's score. The fifth section is typically used to validate and test both new questions and new formats. The LSAT tests

1. Reading comprehension (1 section)
2. Logical reasoning (2 sections)
3. Analytical reasoning (1 section)

Remember that you are required to complete all five sections and are not told which four are official, i.e, which will determine your grade. Note that the LSAT does NOT test business law or other legal topics. The LSAT is designed to test the skills that are thought to be of importance in law school. These skills include: analyzing and evaluating the reasoning and arguments of others; reading and comprehending difficult texts; and the ability to organize, manage, and make inferences from information.

The final part of the LSAT is a 35-minute writing exercise. You are asked to write a short essay on a defined topic. Rather than grade the writing sample, the administrators send a copy to law schools to which you apply, along with your scores on the multiple-choice sections of the exam.

There are numerous LSAT preparation books, courses, etc. We recommend that you use some form of assistance to become better acquainted with the examination. The LSAT does test basic aptitudes and skills that are developed over a long period of time. Thus, you cannot cram for it. However, any review (familiarity) is better than going in "cold." Carefully planned programs to increase reading comprehension and verbal reasoning (e.g., logic courses) may be most helpful.

Multistate Bar Examination

The Multistate Bar Examination has been developed by the National Conference of Bar Examiners for those state bars that choose to use it. Fifty-four jurisdictions now participate in the program.

The examination is 6 hours long and consists of 200 multiple-choice questions on the following topics: Contracts (33 questions); Torts (33); Constitutional Law (31); Criminal Law and Procedure (31); Evidence (31); and Real Property (31). There are also 10 pretest questions that are not used for scoring purposes. More information can be found at www.ncbex.org.

STUDY UNIT ONE
THE AMERICAN LEGAL SYSTEM

Law emerges from a process in which a government produces a set of rules enforceable through sanctions. Thus, the law is a system of social control that recognizes and enforces rights and duties, but it is not the exclusive method of social control. Other controls include religion, morality, custom, societal norms, and family beliefs. The law is dynamic because it must respond to changes in society.

The rights and correlated duties enforced by the law affect individuals and their relation to one another. A **right** is a legal claim that does not interfere with a protected interest; a **duty** is a legal obligation not to interfere with the protected interest. The fundamental types of individual rights are personal rights and property rights. **Personal rights** are those rights one possesses by virtue of being a person but may also arise from contract. **Property rights** are rights in a thing that can be disposed of or transferred. Property rights may relate to real property or personal property.

Law embodies **ethical precepts** but is not coextensive with them. Thus, what is unethical may not be illegal, and nonlegal sources of ethical guidance must be considered. Of course, the world's religions are one such source, and philosophy is another. For example, the philosopher Immanuel Kant devised the **categorical imperative**, an approach to any ethical decision that asks what the consequences would be if all persons in the same circumstances (category) behaved similarly. **Natural law** concepts (see the next page) are a source of ethical standards because they postulate that certain human rights are fundamental, such as life, liberty, and the pursuit of happiness, rights mentioned in the Declaration of Independence. Under this view, a business decision should be evaluated based on how it affects the rights of groups, e.g., consumers or employees. According to **utilitarian ethics**, a decision is good if it maximizes social utility, that is, provides the greatest good for the greatest number of people. Various concepts of the **social responsibility** of business have evolved from a greater awareness of ethical obligations. A limited view is espoused by the economist **Milton Friedman**. He argues that a business must stay "within the rules of the game," i.e., engage in "open and free competition without deception or fraud," but is otherwise obligated only to earn profits. A second view is that businesses must consider the interests of all **stakeholders**, some of whom in a given situation may have interests paramount to the interest of shareholders. A third view is that major corporations have **citizenship** responsibilities, for example, to protect the environment or promote human rights.

The study of law is **jurisprudence**. Over time, differing schools of jurisprudence have emerged. The **natural law school** believes the standard for human conduct consists of laws founded on preordained rights. It believes that God or nature, not humanity, is the source of all law. The **historical school** defines law as those rules that have been developed in society and tested over time. This school believes that changes in the norms of society will gradually be reflected in the law. **Legal positivism** treats law as existing only in the positive sense; that is, law is a product only of an authorized process of a legitimate governmental authority. Adherents to this school propose that no law exists without government, and all valid laws should be obeyed and enforced without regard to any other standard. The **power or command school** considers all law to result from power. This school holds that the law is the set of rules established and enforced by those who exercise power. The **legal realism school** is pragmatic. It proposes that law should be dynamically directed toward meeting the changing needs of society. The **law and economics school** promotes market efficiency as a fundamental issue in legal decision making. The costs and benefits of a proposed rule are weighed in determining its desirability.

A primary function of the legal system is to **resolve disputes** while maintaining stability and predictability in society and permitting orderly change. The legal system must balance competing interests, for example, economic growth and environmental protection. It must therefore provide a civilized forum in which individuals may settle their disputes. Effective dispute resolution mechanisms, in turn, result in substantial predictability in societal relations. When a person interacts with others in society in any capacity, (s)he may anticipate with reasonable certainty that standards of acceptable conduct will be enforced. This expectation is commonly referred to as law and order, and includes the protection of public health and safety. To achieve this purpose, rules must be enforced. Thus, the legal system penalizes wrongdoers. Penalties are an important component of an effective legal system.

Another central function of the legal system is **preservation of the state**. It ensures that changes in the political system are brought about by political action, not by revolution or rebellion.

In the American legal system, power is allocated between the central (federal) government and the state governments (county and city governments are subdivisions of each state government). This division is mandated by the **U.S. Constitution**. Federal and state governments possess three branches: executive (president, governor), legislative (Congress, state legislature), and judicial (courts). The U.S. Constitution allocates federal power among the three branches of government. **Congress**, the legislative branch, has the power to enact laws. The judiciary branch has the power to interpret the law and decide cases and controversies. Importantly, the courts also determine whether actions of the other branches of government are constitutional. This power is referred to as **judicial review**. The **President**, as the head of the executive branch, has the power to ensure that the laws be faithfully executed.

The allocation of authority among the three separate branches of government is known as the **separation of powers**. It prevents excessive accumulation of power in any one branch, and it enables each branch to exercise its constitutional responsibilities without undue influence by the other branches. Most state constitutions are comparable to the U.S. Constitution with respect to separation of powers. Nevertheless, some overlap exists. For example, the power to legislate (make law) is vested in the legislative branch. However, the judiciary is often said to make law when it interprets statutes or the Constitution. Judges also make law when they decide cases by applying common-law principles to issues for which no statutory law has been enacted. Similarly, the executive branch exercises both rulemaking and adjudicatory powers in issuing regulations or licensing.

Initially, judge-made law, or **common law**, was the primary source of U.S. law, but since the twentieth century, enacted law has become the primary source of new law. **Enacted law** includes federal and state constitutions, federal treaties, federal and state statutes, executive orders and proclamations by the President or state governor, administrative rules and regulations, and local ordinances. The **Supremacy Clause** of the U.S. Constitution provides that, when federal law and state law conflict, federal law prevails. However, most of American law is state law. Each state has its own statutes containing laws enacted by its legislature. Thus, there are at least 50 bodies of state contract law, corporation law, real property law, etc. Moreover, both federal and state governments have administrative agencies with the power to promulgate and enforce rules and regulations. Day-to-day operation of the federal and state governments rests largely in the hands of administrative agencies (Study Unit 5). Each state also has its own court system that continuously develops the state's body of common law and case law.

The American legal system is built upon a common-law system first developed in England. It relies heavily on the judiciary as a source of law and on the **adversarial method** for adjudication of disputes. The judiciary in a common-law system develops a body of law that serves as **precedent** for determination of later controversies. Common law is synonymous with case law or judge-made law. Under the common-law system, the principle of **stare decisis** requires that cases before a court be decided in the same manner as prior cases presenting similar facts and legal issues. Stare decisis is a method to ensure that the legal system is consistent. It promotes efficiency for citizens, lawyers, and the judiciary by providing guidelines (prior decisions) for deciding new cases, but its requirements are not absolute. Courts hesitate to overrule an earlier decision but are expected to do so in appropriate circumstances. When the rule of law in an earlier case is overruled by a later decision, a new precedent is established. This precedent is then followed by the lower courts in subsequent disputes. Thus, common law promotes efficiency and stability and also allows sufficient flexibility to accommodate social change. The common law or case law that results from application of stare decisis can be modified by legislation.

Some additional classifications of law in the American legal system are substantive vs. procedural, criminal vs. civil, public vs. private, and law vs. equity. **Substantive law** is the body of constitutional directives, statutes, administrative rules, and common-law principles that define rights and duties. **Procedural law** governs how the judicial or administrative process is accessed and operates. In other words, substantive law creates rights and obligations, but procedural law describes how a party enforces rights or settles obligations. **Criminal law** protects society's interests by defining offenses against the public and providing for their punishment by a governmental body. Thus, a crime is a violation of a duty owed to the public that is prosecuted by representatives of the public. **Civil law** provides an injured party the opportunity to bring suit seeking private remedies to compensate for his/her injury. Thus, criminal violations are deemed to be wrongs against society as a whole, whereas civil violations are noncriminal injuries to specific private parties. However, the same behavior may violate both civil law and criminal law. **Public law** primarily concerns the organization of government and its relation to the people. **Private law** defines the legal relationships among private individuals. Some major areas of public law are constitutional law, criminal law, and administrative law. Private law includes contract law, property law, tort law, and the law of business organizations. The historical distinction between **law and equity** arose because the English common law courts could not furnish sufficiently flexible remedies for the legal needs of the population.

Thus, courts of equity were created with power to order remedies when laws were not sufficient. For example, a court of equity could issue an injunction ordering a party to do or not do an act. It could also decree specific performance of a land contract. The primary remedy at law was an action for damages. Procedure also varied in equity courts because jury trials were not allowed. Another distinctive feature of equity is the application of such **equitable maxims** as the clean hands doctrine ("One who comes into equity must do so with clean hands"). Hence, a plaintiff complaining about waste of corporate assets lacks the necessary clean hands to seek equitable relief if (s)he also has engaged in improper conduct. Modern judicial systems no longer have separate courts of law and equity. But the distinction still exists with regard to remedies, procedure, and the application of equitable maxims.

QUESTIONS

1.1 Nature of Law

1. The word "law" has many definitions. Some of these definitions are broader than others. Which of the following is a definition of law?

A. The Old Testament.

B. Constitutions, treaties, statutes, regulations, and case law.

C. The enterprise of subjecting human conduct to the governance of rules.

D. All of the answers are correct.

Answer (D) is correct. *(Publisher, adapted)*

REQUIRED: The definition(s) of law.

DISCUSSION: "Law" has a variety of meanings. Many believe the law is based on universal principles recorded as absolute standards. Some scholars define law in terms of its manifestations: constitutions, treaties between nations, statutes, administrative regulations issued by the executive branch, and case (judge-made) law. Professor Lon Fuller, a 20th century legal scholar, defined law as "the enterprise of subjecting human conduct to the governance of rules."

2. The term "business ethics" refers to the study of

A. The increase or decrease of a corporation's budget.

B. Good/bad or just/unjust human conduct in a business environment.

C. The feasibility of expanding business facilities.

D. The increase of corporate productivity.

Answer (B) is correct. *(Publisher, adapted)*

REQUIRED: The definition of business ethics.

DISCUSSION: Many business decisions need to be justified as right or wrong. Ethical principles are derived from personal beliefs, religion, and culture. Business ethics is the study of whether a business decision is morally right or wrong. However, most managerial and accounting decisions are ethically neutral, at least in the narrow sense of being right or wrong rather than correct or incorrect.

3. None of the many attempts to define law have gained universal acceptance. The definition least likely to be acceptable in the context of the American experience is that law is a

A. Means of promoting the interests of society through the use of sanctions.

B. Set of principles, standards, and rules applied by courts to controversies.

C. Limit on personal liberty.

D. Group of ethical precepts backed by the power of the state.

Answer (D) is correct. *(Publisher, adapted)*

REQUIRED: The definition of law that is least likely to be acceptable in the U.S.

DISCUSSION: Ethical precepts affect the law, but law and ethics are not the same in American society. For example, a manufacturer of a defective product may be held liable even though it exercised utmost care. This liability furthers social policy. Conversely, conduct unethical under community standards may be subject to neither civil nor criminal sanctions. For example, a duty to aid an injured person is not a legal one.

Answer (A) is incorrect. H.E. Willis in *Introduction to American Law* defines law as "a scheme of social control that delimits personal liberty for the protection of social interests." Answer (B) is incorrect. The American Law Institute has defined law as "the body of principles, standards, and rules that the courts of a particular state apply in the decision of controversies brought before them." Answer (C) is incorrect. H.E. Willis in *Introduction to American Law* defines law as "a scheme of social control that delimits personal liberty for the protection of social interests."

4. One fundamental legal maxim is that ignorance of the law is

A. Usually a good excuse.

B. A legal defense for nonresident aliens.

C. An acceptable excuse for a corporation because it is an artificial entity.

D. No excuse.

Answer (D) is correct. *(D. Woods)*
REQUIRED: The true statement of the maxim about ignorance of the law.
DISCUSSION: Ignorance of the law is no excuse. People have a duty to find out what the law is and to comply with it. However, ignorance of the law may be a mitigating factor, e.g., if a person is taking advantage of another person's ignorance of the law.

5. Jurisprudence is the science or philosophy of law. Which school of jurisprudence adheres to the belief that law is based on ultimate principles that transcend society and its customs?

A. Legal realism.

B. Natural law.

C. Legal positivism.

D. Historical.

Answer (B) is correct. *(Publisher, adapted)*
REQUIRED: The jurisprudential theory that bases law on ultimate principles.
DISCUSSION: The natural law philosophy is based on the belief that ideal concepts of law exist outside of human culture and are knowable through the proper application of human reason. Some find the source of natural law in divine revelation. Others discover it in the inherent nature of humanity or the natural order of the universe.
Answer (A) is incorrect. Legal realism views law pragmatically as a process. It is concerned with which law is really in force. Answer (C) is incorrect. Legal positivists view law as resulting from an authorized process of a legitimate governmental authority. They believe that law does not exist without government. Answer (D) is incorrect. It treats law as custom evolved over a long period.

6. The law performs a variety of functions. Which of the following is not accepted as a function of law in modern American society?

A. Ensuring public safety by punishing persons who deviate from accepted norms.

B. Maintaining a system of social order while facilitating living in a society.

C. Resolving disputes between groups and individuals in a systematic way.

D. Protecting the public order by shaping society so that it complies with the moral values of the elected officials.

Answer (D) is correct. *(Publisher, adapted)*
REQUIRED: The false statement concerning a function of law.
DISCUSSION: Functions of the law include maintaining the social order, resolving disputes, and ensuring public safety. However, elected and other officials have a duty to uphold the law irrespective of their personal views.
Answer (A) is incorrect. The law serves to ensure public safety. Punishing those who injure others is one means of conforming unacceptable conduct. Answer (B) is incorrect. Maintaining social order is a vital role of the legal system. The law introduces stability and predictability into all aspects (political, economic, social) of society by prohibiting conduct harmful to social order and providing sanctions for violations of those prohibitions. Answer (C) is incorrect. The courts systematically interpret and apply the law to resolve the disputes brought before them.

1.2 Sources of Law

7. Allocation of power is a fundamental purpose of a constitutional arrangement. Which of the following is a true statement about the ways in which the U.S. Constitution allocates power?

A. The federal government cannot exercise powers not specifically enumerated.

B. Powers not specifically delegated to the federal government or to the states are reserved to the federal government.

C. State statutes control whenever not in direct conflict with federal statutes.

D. Federal law prevails if federal and state statutes conflict.

Answer (D) is correct. *(Publisher, adapted)*
REQUIRED: The allocation of powers between the federal government and the states.
DISCUSSION: When state and federal law conflict, federal law controls if a federal issue is involved.
Answer (A) is incorrect. The federal government also has implied powers that are necessary and proper for exercising the enumerated powers. Answer (B) is incorrect. The powers not specifically delegated, or implied by such a delegation, to the federal government are reserved to the states or to the people. Answer (C) is incorrect. Even if state statutes do not directly conflict with federal statutes, state law is invalid if material uniform regulation is required, the federal government has preempted the field, or the state statute otherwise violates the U.S. Constitution.

8. In the American legal system, forms of binding legal authority include

A. Constitutions, statutes, and regulations.

B. Attorney general opinions, executive orders, and treaties.

C. Authoritative pronouncements by designated legal authorities such as the National Conference of Commissioners on Uniform State Laws.

D. Advisory opinions of the U.S. Supreme Court.

Answer (A) is correct. *(Publisher, adapted)*

REQUIRED: The sources of law that provide binding legal authority.

DISCUSSION: The federal and state constitutions, statutes enacted by Congress and state legislatures, and regulations issued by administrative agencies are all forms of binding legal authority. A constitution is the highest form of legal authority and must be followed. Statutes are also binding upon courts, and regulations will be followed if in conformity with the related statute.

Answer (B) is incorrect. Attorney general opinions provide only advisory authority. Answer (C) is incorrect. Pronouncements by respected legal scholars may be highly persuasive, but courts are not compelled to comply with them. Answer (D) is incorrect. The Supreme Court does not issue advisory opinions.

9. The power of judicial review

A. Is expressly conferred by the U.S. Constitution.

B. Is limited to review of actions of the executive branch.

C. Enables courts to review laws enacted by legislative bodies and to declare them unconstitutional.

D. Refers to liberal interpretation of remedial statutes.

Answer (C) is correct. *(Publisher, adapted)*

REQUIRED: The true statement concerning the doctrine of judicial review.

DISCUSSION: Both state and federal courts have the power to review actions of the legislative and executive branches of the government, to determine whether those actions are in accordance with the Constitution, and, if not, to declare the actions void.

Answer (A) is incorrect. The power of judicial review is not expressly conferred by the U.S. Constitution; it is implied. Answer (B) is incorrect. The power of judicial review also extends to actions of the legislative branch. Answer (D) is incorrect. Judicial review is not the same as statutory construction.

10. Which of the following is ordinarily not considered to be a desirable characteristic of law?

A. The law should be certain.

B. The law should be flexible.

C. The law should have retroactive effect.

D. The law should be known by those required to comply with it.

Answer (C) is correct. *(Publisher, adapted)*

REQUIRED: The least desirable characteristic of the law.

DISCUSSION: Retroactive application of law often conflicts with the principle of certainty and the goal of fair notice. For example, if a criminal statute is given retroactive effect, action known to be rightful at the time it was taken is subsequently punished. Thus, one could not be certain what conduct is lawful. For this reason, the Constitution prohibits ex post facto criminal laws.

Answer (A) is incorrect. The law should be reasonably certain and reliable. Modern commercial practices, for instance, are based upon the assurance that contracts will be enforceable in the future according to the same principles applied today. Answer (B) is incorrect. The law should be able to adjust to new conditions. Thus, when the reason for a law ceases to exist, the law should cease to exist. Moreover, new law should be enacted when new problems are not addressed by old law. Answer (D) is incorrect. An educated citizenry should at least know the general principles underlying a society's legal system. Although no one knows all the law, access to it is available either directly or through experts (lawyers).

11. The principal law-making bodies in the American legal system are the legislatures. The laws enacted are subject to judicial interpretation. This judicial function is known as

A. Statutory construction.

B. Adjudication.

C. Judicial review.

D. Judicial legislation.

Answer (A) is correct. *(Publisher, adapted)*

REQUIRED: The term for the judicial interpretation of laws.

DISCUSSION: Statutory construction is the judicial function by which courts determine the meaning of statutes. The purpose is not to make law but to resolve ambiguities in the statutes as written.

Answer (B) is incorrect. Adjudication is the judicial function of resolving disputes. Answer (C) is incorrect. Judicial review is the power of courts to review the constitutionality of acts by the other branches of government. The term is also used to describe the power of appellate courts to review the decisions of lower courts and administrative agencies. Answer (D) is incorrect. The process of interpreting statutes is not a law-making function; it is simply a determination of the meaning of the statute.

12. In the complex legal system of the United States, there is a hierarchy of laws. Which of the following has the greatest authority?

A. Constitution of the U.S.

B. Treaties of the U.S.

C. Statutes of the U.S.

D. Regulations of the U.S.

Answer (A) is correct. *(Publisher, adapted)*
REQUIRED: The most authoritative U.S. law.
DISCUSSION: The U.S. Constitution is the supreme law in the United States. All other federal laws are made pursuant to the authority granted in the Constitution.
Answer (B) is incorrect. Treaties of the U.S. have less authority than the Constitution. Answer (C) is incorrect. Statutes of the U.S. have less authority than the Constitution of the U.S. Answer (D) is incorrect. Administrative agencies issue regulations under statutory authority.

13. Which of the following is a false statement about the ranking of federal and state laws?

A. When federal statutes regulate a given subject, state law is not necessarily preempted.

B. Even if no federal law has been enacted on a subject, the state law may be invalid.

C. If a federal and a state statute regulate the same subject matter, the state statute is always invalid.

D. If the federal statute relates to a power delegated to the federal government by the Constitution and the state statute is validly enacted under the state constitution, the federal statute prevails.

Answer (C) is correct. *(Publisher, adapted)*
REQUIRED: The false statement about ranking federal and state law.
DISCUSSION: If the subject matter of a federal law is within the constitutional powers of the federal government, a conflicting state law is invalid under the supremacy clause of the U.S. Constitution. However, federal regulation of a matter does not necessarily preclude state regulation of the same subject matter, e.g., securities regulation. But state regulation must not be unreasonably burdensome to the federal interest.
Answer (A) is incorrect. Nonconflicting federal and state laws often coexist. Answer (B) is incorrect. A state law may concern a subject that requires uniform national regulation or may violate the Constitution. Answer (D) is incorrect. A conflicting state statute would be invalid. If the laws do not conflict, both are usually valid.

14. Which classification of state law has the least authority?

A. The state's constitution.

B. Statutes.

C. Common law.

D. Regulations.

Answer (C) is correct. *(Publisher, adapted)*
REQUIRED: The state law that has the least authority.
DISCUSSION: The constitution of a state is the primary legal authority for that state. Validly enacted statutes and regulations are next in the hierarchy. Cases decided by courts (common law) must defer to a statute or regulation.
Answer (A) is incorrect. The state's constitution has greater authority than case (common) law. Answer (B) is incorrect. Statutes have greater authority than case (common) law. Answer (D) is incorrect. Regulations have greater authority than case (common) law.

15. The legal and the medical professions' ethics standards are established by

A. Congress.

B. Federal administrative agencies.

C. State bars and medical boards.

D. State legislatures.

Answer (C) is correct. *(Publisher, adapted)*
REQUIRED: The governing bodies of the legal and the medical professions.
DISCUSSION: Business associations have codes of ethics that are voluntary and not binding or enforceable. The legal and the medical professions' codes of ethics are different from those of business groups because they are enforceable by state bars and medical boards. A person must be licensed to practice law or medicine but usually not to participate in a trade or business.

1.3 Common Law

16. The principle that gives past judicial decisions binding authority in similar cases is known as

A. The rule of dictum.

B. Stare decisis.

C. Judicial review.

D. Civil law system.

Answer (B) is correct. *(Publisher, adapted)*
REQUIRED: The principle that gives past cases binding authority.
DISCUSSION: In a common-law legal system, past judicial decisions are binding in present cases with similar fact patterns. This principle is known as stare decisis.
Answer (A) is incorrect. Dictum is a statement in a judicial opinion that is unnecessary for the decision of the case. Answer (C) is incorrect. Judicial review is the power of courts to review the constitutionality of acts of government. Answer (D) is incorrect. A civil law system is based on enacted laws only. There is no common law. In the United States, only Louisiana uses a civil law system.

17. The American legal system is based on common law. The essence of the common law is that cases decided by courts become binding precedent under the doctrine of stare decisis for later decisions in similar cases by the same court or by lower courts within the same system. Just what rule of law a given case stands for is often a difficult question. This rule (the holding of a case) is derived from the

A. Transcript of the trial.

B. The dissenting opinion.

C. Dicta in the opinion.

D. Precise issues that had to be decided to reach the result in the case.

Answer (D) is correct. *(Publisher, adapted)*

REQUIRED: The source to determine the rule of law for which a given case stands.

DISCUSSION: Only statements of law contained in the opinion and relating to issues that had to be decided to resolve the dispute have binding legal authority. They constitute the holding of the case.

Answer (A) is incorrect. Only opinions of reported cases are used as precedent. Each reported case contains a written opinion by the judge(s) that summarizes the case and the legal decision. Answer (B) is incorrect. The statement of law made by the majority of the court provides the rule of the case. Nevertheless, dissenting opinions may be persuasive and representative of future trends. Answer (C) is incorrect. Dicta are statements relating to issues that did not have to be resolved to decide the case.

18. A fundamental characteristic of the American legal system is that it is adversarial. The best description of such a system is that

A. Truth is best served by an independent investigation of the facts by the judicial decision maker.

B. Justice is best served if the respective sides to a dispute are represented by advocates whose interests are in conflict and who have a full opportunity to be heard by an impartial tribunal.

C. The court appoints attorneys to represent the respective sides.

D. A person is a poor advocate of his/her own position in a legal dispute.

Answer (B) is correct. *(Publisher, adapted)*

REQUIRED: The best description of an adversarial legal system.

DISCUSSION: An adversarial legal system incorporates an assumption that the truth may best be determined by competition between opposing viewpoints. It attempts to direct the energy of partisanship to ensure that each side of a dispute is as well represented as possible.

Answer (A) is incorrect. The adversarial system assumes that the interested parties are best able to investigate and present the facts and legal arguments related to a dispute. Answer (C) is incorrect. Courts rarely appoint attorneys except to protect the rights of defendants in criminal cases. Answer (D) is incorrect. A party to a legal dispute who stands to gain or lose something significant is presumed to be motivated to present the best case for his/her position.

19. Plaintiff brought a suit in equity to dissolve a corporation of which she was a major shareholder. The petition alleged that corporate assets were being wasted through certain improper actions of management and the other shareholders. Plaintiff conceded that she had also engaged in certain wrongful conduct regarding use of corporate assets. Which of the following is true?

A. A court applying equitable rules should dismiss the suit.

B. The court may issue an injunction to prohibit future criminal conduct of the kind alleged.

C. The plaintiff's rights should be vindicated on the merits of the case regardless of her wrongful actions.

D. The court should only apply rules of law to the case.

Answer (A) is correct. *(Publisher, adapted)*

REQUIRED: The true statement concerning a suit brought in equity.

DISCUSSION: A suit brought in equity is subject to notions of what is just. An equity court applies equitable maxims such as the clean hands doctrine ("One who comes into equity must do so with clean hands"). A plaintiff complaining about waste of corporate assets lacks the necessary clean hands to seek equitable relief if she has also engaged in sufficiently improper conduct.

Answer (B) is incorrect. Criminal conduct is already prohibited by statutes. Answer (C) is incorrect. The plaintiff in equity must have clean hands. Answer (D) is incorrect. A suit in equity is brought when legal rules are inadequate to do justice.

20. The distinction between law and equity has both historical and practical significance for today's legal system. Which of the following is the true statement concerning the distinction?

A. The American legal system is composed of separate courts of law and equity.

B. An action for damages is not equitable.

C. Suits in equity are tried before juries.

D. Equitable remedies and remedies at law are the same.

Answer (B) is correct. *(Publisher, adapted)*

REQUIRED: The true statement concerning the distinction between law and equity.

DISCUSSION: The historical distinction between law and equity arose because the English common law courts could not furnish sufficiently flexible remedies for the legal needs of the population. Courts of equity with power to give remedies when laws were not sufficient were instituted. The action for damages was and is essentially a legal (as opposed to an equitable) remedy.

Answer (A) is incorrect. The same court may exercise both legal and equitable powers. Answer (C) is incorrect. Suits in equity are not tried before juries, but suits in law are tried before juries if the parties so choose. Answer (D) is incorrect. Equity and law give different remedies.

1.4 Classifications of Law

21. Which of the following is false regarding the distinction between substantive and procedural law?

A. Procedural law governs the manner in which rights are asserted or duties are imposed.

B. Substantive law recognizes rights and imposes duties.

C. A court always applies the procedural rules of its own jurisdiction.

D. Courts always apply the substantive law of the forum but may apply procedural rules of another jurisdiction.

Answer (D) is correct. *(Publisher, adapted)*

REQUIRED: The false statement concerning the distinction between substantive and procedural law.

DISCUSSION: Substantive law defines rights, whereas procedural law is concerned with measures to implement those rights. An example of a substantive right is a right to recover when injured by the negligence of another. An example of a procedural rule is one that limits when and where a suit may be brought. If a law is deemed substantive, the court may apply the law of another jurisdiction (e.g., if the case arose out of a transaction in another jurisdiction). If the law is considered procedural, the forum court will usually apply its own law.

22. The distinction between civil and criminal law determines the type of remedies, the parties, and the procedure in a legal proceeding. Which is the true statement concerning this distinction?

A. Criminal law governs felonies, misdemeanors, and torts.

B. A civil action normally involves a dispute between private persons with regard to duties imposed by law or adopted under a contract.

C. A criminal action is prosecuted by a governmental entity against a person who has committed a tort.

D. A civil action is brought by civil authorities for the breach of a duty imposed by law.

Answer (B) is correct. *(Publisher, adapted)*

REQUIRED: The true statement concerning the distinction between civil and criminal law.

DISCUSSION: A criminal prosecution is brought by governmental authorities for an injury to society as a result of a breach of duty imposed upon all persons by the law. A civil action may also involve a breach of a duty imposed by the law upon all persons, but the injury is deemed to be private and is enforced by a private person rather than a governmental entity. A civil action may also involve the breach of a duty arising from agreement between the parties.

Answer (A) is incorrect. A tort is not necessarily a crime. Answer (C) is incorrect. A tort is usually considered a breach of a private duty imposed by the law on all persons. It is not a crime but rather gives rise to a remedy in a civil action. Answer (D) is incorrect. Civil actions are usually brought by private persons.

23. Remedies available in criminal actions include

A. Fines.

B. Punitive damages.

C. Declaratory judgments.

D. Injunctions.

Answer (A) is correct. *(Publisher, adapted)*

REQUIRED: The remedy available in a criminal action.

DISCUSSION: The remedies available in a criminal action range from capital punishment (death) to imprisonment and fines of varying magnitude. They are imposed for breaches of duties imposed upon all persons that are regarded as wrongs to society and are enforced by the appropriate governmental entity.

Answer (B) is incorrect. Punitive damages are a civil remedy available as a penalty for extreme or aggravated behavior. Answer (C) is incorrect. A declaratory judgment (a noncoercive form of relief that states the rights and duties of the parties) is a civil remedy. Answer (D) is incorrect. An injunction is a civil remedy, whether temporary or permanent, commanding a person to do or refrain from doing some action. Criminal actions are already forbidden by law.

24. Which of the following is not a remedy available in a civil proceeding?

A. Compensatory damages.

B. Temporary restraining orders.

C. Declaratory relief.

D. Imprisonment.

Answer (D) is correct. *(Publisher, adapted)*
REQUIRED: The remedy not available in a civil proceeding.
DISCUSSION: Criminal law punishes wrongdoing. Civil law is designed to compensate for injury. Imprisonment is therefore a criminal remedy and not available in a civil proceeding.
Answer (A) is incorrect. Compensatory damages are usually available in civil proceedings. Answer (B) is incorrect. Temporary restraining orders (short term injunctions that restrain or command an action until a hearing can be convened) are available in civil proceedings. Answer (C) is incorrect. Declaratory relief is a civil remedy by which rights and duties of the parties are stated.

25. Which of the following is public rather than private law?

A. Contract law.

B. Constitutional law.

C. Property law.

D. Tort law.

Answer (B) is correct. *(Publisher, adapted)*
REQUIRED: The branch of law that is classified as public rather than private.
DISCUSSION: Public law concerns the structure and powers of governing bodies and their relationship with the population. It includes administrative and criminal law as well as constitutional law. In the American system, constitutional law concerns the rights of the people and the allocation of authority between the federal and state systems and among the legislative, executive, and judicial branches at both levels. Private law concerns the relations among private individuals or entities. Contracts, torts, property, agency, and business organizations fall within the scope of private law.

26. Which of the following is a true statement about tort and contract law?

A. Contract liability is enforced by private persons, whereas tort liability is enforced by a governmental entity.

B. Tort and contract law are similar in that each is concerned with civil duties.

C. A tort is a crime because it is a violation of a duty imposed by law upon all individuals within the society.

D. Contract law involves only enforcement of duties assumed with respect to property.

Answer (B) is correct. *(Publisher, adapted)*
REQUIRED: The true statement regarding the distinction between tort and contract law.
DISCUSSION: A tort is a breach of a civil duty imposed by the law upon all persons. A breach of contract is the breach of a duty imposed by agreement. Torts and contracts are two types of private law. Both compensate a party for a loss resulting from the defendant's wrong.
Answer (A) is incorrect. Liability in both tort and contract is enforced by private persons. Answer (C) is incorrect. Torts give rise to private liability, but crimes give rise to public liability. The injury caused by a crime is deemed to be done to all individuals in the society, whereas the harm caused by a tort is essentially private. Answer (D) is incorrect. Contract law encompasses almost any matter on which two persons agree, e.g., providing services.

27. The legal environment of business includes relationships between business and groups of persons or entities. These include customers, employees, investors, suppliers, creditors, competitors, the public, and government. Probably the most significant is the relationship of business to

A. Investors.

B. Customers.

C. The public.

D. Government.

Answer (D) is correct. *(Publisher, adapted)*
REQUIRED: The most significant relationship within the legal environment of business.
DISCUSSION: The relationship of business and government is the most significant because it has the greatest effect on the other relationships. That relationship includes the laws that regulate the other relationships.

28. The legal environment of business

A. Is limited to environmental law that regulates the relationship between business and the public.

B. Only includes profit-making organizations.

C. Includes the statutory regulation of business but does not include the impact of the common law on business.

D. Concerns all the ways in which the law affects business.

Answer (D) is correct. *(Publisher, adapted)*

REQUIRED: The true statement about the legal environment of business.

DISCUSSION: The legal environment of business includes traditional legal topics such as business associations, contracts, and agency. In addition, the legal environment includes all laws, regulations, and rules that are promulgated by any governmental body or agency and affect the business firm.

Answer (A) is incorrect. The legal environment of business includes all laws that affect business. Environmental law is included. Answer (B) is incorrect. The legal environment includes all business organizations regardless of their purposes. Thus, labor unions, political parties, and public service entities are included. Answer (C) is incorrect. The legal environment includes both statutory and common law regulation of business.

29. Ethical standards that apply when dealing with people in a business relationship are described as

A. Intimate ethics.

B. Marketplace ethics.

C. Community ethics.

D. Individualist ethics.

Answer (B) is correct. *(Publisher, adapted)*

REQUIRED: The ethical standard applicable when dealing with a person in a business relationship.

DISCUSSION: Marketplace ethics concern ethical standards in a business relationship. A person's ethical standards of honesty and loyalty are usually lower in these circumstances than in interactions with friends and family.

Answer (A) is incorrect. A person holds him/herself to an intimate ethics standard when dealing with a close relative, family friend, or neighbor. Answer (C) is incorrect. Community ethics emphasize limiting the individual's rights for the benefit of society. Answer (D) is incorrect. Individualist ethics emphasize that the individual's rights are superior to society's interests.

PASS THE CMA EXAM
with less time and effort
GLEIM®
CMA REVIEW SYSTEM:
• A Personal Counselor to help you develop a personalized study plan
• Study almost anywhere - including while commuting
• Review material guaranteed to be current for 18 months
• Emulates the look and feel of the Exam
SUCCESS GUARANTEED!!
GLEIM
KNOWLEDGE TRANSFER SYSTEMS®
gleim.com/cma • 800.874.5346

STUDY UNIT TWO
THE AMERICAN COURT SYSTEM

The judicial system in the United States is based on a **dual court structure** consisting of federal and state courts. This structure is mandated by the U.S. Constitution, which divides power between the federal and state governments. Retention of power by the states despite establishment of a national authority is a hallmark of **federalism**.

Separate state and federal court systems were established to address specific concerns. When the Constitution was written, the states feared an unduly powerful federal court system. However, in recognition of the provinciality of each state's court system, a concurrent but limited federal system was also developed. Thus, the U.S. has 52 court systems: one for each of the 50 states, one for the District of Columbia, and the federal system. Accordingly, each person in the United States is subject to the law of both the state in which (s)he is a resident and federal law. Moreover, each person is subject to the law of each state with which (s)he has **minimum contacts**. These contacts must be sufficient so that, in the context of the particular case, traditional concepts of fairness are not offended if (s)he is involuntarily subjected to that state's jurisdiction.

The U.S. legal system is based on the principle of **stare decisis**, which requires examination of prior, factually similar cases to determine whether an issue currently before a court has already been decided and whether the same decision should be made again. Application of stare decisis in the dual court structure is complex. A decision by the Supreme Court with regard to a **federal question**, i.e., any case arising under the Constitution, federal statutes, or treaties of the U.S., is binding on all other courts, state or federal. The U.S. Constitution is the supreme law of the land, and a state court must apply a federal law if that law is in direct conflict with the state law. A decision by a lower federal court on a federal question is not binding on a state court. Nevertheless, such a decision will be considered very carefully by the state court. A state court decision on a federal question is not binding on a federal court. Furthermore, a decision by a U.S. court of appeals is not binding on federal district courts beyond the geographical area of the U.S. over which it presides (circuit).

Questions of state law come before a federal court when it exercises **diversity jurisdiction**, that is, when the parties have differing state citizenship and the case presents no federal question. In such a case, the federal court must apply state substantive law, including the case law as determined by the state's highest tribunal. Diversity jurisdiction is based on Article III, Section 2, of the Constitution, under which federal courts have **subject-matter jurisdiction** (power to decide a specific type of case) over controversies between citizens of different states. In the important case of *Erie Railroad Co. v. Tompkins*, 304 U.S. 64 (1938), the Supreme Court held that federal courts must apply state law in a diversity case. Thus, there is no federal common law with respect to state law issues.

A state court decision is binding on all lower courts within the state; for example, a decision by the Florida Supreme Court is binding on all courts in Florida. However, a state court decision is not binding on the courts of other states, unless the law of one state requires application of the law of another state. Some legal issues cross state lines. A diversity action is an example. Thus, if two truck drivers, each from a different state, collide in a third state, the **choice of law (conflict of law) rules** of the state where suit is filed may dictate that another state's law applies. Once the choice of law analysis indicates which state substantive law will provide the rule of decision, the court must apply the law of that state as interpreted by its highest tribunal.

Under the **Full Faith and Credit Clause** of the Constitution, each state is required to respect the final judgments of courts in other states. It provides that "full faith and credit shall be given in each state to the public acts, records, and judicial proceedings of every other state." For example, a judgment by a New Jersey court awarding damages for breach of contract that has been fully, fairly, and finally litigated cannot be relitigated in Texas.

The primary function of a court is to decide controversies between parties to a lawsuit. The parties are **litigants**, and the court's decision is a **judgment**. The judge is the presiding officer of the court and controls the proceedings. **Trial judges** preside over trials, and **appellate judges** review the work of trial judges. **Attorneys** are officers of the court. As such, they must strive to ensure that the proceedings are conducted in an orderly and dignified manner and that the issues are tried on their merits only.

Each court is empowered to decide certain types of cases. As noted previously, the dual court structure consists of two systems: state and federal. Each system has two primary functions: trial and appeal. **Jurisdiction** is the authorized power of a court to hear a case and render a binding decision. A court with **original jurisdiction** has the power to hear, consider, and decide a case when it is first brought into the system. Original jurisdiction is normally exercised by trial courts, which determine questions of both law and fact in a particular case. **Questions of fact** concern what happened. **Questions of law** concern such issues as the relevance of facts, the admissibility of evidence to prove the facts, the choice of rules of law applicable to the facts, the manner in which the rules of law should be applied, and the sufficiency of the evidence to meet a party's burden of proof. **Appellate jurisdiction** is authority to review decisions of trial courts or lower appellate courts. Appellate courts primarily review the correctness of findings of law made at the trial level, but they also review the legal sufficiency of findings of fact. However, they do not decide whether the trial court's findings of fact were correct. If a factual finding was supported by **substantial evidence** in the record and was not clearly erroneous, the trial court's determination will stand.

A court must have both subject-matter jurisdiction and personal jurisdiction. **Subject-matter jurisdiction** is the authority of the court to hear and determine a particular category or type of case. **Personal jurisdiction** is the authority of a court to render a judgment in a case that affects the interest of particular persons. Jurisdiction may be further categorized as general or limited (special). A court of **general jurisdiction** has the power to hear and decide all controversies involving legal rights and duties. An example of a court of general jurisdiction is a U.S. district court. A court of **limited or special jurisdiction** has authority to hear and decide only those cases that fall within a particular class. For example, a small claims court may hear defined cases having a small amount in controversy, such as $1,500.

In the federal system, lawsuits ordinarily begin in **U.S. district courts**, which are the principal trial courts. Each state is divided into federal districts, with at least one district in each state. The subject-matter jurisdiction of U.S. district courts extends to cases in which the U.S. is a party, that involve a federal question, or that involve diversity of citizenship. When a lawsuit concerns either the violation or the interpretation of a federal statute, the appropriate U.S. district court has subject-matter jurisdiction. For example, if an investor alleges that an accounting firm violated federal securities laws by aiding and abetting securities fraud with regard to misstated information contained in overly optimistic profit reports, a question under a federal statute exists, and the appropriate U.S. district court will have subject-matter jurisdiction. Prosecution of federal crimes also involves application and interpretation of federal statutes. The U.S. is a party as the prosecutor, and the case should be tried in the appropriate U.S. district court. When the parties are from different states (i.e., have **diversity of citizenship**) and the dispute involves an **amount in controversy** exceeding the jurisdictional amount (currently $75,000), the U.S. district courts also have subject-matter jurisdiction. Diversity jurisdiction is concurrent; that is, state courts also have jurisdiction to hear cases between citizens of different states when the amount in controversy exceeds $75,000. If the amount in controversy is below the jurisdictional amount, state courts have exclusive jurisdiction, even if the parties' citizenship is diverse (unless a federal question is at issue).

Disputes decided by United States district courts can be appealed directly to the **U.S. courts of appeals**. Most U.S. district courts are grouped into federal circuits according to their geographic locations. Eleven of the circuits are geographical groupings of states. Another circuit is in the District of Columbia. The **Federal Circuit** is a nongeographic circuit that reviews special cases, such as decisions of the U.S. Court of International Trade, the U.S. Court of Federal Claims, and the U.S. Patent and Trademark Office. The court of appeals for each of the 12 geographic circuits oversees the work of the U.S. district courts in the circuit. The function of the appellate courts is to examine the record of a case on appeal and determine whether the trial court committed reversible error. **Reversible error** substantially affects the legal rights and obligations of a party. If uncorrected, reversible error results in a miscarriage of justice. If the appellate court finds reversible error, it may reverse or set aside the lower court's decision, or it may remand the case for a new trial. Normally, a written opinion containing the reasons for a court's decision or judgment is rendered. However, the U.S. courts of appeals do not hear witnesses. They merely review the record of the trial below. Attorneys representing each side usually submit written briefs and make oral arguments.

The highest tribunal in the federal court system is the **Supreme Court of the United States**. Under the Constitution, it has **appellate jurisdiction** "with such exceptions and under such regulations as the Congress shall make." Thus, a primary function of the Supreme Court is to review decisions of the U.S. courts of appeals and, in some instances, the highest state courts or other tribunals. Congress has provided two avenues for invoking Supreme Court appellate jurisdiction. One is mandatory jurisdiction, which applies to very few cases. An appeal by right exists when a party appeals directly to the Supreme Court from a U.S. district court decision rendered pursuant to an act of Congress that requires the case to be heard by a three-judge panel, and such court grants or denies injunctive relief. All other appeals to the Supreme Court fall within its discretionary jurisdiction. A party may file a petition for a **writ of certiorari** after a decision by a U.S. court of appeals in any civil or criminal case. The petition is circulated among the nine justices of the court, of whom at least four must vote in favor of review. When a writ of certiorari is granted, the case is scheduled for a formal hearing.

Furthermore, the Supreme Court's discretionary appellate jurisdiction extends, in rare circumstances, to cases involving substantial federal questions that are appealed from the highest courts of the states. The Supreme Court also has **original jurisdiction** narrowly defined in the Constitution for "all cases affecting ambassadors, other public ministers and consuls, and those in which a state shall be a party." Fewer than 100 cases are decided by the U.S. Supreme Court each year.

Congress has established federal specialty courts to adjudicate narrowly defined types of disputes. The **U.S. Court of Federal Claims** has jurisdiction solely over claims against the U.S. government. Such claims may be founded on breaches of contract, tax refund suits, claims for compensation for the taking of property, any other claim based on the Constitution, an act of Congress, or a regulation issued by the executive branch of the government. The **U.S. Court of International Trade** has jurisdiction over issues involving import transactions. This court resolves disputes between the United States Customs Service (an administrative agency) and importers of goods who must pay a duty or tax on certain goods. The **U.S. Tax Court** is a court of national jurisdiction that resolves controversies with respect to income taxes, gift tax, and estate tax. The **U.S. bankruptcy courts** were formed by the Bankruptcy Act and are discussed in Study Unit 20. One U.S. bankruptcy court is attached to each U.S. district court to hear and decide bankruptcy cases within that district.

The **state court system** is independent of the federal courts. The following, in ascending order of authority, are the components of a typical four-tier state judicial system: (a) specialty courts of limited jurisdiction, (b) trial courts of general jurisdiction, (c) intermediate appellate courts (not available in all states), and (d) the court of last resort (usually called a supreme court). Examples of specialty courts of limited jurisdiction include justice of the peace court, police magistrate court, municipal court, small claims court, juvenile court, domestic relations court, and probate/surrogate court. A state's courts have jurisdiction (the power and authority to hear a case) over all disputes involving the state's constitution, statutes, and common law.

The **principal state trial courts** are courts of general jurisdiction. They are empowered to hear all cases except those expressly assigned to the aforementioned specialty courts. Virtually all significant cases involving contract law, criminal law, corporate law, etc., originate in the general trial courts. The general trial courts maintain formal records of their proceedings as a due process safeguard; that is, a record is preserved so as to permit review on appeal. All states have one or more **appellate courts** that hear appeals from judgments and orders rendered in the trial courts. Appellate jurisdiction empowers the higher state tribunal to correct legal errors of an inferior or lower-level court and to revise their judgments and orders. The final route of appeal within the state court system is the **state supreme court**. Review by a state supreme court is usually discretionary.

QUESTIONS

2.1 The Dual Court Structure

1. The American legal system is a federal system. Accordingly, allocation of power between the respective state court systems and the federal courts is crucial. Under the U.S. Constitution,

A. Federal courts have unlimited jurisdiction.

B. The court of last resort of the state is the final authority in resolving issues regarding that state's law.

C. The federal courts must apply federal case law in diversity cases pursuant to the decision in *Erie Railroad Co. v. Tompkins*.

D. The U.S. Supreme Court is the final authority on all questions of state and federal law.

Answer (B) is correct. *(Publisher, adapted)*

REQUIRED: The true statement concerning the allocation of judicial power.

DISCUSSION: Broad but limited powers of the federal government and its courts is an aspect of federalism. The U.S. Supreme Court is the final authority on all federal matters. With regard to matters left to the province of the states (those not involving any federal question), the federal courts must defer to the authoritative determinations of the courts of last resort in the respective states.

Answer (A) is incorrect. Federal courts have broad but specifically limited jurisdiction. Answer (C) is incorrect. The *Erie* decision requires federal courts to apply the state's statutory and common law in diversity cases. Answer (D) is incorrect. The U.S. Supreme Court must defer to the highest court of the state on questions of state law.

2. The landmark Supreme Court decision in *Erie Railroad Co. v. Tompkins* (1938) had a great impact on the allocation of judicial power between the state and federal courts because it

A. Permitted the development of a federal general common law.

B. Permitted federal courts to apply state statutory law in diversity cases.

C. Permitted state courts to decide federal questions.

D. Required federal courts to apply unwritten state law in diversity cases.

Answer (D) is correct. *(Publisher, adapted)*

REQUIRED: The effect of the *Erie* decision on the allocation of judicial power.

DISCUSSION: The Judiciary Act of 1789 provided for federal courts to apply the appropriate state law in diversity cases. An early decision of the Supreme Court, *Swift v. Tyson*, held that federal courts were not bound to apply state common law in diversity cases. As a consequence, a federal general common law began to develop. Reasoning that the Constitution did not give to federal courts the power to declare state law, the *Erie* court held that they must apply the substantive law of the state in a diversity case. Thus, there is no federal common law with respect to state issues.

Answer (A) is incorrect. *Erie* abolished federal general common law. Answer (B) is incorrect. Federal courts must now apply state common law and statutory law in diversity cases. Answer (C) is incorrect. State courts had concurrent jurisdiction over some federal questions before *Erie*.

3. One night, Paula Plaintiff was walking along a path adjacent to railroad tracks. As a train passed, something protruding from it struck and injured Plaintiff, causing her personal injuries resulting in $80,000 of medical expenses. Plaintiff, a resident of State Y where the incident occurred, wishes to sue the railroad company, which has its principal place of business and is incorporated in State X. The applicable laws of States X and Y differ. Which of the following is true?

A. Plaintiff must sue in State X for jurisdictional reasons.

B. Plaintiff may sue in federal court if she wishes to have the case tried under the federal common law of torts.

C. Plaintiff must sue in State X if she wishes to have that state's law applied.

D. Plaintiff may sue in State X, State Y, or federal court, but the same law will probably be applied.

Answer (D) is correct. *(Publisher, adapted)*

REQUIRED: The true statement about jurisdiction and choice of law.

DISCUSSION: This question is based on the facts of *Erie Railroad Co. v. Tompkins*, a Supreme Court decision significant for the allocation of power between the federal and state systems. The injury occurred in State Y, and the defendant is subject to suit there. The defendant corporation has a principal place of business and is incorporated in State X. Because the parties have diverse citizenship, the action can be brought in federal court because the jurisdictional amount is sufficient (the amount in controversy must exceed $75,000).

A federal court will follow the conflict of law rules of the state in which it is located. Most states apply the law of the state having the most significant relationship to the case. In a tort case, the traditional rule is to apply the substantive law of the place of injury.

Answer (A) is incorrect. Plaintiff can also sue in State Y or federal court. Answer (B) is incorrect. Federal courts apply state law in diversity cases. Answer (C) is incorrect. State X's courts would probably apply State Y's substantive law.

4. The court system in the United States consists of

A. A federal system and a state court system that provides for uniformity among the 50 states regarding nonfederal issues.

B. State and federal courts.

C. Courts that apply substantive law and others that apply procedural law.

D. Federal courts, which may decide any kind of dispute.

Answer (B) is correct. *(Publisher, adapted)*

REQUIRED: The true statement describing the U.S. court system.

DISCUSSION: The United States has a dual court system. The federal government has its own court system, as does each of the 50 states and the District of Columbia. This dual system is an aspect of federalism, which requires an allocation of powers between the federal and state governments.

Answer (A) is incorrect. Although the U.S. has a dual system, there is no uniformity among the court systems of the 50 states. Each state is sovereign regarding state law matters. Answer (C) is incorrect. All courts apply both substantive law, which defines rights and duties, and procedural law, which provides the means to apply the substantive law. Answer (D) is incorrect. A federal court may not decide a case if the parties are from the same state and no federal question is at issue.

5. In the U.S., which of the following is a true statement about trial courts?

A. The principal function of trial courts is to resolve disputes through determination of factual issues and application of the law to the facts thus found.

B. Juries are exclusively responsible for determination of the facts at trial.

C. The function of the trial court judge is to preside over all proceedings and to determine issues of law but not of fact.

D. The trial court judge determines all issues of law and fact in civil cases.

Answer (A) is correct. *(Publisher, adapted)*

REQUIRED: The true statement about the functions of trial courts.

DISCUSSION: The main service performed by the trial court is to act as a trier of fact. Trial court procedure primarily involves defining and resolving factual issues. A trial is never conducted unless a factual issue remains in the case. Appellate courts almost exclusively decide questions of law.

Answer (B) is incorrect. The jury is the primary fact-finding body, but the court (judge) must act as a trier of both law and fact in the many cases not involving juries. Answer (C) is incorrect. In a case heard without a jury, the judge is the trier of fact. Answer (D) is incorrect. If the case is tried by a jury, the jurors will determine the facts.

6. The functions of an appeals court include

A. Rendering decisions with precedential value, but only if made by the highest court in the system.

B. Reviewing actions of lower courts within the same system.

C. Reviewing errors of law and substituting new findings of fact.

D. Exercising exclusive jurisdiction over suits in equity.

Answer (B) is correct. *(Publisher, adapted)*

REQUIRED: The true statement of a function of an appeals court.

DISCUSSION: An appeals court is chiefly concerned with reviewing decisions made by lower courts within the same system. Due process requires that, in almost all cases, litigants have access to at least one appeal.

Answer (A) is incorrect. Decisions of lower-level appellate courts also have precedential effect. Moreover, reported trial court opinions may have some value as precedent. Answer (C) is incorrect. Although appeals courts also review the legal sufficiency of the evidence, they do not usually make new findings of facts. Answer (D) is incorrect. Our legal system observes no administrative distinction between suits in law and suits in equity.

7. Subject-matter jurisdiction is the court's

A. Power over the person of the defendant.

B. Power over a thing that allows it to seize and hold the object for some legal purpose.

C. Jurisdiction based on a person's interest in property.

D. Power to hear a particular category of cases.

Answer (D) is correct. *(Publisher, adapted)*

REQUIRED: The definition of subject-matter jurisdiction.

DISCUSSION: Subject-matter jurisdiction is the court's power to hear a particular type of case. Subject-matter jurisdiction is defined by constitutions and statutes.

Answer (A) is incorrect. Power over the person of the defendant is in personam jurisdiction. Answer (B) is incorrect. Power over a thing is referred to as in rem jurisdiction. Answer (C) is incorrect. Jurisdiction based on a person's interest in property is quasi in rem jurisdiction.

2.2 The Federal Court System

8. Which of the following is a true statement about the organization of the federal court system?

A. It has three levels of courts.

B. The United States district courts have greater authority than any federal court except the U.S. Supreme Court.

C. United States district courts are primarily appellate courts.

D. Any of the United States courts of appeals may review the decisions of any of the district courts.

Answer (A) is correct. *(Publisher, adapted)*

REQUIRED: The true statement about the organization of the federal court system.

DISCUSSION: The federal court system has three levels. The district courts are trial courts at the lowest level. The courts of appeals constitute the middle level. They are courts of review. At the top level is the Supreme Court. It principally reviews decisions of the courts of appeals.

Answer (B) is incorrect. The courts of appeals have power to review decisions of the district courts. Answer (C) is incorrect. The district courts are trial courts, not appellate courts. Answer (D) is incorrect. Each court of appeals reviews decisions of the district courts in its circuit. However, the Court of Appeals for the Federal Circuit hears specialized appeals, e.g., of patent, trademark, and copyright cases.

9. The federal judicial power is articulated in the Constitution. Under the Constitution,

A. The principal courts in the federal system are the U.S. district courts, the U.S. courts of appeals, and the Supreme Court.

B. Congress has power to limit the jurisdiction of the federal courts.

C. Federal judges hold office for specific terms of years.

D. Federal courts have unlimited subject-matter jurisdiction.

Answer (B) is correct. *(Publisher, adapted)*

REQUIRED: The true statement concerning the federal judicial power.

DISCUSSION: Article III, Section I, of the U.S. Constitution provides, "The judicial power of the United States shall be vested in one Supreme Court, and in such inferior courts as the Congress may from time to time ordain and establish." Because Congress has the power to establish the lower federal courts, the Supreme Court has held that it also has the power to limit their jurisdiction. Article III also gives Congress the power to regulate the Supreme Court's appellate jurisdiction.

Answer (A) is incorrect. Only the U.S. Supreme Court is expressly established by Article III of the Constitution. Answer (C) is incorrect. Article III provides that federal judges shall hold their offices during good behavior and not for a specific term of years. Answer (D) is incorrect. Federal courts have limited subject-matter jurisdiction.

10. Federal courts have broad but limited jurisdiction. In which instance would the federal courts not always have jurisdiction?

A. In a case arising under the U.S. Constitution.

B. In an admiralty case.

C. In a case in which the controversy is between two states.

D. In a controversy between citizens of different states.

Answer (D) is correct. *(Publisher, adapted)*

REQUIRED: The cases in which the federal courts have partial jurisdiction and the states have full jurisdiction.

DISCUSSION: A controversy between citizens of different states (diversity cases) may always be brought in one of the state courts. The judicial power of the United States also extends to diversity cases but only those in which the amount in controversy exceeds $75,000.

11. Curt Smith, a citizen of Florida, is injured in an auto accident in Miami. The driver of the other vehicle is a citizen of New York. Smith wishes to recover the $6,000 he incurred for medical expenses and repairs to his car. Can Smith bring an action in federal court based on diversity of citizenship?

A. No, because a citizen of one state cannot sue a citizen of another state in federal court.

B. No, because the suit would not involve a federal statute.

C. No, because diversity suits in federal court must involve more than $75,000.

D. Yes, because he and the driver of the other car are citizens of different states.

Answer (C) is correct. *(Publisher, adapted)*

REQUIRED: The requirements for bringing a diversity action in federal court.

DISCUSSION: A person can bring an action in federal court based on diversity of citizenship if (1) the plaintiff and the defendant are citizens of different states, and (2) the amount involved exceeds $75,000. In this case, Smith's action would fail because it does not involve the required minimum amount.

Answer (A) is incorrect. A citizen of one state can sue a citizen of another state in federal court if the requirements are met. Answer (B) is incorrect. Violation of a federal statute is not required in a diversity action. Answer (D) is incorrect. Diversity of citizenship alone is not sufficient. The amount in controversy must also exceed $75,000.

12. The United States courts of appeals

A. Have been established pursuant to congressional enactment.

B. Are expressly established by the Constitution.

C. Hear only cases appealed from U.S. district courts.

D. Hear cases only if more than $75,000 is in controversy.

Answer (A) is correct. *(Publisher, adapted)*

REQUIRED: The true statement concerning the United States courts of appeals.

DISCUSSION: The Constitution gives Congress the right to establish inferior federal courts in both Article I and Article III. Congress could dispense with the lower federal courts altogether.

Answer (B) is incorrect. There is no express mention of the courts of appeals in the Constitution. Answer (C) is incorrect. The courts of appeals do have some original jurisdiction, e.g., over the actions of certain administrative agencies. Answer (D) is incorrect. Federal courts have jurisdiction over all federal question cases.

13. The U.S. Supreme Court derives its powers from the Constitution. The Constitution establishes

A. The grant of certiorari jurisdiction to the U.S. Supreme Court.

B. That the Supreme Court has extensive original jurisdiction, which it shares concurrently with the lower federal courts.

C. Nine as the number of Supreme Court justices.

D. No express provision for judicial review.

Answer (D) is correct. *(Publisher, adapted)*

REQUIRED: The true statement concerning the U.S. Supreme Court.

DISCUSSION: Judicial review is the process by which the actions of the other branches of government are scrutinized by the appropriate court to determine their constitutionality. If the courts declare such an action to be unconstitutional, it is null and void. The authority for judicial review is not expressly granted in the Constitution. It arose from the Supreme Court's decisions interpreting the Constitution.

Answer (A) is incorrect. The Constitution does not mention certiorari (discretionary) jurisdiction. This appellate jurisdiction is conferred by statute. Answer (B) is incorrect. The Supreme Court's original jurisdiction is narrow and rarely exercised. Answer (C) is incorrect. The Constitution does not establish the number of justices that sit on the Supreme Court. The number is determined by federal statute.

14. The U.S. Supreme Court, a court that is "infallible because final," is the ultimate arbiter of law within the federal system. The Supreme Court

A. May function as a trial court in some cases.

B. Has no discretionary appellate jurisdiction.

C. Exercises mandatory appellate jurisdiction in several important classes of cases.

D. Has no original jurisdiction.

Answer (A) is correct. *(Publisher, adapted)*

REQUIRED: The true statement concerning the U.S. Supreme Court.

DISCUSSION: The Constitution gives the Supreme Court original or trial jurisdiction in certain cases, e.g., in cases involving foreign ministers and ambassadors. In practice, the Supreme Court's original jurisdiction is held concurrently with the lower federal courts (except for controversies between two or more states), and the Supreme Court refuses to exercise it.

Answer (B) is incorrect. Virtually all Supreme Court cases are heard at the discretion of the justices. Answer (C) is incorrect. The Supreme Court exercises mandatory appellate jurisdiction only in controversies between states. Answer (D) is incorrect. The Supreme Court has original jurisdiction in cases affecting ambassadors and similar persons and in cases in which a state is a party.

2.3 The State Court System

15. The subject-matter jurisdiction of state courts

A. Does not extend to cases arising under the U.S. Constitution.

B. Does not extend to cases involving persons residing in different states.

C. Extends to all cases except those over which the federal courts have exclusive jurisdiction.

D. Extends to all cases having "minimum contacts" with the particular state.

Answer (C) is correct. *(Publisher, adapted)*

REQUIRED: The true statement concerning subject-matter jurisdiction of state courts.

DISCUSSION: The states may exercise any powers not exclusively exercised by the federal government. Thus, the state courts may hear any case except one over which the federal courts have exclusive jurisdiction, e.g., bankruptcy, federal taxation, customs, and patent cases.

Answer (A) is incorrect. The jurisdiction of state and federal courts over cases arising under the U.S. Constitution is concurrent. Answer (B) is incorrect. Both state and federal courts have jurisdiction over diversity cases. But, unless the amount in controversy exceeds $75,000, the state courts have exclusive jurisdiction. Answer (D) is incorrect. Whether a person has "minimum contacts" with a state is relevant to the determination of personal, not subject-matter, jurisdiction.

16. A typical state court system includes all but which of the following?

A. A court of last resort.

B. Intermediate-level appeals courts.

C. Small claims courts.

D. Bankruptcy courts.

Answer (D) is correct. *(Publisher, adapted)*
REQUIRED: The court not found in a typical state court system.
DISCUSSION: Proceedings in bankruptcy are within the exclusive jurisdiction of the federal courts. Article I of the Constitution gives Congress the power to enact uniform laws on the subject of bankruptcy throughout the U.S.
Answer (A) is incorrect. Each state has a supreme court or court of last resort that is the final authority within that state on matters of state law. Answer (B) is incorrect. Most states have an intermediate level of appeals courts. Such courts typically handle the bulk of mandatory appeals from the trial courts within the system. Answer (C) is incorrect. The typical state court system includes small claims courts that hear minor claims in an informal and relatively inexpensive manner.

17. Which of the following statements regarding state courts is true?

A. Under the Supremacy Clause of the Constitution, state courts must uphold a federal law that conflicts with state law.

B. The U.S. Supreme Court has no authority to overrule the decisions of state supreme courts.

C. State courts cannot hear cases that involve questions of federal law.

D. A case begun in a state court cannot be transferred to a federal court.

Answer (A) is correct. *(Publisher, adapted)*
REQUIRED: The true statement regarding state courts.
DISCUSSION: Under the Supremacy Clause, a state statute is invalid if it is in direct conflict with a federal law. Hence, a state court must uphold a federal law if that law is in direct conflict with a state statute.
Answer (B) is incorrect. Under the doctrine of judicial review, the U.S. Supreme Court has the authority to overrule a state supreme court if the case involves a question of federal law. Answer (C) is incorrect. Many claims arising under federal law may be tried in state courts. Answer (D) is incorrect. If certain conditions are met, a case can be transferred (removed) from state to federal court.

18. Most state court systems include small claims courts for the resolution of minor disputes. In small claims court,

A. Appeals cannot be taken.

B. Jurisdictional amounts are not established.

C. The ordinary rules of civil procedure are often not followed.

D. Lawyers are never permitted.

Answer (C) is correct. *(Publisher, adapted)*
REQUIRED: The true statement about practices in a small claims court.
DISCUSSION: Small claims litigation varies from state to state, but an essential purpose of these courts is to assure affordability by expediting the resolution of minor legal disputes through a more informal civil procedure than that otherwise available. Formal pleadings, discovery, and evidentiary rules are dispensed with, and the judge often assumes the role of mediator between parties who represent themselves.
Answer (A) is incorrect. Some states permit appeals from small claims decisions. Answer (B) is incorrect. A low jurisdictional amount (e.g., $1,500) is established. Larger claims are litigated in regular courts. Answer (D) is incorrect. Some states permit representation by attorneys.

2.4 Federal Specialty Courts

19. The federal court system is a complex structure that includes numerous specialized courts. Which of the following is a national trial court?

A. U.S. district court.

B. Court of Appeals for the Federal Circuit.

C. U.S. Court of Federal Claims.

D. U.S. bankruptcy court.

Answer (C) is correct. *(Publisher, adapted)*
REQUIRED: The specialized federal court that functions as a national trial court.
DISCUSSION: The U.S. Court of Federal Claims is a trial-level court with nationwide jurisdiction. It hears cases involving monetary claims against the United States, including certain tax cases.
Answer (A) is incorrect. The jurisdiction of the district courts is usually limited to defendants subject to the jurisdiction of the courts of the state where the district court is located. Answer (B) is incorrect. It is an intermediate-level appellate court that hears appeals in certain specialized cases, e.g., from the Court of Federal Claims and the Court of International Trade. Answer (D) is incorrect. The bankruptcy courts are adjuncts to the district courts.

20. The Tax Court of the United States

A. Has removal jurisdiction with regard to tax cases originally filed in U.S. district court.

B. Has appellate jurisdiction of tax cases originating in the U.S. Court of Federal Claims.

C. Hears tax cases without juries.

D. Is not a true court but an administrative body within the Treasury Department.

Answer (C) is correct. *(Publisher, adapted)*

REQUIRED: The true statement concerning the Tax Court.

DISCUSSION: The Tax Court of the United States is established by Section 7441 of the Internal Revenue Code under Article I of the U.S. Constitution. It hears exclusively federal tax cases without juries. A jury trial of a federal tax case is available in a U.S. district court.

Answer (A) is incorrect. Removal jurisdiction applies to the removal of certain cases from state courts to federal district courts. Answer (B) is incorrect. Monetary claims brought against the United States in the U.S. Court of Federal Claims are appealed to the Court of Appeals for the Federal Circuit. Answer (D) is incorrect. The Tax Court is a court of record under Article I.

21. The federal judiciary includes the United States district courts. They

A. Are the exclusive trial courts in the federal court system.

B. Hear appeals from the U.S. Court of Federal Claims and the U.S. Tax Court.

C. Have removal jurisdiction in appropriate cases.

D. Have exclusive jurisdiction of claims against the U.S. government.

Answer (C) is correct. *(Publisher, adapted)*

REQUIRED: The true statement concerning the U.S. district courts.

DISCUSSION: If a civil action could originally have been brought in a district court and if the case has not yet gone to trial, a nonresident defendant in a state court may have the case automatically removed to the appropriate U.S. district court.

Answer (A) is incorrect. The Tax Court, the U.S. Court of Federal Claims, and the bankruptcy courts are also trial courts within the federal system. Answer (B) is incorrect. Appeals from the U.S. Court of Federal Claims are heard by the Court of Appeals for the Federal Circuit. Appeals from the Tax Court are heard by the Circuit Courts of Appeals. Answer (D) is incorrect. Nontort claims against the U.S. government are heard by the U.S. Court of Federal Claims.

STUDY UNIT THREE
CIVIL LITIGATION AND PROCEDURE

Civil litigation is an adversarial proceeding in which a party, the **plaintiff**, may sue another party, the **defendant**, to obtain redress for a wrong committed by the defendant. Civil litigation is primarily compensatory and awards monetary judgments for losses caused by injury to legally recognized interests. Hence, it differs from a criminal proceeding, which is primarily undertaken for punishment or deterrence. In a civil action, the plaintiff seeks to force the defendant either to act or to refrain from acting in a specified manner, or to pay monetary damages as a result of a prior act or omission. In some cases, the plaintiff may seek a declaration of the rights of the parties to a dispute as a means of determining whether expected future conduct will be wrongful and likely to result in liability. The two primary types of civil proceedings are in contract and in tort. In a **civil suit in contract**, a party alleges that another party breached an enforceable agreement. In a **civil suit in tort**, a party alleges that another party breached a legal duty arising from society's expectations of acceptable conduct and that the breach caused injury to the person or property of the complaining party. Civil litigation is a court-supervised proceeding in which the opposing parties seek to demonstrate that their respective views of the law or the facts are correct and that they are entitled to prevail. The plaintiff and the defendant, through their attorneys, present their contrary views of the facts and the law to a theoretically impartial judge and, in many cases, a jury. This study unit focuses on civil litigation in federal courts. Civil litigation in state courts varies somewhat from state to state, although procedural laws similar to those of federal courts are used.

An injury of a person by another does not necessarily give the victim a cause of action. A **cause of action** is a **claim** sufficient in law and fact to demand judicial attention. It is the right by which a party may institute a judicial proceeding. This right belongs to a particular person or class of persons and is said to accrue or to exist at the moment when the injury occurs. The holder of this right has **standing** to sue. Thus, to proceed, a plaintiff must demonstrate a cause of action. The plaintiff initiates the lawsuit by filing with the court a statement called a **complaint** setting forth the cause of action. If the complaint fails to state a proper cause of action, it will be dismissed. The complaint must contain sufficient facts to inform the court and the defendant of the nature of the plaintiff's case. Ordinarily, the plaintiff will have the burden of proving the facts constituting his/her cause of action. If a plaintiff fails to meet his/her burden of proof, the defendant will prevail in the suit. In civil cases, a party's **burden of proof** is met if an assertion is supported by a preponderance of the evidence. In contrast, the prosecution's burden of proof in a criminal case is to establish guilt beyond a reasonable doubt. A further requirement is that a plaintiff file suit in a timely manner, that is, typically within a specified number of years, depending upon the type of lawsuit. For example, the typical **statute of limitations** allows 5 years to bring an action on a breach of contract. A plaintiff who waits too long to sue after (s)he is wronged loses the right to assert a claim even if it is otherwise meritorious.

Jurisdiction is the power of a court to hear a case and render an enforceable decision. Without proper jurisdiction, a court's judgment is void. A court must have both subject-matter jurisdiction and one of the following:

- Personal jurisdiction
- In rem jurisdiction
- Quasi in rem jurisdiction

Subject-matter jurisdiction exists if the lawsuit is of the type the court is empowered to hear. **Personal (in personam) jurisdiction** is the power of a court to render a binding decision affecting the interests of specific parties in a case. Personal jurisdiction is obtained over the plaintiff when the plaintiff files the complaint. Filing is deemed to be a voluntary submission to the power of the court. Jurisdiction over the defendant is usually obtained by **service of process**, that is, by serving the defendant with a copy of the complaint and a summons. Procedural statutes provide for constructive or substituted service of process. **In rem jurisdiction** is a state's jurisdiction over property located in the state. The legal proceeding is directed against the property itself. Hence, binding disposition as to the interest of a party in the property might result even when the court lacks personal jurisdiction over the party. **Quasi in rem jurisdiction** (attachment jurisdiction) is based on a defendant's interest in property located in a state, although the action is directed against a person (defendant) and is unrelated to the property.

To obtain personal jurisdiction over non-residents, most states have enacted **long-arm statutes** that local courts apply when the cause of action is generated locally or affects local plaintiffs. The U.S. Supreme Court has authorized long-arm jurisdiction if the contacts of the nonresident defendant with the forum state are such that exercise of jurisdiction does not offend traditional notions of fair play and substantial justice. The contacts described by the Supreme Court are often referred to as **minimum contacts**. Most long-arm statutes define minimum contacts. Typically, they provide that minimum contacts include any business whatsoever conducted within the state, including advertising. The use of the **Internet** for business purposes has created novel jurisdictional issues. The evolving approach is the **sliding-scale standard**. Doing substantial business over the Internet, such as making sales and entering into contracts, meets jurisdictional requirements, whereas mere passive advertising does not. Depending on the facts, a degree of interactivity with a website may or may not meet the test. The **venue** of a lawsuit is the location of the proceedings. Thus, it addresses the choice of the county or district within a court system's territory where a case may be heard. The party's right to have the action brought and heard in a convenient forum is the crux of the venue decision. For example, under the federal venue statute for diversity cases, a civil action may be brought in a judicial district where (1) any defendant resides (if all reside in the same state), (2) a substantial part of the events or omissions giving rise to the claim occurred, or the property that is the subject of the action is situated, or (3) any defendant is subject to personal jurisdiction if there is no other district in which suit may be brought. The venue statute for federal question cases is the same except that (3) is replaced by any district where any defendant may be found if there is no district in which the action may be brought.

In a **class action suit**, one or more members of a class may sue or be sued as representative parties on behalf of all members only if (1) the class is so numerous that joinder of all members is impracticable; (2) there are questions of law or fact common to the class; (3) the claims or defenses of the representative parties are typical of the claims or defenses of the class; and (4) the representative parties will fairly and adequately protect the interests of the class. Thus, a class action involves similarly situated persons who have been injured by the same defendant or who may be liable to the same plaintiff. A class action usually involves matters in which no one member of the class would have a sufficient financial interest to warrant litigation. However, combining the interests of all members of the class makes litigation feasible.

Pleadings are filed in the first stage of civil litigation. Pleadings normally consist of filing paper or electronic documents. The pleadings notify the parties and the courts about the nature of the case. Pleadings are statements, in logical and legal form, of the law and facts that constitute the plaintiff's cause of action and the defendant's grounds for defense. The pleadings affirm or deny certain matters of fact or other statements by the parties in support of their respective arguments. The pleadings traditionally consist of the following: (1) complaint, (2) answer, (3) counterclaim, (4) crossclaim, and (5) reply. The plaintiff initiates the lawsuit by filing the complaint with the clerk of the court. The complaint must contain a short and plain statement of the (1) claim showing that the pleader is entitled to relief and (2) grounds for the court's jurisdiction. It also should contain a demand for relief.

After the defendant is served a copy of the summons and complaint, the defendant must file a response with the court to avoid a **judgment by default**. In general, a responsive pleading must (1) state in short and plain terms the party's defenses to claims and (2) admit or deny allegations. The response ordinarily is an answer or a motion. An **answer** may contain either a general denial or specific denials of the allegations contained in the complaint. Under federal rules, the answer must contain one or more affirmative defenses if they are applicable. The answer also may contain a counterclaim against the plaintiff. A **counterclaim** asserts an independent cause of action of the defendant against the plaintiff. The purpose of a counterclaim is either to oppose or to offset the plaintiff's claim. Furthermore, a defendant may file a motion instead of an answer. A **crossclaim** may be asserted against a co-party (a fellow defendant or plaintiff). After a counterclaim, the plaintiff files a **reply**, a pleading similar to an answer. In federal courts, an answer is filed in response to a complaint, counterclaim, or crossclaim. A reply to answer is filed only if ordered by the court. A **motion** is an application to the court requesting an order or a ruling in favor of the applicant. In modern practice, many pretrial motions may be filed. Pretrial motions are used to determine issues in a case and to gain strategic advantages. Pretrial motions may (1) challenge the existence of subject-matter or personal jurisdiction; (2) challenge venue; (3) challenge service of the complaint; (4) seek a more definite statement; (5) move to strike an insufficient defense or any inappropriate matter; (6) assert a failure to join a required party; (7) allege failure to state a claim upon which relief may be granted, i.e., a failure to state a cause of action (also known as a demurrer); (8) move for judgment on the pleadings; (9) request additional discovery; and (10) request summary judgment. During the pleadings and at any time prior to the verdict, either party to the lawsuit may make a motion for summary judgment. In a motion for **summary judgment**, a party argues that, based on the pleadings and discovery (a compelled disclosure of facts by the parties), the moving party is entitled to a judgment under the law. In other words, the evidence is so clear that the moving party is legally entitled to prevail. In federal courts, a party claiming relief may move for a summary judgment at any time after 20 days have passed from commencement of the case. A defending party may file this motion at any time.

In preparing for trial and to encourage early settlement, each party has the right to learn as much as possible about the adversary's case before trial. Discovery serves this purpose. **Discovery** assists the parties in determining the extent and content of evidence, who the potential witnesses are, and what specific issues may be relevant. Discovery also helps to preserve relevant evidence that might otherwise be lost, and prevents surprise at trial. Surprise is undesirable because lack of preparation inhibits the truth-ascertainment process. That is, a party may not have time to fashion the most effective argument if confronted with new evidence during a trial. Indeed, in federal courts, each party to a civil suit must disclose, without being asked, (1) the names and contact data of persons who are likely to have discoverable information, (2) copies or descriptions of documents or other tangibles that the party controls, and (3) insurance agreements. Discovery not only assists the parties in preparing their arguments but also narrows the issues to be resolved. In all jurisdictions, the scope of discovery in civil litigation is broad (less extensive discovery is undertaken in criminal cases).

Although the permissible limits of discovery are set by statute and overseen by the trial judge, the actual process is conducted by lawyers, not the court. Discovery can consume days, weeks, or even months. It may proceed in several ways:

1. **Interrogatories** are written answers made under oath to written questions.
2. **Requests for admissions** are used to ascertain the authenticity of a document or the truth of an assertion.
3. **Requests for production** involve the inspection of documents, electronically stored information, and property.
4. **Depositions** consist of out-of-court testimony made orally under oath by the opposing party or other witnesses.
5. **Requests for mental and physical examinations.**

In the federal system and most states, a **pretrial conference** is conducted for all civil suits. A pretrial conference is a meeting of the judge and all attorneys that has two primary purposes: (1) to shorten the trial by refining or narrowing the issues and (2) to encourage settlements. At the end of a pretrial conference, if no settlement has been reached, the judge sets a date for the trial. In the absence of a settlement, the judge will enter a pretrial order containing all of the amendments to the pleadings, stipulations regarding the facts, and other matters agreed to in the pretrial conference. This pretrial order controls the remainder of the trial. For example, witnesses not listed and approved at the pretrial conference will ordinarily not be allowed to testify.

Once the case has proceeded through discovery and survived any pretrial motions, it is set for trial if no settlement has occurred. The most basic function of a **trial** is to settle disputes. The litigants have their day in court to present their evidence and legal theories. A judge presides over the trial to ensure that only proper legal arguments and evidence are presented. Thus, the primary role of the judge is to maintain order in the adversarial process and to provide authoritative decisions on issues of law. In federal courts, the Seventh Amendment to the U.S. Constitution requires trial by jury in civil cases. This provision does not apply to the states. However, state constitutions provide for jury trials in most civil cases. The function of the **jury** is to resolve factual disputes (unless a jury trial either is unavailable or has been waived, in which case the judge assumes this function). At the end of a trial, a verdict is announced. The court then pronounces judgment, usually in accordance with the verdict.

In a jury trial, the initial step is to select the jury. The jury selection process, called a **voir dire**, gives each party an opportunity to challenge the selection of any prospective juror if that juror cannot evaluate the evidence impartially. Attorneys representing each party are allowed an unlimited number of challenges for cause and a limited number of peremptory challenges. A **peremptory challenge** permits a party to dismiss a prospective juror without cause. In a federal court, however, the process differs because the judge selects the jury.

After the jury has been selected, each attorney makes an **opening statement**. The plaintiff's attorney customarily makes the first opening statement. The purpose of the opening statement is to describe the case and to indicate the types of evidence to be offered. However, the opening statements are not evidence. The plaintiff has the initial burden of proof and must introduce evidence to support the allegations set forth in the complaint. If the plaintiff fails to meet the burden of proof at the outset, the defendant can move for the judge to dismiss the case even if the defendant has not yet presented evidence at trial.

The two primary kinds of evidence are testimony of a witness and physical evidence. A witness swears (or affirms under penalty of perjury) that (s)he will tell the truth. The witness then offers testimony upon direct examination. **Direct examination** is the initial questioning of a witness by the party who called the witness. **Cross-examination** is the questioning of a witness by a party other than the one who called the witness. Cross-examination is limited to the scope of the direct examination. The party that originally introduced the witness may then question the witness on redirect examination to clarify points raised on cross-examination. During the trial, the judge rules on the admission or exclusion of both physical and testimonial evidence. The **trial record** is made up of the pleadings and a transcript of the entire trial court proceedings. As a result of an objection and an offer of proof, the record also may refer to certain evidence not heard by the jury that the judge has ruled inadmissible. Objections play an extremely important role. An **objection** indicates to the court that it may be making a mistake by either allowing or disallowing certain activity in the trial. If an attorney fails to object, the client loses the right to raise that issue on appeal. The plaintiff rests [i.e., announces that (s)he has finished presenting evidence] after completing the presentation of witnesses and physical evidence.

When the plaintiff rests in a jury trial, the defendant may make a motion for a **directed verdict**. To grant this motion, the judge must be convinced that, after considering all the evidence with all reasonable inferences drawn most favorably to the plaintiff, the evidence is so clearly in the defendant's favor that reasonable minds could not differ. If the defendant's motion is granted, a **judgment of nonsuit** is entered in favor of the defendant. In a federal court, after a party has been fully heard on an issue, the other party may make a **motion for judgment as a matter of law** on that issue. This motion is allowed at any time before submission of the case to the jury. After all evidence is presented, either side may move for a directed verdict. If it is denied, the attorneys make **closing arguments**. Each attorney will review the evidence produced by his/her side and emphasize its adequacy and credibility. (S)he will also point out the weaknesses in the other side's case. Closing arguments are not evidence.

After closing arguments, the judge normally **instructs the jury**. The jury usually determines the facts in the case, applies the law as instructed by the judge, and reaches a decision called a **verdict** for the plaintiff or the defendant. In jury cases, when the jury has reached its verdict, it returns to the courtroom and, in the presence of the judge, announces the decision. A **general verdict** simply declares which party prevails and does not include any special findings of fact. A **special verdict** consists of answers to specific factual questions posed by the judge without an attempt to reach a decision for either party. The judge then applies the law to the facts found. If there is no jury, the judge renders the verdict.

The final phase in a trial is the rendering of the **judgment**. Two types of relief may be provided by a judgment:

1. An award may be made to the prevailing party of cost, damages, or restoration of property.
2. The defendant may be ordered (enjoined) to act or refrain from acting.

After a judgment is entered, a **motion for a new trial** may be made by either party. A motion for a new trial argues that a serious legal error was made by the judge during the first trial. If a motion for a new trial is granted, the case is again put on the trial calendar. If the motion is dismissed, the moving party may appeal. Often, after the judgment in a jury trial is entered, the losing party will make a motion for **judgment notwithstanding the verdict** (often called a JNOV after the Latin initials for this phrase). In this motion, the losing party argues that (s)he is entitled to a judgment under the law even though the jury rendered a contrary verdict. A judge will grant the motion and enter the judgment for the losing party only when no substantial evidence supports the decision by the jury. "Substantial," in this context, refers not only to the weight of the evidence but also to its relevance to an issue to be resolved. In federal courts, a party that previously moved for a **judgment as a matter of law** may renew the motion within 10 days after entry of judgment.

The typical tool for enforcing legal relief is a writ of execution. A **writ of execution** is a court order enforcing the judgment.

After the entry of the judgment, either party may file an appeal to a higher court. The appealing party is the **appellant**, and the party appealed against is the **appellee**. The loser is more likely to file an appeal, but sometimes the winner appeals, alleging that the damages awarded were inadequate. In the appellate process, the higher court does not retry the case. No evidence is allowed and no jury is empaneled. The appellate court reviews the trial record to determine whether any errors of law or procedure were made. Typically, the appellate court also listens to oral arguments. The attorneys for the parties submit written briefs to support their arguments. Common reasons for appeal are that the trial court erred in one of the following aspects of the trial:

1. Admitting or excluding testimony
2. Ruling on motions
3. Misstating the law during jury instructions
4. Interpreting state or federal statutes

After consideration of the record, the arguments presented, and the briefs, the appellate court announces its decision in writing.

Efficiency and fairness demand an end to litigation. Outside the context of the initial action and any appeals therefrom, a party may not relitigate either a claim or an issue that was actually litigated and determined. However, this initial litigation must have resulted in a valid and final judgment on the merits by a court of competent jurisdiction. Such a claim or issue is said to be res judicata. **Res judicata** means "the matter is decided." If the court in which the judgment is rendered properly exercised jurisdiction, courts in other jurisdictions are required to enforce the judgment. It does not establish a binding precedent in the jurisdiction enforcing the judgment. The **full faith and credit clause** in Article IV of the U.S. Constitution requires each state to give full faith and credit to the public acts, records, and judicial proceedings of other states. It permits a final judgment entered in a court in one state to be enforced in other jurisdictions without retrying the case.

Alternative dispute resolution (ADR) is a nonjudicial method of resolving civil disputes. Rather than filing a lawsuit, the adverse parties agree to allow a neutral third party to hear the dispute. ADR may be used because the regular courts are overcrowded, civil litigation is very expensive, or public policy and economic concerns favor ADR over litigation.

The common forms of ADR are arbitration, mediation, minitrials, and conciliation, but other forms have been developed. **Arbitration** involves third-party intervention. Arbitrators are empowered to make binding decisions. **Mediation** also involves third-party intervention, but the goal is to persuade those involved to settle the dispute themselves. Mediators make suggestions and do not make decisions. **Minitrials** are informal, off-the-record proceedings. No single procedural model of the minitrial has been universally adopted. One possibility is for the lawyers to present their cases to neutral third-party experts. Another possibility is for each side to argue its case before a decision maker on the other side. The goal is that, after both sides have been heard informally, the parties will agree to a settlement without a long and costly trial. **Conciliation** is an informal process whereby a third party is selected by the adversarial parties to facilitate a negotiated agreement. The settlement may result informally because of the conciliation itself or through subsequent formal mediation.

Conciliation is frequently used in extremely volatile conflicts. It differs from mediation in that the conciliator does not make suggestions for solving the problems causing the dispute. The **summary jury trial** is used in many federal courts. The jury's decision is not binding, but provides a basis for subsequent mandatory negotiations. **Early neutral case evaluation** entails submission of the cases of the opposing parties to a neutral expert who assesses their merits. The assessment is then used as a framework for negotiation. ADR has reached the Internet through **online dispute resolution** services offered in forums that provide negotiation and mediation assistance, usually concerning disagreements about sales of goods online or domain names.

QUESTIONS

3.1 Preliminary Issues

1. A statute of limitations compels a plaintiff to bring an action within a reasonable time. It prevents unfairness to defendants, avoids state claims, and encourages litigation while witnesses and evidence are still available. The typical statute

A. Begins to run when the last element constituting the cause of action occurs.

B. Requires that litigation be completed before it expires.

C. Begins to run when the first element constituting the cause of action occurs.

D. Permits tolling only for the plaintiff's incapacity.

Answer (A) is correct. *(Publisher, adapted)*

REQUIRED: The true statement about the application of a statute of limitations.

DISCUSSION: A statute of limitations applies to most civil and criminal actions. It codifies the common law principle of laches: Undue delay in bringing a suit, with consequent prejudice to the other party, results in forfeiture of the right. The statutory period begins to run when the plaintiff's right to bring suit arises, that is, when the last element constituting the cause of action occurs.

Answer (B) is incorrect. Filing the complaint tolls (suspends) the statute. Answer (C) is incorrect. The period begins to run when the last element occurs. Answer (D) is incorrect. The running of the statute is suspended (tolled) for various reasons, e.g., insanity, absence of the defendant from the jurisdiction, court order, or minority of the plaintiff.

2. Before a party may seek judicial relief, (s)he must establish not only that the particular court has subject matter and personal jurisdiction but also that the case is appropriate for judicial resolution. Which is the false statement concerning justiciability of controversies?

A. In the federal system, a court may not hear a case unless it presents a "case or controversy" within the meaning of the U.S. Constitution.

B. Courts refuse to decide collusive suits because the adversary system requires that the opposing parties have a genuine dispute with substantial consequences for each side.

C. A party must have standing.

D. Moot issues are justiciable.

Answer (D) is correct. *(Publisher, adapted)*

REQUIRED: The false statement about justiciability of controversies.

DISCUSSION: The adversary system is based on the theory that courts function best when the parties before it have a genuine dispute the resolution of which has actual consequences for each. If the issues of a case have become moot with the passage of time, a court will normally not regard the case as fit for decision on the merits.

Answer (A) is incorrect. Article III of the Constitution provides that the judicial power may be exercised only when a "case or controversy" exists, i.e., a genuine dispute with legal consequences. Answer (B) is incorrect. The court will not hear the case if the participation of one party has been procured by the adverse party solely to obtain a forum. Answer (C) is incorrect. A party must have standing to bring a cause of action; i.e., the party must claim a direct and immediate injury.

3. A state court is least likely to have jurisdiction over the person of the defendant when (s)he

A. Has no contacts with the forum state but is personally served with process in another state.

B. Has a residence in the forum state, and process is served at the residence.

C. Consents even though no other basis for jurisdiction exists.

D. Cannot be located, and the plaintiff in a divorce action advertises in a local newspaper.

Answer (A) is correct. *(Publisher, adapted)*

REQUIRED: The method of acquiring personal jurisdiction least likely to be effective.

DISCUSSION: Service of process (a copy of the summons and of the complaint) on a person within the forum state is effective to gain jurisdiction. Personal service outside the state is ineffective unless the defendant has minimum contacts with the jurisdiction.

Answer (B) is incorrect. When a defendant has a domicile in the forum state, leaving the summons and complaint at that place with a person of mature years is usually sufficient. Answer (C) is incorrect. A defendant may always consent to personal jurisdiction. Answer (D) is incorrect. Serving process by mail sent to the defendant's last known address and advertising periodically in a publication of general circulation (constructive service) may provide adequate notice when the person cannot be located.

4. Lu Walker lived in Georgia. Returning by automobile from Texas, while traveling on a Florida highway, Walker struck a vehicle driven by Harley Kell, a Florida resident on his way to Alabama. After stopping for repairs, Walker left Florida, never to return. Walker had no other contacts with the state. If Kell wishes to sue Walker for negligence, he

A. Must bring the action in a Georgia state court.

B. Must bring the action in federal court.

C. May bring the suit in a state court in Georgia or Florida or in a federal court, but Georgia law will apply.

D. May bring the action in Florida under Florida law.

Answer (D) is correct. *(Publisher, adapted)*

REQUIRED: The court where suit may be filed when negligence is committed by an out-of-state defendant.

DISCUSSION: Long-arm statutes solve the problem of personal jurisdiction over nonresidents who commit torts while temporarily in the state. Although the defendant's contact with the state may have consisted solely of an automobile accident, the typical long-arm statute allows extension of jurisdiction provided that the suit arose out of the contact. Kell's action in Florida would probably be tried under Florida law because the injury and the minimum contact occurred in Florida.

Answer (A) is incorrect. The lawsuit could be brought in Florida or Georgia (where the defendant resides) or even in federal court if the damages exceed $75,000. Answer (B) is incorrect. The lawsuit could be brought in Florida or Georgia (where the defendant resides) or even in federal court if the damages exceed $75,000. Answer (C) is incorrect. Florida law will probably apply. The minimum contact and the injury occurred in Florida, and it has the greatest interest in having its law applied.

5. An essential guarantee in the American legal system is that a litigant must have timely notice and a reasonable opportunity to be heard before a court may affect his/her rights. Which of the following is true with regard to the notice requirement?

A. The U.S. Supreme Court has held that a defendant in a civil suit must in every case receive either personal notice or notice by mail of a pending action.

B. The U.S. Supreme Court has held that the proper form of notice is what is reasonable in the circumstances.

C. Most state statutes do not provide for notice by substituted service or by publication in appropriate circumstances.

D. The principal constitutional underpinning for the right to notice lies in the Equal Protection Clause.

Answer (B) is correct. *(Publisher, adapted)*

REQUIRED: The true statement about the requirement of notice.

DISCUSSION: Before a court may exert personal jurisdiction over a defendant, due process requires that (s)he be served with appropriate notice. The Supreme Court has held that the requirements of due process are met if notice is given that is reasonable in the circumstances. The circumstances might dictate that actual notice be given. In other cases, when the whereabouts or identity of the parties is unknown, notice by publication may suffice.

Answer (A) is incorrect. The U.S. Supreme Court has adopted only a reasonableness standard with respect to notice. Answer (C) is incorrect. Most state statutes do provide for substituted service and notice by publication. Substituted service of process involves leaving a copy of the complaint and a summons with a person of mature years at the residence of the defendant. Notice by publication involves a legal notice in a paper of general circulation when the location of the defendant is unknown. Answer (D) is incorrect. The Due Process Clause is the constitutional basis for the notice requirement.

6. An essential preliminary step before a court may take up a dispute is to determine whether that court is the proper venue for adjudication of the case.

A. The concept of the inconvenient forum (forum non conveniens) permits a court with jurisdiction to decline to exercise it.

B. A defect in venue is assertable at any time before the conclusion of litigation.

C. Venue is proper only in the location that is the most convenient for the parties, the witnesses, and the court.

D. Venue is a concern only in federal courts.

Answer (A) is correct. *(Publisher, adapted)*

REQUIRED: The true statement about venue.

DISCUSSION: When a court has jurisdiction over the subject matter and the parties, the court will customarily exercise it. The doctrine of the inconvenient forum is an exception to a court's duty to exercise its jurisdiction. If bringing suit in the forum state would seriously inconvenience the courts, parties, or witnesses, and if a more convenient forum is available elsewhere, the forum court may dismiss the suit without prejudice to the plaintiff's rights to bring the action in another court.

Answer (B) is incorrect. A defect in venue must be objected to at an early stage in litigation for it not to be waived. Answer (C) is incorrect. The venue rules do not attempt to locate the action in the best forum, only a reasonably convenient one. Answer (D) is incorrect. Every state has rules concerning the appropriate venue for an action.

7. A fundamental problem in adjudicating disputes is the choice of the law to be applied by the court. The problem is especially acute when a court in one state must decide a case involving either a party domiciled in another state or a cause of action that arose in another state. State choice-of-law rules

A. Ordinarily follow the law of the place of the injury in tort actions.

B. Are usually based on some variation of interest analysis.

C. Apply the law of the forum state in a state court.

D. Forbid parties to choose the applicable law in transactions governed by the UCC.

Answer (B) is correct. *(Publisher, adapted)*
REQUIRED: The true statement about state choice-of-law rules.
DISCUSSION: For lawsuits involving parties from more than one jurisdiction, courts have evolved conflict-of-law (choice-of-law) rules to determine which law to apply. The majority of states follow the interest analysis approach, which requires an application of the minimum contacts doctrine and a determination of which jurisdiction has the greatest relationship to the facts and parties. The substantive law of that jurisdiction is then used.
Answer (A) is incorrect. Although the traditional rule in tort actions was to follow the law of the place of the injury, today the trend is to use some form of interest analysis. Answer (C) is incorrect. The court will always apply its own procedural law but not necessarily its own substantive law. Answer (D) is incorrect. The UCC permits parties to choose the applicable law subject to a reasonable relationship test.

8. The class action suit permits numerous persons with individually insignificant claims to vindicate their rights. Which of the following is ordinarily a requirement for class action suits?

A. Members of the class who do not actively participate in the lawsuit are not bound by the judgment.

B. Questions of law but not of fact must be common to all members of the class.

C. All members of the class must be named as parties.

D. The class must be represented by parties whose claims are typical.

Answer (D) is correct. *(Publisher, adapted)*
REQUIRED: The class action requirement ordinarily applicable.
DISCUSSION: In a class action suit, questions of law and fact must ordinarily be common to everyone in the class, the class must be too large for all members to be named as parties, the claims of class representatives must be typical, and the representatives must fairly and adequately represent the class. The Supreme Court has also said that notice must be given to all members of the class when they can be "identified through reasonable efforts."
Answer (A) is incorrect. Members of the class who are notified of the class action are bound by the judgment unless they ask to be excluded when first notified. Answer (B) is incorrect. Questions of both law and fact must be common. Answer (C) is incorrect. The class is too numerous for all plaintiffs to be named.

3.2 Pleadings and Pretrial Motions

9. The initial stage of a civil lawsuit involves the filing of pleadings by the respective parties. The purpose of pleadings is to give notice to the parties and to the court of the assertions of each side and to assist in the determination of the issues. The complaint is the first pleading filed and has the effect of initiating the lawsuit. The complaint should include all except which of the following?

A. A short statement of the jurisdictional facts.

B. A request for relief.

C. An exact listing of what the plaintiff must prove couched in precise legal terminology.

D. A short and plain statement of the basis for the plaintiff's claim.

Answer (C) is correct. *(Publisher, adapted)*
REQUIRED: The item not required to appear in a complaint.
DISCUSSION: Modern pleading rules have considerably simplified the task of the parties to a lawsuit. The complaint does not need to include any detailed listing of proof or be phrased in legal terminology.
Answer (A) is incorrect. The complaint should indicate facts sufficient to establish both the subject-matter jurisdiction and personal jurisdiction of the court. Answer (B) is incorrect. The complaint should indicate the nature of the relief sought by the claimant. Answer (D) is incorrect. The complaint should include sufficient facts to enable the court and the opposing party to understand the basis for the plaintiff's claim.

10. The rules of civil procedure provide numerous occasions for the parties to make motions to the court. A motion is essentially an application to the court for an order. Motions appropriate at the pleading stage include a motion

A. For a directed verdict.

B. To dismiss for failure to state a claim upon which relief could be granted.

C. To strike evidence.

D. For a new trial.

Answer (B) is correct. *(Publisher, adapted)*

REQUIRED: The motion appropriate at the pleading stage.

DISCUSSION: A motion to dismiss for failure to state a claim is appropriate at the pleading stage because it tests the legal sufficiency of the opponent's claim for relief. It will be granted if the claim does not state an injury for which the law will give a remedy.

Answer (A) is incorrect. A motion for a directed verdict is appropriate only after the defendant's evidence is presented. Answer (C) is incorrect. A motion to strike evidence is appropriate only at trial. Answer (D) is incorrect. A motion for a new trial would only be appropriate during or after trial.

11. The rules of civil procedure permit a case to be disposed of in appropriate circumstances during or at the conclusion of the pleading stage. One such vehicle for early resolution of the case is the summary judgment. A summary judgment is

A. Granted if a genuine issue of material fact remains.

B. Considered the same as a judgment on the pleadings.

C. Decided on the merits.

D. Not granted as to only a portion of a case.

Answer (C) is correct. *(Publisher, adapted)*

REQUIRED: The true statement about a summary judgment.

DISCUSSION: At any time before the beginning of the trial, the court may grant a motion for summary judgment. The early disposition of the case in this manner is based upon the absence of any genuine dispute of material fact between the parties. Pleadings, affidavits, and testimony are considered. The judgment rendered is on the merits of the case, not on a procedural or technical ground.

Answer (A) is incorrect. Summary disposition is not permissible when a genuine issue of material fact remains to be determined by the trier of fact. Answer (B) is incorrect. A judgment on the pleadings is rendered solely on the basis of what appears on the face of the pleadings. Answer (D) is incorrect. A summary judgment may be partial; e.g., it may be rendered with regard to the issue of liability, with trial going forward on the issue of damages.

3.3 Discovery and Pretrial Conference

12. If a case has survived the pleading stage, the next procedural step is discovery. Discovery serves each of the following purposes except

A. Providing an opportunity to preserve relevant information.

B. Eliminating issues between the parties by agreement.

C. Compelling a party to disclose relevant information in his/her possession.

D. Permitting a party to develop his/her own case to the fullest while preserving the element of surprise.

Answer (D) is correct. *(Publisher, adapted)*

REQUIRED: The purpose not served by discovery.

DISCUSSION: A principal purpose of discovery is to avoid surprise. In theory, each side is entitled to notice of the content of the other side's case to provide an opportunity to prepare to meet it. Surprise undermines the basis of the adversarial system, which emphasizes permitting each side to present the best possible case. A secondary purpose of discovery is to facilitate settlements and reduce court workloads.

Answer (A) is incorrect. Discovery enables preservation of evidence, e.g., testimony that might be lost if the witness became unavailable. Answer (B) is incorrect. Discovery can help refine the issues so that only those in genuine dispute are considered at the trial. Answer (C) is incorrect. An adversary can be compelled to disclose relevant information in his/her possession.

13. Permissible methods of discovery under the federal rules of civil procedure do not include

A. Depositions.

B. Physical or mental examinations without a court order.

C. Written requests for admissions.

D. Interrogatories addressed to parties.

Answer (B) is correct. *(Publisher, adapted)*

REQUIRED: The impermissible method of discovery.

DISCUSSION: Physical and mental examinations are a permissible method of discovery only if made pursuant to a court order. Such an examination involves a substantial invasion of the person.

Answer (A) is incorrect. A deposition is a proper method of discovering and preserving information by the examination of a person. A court order is not required. Answer (C) is incorrect. One may make a formal written request for an admission by the opposing party. A bad faith refusal to admit may result in an imposition of sanctions by the judge. Answer (D) is incorrect. One may submit written questions (called interrogatories) to the opposing party to solicit relevant information.

14. The pretrial conference is a valuable aid to the efficient administration of the trial phase. At the pretrial conference, the trial judge and the attorneys consider a variety of matters not including

A. Sharpening and simplifying the issues.

B. Limiting the number of witnesses and testimony.

C. Exploring the possibility of an out-of-court settlement.

D. Extending the suit to embrace other claims.

Answer (D) is correct. *(Publisher, adapted)*

REQUIRED: The matter not properly considered at the pretrial conference.

DISCUSSION: The pretrial conference is informal. The attorneys and the judge endeavor to dispose of the case without trial or to simplify the issues and in general provide guidelines for the most efficient presentation of the respective cases at trial. The result of the conference is a pretrial order that governs the subsequent conduct of litigation. The presentation of other claims would not be appropriate at the conference.

Answer (A) is incorrect. It represents a proper function of the pretrial conference. Answer (B) is incorrect. It represents a proper function of the pretrial conference. Answer (C) is incorrect. It represents a proper function of the pretrial conference.

3.4 The Trial

15. Trial by jury in a civil case

A. Is not available in a federal court for most suits at common law.

B. Is available in a federal court if the suit is filed in equity.

C. Is guaranteed by the typical state constitution whether the suit is legal or equitable.

D. Is guaranteed in federal courts for suits at common law.

Answer (D) is correct. *(Publisher, adapted)*

REQUIRED: The true statement about trial by jury in a civil case.

DISCUSSION: The Seventh Amendment, which applies directly to the federal government, provides for trial by jury in suits at common law (but not equity) if "the value in controversy shall exceed $20."

Answer (A) is incorrect. A jury trial is usually available. Answer (B) is incorrect. Suits filed in equity are not tried before juries in either the federal or the state courts. The right to a jury trial in a civil suit at common law is not guaranteed in a state court absent a provision in the state constitution. Answer (C) is incorrect. Suits filed in equity are not tried before juries in either the federal or the state courts. The right to a jury trial in a civil suit at common law is not guaranteed in a state court absent a provision in the state constitution.

16. If a case is tried before a jury, a jury must be selected prior to the making of opening statements. During jury selection,

A. The attorneys will conduct the venire examination of prospective jurors.

B. Each side has an unlimited number of peremptory challenges.

C. Each side has a limited number of challenges for cause.

D. The attorneys will conduct a voir dire examination of prospective jurors.

Answer (D) is correct. *(Publisher, adapted)*

REQUIRED: The true statement about jury selection.

DISCUSSION: Before the jury may be selected, the respective attorneys will customarily engage in an examination of the prospective jurors to discover possible prejudices. This is known as the voir dire examination.

Answer (A) is incorrect. The venire is the panel of prospective jurors. Answer (B) is incorrect. Peremptory challenges are limited in each jurisdiction by statute. A peremptory challenge permits a party to dismiss a prospective juror without cause. Answer (C) is incorrect. If one side can establish a legally recognized basis for challenging a juror, that juror must be dismissed for cause. The number of challenges for cause is unlimited.

17. The opening statements introduce the evidential phase of the trial. The first opening statement is

A. Evidence in the case.

B. Customarily made by the plaintiff's attorney.

C. Customarily made by the defendant's attorney.

D. Customarily made by the trial judge.

Answer (B) is correct. *(Publisher, adapted)*

REQUIRED: The true statement regarding the opening statements.

DISCUSSION: As a matter of custom, the plaintiff's attorney makes the first opening statement.

Answer (A) is incorrect. The purpose of an opening statement is to provide a summary of that side's case. It is not considered evidence. Answer (C) is incorrect. The attorneys for the parties to the suit make the opening statements, with the plaintiff's attorney customarily making his/hers first. Answer (D) is incorrect. The attorneys for the parties to the suit make the opening statements, with the plaintiff's attorney customarily making his/hers first.

18. Following the opening statements, the trial enters its evidentiary phase. Each side has an opportunity to present evidence to support its assertions or rebut those of the opponent. The presentation of evidence will be made in accordance with the rules of evidence in effect in the forum jurisdiction.

A. Each side has the right to examine and cross-examine its own witnesses.

B. One may not ask leading questions of one's own witnesses in any situation.

C. The scope of the cross-examination is limited to the scope of the direct examination.

D. One may not call an adverse party as a witness in a civil action.

Answer (C) is correct. *(Publisher, adapted)*

REQUIRED: The true statement about the presentation of evidence at trial.

DISCUSSION: After one side has directly examined a witness, the other side has a right to cross-examine. Cross-examination is limited to the scope of the direct examination for purposes of judicial economy. Matters beyond the scope of the direct examination may be brought out in the cross-examiner's own case.

Answer (A) is incorrect. One is not permitted to cross-examine one's own witnesses. Answer (B) is incorrect. One may ask leading questions (those highly suggestive of the answer) of one's own witnesses if the witnesses turn out to be hostile or adverse. Answer (D) is incorrect. In a civil action, an adverse party may be called to testify. No civil law privilege precludes the party from witnessing against him/herself.

19. Evidence that has a logical tendency to prove or disprove a proposition in the case is

A. Material.

B. Probative.

C. Relevant.

D. Competent.

Answer (B) is correct. *(Publisher, adapted)*

REQUIRED: The term describing evidence that has a logical tendency to prove or disprove a proposition.

DISCUSSION: Admissible evidence must be probative. It must have a logical tendency to prove or disprove a material proposition in the case. This and other terms used to determine when evidence is admissible have a tendency to overlap.

Answer (A) is incorrect. Materiality refers to the importance of evidence and its relationship to the case. Answer (C) is incorrect. Relevancy embraces both probativeness and materiality; evidence must relate to a substantive legal issue in the case. Answer (D) is incorrect. A confidential communication between an attorney and a client might not be admissible because it is subject to an exclusionary rule; i.e., it is not competent.

20. Hearsay

A. Cannot consist of evidence of statements made in a court.

B. May be statements made verbally or nonverbally.

C. Is admissible but not discoverable.

D. Is discoverable but not admissible.

Answer (B) is correct. *(Publisher, adapted)*

REQUIRED: The true statement about hearsay.

DISCUSSION: Hearsay is a statement, other than one made by the declarant while testifying, offered in evidence to prove the truth of the matter asserted. The statement alluded to may be a verbal or a nonverbal statement. It might include body language or written statements.

Answer (A) is incorrect. Hearsay might involve a statement made in a courtroom at an unrelated trial or hearing. Answer (C) is incorrect. Anything that is admissible is also discoverable under the rules of discovery. Answer (D) is incorrect. Hearsay is discoverable only if it relates to the subject matter of the pending litigation and is not privileged. Hearsay may be admissible if one of the numerous exceptions to the hearsay rule is applicable.

21. Which is the true statement about directed verdicts?

A. A verdict may not be directed when the case is tried with a jury because the right to a jury trial includes the right to a jury verdict.

B. A party who seeks and fails to obtain a directed verdict loses his/her case.

C. A party who has successfully sought a directed verdict will have the benefit of a final decision on the merits.

D. A judge may not direct a verdict upon the motion of the plaintiff.

Answer (C) is correct. *(Publisher, adapted)*

REQUIRED: The true statement about directed verdicts.

DISCUSSION: A directed verdict (a judgment as a matter of law in federal courts) is a decision by a judge that, in light of the evidence presented, no reasonable person could decide the case in any other way. A directed verdict is a decision on the merits, and when appeals are exhausted, the decision will be final.

Answer (A) is incorrect. The right to a jury trial does not include the right to a jury verdict. A verdict may be directed when the case is tried before a jury if the judge determines that no genuine issue of fact remains to be decided by the jury. Answer (B) is incorrect. If the motion for a directed verdict is denied, the case proceeds in its normal course. Answer (D) is incorrect. Either side may move for a directed verdict.

22. In his/her instructions to the jury, the judge is required to do all except which of the following?

A. Specify the type of verdict to be rendered.

B. Explain the law to be applied.

C. Define the issues to be determined.

D. Limit the time of deliberation.

Answer (D) is correct. *(Publisher, adapted)*

REQUIRED: The purpose not served by the judge's instructions to the jury.

DISCUSSION: A judge may not specify an exact time limit for the jury's deliberations. The jury instructions are limited essentially to explaining the law to be applied, defining the issues to be decided, and specifying the type of verdict to be rendered. There are general verdicts (who wins) and special verdicts (answers to specific factual questions).

23. Judgments for monetary damages

A. Have an indefinite duration.

B. May be enforced by execution.

C. Cannot be discharged in bankruptcy.

D. Expire after 20 years and may not be renewed.

Answer (B) is correct. *(Publisher, adapted)*

REQUIRED: The true statement about judgments for monetary damages.

DISCUSSION: A party who has recovered a civil judgment for damages may, if the defendant fails to pay, have recourse to judicial process to seize, sell, and receive the proceeds from property of the defendant, i.e., execute the judgment. Discovery may be used if desired.

Answer (A) is incorrect. Judgments normally have an initial statutory duration (e.g., 20 years), although they are usually renewable. Answer (C) is incorrect. Most civil judgments may be discharged in bankruptcy. Answer (D) is incorrect. Judgments are customarily renewable.

3.5 Appeal

24. An appeals court may not reverse a decision on evidence offered and objected to at trial if

A. The evidence was wrongly excluded.

B. The evidence was wrongly admitted.

C. The record contained no statement of what evidence was excluded or what specific objection was made to evidence that was admitted.

D. Evidence in a case tried without a jury was wrongly excluded.

Answer (C) is correct. *(Publisher, adapted)*

REQUIRED: The circumstance under which an appeals court may not reverse a decision on the admissibility of evidence.

DISCUSSION: An appeals court must make its decisions based upon the record made in the lower court, the briefs filed by the parties in the appeal, and the oral arguments presented. Accordingly, a party who objects to the admission or exclusion of evidence at trial must make a specific objection for insertion in the record if (s)he wishes to appeal the lower court's ruling on the objection at a later time.

Answer (A) is incorrect. It is a proper basis for reversal on appeal provided the objection was properly taken and the error was harmful. Answer (B) is incorrect. It is a proper basis for reversal on appeal provided the objection was properly taken and the error was harmful. Answer (D) is incorrect. It is a proper basis for reversal on appeal provided the objection was properly taken and the error was harmful.

25. The principle of res judicata

A. Prevents relitigation of a cause of action that has been fully, fairly, and finally decided on the merits by a court of competent jurisdiction.

B. Is synonymous with comity.

C. Is the basis for requiring that the subject matter of a suit (the res) be located within the forum state in order for the court to have in rem jurisdiction.

D. Permits a court to adjudicate disputes.

Answer (A) is correct. *(Publisher, adapted)*

REQUIRED: The true statement about the principle of res judicata.

DISCUSSION: Res judicata is the principle by which a reasonable end is mandated for litigation. It provides that a litigant may have his/her day in court but that this right is limited by concern for the efficient use of judicial resources and fairness to the other parties.

Answer (B) is incorrect. Comity is the respect that one sovereign gives to the legislative, executive, or judicial actions of another. Answer (C) is incorrect. Res judicata is a bar to excessive litigation, not a limit on the court's jurisdiction over property. Answer (D) is incorrect. Res judicata does not provide a court with the authority to adjudicate; it limits the power of parties to relitigate a case.

26. After the trier of fact enters a verdict, and assuming that motions for directed verdicts or for new trials have been denied, the judge will enter a judgment. Under the Full Faith and Credit Clause of the Constitution,

A. A final judgment of a court of competent jurisdiction is effective only within the state in which rendered.

B. The federal rights of U.S. citizens are protected from abridgement by the states.

C. The judicial proceedings of one state must be respected by other states.

D. State statutes, not judgments, are enforceable in every state.

Answer (C) is correct. *(Publisher, adapted)*

REQUIRED: The true statement about the effect of final judgments under the Full Faith and Credit Clause.

DISCUSSION: Article IV of the U.S. Constitution states that "full faith and credit shall be given in each state to the public acts, records and judicial proceedings of every other state." This clause has been interpreted most often to apply to final judgments rendered in courts of competent jurisdiction. The Full Faith and Credit Clause is a necessary protection in a federal system because it facilitates the enforcement of judgments without relitigation when a defendant or his/her property is not in the state in which the judgment was rendered.

Answer (A) is incorrect. The final judgment of a court of competent jurisdiction is effective in every state. Answer (B) is incorrect. The Privileges and Immunities Clause guarantees federal rights of citizens against abridgment by the states. Answer (D) is incorrect. The Full Faith and Credit Clause is seldom applied to state statutes.

27. The border of State X with State Y is a river. Plaintiff, an X corporation, owned land on the X side and defendant, a Y corporation, owned the opposite property on the Y side. Over the years the river changed course, thereby enlarging defendant's holdings and decreasing plaintiff's. Accordingly, plaintiff sued in a State Y court to obtain title to the property that had changed hands as a result of the shift. All issues, including jurisdiction, were fully, fairly, and finally litigated in the courts of State Y. Plaintiff lost after a determination that the disputed land was in State Y. Plaintiff then brought suit in the courts of State X, from which the case was removed to federal court. Which of the following is true?

A. Plaintiff should prevail if it disputes removal.

B. Defendant should prevail on the grounds of res judicata.

C. Plaintiff should prevail if it can show that State Y had no jurisdiction because the land was in State X.

D. Defendant should win because collateral attack of judgments is never allowed.

Answer (B) is correct. *(Publisher, adapted)*

REQUIRED: The outcome of a collateral attack on a final judgment.

DISCUSSION: Once a claim has been finally decided by a court of competent jurisdiction, the matter is res judicata; i.e., the dispute is settled by judgment and may not be litigated further (although it may be appealed). The Full Faith and Credit Clause is the constitutional embodiment of this principle. The courts should give full faith and credit to a final judgment of another state's court. If the court in State Y lacked jurisdiction (e.g., because the disputed realty was not located in State Y), res judicata would be inapplicable. But State Y courts are competent to rule on the question of their own jurisdiction, and defendant was therefore not required to relitigate the merits of the case.

Answer (A) is incorrect. Removal to a federal court is appropriate in a diversity case. Answer (C) is incorrect. The State Y courts have jurisdiction to determine their boundaries and the issue of jurisdiction was litigated. Answer (D) is incorrect. If jurisdiction had not been litigated in State Y, and if the federal court had determined that the State Y court had no jurisdiction, its final judgment would not have been entitled to full faith and credit.

3.6 Alternative Dispute Resolution

28. Arbitration is a nonjudicial dispute resolution mechanism. Arbitration is a(n)

A. Synonym for mediation.

B. Method whereby the parties to a controversy may resolve their dispute by agreeing to be bound by the decision of an impartial third party.

C. Action usually confined to labor management issues.

D. Proceeding normally conducted under governmental auspices.

Answer (B) is correct. *(Publisher, adapted)*

REQUIRED: The true statement about arbitration.

DISCUSSION: Arbitration is used as an alternative to a traditional trial in court. It provides speedy, less expensive, and often more expert resolution of conflicts. Settlement of disputes by arbitration arises from an agreement between the parties to be bound by the decision of an impartial third person who is often a professional arbitrator and an expert in the particular field.

Answer (A) is incorrect. Arbitration is binding under the parties' agreement, whereas mediation is merely advisory. Mediation is frequently employed in labor-management conflicts. Answer (C) is incorrect. Arbitration can extend to any matter upon which the parties may reach a binding agreement. Answer (D) is incorrect. Arbitration is normally conducted privately rather than under governmental auspices.

29. Arbitrators render decisions

A. In accordance with precedent.

B. After hearings conducted with fewer formalities than in judicial proceedings.

C. As nonbinding recommendations to the parties.

D. After required public hearings.

Answer (B) is correct. *(Publisher, adapted)*

REQUIRED: The true statement about decision making by arbitrators.

DISCUSSION: One of the advantages of arbitration is that it may be conducted without the complex rules of procedure and evidence required in litigation. Many arbitration proceedings follow the adversarial model but not with the same strictness as court proceedings.

Answer (A) is incorrect. An arbitrator, unlike a judge, is not bound by decisions in past cases. Answer (C) is incorrect. An arbitration decision is binding upon the parties based upon their agreement, subject to judicial review. Answer (D) is incorrect. Arbitration hearings may be conducted privately.

30. Which of the following alternative dispute resolution methods is nonbinding and involves a third party that proposes possible solutions for the disputants' consideration?

A. Consensual arbitration.

B. Conciliation.

C. Mediation.

D. Compulsory arbitration.

Answer (C) is correct. *(Publisher, adapted)*

REQUIRED: The nonbinding dispute resolution method involving a third party who offers solutions.

DISCUSSION: Mediation is a nonbinding method of dispute resolution. Mediation involves the use of a third party, the mediator, who is selected by the disputants. The disputants attempt to reach an agreement with the help of the mediator. The mediator employs the techniques used in conciliation but also proposes potential solutions to the problem.

Answer (A) is incorrect. Arbitration is binding, even if voluntary. Answer (B) is incorrect. A conciliator acts as an intermediary rather than one who suggests solutions to problems. Answer (D) is incorrect. Compulsory arbitration is required by statute and is binding.

31. Which of the following is not a function of a conciliator?

A. Rendering binding decisions.

B. Explaining issues to the disputants.

C. Serving as an intermediary.

D. Improving communications between the disputants.

Answer (A) is correct. *(Publisher, adapted)*

REQUIRED: The activity that is not a function of a conciliator.

DISCUSSION: A conciliator is the third party selected by disputants to aid in the resolution of a dispute by using conciliation techniques. Conciliation, unlike arbitration, does not result in a binding decision.

Answer (B) is incorrect. Explaining issues is a function of a conciliator. Answer (C) is incorrect. Acting as an intermediary is a function of a conciliator. Answer (D) is incorrect. Improving communications is a function of a conciliator.

STUDY UNIT FOUR
CONSTITUTIONAL LAW AND BUSINESS

A **constitution** defines the formation and operation of a system of government. It establishes an institutional structure, allocates power among the levels and branches of government, and imposes limits upon the powers to be exercised. Furthermore, a constitution enumerates or implies the rights and liberties of the people and provides an orderly mechanism for responding to societal change. Because the U.S. Constitution is intentionally flexible, it is sometimes referred to as a living or organic document -- one for the future as well as the present.

This study unit focuses on the **U.S. Constitution**. It was adopted on September 17, 1787, and declares in the **Supremacy Clause**, found in Article VI, that "this Constitution shall be ... the supreme law of the land." The Constitution provides the foundation and framework of the U.S. government in its seven **articles** and 27 **amendments**. Its first three articles establish the three branches of the federal government: the executive, the legislative, and the judicial. The first 10 amendments, adopted in 1791, are known as the **Bill of Rights**. The protections listed in the Bill of Rights are given the highest constitutional priority because they guarantee individual liberties. They articulate fundamental rights that are substantially immune from governmental action.

The U.S. constitutional framework reflects a **separation of powers** that creates a system of checks and balances. For example, the President is limited to two 4-year terms, and the President, Vice-President, and all civil officers of the U.S. may be removed from office by Congress for "high Crimes and Misdemeanors." Moreover, major appointments by the President, including but not limited to federal judges and cabinet officers, must be confirmed by the Senate. Acts of Congress may be vetoed by the President, and the constitutionality of executive and legislative acts is subject to **judicial review** by the courts. In turn, Congress regulates the appellate jurisdiction of the Supreme Court and establishes the "inferior Courts."

The Constitution entrusts certain powers to the **federal government** alone. Other powers are reserved to the states, and still others may be exercised concurrently by both state and federal governments. When powers may be exercised concurrently, the issue of federal **preemption** arises. If Congress intends for its action to exclude state action, the federal law or regulation is said to preempt a conflicting state law or regulation (for example, the California law legalizing marijuana use for medical purposes has been held to be preempted by the federal Controlled Substances Act of 1970). The federal powers derive from a grant by the people. Thus, the federal government has limited, enumerated, and delegated powers. These **enumerated or express powers** are supplemented by the implied power to do all things **"necessary and proper"** to exercise the express powers. Drawing a clear line separating the constitutional powers of the states and those of the federal government is often difficult. However, each jurisdiction is required to exercise its powers so as not to interfere with the free and full exercise of the powers of others. This allocation of power among the federal government and state governments is a hallmark of **federalism**.

The Constitution grants limited governmental power to regulate the individual rights and liberties of the people, but federal regulation of economic activity is very extensive. The **Commerce Clause** of the Constitution grants Congress the power to regulate business activity with foreign nations and among the several states. The Supreme Court has construed this language to permit the federal government to regulate intrastate (local) commercial and noncommercial activities that affect **interstate commerce**. The Commerce Clause, as broadly interpreted, empowers Congress to enact laws affecting any business activity that has a substantial effect, either positive or negative, on interstate commerce. Federal regulation is permissible even if the object of the regulation never enters the stream of interstate commerce. Congress may regulate any activity that has a mere possibility of affecting interstate commerce. Federal legislation purportedly under the Commerce Clause is declared invalid only if either of the following is clearly true:

1. Congress has no rational basis for finding that the regulated activity affects interstate commerce. This approach is called the **rational basis test**.
2. A reasonable connection between the regulatory means selected and the asserted ends does not exist.

However, the Supreme Court has narrowed federal regulatory power under the Commerce Clause. For example, the Gun-Free School Zones Act of 1990 was struck down in 1995 as unrelated to commerce. Moreover, parts of the Violence Against Women Act of 1994, which allowed women to seek a remedy in federal court when they were victims of gender-based violence, were declared unconstitutional in 2000 on the grounds that the Commerce Clause did not pertain to noneconomic criminal acts.

The Commerce Clause not only contains an express grant of federal power over interstate commerce but also serves to invalidate **state laws** that give local business an unfair advantage over interstate business. The basic rule is that any state regulation imposed merely for economic or resource protection is a per se (on its face) violation of the Commerce Clause and is unconstitutional. The Supreme Court has set forth the following standards:

1. If a state statute discriminates against interstate commerce, it is invalid unless Congress consents to it, regardless of whether the burden would otherwise be permitted.
2. If a state statute is nondiscriminatory, a balancing test is used to determine whether the burden on interstate commerce is unreasonable in light of the strength of the state interest.
3. The Commerce Clause does not prevent a state from purchasing solely from its own citizens or from granting subsidies only to its own residents.

The power to regulate **foreign commerce** is vested exclusively in the federal government and extends to all aspects of foreign trade. State and local governments may not regulate foreign commerce.

General **taxing powers** are granted to Congress by the Constitution. The **Sixteenth Amendment** states, “Congress shall have power to lay and collect taxes on incomes, from whatever source derived, without apportionment among the several states, and without regard to any census or enumeration.” The purpose of federal taxation is to raise revenue to enable the government to, among other things, regulate business and provide for the general welfare, provide for the common defense of the people, and pay national debts. The power enjoyed by the federal government to lay and collect taxes is very broad but is subject to three major restrictions. (1) Direct taxes other than income taxes must be allocated among the states in proportion to population; (2) goods exported from the states must not be taxed; and (3) all duties, imposts, or excises must be uniform nationwide.

Ordinarily, a tax will be upheld as long as the motive of Congress and the effect of its legislative action are to secure revenue for the benefit of the federal government. However, tax laws are also enacted to achieve various economic and social objectives. For example, the progressive tax rate structure and statutory deductions, exemptions, and credits may serve to redistribute wealth.

Under its **spending power**, Congress has authority to pay the debts and provide for the common defense and general welfare of the United States. Thus, Congress has broad authority to spend for the public welfare. The spending power is therefore an important indirect regulatory tool. Federal spending not only directly affects economic activity but also may be used to achieve regulatory objectives indirectly, for example, by establishing conditions for receipt of federal funds.

Congress also has the power to borrow money on the credit of the U.S. and to **coin money** and regulate its value. Congress has used these powers to create the Federal Reserve system and other agencies. They give the federal government substantial power over the money supply, interest rates, and other matters of national economic importance.

An inherent power of the federal and state governments is **eminent domain**, which is the power to take private property for public use. Under the **Takings Clause** of the **Fifth Amendment**, the federal government may not take private property for public use "without just compensation." These restrictions on eminent domain with regard to use and compensation have been extended to state governments through the **Due Process Clause** of the **Fourteenth Amendment**. The classic measure of compensation is the fair market value of the property at the time of the taking. However, if the effect of the taking is merely a diminution of property value, the measure of compensation is the change in fair market value. Before a governmental entity is required to pay compensation, an actual taking of private property must have occurred. A taking need not be physical. Mere governmental regulation of the property does not normally constitute a taking. However, the greater the economic impact of the regulation on the owner, the more likely the regulation will be deemed a taking. Furthermore, a private party, such as a local housing authority, may be delegated the power of eminent domain if it is used for a public purpose.

The Supreme Court extended the application of eminent domain to property taken for private use in the case of *Kelo v. City of New London* (2005). The Court found sufficient public benefits would accrue as part of the private redevelopment plan to justify extending the availability of the states' power of eminent domain.

States may regulate business as long as Congress has not occupied the field, that is, as long as Congress has not preempted state regulation of an activity. States are sovereigns. They are not limited to passing laws that are specifically permitted by the Constitution. Nevertheless, states' power to regulate is limited. A state may not regulate any subject matter over which the federal government has exclusive power, such as coining money or declaring war, or in a manner that will place an undue burden on interstate commerce.

States have inherent **police power** to enact laws that regulate public health and safety and that promote public welfare and morals. A state's police power is not limited to regulation of crime but is a broad inherent authority to pass laws even if they affect or indirectly regulate economic activity. Courts apply a five-step constitutional analysis of a state statute. A "yes" answer to any one of the following questions indicates that the statute is invalid. A "no" answer to all questions indicates the statute is probably valid.

1. Does the state law regulate activity subject to an exclusive federal power?
2. Has Congress occupied the field?
3. Is the statute outside the scope of a state's police power?
4. Does the statute violate any person's constitutional rights?
5. Does the statute impermissibly discriminate or burden interstate commerce?

The Constitution provides that "no state shall pass any law impairing the obligation of contracts." The **Contracts Clause** is not intended to prohibit states from a valid exercise of police power, but it prevents retroactive modification of private contracts and public charters, for example, a charter of incorporation. It does not apply to the federal government, although the due process clause of the Fifth Amendment restricts federal power to impair contracts.

An additional provision of the federal constitution that places limits on state economic regulation is the **Import-Export Clause**, which prohibits states from imposing any tax on imported or exported goods or on any commercial activity connected with them, except with Congressional consent. The clause prohibits states from imposing any tax on any goods once they have entered the export stream.

The Supreme Court has upheld the power of state governments to impose **taxes**. Below is a four-step constitutional framework for determining the validity of a state tax:

1. Does the state tax apply to an activity with a substantial nexus or connection with the taxing state?
2. Is the state tax fairly apportioned?
3. Is the state tax nondiscriminatory against interstate commerce?
4. Is the state tax fairly related to services or benefits provided by the state?

Even if a state meets the foregoing requirements, a tax may be deemed unconstitutional under the Due Process Clause or the Equal Protection Clause.

The Constitution places **limitations** on federal and state powers for the protection of individual rights. The judicial branch reviews whether governmental power, as exercised, violates a right protected by the Constitution. The vast majority of constitutional protections apply only with regard to federal or state governmental action. **State action** includes any action of the federal and state government, including their subdivisions. Ordinarily, to declare an action unconstitutional, the action must be attributable to the government. Only the **Thirteenth Amendment**, which abolished slavery and involuntary servitude, applies to actions of private individuals. However, state action can be found in activities of private individuals when they engage in public functions or have a significant government involvement. State action exists whenever a state affirmatively facilitates, condones, encourages, or authorizes acts of discrimination by its citizens.

The Constitution requires state and federal governments to respect the right of persons to **due process** under the law. The **Fifth Amendment** provides a limitation on federal power by providing that no person shall be "deprived of life, liberty, or property, without due process of law." The **Fourteenth Amendment** provides a similar limitation on state power. Due process of law means that both government regulation and its administration must be reasonable and fair. Due process embraces two issues: (a) **substantive due process**, which is a court's inquiry into the wisdom and utility of state action, and (b) **procedural due process**, such as reasonable notice, a hearing, and the right to counsel.

Under the Fourteenth Amendment, a state is prohibited from denying to any person within its jurisdiction the equal protection of the laws. The **Equal Protection Clause** of the Fourteenth Amendment applies only to the states. However, the **Due Process Clause** of the Fifth Amendment has been interpreted to extend the equal protection guarantee to actions of the federal government. Equal protection means that similarly situated persons must be treated similarly, absent a rational and reasonable ground for treating them differently that furthers a legitimate government interest. Judicial interpretation and application of the equal protection clause has had a profound effect on American society. Probably its most famous application was in ***Brown v. Board of Education* (1954)**, in which the Supreme Court held that segregation by race in public school assignments was an unconstitutional denial of the equal protection of the laws. The Supreme Court applies three levels of scrutiny to determine whether regulation, either state or federal, is valid under the equal protection clause of the Constitution. **Strict scrutiny** is applied when legislation affects fundamental rights, e.g., voting, privacy, travel, free speech, and freedom of religion. Strict scrutiny is also applied when classifications of persons are inherently suspect, e.g., those based on race, religion, or national origin. Any legislation subject to strict scrutiny must be necessary to promote a compelling governmental interest. The **intermediate scrutiny test** requires that legislation have a substantial relationship to achievement of an important governmental objective. Intermediate scrutiny is applied to quasi-suspect classifications, such as gender and legitimacy. The **rational relationship test** is the lowest level of scrutiny. Courts will declare legislation unconstitutional only if clear and convincing evidence shows no reasonable basis for the legislation. The strong presumption is that such legislation is constitutional.

Governments are prohibited from enacting ex post facto laws and bills of attainder. An **ex post facto law** retroactively alters criminal law with respect to offenses or punishments in a substantially prejudicial manner. In other words, an ex post facto law makes an act that was not a crime when it was committed criminally punishable. A **bill of attainder** imposes punishment without a judicial trial upon persons who are designated by name or defined in terms of past conduct.

The first 10 amendments to the Constitution are known as the **Bill of Rights**. The first eight amendments set forth specific limits on the power of the federal government to interfere with basic freedoms. The **Ninth Amendment** declares that the enumeration of rights in the Constitution does not "deny or disparage others retained by the people." The **Tenth Amendment** states that all powers not delegated to the federal government or expressly denied to the states by the Constitution "are reserved to the States respectively, or to the people." The Bill of Rights does not apply directly to the states. However, the courts, by judicial interpretation, have held that most of the protections in the Bill of Rights are incorporated in the Due Process Clause of the Fourteenth Amendment. The **Fourteenth Amendment** provides, "No state shall make or enforce any law which shall abridge the **privileges** or **immunities** of citizens of the United States; nor shall any State deprive any person of life, liberty, or property, without due process of law, nor deny to any person within its jurisdiction the equal protection of the laws." The effect of the **incorporation doctrine** is that most of the Bill of Rights is applicable to the states. These rights include (1) free exercise of religion, (2) freedom of speech (including political speech by corporations and symbolic speech), (3) freedom of the press, (4) the right of assembly, and (5) the right to petition the government for redress of grievances. The Fourth Amendment protects individuals and corporations from unreasonable searches and seizures. The Fifth Amendment (1) prohibits the federal government from depriving any person of life, liberty, or property without due process of law; (2) provides protection against compulsory self-incrimination (i.e., the right to remain silent); (3) prohibits double jeopardy; and (4) requires just compensation when property is taken for a public purpose.

A **right to privacy** is not mentioned in the Constitution. Nevertheless, the Supreme Court has held that it is implied in the Bill of Rights. Concerns about privacy, especially given the proliferation of computerized information, has resulted in much legislation. For example, the **Freedom of Information Act of 1966** permits individuals access to government-held information that concerns them. The **Privacy Act of 1974** requires that federal agencies safeguard and ensure the reliability of information held concerning individuals. Individuals also have the right to know what data are being assembled and how it will be used, the right to correct misstated data, and the right not to have data used for anything other than the purpose for which it was gathered. The **Right to Financial Privacy Act of 1978** prevents sharing of a financial institution's customer records with the federal government without the customer's consent. Other federal legislation regulates the sharing of cable subscriber data, prohibits states from selling or disclosing drivers' personal information, and prohibits disclosure of personal medical data without consent.

The Supreme Court has extended First Amendment protection to **commercial speech**. The court concluded that consumers and society in general would benefit from the free flow of purely commercial information consisting of truthful data about a lawful activity. Commercial speech, however, is afforded less protection than the noncommercial variety. A narrowly drawn restriction has been held valid if it directly advances a substantial governmental interest. A four-part analytical framework is used in commercial speech cases:

1. The speech must concern lawful activity and not be misleading to come within the First Amendment.
2. The governmental interest must be substantial to permit regulation.
3. If both of the foregoing are true, the court must determine whether the governmental regulation directly advances the governmental interest.
4. The court must decide whether the regulation is "narrowly tailored" to advance the governmental interest. Thus, it should not be more extensive than necessary.

QUESTIONS

4.1 Nature and Overview of the U.S. Constitution

1. The U.S. Constitution

A. Like the British Constitution consists of well-established tradition rather than a written document.

B. Consists of seven articles and 27 amendments.

C. Consists of three articles and the Bill of Rights.

D. Is usually considered to include the Bill of Rights, which is actually an Act of Congress and not an amendment.

Answer (B) is correct. *(Publisher, adapted)*

REQUIRED: The nature of the U.S. Constitution.

DISCUSSION: The U.S. Constitution consists of seven articles and 27 amendments. Articles I, II, and III establish the powers and organization of the legislative, executive, and judicial branches, respectively, of the federal government. Article IV is the states' relations article. Article V provides an amendment procedure. Article VI contains the supremacy clause. Article VII pertains to ratification. The amendments cover matters ranging from personal rights to the right of 18-year-olds to vote.

Answer (A) is incorrect. The U.S. Constitution has been formally enacted. Answer (C) is incorrect. The first 10 of the 27 amendments are commonly referred to as the Bill of Rights. Answer (D) is incorrect. The first 10 of the 27 amendments are commonly referred to as the Bill of Rights.

2. The U.S. Constitution defines the powers of the federal government. Which of the following is a false statement concerning the scope of those powers?

A. Congress has the power to make all laws that are necessary and proper for carrying into effect the enumerated powers conferred by the Constitution upon the U.S. government.

B. Powers not delegated to the states by the Constitution or prohibited by it are reserved to the United States exclusively.

C. The states have an implicit police power to provide for the general health, safety, welfare, and morals.

D. The powers not delegated to the United States by the Constitution or prohibited by it to the states are reserved to the states, respectively, or to the people.

Answer (B) is correct. *(Publisher, adapted)*
REQUIRED: The false statement concerning the powers of the federal government.
DISCUSSION: Article I, Section 8, expressly gives Congress the power to legislate in areas that affect business. Examples are the right to collect taxes, to regulate interstate commerce, and to enact a bankruptcy law. Implied powers are not specified in the Constitution but are "necessary and proper" for carrying out the express powers. Examples of the federal government's implied powers are the right to establish a central bank (the Federal Reserve system) and to prohibit racial discrimination in public accommodations. If the Constitution does not expressly delegate powers to the federal government or prohibit states from exercising them, they are reserved to the states or to the people. An example is a state's police power to limit the personal freedom and property rights of persons for the protection of the public safety, health, welfare, and morals.

4.2 Federal Economic Regulation

3. Assume that a state on the Eastern seaboard prohibits commercial fishing in its coastal waters by nonresidents. A federal statute licenses commercial fishing vessels for operations in coastal waters. The state statute is

A. Invalid under the Commerce Clause.

B. Valid as a legitimate exercise of the state police power.

C. Invalid under the Supremacy Clause of the U.S. Constitution.

D. Valid under "the new federalism."

Answer (C) is correct. *(Publisher, adapted)*
REQUIRED: The validity of a state statute that conflicts with a federal statute.
DISCUSSION: The U.S. Constitution provides that the Constitution and laws made under it are the supreme law of the land. When state and federal statutes are in direct conflict, the federal statute will prevail.
Answer (A) is incorrect. The Constitution gives the federal government the power to regulate commerce between the states, but it does not prohibit regulation of commerce by the states. However, state regulation may not directly conflict with federal law and may not place an undue burden on interstate commerce. Answer (B) is incorrect. The conflict with federal law invalidates the state statute. Answer (D) is incorrect. Under the concept of federalism, a Supremacy Clause is vital to avoid conflict.

4. The Commerce Clause of the U.S. Constitution provides that "Congress shall have power to regulate commerce with foreign nations and among the several states and with the Indian tribes." This federal power

A. Has been liberally interpreted to give Congress very extensive authority to regulate economic activity.

B. Has the effect of preempting all state authority over commercial activity.

C. Applies only to interstate or international commerce and not to intrastate commerce.

D. Does not apply to intrastate commerce.

Answer (A) is correct. *(Publisher, adapted)*
REQUIRED: The true statement concerning the Commerce Clause.
DISCUSSION: The Commerce Clause has been the basis for an expansion of federal power. If an activity affects interstate commerce, Congress has power to regulate. Congress also has power over the channels of interstate commerce and substantial power even after the interstate commerce comes to an end.
Answer (B) is incorrect. Federal power to regulate commerce is held concurrently with the states. The states may regulate commerce provided the regulation does not conflict with federal law and does not unduly burden interstate commerce. Answer (C) is incorrect. The Commerce Clause applies to intrastate activity that affects interstate commerce. Answer (D) is incorrect. The Commerce Clause applies to intrastate activity that affects interstate commerce.

5. A local restaurant located on an interstate highway refuses to serve people of the Pentecostal faith. The Civil Rights Act of 1964 specifically prohibits discrimination in restaurants on the basis of race, color, religion, national origin, or sex. If a Pentecostal patron sues, (s)he will win because

A. The Fourteenth Amendment guarantees equal protection.

B. The Commerce Clause expressly grants Congress power to regulate local businesses.

C. State action is present because food is served to the residents of the state.

D. The Commerce Clause gives Congress the power to regulate interstate commerce; discrimination impedes interstate commerce.

Answer (D) is correct. *(D.L. Mescon)*

REQUIRED: The basis for prohibiting religious discrimination in public accommodations.

DISCUSSION: Article I, Section 8, of the Constitution gives Congress the power to regulate interstate commerce. The Supreme Court has upheld Congressional power to regulate discrimination under the interstate Commerce Clause when Congress has determined that discrimination impedes interstate commerce.

Answer (A) is incorrect. The Fourteenth Amendment equal protection guarantee applies only to action by a government. Answer (B) is incorrect. Article I, Section 8, gives Congress the power to regulate interstate, not intrastate, commerce. Answer (C) is incorrect. "State action" requires some governmental involvement.

6. Congress enacted a statute regulating the design, size, and movement of oil tankers. A state also enacted a statute governing those matters with regard to oil tankers operating in its waters, but the state requirements were stricter. Various oil companies brought an action against the state, asserting that its regulation was unconstitutional. Which of the following is the best basis for the court's decision on behalf of the plaintiffs?

A. The Commerce Clause.

B. Separation of powers.

C. The preemption doctrine.

D. State police power.

Answer (C) is correct. *(Publisher, adapted)*

REQUIRED: The best basis for deciding a case involving state and federal regulation of the same matter.

DISCUSSION: Laws made by authority of the Constitution are the supreme law of the land. State statutes that conflict with such laws are invalid if the conflict is direct and substantial or if the federal government has expressly or impliedly preempted the field. Preemption will apply when the scheme of federal regulation is so pervasive that it leaves no room for state supplementation, or when the federal interest is so completely dominant that it precludes enforcement of the state law. In the case of oil tanker design, Congress plainly intended to set a uniform national standard. That intent would be frustrated by enforcing the state law.

Answer (A) is incorrect. The Commerce Clause permits state regulation of interstate commerce that is not unduly burdensome. Answer (B) is incorrect. The separation of powers is the balance among the legislative, executive, and judicial branches of government. This case involves a supremacy question. Answer (D) is incorrect. The state's power to regulate public safety, health, welfare, and morals is preempted by the overriding federal interest.

7. An Arizona statute makes illegal the operation of a train of more than 14 passenger cars or 70 freight cars within the state. The stated purpose of the law is to reduce railroad accidents within the state. Almost every other state permits the operation of longer trains. The Supreme Court would most likely

A. Allow the statute to stand because it is a safety measure.

B. Declare the statute unconstitutional because only the federal government has the authority to enact laws to regulate interstate commerce.

C. Conduct its own fact-finding to determine if the statute does have a rational relation to the objective stated by the legislature.

D. Balance the benefit to the state against the burden placed on interstate commerce and strike down the statute if its contribution to safety is less than its detrimental effect on interstate commerce.

Answer (D) is correct. *(Publisher, adapted)*

REQUIRED: The true statement about a state's power to regulate activities affecting interstate commerce.

DISCUSSION: The Supreme Court gives a greater degree of deference to a state statute that affects interstate commerce if the statute rationally protects a legitimate state objective, such as the safety of the state's citizens. However, even a statute enacted to protect the state's citizens will usually be subject to a balancing test. The Court will weigh the benefit to the state against the burden imposed on interstate commerce. If the statute is determined to have only a marginal impact on safety, it will usually be invalidated.

Answer (A) is incorrect. Even a statute enacted to protect public safety will be invalidated if the benefit to the public does not outweigh the burden placed on interstate commerce. Answer (B) is incorrect. A state has limited authority under its police power to enact statutes that will have an incidental impact on interstate commerce. Answer (C) is incorrect. The Supreme Court will not conduct its own inquiry into the facts of a case. It will customarily defer to the finding of facts by the state legislature.

8. The Constitution does not explicitly grant the federal government the power of eminent domain. The federal government's authority to exercise this power is derived from the

A. Fifth Amendment clause stating that private property shall not be taken for public use without just compensation.

B. Fourteenth Amendment clause stating that no state may deprive any person of life, liberty, or property without due process of law.

C. Doctrine of preemption.

D. Supremacy Clause.

Answer (A) is correct. *(Publisher, adapted)*

REQUIRED: The source of the federal government's power of eminent domain.

DISCUSSION: Eminent domain is a government's authority to take property for public use. The Constitution states that the federal government may not take private property for public use if just compensation is not given. Thus, the courts have interpreted this Fifth Amendment prohibition as the source of an implied power of eminent domain.

Answer (B) is incorrect. The Fourteenth Amendment applies to the states. Answer (C) is incorrect. The doctrine of preemption states that, if the federal government legislates in an area, a state is precluded from regulating the matter by the Supremacy Clause. Answer (D) is incorrect. The Supremacy Clause of Article VI applies to conflicts between state and federal regulation.

9. To reduce drunk driving on the nation's highways, Congress enacted a statute denying federal highway funds to any state with a minimum drinking age less than 21. Georgia challenged the statute on the grounds that it is an unconstitutional interference with its police power. In reviewing the statute, the Supreme Court will probably hold that it is

A. Constitutional, even if a direct congressional establishment of a national minimum drinking age would be unconstitutional.

B. Unconstitutional, because it is an attempt to indirectly accomplish an objective that cannot be accomplished directly.

C. Unconstitutional, because it induces the states to pass laws that violate the constitutional rights of their citizens.

D. Constitutional, because Congress has the authority to set a minimum national drinking age.

Answer (A) is correct. *(Publisher, adapted)*

REQUIRED: The constitutionality of a statute that indirectly accomplishes legislative goals through the use of the federal spending power.

DISCUSSION: Congress derives its spending power from Article I, Section 8. The Supreme Court has held that Congress can deny federal highway funds to any state that allows persons below a certain age to purchase alcoholic beverages, even if a statute establishing a minimum national drinking age would be unconstitutional.

Answer (B) is incorrect. Congress can constitutionally use its spending power to achieve objectives that it cannot attain directly. Answer (C) is incorrect. Setting a minimum drinking age is not a violation of the constitutional rights of the state's citizens. Answer (D) is incorrect. Congress does not have the authority under the Constitution to set a minimum national drinking age.

10. Both state and federal governments take private property for public use. Which of the following would most likely be considered a "taking"?

A. A zoning regulation that impairs an owner's use of his/her property.

B. A landmark preservation scheme that prevents an owner from altering a building considered to be historically significant.

C. A regulation enacted to protect the environment that causes a diminution of the value of property.

D. A permanent physical occupation of the property by a government that causes only a minor interference with the owner's use.

Answer (D) is correct. *(Publisher, adapted)*

REQUIRED: The item that constitutes a "taking."

DISCUSSION: The Supreme Court has held that a permanent physical occupation of private property is a taking, no matter how minor the interference with the owner's use. The Court has stated that the occupation of private property is "qualitatively more intrusive than perhaps any other category of property regulation" and therefore constitutes a taking even if its economic impact on the property's owner is minimal.

Answer (A) is incorrect. A zoning regulation is usually not a taking unless it is "clearly arbitrary and unreasonable." Answer (B) is incorrect. Although the owner of an individual building can be prevented from altering the building in a way that would destroy its historical significance, it is not a taking. Answer (C) is incorrect. The Court will usually not strike down a regulation enacted to protect the public welfare, even if the value of an owner's property is diminished.

4.3 Limitations on State Economic Regulation

11. Under the Constitution, state governments have the power to protect the health, safety, or general welfare of state residents. This power is known as

A. State sovereignty.

B. State police power.

C. Eminent domain.

D. State supremacy.

Answer (B) is correct. *(Publisher, adapted)*

REQUIRED: The term for a state's power to safeguard the health, safety, or welfare of its citizens.

DISCUSSION: The term applied to the power granted to states to protect the health, safety, or welfare of state citizens is "state police power." An action by a state under its police power is ordinarily valid under federal law unless it violates a specific limitation imposed by the U.S. Constitution. For example, a state law that interferes with the flow of interstate commerce may be held unconstitutional even if it is intended as a safety measure.

Answer (A) is incorrect. State sovereignty is the right of states to enact their own laws to the extent that they do not conflict with federal law. Answer (C) is incorrect. Eminent domain is the power of federal and state governments to take private property for public use. Answer (D) is incorrect. The term supremacy ordinarily refers to the supremacy of federal law over conflicting state law.

12. The taxing power is the means by which a government obtains revenue to pay its expenses. Which of the following is a true statement about this essential power?

A. Taxpayers usually have standing to sue the government based on the amount of taxes paid.

B. The taxation of interstate commerce by state and local governments is permitted under the Commerce Clause.

C. Taxation is an inappropriate means of implementing social policy.

D. Taxation is an insignificant regulatory tool.

Answer (B) is correct. *(Publisher, adapted)*

REQUIRED: The true statement about the taxing power.

DISCUSSION: Interstate commerce is not the exclusive domain of the federal taxing authorities. State and local governments may levy property, income, sales, or other taxes in the appropriate circumstances. According to the Supreme Court, such taxation is valid when (1) the nexus between the tax and the activity taxed is sufficient, (2) the tax is fairly apportioned, (3) the tax does not discriminate against interstate commerce, and (4) the tax is fairly related to services provided by the taxing authority.

Answer (A) is incorrect. Payment of taxes seldom gives the taxpayer standing to challenge the use of governmental funds. Answer (C) is incorrect. Taxes have often been imposed to further social policies. Answer (D) is incorrect. Taxation is a principal means of regulating business. Tax credits and depreciation allowances are obvious examples.

13. Minnesota enacted a statute requiring employers who closed down their operations in the state to pay pension benefits to any employee who had worked for the company for more than 10 years. This statute applied to any pension plan the company might have and was intended to apply retroactively. The Supreme Court would most likely declare this statute to be a violation of the

A. Commerce Clause.

B. Contracts Clause.

C. Supremacy Clause.

D. Due Process Clause of the Fourteenth Amendment.

Answer (B) is correct. *(Publisher, adapted)*

REQUIRED: The constitutional basis for invalidating the state statute described.

DISCUSSION: The Contracts Clause is found in Article I, Section 10. It prohibits states from passing any laws impairing the obligation of contracts. Under their police power, states are allowed to make minor modifications to contracts. However, the Court has held that states cannot make substantial modifications to contracts unless (1) there is an emergency; (2) the statute is enacted to protect a basic societal interest, not a favored group; (3) the relief is appropriately tailored to the emergency; (4) the modification is reasonable in scope; and (5) the statute is limited to the duration of the emergency.

Answer (A) is incorrect. Unless the Minnesota statute has some impact on interstate commerce, the Commerce Clause will not apply. Answer (C) is incorrect. Unless the Minnesota statute directly conflicts with a federal statute, the Supremacy Clause will not apply. Answer (D) is incorrect. The Due Process Clause of the Fourteenth Amendment incorporates most of the rights guaranteed by the Bill of Rights and makes them applicable to the states. Unless the statute is found to violate such a right, the Due Process Clause will not apply.

4.4 Limitations on Federal and State Powers

14. Under the doctrine of judicial review, the Supreme Court exercises power to decide whether a statute enacted by Congress is unconstitutional. The basis of this power is

A. The Necessary and Proper Clause of Article I.

B. The Privileges and Immunities Clause of Section 1 of the Fourteenth Amendment.

C. Chief Justice John Marshall's interpretation of the Constitution in *Marbury v. Madison*.

D. Common law.

Answer (C) is correct. *(Publisher, adapted)*

REQUIRED: The source of the Supreme Court's power of judicial review.

DISCUSSION: The Constitution does not expressly grant the Supreme Court authority to interpret the Constitution or to decide whether acts of the other branches of the federal government are in conflict with the Constitution. In deciding the case of *Marbury v. Madison*, Chief Justice Marshall declared that a statute expanding the Supreme Court's original jurisdiction was unconstitutional. He asserted, "It is emphatically the province and duty of the judicial department to say what the law is."

Answer (A) is incorrect. The Necessary and Proper Clause gives Congress the power to make laws "necessary and proper" to carry out the powers given to it by the Constitution. Answer (B) is incorrect. The Privileges and Immunities Clause of the Fourteenth Amendment was intended as a restraint on state government action against individuals. Answer (D) is incorrect. The power of judicial review is not derived from common law.

15. A Maryland statute makes illegal the publishing of statements critical of elected state officials. A newspaper claims that the law violates the First Amendment's guarantee of free speech. The Maryland Supreme Court holds that the law is constitutional. What action can the U.S. Supreme Court take?

A. None. The U.S. Supreme Court does not have the authority to review the decisions of state courts.

B. None. Under the doctrine of state sovereignty, states can pass laws to govern the conduct of their citizens.

C. The U.S. Supreme Court can review the decision of the state court but has no power to overrule the decision.

D. The U.S. Supreme Court can review the decision of the state court and overrule it if the decision violates federal law.

Answer (D) is correct. *(Publisher, adapted)*

REQUIRED: The Supreme Court's authority over state courts.

DISCUSSION: The Supreme Court exercises the power of judicial review with regard to not only the actions of the executive and legislative branches of the federal government but also decisions of state courts that involve questions of federal law. In this case, the issue is free speech, a federal issue. Thus, the U.S. Supreme Court may review the decision.

Answer (A) is incorrect. The U.S. Supreme Court exercises authority to review the decisions of state courts that involve questions of federal law. Answer (B) is incorrect. Under the doctrine of state sovereignty, states can pass laws that do not conflict with existing federal law. Answer (C) is incorrect. The U.S. Supreme Court does have such power if the decision involves a question of federal law.

16. Citizens from Rochester, New York bring a lawsuit against Penfield, an adjacent unincorporated municipality. The citizens allege that Penfield's zoning regulations effectively prevent persons of low and moderate income from living in Penfield in violation of the Fourteenth Amendment. The Supreme Court will most likely

A. Dismiss the suit unless the plaintiffs can show that the Penfield zoning regulation caused them some personal injury.

B. Permit the suit to continue because it involves a constitutional issue.

C. Dismiss the suit because the plaintiffs, as residents of Rochester, lack standing to challenge Penfield's zoning regulation.

D. Permit the suit to continue because it involves a civil rights issue.

Answer (A) is correct. *(Publisher, adapted)*

REQUIRED: The most likely application of the doctrine of standing in constitutional litigation.

DISCUSSION: The doctrine of standing, derived from the case or controversy requirement for federal jurisdiction, requires that an individual or a group seeking to bring a lawsuit based on a perceived constitutional violation must show that the violation has caused an injury in fact to them. In addition, the plaintiff(s) must show that the injury would be redressed by a favorable decision.

Answer (B) is incorrect. The persons bringing the suit must also demonstrate that they have standing. Answer (C) is incorrect. The litigants need not be residents of the municipality to bring a suit based on a constitutional issue. Answer (D) is incorrect. The nature of the controversy does not confer standing to bring a lawsuit. The litigants must still meet the requirements of standing.

17. Arizona is a major producer of grapefruit. The Arizona legislature passed a law restricting the importation of grapefruit from California. In ruling on the constitutionality of this law, the Supreme Court would most likely

A. Defer to the state legislature and allow the law to stand under the doctrine of state sovereignty.

B. Declare the law to be unconstitutional per se because of its discriminatory nature.

C. Declare the law to be unconstitutional unless Arizona can show a compelling state interest that outweighs the burden on interstate commerce.

D. Allow California to pass a law restricting the importation of grapefruit from Arizona as a retaliatory measure.

Answer (C) is correct. *(Publisher, adapted)*

REQUIRED: The most likely ruling about the state's restriction on the importation of a product from another state.

DISCUSSION: The Supreme Court strictly scrutinizes state laws that discriminate against commerce from other states. If the state shows a compelling state interest (such as protecting the safety of the state's citizens), the Court balances the benefit to the state against the burden to interstate commerce.

Answer (A) is incorrect. The Supreme Court has the power to invalidate state laws that violate the Constitution. Answer (B) is incorrect. State laws restricting the importation of products from competing states are not unconstitutional per se. Instead, the Court will apply the balancing test described above. Answer (D) is incorrect. The Court will not uphold retaliatory protectionist legislation. As Justice Cardozo stated, "The Constitution was framed upon the theory that the peoples of the several states must sink or swim together...."

18. The constitutional guarantee of due process,

A. As stated in the Fifth Amendment, prohibits any state from depriving any person of life, liberty, or property without due process of law.

B. As stated in the Fourteenth Amendment, prohibits the federal government from depriving any citizen of the United States of life, liberty, or property without due process of law.

C. As stated in the Fourteenth Amendment, prohibits any state from depriving any person of life, liberty, or property without due process of law.

D. As stated in the Fifth Amendment, prohibits the federal government from depriving states of their rights without due process of law.

Answer (C) is correct. *(Publisher, adapted)*

REQUIRED: The true statement concerning due process.

DISCUSSION: The Fourteenth Amendment provides that a state may not deprive a person of his/her rights (life, liberty, or property) in an unfair and unjust manner (denial of due process). This amendment applies specifically to the states, not the federal government. It also extends its protection to all persons, not just to individuals or citizens.

Answer (A) is incorrect. The due process guarantee found in the Fifth Amendment applies only against the federal government. Answer (B) is incorrect. The Due Process Clause in the Fourteenth Amendment applies specifically against the states and protects any persons (not only citizens). Answer (D) is incorrect. The Fifth Amendment protects any person (not states) from deprivation of life, liberty, or property by the federal government without due process.

19. Amanda is in her junior year at Clearview, a public high school. The assistant dean has just found a loaded gun in Amanda's locker, an offense punishable by suspension for 10 days. Which of the following statements is true?

A. Amanda does not have a property interest in continued attendance at her school.

B. Amanda is entitled to notice and a chance to respond before being suspended, but no formal evidentiary hearing is required.

C. Amanda is entitled to notice, a chance to respond, and a formal evidentiary hearing before being suspended.

D. In principle, Amanda's due process rights are not waivable.

Answer (B) is correct. *(Publisher, adapted)*

REQUIRED: The type of process required when a public school suspends a student.

DISCUSSION: Prior to suspending a student from a public school, the authorities must provide him/her notice and a chance to respond to the charges. Due process is required because continued attendance at a public school is a legitimate claim or entitlement under state law and therefore a property interest protected by the Fourteenth Amendment.

Answer (A) is incorrect. Continued attendance at a public school is considered a property interest. Answer (C) is incorrect. In these circumstances, only an informal hearing is required. Answer (D) is incorrect. In principle, due process rights are subject to waiver if the waiver is voluntary and made knowingly.

20. Assume a state passes a law providing that a police officer may stop a person who is driving in such a way that (s)he appears to be drunk; administer a breath test to that person; and, if the test shows that the person has a blood alcohol content of 0.15% or more, immediately revoke that person's driver's license for 1 year. The law includes nothing about a hearing. If a court holds this law to be unconstitutional, the reason will probably be that the law violates the

A. Due Process Clause of the Fourteenth Amendment.

B. First Amendment.

C. Equal Protection Clause of the Fourteenth Amendment.

D. Administrative Procedure Act of the state.

Answer (A) is correct. *(D. Levin)*

REQUIRED: The provision of the U.S. Constitution that is violated by a state statute authorizing revocation of a driver's license without provision for a hearing.

DISCUSSION: The right to drive is a form of liberty that is protected from state deprivation by the Due Process Clause of the Fourteenth Amendment. Although a person's driver's license may be revoked for driving with excessive alcohol in his/her blood, such revocation cannot constitutionally be accomplished without affording the driver notice and an opportunity to be heard.

Answer (B) is incorrect. Driving is not considered a right protected under the First Amendment. Answer (C) is incorrect. The statute does not treat similarly situated persons in a dissimilar way. Answer (D) is incorrect. An administrative procedures act typically relates to regulations.

21. The constitutional guarantee of equal protection,

A. As stated in the Fourteenth Amendment, prohibits any state from denying any person the equal protection of the laws.

B. As stated in the Fifth Amendment, prohibits the federal government from denying to any person the equal protection of the laws.

C. As stated in the Fifth Amendment, prohibits any state from denying any person the equal protection of the laws.

D. As stated in the Fourteenth Amendment, prohibits the federal government from denying to any person the equal protection of the laws.

Answer (A) is correct. *(Publisher, adapted)*

REQUIRED: The true statement concerning equal protection.

DISCUSSION: The Equal Protection Clause of the Fourteenth Amendment prohibits state action that denies any person (not just a citizen) equal protection. Equal protection means that similarly situated persons must be treated the same unless sufficiently strong reasons justify dissimilar treatment.

Answer (B) is incorrect. The Fifth Amendment contains no express equal protection clause. It has been interpreted, however, to contain an implicit equal protection guarantee applicable against the federal government. Answer (C) is incorrect. The Fifth Amendment applies against the federal government, not the states. Answer (D) is incorrect. The Fourteenth Amendment applies against the states, not the federal government.

22. The constitutional guarantee of equal protection

A. Requires that all citizens of the United States be treated in the same manner.

B. Is enforced with regard to gender-based classifications by means of a strict scrutiny test.

C. Is enforced by means of a strict scrutiny test when the basis for classification is race or national origin.

D. Permits the establishment of any classification of persons so long as it meets the rational basis test.

Answer (C) is correct. *(Publisher, adapted)*

REQUIRED: The true statement concerning equal protection.

DISCUSSION: If state action results in different treatment of classes of persons and the basis for classification is inherently "suspect," the courts apply a "strict scrutiny" test that can be passed only if the state shows that a "compelling" state interest was involved. Classifications based upon race or national origin are regarded as "suspect."

Answer (A) is incorrect. Equal protection prohibits discriminations having an inadequate basis in public policy. Answer (B) is incorrect. Gender-based classifications are subject to an intermediate level of scrutiny. Answer (D) is incorrect. Although many classifications require only a rational basis, certain classifications are subject to more stringent examination.

23. The Privileges and Immunities Clause of Article IV, Section 2,

A. Applies to all constitutional rights, both fundamental and otherwise.

B. Prevents states from discriminating against citizens of other states.

C. Does not apply if the state is a participant in a market.

D. Applies to corporations as well as to natural citizens.

Answer (B) is correct. *(Publisher, adapted)*

REQUIRED: The true statement regarding the Privileges and Immunities Clause.

DISCUSSION: The Privileges and Immunities Clause of Article IV, Section 2 (as distinguished from the Privileges and Immunities Clause of the Fourteenth Amendment), was designed to prevent states from discriminating against residents of other states. As the Supreme Court stated in *Toomer v. Witsell*, the clause "was designed to insure to a citizen of State A who ventures into State B the same privileges which the citizens of State B enjoy."

Answer (A) is incorrect. The Supreme Court has held that the Privileges and Immunities Clause applies only to fundamental rights. Answer (C) is incorrect. The Privileges and Immunities Clause applies even if the state participates in the markets it is attempting to regulate. Answer (D) is incorrect. The Privileges and Immunities Clause does not protect corporations.

4.5 The Bill of Rights and Business

24. The Bill of Rights consists of the first 10 amendments to the U.S. Constitution. These amendments state a variety of fundamental rights that

A. Apply directly and expressly to both the federal and the state governments.

B. Apply directly and expressly to the federal government only.

C. Apply directly and expressly to the federal government and are fully incorporated within the Fourteenth Amendment's Due Process Clause.

D. Do not apply expressly or directly to state governments. Citizens of the several states must look to their respective state constitutions for guarantees of rights enumerated in the Bill of Rights.

Answer (B) is correct. *(Publisher, adapted)*

REQUIRED: The true statement concerning the Bill of Rights.

DISCUSSION: The U.S. Supreme Court has held that the Bill of Rights applies expressly and directly only to the federal government. However, most of the guarantees in the Bill of Rights are indirectly applicable to the states through incorporation in the guarantee of due process stated by the Fourteenth Amendment.

Answer (A) is incorrect. The Bill of Rights applies only indirectly to state governments. Answer (C) is incorrect. A majority of the Supreme Court has never held that all the guarantees stated in the Bill of Rights are embraced within the single guarantee of due process that the states must respect under the Fourteenth Amendment. Answer (D) is incorrect. The majority of individual rights guaranteed in the Bill of Rights have been held to be embraced within the Due Process Clause of the Fourteenth Amendment and thus are applicable to the states.

25. A corporation is an artificial person, existing only in contemplation of law. Nevertheless, this artificial person possesses many of the rights and is subject to many of the obligations of a natural person. Which of the following states a right or rights that can be exercised only by an individual?

A. The right to contract and to own and transfer property.

B. The right to due process, the equal protection of the laws, and freedom from unreasonable searches and seizures.

C. The right to protection from self-incrimination, and the privileges and immunities of citizens in the several states.

D. The right to sue or be sued, to pay taxes, and to be treated as a citizen for some purposes.

Answer (C) is correct. *(Publisher, adapted)*

REQUIRED: The right(s) exercisable only by a natural rather than a corporate person.

DISCUSSION: The Fifth Amendment's provision that no person "shall be compelled in any criminal case to be a witness against himself" has not been applied to corporations. Thus, an officer or a director can be compelled to give testimony that incriminates the corporation, and a corporation's records can be subpoenaed. The Privileges and Immunities Clause of Article IV, Section 2 (as distinguished from the privileges and immunities clause of the 14th Amendment), was designed to prevent states from discriminating against residents of other states. As the Supreme Court stated in *Toomer v. Witsell*, the clause "was designed to ensure to a citizen of State A who ventures into State B the same privileges which the citizens of State B enjoy." The privileges and immunities clause does not protect corporations.

Answer (A) is incorrect. Corporations would have little reason for being if they had no contractual capacity and could not hold, buy, and sell property. Answer (B) is incorrect. These constitutional protections do apply to corporations. Answer (D) is incorrect. Along with the right to contract and to buy and sell property is the right to sue and be sued. The corporation also is a taxable entity and is regarded as a citizen of the state of incorporation.

26. Freedom of the press is guaranteed in the U.S. Constitution. This fundamental right is interpreted to

A. Provide a constitutional shield for communications between members of the news media and their informants.

B. Impose a different standard of liability in defamation cases brought against the news media.

C. Permit the existence of prior restraints on publication if a showing of probable cause is made.

D. Protect publications that are considered not to be obscene under the "redeeming social value" standard.

Answer (B) is correct. *(Publisher, adapted)*

REQUIRED: The true statement concerning the interpretation of freedom of the press.

DISCUSSION: A free press is considered essential to safeguarding liberty; thus, the news media have greater leeway under defamation law than private persons. If the plaintiff is a public figure or a public person with respect to the subject of the alleged defamation, the plaintiff must prove the usual elements of the tort of defamation. In addition, the plaintiff must prove that the defendant acted with "actual malice."

Answer (A) is incorrect. Some states have enacted "shield" laws, but no First Amendment requirement safeguards members of the news media from the duty to answer questions during legal proceedings. Answer (C) is incorrect. The First Amendment usually prohibits the imposition of any system of censorship or prior restraints. Answer (D) is incorrect. Obscenity is defined by reference to "contemporary community standards." "Redeeming social value" is no longer the test.

27. A state statute declared the advertising of the prices of prescription drugs by a licensed pharmacist to be unprofessional conduct. The statute was

A. Upheld because commercial speech is unprotected by the First Amendment.

B. Struck down because commercial speech is protected to the same extent as noncommercial speech.

C. Upheld as a reasonable exercise of the police power.

D. Struck down because commercial speech is protected if it concerns a lawful activity and is not misleading.

Answer (D) is correct. *(Publisher, adapted)*

REQUIRED: The constitutionality of banning advertising by pharmacists of prices of prescription drugs.

DISCUSSION: The Supreme Court has extended First Amendment protection to commercial speech. In the case on which this question is based, the court concluded that consumers and society in general would benefit from the free flow of purely commercial information consisting of truthful data about a lawful activity. Commercial speech, however, is afforded less protection than the noncommercial variety: A narrowly drawn restriction has been held valid if it directly advances a substantial governmental interest. For example, placing restraints on the erection of commercial billboards has been upheld, but a general ban on noncommercial billboards in the same ordinance was deemed unconstitutional.

Answer (A) is incorrect. Commercial speech is protected. Answer (B) is incorrect. Commercial speech is less protected. Answer (C) is incorrect. The vital interests protected by the First Amendment were held to outweigh the state's interest in regulating the professional conduct of pharmacists.

28. Dixie was the sole owner of a small proprietorship. She transferred daily accounting records of the business to a lawyer for the preparation of a tax return. The IRS attempted to subpoena the records. What will be the result?

A. Dixie will prevail if she pleads an unreasonable search and seizure.

B. Dixie will prevail if she pleads a reasonable expectation of privacy.

C. The IRS will prevail even if the items are personal diaries in the possession of the defendant.

D. The IRS will prevail against a self-incrimination defense.

Answer (D) is correct. *(Publisher, adapted)*

REQUIRED: The result of a government attempt to obtain business records.

DISCUSSION: The Fourth Amendment prohibition against unreasonable searches and seizures is related to the Fifth Amendment protection against self-incrimination. The use of a person's private papers as evidence against him/her is a form of self-incrimination. However, private papers are defined narrowly to include only those in which the accused had a reasonable expectation of privacy. Business papers prepared in the ordinary course of business receive no constitutional protection because they are regarded as transactional rather than personal documents.

Answer (A) is incorrect. The attempt to obtain business records material to a lawsuit is not unreasonable under the Fourth Amendment. Answer (B) is incorrect. Daily accounting records are transactional, not personal. Answer (C) is incorrect. Personal diaries and letters are constitutionally protected.

STUDY UNIT FIVE
ADMINISTRATIVE LAW

Administrative law is the branch of **public law** that governs the powers and procedures of administrative agencies, including judicial review of agency action. Administrative agencies, also known as regulatory agencies, are governmental bodies responsible for the supervision and administration of particular activities or areas of public interest. An **administrative agency** is any public officer, bureau, authority, board, or commission that has the power to make rules and render decisions. The term excludes legislatures, the judiciary, and nongovernmental activities. The administrative process relies upon federal and state agencies staffed by specialists to develop and enforce rules and regulations that address issues not easily resolved by the three formal branches of government. Legislative bodies have discovered that a delegation of their powers and functions to agencies results in more effective government. Most agencies are formed by an act of legislation called an **enabling statute**, which sets forth an agency's purposes and establishes its organization. However, the executive branch of a government can, by executive order, form an agency to address a problem. The Environmental Protection Agency (EPA) was formed in this manner. Enabling legislation authorizes agencies to make and enforce rules and regulations to solve one or more problems subject to certain guidelines outlined in the enabling statute. This study unit focuses on the formation and operation of federal agencies, but each state and local government is empowered to establish its own agencies as well.

Agencies can be categorized as regulatory or nonregulatory. They may also be categorized as executive or independent. **Regulatory agencies** make rules, adjudicate disputes, and impose sanctions if necessary. These agencies regulate economic activity of both individuals and businesses. Examples include the Federal Trade Commission (FTC), the Securities and Exchange Commission (SEC), and the Federal Communications Commission (FCC). **Nonregulatory agencies** conduct investigations or administer benefits such as workers' compensation, pensions, and government insurance. Examples of nonregulatory agencies include the Federal Bureau of Investigation (FBI) and the Social Security Administration (SSA). **Executive agencies** are those within the departments of the President's cabinet or the Executive Office of the President. Heads of these agencies are appointed by and serve at the pleasure of the President. Consequently, they tend to be more responsive to political influences than the heads of **independent agencies**. The latter often consist of boards or commissions whose members (1) are appointed by the President with the advice and consent of the Senate, (2) serve for a fixed term, and (3) are removable only for cause. Examples of executive agencies include the Food and Drug Administration, the Internal Revenue Service, and the Occupational Safety and Health Administration. Examples of independent agencies include the Federal Reserve System, the National Labor Relations Board, and the Federal Deposit Insurance Corporation. (The FTC, FCC, SEC, and SSA, mentioned earlier, are also among the numerous independent agencies.)

Agencies combine many of the **functions of the three branches of government**. These functions include (a) rulemaking, (b) investigating, (c) supervising, (d) advising, (e) prosecuting, and (f) adjudicating. Whether an agency performs any or all of these functions depends upon the nature and scope of the specific powers delegated to the agency by the enabling act or the executive order. Moreover, each branch of the political system has some degree of control over an agency. The executive branch may nominate the top official of an agency or make budgetary recommendations. The legislative branch may control administrative activity by amending an agency's authority, by abolishing it, or by enacting budgetary measures. The legislature also can enact laws that nullify rules and regulations issued by an agency. In addition, **The Small Business Regulatory Enforcement Act of 1996** requires agencies to submit their rules to Congress prior to their effective date. Congress may then, by joint resolution passed within 60 days, disapprove the rules. The 1996 act authorizes the courts to enforce the Regulatory Flexibility Act of 1980, which requires agencies to analyze the effects of new regulations when they have a significant impact upon a substantial number of small entities. Thus, agencies must consider cost and less burdensome alternative measures. The 1996 act also established the National Enforcement Ombudsman to handle comments from owners of small businesses, and created regional boards to rate the agencies and publish the resulting findings. The judicial branch provides a check on an agency by exercising the power of **judicial review**. Thus, a court may determine whether rules and regulations adopted by an agency exceed its delegation of authority and satisfy the due process and other requirements of the U.S. Constitution. Although an agency has broad discretion in issuing rules and regulations, it must not act outside the scope of power delegated to it. Exceeding the scope of power is known as **ultra vires** and is unconstitutional and void.

The federal **Administrative Procedure Act (APA)** establishes uniform procedures for rulemaking and adjudication. The APA also sets forth specific grounds for judicial review of agency action. To the extent the enabling statute is silent regarding rulemaking, adjudication, or judicial review procedures, the provisions of the APA fill the gap. In 1966, Congress amended the APA by enacting the **Freedom of Information Act (FOIA)**. The FOIA requires that information in the possession of federal agencies be made available to the public upon request unless it is exempted. Some exemptions include national defense matters, internal personnel rules, trade secrets, personal or commercial financial data, and records gathered by law enforcement agencies. The FOIA was amended in 1996 to require that agency records be available electronically within one year of their creation. In 1976, Congress again amended the APA by passing the **Government in the Sunshine Act**, often called the open meeting law. Its objective is to ensure that every portion of every meeting of an agency is open to public observation. However, certain agency meetings are exempt, including staff meetings and those pertaining to the matters listed above. Furthermore, each state has its own equivalent of the APA.

The **Federal Register Act** established the **Federal Register System**, which oversees the publication of federal agency information. This system publishes three important reference sources available in most large public or university libraries. The ***Government Manual*** lists the names and addresses of all U.S. government agencies. The ***Federal Register*** is published daily in a newspaper format to provide notice of all federal agencies' official acts, including information about Presidential proclamations, agency hearings, proposed and adopted regulations, and amendments thereto. Thus, under the APA, an agency's substantive regulation is not enforceable unless it has been published in the *Federal Register*. Such publication constitutes constructive notice or knowledge imputed to interested parties as a matter of law.

To alleviate the harshness of constructive notice, federal agencies also are encouraged to publish proposed rules in trade journals likely to be read by the business community. The ***Code of Federal Regulations (CFR)*** is a publication of all final rules of all federal agencies. The rules published in the CFR have the force and effect of law. State equivalents of the Federal Register Act provide for publication of state agency regulations.

Legislative rules are laws. But they must be consistent with the enabling statute, the APA, and the Constitution. Suggestions for new and amended rules are submitted by members of Congress, their constituents, professors, businesspeople, trade groups, and politically active organizations. The resulting rulemaking process under the APA may be informal, formal, or hybrid. Most agencies use the **informal rulemaking** procedure provided for by the APA. It involves publication of notice of the proposed rule in the *Federal Register*, affording interested persons an opportunity to submit written comments. After at least 30 days of public comment and review, the agency's final rule is published in the *Federal Register*. In addition, the agency must publish a concise general statement explaining the basis and purpose of the rule. However, the 30-day period can be shortened in the event of an emergency. Informal rulemaking is sometimes referred to as **notice and comment** rulemaking.

Agencies also may issue interpretive and procedural rules, but these need not be enacted in accordance with the APA and are not binding.

The **formal rulemaking** procedures under the APA require a formal hearing to provide an opportunity for interested persons to testify and cross-examine witnesses, much like a trial, before a rule is adopted. After the hearing, the agency makes public its findings of fact, conclusions of law, and decision concerning adoption of a formal rule. These three documents constitute the record. The formal rule must be supported by **substantial evidence** based on the record. This standard requires that the evidence in the record be sufficient for a reasonable person reviewing it to reach the same conclusion as the agency. Formal rulemaking is expensive and time-consuming, and Congress rarely mandates its use.

Hybrid rulemaking is a combination of formal and informal rulemaking. The notice and comment aspects of informal rulemaking are combined with opportunity for oral testimony as opposed to mere submission of written comments. As with formal rulemaking, the substantial evidence standard is applied.

Every final agency action resulting in an order other than rulemaking is an adjudication. The activities that constitute an **adjudication** range from issuing licenses to full-blown hearings that are similar to court trials. When an agency acts as an adjudicative body, it is essentially performing judicial functions. Most agency decisions are adjudications, the majority of which involve informal action. Ordinarily, agency authorities request that a person voluntarily attend a very informal hearing, much like an interview. Because the APA provides little guidance for informal adjudications, agencies do not have consistent procedures for them. However, the U.S. Supreme Court has interpreted the Fifth Amendment in the context of informal adjudications to include the right to **procedural fairness**. An individual is entitled to reasonable notice that his/her rights are about to be affected by agency action and to be informed of his/her right to a hearing prior to any further agency action.

Formal adjudication is required by the APA only when the enabling or related statute requires an adjudication on the record after opportunity for an agency hearing. Discovery is limited in these proceedings, but a respondent does have access to all relevant, unprivileged information contained in agency files. The presiding official at a formal adjudication is an **administrative law judge (ALJ)**. Theoretically, the ALJ is legally independent of agency prosecutors, investigators, and rulemakers.

Formal adjudications are subject to the constitutional standards of due process, which include the rights to (1) notification of charges and hearings, (2) representation by an attorney, (3) an impartial ALJ, (4) presentation of evidence, (5) cross-examination of the witnesses of the agency, and (6) a decision based on the regulation.

The APA requires an agency to provide opportunity for settlement with respect to both formal and informal adjudications. Consequently, most disputes are resolved through settlement. The respondent and the agency usually agree to a consent order that reflects the terms of the compromise.

Judicial review is the process by which agency action is scrutinized by the appropriate court. The purpose is to ensure that an agency does not exceed its grant of delegated authority. A case is heard by the proper court only after a party has established that (s)he is an aggrieved party who has **standing**, the party has **exhausted administrative remedies**, and the court is satisfied that the dispute is **ripe**, or ready for decision. However, a court cannot interfere with the discretion delegated to an agency. Hence, judicial review of formal agency action applies the **substantial evidence** rule. The reviewing court will set aside the agency action only if the conclusions are unsupported by substantial evidence from the record as a whole. Courts reviewing informal agency action apply the **arbitrary and capricious** standard. Under this approach, the court will overrule the agency only if it made a clear error in judgment. The judiciary's reluctance to interfere with an agency's interpretation of facts, particularly involving areas of the agency's specialization, is called **agency deference**. Nevertheless, the reviewing court may freely substitute its own judgment for that of the agency as to questions of law, such as statutory interpretation.

The **doctrine of standing** provides that only the injured party may sue. The Supreme Court has held that a person must demonstrate that (s)he has suffered a direct injury as a result of the agency action in order to meet the standing requirement. Furthermore, the interest that the injured party seeks to protect must be within the range of interests protected by the Constitution, a statute, or a regulation. Even if a party has standing, (s)he must exhaust all available administrative remedies before filing suit. Agencies have internal procedures for appealing an adverse decision, and judicial review is usually available only for final actions by an agency. The **exhaustion doctrine** permits an agency to discover and correct its own errors, thereby minimizing the need for judicial review. The doctrine avoids premature interruption of the administrative process.

The **ripeness** requirement prevents a court from reviewing agency action unless the agency has acted officially and made a final decision. Once an agency takes final action, unless contrary to statute, it may be appealed to a proper federal court. Some statutes specifically provide for appeal only to a particular federal court. For example, specified adjudications may be appealable only to a U.S. court of appeals, whereas others may be made to U.S. district courts. After proper judicial review, a court may declare agency action illegal and may order the agency either to act or to refrain from acting. If agencies or administrators are sued for monetary damages by those subject to their administrative rules, regulations, and decisions, the defenses asserted include **sovereign immunity** and the discretionary function defense. The latter is effective when an administrator's action was in good faith and in the exercise of his/her discretionary powers.

QUESTIONS

5.1 Origin and Purpose of Administrative Agencies

1. Administrative law is

A. The substantive law produced by an administrative agency.

B. Found only in statutes.

C. Any law regarding the powers and procedures of an administrative agency.

D. Produced only by an independent administrative agency.

Answer (C) is correct. *(Publisher, adapted)*

REQUIRED: The true statement about administrative law.

DISCUSSION: Broadly defined, administrative law is any law regarding the powers and procedures of administrative agencies. For example, the federal Administrative Procedure Act (APA) establishes the procedures that govern the carrying out of the various functions (rulemaking, adjudication) of a federal agency.

Answer (A) is incorrect. Administrative law is also found in constitutions, statutes, agency decisions, and court opinions. Answer (B) is incorrect. Administrative law is also found in constitutions, statutes, agency decisions, and court opinions. Answer (D) is incorrect. Executive agencies also produce administrative law.

2. The best description of an administrative agency is that it is a governmental board, commission, officer, bureau, or department

A. Independent of the executive, legislative, or judicial branches of government.

B. With the power to make rules and adjudicate disputes affecting private rights.

C. Within only the executive branch of the federal or a state government.

D. With power only to enforce the law.

Answer (B) is correct. *(Publisher, adapted)*

REQUIRED: The best description of an administrative agency.

DISCUSSION: An administrative agency is a public board, commission, officer, etc. (other than a judicial or legislative body) with limited power to enforce the law, make rules, and adjudicate disputes involving private rights and duties. It may be independent (SEC, FTC, FCC) or executive (OMB, cabinet departments).

Answer (A) is incorrect. Some agencies are within the executive branch and some are independent. Answer (C) is incorrect. Some agencies are within the executive branch and some are independent. Answer (D) is incorrect. Agencies also have other powers, e.g., to make rules.

3. Congress forms administrative agencies to regulate various industries and businesses. Which of the following is not a valid reason for the formation of an agency?

A. To regulate technologically complex industries.

B. To improve efficiency and provide greater flexibility.

C. To increase the power of the legislative branch at the expense of the executive branch.

D. To provide specialized expertise in regulating large industries.

Answer (C) is correct. *(Publisher, adapted)*

REQUIRED: The invalid reason for formation of an administrative agency.

DISCUSSION: Congress has neither the time nor the expertise to regulate all aspects of business. Congress therefore forms administrative agencies and delegates the authority to make rules and to regulate the activities of businesses and industries. Agency experts can devote all their efforts to investigation, rulemaking, and adjudication in one problem area, which provides greater efficiency and flexibility. Agencies are not formed to draw power away from the executive branch.

4. All of the following are criticisms generally made of federal regulatory agencies and policies except

A. Taxes imposed by agencies being too high.

B. Political considerations influencing policies and rules.

C. Regulatory rules being rigid and hard to change.

D. Regulations increasing the cost of products and services.

Answer (A) is correct. *(CMA, adapted)*

REQUIRED: The item not a criticism of federal regulatory agencies and policies.

DISCUSSION: Federal administrative agencies belong to the executive branch of government. They have quasi-legislative powers (rulemaking authority pursuant to enabling statutes enacted by Congress), quasi-judicial powers (the ability to adjudicate certain disputes within their jurisdiction), and quasi-executive powers (for example, to investigate and prosecute violations). However, no federal agency has taxing authority, a power reserved to Congress. Moreover, all bills for raising revenue must originate in the House of Representatives.

5. Which of the following is a true statement about administrative agencies?

A. Independent agencies tend to be less subject to political control.

B. Executive agencies include the Internal Revenue Service (IRS) and the Securities and Exchange Commission (SEC).

C. Independent agencies include the Food and Drug Administration (FDA) and the Occupational Safety and Health Administration (OSHA).

D. The heads of executive agencies usually serve for fixed terms and can be removed only for cause.

Answer (A) is correct. *(Publisher, adapted)*

REQUIRED: The true statement about executive and independent agencies.

DISCUSSION: Executive agencies are those within the departments of the President's cabinet or the Executive Office of the President. Heads of these agencies are appointed by and serve at the pleasure of the President. Consequently, they tend to be more responsive to political influences than the heads of independent agencies. The latter often consist of boards or commissions whose members (1) are appointed by the President with the advice and consent of the Senate, (2) serve for a fixed term, and (3) are removable only for cause.

Answer (B) is incorrect. The SEC is an independent agency. Answer (C) is incorrect. The FDA (Department of Health and Human Services) and OSHA (Department of Labor) are executive agencies. Answer (D) is incorrect. It states a characteristic of independent, not executive, agencies.

6. Which one of the following forms of law is created when regulatory agencies transform statutes into regulations and enforcement procedures?

A. Constitutional law.

B. Statutory law.

C. Administrative law.

D. Judicial law.

Answer (C) is correct. *(CMA, adapted)*

REQUIRED: The law created when regulatory agencies transform statutes into regulations and enforcement procedures.

DISCUSSION: Administrative law is promulgated by the executive branch under a general grant of authority to an agency to regulate an industry. Administrative law may also be promulgated under a specific grant of authority to an agency to make detailed rules to achieve the objectives of a statute. For example, the IRS makes rules to carry out specific statutes but is not given the general authority to make rules for the collection of revenue. Administrative law may not go beyond the scope of the statutes under which it is promulgated.

Answer (A) is incorrect. Constitutional law is the fundamental law of a jurisdiction. Answer (B) is incorrect. Statutory law is a body of detailed enactments by the legislative branch upon which administrative law is based. Answer (D) is incorrect. Judicial (common) law is created by the courts through the adjudication of cases and the publication of the resulting opinions.

5.2 Control of Administrative Agencies

7. Which of the following statements best describes how regulatory agencies of the U.S. government are restricted in the adoption of specific regulations?

A. Regulations must be consistent with standards established in the legislation that created the agency.

B. The agencies must first conduct a study showing that the benefits of a proposed regulation exceed its costs.

C. Businesses subject to the regulation must be given notice 1 year before the regulation will be put into effect.

D. The President of the United States must sign the regulation before it becomes effective.

Answer (A) is correct. *(CMA, adapted)*

REQUIRED: The statement best describing a restriction on the adoption of regulations by regulatory agencies.

DISCUSSION: Regulatory agencies are given the authority to prescribe regulations for implementing statutes. These regulations must be consistent with the standards established by the statute which created the regulatory authority.

Answer (B) is incorrect. Cost-benefit analysis is not a requirement for the promulgation of a regulation. Answer (C) is incorrect. The Administrative Procedure Act requires publication of the rule at least 30 days before its effective date. Answer (D) is incorrect. The President may approve a statute by signing it, but (s)he is not required to sign regulations for them to become effective.

8. Rulemaking by a federal administrative body

A. Is not governed by the Administrative Procedure Act, which is concerned only with adjudicatory action.

B. Is required to meet the same procedural standards as adjudication.

C. Is subject to the Administrative Procedure Act, which is concerned with both rulemaking and adjudicatory action.

D. Does not involve public proceedings, even if the rules are legislative.

Answer (C) is correct. *(Publisher, adapted)*

REQUIRED: The true statement concerning rule-making by an administrative body.

DISCUSSION: The Administrative Procedure Act (APA) governs both rulemaking and adjudicatory action by federal administrative agencies. In general, it provides that rule-making must proceed in an orderly manner allowing those affected by the regulatory process to have notice of, and an opportunity to contribute to, the enactment of regulations. When an agency proposes a regulation, general notice must be published in the *Federal Register*.

Answer (A) is incorrect. The APA is concerned with adjudication and rulemaking. Answer (B) is incorrect. The procedural standards for rulemaking are not as stringent as those for adjudication. Answer (D) is incorrect. Notice of proposed rulemaking must be given and the public must be allowed to participate if the rules are legislative, that is, if they fill the gaps in a statute.

9. The Administrative Procedure Act (APA) was enacted in 1946 as a response to criticism of the discretion and power that Congress had granted to administrative agencies. Its main function is to

A. Provide the authority for administrative agencies to make laws.

B. Provide for congressional review of the rules issued by administrative agencies.

C. Provide a legislative veto power to Congress so that Congress can overrule laws created by administrative agencies.

D. Specify the procedures agencies must follow in making rules and establish standards for judicial review of agency action.

Answer (D) is correct. *(Publisher, adapted)*

REQUIRED: The function of the Administrative Procedure Act.

DISCUSSION: The Administrative Procedure Act applies to all federal agencies and serves to standardize the procedures by which those agencies make laws. It supplements but does not supersede stricter procedural requirements imposed on an agency by Congress in the agency's enabling legislation. The APA applies in cases in which the agency's enabling legislation is silent as to the procedures to be followed in creating laws. The APA also establishes standards for judicial review of agency action.

Answer (A) is incorrect. The authority for agencies to make rules is determined by the statute establishing the agency. Answer (B) is incorrect. The APA does not provide for congressional review of rules made by agencies. Answer (C) is incorrect. Legislative vetoes of agency actions have been ruled unconstitutional by the Supreme Court. Congress can veto agency rules only by passing legislation subject to the President's veto power.

10. There are three types of administrative rules: procedural, interpretive, and legislative. Which, if any, of these rules are subject to the rulemaking requirements of the Administrative Procedure Act (APA)?

A. Procedural rules.

B. Interpretive rules.

C. Legislative rules.

D. All three types of rules are subject to the APA's rulemaking procedures.

Answer (C) is correct. *(Publisher, adapted)*

REQUIRED: The administrative rules to which the APA applies.

DISCUSSION: Legislative rules are those issued by an administrative agency under the authority delegated to it by Congress. These rules have the force of law and are binding on the agency, the courts, and the public. Such rules are subject to the rulemaking requirements of the APA. For example, the rule requiring warning labels on cigarette packages is a legislative rule.

Answer (A) is incorrect. The APA's requirements do not apply to procedural rules. Procedural rules govern the administrative agency's own conduct. Answer (B) is incorrect. Interpretive rules are statements by an agency that express the agency's understanding and interpretations of the statutes it administers. Answer (D) is incorrect. Only legislative rules are governed by the APA.

11. In accordance with the Federal Register Act of 1935,

A. The *Federal Register* prints the names and addresses of all governmental agencies.

B. The *Government Manual* contains all federal regulations currently in force.

C. The *Code of Federal Regulations* (CFR) is published daily to provide notice of proposed regulations.

D. A three-part *Federal Register* system was established.

Answer (D) is correct. *(Publisher, adapted)*

REQUIRED: The true statement about the Federal Register Act.

DISCUSSION: The *Federal Register, Government Manual*, and the *Code of Federal Regulations* are the parts of the system. They provide current information about federal agencies and regulations.

Answer (A) is incorrect. The *Federal Register*, published every business day, gives information about such matters as agency hearings, presidential proclamations, and proposed regulations. Answer (B) is incorrect. The *Government Manual* is published annually to provide the names and addresses of and other pertinent data about federal agencies. Answer (C) is incorrect. The CFR includes all current regulations arranged by agency.

12. In the exercise of their investigatory functions, administrative agencies may conduct inspections and searches. Which of the following warrantless searches by an agency would be considered unreasonable under the Constitution?

A. A safety inspector searches a junkyard that dismantles cars. Because of the high incidence of car theft, the industry is highly regulated under a statute that authorizes warrantless searches and requires maintenance of certain records. The junkyard owner did not consent to the search.

B. An inspector arrives to search the records of a store that sells rifles and other firearms. The owner denies the inspector access to the records of gun sales.

C. An inspector arrives to search a clothing store for workplace dangers. The store manager refuses to admit the inspector.

D. An inspector arrives to search a shoe factory for workplace hazards. The factory superintendent consents to the search.

Answer (C) is correct. *(S. Willey)*

REQUIRED: The warrantless administrative agency search not in compliance with the Fourth Amendment.

DISCUSSION: The Fourth Amendment prohibits unreasonable searches and seizures of information by administrative agencies. Warrantless searches are ordinarily considered reasonable if the party voluntarily consents to the search; the search is conducted in an emergency; the business is in a highly regulated industry, warrantless searches are necessary to follow the regulatory scheme, and the search have a properly defined scope (e.g., liquor and firearms); or the business is hazardous (e.g., a coal mine), and a statute expressly provides for warrantless searches. Because a clothing store is not in a hazardous industry or one in which warrantless searches are automatically valid, the inspector must have a warrant in this nonemergency situation if the store manager does not voluntarily agree to the search.

Answer (A) is incorrect. The U.S. Supreme Court held that the search was reasonable. The Court found that the state had a substantial interest in regulating such businesses, that warrantless searches were necessary to serve the state's interest, and that the statute was a substitute for a warrant because it gave notice that inspections would be made regularly. Answer (B) is incorrect. Warrantless searches are automatically valid in the firearms industry. Answer (D) is incorrect. Consent validates a search.

5.3 Rulemaking

13. The authority of an agency to make law is typically determined by

A. The Administrative Procedure Act (APA).

B. The executive branch.

C. The statute that created the agency.

D. The agency itself.

Answer (C) is correct. *(Publisher, adapted)*

REQUIRED: The source of an agency's authority to legislate.

DISCUSSION: The authority of an agency to make law is typically determined by the statute that creates the agency. The legislative branch, in writing the statute, provides standards and guidelines that limit and direct the authority to be exercised by the agency.

Answer (A) is incorrect. The APA does not provide the authority for the agency to make rules, but governs the procedures to be followed. Answer (B) is incorrect. The executive branch of government does not determine an agency's authority to make rules. Answer (D) is incorrect. Agencies do not have inherent authority to make law. Their authority is delegated by Congress and is determined by the legislative statute establishing the agency.

14. Many agencies promulgate regulations that have the force and effect of law. This process is known as

A. Rulemaking.

B. Enforcement.

C. Adjudication.

D. Delegation.

Answer (A) is correct. *(Publisher, adapted)*

REQUIRED: The term for the promulgation of regulations by agencies.

DISCUSSION: The process by which agencies promulgate regulations that have the force and effect of law is known as rulemaking. The Administrative Procedure Act (APA) defines a rule as "an agency statement of general or particular applicability and future effect designed to interpret, complement, or prescribe law or policy." In promulgating regulations, agencies must follow the procedures provided in their enabling legislation and in the APA.

Answer (B) is incorrect. Enforcement is the execution of existing laws. Answer (C) is incorrect. Adjudication is an administrative proceeding conducted by an agency to determine if a statute or regulation has been violated. Answer (D) is incorrect. Delegation is the transfer of power by a branch of government that vests authority in an agency.

15. The Administrative Procedure Act sets forth two methods of rulemaking by administrative agencies: formal and informal. The major difference between these two methods is that

A. Formal rulemaking requires that the agency creating the rule publish a notice of proposed rulemaking in the *Federal Register*.

B. Formal rulemaking requires that the agency conduct formal hearings at which all its evidence justifying its proposed regulation is presented.

C. Informal rulemaking requires that the agency hold public hearings.

D. The formal method is more efficient because it allows any objection to the rule to be taken into consideration prior to the rule's final adoption.

Answer (B) is correct. *(Publisher, adapted)*

REQUIRED: The difference between formal and informal rulemaking.

DISCUSSION: Formal and informal rulemaking are similar in most respects. Both require publication of the proposed rulemaking in the *Federal Register* so that the public can participate in the proceedings. The major difference is that formal rulemaking requires that the agency hold formal trial-type hearings. Informal rulemaking permits but does not require the agency to hold public hearings.

Answer (A) is incorrect. Both formal and informal rulemaking require that the agency publish notice. Answer (C) is incorrect. An agency conducting informal rulemaking may hold public hearings, but it is not required to do so. Answer (D) is incorrect. The informal method is more efficient because lack of required hearings minimizes opportunities for delay.

16. Which of the following is a true statement about legislative and interpretive rules issued by an administrative agency?

A. Interpretive rules are not subject to judicial review.

B. The making of interpretive rules is subject to the notice and public participation requirements.

C. Legislative rules are not subject to judicial review.

D. The making of legislative rules is subject to the notice and public participation requirements.

Answer (D) is correct. *(Publisher, adapted)*

REQUIRED: The true statement about legislative and interpretive rules.

DISCUSSION: Legislative rules issued by an administrative agency are substantive in that they are intended to fill the gaps in a statute passed by the legislative branch. The power to issue such regulations may be express or implied. Rulemaking of this kind is subject to a notice requirement. Notice of the time, place, and nature of the proceedings and of the substance of the proposed rule must be published in the Federal Register. Also, the agency must permit the public to participate in the process through submission of written or oral arguments and data. Legislative rules are not judicially reviewable under a "correctness" standard. They are presumed valid and will be struck down only if the agency has made an error of law.

Answer (A) is incorrect. Interpretive rules are judicially reviewable. Answer (B) is incorrect. Adoption of interpretive rules, general statements of policy, and the agency's own organization and procedures are not subject to the notice and public participation requirements. Answer (C) is incorrect. Legislative rules are judicially reviewable.

5.4 Adjudication

17. In the exercise of its adjudicatory power, an administrative agency

A. Unlike a court, need not observe procedural due process.

B. Is required to observe procedural due process.

C. Is represented at a hearing by an administrative law judge whose functions within the agency include both investigation and adjudication of disputes.

D. Must afford parties who come before it in adjudicatory hearings the full panoply of procedural rights available in a judicial proceeding.

Answer (B) is correct. *(Publisher, adapted)*

REQUIRED: The true statement concerning the adjudicatory power of an administrative agency.

DISCUSSION: The due process clauses of the 5th and 14th Amendments apply to the deprivation of rights by federal or state action, regardless of whether the process is judicial or quasi-judicial. Procedural due process requires that certain fair and reasonable formalities be followed in administrative adjudications.

Answer (A) is incorrect. An administrative agency is bound by the Due Process Clause. Answer (C) is incorrect. To insure his/her impartiality, an administrative law judge would be prohibited from investigating disputes. Answer (D) is incorrect. Procedural protection of parties' rights is limited in administrative adjudications, given the enormous number of cases heard by administrative agencies.

18. An administrative agency has authority to perform judicial functions. Which of the following statements regarding adjudication is false?

A. Agency adjudication is intended to settle factual disputes among a relatively small group of parties.

B. An administrative agency's adjudications are concerned with general policy to a greater extent than a court's.

C. A party required to appear before an agency investigative hearing is entitled to be represented by an attorney.

D. A defendant in an agency formal adjudicatory action has the right to a jury trial.

Answer (D) is correct. *(Publisher, adapted)*

REQUIRED: The false statement regarding adjudication.

DISCUSSION: Under their adjudicatory powers, administrative agencies perform many of the same functions as courts. However, the Supreme Court has ruled that a defendant in an adjudicatory action does not have a right to a jury trial.

Answer (A) is incorrect. Agency adjudication is not intended to settle general controversies involving the public at large. Answer (B) is incorrect. An agency hearing is more likely to be concerned with general conditions, and the administrative law judge is more likely to consider the effect of a decision on the public. Answer (C) is incorrect. Parties have rights to receive notice, to be represented by attorneys, to present evidence, and to cross-examine opposing witnesses.

19. Adjudication is a quasi-judicial function performed by administrative agencies. Adjudicatory hearings resemble a trial and are conducted by an administrative law judge (ALJ). Regarding adjudicatory hearings, which of the following statements is true?

A. Adjudicatory hearings follow much less restrictive rules of evidence than trials in other courts.

B. The ALJ can impose a criminal penalty.

C. The decision of the ALJ in the adjudicatory hearing is final and cannot be appealed.

D. The Administrative Procedure Act (APA) does not apply to adjudicatory hearings.

Answer (A) is correct. *(Publisher, adapted)*

REQUIRED: The true statement regarding adjudicatory hearings.

DISCUSSION: One of the major differences between adjudicatory hearings and court trials is that the former follow much less restrictive rules of evidence. Agencies need not follow common-law rules that tend to restrict the types of evidence a court may consider. For example, the hearsay rule need not be observed. However, the legal residuum rule requires that a finding of fact be based upon at least some evidence that would be admissible in a court.

Answer (B) is incorrect. Administrative agencies do not have the power to impose criminal penalties on violators. Answer (C) is incorrect. The decision handed down by an ALJ can be appealed to a higher level of the agency. Moreover, final agency action can be judicially reviewed. Answer (D) is incorrect. The APA does provide rules governing adjudicatory hearings.

5.5 Judicial Review

20. As part of the administrative law process, which of the following is a major function of judicial review?

A. Providing political oversight, control, and, in general, shaping and influencing regulatory programs and their basic policies.

B. Assuring that the agency is acting in accordance with the enabling legislation.

C. Correcting deficiencies contained in the relevant legislation.

D. Re-examination of findings of fact contained in agency determinations.

Answer (B) is correct. *(CPA, adapted)*

REQUIRED: The major function of judicial review in administrative law.

DISCUSSION: An administrative agency operates within the guidelines established by the enabling legislation. The rulemaking power of the agency is dependent upon the enabling statute or the statute it is directed to enforce. Rules made within the guidelines established by the statute have the force and effect of law. Whether the agency has acted within these limitations is a question of law that a court may decide. A second major judicial review function is to determine that due process has been observed.

Answer (A) is incorrect. It states a function of the legislative rather than the judicial branch of government. Answer (C) is incorrect. It states a function of the legislative rather than the judicial branch of government. Answer (D) is incorrect. Judicial review of an agency's findings of fact is ordinarily limited to whether the findings were supported by substantial evidence in the record.

21. In reviewing agency action, courts practice considerable self-restraint for all except which of the following reasons?

A. Complexity of the substantive questions and recognition of the special competence of agencies in handling them.

B. Impracticability of reviewing more than a small fraction of agency decisions.

C. Respect for the concept of separation of powers.

D. Lack of jurisdiction.

Answer (D) is correct. *(Publisher, adapted)*

REQUIRED: The reason that is not a basis for a court to exercise self-restraint in reviewing agency action.

DISCUSSION: The judicial branch of government has the power of judicial review to inquire into the constitutional propriety of actions of the executive branch. Lack of jurisdiction is ordinarily not a basis for the courts' exercise of self-restraint in reviewing agency action.

Answer (A) is incorrect. Judicial self-restraint is necessary given the highly technical expertise often required to deal with the subject matter of agency action. Answer (B) is incorrect. Court dockets are already overloaded, and courts can review only a few agency actions. Answer (C) is incorrect. Too much activity by the court would infringe upon the proper exercise of executive authority and therefore violate the constitutional separation of powers.

22. In reviewing an adjudicatory decision by an administrative agency, a court will invalidate the agency action

A. If the circumstances required a formal hearing and no jury was provided to act as a trier of fact.

B. If the agency's determination of facts was incorrect.

C. Unless the agency's determination was supported by substantial evidence in the record.

D. Only if the agency exceeded the authority conferred upon it by the enabling statute.

Answer (C) is correct. *(Publisher, adapted)*

REQUIRED: The basis for judicial invalidation of agency action.

DISCUSSION: The reviewing court is not as well equipped as the agency to make findings of fact, and it will not substitute its judgment for that of the agency on factual questions. Instead, it will inquire whether as a matter of law the agency's findings of fact are supported by substantial evidence in the record. Substantial evidence is evidence from which a reasonable person might reach the same conclusion as the agency. It need not be a preponderance of or greater weight of the evidence.

Answer (A) is incorrect. Juries never serve as triers of fact in agency proceedings. Answer (B) is incorrect. The reviewing court does not ask whether the agency's finding was incorrect, only whether the finding was supported by substantial evidence. Answer (D) is incorrect. Other grounds exist for reviewing agency action, e.g., compliance with procedural due process.

23. In reviewing an administrative agency's decision, a court will usually

A. Accept jurisdiction whether or not all administrative appeals have been exhausted.

B. Make its own independent determinations of fact.

C. Make a redetermination as to the credibility of witnesses who testified before the agency.

D. Affirm the decision of the agency if it is both reasonable and rational.

Answer (D) is correct. *(CPA, adapted)*

REQUIRED: The true statement about judicial review of agency action.

DISCUSSION: When reviewing adjudication by an agency, a court will not substitute its judgment for that of the agency on questions of fact. The standard of review is not "correctness" but whether the record contains substantial evidence that a reasonable and rational person might accept as adequate.

Answer (A) is incorrect. Administrative remedies must usually be exhausted (the agency action must be final) before the court may take jurisdiction. Answer (B) is incorrect. The reviewing court is essentially an appeals court and will not make independent findings of fact. Answer (C) is incorrect. The reviewing court has not seen and heard the witnesses and tried the case and is thus in no position to make a factual determination regarding the credibility of witnesses.

24. Able Corporation was charged with a violation of the Federal Trade Commission Act. Harp, an FTC examiner, concluded that Able had violated the Act and made adverse determinations on several issues. Able believes Harp has been arbitrary in several of the determinations and clearly incorrect in others. Able

A. Must accept the determination unless it was denied due process.

B. Should immediately proceed in the local state court to obtain injunctive relief ordering Harp to reopen the case and redetermine his conclusions.

C. Should appeal immediately to the local federal district court to overturn the determination.

D. Must exhaust the available administrative remedies before relief in court can be sought.

Answer (D) is correct. *(CPA, adapted)*

REQUIRED: The appropriate action by a person who wishes to overturn a decision by an administrative agency.

DISCUSSION: Exhaustion of administrative remedies is necessary prior to judicial review. In part, this principle is based on the need for efficiency: interruption of the administrative process may be wasteful of time and resources. The deference of courts to the superior expertise of the agency also plays a role. Moreover, the exhaustion of remedies requirement reflects the separation of powers concept. Executive branch autonomy is respected until the agency has completed its action or clearly exceeded its authority.

Answer (A) is incorrect. A plaintiff may seek judicial review on many grounds other than violation of due process. Answer (B) is incorrect. Judicial review of an FTC action would be appropriate in a federal court but only when administrative remedies are exhausted. Answer (C) is incorrect. Judicial review of an FTC action would be appropriate in a federal court but only when administrative remedies are exhausted.

25. Judicial review of administrative action

A. Is not available when that action was adjudicatory in nature under the theory of res judicata.

B. Is permitted regardless of whether administrative remedies are exhausted.

C. Is subject to the ripeness doctrine.

D. Extends more often to review of questions of fact than of law since the administrative agency is deemed to have great expertise in the enforcement of the enabling legislation.

Answer (C) is correct. *(Publisher, adapted)*

REQUIRED: The true statement concerning judicial review of administrative action.

DISCUSSION: A court will not review agency action unless the issues are ripe for judicial determination. The agency must have issued a final determination and administrative remedies must have been exhausted.

Answer (A) is incorrect. Agency action is not subject to the res judicata doctrine. The agency is not a court. Also, judicial review is an appellate process. Answer (B) is incorrect. Judicial review is not permitted when the litigant can still pursue a remedy within the administrative structure. Answer (D) is incorrect. Judicial review of administrative action extends to questions of law rather than fact. The agency is better equipped for factual determination than the court.

STUDY UNIT SIX
CRIMINAL LAW AND PROCEDURE

The primary objective of **criminal law** is to protect the public. It is one of society's most important mechanisms for causing the behavior of its citizens to conform to established norms. Criminal law is almost exclusively statutory. The **Model Penal Code (MPC)** is an important general reference in criminal law developed by the American Law Institute (ALI). The ALI is an organization of lawyers, judges, and scholars that publishes restatements of the general common law of the U.S. as well as model statutes. Although not authoritative, the MPC is the basis for many state criminal codes. A **crime** is a public wrong committed against the state, as distinguished from a **tort**, which is a civil wrong to an individual. The same activity may be subject to criminal action by the state and a civil suit by the victim. An example is a battery. A critical difference lies in the **burden of proof**. A plaintiff in a civil action must prove all the elements of recovery by a preponderance, or greater weight, of the evidence. The state must prove all the elements of a crime **beyond a reasonable doubt**, a much higher standard. The **rules of evidence** are designed to ensure that the evidence offered at trial is relevant, reliable, and not unfairly prejudicial.

Virtually all crimes require a physical act and most require criminal intent. Concurrence of a wrongful act with a wrongful intent or state of mind is usually required. **Strict liability** crimes do not require a mental element. The conduct itself, even if innocently engaged in, results in criminal liability. For example, health code violations, statutory rape, bigamy, and speeding are strict liability crimes. No fault needs to be proven. Criminal liability requires the defendant to have performed a voluntary physical act. This act may be one of commission or omission. A criminal act of omission occurs when a person has a legal duty to act and does not, for example, failing to file a tax return. The performance of the criminal act is the **actus reus** (the guilty act). A thought is not an act. Bad thoughts alone, therefore, do not constitute a crime. Criminal intent is a state of mind by which the person intends either the act or the act and its consequences. This mental state is the **mens rea**. Crimes that include a mental element are classified according to whether they require objective fault or subject fault. **Objective fault** involves (1) carelessness, (2) negligence, or (3) having reason to know that certain conduct is prohibited. The standard is the state of mind of an ordinary reasonable person, not the defendant's actual mental state. Examples of crimes requiring objective fault are (1) negligent homicide, (2) careless driving, and (3) receiving stolen property having reason to know it was stolen. **Subjective fault** is an actual state of mind. It may be (1) purposeful (intentional), (2) knowing, or (3) reckless. **Purposeful fault** is a conscious intent to do the wrongful act or effect the wrongful result. An example is larceny. An element of this crime is an intent to deprive another of property by taking it and carrying it away. **Knowing fault** is knowledge that conduct is of a wrongful type or almost certain to lead to a wrongful outcome. An example is receiving stolen property knowing it to be stolen. **Reckless fault** is a conscious indifference to a serious risk of wrongful conduct or a wrongful result. An example is reckless homicide resulting from reckless operation of a motor vehicle. Subjective fault is usually required to be proved under criminal law. Motive does not determine criminal liability. Thus, a person may possess an ethical motive for committing an act and still be guilty of a crime, e.g., mercy killing.

Crimes are classified by degree of seriousness as felonies or misdemeanors. A **felony** is a crime punishable by death or incarceration for more than a year in a prison. A **misdemeanor** is a lesser crime, punishable by a fine and/or incarceration for less than 1 year in a jail or detention center. An **inchoate crime** is committed in preparation for what may be a serious offense. The inchoate crime is a complete offense in itself even if the serious offense is never completed. The inchoate offenses are attempt, aiding and abetting, solicitation, and conspiracy. **Attempt** is commission of a substantial step toward committing a crime. **Aiding and abetting** is actively assisting another to commit or attempt to commit a crime. **Solicitation** is encouragement of another to commit a crime. **Conspiracy** is agreement to reach an illegal objective, when at least one overt act has occurred in its furtherance.

The MPC states five classifications of crimes. Those creating **danger to the person** include (1) murder, (2) manslaughter, (3) reckless homicide, (4) robbery, (5) sex offenses, (6) assault, and (7) kidnapping. Crimes **against property** include (1) business frauds, (2) forcible robbery, (3) burglary, (4) arson, (5) larceny, and (6) forgery. Crimes **against the family** include (1) bigamy, (2) child abuse, and (3) incest. Crimes against **public administration** include (1) bribery, (2) resisting arrest, (3) escape, (4) perjury, and (5) obstructing justice. Crimes **against public order and decency** include (1) drunkenness, (2) prostitution, (3) loitering, and (4) disorderly conduct.

For a defendant in a criminal case to be held criminally liable, (s)he must have engaged in unjustified criminal behavior with criminal intent. Many defenses raised in a criminal case attempt either to rebut the proof of the requisite criminal state of mind or to prove that the cause of the behavior was sufficient to excuse or justify it. One common **defense** is that the act was **involuntary**. Criminal liability ordinarily attaches only to voluntary behavior. Thus, no criminal liability is usually imposed in the case of reflex actions, sleepwalking, seizures, blackouts, or similar circumstances. The **insanity** defense is used whenever a mental disease or defect is asserted to have resulted in a lack of control over a defendant's actions. The defendant has the burden to prove the insanity defense. The defense of **duress** is available when the defendant is coerced by another person. The coercion must be a threat of imminent death or serious bodily harm to the defendant or to another. Duress is not a defense to an otherwise unlawful intentional killing of a person. An honest **mistake of fact** can be a defense to a specific intent crime. For example, a person might take property that (s)he honestly mistakes for his/her own. However, a **mistake of law** is ordinarily not a defense, even if the ignorance or mistake was reasonable. Nevertheless, some state statutes now permit a defense when the mistake is by one charged with responsibility for the interpretation, administration, or enforcement of the law. Furthermore, **consent** of an alleged victim also is normally not a defense. However, if it negates an element of the crime, consent is a complete defense. For example, proof that an adult victim consented to intercourse is a defense to a charge of rape. The consent must be knowingly and voluntarily given without duress or fraud. The defense of **entrapment** arises if the intent to commit a crime originates with the activities of law enforcement officers and not the defendant. The defense of entrapment requires proof of two elements: the criminal plan originated with law enforcement officers, and the defendant was not predisposed in any way to commit the crime. The law recognizes two types of intoxication as a defense: voluntary and involuntary. **Voluntary intoxication** is a defense to some crimes because the ability to form the required intent is negated by the effect of a drug. **Involuntary intoxication** occurs when a person either was unaware that a substance contained a drug or was physically forced to ingest a drug or a substance containing a drug. Involuntary intoxication is ordinarily a defense if its effect was to make the defendant unable to understand that the act was wrong.

Under certain circumstances, a defendant may raise the issue of **just cause** to excuse guilt. For example, a person who is without fault may plead self-defense to justify the use of deadly force or force that appeared reasonably necessary to protect him/herself from an imminent threat of death or great bodily harm. The period specified in a **statute of limitations** prevents prosecution of most crimes after such period expires. A notable exception is murder.

Criminal procedure generally refers to the constitutional protection given to the criminally accused to prevent potential abuse of government power. The primary sources of criminal procedure are the U.S. Constitution, state constitutions, state statutes governing police activities, court procedures, and sentencing matters. Constitutional limitations embodied in criminal procedure are intended to protect the individual liberties enjoyed by all persons in the United States. U.S. Constitutional protections relevant to criminal procedure include provisions in the Fourth, Fifth, Sixth, and Eighth Amendments. These rights have been applied to the states through the due process clause of the Fourteenth Amendment. Thus, (1) probable cause is required for a warrant, (2) a warrant must specifically describe the place to be searched and the persons or things to be seized, and (3) the people are to be secure against unreasonable searches and seizures **(Fourth Amendment)**. No person should be (1) subject to double jeopardy for the same criminal offense; (2) forced to incriminate him/herself in a criminal case (not applicable to corporations); or (3) deprived of life, liberty, or property without due process **(Fifth Amendment)**. The accused has the right (1) to a speedy, public trial by jury where the crime was committed; (2) to be informed of the cause of action; (3) to confront witnesses; (4) to have compulsory process for calling witnesses; and (5) to have counsel **(Sixth Amendment)**. Excessive bail and fines must not be imposed or cruel and unusual punishments inflicted **(Eighth Amendment)**. Accordingly, the **exclusionary rule** requires that any evidence obtained by law enforcement officers using methods that violate a person's constitutional rights be excluded from evidence in a criminal prosecution against that person. The exclusionary rule is a procedural rule of evidence used to protect civil liberties by deterring unlawful conduct by government officials. It often applies to evidence that is the direct product of unconstitutional police action, e.g., coerced confessions or evidence seized in an illegal search. The exclusionary rule also requires exclusion of evidence obtained indirectly as a result of a violation of constitutional rights (the "fruit of the poisonous tree" doctrine). However, the federal courts recognize numerous exceptions to the exclusionary rule.

Probable cause is required by the Constitution for a proper arrest or issuance of a valid search warrant. Probable cause for arrest means more than mere suspicion. Probable cause to **arrest** refers to the quantity of evidence that would lead a reasonable person to believe that the defendant probably committed a crime. Probable cause for issuance of a **search warrant** permits officers to search certain places and arrest certain persons or seize certain things if they can demonstrate to a judge or magistrate that the persons, places, or things are significantly connected with criminal activity. Recognizing the delicate balance between individual rights and the need for adequate law enforcement, courts have carved out various exceptions to the search warrant requirements. In a **search incident to a lawful arrest**, the officer may search for and remove any weapons that the arrestee may use to escape or resist arrest. The officer also may search for and seize evidence to prevent its concealment or destruction. In a **search of a motor vehicle**, a law enforcement officer who makes a lawful arrest of the occupant of an automobile may, as a contemporaneous incident of the arrest, search its passenger compartment. In a **search of a person in the presence of an arrestee**, when a potential accomplice of an arrestee is located on the premises where the arrest was made, courts have held that police may search the potential accomplice and the area within the potential accomplice's immediate control.

In a **search incident to detention**, a law enforcement officer may conduct a limited warrantless search of a person detained only for investigation, provided that the search is very limited; the detainee attempts to destroy evidence and the evidence is readily destructible; or probable cause existed to arrest the detainee even though (s)he was merely detained. In a **consent search**, a law enforcement officer may search a person, his/her premises, or his/her belongings without a warrant if the person consents. By giving consent, an individual relinquishes any right to object later on constitutional grounds. Evidence seized as a result of the search is admissible in court despite the lack of a warrant and of probable cause to search. The consent cannot be coerced by explicit or implicit threats.

Still another exception is the **plain view** doctrine, which permits alert law enforcement officers to obtain admissible evidence when it has been left in open and plain view. The observation and seizure of the evidence may, in most cases, be made without having probable cause or obtaining a warrant.

An **arrest** in criminal law is the apprehension or detention of a person so that (s)he may be available to answer for an alleged or supposed crime. A valid arrest permits an officer to deprive a person of freedom and initiates a process of the court system that may ultimately result in fine, imprisonment, or both. An arrest constitutes seizure of the person and must therefore meet the constitutional requirements of the Fourth Amendment of the U.S. Constitution. The remedy for an unlawful arrest is a civil suit for money damages. A law enforcement officer may arrest a person without a warrant when (s)he has reasonable grounds to believe that a felony has been committed by the arrestee. An officer also may make a warrantless arrest for a misdemeanor committed in his/her presence. Whenever a state or federal law enforcement officer makes an arrest or otherwise deprives an individual of freedom of action in any significant way, the officer is required to give the accused certain warnings about his/her constitutional rights. These mandatory warnings are called Miranda rights after the 1966 Supreme Court case *Miranda v. Arizona*.

The next procedural step is **booking** (fingerprinting and photographing the suspect, etc.). If charges are not dropped, the suspect makes an **initial appearance** to be informed of the charges. If necessary, a defense attorney is appointed and bail is set or denied. The case then proceeds to the **preliminary hearing** at which a probable cause determination is made. The case is then reviewed by a **grand jury** or a **magistrate** to determine whether the evidence is sufficient to try the suspect. If it is, an indictment (by a grand jury) or an information (by a magistrate) is issued, and the suspect is **arraigned** (informed of the charges and asked to enter a plea). The case then goes to **trial** if a **plea bargain** is not reached. If the suspect pleads guilty or is convicted at trial, **sentencing** follows. An **appeal** from a guilty verdict is always allowed.

White-collar crime generally refers to nonviolent crime committed in the business context, often by members of the managerial or professional class. Some examples are embezzlement, bribery, and fraud. In 1970, Congress passed the Organized Crime Control Act, which includes the Racketeer Influenced and Corrupt Organizations Act (RICO). **RICO** was enacted primarily to combat organized crime's control of legitimate businesses. Recently, it has been used against classic white-collar crime. For RICO to apply, a **pattern of racketeering activity** must be established. A pattern is at least two related racketeering acts (predicate offenses) within a 10-year period. RICO provides for both criminal and civil penalties. **Predicate offenses** include violations of state and federal laws, such as mail fraud, wire fraud, or bribery. For example, federal law prohibits using the mails, wire (e.g., telephone), radio, or television to defraud the public. See Study Unit 22 for materials on computer crime and Study Unit 33 for the **actions criminalized** under the **securities acts**.

A **corporation** may be held criminally liable for its acts and for strict liability crimes. That an act or omission constituting the offense was *ultra vires*, or outside the corporation's legal authority, is immaterial. A corporation may be charged with a crime for either an act or an omission by which it fails to discharge a legal duty. Corporations may be criminally liable for the acts of their directors, officers, employees, or agents. Although a corporate crime is based on the acts of individuals, a corporation is a separate entity and as such is liable as a principal for its crimes. Furthermore, individuals responsible for a legal duty imposed on the corporation are accountable for its reckless omission of the required act. A corporation also may be indicted for a crime for which a specific intent is an element, e.g., conspiracy. The intent of its employees or agents may be imputed to the corporation. A corporation may be punished by a fine or by seizure of property. In addition, a corporation may be ordered to pay restitution.

The **Federal Organizational Corporate Sentencing Guidelines** require a corporation to institute a reasonable **compliance program** to prevent violations. A base corporate fine for an offense is determined using (1) an amount in the offense-level fine table; (2) the organization's gain; or (3) the loss to the extent caused intentionally, purposefully, or recklessly. But a fine may be substantially reduced if the entity's compliance program is effective or substantially increased if it is not.

QUESTIONS

6.1 Introduction to Criminal Law

1. Thievery is a violation of

A. The ethics of excellence.

B. Community ethics.

C. Individualist ethics.

D. The ethics of duty.

Answer (D) is correct. *(Publisher, adapted)*
REQUIRED: The ethical system that prohibits crimes.
DISCUSSION: Ethical systems may be considered to establish either ethics of duty or ethics of excellence. Ethics of duty emphasize obeying the law. If the law is violated, punishment will occur. Thievery is a violation of the ethics of duty because the law prohibits such conduct.
Answer (A) is incorrect. The ethics of excellence consist of the goals, aspirations, and standards of perfection a person sets out for him/herself. Answer (B) is incorrect. Community ethics place the emphasis on the good of society, with individual rights being limited for the benefit of society. Answer (C) is incorrect. Individualist ethics hold the individual interest to be superior to society's.

2. Which of the following statements is false regarding the thinking that underlies the modern body of criminal law?

A. One objective of criminal law is to deter future wrongs from being committed against society.

B. General objectives of criminal law include retribution and the restraint and rehabilitation of perpetrators.

C. If a person is found guilty of committing a crime, (s)he is adjudicated criminally liable to the victim for any damages that the victim may have personally sustained.

D. If a person is found guilty of committing a crime, (s)he may be required to pay a fine or may be incarcerated, or both.

Answer (C) is correct. *(Publisher, adapted)*
REQUIRED: The false statement about the underlying theoretical basis of criminal law.
DISCUSSION: In theory, crimes are wrongs committed against society as a whole. Accordingly, one who is found guilty in a criminal proceeding is liable to society. Thus, a criminal proceeding does not seek to compensate the specific victims of crimes. The victim's personal remedy rests in the form of a separate civil action against the criminal wrongdoer.
Answer (A) is incorrect. This states one of the four general objectives of the criminal law system: deterrence, retribution, restraint, and rehabilitation. Answer (B) is incorrect. This states three of the four general objectives of the criminal law system: deterrence, retribution, restraint, and rehabilitation. Answer (D) is incorrect. Monetary damages and incarceration are manifestations of deterrence, retribution, and restraint.

3. In what way is criminal law most distinguishable from tort law?

A. The criminal defendant is presumed innocent until proven guilty.

B. Guilt must be proven by a preponderance of the evidence.

C. A crime is a violation of public law and is prosecuted in the name of the state.

D. Punishment of a crime may be by imposition of a fine.

Answer (C) is correct. *(Publisher, adapted)*

REQUIRED: The way in which criminal law most differs from tort law.

DISCUSSION: A crime is a breach of a duty imposed by the state upon all persons. It is a violation of a public rather than private law and is accordingly prosecuted by and on behalf of the state. Tort law is private law. A tort action is brought by the victim in his/her own name. Criminal law protects society. Tort law safeguards individual rights.

Answer (A) is incorrect. In a civil case, the liability of the defendant is also not presumed. Answer (B) is incorrect. It states the burden of proof in a civil case. The prosecution must prove a criminal defendant's guilt beyond a reasonable doubt. Answer (D) is incorrect. A fine in a criminal case is analogous to the imposition of punitive damages in a tort action.

4. In a criminal action, the state prosecutes the defendant for violation of a duty to society the breach of which requires punishment. Which of the following is a true statement about the elements of a crime?

A. The defendant has the burden of disproving at least one element of the crime charged.

B. The elements of a crime generally do not include the state of mind of the accused.

C. The prosecution must generally prove both an actus reus (wrongful action) and a mens rea (criminal intent).

D. The prosecution must generally prove only that a specific act was committed by the defendant.

Answer (C) is correct. *(Publisher, adapted)*

REQUIRED: The true statement about the elements of criminal law.

DISCUSSION: Most crimes are defined in terms of two elements: a wrongful action or failure to act (actus reus) and a mental state or criminal intent (mens rea). For example, first-degree murder requires proof of premeditation as well as the act of homicide. Some crimes, however, may be defined without regard to the mental state of the accused.

Answer (A) is incorrect. The burden of proof in a criminal action is on the state. The defendant is always presumed innocent. When the defense by reliable proof (either direct evidence or by cross-examination) raises a reasonable doubt as to the prosecution's charges, the verdict must be for the defendant. Answer (B) is incorrect. An actus reus and a mens rea must usually be proven. Answer (D) is incorrect. An actus reus and a mens rea must usually be proven.

6.2 Classification of Crimes

5. Jim is employed by First Bank in its operations department. Jim's job entails writing computer programs for different banking applications. While working on a program that calculates the interest earned by customers and allocates it to their individual accounts, Jim realizes that rounding differences involve substantial amounts. Jim writes a program to credit all rounding differences to his personal account. If Jim is caught and tried in a criminal action, he will be convicted of

A. Embezzlement.

B. Robbery.

C. Larceny.

D. Burglary.

Answer (C) is correct. *(Publisher, adapted)*

REQUIRED: The type of crime committed.

DISCUSSION: Larceny is the wrongful or fraudulent taking and carrying away of the personal property of another. Interest earned by the customers is personal property. The wrongful allocation of interest is the taking and carrying away necessary to prove larceny.

Answer (A) is incorrect. Embezzlement occurs when property is entrusted to a person who subsequently converts the property to his/her own use. Answer (B) is incorrect. Robbery involves the use of force or fear to take property from another unlawfully. Answer (D) is incorrect. The traditional common-law definition of burglary requires breaking and entering into the dwelling of another at night with intent to commit a felony.

6. In what way is criminal deceit distinguishable from both larceny and embezzlement?

A. The accused obtains possession of the victim's property.

B. The accused obtains possession of the victim's property with his/her consent.

C. The accused is entrusted with the victim's property.

D. The accused obtains title to the victim's property.

Answer (D) is correct. *(Publisher, adapted)*

REQUIRED: The characteristic distinguishing criminal deceit from larceny and embezzlement.

DISCUSSION: The crime of deceit or false pretenses is similar to the tort of fraud. It consists of a misrepresentation of a material past or existing fact that the defendant knew to be false and uttered with an intent to deceive. The victim must surrender money or property in reliance on the misrepresentation. Deceit results in obtaining title to, as well as possession of, money or property.

Answer (A) is incorrect. Possession is obtained in all three crimes. Answer (B) is incorrect. The victim gives consent in embezzlement and deceit but not larceny. Answer (C) is incorrect. No entrustment occurs in larceny or deceit.

7. Which of the following is a true statement about the crime of receiving stolen property?

A. The property may consist of money or tangible property but not stock certificates or credit cards.

B. In most states, the person who stole the property is also guilty of receiving it.

C. The elements of knowledge and intent must be proven.

D. In most states, the person who stole the property may be convicted of larceny or receiving stolen property.

Answer (C) is correct. *(Publisher, adapted)*

REQUIRED: The true statement about the crime of receiving stolen property.

DISCUSSION: To be convicted, the defendant must have received property knowing or having reason to know it to be stolen and with a fraudulent intent to deprive the lawful owner of the property. In some cases, the belief that the property was stolen has been found sufficient to convict even though the property had not in fact been stolen.

Answer (A) is incorrect. Any form of property may be involved. Answer (B) is incorrect. In most states, the person who stole the property cannot be convicted of receiving stolen property. In a minority of states, one may be convicted of either larceny or receiving stolen property but not both. Answer (D) is incorrect. In most states, the person who stole the property cannot be convicted of receiving stolen property. In a minority of states, one may be convicted of either larceny or receiving stolen property but not both.

8. Which of the following constitutes forgery?

A. A student signs his/her name to a scholarly paper that (s)he did not write.

B. One spouse signs the name of the other to a check without permission.

C. An artist orally makes a false representation that (s)he created a specific work.

D. An agent signs the name of his/her principal to a deed with permission.

Answer (B) is correct. *(Publisher, adapted)*

REQUIRED: The activity constituting the crime of forgery.

DISCUSSION: The crime of forgery entails making or altering a writing with fraudulent intent so that the legal rights and obligations of another person are apparently affected. Signing another's name to a check without permission evidences a fraudulent intent. Marriage to the other person is not a defense to forgery.

Answer (A) is incorrect. The falsification must be one with apparent legal significance such as a check, promissory note, or deed. Answer (C) is incorrect. Forgery cannot be oral. Answer (D) is incorrect. If signing is with permission, fraudulent intent cannot be proven.

9. Computer crimes ordinarily are not new crimes per se, but are old crimes that involve a computer. Which of the following traditional crimes generally will not arise with the assistance or use of a computer?

A. Larceny.

B. Criminal fraud.

C. Embezzlement.

D. Burglary.

Answer (D) is correct. *(Publisher, adapted)*

REQUIRED: The traditional crime not arising from computer use.

DISCUSSION: The traditional common-law definition is that burglary is breaking and entering into the dwelling of another at night with the intent to commit a felony. Because physical entry is required, a computer is not normally associated with burglary.

Answer (A) is incorrect. Larceny involves the wrongful taking, obtaining, and conversion of another's property and are easily committed with a computer. Answer (B) is incorrect. Criminal fraud involves the wrongful taking, obtaining, and conversion of another's property and are easily committed with a computer. Answer (C) is incorrect. Embezzlement involves the wrongful taking, obtaining, and conversion of another's property and are easily committed with a computer.

10. The attempt to commit a crime is an inchoate crime. Which of the following is true?

A. Attempt is similar to conspiracy in that some action in furtherance of the substantive crime is necessary

B. Intent to commit a crime constitutes an attempt.

C. A person may be separately charged and convicted of both attempt and the substantive crime committed.

D. Impossibility is a defense to the crime of attempt.

Answer (A) is correct. *(Publisher, adapted)*

REQUIRED: The true statement about the crime of attempt.

DISCUSSION: A person may be charged with a crime even though (s)he has not committed the intended offense. (S)he may be tried for such inchoate crimes as conspiracy, attempt, solicitation, or aiding and abetting. Aiding and abetting is the giving of assistance in the commission or concealment of a crime. The elements of the crime of attempt are an intent to commit a crime and some action in furtherance thereof. Unlike conspiracy, one person may commit the crime of attempt.

Answer (B) is incorrect. Some action in furtherance of the crime is needed. Answer (C) is incorrect. Unlike conspiracy, the two crimes merge. Answer (D) is incorrect. Impossibility, e.g., breaking into a building to steal something that was not there, is not a defense to the crime of attempt.

11. A substantive criminal offense and the conspiracy to commit that offense are separate crimes. Which of the following statements is true?

A. Without more, a conspiracy is found when two or more persons have agreed to commit a crime.

B. The same person cannot be convicted of both the substantive offense and conspiracy.

C. Oral or written statements are necessary to a conspiracy.

D. A conspirator who took no action may be convicted.

Answer (D) is correct. *(Publisher, adapted)*

REQUIRED: The true statement about the crime of conspiracy.

DISCUSSION: To constitute a conspiracy, an agreement between two or more persons to commit a crime must be furthered by some action on the part of at least one conspirator. Even though the substantive crime is not committed or the attempt is not completed, such action will be sufficient to impose criminal liability on all parties to the conspiratorial agreement.

Answer (A) is incorrect. Overt action in support of the agreement must be undertaken, e.g., setting money aside in a bank account for a bribe. Answer (B) is incorrect. The crimes do not merge. Conviction for both is possible. Answer (C) is incorrect. Nonverbal communication (e.g., handshake) may suffice for an agreement, or the facts of the case may support an inference of conspiracy.

6.3 Defenses and Justification

12. Al Butler, a mechanic, worked for Ernie's Auto. The agreement was that Butler would be paid 50% of amounts received by Ernie attributable to Butler's labor. Immediately after Ernie was paid cash for a major overhaul performed by Butler, Butler requested 50%. Ernie maintained that Butler would not be paid until the following Friday. Argument ensued, guns appeared, and shots were fired. Butler took Ernie's wallet, removed half the money, and left. Acquittal of Butler for robbery would most likely be based on

A. Assumption of risk.

B. Lack of intent.

C. Justification.

D. None of the answers are correct.

Answer (B) is correct. *(Publisher, adapted)*

REQUIRED: The most likely basis for acquittal of a robbery charge.

DISCUSSION: Robbery is a subjective-fault crime. The state must prove beyond a reasonable doubt that the accused intended to take another's personal property against that person's will. The defendant's mistaken belief that he had a claim or right to the property negates the felonious intent. Thus, the most likely basis for acquittal is the defense that a required element of the crime cannot be proved beyond a reasonable doubt.

Answer (A) is incorrect. Assumption of risk by a victim provides neither a defense to, nor justification for, a crime. Answer (C) is incorrect. A justification or excuse applies when each element of a crime is proved. In this case, the subjective-fault element was lacking. Answer (D) is incorrect. The defense of mistake of fact would most likely negate an element of the crime charged.

13. When June and her child were stopped at an intersection, Bart jumped in her car and placed a knife against her back. After cutting off some of her hair, Bart said he would harm the child unless June picked up a package at a designated house. Within a block of driving away from the house, Bart fled as June pulled over in response to flashing police car lights. If June is tried for unlawful possession of cocaine (found in the package) with intent to distribute, which of the following applies?

A. Justification of necessity.

B. Self-defense justification.

C. Involuntary act defense.

D. Defense of duress.

Answer (D) is correct. *(Publisher, adapted)*

REQUIRED: The applicable justification as defense for a criminal act.

DISCUSSION: Elements of the duress defense are (1) an immediate threat of serious bodily harm to the defendant or another, (2) reasonable apprehension that the threat would be carried out, and (3) lack of a reasonable opportunity to escape the threatened harm.

Answer (A) is incorrect. Necessity excuses otherwise criminal conduct as a result of pressure from natural forces. Answer (B) is incorrect. Self-defense applies when the defendant applied force to a person. Answer (C) is incorrect. Involuntary acts are ones such as reflexive acts, not ones over which the person has mental control.

6.4 Criminal Procedure

14. Criminal law uses procedural rules that may differ from those of the civil law. In the trial of a criminal case,

A. The prosecution can obtain a conviction on appeal.

B. Guilt must be proven by a preponderance of the evidence.

C. The accused is presumed to be innocent.

D. The prosecution may call the defendant as a witness.

Answer (C) is correct. *(Publisher, adapted)*

REQUIRED: The true statement about criminal procedure in American courts.

DISCUSSION: American concepts of due process provide many protections for the accused. One very important protection is that the defendant is presumed to be innocent.

Answer (A) is incorrect. The defendant can successfully appeal a guilty verdict, but the state cannot obtain an appellate reversal of a not guilty verdict. Once acquitted, an accused cannot be placed in jeopardy (charged) again for the same offense. Answer (B) is incorrect. The state must prove the guilt of the accused beyond a reasonable doubt. This rule minimizes the possibility of convicting an innocent person. Answer (D) is incorrect. The Fifth Amendment states that no person "shall be compelled in any criminal case to be a witness against himself."

15. Which of the following protections is provided to defendants in criminal cases in federal but not necessarily in state courts?

A. The right against self-incrimination.

B. Double jeopardy safeguard.

C. Due process.

D. Grand jury indictment.

Answer (D) is correct. *(Publisher, adapted)*

REQUIRED: The protection given a criminal defendant in federal but not necessarily in state court.

DISCUSSION: All states do not require a grand jury indictment in criminal cases, but the Fifth Amendment requires it in federal courts. A grand jury is a panel of jurors who do not determine guilt but merely whether probable cause of guilt is sufficient to issue charges against a person. In many state cases, criminal charges result from an "information" (charges) filed by a prosecuting officer.

16. After being arrested, an individual must be charged with a specific crime before being brought to trial. A charge issued by a grand jury is

A. An indictment.

B. An information.

C. An arraignment.

D. A complaint.

Answer (A) is correct. *(Publisher, adapted)*

REQUIRED: The name for a criminal charge issued by a grand jury.

DISCUSSION: After an individual is arrested, a grand jury or a magistrate determines if the evidence is sufficient to justify a trial. If the evidence is deemed to be sufficient, a formal charge is issued against the individual. A charge made by a grand jury is an indictment. An indictment may only be handed down for a felony.

Answer (B) is incorrect. An information is issued by a magistrate or prosecutor in most misdemeanor cases. Occasionally, an information is issued in a felony case. Answer (C) is incorrect. An arraignment is the proceeding in which the individual is formally charged with a specific crime. Answer (D) is incorrect. A complaint is the document filed by a plaintiff to initiate a civil lawsuit.

17. Del Defendant was charged with criminal trespass. The trial by a six-member jury ended in a mistrial. The case was subsequently postponed for two terms of court. After Defendant moved to determine when he would be brought to trial, the state moved to release him from custody while retaining the right to prosecute at its discretion. This motion was granted. On appeal, Defendant should win because

A. His right to a speedy trial was denied.

B. His right to a trial by a 12-person jury was denied.

C. Once released from custody, he cannot be tried.

D. He cannot be tried twice for the same offense.

Answer (A) is correct. *(Publisher, adapted)*

REQUIRED: The constitutional basis for a criminal defendant's successful appeal.

DISCUSSION: In the actual case, the Supreme Court held that indefinite postponement of the trial without stated justification and over the objection of the defendant violated the right to a speedy trial. The Sixth Amendment states, "In all criminal prosecutions, the accused shall enjoy the right to a speedy and public trial." This protection has been incorporated in the Fourteenth Amendment's Due Process Clause ("nor shall any state deprive any person of life, liberty, or property, without due process of law") and thus applies to the states.

Answer (B) is incorrect. No specified number of jurors is constitutionally required. Answer (C) is incorrect. Release from custody while awaiting trial is a common action, e.g., out on bail. Answer (D) is incorrect. A mistrial declared by necessity is an exception to the double jeopardy safeguard.

18. In criminal cases, the U.S. Constitution has been interpreted to

A. Prohibit capital punishment.

B. Require court appointment of an attorney for a defendant in certain instances.

C. Permit questioning of the accused by the police without prior warning of his/her right to remain silent.

D. Prohibit questioning of the accused by the police when (s)he has not consulted with an attorney.

Answer (B) is correct. *(Publisher, adapted)*

REQUIRED: The correct interpretation of the Constitution regarding the rights of the accused.

DISCUSSION: In *Gideon v. Wainwright*, the Supreme Court held that a criminal defendant who could not afford counsel had a right to a court-appointed attorney in a case involving a possible prison sentence. The scope of this holding has been narrowed by more recent decisions, for example, by a ruling that indigents are not entitled to counsel for discretionary appeals.

Answer (A) is incorrect. Capital punishment has been held not to be inherently cruel and unusual under the Eighth Amendment. Answer (C) is incorrect. The police must warn the accused that (s)he has the right to remain silent and the right to consult with an attorney (Miranda rights). Answer (D) is incorrect. The accused may waive his/her right to consult with an attorney.

6.5 Search Warrants, Exceptions, and Arrest

19. Unreasonable searches and seizures are prohibited by the Fourth Amendment of the U.S. Constitution. Which of the following is a true statement about its implications for criminal law?

A. The Fourth Amendment is the basis for the exclusionary rule.

B. A valid search and seizure requires a warrant.

C. Search warrants may be issued only upon reasonable suspicion.

D. The manner in which evidence is obtained does not affect its admissibility.

Answer (A) is correct. *(Publisher, adapted)*

REQUIRED: The true statement about the Fourth Amendment.

DISCUSSION: The Fourth Amendment states, "The right of the people to be secure in their persons, houses, papers, and effects, against unreasonable searches and seizures, shall not be violated." If a search and seizure violates the Fourth Amendment, the exclusionary rule (a rule of court) prohibits introduction of the evidence thus obtained in a criminal case brought against the party whose rights were infringed. The Supreme Court, however, has allowed numerous exceptions to the rule.

Answer (B) is incorrect. A warrantless search and seizure may be made with consent of an accused or in the course of a lawful arrest. Answer (C) is incorrect. A search warrant requires probable cause, supported by a sworn statement particularly describing the place to be searched and the persons or things to be seized. Answer (D) is incorrect. Even though it is subject to many exceptions, the exclusionary rule is still in force.

20. The Fifth Amendment to the U.S. Constitution protects a person accused of a crime by providing a privilege to avoid self-incrimination (compelled testimony against him/herself). This privilege is the basis for the "Miranda rights" required to be given to criminal suspects prior to custodial interrogation. The landmark Supreme Court case of *Miranda v. Arizona* is the origin of the requirement. Which of the following is not a Miranda right?

A. The individual has the right to counsel before answering any question.

B. The individual has the right to counsel even if (s)he cannot afford an attorney.

C. The individual has the right to remain silent.

D. The individual has the right to represent him/herself in a criminal trial.

Answer (D) is correct. *(Publisher, adapted)*

REQUIRED: The element not included among the Miranda rights.

DISCUSSION: Although an individual has the right to represent him/herself in a criminal trial, the decision in *Miranda v. Arizona* does not require law enforcement officers to advise the individual of this right prior to questioning. The Miranda rights are rights of the individual that are pertinent to the decision to answer or not answer questions by law enforcement officers.

Answer (A) is incorrect. The individual has the right to counsel before answering any question. Answer (B) is incorrect. The individual has the right to counsel even if (s)he cannot afford an attorney. Answer (C) is incorrect. The individual has the right to remain silent.

6.6 White-Collar Crime

21. Embezzlement is a white-collar crime that was not recognized by common law. In a prosecution for embezzlement,

A. The intent of the defendant to return the property is usually a complete defense.

B. The state must only show that a fiduciary has converted or appropriated the property.

C. The elements state must prove are the same elements as for larceny.

D. Entrustment is a crucial element of the prima facie case.

Answer (D) is correct. *(Publisher, adapted)*

REQUIRED: The true statement about the elements of the crime of embezzlement.

DISCUSSION: White-collar crimes encompass those committed in a commercial setting by persons holding a position of authority within a business organization. These crimes typically are not associated with the use of force or violence. Embezzlement is the fraudulent conversion or appropriation of the property of another by a fiduciary to whom it was lawfully entrusted. The fiduciary (a bailee, employee, trustee, etc.) must usually be shown to have had a fraudulent intent to deprive the rightful owner of his/her property.

Answer (A) is incorrect. It states a minority rule. Answer (B) is incorrect. Proof of fraudulent intent is normally needed. Answer (C) is incorrect. Common larceny does not include the element of entrustment.

22. The crime of bribery

A. Applies only to attempts to influence public officials.

B. Is committed by the offeror only.

C. Is a kind of extortion.

D. Must involve an immediate transfer of money or property.

Answer (B) is correct. *(Publisher, adapted)*

REQUIRED: The true statement about the scope of the crime of bribery.

DISCUSSION: The crime of bribery consists of giving something of value to unlawfully influence either a public official (domestic or foreign) or a private person. The crime is committed by the offeror. Acceptance of a bribe by an offeree is a distinct crime. The Foreign Corrupt Practices Act of 1977 prohibits bribery of foreign officials and certain other parties. Commercial bribery usually involves theft of trade secrets (in itself a federal crime under the Economic Espionage Act of 1996), obtaining new business, or preventing exposure of product defects.

Answer (A) is incorrect. Bribery applies to public and private persons. Answer (C) is incorrect. Extortion involves coercion as opposed to inducement. Answer (D) is incorrect. The transfer may be prospective and consist of anything of value.

23. Computer Shop sold a used computer knowingly and intentionally misrepresenting that it was new. Which of the following statements is true?

A. Computer Shop has committed an act of criminal fraud.

B. The buyer would have to elect between bringing criminal charges and filing a civil suit, because Computer Shop cannot be charged twice with the same offense.

C. In a criminal suit against Computer Shop, the buyer can be awarded a remedy of actual and punitive damages.

D. In the interests of judicial economy, criminal and civil suits based on this activity can be consolidated into one case.

Answer (A) is correct. *(M. Levin)*

REQUIRED: The true statement about an intentional misrepresentation by a seller.

DISCUSSION: Criminal fraud essentially consists of any word or deed by which one party deceives another causing a loss to the deceived person. It can take a variety of forms. It is similar in its elements to the tort of deceit. A government official can initiate criminal proceedings, and the deceived victim can bring a separate civil suit for money damages.

Answer (B) is incorrect. The constitutional protection (Fifth Amendment) regarding double jeopardy prohibits trying a defendant on a criminal charge of which (s)he has previously been convicted or acquitted. It does not affect a civil suit based on the same events. Answer (C) is incorrect. Actual and punitive damages are civil awards, not criminal sanctions. Answer (D) is incorrect. The two suits cannot be consolidated; they involve different wrongs and are subject to different standards of proof.

24. Rob Leslie induced people to invest their savings in a business venture that he represented to be risky. Because the planned venture never became operational, Leslie never applied the investors' funds in the way he promised. Instead, he used the funds to pay for his personal expenses. The investors wanted the state to charge Leslie with fraud, but state prosecutors declined. What was the most probable reason for that decision?

A. The investors were not justified in relying on Leslie's statements about the proposed business venture.

B. Leslie did not induce the people to invest since each made his/her independent decision.

C. No proof is available to show that Leslie had fraudulent intent when he talked with the investors.

D. Leslie's statements to investors about the proposed business venture did not include facts.

Answer (C) is correct. *(E. Arnold)*

REQUIRED: The first element necessary to prove fraud.

DISCUSSION: Fraud is often claimed and rarely proved because of the requirement of wrongful intent at the time the defendant acted. These facts show no criminally fraudulent intent at the time Leslie accepted the investors' funds. A tort action may be appropriate, however.

Answer (A) is incorrect. The facts do not indicate whether reliance was justifiable. Answer (B) is incorrect. The facts state Leslie did induce the investors to invest. Answer (D) is incorrect. Leslie gave the investors facts about risk.

25. Damiano borrowed money for currency speculation from several lenders and issued promissory notes in return. She promised to pay the notes in 90 days at 150% of the amount lent. She paid some notes in full after 45 days by using funds borrowed from other lenders. She collected millions but made no investments and continued to pay old notes with funds obtained from new lenders. What is the best characterization of Damiano's activities?

A. A pyramid scheme.

B. Embezzlement.

C. A legal Ponzi investment.

D. A tort but not a crime.

Answer (A) is correct. *(Publisher, adapted)*

REQUIRED: The best term for the activities described.

DISCUSSION: A pyramid scheme is a form of criminal deceit. It entails using the funds obtained from subsequent investors to pay off the initial investors who were promised a large return in a short time. The resources obtained from additional investors are then used to pay the prior investors. The scheme fails when no new investors can be found, that is, when the base of the pyramid can no longer be expanded.

Answer (B) is incorrect. Embezzlement involves lawful entrustment to a fiduciary. Answer (C) is incorrect. Pyramid schemes are generally unlawful. The facts of this question are similar to a famous case, *Cunningham, Trustee of Ponzi v. Brown*. Thus, it is also called a Ponzi scheme. Answer (D) is incorrect. Both a tort and a crime were committed.

26. In general, the provisions of RICO prohibit

A. Specific acts of racketeering, such as murder or trafficking in stolen property.

B. Organized crime from operating legitimate businesses.

C. Organized crime from operating illegitimate businesses.

D. Operation of any business with funds obtained through a pattern of racketeering acts.

Answer (D) is correct. *(R. Welton)*

REQUIRED: The true statement about the scope of RICO.

DISCUSSION: RICO prohibits (1) direct or indirect investment of funds obtained through a pattern of racketeering acts in a business, (2) the acquisition or control of a business through a pattern of racketeering acts, (3) participation in an enterprise through a pattern of racketeering acts, or (4) a conspiracy to do (1), (2), or (3).

Answer (A) is incorrect. RICO does not prohibit acts of racketeering, per se. Answer (B) is incorrect. RICO does not prohibit the mere ownership or operation of a business by organized crime. Answer (C) is incorrect. RICO does not prohibit the mere ownership or operation of a business by organized crime.

27. The Racketeer Influenced and Corrupt Organizations Act (RICO) concerns, among other things, connections between organized crime and business. The act

A. Is invoked only in prosecutions of organized crime figures.

B. Applies only to illegitimate business activities.

C. Permits the confiscation of legitimate businesses.

D. Creates accounting requirements for businesses that report to the SEC.

Answer (C) is correct. *(Publisher, adapted)*

REQUIRED: The true statement about the RICO Act.

DISCUSSION: Under RICO, profits from racketeering activities may be forfeited. The statute not only makes racketeering a federal offense, but also permits tracing of the proceeds to legitimate enterprises. These businesses can be seized, thus reducing the effect of organized crime on legal business activities.

Answer (A) is incorrect. The civil provisions of the act have been applied to activities of persons not related to organized crime. Answer (B) is incorrect. RICO allows the seizure of legal businesses purchased with funds obtained through illegal activities. Answer (D) is incorrect. The Foreign Corrupt Practices Act created these requirements.

28. Under the Racketeer Influenced and Corrupt Organizations Act (RICO), an injured party who is not a governmental entity

A. Cannot bring suit.

B. May bring suit for treble damages.

C. May bring suit for punitive damages.

D. May bring suit to recover only the amount of the actual injury plus any court costs.

Answer (B) is correct. *(R. Welton)*

REQUIRED: The true statement about RICO actions by private parties.

DISCUSSION: An injured party who is not a governmental entity may bring suit under the civil provisions of RICO for treble damages (three times the actual loss). In addition, the party may also recover court costs and reasonable attorney's fees.

Answer (A) is incorrect. RICO permits a civil remedy. Answer (C) is incorrect. The plaintiff may not recover punitive damages in addition to treble damages, which are themselves intended as a penalty. Answer (D) is incorrect. The plaintiff may recover attorney's fees, court costs, and treble damages.

6.7 Criminal Liability of Corporations

29. A corporation is a separate legal entity that may sue and be sued, own property, and engage in many of the same activities as individuals. A corporation

A. Can have no criminal liability because it cannot form the necessary intent.

B. May be criminally liable for the acts of its agents.

C. Can have no criminal liability because it acts only through agents.

D. Is criminally punishable in the same manner as an individual.

Answer (B) is correct. *(Publisher, adapted)*

REQUIRED: The true statement about the criminal liability of a corporation.

DISCUSSION: Corporations are held criminally liable for the acts of their agents within the scope of their employment, for example, for violations of regulatory statutes (antitrust, tax, and security laws). For a corporation to possess the requisite mens rea and actus reus for criminal liability, the mental intentions and physical acts of the corporation's agents (including employees) must be imputed to it because the corporation is an artificial person.

Answer (A) is incorrect. Criminal liability is imposed on the basis of the intent of its officers. Answer (C) is incorrect. Criminal liability is imposed on the basis of the acts of its officers. Answer (D) is incorrect. A corporation cannot be imprisoned.

30. Paul Place was the chief executive of Nadir Company, a large retail food chain. An FDA inspection pursuant to the federal Food, Drug, and Cosmetic Act revealed unsanitary conditions in a warehouse. When notified by the FDA, Place consulted with Nadir's vice-president for legal affairs, who gave assurances that the divisional vice-president with responsibility for the warehouse would take corrective action. A subsequent inspection disclosed that the problem had not been corrected. Nadir and Place were subsequently indicted under the Act for introducing adulterated articles into interstate commerce. Place is

A. Not liable in the absence of any awareness of some wrongdoing.

B. Not liable because only corporate liability can be imposed for corporate crime.

C. Strictly liable because he has a responsible relation to the situation and the authority to deal with it.

D. Liable solely by reason of occupying the chief executive's position.

Answer (C) is correct. *(Publisher, adapted)*

REQUIRED: The true statement about an individual's liability for corporate action.

DISCUSSION: The Food, Drug, and Cosmetic Act imposes strict liability for the introduction of misbranded and adulterated articles into interstate commerce. The defendant need not have had a "consciousness of wrongdoing" or criminal intent to be found guilty. Normally, when the criminal prosecution is not based on strict liability, the corporate officer is criminally liable only if (s)he knew of the wrongdoing (had the requisite intent). In the case on which this question is based, liability attached to a corporate official who had a "responsible relation to the situation" and "by virtue of his/her position had authority and responsibility to deal with the situation." Thus, Place's guilt was not based solely on occupying a certain position in the corporation.

Answer (A) is incorrect. The applicable statute imposes strict liability regardless of intent. Answer (B) is incorrect. Individuals are also liable. "The only way in which a corporation can act is through the individuals who act on its behalf." Answer (D) is incorrect. "A responsible share in the transaction that the statute outlaws" also is required.

STUDY UNIT SEVEN
TORT LAW

A **tort** is a private wrong (civil, not criminal) resulting in a breach of a legal duty derived from society's expectations regarding conduct. Thus, the duty does not arise out of a contract between the parties. A person whose rights have been compromised and who has suffered injury may bring a civil action to recover monetary damages. Such rights and duties may derive from either statutory law or common law. The purpose of tort law is to compensate the injured party, not to punish the wrongdoer as in criminal law. However, punitive damages may be awarded if the defendant's conduct was willful, malicious, or particularly repugnant. Moreover, conduct that unreasonably interferes with someone else's interests is frequently both a tort and a crime.

Torts consist of intentional torts to the person (including his/her right of dignity) or to property, torts involving business relations, negligent torts, and strict liability torts. To recover damages for an **intentional tort**, the plaintiff usually must prove an act by the defendant, intent, and causation. The **act** is an intentional movement by the defendant. **Intent** is found if an actor desires to cause the consequences of his/her conduct, and (s)he believes that those consequences are substantially certain to result from it. The intent to commit a tort against one person may be transferred to another person injured by the act. The element of **proximate cause** limits an actor's liability to results proximately caused by, or connected with, one's conduct.

Intentional torts to the person include **battery**, which is the intentional, unprivileged, and unwanted touching of another person. They also include **assault**, an act by the defendant that causes a reasonable apprehension in the plaintiff of immediate harmful or offensive touching, such as an attempted battery. The plaintiff who attempts to prove the tort of assault must have been aware of the defendant's conduct and reasonably believed him/herself to be threatened. Although assault is an intentional tort, the defendant need not actually have intended to harm the plaintiff. The plaintiff must prove only that the defendant intended his/her conduct and that a reasonable person in the position of the plaintiff would, under the circumstances, have feared for his/her own safety as a result.

The tort of **false imprisonment** is intentionally causing the confinement of another without consent of legal justification. Actual physical force is not required. The mere threat of physical harm may suffice. **Intentional infliction of emotional distress** is sometimes called the tort "outrage." This tort may be defined as an act or the use of words by a person with the intent of causing another person to experience severe emotional anguish. The elements are an act by the defendant amounting to extreme and outrageous conduct, intent to cause the plaintiff to suffer severe emotional distress, causation, and damages. Outrageous conduct is conduct that transcends the bounds of human decency.

Defamation is an unprivileged publication of false statement about a person that is injurious to his/her good name or reputation. Defamation tends to adversely affect a person's interest in his/her reputation. This may result from impeaching the person's honesty, integrity, virtue, sanity, or the like. The plaintiff must establish that a reasonable listener, reader, or viewer would understand that the defamatory statement referred to the plaintiff. A statement is not actionable unless it has been published. **Publication** is communication to a third person who understood it. The communication to the third person may be made either **intentionally or negligently**. Once publication is established, it is no defense that the defendant did not know that (s)he was defaming the plaintiff. Intent to publish, not intent to defame, is the **requisite intent** for liability. Defamation may be libel or slander. **Libel** is a defamatory statement in writing or some other permanent form, including television and radio recordings and emails. **Slander** is spoken defamation. It is distinguished from libel in that it is less permanent and less physical in form. Determining whether a defamation is libel or slander may be difficult. The courts generally consider several factors to make the determination. Thus, the more permanent, the broader the area of publication, and the more premeditated, the more likely the statement will be libel.

In most jurisdictions, **truth** is an absolute defense to defamation regardless of the defendant's intent. But the defendant also may assert a privilege. For example, a **constitutional privilege** applies to defamation of a public figure or official regarding his/her conduct, fitness, or role in that capacity. In these cases, the plaintiff must prove **malice**. It must be proven that the defendant (a) knew that the statement was false or (b) recklessly disregarded its truth or falsity. If the plaintiff is a private party, malice need not be proven when defamatory statements are about **matters of public concern** if the defamation is apparent to a reasonable person. Plaintiff must prove only that defendant was negligent regarding its truth or falsity. An **absolute privilege** applies to statements made during the course of legislative, judicial, and executive proceedings. It also applies to communications between spouses. A **qualified privilege** applies to (1) letters of reference, (2) reports of public proceedings, (3) defense of the publisher's own interests (e.g., response by a debtor to a debt collector), and (4) communications between parties with a common interest (e.g., between two members of a board of directors about company business).

The Communications Decency Act of 1996 (CDA) immunizes Internet service providers (ISPs) of liability for defamatory materials placed online by another information content provider. Hence, an ISP is not deemed to be a publisher or speaker. Moreover, an ISP cannot disclose customer information without a court order. A defamed party may therefore need to sue the unknown person to obtain an order compelling disclosure. Employers do not receive immunity under the CDA. Thus, they may be liable for defamatory material on electronic bulletin boards, etc., that they maintain.

Invasion of privacy includes appropriation, publicity given to private life, placing a person in a false light, and intrusion. **Appropriation** (the right of publicity) is the use of another's name or likeness for the benefit of the defendant, for example, using a celebrity's picture in advertising without authorization. **Publicity given to private life** (public disclosure of private facts) results in liability if a matter that is highly offensive to a reasonable person and is not of legitimate concern to the public is publicized. An example is a newspaper article reporting that a person who is not a public figure and has not been involved in recent newsworthy actions served a prison sentence many years ago.

Thus, publication in this context requires making private facts public knowledge, not mere communication to another person. Moreover, the tort may be committed even though the publicized information is truthful. **Publicity placing a person in a false light** results in liability if (1) the false light would be highly offensive to a reasonable person, (2) the defendant knew of the falsity of the publicized matter, and (3) the defendant knew of the false light in which the plaintiff would be placed. This tort often overlaps defamation because the information must be false. However, it must be publicized, not merely published. Moreover, it need not be defamatory if it is "highly-offensive to a reasonable person." An example is the defendant's inclusion of the plaintiff's name in a newspaper ad listing supporters of a political candidate when in fact the plaintiff favors a rival candidate. **Intrusion upon seclusion**, whether in a physical sense or otherwise, is an invasion of the solitude or private affairs or concerns of another. The defendant is liable if the intrusion would be highly offensive to a reasonable person. Intrusion may include such actions as physical entry into the plaintiff's home, unauthorized electronic surveillance, or unconsented to examination of private papers.

Improper use of legal procedure is an unjustified resort to the legal system. It may result in the torts of malicious prosecution, wrongful civil proceedings, or abuse of process. The tort of **malicious prosecution** of a criminal action involves proof of four elements: (1) the prosecution was without probable cause, (2) the proceedings ended favorably for the person bringing the malicious prosecution suit, (3) the initiator of the proceedings acted with malice (for an improper purpose), and (4) damages. However, a criminal prosecutor acting in his/her official capacity is absolutely immune from tort suits for malicious prosecution. The tort of **wrongful use of civil proceedings** is the civil equivalent of the tort of malicious prosecution. **Abuse of process** is the use of criminal or civil legal proceedings for a primary purpose other than that for which they are intended. An example is bringing a suit complaining of a nuisance on a neighbor's property as a means of compelling him/her to sell the land. An abuse of process suit may be successful even though probable cause existed and the legal proceedings did not end favorably for the person suing for abuse of process. The defenses to invasion of privacy claims are the same as those to claims of defamation.

Torts that involve **interference with property rights** include trespass to land, nuisance, trespass to chattels, and conversion. **Trespass to land** is the unauthorized entry of a person or thing into the land of another. The basis of the tort is the right to the exclusive possession of land. The elements are actual physical invasion of land without the plaintiff's consent, defendant's intent to bring about such invasion, and causation (the invasion was produced by defendant's conduct). Most courts hold that, if a person is on land, intends to be on that land, and does not have permission to be there from the person(s) with the possessory interest in the land, (s)he is liable for trespass even if his/her presence is based on a good-faith mistake, such as ignorance of boundary lines or ownership. Actual damages need not be proven to bring and win a suit for trespass.

Nuisance is unlawful and unreasonable interference with the use and enjoyment of another landowner. Nuisances typically involve noise, odors, or similar activity rather than physical invasion. Determining the presence or absence of nuisance requires courts to balance the competing interests of the parties' respective uses of their property. Nuisances are either private or public. To recover under a theory of **private nuisance**, the landowner or occupant must establish a substantial lessening of the enjoyment of his/her land by the alleged nuisance and, if successful, may obtain damages or injunctive relief. A **public nuisance** is activity that harms members of the public, not necessarily their property. A suit to abate a public nuisance must usually be brought by a government agency, but private parties may obtain damages or injunctive relief if they suffer harm beyond that experienced by the general public.

Trespass to chattels is the intentional and harmful interference with possession of personal property without the consent of the rightful possessor. Personal property is any movable or portable property. The tort usually involves temporary use of, or slight harm to, an item of property. The plaintiff's damages ordinarily equal the value of the loss of use of the item plus any diminution of value caused by defendant's use.

Conversion consists of treating personal property in a manner that is utterly inconsistent with the true owner's rights. Conversion is an intentional exercise of dominion or control that so seriously interferes with the rights of the true owner that the defendant is liable for its full value at the time of conversion. Some examples are theft, destroying the property of another, delivering property to the wrong person, and illegally acquiring possession of property and refusing to return it when rightfully requested to do so. Upon payment of a judgment, the converter becomes the owner of the converted property. Thus, suit is appropriate only when the defendant has so seriously damaged or interfered with the plaintiff's possession that a forced sale is justified. However, the owner of converted property may seek to have the actual property returned. In such a case, the court may issue an order called a **writ of replevin**.

A wrongfully injured business entity is as entitled to compensation as an individual. If the wrongful activity continues and the injured business cannot be compensated by money, a court may issue an injunction against the wrongdoer to restrain the activity. Thus, the courts apply common-law tort theory to provide relief from unfair and tortious business practices, such as **interference with business relations**. Two significant variations of this tort are interference with **contractual relations** and interference with **employer-employee** relations. The law clearly recognizes that parties to a valid contract have a reasonable expectation of performance. Tort law protects the interests of contracting parties from interference by others. Third parties may wrongfully interfere with contractual relations at two stages: (1) at the outset by interfering with the formation of a contract and (2) after the contract is in existence by interfering with its performance.

A tort is committed at the earlier stage when an individual or a firm acts with **malice** to induce another not to enter into a contract with the plaintiff. Malice is an intent to cause harm. Interference with the **formation** of a contract must (1) be intentional, (2) result in a present or potential economic or business advantage to the interfering party, and (3) be unjustified and without privilege. If an inducement not to enter into a contract serves a legitimate end and no improper means are used, the action is justifiable or privileged, and there is no tort.

Any unprivileged interference by a third party that **inhibits performance** of an existing contract gives rise to a cause of action in tort. Bona fide competition never justifies inducing another party to breach an existing contract.

A **contract for employment** is a valuable property right. Inducing an employee to change employers may be tortious whether the initial employment relationship was established orally or in writing or whether it was for a specified term or at will. The hiring away of an employee from a competitor is tortious if the interfering person both induces the employee to leave and intends to injure the original employer.

Defamation is a false statement that wrongfully harms another's reputation, name, or character. Thus, **disparagement of business reputation or property** is actionable because an enterprise is entitled to compete freedom from wrongful attacks on its reputation or its products. **Disparagement of property** includes the common-law torts of slander of title and slander of quality. **Slander of title** is unprivileged publication of untrue statements about the validity of another's title or interest in any kind of property. **Slander of quality** is the unprivileged publication of a false statement that another's product lacks the characteristics its vendors claim it has or that the product is unfit for the purposes for which it is being sold. A single improper publication often constitutes both disparagement of property and defamation.

Misrepresentation is one of the more common torts. **Intentional misrepresentation (fraud)** consists of the following elements: (1) defendant's misrepresentation of a material fact, (2) defendant's knowledge of the falsity or reckless disregard for the truth (scienter), (3) defendant's intent to induce plaintiff's reliance, (4) plaintiff's reasonable reliance on defendant's misrepresentation, and (5) damages. However, with certain exceptions, a party has no duty to disclose a material fact or opinion. The business tort of **palming off** involves fraudulent marketing by intentionally misrepresenting the source or manufacturer of a product or imitating the physical appearance or packaging of a product. Under **negligent misrepresentation**, the defendant owes a duty of care only to those persons to whom the representation was made and to those persons defendant knew would rely on it.

Trademark infringement is committed when an intentional or unintentional use is made of a trademark that is identical or confusingly similar to a previously established and distinctive trademark of another firm. A **trademark** is any word, name, symbol, or device, or any combination thereof, adopted and placed on a product or its container to identify its originator and differentiate the product. A trademark belongs to, and may be used exclusively by, the firm that first uses it, but only in connection with the class or category of goods that the firm produces. Other firms may use a similar mark with a noncompeting class of goods. Trademarks may, but need not, be registered with a state or with the federal government to obtain protection from infringement. To maintain a trademark, the holder must actively prevent its misuse and unauthorized use. If the public regards a registered trademark as a general class of goods as opposed to a single brand, registration and the right to sue for trademark infringement may be lost. The principal federal statute regarding trademarks is the **Lanham Trademark Act of 1946**. This act was amended by the Federal Trademark Dilution Act of 1995, which protects distinctive or famous trademarks, whether or not the unauthorized use is on a competing or related product or is likely to be confusing to customers.

Trade dress is the unique shape, image, appearance, or packaging of a product, e.g., the Coca-Cola bottle. Trade dress is protected from infringement if it is distinctive (inherently or through acquisition of a secondary meaning as a result of advertising and other promotional efforts) and not functional, and its imitation by a competitor would cause consumer confusion.

Trade name infringement is the wrongful appropriation of a trade name when confusion or uncertainty may result. A trade name is a name or phrase, the use of which has caused the name to become intimately associated with the overall image of a particular business. A trade name is not necessarily the firm's legal name.

Patent infringement is the act of infringing on the tangible or intangible rights secured by a patent. A patent confers on its owner a statutory right to exclude others from making, selling, or using a patented product, process, or invention. A patent holder may bring suit to enjoin infringement and seek damages. A utility patent usually lasts 20 years from the date of application and is not renewable. A design patent has a duration of 14 years.

Copyright infringement involves an unprivileged actual copying of a copyrighted work. A copyright is an exclusive right given to an author that allows him/her to control the publication, reproduction, or use of a creative work, such as a writing, a recording, or any other expression fixed in a tangible medium. To obtain full federal copyright protection, the copyright should be registered with the U.S. Copyright Office. Notice need not be given on every copy. A copyright runs for the **author's** lifetime plus 70 years. If the copyright owner is a **publisher**, the duration is 95 years from the date of publication or 120 years from the date of creation, whichever period elapses first. However, the **fair use doctrine** permits a person, without the owner's consent, to use excerpts from copyrighted work if the copying is within the bounds of fair use. When infringement occurs, various remedies are available, including injunctions to prevent further copying, actual damages, and receipt of actual profits earned by the infringer.

Misappropriation is the unlawful taking of the product or idea of another and making use of it as though it were one's own. A plaintiff suing for misappropriation of unsolicited ideas must prove that (1) the information was presented to the defendant with the clear expectation that the presenter would be compensated for its use, (2) the presenter has a protected property interest in the proposal, and (3) the business use of this idea was wrongful.

Violation of trade secrets occurs when a party discloses or uses another's trade secret without privilege. A trade secret is any information protected by a business because it provides a particular economic advantage. A firm is allowed to emulate another's business methods and process, provided that the information is derived solely by legitimate means, such as reverse engineering. However, gaining access to another's trade secret dishonestly, for example, through industrial espionage, bribery, or abuse of a confidence, results in tort liability. To recover for violation of a trade secret, the plaintiff must prove the alleged trade secret exists, the defendant wrongfully obtained the secret from the plaintiff, and harm will result from actual or threatened misappropriation. Moreover, many states and the federal government (in the **Economic Espionage Act of 1996**) make theft of trade secrets a crime.

Negligence is an unintentional tort. It is the most common action in tort. The **Restatement (Second) of Torts** published by the American Law Institute is a general restatement of the common law of torts. It defines **negligence** as "conduct which falls below the standard established by law for the protection of others against unreasonable risk of harm." The tort of negligence has the following elements: (1) The defendant owed a **duty** to conform to a specific standard of conduct for the protection of the plaintiff against unreasonable risk of injury, (2) the defendant **breached** that duty, (3) the breach was the actual and proximate **cause** of plaintiff's injury, and (4) **damage** to the plaintiff's person or property resulted. Although views diverge as to who owes a duty of care and when such duty arises, the consensus is that, when a person engages in any activity, (s)he is under a legal duty to act as an ordinary, prudent, reasonable person. However, this duty is not affirmative. The general rule is that a person has no legal duty or obligation to rescue or aid another person in distress (it is, of course, an ethical responsibility). One may even begin to assist another and then abandon the effort. However, liability will result if a rescuer's actions leave the victim in a worse situation. Furthermore, a special relationship, e.g., parent-child, employer-employee, or common carrier-passenger, may impose an affirmative duty.

The concept of **proximate cause** limits the class of plaintiffs to which the duty of care is owed. Accordingly, the defendant's conduct must be not only the actual cause but also the proximate (legal) cause of the harm suffered by the plaintiff. The result of this doctrine is that liability is not imposed for all consequences of a negligent act but rather for those with a relatively close connection. Under the Restatement, the fact that the defendant neither foresaw nor should have foreseen the extent of the harm or the manner in which it occurred does not preclude liability. However, a court may find for the defendant if, "after the event and looking back from the harm to the actor's negligent conduct, it appears to the court highly extraordinary that it should have brought about the harm."

The **reasonable person standard** is an objective standard with regard to the duty of care. It is interpreted according to the circumstances. For example, persons who practice a profession or trade that requires special expertise must exercise the degree of care and skill of a member of the profession in good standing in the same or similar localities. Similarly, a child is held to the standard of a reasonable child of like age, intelligence, and experience in the same situation.

The duty owed by a possessor of land traditionally has depended on the nature of the party who enters the premises. An **invitee** is one who enters the premises in response to an express or implied invitation from the possessor. The duty owed to an invitee is to inspect the premises and remedy any dangerous conditions or to warn of known dangers. A **licensee** is one who enters the land with the possessor's permission, express or implied, for his/her own purposes or business rather than for the possessor's benefit. The duty owed to the licensee is to warn of known dangerous conditions. A **trespasser** enters or remains on the land of another without permission or privilege. The duty owed to a trespasser is to not injure intentionally. Upon discovery of the presence of a trespasser, the landowner must exercise reasonable care to warn the trespasser or make safe conditions that may be concealed, unsafe, or artificial and that involve risk of death or serious bodily harm. A landowner owes no duty to an **undiscovered trespasser**.

A substantial minority of states have abandoned the traditional approach. They apply general negligence law in cases involving injury to persons entering land. Thus, the owner (or occupier) must act with **reasonable care** to maintain the property in a reasonably safe condition, given all the circumstances. These include (1) probability of injury, (2) its degree, and (3) the burden on the parties of avoiding the risk.

Whether the duty of care is breached in an individual case is a question for the trier of fact. To prove that a breach of duty has occurred, the plaintiff may present both direct and circumstantial evidence, including custom or usage, an applicable statute, or the res ipsa loquitur doctrine. For example, violation of a statute proscribing a specified activity is **negligence per se**. If the statute protects a class of which the plaintiff is a member, a violation is deemed to be negligence with no further proof. This rule applies in a majority of states.

The doctrine of **res ipsa loquitur** ("the thing speaks for itself") is useful when the circumstances make proof difficult because the defendant is the only party with knowledge of how the harm was caused. According to the Restatement (Second) of Torts, three elements must be shown to invoke the doctrine: "The event is of a kind that ordinarily does not occur in the absence of negligence; other responsible causes, including the conduct of the plaintiff and third persons, are sufficiently eliminated by the evidence; and the indicated negligence is within the scope of the defendant's duty to the plaintiff." When res ipsa loquitur is established, the burden of proof shifts, and the defendant must prove (s)he was not negligent.

The plaintiff's evidence must establish a causal connection between the injury and the defendant's act. This act must have been the cause in fact and the proximate cause of plaintiff's injury. **Cause in fact** exists when the injury would not have occurred "but for" the defendant's act or omission. The "but for" test must be supplemented, however, when multiple causes inflicted the injury. In this case, the defendant will be liable if his/her act was a **substantial factor** in bringing about the harm, even if other causes were sufficient to cause the entire injury. An **intervening cause** occurs after the defendant's negligence and alters the consequences. Ordinarily, it does not absolve the defendant of liability if it is reasonably foreseeable. An intervening cause that is not a foreseeable or normal consequence of the defendant's negligence is a **superseding cause**. It severs the causal connection between the initial wrongful act and the ultimate injury.

The final element of plaintiff's case is proof of **damages**. They may be mental as well as physical, and the plaintiff is to be compensated for all his/her damages, past, present, and future. The purpose is to put him/her in the same economic position as if the wrong had not occurred. However, the plaintiff has a **duty to mitigate** or avoid damages and cannot recover for harm that could reasonably have been avoided. **Punitive damages** may be awarded if the defendant's conduct was reckless or malicious.

Even if a plaintiff has established the elements of negligence, (s)he may nevertheless be denied recovery if the defendant has a valid defense. A defense involving the doctrine of contributory negligence is available in a minority of jurisdictions. **Contributory negligence** involves a failure by the plaintiff to exercise due care for his/her own safety that is a contributing cause of plaintiff's injury, which bars the plaintiff from recovering any damages from the defendant. However, under the doctrine of **last clear chance**, if the defendant had the last opportunity to avoid injury to the plaintiff but did not do so, the contributory negligence of the plaintiff does not bar recovery for damages. The severity of this doctrine has caused most jurisdictions to adopt the principle of **comparative negligence**. It requires the judge or jury to apportion damages between the plaintiff and the defendant on the basis of relative fault. The defense of **assumption of the risk** arises when the plaintiff voluntarily assumes a known risk. This defense is similar to consent as a defense to an intentional tort. Assumption of the risk may be express or implied. A **Good Samaritan statute** protects those who voluntarily give aid to those in peril (for example, emergency workers rendering assistance to victims of a natural disaster). Protected parties will be liable only if they behaved recklessly.

A **dram shop act** imposes liability without negligence on owners and servers of drinking establishments (and possibly on social hosts of private functions) when a person becomes intoxicated at the establishment (or is already intoxicated when served) and then causes harm to another.

A person who engages in an **inherently or imminently dangerous activity** is liable for all injuries proximately caused by the activity, regardless of negligence or intent. In contrast, intentional and unintentional torts require proof of fault. Under the theory of **strict liability**, the law has determined that certain types of otherwise socially accepted activity pose sufficient risk of harm, regardless of how carefully conducted, to impose liability without regard to fault. To establish strict liability, the following elements must be proved: an absolute duty of the defendant to make the activity safe, breach of that duty, injury to the plaintiff caused by the breach, and damage to the plaintiff's person or property. For example, keepers of wild or domestic animals are strictly liable for the damage done by the trespass of their animals, and owners of wild animals are strictly liable for injuries caused by any animal that cannot be fully tamed. However, if an owner, such as a zookeeper, is under a public duty to keep animals, negligence must be shown. Moreover, the owner of a domestic animal is not strictly liable for injuries that it causes unless (s)he has knowledge of a particular animal's vicious propensity.

Ordinarily, a person is liable without fault for injury to the person or property of another caused by an **ultrahazardous activity** that is inappropriate to the particular locale. An activity is ultrahazardous if it involves a risk of serious harm to persons or property; cannot be performed with complete safety, regardless of the precautions taken; and is not commonly conducted in the locale. Common examples of ultrahazardous activities include blasting, fumigating, and manufacturing highly flammable products.

Workers' compensation statutes impose strict liability without fault on employers of accidentally injured workers. Liability is imposed provided that the necessary nexus exists between the injury and the employer. An injured employee may receive benefits, even if the injury resulted from his/her own negligence or intentional disregard for established safety procedures. Workers' compensation statutes are intended as humanitarian legislation, designed to protect workers and benefit society. Their rationale is that persons who enjoy the products of a business should ultimately pay the costs of accidents incident to the manufacture and distribution of a product, regardless of who is at fault. Injured employees are guaranteed predetermined amounts for payments covering medical costs, wage loss, and survivorship benefits. The award is an exclusive remedy. Absent an intentional injury by the employer, the employee cannot bring suit against the employer for additional recovery. However, an employee can sue a negligent third party that caused the job-related injury.

Products liability is a doctrine that holds a manufacturer, wholesaler, retailer, or lessor liable if a defective product is placed into the market and causes injury to a protected party. The liability may be based on the legal theories of negligence, contract, warranty, or strict liability. The law shifts the burden of loss from the injured buyer, user, lessee, or bystander to those capable of avoiding or bearing it. To recover under a negligence theory, a plaintiff ordinarily must prove negligent design, a manufacturing flaw, failure to inspect, or failure to warn. However, a plaintiff need not be in **privity of contract** with the defendant. Wholesalers, retailers, and lessors have a responsibility to inspect for defects if they have reason to believe a product is likely to be defective. The manufacturer or distributor of a product is liable for negligence only if it fails to exercise reasonable care under the circumstances. Extraordinary care is not required.

Warranties establish the characteristics of a product that the purchaser or other plaintiff is entitled to and relies on. A plaintiff is entitled to damages upon proof that an express warranty was made or a warranty was implied, the product does not conform to the standard entitled by the warranty, and the plaintiff suffered harm as a result of the breach of warranty. No proof is necessary that the manufacturer, seller, or lessor was at fault.

If negligence cannot be proved and the manufacturer, seller, or lessor has made no warranty, an injured plaintiff, who need not be in privity of contract with the defendant and may simply be a bystander, may rely on a theory of **strict liability in tort** to recover for injuries due to a defective product. A seller is strictly liable in tort when it places an article on the market, knowing that the article is to be used without inspection for defects, and the article proves to have a defect that causes injury to a human being. **Section 402A of the Restatement (Second) of Torts** provides that a seller (manufacturer, distributor, retailer, lessor, etc.) of any product in a defective condition unreasonably dangerous to the user or consumer or to his/her property is subject to liability for physical harm thereby caused to the ultimate user or consumer or to his/her property if (a) the seller is engaged in the business of selling such a product, and (b) it is expected to and does reach the user or consumer without substantial change in the condition in which it is sold. A defective product is one that does not meet reasonable consumer expectations as to safety or for which an economically feasible and less dangerous alternative was available but not produced. Section 402A reflects a public policy that favors consumer protection, opposes permitting a seller to escape liability solely because of lack of privity, and regards sellers as better able to bear the costs of defective products. In some states, a **statute of repose** precludes a remedy for damages caused by a defective product after a specified period.

Moreover, when a specific defendant cannot be identified (e.g., when a specific manufacturer of a drug cannot be ascertained years after its use), some courts impose **market-share liability** (apportion damages among all sellers in proportion to market share).

The **Restatement (Third) of Torts: Products Liability** attempts to update products liability law by defining the types of defects and stating a specific test of liability for each, regardless of the legal theory underlying a specific plaintiff's case. A **manufacturing defect** is a departure from the product's "intended design even though all possible care was exercised" in its preparation and marketing. Strict liability is imposed even if the defendant behaved reasonably. A **defect in design** arises when the foreseeable risks could have been reduced or avoided by adoption of a "reasonable alternative design" and omitting that alternative rendered the product "not reasonably safe." This test emphasizes the actual design and the alternative and whether the harm was reasonably preventable. A **defect in instructions or warnings** occurs when the foreseeable risks could have been reduced or avoided by providing "reasonable instructions or warnings," and omitting them rendered the product "not reasonably safe." **Defenses** in product liability cases include product misuse, assumption of the risk, commonly known danger (such as that attending use of firearms), or knowledgeable user. (A warning is not needed if a danger should be known by a plaintiff in a given occupation.) Moreover, the Restatement (Third) of Torts and most courts apply **comparative negligence** principles in products liability cases.

QUESTIONS

7.1 Introduction to Torts

1. Which of the following is tortious conduct?

A. Beth agrees to sell 100 whistles to May for $1 each. On the day of delivery, Beth tenders 50 whistles.

B. Andre intentionally fails to report a substantial amount of income subject to federal tax.

C. Pops promises to give David a car for his birthday but forgets to.

D. Myra abducts Reginald at gunpoint and holds him for ransom.

Answer (D) is correct. *(Publisher, adapted)*

REQUIRED: The action that constitutes a tort.

DISCUSSION: In *Handbook of the Law of Torts*, Prosser defines a tort as "a civil wrong other than breach of contract for which the court will provide a remedy in the form of an action for damages." A tort involves civil liability for conduct affecting another person that society (through its judges and legislatures) views as wrongful. Tort law evolves to reflect changing circumstances. New torts are recognized, old ones are modified, and some are no longer actionable. Enforcement is by way of a lawsuit brought by the person whose injury was caused by the wrongful conduct. When Myra committed the crime of kidnapping, she also became civilly liable for the tort of false imprisonment: intentional confinement of another without legal justification. She should be tried separately for her criminal conduct.

Answer (A) is incorrect. Beth breached a contract. Answer (B) is incorrect. Andre committed a federal crime. Answer (C) is incorrect. A breach of a promise to make a gift is ordinarily not actionable, and even if it were, it would be an action under the law of contracts.

2. In what way is the law of torts similar to criminal law?

A. Enforcement is by the state, not the individual.

B. A tort is a breach of a duty imposed by the state.

C. The primary purpose is to compensate injured persons.

D. The defendant must have acted with a wrongful intent.

Answer (B) is correct. *(Publisher, adapted)*

REQUIRED: The similarity between torts and crimes.

DISCUSSION: A tort is the breach of a duty owed by one person to another. Unlike contractual duties, which are voluntarily assumed, tort law is imposed by the state on all its citizens. Tort law is mainly state law. In this respect, a tort is like a crime, and many torts arise from the same circumstances that produce criminal liability.

Answer (A) is incorrect. The party injured by a tort must sue for damages. In a criminal case, the state prosecutes the wrongdoer. Answer (C) is incorrect. The primary purpose of criminal law is to protect the public by punishing the wrongdoer; the purpose of tort law is to compensate the injured party. Answer (D) is incorrect. Tort liability may be imposed when the defendant had good intentions, for example, in strict liability cases.

7.2 Intentional Torts to the Person

3. Paul is charged with battery. The plaintiff was struck in the face by Paul's golf club. In which situation is Paul least likely to be liable for battery?

A. Paul had been hypnotized at a party and ordered by the hypnotist to strike the person he disliked the most.

B. Paul was suffering from an epileptic seizure and had no control over his motions.

C. Paul was heavily intoxicated and was swinging the club without realizing that the plaintiff was near him.

D. Paul, who had just awakened from a deep sleep, was not fully aware of what was happening and mistakenly thought the plaintiff was attacking him.

Answer (B) is correct. *(Publisher, adapted)*

REQUIRED: The situation in which the defendant is least likely to be liable for battery.

DISCUSSION: To be liable for the tort of battery, Paul must commit an act of his/her own volition that brings about harmful or offensive contact with the plaintiff. A person who commits the touching of another during an epileptic seizure is not liable for battery because it is not willful or voluntary.

Answer (A) is incorrect. An act done under hypnosis is considered a voluntary act. Answer (C) is incorrect. Intoxication is not an excuse. Paul is chargeable with having voluntarily put himself in a state of intoxication. Answer (D) is incorrect. The act of striking was intentional, and the mistaken thought is not a defense.

Questions 4 and 5 are based on the following information. Brother and Sister, walking on a city sidewalk, were frightened by a car swerving in and out of traffic. They climbed over a fence to get onto the adjacent property, owned by Defendant. The fence was posted with a large sign, "No Trespassing." Defendant saw Brother and Sister and came toward them with his large watchdog on a long leash. The dog rushed at Sister. Defendant had intended only to frighten Brother and Sister, but the leash broke and, before Defendant could restrain the dog, the dog bit Sister.

4. If Brother asserts a claim based on assault against Defendant, will Brother prevail?

A. Yes, because the landowner did not have a privilege to use excessive force.

B. Yes, if Brother reasonably believed that the dog might bite him.

C. No, if the dog did not come in contact with him.

D. No, if Defendant was trying to protect his property.

Answer (B) is correct. *(Publisher, adapted)*

REQUIRED: The circumstance under which Brother will prevail on a claim of assault.

DISCUSSION: An assault is an intentional act by a defendant that produces a reasonable apprehension of a harmful or offensive contact to the plaintiff. The apprehension of an unlawful touching is required to be reasonable only; i.e., it need not actually occur or even be possible.

Answer (A) is incorrect. Brother will prevail on an assault theory regardless of the degree of force. Answer (C) is incorrect. Assault does not require an actual touching (only the apprehension of a touching). Answer (D) is incorrect. While Defendant is entitled to use reasonable force to protect his property, he is also under a duty to request the trespassers to leave before using force of any kind.

5. If Sister asserts a claim based on battery against Defendant, will Sister prevail?

A. Yes, because Defendant intended that the dog frighten Sister.

B. Yes, because the breaking of the leash establishes liability under res ipsa loquitur.

C. No, because Sister made an unauthorized entry on Defendant's land.

D. No, because Defendant did not intend to cause any harmful contact with Sister.

Answer (A) is correct. *(Publisher, adapted)*

REQUIRED: The circumstances under which Sister will prevail, and the reason she will prevail, in a claim based on battery.

DISCUSSION: The intent to commit the assault (causing a reasonable apprehension of contact by the dog) is transferred to the battery (the actual harmful or offensive touching by the dog). Therefore, Defendant is liable for battery.

Answer (B) is incorrect. Res ipsa loquitur ("the thing speaks for itself") is a legal doctrine that permits the finding of a tort from circumstantial evidence. It is inapplicable here because direct evidence is available. Answer (C) is incorrect. An owner of land has a duty to avoid intentional torts even to trespassers. Answer (D) is incorrect. Defendant's intent to commit the assault is transferred to the battery.

6. In a tort action based on defamation, a defendant may plead

A. An absolute privilege if (s)he is a former employer asked by a prospective employer for information about the plaintiff's character.

B. A conditional privilege if (s)he is a witness called to testify about the plaintiff in a suit to which the plaintiff was not party.

C. A constitutional privilege if (s)he is a public figure.

D. The truth of the defamatory statement even though it was uttered with malicious intent.

Answer (D) is correct. *(Publisher, adapted)*

REQUIRED: The defense that a defendant may plead in a defamation suit.

DISCUSSION: In most jurisdictions, truth is an absolute defense to defamation regardless of the defendant's intent. A few require truth plus good motive. In some cases, however, the plaintiff may be able to avoid this defense by pleading and proving invasion of privacy.

Answer (A) is incorrect. In these circumstances, the privilege is only qualified or conditional. The limited privilege is lost if the defendant acts maliciously or abusively. Answer (B) is incorrect. An absolute (not conditional) privilege is given to participants in judicial proceedings. Answer (C) is incorrect. The constitutional privilege is extended to statements about (not by) public figures uttered without malice (knowledge of falsity or reckless disregard for the truth).

7. Store's private security guard saw Fran put a lipstick into her purse and leave the store without paying for it. The guard caught Fran, threw her to the ground, and held her down until the police came. Fran sued Store for false imprisonment. Will she likely win?

A. No, because the guard acted on reasonable belief.

B. No, because Fran had shoplifted the lipstick.

C. Yes, because a private security guard has no right to detain a person in the parking lot.

D. Yes, because the guard used unreasonable force and an unreasonable means of detention.

Answer (D) is correct. *(E. Arnold)*

REQUIRED: The true statement regarding the tort of false imprisonment.

DISCUSSION: Merchants have a qualified privilege to detain suspected shoplifters. If merchants or their agents abuse the privilege by using unreasonable means of detention, however, they lose the privilege and incur liability for false imprisonment. In this case, the guard used excessive force in detaining Fran.

Answer (A) is incorrect. A reasonable basis for asserting the privilege fails in light of the unreasonable detention. Answer (B) is incorrect. The act of shoplifting does not provide a basis for an unreasonable detention. Answer (C) is incorrect. The guard, as the merchant's agent, does have a qualified privilege to detain a shoplifter.

8. Lowe Ricard posed as a trick-shot artist with the Great Wild West Show. He asked Jane Witt to try out as his partner. Witt stood 75 feet away with a lighted cigarette between her lips. Ricard shot three cigarettes out of her mouth. He told her to report to the Wild West Show's headquarters. Witt reported but was informed that Ricard had been discharged months before because of failing eyesight and mental instability. Witt became hysterical, requiring sedation and hospitalization for a severe nervous reaction. Witt's best chance of recovering from Ricard is

A. As added damages in an assault action.

B. As added damages in a battery action.

C. On the basis that perpetrators of "sick" jokes should have to pay for the damages caused by their jokes.

D. On the basis of the tort of intentional infliction of severe emotional distress.

Answer (D) is correct. *(Publisher, adapted)*

REQUIRED: The plaintiff's best chance of recovering for her emotional distress.

DISCUSSION: The tort of intentional infliction of emotional distress involves intentional conduct by the defendant that is so outrageous and so far beyond the bounds of civilized behavior as to cause the plaintiff extreme emotional suffering. Ricard's intentional actions could meet the outrageous conduct requirement, and Witt's hospitalization was indicative of severe emotional distress.

Answer (A) is incorrect. There is no indication that Witt had any apprehension of bodily contact at the time of the shooting. Answer (B) is incorrect. There is no indication of contact to which Witt did not consent. Answer (C) is incorrect. It does not state a legal basis for recovery.

9. The tort of invasion of privacy may take a number of forms. In which case will the defendant most likely prevail?

A. Defendant newspaper published that Plaintiff, a local political candidate, had been convicted of burglary many years before.

B. Defendant landlord installed a two-way mirror in the plaintiff's bedroom through which he secretly viewed the plaintiff's activities.

C. Defendant newspaper published an editorial opposing abortion, naming Plaintiff as supporting it. Plaintiff is president of a pro-life group.

D. Defendant newspaper published that the plaintiff retiree had served time in prison 20 years ago but had ever since been a valuable member of the community.

Answer (A) is correct. *(Publisher, adapted)*

REQUIRED: The action for invasion of privacy in which defendant will most likely prevail.

DISCUSSION: Invasion of privacy consists of four separate torts: appropriation, intrusion, public disclosure of private facts, and false light in the public eye. Appropriation involves using the plaintiff's name or likeness for commercial gain. Public disclosure of private facts results in liability when offensive publicity is given to private information. A political candidate's criminal record is of legitimate public interest, and public figures receive less protection than private citizens in both defamation and invasion of privacy actions.

Answer (B) is incorrect. Intrusion is an unreasonable interference with a person's solitude or seclusion. Answer (C) is incorrect. False light in the public eye is unreasonable and offensive publicity attributing to the plaintiff views (s)he does not hold or traits (s)he does not have. Answer (D) is incorrect. It is an example of public disclosure of private facts (not newsworthy and lacking legitimate public interest).

10. Edmond was a butler in the home of Ville, the local district attorney. On September 17, Ville's wife, Mercedes, questioned Edmond about the loss of certain jewelry. The next day Ville filed a criminal complaint against Edmond. Edmond consented to a search of his belongings, but nothing was found. Ville charged Edmond with grand theft because Edmond was the only nonfamily member living in the house. Edmond was arrested, tried, and found not guilty. If Edmond brings a civil action against Ville,

A. Edmond will succeed on a theory of malicious prosecution.

B. Edmond will win on a theory of intentional infliction of emotional distress.

C. Ville will prevail if the claim is based on malicious prosecution.

D. Edmond will win on a theory of false imprisonment.

Answer (C) is correct. *(Publisher, adapted)*

REQUIRED: The one who will prevail in an action for malicious prosecution of a criminal action and the theory upon which he will win.

DISCUSSION: To prevail on the tort theory of malicious prosecution, the plaintiff must show that the defendant initiated criminal proceedings against him/her, the case ended favorably for the plaintiff, there was no probable cause for prosecution, and the defendant acted with malice. However, a prosecutor, such as Ville, is usually privileged and may not be sued for malicious prosecution. Such immunity is deemed to be necessary to allow a prosecutor to perform his/her public functions. Otherwise, lawsuits or the threat thereof might hinder or prevent the execution of his/her duties. For example, a threat of suit might deter a meritorious prosecution.

Answer (A) is incorrect. Ville is privileged as a district attorney. Answer (B) is incorrect. To prevail, the plaintiff would have to show that the defendant's conduct was intended to cause severe emotional distress and was so outrageous that it exceeded all civilized limits. Answer (D) is incorrect. A legal arrest cannot be the basis for false imprisonment even if the individual is not guilty.

7.3 Intentional Torts to Property

11. Without permission, Olivia drove Portia's car to the beach. Before returning the vehicle later the same day, Olivia scraped it against a pole, causing minor damage to the fender. Olivia will be liable to Portia on the theory of

A. Conversion, for the actual damages.

B. Conversion, for the full value of the property.

C. Trespass to personal property, for the full value of the property.

D. Trespass to personal property, for actual damages.

Answer (D) is correct. *(Publisher, adapted)*

REQUIRED: The basis for and nature of recovery for temporarily dispossessing plaintiff of personal property.

DISCUSSION: The tort of trespass to personal property is the intentional and unjustifiable taking or damaging of personal property possessed by someone else. Recovery is for the actual harm done to the property or for the loss of possession.

Answer (A) is incorrect. For conversion, the interference must be so serious that it would be appropriate for the defendant to pay the full value of the property to the plaintiff in damages. Because the car was returned with minor damage on the same day, the interference would not be treated as a forced sale of the car. Answer (B) is incorrect. For conversion, the interference must be so serious that it would be appropriate for the defendant to pay the full value of the property to the plaintiff in damages. Because the car was returned with minor damage on the same day, the interference would not be treated as a forced sale of the car. Answer (C) is incorrect. Liability is for actual loss.

12. DeAnn is a defendant in a suit brought for trespass to real property. She will most likely prevail in which situation?

A. The limbs of a tree on DeAnn's land extend over the boundary line into the air above Bonita's property.

B. While walking on her own wooded land, DeAnn became lost and walked onto Neighbor's land.

C. Mike shoved DeAnn over a fence and into Irv's yard.

D. DeAnn dug a tunnel from her house, under Larry's land to Gary's property.

Answer (C) is correct. *(Publisher, adapted)*

REQUIRED: The case in which defendant is not liable for trespass to real property.

DISCUSSION: Trespass to real property is an intentional and unjustifiable entry onto land possessed by someone else, causing an object or a third person to do so, remaining on the land, or failing to remove from the land an object that one is under a duty to remove. Given that DeAnn did not enter Irv's yard of her own volition, she is not liable for trespass. Mike is liable, however, because he caused a third person to enter the land.

Answer (A) is incorrect. The land includes the airspace above it (to a limited height). DeAnn has either caused an object to enter Bonita's property or failed to remove it. Answer (B) is incorrect. DeAnn intentionally stepped on Neighbor's land. Answer (D) is incorrect. The land includes the ground below it.

Questions 13 and 14 are based on the following information. In 1964, Bacon Company paid $30,000 for a 150-acre tract of agricultural land well suited for a pig farm lot. The tract was 10 miles from the city of Jefferson, then a community of 50,000 people, and 5 miles from the nearest home. By 2003, the city limits extended to Bacon Company's feed lot, and the city had a population of 350,000. About 10,000 people live within 3 miles of the pig farm operation. The Bacon Company land is outside the city limits, and no zoning ordinance applies. The Bacon Company land is now worth $300,000, and $25,000 has been invested in buildings and pens. Bacon Company, conscious of its obligations to its neighbors, uses the best and most sanitary feed lot procedures, including chemical sprays, to keep down flies and odors, and frequently removes manure. Despite these measures, residents of Jefferson complain of flies and odors. An action has been filed by five individual homeowners who live within half a mile of the Bacon Company pig farm lot. The plaintiffs' homes are valued currently at $40,000 to $110,000 each. Flies in the area are five to ten times more numerous than in other parts of Jefferson, and extremely obnoxious odors are frequently carried by the wind to the plaintiffs' homes. The flies and odors are a substantial health hazard.

---

13. If the plaintiffs assert a claim based on private nuisance, the plaintiffs will

A. Prevail because Bacon Company's activity unreasonably interferes with the plaintiffs' use and enjoyment of their property.

B. Prevail because Bacon Company's activity constitutes an inverse condemnation of their property.

C. Not prevail because Bacon Company had operated the feed lot for more than 35 years.

D. Not prevail because Bacon Company uses the most reasonable procedures to keep down flies and odors.

Answer (A) is correct. *(MBE, adapted)*

REQUIRED: The outcome of asserting a claim based on private nuisance.

DISCUSSION: Private nuisance involves a substantial and unreasonable interference with the use and enjoyment of the land of another. Flies, extremely obnoxious odors, and a substantial health hazard constitute a substantial interference with an ordinary person's use and enjoyment of his/her own property.

Answer (B) is incorrect. Condemnation is the taking of property for public purposes by the government. Answer (C) is incorrect. Bacon Company will lose even though it has been in operation for a long time if its operations substantially and unreasonably interfere with the use and enjoyment of the neighboring properties. Answer (D) is incorrect. The Bacon Company may be liable without fault or any intent to do harm.

14. If the plaintiffs assert a claim based on public nuisance, the plaintiffs will

A. Prevail if the plaintiffs have sustained harm different from that suffered by the public at large.

B. Prevail if Bacon Company's acts interfere with any person's enjoyment of his/her property.

C. Not prevail because only the state may bring an action based on public nuisance.

D. Not prevail because the plaintiffs came to the nuisance.

Answer (A) is correct. *(MBE, adapted)*

REQUIRED: The possibility of recovery on a claim based on public nuisance.

DISCUSSION: A public nuisance is an act that unreasonably interferes with the health, safety, or property rights of the community at large. A private party may recover only if (s)he has sustained a unique form of harm not suffered by the public at large, e.g., if the smell was a nuisance to the public but the flies were a health hazard only to the neighbors who are suing.

Answer (B) is incorrect. Interference with enjoyment of property is not sufficient to sustain a claim based on public nuisance. Answer (C) is incorrect. Private parties may bring actions based on public nuisance if they have suffered a unique harm. Answer (D) is incorrect. Coming to the nuisance is not a defense if the plaintiffs purchased in good faith and without the intent to acquire a lawsuit. Nuisance is a form of trespass against the plaintiff that is not affected by which property was developed first.

7.4 Torts Involving Business Relations

NOTE: Also see Study Unit 36, "Antitrust," Study Unit 37, "Consumer Protection," and Study Unit 40, "Accountants' Legal Responsibilities."

15. Dont Products sells notions door to door. Tiff Co. is its primary competitor. In order to increase its own sales and to reduce Dont's sales, Tiff initiated a successful campaign to recruit most of Dont's sales people, who are not under contract for a specified time. In a suit brought by Dont, Tiff will

A. Lose because it acted with malice when inducing Dont's employees to terminate their employment.

B. Lose because the contractual relation interfered with was current rather than prospective.

C. Win because the employees' contracts were terminable at Dont's will.

D. Win because it is not a tort to offer someone a better job.

Answer (A) is correct. *(Publisher, adapted)*

REQUIRED: The outcome of a suit against a firm that recruited a competitor's employees.

DISCUSSION: Malicious interference with the contractual relationship between an employer and an employee is a tort. Malice in this context means that the conduct was intentional. When there is no contractual obligation between the employee and employer (terminable at will), malice also includes intent to injure the plaintiff. Tiff's recruitment of Dont's personnel was to gain a competitive advantage at the expense of Dont and to damage Dont's economic condition. Tiff would lose.

Answer (B) is incorrect. Tiff should lose because it acted maliciously, not because the contractual relation was current. Answer (C) is incorrect. Tiff should lose since its motive was to injure Dont. Answer (D) is incorrect. Enticing an employee away is a tort if the purpose is to injure the competitor (or if it interferes with a contract).

16. Supplier has a contract with Factory to provide its needs for gidgets. Fabriken, a major competitor of Factory, hoping to disrupt Factory's production schedule, induces one of Supplier's subcontractors to delay delivery of materials necessary for the production of gidgets. As a result, Factory sustains millions of dollars in losses when the gidgets are not promptly delivered. On what theory could Factory prevail in an action against Fabriken?

A. Interference with contractual relations.

B. Fraud.

C. Breach of contract.

D. Factory has no action against Fabriken.

Answer (A) is correct. *(Publisher, adapted)*

REQUIRED: The theory upon which Factory could prevail in an action against Fabriken.

DISCUSSION: Factory appears to have an action based on intentional interference with contractual relations. Factory must show that it had a valid and enforceable contract with Supplier, Fabriken intentionally caused a material interference with the contract relationship, and the interference proximately caused plaintiff's damages.

Answer (B) is incorrect. There is no evidence that a false representation was made or was relied upon. Answer (C) is incorrect. Fabriken did not contract with Factory and could not have breached a contract. Answer (D) is incorrect. Fabriken intentionally interfered with contractual relations.

17. Competitor runs an ad in the newspaper in which it states that Seller's product has a serious design defect. As a result, Seller's sales slide.

A. Competitor has committed the tort of disparagement or trade libel if the statement is false.

B. Competitor has committed the tort of disparagement or trade libel only if it knew of the falsehood of the statement or acted with reckless disregard for the truth.

C. Competitor has committed the tort of interference with contractual relations.

D. Seller may sue Competitor for the tort of deceit.

Answer (B) is correct. *(Publisher, adapted)*

REQUIRED: The liability for publicly degrading a competitor's product.

DISCUSSION: An action for disparagement (called trade libel) may be based upon an intentional false or reckless statement made concerning the quality of another's product. (A few states base the tort on negligent misrepresentation.) The intent of the defendant is usually crucial. If Competitor's statement was honestly made, even though mistaken, an action for disparagement would not be available.

Answer (A) is incorrect. Disparagement usually requires an intentional or reckless falsehood. Answer (C) is incorrect. An action for interference with contractual relations would exist only if the defendant had hindered performance of an enforceable contract. Answer (D) is incorrect. Justifiable reliance on a false representation is required for an action for deceit (fraud).

18. The tort of intentional misrepresentation (fraud) consists of the following elements: a material misrepresentation with scienter and an intent to induce reliance that proximately causes damages to the plaintiff who reasonably relied upon the misrepresentation. Which is the true statement concerning this tort?

A. When one party to a transaction knows that the other has no knowledge of a material fact, failure to disclose the fact is intentional misrepresentation.

B. Scienter exists only if the defendant made a false representation with actual knowledge of its falsity.

C. The plaintiff may not prove justifiable reliance if the false representation was one of opinion rather than of fact.

D. The plaintiff may show that (s)he justifiably relied upon the false representation even though (s)he has not investigated the factual statement.

Answer (D) is correct. *(Publisher, adapted)*

REQUIRED: The true statement concerning the tort of intentional misrepresentation.

DISCUSSION: To recover for the tort of intentional misrepresentation (fraud, deceit), a plaintiff must prove justifiable reliance upon the false representation of a material fact (that it was a substantial factor influencing his/her decision). The plaintiff may rely on the representations without investigation unless the falsity of the representations could be discovered without an unreasonable (costly, difficult, etc.) investigation.

Answer (A) is incorrect. Failure to disclose a material fact is not intentional misrepresentation if it was not done to induce reliance and if the fact was obvious or could have been discovered by reasonable inspection. Answer (B) is incorrect. Scienter also exists if the defendant made a false representation with reckless regard as to its truth. Answer (C) is incorrect. In certain instances, a plaintiff may justifiably rely upon an opinion, e.g., that of an expert.

19. Sly offered Merry Lamb a watch for $100 and falsely represented that it was studded with diamonds, which would make its retail value $650. In reliance on Sly's statement, Merry paid $100 for the watch. She later learned that its stones were fake and its retail value was only $100. In a tort action based on fraud, what will be the measure of Merry's damages in the majority of states?

A. $0

B. $100

C. $550

D. $650

Answer (C) is correct. *(Publisher, adapted)*

REQUIRED: The measure of fraud damages under the majority rule.

DISCUSSION: The majority of states adhere to the "loss-of-bargain" theory, under which the measure of damages is the difference between the value received and the value as represented. Given that the watch was stated to be worth $650 and was actually worth only $100, damages will equal $550. The minority view is that damages should be based on plaintiff's "out-of-pocket" loss. Because Merry paid $100 for a watch worth $100, applying the minority rule would result in no damages. The misrepresentation was of a fact. In contrast, a misrepresentation as to value is usually considered an opinion.

20. Bippo is a successful marketer of a ballpoint pen whose form and design are distinctive and well known to the general public. Bippo's patent for its pen has expired, and a pen very similar in form and design has appeared on the market. The imitator has stamped its own trade name on the product. What will be the outcome if Bippo sues in tort?

A. Bippo will win because the product has acquired a secondary meaning.

B. Bippo will lose because the public is not likely to be confused by the imitation.

C. Bippo will lose because courts do not recognize palming off as a tort.

D. Bippo will win because it imitated the appearance of a highly advertised product.

Answer (B) is correct. *(Publisher, adapted)*

REQUIRED: The outcome of a suit by a manufacturer against an imitator of its product.

DISCUSSION: Palming off has two elements: The original product has a secondary meaning, and the imitation and the original are so similar that the public may confuse the two. Secondary meaning is the association by the public of a manufacturer with its product. But if the imitator does not fraudulently market the product and if the public is not likely to confuse the imitation with the original, tort liability will not be imposed.

Answer (A) is incorrect. The public must also be likely to confuse the original with the copy. Answer (C) is incorrect. Palming off is one of several torts in the category of unfair trade practices. Answer (D) is incorrect. One may imitate the form and design of a product not under patent protection if the public is not likely to confuse the two.

21. In which case is the defendant (D) most likely to prevail in a suit by the plaintiff (P) for infringement of a trademark or trade name?

A. D sells a soft drink called Coke.

B. D uses a trademark that P registered with the U.S. Patent Office. P did not affix the trademark to the goods but affixed it to a tag attached to the goods.

C. D sells a beer it describes as "light" beer.

D. D sells a cough syrup called Smith's with two bearded men pictured on the container.

Answer (C) is correct. *(Publisher, adapted)*

REQUIRED: The instance that is probably not an infringement of a trademark or trade name.

DISCUSSION: A trademark is a distinctive design, word, symbol, mark, picture, etc., affixed to a product and adopted by its seller or manufacturer to identify the product's source. A trade name is generally regarded as referring to a business and the goodwill it has generated, for example, Exxon. In general, trademark protection is not given to a term that is generic or commonly descriptive. "Light" has been used in the beer industry for years to describe a certain set of characteristics; thus, it is not protected.

Answer (A) is incorrect. "Coke" is associated in the public mind with products of a particular company, and it has acquired a secondary meaning. Answer (B) is incorrect. Placement on a tag, label, container, or associated display suffices. Answer (D) is incorrect. Common personal names or place names can be trademarked if accompanied by a distinctive design or logo.

22. Under the Patent Act, "Whoever invents or discovers any new and useful process, machine, manufacture, or composition of matter, or any new and useful improvement thereof, may obtain a patent therefor." Which of the following is true?

A. A stand-alone computer program may be copyrighted but not patented.

B. After June 1995, the duration of a new patent will be 20 years. It may be renewed.

C. A genetically engineered bacterium is not protected.

D. The only requirement for a process, machine, manufacture, or composition of matter to be patentable is novelty (not in conflict with an existing patent).

Answer (A) is correct. *(Publisher, adapted)*

REQUIRED: The true statement about federal patent law.

DISCUSSION: A single computer program can be copyrighted but not patented. Methods of calculation, fundamental truths, principles, laws of nature, ideas, and the like are not patentable. However, a process that includes a computer program is patentable.

Answer (B) is incorrect. Under current law, the right to a patent lasts for a nonrenewable term of 20 years from the date the patent application is filed. Upon expiration, the invention enters the public domain. Answer (C) is incorrect. Such a bacterium is human-produced (not naturally occurring) and therefore patentable. Answer (D) is incorrect. The process, etc., must have utility and be nonobvious as well as novel.

23. M.A. Genius invented, manufactures, and distributes a flashlight needing no batteries if used in direct sunlight. Genius did not apply for a patent. Novelco bought one at a retail store, analyzed and copied it, and now sells an identical product under its own name. Which of the following is true?

A. Genius can enjoin Novelco's activities on the basis of a trade secret violation.

B. Genius can enjoin Novelco's activities because it clearly meets the novelty, utility, and nonobviousness criteria.

C. If Novelco continues to make and sell the solar flashlights, it will have to pay Genius a royalty.

D. Novelco has not violated any legal duty owed to Genius.

Answer (D) is correct. *(M. Levin)*

REQUIRED: The protection afforded to ideas and their representation in new products.

DISCUSSION: Society's interest in free competition is so strong that copying a competitor's product is lawful unless a trademark, trade secret, patent, or copyright is infringed. If a product is not protected by a patent, competitors can use information gained through "reverse engineering."

Answer (A) is incorrect. Trade secrets receive only limited protection. If a competitor can discover a secret through independent means not involving a misappropriation, the owner has no protection against duplication. Answer (B) is incorrect. Patentability affords no protection unless a patent is obtained. Answer (C) is incorrect. Genius cannot claim a royalty if he has no exclusive right to his product.

24. Trade secrets receive a substantial measure of protection under the tort law. Assuming no patent protection, in which case will the defendant (D) prevail against the plaintiff (P)?

A. D offers a lucrative job to Albert, who is employed by P, a competitor in the electronics industry. Albert has specialized knowledge of certain components developed by P and highly useful to D but has no contract with P.

B. D's R&D department discovers an old article in an obscure technical journal written by a researcher who helped formulate P's product. The article enables D to produce an identical product at a lower price.

C. P required a unique machine for its process. Accordingly, it asked Judy to manufacture the equipment according to P's design but to keep the specifications confidential. D paid Judy for the machine's plans.

D. D conducted aerial surveillance of P's plant site during its construction phase. The site was surrounded by a fence, and the grounds were patrolled by security people. The only gate was guarded 24 hours a day. The reconnaissance revealed details about a new process.

Answer (B) is correct. *(Publisher, adapted)*

REQUIRED: The means of discovering a trade secret not resulting in liability.

DISCUSSION: A trade secret is information of economic value to a business that it wishes to keep confidential. The courts protect this interest even though the trade secret cannot be copyrighted or patented. A competitor is not prevented, however, from obtaining the knowledge by lawful means, such as independent research, purchase of the product in the open market, or the plaintiff's voluntary disclosure or failure to take reasonable precautions.

Answer (A) is incorrect. Albert may work for D but can be enjoined on the grounds of unfair competition from revealing P's trade secrets. Answer (C) is incorrect. Industrial espionage is tortious. In this case, the plaintiff took reasonable precautions to protect its secrets. Answer (D) is incorrect. Industrial espionage is tortious. In this case, the plaintiff took reasonable precautions to protect its secrets.

25. A copyright is one means of protecting intellectual property consisting of "original works of authorship in any tangible medium of expression, now known or later developed" (Copyright Act). Which of the following is true?

A. A book written in 2003 may be copyrighted only until 2053.

B. Protection begins when the copyright is registered in the appropriate state office.

C. Conveyance of a copyright may be oral or in writing. A copyright may also pass by will or intestate succession.

D. A college professor who copies a few pages from a copyrighted book and distributes them to the five members of a graduate seminar has not committed infringement.

Answer (D) is correct. *(Publisher, adapted)*

REQUIRED: The true statement about the protection afforded by the Copyright Act.

DISCUSSION: The Copyright Act permits fair use of the copyrighted material "for purposes such as criticism, comment, news reporting, teaching (including multiple copies for classroom use), scholarship, or research." Whether a use is fair depends upon factors such as the effect on the market for the work, the substantiality of the portion used in relation to the whole work, the nature of the copyrighted work, and the purpose and character of the use, including whether the use is commercial or for a nonprofit educational purpose. The professor's use therefore appears to be fair.

Answer (A) is incorrect. The duration of the copyright is the life of the author plus 70 years. If the copyright owner is a publisher, the duration is 95 years from the date of publication or 120 years from the date of creation, whichever period elapses first. Answer (B) is incorrect. Copyrights need not be registered to give protection. However, the work must be registered with the U.S. Copyright Office before the owner can sue in federal court for infringement. Answer (C) is incorrect. Conveyance must be in writing and be signed by the owner of the rights or his/her agent.

7.5 Negligence

26. In a negligence case, the finder of fact (either the judge or a jury) must determine whether the defendant's conduct breached the duty to exercise the care required in the circumstances. The standard to which the defendant's behavior is compared is that of the hypothetical ordinary reasonable person. The application of the standard is subject to the particular circumstances of the case, but the same criterion is applied regardless of the defendant's

A. Superior skill or knowledge.

B. Mental deficiency.

C. Infancy (under age of majority).

D. Physical disability.

Answer (B) is correct. *(Publisher, adapted)*
REQUIRED: The factor that does not alter the standard used to determine negligence.
DISCUSSION: A person who is insane or otherwise mentally deficient is expected to conduct him/herself as would an ordinary reasonable person in the circumstances who is not mentally deficient. Reasons include the difficulty of distinguishing mental deficiency from the ordinary variations of emotions and intellect; the difficulty of proving and the ease of feigning mental deficiency; and the belief that liability will be an incentive to guardians to look after the mentally deficient.
Answer (A) is incorrect. One who has or claims superior knowledge or skill is held to a higher standard. Answer (C) is incorrect. Children are not expected to have the same maturity of judgment as an adult. Answer (D) is incorrect. A handicapped person is expected to act as would a reasonable person with the same impairment.

27. In which case will the defendant be liable for the tort of negligence?

A. Dyana throws a baseball intending to hit her brother and strikes a passerby.

B. While playing golf, Dee swings a club on the fairway. Because of a design defect, the head of the club flies off and strikes a fellow golfer standing 20 yards away.

C. Dari takes medication that she knows causes drowsiness at the maximum dosage. Dari takes this dose prior to flying her aircraft. Her lack of alertness causes a crash in which a passenger is injured.

D. While driving her car, Diana, without warning, has a sudden, stabbing chest pain that causes her to lose control and crash into another vehicle.

Answer (C) is correct. *(Publisher, adapted)*
REQUIRED: The instance that meets the definition of negligence.
DISCUSSION: The Restatement (Second) of Torts defines negligence as "conduct that falls below the standard established by law for the protection of others against unreasonable risk of harm." This standard is that of a reasonable person acting with the care due in the circumstances. A person who knowingly pilots an aircraft after taking medication she knows will impair her capacities has behaved negligently.
Answer (A) is incorrect. Dyana has committed the intentional tort of battery. The intent to strike one person is transferred to the individual actually hit. Answer (B) is incorrect. Unless Dee had reason to know that the club was defective, she has no liability. She could not have prevented the harm by the exercise of reasonable care. Answer (D) is incorrect. Assuming the heart attack was unforeseeable, Diana will not be liable in tort.

28. Bea Bystander was walking on the streets of Big Town when she turned a corner and found Vince Victim lying on the sidewalk having what appeared to be a heart attack. Bystander loosened Victim's tie but then, deciding not to get involved, left the scene without calling for help. Victim survived but suffered a permanent disability as a consequence of not receiving immediate aid. If Victim asserts a claim against Bystander, will he prevail?

A. Yes, because a reasonably prudent person would have aided Victim.

B. Yes, because, by beginning the rescue, Bystander assumed a duty to aid.

C. Yes, because Victim is a foreseeable plaintiff.

D. No, because Bystander did not make Victim's situation any worse.

Answer (D) is correct. *(Publisher, adapted)*
REQUIRED: The liability for failure to render assistance to an endangered person.
DISCUSSION: The general rule is that a person has no legal duty or obligation to rescue or aid another person in distress (it is, of course, a moral responsibility). One may even begin to assist another and then abandon the effort. However, liability will result if a rescuer's actions leave the victim in a worse situation.
Answer (A) is incorrect. The law imposes no affirmative duty to act for the benefit of another person. Answer (B) is incorrect. One does not assume a duty to aid another unless, by beginning a rescue, one has prevented or deterred another from giving assistance. Answer (C) is incorrect. Bystander owed no legal duty to Victim, and her act did not cause the injury to Victim.

29. Which is the true statement concerning the duty owed by the possessor of land to those who enter it?

A. The possessor owes no duty to undiscovered trespassers and to anticipated trespassers.

B. The owner or occupier of the property owes to a social guest the duty owed to an invitee.

C. The duty extended to a licensee includes warning of concealed and dangerous conditions known to the possessor of the property, the use of ordinary care in active operations upon the property, and the making of reasonable inspections to discover dangerous conditions and to make them safe.

D. The owner or occupier of land owes the highest duty to invitees.

Answer (D) is correct. *(Publisher, adapted)*

REQUIRED: The true statement concerning the duty of care owed by a possessor of land.

DISCUSSION: Under the law of negligence, the duty owed by a possessor of land varies with the legal status of parties who enter the land. Invitees (persons expressly or impliedly invited onto the property for the possessor's business interest or members of the public if the property is held open to the public) receive the greatest protection.

Answer (A) is incorrect. A possessor owes no duty to an undiscovered trespasser, but (s)he does owe a duty not to harm anticipated trespassers intentionally (e.g., not to set traps, etc.). Answer (B) is incorrect. A social guest is a licensee who is owed a duty of reasonable care (in active operations and by warning of dangers of which the possessor should know) but not the duty to inspect for defective conditions. Answer (C) is incorrect. It describes the duty owed to an invitee, not a licensee.

30. While shopping with his mother at the Supermarket, 14-year-old Ronald dropped a banana peel on the floor in the produce department. Three hours later, Mr. Customer slipped on the peel and broke his leg. Which of the following is true?

A. Customer can probably recover from Supermarket if it has failed to frequently inspect and clear the floor of foreign objects.

B. Customer could not recover from Ronald because he is a minor.

C. If Supermarket did not have actual knowledge of the condition, it cannot be held liable.

D. If Supermarket cleans and waxes its floor each night, it cannot be held liable.

Answer (A) is correct. *(M. Levin)*

REQUIRED: The standard of care that a business owes to an invitee.

DISCUSSION: A high degree of care is owed to a business visitor (an invitee). The possessor of the property has a duty to exercise reasonable care to protect the invitee against dangerous conditions. Because slips and falls of this kind often occur in a grocery store setting, reasonable prudence requires that the floor be frequently inspected and that such hazards be promptly eliminated (3 hours is much too slow). If the store's employee had caused the dangerous condition or allowed it to continue after discovery, the store would be liable without regard to the elapsed time.

Answer (B) is incorrect. Infancy is not a tort defense, although it may be a mitigating factor. Answer (C) is incorrect. The defendant has an affirmative duty to make the premises safe for an invitee. Lack of actual knowledge would be a defense only against a trespasser or licensee. Answer (D) is incorrect. Reasonable care requires more than a once-a-day cleaning in such circumstances.

31. Fraternity is a rowdy group. During its convention at Ace Hotel, the members littered both the inside and the outside of the hotel with debris and bottles. Hotel employees patrolled the hallways telling the guests to refrain from such conduct. Owner was out of town and was not aware of the problems that were occurring. During the convention, as Smith walked past the Ace Hotel on the sidewalk, he was injured by an ashtray thrown out of a window of the hotel. Smith sued the owner of Ace Hotel. Will Smith prevail?

A. Yes, because a property owner is strictly liable for acts on the premises that cause harm to persons using the adjacent public sidewalks.

B. Yes, if the person who threw the ashtray cannot be identified.

C. No, if the owner had no personal knowledge of the conduct of the hotel guests.

D. No, if the trier of fact determines that the hotel employees had taken reasonable precautions to prevent such an injury.

Answer (D) is correct. *(Publisher, adapted)*

REQUIRED: The liability of a hotel owner for injuries caused by hotel employees or guests.

DISCUSSION: The owner of land has a duty to undertake reasonable precautions to prevent injury to persons off the land as a result of activities of the landowner or his/her guests. If the trier of fact determines that the employees had exercised due care to prevent the injury, then Smith will not prevail.

Answer (A) is incorrect. A property owner is not strictly liable for acts on his/her premises that cause harm to persons off the premises. The owner is required to exercise only reasonable care. Answer (B) is incorrect. Whether the person who threw the ashtray can be identified will not affect the owner's liability. Answer (C) is incorrect. The owner needs no personal knowledge to be held liable if his employees had the knowledge.

32. Kay owns a large department store. In the rear is a freight elevator used by the employees of the shipping and receiving departments. A state statute for the protection of employees requires that all such elevators have a specified safety device. Employee Ben and supplier Chris are injured as a result of a failure to install the device. Which of the following is true?

A. As a result of the statute, Kay is negligent per se with regard to Ben but not Chris.

B. As a result of the statute, Kay is negligent per se with regard to Chris but not Ben.

C. Res ipsa loquitur applies.

D. Res ipsa loquitur applies only to Chris.

Answer (A) is correct. *(Publisher, adapted)*

REQUIRED: The consequence of a defendant's failure to adhere to a statute.

DISCUSSION: One means of establishing breach is to prove that the defendant committed an unexcused violation of a statute intended to protect the class of persons to which the plaintiff belongs. The statute defines the standard of conduct of the ordinary reasonable person. In the majority of states, Kay, absent a sufficient excuse, would be irrebuttably presumed negligent toward its employee Ben.

Answer (B) is incorrect. Chris did not belong to the class the legislature named and could not rely on the statute to prove negligence. Answer (C) is incorrect. Res ipsa loquitur ("the thing speaks for itself") does not apply. It is useful when the circumstances make proof difficult because the defendant is the only party with knowledge of how the harm was caused. Answer (D) is incorrect. Res ipsa loquitur ("the thing speaks for itself") does not apply. It is useful when the circumstances make proof difficult because the defendant is the only party with knowledge of how the harm was caused.

33. Plaintiff customer was injured when he fell in Defendant's store one Sunday. A local ordinance requires Sunday closing. Plaintiff sues Defendant for damages. What is the effect of the statute?

A. Defendant's violation of the statute was negligence per se.

B. Defendant will prevail if the statute was not intended to prevent the kind of harm incurred by Plaintiff.

C. Violation of a criminal statute always establishes a presumption of a duty and breach of that duty.

D. Compliance with a criminal statute establishes that the duty of due care has not been breached.

Answer (B) is correct. *(Publisher, adapted)*

REQUIRED: The effect of a violation of an ordinance upon a defendant's liability in tort.

DISCUSSION: A statute providing a criminal penalty may be used to establish the required duty of care and establish that the duty has been breached. Plaintiff must show that he is a member of the class intended to be protected by the statute and that the statute was intended to prevent the kind of injury that he sustained. However, the kind of harm intended by a Sunday closing law does not embrace the physical injuries from a fall.

Answer (A) is incorrect. The harm to be prevented by the ordinance was not that suffered by the plaintiff. Answer (C) is incorrect. Although many courts hold that the violation of an applicable criminal statute produces a conclusive presumption, some hold it to be only rebuttable evidence of negligence. Answer (D) is incorrect. Compliance with an applicable criminal statute does not establish that due care has been exercised.

34. Agnes and Buford went camping to celebrate their 50th wedding anniversary. While eating under the moonlit sky, Agnes and Buford conversed about days gone by. Suddenly the mood was spoiled when Buford discovered a rat's ear in the bottom of his can of Best-of-the-Rest baked beans. Buford wants to sue Best-of-the-Rest. Buford's best theory of liability is

A. Respondeat superior.

B. Strict liability for design defects.

C. Res ipsa loquitur.

D. Assumption of the risk.

Answer (C) is correct. *(K. Wilburn)*

REQUIRED: The best theory of liability for discovery of a foreign object in a sealed container.

DISCUSSION: The doctrine of res ipsa loquitur ("the thing speaks for itself") is useful when the circumstances make proof difficult because the defendant is the only party with knowledge of how the harm was caused. According to the Restatement (Second) of Torts, three elements must be shown to invoke the doctrine: "The event is of a kind that ordinarily does not occur in the absence of negligence; other responsible causes, including the conduct of the plaintiff and third persons, are sufficiently eliminated by the evidence; and the indicated negligence is within the scope of the defendant's duty to the plaintiff." When res ipsa loquitur is established, the burden of proof shifts, and the defendant must prove (s)he was not negligent.

Answer (A) is incorrect. Respondeat superior is used to hold an employer liable for the acts of an employee committed within the course and scope of employment. Answer (B) is incorrect. Strict liability for design defects applies when the product is in the condition intended by the manufacturer but was designed in a way that makes it unreasonably dangerous in normal use. Answer (D) is incorrect. Assumption of the risk is a defense to a tort action for negligence.

35. After repairing the roof of Orissa's home, Rex Roofer left his 20-foot ladder against the side of the house. Orissa and her family were away on a trip. During the night, a thief using the ladder entered an upstairs window and stole some valuable jewels. In her claim against Roofer, Orissa will

A. Prevail because, by leaving the ladder, Roofer became a trespasser on Orissa's property.

B. Prevail because, by leaving the ladder, Roofer created the risk that a person might unlawfully enter the house.

C. Not prevail because the act of the thief was a superseding cause.

D. Not prevail because Orissa's claim is limited to damages for breach of contract.

Answer (B) is correct. *(Publisher, adapted)*

REQUIRED: The liability of a roofer for leaving a ladder which was used for burglary.

DISCUSSION: Liability for negligence requires a foreseeable risk of harm that could have been avoided. A reasonable person could foresee that someone might use the ladder to enter the house. Thus, Roofer owed a duty to Orissa to exercise due care to avoid the risk.

Answer (A) is incorrect. Leaving his ladder on the premises overnight probably did not make Roofer a trespasser (he was probably a licensee). Answer (C) is incorrect. The act of the thief was reasonably foreseeable; therefore, it is not a superseding cause. Answer (D) is incorrect. A duty of reasonable care exists regardless of contractual relations.

36. In which case is M liable?

A. M was filling a sinkhole in a highway but had not erected a barrier. Motorist saw the danger but plunged into the sinkhole at 60 mph when her brakes failed. A barrier could not have stopped the vehicle.

B. M negligently failed to install a fire escape. While sleeping, M's guest died of smoke inhalation in a fire set by an arsonist.

C. M, B, and C became separated while hunting. Thinking they were firing at a deer, M and C negligently discharged their firearms in B's direction. Each shot gave B a fatal wound.

D. Motorist was driving 50 mph in a 55 mph zone after having her brakes repaired by M. When a child darted in front of the car, the brakes failed and the child was killed. Motorist would not have been able to stop in time if the brakes had worked.

Answer (C) is correct. *(Publisher, adapted)*

REQUIRED: The case in which M's conduct is a cause in fact of the plaintiff's injury.

DISCUSSION: An element of the tort of negligence is causation. The act of the defendant must have actually caused the injury of the plaintiff (cause in fact). The act is an actual cause of the injury if one can say that "but for" the defendant's negligence, no injury would have occurred. The "but for" test must be supplemented, however, when concurring causes inflicted the plaintiff's injury. For example, M could argue that B's death would have occurred without M's action. Under the "substantial factor" test, however, both M and C will nevertheless be liable because both contributed substantially to B's death.

37. To establish a prima facie case of negligence, the plaintiff must show that defendant's act proximately caused the injury complained of. Which of the following is true?

A. The purpose of the proximate cause doctrine is to extend defendant's liability.

B. Proximate cause is synonymous with actual cause.

C. If a plaintiff's injury is inflicted by an intervening force, a defendant will usually be liable if his/her conduct was a direct cause in fact of the injury even though the nature both of the harm and of the force was not foreseeable.

D. According to the Restatement (Second) of Torts, a court may find for the defendant if, after the event and looking back, it appears highly extraordinary that his/her conduct should have caused the plaintiff's injury.

Answer (D) is correct. *(Publisher, adapted)*

REQUIRED: The true statement about the proximate cause doctrine.

DISCUSSION: In addition to actual cause, the defendant's negligence must also be the proximate cause of the plaintiff's injury. A factor in deciding whether an act was the proximate cause of an injury is foreseeability. An actual cause may not be a legal cause when, after the event and looking back, it appears to the court highly extraordinary that the defendant's action should have brought about the harm. In a famous case, the defendant drove a car into another car. Explosives in the second car detonated, blowing out windows in a faraway building. The defendant's act was held not to be a proximate cause of the injury caused by the flying glass.

Answer (A) is incorrect. Proximate cause limits liability. Answer (B) is incorrect. Every proximate cause is an actual cause but not vice versa. Answer (C) is incorrect. An intervening force occurring after the defendant's act may have a significant effect on the plaintiff's injury and relieve the defendant of liability.

38. Proof of damages is an essential element of the prima facie case of the tort of negligence. The purpose of tort damages is to make the plaintiff whole, to place him/her in the position in which (s)he would have been if there had been no injury. Plaintiff may therefore recover for all damages including

A. Reasonable attorney's fees.

B. Health care costs, except for those which have been mitigated by receipt of benefits from collateral sources; e.g., health insurance payments.

C. Punitive damages.

D. An award for impaired earning capacity discounted to present value.

Answer (D) is correct. *(Publisher, adapted)*

REQUIRED: The true statement concerning the award of damages in a negligence case.

DISCUSSION: If the defendant's actions have resulted in injury to the plaintiff such that future earning capacity is impaired, a lump-sum award compensating for this reduced earning capacity would be a proper element of damages. To avoid an excess award, the lump sum would represent the present value of the stream of lost future income discounted at an appropriate interest rate.

Answer (A) is incorrect. The fees of attorneys are not considered properly recoverable in negligence, unless provided by statute. Answer (B) is incorrect. Damages are awarded regardless of payment of benefits from collateral sources. Answer (C) is incorrect. Punitive damages may be awarded only when a defendant was grossly negligent or acted in a willful and wanton manner.

39. Mort Morpheus parked his car on the railroad tracks in a contributory negligence state. Casey Jones was operating the train at a safe speed when he saw Morpheus's car parked on the tracks ahead. Because Casey was eating, by the time he could put his foot down and apply the brakes, it was too late. In an action brought by Morpheus against Jones and the railroad,

A. Contributory negligence will be a complete defense.

B. Morpheus might prevail under the last-clear-chance doctrine.

C. Contributory negligence of the plaintiff will reduce his award proportionate to his negligence.

D. The railroad will have no liability because the engineer had the last clear chance to avoid the accident.

Answer (B) is correct. *(Publisher, adapted)*

REQUIRED: The effects of the contributory negligence and last-clear-chance doctrines.

DISCUSSION: In those states that continue to recognize the defense of contributory negligence, if the negligence of the plaintiff contributed to his/her damages, plaintiff will be absolutely barred from recovery. Morpheus's negligence contributed to his loss. The last-clear-chance doctrine applies when, despite plaintiff's prior negligence, injury could have been avoided if defendant had acted with reasonable care. Because Jones had the "last clear chance" to avoid the accident, Morpheus may prevail against the engineer and the railroad.

Answer (A) is incorrect. The last-clear-chance doctrine removes the bar of contributory negligence. Answer (C) is incorrect. This is the result under the theory of comparative (not contributory) negligence. Answer (D) is incorrect. If Jones is liable, the railroad will also be liable as his employer.

40. Hemlock Holmes lives in a contributory negligence state. Holmes drank four ounces of straight gin in 30 minutes and became intoxicated. Then, on an unlighted street, he walked without looking from between two parked cars in front of a speeding car. The driver was unable to stop before hitting Holmes. Holmes has sued the driver to recover for his damages. Will he win?

A. Yes, to the extent the driver's speeding contributed to Holmes's injuries.

B. Yes, because the driver had the last clear chance to prevent the injury.

C. No, because Holmes contributed to his own injury.

D. No, because Holmes had the last clear chance to prevent the injury.

Answer (C) is correct. *(E. Arnold)*

REQUIRED: The true statement about the implications of contributory negligence.

DISCUSSION: Contributory negligence is an absolute bar to recovery by a plaintiff. It is conduct on plaintiff's part that is below the standard required for his/her own protection and that legally contributes to the harm. Holmes's self-induced intoxication rendered him unable to properly attend to his own safety on the streets.

Answer (A) is incorrect. Liability is not apportioned in contributory negligence states. Answer (B) is incorrect. The facts suggest that the driver had no last clear chance to avoid the impact. Answer (D) is incorrect. The last-clear-chance doctrine does not apply to plaintiffs (it applies to defendants).

41. Hemlock Holmes lives in a comparative negligence state. Holmes drank four ounces of straight gin in 30 minutes and became intoxicated. Then, on an unlighted street, he walked without looking from between two parked cars in front of a speeding car. The driver was unable to stop before hitting Holmes. Holmes has sued the driver to recover for his damages. Will he prevail?

A. Yes, to the extent the driver's speeding contributed to Holmes's injuries.

B. Yes, because the driver had the last clear chance to prevent the injury.

C. No, because Holmes contributed to his own injury.

D. No, because Holmes had the last clear chance to prevent the injury.

Answer (A) is correct. *(E. Arnold)*

REQUIRED: The true statement about comparative negligence.

DISCUSSION: The comparative negligence doctrine offers a compromise solution to the "either/or" solution of contributory negligence with its accompanying harsh results. States that recognize the doctrine apportion damages based on the plaintiff's and the defendant's respective degrees of fault. The majority of such states, however, do not allow recovery if the plaintiff's negligence contributed to 50% or more of the injury.

Answer (B) is incorrect. The driver was unable to stop before striking Holmes. Answer (C) is incorrect. Holmes's contribution to his own injuries does not prevent recovery. Answer (D) is incorrect. Even with a last chance to prevent the accident, Holmes can use comparative negligence to recover for the driver's contribution to his injuries.

42. Plaintiff and Defendant went on a social outing to Defendant's fish camp. Defendant warned Plaintiff that she should not go onto an unfinished pier and that the boards at the end were not closely spaced. Plaintiff heard the warning but continued on without replying. After reaching the end of the pier, she started back, choosing her steps carefully. A loose board then gave way and she fell, tearing ligaments in her knee. The best argument by Defendant is

A. Express assumption of the risk.

B. Implied assumption of the risk.

C. Contributory negligence.

D. Lack of proximate cause.

Answer (B) is correct. *(Publisher, adapted)*

REQUIRED: The best defense of a defendant who has expressly warned plaintiff.

DISCUSSION: Assumption of the risk is a complete defense to negligence. Only a few of the comparative negligence jurisdictions have abolished it. The elements of this defense are a risk of harm caused by the defendant's conduct, actual knowledge of the risk, and a voluntary choice to remain within the area of risk. Defendant's pier was in an unsafe condition, Plaintiff actually knew of the risk, and Plaintiff voluntarily chose to continue walking on the pier.

Answer (A) is incorrect. Express assumption of risk involves an agreement in advance, by contract or otherwise, whereby the plaintiff expressly agrees to accept a risk. Answer (C) is incorrect. Plaintiff voluntarily assumed the risk. After she ventured onto the pier, she exercised due care, so the defense of contributory negligence is not available. Answer (D) is incorrect. The defective condition of the pier was evidently a legal (proximate) as well as a direct cause of the injury.

7.6 Strict Liability

43. Gerald, an 18-year-old high school student, stole a tiger cub from a zoo and took it home. Although Gerald built a large, apparently secure cage for the cub in his bedroom and otherwise took excellent care of it, the cub escaped from the cage and bit Edward, Gerald's neighbor. Edward sued Gerald to recover damages. If Edward wins the lawsuit, the court will probably rely on the doctrine of

A. Negligence.

B. Quasi-contract.

C. Express contract.

D. Strict liability.

Answer (D) is correct. *(D. Levin)*

REQUIRED: The appropriate theory of liability for damages caused by a wild animal.

DISCUSSION: Courts impose strict liability (liability without fault) on a defendant after considering such factors as (1) whether the activity is likely to injure others even though the defendant uses reasonable or even great care, (2) whether the gravity of the harm is likely to be great, (3) whether the activity is uncommon or not appropriate to the area, and (4) whether the activity is of value to the community. If one keeps a wild animal and the animal injures someone, the keeper is strictly liable, regardless of the care exercised or whether the animal trespassed on another's land.

Answer (A) is incorrect. Gerald exercised reasonable care for the safety of others. Answer (B) is incorrect. The circumstances do not justify the remedy of quasi-contract; Gerald has not been unjustly enriched at the expense of Edward. Answer (C) is incorrect. Gerald and Edward have not entered into a contract.

44. Strict liability in tort is imposed for abnormally dangerous activities. In which case will defendant Q, who is not at fault, most likely prevail?

A. Q stores a large quantity of flammable liquid in the heart of a city. The liquid explodes and destroys a city block.

B. Q dynamites rock during construction of a building, breaking glass a mile away.

C. Q drills for oil in a residential area, causing pollution of a neighbor's well.

D. Q stores dynamite in the middle of a city. There is no explosion, but the wall of the building where the dynamite is stored crumbles and falls on a pedestrian.

Answer (D) is correct. *(Publisher, adapted)*

REQUIRED: The situation in which strict liability is least likely to be imposed.

DISCUSSION: Whether activity is abnormally dangerous depends on the probability of harm to the person, land, or property of others; the gravity of the harm; the inability to eliminate risk by the exercise of reasonable care; the rarity of the activity; the inappropriateness of the activity to the place where it is carried on; and the value of the activity to the community. Strict liability is imposed if the possibility of the kind of injury suffered was what made the activity abnormally dangerous in the first place. Since the crumbling of the wall without an explosion was not why storing dynamite in the city was abnormally dangerous, there is no strict liability for the injury to the pedestrian.

45. Liability without fault is most likely to be imposed when the plaintiff was

A. Injured during the course and within the scope of her employment as a lathe operator in the defendant's machine shop.

B. Bitten by a horse on the defendant's property. The animal had been raised as a pet and had previously been perfectly docile.

C. Intentionally injured by himself during employment.

D. Injured in the crash of the defendant's private plane.

Answer (A) is correct. *(Publisher, adapted)*

REQUIRED: The case in which strict liability is most likely to be imposed.

DISCUSSION: Workers' compensation laws in all states provide compensation to injured employees without regard to the fault of the employer or employee. The employee must show only that (s)he was injured during the course and scope of employment. The recovery is fixed by statute. The employee may not sue the employer in regular court but is not barred from legal action against third parties.

Answer (B) is incorrect. Strict liability is not generally imposed for the actions of domesticated animals that are not trespassers and have not previously shown dangerous propensities. Answer (C) is incorrect. Intentional self-infliction of injury is a bar to recovery even under workers' compensation laws. Answer (D) is incorrect. Flying an aircraft is not considered abnormally dangerous.

46. Some states have enacted no-fault automobile insurance statutes. The typical statute

A. Removes all claims for automobile accident injuries from the courts to an administrative agency.

B. Provides that, if the law applies, the injured party will collect from his/her insurer if the amount of damages is less than a specified amount.

C. Allows for recovery in amounts comparable to average damage awards by courts in similar cases.

D. Excludes from coverage personal injury to individuals not traveling in a vehicle involved in the accident.

Answer (B) is correct. *(Publisher, adapted)*

REQUIRED: The effect of no-fault automobile insurance statutes.

DISCUSSION: A no-fault automobile insurance statute essentially tries to do for damages arising from automobile accidents what workers' compensation laws do for work-related injuries. If the claim is within the statute, the injured party need not prove fault but may automatically receive a certain amount, usually less than that recoverable in court.

Answer (A) is incorrect. Claims for damages above a certain threshold amount may still be litigated in court. Answer (C) is incorrect. No-fault awards are limited by statute and are generally lower than those awarded by courts. Answer (D) is incorrect. Persons not traveling in a vehicle are covered by the vehicle's insurance.

7.7 Products Liability

47. A manufacturer who fails to exercise due care in the manufacture or handling of a product may be held liable for negligence. A defendant manufacturer will prevail, however, when the

A. Negligence was in the design of the product.

B. Product was assembled improperly.

C. Product was designed to be safe for proper use but not for an unforeseeable improper use.

D. Conduct complained of was merely a failure to warn.

Answer (C) is correct. *(Publisher, adapted)*

REQUIRED: The manufacturer's defense to a negligence action.

DISCUSSION: A manufacturer is negligent if its breach of a legal duty to exercise reasonable care proximately caused injury to the plaintiff. A manufacturer may be liable when the product is unsafe as a result of negligence in its manufacture. Liability will also be found when the design of the product makes it unreasonably dangerous for the uses for which it is manufactured even though all reasonable care is taken in manufacture, assembly, testing, and inspection. The manufacturer also has a duty to use reasonable care to warn when the product is known to be dangerous for the use for which it is supplied, and there is no reason to believe that users will be aware of the danger. However, no liability arises when a product is designed to be reasonably safe for proper and foreseeable improper uses but not for unforeseeable improper uses.

48. A retailer of a defective product that causes injury to the plaintiff will most likely prevail in an action based on negligence when the

A. Defect was in the product's manufacture, although the defendant represented the product as its own.

B. Retailer merely failed to inspect because inspection is the duty of the manufacturer.

C. Retailer merely failed to warn of the danger.

D. Fault was in the design or construction of the product.

Answer (D) is correct. *(Publisher, adapted)*

REQUIRED: The circumstance in which a retailer is most likely to prevail in a negligence action.

DISCUSSION: Negligence is usually a poor theory on which to base recovery from a retailer. The design and manufacture of the product are seldom under the retailer's control, and the retailer may have no more knowledge of the product than the buyer, especially when it is packaged in a sealed container.

Answer (A) is incorrect. The retailer is subject to the same standards as a manufacturer when it holds the product out as its own. Answer (B) is incorrect. Whereas a retailer usually has no duty to inspect or warn, circumstances may arise that alert the retailer to a possible defect and create a duty to inspect and/or warn. For example, a failure of refrigeration may create a duty on the part of a grocer to inspect and warn about its perishables. Answer (C) is incorrect. Whereas a retailer usually has no duty to inspect or warn, circumstances may arise that alert the retailer to a possible defect and create a duty to inspect and/or warn. For example, a failure of refrigeration may create a duty on the part of a grocer to inspect and warn about its perishables.

49. Under the Restatement (Second) of Torts, to establish a cause of action based on strict liability in tort for personal injuries resulting from using a defective product, one of the elements the plaintiff must prove is that the seller (defendant)

A. Failed to exercise due care.

B. Was in privity of contract with the plaintiff.

C. Defectively designed the product.

D. Was engaged in the business of selling the product.

Answer (D) is correct. *(CPA, adapted)*

REQUIRED: The element a plaintiff must prove in a strict liability case.

DISCUSSION: In a strict liability suit against a seller of a product, a plaintiff who has suffered physical harm or property damage must prove that the product was defective, the defect rendered it unreasonably dangerous, the unreasonably dangerous condition of the product caused the harm or damage, the seller was a merchant engaged in the business of selling the particular product, and the product reached the user or consumer without substantial change from the condition in which it was sold.

Answer (A) is incorrect. In an action based on strict liability, the plaintiff need not prove any defendant was at fault. Answer (B) is incorrect. An ultimate user or consumer may bring an action based on strict liability even though (s)he was not in privity with the defendant seller. Answer (C) is incorrect. In an action based on strict liability, the plaintiff need not prove any defendant was at fault.

50. Merton Morgan is suing the manufacturer, wholesaler, and retailer for bodily injuries caused by a power saw Morgan purchased. Under the Restatement (Second) of Torts, which of the following statements is true under the theory of strict liability?

A. The manufacturer will avoid liability if it can show it followed the custom of the industry.

B. Morgan may recover even if he cannot show any negligence was involved.

C. Contributory negligence on Morgan's part will always be a bar to recovery.

D. Privity will be a bar to recovery insofar as the wholesaler is concerned if the wholesaler did not have a reasonable opportunity to inspect.

Answer (B) is correct. *(CPA, adapted)*

REQUIRED: The true statement under the theory of strict liability.

DISCUSSION: In an action based on strict liability in tort, the plaintiff need not show that the manufacturer was negligent. No proof is required that a breach of a legal duty to exercise reasonable care proximately caused the plaintiff's injury.

Answer (A) is incorrect. Under strict liability, the loss is shifted to the industry even if its custom results in the defective product. Answer (C) is incorrect. Although contributory negligence (the plaintiff did not act reasonably to protect him/herself) has been accepted as an absolute defense in a few states, many states have adopted comparative fault or comparative negligence rules. Answer (D) is incorrect. Any reasonably foreseeable plaintiff may generally sue. A duty to inspect may form part of a negligence theory-based suit.

51. Purchaser informed Storekeeper that she wanted to buy a reconditioned paper shredder for use in her business. The reconditioned shredder had been manufactured by Power Shredder Company. The week after the shredder was purchased, Employee, who works for Purchaser, was injured while shredding paper when the shaft holding the shredder blade came loose after a bearing gave way. Employee asserts a claim based on strict liability in tort against Power Shredder. Under the Restatement (Second) of Torts, Employee will probably

A. Recover if the shaft that came loose was a part of the shredder when it was new.

B. Recover because Power Shredder was in the business of manufacturing dangerous machines.

C. Not recover because Employee was not the buyer of the power shredder.

D. Not recover because the shredder had been rebuilt by Storekeeper.

Answer (D) is correct. *(Publisher, adapted)*

REQUIRED: The outcome of a suit by an injured employee whose employer purchased defective reconditioned goods.

DISCUSSION: If Employee asserts a claim based on strict liability in tort, he will probably not recover because the shredder did not reach the user in substantially the same condition as when it was manufactured. Power Shredder Company should not be held strictly liable for selling a product containing a defect that made it unreasonably dangerous if the defect may have occurred later.

Answer (A) is incorrect. The substantial change in the shredder (reconditioning or rebuilding) eliminates a necessary condition for strict liability. Answer (B) is incorrect. Strict liability is based on the existence of a defect that makes a product unreasonably dangerous. Power Shredder is not absolutely liable for every injury caused by its machines. Answer (C) is incorrect. Strict liability may be asserted by a plaintiff who is a user, consumer, or foreseeable bystander.

52. Landon Motor Company sells minibikes for off-the-road use. The owner's manual and a sticker on each bike sold state in bold print that the bike should not be used on public roads. A child riding a Landon minibike was injured on a public road after being told by her parents not to ride in the street. Did Landon breach an ethical duty to the consumer?

A. Yes. A manufacturer is strictly liable for the harm caused by its products.

B. Yes. A manufacturer is absolutely liable for the harm caused by its products.

C. No. A manufacturer is not strictly liable for the products it put in the stream of commerce.

D. No. The bold print in the owner's manual was sufficient to satisfy the duty to warn.

Answer (D) is correct. *(Publisher, adapted)*

REQUIRED: The ethical duty a manufacturer owes to the consumer.

DISCUSSION: When a product is not defectively manufactured and warnings concerning its appropriate use are adequate, a manufacturer is not liable for an accident and resulting injuries. In *Baughn v. Honda Motor Co.,* a case from the state of Washington, Honda designed a minibike for use on dirt roads. A sticker on the bike stated that it was only for off-the-road use. A similar statement appeared in the owner's manual. The court held that the warnings were adequate to protect Honda from liability.

Answer (A) is incorrect. A manufacturer is held strictly liable for products that are unreasonably dangerous when the product is placed in the consumer's hands without giving adequate warnings to the consumer regarding safe use. Landon gave adequate notice by placing a sticker on the minibike and by boldly printing instructions in the owner's manual. Answer (B) is incorrect. The law imposes strict, not absolute, liability. Answer (C) is incorrect. A manufacturer is strictly liable when the product sold to the consumer is not accompanied by adequate instructions as to how to use the product safely.

53. Under the Restatement (Third) of Torts: Products Liability, strict liability is imposed for which type of product defect?

A. Manufacturing.

B. Design.

C. Instructions.

D. Warnings.

Answer (A) is correct. *(Publisher, adapted)*

REQUIRED: The product defect resulting in strict liability.

DISCUSSION: The Restatement (Third) of Torts: Products Liability clarifies and expands products liability law by defining the types of defects and stating a specific test of liability for each, regardless of the legal theory underlying a specific plaintiff's case. A manufacturing defect is a departure from the product's "intended design even though all possible care was exercised" in its preparation and marketing. Strict liability is imposed even if the defendant behaved reasonably.

Answer (B) is incorrect. Recovery for a design defect requires that the plaintiff prove the existence of a reasonable alternative design and that the harm was reasonably preventable. Answer (C) is incorrect. Recovery for a defect in warnings or instructions requires that the plaintiff prove that the "foreseeable risks of harm could have been reduced or avoided by reasonable instructions or warnings by the seller or other distributor, or a predecessor in the commercial chain of distribution, and the omission renders the product not reasonably safe" [Restatement (Third) of Torts]. A court considers the nature of expected users and the content, comprehensibility, and "intensity of expression" of the warnings and instructions. Answer (D) is incorrect. Recovery for a defect in warnings or instructions requires that the plaintiff prove that the "foreseeable risks of harm could have been reduced or avoided by reasonable instructions or warnings by the seller or other distributor, or a predecessor in the commercial chain of distribution, and the omission renders the product not reasonably safe" [Restatement (Third) of Torts]. A court considers the nature of expected users and the content, comprehensibility, and "intensity of expression" of the warnings and instructions.

54. Julia rented a new automobile from Mack's Auto Leasing Service. While operating the vehicle in a lawful manner and wearing her shoulder harness, Julia was injured when a defective steering mechanism caused her to lose control. To recover under a strict liability in tort theory, Julia

A. Must show that the automobile was inherently dangerous.

B. May be able to recover even though no sale was made.

C. Need not establish causation.

D. May not sue the manufacturer.

Answer (B) is correct. *(Publisher, adapted)*

REQUIRED: The true statement about the elements of the plaintiff's case in a product liability action.

DISCUSSION: Ordinarily, a product liability case involves a suit by an injured plaintiff against some seller in the chain of distribution, most often the manufacturer. Many courts, however, have extended the doctrine to lessors and bailors of defective goods. They reason that the danger to the public from defectively maintained motor vehicles placed on the highways by lessors is substantially the same as the danger from defective manufacture by a seller or manufacturer.

Answer (A) is incorrect. Julia must show that the product was unreasonably (not inherently) dangerous. Answer (C) is incorrect. The plaintiff must establish a causal connection between her injuries and the defect. Answer (D) is incorrect. Julia may sue the manufacturer even though no privity of contract is present.

STUDY UNIT EIGHT
CONTRACTS: THE AGREEMENT

No part of American law is more pervasive than contract law. Literally billions of contract-based agreements to transfer property and services are negotiated by individuals, businesses, and governments. Promise-keeping is essential for planning in a modern society. Without a legal system committed to enforcement of private contractual agreements, everyday transactions in a free-enterprise economy would be impossible. Contemporary contract law allows parties to enter into private agreements with others with assurance that these agreements are enforceable against a party that fails to perform. The principles of contract law may be organized into the categories of formation, performance, and enforcement.

The two major sources of contract law are the **common law of contracts** and **Article 2 of the Uniform Commercial Code (UCC)**. American common law evolved from English common law. The common law consists of past judicial decisions that serve as binding precedents in subsequent cases having similar fact patterns. This principle is **stare decisis**. By its nature, common law is constantly evolving to meet the needs of society. It is primarily **state common law** that applies to contracts other than those for the sale of goods. The **Restatement (Second) of Contracts** compiled by the American Law Institute is a respected but nonauthoritative source of the common law.

According to the Restatement, a contract is "a promise or a set of promises for the breach of which the law gives a remedy, or the performance of which the law in some way recognizes a duty."

The need for greater uniformity of commercial law among the states has resulted in the publication of many proposed uniform acts by the National Conference of Commissioners on Uniform State Laws (NCCUSL). Its most successful product is the UCC (also sponsored by the American Law Institute), which has been adopted in full by every state except Louisiana. UCC Article 2 applies to contracts for the sale of goods. **Goods** are defined as tangible, movable personal property. Article 2 removes transactions in goods from the common law by establishing a uniform set of rules in every state to facilitate commercial transactions and provide a reasonable basis for resolving problems. However, Article 2 does not replace all common-law contract rules. When Article 2 does not provide a specific rule that addresses the particular problem, the relevant common law rule applies to a sale of goods. Thus, Article 2 replaces only those rules that do not facilitate commercial transactions.

Another effect of Article 2 is that, beginning with the adoption of the UCC, courts have applied code rules to decide noncode cases. Courts thereby modify the common law by incorporating the code rule into the common law of contracts. This process has narrowed, and will continue to narrow, the differences between the rules of Article 2 and the traditional common-law of contracts. For current purposes, the specific rules of Article 2 apply to transactions involving sales of goods, and common-law principles apply when the UCC is silent or when the contract does not involve goods.

A basic principle of contract law is **freedom of contract**. It emphasizes that the contracting parties, not courts, form the contract according to their own will. A court's role is to determine the existence of a contract and enforce it according to its terms, largely without regard to fairness. However, courts have increasingly responded to changed circumstances and have modified the approach to formation and enforcement of contracts in two important ways. First, courts have substantially relaxed the technical requirements of contract formation. Greater emphasis now is on the objective intent of the parties and the court's ability to determine an appropriate remedy. Second, courts have demanded that, to be enforceable, an agreement must not be manifestly unfair. These changes have made both contract formation and contract avoidance easier.

Contract law has a basic vocabulary. For example, contracts are classified in several important ways. A **valid contract** is one that meets all the legal requirements of a binding agreement. These four requirements are an agreement consisting of (1) an offer and acceptance (including mutuality of assent), (2) an exchange of legal consideration, (3) capacity of the parties to the agreement, and (4) legality of purpose. A **void contract** lacks an essential requirement and has no legal effect. A **voidable contract** is an agreement that one party may either enforce or void without being in breach of contract. It arises when a contract is formed but may not be enforceable because of a legal defense. An example is an oral contract that is of a type required to be in writing. Contracts also may be classified as (1) express or implied, (2) unilateral or bilateral, (3) executory (unperformed) or executed, (4) formal or informal, (5) implied in fact or implied in law (also called a quasi-contract), and (6) enforceable or unenforceable.

The subject of contract law is covered in this and the next four study units. The explanations for the answers in these study units are based almost entirely on common law.

A few questions concern sales of goods because that area is closely related to general contract law. Contracts for the sale of goods are covered in Study Units 13 and 14.

The most basic element of a contract is a voluntary agreement by the parties. **Agreement** requires the mutual assent of the contracting parties reached through an offer by the offeror and acceptance by the offeree. An **offer** is a statement or other communication that, if not terminated, confers upon the offeree the power of acceptance. An offer need not be in any particular form to be valid but it must (1) be communicated to an offeree, (2) manifest an intent to enter into a contract, and (3) be sufficiently definite and certain.

Offers are either unilateral or bilateral. A **unilateral offer** is a promise made in exchange for an act. No contract is formed until the offeree performs the bargained-for act. A **bilateral offer** is a promise that invites a return promise. Most offers and most contracts are bilateral. Thus, when uncertainty exists, courts usually presume the contract to be bilateral. Bilateral agreements involve an exchange of two promises, but a unilateral agreement is one in which only one party makes a promise.

Communication of an offer may be done in various ways and may occur over time. But, at some moment in the formation of a contract, each party expresses an intent to enter into a legally binding and enforceable agreement. Whether an offer has been made is determined by an **objective standard** that uses the following test: Would a reasonable person assume that the power of acceptance had been conferred upon him/her? An offer must be made with serious intent, not in anger, great excitement, or jest. An offer can exist whether or not the offeror intended that it exist as long as it manifests an intent to contract. Offers may be communicated by conduct rather than words. The conduct must be such that a **reasonable person** would infer that an offer arose. An offer may be made to an individual or to the public at large. However, no person can accept an offer unless or until (s)he has knowledge that the offer exists.

Language constituting an offer should be distinguished from that merely **soliciting or inviting offers**. Communications between parties may simply be preliminary negotiations concerning a possible contract. A party may initiate negotiations by suggesting the general nature of a possible contract. That party may then wait for the second party to make a specific offer. Such an invitation to negotiate does not constitute an offer. Phrases such as the following are not offers: (1) Would you be interested in ..., (2) I may be willing to ..., (3) I'll probably take ..., (4) I hear you are looking for ..., and (5) Are you interested in ... As usually worded, advertisements, circulars, price tags, and catalogs are not offers but merely invitations to submit offers. However, an **advertisement** may constitute an offer. Clear, definite, and explicit language leaving nothing open for further negotiation constitutes an offer that empowers the offeree to accept and form an agreement.

An offer also must be **definite and certain**. If an offer is indefinite or vague or lacking an essential provision, no agreement arises from an attempt to accept it because the courts cannot tell what the parties are binding themselves to do. However, minor details left for future determination do not make an agreement too vague to be an offer. A fundamental concept of contract law is that contracts should be made by the parties, not courts. Ordinarily, a contract must be reasonably definite as to all of its material terms and must set forth clearly all rights and duties of the parties. Nevertheless, the circumstances may imply an omitted term. For example, if an offer does not specify the time of performance, courts will usually determine that performance within a reasonable time is intended. Moreover, a requirements or output contract is valid. A **requirements contract** is one in which the seller agrees to supply all the buyer needs. An **output contract** is one in which the buyer agrees to purchase all the seller produces. Under common law and UCC 2-306, requirements and output contracts are enforceable if the buyer or seller, respectively, acts in good faith and does not vary substantially from the estimated or normal quantity. The definiteness criterion is met because the requirements or output term is defined by the reasonable needs of the buyer's or seller's business, not by the whim or will of any party.

An offer does not remain effective forever. The **offer will terminate** under any of the following circumstances: (1) revocation by the offeror, (2) rejection or counteroffer by the offeree, (3) death or incompetency of either the offeror or offeree, (4) destruction of the specific subject matter to which the offer relates, (5) subsequent illegality of the offer, or (6) lapse of a specified or reasonable time. Items (3) through (6) are sometimes referred to as terminations by **operation of law**. A counteroffer is a response by the offeree that makes the original offeror a new offer. A **counteroffer** has the same effect as a rejection and terminates the earlier offer. Because the offeror is considered the master of the offer, (s)he has the power to revoke an offer at any time prior to acceptance. To be effective, a revocation of an offer must be communicated to the offeree prior to acceptance. The revocation is effective when received by the offeree. However, an **option contract** limits the offeror's power to revoke the offer. If the offeree exchanges something of legal value for the offeror's promise to hold the offer open for a specified period, the offeror is precluded from revoking the offer during the stated option period. The option itself is a valid and binding contract. Under the **firm offer rule** of UCC 2-205, a party who is a merchant with respect to a sale of goods is bound to keep an offer to buy or sell the goods open for a period **not in excess of 3 months**, provided the merchant gives an assurance in a signed writing that the offer will be held open.

Acceptance of an offer is essential to the formation of a contract. An agreement consists of an offer and an acceptance. To be effective, an acceptance must relate to the terms of the offer. The acceptance must be positive, unequivocal, and unconditional. It may not change, subtract from, add to, or qualify in any way the terms of the offer. This principle is the **mirror image rule**. As the term indicates, the acceptance must mirror or reflect the offer and not change it. The common-law mirror image rule has been modified by UCC 2-207 (Study Unit 13). An acceptance can be made only by an offeree and may consist of verbal, written, or any other implicit or explicit communication of a return promise to the offeror. A unilateral offer is accepted by performance. If the offer requires acceptance to be communicated in a particular manner, such as in writing, the acceptance must be communicated in the manner specified to be effective. The offer may specify that acceptance is to be communicated face to face or by telephone, mail, email, fax, or some other medium. If the offer does not indicate any particular means of acceptance, communication of acceptance to the offeror may be by any reasonable means. A medium of acceptance is reasonable if it is (1) the one used by the offeror; (2) customary in similar transactions; and (3) appropriate under the circumstances, considering any prior dealings between the offeror and offeree or the usage of trade. Under the **deposited acceptance**, or **mailbox, rule**, the acceptance is effective and a contract arises at the moment of dispatch if the offeree has used an authorized medium of acceptance and the offer is still open. An offeror who wishes to avoid the risk of a delayed or lost acceptance may specify that the acceptance be received by the offeror at the offeror's place of business on or before a specified date. If the offer specifies a time for acceptance, the acceptance must be communicated within that time.

QUESTIONS

8.1 Nature and Classification of Contracts

1. Contract law has undergone considerable change in response to social, economic, and political shifts since the nineteenth century. Which of the following is a characteristic of modern contract law?

A. Contract formation has become more difficult.

B. Greater freedom of contract is permitted.

C. Once a contract is formed, the parties are less likely to be excused from performance.

D. The principles of caveat emptor and laissez-faire are less influential.

Answer (D) is correct. *(Publisher, adapted)*

REQUIRED: The status of contract law after a century of change.

DISCUSSION: In the nineteenth century, contract theory was dominated by the notions of caveat emptor ("let the buyer beware") and laissez-faire (the idea that economic activity should be unregulated or "left alone" by government). In today's complex society, contract law has changed in response to disparity of bargaining power between buyers and sellers, government influence in commercial matters, and social reality.

Answer (A) is incorrect. In 19th-century contract law, contract formation and excuse from performance were more difficult. Autonomy in contracting was the ideal. Today, freedom to drive a hard bargain has been curtailed, means of escaping liability are more numerous, and contracts are more readily found to exist. Answer (B) is incorrect. Modern contract law is more likely to protect parties from the consequences of their agreements when disparities of power between the parties are great. Answer (C) is incorrect. Means of escaping liability are more numerous today.

2. Which of the following is not a required element of a contract?

A. Legality.

B. Consideration.

C. Legal capacity.

D. A writing.

Answer (D) is correct. *(Publisher, adapted)*

REQUIRED: The item that is not a required element of a contract.

DISCUSSION: The four essential elements of a contract are an agreement (offer and acceptance), consideration, legal capacity of the parties to contract, and a legal objective or purpose. A writing is not required to enter into a contract. However, some contracts are not enforceable unless a writing evidences the contract.

Answer (A) is incorrect. Legality is a required element of a contract. Answer (B) is incorrect. Consideration is a required element of a contract. Answer (C) is incorrect. Legal capacity is a required element of a contract.

3. When a client accepts the services of an accountant without an agreement concerning payment, the result is

A. An implied-in-fact contract.

B. An implied-in-law contract.

C. An express contract.

D. No contract.

Answer (A) is correct. *(CPA, adapted)*

REQUIRED: The type of contract formed when a client accepts an accountant's services.

DISCUSSION: Enforceable contracts may be formed without an express agreement of terms if the facts of the situation indicate (imply) an objective intent of both parties to contract. Objective intent means the apparent intent of an ordinary, reasonable person and not the actual (subjective) intent. When a client accepts the services of an accountant, there is an implied agreement to pay for them. Because the facts indicate a contract was formed, it is an implied-in-fact contract.

Answer (B) is incorrect. A contract implied in law prevents unjust enrichment of one party when the facts do not indicate both parties intended to form a contract. Answer (C) is incorrect. An express contract is one in which the terms (such as payment) are specifically agreed upon. Answer (D) is incorrect. A contract implied in fact was formed.

4. Which of the following represents the basic distinction between a bilateral contract and a unilateral contract?

A. Specific performance is available if the contract is unilateral but not if it is bilateral.

B. Only one promise is involved if the contract is unilateral, but two are involved if it is bilateral.

C. The statute of frauds applies to a bilateral contract but not to a unilateral contract.

D. Rights under a bilateral contract are assignable, whereas rights under a unilateral contract are not assignable.

Answer (B) is correct. *(CPA, adapted)*

REQUIRED: The basic distinction between a unilateral and a bilateral contract.

DISCUSSION: In a bilateral contract, the promise of one party to perform is consideration for the promise of the other. In a unilateral contract, one party makes a promise in exchange for the other party's act, instead of in exchange for a promise from the other party (as in a bilateral contract). Thus, a unilateral contract involves only one promise, but a bilateral contract involves two promises.

Answer (A) is incorrect. The availability of specific performance is not affected by the distinction between unilateral and bilateral contracts. They may apply to either a unilateral or bilateral contract. Answer (C) is incorrect. The applicability of the statute of frauds is not affected by the distinction between unilateral and bilateral contracts. They may apply to either a unilateral or bilateral contract. Answer (D) is incorrect. The assignability of rights is not affected by the distinction between unilateral and bilateral contracts. They may apply to either a unilateral or bilateral contract.

5. On the first day of the month, Thomas and Moore orally agreed that Thomas was to deliver to Moore's place of business a case of fruit on each Monday of the current month. Moore was to pay the $100 price on the first of the following month. On the 15th of the month, the agreement should be classified as

A. Executed.

B. Executory.

C. Unexecuted because the agreement was oral.

D. Cancelable at any time.

Answer (B) is correct. *(Publisher, adapted)*

REQUIRED: The classification of a partially performed oral contract.

DISCUSSION: An executed contract is one in which the parties have completed their performance. A contract is executory to the extent it has not been fully performed. As of the 15th, Thomas had partially performed, but Moore had not performed at all. The contract was therefore executory.

Answer (A) is incorrect. Both parties had not completed performance. Answer (C) is incorrect. "Executory" and "executed" refer to the performance of the contract, not to its form. Although "executed" in ordinary usage may mean signed, an oral contract can never be executed in this sense. Answer (D) is incorrect. The entire contract is enforceable. No provisions allow for it to be canceled.

6. Certain contracts have absolutely no effect and are not recognized under law. If two or more parties enter into such an agreement, it is

A. Valid.

B. Void.

C. Voidable.

D. Unenforceable.

Answer (B) is correct. *(Publisher, adapted)*

REQUIRED: The term for contracts that are not effective or recognized under law.

DISCUSSION: Contracts that are of no effect and not recognized under law are void. Neither party has a legal obligation to the other based on the contract. The parties may go through with their performance, but the law provides no remedy for a breach.

Answer (A) is incorrect. Remedies are available if a valid contract is breached. Answer (C) is incorrect. A voidable contract is valid but enforceable by only one party. For example, a contract entered into by fraud may be enforced by the innocent party but not by the fraudulent party. Answer (D) is incorrect. An unenforceable contract has been validly formed but cannot be enforced because of a flaw.

7. Spring agreed to buy Summer's car. Because the actual purchase was not to occur for several months, they drafted a lengthy agreement that specified all of the rights and obligations of each of the parties. They hired an attorney to review this two-page, single-spaced document. After the attorney suggested a few changes, the document was retyped and signed. The contract is

A. A formal contract.

B. An executed contract.

C. A simple contract.

D. An implied contract.

Answer (C) is correct. *(Publisher, adapted)*

REQUIRED: The type of contract.

DISCUSSION: Formal contracts are those the law has historically treated specially based on their form. In early law, formal contracts included contracts for which a personal seal was required. They also include negotiable instruments and contracts of record (those entered into the records of a court). All other contracts are simple contracts, even if in writing and evidenced by a document.

Answer (A) is incorrect. Typing a lengthy document does not make a contract formal. Answer (B) is incorrect. An executed contract has been fully performed by both parties. Answer (D) is incorrect. This contract is an express contract. The terms of an implied contract are inferred from surrounding circumstances.

8.2 Offer

8. For an offer to confer the power to form a contract by acceptance, it must have all of the following elements except

A. Be communicated to the offeree in a communication made or authorized by the offeror.

B. Be sufficiently definite and certain.

C. Be communicated by words to the offeree by the offeror.

D. Manifest an intent to enter into a contract.

Answer (C) is correct. *(CPA, adapted)*

REQUIRED: The element not needed for an offer to confer the power to form a contract by acceptance.

DISCUSSION: Offers may be made orally, in writing, or through any means of nonverbal communication. The manner of communication of offers is not important provided they are communicated as intended by the offeror.

9. Carol used her dictating machine to record the text of an offer she intended to make to Deanna. Irvin, her secretary, transcribed the tape. During lunch and before the offer had been mailed, Irvin saw Deanna and told her about it. Deanna promptly mailed an acceptance to Carol. What was the effect of this attempted acceptance?

A. No contract was formed because the offer was not communicated to the offeree.

B. No contract was formed because the offer was not communicated to the offeree by the means chosen by the offeror.

C. A contract was formed because Irvin was Carol's agent.

D. A contract was formed because Carol intended to make an offer and Deanna learned of the offer in time to make a valid acceptance.

Answer (B) is correct. *(Publisher, adapted)*

REQUIRED: The effect of communication of an offer by a means not intended by the offeror.

DISCUSSION: An offer is not effective until it is communicated to the offeree. The communication, however, must be by a means chosen by the offeror. Carol evidently intended to communicate the offer by mail. When the offeree learned of the offer in an unauthorized manner, she could only make an offer, not a valid acceptance.

Answer (A) is incorrect. The offer was actually communicated but not as intended by the offeror. Answer (C) is incorrect. The facts do not indicate that Irvin was an agent for purposes of communicating offers. Answer (D) is incorrect. The offer must be communicated as intended by the offeror.

10. The following conversation took place between Mary and Ed. Mary: "Ed, if you wanted to sell your table, what would you ask for it?" Ed: "I suppose $400 would be a fair price." Mary: "I'll take it, if you will have it refinished." Ed: "Sold." Thus,

A. Ed's statement, "I suppose $400 would be a fair price," constituted an offer.

B. Mary's reply, "I'll take it, if you will have it refinished," was a conditional acceptance, terminating Ed's offer.

C. No contract resulted because Ed never stated he would actually sell the table for $400.

D. A contract was formed when Ed said, "Sold."

Answer (D) is correct. *(CPA, adapted)*

REQUIRED: The contractual implication of the statements.

DISCUSSION: An offer usually makes a promise and requests a return promise or act. Mary's first question was merely a request for information. It contained no promissory language and evidenced no intention to be bound, so it could not have been construed as an offer. Ed's first reply was at best a negotiatory statement and likewise contained no language construable as an offer. Mary's second statement effectively contained a promise to pay $400 for the table if Ed had it refinished. Mary thereby manifested an intention to be bound if Ed made a return promise or performed a certain act. Ed's response of "sold" was an acceptance and formed a contract.

Answer (A) is incorrect. Ed's first reply lacked the necessary elements of an offer. Answer (B) is incorrect. Mary's second statement was an offer. Answer (C) is incorrect. Ed impliedly acquiesced to a sale at the price he quoted and upon the condition stated in Mary's offer.

11. Mildred saw a vase in a store. A tag on the vase said, "Genuine Crystal, $125." Mildred said to the owner of the shop, "I'll buy this vase for $125." Milford, the owner of the shop, refused to sell the vase. In a lawsuit brought by Mildred against Milford,

A. Mildred will win because a contract was formed when she said she would buy the vase.

B. Mildred will win because the vase was a unique chattel.

C. Milford will win because he rejected Mildred's offer.

D. Milford will win because the contract was not written.

Answer (C) is correct. *(E. Rahm)*

REQUIRED: The effect of a customer's attempt to purchase at an advertised price.

DISCUSSION: Advertisements or price quotations made to the public are not offers. Advertisements (in any format) are usually only invitations to negotiate. They are not considered offers because they contain no words of promise, they are addressed to the public (the quantity accepted could exceed the supply), and they are usually indefinite.

Answer (A) is incorrect. The tag was not the offer. The offer was made when Mildred said she would purchase the vase for $125. Answer (B) is incorrect. The uniqueness of the item is irrelevant to contract formation. Answer (D) is incorrect. No contract was formed.

12. Bea Barnes held an annual auction at her farm to sell tools, animals, and leftover crops. Ana Adam bid $50 for a plow, and no one bid against her. The auctioneer did not accept Adam's bid and stated that the plow would not be sold for such a low price. What is the legal effect of the bid and its rejection?

A. Adam's bid constituted an acceptance, which formed a valid contract.

B. Adam's bid was only an offer.

C. The plow could not be withdrawn from the auction.

D. Two bids must be made before an auction is deemed to be without reserve.

Answer (B) is correct. *(Publisher, adapted)*

REQUIRED: The legal effect of the auctioneer's rejection of a bid.

DISCUSSION: Putting property up for auction is an invitation to negotiate. The purchasers make offers by bidding. The auctioneer accepts an offer by the falling of the hammer or an announcement that the property is sold. Adam's bid was only an offer, so no contract was formed.

Answer (A) is incorrect. The bid is only an offer, which need not be accepted by the auctioneer. Answer (C) is incorrect. Property subject to an auction can be withdrawn at any time prior to acceptance of a bid, unless the auction is "without reserve." If an auction is "without reserve," property may not be withdrawn, and the highest bid must be accepted after the auction has begun. Answer (D) is incorrect. The number of bids is irrelevant.

13. Carson Corp., a retail chain, asked Alto Construction to fix a broken window at one of Carson's stores. Alto offered to make the repairs within 3 days at a price to be agreed on after the work was completed. A contract based on Alto's offer will fail because of indefiniteness as to the

A. Price involved.

B. Nature of the subject matter.

C. Parties to the contract.

D. Time for performance.

Answer (A) is correct. *(CPA, adapted)*

REQUIRED: The contractual element the absence of which renders the offer indefinite.

DISCUSSION: An agreement is not enforceable as a contract unless essential terms are agreed upon with reasonable certainty. A contract must be definite and complete. Essential terms usually include the names of the parties, subject matter and quantity, price, and time and place for performance. No basis for an objective computation of the price was agreed to by the parties. An agreement to agree does not establish an enforceable obligation at common law.

Answer (B) is incorrect. The offer describes the nature of the subject matter with reasonable certainty. Answer (C) is incorrect. The offer describes the parties to the contract with reasonable certainty. Answer (D) is incorrect. The offer describes the time for performance with reasonable certainty.

14. Gudrun owned a 2,000-acre country estate. She signed a written agreement with Johann, selling the house on the property and "a sufficient amount of land surrounding the house to create a park." The price was stated to be $200,000. When Gudrun refused to honor the agreement, Johann sued. Who will prevail and why?

A. Gudrun will win because the agreement is not reasonably definite.

B. Johann will win because the quantity of land is implied.

C. Johann will win because the parties intended to make a contract.

D. Gudrun will win because no financing term was included in the agreement.

Answer (A) is correct. *(Publisher, adapted)*

REQUIRED: The result when a contract for the sale of land does not state the quantity.

DISCUSSION: For an agreement between the parties to be enforceable, it must be reasonably definite and certain (not ambiguous). A court must be able to determine with reasonable accuracy what the parties agreed upon. In this case, the writing is not reasonably clear as to what amount of land Gudrun agreed to sell.

Answer (B) is incorrect. Some objective basis must exist for measuring the implied term. The court has no means of determining how much land is needed for a park. Answer (C) is incorrect. A court must be able to determine with reasonable accuracy what the parties agreed upon. Answer (D) is incorrect. The quantity term is more significant than the financing term. The price is given and payment in cash (or its equivalent) is implied.

15. Which of the following agreements is unenforceable because of indefiniteness?

A. The seller agrees to supply all of the buyer's requirements for tents for the next year.

B. The buyer agrees to purchase all of the seller's output of cotton in the next season.

C. The buyer agrees to purchase all of the seller's output of ice cream and to deal exclusively in the seller's goods.

D. The seller agrees to supply a quantity of pears dependent upon the buyer's will.

Answer (D) is correct. *(Publisher, adapted)*

REQUIRED: The contract unenforceable for indefiniteness.

DISCUSSION: Historically, requirements and output contracts were unenforceable because they were too indefinite; i.e., the quantity was not determined. A requirements contract is one in which the seller agrees to supply all the buyer needs. An output contract is one in which the buyer agrees to purchase all the seller produces. Under current common law and UCC 2-306, requirements and output contracts are valid and enforceable. Both parties are required to act in good faith and not vary substantially from the estimated or normal quantity. The definiteness criterion is met because the output or requirements term is defined by the reasonable needs of the seller's or buyer's business, not by the whim or will of any party.

Answer (A) is incorrect. Under the modern approach, requirements and output contracts do not fail for indefiniteness. Agreements for exclusive dealing that are lawful under federal antitrust statutes are also recognized by UCC 2-306. Answer (B) is incorrect. Under the modern approach, requirements and output contracts do not fail for indefiniteness. Agreements for exclusive dealing that are lawful under federal antitrust statutes are also recognized by UCC 2-306. Answer (C) is incorrect. Under the modern approach, requirements and output contracts do not fail for indefiniteness. Agreements for exclusive dealing that are lawful under federal antitrust statutes are also recognized by UCC 2-306.

16. Quick Corp. mailed a letter to Blue Co. on May 1, offering a 3-year franchise dealership. The offer stated the terms in detail and, at the bottom, stated that the offer would not be withdrawn prior to June 5. Which of the following is true?

A. The offer cannot be assigned to another party by Blue.

B. A letter of acceptance sent on June 5 and received by Quick on June 6 does not form a valid contract.

C. The offer is an irrevocable option that cannot be withdrawn prior to June 5.

D. The statute of frauds does not apply to the proposed contract.

Answer (A) is correct. *(CPA, adapted)*

REQUIRED: The true statement about an offer of a franchise dealership.

DISCUSSION: Offers are never assignable except by express approval of the offeror. An attempted acceptance by an assignee would operate as an offer. In contrast, a contract is assignable unless prohibited by express agreement or implication because of its personal nature.

Answer (B) is incorrect. The acceptance was effective when mailed on June 5. An acceptance forms a contract when dispatched by any reasonable means. Answer (C) is incorrect. An option is not formed by an offer alone. An option is itself a contract requiring consideration, offer and acceptance, etc. Answer (D) is incorrect. The statute of frauds applies because the contract cannot be performed within 1 year of its making.

17. Which of the following statements concerning the effectiveness of an offeree's rejection and an offeror's revocation of an offer are ordinarily true?

	An Offeree's Rejection Is Effective When	An Offeror's Revocation Is Effective When
A.	Received by offeror	Sent by offeror
B.	Sent by offeree	Received by offeree
C.	Sent by offeree	Sent by offeror
D.	Received by offeror	Received by offeree

Answer (D) is correct. *(CPA, adapted)*

REQUIRED: The true statements about effectiveness of an offeree's rejection and an offeror's revocation.

DISCUSSION: The general rule is that a revocation of an offer is effective when received by the offeree. Receipt occurs when the revocation comes into the possession of the offeree or his/her agent or when it is delivered to his/her office. Similarly, a rejection must actually be received to be effective. Only an acceptance can be effective upon dispatch.

18. The president of Deal Corp. wrote to Boyd, offering to sell the Deal factory for $300,000. The offer was sent by Deal on June 5 and was received by Boyd on June 9. The offer stated that it would remain open until December 20. The offer

A. Constitutes an enforceable option.

B. May be revoked by Deal anytime prior to Boyd's acceptance.

C. Is a firm offer under the UCC but will be irrevocable for only 3 months.

D. Is a firm offer under the UCC because it is in writing.

Answer (B) is correct. *(CPA, adapted)*

REQUIRED: The proper interpretation of an offer stating it will be held open for a specified time.

DISCUSSION: Revocation of an offer may be by any method sufficient to give reasonable notice to the offeree. The statement that the offer would be held open was not binding because it was not supported by consideration. Under the UCC, however, a firm offer by a merchant for the sale of goods can be irrevocable.

Answer (A) is incorrect. Boyd gave no consideration to support the promise to keep the offer open. Answer (C) is incorrect. The UCC's firm offer rule does not apply to a sale of realty. Answer (D) is incorrect. The UCC's firm offer rule does not apply to a sale of realty.

19. Baker Corporation sent a letter to Sampson Company in which Baker offered to purchase 10 acres of certain real estate from Sampson for $4,000. Sampson responded that it would sell eight of these acres for that price. Baker and Sampson have created

A. A contract for sale of eight acres for $4,000.

B. A contract for sale of 10 acres for $4,000.

C. A contract to sell eight acres for $3,200.

D. No contract via these communications.

Answer (D) is correct. *(CPA, adapted)*

REQUIRED: The effect of the differing statements about the quantity term.

DISCUSSION: The response to the offer contained a different term, thus constituting a counteroffer rather than an acceptance. There is no contract unless Baker accepts Sampson's counteroffer. Under common law, any variation of an offer by the offeree would preclude an acceptance, especially if the variation is material. Differences in quantity and price are material.

20. Ann Mayer wrote Tom Jackson and offered to sell Jackson a building for $200,000. The offer stated it would expire 30 days from July 1. Mayer changed her mind and does not wish to be bound by the offer. If a legal dispute arises between the parties regarding whether there has been a valid acceptance of the offer, which of the following is true?

A. The offer cannot be legally withdrawn for the stated period of time.

B. The offer will not expire prior to the 30 days even if Mayer sells the property to a third person and notifies Jackson.

C. If Jackson phoned Mayer on August 1 and unequivocally accepted the offer, a contract would be formed, provided Jackson had no notice of withdrawal of the offer.

D. If Jackson categorically rejects the offer on July 10, Jackson cannot validly accept within the remaining stated period of time.

Answer (D) is correct. *(CPA, adapted)*

REQUIRED: The true statement as to termination of an offer.

DISCUSSION: Rejection of an offer terminates it. An offeree cannot accept an offer after rejection is effective. An attempted acceptance after rejection is a new offer.

Answer (A) is incorrect. The offer may be legally withdrawn at any time prior to acceptance even though it states it will be held open for a specified period. It is not a firm offer under the UCC because it is not for a sale of goods. Answer (B) is incorrect. Notice to the offeree of sale of the property to a third person has the effect of terminating the offer. Answer (C) is incorrect. Acceptance on August 1 would be ineffective. The time provided for acceptance expires on July 31.

21. On January 1, Lemon wrote Gina Martin offering to sell Martin a ranch for $80,000 cash. Lemon's letter indicated that the offer would remain open until February 15 if Martin mailed $100 by January 10. On January 5, Martin mailed $100 to Lemon. On January 30, Martin telephoned Lemon stating that she would be willing to pay $60,000 for the ranch. Lemon refused to sell at that price and immediately placed the ranch on the open market. On February 6, Martin mailed Lemon a letter accepting the original offer to buy the ranch at $80,000. The following day, Lemon received Martin's acceptance. At that time, the ranch was on the market for $100,000. Which of the following is true?

A. Martin's mailing of $100 to Lemon on January 5 failed to grant an option.

B. Martin's call on January 30 automatically terminated the January 1 offer.

C. Placing the ranch on the market constituted an effective revocation of the offer of January 1.

D. Martin's letter of February 6 formed a binding contract based on the original terms of Lemon's January 1 letter.

Answer (D) is correct. *(CPA, adapted)*

REQUIRED: The effect of a counteroffer when an option contract exists.

DISCUSSION: Martin's telephone call was a counteroffer because it varied the price term of the offer. Although a counteroffer normally is a rejection of the offer, the option contract was not affected. Martin could still accept under the terms of the option. Furthermore, even an outright rejection will not terminate the option unless the principle of estoppel applies.

Answer (A) is incorrect. Mailing the $100 by January 10 furnished the consideration necessary to enforce the promise to hold the option open. Answer (B) is incorrect. The telephone call did not affect Lemon's contractual obligation to hold the offer open. Answer (C) is incorrect. Lemon had no power to rescind the contract unilaterally.

22. An offer is not terminated by operation of law solely because the

A. Offeror dies.

B. Offeree is adjudicated insane.

C. Subject matter is destroyed.

D. Subject matter is sold to a third party.

Answer (D) is correct. *(CPA, adapted)*

REQUIRED: The event that does not terminate an offer by operation of law.

DISCUSSION: By certain events, an offer is automatically terminated: incapacity (death or adjudicated insanity) of either party, destruction of the subject matter, and supervening illegality. Sale of the subject matter does not automatically terminate the offer. But if the offeree receives actual notice of the sale, the sale is effective as a revocation.

Answer (A) is incorrect. By law, an offer is terminated when the offeror dies. Answer (B) is incorrect. By law, an offer is terminated when the offeree is adjudicated insane. Answer (C) is incorrect. By law, an offer is terminated when the subject matter is destroyed.

8.3 Acceptance

23. An agreement is an essential element of a contract. Ordinarily, the required mutual assent is achieved by means of an offer and an acceptance. Acceptance

A. Requires a subjective intent to accept.

B. Is never accomplished by silence.

C. Requires manifestation of an intent to accept.

D. May ordinarily be made by anyone with knowledge of the offer.

Answer (C) is correct. *(Publisher, adapted)*

REQUIRED: The true statement about acceptance.

DISCUSSION: Mutual assent requires that a valid offer be accepted by the intended offeree in a manner stipulated by the offeror. The overt manifestation of the offeree's assent should signify an intent to accept. For example, performance of an act requested by an offer does not result in a contract if the offeree had not yet learned of the offer.

Answer (A) is incorrect. Acceptance requires an objective, not subjective, intent to accept. Answer (B) is incorrect. Silence may be an effective method of acceptance in cases in which both parties intend it as such. Answer (D) is incorrect. Only the intended offeree may accept. There is no mutual assent unless both parties agree to contract.

24. An offer may be accepted

A. By an assignee of the designated offeree.

B. Only by a specific individual named in the offer.

C. By anyone who learns of its existence prior to acceptance by the designated offeree.

D. Only by the designated offeree.

Answer (D) is correct. *(Publisher, adapted)*

REQUIRED: The person who may accept an offer.

DISCUSSION: The offeror has the right to specify who may accept the offer. When an offer designates a specific offeree, only that person may accept. When an offer designates a specific group of offerees, only members of that group may accept. Some offers, however, may be extended to the general public.

Answer (A) is incorrect. An offer can be accepted only by a person who is designated as an offeree by the offeror. It may not be assigned. Answer (B) is incorrect. Offers may be made to the members of a group, to the general public, or to persons that are not individuals, such as corporations. Answer (C) is incorrect. An offer can be accepted only by a person who is designated as an offeree by the offeror. It may not be assigned.

25. In which of the following instances may silence by the offeree constitute acceptance?

A. The offeror stated that silence would constitute an acceptance, and the offeree intended to reject the offer but forgot.

B. During the course of prior business dealing, the offeree has always sent a rejection if the items were not wanted. The offeror always shipped the items if such a rejection was not received.

C. An offeree receives unordered goods in the mail along with a letter from the sender stating that the offeree must return them if they are not wanted.

D. The offeree tells the offeror that (s)he will accept or reject on the next morning. (S)he intends to reject but fails to respond to the offeror.

Answer (B) is correct. *(Publisher, adapted)*

REQUIRED: The instance in which silence may constitute an acceptance.

DISCUSSION: Silence rarely constitutes an acceptance of an offer. Some surrounding facts or circumstances must indicate that the offeree intended silence as an acceptance. A prior course of business dealing might furnish the required inference that silence was intended as acceptance.

Answer (A) is incorrect. The offeror cannot require the offeree to respond to avoid a contract. Answer (C) is incorrect. Federal law provides that unordered goods received in the mail may be retained by the recipient without any obligation to pay. Answer (D) is incorrect. Silence will constitute an acceptance only if it was so intended by the offeree. If the offeree retains goods and uses them for his/her benefit, however, silence plus the use of goods can constitute an acceptance.

26. Under common law, an acceptance of an offer for a bilateral contract is effective

A. Even though it adds to, or subtracts from, the terms of the offer.

B. Only if it is the mirror image of the offer.

C. Only if it is expressed in words.

D. Even though it alters or qualifies a term of the offer.

Answer (B) is correct. *(Publisher, adapted)*

REQUIRED: The true statement about effectiveness of an acceptance of a bilateral offer.

DISCUSSION: The common-law rules regarding acceptance apply to all transactions except those governed by the UCC provisions related to sales of goods. Under common law, the acceptance of a bilateral offer may not add to, subtract from, alter, or qualify any term in the acceptance. The terms of the acceptance must reflect the exact terms of the offer.

Answer (A) is incorrect. A purported acceptance that departs from the offer is conditional or a "counteroffer" and does not form a contract. Answer (C) is incorrect. An acceptance can be implied from nonverbal conduct. Answer (D) is incorrect. A purported acceptance that departs from the offer is conditional or a "counteroffer" and does not form a contract.

27. Nix sent Castor a letter offering to employ Castor as controller of Nix's automobile dealership. Castor received the letter on February 19. The letter provided that Castor would have until February 23 to consider the offer and, in the meantime, Nix would not withdraw it. On February 20, Nix, after reconsidering the offer to Castor, decided to offer the job to Vick, who accepted immediately. That same day, Nix called Castor and revoked the offer. Castor told Nix that an acceptance of Nix's offer was mailed on February 19. Under the circumstances,

A. Nix's offer was irrevocable until February 23.

B. No contract was formed between Nix and Castor because Nix revoked the offer before Nix received Castor's acceptance.

C. Castor's acceptance was effective when mailed.

D. Any revocation of the offer would have to be in writing because Nix's offer was in writing.

Answer (C) is correct. *(CPA, adapted)*

REQUIRED: The effect of revocation communicated after acceptance was dispatched.

DISCUSSION: An acceptance is effective when dispatched by the same mode used to transmit the offer, unless the offer stipulated otherwise. Revocation of an offer received after effective acceptance does not cancel the contract formed on acceptance.

Answer (A) is incorrect. No consideration supported the offer to hold it open. Answer (B) is incorrect. The attempted revocation was received by the offeree only after acceptance was effective (on dispatch). Answer (D) is incorrect. Revocation may be communicated by any means and is effective, if at all, when received by the offeree.

28. Jackson paid Brady $100 for a 90-day option to purchase Brady's 160-acre farm for $32,000. The option agreement was in writing and signed by both parties. The agreement referred only to the option, its period, a legal description of the farm, and the purchase price. Jackson wrote Brady 30 days later: "I hereby exercise my option to purchase your farm for $32,000 subject to closing details to be worked out by you and my attorney." Jackson's letter

A. Rejects Brady's offer and terminates the option agreement.

B. Accepts Brady's offer, leaving customary details to be worked out during formalization of the contract.

C. Accepts Brady's offer, leaving a matter to be negotiated during formalization of the contract.

D. Does not affect the option agreement.

Answer (B) is correct. *(CPA, adapted)*

REQUIRED: The effect of an acceptance of an offer to sell real property subject to working out details of closing.

DISCUSSION: Jackson's letter exercising the option effectively accepts the offer. The letter does not state additional or different terms from those contemplated by the offer, so it is not a counteroffer. The details of closing can be left to be worked out later without affecting the validity of the contract.

Answer (A) is incorrect. The letter operates as an effective acceptance. Even if it operated as a rejection, the letter would not terminate the option because consideration had been given to hold it open for 90 days. Answer (C) is incorrect. Acceptance was made and no additional matters are to be negotiated; only a few closing details are to be worked out. Answer (D) is incorrect. The acceptance represents an exercise of the option.

29. On February 12, Harris sent Fresno a written offer to purchase Fresno's land. The offer included the following provision: "Acceptance of this offer must be by registered or certified mail, received by Harris no later than February 18 by 5:00 p.m. CST." On February 18, Fresno sent Harris a letter accepting the offer by private overnight delivery service. Harris received the letter on February 19. Which of the following statements is true?

A. A contract was formed on February 19.

B. Fresno's letter constituted a counteroffer.

C. Fresno's use of the overnight delivery service was an effective form of acceptance.

D. A contract was formed on February 18 regardless of when Harris actually received Fresno's letter.

Answer (B) is correct. *(CPA, adapted)*

REQUIRED: The result of acceptance by a means other than that required in the offer.

DISCUSSION: The offeror is the master of the offer. To the extent (s)he expressly limits what constitutes effective acceptance, it is limited under both common law and the UCC. Thus, Fresno's failure to respond in a timely manner by the stipulated method nullified the attempted acceptance. The letter therefore constituted a counteroffer.

30. On November 1, Yost sent a telegram to Zen offering to sell a rare vase. The offer required that Zen's acceptance telegram be sent on or before 5:00 p.m. on November 2. On November 2 at 3:00 p.m., Zen sent an acceptance by overnight mail. It did not reach Yost until November 5. Yost refused to complete the sale to Zen. Is there an enforceable contract?

A. Yes, because the acceptance was made within the time specified.

B. Yes, because the acceptance was effective when sent.

C. No, because Zen did not accept by telegram.

D. No, because the offer required receipt of the acceptance within the time specified.

Answer (C) is correct. *(CPA, adapted)*

REQUIRED: The result when acceptance of an offer for the sale of goods is sent by an unauthorized means.

DISCUSSION: The UCC governs because the contract would be for the sale of goods. The deposited acceptance rule is that acceptance is effective when dispatched by any means reasonable in the circumstances. But if the offer requires that acceptance be by a stated mode, purported acceptance by a different mode is not effective on dispatch.

Answer (A) is incorrect. Acceptance was transmitted by a mode other than that explicitly required as part of the offer. Answer (B) is incorrect. Acceptance was transmitted by a mode other than that explicitly required as part of the offer. Answer (D) is incorrect. It is an inaccurate statement of fact.

31. Able Sofa, Inc., sent Noll a letter offering to sell Noll a custom-made sofa for $5,000. Noll immediately sent a telegram to Able purporting to accept the offer. However, the telegraph company erroneously delivered the telegram to Abel Soda, Inc. Three days later, Able mailed a letter of revocation to Noll that was received by Noll. Able refused to sell Noll the sofa. Noll sued Able for breach of contract. Able

A. Would have been liable under the deposited acceptance rule only if Noll had accepted by mail.

B. Will avoid liability because it revoked its offer prior to receiving Noll's acceptance.

C. Will be liable for breach of contract.

D. Will avoid liability because of the telegraph company's error.

Answer (C) is correct. *(CPA, adapted)*

REQUIRED: The effect of an acceptance lost by the transmitting agency.

DISCUSSION: Assuming the offer did not specify a means of acceptance, the contract was formed when Noll sent the acceptance by telegraph. If the contract is for the sale of goods (a sofa), acceptance may be by any means reasonable under the circumstances and will be effective upon dispatch (UCC 2-206). This rule is gaining acceptance under common law also. A properly dispatched acceptance is effective upon dispatch, and the risk of its loss or delay is on the offeror. Hence, the negligence of the telegraph company does not excuse the offeror's failure to perform.

Answer (A) is incorrect. The UCC's deposited acceptance rule permitted Noll to accept by any reasonable means. Answer (B) is incorrect. The attempted revocation came after the acceptance was effective. Answer (D) is incorrect. The offeror bears the risk that the transmitting agency may lose or delay the acceptance.

Questions 32 and 33 are based on the following information. On April 2, Jet Co. wrote to Ard, offering to buy Ard's building for $350,000. The offer contained all of the essential terms to form a binding contract and was duly signed by Jet's president. It further provided that the offer would remain open until May 30 and an acceptance would not be effective until received by Jet. On April 10, Ard accepted Jet's offer by mail. The acceptance was received by Jet on April 14.

32. For this item only, assume that on April 11, Jet sent a telegram to Ard revoking its offer and that Ard received the telegram on April 12. Under the circumstances,

A. A contract was formed on April 10.

B. A contract was formed on April 14.

C. Jet's revocation effectively terminated its offer on April 12.

D. Jet's revocation effectively terminated its offer on April 11.

Answer (C) is correct. *(CPA, adapted)*

REQUIRED: The outcome when an acceptance and a revocation are attempted.

DISCUSSION: The offer expressly stated that an acceptance would be effective only upon receipt. The acceptance was received on April 14. However, Jet's revocation was effective when received by the offeree on April 12. Thus, the offer had been terminated before the acceptance could have formed a contract.

Answer (A) is incorrect. The offer stated that receipt was necessary to acceptance. Answer (B) is incorrect. The offer was terminated on April 12. Answer (D) is incorrect. Revocation is effective when received.

33. For this item only, assume that on April 13, Ard sent a telegram to Jet withdrawing the acceptance and rejecting Jet's offer and that Jet received the telegram on April 15. Under the circumstances,

A. A contract was formed on April 14.

B. A contract was formed on April 10.

C. Ard's rejection effectively terminated Jet's offer on April 13.

D. Ard's rejection effectively terminated Jet's offer on April 15.

Answer (A) is correct. *(CPA, adapted)*

REQUIRED: The legal effect of sending a rejection and an acceptance.

DISCUSSION: The offer stipulated that acceptance would be effective only upon receipt, an event that occurred on April 14. A rejection is effective only upon receipt. But because the acceptance formed a contract on April 14, the receipt of the rejection on April 15 had no effect.

Answer (B) is incorrect. The offer specified that acceptance would be effective on receipt, not dispatch. Answer (C) is incorrect. A rejection is effective, if at all, on the date of receipt. Answer (D) is incorrect. The rejection had no effect in that a contract had already been formed.

34. Tom Payne had a toothache, so he visited Dennis Dentist, DDS, during his lunch hour. Although the visit was Payne's first, Dentist accepted him as a patient without discussion of the cost of dental services. Dentist extracted a tooth and sent Payne a bill for $600. Payne was outraged and asserted that a contract was never formed. Payne was

A. Not liable because he never made an offer for Dentist to accept.

B. Not liable because he never accepted any offer.

C. Liable for the $600 because he accepted Dentist's services.

D. Liable only for a reasonable amount.

Answer (D) is correct. *(Publisher, adapted)*

REQUIRED: The liability of the recipient of services absent an express agreement about the cost.

DISCUSSION: A person who accepts the services of another known to be in the business of providing services for a fee is liable for the reasonable value of the services. This contract is implied; the intent of the parties is inferred from the circumstances. The reasonable value is measured by what others in the locality charge, i.e., the market price.

Answer (A) is incorrect. Although who is implied to have made the offer and the acceptance is unclear, either Payne or Dentist made an offer and the other accepted. Answer (B) is incorrect. Although who is implied to have made the offer and the acceptance is unclear, either Payne or Dentist made an offer and the other accepted. Answer (C) is incorrect. Payne is liable for $600 only if it is a reasonable amount based on charges by other dentists in the area.

35. The mailbox rule ordinarily makes acceptance of an offer effective at the time the acceptance is dispatched. The mailbox rule does not apply if

A. Both the offeror and offeree are merchants.

B. The offer proposes a sale of real estate.

C. The offer provides that an acceptance shall not be effective until actually received.

D. The duration of the offer is not in excess of 3 months.

Answer (C) is correct. *(CPA, adapted)*

REQUIRED: The circumstance in which the mailbox rule is inapplicable.

DISCUSSION: Acceptance is effective upon dispatch by the same mode used to transmit the offer. The UCC provides that acceptance may be by any means reasonable under the circumstances and is effective upon dispatch. But an offeror may stipulate the moment when acceptance will be effective.

Answer (A) is incorrect. Neither the common law nor the UCC exempts merchants from the mailbox rule. Answer (B) is incorrect. The rule applies whether the subject matter is personalty or realty. Answer (D) is incorrect. Whether an acceptance is effective on dispatch or receipt is a function of what method is authorized, not the duration of the offer.

STUDY UNIT NINE
CONTRACTS: CONSIDERATION

Consideration is the primary basis for the enforcement of agreements in contract law. It is a thing of value each party to a contract agrees to give in exchange for the benefit received. Ordinarily, if a promise is not supported by consideration, it is not enforceable. One requirement of consideration is **mutuality of obligation**. Both parties must give consideration. Consequently, something of legal value must be given in a bargained-for exchange when the parties intend an exchange. The two required elements of consideration are legal sufficiency (something of legal value) and bargained-for exchange. Consideration is legally sufficient to render a promise enforceable if the promisor receives a legal benefit or the promisee incurs a legal detriment. To incur a legal detriment, the promisee must do (or promise to do) something that (s)he is not legally obligated to do or refrain from doing (or promise to refrain from doing) something (s)he is legally entitled to do. A cause-and-effect relationship must exist between the promise made by one party and the detriment incurred by the other. The promise must induce the detriment. When a promisee suffers a legal detriment, the promisor gains a directly related legal benefit.

An important distinction is drawn between legal and actual benefits and detriments. Most people expect an actual benefit when entering into a contract. However, consideration exists when the promisee incurs a **legal detriment** or the promisor receives a **legal benefit**. By defining consideration in terms of legal rather than actual benefits and detriments, the courts have left the issue of economic value or actual benefit to the contracting parties. Thus, the terms "sufficient consideration" and "consideration" tend to be treated as synonymous by the courts.

The **Restatement (Second) of Contracts** defines consideration as something bargained for, and given in exchange for, the promise. It will consist of one of the following:

- An act other than a promise
- A forbearance to act
- Formation, modification, or destruction of a legal relation
- A return promise

The following are additional important matters to understand in connection with consideration:

- Promises that impose no actual obligation on the promisor are **illusory** and do not constitute consideration.
- Under the bargain theory, **past consideration** (an act prior to contract formation) and **moral consideration** (a pre-existing moral obligation) are not valid forms of consideration. But the Restatement treats a moral obligation as consideration if necessary to prevent injustice.
- A person who performs or promises to perform an act that (s)he is already under a **pre-existing duty** to perform has not given consideration for another party's promise.
- A new promise to pay a debt discharged in **bankruptcy** is enforceable if the federal statutory requirements are met.
- A new promise to perform a **voidable obligation** is enforceable. An example is the promise of a person who has reached legal adulthood to pay a debt incurred when (s)he was a minor.
- A new promise to pay a debt barred by the **statute of limitations** is enforceable if written. But the writing is not needed if partial payment has been made.

Many courts recognize an exception to the pre-existing duty rule. For example, the Restatement provides that the parties may **modify an executory contract** without the requirement of consideration if the modification is fair and equitable in light of surrounding facts that were not anticipated by either party when the contract was entered into.

The pre-existing duty rule also applies in the context of **debtor-creditor relationships**. Parties frequently attempt to settle **disputed and undisputed debts**. The part payment of an undisputed debt is not consideration for a promise by the creditor to accept the part payment as payment in full. However, the part payment rule does not apply when an honest dispute occurs about the existence of a debt or its amount.

Most contracts are supported by bargained-for consideration. However, on rare occasions, an agreement will lack consideration and yet still be enforceable on the basis of a legal rationale, such as promissory estoppel, quasi-contract, or public policy.

Promissory estoppel is an alternative to consideration but is used only to avoid injustice. Promissory estoppel involves a gratuitous promise by a promisor who does not expect the promisee to accept an offer by performing an act or making a return promise. The bargain element is lacking because no bargain is intended. Section 90 of the Restatement sets forth the three requirements of the doctrine of promissory estoppel:

1. A promise that the promisor should reasonably expect to induce action or forbearance by the promisee
2. Action or forbearance by the promisee that is induced by the promise
3. Enforcement of the promise as the only means of avoiding injustice

A **quasi-contract** is a contract implied in law to impose an obligation on a person to prevent unjust enrichment. The parties to a quasi-contract make no promises and reach no agreement. However, one of the parties is substantially benefited at the expense of the other.

Still another substitute for consideration is **public policy**. Courts sometimes cite public policy to support enforcement of a promise despite lack of bargained-for consideration, promissory estoppel, or quasi-contract. For example, when a debtor promises to pay a debt even when the collection is barred by the **statute of limitations**, the courts hold the promise to be enforceable without consideration.

Under Article 2 of the UCC, a **firm offer**, that is, a written offer signed by a **merchant** to buy or sell goods, is not revocable for lack of consideration during the time within which it is stated to be open, not to exceed 3 months. In several instances, Article 2 eliminates the requirement of consideration under common law, for example, a good-faith modification of a contract for the sale of goods.

QUESTIONS

9.1 Consideration

1. In determining whether the consideration requirement to form a contract has been satisfied, the consideration exchanged by the parties to the contract must be

A. Of approximately equal value.

B. Legally sufficient.

C. Exchanged simultaneously by the parties.

D. Fair and reasonable under the circumstances.

Answer (B) is correct. *(CPA, adapted)*

REQUIRED: The nature of the consideration required to support an enforceable contract.

DISCUSSION: Consideration must be legally sufficient and intended as a bargained-for exchange. A promisee has provided legally sufficient consideration if (s)he incurs a legal detriment or if the promisor receives a legal benefit.

Answer (A) is incorrect. Legally sufficient consideration exchanged may be disparate in value. Answer (C) is incorrect. As long as a genuine bargained-for exchange is intended, the consideration need not be simultaneously exchanged. Answer (D) is incorrect. The amount of consideration is set in the market, not the courts. But extreme disparity of value may evidence fraud, unconscionability, a gift, etc.

2. Harry promised to sell his guitar to Harriet, who promised to pay him $1,000. After Harriet tendered payment, Harry reneged on his promise, so Harriet filed suit. Which of the following is true?

A. The consideration for Harry's promise is both a legal detriment to Harriet and a legal benefit to Harry.

B. This contract is unilateral, so only Harry is bound.

C. Harriet cannot enforce Harry's promise because she neither incurred a legal detriment nor received a legal benefit.

D. In a bilateral contract, each party is bound only if each receives a legal benefit and incurs a legal detriment.

Answer (A) is correct. *(Publisher, adapted)*

REQUIRED: The true statement about the consideration requirement in a contract.

DISCUSSION: The contract is bilateral because each party has made a promise. The consideration necessary to support the enforceability of a promise may consist of either a legal detriment to the promisee or a legal benefit to the promisor. Both will usually be found, but either is legally sufficient. Harriet's promise to pay is a legal detriment to her because she had no prior obligation to pay $1,000. It is also a legal benefit to Harry because he had no prior legal right to the money.

Answer (B) is incorrect. Each party made a promise. Answer (C) is incorrect. Harriet incurred a detriment by becoming obligated to pay $1,000. She received a benefit because she obtained a right to the guitar. Answer (D) is incorrect. The promisor is bound when either the promisee incurs a legal detriment or the promisor receives a legal benefit. Both are not needed.

3. Lydia promised to pay Lavinia $10,000 if she stopped smoking for 1 year. Lavinia stopped and brought suit when Lydia failed to pay. Who will win?

A. Lydia will win because she received no actual benefit.

B. Lydia will win because Lavinia incurred no actual detriment.

C. Lydia will win because Lavinia incurred no legal detriment.

D. Lavinia will win because Lydia received a legal benefit.

Answer (D) is correct. *(Publisher, adapted)*

REQUIRED: The outcome of a suit turning upon whether forbearance from an act is consideration.

DISCUSSION: A unilateral contract was formed when the promisee stopped performing an act that she had a legal right to perform, i.e., smoking for 1 year. The promise to pay is enforceable because it was supported by consideration that was a legal detriment to the promisee (not smoking). The consideration was also a legal benefit to the promisor because she obtained a forbearance to which she had no previous legal right.

Answer (A) is incorrect. Consideration is legally sufficient if the promisor receives a legal rather than an actual benefit or if the promisee incurs a legal rather than an actual detriment. Answer (B) is incorrect. Consideration is legally sufficient if the promisor receives a legal rather than an actual benefit or if the promisee incurs a legal rather than an actual detriment. Answer (C) is incorrect. Lavinia gave up a legal right.

4. Dye sent Hill a written offer to sell a tract of land for $60,000. They were engaged in a separate dispute. The offer stated that it would be irrevocable for 60 days if Hill would promise to refrain from suing Dye during this time. Hill promptly delivered a promise not to sue during the term of the offer. Dye subsequently decided that the possible suit by Hill was groundless. Dye then phoned Hill and revoked the offer. Hill mailed an acceptance. Dye did not reply. Under the circumstances,

A. Dye's offer was supported by consideration and was not revocable when accepted.

B. Dye's written offer would be irrevocable even without consideration.

C. Dye's silence was an acceptance of Hill's promise.

D. Dye's revocation, not being in writing, was invalid.

Answer (A) is correct. *(CPA, adapted)*

REQUIRED: The effect of a promise to keep an offer open if the offeree promised to forgo a lawsuit.

DISCUSSION: Hill's promise not to sue during the term of the offer formed an option contract. That is, Hill's promise to forgo a legal right was consideration for Dye's promise not to revoke the offer for 60 days. Consequently, Dye's attempted revocation was ineffective, and Hill's acceptance within the 60-day period resulted in a contract.

Answer (B) is incorrect. An offer to sell realty is not irrevocable solely because it is in writing. Answer (C) is incorrect. Dye's silence was legally irrelevant because Hill's actions were sufficient to establish a contract. Answer (D) is incorrect. A written revocation would likewise have been invalid.

5. In deciding whether consideration necessary to form a contract exists, a court must determine whether

A. The consideration given by each party is of roughly equal value.

B. There is mutuality of consideration.

C. The consideration has sufficient monetary value.

D. The consideration conforms to the subjective intent of the parties.

Answer (B) is correct. *(CPA, adapted)*

REQUIRED: The requirement of consideration to support an enforceable contract.

DISCUSSION: An essential aspect of consideration is that it be bargained for, and given in exchange for, the consideration provided by the other party. That is, consideration is mutual.

Answer (A) is incorrect. Consideration may be unreasonable, disproportionate, inadequate, or unfair if it is mutual and bargained for. If an agreement is unconscionable, a court considers inadequate value. Also, a promise supported by nominal consideration (e.g., "$1 and other valuable consideration") may be treated as a gift. Answer (C) is incorrect. Consideration may be unreasonable, disproportionate, inadequate, or unfair if it is mutual and bargained for. If an agreement is unconscionable, a court considers inadequate value. Also, a promise supported by nominal consideration (e.g., "$1 and other valuable consideration") may be treated as a gift. Answer (D) is incorrect. Courts look at the external or objective manifestations of the parties' intent.

6. Gus Parker owned a race horse that had not made a good showing in the last 10 races. Disgusted with the horse, Parker stated that he would sell the horse for $25. Sam Hood immediately said that he would accept the horse for $25. Parker agreed to accept $25 after the afternoon's race in which Parker was obligated to participate. The horse won the race, and Parker decided that he did not really want to sell the horse. Which of the following is true?

A. The contract is unenforceable because the consideration is not adequate.

B. The courts will review whether the consideration is good consideration.

C. $25 constitutes sufficient consideration.

D. The sufficiency of the consideration depends on whether Parker was serious.

Answer (C) is correct. *(Publisher, adapted)*

REQUIRED: The true statement about the adequacy of the consideration.

DISCUSSION: Courts will usually not review the value or the adequacy of consideration. The $25 is adequate consideration if that is the amount bargained for, whether or not it is a fair value.

Answer (A) is incorrect. The amount of $25 was bargained for and is adequate consideration. Answer (B) is incorrect. Courts will usually not review whether consideration is adequate. The term "good consideration" has historically referred to a promise founded on love or affection. Answer (D) is incorrect. The sufficiency or adequacy of consideration does not depend on the seriousness of the offer. Whether the offer was in jest would bear on whether a meeting of the minds had occurred.

7. Tim Carlton was swimming at the beach when he happened to see Fay Hudson struggling in the water. Carlton saved Hudson's life. Hudson was so grateful that she promised Carlton a job for the rest of his life. Carlton went to work for Hudson, but a few months later Hudson found that she did not get along with Carlton and demanded Carlton's resignation. The contract is

A. Unenforceable because it was not definite enough.

B. Unenforceable because Carlton did not give consideration.

C. Enforceable because Hudson gave consideration in the form of job security.

D. Enforceable because there was mutuality of assent.

Answer (B) is correct. *(Publisher, adapted)*

REQUIRED: The enforceability of a contract for life employment.

DISCUSSION: A contract for life employment is ordinarily terminable at the option of the employee (one cannot be required to perform personal services). But the employer can be bound not to terminate the contract without good cause if the employee has given consideration. Saving Hudson was "past consideration." Past consideration, that is, an act performed before the making of the agreement, does not satisfy the consideration requirement for the formation of a contract.

Answer (A) is incorrect. A contract for life employment states a definite enough period of time. Answer (C) is incorrect. The contract is unenforceable based on lack of consideration. Answer (D) is incorrect. Although there is mutuality of consent, Carlton gave no consideration.

8. Which of the following requires consideration to be binding on the parties?

A. Material modification of a contract involving the sale of real estate.

B. Ratification of a contract by a person after reaching the age of majority.

C. A written promise signed by a merchant to keep an offer to sell goods open for 10 days.

D. Material modification of a sale of goods contract under the UCC.

Answer (A) is correct. *(CPA, adapted)*

REQUIRED: The transaction that must be supported by consideration to be enforceable.

DISCUSSION: Common law requires that a material modification to a contract be supported by new bargained-for consideration.

Answer (B) is incorrect. A minor's contract is ratified after majority by mere express or implied affirmation, e.g., by using or retaining the subject matter. Answer (C) is incorrect. Under the UCC, such a promise is enforceable without consideration. Answer (D) is incorrect. The UCC does not require consideration as a condition to enforcement of a good faith oral modification of a contract for the sale of goods.

9. Culler Construction Company agreed with the City of Orange Key to build a road. The project was to begin on December 1. One week after work began, a hurricane struck the site, washing away so much land that the construction would be twice as expensive. As a result, Culler refused to continue the job unless Orange Key paid a large sum in addition to the initial contract price. A promise by Orange Key to pay more than the original price is

A. Unenforceable because Orange Key received no additional legal benefit.

B. Unenforceable because Culler incurred no additional legal detriment.

C. Unenforceable because of the pre-existing contractual obligation.

D. Enforceable because Culler encountered unforeseeable difficulties.

Answer (D) is correct. *(Publisher, adapted)*

REQUIRED: The enforceability of a promise to pay more than the contract price.

DISCUSSION: If Culler had simply made a bad bargain or had met foreseeable difficulties, such as labor problems, equipment malfunctions, or materials price increases, Orange Key's additional promise would have been unenforceable for lack of consideration. Culler was already contractually obligated to perform the promised act. Unforeseen difficulties, however, are an exception to this principle. Because Culler could not reasonably have anticipated a hurricane in December, the promise to pay additional compensation would probably be enforceable.

Answer (A) is incorrect. Orange Key received an additional legal benefit and Culler incurred an additional legal detriment. The former received the right to the provision of, and the latter assumed the obligation to provide, a post-hurricane performance, one that the parties could not reasonably have anticipated when they concluded their original bargain. Answer (B) is incorrect. The contract is enforceable. Culler's new legal detriment was post-hurricane performance. Answer (C) is incorrect. There is an exception to the rule for unforeseen difficulties.

10. Adele borrowed $1,000 from Beatrice and signed a promissory note due on January 1. On December 1, Beatrice agreed to accept immediate payment of $800 in full satisfaction of the debt. In January, Beatrice sought to receive the $200 unpaid balance. What will be the result?

A. Adele will win because she provided consideration for Beatrice's new promise.

B. Adele will win because the debt was unliquidated.

C. Beatrice will win because of the pre-existing contractual obligation rule.

D. Beatrice will win because the debt was liquidated.

Answer (A) is correct. *(Publisher, adapted)*

REQUIRED: The result when a creditor accepts partial payment prior to the due date.

DISCUSSION: The debt was liquidated (undisputed in amount). Because a debtor has a pre-existing contractual obligation to pay the full amount, a creditor's promise to accept partial payment in full satisfaction is unenforceable for lack of consideration unless the debtor furnishes new or different consideration, such as payment before the due date. Beatrice had no right to early payment, so she received a new legal benefit. Adele was under no obligation to make early payment, so she incurred a new legal detriment. Adele can therefore enforce Beatrice's promise to accept a lesser amount in full satisfaction of the debt.

Answer (B) is incorrect. The debt was liquidated (not subject to honest dispute). Answer (C) is incorrect. Adele provided new consideration. Answer (D) is incorrect. Adele provided new consideration.

11. In which of the following situations does the first promise serve as valid consideration for the second promise?

A. A police officer's promise to catch a thief for a victim's promise to pay a reward.

B. A builder's promise to complete a contract for a purchaser's promise to extend the time for completion.

C. A debtor's promise to pay $500 for a creditor's promise to forgive the balance of a $600 liquidated debt.

D. A debtor's promise to pay $500 for a creditor's promise to forgive the balance of a $600 disputed debt.

Answer (D) is correct. *(CPA, adapted)*

REQUIRED: The promise that serves as valid consideration.

DISCUSSION: A promise unsupported by consideration ordinarily is unenforceable. Consideration must be legally sufficient and provided in a bargained-for exchange. Legal sufficiency is found in the promisee incurring a legal detriment or the promisor receiving a legal benefit. The debtor's promise to pay part of a disputed liability incorporates legally sufficient consideration: the legal detriment of forgoing the dispute.

Answer (A) is incorrect. A pre-existing legal duty does not constitute consideration. Answer (B) is incorrect. The builder already was obligated to perform the promise. Answer (C) is incorrect. The debtor's promise to pay a liquidated (undisputed) debt was to perform a pre-existing obligation.

12. Denise Smolen hired David Vause to construct an exercise center in her home. After completing the job, Vause sent her a bill for $3,000. Based on the cost of similar work done for several of her neighbors, Smolen stated that $2,000 was a fair price. Vause said that the market rate for quality work was $3,000 but that he would accept $2,500. Smolen agreed and remitted a $2,500 check in full payment of the debt. The parties have

A. Compromised a liquidated debt.

B. Concluded a composition with a creditor.

C. Reached an accord and satisfaction.

D. Reached an accord without satisfaction.

Answer (C) is correct. *(Publisher, adapted)*

REQUIRED: The description of an agreement to settle a disputed debt and the subsequent payment.

DISCUSSION: The parties had an honest dispute as to the amount of the debt. The agreement to compromise was an accord. The payment of the agreed amount was a satisfaction. The accord and satisfaction is enforceable because of mutuality of consideration: Vause's acceptance of a lesser amount is consideration for Smolen's payment of a greater amount and vice versa.

Answer (A) is incorrect. The debt was unliquidated or honestly disputed. Answer (B) is incorrect. A composition is an agreement among a debtor and two or more creditors to accept lesser sums from the debtor in full satisfaction of their claims. Answer (D) is incorrect. The remittance of the check was the satisfaction.

13. Adolf Anderssen performed accounting services for Carla Jung and sent her a bill for $500. She responded in good faith that the value of the services was $300 but that she was willing to pay $375 to avoid litigation. Accordingly, she sent Anderssen a check for that amount marked "payment in full." Anderssen received the check, crossed out the notation "payment in full," cashed it, and filed suit in small claims court for $125 and costs. If he desired to recover the full $500, Anderssen's best course of action was

A. To keep the check instead of cashing it.

B. To cash the check without crossing out the satisfaction recital.

C. To follow the course of action he actually chose.

D. To return the check.

Answer (D) is correct. *(Publisher, adapted)*

REQUIRED: The creditor's best course of action upon receipt of a check marked "payment in full."

DISCUSSION: A debt is unliquidated if a genuine controversy exists as to its amount. Tender of the check by Jung was an offer of settlement that Anderssen effectively accepted by cashing it. Returning the check would have been an unequivocal rejection of the offer. If the debt had not been disputed, cashing a check for a lesser sum (even if marked "payment in full") would not have been an acceptance of an offer to settle for the lesser amount.

Answer (A) is incorrect. Holding the check beyond a reasonable time for returning it would also have been an acceptance of Jung's offer. Answer (B) is incorrect. Whether the recital is crossed out does not affect the legal significance of cashing the check. Answer (C) is incorrect. The action Anderssen took is treated as acceptance of the lesser sum.

9.2 Substitutes for Consideration

14. Which of the following will be legally binding despite lack of consideration?

A. An employer's promise to make a cash payment to a deceased employee's family in recognition of the employee's many years of service.

B. A promise to donate money to a charity on which the charity relied when incurring large expenditures.

C. A modification of a signed contract to purchase a parcel of land.

D. A merchant's oral promise to keep an offer open for 60 days.

Answer (B) is correct. *(CPA, adapted)*

REQUIRED: The promise enforceable absent consideration.

DISCUSSION: A requirement for enforceability of an agreement is legally sufficient consideration or a substitute for it. One substitute is promissory estoppel: A promise that induces action or forbearance that the promisor should reasonably have expected is enforceable absent consideration if it is the only way to avoid injustice. The doctrine has been applied to promises to charitable organizations.

Answer (A) is incorrect. Past actions are not legally effective as consideration for a new promise. Answer (C) is incorrect. Modification of a real estate contract needs consideration. Modification of a contract for the sale of goods for $500 or more does not. Answer (D) is incorrect. The merchant's firm-offer rule under the UCC applies to a written commitment.

15. Sam Student was hit by a car while he was crossing the street and was knocked unconscious. Fast Ambulance Service and Towing (FAST) took him to the hospital while he was still unconscious. What is Sam's liability for FAST's fee?

A. Not liable because no contract was formed.

B. Liable under an implied-in-fact contract theory.

C. Liable under the UCC.

D. Liable under quasi-contract (implied-in-law contract) theory.

Answer (D) is correct. *(R. Cherry, Jr.)*

REQUIRED: The liability of the recipient of emergency services.

DISCUSSION: FAST should recover the reasonable value of its services (not the potential contract price) under the theory of quasi-contract. Liability is imposed to prevent unjust enrichment because no other basis of recovery is available.

Answer (A) is incorrect. The fee is recoverable under quasi-contract theory. Answer (B) is incorrect. An implied-in-fact contract is inferred from the actions of the parties. An unconscious person cannot manifest contractual intent. Answer (C) is incorrect. The UCC does not apply.

16. Which promise is enforceable in most states?

A. A creditor's promise to accept a lesser sum than due.

B. A written promise to pay a debt barred by the statute of limitations.

C. A promise to perform an illegal act.

D. A promise to pay a debt after the discharge of the debt in bankruptcy was granted.

Answer (B) is correct. *(Publisher, adapted)*

REQUIRED: The promise that is enforceable in most states.

DISCUSSION: A new promise to pay a debt barred by the statute of limitations requires no consideration to be enforceable because it is only the waiver of a defense. Some courts, however, take the view that consideration is supplied by the old debt. Nevertheless, most states require the new promise to be in writing.

Answer (A) is incorrect. A promise to accept a lesser sum must be supported by additional consideration. Answer (C) is incorrect. Legality is an essential element of a contract. Answer (D) is incorrect. The new promise (a reaffirmation agreement) must be made before the discharge is granted. Also, the debtor has 30 days to revoke the agreement after it becomes enforceable.

17. Which of the following does not require consideration to be effective and binding?

A. Waiver of a breach.

B. Mutual rescission.

C. Modification of a contract.

D. Composition with creditors.

Answer (A) is correct. *(Publisher, adapted)*

REQUIRED: The contractual action that does not require consideration to be effective.

DISCUSSION: Most contractual actions require consideration because they involve either the formation or the modification of a contract. Waiver of remedies prior to breach is a modification of a contract and needs consideration unless the agreement is within the UCC. However, once a breach has been committed, remedies may be waived without any consideration.

Answer (B) is incorrect. The cancelation of a contract by mutual rescission is a modification needing consideration. The mutual promises to rescind usually constitute the required consideration. Answer (C) is incorrect. Modification of a contract is itself a contract and thus needs consideration. Answer (D) is incorrect. A composition with creditors is a contract for which the consideration is the creditors' mutual promises.

STUDY UNIT TEN
CONTRACTS: CAPACITY, LEGALITY, MUTUALITY, AND STATUTE OF FRAUDS

Parties to a contract must possess legal capacity. **Capacity** is the mental ability to make a rational decision, which includes the ability to perceive and appreciate all relevant facts. Three classes of parties are legally limited in their capacity to contract: minors (also known as infants), mentally incompetent persons, and intoxicated parties. For public policy reasons, parties in these three groups are protected from the enforcement of most contracts against them.

Under the common law, persons are classified as **minors** until they reach the age of 21 years. By statute, the current age of majority is 18 in most jurisdictions. A minor may enter into a contract, but it is voidable and may be revoked or disaffirmed by the minor at any time after formation and for a reasonable time after (s)he reaches majority. Disaffirmation requires no formality. The contract may be disaffirmed orally, in writing, or by conduct indicating repudiation. Ratification consists of words or conduct indicating affirmance of the contract and can occur only after the minor reaches majority. If a contract is for items essential for the minor's welfare **(necessaries)**, it can be disaffirmed, but a quasi- or implied-in-law contract will be substituted. A **quasi-contract** requires the payment of the reasonable value of the necessary rather than the contract price. What is considered a necessary is not settled. In general, courts regard those items reasonably needed to maintain the minor in his/her station in life as necessaries. Included are food, shelter, clothing, medical services, and perhaps some educational or training expenses. Many courts declare that, if the minor is unemancipated and living with parents or other guardian, nothing purchased by the minor is a necessary.

A contract made by an **incompetent person** may be treated similarly to one made by a **minor**. If a person has been adjudged incompetent by a court, a guardian is appointed to handle the ward's affairs. Any contract with the incompetent person is **void** and of no legal effect. The contract of a party that factually lacked mental capacity but has not been adjudicated incompetent is **voidable** by the incompetent party or a guardian appointed later. However, one who deals with an incompetent party in good faith is entitled to restitution. Incompetent parties are liable in quasi-contract for necessaries furnished. A contract by an intoxicated person may be valid or voidable. To be voidable, the person must be intoxicated to the extent necessary to lack contractual capacity.

Legality is an essential requirement for an agreement to be valid and enforceable. When formation or performance of an agreement violates a criminal law, constitutes a tort, or is determined by the court to be contrary to **public policy**, the agreement is illegal and unenforceable. An agreement that is "contrary to public policy" has a negative impact on society at large that outweighs the interests of the parties. This principle reflects a balancing by the courts of freedom of contract and the public interest. Examples of agreements that have been found to violate public policy are (1) agreements that unduly restrain marriage; (2) surrogate-mother agreements; (3) agreements that unduly restrain competition; (4) broad exculpatory clauses (those excusing a party from liability for his/her torts); (5) contracts calling for immoral acts; and (6) agreements found to be unfair, oppressive, or unconscionable. An unconscionable agreement (or clause) is one shocking to the conscience and unjust, not merely unfair. **Procedural unconscionability** arises from the way the agreement is reached, for example, as a result of incomprehensible language or a disparity in the parties' bargaining power (e.g., the **adhesion contract**, one presented to a weaker party who must adhere to its terms without any bargaining). **Substantive unconscionability** concerns shockingly unjust terms, such as those that deprive a party of a remedy for the other's breach or leave a party with no benefit from the contract. Decisions about which agreements violate public policy constantly change to reflect society's beliefs about what is acceptable contractual behavior. Each state has its own standards of public policy. Thus, a contract that is contrary to public policy in one state may be valid in another. Some common agreements that violate statutes are (1) loans with interest rates exceeding those allowed by usury laws, (2) gambling, (3) noncompliance with licensing requirements, and (4) antitrust infractions. Agreements to perform any activity prohibited by federal or state statutes are illegal and unenforceable.

As discussed in Study Unit 8, the primary element of a valid contract is an agreement consisting of an **offer and acceptance**. The initial test for formation of an agreement is objective intent. A second level of analysis is then needed to determine whether the manifestation of **mutual assent** was subjectively an act of free will. If a party's assent to a contract is not genuine, (s)he may void the contract. Certain occurrences during the bargaining process prevent genuine, mutual assent. They include (1) fraud, (2) mistake, (3) duress, and (4) undue influence.

The essence of **fraud** is that one party intentionally deceives and thereby takes advantage of another. The elements of actionable fraud may vary from state to state, but the following are usually required:

- A false representation or the concealment of a material fact
- Intent to misrepresent (scienter)
- Intent to induce reliance
- Reasonable or justifiable reliance by the injured party
- Damage resulting from the misrepresentation

When a misrepresentation is fraudulent, the injured party may, as an alternative to voiding the contract, recover damages. However, if the misrepresentation was not intentional and therefore not fraudulent, the remedy available to the injured party is rescission.

Innocent misrepresentation is a false representation of a material fact intended to be relied upon and reasonably relied upon. It can be oral, written, or implied from conduct.

A **mistake** is an unintended act, omission, or error that arises in the formation, execution, or performance of a contractual relationship. Under some circumstances, a mistake will require that a contract be set aside on the grounds of absence of genuine assent. In contract formation, mistakes can occur in two forms: unilateral or individual mistake and bilateral or mutual mistake.

If only one party to a contract acts on the basis of a mistaken assumption, the mistake is **unilateral**. In general, when a party enters into a contract under a mistaken belief, that party is not relieved from contractual obligation. An important exception is that, if the other party knew of the mistake or it is so obvious that a reasonable person would have noticed, the unilateral mistake may justify rescission. **Mutual mistake** occurs when both parties are mistaken about the same material fact. A **material fact** is one that is important and central to the contract. It is a basis of the bargain. **Mutual mistake** is grounds for rescission or a sufficient defense in an action on the contract.

Genuine assent requires the parties to exercise free will in the formation of agreements. Assent to a contract is not genuine if obtained by duress. **Duress** occurs when one party, by means of threats or actions, instills fear or apprehension in the other party so as to deny that party's exercise of free will. The essence of duress is the threat of one party to do some wrongful act unless the other party enters into a contract. Duress may consist of threats of physical force or economic duress.

If one party to a contract dominates the other party so as to deprive that party of free will, the contract may be voidable as a result of **undue influence**. A claim of undue influence primarily focuses on the underlying relationship of the parties. The relationship that is most often subject to such a claim is a fiduciary relationship, such as between a trusted lawyer, doctor, relative, or guardian and a weaker party.

Unless contrary to statute, an oral contract is as enforceable as a written contract. However, the **statute of frauds** requires that some contracts be in writing to be enforceable. Contracts subject to the statute of frauds are said to be within the statute and must therefore comply with its requirements to be enforceable. Ordinarily, if the statute of frauds requires that a contract be in writing, any modification of that contract also must be in writing. The primary purpose of the statute is to promote the reliability of evidence that an alleged contract actually exists. To accomplish this purpose, the statute of frauds requires the agreement or some memorandum or note of it to be in writing and signed by the party to be bound by its terms. The basic requirements of a written memorandum are (1) the names of the parties, (2) the terms and conditions of the contract, (3) a reasonably certain description of the subject matter, (4) the signature of the party to be bound, and (5) a recitation of the consideration. Under the **Uniform Electronic Transactions Act (UETA)**, an electronic signature satisfies a requirement for a signature, an electronic record satisfies a requirement for a writing, and a contract is not denied legal effect solely because an electronic record was used in its formation. The federal law is the **Electronic Signatures in Global and National Commerce Act of 2000**, which applies to transactions in or affecting interstate or foreign commerce. It provides that signatures, contracts, or other records related to those transactions are not invalid solely because they are in electronic form. Although their statutes may vary slightly, most states require the following types of contracts to be in writing:

- Contracts involving an interest in land
- Contracts that by their terms cannot possibly be performed within 1 year
- Collateral (secondary) promises by which a person promises to answer for the debt or duty of another (the suretyship provision)
- Promises made in consideration of marriage
- Contracts for the sale of goods for $500 or more (UCC Article 2)

Usually, a contract within the statute of frauds that is not in writing is unenforceable by either party. However, it may be voluntarily performed by the parties. If a contract is already executed, neither party can rescind the contract on the grounds of noncompliance with the statute.

QUESTIONS

10.1 Capacity

1. Egan, a minor, purchased Baker's used computer for Egan's personal use. Egan paid $200 down on delivery and was to pay $200 30 days later. Twenty days later, the computer was damaged seriously as a result of Egan's negligence. Five days after the damage occurred and 1 day after Egan reached the age of majority, Egan attempted to disaffirm the contract with Baker. Egan will

A. Be able to disaffirm despite the fact that Egan was not a minor at the time of disaffirmance.

B. Be able to disaffirm only if Egan does so in writing.

C. Not be able to disaffirm because Egan had failed to pay the balance of the purchase price.

D. Not be able to disaffirm because the computer was damaged as a result of Egan's negligence.

Answer (A) is correct. *(CPA, adapted)*

REQUIRED: The true statement about disaffirming a contract made by a minor.

DISCUSSION: Most contracts entered into by a minor may be disaffirmed if (s)he acts during minority or a short time thereafter. Tender of the goods is usually required. However, a minor may disaffirm even though (s)he cannot return the property or can return it only in damaged condition.

Answer (B) is incorrect. A writing was not required to disaffirm the voidable contract. Note that a minor's power to disaffirm is not dependent on the UCC. Answer (C) is incorrect. Payment of the balance would be performance, which is not a condition for disaffirming. Answer (D) is incorrect. Egan may still disaffirm the contract but may be liable for negligence in tort.

2. Joe Minorca purchased a motorcycle from Big Rig Company on May 1. Joe's birthday is June 17, at which time he will have attained his majority. Which of the following actions is ineffective as a ratification of the contract of purchase?

A. On June 21, Joe gave the property to his sister.

B. On June 20, Joe made an oral promise to honor the contract.

C. On June 16, Joe remitted an installment payment.

D. As of November 17, Joe was still using the vehicle.

Answer (C) is correct. *(Publisher, adapted)*

REQUIRED: The action ineffective to constitute ratification of a minor's contract.

DISCUSSION: Contracts of minors are usually voidable at the option of the minor. Upon attainment of the age of majority, however, the minor can ratify the contract. After ratification, (s)he will be bound from the inception of the contract. An attempt to ratify while still a minor is not effective. One who lacks contractual capacity clearly lacks the capacity to ratify. Performance of the contract by making installment payments may be a ratification but only if done after the minor comes of age.

Answer (A) is incorrect. Making the gift is an implied ratification. It is inconsistent with an intention to disaffirm. Answer (B) is incorrect. An express promise, whether oral or written, is sufficient to bind an adult to a contract formed during his/her minority. Answer (D) is incorrect. Failure to disaffirm within a reasonable time after reaching one's majority is ratification.

3. The age of majority in the State of Gibraldi is 21. At the age of 20, Carol decided to leave school to seek employment sufficient to support herself. She therefore concluded an agreement with The Employment Agency (TEA) to pay a fee if it located a job for her. TEA did find a job, but Carol refused to pay. At the time of her refusal, Carol was still 20. In an action against Carol, TEA will most likely

A. Lose, because Carol was a minor when she contracted.

B. Lose, because Carol disaffirmed while still a minor.

C. Win, because Carol is liable as an emancipated minor.

D. Win, because Carol is liable for necessaries.

Answer (D) is correct. *(Publisher, adapted)*

REQUIRED: The outcome of an action against a minor for an employment agency's fee.

DISCUSSION: Minors are liable for necessaries such as food, clothing, shelter, medicine, and tools of a trade. Other items may be considered necessaries depending upon the circumstances. This rule protects the minor: A person may be unwilling to contract to supply necessaries to a minor who is not liable on the agreement. Nevertheless, a minor may still disaffirm a contract for necessaries. In that event, the minor will be liable in quasi-contract for the reasonable value of the necessaries, not for the contract price.

Answer (A) is incorrect. Minors are liable for the reasonable value of necessaries. Answer (B) is incorrect. Carol could disaffirm the contract but not avoid liability in quasi-contract. Answer (C) is incorrect. The facts do not indicate that Carol was legally emancipated. Minors who are emancipated in the sense of being free of parental constraint still lack contractual capacity.

10.3 Reality of Mutual Assent

14. To prevail in a common-law action for fraud in the inducement, a plaintiff must prove that the

A. Defendant was an expert with regard to the misrepresentations.

B. Defendant made the misrepresentations with knowledge of their falsity and with an intention to deceive.

C. Misrepresentations were in writing.

D. Plaintiff was in a fiduciary relationship with the defendant.

Answer (B) is correct. *(CPA, adapted)*
REQUIRED: The element(s) of a prima facie case of fraud in the inducement.
DISCUSSION: Elements of fraud are a false representation of a material fact, scienter (knowledge of the falsehood or reckless disregard for its truth), intent to deceive, and reliance on the false representation that is both justifiable and detrimental. Fraud in the inducement occurs when the underlying consideration (something of legal value offered in an exchange) is misrepresented. Such an agreement is voidable.

15. Sardy, a famous football player, was asked to autograph a pad of paper held by Maple. Unknown to Sardy, Maple had carefully concealed a contract for the sale of Sardy's home to Maple in the pad that Sardy signed. If Maple seeks to enforce the contract, Sardy's best defense to have the contract declared void would be

A. Fraud in the inducement.

B. Fraud in the execution.

C. Mistake.

D. Duress.

Answer (B) is correct. *(CPA, adapted)*
REQUIRED: The term for misleading someone as to the contents of a document.
DISCUSSION: When the content of an agreement or the nature of a document is purposely misrepresented to a party, fraud in the execution has occurred, and the agreement is void. It is fraudulent if it is based on a false representation, made with knowledge that it is false, and intended to induce another to act, and if the affected party acts in justifiable reliance thereon.
Answer (A) is incorrect. Fraud in the inducement occurs when the consideration (something of legal value offered in an exchange) is misrepresented. Such an agreement is voidable. Answer (C) is incorrect. This case involved intentional deceit. Answer (D) is incorrect. Duress entails a wrongful threat that induces fear sufficient to overcome one's free will.

16. Steele, Inc., wanted to purchase Kalp's distribution business. On March 15, 2003, Kalp provided Steele with copies of audited financial statements for the period ended December 31, 2002. The financial statements reflected inventory in the amount of $1.2 million. On March 29, 2003, Kalp discovered that the December 31 inventory was overstated by at least $400,000. On April 3, 2003, Steele, relying on the financial statements, purchased all of Kalp's business. On April 29, 2003, Steele discovered the inventory overstatement. Steele sued Kalp for fraud. Which of the following statements is true?

A. Steele will lose because it should not have relied on the financial statements.

B. Steele will lose because Kalp was unaware that the financial statements were incorrect when it gave them to Steele.

C. Steele will prevail because Kalp had a duty to disclose that the inventory was overstated.

D. Steele will prevail but will not be able to sue for damages.

Answer (C) is correct. *(CPA, adapted)*
REQUIRED: The true statement about failure to disclose a known error.
DISCUSSION: Neither party to a contract has a duty to disclose facts. Each is responsible to exercise ordinary business sense in his/her dealings. But a fraud action might be based on failure to disclose material facts when (1) there is a fiduciary relationship between the parties, (2) one party could not reasonably discover a fact known to the other, or (3) a person who misstates an important fact subsequently learns of it. Kalp had an affirmative duty to disclose the overstated inventory to Steele.
Answer (A) is incorrect. Reliance on audited financial statements is both common and reasonable. Answer (B) is incorrect. Kalp, having provided the statements, effected a representation. When (s)he learned that it was false, (s)he incurred an affirmative duty to disclose that it was a misstatement. Answer (D) is incorrect. When one party induces a contract by fraud, the other party may elect to rescind or to sue for damages.

4. Green was adjudicated incompetent by a court having proper jurisdiction. Which of the following statements is true regarding contracts subsequently entered into by Green?

A. All contracts are voidable.

B. All contracts are valid.

C. All contracts are void.

D. All contracts are enforceable.

Answer (C) is correct. *(CPA, adapted)*
REQUIRED: The consequence of an adjudication of mental incompetence.
DISCUSSION: An incompetent person is one whose mental capacity is such that (s)he is unable to understand the nature and consequences of his/her acts. If a person is adjudicated insane or otherwise incompetent before a contract is entered into, the contract is void and cannot be ratified (even after the person is later adjudged competent).

5. Payne entered into a written agreement to sell a parcel of land to Stevens. At the time the agreement was executed, Payne had consumed alcoholic beverages. Payne's ability to understand the nature and terms of the contract was not impaired. Stevens did not believe that Payne was intoxicated. The contract is

A. Void as a matter of law.

B. Legally binding on both parties.

C. Voidable at Payne's option.

D. Voidable at Steven's option.

Answer (B) is correct. *(CPA, adapted)*
REQUIRED: The capacity to contract when intoxicated.
DISCUSSION: A contract entered into by a person when intoxicated is not void. It is voidable by that person only if his/her reason and judgment were impaired to the extent that (s)he did not understand the legal consequences of his/her actions. If so, (s)he may disaffirm the contract even if the intoxication was voluntary and unknown to the other party.
Answer (A) is incorrect. Intoxication of one or more of the parties does not void contract formation. Answer (C) is incorrect. Payne understood the nature and terms of the contract. Answer (D) is incorrect. Stevens was bound by the contract. Awareness of Payne's intoxication is irrelevant.

10.2 Legality

6. The Acme Corporation is having a "Happy Holiday Giveaway." To win, a person must guess the number of marbles in a large jar. No purchase is necessary. This contest is probably not illegal because what element is lacking?

A. A prize.

B. Consideration.

C. Chance.

D. The illegality of the lottery in most states.

Answer (B) is correct. *(J. Norwood)*
REQUIRED: The element lacking to make the contest illegal.
DISCUSSION: To be illegal, this promotion would need to have the three characteristics of a wager: a prize, consideration, and determination of the outcome by chance. If all three are present, the contest is illegal and the contract is unenforceable. Because the participants in the promotion were not required to give up anything of value to participate, the element of consideration is lacking.
Answer (A) is incorrect. There was a prize to be won. Answer (C) is incorrect. The possibility of success depends upon chance. Answer (D) is incorrect. Most forms of gambling remain illegal in states that have state-operated lotteries.

7. Phil Fairbanks was approached by Nickle Corporation to write the history of Nickle for $15,000. The president of Nickle told Fairbanks the job was his if he would agree to cleverly defame Nickle's leading competitor, Mogul Corporation, using sly innuendo and clever distortion of the facts. Fairbanks wrote the history. It turned out that the Mogul passages were neither sly nor clever, although they were defamatory, and Mogul obtained a judgment against Nickle. Fairbanks is seeking to collect the final $5,000 installment of the contract. Nickle refuses to pay and seeks to recover the $10,000 it has paid. In the event of a lawsuit,

A. Fairbanks will recover $5,000.

B. The court will deny relief to either Fairbanks or Nickle.

C. Nickle will recover $10,000.

D. Fairbanks will recover in quantum meruit for the value of his services.

Answer (B) is correct. *(CPA, adapted)*
REQUIRED: The outcome of a suit based on an agreement to commit defamation.
DISCUSSION: A promise to commit a tort or to induce a tort is unenforceable on public policy grounds. The general principle is that neither party to an illegal bargain can use the judicial process to compel performance, obtain damages, or recover performance or its value.

8. When Lynx, Inc., hired Parr, Parr signed an employment contract prohibiting Parr from competing with Lynx during and after employment. While employed, Parr acquired knowledge of many of Lynx's trade secrets. Which of the following statements is correct?

A. Parr has the right to compete with Lynx upon resigning from Lynx.

B. Parr has the right to compete with Lynx only if fired from Lynx.

C. In determining whether Parr may compete with Lynx, the court should not consider Parr's ability to obtain other employment.

D. In determining whether Parr may compete with Lynx, the court should consider, among other factors, whether the agreement is necessary to protect Lynx's legitimate business interests.

Answer (D) is correct. *(CPA, adapted)*

REQUIRED: The rights under a covenant not to compete.

DISCUSSION: A covenant not to compete may violate the public policy to preserve and promote competition. Such an agreement must be ancillary to an otherwise enforceable agreement (not the sole object of the contract). It should state reasonable time, geographic area, and scope restrictions. Moreover, the covenant should not unduly burden the public interest or the party who is prevented from competing. The hardship factor is especially important if the covenant is part of an employment contract. If the restraint is unreasonable, a court may void the provision or reformulate it.

Answer (A) is incorrect. Whether Parr resigns is irrelevant to the enforceability of the covenant. Answer (B) is incorrect. Whether Parr is fired is irrelevant to the enforceability of the covenant. Answer (C) is incorrect. The ability to find other employment is a factor in determining how heavily the covenant will weigh upon the employee.

9. Bill Cratchett leased an apartment from Grendel. Cratchett was a person of limited means in a locality where low-income housing was scarce. Shortly after signing the agreement, he fell in an unlit stairwell when a step unexpectedly gave way. In a suit for damages, Grendel relied on a clause in the lease stating, "Tenant agrees to hold Owner harmless from any claims for damages no matter how caused." Cratchett should

A. Win because the exculpatory clause was unenforceable as a violation of public policy.

B. Win because the lease was a contract of adhesion.

C. Lose because nothing indicates that the lease was unconscionable as a whole.

D. Lose because exculpatory clauses are usually upheld in the interest of freedom of contract.

Answer (A) is correct. *(Publisher, adapted)*

REQUIRED: The outcome of the lessee's suit when the lease contained an exculpatory clause.

DISCUSSION: A bargain may fail to meet the legality requirement for enforceability if it constitutes a violation of public policy even though no crime, tort, or violation of a statute is contemplated. An exculpatory clause is viewed with disfavor by the courts because it may enable a person to escape paying damages for wrongful conduct. The clause is most likely invalid when the parties have unequal bargaining power and the terms have been imposed upon one party by the other.

Answer (B) is incorrect. Most standard-form contracts (contracts of adhesion) are enforceable. Answer (C) is incorrect. An outrageously unfair (unconscionable) clause may be invalidated even though the agreement as a whole is fair. Answer (D) is incorrect. The need for freedom and stability of contract may be outweighed by the public interest in compensating injured parties.

10. Adhesion contracts are sometimes held to be unconscionable, but their use is often justified. An adhesion contract is most appropriate if a seller

A. Has few transactions.

B. Drafts a standard contract containing extremely favorable terms and refuses to negotiate with buyers who wish to alter its terms.

C. Thereby realizes efficiencies that reduce transaction costs.

D. Has substantially greater bargaining power than the buyer.

Answer (C) is correct. *(Publisher, adapted)*

REQUIRED: The justification for adhesion contracts.

DISCUSSION: Many businesses could function only on a small scale if all adhesion contracts were prohibited. Their use permits large businesses to avoid the costs associated with negotiating the terms of individual transactions. Consequently, the transaction costs of inexpensive goods and services are reduced.

Answer (A) is incorrect. Adhesion contracts are most appropriate when a company has many similar transactions. Answer (B) is incorrect. Courts often hold adhesion contracts to be unconscionable when buyers have little or no meaningful choice with regard to the terms. Answer (D) is incorrect. Courts often hold adhesion contracts to be unconscionable when buyers have little or no meaningful choice with regard to the terms.

11. A state statute establishes a maximum interest rate of 10% for loans or forbearance of money when the debtor is not a corporation. Arrears and Buck, a large retailer, effectively charges consumers an annual rate of 18% on the unpaid balances of their purchases.

A. Arrears and Buck is guilty of usury.

B. The time-price doctrine may apply.

C. Arrears and Buck's rates violate public policy.

D. Arrears and Buck's rates are unconscionable.

Answer (B) is correct. *(Publisher, adapted)*

REQUIRED: The effect on consumer interest rates of a usury statute.

DISCUSSION: Because of the need for more consumer credit, courts developed the time-price differential theory to exempt consumer credit sales from the effect of usury statutes, which limit the interest that may be charged for a loan of money. The cash price is in theory the lowest price at which the seller will make the sale. The time-price is the higher price charged for a credit sale, the difference being attributable to the greater risk borne by the seller. Under the time-price theory, the difference is not interest, the transaction is not a loan, and the usury statute is not violated.

Answer (A) is incorrect. Consumer credit sales may be exempt under the time-price doctrine. Answer (C) is incorrect. Arrears and Buck's rates reflect modern consumer credit reality. Answer (D) is incorrect. Arrears and Buck's rates reflect modern consumer credit reality.

12. West, an Indiana real estate broker, misrepresented to Zimmer that West was licensed in Kansas under the Kansas statute that regulates real estate brokers and requires all brokers to be licensed. Zimmer signed a contract agreeing to pay West a 5% commission for selling Zimmer's home in Kansas. West did not sign the contract. West sold Zimmer's home. If West sued Zimmer for nonpayment of commission, Zimmer would be

A. Liable to West only for the value of services rendered.

B. Liable to West for the full commission.

C. Not liable to West for any amount because West did not sign the contract.

D. Not liable to West for any amount because West violated the Kansas licensing requirements.

Answer (D) is correct. *(CPA, adapted)*

REQUIRED: The recovery for services rendered in violation of a regulatory statute.

DISCUSSION: A person who performs services without obtaining a statutorily required license may recover only if the statute is solely a revenue measure. If the legislative intent was to protect the public from incompetent work by unqualified persons, the statute is regulatory and the contract is unenforceable even if the defendant was benefited and the work performed was satisfactory.

Answer (A) is incorrect. A court will not give any remedy to a party who violates a regulatory statute. West will not recover in quasi-contract, although Zimmer was unjustly enriched. Answer (B) is incorrect. A violator of a regulatory statute is not permitted any recovery. Answer (C) is incorrect. The contract is not subject to the statute of frauds. (It is not a contract to sell real property.) If it were, failure of West to sign would not relieve Zimmer of liability.

13. Gala leases her B-25 to pilots for recreational flying. One Saturday morning, Hanna called and offered to rent the B-25 for the day. Gala agreed. Unknown to her, Hanna had been hired by Lana to use the aircraft to fly at an extremely low altitude over a crowded stadium that afternoon. The flight would violate state and federal law. Who may enforce the agreement?

A. Only Gala.

B. Only Hanna.

C. Only Lana.

D. None of the answers are correct.

Answer (A) is correct. *(Publisher, adapted)*

REQUIRED: The person who can enforce the agreement.

DISCUSSION: When one party to an agreement has no knowledge that what (s)he is to supply is intended for an illegal use, (s)he may enforce the agreement. The party intending the illegal use may not. The latter restriction is based on the argument that the bargain would facilitate accomplishment of an illegal objective. Rental of an aircraft, for example, is in itself lawful. In the circumstances, however, it would facilitate achievement of an illegal objective.

Answer (B) is incorrect. The contract could be completed without violating the law. However, a party intending illegal activity may not enforce the contract. Answer (C) is incorrect. The contract could be completed without violating the law. However, a party intending illegal activity may not enforce the contract. Answer (D) is incorrect. Gala may enforce the agreement.

17. To prevail in a common-law action for innocent misrepresentation, the plaintiff must prove

A. The defendant made the false statements with a reckless disregard for the truth.

B. The misrepresentation was in writing.

C. The misrepresentation concerned material facts.

D. Reliance on the misrepresentation was the only factor inducing the plaintiff to enter into the contract.

Answer (C) is correct. *(CPA, adapted)*

REQUIRED: The necessary element of a claim of innocent misrepresentation.

DISCUSSION: Innocent misrepresentation is a false statement of a fact that is intended to induce reliance and that actually and reasonably results in reliance that is detrimental. The fact misrepresented must be material to (i.e., a basis of, important, or central to) the bargain.

Answer (A) is incorrect. Making false statements with a reckless disregard for the truth is constructive intent to defraud, not innocent misrepresentation. Answer (B) is incorrect. The misrepresentation may be expressed orally or in writing, or it may be implied by conduct. Answer (D) is incorrect. Reliance on the misrepresentation must be reasonable, but it need not be the only factor inducing contract formation.

18. Which of the following types of mistakes ordinarily will not allow a contract to be rescinded?

A. Mutual mistake of fact.

B. Unilateral mistake of fact known to the other party.

C. Mistake of law.

D. Mistake as to the existence of the object of the contract.

Answer (C) is correct. *(Publisher, adapted)*

REQUIRED: The type of mistake that will not allow a contract to be rescinded.

DISCUSSION: A mistake of law is based on either a lack of knowledge of the law or an incorrect interpretation of the law. Ordinarily, a contract may not be rescinded on such a basis because everyone is deemed to know the law.

Answer (A) is incorrect. A mutual mistake of material fact is a basis for rescinding a contract. Answer (B) is incorrect. A contract can be rescinded if a unilateral mistake is material and the other party either knew of the mistake or should have known given the surrounding facts. Answer (D) is incorrect. A mistake as to the existence of the object of the contract totally defeats its purpose and permits it to be rescinded.

19. Blume owns three motorcycles: a 1996 Kawasaki, a 1999 Honda, and a 1995 Honda. Rich is interested in purchasing a motorcycle. If Blume makes a written offer to sell and Rich accepts, in which case is the agreement enforceable?

A. Blume, meaning to offer the 1995 Honda, inadvertently wrote Kawasaki instead. Rich accepted in good faith.

B. Blume, meaning the 1995 model, offered to sell the Honda. Rich, meaning the 1999 model, accepted in good faith.

C. Blume, meaning to offer the Kawasaki, inadvertently wrote Honda instead. Rich, realizing from the price offered that an error had been made, accepted in hopes of getting a bargain.

D. Blume, meaning the 1995 Honda, offered to sell "the motorcycle." Rich, knowing only that Blume owned a 1996 Kawasaki, accepted in good faith.

Answer (A) is correct. *(Publisher, adapted)*

REQUIRED: The contract offer that could be validly accepted with a mistake in the language.

DISCUSSION: A contract is voidable (1) when it is based upon a mutual mistake regarding a material fact that induced the making of the contract; (2) when it arises from different, good faith interpretations of a material ambiguity in the contractual language; or (3) when one party makes a material mistake about which the other knew or should have known. In these cases, the requisite meeting of the minds is deemed not to have occurred. If Blume offered to sell the Kawasaki and neither the price nor anything else in the transaction alerted Rich to the error, the acceptance was binding despite the unilateral mistake in the description of the subject matter.

Answer (B) is incorrect. The mutual mistake about a material fact that induced the making of the contract renders the contract voidable. Answer (C) is incorrect. No contract is formed when one party knows or has reason to know of the other's unilateral mistake. Answer (D) is incorrect. The mutual mistake about a material fact that induced the making of the contract renders the contract voidable.

20. On April 6, Apple entered into a signed contract with Bean, by which Apple was to sell Bean an antique automobile, having a fair market value of $150,000, for $75,000. Apple believed the auto was worth only $75,000. Unknown to either party, the auto had been destroyed by fire on April 4. If Bean sues Apple for breach of contract, Apple's best defense is

A. Unconscionability.

B. The transfer of the risk of loss to Bean.

C. Lack of adequate consideration.

D. Mutual mistake.

Answer (D) is correct. *(CPA, adapted)*

REQUIRED: The result when the parties do not know that the subject matter has been destroyed.

DISCUSSION: A mistake of material fact made by both parties is grounds for rescission or is a sufficient defense in an action on the contract. Existence of the subject matter of the contract is a material fact.

Answer (A) is incorrect. An agreement is unconscionable if it is so unfair as to be oppressive, but the facts do not suggest that Bean took unfair advantage of Apple. Answer (B) is incorrect. The seller initially has the risk of loss. No event occurred that transferred the risk to Bean. Answer (C) is incorrect. Courts seldom inquire into the adequacy or value of consideration.

21. Kent contracted to provide Maco consulting services at an hourly rate of $20. The fair market value of the services was $90 per hour. Kent agreed to the $20 rate because he was having serious financial problems. At the time the agreement was negotiated, Maco was aware of Kent's financial condition and refused to pay more for Kent's services. Kent has now sued to rescind, claiming duress. Under the circumstances, Kent will

A. Win, because Maco refused to pay the fair market value of Kent's services.

B. Win, because Maco was aware of Kent's serious financial problems.

C. Lose, because Maco's actions did not constitute duress.

D. Lose, if Maco cannot prove that Kent, at the time, had no other offers to provide consulting services.

Answer (C) is correct. *(Publisher, adapted)*

REQUIRED: The result of a suit asserting duress as a defense to a services contract.

DISCUSSION: Duress sufficient to render a contract voidable is a threat that is so coercive that the victim has no reasonable alternative but to enter into the contract. Duress may result from extreme economic pressure, but taking advantage of another's financial difficulty is not enough. Kent will lose because Maco made no improper threat; it did not exert extreme economic pressure on Kent. Even if Kent was coerced by threat, on these facts, Maco was not the source.

Answer (A) is incorrect. Legal sufficiency of consideration does not depend on its relative value. Duress is not a function of the adequacy of consideration. Answer (B) is incorrect. Coercive threat, not awareness of financial problems, is the basis for duress. Answer (D) is incorrect. Kent has the burden to prove the defense. Although Kent may have felt pressured to enter the contract, Maco did not exert the coercive pressure.

22. If a person is induced to enter into a contract by another person because of the close relationship between the parties, the contract may be voidable under which of the following defenses?

A. Fraud in the inducement.

B. Unconscionability.

C. Undue influence.

D. Duress.

Answer (C) is correct. *(CPA, adapted)*

REQUIRED: The defense under which a contract may be voidable if the parties have a close personal relationship.

DISCUSSION: A valid contract requires mutual assent, that is, a true or genuine meeting of the minds of the contracting parties. No serious misconduct must have occurred, and no party must have taken unfair advantage of another, during the formation of the contract. A valid contract is an exercise of free will of the parties and not the result of threats, other forms of coercion, wrongful persuasion, innocent misrepresentation, mistake, or fraud. Thus, a fiduciary or other close personal relationship between the contracting parties may give rise to a claim of undue influence. When one party dominates the other party so as to deprive him/her of free will, the contract is voidable as a result of undue influence, the essence of which is wrongful persuasion rather than coercion.

Answer (A) is incorrect. Fraud in the inducement is the result of a contracting party's being deceived about some material aspect of the underlying consideration, such as the quality of the goods or services. Answer (B) is incorrect. An unconscionable contract lacks fundamental fairness in its purpose or effect, showing no regard for conscience. Such contracts are declared by the courts to be against public policy and are unenforceable. Answer (D) is incorrect. Duress occurs when one party, by means of threats or actions, instills fear or apprehension in the other party so as to deny that party's exercise of free will.

10.4 Statute of Frauds

23. With regard to an agreement for the sale of real estate, the statute of frauds

A. Does not require that the agreement be signed by all parties.

B. Does not apply if the value of the real estate is less than $500.

C. Requires that the entire agreement be in a single writing.

D. Requires that the purchase price be fair and adequate in relation to the value of the real estate.

Answer (A) is correct. *(CPA, adapted)*

REQUIRED: The result when a contract is within the statute of frauds.

DISCUSSION: An agreement for the sale of real property is within the statute of frauds. To be enforceable, it must satisfy requirements of the statute: A written memorandum must name the parties, describe the subject matter, state the essential terms, recite the consideration, and be signed by the party to be charged. Other parties need not sign it.

Answer (B) is incorrect. The value of real estate is not determinative. The UCC does not apply to real property. Answer (C) is incorrect. The agreement may be in several writings if evidence indicates they all relate to the same transaction and one is signed. Answer (D) is incorrect. The statute of frauds does not address adequacy of consideration.

24. Don and Peter each signed a memorandum stating that Don agreed to sell and Peter agreed to purchase a tract of land. The memorandum did not recite the purchase price. Don relies upon the statute of frauds as a defense to performance. If Peter offers evidence that the parties agreed upon a purchase price of $75,000 just prior to signing, Peter should

A. Succeed, because Don is prohibited from denying that the agreed price is a fair one, which will be implied by law as a term of the written memorandum.

B. Succeed, because the law implies that the parties contracted for the reasonable value of the land, even if it is not that orally agreed upon.

C. Fail, because the price agreed upon is an essential element of the contract and must be in writing.

D. Fail, because the evidence does not show that the price agreed upon is in fact the reasonable market value of the land.

Answer (C) is correct. *(Publisher, adapted)*

REQUIRED: The effect of the omission of the price term from the writing.

DISCUSSION: The statute of frauds requires that a contract to sell or purchase an interest in real property be in writing, be signed by the party to be charged, and contain a recitation of the material terms of the agreement. Peter should fail because the consideration for the sale of the realty is not stated in the writing evidencing the agreement. The statement of consideration is a material term of the contract. This rule contrasts with the UCC provision regarding a contract for the sale of goods. Under the UCC, a reasonable price may be substituted for an omitted price term if there is sufficient evidence that the parties intended to contract.

Answer (A) is incorrect. A court will not infer the price term of a contract for the sale of real property. Answer (B) is incorrect. A court will not infer the price term of a contract for the sale of real property. Answer (D) is incorrect. Peter will fail as a result of the insufficiency of the writing, not because the agreed price is not the reasonable market value. A court will seldom inquire into the reasonableness of consideration.

25. Under the statute of frauds, an agreement not able to be performed within 1 year of its making is unenforceable unless in writing and signed by the party to be charged. Assuming the other elements of a contract are present, which of the following oral promises is not enforceable?

A. Tanya promises to support Ultima for the rest of her life.

B. On January 1, Vance promises to act as Wally's agent for 1 year ending on the following January 1.

C. Xenia promises to serve as legal counsel for Yvonne's company for 2 years.

D. Zoe agrees to serve as Ava Company's vice-president for 1 year if Bee will sit on the board of directors for 18 months. Zoe has completed performance.

Answer (C) is correct. *(Publisher, adapted)*

REQUIRED: The oral promise unenforceable under the statute of frauds.

DISCUSSION: An oral contract that cannot be performed within 1 year (beginning the day after the contract is entered into) is unenforceable. An oral promise to serve for 2 years is within the statute and thus unenforceable.

Answer (A) is incorrect. Ultima's life might end within a year and thus the contract could be completed before the statute of frauds is required. Courts usually construe the provision so that a possibility of performance within 1 year takes a contract outside the statute. Answer (B) is incorrect. The contract is to be performed within the year running from January 2 (the day after the contract was formed) to the following January 1. Answer (D) is incorrect. The majority view is that complete performance by one party renders the contract enforceable against the other party.

26. On May 1, Dix and Wilk entered into an oral agreement by which Dix agreed to purchase a small parcel of land from Wilk for $450. Dix paid Wilk $100 as a deposit. The following day, Wilk received another offer to purchase the land for $650, the fair market value. Wilk immediately notified Dix that Wilk would not sell the land for $450. If Dix sues Wilk for specific performance, Dix will

A. Prevail, because the amount of the contract was less than $500.

B. Prevail, because the contract was partially performed.

C. Lose, because the fair value of the land is over $500.

D. Lose, because the agreement was not in writing and signed by Wilk.

Answer (D) is correct. *(CPA, adapted)*

REQUIRED: The enforceability at law of an oral agreement to sell land.

DISCUSSION: A contract for the sale of an interest in real property must be in writing and signed by the party to be charged. The writing must state the essential terms of the transaction, not all details.

Answer (A) is incorrect. The statute of frauds sets no dollar minimum regarding sales of realty. Answer (B) is incorrect. Payment of a deposit is not part performance sufficient to make the oral agreement enforceable. The part performance exception is intended to prevent injustice when the buyer has substantially changed his/her position, e.g., by taking possession or making improvements. Answer (C) is incorrect. The statute of frauds sets no dollar minimum regarding sales of realty.

27. Under the statute of frauds, a contract for the sale of an interest in land must be in writing to be enforceable. This rule applies to

A. A 1-year lease.

B. A real estate mortgage.

C. Minerals to be severed by the seller.

D. Growing crops.

Answer (B) is correct. *(Publisher, adapted)*

REQUIRED: The sale to which the statute of frauds applies.

DISCUSSION: Interests in land include real estate and contracts that affect ownership in real estate. Contracts to sell real estate, long-term leases, real estate mortgages, and easements are interests in land.

Answer (A) is incorrect. Most states require a lease to be in writing only if it is for more than 1 year. Answer (C) is incorrect. If the seller is to sever the minerals, the contract is for the sale of goods, not an interest in land. Answer (D) is incorrect. The sale of growing crops apart from the land and capable of severance without material harm to the land is a sale of goods.

28. On June 1, Year 1, Decker orally guaranteed the payment of a $5,000 note Decker's cousin owed Baker. On June 3, Year 1, Baker wrote Decker confirming Decker's guarantee. Decker did not object to the confirmation. On August 23, Year 1, Decker's cousin defaulted on the note. Which of the following statements is true?

A. Decker is liable under the oral guarantee because Decker did not object to Baker's June 3 letter.

B. Decker is not liable under the oral guarantee if it expired more than 1 year after June 1.

C. Decker is liable under the oral guarantee because Baker demanded payment within 1 year of the date the guarantee was given.

D. Decker is not liable under the oral guarantee because Decker's promise was not in writing.

Answer (D) is correct. *(CPA, adapted)*

REQUIRED: The true statement concerning an oral guarantee confirmed by the person to whom it was made.

DISCUSSION: A contract within the statute of frauds is unenforceable against a party who did not sign a writing expressing its essential terms. An agreement to answer for the debt of another is within the statute, as is one that cannot be performed within a year of contract formation. The guarantee agreement might have been fully performed by May 31, Year 2.

Answer (A) is incorrect. Failure to act does not bind a person to contractual performance, except in certain instances under the UCC. Answer (B) is incorrect. The guarantee agreement could have been fully executed within a year of its making, so the 1-year rule of the statute of frauds does not apply. Answer (C) is incorrect. The guarantee agreement could have been fully executed within a year of its making, so the 1-year rule of the statute of frauds does not apply.

29. Certain contracts to answer for the debt or default of another must be evidenced by a writing. Which of the following oral promises is within this provision of the statute of frauds?

A. Iona promises Jonna to pay her rent if Jonna does not receive her paycheck by the end of the month.

B. Ken is to build houses for Luana. When Ken fails to pay for certain added materials, Luana promises the supplier to pay Ken's current and future debts if Ken does not. Luana has a contract to sell the houses by a certain date to Mara.

C. Nona tells Jackson, "Sell Phoebe $200 worth of supplies for school and send me the bill."

D. Queenie tells Rhoda, "Sell Sue $400 worth of lumber. If she doesn't pay, send me the bill."

Answer (D) is correct. *(Publisher, adapted)*

REQUIRED: The promise not enforceable without a writing.

DISCUSSION: The suretyship section of the statute of frauds provides that a secondary promise to answer for the debt or default of another must be written. Queenie's promise to Rhoda is secondary. She will be liable only if Sue, the primary obligor, fails to pay.

Answer (A) is incorrect. The promise must be made to the creditor, not the debtor. Answer (B) is incorrect. The "leading-object" or "main-purpose" rule is an exception. A promise primarily for one's own benefit is not required to be written even though the debtor is also benefited. Luana has apparently guaranteed Ken's debts to avoid defaulting on her own contract with Mara. Answer (C) is incorrect. The promisor has incurred a direct obligation, not a secondary one.

30. Nolan agreed orally with Train to sell Train a house for $100,000. Train sent Nolan a signed agreement and a down payment of $10,000. Nolan did not sign the agreement but allowed Train to move into the house. Before closing, Nolan refused to go through with the sale. Train sued Nolan to compel specific performance. Under the provisions of the statute of frauds,

A. Train will win because Train signed the agreement and Nolan did not object.

B. Train will win because Train made a down payment and took possession.

C. Nolan will win because Nolan did not sign the agreement.

D. Nolan will win because the house was worth more than $500.

Answer (B) is correct. *(CPA, adapted)*

REQUIRED: The enforceability of a partly performed oral real property contract of sale.

DISCUSSION: An agreement for the sale of land is within the statute of frauds and is not enforceable against a party who did not sign a written memorandum containing the essential terms. However, under the part performance doctrine, specific performance may be granted the purchaser if (s)he paid part of the consideration and either took possession of the property or made valuable improvements to the land.

Answer (A) is incorrect. The party to be charged must have signed the agreement. Answer (C) is incorrect. Partial performance is sufficient such that specific performance may be decreed. Answer (D) is incorrect. Only if an agreement is for the sale of goods is a threshold amount of $500 or more significant to a signed writing requirement.

STUDY UNIT ELEVEN
CONTRACTS: INTERPRETATION, CONDITIONS, DISCHARGE, AND REMEDIES

Courts do not make contracts, but they are responsible for construing (interpreting) the intent of the contracting parties. The following are basic **rules of construction (interpretation)** for contract disputes:

1. The contract is interpreted as a whole.
2. All writings that are part of the same transaction are interpreted together.
3. When the language of the contract is inconsistent, written provisions take priority over printed or typed provisions, and typed provisions take priority over printed provisions.
4. When words conflict with figures or numerals, words prevail.
5. Words used in a contract are given their plain meaning. (Most states have enacted **plain language laws** that require legal writing to be clear and coherent and to use words with common meanings. Federal agencies must follow similar guidelines.)
6. Technical terms and words of art are assigned their technical meanings when used in a technical transaction.
7. The interpretation of words and other conduct considers all surrounding circumstances, especially the parties' principal purpose.
8. Courts give consideration to express terms, course of performance, course of dealing, and usage of trade in that sequence.
9. An interpretation that gives an agreement full force and effect is preferred over one that renders all or part of it unreasonable, unlawful, or void.
10. An interpretation that favors a public interest is preferred over one that favors a private interest.
11. Courts will supply a term to save an agreement but not to make an agreement for the parties.
12. When a contract is ambiguous and two reasonable interpretations are possible, the ambiguity is interpreted more strictly against the party who drafted it.
13. Ordinarily, and unless it specifically states otherwise, a contract is governed by the law of the state having the most significant contacts with the transaction.
14. If it is reasonable to do so, the parties' expressions of intent are interpreted as consistent with each other and any course of performance, course of dealing, and usage of trade.
15. Specific terms are weighted more heavily than general terms.
16. Added or specifically negotiated terms are given greater consideration than default or general terms.

Often, parties to a contract make a variety of oral and written statements during complex and extended negotiations. Ultimately, they reach final agreement and reduce their contract to writing. The parol evidence rule is a substantive rule of law that helps to determine the content of a written agreement. Under the **parol evidence rule**, evidence of a prior oral or written agreement or a contemporaneous (occurring at the same time) oral agreement is inadmissible if offered to contradict or modify the terms of a written contract meant to be entire (an integrated contract). This rule promotes certainty by giving binding effect, as far as is reasonable, to a signed writing intended as the final and complete expression of the rights and duties of the parties. It applies to all written contracts, whether or not the statute of frauds requires them to be in writing. However, parol evidence may be admitted to (1) resolve an ambiguity in a purported complete integration; (2) establish illegality, fraud, duress, lack of consideration, or other defense to the contract; (3) correct errors; (4) establish the existence of a condition precedent to the existence of the contract; and (5) prove a subsequent modification of the contract or the creation of a separate contract. Moreover, although a partially integrated agreement may not be contradicted, it may be supplemented with consistent additional terms from prior negotiations or agreements, whether written or oral. It also may be supplemented with evidence of course of dealing, course of performance, and usage of trade.

In practice, parties to a contract commonly insert a clause, called a **merger clause**, stating that the writing constitutes their entire and final agreement and that all prior negotiations and agreements are merged in the writing. Courts give great weight to this type of clause.

Despite its name, the parol evidence rule is neither an exclusionary rule of evidence nor a rule of contract construction or interpretation. Instead, it is a completed-document rule that applies only to integrated contracts. The parol evidence rule is part of the common law of contracts and is included in Article 2 of the UCC.

Contractual promises may be classified as unconditional or conditional. In a **conditional promise**, the promisor's duty to perform arises only if the condition occurs. However, it becomes **unconditional** if the condition is met. A **condition** is an act, event, or set of facts that, unless excused, must occur prior to the time a party is required to perform under the conditional promise. Thus, a condition triggers, limits, or extinguishes an absolute contractual duty to perform. It may be the occurrence or the nonoccurrence of a specific event. Conditions may be express, implied-in-fact, implied-in-law, precedent, subsequent, or concurrent.

An **express condition** is explicitly set forth in language, usually preceded by such terms as "provided that," "on condition that," "after," "while," "upon," or "as soon as." A particular form or term is not necessary to create an express condition. However, a clear intention that a promise be conditioned must be evidenced. An example of a very common express condition is that performance by one party must be to the **personal satisfaction** of the other. To resolve disputes about personal satisfaction, the courts have developed rules involving two categories of personal satisfaction cases:

1. Matters of personal taste, opinion, or judgment, to which the courts apply a **subjective** standard
2. Matters involving mechanical fitness, marketability, or utility, to which they apply an **objective** standard

Implied conditions (constructive conditions) are not expressly stated in the contract but are inferred from the parties' intent or are read into the contract by a court. **Implied-in-fact conditions** are not stated in express language but are understood to be part of the agreement. **Implied-in-law conditions** are not contained in the language of the contract or necessarily implied by the terms of the contract, but they are imposed by operation of law to serve justice and promote fairness.

Conditions also are classified based on their time of occurrence. A **condition precedent** is an event that must occur before contractual performance is due, for example, payment only after delivery of goods. Unless the condition is fulfilled, no duty of performance exists. A **condition subsequent** is an event that operates to terminate an existing duty to perform and a right to compensation for breach of contract, for example, return of nonconforming goods. **Concurrent conditions** arise when the parties to a contract must render performance simultaneously, that is, when each party's absolute duty to perform is conditioned on the other party's absolute duty to perform. For example, payment is often conditioned upon the simultaneous delivery of goods.

Most, if not all, contracting parties expect to give and receive the promised performance. However, performance of a contractual duty is only one method of discharging contractual obligations. **Discharge** of a contractual duty may occur by (1) performance; (2) impossibility, impracticability, or frustration; (3) breach by one or both parties; (4) agreement of the parties; and (5) operation of law. A duty that has been discharged is no longer enforceable.

Performance is the most common method of discharging a contractual duty. Many things can happen between the time that a contract is formed and the time that performance must occur. Intervening events may make performance extremely difficult or financially prohibitive. However, courts adhere to the theory that, unless expressly provided for in the contract, intervening events rarely constitute an excuse for nonperformance.

Exceptions to the rule of strict performance include impossibility, impracticability, and frustration. Usually, the courts will apply the doctrine of **impossibility** only when they perceive that circumstances have changed so radically since the contract was formed that the parties could not reasonably have contemplated and expressly provided for the new conditions. For this doctrine to apply, the impossibility must be objective. If the duty could be performed by someone but not by the promisor, the doctrine does not apply. On other occasions, courts may allow discharge based on **impracticability**. The Restatement (Second) of Contracts and the UCC adopt a more lenient standard than objective impossibility. They permit discharge when a party's performance is rendered impracticable without his/her fault as a result of the occurrence of an event, the nonoccurrence of which was a basic assumption of the contract. This rule applies unless the circumstances or the contract's language indicate differently. A fundamental issue is therefore whether the promisor expressly or impliedly assumed the risk of such an event. An example is a severe shortage of raw materials caused by war, local crop failure, or unforeseen closure of major suppliers. Such events may result in a great increase in cost or in an inability to obtain the necessary supplies. The doctrine of **frustration of purpose** permits discharge of parties even though performance is still possible. Frustration occurs when an unforeseeable intervening event substantially frustrates a party's principal purpose, through no fault of the party seeking such relief.

Breach of contract is the failure of a party to perform a duty imposed by a contract. A **nonmaterial breach** does not deprive the nonbreaching party of the benefit of the bargain and does not discharge that party. Nevertheless, the nonbreaching party has a cause of action for damages. In these circumstances, **substantial performance** has occurred. All essential terms of the contract have been performed, and its central purpose has been achieved. A **material breach** is an unexcused failure to perform substantially the obligations arising from a contract. Thus, an aggrieved party is deprived of what (s)he actually bargained for. A material breach relieves the nonbreaching party from any obligation to perform and gives a right to seek damages or other appropriate relief as a remedy for the breach. However, legal opinion differs as to when the discharge of the nonbreaching party should occur. The traditional theory is that a material breach immediately discharges the injured party, even if performance is still possible. The modern trend allows the injured party to suspend performance while the breaching party uses any time remaining under the contract to cure the defective performance. If the breaching party does not cure the defect, the injured party's performance is discharged when the time for performance expires. When a party to a contract informs the other prior to the time set for performance that (s)he has no intention to perform the contract, nearly all courts allow the aggrieved party to suspend performance. This **anticipatory breach** is deemed to occur only when a party's repudiation of the contract is absolute and clear.

A contract may be discharged by **agreement** of the parties. The parties to a contract may agree to rescind the agreement prior to performing or alter their performance obligation in some manner. Ordinarily, the parties may cancel the contract at any time by mutual agreement. This agreement is a **mutual rescission**. A **novation** cancels an existing contract and replaces it with a new one. Although a novation may sometimes replace one of the original parties, the execution of a **substituted contract** merely replaces the contract while retaining the original parties. Parties also may discharge an existing contract by an accord and satisfaction, release, or waiver. Sometimes, contractual obligations are discharged by law regardless of the will of the parties. Discharge by **operation of law** may occur, for example, as a result of merger, bankruptcy, or operation of a statute of limitations.

When a party to a contract breaches it by failing to perform a contractual obligation, the law provides a remedy for the injured party. The primary objective of contract **remedies** is to compensate the nonbreaching party for loss resulting from the breach. The nonbreaching party is entitled to protection of three interests: an **expectation** interest (the benefit bargained for), a **reliance** interest (recovery of a loss suffered by relying on the other party to perform), and a **restitution** interest (recovery of the benefits conferred on the other party). **Damages** for breach of contract is the most common judicial remedy. Damages are classified variously. **Nominal damages** are awarded when a breach of contract is proved, but the nonbreaching party is unable to prove any actual loss. **Punitive damages** are designed to punish a wrongdoer and set an example for others, but a court rarely awards punitive damages in a breach of contract suit. **Compensatory damages** constitute the amount of money necessary to compensate the nonbreaching party for the breach. To recover compensatory damages, the plaintiff must be able to prove the amount of damages with reasonable certainty. Damages for lost profits and mental stress are difficult to prove. **Consequential (special) damages** are granted in addition to compensatory damages when they are **foreseeable** to a reasonable person at the time the contract was entered into. A **liquidated damages** clause provides for a predetermined amount to be paid in the event of a breach. Its purpose is to ensure that a reasonable estimate of probable damages is available in case of breach. When a breach of contract occurs, the injured party is required to take reasonable steps to **mitigate** or lessen the damages that may result. An injured party may not recover damages for losses that (s)he could have avoided without undue risk, burden, or humiliation.

Rescission is the appropriate remedy in three situations: (1) a mutual mistake; (2) a unilateral mistake due to fraud, duress, or undue influence; or (3) a material breach. Rescission is the cancelation of a contract and the return of the parties to the positions they would have occupied if the contract had not been formed.

When the damages remedy is inadequate, a court may, at its discretion, provide the equitable remedy of **specific performance**. It is ordinarily granted when the property that is the subject of a contract is unique, for example, real property or personal property, such as a patent, rare painting, or stock in a company that is not publicly traded. However, specific performance is not a remedy for breach of a contract to provide personal services. An **injunction** is another equitable remedy. For example, although the contract for personal services will not be specifically enforced, a court might enjoin the breaching party from performing similar services for another employer, provided that the defendant is not deprived of reasonable means of earning a living. Still another equitable remedy is **reformation** by which a court revises an imperfectly drafted contract to reflect the true intentions of the parties.

QUESTIONS

11.1 Interpretation and Parol Evidence Rule

1. Under the parol evidence rule, oral evidence will be excluded if it relates to

A. A contemporaneous oral agreement relating to a term in the contract.

B. Failure of a condition precedent.

C. Lack of contractual capacity.

D. A modification made several days after the contract was executed.

Answer (A) is correct. *(CPA, adapted)*

REQUIRED: The inadmissible parol evidence.

DISCUSSION: The parol evidence rule applies to oral or written statements made prior to, or contemporaneously with, a written contract which the parties intended as the complete agreement. Extrinsic evidence of the prior or contemporaneous statement is inadmissible to contradict or otherwise vary the integrated writing.

Answer (B) is incorrect. Failure of a condition precedent does not vary written contract terms and is admissible. Answer (C) is incorrect. Lack of contractual capacity affects validity of the contract, rather than the meaning of a contract term. Answer (D) is incorrect. The evidence is not of a statement prior or contemporaneous to the written contract.

2. A ship came into port to receive a shipment of goods. The insurance policy provided that the policy would not be enforceable or effective while the ship was in port loading. The ship was fully loaded during the day and remained in port during the night while waiting for a storm to blow over. During the night, the storm worsened, and the ship was totally destroyed. A question has arisen about whether the insurance policy covers the damage because the ship was not actually in the loading process but was in port for the purpose of loading. Evidence of oral conversations at the time the contract was formed concerning this issue

A. Is prohibited by the parol evidence rule.

B. Is prohibited because all terms in insurance contracts are required to be in writing.

C. May be used only if all parties agree.

D. May be used to explain the meaning of a contractual provision as an exception to the parol evidence rule.

Answer (D) is correct. *(Publisher, adapted)*

REQUIRED: The ability to use oral evidence to interpret a provision in a contract.

DISCUSSION: The parol evidence rule excludes evidence of prior or contemporaneous oral or written agreements that would add to, vary, or contradict the terms of a written agreement meant to be entire. However, there is an exception for oral evidence to explain ambiguous terms in the agreement.

Answer (A) is incorrect. The oral evidence will be admissible as an exception to the rule. Answer (B) is incorrect. There is no common-law requirement that all terms in insurance contracts be in writing, but certain statutes may so provide. Answer (C) is incorrect. The oral evidence may be used to explain an ambiguous term regardless of whether all parties agree.

3. Ward is attempting to introduce oral evidence in an action relating to a written contract between Ward and Weaver. Weaver has pleaded the parol evidence rule. Ward will be prohibited from introducing parol evidence if it relates to

A. A modification made several days after the contract was executed.

B. A change in the meaning of an unambiguous provision in the contract.

C. Fraud in the inducement.

D. An obvious error in drafting.

Answer (B) is correct. *(CPA, adapted)*

REQUIRED: The circumstance in which oral evidence will be excluded.

DISCUSSION: The parol evidence rule applies to all prior or contemporaneous oral or written agreements that would tend to modify the terms of a written agreement intended to be complete. The purpose of the rule is to determine the limits of the contract. If the parties meant their written agreement to be entire, only terms incorporated directly or by reference are part of the contract as it existed at the time it was set forth in writing and signed. Thus, unless the parol evidence concerns a later modification or an ambiguity, a mistake, or lack of reality of assent (fraud, duress, etc.), it will be excluded.

Answer (A) is incorrect. Evidence of a subsequent modification is not excluded. The rule is intended only to protect the contract as it existed when it was made. Answer (C) is incorrect. Evidence of ambiguities, fraud, duress, obvious errors, etc., may be admitted. Answer (D) is incorrect. Evidence of ambiguities, fraud, duress, obvious errors, etc., may be admitted.

11.2 Conditions

4. A condition in a contract for the purchase of real property that makes the purchaser's obligation dependent upon obtaining a given dollar amount of conventional mortgage financing

A. Can be satisfied by the seller if the seller offers the buyer a demand loan for the amount.

B. Is a condition subsequent.

C. Is implied as a matter of law.

D. Requires the purchaser to use reasonable efforts to obtain the financing.

Answer (D) is correct. *(CPA, adapted)*

REQUIRED: The legal effect of a condition in a contract.

DISCUSSION: When the obligation of a contracting party is conditioned upon the occurrence of an event and (s)he has some power over the occurrence, the party is required to act in good faith to fulfill the condition. Acting in good faith includes using reasonable efforts to obtain the financing.

Answer (A) is incorrect. The condition calls for conventional mortgage financing, which involves repayment of the loan in installments over a substantial number of years. A demand loan is payable in full upon the creditor's demand and does not satisfy the condition. Answer (B) is incorrect. The condition is precedent. It must occur before the purchaser becomes bound. Answer (C) is incorrect. The condition must be expressed.

5. On July 25, Post Corp. engaged Bigg, a CPA, to audit Post's July 31 financial statements and to issue a report in time for the annual shareholders' meeting to be held on September 5. Notwithstanding Bigg's reasonable efforts, the report was not ready until September 7 because of delays by Post's staff. Post refused to accept or to pay for the report. In the event Bigg sues Post, what is the probable outcome?

A. The case would be dismissed because it is unethical for a CPA to sue for a fee.

B. Bigg will be entitled to recover in quasi-contract for the value of the services.

C. Bigg will not recover. The completion by September 5 was a condition precedent to recovery.

D. Bigg will recover because the delay by Post's staff prevented Bigg from performing on time.

Answer (D) is correct. *(CPA, adapted)*

REQUIRED: The probable outcome of a suit by a CPA for payment for services rendered.

DISCUSSION: Completion by September 5 was a condition precedent to Post's performance. Thus, Post was not required to perform (pay Bigg) unless the September 5 date was met. However, a contracting party is under an obligation not to prevent the other from performing. Post kept Bigg from meeting the September 5 date, and Post is liable to Bigg.

Answer (A) is incorrect. It is not unethical for a CPA to sue for a fee. Answer (B) is incorrect. Bigg is entitled to recover on the contract. Answer (C) is incorrect. Bigg will recover. Post's employees prevented performance by September 5.

6. Mary agrees to sell her home to Marisol for $100,000. The contract is silent regarding the time of payment and the time of delivery of the deed. Thus, payment or tender of the price is a condition of tender or delivery of the deed and vice versa. The conditions involved are

A. Implied in fact.

B. Implied in law.

C. Subsequent.

D. Express.

Answer (B) is correct. *(Publisher, adapted)*

REQUIRED: The classification of the conditions.

DISCUSSION: In these circumstances, the law will impose mutually dependent and concurrent conditions to reach an equitable result even though the actual language of the contract neither implies conditions nor states them expressly and even if the parties have not understood the conditions to be part of their agreement.

Answer (A) is incorrect. A condition implied in fact is part of the basis of the parties' bargain but not stated expressly. Such a condition is implied by the language of the contract. Answer (C) is incorrect. A condition subsequent is an event that terminates an existing contractual duty. Answer (D) is incorrect. An express condition is stated as part of the agreement.

11.3 Discharge

7. Oscar Orange owes Blue $1,000. Under the terms of their agreement, $1,000 is due at noon on January 27 at Blue's place of business. If Orange tenders $1,000 in cash at the agreed place

A. On January 28, he will be discharged if Blue refuses to accept.

B. At noon on January 27, he will be discharged if Blue refuses to accept.

C. At noon on January 27, and Blue refuses to accept, Orange remains liable for $1,000 but not for interest subsequently accrued.

D. At noon on January 27, Blue must accept the payment and apply it to the $1,000 debt even if Orange is indebted to Blue on another account.

Answer (C) is correct. *(Publisher, adapted)*

REQUIRED: The true statement about the consequences of tender.

DISCUSSION: Tender is an offer by a party to a contract to perform according to its terms. The party tendering must be ready, willing, and able to perform. If the other party refuses to accept the tender, the debt is not discharged, but any lien is extinguished, no more interest will accrue, and the tendering party will be relieved of court costs if sued on the debt.

Answer (A) is incorrect. Rejection of tender of late payment will not discharge the debt but prevents further accrual of interest and precludes court costs and damages in a later suit. Answer (B) is incorrect. The debt is not discharged. Answer (D) is incorrect. If the debtor has two or more accounts with the creditor and does not specify application of the tendered payment, the creditor may apply it as (s)he wishes.

8. Parc hired Glaze to remodel and furnish an office suite. Glaze submitted plans that Parc approved. After completing all the necessary construction and painting, Glaze purchased minor accessories that Parc rejected because they did not conform to the plans. Parc refused to allow Glaze to complete the project and refused to pay Glaze any part of the contract price. Glaze sued for the value of the work performed. Which of the following statements is true?

A. Glaze will lose because Glaze breached the contract by not completing performance.

B. Glaze will win because Glaze substantially performed and Parc prevented complete performance.

C. Glaze will lose because Glaze materially breached the contract by buying the accessories.

D. Glaze will win because Parc committed anticipatory breach.

Answer (B) is correct. *(CPA, adapted)*

REQUIRED: The effect of minor deviations from a substantially completed construction contract.

DISCUSSION: If performance is only marginally deficient and the obligor acts in good faith, (s)he has substantially performed and is entitled to receive damages or the contract price minus the cost of correction. If the cost of correction is excessive, the obligor (Glaze) is entitled to receive the contract price minus the diminished value. The doctrine does not apply when the substantially performing party has not acted in good faith. Some courts would nevertheless allow recovery, under quasi contract or quantum meruit theory, of the value of work and materials that substantially contributed value to the property.

Answer (A) is incorrect. Despite a technical immaterial breach, Glaze in good faith substantially performed the contract. Tender of complete performance was rejected by Parc. Answer (C) is incorrect. Purchase of the accessories may not have even been an immaterial breach. Parc was not denied the benefit of the bargain. Answer (D) is incorrect. The contract was substantially executed by Glaze. Anticipatory breach does not apply. Also, there was no unequivocal repudiation by Glaze.

9. On Monday, Harry Lime entered into a contract to sell some real estate to Holly Martins, borrowed $10,000 from Welles, agreed to teach a weekend seminar at the Vienna School of Business, and agreed to ship 100 textbooks to Alida College. Before he could perform under any of these agreements, Harry died. His estate has not satisfied any of these obligations. Harry's estate will prevail in an action brought by

A. Welles.

B. Vienna.

C. Holly.

D. Alida.

Answer (B) is correct. *(Publisher, adapted)*
REQUIRED: The party that will lose in an action against a promisor's estate for nonperformance.
DISCUSSION: Lime promised to teach a seminar for Vienna. Nonperformance of this contract is excused by impossibility because it called for the personal services of the promisor. Failure to perform duties that are delegable to others is not excused. The estate is able to convey the real estate to Holly, pay the money owed to Welles, and ship goods to Alida.

10. On May 25, Smith contracted with Jackson to repair Smith's cabin cruiser. The work was to begin on May 31. On May 26, the boat was destroyed by arson. Which of the following statements regarding the contract is true?

A. Smith is not liable to Jackson because of mutual mistake.

B. Smith is liable to Jackson for the profit Jackson would have made under the contract.

C. Jackson is not liable because performance is impossible.

D. Jackson is liable to repair another boat owned by Smith.

Answer (C) is correct. *(CPA, adapted)*
REQUIRED: The parties' liability when the subject matter of a contract is destroyed.
DISCUSSION: Nonperformance is excused when circumstances change so radically that performance is objectively impossible; i.e., nobody could perform the duty. Impossibility occurs when the subject matter of, or an item or commodity essential to, the contract is destroyed. The impossibility must arise after, and could not have been reasonably contemplated at, contract formation.
Answer (A) is incorrect. Mutual mistake is present at, not after, contract formation. It would apply if, unbeknownst to the parties, the boat was destroyed before formation. Answer (B) is incorrect. To the extent the doctrine of impossibility applies, performance by both parties is excused, and the contract is canceled. Answer (D) is incorrect. Under the doctrine of impossibility, duties are discharged, not substituted. But performance of a promise to supply a commodity is not impossible when an alternative supply is available.

11. In September, Cobb Company contracted with Thrifty Oil Company for the delivery of 100,000 gallons of heating oil at the price of $.75 per gallon at regular specified intervals during the forthcoming winter. Due to an unseasonably warm winter, Cobb took delivery on only 70,000 gallons. In a suit against Cobb for breach of contract, Thrifty will

A. Lose, because Cobb acted in good faith.

B. Lose, because both parties are merchants and the UCC recognizes commercial impracticability.

C. Win, because this is a requirements contract.

D. Win, because the change of circumstances could have been contemplated by the parties.

Answer (D) is correct. *(CPA, adapted)*
REQUIRED: The liability when a contract to purchase a commodity is partly performed due to reduced demand.
DISCUSSION: Performance was not conditioned on customer usage or demand. The doctrines of impossibility, impracticability, and frustration of purpose excuse performance only if a supervening circumstance was not reasonably contemplated or foreseeable when the contract was made. Unseasonably warm weather is not such a circumstance; it is an ordinary business risk.
Answer (A) is incorrect. Lack of good faith is a bar to certain legal defenses and remedies, but good faith is expected of parties in performing contractual promises. The reward is return performance, not excuse. Answer (B) is incorrect. Commercial impracticability excuses nonperformance only when the nonoccurrence of the contingency was a basic assumption on which the contract was made. Answer (C) is incorrect. The buyer agrees to purchase all the supplies needed in a requirements contract, not a stipulated quantity.

12. Axel rented from Lester a room overlooking the main thoroughfare of Coastal City. The purpose of the transaction, known to Lester, was to provide Axel with a view of a large parade that was a highlight of the holiday season. Unexpectedly, a late-season hurricane struck Coastal City, causing cancelation of the event. Axel refuses to pay the agreed rental. If Lester sues, who should prevail?

A. Lester, because the subject matter of the contract was not destroyed.

B. Lester, because the lease was commercially practicable.

C. Axel, because of frustration of purpose.

D. Axel, because the contract was impossible to perform.

Answer (C) is correct. *(Publisher, adapted)*

REQUIRED: The outcome of a suit on a contract when a supervening event prevented fulfillment of its purpose.

DISCUSSION: The frustration of purpose doctrine applies. Axel's principal purpose was substantially frustrated without his fault by the occurrence of an event the nonoccurrence of which was a basic assumption on which the contract was made. Because he did not assume the risk of cancelation, Axel is discharged.

Answer (A) is incorrect. Fulfillment of the purpose that both parties contemplated was impossible. Answer (B) is incorrect. Nothing indicates that Axel had a commercial interest in the rental. Answer (D) is incorrect. Renting the room was still possible.

13. Whether a breach is material is vital for determining the rights and duties of the parties to a contract. A breach is usually deemed not to be material and will not discharge the nonbreacher when the

A. Breach is intentional but minor.

B. Contract specifies that time is of the essence and performance is delayed.

C. Cost to correct the breach is substantial in relation to the contract price.

D. Injured party receives substantially all of the benefits reasonably anticipated.

Answer (D) is correct. *(Publisher, adapted)*

REQUIRED: The instance in which breach is not material.

DISCUSSION: Courts consider numerous factors to determine whether a breach is material: whether the nonbreaching party has received substantially all the benefits bargained for, whether money damages will adequately compensate for the breach, the quantitative measure of the breach, its timing, what the contract states to be material, whether the failure of performance was intentional, whether the breaching party acted in good faith, and the degree of unjust enrichment if the injured party is not required to perform.

Answer (A) is incorrect. Lack of good faith usually results in a holding of materiality. Answer (B) is incorrect. Within limits, the parties may specify what is material. Failure to perform promptly when time is of the essence will often deprive the other party of the contractual benefits bargained for. Answer (C) is incorrect. One indication of a material breach is that the cost to correct is substantial in relation to the contract price.

14. Which of the following actions if taken by one party to a contract generally will discharge the performance required of the other party to the contract?

A. Material breach of the contract.

B. Delay in performance.

C. Tender.

D. Assignment of rights.

Answer (A) is correct. *(Publisher, adapted)*

REQUIRED: The action that discharges the performance required of the other party.

DISCUSSION: A material breach is an unjustified failure to perform substantial obligations arising from promises in a contract, such that one party is deprived of what (s)he bargained for. A material breach discharges the nonbreaching party from any obligation to perform under the contract and entitles that party to seek damages or other appropriate relief as a remedy for the breach.

Answer (B) is incorrect. A delay in performance may not be material. A nonmaterial breach does not discharge the nonbreaching party but may be the basis of a suit for damages. Answer (C) is incorrect. One party's tender of performance, if repudiated, discharges the tendering party. Answer (D) is incorrect. Most contract rights are assignable. Hence, an assignment of rights does not ordinarily discharge another party's duty to perform.

15. Which of the following will release all original parties to a contract but will, in every instance, maintain a contractual relationship between the original parties?

	Novation	Substituted Contract
A.	Yes	Yes
B.	Yes	No
C.	No	Yes
D.	No	No

Answer (C) is correct. *(Publisher, adapted)*

REQUIRED: The contract(s), if any, that cancels performance but maintains a contractual relationship between the original parties in every instance.

DISCUSSION: The parties to a contract may discharge each other from performance without being in breach of contract. A substituted contract is a new contract agreed to by contracting parties in satisfaction of their duties under an original contract. The substituted contract discharges the original duties and imposes new duties between the same contracting parties. A novation may substitute a new party for an original party (either the promisor or promisee).

16. Keats Publishing Company shipped textbooks and other books for sale at retail to Campus Bookstore. An honest dispute arose over Campus's right to return certain books. Keats maintained that the books in question could not be returned and demanded payment of the full amount. Campus relied upon trade custom, which indicated that many publishers accepted the return of such books. Campus returned the books in question and paid for the balance with a check marked "Account Paid in Full to Date." Keats cashed the check. Which of the following is a true statement?

A. Keats is entitled to recover damages.

B. The cashing of the check constituted an accord and satisfaction.

C. The pre-existing legal duty rule applies, and Keats is entitled to full payment.

D. The custom of the industry argument would have no merit in a court of law.

Answer (B) is correct. *(CPA, adapted)*

REQUIRED: The true statement regarding a genuine dispute over the amount of a debt.

DISCUSSION: The cashing of the check marked "Account Paid in Full to Date" operated as an acceptance of an agreement to settle a genuine controversy. Each party's implied promise not to sue supplies the consideration needed to enforce the agreement. This substitution of performance is called an accord and satisfaction. If the amount of the debt is undisputed, however, an attempt to perform the duty of payment by the tender and acceptance of a lesser sum is invalid for lack of consideration.

Answer (A) is incorrect. Keats accepted the substituted performance by cashing the check. Answer (C) is incorrect. The amount of the debt (duty) was genuinely disputed. Answer (D) is incorrect. Trade custom would bear upon whether the dispute was genuine.

17. In 1971, Dart bought an office building from Graco under a written contract signed only by Dart. In 2003, Dart discovered that Graco made certain false representations during their negotiations concerning the building's foundation. Dart could have reasonably discovered the foundation problems by 1977. Dart sued Graco claiming fraud in the formation of the contract. Which of the following statements is true?

A. The parol evidence rule will prevent the admission into evidence of proof concerning Dart's allegations.

B. Dart will be able to rescind the contract because both parties did not sign it.

C. Dart must prove that the alleged misrepresentations were part of the written contract because the contract involved real estate.

D. The statute of limitations would likely prevent Dart from prevailing because of the length of time that has passed.

Answer (D) is correct. *(CPA, adapted)*

REQUIRED: The defense to a breach of contract claim based on misrepresentation.

DISCUSSION: Even if the misrepresentations were intentional, fraud would have resulted in a contract that was voidable rather than void and nonexistent. Statutes of limitations vary from state to state. The actionable period usually begins when a contract is breached, but not later than when the alleged breach could reasonably have been discovered. Although the period is sometimes longer for a claim based on fraud, it is improbable that it would exceed 26 years. A claim is barred when a statute of limitations period has expired even if the basis of the claim is otherwise sufficient.

Answer (A) is incorrect. Although the rule does not prevent admission of evidence of fraud, the claim is barred by the statute of limitations, even if there was fraud. Answer (B) is incorrect. Compliance with the statute of frauds requires the signature of the party charged with liability, not of both parties. Answer (C) is incorrect. Although the statute of frauds is not intended to be used as a shield for fraud, the claim (even if meritorious) is barred by the statute of limitations.

18. Mort owes $10,000 to O, $20,000 to P, $20,000 to Q, and $50,000 to R. He is insolvent and has net assets of $50,000. O, P, Q, and R have agreed with Mort and each other to accept proportionate distributions in full satisfaction of the claims. Which of the following is true?

A. The agreement is invalid for lack of consideration.

B. Once the creditors began negotiations, none could attach the debtor's assets.

C. If O were not a party to the agreement, (s)he would nevertheless be bound.

D. The agreement is a valid composition with creditors.

Answer (D) is correct. *(Publisher, adapted)*

REQUIRED: The true statement about an agreement among creditors to accept lesser sums.

DISCUSSION: A composition with creditors is a common-law contractual undertaking between the debtor and the creditors. The participating creditors agree to extend time for payment, take lesser sums in satisfaction of the debts owed, or accept some other plan of financial adjustment. Under general contract law, the original debts will not be discharged until the debtor has performed the new obligations.

Answer (A) is incorrect. The consideration for the promise of one creditor to accept less than the amount due is found in the similar promises of the other creditors. Answer (B) is incorrect. A disadvantage of a composition is that, prior to agreeing to the contract, the creditors may still seek to seize (attach) the debtor's property. Answer (C) is incorrect. A creditor who does not participate in the composition is not bound by it.

11.4 Remedies

19. Which of the following is a measure of compensatory damages likely to be applied in a majority of jurisdictions?

A. The seller of land breaches a contract. The buyer recovers the difference between the market price and the contract price.

B. The seller of textbooks contracts to deliver 100 books at $20 each. When the seller fails to deliver, buyer pays $25 each to another seller. Damages are $2,500.

C. A company agrees to construct a pool. Before work begins, the owner breaches. Damages equal the contract price.

D. A company agrees to construct a tennis court but abandons work when the project is one-third complete. The damages are the value of completed tennis courts.

Answer (A) is correct. *(Publisher, adapted)*

REQUIRED: The measure of compensatory damages recognized in a majority of states.

DISCUSSION: Compensatory damages for breach of a contract to sell land are usually measured as market price minus contract price regardless of whether the breaching party is the buyer or seller. This gives the injured party "the benefit of the bargain" by placing him/her in the position (s)he would have been in had the contract been performed.

Answer (B) is incorrect. Market price ($2,500) minus contract price ($2,000) is the usual measure of damages ($500) when the contract is for the sale of goods. Answer (C) is incorrect. When a construction contract is breached by the owner prior to the start of work, the measure of damages is usually the profit expected to be earned by the builder (contract price minus cost of construction). Answer (D) is incorrect. When the builder abandons the work before substantial completion, damages equal the cost to complete.

20. The Johnson Corporation sent its only pump to the manufacturer to be repaired. It engaged Travis, a local trucking company, to deliver the pump and to redeliver it to Johnson promptly upon completion of the repair. Travis did not know that Johnson's entire plant was inoperative without the pump. Travis delayed several days in returning the repaired pump. During the time it expected to be without the pump, Johnson incurred $5,000 in lost profits. At the end of that time, Johnson rented a replacement pump at $200 per day. What is Johnson entitled to recover from Travis?

A. The $200-a-day cost incurred in renting the pump.

B. The $200-a-day cost incurred in renting the pump plus the lost profits.

C. Actual damages plus punitive damages.

D. Nothing, because Travis is not liable for damages.

Answer (A) is correct. *(CPA, adapted)*

REQUIRED: The damages the plaintiff is entitled to recover because of the late delivery.

DISCUSSION: The failure of Travis to perform with reasonable promptness was a breach of contract for which Johnson could recover monetary damages. Johnson may recover its general damages, which were those likely and foreseeable as a result of the breach (the pump rental costs).

Answer (B) is incorrect. Special damages, those flowing from some unique aspect of the case, are recoverable only if the defendant knew or should have known at the time of contracting of the possibility of their incurrence. By not informing Travis that the plant would be inoperative without the pump, Johnson was precluded from recovering lost profits. Answer (C) is incorrect. Punitive damages are normally not granted in contracts cases. Answer (D) is incorrect. Travis is liable for general damages as a result of breaching the contract.

21. Master Mfg., Inc., contracted with Accur Computer Repair Corp. to maintain Master's computer system. Master's manufacturing process depends on its computer system operating properly at all times. A liquidated damages clause in the contract provided that Accur pay $1,000 to Master for each day that Accur was late responding to a service request. On January 12, Accur was notified that Master's computer system failed. Accur did not respond to Master's service request until January 15. If Master sues Accur under the liquidated damage provision of the contract, Master will

A. Win, unless the liquidated damage provision is determined to be a penalty.

B. Win, because liquidated damage provisions are never enforceable.

C. Lose, because Accur's breach was not material.

D. Lose, because liquidated damage provisions violate public policy.

Answer (A) is correct. *(CPA, adapted)*

REQUIRED: The effect of a liquidated damages clause.

DISCUSSION: The parties to a sales contract may stipulate an amount in the contract that the parties agree to be a reasonable estimate of the damages owing to one in the event of a breach by the other. To be enforceable, the liquidated damages amount must constitute a reasonable forecast of the damages likely to result from the breach. The amount must have a reasonable relationship to the loss expected to result from the breach. If the liquidated damages provision was motivated by a desire to deter a breach as opposed to a good faith effort to estimate probable damages, the provision will be deemed to be a penalty and will be declared void.

Answer (B) is incorrect. Liquidated damage provisions are enforceable only if they reasonably forecast the damages likely to result from a breach. Answer (C) is incorrect. Accur's delay was a material breach. Answer (D) is incorrect. Contracting parties are encouraged to fashion their own reasonable remedies. Public policy favors reasonable liquidated damages clauses.

22. The amount of monetary damages recoverable by the nonbreaching party when a contract is breached is determined by

	Forseeability of Damages	Mitigation of Damages
A.	Yes	Yes
B.	Yes	No
C.	No	Yes
D.	No	No

Answer (A) is correct. *(Publisher, adapted)*

REQUIRED: The factor(s), if any, determining monetary damages when a contract is breached.

DISCUSSION: The right to recover compensatory money damages for breach of contract is always available to the nonbreaching party. The purpose of compensatory damages is to place the injured party in as good a position as (s)he would have occupied had the contract been performed as agreed. Compensating damages also may include incidental damages arising directly out of the breach. However, contract law imposes the doctrines of forseeability of damages and mitigation of damages as limitations on recovery for breach of contract. The forseeability of damages requirement ensures that damages are recoverable only to the extent the party in breach knew, or should have known at the time the contract was formed, of special circumstances of the injured party beyond the contract likely to result in damages if the contract is breached. These damages are special or consequential and are in addition to compensatory damages. When a breach of contract occurs, the injured party is required to make reasonable efforts to mitigate or avoid the damages. An injured party may not recover for losses that (s)he could have avoided by ordinary means, for example, by obtaining substitute goods or services from another source at a reasonable price.

23. Which of the following is a true statement about the award of attorney's fees in a contracts case as an element of damages?

A. Attorney's fees are routinely awarded as court costs.

B. Attorney's fees provided for in the contract are treated as punitive damages and disallowed.

C. Attorney's fees are only awarded pursuant to express statutory authorization.

D. The general rule is that each party pays his/her own attorney's fees.

Answer (D) is correct. *(Publisher, adapted)*

REQUIRED: The true statement about payment of attorney's fees.

DISCUSSION: The parties to litigation are normally required to pay their own attorney's fees. Specific statutes sometimes provide an incentive for a private party to vindicate a right or enforce a duty by providing for an award of attorney's fees. Also, the parties to a contract, as a form of liquidated damages, may provide for payment of attorney's fees by the losing party. Finally, the powers of a court of equity include the ability to make such an award in appropriate circumstances.

Answer (A) is incorrect. Attorney's fees are not routinely treated the same as court costs. Answer (B) is incorrect. Attorney's fees may be provided for in a contract, but they are not treated as punitive. Answer (C) is incorrect. Attorney's fees may be authorized by contract or by court order.

24. K contracted to sell H a building for $310,000. The contract required H to pay the entire amount at closing. K refused to close the sale. H sued K. To what relief is H entitled?

A. Punitive damages and compensatory damages.

B. Specific performance and compensatory damages.

C. Consequential damages or punitive damages.

D. Compensatory damages or specific performance.

Answer (D) is correct. *(CPA, adapted)*

REQUIRED: The relief available for breach of a contract to sell realty.

DISCUSSION: The equitable remedy of specific performance is available only when damages are inadequate to remedy a breach of contract, usually when the subject matter is unique. Land is usually considered not interchangeable; it is unique. But a plaintiff may accept compensatory damages in lieu of specific performance.

Answer (A) is incorrect. Punitive damages are seldom awarded in contracts cases. Answer (B) is incorrect. The common law election of remedies doctrine requires the plaintiff to choose one of alternative remedies. However, remedies are cumulative under Article 2 of the UCC. Answer (C) is incorrect. Punitive damages are seldom awarded in contracts cases.

25. Which of the following is not a traditional remedy for breach of a contract?

A. Rescission and restitution.

B. Injunction.

C. Reformation.

D. Punitive damages.

Answer (D) is correct. *(Publisher, adapted)*

REQUIRED: The remedy not usually available for breach of a contract.

DISCUSSION: The purpose of damages and other contractual remedies is to place the parties in the same position as if the contract had been performed, not to punish a breaching party. Punitive damages are intended to punish especially wrongful conduct and deter future wrongs. Thus, they may be awarded in tort actions. When they are permitted in contracts cases, the facts often involve tortious behavior.

Answer (A) is incorrect. Rescission (the return of the parties to their position before entering into the contract) is a standard remedy for breach. Restitution is an equitable remedy whereby a court requires a benefited party to indemnify one who has rendered a performance even though no contract exists between them. Answer (B) is incorrect. An injunction (a court's order to do or not do some act) is a contract remedy. Answer (C) is incorrect. Reformation is an equitable remedy whereby a written agreement is rewritten by a court to reflect the actual agreement of the parties.

26. Which of the following remedies is available to a party who has entered into a contract in reliance upon the other contracting party's innocent misrepresentations as to material facts?

	Compensatory Damages	Punitive Damages	Rescission
A.	No	No	No
B.	Yes	No	Yes
C.	No	No	Yes
D.	Yes	Yes	No

Answer (C) is correct. *(CPA, adapted)*

REQUIRED: The relief available in an action for innocent misrepresentation.

DISCUSSION: Innocent misrepresentation is false representation of a material fact, intended to induce reliance, justifiably and detrimentally relied upon. It differs from fraud in that knowledge of the falsity or reckless disregard for truth is not present. The only remedy customarily available absent fraud is rescission: cancelation of the agreement and restoration of the parties to their positions prior to contracting. Compensatory damages are not available when misrepresentation is innocent, and punitive damages are seldom allowed in contracts cases.

Answer (A) is incorrect. Rescission is the usual remedy. Answer (B) is incorrect. Compensatory damages are not available when misrepresentation is innocent, punitive damages are seldom allowed in contracts cases, and rescission is an available remedy. Answer (D) is incorrect. Compensatory damages are not available when misrepresentation is innocent, punitive damages are seldom allowed in contracts cases, and rescission is an available remedy.

27. The Hathaways contracted with Stan Smith to build a house. Part way through the project, before even putting up the roof, Smith decided the contract was uneconomical and quit. Because Smith had spent a considerable amount of time on the job, he demanded payment. Which statement about the parties' rights and duties is true?

A. The breach is immaterial, so Smith is entitled to a proportionate part of the contract price.

B. If the breach is material, the Hathaways are discharged from any obligation under the contract.

C. If the contract is substantially performed, the Hathaways are liable for the full contract price.

D. Because he partly performed, Smith is entitled to the reasonable value of his services.

Answer (D) is correct. *(Publisher, adapted)*

REQUIRED: The rights and duties of the parties under a partially executed contract.

DISCUSSION: A party who breaches prior to substantial performance is usually not entitled to any remedies under the contract. This result assumes the other parties receive no benefit from the part performance. However, the courts tend to provide for the reasonable value of a person's services if (s)he has received nothing and the other party has benefited. This equitable remedy, called quasi-contract, is a setoff and does not relieve the breaching party from liability for damages for breach of contract.

Answer (A) is incorrect. The breach is material. It defeats the essential purposes of the contract. Answer (B) is incorrect. The Hathaways are not discharged from liability to Smith for the reasonable value of his services. Answer (C) is incorrect. If the contract is substantially performed, the Hathaways are liable for a proportionate amount of the contract, not the full contract price.

28. The remedy of quasi-contract is available

A. Although no contract was ever formed.

B. In addition to any contractual remedies.

C. Only when the specific benefit given can be recovered.

D. Regardless of whether unjust enrichment has occurred.

Answer (A) is correct. *(Publisher, adapted)*

REQUIRED: The true statement about the remedy of quasi-contract.

DISCUSSION: When one person has bestowed a benefit on another in circumstances such that failure to give a remedy would constitute unjust enrichment, a court may allow a recovery in quasi-contract although no contract was formed or attempted to be formed.

Answer (B) is incorrect. A remedy in quasi-contract is given instead of a contractual remedy. Answer (C) is incorrect. If the particular benefit provided can be specifically restored, it is recoverable in quasi-contract. Otherwise, the reasonable value of the benefit is the measure of the remedy. Answer (D) is incorrect. Unjust enrichment is the essence of the remedy.

29. Johnson and Harris entered into an agreement in which Johnson was to build a drainage canal for Harris. The contract contained a clause providing that either party's sole remedy under the contract was arbitration. If either Johnson or Harris breaches the contract, which is the effect of the arbitration clause?

A. Required arbitration is not enforceable because everyone is entitled to use the court system.

B. The clause is enforceable as the parties' sole remedy.

C. Any decision of an arbitrator must be reviewed by a court before the decision can be specifically enforced.

D. The clause is void as against public policy.

Answer (B) is correct. *(Publisher, adapted)*

REQUIRED: The effect of an arbitration clause in a contract.

DISCUSSION: A clause providing that arbitration is the parties' sole remedy in the event of breach is enforceable. The parties may agree to limit their remedies under contract if reasonable. Arbitration has become quite common, and the arbitrator's decision in a case is enforceable. The decision may, in limited circumstances, be judicially reviewed subject to the state arbitration statute.

Answer (A) is incorrect. Although everyone is entitled to use the court system, this right can be waived. Answer (C) is incorrect. The decision of the arbitrator is final although it is subject to review by a court. Answer (D) is incorrect. Arbitration clauses are encouraged to reduce the caseload of courts.

STUDY UNIT TWELVE
CONTRACTS: THIRD-PARTY RIGHTS AND DUTIES

To possess contractual rights, a person ordinarily must be a party to the contract. The parties are said to be in **privity of contract**. Requiring privity is consistent with the theory that contracts are binding only on those who intend to be bound. However, certain third parties may obtain legal rights to performance of a contract to which (s)he was not originally a party. They include intended third-party beneficiaries to whom contracting parties intended to give rights under the contract at the time of formation. They also include assignees to whom rights subsequently are transferred following formation of a contract.

The crucial inquiry in determining whether a third person is entitled to enforce a contract as a **third-party beneficiary** is whether the primary parties objectively intended to benefit the third person. An **intended beneficiary** is a party who can sue the promisor directly for breach of a contract made for the beneficiary's benefit, but enforcement is denied to one who is merely an incidental beneficiary. An **incidental beneficiary** is a person not intended to be benefited directly.

Intended third-party beneficiaries include creditor beneficiaries and donee beneficiaries. If a promisee's main purpose in making a contract is to discharge a debt (s)he owes to a third party, that party is a **creditor beneficiary**. In contrast, if a promisee's main purpose is to confer a benefit on a third party as a gift, that party is a **donee beneficiary**. The most common donee beneficiary contract is a life insurance policy. In a typical insurance contract, the designated beneficiary is a donee beneficiary. However, an insurance policy beneficiary may be a creditor beneficiary if the purpose of the policy is to pay a debt owed by the insured to the stated beneficiary.

A third party cannot enforce a contract against the **original parties** until his/her rights in the contract have **vested.** A third party's rights are deemed to vest when they are fixed, accrued, or absolute, not contingent. Until the rights vest, the original parties may modify or rescind the contract without the consent of the third party. State laws on vesting of third-party beneficiary rights vary substantially. Under the Restatement, vesting occurs when (1) the third party learns of the contract made for his/her benefit and changes position to his/her detriment in reliance, (2) the intended beneficiary commences an action against the promisor for any refusal or failure to perform or for defective performance of the contract, or (3) the intended beneficiary consents to receive performance of the promisor in response to a request by the promisor or promisee.

Whether a beneficiary may enforce the beneficial promise depends on the **enforceability of the contract** between the **promisor and the promisee**. The promisor may assert against the beneficiary any defense that the promisor could have asserted against the promisee if the promisee had sought to enforce the contract. Such **defenses** may consist of, but are not limited to, (1) fraud, (2) duress, (3) mistake, (4) absence of mutual assent, (5) incapacity, (6) lack of consideration, (7) illegality, and (8) violation of the statute of frauds. This rule emphasizes that a third party's rights are derivative, i.e., the same as the promisee's. However, the beneficiary's rights sometimes may be greater than the promisee's, for example, when an insurer seeks to avoid making payments for a loss caused by intentional wrongdoing of the promisor.

Third-party rights also may arise from an **assignment**. With few exceptions, a party to a contract may assign his/her rights. Contract rights are a form of property, and an important attribute of property is **transferability**. The party assigning contract rights is the **assignor**, and the person to whom the assignment is made is the **assignee**. The **obligor** is the person who has a duty to perform. The **obligee** is the person to whom the duty is owed. When rights under a contract are assigned unconditionally, the interest of the assignor is extinguished. Moreover, this assignment ordinarily can be made in any form. Any act or statement, written or oral, that indicates an intention to transfer a right is sufficient. However, the general statute of frauds provision of the UCC (Article 1-206) states that a contract for the sale of personal property is not enforceable beyond $5,000 without a writing. (But other rules apply to securities, security agreements, and sales of goods.) The law also permits a **partial assignment** under which an assignor transfers a clearly defined portion of the subject matter to an assignee and retains a portion for him/herself.

In some cases, contract rights cannot be assigned. Future rights under an existing contract are freely assignable in the present, but future rights in a not-yet-existing contract may not be assigned. Furthermore, contract rights may not be assigned if a statute or public policy forbids assignment or if the contract expressly states that it cannot be assigned. However, some contract prohibitions on assignment are not effective. Thus, a contract cannot prevent assignment of a right to receive money, and the assignment of negotiable instruments cannot be prohibited. Under the UCC, in a contract for the sale of goods, the right to receive damages for breach of contract or payment of an account owed may be assigned even if the contract prohibits assignment.

Among the rights that are not assignable are those that are highly personal, such as the right of a student to a scholarship or the right of a CPA to a position in his/her firm. Moreover, the right to receive **personal services** is not assignable. For example, the right to be represented by an attorney may not be assigned to another client. Another class of rights that may not be assigned consists of those that result in a material increase or alteration of the duties or risk of the obligor. For example, a person selling a building may not assign his/her rights under an insurance policy to the purchaser without the consent of the insurance company.

An assignment is effective between the assignor and the assignee without any notice to the obligor. However, until the obligor receives **notice** of the assignment, (s)he owes no duty to the assignee. Absent notice, payment or other performance that the obligor renders to the assignor discharges the original contract obligation to the extent of the payment or performance. The assignee cannot sue the obligor and force a repeat performance. His/her remedy is to bring suit against the assignor.

The assignee of a contract acquires all the **rights possessed by the assignor** and no more. A serious limitation of an assignment is that any claims and defenses that the obligor might have asserted against the assignor also can be asserted against the assignee in the event of an action for enforcement. Hence, the assignee "stands in the shoes" of the assignor.

An assignment is effective with or without consideration. When **made for consideration**, the assignment is **not revocable** by the assignor, and the assignor makes **implied warranties** to the assignee: (1) The right, as assigned, actually exists and is subject to no limitations or defenses against the assignor, except those stated or apparent; (2) any writing given or shown to the assignee as evidence of the right is genuine and is what it purports to be; and (3) the assignor will do nothing to affect or impair the value of the assignment, and (s)he has no knowledge of any fact that would do so. The assignor does not warrant that the obligor will fulfill his/her obligation.

Rights are assigned. Duties are delegated. No formalities are required for a valid **delegation of duties**. The delegator's expressed intention suffices. **Delegation** means that a person under a duty of performance (a **delegator** and **obligor**) authorizes another person (a **delegatee** who also becomes an **obligor** upon acceptance of the duty) to render the required performance. The delegatee's performance must be substantially similar to the performance by the delegator. Duties that may be delegated include the duty to (1) pay money, (2) manufacture ordinary goods, (3) build according to a set of plans and specifications, or (4) deliver standard merchandise. Duties may not be delegated if performance by the delegatee would (1) materially change the expectations of the obligee, (2) involve a special trust, or (3) involve personal judgment and skill.

The terms of a contract may restrict either party's right to delegate duties. These provisions are **strictly construed**. Of paramount importance is that a valid delegation of duties does not relieve the delegator of his/her obligations under the contract. When the delegatee gives a promise to the delegator that will directly benefit the obligee, that promise is a **third-party beneficiary contract** and renders the delegatee liable to the obligee. The general rule is that the obligee can sue both the delegatee and the delegator. For example, if Able contracts with Baker to construct a building and Able subsequently contracts to have Carr construct the building for Baker, a failure by Carr to do so would allow Baker to sue Able or Carr, or both.

QUESTIONS

12.1 Third-Party Beneficiaries

1. Graham contracted with the City of Harris to train and employ high school dropouts residing in Harris. Graham breached the contract. Long, a resident of Harris and a high school dropout, sued Graham for damages. Under the circumstances, Long will

A. Win, because Long is a third-party beneficiary entitled to enforce the contract.

B. Win, because the intent of the contract was to confer a benefit on all high school dropouts residing in Harris.

C. Lose, because Long is merely an incidental beneficiary of the contract.

D. Lose, because Harris did not assign its contract rights to Long.

Answer (C) is correct. *(CPA, adapted)*

REQUIRED: The rights of a third party when breach resulted in nonreceipt of the anticipated benefit.

DISCUSSION: Long was neither a party to the contract nor an assignee of rights under it. The right to enforce the contract is denied to Long, a mere incidental beneficiary. The contract was not intended primarily to benefit Long, but rather the city.

Answer (A) is incorrect. Long is not an intended beneficiary, i.e., one of the parties intended to benefit directly and personally from the contract. Answer (B) is incorrect. The primary intent of the contract was not to confer benefit on any particular person within the class, although one might incidentally receive personal benefit. Answer (D) is incorrect. Long would have standing to sue if he were a donee or creditor beneficiary.

2. Allied is indebted to Ferco. A contract between Bell and Allied provides that Bell is to purchase certain goods from Allied and pay the purchase price directly to Ferco until Allied's obligation is satisfied. Without justification, Bell failed to pay Ferco, and Ferco sued Bell. Ferco will

A. Not prevail, because Ferco lacked privity of contract with either Bell or Allied.

B. Not prevail, because Ferco did not give any consideration to Bell.

C. Prevail, because Ferco was an intended beneficiary of the contract between Allied and Bell.

D. Prevail, provided Ferco was aware of the contract between Bell and Allied at the time the contract was entered into.

Answer (C) is correct. *(CPA, adapted)*

REQUIRED: The rights of a creditor who is also a third party to, and a payee under, a contract with the debtor.

DISCUSSION: A creditor beneficiary has standing to enforce a contract to which (s)he is a third party. Given that the intent of the promisee (Allied) in entering into the contract with Bell was specifically to have return performance (payment) to discharge the debt to a third party (Ferco), the third party is a creditor beneficiary.

Answer (A) is incorrect. Ferco was an intended beneficiary of the contract. Answer (B) is incorrect. An intended beneficiary may enforce a contract enforceable between the parties. A prerequisite element of the contract was consideration, but not from Ferco. Answer (D) is incorrect. Creditor awareness is not sufficient. The parties to the contract must have intended direct benefit to the third party.

3. Egan contracted with Barton to buy Barton's business. The contract provided that Egan would pay the business debts Barton owed Ness and that the balance of the purchase price would be paid to Barton over a 10-year period. The contract also required Egan to take out a decreasing term life insurance policy naming Barton and Ness as beneficiaries to ensure that the amounts owed Barton and Ness would be paid if Egan died. Which of the following would describe Ness's status under the contract and insurance policy?

	Contract	Insurance Policy
A.	Donee beneficiary	Donee beneficiary
B.	Donee beneficiary	Creditor beneficiary
C.	Creditor beneficiary	Donee beneficiary
D.	Creditor beneficiary	Creditor beneficiary

Answer (D) is correct. *(CPA, adapted)*

REQUIRED: The status of a seller's creditor regarding the business sale contract and credit life insurance policy.

DISCUSSION: Ness is a beneficiary although a third party to both contracts. When the contracting parties entered into the sale contract (Egan and Barton) and the insurance contract (Egan and insurer), they specifically intended that the contracts directly benefit a third party by providing for discharge of debt to the third party. Ness is a creditor beneficiary of both contracts. Ness is not a donee beneficiary. The intended payment is not a gift.

4. Pete Fenwar purchased a used car from Zippy Auto Sales. Zippy provided a financing package that was to include liability insurance. Several days later, Fenwar, while driving the car, ran a red light and injured Myrtle. If Zippy failed to obtain the liability insurance, from whom can Myrtle recover?

A. Only Fenwar.

B. Only Zippy Auto Sales.

C. Only the finance company with which Zippy made financing arrangements.

D. Both Fenwar and Zippy.

Answer (D) is correct. *(Publisher, adapted)*

REQUIRED: The person(s) liable when a third party contracted to provide liability insurance for defendant.

DISCUSSION: Myrtle is an intended third-party beneficiary of the contract between Fenwar and Zippy. Although Myrtle was not specifically named or identified in the contract, she is a member of the class of persons who were to benefit from the liability insurance that Zippy promised. Thus, she can recover from Zippy for breach of contract. She can recover from Fenwar for the tort of negligence.

Answer (A) is incorrect. Zippy is liable for breach of contract. Answer (B) is incorrect. Fenwar is liable for his negligent act. Answer (C) is incorrect. The finance company made no contractual promises to obtain the insurance.

12.2 Assignment

5. One of the criteria for a valid assignment of a sales contract to a third party is that the assignment must

A. Not materially increase the other party's risk or duty.

B. Not be revocable by the assignor.

C. Be supported by adequate consideration from the assignee.

D. Be in writing and signed by the assignor.

Answer (A) is correct. *(CPA, adapted)*

REQUIRED: The general requisite to assignment.

DISCUSSION: Contracts are generally assignable but not if the other party's risk or duty would materially increase. Assignment is effective by any statement or other act indicating intent to presently transfer a right.

Answer (B) is incorrect. A gratuitous assignment is revocable unless an exception applies. Answer (C) is incorrect. Assignment can be effective absent consideration. Answer (D) is incorrect. Formality is not required for effective assignment. But if the statute of frauds otherwise applies, a writing is required.

6. Yost contracted with Egan for Yost to buy certain real property. If the contract is otherwise silent, Yost's rights under the contract are

A. Assignable only with Egan's consent.

B. Nonassignable because they are personal to Yost.

C. Nonassignable as a matter of law.

D. Generally assignable.

Answer (D) is correct. *(CPA, adapted)*

REQUIRED: The assignability of rights in a contract to buy real property.

DISCUSSION: Rights in a contract to buy real property, as in other contracts, are generally assignable. The other party's duties or risks must not be materially increased. When real property rights are transferred, the statute of frauds requires a writing.

Answer (A) is incorrect. Generally, unless the contract so requires, consent of a party is not required for assignment. Answer (B) is incorrect. If the contract involves unique personal services, assignment without consent will be ineffective. This contract does not involve unique personal services. Answer (C) is incorrect. No exception to the principle favoring assignability applies.

7. Which of the following is not subject to assignment?

A. Salary not yet earned.

B. A contract to sell specially manufactured goods.

C. Compensation from contracts not yet entered into.

D. A construction contract.

Answer (C) is correct. *(Publisher, adapted)*

REQUIRED: The improper subject matter for an assignment.

DISCUSSION: Although compensation is usually assignable, compensation from contracts that have not yet been entered into is not assignable. It is considered a mere expectancy; the assignor has no property right to assign until the contract is actually formed.

Answer (A) is incorrect. Wages and salary can be assigned even if not yet earned as long as the person is currently in a position to earn them. This kind of assignment is often restricted by statute. Answer (B) is incorrect. Contracts to sell goods are assignable whether or not the goods are specially manufactured. Answer (D) is incorrect. Construction contracts are commonly assignable; e.g., a general contractor usually assigns part of the contract to subcontractors.

8. Betty contracts to purchase 200 books from Ralph, a book collector, for $5,000. The contract provides that "this contract shall not be assigned." Subsequently, Ralph assigned to Alice his right to receive the $5,000 from the contract. Which of the following statements is true?

A. Ralph delegated his duty to deliver the books.

B. Ralph breached the contract.

C. Ralph has not breached the contract with Betty.

D. The assignment was void.

Answer (C) is correct. *(Publisher, adapted)*

REQUIRED: The legal effect of the covenant not to assign the contract.

DISCUSSION: Under the UCC, absent circumstances suggesting otherwise, a clause prohibiting the assignment of "the contract" will be construed as barring only the delegation of the assignor's duties.

Answer (A) is incorrect. Ralph did not breach the contract by assigning his right to receive payment. Answer (B) is incorrect. Ralph did not breach the contract by assigning his right to receive payment. Answer (D) is incorrect. The assignment of rights was effective.

9. Ordinarily, which of the following transfers will be valid without consent of the other parties?

A. Assignment by the lessee of a lease contract if rent is a percentage of sales.

B. Assignment by a purchaser of goods of the right to buy on credit without giving security.

C. Assignment by an architect of a contract to design a building.

D. Assignment by a patent holder of the right to receive royalties.

Answer (D) is correct. *(CPA, adapted)*

REQUIRED: The transfer valid without the consent of the other parties.

DISCUSSION: Unless agreed otherwise, most contract rights can be assigned. If exercising the rights calls for personal skill or judgment, they may not be assigned. Also, assignment that materially changes a duty, increases risk, or reduces opportunity for repeat performance is ineffective. Assignments may be against public policy, for example, a statutory prohibition of the assignment of future wages. Assignment of a right to receive money or goods, however, is usually valid. The right to receive royalties is therefore assignable.

Answer (A) is incorrect. The lessor's risk is materially changed. Answer (B) is incorrect. The assignee may not be as creditworthy as the assignor, and the seller's bad debt risk could increase. Answer (C) is incorrect. Personal service contracts generally cannot be assigned.

10. Alice sells Monica a mink coat for $1,000, due on July 4. Alice assigns the debt to Lola as a gift. On July 4, Monica tells Lola that because of financial reversals she cannot pay. Moreover, the fur has been lost in a fire. In this case, Lola has a legal right to collect $1,000 from

A. Monica.

B. Alice.

C. Either Monica or Alice.

D. Neither party.

Answer (A) is correct. *(J. Norwood)*

REQUIRED: The rights of the assignee against the debtor and the assignor.

DISCUSSION: If the debtor fails to pay the assignee, the assignee has rights against the debtor but no recourse against the assignor, unless the assignor guaranteed that the debt would be paid. Even though no consideration was given, Lola is the assignee and has a right to collect on the debt from Monica.

Answer (B) is incorrect. Lola has no rights against the assignor (Alice) in the absence of consideration and a guarantee that the debt would be paid. Answer (C) is incorrect. Lola has no rights against the assignor (Alice) in the absence of consideration and a guarantee that the debt would be paid. Answer (D) is incorrect. Lola does have rights against the debtor.

11. Seller delivers goods to Buyer who agrees to pay the $5,000 price in 60 days. Seller transfers its right to receive the price to Bank at a 10% discount. Which of the following is false?

A. Upon receipt of notice of the assignment, Buyer (the obligor) must pay Bank to discharge its obligations.

B. Seller (the assignor) has no right to make further assignments or collect payments for its own benefit.

C. Seller is obligated to pay the assignee in the event the obligor fails to pay, unless the assignment was specifically without recourse.

D. After notice of the assignment, Bank (the assignee) can sue Buyer directly if Buyer does not pay.

Answer (C) is correct. *(Publisher, adapted)*

REQUIRED: The false statement about the transfer of a contract right for consideration.

DISCUSSION: Most rights acquired by contract may be transferred by the owner (the assignor) to another person (the assignee). The assignee receives all the rights assigned but is subject to the defenses the obligor has against the assignor. An assignor who receives consideration impliedly warrants that the claim is genuine and that the assignor has not impaired and will not impair the value of the assignment, but not that the claim will be paid. Thus, if the obligor does not pay the assignee, there is no recourse against the assignor unless the assignment is agreed to be with recourse.

Answer (A) is incorrect. After notice and a reasonable opportunity to verify the assignment, the obligor must honor the assignment (by paying the assignee) or risk having to pay twice. Answer (B) is incorrect. An assignor who receives consideration impliedly warrants that (s)he will not impair the value of the assignment. Also, an assignor who receives payment after the assignment must account to the assignee. Answer (D) is incorrect. The assignee may enforce his/her rights against the debtor (the obligor) by direct action.

12. Quick Corp. has $270,000 of outstanding accounts receivable. On March 10, Quick assigned a $30,000 account receivable due from Pine, one of Quick's customers, to Taft Bank for value. On March 30, Pine paid Quick the $30,000. On April 5, Taft notified Pine of the March 10 assignment from Quick to Taft. Taft is entitled to collect $30,000 from

A. Either Quick or Pine.

B. Neither Quick nor Pine.

C. Pine only.

D. Quick only.

Answer (D) is correct. *(CPA, adapted)*

REQUIRED: The party liable on an assigned receivable paid prior to the assignee's notice to the debtor.

DISCUSSION: This contract was an assignment of the account receivable. The assignee (Taft) became the owner of the receivable (rather than a holder for security purposes) and was the only party entitled to payment. The debtor (Pine) was entitled to notice of the assignment so it would know whom to pay. Until given this notice, it was entitled to pay Quick and be relieved of the debt. Quick, the assignor, must account to the assignee. Quick holds the amount paid as trustee for Taft.

Answer (A) is incorrect. Only Quick is liable. Answer (B) is incorrect. The assignee may look to the assignor to account for the performance. Note that, if the assignment had been gratuitous, the assignor taking performance would have revoked the assignment. Answer (C) is incorrect. Given that the obligor (Pine) was without notice of the assignment, (s)he was discharged to the extent of performance rendered to the assignor.

13. Abe Walton owed $10,000 to Ted Grant. Grant assigned his claim against Walton to the Line Finance Company for value on October 15. On October 25, Al Hayes assigned his matured claim for $2,000 against Grant to Walton for value. On October 30, Line notified Walton of the assignment of the $10,000 debt owed by Walton to Grant. Line has demanded payment in full. Insofar as the rights of the various parties are concerned,

A. Walton has the right of a $2,000 setoff against the debt that he owed Grant.

B. Walton must pay Line in full but has the right to obtain a $2,000 reimbursement from Grant.

C. Line is a creditor beneficiary of the debt owed by Walton.

D. The claimed setoff of the Hayes claim for $2,000 is invalid because it is for an amount less than the principal debt.

Answer (A) is correct. *(CPA, adapted)*

REQUIRED: The rights of the parties when an assignor-creditor becomes a debtor of the original obligor.

DISCUSSION: Grant was the original creditor (obligee) of Walton. By assignment from Hayes, Walton became a creditor of Grant after Grant had assigned his claim against Walton to Line but before Walton was notified of the transfer. In the absence of the assignment to Line, Walton could have pleaded a $2,000 right of setoff against Grant as a result of the Hayes assignment. An assignee (Line) receives the assignor's (Grant's) rights subject to any defenses, rights of setoff, or counterclaims assertable by the obligor (Walton) against the assignor that arise prior to the receipt of notice of the assignment. Hence, Walton has a right of setoff against Line.

Answer (B) is incorrect. Walton owes only $8,000 to Line after the setoff. Answer (C) is incorrect. Walton and Grant presumably did not intend to benefit Line when they contracted. Line is only an assignee, not a beneficiary. Answer (D) is incorrect. A setoff is possible against all or part of the claim.

14. On May 2, Kurtz Co. assigned to City Bank for $65,000 its entire interest in a $70,000 account receivable due in 60 days from Long. On May 4, City notified Long of the assignment. On May 7, Long informed City that Kurtz had committed fraud in the transaction out of which the account receivable arose and that payment would not be made to City. If City commences an action against Long and Long is able to prove Kurtz acted fraudulently,

A. Long will be able to successfully assert fraud as a defense.

B. City will be entitled to collect $65,000, the amount paid for the assignment.

C. City will be entitled to collect $70,000 because fraud in the inducement is a personal defense that was lost on May 2.

D. City will be entitled to collect $70,000 because Long's allegation of fraud arose after notice of the assignment.

Answer (A) is correct. *(CPA, adapted)*

REQUIRED: The outcome if the debtor asserts a defense against the assignee that is effective against the assignor.

DISCUSSION: The assignee (City) has the same rights but is subject to the same defenses as the assignor (Kurtz) in an action against the debtor (Long). Accordingly, if the defense of fraud would be effective against Kurtz, it will also succeed against City. City's recourse is against Kurtz. Moreover, fraud in the inducement has the status of a personal defense only under the law of negotiable instruments. A personal defense is one that can be asserted between the original parties but not against a holder in due course of the instrument. The facts do not indicate that a negotiable instrument was transferred or that City was a holder in due course.

15. McDonald was entitled to insurance proceeds from an insurance company. McDonald assigned the contract right to Mohawk on July 1. In need of additional funds, McDonald also assigned this contract right to Niagara on July 15 and to Shapiro on August 1. Mohawk neglected to notify the insurance company, but Niagara sent a written notice of the assignment to the insurance company. Shapiro also sent the insurance company a written notice, which was lost after its receipt by the general manager. Which of the following has priority in the contract right?

A. Mohawk.

B. Niagara.

C. Shapiro.

D. McDonald.

Answer (A) is correct. *(Publisher, adapted)*

REQUIRED: The assignee with priority in a contract right that was the subject of successive assignments.

DISCUSSION: When contract rights are successively assigned to different assignees, the first assignee has priority (unless the assignment was made without consideration). Once the assignment has been made, the assignor has nothing left to assign. A minority rule provides that the first to give notice to the obligor (insurance company) has priority, but this is not the general rule.

Answer (B) is incorrect. Niagara was an assignee subsequent to Mohawk. Whether notice is given does not affect priority in most states. Answer (C) is incorrect. Shapiro was an assignee subsequent to Mohawk. Answer (D) is incorrect. The assignor has absolutely no rights to the insurance proceeds. An assignor who receives the assigned proceeds is treated as a trustee and must hold them for the assignee.

16. Stevens sells personal property to Baurer for $1,700 due in 30 days from the date of delivery. Stevens assigns the account to Adams without consideration. Which action precludes revocation by Stevens?

A. Death or bankruptcy of Stevens.

B. Subsequent assignment of the same rights by Stevens to George.

C. Notice to Adams by Stevens of revocation.

D. Assignment by Adams to Ansel for consideration.

Answer (D) is correct. *(Publisher, adapted)*

REQUIRED: The act precluding revocation of an assignment made without consideration.

DISCUSSION: Assignments need not be supported by consideration, but, as in other situations involving gratuitous promises or executory gifts, revocation is possible. An assignment without consideration is revoked by (1) operation of law upon the death, insanity, or bankruptcy of the assignor; (2) the subsequent assignment of the same rights by the assignor; or (3) notice of revocation given by the assignor to the assignee. If the assignee has collected from the obligor or made a further assignment for consideration, the revocation is not effective.

Answer (A) is incorrect. Death or bankruptcy revokes a gratuitous assignment. Answer (B) is incorrect. Subsequent assignment of the same rights revokes a gratuitous assignment. Answer (C) is incorrect. Notice to Adams by Stevens revokes a gratuitous assignment.

17. On February 1, Burns contracted in writing with Nagel to sell Nagel a used car. The contract provided that Burns was to deliver the car on February 15 and Nagel was to pay the $800 purchase price not later than March 15. On February 21, Burns assigned the contract to Ross for $600. Nagel was not notified of the assignment. Which of the following statements is true?

A. By making the assignment, Burns implicitly warranted that Nagel would pay the full purchase price.

B. The assignment to Ross is invalid because Nagel was not notified.

C. Ross will not be subject to any contract defenses Nagel could have raised against Burns.

D. By making the assignment, Burns implicitly warranted a lack of knowledge of any fact impairing the value of the assignment.

Answer (D) is correct. *(CPA, adapted)*

REQUIRED: The true statement concerning contract assignment.

DISCUSSION: When an assignment is made for value, the Restatement of Contracts states that the assignor makes three implied warranties to the assignee: (1) The assignor will do nothing to affect or impair the value of the assignment, and (s)he has no knowledge of any fact that would do so; (2) the right, as assigned, actually exists and is subject to no limitations or defenses good against the assignor, except those stated or apparent; and (3) any writing given or shown to the assignee as evidence of the right is genuine and is what it purports to be.

Answer (A) is incorrect. The assignor makes no implied warranty that the debtor is solvent or will pay. Answer (B) is incorrect. An assignment can be effective absent notice to the obligor (Nagel). Answer (C) is incorrect. Any defenses that the obligor might have asserted against the assignor can also be asserted against the assignee.

12.3 Delegation

18. On April 1, Neptune Fisheries contracted in writing with West Markets to deliver to West 3,000 pounds of lobsters at $4.00 a pound. Delivery of the lobsters was due May 1, with payment due June 1. On April 4, Neptune entered into a contract with Sea Farms, which provided: "Neptune Fisheries assigns all the rights under the contract with West Markets dated April 1 to Sea Farms." The April 4 contract was

A. Only an assignment of rights by Neptune.

B. Only a delegation of duties by Neptune.

C. An assignment of rights and a delegation of duties by Neptune.

D. An unenforceable third-party beneficiary contract.

Answer (C) is correct. *(CPA, adapted)*

REQUIRED: The legal effect of a general assignment.

DISCUSSION: The UCC, like the common law, recognizes that general language such as "I hereby assign my contract" effects both an assignment of the rights and a delegation of the duties.

Answer (A) is incorrect. Such general language also effects a delegation of the duties under the contract. Answer (B) is incorrect. The expressed intention is effective to assign the rights. Answer (D) is incorrect. The beneficiary is not a party to such a contract. One might have characterized Sea as an incidental beneficiary of the April 1, not the April 4, contract.

19. Wilcox Co. contracted with Ace Painters, Inc. for Ace to paint Wilcox's warehouse. Ace, without advising Wilcox, assigned the contract to Pure Painting Corp. Pure failed to paint Wilcox's warehouse in accordance with the contract specifications. The contract between Ace and Wilcox was silent with regard to a party's right to assign it. Which of the following statements is true?

A. Ace remained liable to Wilcox despite assigning the contract to Pure.

B. Ace would not be liable to Wilcox if Ace had notified Wilcox of the assignment.

C. Ace's duty to paint Wilcox's warehouse was nondelegable.

D. Ace's delegation of the duty to paint Wilcox's warehouse was a breach of the contract.

Answer (A) is correct. *(CPA, adapted)*

REQUIRED: The delegability of a contractual duty to paint a warehouse, and the liability after delegation.

DISCUSSION: A general indication of contract assignment effects assignment of rights and delegation of duties, unless an exception applies. Painting a warehouse generally is not so personal that performance by a delegatee in itself would materially change the expectations of the obligee. Because assignment was not prohibited, it was valid and not a breach. But the delegator remains liable on the contract to the obligee.

Answer (B) is incorrect. Notice of delegation to an obligee does not relieve the delegator of liability (unless the contract so provided). Answer (C) is incorrect. The contract did not prohibit delegation, and painting a warehouse is not a unique skill. Also, the duty did not involve special trust. Painting of a warehouse by a delegatee would normally be substantially similar to that of the delegator, such that material expectations of the obligee would not change by delegation. Answer (D) is incorrect. Delegation itself would constitute breach only if a valid contract term prohibited it.

20. A CPA was engaged by Jackson & Wilcox, a small retail partnership, to audit its financial statements. The CPA discovered that, because of other commitments, the engagement could not be completed on time. The CPA therefore unilaterally delegated the duty to Vincent, an equally competent CPA. Under these circumstances, which of the following is correct?

A. The duty to perform is delegable in that it is determined by an objective standard.

B. If Jackson & Wilcox refuses to accept Vincent because one of the partners personally dislikes Vincent, Jackson & Wilcox has breached the contract.

C. Jackson & Wilcox must accept the delegation if Vincent is equally competent.

D. The duty to perform the audit engagement is nondelegable, and Jackson & Wilcox need not accept Vincent as a substitute.

Answer (D) is correct. *(CPA, adapted)*

REQUIRED: The effect of the unilateral delegation by a CPA of the duty to audit financial statements.

DISCUSSION: Personal service contracts, or those involving confidential relationships, are not assignable or delegable. Performance by different auditors will not necessarily be substantially the same because of the delicate nature of the relationship and the professional judgments involved. Hence, Jackson & Wilcox need not accept Vincent as a substitute.

Answer (A) is incorrect. The duty to perform the audit engagement is nondelegable. An objective standard is difficult to establish for audits because professional judgment and confidentiality are very significant factors. Answer (B) is incorrect. Jackson & Wilcox has no duty to accept another CPA. The motives of the partners are irrelevant. Answer (C) is incorrect. The competence of the delegates is also irrelevant.

21. Charles Land offered to sell his business to Donald Bright. The assets consisted of real property, merchandise, office equipment, and the rights under certain contracts to purchase goods at an agreed price. In consideration for receipt of the aforementioned assets, Bright was to pay $125,000 and assume all business liabilities owed by Land. Bright accepted the offer, and a written contract was signed by both parties. Under the circumstances, the contract

A. Represents an assignment of all the business assets and rights Land owned and a delegation of whatever duties Land was obligated to perform.

B. Must be agreed to by all Land's creditors and the parties who had agreed to deliver goods to Land.

C. Frees Land from all liability to his creditors once the purchase is consummated.

D. Is too indefinite and uncertain to be enforced.

Answer (A) is correct. *(CPA, adapted)*

REQUIRED: The legal effect of a contract to sell a business.

DISCUSSION: The sale of an entire business necessarily involves the assignment of certain rights and the delegation of various duties. Bright will own the physical assets, be able to assert Land's rights under the purchase contract, and be responsible for liabilities and performance.

Answer (B) is incorrect. This assignment of rights and delegation of duties need not be agreed to by the creditors or suppliers. A debtor may delegate the simple duty to pay money and other nonpersonal duties, especially because (s)he remains liable unless a novation is made. Answer (C) is incorrect. Land remains liable to the creditors if Bright does not pay. Answer (D) is incorrect. The contract is sufficiently definite. The rights and liabilities can be precisely ascertained.

22. Omega Corp. owned a factory that was encumbered by a mortgage securing Omega's note to Eagle Bank. Omega sold the factory to Spear, Inc., which assumed the mortgage note. Later, Spear defaulted on the note, which had an outstanding balance of $15,000. To recover the outstanding balance, Eagle

A. May sue Spear only after suing Omega.

B. May sue either Spear or Omega.

C. Must sue both Spear and Omega.

D. Must sue Spear first and then proceed against Omega for any deficiency.

Answer (B) is correct. *(CPA, adapted)*

REQUIRED: The recourse against delegator and delegatee.

DISCUSSION: Delegation did not relieve Omega of its payment obligation under the note. The delegatee assumes the performance duty when (s)he receives consideration for the promise to perform that directly benefits the obligee. The obligee is a creditor beneficiary of the assumption contract. The obligee may sue for breach of either contract.

Answer (A) is incorrect. The right of the creditor beneficiary of the assumption contract to enforce it is not conditioned on first suing on the contract assumed. Answer (C) is incorrect. An obligee has no implied obligation to sue a delegatee as a condition to enforcing contract rights. Answer (D) is incorrect. An obligee has no implied obligation to sue a delegatee as a condition precedent to enforcing contract rights.

23. Baxter, Inc. and Globe entered into a contract. After receiving valuable consideration from Clay, Baxter assigned its rights under the contract to Clay. In which of the following circumstances would Baxter not be liable to Clay?

A. Clay released Globe.

B. Globe paid Baxter.

C. Baxter released Globe.

D. Baxter breached the contract.

Answer (A) is correct. *(CPA, adapted)*

REQUIRED: The assignor's liability to the assignee.

DISCUSSION: When Baxter unconditionally assigned its rights to Clay, Baxter no longer had rights in the contract. But Clay has rights, as assignee, against Baxter (1) if Baxter breaches the assignor's warranties (in that the rights were transferred for value) or (2) if Baxter accepts performance of the contract. But if Clay releases Globe from obligation to perform the contract, there is no basis for holding liable the assignor of the right to receive performance. Keep the parties straight.

Answer (B) is incorrect. If Globe, without notice of the assignment, paid the assignor, the assignee has recourse against the assignor. Answer (C) is incorrect. Baxter, by impairing the value of the assignment, would breach the assignor's implied warranty. Answer (D) is incorrect. Baxter would be liable for breach of the assignor's implied warranty if that breach would impair the value of the contract or subject it to defense.

STUDY UNIT THIRTEEN
SALE OF GOODS: THE SALES CONTRACT, INTERPRETATION, AND RISK OF LOSS

Contracts for the **sale of goods** are governed by common-law principles applicable to all contracts. Nevertheless, **Article 2 of the UCC** has modified many of these principles. Some of its rules were covered in previous Study Units. A **sale** is defined as "the passing of title from the seller to the buyer for a price." **Goods** are tangible things that are movable at the time of their identification to the contract. If a contract involves a combination of goods and services, courts decide whether Article 2 applies by determining which is the predominant factor. Two controversial issues of this kind have been resolved through legislation. The serving of food or drink by a merchant is a sale of goods, but a blood transfusion is deemed to be a sale of services.

Article 2 also may apply to goods associated with **real property**. For example, sales of minerals or the like or a structure or its materials to be removed from realty is subject to Article 2 if the seller is to sever the items. If the buyer is to sever the items, a contract for their sale is governed by real property law, not the UCC. However, growing crops, timber to be cut, and other things attached to realty that can be severed without material harm (but not minerals or the like or a structure or its materials) are treated as goods regardless of who severs them.

A **lease** of goods does not involve a transfer of title to the goods and is not regulated under Article 2. **Article 2A** of the UCC covers all leases and subleases of goods, but most of its provisions are the same as or similar to those in Article 2. Significant differences are noted in this discussion. Otherwise, the rules stated apply to both leases and sales of goods with minor changes in terminology (e.g., "sale" to "lease" or "seller" to "lessor"). A **lease** or sublease transfers the right to possession and use of goods for a term in exchange for consideration. A **lessee** acquires the right, and the **lessor** is the transferor of the right. Moreover, rules may vary for some leases, notably consumer and finance leases. A **consumer lease** is one that a lessor regularly engaged in the business of leasing or selling makes to an individual who takes for consumer purposes if the payments (excluding options) are less than an amount stipulated by statute. A consumer lessee may have additional rights, such as receipt of reasonable attorney's fees, if a court finds that the lease is unconscionable. A **finance lease** is a three-party arrangement (supplier, lessor, lessee) in which the lessor ordinarily is a financier and does not select, manufacture, or supply the goods. Under a finance lease (one that is not also a consumer lease), the lessee's promises become irrevocable and independent when the lessee accepts the goods (UCC 2A-407). Thus, the lessee has a duty to perform under a finance lease even if the lessor does not. Furthermore, a lessor-financier does not make implied warranties of merchantability or fitness for a particular purpose.

The relevant treaty for international sales is the **United Nations Convention on Contracts for the International Sale of Goods (CISG)**. Unlike Article 2, it does not apply to consumer transactions. However, its provisions are similar to those of Article 2.

Article 2 extends to the sale of goods between any buyer and any seller, but special rules govern sales contracts involving merchants. A **merchant** is someone who deals in the practices or goods involved in the transaction or otherwise holds him/herself out as having knowledge or skill peculiar to those goods or practices. A person may have the status of a merchant by employing an agent, broker, or other intermediary who is a merchant with respect to the goods. Thus, a person is a merchant when (s)he, acting in a mercantile capacity, possesses or uses an expertise specifically related to the goods being sold. Merchants are held to a higher standard than nonmerchants.

A sales contract is like any other contract in most respects. The elements of offer and acceptance (including mutuality of assent), consideration, competent parties, and legal purpose must be present. In addition, each contract for the sale of goods must be entered into and performed in **good faith**, and no contract or any part of a contract will be enforceable if it is found to be **unconscionable** (so one-sided as to indicate a lack of meaningful choice by one of the parties). But the common law and Article 2 have important differences. At common law, an offer is required to be definite and complete. Under the UCC, a contract for the sale of goods may be created in any manner sufficient to show agreement. Another important distinction is the **firm offer** rule. A written and signed offer by a merchant giving assurances that it will be held open is irrevocable for the stated period without consideration. If no period is stated, it is irrevocable for a reasonable time. In either case, the maximum period is 3 months. (Under the **CISG**, a firm offer may be oral. Also, an offer is deemed irrevocable if the offeree reasonably relies on it.) The firm offer rule eliminates the need for an option contract to keep an offer open. Still another distinction is that one or more **open terms** do not prevent contract formation if the parties have expressed their intent to contract and a reasonably certain basis for granting a remedy exists. However, if the **quantity term** is left open, a court has no reasonable basis to grant a remedy. Thus, a contract will not be formed. Exceptions are made for a **requirements** contract (an agreement by the seller to supply the requirements of the buyer) and an **output** contract (an agreement by the buyer to buy all of the seller's output). The amounts must not be unreasonably disproportionate to a stated estimate or to normal or comparable prior amounts. If the **price term** is not specified, it is a reasonable price at the time for delivery. (The **CISG** requires specification of price or a provision for its specification.) When the **payment terms** are not specified, payment is due at the time and place at which the buyer is to receive the goods. When the **delivery term** is not specified, the buyer normally takes delivery at the seller's place of business unless, at the time of contract formation, the parties know where the goods are located, presumably the place of delivery. If the **time for shipment or delivery** is not specified, it is a reasonable time.

Unless otherwise indicated, an offer invites **acceptance** in any manner and by any medium reasonable under the circumstances. If the offer indicates that a particular **medium of acceptance** must be used, only the indicated medium is authorized. Such a requirement must be unambiguously indicated to the offeree. If the offer does not require a particular manner or medium for acceptance, the UCC permits acceptance by either a **prompt promise to ship or a prompt or current shipment** of the goods to the buyer. (The **CISG** provides for contract formation when the offeror receives the acceptance, but the offer becomes irrevocable when the acceptance is sent. Also, unlike the UCC, acceptance by performance does not require notice within a reasonable time.) Furthermore, Article 2 abandons the rule requiring the acceptance to mirror the offer because contracts are routinely entered into using standardized business forms. Forms used by buyers and sellers are unlikely to match exactly. Thus, if the offeree's response to an offer indicates a definite acceptance, a contract is formed, even if the acceptance includes **additional or different terms**. Nevertheless, if the acceptance is **expressly conditional** upon different or additional terms, it is not an acceptance but a **counteroffer**.

The additional terms are treated as **proposals** for addition to the contract. **Between merchants**, the terms become part of the contract unless (1) they **materially alter** the contract, (2) the offer **expressly limited acceptance** to the terms of the offer, or (3) the **offeror timely objects** to the modified terms. Under common law, ambiguity or uncertainty results in no contract. Article 2 determines the intent of the parties. If the words or actions of the parties indicate an intent to form an agreement, Article 2 attempts to resolve disputes by forming a contract. The **CISG** treats most differences in terms as material alterations.

Consideration is required for contracts covered by Article 2, with two important exceptions: (1) agreement modifying contracts and (2) firm offers by merchants. Under Article 2, **contract modifications** need **no consideration** to be binding. However, if a written agreement signed by the parties excludes oral modifications, a contract may be modified only by written agreement. Moreover, any modification that brings the contract within some section of the UCC's **statute of frauds** must be in writing to be enforceable. A modification also may be in the form of a waiver. A **waiver** regarding an unperformed part of a contract may be **retracted** by reasonable notice received by the other party unless such retraction would be unjust in view of a material change in position in reliance on the waiver (UCC 2-209). Article 2A does not state whether a modified lease contract must comply with the statute. Also, under the UCC's **parol evidence rule**, the terms of any contract set forth in a writing intended by the parties to be a final expression of their agreement cannot be contradicted by evidence of any prior agreement or contemporaneous oral agreement. However, the UCC requires that the meaning of any agreement evidenced by the actions and language of the parties must be interpreted in accordance with (1) commercial practices and (2) such circumstances as (a) course of dealing, (b) usage of trade, and (c) course of performance.

Article 2's (2A's) **statute of frauds** provides that contracts for the sale (lease) of goods for a price of $500 ($1,000) or more are not enforceable absent a writing signed by the party to be held liable. Unlike common law, the UCC provides that all the essential terms of the contract need not be included in the writing if it is sufficient to indicate that a contract was made. But the contract will not be enforceable beyond the **quantity shown** in the writing. Furthermore, under Article 2 (but not 2A), **between merchants**, if one party, within a reasonable time after an oral agreement, sends a written confirmation that binds the sender, it also will bind the recipient barring an objection within 10 days of receipt. Article 2 also provides for additional exceptions when (1) the **goods are to be specially made** for the buyer (and are not suitable for sale in the ordinary course of business), and the seller has made either a substantial beginning in their manufacture or commitments for their purchase before a notice of repudiation is received from the buyer; (2) the goods are actually **received and accepted or payment has been made**; and (3) a party **admits in pleadings or in court** that a contract for the sale of goods exists. (The **CISG** has no statute of frauds.)

A sale of goods is the transfer of title from the seller to the buyer. At common law, **title** is a fundamental concept. Ordinarily, the **risk of loss** (the financial risk and responsibility for damage) depends on who has title, but the importance of title has been reduced under the UCC. Before any interests in specific goods can pass from the seller to the buyer, (1) the goods must be in existence, and (2) they must be identified to the contract. **Identification** means designating goods as the subject matter of the contract. Title to goods passes from the seller to the buyer in any manner and on any conditions explicitly agreed to by the parties. **Unless agreed otherwise**, title passes to the buyer at the time and place at which the seller satisfies its obligation to make a physical delivery of the goods (as determined under the contract and the UCC). If the contract requires or authorizes the seller to send the goods to the buyer but does **not require delivery at the destination**, title passes to the buyer at the time and place of **shipment**. If the contract requires **delivery at the destination**, title passes on tender of delivery there. If delivery is to be made **without moving the goods**, unless the parties explicitly agree otherwise, passage of title depends on whether **documents of title** are to be delivered. If the seller is to deliver a document of title, title passes at the time when and the place where (s)he delivers such documents. However, if the goods are already identified at the time of contracting, and no documents are to be delivered, title passes at the time and place of contracting. Moreover, a **rejection** or other refusal by the buyer to receive or retain the goods, whether or not justified, or a **justified revocation of acceptance** revests the title in the seller.

Parties to a sales contract use specific **shipping terms** to indicate whether a contract is a shipment or a destination contract. The most common shipping terms are FOB (free on board), FAS (free alongside), CIF (cost, insurance, freight), C&F (cost and freight), and delivery ex-ship.

Two fundamental principles related to transfer of property are retained by Article 2. A **thief has no title** and therefore cannot transfer title to a purchaser. However, if a seller has **voidable title**, (s)he has the power to transfer good title to a **good-faith purchaser for value**. Under Article 2A, a lessee receives whatever leasehold interest the lessor had the power to convey. A good faith purchaser (1) pays a valuable consideration, (2) has no notice or knowledge of a defect in the transferor's title, and (3) acts in good faith concerning the purchase. Thus, a voidable title becomes valid in the hands of a good-faith purchaser. Even if voidable title was obtained by (1) fraud punishable as larceny, (2) issuance of a bad check, (3) deceiving the transferor about the identity of the transferee, or (4) agreeing to a cash sale but not paying the price. Article 2 also provides that any **entrusting** of goods to a merchant who deals in goods of that kind gives the merchant the power to transfer all rights of the entruster to a **buyer in the ordinary course of business**. Such a person buys (1) in good faith, (2) without knowledge that the sale violates the interests of a third party in the goods, (3) in the ordinary course, and (4) from a person in the business of selling goods of that kind (but not a pawnbroker). Under Article 2A, a lessee-merchant (the entrustee) can transfer the lessor's rights to a buyer or sublessee in the ordinary course of business.

A buyer who has not yet acquired title to goods nevertheless has an **insurable interest** in identified goods. Moreover, the seller has an insurable interest in goods as long as title to, or any security interest in, the goods remains in the seller. Under Article 2A, a lessor has an insurable interest until an option to buy has been exercised and risk of loss has passed to the lessee.

When goods are lost, damaged, or destroyed without fault of either the seller or the buyer, one or the other must absorb the loss or collect from the person responsible for the damage. The parties to a sales contract may decide who is to bear the **risk of loss** or how it will be shared. Otherwise, the UCC assigns it to the party most likely to control and insure the goods or most able to prevent the loss. For example, in the absence of breach of contract, if the seller (lessor or, in a finance lease, the supplier) is a **merchant**, risk of loss passes to the buyer (lessee) only upon taking physical possession of the goods. If the seller (lessor or supplier) is a **nonmerchant**, risk of loss passes to the buyer (lessee) upon tender of delivery. In **destination contracts**, the risk of loss passes to the buyer when the goods have reached the destination and have been duly tendered to the buyer. In **shipment contracts**, the risk of loss passes to the buyer when the seller delivers the goods to the carrier for shipment. If goods are held by a warehouser or other bailee and are **not to be shipped or moved** as part of the contract, risk passes to the buyer upon (1) the buyer's receipt of a negotiable document of title covering the goods, (2) an acknowledgment by the bailee of the buyer's right to the goods, or (3) the lapse of a reasonable amount of time. In a lease, risk of loss passes on acknowledgment by the bailee of the lessee's rights. If goods are sufficiently defective for the buyer to have a **right to reject** them, the risk of loss does not pass to the buyer until the defects are cured or the buyer accepts the goods despite the defects. When a buyer rightfully **revokes acceptance**, the seller is deemed to have had the risk of loss from the inception of the contract in an amount equal to any deficiency in the buyer's insurance coverage. After a **seller has identified conforming goods** to the contract, the **buyer may repudiate or otherwise breach** the contract before the risk of loss has passed. In this case, any loss occurring within a commercially reasonable time after the seller learns of the breach falls on the buyer to the extent of any deficiency in the seller's **insurance coverage**.

Conditional sales include a sale on approval and a sale or return. In a **sale on approval**, the risk of loss does not pass from the seller until the buyer accepts. In a **sale or return**, the transaction is treated as an ordinary sale for purposes of risk. The buyer takes the goods to resell them but may return those that remain unsold. If the goods are returned, the buyer bears the risk of loss while they are in transit.

QUESTIONS

13.1 Sales: Fundamentals

1. The distinction between contracts that are covered by the UCC and those that are not is

A. Basically dependent upon whether the subject matter of the contract involves the purchase or sale of goods.

B. Based upon the dollar amount of the contract.

C. Dependent upon whether the statute of frauds is involved.

D. Of relatively little or no importance because the laws are invariably the same.

Answer (A) is correct. *(CPA, adapted)*

REQUIRED: The distinction between contracts covered by the UCC and those that are not.

DISCUSSION: The UCC covers contracts for the purchase or sale of goods (UCC 2-102), and Article 2 of the UCC governs most of these transactions. If a contract is not for the sale or purchase of goods, it is rarely covered by the UCC.

Answer (B) is incorrect. The application of the UCC is a function of the subject matter of the contract, not its dollar amount. Answer (C) is incorrect. The application of the UCC is a function of the subject matter of the contract, not its involvement with the statute of frauds. Answer (D) is incorrect. The distinction is of great importance. The UCC made substantial changes in prior legislation and the common law. Furthermore, the UCC allows buyers and sellers substantial, but not unlimited, freedom of contract to modify the UCC's general rules (UCC 1-102).

2. Which of the following is excluded from the UCC's definition of goods?

A. Minerals (including oil and gas) to be extracted by the seller.

B. Investment securities.

C. Growing crops and timber.

D. The unborn young of animals.

Answer (B) is correct. *(Publisher, adapted)*

REQUIRED: The items excluded from the definition of goods.

DISCUSSION: UCC 2-105 defines goods as all things (including specially manufactured goods) that are movable at the time of identification to the contract for sale other than the money in which the price is to be paid, investment securities (Article 8), and things in action.

Answer (A) is incorrect. Minerals are considered goods if they are to be extracted by the seller. Answer (C) is incorrect. Goods include growing crops and timber. Answer (D) is incorrect. Goods include the unborn young of animals.

3. Regarding the scope of Article 2 of the UCC, when a contract involves a mixed transaction, such as a sale of goods combined with the rendition of services, which of the following statements is true?

A. The courts ordinarily will apply Article 2 to any contract that involves goods.

B. The courts ordinarily will apply Article 2 when the contract's focus or predominant feature is the sale of goods.

C. The courts ordinarily will not apply Article 2 to any contract that involves the rendition of services.

D. Applicability of Article 2 depends on the dollar amount of the contract.

Answer (B) is correct. *(J. Pittman)*

REQUIRED: The coverage of a mixed goods and services contract by UCC Article 2.

DISCUSSION: Article 2 of the UCC applies to transactions in (sales of) goods (UCC 2-101). Sales of services are not covered. When the contract involves a mixed transaction, the courts ordinarily will apply Article 2 if the predominant feature of the contract as a whole is the sale of goods, with services incidentally involved. The issue arises, for example, when a hospital gives a blood transfusion or a beautician dyes the hair of a customer.

Answer (A) is incorrect. Article 2 does not apply to transactions intended to operate only as security transactions, bailments, or gifts. Answer (C) is incorrect. If a sale of goods is the major part of the contract, courts will apply Article 2 even though the contract also involves services. Answer (D) is incorrect. The applicability of Article 2 does not depend on the dollar amount of the contract.

4. Article 2A of the Uniform Commercial Code governs leases of goods, including consumer and finance leases. Under Article 2A,

A. A consumer lease is any lease to an individual who takes goods for consumer purposes.

B. In a finance lease, the lessor rather than the supplier impliedly warrants the merchantability of the goods.

C. In a consumer lease arrangement, the lessor ordinarily does not select, manufacture, or supply the goods.

D. The lessee's promises in a finance lease that is not a consumer lease must be performed even if the lessor breaches the contract.

Answer (D) is correct. *(Publisher, adapted)*

REQUIRED: The true statement about a lease of goods.

DISCUSSION: A finance lease is a three-party arrangement (supplier, lessor, lessee) in which the lessor ordinarily is a financier and does not select, manufacture, or supply the goods. Under a finance lease (one that is not also a consumer lease), the lessee's promises become irrevocable and independent when the lessee accepts the goods (UCC 2A-407). Thus, the lessee has a duty to perform under a finance lease even if the lessor does not.

Answer (A) is incorrect. In a consumer lease, a lessor regularly engaged in the business of leasing or selling leases goods to an individual who takes for personal, family, or household purposes. However, the payments (excluding options) must be less than the amount stipulated in the applicable statute. Answer (B) is incorrect. In a lease of goods, a lessor-financier does not make implied warranties of merchantability and fitness for a particular purpose. Hence, the lessee must rely on the supplier for warranty protection. Answer (C) is incorrect. The lessor ordinarily does not select, manufacture, or supply the goods in a finance lease arrangement.

5. I. M. Cruck sold refrigerators door to door. Cruck called on Ms. Kalik, a welfare recipient with four small children. Convinced by the sales talk, Kalik signed a form contract that clearly stated the terms of the agreement. After adding credit charges, insurance, and tax, the total price came to more than $1,200. The retail value of the appliance was $300. After paying $600, Ms. Kalik defaulted. Ms. Kalik then sued and prevailed on the theory of

A. Duress.

B. Unconscionability.

C. Fraud.

D. Misrepresentation.

Answer (B) is correct. *(Publisher, adapted)*

REQUIRED: The legal theory allowing a buyer to prevail when the price and value of a good are greatly disparate.

DISCUSSION: UCC 2-302 provides that a court may refuse to enforce an unconscionable contract, it may enforce the remainder without the offending clause, or it may limit the application of any such clause so as to avoid any unconscionable result. The term unconscionable is not defined, but the purpose of the section is to prevent oppression and unfair surprise and to avoid results shocking to the conscience. In a case with similar facts, the court reformed the agreement to set the price term equal to the amount already paid.

13.2 Formation of Sales Contracts

6. Patch, a frequent shopper at Soon-Shop Stores, received a rain check for an advertised sale item after Soon-Shop's supply of the product ran out. The rain check was in writing and stated that the item would be offered to the customer at the advertised sale price for an unspecified period of time. A Soon-Shop employee signed the rain check. When Patch returned to the store one month later to purchase the item, the store refused to honor the rain check. Under UCC Article 2, will Patch win a suit to enforce the rain check?

A. No, because one month is too long a period of time for a rain check to be effective.

B. No, because the rain check did not state the effective time period necessary to keep the offer open.

C. Yes, because Soon-Shop is required to have sufficient supplies of the sale item to satisfy all customers.

D. Yes, because the rain check met the requirements of a merchant's firm offer even though no effective time period was stated.

Answer (D) is correct. *(CPA, adapted)*

REQUIRED: The result of a suit under UCC Article 2 to enforce a rain check.

DISCUSSION: The rain check meets the requirements of the firm offer rule regardless of the lack of a stated time period. A firm offer is an assurance, in writing and signed by a merchant, that the offer will remain open. A firm offer remains open during the time stated, even if it is not supported by consideration. If no time is stated, the time is a reasonable time. But in no event may the period of irrevocability exceed 3 months. Soon-Shop (acting through its agent) is a merchant that signed a writing containing an undertaking to keep an offer open. One month appears to be a reasonable time. Consequently, Patch will win.

Answer (A) is incorrect. The rain check may be valid for up to 90 days. Answer (B) is incorrect. A stated effective time period is not necessary. Answer (C) is incorrect. Soon-Shop is not required to have sufficient supplies of sale items to satisfy all customers. However, to avoid violating FTC rules against bait-and-switch advertising, it should have a reasonable amount of the advertised item available for sale.

7. Under UCC Article 2, and unless otherwise agreed to, the seller's obligation to the buyer is to

A. Deliver the goods to the buyer's place of business.

B. Hold conforming goods and give the buyer whatever notification is reasonably necessary to enable the buyer to take delivery.

C. Deliver all goods called for in the contract to a common carrier.

D. Set aside conforming goods for inspection by the buyer before delivery.

Answer (B) is correct. *(CPA, adapted)*

REQUIRED: The seller's obligation to the buyer under the UCC.

DISCUSSION: Absent an agreement otherwise, the seller is not obligated to deliver the conforming goods to the buyer but merely needs to hold them for the buyer's disposition.

Answer (A) is incorrect. Absent an agreement otherwise, a seller has no duty to deliver the conforming goods to the buyer. Answer (C) is incorrect. Absent an agreement otherwise, a seller has no duty to deliver the conforming goods to a common carrier. Answer (D) is incorrect. Absent an agreement otherwise, a seller need not hold the conforming goods aside for inspection before delivery.

8. Doral, Inc., contacted Ace Lumber Company to acquire a 75-day option (firm offer) to buy the lumber it needed to expand its building. Doral supplied a form contract that included the option. Ace Lumber signed at the physical end of the contract but did not sign elsewhere. The price of lumber has risen drastically and Ace wants to avoid its obligation. Which of the following is best defense?

A. Such an option is invalid if its duration is for more than 2 months.

B. The option is not supported by any consideration on Doral's part.

C. Doral is not a merchant.

D. The promise of irrevocability was contained in a form supplied by Doral and was not separately signed by Ace.

Answer (D) is correct. *(CPA, adapted)*

REQUIRED: The best defense of a merchant to avoid being legally bound under a firm offer.

DISCUSSION: Under the firm offer rule of UCC 2-205, if a merchant in a signed writing states that an offer will be held open, the offer may not be revoked during the time stated even if no consideration was given to hold it open. If the offeree supplies the form, however, the firm offer must be separately signed. Ace's best defense is to assert that the firm offer rule does not apply because Ace did not separately sign the promise to hold the offer open. The purpose of this rule is to protect an offeror who is unaware that the offeree's form contains the firm offer term.

Answer (A) is incorrect. Such an option is valid for the time stated or, if no time is stated, for a reasonable time, but in no event for more than 3 months. Answer (B) is incorrect. A firm offer made by a merchant need not be supported by consideration. Answer (C) is incorrect. The firm offer rule requires only that the offeror (Ace) be a merchant.

9. A sheep rancher agreed, in writing, to sell all the wool shorn during the shearing season to a weaver. The contract failed to establish the price and a minimum quantity of wool. After the shearing season, the rancher refused to deliver the wool. The weaver sued the rancher for breach of contract. Under UCC Article 2, will the weaver win?

A. Yes, because this was an output contract.

B. Yes, even though both price and quantity terms were omitted.

C. No, because quantity cannot be omitted for a contract to be enforceable.

D. No, because the omission of price and quantity terms prevents the formation of a contract.

Answer (A) is correct. *(CPA, adapted)*

REQUIRED: The result of a suit under UCC Article 2 concerning an output contract.

DISCUSSION: An agreement by a buyer to purchase the entire output of a seller's product for a specified period, or an agreement by a seller to supply a buyer with all of the buyer's requirements of specified goods, is enforceable under both the UCC and the Restatement of Contracts. The courts apply an objective standard based upon good faith by both parties. A buyer cannot expand his/her operations extraordinarily and demand that the seller supply all of his/her requirements, and the seller's output cannot be unreasonably disproportionate to the normal previous output. Accordingly, the contract does not fail for lack of a quantity term. Furthermore, it does not fail for lack of a price term. The UCC permits a contract for the sale of goods to be made "in any manner sufficient to show agreement." Most terms of a sales contract may be implied, including price. Under the UCC, the price is a reasonable price at the time of delivery if nothing is said as to price. Thus, the weaver will prevail in a suit under UCC Article 2.

Answer (B) is incorrect. The weaver will prevail despite the omission of a price term or a specific quantity term. Answer (C) is incorrect. An output contract is enforceable under common law or the UCC. Moreover, in a contract for the sale of goods under the UCC, a price may be implied. Answer (D) is incorrect. An output contract is enforceable under common law or the UCC. Moreover, in a contract for the sale of goods under the UCC, a price may be implied.

10. Casassa, a merchant in San Francisco, under the terms of a nonshipment contract, agrees to sell 50 cases of packaged macaroni to Paoli, a restaurant owner whose business is in San Jose. At the time of contracting for the sale, both parties are aware that these identified goods are in a warehouse in Fresno. The place for delivery is not specified in the agreement. On the basis of these facts, the place for delivery is

A. San Francisco.

B. San Jose.

C. Fresno.

D. Indefinite, and the contract is unenforceable.

Answer (C) is correct. *(L. Fischl)*

REQUIRED: The place of delivery if the delivery term is omitted in a contract for the sale of goods.

DISCUSSION: A contract for the sale of goods may not expressly designate a place of delivery, and none may be provided by course of dealing, usage of trade, or course of performance. In this case, UCC 2-308 provides that the seller's place of business (if none, his/her residence) will be the place of delivery. However, if the goods are known to be located elsewhere (Fresno) than the seller's place of business, the other location is the place of delivery.

Answer (A) is incorrect. The seller's place of business is the proper place for delivery in the absence of a designation or unless the goods are known to be elsewhere. Answer (B) is incorrect. The seller's place of business is the proper place for delivery in the absence of a designation or unless the goods are known to be elsewhere. Answer (D) is incorrect. If the parties intended to contract and the basis for a remedy exists, the contract will not fail for indefiniteness even if some terms are left open (UCC 2-204).

11. Taylor signed and mailed a letter to Peel that stated: "Ship promptly 600 dozen grade A eggs." Taylor's offer

A. May be accepted only by a prompt shipment.

B. May be accepted by either a prompt promise to ship or prompt shipment.

C. Is invalid because the price term was omitted.

D. Is invalid because the shipping term was omitted.

Answer (B) is correct. *(CPA, adapted)*

REQUIRED: The true statement about the validity of acceptance of an offer to buy goods for prompt shipment.

DISCUSSION: Unless otherwise unambiguously indicated by the language or circumstances, an order to buy goods for prompt or current shipment invites acceptance either by a prompt promise to ship or by prompt shipment (UCC 2-206). Notice need not be given when prompt shipment is made. However, if acceptance is by preparation of the goods for later shipment, notice should be given to avoid lapse of the offer. But if the offer clearly requires shipment as the method of acceptance, a promise to ship is not a valid acceptance.

Answer (A) is incorrect. Acceptance may also be by a prompt promise to ship. Answer (C) is incorrect. "Even though one or more terms are left open, a contract for sale does not fail for indefiniteness if the parties have intended to make a contract and there is a reasonably certain basis for giving an appropriate remedy." Answer (D) is incorrect. "Even though one or more terms are left open, a contract for sale does not fail for indefiniteness if the parties have intended to make a contract and there is a reasonably certain basis for giving an appropriate remedy."

12. Cookie Co. offered to sell Distrib Markets 20,000 pounds of cookies at $1.00 per pound, subject to certain specified terms for delivery. Distrib replied in writing as follows:

> "We accept your offer for 20,000 pounds of cookies at $1.00 per pound, weighing scale to have valid city certificate."

Under the UCC,

A. A contract was formed between the parties.

B. A contract will be formed only if Cookie agrees to the weighing scale requirement.

C. No contract was formed because Distrib included the weighing scale requirement in its reply.

D. No contract was formed because Distrib's reply was a counteroffer.

Answer (A) is correct. *(CPA, adapted)*

REQUIRED: The effect of a merchant's adding a term in an unconditional acceptance.

DISCUSSION: Additional or different terms in an unconditional, definite, and seasonable acceptance of an offer for a sale of goods are construed as proposals for addition to the contract. But, between merchants, such terms become part of the contract unless (1) the offer expressly limits acceptance to its terms, (2) the additional or different terms materially alter the offer, or (3) the offeree objects within a reasonable time (UCC 2-207). Hence, the weighing scale term becomes part of the agreement unless objected to in a reasonable time.

Answer (B) is incorrect. An additional term in an unconditional acceptance of an offer for a sale of goods does not constitute a rejection and counteroffer. Thus, a contract was formed regardless of whether either of the parties is a merchant. Answer (C) is incorrect. An additional term in an unconditional acceptance of an offer for a sale of goods does not constitute a rejection and counteroffer. Thus, a contract was formed regardless of whether either of the parties is a merchant. Answer (D) is incorrect. An additional term in an unconditional acceptance of an offer for a sale of goods does not constitute a rejection and counteroffer. Thus, a contract was formed regardless of whether either of the parties is a merchant.

13. Which of the following statements is true with regard to an auction of goods?

A. The auctioneer may withdraw the goods at any time prior to completion of the sale unless the goods are put up without reserve.

B. A bidder may retract a bid before the completion of the sale only if the auction is without reserve.

C. A bidder's retraction of a bid will revive the prior bid if the sale is with reserve.

D. In a sale with reserve, a bid made while the hammer is falling automatically reopens the bidding.

Answer (A) is correct. *(CPA, adapted)*

REQUIRED: The true statement about an auction of goods.

DISCUSSION: An auction is with reserve unless the goods are explicitly offered without reserve. When goods are auctioned with reserve, the auctioneer may withdraw them at any time before (s)he announces completion of the sale. In an auction without reserve, the goods may not be withdrawn after the auctioneer calls for bids unless no bid is made (UCC 2-328).

Answer (B) is incorrect. Whether the sale is with or without reserve, a bid is an offer and may be retracted until the auctioneer announces acceptance and completion of the sale. However, a retraction does not revive any previous bid. The bidding would start over. Answer (C) is incorrect. Whether the sale is with or without reserve, a bid is an offer and may be retracted until the auctioneer announces acceptance and completion of the sale. However, a retraction does not revive any previous bid. The bidding would start over. Answer (D) is incorrect. When a bid is made while the hammer is falling (the act of acceptance), the auctioneer may reopen the bidding or declare the goods sold under the bid on which the hammer was falling.

13.3 Modification, Interpretation, and the Statute of Frauds

14. An oral agreement concerning the sale of goods entered into without consideration is binding if the agreement

A. Is a firm offer made by a merchant who promises to hold the offer open for 30 days.

B. Is a waiver of the nonbreaching party's rights arising out of a breach of the contract.

C. Contradicts the terms of a subsequent written contract that is intended as the complete and exclusive agreement of the parties.

D. Modifies the price in an existing, enforceable contract from $525 to $475.

Answer (D) is correct. *(CPA, adapted)*

REQUIRED: The circumstance in which an oral modification is binding.

DISCUSSION: An oral modification of a contract for the sale of goods does not require consideration to be binding. But the UCC's statute of frauds section (UCC 2-201) must be satisfied if the contract "as modified" is within its provisions (UCC 2-209). Because the contract as modified is for less than $500, UCC 2-201 is inapplicable, no writing is required, and the oral agreement is enforceable.

Answer (A) is incorrect. A firm offer must be contained in a signed writing (UCC 2-205). Answer (B) is incorrect. A waiver may be retracted by reasonable notice received by the other party unless such retraction would be unjust in view of a material change in position in reliance on the waiver (UCC 2-209). Answer (C) is incorrect. The parol evidence rule would exclude proof of a prior oral agreement that would modify the terms of a written agreement meant to be entire.

15. Filmore purchased a TV set from Allison Appliances, an authorized dealer, for $499. The written contract contained the usual 1-year warranty as to parts and labor as long as the set was returned to the manufacturer or one of its authorized dealers. The contract also contained an effective disclaimer of any express warranty protection, other than that included in the contract. It further provided that the contract represented the entire agreement and understanding of the parties. Filmore claims that during the bargaining process Surry, Allison's agent, orally promised to service the set at Filmore's residence if anything went wrong within the year. Which of the following would be Allison's best defense?

A. The statute of frauds.

B. The parol evidence rule.

C. All warranty protection was disclaimed other than the express warranty contained in the contract.

D. Surry, Allison's agent, did not have express authority to make such a promise.

Answer (B) is correct. *(CPA, adapted)*

REQUIRED: The best defense to liability on an oral agreement made during negotiations.

DISCUSSION: The writing stated that it was the entire agreement of the parties (an integration). "A writing intended by the parties as the final expression of their agreement with respect to such terms as are included therein may not be contradicted by evidence of any prior agreement or of a contemporaneous oral agreement" (UCC 2-202). Here, the contemporaneous oral agreement contradicted the term providing for servicing of the set upon return to the manufacturer or authorized dealer. Hence, the parol evidence rule is the seller's best defense.

Answer (A) is incorrect. The price is less than $500, so the contract is not within the statute of frauds. Answer (C) is incorrect. Under UCC 2-316, words or conduct granting and negating an express warranty are construed whenever reasonable as consistent with each other. However, negation is inoperative to the extent such construction is unreasonable. Surry's oral express warranty was in conflict with the words of the written contract, and UCC 2-316 would negate the disclaimer. But UCC 2-316 is subject to the parol evidence rule. Answer (D) is incorrect. Surry presumably had at least apparent authority.

16. The UCC provides rules of construction that allow unclear contracts to be read in the context of commercial practices and other surrounding circumstances. When the application of these rules results in a conflict, what hierarchy does the UCC establish with regard to the following?

1. Course of performance
2. Course of dealing
3. Usage of trade
4. Express terms

A. 3, 4, 2, 1

B. 4, 2, 3, 1

C. 4, 1, 2, 3

D. 2, 4, 1, 3

Answer (C) is correct. *(Publisher, adapted)*

REQUIRED: The order of priority among rules of construction.

DISCUSSION: Course of performance refers to the repeated prior occasions for performance of the same contract. Course of dealing is a sequence of previous conduct between the parties. Usage of trade is any practice or method of dealing having such regularity of observance in a place, vocation, or trade as to justify an expectation that it will be observed with respect to the transaction in question (UCC 1-205). Express terms control the contract. But when not clear, course of performance or dealing and usage of trade may be used to explain the terms of an agreement and will be interpreted as consistent with each other whenever possible. If not consistent with each other, the hierarchy of 4,1,2,3 controls.

Answer (A) is incorrect. Express terms control. Answer (B) is incorrect. Course of performance and course of dealing have priority over usage of trade. Answer (D) is incorrect. Express terms control.

17. To satisfy the UCC statute of frauds, a written agreement for the sale of goods must

A. Contain payment terms.

B. Be signed by both buyer and seller.

C. Be sufficient to show that a contract for sale has been made.

D. Refer to the time and place of delivery.

Answer (C) is correct. *(CPA, adapted)*

REQUIRED: The element necessary for a writing to satisfy the UCC statute of frauds.

DISCUSSION: A writing must be sufficient to indicate that a contract for sale has been made between the parties and signed by the party sought to be bound or his/her authorized agent or broker. A writing is not insufficient because it omits or misstates a term agreed upon, but it will not be enforceable beyond the quantity of goods shown (UCC 2-201).

Answer (A) is incorrect. A writing in which some terms are omitted may be sufficient if a contract is intended and a reasonable basis for establishing a remedy exists. In these circumstances, the UCC supplies most missing terms. Answer (B) is incorrect. The writing need be signed only by the party against whom enforcement is sought. Answer (D) is incorrect. A writing in which some terms are omitted may be sufficient if a contract is intended and a reasonable basis for establishing a remedy exists. In these circumstances, the UCC supplies most missing terms.

18. Mayker, Inc., and Oylco contracted for Oylco to be the exclusive provider of Mayker's fuel oil for 3 months. The stated price was subject to increases of up to a total of 10% if the market price increased. The market price rose 25% and Mayker tripled its normal order. Oylco seeks to avoid performance. Oylco's best argument in support of its position is that

A. There was no meeting of the minds.

B. The contract was unconscionable.

C. The quantity was not definite and certain enough.

D. Mayker ordered amounts of oil unreasonably greater than its normal requirements.

Answer (D) is correct. *(CPA, adapted)*

REQUIRED: The best argument for avoiding performance on a requirements contract.

DISCUSSION: Requirements and output contracts are enforceable under UCC 2-306 provided that the parties act in good faith and demand or tender reasonable quantities. Absent stated estimates, normal or otherwise comparable prior requirements or output will provide the standard of reasonableness. No estimates were made, so if Mayker orders excessive amounts, it will have violated its duties, and Oylco may be able to avoid performance.

Answer (A) is incorrect. Under the UCC, an agreement that one party will supply the other's requirements for a specified period within a given price range suggests a meeting of the minds (formation of a contract). Hence, Oylco's best argument is breach, not failure to reach an agreement. Answer (B) is incorrect. The difference between 10% and 25% above contract price is not so oppressive and unfair as to render the contract unconscionable. Answer (C) is incorrect. The contract does not fail for indefiniteness, given that the parties must act in good faith and demand or tender reasonable quantities.

19. EG Door Co., a manufacturer of custom exterior doors, verbally contracted with Art Contractors to design and build a $2,000 custom door for a house that Art was restoring. After EG had completed substantial work on the door, Art advised EG that the house had been destroyed by fire and Art was canceling the contract. EG finished the door and shipped it to Art. Art refused to accept delivery. Art contends that the contract cannot be enforced because it violated the statute of frauds by not being in writing. Under UCC Article 2, is Art's contention correct?

A. Yes, because the contract was not in writing.

B. Yes, because the contract cannot be fully performed due to the fire.

C. No, because the goods were specially manufactured for Art and cannot be resold in EG's regular course of business.

D. No, because the cancelation of the contract was not made in writing.

Answer (C) is correct. *(CPA, adapted)*

REQUIRED: The situation in which a contract for the sale of goods for $500 or more is enforceable without a writing.

DISCUSSION: Most contracts for the sale of goods for $500 or more are unenforceable unless evidenced by a writing. It should (1) indicate that a contract has been made, (2) specify the quantity of goods, and (3) be signed by the party to be held liable. However, an oral contract is enforceable when, for example, (1) the goods are to be specially made for the buyer, (2) they are not suitable for sale to others in the ordinary course of the seller's business, and (3) the seller has made a substantial beginning of their manufacture or commitments for their procurement before a notice of repudiation is received from the buyer.

Answer (A) is incorrect. The verbal agreement for the special manufacture of goods is an exception to the statute of frauds. Answer (B) is incorrect. Courts do not excuse a contract party from performance on the basis of commercial impracticability unless the circumstance is beyond the reasonable expectation of both parties. The fire was not an unforeseeable occurrence when the contract was made. Answer (D) is incorrect. The statute of frauds does not require the cancelation of a contract to be in writing.

13.4 Passage of Title

20. Assume that the parties have entered into a contract for the sale of goods. Which of the following is a false statement under the UCC?

A. Retention of title by the seller to goods delivered to the buyer is, in effect, a reservation of a security interest.

B. Title to goods may pass under a contract for sale prior to identification to the contract.

C. Title can pass to the buyer when the seller completes physical delivery of the goods if a document of title is to be delivered at a different time or place.

D. Identification of the goods to the contract gives the buyer an insurable interest in the goods even before delivery.

Answer (B) is correct. *(Publisher, adapted)*

REQUIRED: The false statement under the UCC.

DISCUSSION: Traditionally, risk is assigned to the party holding title. However, under the UCC, risk of loss is not assigned on the basis of title. Under UCC 2-401, the earliest time title may pass is when the goods have been identified to the contract. Subject to this limitation, title passes when the contracting parties intend. Absent an expression of their intent, it passes in accordance with UCC rules.

Answer (A) is incorrect. The seller is essentially treated as a secured party if a sale of goods has taken place and the title has been reserved by the seller. Answer (C) is incorrect. It correctly describes when title passes if the goods must be physically moved. Answer (D) is incorrect. Identification does give the buyer a special property interest that also results in an insurable interest. If the seller becomes insolvent, under some circumstances the buyer may be able to recover the goods.

21. Pulse Corp. maintained a warehouse where it stored its manufactured goods. Pulse received an order from Star. Shortly after Pulse identified the goods to be shipped to Star, but before moving them to the loading dock, a fire destroyed the warehouse and its contents. With respect to the goods, which of the following statements is true?

A. Pulse has title but no insurable interest.

B. Star has title and an insurable interest.

C. Pulse has title and an insurable interest.

D. Star has title but no insurable interest.

Answer (C) is correct. *(CPA, adapted)*

REQUIRED: The true statement about title to and an insurable interest in goods.

DISCUSSION: Unless otherwise explicitly agreed to, title passes to the buyer at the time and place at which the seller completes performance of physical delivery of the goods. The seller has an insurable interest in goods as long as title to, or any security interest in, the goods remains with the seller. A buyer of goods has an insurable interest in them when they are identified to the contract.

Answer (A) is incorrect. The seller has an insurable interest when it has title to the goods. Answer (B) is incorrect. The buyer has no title. The seller has not completed physical delivery. Answer (D) is incorrect. The buyer has an insurable interest. The goods have been identified to the contract.

22. Which of the following is a true statement concerning a contract for the sale of goods which contains no express provision on passage of title?

A. If delivery is to be made without moving the goods and the seller is to deliver a document of title, title passes at the time and the place the parties entered into their contract.

B. If delivery is to be made without moving goods that are already identified to the contract and no documents are to be delivered, title will pass when the buyer takes physical possession.

C. Reservation of a security interest by the seller is a retention of title.

D. If the contract requires the seller to deliver the goods at a named destination, title will pass to the buyer on tender there.

Answer (D) is correct. *(Publisher, adapted)*

REQUIRED: The true statement concerning passage of title under the UCC.

DISCUSSION: Most provisions of the UCC apply regardless of title. For some purposes, however, (e.g., the probate of an estate, assessment of taxes, or certain accounting purposes) it is still necessary to determine who has title. Passage-of-title rules depend upon whether the goods are to be moved, where delivery is to be made, and whether documents of title are to be exchanged. If the contract requires the seller to ship the goods to a given destination, title is considered to pass upon tender to the buyer at that point (UCC 2-401).

Answer (A) is incorrect. If the goods are not to be moved and the seller is to deliver a document of title, title passes upon delivery of the document. Answer (B) is incorrect. If the goods are not to be moved, they are already identified to the contract, and no documents are to be delivered, then title passes at the time and place of contracting. Answer (C) is incorrect. The UCC treats even an express retention of title as being no more than a reservation of a security interest if the goods have been delivered to the buyer.

23. On May 2, Lace Corp., an apparel wholesaler, offered to sell clothing worth $3,000 to Parco, Inc., a clothing retailer. The offer was signed by Lace's president and provided that it would not be withdrawn before June 1. It also included the shipping terms: "FOB -- Parco's warehouse." Parco accepted Lace's offer. If Lace inadvertently ships the wrong apparel to Parco and Parco rejects them two days after receipt, title to the goods will

A. Pass to Parco when they are identified to the contract.

B. Pass to Parco when they are shipped.

C. Remain with Parco until the goods are returned to Lace.

D. Revert to Lace when they are rejected by Parco.

Answer (D) is correct. *(CPA, adapted)*

REQUIRED: The true statement about passage of title when a seller ships nonconforming goods.

DISCUSSION: A rejection or other refusal by the buyer to receive or retain the goods, whether or not justified, or a justified revocation of acceptance, revests title to the goods in the seller. Such revesting occurs by operation of law.

Answer (A) is incorrect. Title passes when the contract is formed if there are documents of title or, if there are none, when the seller completes its delivery obligation (in this case, by putting and holding them at the warehouse). Answer (B) is incorrect. Title passes when the contract is formed if there are documents of title or, if there are none, when the seller completes its delivery obligation (in this case, by putting and holding them at the warehouse). Answer (C) is incorrect. Title did pass but it reverted to the seller upon rejection.

24. On Monday, Gullible George is induced to sell a computer to Fraudulent Freddy on the basis of Freddy's misrepresentation that he is Wealthy Walter. That same day, Freddy resells the computer to Innocent Ivan, a good faith purchaser for value. On Tuesday, Gullible George sells an electronic typewriter to Dishonest David who pays for the goods with a check that is later dishonored by the payor (drawee) bank. Before the check is dishonored, David sells the typewriter to Innocent Irene, a good faith purchaser for value. On the basis of these facts,

A. George's best remedy is to recover the value of the goods from Freddy and David in a tort action for deceit.

B. George is entitled to recover the computer from Ivan, but he is not entitled to recover the typewriter from Irene.

C. George is entitled to recover the typewriter from Irene, but he is not entitled to recover the computer from Ivan.

D. George is entitled to recover the computer from Ivan and the typewriter from Irene.

Answer (A) is correct. *(L. Fischl)*

REQUIRED: The effect of a transfer by a person with voidable title to a good faith purchaser for value.

DISCUSSION: In general, a purchaser of goods acquires only the title that his/her transferor had or had power to transfer. Under UCC 2-403, a purchaser who deceived the transferor as to his/her identity or procured delivery of the goods in exchange for a check that is later dishonored has a voidable rather than a void title. The transferor can recover the goods (or damages) from the wrongdoer. However, a person with voidable title may transfer good title to a good faith purchaser for value. Hence, George cannot recover from Ivan or Irene, each of whom has good title.

Answer (B) is incorrect. Ivan, a good faith purchaser for value, acquired good title from Freddy, whose title was voidable, not void, despite the fraud he perpetrated to induce the purchase from George. Answer (C) is incorrect. Irene, a good faith purchaser for value, acquired good title from David, whose title was voidable, not void, despite his receipt of delivery of the typewriter in exchange for a check that was later dishonored. Answer (D) is incorrect. Ivan, a good faith purchaser for value, acquired good title from Freddy, whose title was voidable, not void, despite the fraud he perpetrated to induce the purchase from George. Additionally, Irene, a good faith purchaser for value, acquired good title from David, whose title was voidable, not void, despite his receipt of delivery of the typewriter in exchange for a check that was later dishonored.

13.5 Risk of Loss

25. Which of the following factors is most important in deciding who bears the risk of loss between merchants when goods are destroyed during shipment?

A. The agreement of the parties.

B. The perishable or nonperishable nature of the goods.

C. The holder of title at the time of the loss.

D. The terms of applicable insurance policies.

Answer (A) is correct. *(CPA, adapted)*

REQUIRED: The most important factor in deciding risk of loss on goods destroyed in transit.

DISCUSSION: The parties to a contract for the sale of goods ordinarily may agree who will have the risk of loss, or they can divide the risk of loss (UCC 2-509 and 2-303). The agreement may be express, or implied from trade usage, course of dealing, or course of performance. Absent contrary agreement, the intent with respect to risk is often determined by shipping and delivery terms. Whether the parties are merchants usually does not affect risk of loss.

Answer (B) is incorrect. The nature of the goods destroyed in transit is irrelevant to risk of loss. However, a merchant buyer who has rightfully rejected perishables may have a duty to resell (UCC 2-603). Answer (C) is incorrect. Under the UCC, risk of loss is never based on title. Answer (D) is incorrect. Insurance coverage is a consideration but is not as significant as the parties' intent or a possible breach.

26. On Monday, Wolfe paid Aston Co., a retailer, $300 for a table. On Thursday, Aston notified Wolfe that the table was ready to be picked up. On Saturday, while Aston was still in possession of the table, it was destroyed in a fire. Who bears the loss of the table?

A. Wolfe, because Wolfe had title to the table at the time of loss.

B. Aston, unless Wolfe is a merchant.

C. Wolfe, unless Aston breached the contract.

D. Aston, because Wolfe had not yet taken possession of the table.

Answer (D) is correct. *(CPA, adapted)*

REQUIRED: The true statement about risk of loss, given that the seller was a merchant.

DISCUSSION: If the parties have no agreement as to risk of loss, no carrier is involved, and the goods are not in the possession of a bailee, "the risk of loss passes to the buyer on his/her receipt of the goods if the seller is a merchant; otherwise, the risk passes to the buyer on tender of delivery" (UCC 2-509). Because Aston is a merchant (a person engaged in selling goods of the kind), risk did not pass to Wolfe on tender of delivery.

Answer (A) is incorrect. The UCC never assigns risk of loss to goods on the basis of title. Answer (B) is incorrect. It is the seller's status that is relevant. Answer (C) is incorrect. Risk of loss would not have passed prior to receipt by Wolfe.

27. If a contract for the sale of goods includes a C&F shipping term and the seller has fulfilled all of its obligations, the

A. Title to the goods will pass to the buyer when the goods are received by the buyer at the place of destination.

B. Risk of loss will pass to the buyer upon delivery of the goods to the carrier.

C. Buyer retains the right to inspect the goods prior to making payment.

D. Seller must obtain an insurance policy at its own expense for the buyer's benefit.

Answer (B) is correct. *(CPA, adapted)*

REQUIRED: The effect of a C&F shipping term if the seller has fully performed.

DISCUSSION: The term CIF means that the price includes the cost of the goods, insurance, and freight to the indicated destination (UCC 2-320). Unless otherwise agreed by the parties, the use of the term CIF also requires the seller to load the goods, pay the freight, obtain the insurance, etc. It also determines that risk of loss passes to the buyer upon shipment unless the parties have agreed otherwise. The term C&F has the same effect except with regard to insurance.

Answer (A) is incorrect. Unless otherwise agreed, title passes under a C&F term at the time and place of shipment. Answer (C) is incorrect. The buyer most likely will have no right to inspect before payment. A CIF or C&F term indicates a shipment contract. The buyer ordinarily must make payment against tender of the required documents, and these will commonly arrive and be tendered while the goods are in transit and before inspection. Answer (D) is incorrect. A C&F term imposes no obligation on the seller regarding insurance.

28. Cey Corp. entered into a contract to sell parts to Deck, Ltd. The contract provided that the goods would be shipped "FOB Cey's warehouse." Cey shipped parts different from those specified in the contract. Deck rejected the parts. A few hours after Deck informed Cey that the parts were rejected, they were destroyed by fire in Deck's warehouse. Cey believed that the parts were conforming to the contract. Which of the following statements is true?

A. Regardless of whether the parts were conforming, Deck will bear the loss because the contract was a shipment contract.

B. If the parts were nonconforming, Deck had the right to reject them, but the risk of loss remains with Deck until Cey takes possession of the parts.

C. If the parts were conforming, risk of loss does not pass to Deck until a reasonable period of time after they are delivered to Deck.

D. If the parts were nonconforming, Cey will bear the risk of loss, even though the contract was a shipment contract.

Answer (D) is correct. *(CPA, adapted)*

REQUIRED: The party bearing the risk of loss when nonconforming goods are shipped and then destroyed while in the buyer's possession.

DISCUSSION: If the contract does not cover risk, the most significant factor in determining who has the risk of loss is whether a breach has occurred. If a tender or delivery of goods is so nonconforming as to give a right of rejection, the risk of loss remains on the seller until cure or acceptance (UCC 2-510). The breaching party therefore has the risk of loss. Even if seller's shipment of nonconforming goods is an accommodation, it is a breach. The result is the same for either a shipment contract or a destination contract.

Answer (A) is incorrect. If the parts are nonconforming, the seller (Cey) bears the risk of loss in either a shipment contract or a destination contract. Answer (B) is incorrect. If a tender or delivery of goods is so nonconforming as to give a right of rejection, the risk of loss remains on the seller until cure or acceptance. Answer (C) is incorrect. The buyer would have had the risk of loss in a shipment contract under which conforming goods had been delivered to the carrier.

29. Which of the following statements applies to a sale on approval under UCC Article 2?

A. Both the buyer and seller must be merchants.

B. The buyer must be purchasing the goods for resale.

C. Risk of loss for the goods passes to the buyer when the goods are accepted after the trial period.

D. Title to the goods passes to the buyer on delivery of the goods to the buyer.

Answer (C) is correct. *(CPA, adapted)*

REQUIRED: The true statement about a sale on approval.

DISCUSSION: A sale is on approval if the goods are delivered to the buyer with an understanding that (s)he may test them for the purpose of determining whether (s)he wishes to purchase them. (S)he may return them without breaching the contract even though they conform to the contract. In a sale on approval, title and risk of loss do not pass to the buyer until acceptance (UCC 2-327). Acceptance may be express or implied, e.g., by not returning the goods in a reasonable period.

Answer (A) is incorrect. In a normal sale on approval, the goods are primarily for the use of the buyer. If the goods are delivered primarily for resale, the transaction is a sale or return, and risk of loss and title pass to the buyer in accordance with the particular delivery situation. Answer (B) is incorrect. The buyer is normally acquiring the goods for his/her own use. Answer (D) is incorrect. In a sale on approval, title and risk of loss do not pass to the buyer until acceptance.

30. Under UCC Article 2, when a contract for the sale of goods stipulates that the seller ship the goods by common carrier, "FOB purchaser's loading dock," which of the parties bears the risk of loss during shipment?

A. The purchaser, because risk of loss passes when the goods are delivered to the carrier.

B. The purchaser, because title to the goods passes at the time of shipment.

C. The seller, because risk of loss passes only when the goods reach the purchaser's loading dock.

D. The seller, because risk of loss remains with the seller until the goods are accepted by the purchaser.

Answer (C) is correct. *(CPA, adapted)*

REQUIRED: The party that bears risk of loss during shipment of goods FOB purchaser's loading dock.

DISCUSSION: The parties to a contract for the sale of goods may agree who will have the risk of loss. In the absence of an express agreement, the intent with respect to risk is determined by shipping and delivery terms. The shipping term FOB purchaser's place of business indicates a destination contract, and the seller bears the risk of loss until the goods reach the buyer's loading dock.

Answer (A) is incorrect. The shipping term FOB purchaser's loading dock is a destination contract and requires the seller to bear the risk of loss until the goods are tendered at destination. Answer (B) is incorrect. When title passes does not determine who has risk of loss during transit. Answer (D) is incorrect. The tender (not acceptance) of delivery of conforming goods passes risk from the seller to the buyer in a destination contract.

STUDY UNIT FOURTEEN
SALE OF GOODS: PERFORMANCE, REMEDIES, AND WARRANTIES

When the parties have made a valid contract for the sale of goods, the **seller is obligated to transfer and deliver** the goods, and the **buyer is obligated to accept and pay** the price in accordance with the contract. The standards by which the **performance** obligation is measured are the agreement and the customs within the industry, supplemented or limited by law. If the goods or the seller's tender of delivery fail in any respect to conform to the contract, the buyer may reject the goods or the tender. This rule is the **perfect tender rule**. A **tender** is an unconditional offer to perform combined with a present ability to do so. The buyer's right to reject nonconforming goods is subject to the seller's right to **cure** (remedy the nonconformity). Cure must normally occur within the **original contract period**, but a reasonable extension is allowed if the rejection is a surprise to the seller. If the parties do not intend that a carrier be used to move the goods, the seller must put and hold conforming goods at the buyer's disposition for a time sufficient for the buyer to take possession. A seller must give the buyer notice to enable the buyer to take possession. If the parties **intend that a carrier be used** to move the goods, the seller must place the goods into the care of the designated carrier (or a reasonable carrier) and make a reasonable contract for their transportation to the buyer. The seller also must obtain and promptly deliver or tender any **documents** required to enable the buyer to take possession. (S)he must then properly notify the buyer of the shipment.

If the terms of the contract require that the **seller deliver the goods at a particular destination**, the seller must, at the destination, put and hold conforming goods at the buyer's disposition. (S)he must give the buyer any reasonably necessary notice of tender and provide the buyer with any **documents of title** required to obtain delivery. In contracts specifying that delivery is FOB (free on board) a particular point, the tender of delivery must be made at that point. For example, if the contract is **FOB shipping point**, the seller need only, at his/her expense and risk, place the goods in the control of such carrier as is described in the contract. If the contract is **FOB destination**, the seller must, at his/her expense and risk, tender delivery of the goods at the particular destination described in the contract. Similarly, if the contract is **FAS** (free alongside ship) **vessel at a named port**, the seller must deliver the goods alongside the vessel in the manner customary in the port of delivery, or on a dock designated by the buyer, and obtain and tender a receipt for the goods. In exchange for the receipt, the carrier is obligated to issue a bill of lading.

When a seller has properly tendered conforming goods, the buyer is obligated to accept them and pay the price. However, the buyer's obligations are conditional on the **right to inspect** the goods. **Acceptance** of goods by the buyer precludes the buyer from exercising the **right of rejection**. Rejection is available to the buyer for any defect unless the perfect tender rule does not apply because of the terms of the contract. Buyers may accept the goods by (1) expressly accepting the shipment by words or conduct, (2) failing to make an effective rejection after a reasonable opportunity to inspect the goods, or (3) performing any act inconsistent with the rights of the seller.

The **legal effect of acceptance** is that the buyer becomes obligated to pay the contract price. Unless agreed otherwise, in noncarrier cases, a sale is for cash, and the price is due at tender. However, when goods are shipped by carrier, the price is due only at the time and place at which the buyer receives the goods. **Tender of payment** by any means currently used in the ordinary course of business, including by check, is sufficient unless the seller demands legal tender (currency) and gives the buyer a reasonable amount of time to obtain it. **Payment made by check** is conditional (not final) until the check is paid upon presentment to the proper bank. If the check is dishonored upon presentment, payment is defeated. In a sale on credit, the credit period runs from the shipment date. A **lessee** pays rent in accordance with the contract for goods accepted (with an allowance for goods rightfully rejected or not delivered).

The **rights of a buyer include inspection** at any reasonable time and place and in any reasonable manner before payment or acceptance. Unless agreed otherwise, the buyer's right to inspect is absolute. However, if the contract provides for (1) delivery COD, (2) payment against documents of title, or (3) the buyer to pay without inspecting the goods, no right of inspection exists prior to payment. If payment is due before inspection, a defect in the goods does not excuse nonpayment unless (1) the defect appears without inspection, or (2) the transaction is fraudulent. Furthermore, the buyer may **subsequently reject the goods or revoke acceptance**. A buyer who fails to inspect the goods within a **reasonable time after receipt** loses the right to inspection. All **expenses** of inspection are borne by the buyer. However, if the goods are rejected for nonconformity, the cost of inspection can be recovered from the seller.

Rejection of nonconforming goods is appropriate when a nonconforming tender occurs. In **single delivery** contracts, if the **tender** is not perfect, the buyer may reject all, accept all, or accept any commercial units and reject the rest. In an **installment contract**, rejection is not permitted unless the defect cannot be cured. Thus, the nonconformity impairs the contract as a whole. A buyer in possession of rejected goods has an obligation to hold them with reasonable care for a time sufficient to permit the seller to remove them. When a seller gives **no instructions** within a reasonable time after notification of rejection, the buyer may reship the goods to the seller, store them for the seller, or resell them for the seller's account. A buyer is awarded a **security interest** in all rejected goods in his/her possession to secure payment of the price paid plus expenses reasonably incurred in handling them after rejection.

Revocation of acceptance may occur when the buyer accepts goods and later discovers they are nonconforming. Revocation is permitted only if the nonconformity substantially impairs the value of the goods to the buyer. The buyer has the same rights and duties as after a rejection. Under the United Nations **Convention on Contracts for the International Sale of Goods (CISG)**, if the facts would permit revocation of acceptance under the UCC, the buyer may treat the contract as fundamentally breached [the buyer is deprived of what (s)he is entitled to under the contract].

The objective in awarding a **remedy** is neither to penalize the breaching party nor to enrich the nonbreaching party. The UCC attempts to place the injured party in approximately the same position (s)he would have occupied had the breaching party properly performed. The seller's breach of contract arises from (1) repudiating (renouncing) all or part of the contract, (2) making a nonconforming tender of delivery, or (3) failing to deliver conforming goods.

After a seller's breach, the buyer, whether or not a merchant, may **cover**. This right to cover means that a buyer who rightfully rejects nonconforming goods or justifiably revokes acceptance has a right to **purchase substitute goods** in the marketplace. Cover is **not mandatory**. The buyer may choose between cover and damages. Moreover, the buyer must act **reasonably and in good faith**. (S)he may recover from the seller any excess of the cover price over the contract price, minus any savings on expenses, and damages.

The buyer also may **sue for damages**. The **buyer's basic remedy** when (s)he rejects or justifiably revokes acceptance, or the seller fails to deliver, is the right to sue for monetary damages. Typically, damages are any difference between the **contract price and the market price**. An alternative is to measure damages by the difference between the contract price and the amount (s)he actually must pay for replacement goods. The buyer is entitled to **incidental damages**. They are expenses reasonably incurred in inspection, receipt, transportation, care, and custody of goods rightfully rejected. They also include other such expenses reasonably related to the breach. In addition, the **buyer** may be entitled to **consequential damages** (e.g., lost profits). Recovery of these damages is allowed if the seller knew or had reason to know, at the time of contracting, of the buyer's general or particular needs. However, the UCC normally does **not** allow recovery of **punitive damages**.

A buyer may **recover goods from an insolvent seller** if (1) the goods have been **identified to the contract**, (2) the seller became insolvent **within 10 days** of receipt of the first installment of the price, and (3) **tender** of any unpaid portion of the price is made and kept open. In unusual cases, a buyer (not a seller) may **seek specific performance**. If the goods are unique and monetary damages are not an adequate remedy, a court may order specific performance. Specific performance is available whenever the subject matter of the sale contract is unique or "in other proper circumstances." For example, an inability to use the cover remedy suggests that specific performance may be appropriate. Thus, the commercial feasibility of replacement determines whether the remedy is available. If reasonable efforts to cover have failed or the circumstances reasonably indicate such a result, the buyer may have a **right of replevin**. But the goods must have been **identified to the contract**. The right of replevin allows the buyer to gain possession of goods wrongly withheld.

When a **buyer breaches the contract**, the UCC provides various **remedies**. For example, the seller may **withhold delivery of goods**. A seller may discontinue performance when the buyer (1) is insolvent, (2) fails to make a payment due on or before delivery, (3) wrongfully rejects goods, (4) wrongfully revokes acceptance, or (5) repudiates the contract.

The seller also may **identify goods to the contract**. A buyer may breach or repudiate a sales contract while the seller is still in possession. In this case, the seller can identify to the contract the conforming goods that are still in his/her possession or control. The seller can do so even if the goods were not identified at the time of the breach. When the goods contracted for are **unfinished** at the time of breach, the seller may proceed in any reasonable manner. For example, the seller may (1) stop work on the goods at once and resell them for scrap or salvage value, or (2) complete manufacture and wholly identify the goods to the contract. The seller must exercise **reasonable commercial judgment** to mitigate the loss and obtain maximum value for the unfinished goods. Thus, if finishing the goods would materially increase the seller's damages, this remedy would not be commercially reasonable.

Another seller's remedy is to **recover goods in transit**. The seller may stop delivery of goods in the possession of a carrier or other bailee when (s)he discovers the buyer to be **insolvent**. Thus, the seller may withhold delivery except for cash, including payment for prior deliveries. Furthermore, the seller may **recover goods from an insolvent buyer**. When a seller discovers that the buyer has received goods on credit and is insolvent, (s)he may recover the goods. Demand must be made **within 10 days** after the buyer's receipt of the goods. No time limit applies if a **misrepresentation of solvency** was made in writing to the seller within 3 months prior to the delivery of the goods. The seller's **right to reclaim** is subject to the rights of a good-faith purchaser or other buyer in the ordinary course of business. Reclamation excludes all other remedies.

When a seller (1) possesses or controls the goods at the time of the buyer's breach or (2) duly reacquires the goods in transit, the seller has the **right to resell**. The resale must be in **good faith** and **commercially reasonable**. The seller can recover any deficiency between the sales price and the contract price, plus incidental damages, minus any savings. **Incidental damages** result from the breach. **Perishable goods** must be sold as rapidly as possible to mitigate damages. A **good-faith purchaser** in a resale takes free of any rights of the original buyer. A **lessor in possession** of the goods after default by the lessee may lease to a third party. If this agreement is in good faith, commercially reasonable, and substantially similar to the original lease, the lessor may recover (1) accrued and unpaid rent up to the beginning of the new lease, (2) any excess of the present value of the total rent on that date over the present value of the rent under the new lease, and (3) incidental damages minus expenses saved.

An unpaid seller can sue to **recover the purchase price plus incidental damages**, but only under specific circumstances. (1) The buyer must have accepted the goods and **not revoked acceptance**, (2) **risk of loss** must have passed to the buyer before conforming goods were lost or damaged, or (3) the buyer must have breached after the goods were **identified to the contract**, and the seller is unable to resell the goods. If a seller sues for the contract price of goods that (s)he has been unable to resell, the goods must be held for the buyer. The seller can resell at any time prior to collection, but the net proceeds from the sale must be credited to the buyer.

A seller who **seeks damages for wrongful repudiation or nonacceptance** may or may not **resell the goods**. In either case, the seller has the option to seek damages equal to the difference between (1) the market price of the goods at the time and place of tender and (2) the unpaid contract price. The seller also may recover any incidental damages. The difference between the contract price and the market price may be too small to place the seller in the same position (s)he would have been in had the buyer fully performed. The proper **measure of damages** in this case is the seller's lost profits, including a reasonable allowance for overhead and other incidental expenses.

A seller can **cancel the contract** if the buyer (1) wrongfully rejects or revokes acceptance of conforming goods duly delivered, (2) fails to make proper payment, or (3) repudiates the contract in whole or in part. The buyer is not discharged. (S)he is considered to be in breach. If the seller's cancelation is not justified, the seller is in breach. The buyer can sue for appropriate damages.

A clause providing that a seller may **accelerate payment or performance** "at will" when (s)he deems him/herself insecure is interpreted to mean it will be exercised only if the seller, in good faith, believes payment or performance is impaired (UCC 1-208).

Remedies available to the buyer or seller include the **right to demand assurances**. If a party has a reasonable basis for believing that performance will not be tendered, (s)he may demand adequate assurance of performance in writing. Until (s)he receives such assurance, the party may **suspend further performance** if suspension is commercially reasonable. If the proper assurances are not provided within a reasonable period **(not over 30 days)**, the party seeking assurance can treat the contract as repudiated. Just what constitutes an adequate assurance depends on the facts.

A buyer or seller may **assert rights after anticipatory repudiation**. Either party, through words, actions, or circumstances, may repudiate the contract with respect to a performance not yet due. If the loss will substantially impair the value of the contract, the injured party may (1) **await performance** for a commercially reasonable time, (2) **resort to any remedy** for breach even though (s)he has also urged the other party to perform (e.g., the injured party may sue at once), or (3) **suspend performance**. The repudiating party's words, actions, or conduct must make it clear that (s)he is unwilling or unable to perform. A repudiating party may, at any time before his/her next performance is due, **retract repudiation** unless the other party has (1) canceled, (2) materially changed his/her position in reliance on the repudiation, or (3) otherwise indicated that (s)he considers the repudiation final.

The buyer and seller also may **modify the contract**. The parties may (1) limit the remedies available to either buyer or seller or (2) provide for an exclusive remedy for either or neither party. Substantial freedom of contract is permitted. However, any remedy must not be **unconscionable** or fail to accomplish its essential purpose.

Furthermore, the parties may agree to **liquidate damages**. They may set an amount in the contract that they agree to be a reasonable estimate of the damages for breach. Such a clause must be reasonable in light of (1) the anticipated losses, (2) the difficulties of proof of loss, and (3) the inconvenience of otherwise obtaining a remedy. To be enforceable, the liquidated damages amount must constitute a **reasonable forecast** of the damages likely to result from the breach. Usually, the provision establishes a ceiling on the defaulting party's liability. If the provision is an effort to deter breach as opposed to a good-faith effort to estimate probable damages, it will be deemed to be a **penalty** and will be declared void. If a liquidated damages clause has been deemed void, recovery will be limited to actual damages proved, if any. If a seller has properly **withheld delivery of goods**, the **buyer** may receive a refund of amounts paid minus any liquidated damages agreed on. If no liquidated damages have been provided for, the **seller** may retain 20% of the value of the total contract price or $500, whichever is less (UCC 2-718). The **buyer's right of restitution** is subject to **offset** to the extent the **seller** establishes either (1) a right to damages other than liquidated damages or (2) an amount of benefits received by the buyer directly or indirectly under the contract.

Suit must be within the **statute of limitations**. Except for a breach of warranty, one party to a contract for the sale of goods may sue another party for breach only if the legal action is started **within 4 years after breach**. The parties may reduce the period, but not to less than 1 year. The parties may not extend the period. A plaintiff also must **notify** the defendant within a reasonable time of the breach or be barred from any remedy. A **breach of warranty** occurs and establishes a cause of action when the seller tenders delivery of the goods. When a warranty explicitly extends to future performances and **discovery of breach is deferred**, the statute of limitations begins to run when the breach is or should have been discovered and not at the time of tender. For example, if a heating system is installed during the summer, discovery of any defect would likely be delayed until winter. The statute of limitations for any breach of warranty would therefore begin in winter.

An innocent party may **rescind the contract** because of fraud in its formation. Such a contract is voidable. A party who rescinds must return the consideration received from the other party. But rescission does not bar a claim for damages or any other remedy. The common-law elements of fraud must be present.

Articles 2 and 2A provide for four principal **warranties**. A warranty assures one party to a contract of the existence of a fact upon which the other party may rely. A warranty gives rise to a duty on the part of the seller (lessor) that the goods (s)he sells (leases) will conform to certain specific qualities, characteristics, or conditions. However, a seller (lessor) may, by appropriate words, disclaim, negate, or modify particular warranties.

Express warranties arise from words or conduct of the seller. To make an express warranty, the seller merely (1) affirms a fact or promise relating to the goods (e.g., "This computer chip has a speed of 3.2 gigahertz"), (2) affirms a fact or promise by describing the goods (e.g., "This computer will outperform all other Core i5 computers"), or (3) provides a sample or model of the goods (e.g., a computer is displayed in a retail store). However, a seller's expression of opinion or sales talk does not constitute an express warranty (e.g., "This computer is a first-class machine with five of the very best features offered"). Nevertheless, an express warranty is likely to be found if the statement is objectively verifiable (e.g., "The machine is brand new"). Disclaimers of express warranties are usually ineffective.

Article 2 also provides for implied warranties. In every sale by a merchant who deals in goods of the kind sold, an **implied warranty of merchantability** is made. Under the UCC, a **merchant** is a person who deals in goods of the kind or otherwise by occupation holds him/herself out as having special knowledge or skill peculiar to the practice or goods involved in the transaction. Thus, a one-time seller not dealing in goods of the type in question is not a merchant. To be merchantable, goods must pass without objection in the trade under the contract description and, in the case of fungible goods, be of fair average quality within the description. They also should be adequately packaged and labeled. The primary test is whether the goods are fit for the ordinary purposes for which such goods are used. The **implied warranty of fitness for a particular purpose** arises whenever the seller (whether or not a merchant) has reason to know (1) that the goods are to be used for a particular purpose, (2) what that purpose is, and (3) that the buyer is relying on the seller's skill and judgment to select suitable goods. In all implied warranty cases, whether the buyer knew of the defect or could have discovered it is irrelevant. Implied warranties are not based on principles of negligence. Sellers are strictly liable for breach of an implied warranty.

Unless agreed otherwise, a contract for the sale of goods contains a **warranty of title**. Sellers warrant that they have good title to the goods sold and that the transfer is rightful. Sellers also represent that the goods are free of security interests or other liens or encumbrances of which the buyer is unaware at the time of contracting. A **lessor** warrants that, for the lease term, no third party's claim or interest (other than for infringement) will interfere with the lessee's enjoyment of the leasehold. Furthermore, a **merchant seller** regularly dealing in goods of the type sold warrants that they are delivered free from any infringement on patent, trademark, copyright, or similar rights. If the buyer is sued for infringement, the seller must be notified. If the seller then demands to defend the suit and agrees to pay expenses and any adverse judgment, the buyer must turn over control or be barred from a remedy against the seller. The same rule applies in leases of goods, except that a **consumer lessee** does not lose the remedy against the lessor because of the lessee's failure to give notice.

Warranties are interpreted as **cumulative** and consistent. If this interpretation is unreasonable, the intent of the parties controls. To determine intent, certain rules are applied. (1) Exact specifications displace inconsistent samples, models, or general descriptions; (2) a sample displaces an inconsistent general description; and (3) express warranties displace inconsistent implied warranties (but not a warranty of fitness for a particular purpose). The **exclusion or modification of warranties** is difficult under the UCC. For practical purposes, a seller cannot disclaim an express warranty. Implied warranties of both merchantability and fitness for a particular purpose may be disclaimed by the use of language such as "with all faults," "as is," or other commonly accepted expressions that alert the buyer to the risk associated with a purchase. In other circumstances, the **warranty of merchantability** may be disclaimed or modified only by specific mention of the word merchantability. Moreover, if the disclaimer is part of a written contract, it must be **stated conspicuously** in the writing. Except when disclaimed by use of words such as "with all faults," the **warranty of fitness for a particular purpose** cannot be excluded except in writing. A **warranty of title** can be excluded or modified only by specific language. A **lessor** may ordinarily exclude or modify a warranty against interference or infringement if the language is specific, written, and conspicuous. However, even when all of the UCC requirements regarding the language and form of a disclaimer have been met, many courts refuse to enforce the disclaimer on the grounds that it is an attempt to avoid fundamental obligations of good faith, diligence, reasonableness, and care. Sellers also attempt to limit available remedies by including a clause in the sales documentation that provides that repairs or replacements, but neither refunds nor consequential damages, are permitted. Furthermore, an **integration clause** is typically included. It states that the entire agreement is contained in the written contract. No oral statements provide a warranty.

All warranties made by a seller to a buyer may automatically extend to certain **third-party beneficiaries**. Article 2 provides three options from which a state may choose to establish which third parties to a sales contract are entitled to recover for breach of express or implied warranties. The narrowest category consists of natural persons who are in the buyer's household or who are guests in the buyer's home and who are reasonably expected to use, consume, or be affected by the goods, and who are injured in person by breach of the warranty. The second option includes third parties who are natural persons reasonably expected to use, consume, or be affected by the goods and who are injured in person by breach of the warranty. The broadest option extends warranty coverage to any person expected to use, consume, or be affected by the goods and who is injured by breach of the warranty. Thus, the third option extends to property damage as well as personal injury.

An express or implied warranty may provide a basis for a **product liability** suit in addition to a cause of action for breach of warranty. For example, a merchant seller of a product is strictly liable in tort to any person who suffers physical harm or property damage if (1) a defect in a product rendered it unreasonably dangerous, (2) the defect caused the harm or damage, and (3) the product reached the user or consumer without substantial change from the condition in which it was sold.

QUESTIONS

14.1 Performance

1. Which of the following is a true statement about the general obligations of the parties to a sale of goods?

A. Tender of delivery is a condition of the buyer's duty to accept the goods.

B. Tender does not entitle the seller to payment.

C. Tender does not entitle the seller to acceptance of the goods.

D. The UCC requires tender as a prerequisite to the buyer's performance, and the parties may not agree otherwise.

Answer (A) is correct. *(Publisher, adapted)*

REQUIRED: The true statement about the general obligations of parties to a sale.

DISCUSSION: The general obligation of a seller is to transfer and deliver. That of the buyer is to accept and pay in accordance with the contract (UCC 2-301). Tender of delivery is a condition to the buyer's duty to accept the goods. Tender entitles the seller to demand buyer's acceptance of the goods and to payment according to the contract (UCC 2-507).

Answer (B) is incorrect. A proper tender does entitle the seller to payment according to the terms of the agreement. Answer (C) is incorrect. The buyer has a duty to accept a proper tender of conforming goods. Answer (D) is incorrect. The parties are free to alter the obligations established by the UCC.

2. A proper tender of delivery requires that the seller

A. Put and hold conforming goods, or nonconforming goods that the seller reasonably believes will be acceptable, at the buyer's disposition.

B. Furnish facilities reasonably suited to the receipt of the goods.

C. Deliver the goods at the buyer's place of business and keep them available for the time reasonably necessary for the buyer to take possession.

D. Put and hold conforming goods at the buyer's disposition and give any necessary notice.

Answer (D) is correct. *(Publisher, adapted)*

REQUIRED: The true statement about a proper tender by the seller.

DISCUSSION: UCC 2-503 states, "Tender of delivery requires that the seller put and hold conforming goods at the buyer's disposition and give the buyer any notification reasonably necessary to enable him to take delivery." The manner, time, and place for tender must be reasonable.

Answer (A) is incorrect. Under the perfect tender rule (UCC 2-601), the goods must conform precisely to the contract. Otherwise, the buyer may rightfully reject them. Answer (B) is incorrect. The buyer must furnish the facilities for receipt, unless otherwise agreed. Answer (C) is incorrect. Unless the parties agree otherwise, the place for delivery is the seller's place of business.

3. Smith contracted in writing to sell Peters a used personal computer for $600. The contract did not specifically address the time for payment, place of delivery, or Peters' right to inspect the computer. Which of the following statements is true?

A. Smith is obligated to deliver the computer to Peters' home.

B. Peters is entitled to inspect the computer before paying for it.

C. Peters may not pay for the computer using a personal check unless Smith agrees.

D. Smith is not entitled to payment until 30 days after Peters receives the computer.

Answer (B) is correct. *(CPA, adapted)*

REQUIRED: The true statement about a contract with terms left open.

DISCUSSION: A contract for the sale of goods is enforceable if missing terms can be supplied. The buyer has a right to inspect the goods before payment unless contract terms waive the right, e.g., a COD or a documentary sale.

Answer (A) is incorrect. Unless otherwise agreed, tender is generally due at the seller's place of business. Answer (C) is incorrect. Tender of payment by check is sufficient, unless the seller demands legal tender (currency) and gives the buyer a reasonable amount of time to obtain it. Answer (D) is incorrect. Unless otherwise agreed, the price is due upon tender of delivery.

4. The buyer's general obligation under a contract for the sale of goods is to accept and pay according to the contract. Unless the parties have agreed otherwise, the UCC states that

A. The buyer must pay before the seller has an obligation to deliver.

B. Payment is due at the time and place at which the goods are to be shipped.

C. When the seller is to ship the goods on credit, the credit period runs from the time of receipt.

D. If the seller demands payment in cash, (s)he must give any reasonably necessary extension of time.

Answer (D) is correct. *(Publisher, adapted)*

REQUIRED: The UCC requirement concerning payment as performance.

DISCUSSION: "Tender of payment is sufficient when made by any means or in any manner current in the ordinary course of business unless the seller demands payment in legal tender (cash) and gives any extension of time reasonably necessary to procure it" (UCC 2-511). The buyer is thus protected from an unexpected demand for cash. A seller who accepts a check is also protected by UCC 2-511: "Payment by check is conditional and is defeated as between the parties by dishonor of the check on due presentment."

Answer (A) is incorrect. Theoretically, tender of delivery and tender of payment are concurrent conditions. As a practical matter, however, delivery and receipt of goods are normally preconditions of the buyer's duty to pay. Answer (B) is incorrect. Payment is due at the time and place buyer is to receive the goods (UCC 2-310). Answer (C) is incorrect. The credit period runs from the time of shipment, unless the invoice is postdated or delayed.

5. Unless otherwise agreed in a contract for the sale of goods, the buyer is obligated to pay at the time and place at which the buyer receives the goods. The duty of the buyer, however, is subject to a right of inspection. If the sale is a "documentary sale," the

A. Buyer has no right of inspection if the seller ships under reservation.

B. Buyer has no right of inspection prior to payment.

C. Buyer is under an obligation to pay only when the goods are delivered even if the documents of title representing the goods are tendered previously.

D. Parties have entered into a CIF contract.

Answer (B) is correct. *(Publisher, adapted)*

REQUIRED: The true statement concerning documentary sales.

DISCUSSION: A contract for the sale of goods involves a documentary sale if it calls for the buyer to pay for the goods when documents of title are tendered, regardless of the time or place of the receipt of the goods. The shipping terms COD and CIF require payment against a tender of documents; FAS and FOB do not. The buyer in a documentary sale would thus not be entitled to inspect the goods before payment unless otherwise agreed (UCC 2-310 and 2-513).

Answer (A) is incorrect. A shipment under reservation specifically allows a buyer a right of inspection, even though the sale is a documentary sale, unless the inspection would be inconsistent with the terms of the contract, e.g., if the contract includes a COD term. Answer (C) is incorrect. In a documentary sale, the duty to pay is upon tender of documents rather than the goods. Answer (D) is incorrect. Not every documentary sale is made pursuant to a CIF contract.

14.2 Excuse for Nonperformance or Substitute Performance

6. Under a contract governed by UCC Article 2, which of the following statements is true?

A. Unless both the seller and the buyer are merchants, neither party is obligated to perform the contract in good faith.

B. The contract will not be enforceable if it fails to expressly specify a time and a place for delivery of the goods.

C. The seller may be excused from performance if the goods are accidentally destroyed before the risk of loss passes to the buyer.

D. If the price of the goods is less than $500, the goods need not be identified to the contract for title to pass to the buyer.

Answer (C) is correct. *(CPA, adapted)*

REQUIRED: The true statement about a contract governed by UCC Article 2.

DISCUSSION: Under the commercial impracticability doctrine, delay in delivery or nondelivery by a seller is not a breach of his/her duty under a contract for sale if performance as agreed has been made impracticable by the occurrence of a contingency the nonoccurrence of which was a basic assumption on which the contract was made. The risk of the unexpected occurrence must not already have been allocated (by agreement or custom) to the party seeking excuse.

Answer (A) is incorrect. The obligation of good faith applies to both merchants and nonmerchants. Answer (B) is incorrect. Provisions in the UCC provide the terms when they are omitted from the agreement. Answer (D) is incorrect. Title does not pass before goods are identified to the contract, without regard to the price.

7. In September, Cobb Company contracted with Thrifty Oil Company for the delivery of 100,000 gallons of heating oil at the price of $.75 per gallon at regular specified intervals during the forthcoming winter. Because of an unseasonably warm winter, Cobb took delivery of only 70,000 gallons. In a suit against Cobb for breach of contract, Thrifty will

A. Lose, because Cobb acted in good faith.

B. Lose, because both parties are merchants and the UCC recognizes commercial impracticability.

C. Win, because this is a requirements contract.

D. Win, because the change of circumstances could have been contemplated by the parties.

Answer (D) is correct. *(CPA, adapted)*

REQUIRED: The result and its basis if a seller sues a buyer for nonacceptance of the agreed quantity.

DISCUSSION: The possibility that the buyer might actually need less than the agreed quantity was a risk that was readily foreseeable at the time of contracting. Unseasonably warm weather was not a contingency, the nonoccurrence of which was a basic assumption of the contract. Nor was the buyer prevented from receiving the benefit of its bargain. Thus, warm weather was an ordinary business risk of the kind ordinarily assumed by a contracting party and accordingly did not excuse Cobb's breach.

Answer (A) is incorrect. Good faith is not an excuse for nonperformance. Answer (B) is incorrect. Absent a specific contractual reference, reasonable commercial understanding would not regard the contract as conditioned upon an assumption about the weather. Answer (C) is incorrect. The contract was for a stipulated quantity, not for the buyer's requirements.

8. Yost Corp., a computer manufacturer, contracted to sell 15 computers to Ivor Corp., a computer retailer. The contract specified that delivery was to be made by truck to Ivor's warehouse. Instead, Yost shipped the computers by rail. When Ivor claimed that Yost did not comply with the contract, Yost told Ivor that there had been a trucker's strike when the goods were shipped. Ivor refused to pay for the computers. Under these circumstances, Ivor

A. Is obligated to pay for the computers because Yost made a valid substituted performance.

B. Is obligated to pay for the computers because title to them passed to Ivor when Ivor received them.

C. May return the computers and avoid paying for them because of the way Yost delivered them.

D. May return the computers and avoid paying for them because the contract was void under the theory of commercial impracticability.

Answer (A) is correct. *(CPA, adapted)*

REQUIRED: The effect of substituting for the agreed-to manner of delivery.

DISCUSSION: If the goods or the seller's tender of delivery fails in any respect to the contract, the buyer may reject the goods or the tender (perfect tender rule). But if neither party is at fault and the agreed-upon manner of delivery of the goods becomes commercially impracticable due to failure of loading or unloading facilities or the unavailability of an acceptable carrier, a substituted manner of performance must be tendered and accepted if commercially reasonable.

Answer (B) is incorrect. The payment obligation is not dependent on when title passes. Answer (C) is incorrect. Under these circumstances, the buyer must accept a substituted manner of performance when the agreed-upon manner of delivery of the goods becomes commercially impracticable. Answer (D) is incorrect. Under these circumstances, the buyer must accept a substituted manner of performance when the agreed-upon manner of delivery of the goods becomes commercially impracticable.

14.3 Buyer's Remedies

9. Under UCC Article 2, which of the following legal remedies would a buyer not have when a seller fails to transfer and deliver goods identified to the contract?

A. Suit for specific performance.

B. Suit for punitive damages.

C. Purchase substitute goods (cover).

D. Recover the identified goods (capture).

Answer (B) is correct. *(CPA, adapted)*

REQUIRED: The legal remedy not available to a buyer when the seller fails to deliver goods.

DISCUSSION: The buyer's basic remedy when the seller fails to deliver goods is the right to sue for monetary damages. The UCC generally does not provide for an aggrieved party to recover punitive damages.

Answer (A) is incorrect. When the goods are unique and monetary damages are not an adequate remedy, a buyer might obtain specific performance. Answer (C) is incorrect. A buyer may generally cover, that is, purchase substitute goods in the marketplace. Answer (D) is incorrect. A buyer may recover goods from a seller that became insolvent within 10 days of receipt of the first installment of the price.

10. Kirk Corp. sold Nix an Ajax freezer for $490. The contract required delivery to be made by June 23. On June 12, Kirk delivered a Sure freezer to Nix. Nix immediately notified Kirk that the wrong freezer had been delivered and indicated that the delivery of a correct freezer would not be acceptable. Kirk wishes to deliver an Ajax freezer on June 23. Which of the following statements is true?

A. Kirk may deliver the freezer on June 23 without further notice to Nix.

B. Kirk may deliver the freezer on June 23 if it first reasonably notifies Nix of its intent.

C. Nix must accept the nonconforming freezer but may recover damages.

D. Nix may always reject the Sure freezer and refuse delivery of an Ajax freezer.

Answer (B) is correct. *(CPA, adapted)*

REQUIRED: The true statement about options after a nonconforming tender of goods.

DISCUSSION: When a buyer rejects delivery for nonconformity and the time for performance has not expired, the seller can notify the buyer of his/her intent to cure and then deliver within the contract period (UCC 2-508). Accordingly, Kirk can promptly notify Nix and make a conforming delivery by June 23.

Answer (A) is incorrect. Cure is ineffective without reasonable notification. Answer (C) is incorrect. The buyer may rightfully reject a tender that fails in any way to conform to the contract. Answer (D) is incorrect. After receiving notice, Nix must accept conforming goods tendered by the contract date.

11. Bush Hardware ordered 300 Ram hammers from Ajax Hardware. Ajax accepted the order in writing. On the final date allowed for delivery, Ajax discovered it did not have enough Ram hammers to fill the order. Instead, Ajax sent 300 Strong hammers. Ajax stated on the invoice that the shipment was sent only as an accommodation. Which of the following statements is true?

A. Ajax's note of accommodation cancels the contract between Bush and Ajax.

B. Bush's order can be accepted only by Ajax's shipment of the goods ordered.

C. Ajax's shipment of Strong hammers is a breach of contract.

D. Ajax's shipment of Strong hammers is a counteroffer, and no contract exists between Bush and Ajax.

Answer (C) is correct. *(CPA, adapted)*

REQUIRED: The true statement about the shipment of goods solely as an accommodation.

DISCUSSION: Shipment of a brand different from that stipulated in the contract was a breach of the contract (UCC 2-601). Bush may accept the goods despite their nonconformity, rightfully reject them, or resort to any of the buyer's other remedies under the UCC. UCC 2-206 and 2-508, allowing accommodation shipments and the ability to cure, are not applicable because a cure must be made within the time for performance in most cases.

Answer (A) is incorrect. The breaching party cannot cancel the contract. Only a mutual rescission or the promised performance will discharge the seller's obligation unless the nonconforming goods are accepted. Answer (B) is incorrect. Bush's order constituted an offer to enter into either a bilateral or unilateral contract. It could be accepted either by a prompt promise to ship or by a prompt shipment. Answer (D) is incorrect. The acceptance had already formed a contract.

12. Mix Clothing shipped 300 custom suits to Tara Retailers. The suits arrived on Thursday, earlier than Tara had anticipated and on an exceptionally busy day for its receiving department. They were perfunctorily examined and sent to a nearby warehouse for storage until needed. On the following day, upon closer examination, it was discovered that the quality of the linings of the suits was inferior to that specified in the sales contract. Which of the following is true insofar as Tara's rights are concerned?

A. Tara must retain the suits because it accepted them and had an opportunity to inspect them upon delivery.

B. Tara had no rights if the linings were of merchantable quality.

C. Tara can reject the suits upon subsequent discovery of the defects.

D. Tara's only course of action is rescission.

Answer (C) is correct. *(CPA, adapted)*

REQUIRED: The true statement regarding the rights of a buyer of nonconforming goods.

DISCUSSION: A buyer has the right to inspect the goods at any reasonable place and time and in any reasonable manner (UCC 2-513). Tara did not have a reasonable opportunity to inspect on the day of the delivery. A buyer may reject nonconforming goods within a reasonable time if the seller is properly notified (UCC 2-602). Also, a buyer who has accepted goods may revoke acceptance within a reasonable time if the acceptance was reasonably induced by the difficulty of discovery (UCC 2-608).

Answer (A) is incorrect. Tara did not have a reasonable opportunity to inspect and may reject the goods within a reasonable time after acceptance or revoke acceptance. Answer (B) is incorrect. If the linings were not as described in the contract, Mix breached the express warranty regardless of merchantability. Answer (D) is incorrect. Tara may also seek any of the other buyer's remedies under the UCC.

13. Dara bought an automobile needing repairs from Chevalier Motors, Inc. (CMI). CMI promised to repair it, but 1 month later had not yet completed the repairs. Dara was using the car anyway (1 month after purchase) when a fire in the dashboard rendered the vehicle inoperable. Dara returned the automobile immediately and orally informed a representative of CMI that she was demanding the purchase price. Dara sent a written notice of rescission 3 months later and filed suit 3 months after that. Who will most likely prevail, and what is the legal theory that best supports the result?

A. CMI, because Dara accepted goods she knew to be nonconforming.

B. CMI, because Dara did not revoke her acceptance within a reasonable time.

C. Dara, because she made a justifiable revocation of acceptance.

D. Dara, because she made a rightful rejection.

Answer (C) is correct. *(Publisher, adapted)*

REQUIRED: The likely result of a suit to recover the purchase price of returned goods.

DISCUSSION: Dara decided to take the goods despite their nonconformity and thus accepted them (UCC 2-606). A buyer may revoke acceptance, however, if certain conditions are met. (1) The goods are nonconforming; (2) the nonconformity substantially impairs their value; and (3) (a) the buyer knew of the nonconformity and acted on the reasonable assumption it would be cured, but it was not seasonably cured; or (b) (s)he did not know, and acceptance was reasonably induced either by the difficulty of discovery or by the seller's assurances. Moreover, revocation is made within a reasonable time (UCC 2-608).

Answer (A) is incorrect. The revocation is effective. Acceptance was predicated upon the reasonable assumption that nonconformity would be cured, and it was not seasonably cured. Answer (B) is incorrect. A reasonable time for revocation normally is longer than that for rejection after tender, notification of breach, or discovery of nonconformity because the remedy will, in most cases, be resorted to only after attempts at adjustment have failed. Answer (D) is incorrect. Acceptance precludes rejection (UCC 2-607).

14. Eli contracted to buy 600 bales of No. 1 quality cotton from Whitney. The contract provided that Eli would make payment prior to inspection. The 600 bales were shipped, and Eli paid Whitney. Upon inspection, however, Eli discovered that the cotton was No. 2 quality. Eli returned the cotton to Whitney and demanded return of the payment. Whitney refused on the ground that there is no difference between No. 1 quality cotton and No. 2 quality cotton. What is Eli's remedy for the nonconforming cotton?

A. Specific performance.

B. Damages measured by the difference between the value of the goods delivered and the value of conforming goods.

C. Damages measured by the price paid plus the difference between the contract price and the cost of buying substitute goods.

D. None. Eli waived any remedies by agreeing to pay before inspection.

Answer (C) is correct. *(Publisher, adapted)*

REQUIRED: The buyer's remedy for nonconformity of goods.

DISCUSSION: Under UCC 2-711 and 2-712, a buyer who has rightfully rejected goods after having prepaid the purchase price may recover as much of the price as has been paid and also use the cover remedy. To cover is to make a timely, good-faith purchase of substitute goods and have as damages the difference between the contract price and the cost of the substitutes.

Answer (A) is incorrect. Under UCC 2-716, specific performance is available only for unique goods "or in other proper circumstances." These goods are not unique, and the circumstances are not otherwise proper for the specific performance remedy. It is likely that No. 1 quality cotton is available elsewhere. Answer (B) is incorrect. Eli is entitled to recover the price prepaid as well as the damages accruing from the cover remedy. Instead of tendering the goods back to Whitney, he could have elected to keep the goods and recovered the difference between the value of the goods delivered and the value they would have had if they had been as warranted. Answer (D) is incorrect. The agreement to prepay is not a waiver of the right to inspect or any of the buyer's remedies.

15. On September 10, Bell Corp. entered into a contract to purchase 50 lamps from Glow Manufacturing. Bell prepaid 40% of the purchase price. Glow became insolvent on September 19 before segregating, in its inventory, the lamps to be delivered to Bell. Bell will not be able to recover the lamps because

A. Bell is regarded as a merchant.

B. The lamps were not identified to the contract.

C. Glow became insolvent fewer than 10 days after receipt of Bell's prepayment.

D. Bell did not pay the full price at the time of purchase.

Answer (B) is correct. *(CPA, adapted)*

REQUIRED: The circumstances that will prevent the buyer from recovering goods from an insolvent seller.

DISCUSSION: A buyer may recover goods from an insolvent seller if the goods have been identified to the contract, the seller became insolvent within 10 days of receipt of the first installment of the price, and tender of any unpaid portion of the price is made and kept open (UCC 2-502). If the lamps have not been identified to the contract, Bell cannot obtain them.

Answer (A) is incorrect. The buyer's right to reach the goods is not dependent upon its status as a merchant. Answer (C) is incorrect. To recover the goods, the seller must have become insolvent within 10 days of receipt of the first installment of the price. Answer (D) is incorrect. Failure to pay the full price will not prevent Bell from obtaining the goods if it makes and keeps open a tender of the unpaid balance of the price.

16. Eagle Corporation solicited bids for various parts it uses in the manufacture of jet engines. Eagle received six offers and selected the offer of Sky Corporation. The written contract specified a price for 100,000 units, delivery on June 1 at Sky's plant, with payment on July 1. On June 1, Sky had completed a 200,000 unit run of parts similar to those under contract for Eagle and various other customers. Sky had not identified the parts to specific contracts. When Eagle's truck arrived to pick up the parts on June 1, Sky refused to deliver claiming the contract price was too low. Eagle was unable to cover in a reasonable time. Its production lines were in danger of shutdown because the parts were not delivered. Eagle would probably

A. Have as its only remedy the right of replevin.

B. Have the right of replevin only if Eagle tendered the purchase price on June 1.

C. Have as its only remedy the right to recover dollar damages.

D. Have the right to obtain specific performance.

Answer (D) is correct. *(CPA, adapted)*

REQUIRED: The remedy right(s) of a buyer of goods.

DISCUSSION: If the goods are unique and monetary damages are not an adequate remedy, the courts may order specific performance of the sales contract. Under the UCC, specific performance is available whenever the subject matter of the sales contract is unique and "in other proper circumstances" (UCC 2-716). Although specific performance is thus not usually available for ordinary goods, courts have found facts such as those in the question to be "other proper circumstances" for ordering it.

Answer (A) is incorrect. Specific performance and/or monetary damages might also be sought. Answer (B) is incorrect. The right to replevin (recover possession of) goods wrongfully withheld is available if the goods are identified to the contract. Answer (C) is incorrect. Replevin and specific performance might also be sought.

14.4 Seller's Remedies

17. When a buyer is in breach of a contract for the sale of goods, the seller may withhold delivery. Which of the following is true?

A. When the breach regarding one installment substantially impairs the value of the whole contract, all undelivered goods may be withheld.

B. The seller who withholds delivery may not proceed with other remedies.

C. The breach justifying withholding delivery of all undelivered goods need not go to the whole contract.

D. Withholding delivery is no longer available once goods are in the hands of a carrier even though the shipping term is FOB destination.

Answer (A) is correct. *(Publisher, adapted)*

REQUIRED: The true statement about a seller's remedy of withholding delivery.

DISCUSSION: A seller may withhold delivery of all the undelivered goods if the buyer breaches the contract as a whole. A breach of the whole contract occurs if default on any installment substantially impairs the value of the whole contract (UCC 2-612). The breach may be by wrongful rejection of an installment, revoking acceptance, not paying when due, repudiating, etc. (UCC 2-703).

Answer (B) is incorrect. Remedies are cumulative. Answer (C) is incorrect. UCC 2-703 requires a breach of the whole contract. Answer (D) is incorrect. Stoppage in transit of any goods is possible when the buyer is found to be insolvent. Carloads, planeloads, truckloads, etc., may be stopped in transit in other circumstances (UCC 2-705).

18. A lessor of goods may be in rightful possession of the leased goods after a default by the lessee. In this circumstance, a lessor

A. Is accountable to the lessee for any profit on any disposition of the goods by the lessor.

B. Who sells the goods is not entitled to damages.

C. May dispose of the goods by a lease agreement and recover damages.

D. May lease the goods to a new lessee who will take subject to the rights of the original lessee.

Answer (C) is correct. *(Publisher, adapted)*

REQUIRED: The effect of a lessor's disposition of leased goods after the lessee's default.

DISCUSSION: A lessor in possession of the leased goods after the lessee's default may lease to a third party. If this agreement is in good faith, commercially reasonable, and substantially similar to the original lease, the lessor may recover (1) accrued and unpaid rent up to the beginning of the new lease, (2) any excess of the present value of the total rent on that date over the present value of the rent under the new lease, and (3) incidental damages minus expenses saved (UCC 2A-527).

Answer (A) is incorrect. UCC 2A-527 states, "The lessor is not accountable to the lessee for any profit made on any disposition." Answer (B) is incorrect. If the lessor disposes of the goods by a lease that does not qualify for the treatment described in the correct answer explanation or by a sale or other means, the lessor may recover damages to the same extent as if the lessor had not disposed of the goods. Answer (D) is incorrect. A subsequent lessee in good faith for value takes free of the initial lease agreement and any rights of the initial lessee, even if the lessor does not comply with Article 2A.

Questions 19 and 20 are based on the following information. On April 5, Anker, Inc., furnished Bold Corp. with Anker's financial statements dated March 31. The financial statements contained misrepresentations indicating that Anker was solvent when it was insolvent. Based on Anker's financial statements, Bold agreed to sell Anker 90 computers, "FOB -- Bold's loading dock." On April 14, Anker received 60 of the computers. The remaining 30 computers are in the possession of the common carrier and in transit to Anker.

19. On April 28, if Bold discovered that Anker was insolvent, then with respect to the computers delivered to Anker on April 14, Bold may

A. Reclaim the computers upon making a demand.

B. Reclaim the computers irrespective of the rights of any subsequent third party.

C. Not reclaim the computers because 10 days have elapsed from their delivery.

D. Not reclaim the computers because it is entitled to recover the price of the computers.

Answer (A) is correct. *(CPA, adapted)*

REQUIRED: The right of a seller if the buyer has misrepresented its solvency.

DISCUSSION: When the seller discovers that the buyer has received goods on credit while insolvent, (s)he may reclaim the goods upon demand made within 10 days after the receipt. But if misrepresentation of solvency has been made to the seller in writing within 3 months before delivery, the 10-day limitation does not apply (UCC 2-702). No other remedies are permitted with respect to goods successfully reclaimed.

Answer (B) is incorrect. Goods in the possession of a good-faith purchaser cannot be reclaimed. Answer (C) is incorrect. The misrepresentation may have been made within 3 months before delivery. In that case, the 10-day limitation is inapplicable. Answer (D) is incorrect. The facts do not indicate that Bold has become entitled to bring an action for the price. Anker has not yet breached. Moreover, Bold is entitled to a reclamation remedy because of Anker's misrepresentation.

20. With respect to the remaining 30 computers in transit, which of the following statements is correct if Anker refuses to pay Bold in cash, and Anker is not in possession of a negotiable document of title covering the computers?

A. Bold may stop delivery of the computers to Anker. Their contract is void because Anker furnished false financial statements.

B. Bold may stop delivery of the computers to Anker despite the passage of title to Anker.

C. Bold must deliver the computers to Anker on credit because Anker has not breached the contract.

D. Bold must deliver the computers to Anker because the risk of loss passed to Anker.

Answer (B) is correct. *(CPA, adapted)*

REQUIRED: The right (duty) of an unpaid seller to stop goods in transit after learning of the buyer's insolvency.

DISCUSSION: When an unpaid seller discovers the buyer is insolvent, it may stop any goods in transit (UCC 2-705). This right may be exercised even when the shipping terms are FOB shipping point and title and risk of loss have passed to the buyer. Once the goods are stopped, Bold may refuse to deliver except for cash (UCC 2-702). If Anker pays cash, including payment for all goods previously delivered, Bold will have no reason to withhold delivery. If the buyer breaches before delivery (e.g., fails to pay an installment or commits fraud), any stoppage in transit must be by carload, truckload, or planeload.

Answer (A) is incorrect. If Anker pays cash, it may enforce the contract against Bold. Answer (C) is incorrect. The buyer's insolvency justifies nondelivery despite the lack of a breach. Answer (D) is incorrect. The buyer's insolvency justifies nondelivery despite the passage of title and risk of loss.

21. Badger Corporation sold goods to Watson. Watson has arbitrarily refused to pay the purchase price. Under what circumstances will Badger not be able to recover the price if it seeks this remedy instead of other possible remedies?

A. If Watson refused to accept delivery and the goods were resold in the ordinary course of business.

B. If Watson accepted the goods but seeks to return them.

C. If the goods sold were destroyed shortly after the risk of loss passed to the buyer.

D. If the goods were identified to the contract, and Badger made a reasonable effort to resell them at a reasonable price but was unable to do so.

Answer (A) is correct. *(CPA, adapted)*

REQUIRED: The circumstances under which the seller will not be able to recover the price.

DISCUSSION: The seller cannot recover the price if the goods have been resold. In that event, Badger's damages would be measured by the difference between the contract price and the resale price, plus any incidental damages, minus expenses saved (UCC 2-706).

22. Lazur Corp. entered into a contract with Baker Suppliers, Inc., to purchase a computer from Baker. Lazur is engaged in the business of selling computers to the general public. The contract required Baker to ship the goods to Lazur by common carrier pursuant to the following provision in the contract: "FOB - Baker Suppliers, Inc., loading dock." Assume that Lazur refused to accept the computer even though it was in all respects conforming to the contract and that the contract is otherwise silent. Under UCC Article 2,

A. Baker can successfully sue for specific performance and make Lazur accept and pay for the word processor.

B. Baker may resell the word processor to another buyer.

C. Baker must sue for the difference between the market value of the word processor and the contract price plus its incidental damages.

D. Baker cannot successfully sue for consequential damages unless it attempts to resell the word processor.

Answer (B) is correct. *(CPA, adapted)*

REQUIRED: The true statement about a seller's remedies after wrongful rejection.

DISCUSSION: Resale of the goods and recovery of damages is a seller's remedy. After the buyer's breach, the resale in good faith and in a commercially reasonable manner permits the seller to recover the difference between the resale price and the contract price, plus any incidental damages allowed under UCC 2-710, minus expenses saved.

Answer (A) is incorrect. Specific performance is a remedy that may be available to a buyer but not a seller of goods. Answer (C) is incorrect. An aggrieved seller has a variety of possible remedies, including but not limited to a suit for damages for nonacceptance or repudiation. In such an action, the measure of damages is the difference between the market price and the unpaid contract price, plus incidental damages, minus expenses saved. If this measure of damages is inadequate, the seller may recover the profit it would have made from full performance by the buyer, plus incidental damages, with due allowance for costs reasonably incurred and payments or proceeds of resale. Answer (D) is incorrect. The UCC expressly provides for an aggrieved buyer, not a seller, to recover consequential (special) damages. But the UCC does not prevent the seller from seeking this common-law remedy. Consequential damages are the losses resulting from the unique facts of the case, assuming the breaching party knew or had reason to know of these circumstances. Resale is not a prerequisite to their recovery.

23. Cara Fabricating Co. and Taso Corp. agreed orally that Taso would custom manufacture a compressor for Cara at a price of $120,000. After Taso completed the work at a cost of $90,000, Cara notified Taso that the compressor was no longer needed. Taso is holding the compressor and has requested payment from Cara. Taso has been unable to resell the compressor for any price. Taso incurred storage fees of $2,000. If Cara refused to pay Taso and Taso sues Cara, the most Taso will be entitled to recover is

A. $92,000

B. $105,000

C. $120,000

D. $122,000

Answer (D) is correct. *(CPA, adapted)*

REQUIRED: The seller's recovery after a buyer's refusal to pay for specially made goods.

DISCUSSION: A seller may recover the contract price ($120,000) and any incidental damages ($2,000) if circumstances reasonably indicate that an effort at resale would be unsuccessful (UCC 2-709). Because the machine was made-to-order and not adaptable to others' use, Pine should be successful in recovering the price. After recovery of the price, seller would be holding the machine for buyer.

14.5 Remedies Available to Both Buyer and Seller

24. Under UCC Article 2, a plaintiff who proves fraud in the formation of a contract may

A. Elect to rescind the contract and need not return the consideration received from the other party.

B. Be entitled to rescind the contract and sue for damages resulting from the fraud.

C. Be entitled to punitive damages provided physical injuries resulted from the fraud.

D. Rescind the contract even if there was no reliance on the fraudulent statement.

Answer (B) is correct. *(CPA, adapted)*

REQUIRED: The legal effect of fraud in the formation of a contract for the sale of goods.

DISCUSSION: UCC 2-721 provides that rescission for fraud does not bar a claim for damages or another remedy.

Answer (A) is incorrect. A party who rescinds must return the consideration received from the other party. Answer (C) is incorrect. The UCC generally does not provide for punitive damages. Answer (D) is incorrect. Proof of fraud is based on its common-law elements, one of which is reliance.

25. A provision in a contract for the sale of goods providing that the seller may accelerate payment at will when (s)he deems him/herself insecure

A. Is void as against public policy and ignored in determining contract rights.

B. Makes the agreement illusory and prevents contract formation.

C. Gives the seller a preferred creditor's status.

D. Is enforceable subject to the good faith belief of the seller.

Answer (D) is correct. *(CPA, adapted)*

REQUIRED: The legal effect of accelerating payment because of the seller's insecurity.

DISCUSSION: A clause providing that a seller may accelerate payment or performance "at will" when (s)he deems him/herself insecure is construed to mean it will only be exercised if the seller, in good faith, believes payment or performance is impaired (UCC 1-208).

Answer (A) is incorrect. Such clauses are valid subject to good-faith belief. Answer (B) is incorrect. An acceleration clause does not make the agreement illusory if it can only be exercised in good faith. Answer (C) is incorrect. Acceleration gives no priority among creditors.

26. On February 15, Mazur Corp. contracted to sell 1,000 bushels of wheat to Good Bread, Inc., at $6.00 per bushel, with delivery to be made on June 23. On June 1, Good advised Mazur that it would not accept or pay for the wheat. On June 2, Mazur sold the wheat to another customer at the market price of $5.00 per bushel. Mazur had advised Good that it intended to resell the wheat. Which of the following statements is true?

A. Mazur can successfully sue Good for the difference between the resale price and the contract price.

B. Mazur can resell the wheat only after June 23.

C. Good can retract its anticipatory breach at any time before June 23.

D. Good can successfully sue Mazur for specific performance.

Answer (A) is correct. *(CPA, adapted)*

REQUIRED: The effect of a buyer's advance notice to the seller of an intent to breach.

DISCUSSION: Under UCC 2-610, when either party repudiates a future performance the loss of which will substantially impair the value of the contract to the other party, the possibilities are to (1) await performance for a commercially reasonable time, (2) resort to any remedies for breach available to a buyer (UCC 2-711) or a seller (UCC 2-703), and (3) suspend performance. Hence, an aggrieved seller may resell the goods and sue the buyer for the difference between the resale price and the contract price (UCC 2-703 and 2-706).

Answer (B) is incorrect. Upon anticipatory repudiation, the seller may immediately resort to any remedies available for breach. Answer (C) is incorrect. Retraction is permitted only until the other party has canceled, materially changed his/her position in reliance on the repudiation, or otherwise indicated that (s)he considers the repudiation final (UCC 2-611). Answer (D) is incorrect. Monetary damages would be an adequate remedy. The goods are not unique.

27. One of the underlying purposes of the UCC is to permit the parties to exercise considerable contractual freedom. With regard to contractual modification or limitation of remedy, however, this freedom is circumscribed. Which is the true statement about the parties' ability to agree about remedies for breach of their contract for the sale of goods?

A. If the parties have limited the remedies available for breach of their contract and unforeseen circumstances cause the limited remedy to fail of its essential purpose, the injured party must adhere to his/her bargain.

B. The limitation of consequential damages for injury to the person in the case of consumer goods and for commercial loss is prima facie unconscionable.

C. The parties may limit the remedies afforded by the UCC but may not agree to remedies in addition to those provided.

D. The damages for breach by either party may be liquidated in the agreement.

Answer (D) is correct. *(Publisher, adapted)*

REQUIRED: The true statement concerning the ability of parties to a contract for the sale of goods to shape their own remedies.

DISCUSSION: The UCC recognizes that it is efficient for parties to agree on remedies for breach and avoid the trouble, expense, and uncertainty of litigation. Under UCC 2-718, damages may be liquidated or specified in the agreement as long as such damages are reasonable in the circumstances.

Answer (A) is incorrect. If an otherwise reasonable remedy agreed to by the parties should fail, the general remedy provisions of the UCC will be available. Answer (B) is incorrect. The limitation of consequential damages for commercial loss is not prima facie unconscionable as it is for injury to a person in the case of consumer goods (UCC 2-719). Answer (C) is incorrect. The parties are permitted to fashion remedies in addition to those provided in the UCC.

28. Devold Manufacturing, Inc., contracted to sell to Hillary Company 3,000 CB radios at $30 each. After delivery of the first 500 radios, a minor defect was discovered, which Hillary incurred costs to correct. Hillary sent Devold a signed memorandum indicating that it would relinquish its right to recover the costs to correct the defect, provided that the remaining radios were in conformity with the terms of the contract and the delivery dates were strictly adhered to. Devold met these conditions. Shortly before the last shipment of radios arrived, Hillary notified Devold that it was not bound by the prior generous agreement and would sue Devold for damages. In the event of litigation,

A. Devold will lose in that Hillary's relinquishment of its rights was not supported by a consideration.

B. Devold will win in that the defect was minor and the substantial performance doctrine applies.

C. Hillary will lose in that the memorandum constituted a waiver of Hillary's rights.

D. Hillary will win in that there was a failure to perform the contract, and Hillary suffered damages as a result.

Answer (C) is correct. *(CPA, adapted)*

REQUIRED: The result and the basis upon which litigation over a defect and its waiver would be decided.

DISCUSSION: Hillary waived its rights under the contract. Under UCC 1-107, any claim or right arising out of a breach may be discharged without consideration by means of a written waiver signed and delivered by the aggrieved party. The waiver cannot be retracted because it affected an executed (completed) part of the contract. UCC 2-209 permits retraction of a waiver only if it affects an executory portion of a contract.

Answer (A) is incorrect. The waiver by Hillary was effective without consideration as long as it was contained in a writing signed and delivered by the aggrieved party. Answer (B) is incorrect. The doctrine of substantial performance would not preclude recovery for damages if no waiver had been made. Substantial performance merely requires the nonbreaching party to go forward with performance. Answer (D) is incorrect. Hillary waived its right to damages.

14.6 Warranties

29. A warranty imposes upon the seller of goods a duty that the goods conform to the promise in the warranty. If they do not, the buyer has an action for breach of warranty. Under the UCC,

A. The warranty of title is an implied warranty.

B. Only express warranties are recognized.

C. Express and implied warranties are treated separately from the warranty of title.

D. Implied warranties are those which result from affirmations of fact or other promises made by the seller.

Answer (C) is correct. *(Publisher, adapted)*

REQUIRED: The true statement about the types of warranties under the UCC.

DISCUSSION: A warranty is a promise or statement about the nature, quality, or performance of goods. In the sale of a product (goods), it is an express or implied promise establishing the characteristics of ownership and level of quality. Under UCC 2-313, express warranties are given by the seller's explicit affirmations of fact or promises. The implied warranties of merchantability (UCC 2-314) and fitness for a particular purpose (UCC 2-315) arise by operation of law and thus arise without intent. The warranty of title is treated separately by the UCC, even though it is inherent in the sales transaction.

Answer (A) is incorrect. The UCC treats it as neither an express nor an implied warranty. Answer (B) is incorrect. The UCC also recognizes a warranty of title and implied warranties. Answer (D) is incorrect. It defines express warranties.

30. The Uniform Commercial Code implies a warranty of merchantability to protect buyers of goods. To be subject to this warranty, the goods need not be

A. Fit for all the purposes for which the buyer intends to use the goods.

B. Adequately packaged and labeled.

C. Sold by a merchant.

D. In conformity with any promises or affirmations of fact made on the container or label.

Answer (A) is correct. *(CPA, adapted)*

REQUIRED: The characteristic that goods need not have under the warranty of merchantability.

DISCUSSION: The implied warranty of merchantability (UCC 2-314) requires that the goods be of a fair quality that would usually be accepted without objection by buyers, be fit for the ordinary purposes for which they are normally used, and be adequately packaged and labeled. There is no implied warranty that goods be fit for all purposes for which the buyer might intend to use them.

31. Olsen purchased a used van from Super Sales Co. for $350. A clause in the written contract in boldface type provided that the van was being sold "as is." Another clause provided that the contract was intended as the final expression of the parties' agreement. After driving the van for 1 week, Olsen realized that the engine was burning oil. Olsen telephoned Super and requested a refund. Super refused but orally gave Olsen a warranty on the engine for 6 months. The engine exploded 3 weeks later. Super's oral warranty

A. Is invalid because the modification of the existing contract required additional consideration.

B. Is invalid because of the Statute of Frauds.

C. Is valid and enforceable.

D. Although valid, proof of its existence will be inadmissible because it contradicts the final written agreement of the parties.

Answer (C) is correct. *(CPA, adapted)*

REQUIRED: The true statement about an oral warranty made subsequent to a contract for sale.

DISCUSSION: The promise made by the seller to the buyer related to the goods and became part of the basis of the bargain and thus constituted a valid and enforceable express warranty (UCC 2-313). The basis of the bargain in this case included a subsequent oral modification, which needs no consideration to be binding (UCC 2-209). It need not be written if the agreement as modified is not within the statute of frauds and the parties have no written agreement excluding an oral modification or rescission (if they do, it is ineffective against a nonmerchant if the merchant's form exclusion is not separately signed).

Answer (A) is incorrect. Additional consideration is not required for modification. Answer (B) is incorrect. The UCC Statute of Frauds applies to sales of goods for at least $500. Answer (D) is incorrect. The parol evidence rule excludes evidence of prior or contemporaneous oral agreements, not of subsequent oral modifications.

32. Which of the following conditions must be met for an implied warranty of fitness for a particular purpose to arise in connection with a sale of goods?

I. The warranty must be in writing.

II. The seller must know that the buyer was relying on the seller in selecting the goods.

A. I only.

B. II only.

C. Both I and II.

D. Neither I nor II.

Answer (B) is correct. *(CPA, adapted)*

REQUIRED: The requirement for a warranty of fitness to be implied.

DISCUSSION: Under UCC 2-315, a warranty of fitness for a particular purpose is implied (unless excluded or modified) when the seller has reason to know (1) the particular purpose for which the goods will be used and (2) that the buyer is relying on the seller's skill or judgment to choose the goods.

Answer (A) is incorrect. No writing is necessary for a warranty implied by operation of law. Answer (C) is incorrect. No writing is necessary for a warranty implied by operation of law. Answer (D) is incorrect. The warranty of fitness is implied when the seller has reason to know the buyer's particular purpose for the goods and the buyer is relying on the seller's skill or judgment to choose the goods.

33. Parks furnished specifications and ordered 1,000 specially constructed folding tables from Metal Manufacturing Company, Inc. The tables were unique in design and had not appeared in the local market. Metal completed the job and delivered the order to Parks. Parks sold about 600 of the tables when Unusual Tables, Inc., sued both Parks and Metal for patent infringement. If Unusual wins, what is the status of Parks and Metal?

A. Metal is liable to Parks for breach of the warranty against infringement.

B. Parks is liable to Metal for damages resulting from an infringement claim.

C. The UCC does not allocate liability for infringement between Parks and Metal.

D. Parks and Metal are jointly and severally liable and, as such, must pay the judgment in equal amounts.

Answer (B) is correct. *(CPA, adapted)*

REQUIRED: The legal status of a buyer and a manufacturer of goods if both are sued for patent infringement.

DISCUSSION: A buyer of goods who furnishes specifications to the seller must hold the seller harmless against an infringement claim if compliance with the specifications results in liability for the seller (UCC 2-312).

Answer (A) is incorrect. The manufacturer is not liable for breach of the warranty against infringement when the buyer furnishes specifications for specially made goods. Answer (C) is incorrect. The UCC requires that Parks hold Metal harmless for infringement. Answer (D) is incorrect. Parks must reimburse any amount Metal is required to pay.

34. Under UCC Article 2, the implied warranty of merchantability

A. May be disclaimed by a seller's oral statement that mentions merchantability.

B. Arises only in contracts involving a merchant seller and a merchant buyer.

C. Is breached if the goods are not fit for all purposes for which the buyer intends to use the goods.

D. Must be part of the basis of the bargain to be binding on the seller.

Answer (A) is correct. *(CPA, adapted)*

REQUIRED: The true statement about the implied warranty of merchantability.

DISCUSSION: Unless the circumstances indicate otherwise, all implied warranties are excluded by expressions like "as is," "with all faults," or other language that in common understanding calls the buyer's attention to the exclusion of warranties and makes plain that there is no implied warranty. With certain exceptions, "to exclude or modify the implied warranty of merchantability or any part of it, the language must mention merchantability and in case of a writing must be conspicuous. To exclude or modify any implied warranty of fitness, the exclusion must be by a writing and conspicuous" (UCC 2-316). A disclaimer of the implied warranty of merchantability may be oral. Moreover, the UCC does not require a buyer to sign a disclosure.

Answer (B) is incorrect. The buyer need not be a merchant. Answer (C) is incorrect. The standard is the ordinary purposes for which such goods are used. Answer (D) is incorrect. This is necessary to an express, but not an implied, warranty.

35. Under UCC Article 2, the warranty of title may be excluded by

A. Merchants or nonmerchants, provided the exclusion is in writing.

B. Nonmerchant sellers only.

C. The seller's statement that it is selling only such right or title as it has.

D. Use of an "as is" disclaimer.

Answer (C) is correct. *(CPA, adapted)*

REQUIRED: The party or method by which the warranty of title may be excluded.

DISCUSSION: Every contract for the sale of goods warrants that the title is good, its transfer is rightful, and that the goods are free of encumbrances not known to the buyer. The warranty of title can be excluded or modified only by specific language or by circumstances giving the buyer reason to know that the transferor has no title or a limited title.

Answer (A) is incorrect. A warranty of title can be orally disclaimed. Answer (B) is incorrect. A merchant seller may disclaim by specific language. Answer (D) is incorrect. A general disclaimer, e.g., by language such as "as is," is ineffective with respect to the warranty of title.

36. Sklar, CPA, purchased two computers from Wiz Corp. Sklar discovered material defects in the computers 10 months after taking delivery. Sklar commenced an action for breach of warranty against Wiz 3 years later. Wiz has raised the statute of limitations as a defense. The original contract between Wiz and Sklar contained a conspicuous clause providing that the statute of limitations for breach of warranty actions would be limited to 18 months. Under the circumstances, Sklar will

A. Win because the action was commenced within the 4-year period as measured from the date of delivery.

B. Win because the action was commenced within the 4-year period as measured from the time Sklar discovered the breach or should have discovered the breach.

C. Lose because the clause providing that the statute of limitations would be limited to 18 months is enforceable.

D. Lose because the statute of limitations is 3 years from the date of delivery with respect to written contracts.

Answer (C) is correct. *(CPA, adapted)*

REQUIRED: The effect of a contractual modification of the statute of limitations.

DISCUSSION: Under UCC 2-725, a 4-year statute of limitations applies to cases involving sales of goods. The parties may reduce (but not extend) the period to not less than 1 year. An action for breach of warranty accrues (the statute begins to run) when tender of delivery is made. But if the warranty explicitly extends to future performance and discovery of breach must await such performance, the action accrues when the breach is or should have been discovered. But suit was brought more than 18 months after both delivery of the goods and discovery of the defects.

Answer (A) is incorrect. When breach occurred is unclear on these facts. The question does not state whether the seller explicitly extended the warranty to future performance. Thus, whether the statute of limitations began to run at delivery of the defects cannot be determined. Nevertheless, the 4-year period provided by UCC 2-725 is inapplicable. Answer (B) is incorrect. When breach occurred is unclear on these facts. The question does not state whether the seller explicitly extended the warranty to future performance. Thus, whether the statute of limitations began to run upon discovery of the defects cannot be determined. Nevertheless, the 4-year period provided by UCC 2-725 is inapplicable. Answer (D) is incorrect. UCC 2-725 states that the limitation period is 4 years from the date of accrual. It applies to oral as well as written contracts for the sale of goods.

NOTE: Refer to Study Unit 37 for questions on the effect of the Magnusson-Moss Act on warranties under the UCC.

37. Vick bought a used boat from Ocean Marina that disclaimed "any and all warranties" in connection with the sale. Ocean was unaware the boat had been stolen from Kidd. Vick surrendered it to Kidd when confronted with proof of the theft. Vick sued Ocean. Who is likely to prevail and why?

A. Vick, because the warranty of title has been breached.

B. Vick, because a merchant cannot disclaim implied warranties.

C. Ocean, because of the disclaimer of warranties.

D. Ocean, because Vick surrendered the boat to Kidd.

Answer (A) is correct. *(CPA, adapted)*

REQUIRED: The party who will prevail, and why, if neither knew the goods were stolen.

DISCUSSION: UCC 2-312 establishes a warranty of title by any seller that can only be excluded or modified by specific language or by the buyer's knowledge of circumstances relating to the title. A general disclaimer of warranty, such as a disclaimer of "any and all warranties," is ineffective regarding the warranty of title. Marina therefore warranted the title by selling the boat to Vick and will bear the loss.

Answer (B) is incorrect. The warranty of title is not an implied warranty. Also, a merchant can disclaim implied warranties. Answer (C) is incorrect. The language must be specific to disclaim the warranty of title. Answer (D) is incorrect. The warranty is made and breached when the title is transferred.

38. Pure Food Company packed and sold quality food products to wholesalers and fancy food retailers. One of its most popular items was "southern style" baked beans. Charles purchased a can of the beans from the Superior Quality Grocery. When Joan, the mother of Charles, bit into a heaping spoonful of the beans at a family outing, her teeth were damaged. Evidence revealed that the beans contained a brown stone. In a subsequent lawsuit by Joan, which of the following is true?

A. Joan can collect against Superior Quality for negligence.

B. Privity will not be a bar in a lawsuit against either Pure Food or Superior Quality.

C. The various sellers involved could have effectively excluded or limited the rights of third parties to sue them.

D. Privity is a bar to recovery by Joan, although Charles may sue Superior Quality.

Answer (B) is correct. *(CPA, adapted)*

REQUIRED: The true statement regarding a lawsuit by a party other than the purchaser of the goods.

DISCUSSION: Under UCC 2-318, a seller's warranty extends, at a minimum, to household members and guests if it is reasonable to expect they may be affected by the goods. The sellers (both Pure Food and Superior Quality) made an implied warranty that the food was fit for eating and contained no foreign objects. Joan can sue on this warranty even though she did not purchase the beans. Under strict liability, privity of contract is unnecessary. An object is considered foreign when it is not reasonably expected by the consumer (e.g., a cherry pit in cherry ice cream).

Answer (A) is incorrect. The facts do not suggest that Superior was negligent. A retailer of a closed container would have no reasonable way of knowing the contents were defective. Answer (C) is incorrect. This liability cannot be excluded. It is imposed as a matter of public policy. Answer (D) is incorrect. Joan may sue either Superior or Pure Food even though she was not in privity with either one. Her son can sue only for the price of the product.

39. Which of the following factors is least important in determining whether a manufacturer is strictly liable in tort for a defective product?

A. The negligence of the manufacturer.

B. The contributory negligence of the plaintiff.

C. Modifications to the product by the wholesaler.

D. Whether the product caused injuries.

Answer (A) is correct. *(CPA, adapted)*

REQUIRED: The least important factor in determining whether a manufacturer is strictly liable in tort.

DISCUSSION: In an action based on strict liability in tort for a defective product the plaintiff need not prove that a breach of a legal duty to exercise reasonable care proximately caused the plaintiff's injury. Rather, the plaintiff must prove that the product was defective, the defect rendered it unreasonably dangerous, the unreasonably dangerous condition of the product caused the plaintiff's harm or damage, the seller was in the business of selling the product, and the product reached the user or consumer without substantial change from the condition in which it was sold.

Answer (B) is incorrect. Whether the plaintiff acted reasonably to protect him/herself may be a factor in the outcome of the suit. Answer (C) is incorrect. Substantial alteration of the product after its sale by the manufacturer may be a defense if the change caused the plaintiff's injury. Answer (D) is incorrect. Plaintiff must prove that physical harm was caused to the ultimate user or consumer or to his/her property as a result of a defective condition of the product that made it unreasonably dangerous.

NOTE: Refer to Study Unit 7 for additional questions on Products Liability and Warranties.

STUDY UNIT FIFTEEN
NEGOTIABLE INSTRUMENTS: TYPES, NEGOTIATION, AND HOLDER IN DUE COURSE

Negotiable instruments law is codified primarily in **Article 3 of the Uniform Commercial Code (UCC)**. **Negotiable instruments** are **formal written contracts** and a form of property used extensively in business transactions as a substitute for money and to extend credit. Such instruments may be repeatedly negotiated. They include notes, certificates of deposit, drafts, and checks. A **promissory note** is a negotiable instrument containing a **promise**. The maker (1) promises unconditionally (2) to pay a fixed amount of money (3) to the order of the payee or to bearer (4) on demand or at some defined future date.

$500.00 Dayton, Ohio May 2, Year 1

Sixty days after date I promise to pay to the order of

Cash

Five hundred Dollars

Miami, Florida

Value received with interest at the rate of nine percent per annum.

This instrument is secured by a conditional sales contract.

No. 11 Due July 1, Year 1 *Mark Maker*

Mark Maker

The **maker** signs, or is identified in, a note as a person undertaking to pay a second person, either an identified person (the payee) or bearer. A **certificate of deposit** (CD) is an instrument containing an acknowledgment by a bank of receipt of money with a promise by the bank to repay it. It typically bears interest. **A CD is a form of promissory note.** It evidences deposit of funds, but it contains an unconditional promise to repay the amount. The bank is the maker, and the payee is generally an individual or a business. The classes of CDs are **demand certificates** (payable on demand) and **time certificates** (payable at a definite time after issue). A **draft** is a negotiable instrument that contains an **order**. Thus, a draft is (1) an unconditional written order (2) by one person, the drawer, (3) to another person, the drawee, (4) to pay a fixed amount of money (5) to a third person, either to an identified person (the payee) or to bearer.

To: Home Commerce Bank
Newtown, FL

May 15, Year 1

Pay to the order of Paul Payee $2,000.00
Two Thousand and xx/100 Dollars
on November 1, Year 1

David Drawer
David Drawer

The **drawer** is a person who signs or is identified in a draft as a person ordering payment. The **drawee** is the person ordered to make payment. The drawee must be obligated to the drawer either by agreement or through a debtor-creditor relationship before becoming obligated to honor the order. Drafts are usually classified as a **time draft** (payable at a definite time in the future) or a **sight draft** (payable on demand upon presentation to the drawee). A time draft is usually presented to the drawee for **acceptance** (agreement to pay) before the instrument's due date. The drawee accepts by writing the acceptance on the instrument. **A check is a form of draft.** It is always drawn on a bank, and it is always a sight draft that is **payable on demand** on or after its date. The drawer is a customer who has an account at a drawee bank. A **postdated check** is a time draft. It bears a date later than the date on which the check is drawn. To facilitate automated check collection, a bank may pay a postdated check when presented and before the stated date unless the drawer gives notice to the bank. A **certified check** is one that the drawee bank has accepted, even if the funds in the drawer's account are insufficient. A **cashier's check** is drawn by a bank on itself. The bank is obligated to itself. A cashier's check is often obtained by a **remitter**, a person not a party to the instrument who purchases it from the issuer, usually to pay a debt to the identified payee. A **traveler's check** is a three-party instrument. The traveler is the drawer, and the bank or other issuer is the drawee. For identification, the traveler signs the traveler's check twice, when the seller issues it and when the traveler cashes it.

Negotiability is strictly a matter of form. To be negotiable, an instrument must meet all of the following requirements:

- Be in **writing** and **signed** by the maker or drawer
- Contain an unconditional **promise** or **order** to pay a **fixed amount of money**, with or without interest or other charges described in the promise or order
- Be **payable on demand or at a definite time**
- Be **payable to order or to bearer** when it is issued or first comes into possession of a holder (but a **check** not payable to order or to bearer is negotiable if it meets the other requirements)
- **Not state any other undertaking or instruction** by the person promising or ordering payment of money (but the instrument may contain an undertaking or power with respect to collateral, an authorization to the holder to confess judgment or dispose of collateral, or the waiver of the benefit of a law)

If an instrument is in **negotiable form**, it may be transferred by **negotiation**. This is the transfer of possession of an instrument, whether or not voluntarily, by a person other than the issuer to a person who, as a result, becomes its holder. A **transfer** is a delivery of an instrument by a nonissuer for the purpose of giving the recipient a right to enforce it. Whether or not a transfer is a negotiation, it vests in the transferee whatever right the transferor had to enforce the instrument. A **holder** is the person in possession if the instrument is payable to bearer. If it is payable to an identified person, the holder is the person in possession only if (s)he is the identified person. Instruments in **bearer form** may be negotiated by **transfer of possession alone**. If the instrument is in **order form**, it must be negotiated by **endorsement by the holder and transfer of possession**. If a holder does **not endorse** an order instrument, a mere transfer occurs. This transfer is an **assignment** of the transferor's rights, and the transferee assigned is subject to **personal** as well as **real defenses**. An instrument is **payable to order** if it is payable to (1) the order of an identified person or (2) an identified person or order. An instrument is **payable to bearer** if it (1) is payable to bearer or the order of bearer, (2) is payable to cash or the order of cash, (3) states no payee, (4) indicates that it is not payable to an identified person, or (5) indicates that the person in possession is entitled to payment.

Endorsement is a signature that negotiates the instrument, restricts payment, or incurs endorser's liability. Endorsements are usually written on the back of the instrument itself. The placement of any endorsement and the **relative liability of endorsers** are presumed to be according to the order in which their signatures appear. A **forged endorsement** ordinarily is ineffective to negotiate an instrument payable to an identified person. Hence, no transferee can be a holder. A **blank endorsement** names no particular endorsee and consists merely of the signature of the endorser (or his/her authorized agent). An instrument payable to order and endorsed in blank becomes **payable to bearer**. A **special endorsement** names the specific party to whom the instrument is payable. Thus, an endorsement "Pay to Grace Smith" or "Pay to the order of Grace Smith" is a special endorsement.

Pay to Grace Smith

Grace Smith

A specially endorsed instrument becomes **payable to the order of the special endorsee** and requires his/her endorsement for further negotiation. Words of negotiability are **not required** in an endorsement. A holder may convert a blank endorsement consisting only of a signature into a special endorsement by writing above the signature of the endorser words identifying the payee (generally the holder). The effect is to convert bearer paper to order paper. The last endorsement determines whether the instrument is order paper or bearer paper. A **restrictive endorsement** attempts to limit or prohibit further negotiation or transfer. Nevertheless, such an endorsement **cannot prevent further negotiation or transfer**. Moreover, a restriction in the form of a **condition** precedent to the endorsee's right to receive payment is ineffective. (NOTE: Conditional language on the face of the instrument, but not in an endorsement, renders it nonnegotiable.)

Pay to Paula Payee, provided
that she completes painting my house
at 100 Safe Street by July Year 1

Emma Endorser

A restrictive endorsement that is effective to limit (not prevent) negotiation is one for deposit or collection (e.g., "for deposit only in my checking account"). This endorsement keeps the instrument within the bank collection process. A **qualified endorsement** (such as "without recourse") disclaims contractual liability on the instrument, but a qualified endorser may incur **warranty liability**.

> Pay to Paul Payee without
> recourse *Mark Maker*

Moreover, qualified endorsement does not destroy negotiability but may lessen marketability. An **unqualified endorsement** usually guarantees payment of the instrument if the primarily liable party does not pay. An **anomalous endorsement** is made by a person who is not the holder. It has no effect on negotiability, but it makes the signer liable as an endorser.

Negotiable instruments cannot effectively substitute for money unless collection is reasonably certain. Reasonable certainty is not possible unless most parties to whom negotiable instruments are negotiated are free of most claims and defenses assertable against prior parties. Thus, the most significant aspect of negotiability is the status of the **holder in due course (HDC)**. Usually, a mere **holder** acquires a negotiable instrument subject to all claims and defenses. However, an HDC (except in consumer credit transactions) takes the instrument free of all personal defenses but subject to real defenses. Among the **personal or contract defenses** are (1) prior payment, (2) theft by the holder, (3) lack or failure of consideration, (4) fraud in the inducement, (5) nonperformance of a condition precedent, (6) slight duress, and (7) unauthorized completion. The **real or universal defenses** are (1) illegality, (2) extreme duress, (3) fraud in the execution, (4) unauthorized signature, (5) lack of legal capacity, (6) infancy, (7) discharge in bankruptcy, and (8) alteration. However, duress, lack of legal capacity, or illegality is a real defense only if, under other law, the obligation is nullified. A holder may become an HDC if these requirements are met:

- The holder took in **good faith**. The requirement of good faith applies only to the holder. Good faith is a subjective and an objective determination. It means honesty in fact and the reasonable observance of commercial standards of fair dealing.
- The holder gave **value** for the instrument.
- The holder took the instrument without any **notice** of defenses to payment, rival claims of ownership, its overdue or dishonored status, or an alteration or unauthorized signature.
- The **authenticity** of the instrument is not questionable because of apparent evidence of forgery or alteration or otherwise because of its irregularity or incompleteness.

Special rules are provided by Article 3 with respect to the requirements for the preferred status of an HDC. In most cases, a party that does not personally qualify may nevertheless succeed to the rights of an HDC if (s)he derives title to the instrument through an HDC. This rule is the **shelter rule**. Its purpose is to broaden the marketability of negotiable instruments. However, a holder may not claim the benefits of the shelter principle if (s)he was a **party to fraud or illegality**.

Because of objections by consumer groups, the Federal Trade Commission (FTC) adopted an **anti-HDC rule**. It abolishes the HDC concept in most **consumer transactions**. Thus, the FTC requires a seller or a lessor of consumer goods or services to include in a consumer credit contract the following prominently printed notice:

NOTICE:
ANY HOLDER OF THIS CONSUMER CREDIT CONTRACT IS SUBJECT TO ALL CLAIMS AND DEFENSES WHICH THE DEBTOR COULD ASSERT AGAINST THE SELLER OF GOODS OR SERVICES OBTAINED PURSUANT HERETO OR WITH THE PROCEEDS HEREOF. RECOVERY HEREUNDER BY THE DEBTOR SHALL NOT EXCEED AMOUNTS PAID BY THE DEBTOR HEREUNDER.

This notice preserves all claims and defenses that a consumer may have, even against a good-faith purchaser for value without notice of any defenses, and effectively cancels HDC status.

QUESTIONS

15.1 Nature of Negotiable Instruments

1. Which of the following instruments is subject to the provisions of the Negotiable Instruments Article of the UCC?

A. A bill of lading.

B. A warehouse receipt.

C. A certificate of deposit.

D. An investment security.

Answer (C) is correct. *(Publisher, adapted)*

REQUIRED: The instrument that is subjected to the provision of the UCC.

DISCUSSION: UCC Article 3 regulates negotiable instruments. The article includes four kinds of negotiable instruments: drafts, checks, promissory notes, and certificates of deposit. Negotiable instruments are formal written contracts used extensively in business as a substitute for money and as a method to extend credit. Every negotiable instrument governed by Article 3 contains an unconditional promise or order to pay money. Other forms of negotiable contracts, such as bills of lading, warehouse receipts, and investment securities, do not order or promise payment of money and are governed by UCC Articles 7 and 8, respectively, and not by UCC Article 3. A certificate of deposit (CD) is a specialized form of promissory note in which a bank acknowledges a receipt of money and promises to repay the money with interest in the future.

Answer (A) is incorrect. A bill of lading is a document evidencing receipt of goods for shipment and is governed by UCC Article 7. Answer (B) is incorrect. A warehouse receipt is a document evidencing receipt of goods for storage and is governed by UCC Article 7. Answer (D) is incorrect. Investment securities are stocks and bonds or other recognized forms of investment regulated by UCC Article 8.

2. Anton promised to pay Beta $10,000 in exchange for an automobile. Accordingly, Anton executed a contract and delivered it to Beta. Beta then transferred the contract to Carl for value. When Beta failed to perform, Anton refused to pay. If Carl sues Anton,

A. Carl will win because he stepped into the shoes of the assignor.

B. Anton will win because the contract is not transferable.

C. Anton will win even if the contract is instead a negotiable instrument.

D. Carl will win if the contract is instead a negotiable instrument and the requirements of Article 3 of the UCC are complied with.

Answer (D) is correct. *(Publisher, adapted)*

REQUIRED: The difference in effect between a contract right and a negotiable instrument.

DISCUSSION: Most contract rights are assignable, and an assignee takes subject to all defenses assertable against his/her assignor. But the taker of a negotiable instrument who conforms to the holder-in-due-course rules of Article 3 of the UCC is not subject to such personal defenses as failure of consideration. Thus, certain good-faith transferees for value of negotiable instruments are protected from the effects of disputes between the original contracting parties.

Answer (A) is incorrect. Although Carl does step into the shoes of the assignor, Anton may assert the same defenses against both the assignor (Beta) and the assignee (Carl) of a contract. Answer (B) is incorrect. Although Anton may win, a right to receive money is transferable. Answer (C) is incorrect. Carl may win if the contract is a negotiable instrument.

3. If an instrument does not meet one of the requirements of negotiability,

A. It will usually be transferable.

B. It will be worthless.

C. It will not be assignable.

D. An innocent transferee will nevertheless take free of the issuer's personal defenses.

Answer (A) is correct. *(Publisher, adapted)*

REQUIRED: The effect of nonnegotiability of an instrument.

DISCUSSION: If a required element of negotiability is not present, special protections provided by the law are not available. Nevertheless, the contract right embodied in the nonnegotiable instrument will usually be transferable because most contract rights, especially the right to receive money, are assignable. But the assignee will take no better right than that held by his/her assignor.

Answer (B) is incorrect. A contract right may have value even if not evidenced by a negotiable instrument. Answer (C) is incorrect. Contract rights are generally assignable. Answer (D) is incorrect. A transferee of a nonnegotiable instrument takes subject to all defenses of the obligor.

15.2 Types of Negotiable Instruments and Parties

4. The following instrument is negotiable:

> April 30, Year 1
>
> I promise to pay, on October 13, Year 1, to the order of Pam Payee $1,000 (One thousand dollars) with interest thereon at the rate of 12% per annum.
>
> *Paula Promisee*
>
> Paula Promisee

The instrument is a

A. Promissory note.

B. Draft.

C. Certificate of deposit.

D. Check.

Answer (A) is correct. *(CPA, adapted)*

REQUIRED: The term identifying the instrument.

DISCUSSION: The instrument is a promissory note because it is a two-party instrument in which the maker unconditionally promises to pay a fixed amount of money to the payee.

Answer (B) is incorrect. A negotiable instrument is a draft if it contains an order. It is a three-party instrument in which one person orders a second person to pay a third person. Answer (C) is incorrect. A certificate of deposit is a written acknowledgment by a bank of receipt of money with a promise to repay. It is one form of note. Answer (D) is incorrect. A check is a type of draft by which a bank is ordered to make the payment on demand.

5. An instrument complies with the requirements for negotiability contained in the UCC article on negotiable instruments. The instrument contains language expressly acknowledging the receipt of $40,000 by Mint Bank and an agreement to repay principal with interest at 11% 6 months from date. The instrument is

A. A banker's acceptance.

B. A banker's draft.

C. A negotiable certificate of deposit.

D. A nonnegotiable instrument because of the additional language.

Answer (C) is correct. *(CPA, adapted)*

REQUIRED: The term for a bank's acknowledgment of receipt of money with an agreement to repay.

DISCUSSION: A certificate of deposit (CD) is an acknowledgment by a bank of receipt of money with an engagement to repay it. The bank is the maker, and the payee is the depositor. Although a CD is essentially a note, it is separately classified because certain laws apply to CDs but not to other notes.

Answer (A) is incorrect. An acceptance is the drawee's signed agreement to pay a draft as presented. As a note, a CD is a two-party instrument and does not require acceptance by a drawee. Answer (B) is incorrect. A teller's check is a draft drawn by a bank (1) on another bank or (2) payable at or through a bank. Answer (D) is incorrect. The additional language is consistent with negotiability. A fixed amount of money is to be paid at a definite time.

6. Gold is holding the following instrument:

> TO: Sussex National Bank
> Suffolk, N.Y.
>
> April 15, Year 1
>
> Pay to the order of Tom Gold $2,000.00
>
> Two Thousand and xx/100 Dollars
>
> on April 9, Year 1
>
> *Lester Davis*
>
> Lester Davis

The instrument is

A. A postdated check.

B. A promissory note.

C. A draft.

D. Payable on demand.

Answer (C) is correct. *(CPA, adapted)*

REQUIRED: The term that identifies the instrument.

DISCUSSION: A draft is a three-party instrument in which one person (the drawer) orders a second person (the drawee) to pay a third person (the payee). With this instrument, Lester Davis (the drawer) is ordering Sussex National Bank (the drawee) to pay Tom Gold (the payee).

Answer (A) is incorrect. This instrument is payable on April 9, Year 1. Thus, it is not postdated because it is payable before its issue date (April 15, Year 1). Answer (B) is incorrect. A promissory note is a two-party instrument in which one person promises to pay another person. Answer (D) is incorrect. The draft is payable on April 9, Year 1, not on demand. A promise is payable on demand if (1) it states that it is payable on demand or at sight, or otherwise indicates that it is payable at the will of the holder, or (2) it states no time for payment. This draft is payable at a definite time because it is payable at a fixed date.

7. Mary issued an instrument in which she directed the Doe State Bank to pay to the order of Rhonda a fixed amount of money 30 days after sight. The instrument was presented, and Doe gave its signed undertaking to pay on the due date. Doe State Bank is

A. The drawer.

B. The payee and the maker.

C. Both the drawee and the acceptor.

D. Both the drawer and the acceptor.

Answer (C) is correct. *(Publisher, adapted)*

REQUIRED: The term(s) for the bank on which a draft is drawn.

DISCUSSION: The instrument is a draft because it contains an order by the drawer (Mary) to a drawee (Doe) to pay money to a payee (Rhonda). A person, usually a drawee, who agrees to pay the draft is an acceptor. Ordinarily, this agreement is signified by writing "accepted" on the instrument along with the date and a signature. Doe is therefore a drawee and an acceptor.

Answer (A) is incorrect. Mary is the drawer. Answer (B) is incorrect. The maker is the person who issues a note. The payee is the person who is to be paid. Answer (D) is incorrect. Mary is the drawer.

8. A trade acceptance usually

A. Is an order to deliver goods to a named person.

B. Provides that the drawer is also the payee.

C. Is not regarded as a negotiable instrument under the UCC.

D. Must be made payable "to the order of" a named person.

Answer (B) is correct. *(CPA, adapted)*

REQUIRED: The true statement about a trade acceptance.

DISCUSSION: A trade acceptance is a special form of negotiable instrument known as a time draft used by sellers as a way to extend credit to buyers of their goods. The seller draws a draft ordering the buyer to pay the seller at some time in the future. The seller is thus both drawer and payee of a trade acceptance.

Answer (A) is incorrect. A trade acceptance is a negotiable instrument and must be payable in money. Answer (C) is incorrect. A trade acceptance is a type of draft. As such, it is recognized as a negotiable instrument under the UCC. Answer (D) is incorrect. A trade acceptance may be payable to order or to bearer.

15.3 Negotiability

9. To be negotiable, an instrument must be written and signed. Which of the following is true?

A. A drawee's signature is required for the negotiability of a draft.

B. A signature may be any symbol intended by a party to authenticate a writing.

C. A signature must be handwritten.

D. A signature must be placed at the end of the instrument.

Answer (B) is correct. *(Publisher, adapted)*

REQUIRED: The true statement about the signature requirement.

DISCUSSION: Under UCC 3-401, "A signature may be made (1) manually or by means of a device or machine, and (2) by the use of any name, including a trade or assumed name, or by a word, mark, or symbol executed or adopted by a person with present intention to authenticate a writing."

Answer (A) is incorrect. Only the drawer's signature is required. Answer (C) is incorrect. A signature may be stamped, printed, typed, or produced by some other mechanical method. Answer (D) is incorrect. The signature may appear almost anywhere, but placement at the end is usual and makes it clear who issued the instrument.

10. An instrument will be negotiable only if it contains an order or promise to pay. Accordingly, an instrument is negotiable if it

A. Authorizes payment to an identified person.

B. Acknowledges an obligation.

C. Omits the word "promise" but states an undertaking to pay.

D. Omits the word "order" but states a request to pay.

Answer (C) is correct. *(Publisher, adapted)*

REQUIRED: The language satisfying the promise or order to pay requirement.

DISCUSSION: Under UCC 3-103, a promise is a written undertaking to pay money signed by the person undertaking to pay. It must be more than an acknowledgment of an obligation. The word "promise" need not be used, however.

Answer (A) is incorrect. An authorization to pay is not an order unless the person authorized is also instructed to pay. Answer (B) is incorrect. An acknowledgment, such as an IOU, is not a promise to pay. Answer (D) is incorrect. An order is an instruction to pay, not a mere request.

11. Under the negotiable instruments article of the UCC, which of the following circumstances would prevent a promissory note from being negotiable?

A. An extension clause that allows the maker to elect to extend the time for payment to a date specified in the note.

B. An acceleration clause that allows the holder to move up the maturity date of the note in the event of default.

C. A note that is signed on behalf of the maker by a person having a power of attorney.

D. A clause that allows the maker to satisfy the note by the performance of services or the payment of money.

Answer (D) is correct. *(CPA, adapted)*

REQUIRED: The circumstances that would prevent a promissory note from being negotiable.

DISCUSSION: To be negotiable, a note must be payable in money and only in money. A note that allows the maker to pay by performing services is not negotiable (UCC 3-104).

Answer (A) is incorrect. To be negotiable, an instrument must be payable on demand or at a definite time. Under UCC 3-108, a promise is "payable at a definite time" if it is payable at a time readily ascertainable when the promise is issued, subject to rights of, for example, prepayment, acceleration, or extension at the holder's option, or extension to a further definite time at the option of the maker. Answer (B) is incorrect. To be negotiable, an instrument must be payable on demand or at a definite time. Under UCC 3-108, a promise is "payable at a definite time" if it is payable at a time readily ascertainable when the promise is issued, subject to rights of, for example, prepayment, acceleration, or extension at the holder's option, or extension to a further definite time at the option of the maker. Answer (C) is incorrect. An agent, such as a person having power of attorney, can sign a negotiable instrument on behalf of a principal.

12. A secured promissory note is nonnegotiable if it provides that

A. Additional collateral must be tendered if there is a decline in market value of the original collateral.

B. Upon default, the maker waives a trial by jury.

C. The maker is entitled to a 5% discount if the note is prepaid.

D. It is subject to the terms of the mortgage given by the maker to the payee.

Answer (D) is correct. *(CPA, adapted)*

REQUIRED: The provision that defeats negotiability of a promissory note.

DISCUSSION: A negotiable instrument must include an unconditional promise or order to pay. When a promise or order is subject to the provisions of another writing, it is conditional (UCC 3-106). A conditional instrument is nonnegotiable because the rights of a holder cannot be ascertained with reasonable certainty from its face. A note that is subject to the terms of a mortgage violates this requirement and is rendered nonnegotiable.

Answer (A) is incorrect. A negotiable instrument may include a promise to maintain or protect collateral. Answer (B) is incorrect. Waiver of a benefit for the advantage or protection of the obligor does not affect negotiability. Answer (C) is incorrect. The requirement of a fixed amount of money does not preclude a provision for specified prepayment discounts.

13. Under the Negotiable Instruments Article of the UCC, which of the following statements is true regarding the requirements for an instrument to be negotiable?

I. The instrument must be in writing, be signed by both the drawer and the drawee, and contain an unconditional promise or order to pay.

II. The instrument must state a fixed amount of money, be payable on demand or at a definite time, and be payable to order or to bearer.

A. I only.

B. II only.

C. Both I and II.

D. Neither I nor II.

Answer (B) is correct. *(CPA, adapted)*

REQUIRED: The true statement regarding the requirements for an instrument to be negotiable.

DISCUSSION: Negotiability is strictly a matter of form. If an instrument is drafted in a specific form, it is a negotiable instrument. To be negotiable, an instrument must be a writing that is signed by the person undertaking to pay or the person giving the instruction to pay. It also must (1) contain an unconditional promise or order to pay a fixed amount of money, (2) be payable on demand or at a definite time, (3) be payable to bearer or to order at the time the instrument is issued or first comes into possession of a holder, and (4) not state any other undertaking or instruction by the person promising or ordering payment.

Answer (A) is incorrect. Only the drawer of a negotiable draft or the maker of a negotiable note, not the drawee or payee, must sign a negotiable instrument. Answer (C) is incorrect. Only the drawer of a negotiable draft or the maker of a negotiable note, not the drawee or payee, must sign a negotiable instrument. Answer (D) is incorrect. To be negotiable, an instrument must state a fixed amount of money, be payable on demand or at a definite time, and be payable to order or bearer.

14. The following instrument is in the possession of Bill North:

> On May 30, Year 1, I promise to pay Bill North, the bearer of this document, $1,800.
>
> *Joseph Peppers*
> Joseph Peppers
>
> Re: Auto Purchase Contract

This instrument is

A. Nonnegotiable because it is undated.

B. Nonnegotiable because it is not payable to order or bearer.

C. Negotiable even though it refers to the contract out of which it arose.

D. Negotiable because it is payable at a definite time.

Answer (B) is correct. *(CPA, adapted)*

REQUIRED: The negotiability of the instrument.

DISCUSSION: The instrument is a nonnegotiable note because it was not payable to order or bearer when it was first issued or came into the possession of a holder (UCC 3-104). It is payable only to Bill North and refers to him specifically as the bearer on its face.

Answer (A) is incorrect. An issue date is not necessary for negotiability. Answer (C) is incorrect. An instrument is nonnegotiable if it is not payable to order or to bearer. Reference to a separate agreement would impair negotiability only if the obligation were made subject to the other agreement. Answer (D) is incorrect. More is required for negotiability than that an instrument be payable at a definite time or on demand.

15. A company has in its possession the following instrument:

$500.00	Dayton, Ohio	October 2, Year 1

Sixty days after date I promise to pay to the order of

Cash

Five hundred dollars

at Miami, Florida

Value received with interest at the rate of nine percent per annum

This instrument is secured by a conditional sales contract.

No. 11 Due December 1, Year 1 *Craig Burke*
Craig Burke

This instrument is

A. Not negotiable until December 1, Year 1.

B. A negotiable bearer note.

C. A negotiable time draft.

D. A nonnegotiable note because it states that it is secured by a conditional sales contract.

Answer (B) is correct. *(CPA, adapted)*

REQUIRED: The type of instrument evidenced by the specified commercial document.

DISCUSSION: The instrument is a signed writing unconditionally promising to pay a fixed amount of money at a definite time to the bearer. It thus meets all of the requirements of negotiability. It is a two-party instrument with a maker and a payee, so it is a promissory note. It is a bearer note because it is payable to the order of cash.

Answer (A) is incorrect. Negotiability is not altered by an instrument's not being payable until some future date. Answer (C) is incorrect. A draft is a three-party instrument involving a drawer, drawee, and payee. Answer (D) is incorrect. A promise or order is unconditional unless it states an express condition to payment, that the promise or order is governed by another writing, or that rights or obligations regarding the promise or order are stated in another writing. A mere reference to another writing does not condition the obligation to pay or affect the note's negotiability.

16.

August 30, Year 1

McHugh Wholesaler, Inc.
Pullman, Washington

Pay to the order of Luft Manufacturing, Inc., three thousand dollars ($3,000) three months after acceptance.

Peter Crandall
Peter Crandall, President
Luft Manufacturing, Inc.

Accepted September 15, Year 1
McHugh Wholesalers, Inc.

By *David Cruz* President

This instrument

A. Would be treated as a promissory note because the drawee is not a bank.

B. Is a negotiable draft.

C. Is not negotiable under Article 3 (Negotiable Instruments) of the Uniform Commercial Code, although it may be negotiable under another article.

D. Is not negotiable because the drawer and the payee are the same person.

Answer (B) is correct. *(CPA, adapted)*

REQUIRED: The true description of the instrument.

DISCUSSION: The instrument is a draft because it is an order by one person (Luft) directing another (McHugh) to pay a third person (Luft). That the third party is the same as the first party is irrelevant. It is negotiable because all of the requirements of negotiability are met. The instrument is written, is signed by the drawer, contains an unconditional order to pay a fixed amount of money at a definite time, is payable to order, and contains no other promises or obligations (UCC 3-104).

Answer (A) is incorrect. A note is a two-party instrument in which one person promises to pay another. Answer (C) is incorrect. The draft is negotiable under Article 3 of the UCC, the sole authority concerning negotiable instruments. Answer (D) is incorrect. The drawer and the payee may be the same person. This is a means of documenting a third person's (McHugh's) promise to pay a debt.

17. An instrument reads as follows:

$10,000	Ludlow, Vermont	February 1, Year 1

I promise to pay to the order of Custer Corp. $10,000 within 10 days after the sale of my two-carat diamond ring. I pledge the sale proceeds to secure my obligation hereunder.

R. Harris

R. Harris

Which of the following statements correctly describes the above instrument?

A. The instrument is nonnegotiable because it is not payable at a definite time.

B. The instrument is nonnegotiable because it is secured by the proceeds of the sale of the ring.

C. The instrument is a negotiable promissory note.

D. The instrument is a negotiable sight draft payable on demand.

Answer (A) is correct. *(CPA, adapted)*

REQUIRED: The statement that describes the instrument.

DISCUSSION: The instrument is a signed writing promising to pay a fixed amount of money to the order of an identified person. A fixed amount of money means it is possible to compute the amount from the face of the instrument. But the obligation to pay and its timing depend on an uncertain event (sale of a ring). The promise is therefore conditional; negotiability requires that it be unconditional. A "definite time" is not limited to one particular date. An instrument payable on or before a stated date is payable on demand until that date and is payable at a fixed date thereafter (if not yet paid).

Answer (B) is incorrect. Existence of security does not condition the obligation to pay or affect the note's negotiability. Answer (C) is incorrect. The promise is conditioned upon the sale of the ring. Answer (D) is incorrect. In a draft, the drawer orders the drawee to pay a third person.

18. A client has an instrument that contains certain ambiguities or deficiencies. In construing the instrument, which of the following is false?

A. If there is doubt whether the instrument is a draft or a note, the holder may treat it as either.

B. Handwritten terms control typewritten and printed terms, and typewritten terms control printed terms.

C. An instrument that does not state any time of payment is not negotiable.

D. That the instrument is antedated will not affect the instrument's negotiability.

Answer (C) is correct. *(CPA, adapted)*

REQUIRED: The false statement about construing an ambiguous or deficient instrument.

DISCUSSION: A promise or order is payable on demand if it does not state any time of payment. A negotiable instrument is, among other things, payable on demand or at a definite time (UCC 3-108).

Answer (A) is incorrect. A person entitled to enforce an ambiguous instrument may treat it as either a draft or a note if the instrument meets the definition of either. Answer (B) is incorrect. Handwritten terms control typewritten and printed (typeset) terms, and typewritten terms control printed terms. Answer (D) is incorrect. An instrument may be either antedated or postdated without affecting its negotiability.

15.4 Negotiation and Endorsements

19. To negotiate an instrument payable to bearer, one must

A. Transfer possession of, and endorse, the instrument.

B. Transfer possession of the instrument.

C. Endorse the instrument.

D. Endorse and transfer possession of the instrument with consideration.

Answer (B) is correct. *(CPA, adapted)*

REQUIRED: The proper means of negotiating a bearer instrument.

DISCUSSION: Under UCC 3-201, negotiation is the voluntary or involuntary transfer of possession of an instrument (other than by the issuer) to a holder. If the instrument is payable to an identified person, it is negotiated by transfer of possession and endorsement by the holder; if the instrument is payable to bearer, it is negotiated by transfer of possession alone.

Answer (A) is incorrect. It states the method of negotiating an instrument payable to an identified person. Answer (C) is incorrect. Negotiation requires transfer of possession. Answer (D) is incorrect. Consideration is not required for negotiation.

20. There are several legally significant differences between a negotiable instrument and a contract right, and the transfer of each. Which of the following statements is true?

A. A negotiable instrument is deemed prima facie to have been issued for consideration, whereas a contract right is not.

B. The transferee of a negotiable instrument and the assignee of a contract right take free of most defenses.

C. Neither can be transferred without a signed writing or by a delivery.

D. The statute of frauds rules apply to both.

Answer (A) is correct. *(CPA, adapted)*

REQUIRED: The true statement comparing negotiable instruments and contract rights.

DISCUSSION: Lack of consideration is a personal defense that is not available against a holder in due course of a negotiable instrument or one who has the rights of a holder in due course. However, an obligor on a contract right may assert such a defense.

Answer (B) is incorrect. The transferee of a negotiable instrument who is not a holder in due course and the assignee of a contract right both take subject to all defenses of the obligor. Answer (C) is incorrect. A contract right can be transferred orally and without delivery. Negotiation of a negotiable instrument requires an endorsement and a transfer of possession if it is payable to an identified person. It requires transfer of possession alone if it is payable to bearer. Answer (D) is incorrect. The statute of frauds applies only to certain contracts. But an instrument must be in writing to be negotiable.

21. Anna Karr transferred a negotiable instrument payable to her order in exchange for value to John Watson. Karr did not endorse the instrument. As a result of the transfer, Watson

A. Obtains such rights as the transferor had in all cases.

B. Can become a holder only if the instrument is endorsed and possession is transferred at the same time.

C. Is presumed to be the owner of the instrument because she gave value.

D. Is entitled to an unqualified endorsement by Karr.

Answer (D) is correct. *(CPA, adapted)*

REQUIRED: The true statement concerning the transfer of a negotiation instrument for value.

DISCUSSION: Because Watson received the instrument from Karr for value, Watson has a specifically enforceable right to Karr's cooperation in negotiating that instrument absent an agreement to the contrary (UCC 3-203). Thus, Watson has a right to Karr's unqualified endorsement of the instrument.

Answer (A) is incorrect. Watson, as transferee, may qualify as a holder in due course and therefore may have rights superior to those of the transferor. Answer (B) is incorrect. Endorsement and transfer of possession need not coincide. Watson will not become a holder, however, until the instrument has been negotiated to him through proper endorsement. Answer (C) is incorrect. Endorsement and transfer of possession of an instrument define its ownership.

22. Herbert is a holder of a check originally payable to the order of Byron or bearer. These endorsements appear on the back:

> *Byron*
>
> Pay to the order of House
>
> *Daugherty*
>
> *House*
>
> *Humble*

Which of the following is true?

A. The check was originally order paper.

B. The check was order paper in Humble's hands.

C. The check is bearer paper in Herbert's hands.

D. Byron's signature was necessary for negotiation.

Answer (C) is correct. *(Publisher, adapted)*

REQUIRED: The true statement about the effect of the endorsements.

DISCUSSION: The instrument was originally bearer paper, and Byron's signature was not necessary for negotiation. Daugherty converted the check to order paper with the special endorsement to House, who negotiated it to Humble with a blank endorsement. By failing to name a payee, House converted the check back to bearer paper. Humble's blank endorsement did not affect the status of the check. Consequently, Herbert holds bearer paper.

Answer (A) is incorrect. The check was originally bearer paper, assuming the bearer language was hand- or typewritten. Answer (B) is incorrect. House converted the check back to bearer paper. Answer (D) is incorrect. Byron held the check when it was bearer paper and thus negotiable by transfer of possession alone.

23. Tim Teff entered Al Archer's office and stole some radios and Archer's wallet containing identification. Subsequently, representing himself as Archer, Teff induced Bob Bane to purchase one of the stolen radios for a fair price. Bane gave Teff his check made out to Archer. Teff endorsed the check "Pay to the order of Crown, Archer" and transferred it to Cal Crown for cash in the amount of the check. Crown endorsed the check "Pay to the order of Fox, Crown" and transferred the check to Fred Fox to be applied to his account. Bane's check was

A. Void from the beginning.

B. Bearer paper when Crown took it.

C. Order paper initially and negotiated by Teff to Crown.

D. Nonnegotiable absent a valid endorsement by the real Archer.

Answer (C) is correct. *(CPA, adapted)*

REQUIRED: The true statement regarding the type of check described in the facts.

DISCUSSION: The check was initially order paper because it was payable to the order of Archer, as opposed to bearer or cash (UCC 3-109). It was negotiated by Teff to Crown when Teff fraudulently endorsed it with Archer's name and delivered it to Crown (UCC 3-201).

Answer (A) is incorrect. The check was not initially void. Bane gave it for consideration of the purchase of the radios. Answer (B) is incorrect. The check was order paper (payable to the order of Crown) when Crown took it. Answer (D) is incorrect. The forged endorsement does not make the check nonnegotiable. If an imposter induces the drawer to issue a check to the imposter by impersonating the payee, an endorsement by anyone (including the impostor) in the name of the payee is effective in favor of any person (e.g., Crown or Fox) who in good faith pays the check or takes it for value or collection (UCC 3-404).

24. The following endorsements appear on the back of a negotiable promissory note payable to Lake Co.:

> Pay to John Smith only
> *Frank Parker*, President of Lake Co.
>
> *John Smith*
>
> Pay to the order of Sharp, Inc. but only if Sharp delivers computers purchased by Mary Harris by March 15, Year 1.
>
> *Mary Harris*

Which of the following statements is true?

A. The note became nonnegotiable as a result of Parker's endorsement.

B. Harris's conditional endorsement caused the note to be nonnegotiable.

C. Smith's endorsement effectively prevented further negotiation of the note.

D. Harris's signature was not required to effectively negotiate the note to Sharp.

Answer (D) is correct. *(CPA, adapted)*

REQUIRED: The true statement concerning negotiability of the instrument.

DISCUSSION: The restrictive endorsement, *Pay to John Smith only*, is an ineffective attempt to prohibit further negotiability. Endorsement by John Smith in blank converts this order instrument to bearer paper, which is negotiable by mere transfer of possession. Thus, Harris's signature was not necessary to negotiate the note.

Answer (A) is incorrect. Restrictive endorsements are generally ineffective to limit negotiability. Answer (B) is incorrect. A conditional endorsement does not hinder negotiability. Answer (C) is incorrect. Smith's endorsement converted negotiable order paper to negotiable bearer paper.

25. Under the Negotiable Instruments Article of the UCC, an endorsement of an instrument "for deposit only" is an example of what type of endorsement?

A. Blank.

B. Qualified.

C. Restrictive.

D. Special.

Answer (C) is correct. *(CPA, adapted)*

REQUIRED: The classification of an endorsement.

DISCUSSION: A restrictive endorsement attempts to restrict or further limit the negotiation of an instrument. An endorsement "for deposit only" locks the instrument into the banking system for deposit and restricts the negotiation of the instrument.

Answer (A) is incorrect. A blank endorsement is an endorsement by the holder that is not a special endorsement. Thus, it identifies no particular payee. Answer (B) is incorrect. A qualified endorsement is used by an endorser to disclaim or limit contractual liability on the instrument. Answer (D) is incorrect. A special endorsement is an endorsement by a holder that identifies the person to whom the instrument is payable.

26. A person who endorses a check "without recourse"

A. Has the same liability as an accommodation endorser.

B. Negates his/her liability only insofar as prior parties are concerned.

C. Modifies the warranty to his/her transferee.

D. Does not promise or guarantee payment of the instrument upon dishonor even if there has been a proper presentment and proper notice has been given.

Answer (D) is correct. *(CPA, adapted)*

REQUIRED: The effect of a "without recourse" endorsement.

DISCUSSION: Under UCC 3-415, unless otherwise specified (such as by words like "without recourse"), every endorser engages that, upon dishonor and any necessary notice of dishonor, (s)he will pay the amount due according to the instrument's terms when it was endorsed. The obligation is owed to a person entitled to enforce the instrument or to a subsequent endorser that paid the instrument. An endorsement "without recourse" is a qualified endorsement that disclaims this contract liability. But it does not eliminate warranty liability.

Answer (A) is incorrect. An accommodation endorser incurs the liability of an endorser who does not use a qualified endorsement. Answer (B) is incorrect. The words negate contract liability to subsequent parties as well. Answer (C) is incorrect. A qualified endorsement does not modify the transfer warranties.

27. Ed Johnson lost a check that he had received for professional services rendered. The instrument on its face was payable to Johnson's order. He had endorsed it on the back by signing his name and printing "for deposit only" above his name. Amy found the check. Which of the following is true?

A. A nonbank party who purchases the instrument commits a tort unless the amount paid is received by the endorser or applied consistently with the endorsement.

B. The endorsement is a blank endorsement, and a holder in due course who cashed it for Amy would prevail.

C. The endorsement prevents further transfer or negotiation by anyone.

D. If Amy simply signs her name beneath Johnson's endorsement, the instrument becomes bearer paper, and a holder in due course would take free of the restriction.

Answer (A) is correct. *(CPA, adapted)*

REQUIRED: The true statement regarding the effect of an endorsement "for deposit only."

DISCUSSION: A restrictive endorsement "for deposit only" puts the burden on most subsequent transferees to comply with the endorsement or to be certain that the endorsement has already been complied with. A person other than a bank, a depository bank (the first bank to receive a check for payment), or a bank that takes the instrument for immediate payment over the counter commits the tort of conversion unless the amount paid is received by the endorser or applied consistently with the endorsement. Conversion is treating personal property in a manner that is completely inconsistent with the rights of the true owner. However, banks later in the collection process are usually exempt from the requirement (UCC 3-206). Hence, a nonbank purchaser of Johnson's check is required to act consistently with the endorsement. (S)he must deposit the check only in Johnson's bank account.

Answer (B) is incorrect. "For deposit only" is a restrictive endorsement (not a blank endorsement), and most subsequent transferees must comply with it. Answer (C) is incorrect. The endorsement merely restricts payment; it does not prevent transfer or negotiation (an endorsement attempting to do so is not effective). Answer (D) is incorrect. The restrictive endorsement prevents the instrument from being changed directly into bearer paper. Furthermore, a subsequent transferee could not qualify as a holder in due course if the restriction had not been complied with.

15.5 Holder in Due Course

28. The status of a holder in due course as opposed to a mere holder of a negotiable instrument

A. Is of little consequence as a practical matter.

B. Eliminates the presentment requirement.

C. Allows the holder in due course to overcome certain defenses that cannot be overcome by a mere holder.

D. Allows the further negotiation of the instrument.

Answer (C) is correct. *(CPA, adapted)*

REQUIRED: The true statement concerning the difference between a holder and a holder in due course.

DISCUSSION: Real defenses are good against both holders and holders in due course; personal defenses are good against holders but not against holders in due course.

Answer (A) is incorrect. That the holder in due course is free of personal defenses of previous holders is a significant advantage. Answer (B) is incorrect. Presentment is required when a secondary party is to be held liable on a negotiable instrument (unless waived or excused under UCC 3-504). A holder in due course is not excused from this requirement. Answer (D) is incorrect. Previous negotiation of an instrument by either a holder or a holder in due course will not defeat the negotiability of that instrument.

29. To the extent that a holder of a negotiable promissory note is a holder in due course, (s)he takes the note free from which of the following defenses?

A. Minority of the maker if it is a defense to enforcement of a contract.

B. Forgery of the maker's signature.

C. Nonperformance of a condition precedent.

D. Discharge of the maker in bankruptcy.

Answer (C) is correct. *(CPA, adapted)*

REQUIRED: The defense not valid against a holder in due course.

DISCUSSION: A holder in due course ordinarily takes an instrument free of all personal defenses, but the holder in due course is still subject to real defenses. Traditional contract defenses, such as nonperformance of a condition precedent, are usually personal defenses and thus not valid against a holder in due course.

30. For a person to be a holder in due course of a promissory note,

A. The note must be payable in U.S. currency to the holder.

B. The holder must be the payee of the note.

C. The note must be negotiable.

D. All prior holders must have been holders in due course.

Answer (C) is correct. *(CPA, adapted)*

REQUIRED: The requirement for HDC status.

DISCUSSION: A holder is a person in possession to whom an instrument has been negotiated. An HDC is a holder of a negotiable instrument that, when issued or negotiated to the holder, does not "bear such apparent evidence of forgery or alteration or is not otherwise so irregular or incomplete as to call into question its authenticity." Furthermore, an HDC must take the instrument for value, in good faith, and without notice of certain disqualifying conditions. These include that the instrument (1) is overdue; (2) has been dishonored; (3) is part of a series of instruments, one of which is in uncured default with respect to payments; (4) contains an unauthorized signature or has been altered; (5) is subject to a claim of a property or possessory right; and (6) is subject to any claim in recoupment (UCC 3-302).

Answer (A) is incorrect. A negotiable note may be payable in foreign money (UCC 3-107). Answer (B) is incorrect. The holder may be, but is not required to be, a maker, payee, drawer, drawee, or endorser. Answer (D) is incorrect. A person who acquires an instrument from a holder may be an HDC.

31. Your client, Robert Rose, has the following instrument in his possession:

> March 1, Year 1
>
> One month from date, I, Charles Wallace, do hereby promise to pay Edward Carlson seven hundred and fifty dollars ($750.00).
>
> *Charles Wallace*

Edward Carlson wrote "pay to the order of Robert Rose" on the back, endorsed the instrument, and delivered it to Rose.

A. Robert Rose is a holder in due course.

B. The instrument is a negotiable promissory note.

C. Edward Carlson is a holder in due course.

D. All defenses, real and personal, are assertable by Wallace against Rose.

Answer (D) is correct. *(CPA, adapted)*

REQUIRED: The true statement regarding the promissory note described.

DISCUSSION: All defenses are assertable by the maker of a promissory note against all parties except a holder in due course. One can qualify for the special status of holder in due course only if the instrument is negotiable. This instrument is not negotiable because it is not payable to order or to bearer. Thus, the transfer by Carlson to Rose is a mere assignment, not a negotiation, and the assignee stands in the shoes of the assignor. Wallace can therefore assert all defenses against Rose (the assignee) that he could have asserted against Carlson (the assignor-payee).

Answer (A) is incorrect. Rose is not a holder in due course. The instrument is not negotiable. Answer (B) is incorrect. The instrument is a nonnegotiable note. Answer (C) is incorrect. Carlson is not a holder in due course. The instrument is not negotiable.

32. Alfredo promises to rebuild the engine in Ernesto's Maserati in exchange for Ernesto's negotiation to him of a promissory note in the amount of $5,000.00. If Alfredo never rebuilds the engine,

A. He cannot qualify as a holder in due course.

B. The maker of the note will sue Alfredo for lack of consideration.

C. The maker of the note will sue Ernesto for lack of consideration.

D. He still qualifies as a holder in due course.

Answer (A) is correct. *(I. Schwartz)*

REQUIRED: The effect of failure to perform a promise given for the negotiation of a promissory note.

DISCUSSION: Under UCC 3-303, the value requirement is met (1) to the extent a promise has been performed; (2) if the transferee acquires a security interest or other nonjudicial lien on the instrument; (3) if the issuance or transfer of the instrument is in payment of, or as security for, an existing obligation of any person, whether or not due; (4) if the issuance or transfer is for another negotiable instrument; or (5) if the issuance or transfer is in exchange for an irrevocable commitment to a third person. Future consideration, such as an executory contractual promise, does not constitute value.

Answer (B) is incorrect. The maker of the note presumably received consideration from the payee, and the facts given do not indicate otherwise. Answer (C) is incorrect. The maker of the note presumably received consideration from the payee, and the facts given do not indicate otherwise. Answer (D) is incorrect. Alfredo has not performed and therefore cannot qualify as a holder in due course. He did not take the note for value.

33. A $5,000 promissory note payable to the order of Neptune is discounted to Chill Bane by blank endorsement for $4,000. Brutus King steals the note from Bane and sells it to Melinda Ott, who promises to pay King $4,500. After paying King $3,000, Ott learns that King stole the note. Ott makes no further payment to King. Ott is

A. A holder in due course to the extent of $5,000.

B. An ordinary holder to the extent of $4,500.

C. A holder in due course to the extent of $3,000.

D. An ordinary holder to the extent of $0.

Answer (C) is correct. *(CPA, adapted)*

REQUIRED: The status of a transferee of an instrument obtained from a thief.

DISCUSSION: To be an HDC, a holder must take for value. An unsecured promise to pay does not constitute value given for a negotiable instrument (another promissory note or draft would constitute value). Prior to receiving notice of a defense against the instrument, Ott has given value to the extent of $3,000 and is an HDC only to that extent.

Answer (A) is incorrect. Ott is an HDC only with respect to the $3,000 value given prior to notice of a defense against the instrument. Answer (B) is incorrect. Negotiability is determined by the face of the instrument. Blank endorsement rendered it bearer paper. Mere transfer of possession to Ott constituted negotiation. Ott is an HDC to the extent of the $3,000 she gave in good faith without notice of defenses. Answer (D) is incorrect. Negotiability is determined by the face of the instrument. Blank endorsement rendered it bearer paper. Mere transfer of possession to Ott constituted negotiation. Ott is an HDC to the extent of the $3,000 she gave in good faith without notice of defenses.

34. A purchaser of a negotiable instrument payable on demand would least likely be a holder in due course if, at the time of purchase, the instrument is

A. Purchased at a discount.

B. Collateral for a loan.

C. Payable to bearer on demand.

D. Overdue by 3 weeks.

Answer (D) is correct. *(CPA, adapted)*

REQUIRED: The characteristic of a negotiable instrument most likely to preclude HDC status.

DISCUSSION: A holder usually cannot qualify as an HDC if (s)he has notice that the instrument is overdue. Under UCC 3-304, a demand instrument is overdue on the earliest of the following: (1) on the day after demand is duly made; (2) if the instrument is a check, 90 days after its date; or (3) if it is not a check, when it has been outstanding for a period of time after its date that is unreasonably long in the circumstances.

Answer (A) is incorrect. The amount of value given is relevant only if it is such that the purchaser took the instrument not in good faith or with notice of a defense or dishonor. Answer (B) is incorrect. An instrument can be collateral for a loan and be negotiable. Answer (C) is incorrect. Both order and bearer paper can be negotiated to an HDC.

35. Silver Corp. sold 20 tons of steel to River Corp. with payment to be by River's check. The price of steel was fluctuating daily. Silver requested that the amount of River's check be left blank so that Silver could fill in the current market price. River complied with Silver's request. Within 2 days, Silver received River's check. Although the market price of 20 tons of steel at the time Silver received River's check was $80,000, Silver filled in the check for $100,000 and negotiated it to Hatch Corp. Hatch took the check in good faith, without notice of Silver's act or any other defense, and in payment of an existing obligation. River will

A. Not be liable to Hatch, because the check was materially altered by Silver.

B. Not be liable to Hatch, because Hatch failed to give value when it acquired the check from Silver.

C. Be liable to Hatch for $100,000.

D. Be liable to Hatch, but only for $80,000.

Answer (C) is correct. *(CPA, adapted)*

REQUIRED: The effect of an unauthorized completion of a check on the drawer's liability to a holder in due course.

DISCUSSION: Hatch took after proper negotiation, in good faith, without notice of the unauthorized completion, and for value (payment of an existing obligation). Mere knowledge that an incomplete instrument has been completed is not notice of a defense. Accordingly, Hatch is a holder in due course, and River is liable for the amount of the check as completed.

Answer (A) is incorrect. When an incomplete instrument has been improperly completed, a subsequent holder in due course may enforce it as completed. Answer (B) is incorrect. A holder takes for value when (s)he takes in payment of an existing obligation. Answer (D) is incorrect. When an incomplete instrument has been improperly completed, a subsequent holder in due course may enforce it as completed.

36. Bond fraudulently induced Teal to make a note payable to Wilk, to whom Bond was indebted. Bond delivered the note to Wilk. Wilk negotiated the instrument to Smith, who purchased it with knowledge of the fraud and after it was overdue. If Wilk qualifies as a holder in due course, which of the following statements is true?

A. Smith has the standing of a holder in due course through Wilk.

B. Teal can successfully assert the defense of fraud in the inducement against Smith.

C. Smith personally qualifies as a holder in due course.

D. Teal can successfully assert the defense of fraud in the inducement against Wilk.

Answer (A) is correct. *(CPA, adapted)*

REQUIRED: The effect of a holder's knowledge of fraud when (s)he has taken from a holder in due course.

DISCUSSION: A person who takes through a holder in due course (HDC) acquires the rights of an HDC unless the transferee engaged in fraud or illegality affecting the instrument (UCC 3-203). This rule is the "shelter principle." Smith was not a party to the fraud. Thus, Smith can assert the rights of Wilk, the HDC.

Answer (B) is incorrect. Smith is an assignee of Wilk's rights as an HDC. Answer (C) is incorrect. Smith knew of the fraud and thus cannot be an HDC. Answer (D) is incorrect. Wilk is an HDC, and fraud in the inducement is a personal defense.

37. Jean bought a radio for $280 from Ace Appliances. Jean signed a promissory note (that stated the holder is subject to all defenses of the maker) and a purchase contract to cover the entire purchase price. The television proved defective so Jean returned it to Ace. One week later, Moe Finance Company demanded the first payment on the promissory note, which it had purchased from Ace without any knowledge that the television was defective.

A. As a holder in due course, Moe Finance is entitled to payment from Jean because it took free of contractual defenses.

B. Jean must seek reimbursement from Ace Appliances for the amount he has to pay to Moe Finance.

C. Jean's liability is not determined by having signed a promissory note instead of a check.

D. Jean cannot be held liable on the promissory note even if Moe Finance qualifies as a holder in due course under Article 3 of the UCC.

Answer (D) is correct. *(Publisher, adapted)*

REQUIRED: The true statement concerning a consumer who buys with a promissory note when the goods are defective.

DISCUSSION: The Federal Trade Commission has issued a regulation protecting consumers who purchase goods in exchange for an installment obligation. Under the regulation, the note is to contain a notice stating that the holder is subject to all claims and defenses of the debtor. This notice prevents a holder of the promissory note from obtaining the rights of a holder in due course. The consumer can thereby assert his/her contractual defenses against such a holder and avoid having to sue the seller separately.

Answer (A) is incorrect. Moe Finance is subject to Jean's contractual defenses regarding the defective television. Without the FTC regulation, Moe Finance could be a holder in due course who would take free of contractual defenses. Answer (B) is incorrect. Jean can assert his defense against Moe Finance and avoid having to seek reimbursement from Ace. Answer (C) is incorrect. The FTC regulation does not apply to a check, which can be transferred to a holder in due course.

38. Under the negotiable instruments article of the UCC, in a nonconsumer transaction, which of the following are real defenses available against a holder in due course?

	Material Alteration	Discharge in Bankruptcy	Breach of Contract
A.	No	Yes	Yes
B.	Yes	Yes	No
C.	No	No	Yes
D.	Yes	No	No

Answer (B) is correct. *(CPA, adapted)*

REQUIRED: The defenses available against a holder in due course in a nonconsumer transaction.

DISCUSSION: Material alteration is a real defense to the extent of the alteration. Bankruptcy also is a real defense. However, breach of contract is a personal defense (UCC 3-305).

39. Cynthia purchased a machine from VCR, Inc., for use in her home. She gave a small down payment and executed a promissory note for the balance. VCR negotiated the note to the Finley Company, which gave value, acted in good faith, and had no notice of any defense against or claim to the note. Subsequently, Cynthia was able to assert a defense of failure of consideration against VCR. If the note did not contain the notice required by the FTC,

A. Finley is not treated as a holder in due course.

B. Finley cannot recover from VCR.

C. Finley will prevail against Cynthia.

D. VCR will prevail against Cynthia.

Answer (C) is correct. *(Publisher, adapted)*

REQUIRED: The effect of omitting the notice required by the anti-holder in due course rule.

DISCUSSION: Subsequent holders of a negotiable instrument issued by a consumer for the purchase of goods are given notice of defenses by a statement required to be printed on all commercial paper to which this rule applies. Failure to include the notice is illegal as an unfair trade practice but has the effect of freeing a holder in due course from personal defenses. Accordingly, the omission would allow Finley to prevail against Cynthia absent any real defense.

Answer (A) is incorrect. The notice would have precluded Finley from being treated as a holder in due course. Answer (B) is incorrect. A holder may recover from an endorser if the maker dishonors the note. Answer (D) is incorrect. The facts state that Cynthia has a defense against VCR.

STUDY UNIT SIXTEEN

NEGOTIABLE INSTRUMENTS: LIABILITY, BANK TRANSACTIONS, AND ELECTRONIC FUND TRANSFERS

Negotiable instruments combine concepts of contracts and property. The parties who deal in negotiable instruments can incur liability for payment based on contract or warranty. Article 3 of the UCC imposes contractual liability on most signers of a negotiable instrument for the face amount. These parties include (1) a maker of a note, (2) a drawer or an acceptor of a draft, (3) an endorser of a note or draft, or (4) a party bound by the signature of an agent authorized to sign a negotiable instrument. The key to contract liability is the party's valid signature on the instrument.

Because an instrument is also a form of property, Article 3 imposes warranty liability on persons who transfer or present an instrument for payment whether or not they sign it.

The contractual liability of parties is either primary or secondary. **Primary parties** are absolutely obligated to pay the instrument. The maker of a note, the issuer of a certificate of deposit (CD) or cashier's check, and the acceptor of a draft (including a check) are primary parties. (A draft has no primarily liable party until acceptance by the drawee.) Primary liability is unconditional. A primary party is liable to the holder of the instrument and can be sued for the face amount immediately when the instrument becomes due. **Secondary parties** are liable when an obligation to pay arises and the primary parties fail to pay the instrument. Secondary parties are conditionally obligated to pay the instrument. Secondary parties are the drawers of a draft and endorsers of notes or drafts. An **accommodation party** is a surety whose liability depends on the capacity in which (s)he signs the instrument. Conditions precedent to holding secondary parties liable are presentment, dishonor, and notice of any dishonor.

Presentment is a timely demand by the holder for acceptance by the drawee or for payment by the maker or acceptor. Presentment may be made by any commercially reasonable means, including in person, by mail, through a clearinghouse, through a collecting bank, or by electronic communication. **Dishonor** of an instrument occurs when proper presentment is made and an acceptance or payment is refused. When proper presentment has been made and dishonor occurs, proper notice of the dishonor must be given by the holder to secondarily liable parties to hold them liable. **Notice of dishonor** can be given in any commercially reasonable manner. Notice by mail is effective when mailed. A collecting bank must give notice of dishonor before its midnight deadline, that is, midnight of the next banking day following the banking day on which the bank received notice of dishonor. Nonbank parties must give notice with regard to dishonor of instruments taken for collection by a collecting bank within 30 days after notice of dishonor. Regarding any other instrument, notice must be given within 30 days after dishonor. **However, the terms of most notes expressly waive the requirements for presentment and notice of dishonor.**

In addition to the signature (contract) liability, the UCC imposes warranty liability on sellers and other transferors. The basic types of warranties concern transfer and presentment. Warranty liability is important because it often exists in the absence of contractual liability. Any person who endorses an instrument and receives consideration makes **transfer warranties** to all subsequent transferees and holders who take the instrument in good faith: (1) The transferor is entitled to enforce the instrument, (2) all signatures are genuine and authorized, (3) the instrument has not been altered, (4) no defense of any party is good against the transferor, and (5) the transferor has no knowledge of insolvency proceedings against the maker, the drawer of an unaccepted draft, or the acceptor. If the endorsement is qualified (without recourse), the effect is to eliminate secondary contract liability but not transfer warranties. If the transfer is without endorsement, the transfer warranties are limited to the immediate transferee. **Presentment warranties** are given only to persons who, in good faith, pay on or accept an instrument. Any person who obtains payment or acceptance of a negotiable instrument and a prior transferor impliedly warrants that (1) the warrantor was entitled to enforce the instrument or authorized to obtain payment or acceptance on behalf of a person entitled to enforce the instrument, (2) the instrument has not been altered, and (3) the warrantor has no knowledge that the signature of the issuer is unauthorized. (The second and third presentment warranties are made only to drawees.) Claims of breach of warranty usually arise in cases involving instruments that have been altered, stolen, or forged. The warranty rules serve to allocate losses to the person who is in the best position to avoid the loss.

The UCC provides a variety of ways in which a party may be **discharged from liability** on an instrument. The most common method is by payment to the holder. A party, including a secondary party, who pays the amount of the instrument to a holder is completely discharged from liability on it. Other parties who may be liable to the party making payment are not discharged. A party also may be discharged from liability on an instrument, in whole or in part, by acts or agreements with other parties that would discharge a simple contract for the payment of money or by one or more of the following: (1) payment or satisfaction, (2) tender of payment, (3) cancelation or renunciation, (4) reacquisition of the instrument by a prior holder if that party cancels endorsements, (5) certification of a check, (6) acceptance of a draft after endorsement, (7) acceptance varying a draft, (8) impairment of right of recourse or of collateral, and (9) fraudulent and material alteration.

UCC Article 4, *Bank Deposits and Collections*, establishes (1) a time frame for collecting and paying checks and (2) a framework for the contractual relationship between banks and their customers. A **check** is a particular type of draft, always drawn on a bank and payable on demand of the payee or other holder. A check is a depositor's order or instruction to the drawee bank to pay a specified amount from the drawer's account. The usual check drawn by an individual or a business is an ordinary check. It is a mainstay of everyday commercial transactions. Other commonly encountered types of checks are certified checks (those accepted by the bank), cashier's checks (those drawn by a bank on itself, that is, the bank is the drawer and drawee), and traveler's checks (those issued by a drawee, with the traveler as drawer).

The relationship between a bank and its customer is multidimensional. By opening a checking account, an individual or a business enters into a **contractual relationship** with the bank. By providing checking services, the bank agrees to honor the checks written by its customers on condition that sufficient funds are available in the account to pay each check. When a drawee bank wrongfully fails to honor a check, it is liable only to its customer for damages. An **agency relationship** also exists between a bank and its depositor. The depository bank acts as a depositor's collection agent when the depositor deposits a check that is drawn on a different bank. Thus, the depository bank may be the **depositary bank** (the first bank in the collection process). Moreover, a **bailment relationship** is established when a merchant places his/her business receipts in a bank's night deposit box. The bank must exercise ordinary care in performing its collection functions and is required to conform with general banking usage as established under the UCC, Federal Reserve regulations, clearinghouse rules, etc.

The **check collection process** is the means by which a check, deposited in one bank (the **depository bank**) but drawn on another (the drawee or **payor bank**), is paid. Any bank in the chain that is not the payor is a **collecting bank**, and an **intermediary** is any bank not the depository or payor. The deposited check is presented directly or through intermediary banks to the payor. If the depository and payor are the same, the check is an **on-us item**. It is deemed to be paid if not dishonored by the opening of the second banking day after receipt. Collection is accomplished by debiting and crediting accounts that banks maintain among themselves, a system of **provisional debits and credits** expected to become final. Thus, when a provisional credit becomes final, such as by payment in cash or by settlement, the bank becomes accountable to its customer for the amount. The **Federal Reserve System** (the Fed) serves as a **clearinghouse**. It facilitates the exchange of checks by banks and the daily settlement of balances. Moreover, most electronic payments are processed by the Fed's automated clearinghouse. An electronic processing service must therefore abide by the Fed's rules, for example, that a debit is reversible for as long as 48 hours. Check processing is facilitated by **electronic presentment**. Pursuant to agreement, clearinghouse rule, or Fed regulation, presentment may be by transmission of an image, or a description, of an item (presentment notice). Under the **Expedited Funds Availability Act of 1987**, funds represented by deposited checks must be available promptly, e.g., within a business day of deposit for a local check (payor is in the same Federal Reserve check-processing region) or five business days for a nonlocal check. Other rules also are provided, for example, next-business-day availability for the first $100 of check deposits, government checks, cashier's and certified checks, and other items not likely to be dishonored. Longer availability periods are allowed for riskier items, such as deposits at nondepository ATMs, in new accounts, or in large amounts (over $5,000).

Banks have a **duty to act seasonably**, which means they must take appropriate action (either pay or dishonor the check) before the midnight deadline. Thus, unless the payor bank dishonors the check or returns it by midnight on the next banking day following receipt, it is accountable for the face amount of the check. The general rule is that, when a bank honors a check properly drawn on the customer's account or certifies a customer's check, it charges (debits) the customer's account for the amount of the check, assuming sufficient funds. However, a bank has no obligation to pay checks in any special order, even to minimize **overdrafts**. A bank also may agree to provide **overdraft protection**, that is, to pay the check and impose a service charge in addition to subtracting the amount from the customer's future deposits. Furthermore, a bank usually must recredit the customer's account when it pays on a **forged signature**. Such a signature on a check has no legal effect as the signature of a drawer, and the bank is responsible for determining whether the signature of a customer's check is genuine.

A bank also is liable to its customer for loss if the bank pays a check that has been **altered as to amount**. The customer's instruction to the bank is to pay the holder the exact amount on the face of the check. When a bank fails to detect an alteration, it is liable to its depositor for the loss because it did not pay as the drawer (customer/depositor) ordered. Nevertheless, a customer's negligence can shift the risk of loss from the bank to the customer. Examples of a bank customer's negligence include leaving large gaps or spaces around numbers or words in a check so that additional numbers and words can be inserted; signing a check and leaving the dollar amount blank to allow someone else to fill in the amount; or failing to make a timely examination of any bank statement that contains forgeries, alterations, or other irregularities.

A bank is not obligated to pay an uncertified check presented more than 6 months from its date of issuance. Banking practice regards a check outstanding for longer than 6 months as a **stale check**. However, if the bank pays in good faith without consulting the customer, it has a right to charge the customer's account for the amount of the check.

A check is not an assignment of funds but merely an order to pay that may be rescinded by the drawer. Article 4 recognizes the right of a bank customer to instruct the drawee bank not to pay a certain check by issuing a **stop-payment order**, either orally or in writing. The stop order does not cancel the check itself. The check is a contract that binds the drawer, and the holder may bring suit on the check against the drawer. An oral stop-payment order is binding on the bank for 14 calendar days. To be binding for a longer time, the order must be confirmed in writing within the 14-day period. A written stop order is effective for 6 months but may be renewed by the depositor in writing. A stop order must be received in time and must contain sufficient information to give the bank reasonable opportunity to act on the order before the bank has either certified or paid the check. A bank that pays the check over the customer's properly instituted stop order will be obligated to recredit the amount to the depositor's account. **Postdated** checks are normally paid regardless of their dates unless a timely notice of postdating is given. Such a note is equivalent to a stop-payment order.

Under the UCC, neither the **death** nor the **incompetency** of a depositor revokes a bank's authority to pay or collect an item, or to account for the proceeds of the collection, until the bank knows of the death or an adjudication of incompetence and has a reasonable opportunity to act on it. Even when a bank knows of its depositor's death, it may pay or certify checks for a period of up to 10 days from the date of death, unless a stop order is issued by a person claiming an interest in the account.

Because of the staggering volume of paper, the check-collection process has been computerized. The result has been to reduce the significance of checks because electronic transfer provides means to make payments and deposit funds without manual transfer of negotiable instruments. Thus, wholesale electronic fund transfers (EFTs) among financial institutions and businesses **(commercial transfers)** are measured in the trillions of dollars. The two major systems are Fedwire (Federal Reserve wire transfer network) and CHIPS (New York Clearing House Interbank Payment System), but private systems are also operated by large banks. The emergence of these EFT systems created a need to refine **consumer protection** legislation. Hence, Congress enacted the **Electronic Fund Transfer Act of 1978 (EFTA)** to regulate electronic banking services. The primary purpose of the EFTA is to provide disclosure to consumers who use such services. These services include automatic teller machines (ATMs), point-of-sale systems (POS), direct deposit and payment, and payment by telephone (PBT). The EFTA applies to banks, savings and loan institutions, and credit unions. It does not cover commercial transfers.

The EFTA requires that the financial institution provide an easily understandable **written contract** explaining the system and the consumer's rights and duties. For each EFT, the financial institution must furnish a **receipt** for the transaction unless it is initiated by telephone. When a receipt is required, it must set forth the (1) amount involved, (2) date of the transaction, (3) type of transfer, (4) identity of the account, (5) identity of any third party from whom or to whom funds are transferred, and (6) location or identification of the electronic terminal involved. The EFTA also requires that the financial institution provide a **statement**, typically monthly, for each account accessible by EFT. The statement must set forth a record of transactions and must include (1) the amount of fees or charges assessed for maintenance of the account, (2) the balances of the account at the beginning and end of the period, and (3) the address and telephone to be used in case of error. Customers have 60 days after receiving a statement to report errors. The financial institution then has 10 days after it receives a report of an error to investigate. If an error is found, the bank has 1 day to correct it. As an alternative, a financial institution may credit a customer's account and then have 45 days to investigate (in contrast with the 10-day limit).

To protect consumers, the EFTA sets limits on **liability**. Consumers are liable for a maximum of $50 for **unauthorized transfers**. A consumer may be liable for up to $500 if (s)he does not notify the bank within 2 business days after (s)he discovers the loss of an EFT card or personal identification number (PIN). If the customer does not give notice within 60 days after receiving a statement showing the transfers, (s)he has unlimited liability.

UCC **Article 4A, *Funds Transfers***, governs certain EFTs not covered in whole or in part by the EFTA. Article 4A has been adopted by most states. Article 4A applies to a funds transfer, meaning a "series of transactions, beginning with the originator's **payment order**, made for the purpose of making payment to the beneficiary." A funds transfer includes subsequent payment orders made by the originator's bank and intermediary banks to execute the original order. Hence, Article 4A does not apply to an instruction to pay made by a beneficiary (a **commercial debit EFT**). The payment order is not, like a check, a separate obligation. It is a request that the receiving bank need not accept unless it has an agreement with the sender. Acceptance of the order results in an obligation to issue a payment order to the next bank in the chain. The **beneficiary's bank accepts** by payment, notice to the beneficiary of receipt of the order, or receipts of payment of the order by the issuing bank. Thus, each bank that issues a payment order is entitled to payment from its predecessor in the chain. However, if the beneficiary's bank does not accept the order, each predecessor sender is excused. Acceptance by the beneficiary's bank ordinarily discharges the originator's debt. If a payment order is unauthorized or erroneous, Article 4A allocates the risk of loss between the originator of the order and its bank. This allocation involves consideration of the **security procedure** agreed to by the customer and the bank for the purpose of verifying that the order is that of the customer and detecting errors. The risk of loss for an **unauthorized order** usually rests with the customer if the security procedure is commercially reasonable and the bank accepted the order in good faith and complied with the procedure and any written agreement or instruction of the customer. Risk of loss passes to the receiving bank, however, if the order was **not** made by a person entrusted to act for the customer in such matters or who obtained access to the customer's transmitting facilities or customer-controlled information (such as software) facilitating breach of the security procedure. The customer also bears the risk of loss for **errors** unless (1) the security procedure was designed for error detection, and (2) the customer complied and the error would have been detected if the bank had complied.

Electronic money may someday supplant traditional currency and coins. For example, **stored-value cards** (such as phone cards) are already in wide use. **Smart cards** contain computer chips rather than magnetized stripes. A smart card therefore can store data and security programs. It not only stores value but also authenticates transactions, such as by means of its digital signature. A potentially important use of smart cards is to transmit funds over the Internet as part of **online banking** transactions. Currently, online (virtual) banks must receive most deposits in traditional ways. A disadvantage of electronic money is that most types are not covered by the insurance offered by the **Federal Deposit Insurance Corporation**. Federal Reserve rules concerning electronic funds transfers **(Regulation E)** do not extend to electronic money transactions. However, users of electronic money are protected by the **Federal Trade Commission Act of 1914** (as amended), which empowers the FTC to protect consumers from "unfair or deceptive acts or practices in or affecting commerce." Furthermore, common law principles, such as those pertaining to contracts, and federal privacy laws should apply. The **Uniform Money Services Act** is intended to standardize laws covering firms that do not accept deposits but engage in such services as (1) check cashing; (2) currency exchange; and (3) issuance of traveler's checks, money orders, and stored-value cards. A state that adopts the UMSA will require licensure of these firms, state examination of their activities, and compliance with reporting and record-keeping provisions, posting of a bond and limitations on the nature of investments to ensure financial safety and soundness, and an annual audit. The UMSA applies to money services whether or not electronic or Internet-based but not to governments, banks, securities dealers, payday loan firms, and certain other entities. Adoption of the UMSA will help authorities to monitor transfers of large amounts of money and to detect money laundering.

QUESTIONS

16.1 Liability of Parties

1. Libby has primary liability on a negotiable instrument. Carl has secondary liability on the negotiable instrument. Consequently,

A. Libby is liable only after the instrument is dishonored.

B. If Carl is a drawer, he will have no liability after acceptance.

C. Libby cannot be the maker of a certificate of deposit.

D. Carl's liability ordinarily arises only after presentment, dishonor, and notice.

Answer (D) is correct. *(Publisher, adapted)*

REQUIRED: The true statement about primary and secondary liability.

DISCUSSION: Makers and acceptors have primary liability. Their liability arises when the instrument comes due. Secondary liability, however, is conditional. The drawer of a draft or an endorser of any negotiable instrument will ordinarily be liable only after a proper demand for acceptance or payment (presentment), a refusal to pay or accept (dishonor), and prompt notice of dishonor. These requirements may be waived.

Answer (A) is incorrect. The only condition precedent to primary liability is maturity of the instrument. Answer (B) is incorrect. The drawer of a draft remains secondarily liable after the drawee's acceptance. Answer (C) is incorrect. The maker of a note or CD is primarily liable.

2. Abe Booth is president of ABC Company. He has signed a promissory note on behalf of the corporation. On which signature below will Abe Booth not be personally liable?

A. Abe Booth.

B. ABC Company
Abe Booth.

C. ABC Company
By Abe Booth
Its President.

D. ABC Company, Abe Booth.

Answer (C) is correct. *(Publisher, adapted)*

REQUIRED: The signature of an agent that does not result in personal liability on a negotiable instrument.

DISCUSSION: An agent who signs his/her own name to a negotiable instrument is personally liable unless both the identity of the principal and the representative capacity are indicated on the face of the instrument (UCC 3-402). By naming the company, stating his title, and using the word "by," Booth avoids personal liability.

Answer (A) is incorrect. Booth has signed as the maker as far as third parties are concerned. There is no indication that he signed for ABC Company. Answer (B) is incorrect. Booth has not indicated that he has signed in a representative capacity. Each signature makes it appear that both ABC Company and Abe Booth are makers. Answer (D) is incorrect. Booth has not indicated that he has signed in a representative capacity. Each signature makes it appear that both ABC Company and Abe Booth are makers.

3. One who signs as an accommodation party to a negotiable instrument

A. Has the same liability on the instrument whether (s)he signs as an accommodation maker or as an accommodation endorser.

B. Has a right of recourse against the party accommodated.

C. Cannot be held liable against a subsequent holder in due course if the party accommodated has a contract (personal) defense against the party to whom the instrument was originally issued.

D. Has no liability to any subsequent taker who knew of the accommodation.

Answer (B) is correct. *(CPA, adapted)*

REQUIRED: The rights and liabilities of an accommodation party.

DISCUSSION: An accommodation party is very much like a surety. (S)he in effect gives security by assuming liability for the person accommodated. Thus, if (s)he must pay on an instrument because of the accommodated party's default, (s)he has the rights of a surety against his/her principal for reimbursement (UCC 3-419).

Answer (A) is incorrect. An accommodation party is liable in the capacity in which (s)he signs. This is the purpose of obtaining the accommodation signature. An accommodation maker is primarily liable, and an accommodation endorser is secondarily liable. Answer (C) is incorrect. A holder in due course takes free of personal (contractual) defenses. The accommodation party cannot assert these defenses because the accommodated party could not. Answer (D) is incorrect. An accommodation party is liable in the capacity in which (s)he signs. This is the purpose of obtaining the accommodation signature. An accommodation maker is primarily liable, and an accommodation endorser is secondarily liable.

4. Which of the following parties makes warranties upon transferring a negotiable instrument?

A. Transferors for consideration.

B. All endorsers.

C. Only unqualified endorsers.

D. All secondary parties.

Answer (A) is correct. *(E. Rubert)*

REQUIRED: The parties subject to warranty liability after transferring a negotiable instrument.

DISCUSSION: Any person who receives consideration for transferring (as opposed to obtaining payment or acceptance of) an instrument makes specific warranties regarding that instrument and may be held liable for any breach of those warranties (UCC 3-416).

Answer (B) is incorrect. Secondary parties (endorsers and drawers) may transfer an instrument without consideration, e.g., as a gift. Answer (C) is incorrect. Qualified endorsers also make warranties about the transferred instrument. An endorsement without recourse (a qualified endorsement) simply disclaims contract liability to subsequent holders if a maker or drawee defaults (UCC 3-415). The qualification does not modify warranty liability. Answer (D) is incorrect. Secondary parties (endorsers and drawers) may transfer an instrument without consideration, e.g., as a gift.

5. An otherwise valid negotiable bearer note is signed with the forged signature of Darby. Art Archer, who believed he knew Darby's signature, bought the note in good faith from Hal Harding, the forger. Archer transferred the note without endorsement to Barker in partial payment of a debt. Barker then sold the note to Charles Chase for 80% of its face amount and delivered it without endorsement. When Chase presented the note for payment at maturity, Darby refused to honor it, pleading forgery. Chase gave proper notice of dishonor to Barker and to Archer. Which of the following statements best describes the situation from Chase's standpoint?

A. Chase cannot qualify as a holder in due course because he did not pay face value for the note.

B. Chase can hold Barker liable on the ground that Barker warranted to Chase that neither Darby nor Archer had any defense valid against Barker.

C. Chase can hold Archer liable on the ground that Archer warranted to Chase that Darby's signature was genuine.

D. Chase cannot hold Harding, the forger, liable on the note because his signature does not appear on it and thus he made no warranties to Chase.

Answer (B) is correct. *(CPA, adapted)*

REQUIRED: The party, if any, who is liable and why.

DISCUSSION: The parties to this note are Harding (the forger of Darby's signature), Archer, Barker, and Chase. The only signature on the note was Darby's forged by Harding. Every transferor of a negotiable instrument for consideration warrants to his/her transferee that no defense of any party is good against him/her (UCC 3-416). Thus, Barker warranted to Chase that neither Darby nor Archer had any defense against Barker. But Darby had a defense of forgery effective even against a holder in due course, and Chase could therefore hold Barker liable.

Answer (A) is incorrect. Chase can qualify as a holder in due course. The purchase of a promissory note at a discount does not mean that value was not paid or that the purchaser had notice of a claim or defense. Answer (C) is incorrect. Archer did not endorse the note. Accordingly, he warranted only to his/her immediate transferee (Barker) that Darby's signature was genuine. Answer (D) is incorrect. Darby's forged signature operates as Harding's own signature, and Harding can be held liable in the capacity of maker of the note (UCC 3-404).

6. When the holder of a negotiable instrument transfers it for consideration by endorsing "without recourse," (s)he

A. Makes no warranty as to title to any subsequent holder.

B. Prevents further negotiability.

C. Makes the same warranties as an unqualified endorser.

D. Becomes immune from recourse to him/her by a subsequent holder.

Answer (C) is correct. *(CPA, adapted)*

REQUIRED: The effect of transferring a negotiable instrument by endorsing it "without recourse."

DISCUSSION: The endorsement "without recourse" is a qualified endorsement that negates secondary contract liability. However, qualified endorsement does not modify transfer warranties.

Answer (A) is incorrect. The qualified endorsement does not eliminate the warranty of title to subsequent holders. Answer (B) is incorrect. Neither the qualified endorsement nor any other endorsement can prevent further negotiability. Answer (D) is incorrect. The qualified endorser is still subject to liability for warranties to subsequent holders.

16.2 Presentment, Dishonor, and Discharge

7. Unless the requirement is waived or expired, presentment of a promissory note for payment is necessary to hold liable

A. The maker.

B. An unqualified endorser.

C. An acceptor.

D. An accommodation maker.

Answer (B) is correct. *(J.C. Folkenroth)*

REQUIRED: The party whose liability on a note is dependent upon previous presentment.

DISCUSSION: Presentment is a demand for payment or acceptance made by (or on behalf of) a person entitled to enforce the instrument. This demand is made (1) to the drawee (e.g., a bank) or a party obliged to pay the instrument (a maker, endorser, etc.); (2) to a bank in the case of a note or accepted draft payable at the bank; or (3) to the drawee to accept a draft. An unqualified endorser undertakes that, upon proper presentment to the primary party, dishonor, and proper notice of dishonor to the endorser (satisfaction of conditions precedent), (s)he will pay the instrument. Thus, an endorser is secondarily liable. Presentment is not necessary to charge a primary party. However, in practice, a note contains a waiver of compliance with the conditions precedent, and the holder may proceed directly against endorsers when payment is made by the maker.

Answer (A) is incorrect. Makers of notes are primarily liable. Answer (C) is incorrect. Only drafts can be accepted. Also, acceptors are primarily liable. Answer (D) is incorrect. Accommodation parties are liable in the capacity in which they sign; hence, accommodation makers are primarily liable.

8. Hoover is a holder in due course of a check that was originally payable to the order of Nelson or bearer and has the following endorsements on its back:

Nelson
Pay to order of Maxwell
Duffy
Without Recourse
Maxwell
Howard

Which of the following statements about the check is true?

A. It was originally order paper.

B. It was order paper in Howard's hands.

C. Maxwell's signature was not necessary for it to be negotiated.

D. Presentment for payment must be made within 30 days after endorsement to hold an endorser liable.

Answer (D) is correct. *(CPA, adapted)*

REQUIRED: The true statement concerning the example check.

DISCUSSION: If an instrument is dishonored, an endorser must pay the amount due according to the terms at the time of endorsement or, if the endorsement was of an incomplete instrument, according to the terms as completed. The endorser is not liable, however, if the endorsement was without recourse, any required notice of dishonor is not given, or the instrument is a draft accepted by a bank post-endorsement. If the endorser is liable under the foregoing rules, this liability is nevertheless discharged if a check is not presented for payment (or given to a depository bank for collection) within 30 days after endorsement.

Answer (A) is incorrect. An instrument payable to order or bearer is order paper unless written. Checks do not commonly have "to bearer" printed on them, so the bearer words must have been written or typed in making the instrument originally bearer paper. Answer (B) is incorrect. The instrument was bearer paper in Howard's hands. Maxwell converted the instrument to bearer paper by endorsing in blank; i.e., Maxwell did not sign "Pay to the order of Howard." Answer (C) is incorrect. The instrument in Maxwell's hands was order paper due to Duffy's special endorsement. Order paper cannot be properly negotiated without both endorsement and transfer of possession.

9. Robb, a minor, executed a promissory note payable to bearer and delivered it to Dodsen in payment for a stereo system. Dodsen negotiated the note for value to Mellon by transfer of possession alone and without endorsement. Mellon endorsed the note in blank and negotiated it to Bloom for value. Bloom's demand for payment was refused by Robb because the note was executed when Robb was a minor. Bloom gave prompt notice of Robb's default to Dodsen and Mellon. No holder of the note was aware of Robb's minority. Which of the following parties will be liable to Bloom?

	Dodsen	Mellon
A.	Yes	Yes
B.	Yes	No
C.	No	No
D.	No	Yes

Answer (D) is correct. *(CPA, adapted)*

REQUIRED: The party(ies) liable on a promissory note.

DISCUSSION: Any person who signs a negotiable instrument is liable on it. A party is primarily liable if (s)he is required to pay by the terms of the instrument itself. Unqualified endorsers are secondarily liable; they are liable only if the party with primary liability fails to honor the instrument, and only if the holder gives timely notice of dishonor. A person who does not endorse an instrument is usually not liable on it. However, a person who transfers a negotiable instrument without endorsement, but for full consideration, warrants to the immediate transferee that (s)he is entitled to enforce the instrument.

Answer (A) is incorrect. Dodsen did not endorse the note. Answer (B) is incorrect. Dodsen did not endorse the note. Answer (C) is incorrect. Mellon, as an HDC, can enforce the instrument against a holder who endorsed the instrument. Timely notice of dishonor was provided.

10. A proper presentment, dishonor, and a prompt notice of dishonor are required to establish the liability of a secondary party. In certain cases, these requirements may be waived or excused. Which of the following is a true statement?

A. A person giving the notice cannot be excused for a delay.

B. If the drawer of a check instructed the drawee not to pay, (s)he and subsequent endorsers are not entitled to presentment and notice.

C. Both presentment and notice of dishonor may be waived.

D. Notice of dishonor, but not presentment, may be waived.

Answer (C) is correct. *(Publisher, adapted)*

REQUIRED: The true statement about waiver or excuse of conditions for secondary liability.

DISCUSSION: Under UCC 3-504, presentment and notice of dishonor may be entirely excused when the party to be charged has waived these requirements expressly or by implication either before or after the instrument is due.

Answer (A) is incorrect. Delay in notice of dishonor is excused when the delay is caused by circumstances beyond the control of the person giving the notice, and (s)he exercised reasonable diligence after the cause of the delay ceased to operate. Answer (B) is incorrect. An endorser in this case is still entitled to presentment unless the endorser has made a waiver or otherwise has no reason to expect or right to require that the instrument be paid. Answer (D) is incorrect. Both presentment and notice of dishonor may be waived.

11. Which of the following actions does not discharge a prior party to a negotiable instrument?

A. Payment of the instrument even if the payment is made with knowledge of a claim by another person.

B. Cancelation of that prior party's endorsement.

C. An oral renunciation of that prior party's endorsement.

D. The intentional destruction of the instrument by a person entitled to enforce the instrument.

Answer (C) is correct. *(CPA, adapted)*

REQUIRED: The action that does not discharge a prior party to a negotiable instrument.

DISCUSSION: A person entitled to enforce the instrument may discharge any party. No consideration is required. It may be done by surrendering the instrument, by intentionally canceling the instrument or the party's signature, by destruction or mutilation, or by striking out the party's signature. It may also be done by agreeing not to sue or otherwise renouncing rights by a signed writing. Thus, a renunciation is ineffective unless in written form.

Answer (A) is incorrect. Payment discharges, to the extent of the payments, the obligation of the party obliged to pay even if that party has knowledge of a claim by another person, unless the person making payment knows that the instrument is stolen or that the payment violates an injunction or unless the person making payment has accepted indemnity against loss from the other claimant. Answer (B) is incorrect. A person entitled to enforce the instrument who cancels a prior party's endorsement discharges that party from liability on the instrument. Answer (D) is incorrect. Destruction of the instrument with intent to cancel it discharges all parties from liability on it.

12. Vex Corp. executed a negotiable promissory note payable to Tamp, Inc. The note was collateralized by some of Vex's business assets. Tamp negotiated the note to Miller for value. Miller endorsed the note in blank and negotiated it to Bilco for value. Before the note became due, Bilco agreed to release Vex's collateral. Vex refused to pay Bilco when the note became due. Bilco promptly notified Miller and Tamp of Vex's default. Which of the following statements is true?

A. Bilco will be unable to collect from Miller because Miller's endorsement was in blank.

B. Bilco will be able to collect from either Tamp or Miller because Bilco was a holder in due course.

C. Bilco will be unable to collect from either Tamp or Miller because of Bilco's release of the collateral.

D. Bilco will be able to collect from Tamp because Tamp was the original payee.

Answer (C) is correct. *(CPA, adapted)*

REQUIRED: The liability of parties to a promissory note when a subsequent holder has impaired collateral.

DISCUSSION: The UCC provides many circumstances in which a party may be discharged from liability on an instrument. One way is the impairment of right of recourse or of collateral. The extent of discharge is limited to the loss resulting to the party from the impairment. Bilco's agreement to release the collateral effected discharge of Tamp and Miller.

Answer (A) is incorrect. Each unqualified endorser is liable on the instrument. The blank endorsement, rather than limiting liability, operates to render the instrument payable to bearer. But Bilco's release of collateral discharged Miller from liability. Answer (B) is incorrect. A prior endorsee, HDC or otherwise, is discharged when a subsequent holder releases collateral. Answer (D) is incorrect. It is an unqualified endorsement that renders a payee liable on the instrument. Also, the release discharged Tamp.

13. A check has the following endorsements on the back:

> *Paul Folk*
> without recourse
>
> *George Hopkins*
> payment guaranteed
>
> *Ann Quarry*
> collection guaranteed
>
> *Rachel Ott*

Which of the following conditions occurring subsequent to the endorsements would discharge all of the endorsers?

A. Lack of notice of dishonor.

B. Late presentment.

C. Insolvency of the maker.

D. Certification of the check.

Answer (D) is correct. *(CPA, adapted)*

REQUIRED: The condition that would discharge all the endorsers of a check.

DISCUSSION: Certification is an unconditional promise by a bank to pay (an acceptance of liability). Prior to certification, a drawee bank is not liable on a check. But once the drawee bank certifies a check, the drawer and all prior endorsers are discharged (UCC 3-414 and 3-415). Moreover, by his qualified endorsement, Paul Folk is not liable on the instrument.

Answer (A) is incorrect. Lack of notice of dishonor impair a right of recourse and discharge secondarily liable endorsers. But the guarantors are primarily liable and are not discharged. Answer (B) is incorrect. Late presentment impair a right of recourse and discharge secondarily liable endorsers. But the guarantors are primarily liable and are not discharged. Answer (C) is incorrect. Insolvency of the maker discharges nobody. A discharge in bankruptcy proceedings, however, effects discharge only of the bankrupt person from liability on the instrument.

16.3 Bank Transactions

14. Blue is a holder of a check originally drawn by Rush and made payable to Silk. Silk properly endorsed the check to Field. Field had the check certified by the drawee bank and then endorsed the check to Blue. As a result,

A. Field is not discharged from liability.

B. Rush alone is discharged from liability.

C. The drawee bank becomes liable, but Silk and Rush also remain liable.

D. Rush is secondarily liable.

Answer (A) is correct. *(CPA, adapted)*

REQUIRED: The effect of certification of a check.

DISCUSSION: Certification is an unconditional promise by a bank to pay (an acceptance of liability). Prior to certification, a drawee bank is not liable on a check. But once the drawee bank certifies a check, the drawer and all prior endorsers are discharged (UCC 3-414 and 3-415). However, a party who endorses subsequent to certification is not discharged. (S)he is secondarily liable.

Answer (B) is incorrect. All prior endorsers are also discharged. Answer (C) is incorrect. The drawer and prior endorsers are discharged. Answer (D) is incorrect. Rush, the drawer, is completely discharged by the certification, regardless of when or by whom acceptance was obtained.

15. Drawer writes a check on Drawee Bank. Drawer has sufficient funds in her account, and the check is in proper form. When Payee presents the check for payment, Drawee refuses to pay. Drawee is liable to

A. Both Drawer and Payee.

B. Neither Drawer nor Payee.

C. Payee but not Drawer.

D. Drawer but not Payee.

Answer (D) is correct. *(Publisher, adapted)*
REQUIRED: The liability of a drawee bank for not paying on a check.
DISCUSSION: A bank has no liability to anyone other than its drawer for refusing to pay on a check. Hence, the bank has no liability whatsoever to Payee. Only if the bank accepted (or certified) the check would it be liable to the holder (UCC 3-413).

16. In general, which of the following statements is true concerning the priority among checks drawn on a particular account and presented to the drawee bank on a particular day?

A. The checks may be charged to the account in any order convenient to the bank.

B. The checks may be charged to the account in any order provided no charge creates an overdraft.

C. The checks must be charged to the account in the order in which the checks were dated.

D. The checks must be charged to the account in the order of lowest amount to highest amount to minimize the number of dishonored checks.

Answer (A) is correct. *(CPA, adapted)*
REQUIRED: The true statement about the priority among checks presented to a bank for payment.
DISCUSSION: In general, the UCC provides that items may be accepted, paid, certified, or charged to the indicated account of its customer in any order convenient to the bank (UCC 4-303).

17. Drawer writes a $1,000 check on her account at Drawee Bank. Drawer has only $975 in the account. If Drawer and Drawee have no agreement concerning overdrafts,

A. Drawee may honor the check and charge Drawer's account for $1,000.

B. Drawee may honor the check and charge Drawer's account for no more than $975.

C. Drawee must pay the full amount of the check.

D. Drawee must pay $975.

Answer (A) is correct. *(Publisher, adapted)*
REQUIRED: The true statement about a bank's rights regarding overdrafts.
DISCUSSION: In the absence of an agreement to permit overdrafts, the bank has no obligation to honor an overdraft. If it chooses to pay the check, the customer has an enforceable implied obligation to reimburse the bank (i.e., effectively a loan). The bank will also have the right to impose a service charge. If the bank and the customer have an agreement permitting overdrafts, the bank will probably charge interest.

18. Robb stole one of Markum's blank checks, made it payable to himself, and forged Markum's signature to it. The check was drawn on the Unity Trust Company. Robb cashed the check at the Friendly Check Cashing Company, which in turn deposited it with its bank, Farmers National. Farmers proceeded to collect on the check from Unity Trust. The theft and forgery were quickly discovered by Markum who promptly notified Unity. None of the parties were negligent. Who will bear the loss, assuming the amount cannot be recovered from Robb?

A. Markum.

B. Unity Trust Company.

C. Friendly Check Cashing Company.

D. Farmers National.

Answer (B) is correct. *(CPA, adapted)*
REQUIRED: The party who will bear the loss when the drawer's signature is forged.
DISCUSSION: Unity must ultimately bear the loss because a drawee bank that pays a check issued over a forged drawer's signature may not charge the customer's account if the customer was not negligent. Also, Unity may hold neither Friendly nor Farmers National (the collecting bank) liable on breach of a presentment warranty. On presentment, one warrants only that (s)he has no knowledge a drawer's signature is forged (UCC 4-208).

19. Jack drew a check, payable to the order of Ellen, for $100. The check was endorsed in blank by Ellen to John, who skillfully altered the amount of the check to $1,000. John then cashed it at his club, which gave value, took in good faith, and had no knowledge or notice of the alteration. The alteration was not detected until Jack received his bank statement. Jack insisted that his bank recredit his account. Which of the following is true?

A. Jack's bank must recredit $1,000 because of the holder in due course doctrine.

B. Jack's bank must recredit only $900 if the drawer did not negligently contribute to the alteration.

C. John is not liable to anyone for any breach of warranty on transfer or presentment because he did not endorse the check.

D. The original tenor rule precludes Jack's bank from debiting his account for $100.

Answer (B) is correct. *(D. Sipes)*

REQUIRED: The effect of a fraudulent and material alteration of a check on its negotiation.

DISCUSSION: The material alteration of an instrument is a real defense that can be asserted even against a holder in due course (UCC 3-407). The holder in due course may enforce the instrument's original terms but is not entitled to the altered terms of the document, provided the drawer was not negligent in contributing to the alteration (UCC 3-406). Jack's bank most likely qualifies as a holder in due course and, as such, may debit Jack's account for only $100 (the check's "original tenor"). The bank must recredit Jack's account for $900 (UCC 4-401).

Answer (A) is incorrect. The bank need only recredit the excess debited to Jack's account because of the alteration. Answer (C) is incorrect. John warranted on transfer and presentment that the check had no fraudulent and material alterations (UCC 3-417). Answer (D) is incorrect. The original tenor rule allows holders in due course to enforce the original terms of an instrument.

20. Cobb gave Garson a signed check with the amount payable left blank. Garson was to fill in, as the amount, the price of fuel oil Garson was to deliver to Cobb at a later date. Garson told Cobb the amount would be no more than $900. Garson did not deliver the fuel oil but filled in the amount of $1,000 on the check. Garson then negotiated the check to Joseph in satisfaction of a $500 debt with the $500 balance paid to Garson in cash. Cobb stopped payment, and Joseph is seeking to collect $1,000 from Cobb. Cobb's maximum liability to Joseph will be

A. $50

B. $500

C. $900

D. $1,000

Answer (D) is correct. *(CPA, adapted)*

REQUIRED: The effect of unauthorized completion on the drawer's liability to a holder in due course.

DISCUSSION: Joseph took after proper negotiation, in good faith, without notice of the unauthorized completion, and for value (payment of an antecedent debt). Mere knowledge that an incomplete instrument has been completed is not notice of a defense. Accordingly, Joseph is a holder in due course (HDC), and Cobb is liable for the amount of the check as completed (UCC 3-407).

Answer (A) is incorrect. When an incomplete instrument has been improperly completed, a subsequent HDC may enforce it as completed. Answer (B) is incorrect. A holder takes for value when (s)he takes in payment of an antecedent claim. Answer (C) is incorrect. When an incomplete instrument has been improperly completed, a subsequent HDC may enforce it as completed.

21. Path stole a check made out to the order of Marks. Path forged the name of Marks on the back and made the instrument payable to himself. He then negotiated the check to Harrison for cash by signing his own name on the back of the instrument in Harrison's presence. Harrison was unaware of any of the facts surrounding the theft or forged endorsement and presented the check for payment. Central County Bank, the drawee bank, paid it. Disregarding Path, which of the following will bear the loss?

A. The drawer of the check payable to Marks.

B. Central County Bank.

C. Marks.

D. Harrison.

Answer (D) is correct. *(CPA, adapted)*

REQUIRED: The person bearing the loss when a bank pays over a forged endorsement.

DISCUSSION: This question involves the forgery of an endorser's signature. Harrison did not qualify as a holder, much less a holder in due course, because the theft and forged endorsement precluded a proper negotiation of the check by the payee. Because Harrison did not acquire title, (s)he breached the presentment warranty of title (UCC 4-208) and is liable to Central County Bank. Harrison's only recourse is against the thief.

Answer (A) is incorrect. The drawer of the check can assert Path's forgery as a defense. Answer (B) is incorrect. Central County Bank can rely on Harrison's warranty of good title. Answer (C) is incorrect. Marks has his own defense of forgery.

22. Gomer obtained checks payable to the order of certain repairmen who serviced various large corporations. He observed the delivery trucks of repairmen who did business with the corporations; then he submitted bills on the bogus letterhead of the repairmen to the corporations. The return envelope for payment indicated a local post office box. When the checks arrived, Gomer would forge the payees' signatures and cash the checks. The parties cashing the checks are holders in due course. Who will bear the loss assuming the amount cannot be recovered from Gomer?

A. The defrauded corporations.

B. The drawee banks.

C. Intermediate parties who endorsed the instruments for collection.

D. The ultimate recipients of the proceeds of the checks even though they are holders in due course.

Answer (A) is correct. *(CPA, adapted)*

REQUIRED: The party who will bear the loss on checks delivered to an impostor.

DISCUSSION: When an impostor causes a drawer to issue a check to him/her and endorses it in the name of the payee, the endorsement is effective against the drawer (UCC 3-404). The drawer is thereby deprived of the real defense of forgery against holders in due course and others. Thus, the defrauded corporations (drawers) will ultimately have to bear the loss.

Answer (B) is incorrect. Drawee banks are not liable until they accept an instrument, and even then, they have recourse against the drawer. Answer (C) is incorrect. The drawer is deprived of the real defense of forgery against holders in due course and others since an impostor caused it to issue the checks. Answer (D) is incorrect. The drawer is deprived of the real defense of forgery against holders in due course and others since an impostor caused it to issue the checks.

23. Smith bought a TV from the ABC Appliance Store and paid for the set with a check. Later in the day, Smith found a better model for the same price at another store. Smith immediately called ABC trying to cancel the sale. ABC told Smith that they were holding him to the sale and had negotiated the check to their wholesaler, Glenn Company, as a partial payment on inventory purchases. Smith telephoned his bank, the Union Trust Bank, and ordered the bank to stop payment on the check. Which of the following statements is true?

A. If Glenn can prove it is a holder in due course, Union Trust must honor Smith's check.

B. Union Trust is not bound or liable for Smith's stop payment order unless the order is placed in writing.

C. If Union Trust mistakenly pays Smith's check 2 days after receiving the stop order, the bank will not be liable.

D. Glenn cannot hold Smith liable on the check.

Answer (C) is correct. *(CPA, adapted)*

REQUIRED: The true statement regarding an oral order to stop payment on a check.

DISCUSSION: An oral order to stop payment is good for 14 days. The drawee bank, however, must be given reasonable time to act on the stop order (UCC 4-403). Because 2 days is probably reasonable time to act on an order to stop payment, the reason the bank will not be liable is that Smith has no defense on the check and will be liable on it. A bank that pays in violation of a stop order succeeds to the rights of the payee (ABC) against the drawer (UCC 4-407).

Answer (A) is incorrect. A drawee bank must honor the order to stop payment and is not liable to any party other than the drawer. Answer (B) is incorrect. An oral order to stop payment is good for 14 days. Answer (D) is incorrect. Smith has no defense on the check and any holder can enforce it.

24. Ajax, Inc., sold a refrigerator to Broadway Bill's Restaurant and accepted Broadway's negotiable promissory note for $450 as payment. The note was payable to Ajax's order 1 year later. Ajax endorsed in blank endorsement and sold it to National Bank for $350. National credited Ajax's checking account with $350, which brought Ajax's balance to $925. Ajax drew checks for a total of $825, which National honored. National then learned that the refrigerator had not been delivered by Ajax. The note is now due and unpaid. National brings suit; Broadway pleads lack of consideration on the note. Which of the following is a valid statement?

A. The discount on the note is so great as to impugn National's taking in good faith.

B. In ascertaining the extent to which value had been given by National, the FIFO rule will apply to the deposit and withdrawals.

C. Broadway has no liability on the note since it never received the refrigerator.

D. Broadway has only secondary liability on the note in question.

Answer (B) is correct. *(CPA, adapted)*

REQUIRED: The valid statement regarding liability on a promissory note to a holder in due course.

DISCUSSION: A holder in due course can assert its rights only to the extent that it has given value (UCC 3-302). A bank is considered to give value on a customer's account only to the extent that the funds have been withdrawn from the bank. The FIFO rule (the first funds in are the first funds out) applies for this purpose. Thus, National gave value only to the extent of $250 because $100 of the deposit still remained in Ajax's account.

Answer (A) is incorrect. A $100 discount on a $450 promissory note is not extraordinary in the financial community. Answer (C) is incorrect. Broadway is liable to National as a holder in due course to the extent of $250 (the value given). Answer (D) is incorrect. Broadway is primarily liable as the maker of a promissory note.

16.4 Electronic Fund Transfers

25. The Electronic Fund Transfer Act (EFTA) is consumer legislation that would not apply to transactions originated through

A. Point-of-sale terminals (POS).

B. Automated tellers (ATM).

C. Machine-generated checks.

D. Transfers by telephone (or pay-by-phone).

Answer (C) is correct. *(Publisher, adapted)*

REQUIRED: The item to which the EFTA is not applicable.

DISCUSSION: An electronic fund transfer is a "transfer of funds, other than a transaction originated by check, draft, or similar paper instrument, initiated through an electronic terminal, telephonic instrument, or computer or magnetic tape so as to order, instruct, or authorize a financial institution to debit or credit an account." The EFTA does not apply to machine-generated checks (negotiable instruments regulated by UCC Articles 3 and 4).

Answer (A) is incorrect. Point-of-sale devices (terminals, other computers, phones, etc.) are within the EFTA. Answer (B) is incorrect. Automated tellers are within the EFTA. Answer (D) is incorrect. Transfers by telephone are within the EFTA.

26. The EFTA requires financial institutions to provide their customers with written documentation of electronic fund transfers at various times. These times include all of the following except

A. On a periodic basis, usually monthly, in the form of a statement.

B. At the time of each use of an automated teller.

C. At the time of each preauthorized credit to an account.

D. At the time of contracting for EFT services.

Answer (C) is correct. *(Publisher, adapted)*

REQUIRED: The occasion not requiring the generation of written documentation of an electronic fund transfer.

DISCUSSION: An individual may arrange with a financial institution to have transfers made to his/her account on a prearranged basis. The financial institution and consumer may agree that written notification will be given only when a scheduled credit is not actually made.

27. Under the EFTA, a financial institution holding a customer's account that may be accessed by electronic means must furnish the customer with periodic statements. If the customer discovers an error, the financial institution must comply with certain procedures prescribed by the act. Which of the following is true?

A. A customer will collect treble damages if the institution is in error.

B. The institution may not require written notice of the error.

C. The institution must recredit the customer's account pending an investigation.

D. After proper notice, the institution is obligated to investigate.

Answer (D) is correct. *(Publisher, adapted)*

REQUIRED: The true statement about the error resolution procedure under the EFTA.

DISCUSSION: The customer has 60 days to give an oral or written notice of errors in its account, but the institution may require written confirmation within 10 business days of receiving an oral notice. The notice obligates the institution to investigate and report within 10 business days. Any error must be corrected within 1 business day after its discovery. Instead, the institution may temporarily recredit the account within 10 business days of receipt of notice. If it chooses this alternative, it has 45 business days from receipt of notice to complete the investigation. If it finds no error, the institution has 3 business days to mail an explanation to the customer. Failure to adhere to the prescribed procedures or a knowing and willful conclusion (despite the evidence) that the account was not erroneous permits the customer to recover treble damages.

Answer (A) is incorrect. Treble damages are available only for failure to follow the rules to resolve an error. Answer (B) is incorrect. Written notice can be required. Answer (C) is incorrect. The institution can investigate first if it finishes within 10 days.

28. Hannah Palindrome became aware of the loss of her automated teller card on Monday evening, March 3. The financial statements mailed to Hannah on April 1, May 1, and June 1 showed a $60 withdrawal on March 4 and a $600 withdrawal on March 9 but no other activity in the account. Assuming that the main provisions of the EFTA apply, Hannah is liable for

A. $660 if she reports the loss on June 15.

B. $50 if she reports the loss on May 15.

C. $600 if she reports the loss on March 21.

D. $50 if she reports the loss on March 19.

Answer (A) is correct. *(Publisher, adapted)*

REQUIRED: The liability of a customer for an unauthorized electronic fund transfer.

DISCUSSION: The consumer's liability is limited to the lesser of $50 or the amount transferred without authorization prior to notifying the financial institution. If the consumer fails to notify the institution within 2 business days after learning of the loss of the means of access, his/her liability is the lesser of $500 or the amount transferred without authorization after 2 business days following discovery of the loss but prior to notification of the institution. If the consumer does not report an unauthorized transfer or error within 60 days of the transmission of a financial statement containing such a transaction or error, the consumer bears the loss. Consequently, if Hannah does not report the loss until June 15, her liability is $660.

29. Under the EFTA, a financial institution will avoid liability to its customer for failure to

A. Make a transfer in the proper amount.

B. Make a timely transfer if the terminal does not have sufficient funds.

C. Credit a deposit of funds.

D. Stop payment on a preauthorized transfer when the customer has given sufficient notice.

Answer (B) is correct. *(Publisher, adapted)*

REQUIRED: The instance in which a financial institution avoids liability under the EFTA.

DISCUSSION: The institution will not be liable when the terminal lacked the cash to complete the transaction or the customer's account had insufficient funds. Except in the case of stop-payment orders, the institution may also defend by proving that an act of nature or a technical malfunction known to the customer at the time (s)he attempted the transaction caused the failure.

STUDY UNIT SEVENTEEN
DOCUMENTS OF TITLE AND LETTERS OF CREDIT

A **bailment** is the legal relationship that results when a person transfers possession of, not title to, personal property to another person who is under a duty to return the property or dispose of it and make an accounting. The transferor is the **bailor**. The party receiving possession is the **bailee**. **Special bailments** involve professional bailees, such as common carriers and warehousers, and are subject to special rules and regulations. Professional bailees, who either store or deliver goods, issue documents of title.

A **document of title** is any record that, in the regular course of business or financing, is treated as adequate evidence that the person in possession is entitled to receive, hold, and sell or otherwise dispose of the document and the goods it covers [UCC 1-201(16)]. Documents of title are governed by Article 7 of the UCC. A document of title is (1) a receipt for goods, (2) a contract between a bailor and a bailee for the storage and transport of the goods (a bailment, e.g., the delivery of personal property in trust to a warehouser or carrier), and (3) evidence of title to the goods. It may be in **written or electronic form**, that is, a record consisting of information stored in an electronic medium. The fundamental types of documents of title are warehouse receipts and bills of lading. These documents may be either **negotiable or nonnegotiable** when in tangible form. An electronic document of title is transferred by a **change in control**. Article 3 of the UCC applies only to negotiable instruments (UCC 3-102). Because a negotiable instrument must contain a promise or order to pay money (UCC 3-104), Article 3 does not apply to documents of title, which ordinarily cover goods.

A document of title in **tangible form** is **negotiable** if it states that the goods are to be delivered either to (1) bearer (a person in possession of the document if it is payable to bearer or endorsed in blank) or (2) the order of a named person. If neither of these statements is in the document, it is not negotiable. Negotiable documents of title are negotiated in much the same manner as negotiable notes, drafts, and checks. **Order** documents of title are negotiated by endorsement and delivery. **Bearer** documents are negotiated by delivery alone. A **blank endorsement** (signature only) of an order document converts it to bearer paper. A **special endorsement**, e.g., endorsement to a specified person, of a bearer document converts it to order paper. Conditional or qualified endorsements do not apply to documents of title. A **forged endorsement** does not result in negotiation. Forgery is a real defense to enforcement. If the document is negotiable, the goods must be delivered to the holder of the document. A **holder** is the person in possession if goods are deliverable to (1) bearer or (2) the order of the person in possession. If the document is **nonnegotiable**, the goods usually must be delivered to the person named in the document. The document itself is not required to obtain the goods if the person requesting them can prove that (s)he is the bailor or an assignee of the rights of the bailor. Carriers and warehousers have **absolute liability** for misdelivery.

A person who takes a document of title by **due negotiation** is in a position similar to that of a holder in due course of a negotiable instrument. A document of title is duly negotiated when it is negotiated as described on the previous page to a holder who purchases it (1) in good faith, (2) without notice of any defense against or claim to it, (3) for value, (4) in the regular course of business or financing, and (5) not in settlement or payment of a money obligation. A holder by due negotiation acquires **title** to the document and the goods and takes **free of claims and defenses** raised by either the bailee or third parties. But certain exceptions apply. The bailee is entitled to compensation for transportation or storage charges, which are usually specified on the document. Furthermore, the holder will not be entitled to the goods in cases in which the **bailor had no authority to deliver the goods** to the bailee carrier or warehouser. Consequently, a document of title issued to a bailor who **stole the goods** does not represent title to the goods. Nevertheless, a **thief can negotiate** a bearer document or an order document that was endorsed in blank. A subsequent holder who takes by due negotiation then acquires **rights superior to the original bailor's**. A **transferee of a document**, whether negotiable or nonnegotiable, to whom the document has been delivered but not duly negotiated, is an **assignee**. The transferee acquires the title and rights his/her transferor had or had actual authority to convey.

According to the **statute of frauds** provision of Article 7, the enforceability of a document of title depends on compliance with writing requirements. Electronic records and signatures have the same standing for this purpose as paper documents and manual signatures. Thus, a holder includes a person **in control of an electronic document**. A person is in control "if a system employed for evidencing the transfer of interests in the electronic document reliably establishes that person as the person to which the electronic document was issued or transferred." Moreover, the electronic alternative to the tangible system must produce only **one authoritative copy**. This copy must be unique, identifiable, and unalterable. The copy also identifies the person in control or the next transferee. The person in control determines the next transferee. Nonauthoritative copies must be readily identifiable as nonauthoritative. One **possible system** is to establish a custodian of electronic documents that records transfers and identifies the person currently in control of a given document. However, the UCC does not prescribe the characteristics of a system or require that only one be developed. Whatever the system, **tangible and electronic documents must be be interchangeable**. One form must be convertible to the other. For example, the person in control of an electronic document may transfer control to its issuer in exchange for a tangible document. This document must state explicitly that it substitutes for the electronic document. A similar procedure is followed to convert a tangible to an electronic document. The person entitled to enforce a tangible document transfers it to the issuer in exchange for an electronic document, which must state that it substitutes for the tangible document.

A **warehouse receipt** is issued by a warehouser to the entity or individual who deposits goods for storage. The depositor is the bailor and the warehouser is the bailee who obtains a **lien** on the goods. A lien is a claim on property of another as security for a debt. It is enforceable by public or private sale. A warehouse receipt need not be in any special form, but it **must state** (1) the location of the warehouse, (2) the date of issue of the receipt, (3) the one to whom the goods are to be delivered, (4) the storage or handling charges, (5) a description of the goods or their container, (6) a statement that advances have been made or liabilities incurred for which the warehouser claims a lien or security interest, (7) the consecutive number of the receipt, and (8) disclosure of the warehouser's ownership interest (if any) in the goods. With respect to the goods, a warehouser must exercise the same amount of care that a **reasonable person** would under like circumstances. The warehouser, like most other bailees, is liable only for those damages caused by **negligence** (lack of due care). Moreover, a warehouser must keep goods covered by each receipt separate, although different lots of **fungible goods** may be commingled. A warehouser may **contractually limit** its liability, but an amount need not be stated per article. This limit does not apply if the warehouser converts the goods to its own use.

A **bill of lading** is a **contract and a receipt**. It is issued by a carrier evidencing the carrier's receipt of goods for shipment. The carrier is a bailee of the goods who obtains a **lien** on the goods enforceable by public or private sale. The lien extends to **proceeds** of the goods if the carrier has the proceeds. The person delivering the goods to the carrier for shipment is the **shipper** and also the **bailor**. The delivery of the goods by the shipper-bailor to a carrier for transport is a **consignment**. The shipper-bailor is the **consignor**. The person to whom the carrier is to deliver the goods at their destination is the **consignee**.

Common carriers are special bailees and are subject to **strict liability** for losses occurring while goods are in transit. However, common carriers are not liable for damage or losses caused by (1) an Act of God, (2) the fault of the shipper, (3) an act of a public enemy, (4) an act of public authority, or (5) the inherent nature of the goods. A carrier may **limit its liability** by contract and notation on the bill of lading. This limit does not apply if the carrier converts the goods to its own use. An **endorser or transferor** of a document of title **warrants to the transferee** that (1) the document is genuine and not a forgery, (2) (s)he has no knowledge of any fact that impairs the document's worth or validity, and (3) his/her transfer or negotiation is rightful and fully effective with respect to the title to the document and the goods it represents.

Letters of credit are widely used in both domestic and international trade and are intended to facilitate the purchase and sale of goods. Use of a letter of credit often involves a buyer and a bank in the buyer's country and a seller and a bank in the seller's country. Article 5 of the UCC governs letters of credit. A letter of credit is (1) a definite undertaking by an **issuer** (such as a bank) (2) to a **beneficiary** (such as a seller) (3) at the request or for the account of an **applicant** (such as a buyer who is a customer of the bank) (4) to honor a **documentary presentation** by payment or delivery of an item of value [UCC 5-102(10)]. A **confirmer**, such as a bank in the beneficiary's country, may serve as an intermediary between the beneficiary and issuer.

No **consideration** is needed to establish a letter of credit, and it may be issued in any form that is a **record** and is **authenticated** (1) by a signature or (2) in accordance with the parties' agreement or the standard practice of financial institutions that regularly issue letters of credit (UCC 5-104). It is **revocable** only if it so provides. After its issuance, a letter of credit may be **amended or canceled** without consent of a beneficiary, applicant, confirmer, or issuer. However, it must be expressly revocable or state that the issuer may amend or cancel without consent (UCC 5-106). If not otherwise indicated, a letter of credit expires **1 year** after its date of issuance. If the letter of credit states it is **perpetual**, it expires **5 years** after issuance (UCC 5-106).

The function of the **traditional or commercial letter of credit** is to finance the movement of goods in commerce and to ensure that the seller will be paid. A letter of credit is legally separate from the **underlying contract** between the issuing bank's customer and the beneficiary. The **issuer** is required to look only to the **terms of the letter of credit**. It is not required to consider the contractual obligations between the parties. Thus, the issuer is concerned with **documents**, not contract performance. An issuer must honor a **presentation of documents** (e.g., a document of title, an invoice, and an issuance policy) that, as determined by standard practice, "appears on its face strictly to comply with the terms and conditions of the letter of credit" (UCC 5-108). If the presentation appears on its face to comply strictly with the letter of credit but a required document is **forged or materially fraudulent**, or honoring the presentation would facilitate a material fraud by the beneficiary, the issuer, in good faith, may honor or dishonor the presentation. However, even in the cases of fraud or forgery, the presentation must be honored if the presenting person belongs to a **protected class**. Examples are (1) a holder in due course of a draft drawn under the letter of credit that was taken after acceptance by the issuer and (2) a confirmer that has honored its confirmation in good faith (UCC 5-109).

The traditional letter of credit is used in connection with a **contract for the sale of goods**. It is typically issued by a bank or other financially responsible entity at the request of a buyer and addressed to the **seller** of the goods. The letter of credit provides **assurance** of prompt payment upon compliance with the conditions specified (typically, mere presentation of the documents). Use of the letter of credit involves the **exchange of documents (and money) through intermediaries**. The following steps illustrate the traditional letter of credit life cycle:

1. A **buyer (applicant)** and the **seller (beneficiary)** agree to terms.
2. The buyer completes an application for a letter of credit and forwards it to the issuing bank.
3. The issuer then forwards the letter of credit to a **confirmer**, which has the rights and obligations of an issuer. A confirmer agrees to honor a presentation under a letter of credit issued by another.
4. The confirmer confirms and forwards the letter of credit to the seller.
5. The seller, having received assurance of payment, arranges for the required method of shipment under its contract with the buyer.
6. The seller then obtains or prepares the documents (documents of title, proof of insurance, and invoice) required under the letter of credit, draws a draft on it, and delivers them to the confirmer.
7. The confirmer inspects the documents, duly negotiates the document of title, and forwards the other documents to the issuer.
8. The confirmer pays the seller in accordance with the letter of credit.
9. When the issuer receives and inspects the documents, it debits the buyer's account.
10. The issuer then forwards the documents to the buyer.
11. The issuer reimburses the confirmer.
12. The buyer takes delivery of the goods from the shipper or warehouser.

The Letter of Credit Cycle

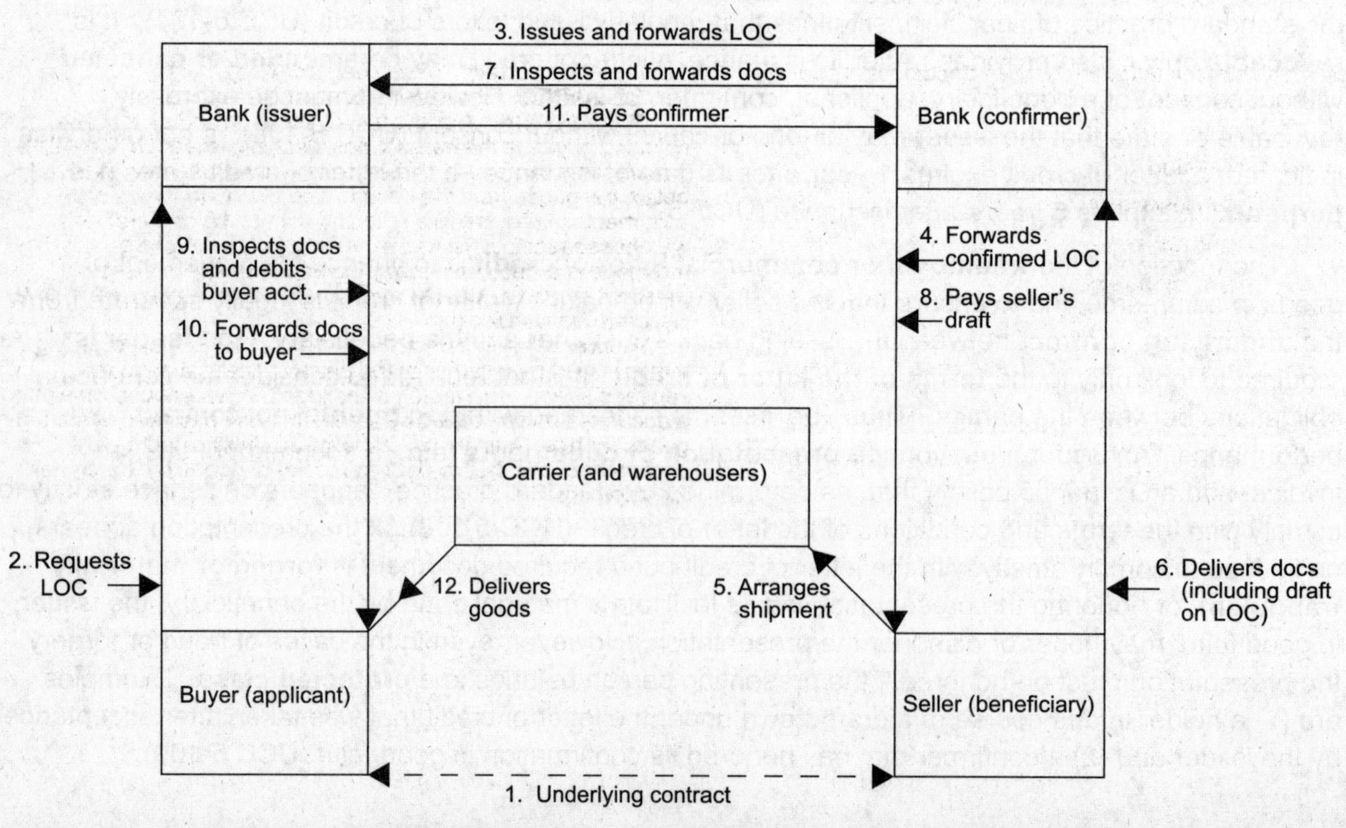

The **standby letter of credit** obligates the issuer to pay only in the event of default by its customer.

EXAMPLE: Cruz, a real estate developer, usually requires the general contractor to provide a completion bond assuring the payment of a fixed amount of money if the project is not completed on schedule. Cruz also can request that the general contractor obtain a letter of credit stating that, upon its failure to perform on schedule, the issuer will pay a draft drawn on the letter of credit. The issuer, who assumes **primary liability**, receives an agreement from the general contractor that (s)he will reimburse it for any expenditure made under the letter and a percentage fee based on the face amount of the letter of credit.

Under a standby letter of credit, the issuer receives no documents of title. Instead, it receives the applicant's promise to reimburse any expenditure made under the letter. Moreover, the issuer **cannot assert defenses** that (1) the applicant has against the beneficiary or (2) the issuer has against the applicant. The issuer must pay when the beneficiary presents a draft and a statement certifying the applicant's nonperformance that strictly conforms with the letter of credit. In exchange for undertaking this obligation to pay, the issuer ordinarily charges a percentage fee based on the face amount of the letter of credit.

QUESTIONS

17.1 Documents of Title

1. Documents of title do not perform which of the following functions?

A. Obligation of repayment.

B. Receipt for a bailment.

C. Contract for storage or shipment.

D. Symbol evidencing ownership of goods.

Answer (A) is correct. *(Publisher, adapted)*

REQUIRED: The function that documents of title do not perform.

DISCUSSION: Documents of title function as receipts for bailments, contracts for storage or shipment, and symbols evidencing ownership of goods. However, a document of title does not encompass an obligation of repayment. An obligation of repayment is generally represented by a note, draft, certificate of deposit, etc.

2. Which of the following is not a document of title covered by Article 7 of the UCC?

A. Destination bill.

B. Warehouse receipt.

C. Bill of lading.

D. Chattel mortgage.

Answer (D) is correct. *(Publisher, adapted)*

REQUIRED: The item not a document of title.

DISCUSSION: A document of title is issued by a bailee covering goods in the bailee's possession or care (UCC 1-201). It represents ownership of the goods and is ordinarily needed to obtain the goods from the bailee. The two major types of documents of title are bills of lading (issued by carriers) and warehouse receipts (issued by warehousers). A chattel mortgage is a document providing for a security interest in personal property. Chattel mortgages are governed by Article 9, *Secured Transactions*.

Answer (A) is incorrect. A destination bill is a bill of lading that is issued by a carrier at the place of destination to the sender's agent. Answer (B) is incorrect. A warehouse receipt is a document of title issued by a person in the business of storing goods for hire. Answer (C) is incorrect. A bill of lading is a document of title that evidences receipt of goods by the carrier for shipment.

3. The procedure necessary to negotiate a document of title depends principally on whether the document is

A. An order document or a bearer document.

B. Issued by a bailee or a consignee.

C. A receipt for goods stored or goods already shipped.

D. A bill of lading or a warehouse receipt.

Answer (A) is correct. *(CPA, adapted)*

REQUIRED: The factor most affecting the negotiation of a document of title.

DISCUSSION: The negotiation of a document of title principally depends on whether the document is an order document or a bearer document. An order document must be endorsed and delivered to be properly negotiated. But delivery suffices to complete the negotiation of a bearer document.

Answer (B) is incorrect. Whether the document is issued by a bailee or a consignee is irrelevant to the negotiation of a document of title. Answer (C) is incorrect. A receipt for goods stored or goods already shipped is irrelevant to the negotiation of a document of title. Answer (D) is incorrect. Bills of lading and warehouse receipts are both documents of title, and negotiation requires the same procedures for both.

4. Under the UCC, a warehouse receipt

A. Will not be negotiable if it contains a contractual limitation on the warehouser's liability.

B. May qualify as both a negotiable warehouse receipt and negotiable commercial paper if the instrument is payable either in cash or by the delivery of goods.

C. May be issued only by a bonded and licensed warehouser.

D. Is negotiable if, by its terms, the goods are to be delivered to bearer or the order of a named person.

Answer (D) is correct. *(CPA, adapted)*

REQUIRED: The true statement about a warehouse receipt.

DISCUSSION: Article 7 of the UCC controls documents of title. A document of title, known as a warehouse receipt, is issued by a person storing goods for hire as a receipt for goods and to represent ownership of the goods. A document of title is negotiable if, by its terms, the goods are to be delivered to the order of a named person or to bearer (UCC 7-104).

Answer (A) is incorrect. Limits on a warehouser's liability do not affect negotiability of a warehouse receipt. Answer (B) is incorrect. Negotiable commercial paper must be payable only in money. Answer (C) is incorrect. The UCC does not require that warehousers be bonded and licensed before they can issue warehouse receipts.

5. Thieves broke into the warehouse of Monogram Airways and stole a shipment of parts belonging to Valley Instruments. Valley had in its possession a negotiable bill of lading covering the shipment. The thieves transported the stolen parts to another state and placed the parts in a bonded warehouse. The thieves received a negotiable warehouse receipt that they used to secure a loan of $30,000 from Reliable Finance. These facts were revealed upon apprehension of the thieves. Regarding the rights of the parties,

A. Reliable is entitled to a $30,000 payment before relinquishment of the parts.

B. Monogram will be the ultimate loser of the $30,000.

C. Valley is entitled to recover the parts free of Reliable's $30,000 claim.

D. Valley is not entitled to the parts but may obtain damages from Monogram.

Answer (C) is correct. *(CPA, adapted)*

REQUIRED: The rights of the parties when goods covered by a document of title are stolen.

DISCUSSION: Under UCC 7-503, a document of title confers no right in goods against a person who before issuance had a legal right in them and who neither delivered nor entrusted them or any document covering them to the bailor with actual or apparent authority to ship, store, or sell or with power to obtain delivery or with power of disposition. Because Valley had a legal right in the goods and did not deliver or entrust them or a document covering them to the bailor (the thieves), the warehouse receipt gave no right to Reliable or anyone else against Valley. It did not represent title to the goods.

Answer (A) is incorrect. Valley may recover the parts from Reliable. Answer (B) is incorrect. The carrier (Monogram) will have no liability if it exercised the degree of care in relation to the goods that a reasonably careful person would have exercised in like circumstances (UCC 7-309). Answer (D) is incorrect. Valley may recover the parts from Reliable. Additionally, the carrier (Monogram) will have no liability if it exercised the degree of care in relation to the goods that a reasonably careful person would have exercised in like circumstances (UCC 7-309).

6. Klep stole several negotiable warehouse receipts, which were deliverable to the order of Apple from the premises of Store Co. Klep endorsed Store's name on the instruments and transferred them to Margo Wholesalers, a bona fide purchaser for value. As between Store and Margo,

A. Store will prevail because the warehouser must be notified before negotiation is effective.

B. Store will prevail because Klep's endorsement prevents negotiation.

C. Margo will prevail because it has taken a negotiable warehouse receipt as a bona fide purchaser for value.

D. Margo will prevail because the warehouse receipt was converted to a bearer instrument by Klep's endorsement.

Answer (B) is correct. *(CPA, adapted)*
REQUIRED: The effect of a forged endorsement on a document of title.
DISCUSSION: A holder to whom a negotiable document of title has been "duly negotiated" acquires title to the document (UCC 7-502). However, negotiation requires an endorsement as well as delivery if the document runs to the order of a named person (UCC 7-501). In addition, the holder must have purchased in good faith, for value, and in the ordinary course of business. Klep's forgery of Store's endorsement does not constitute negotiation and provides Store a real defense against Margo even though Margo was a bona fide purchaser for value.
Answer (A) is incorrect. Negotiation does not require notification of the warehouser. Answer (C) is incorrect. The warehouse receipt was not duly negotiated. Answer (D) is incorrect. A forged endorsement does not convert a warehouse receipt into a bearer instrument.

7. Woody Pyle, a public warehouser, issued Merlin a negotiable warehouse receipt for fungible goods stored. Pyle

A. May not limit the amount of his liability for his own negligence.

B. Will be absolutely liable for any damages in the absence of a statute or a provision on the warehouse receipt to the contrary.

C. May commingle Merlin's goods with similar fungible goods of other bailors.

D. Is obligated to deliver the goods to Merlin despite Merlin's improper refusal to pay storage charges due.

Answer (C) is correct. *(CPA, adapted)*
REQUIRED: The true statement about a warehouser's rights and duties.
DISCUSSION: Unless otherwise provided by the receipt, "A warehouseman must keep separate the goods covered by each receipt so as to permit at all times identification and delivery of those goods except that different lots of fungible goods may be commingled" (UCC 7-207).
Answer (A) is incorrect. Damages may be limited by the warehouse receipt or storage agreement (UCC 7-204). Answer (B) is incorrect. Unless otherwise agreed, Pyle is not liable for damages that could not have been avoided by the exercise of such care as a reasonably careful person would have exercised in the circumstances (UCC 7-204). Answer (D) is incorrect. A warehouser has a lien on the goods that may be enforced by a public or private sale (UCC 7-209 and 7-210).

8. Field Corp. issued a negotiable warehouse receipt to Hall for goods stored in Field's warehouse. Hall's goods were lost due to Field's failure to exercise such care as a reasonably careful person would under like circumstances. The state in which this transaction occurred follows the UCC rule with respect to a warehouser's liability for lost goods. The warehouse receipt is silent on this point. Under the circumstances, Field is

A. Liable because it is strictly liable for any loss.

B. Liable because it was negligent.

C. Not liable because the warehouse receipt was negotiable.

D. Not liable unless Hall can establish that Field was grossly negligent.

Answer (B) is correct. *(CPA, adapted)*
REQUIRED: The liability of a warehouser that failed to exercise reasonable care.
DISCUSSION: A warehouser is liable for damages for loss of, or injury to, goods caused by its failure to exercise reasonable care (UCC 7-204). Field's negligence in failing to exercise the care of a reasonable person makes Field liable for the lost goods.
Answer (A) is incorrect. Warehousers are not liable for losses caused by events beyond their control, provided that due care was exercised. Answer (C) is incorrect. Negotiability of the warehouse receipt is irrelevant to the warehouser's liability. Answer (D) is incorrect. Hall need not prove gross negligence, only simple negligence.

9. Which of the following is not a warranty made by the seller of a negotiable warehouse receipt to the purchaser of the document?

A. The document transfer is fully effective with respect to the goods it represents.

B. The warehouser will honor the document.

C. The seller has no knowledge of any facts that would impair the document's validity.

D. The document is genuine.

Answer (B) is correct. *(CPA, adapted)*
REQUIRED: The warranty not made by the seller of a negotiable warehouse receipt.
DISCUSSION: The seller of a negotiable warehouse receipt does not guarantee that the warehouser will honor the document.

10. Under Article 7 of the UCC, which of the following statements is(are) true regarding a common carrier's duty to deliver goods subject to a negotiable bearer bill of lading?

I. The carrier may deliver the goods to any party designated by the holder of the bill of lading.

II. A carrier who, without court order, delivers goods to a party claiming the goods under a missing negotiable bill of lading is liable to any person injured by the misdelivery.

A. I only.

B. II only.

C. Both I and II.

D. Neither I nor II.

Answer (C) is correct. *(CPA, adapted)*

REQUIRED: The true statement(s), if any, about the delivery of goods by a common carrier.

DISCUSSION: A bill of lading is a document issued by a carrier evidencing the receipt of goods for shipment. It may be in negotiable or nonnegotiable form. If negotiable, the bill may be an order or a bearer instrument. UCC Article 7 requires the carrier under a negotiable bearer instrument to deliver the goods to the holder of the document or his/her agent or assignee. A negotiable bearer bill of lading may be negotiated by delivery without endorsement. To receive the goods, the consignee must tender the document. A carrier who delivers goods without surrender of the negotiable bill of lading is strictly liable to any person rightfully entitled to the goods.

11. Under Article 7 of the UCC, which of the following acts may excuse or limit a common carrier's liability for damage to goods in transit?

A. Vandalism.

B. Power outage.

C. Willful acts of third parties.

D. Providing for a contractual dollar liability limitation.

Answer (D) is correct. *(CPA, adapted)*

REQUIRED: The act that may excuse or limit a common carrier's liability for damage to goods in transit.

DISCUSSION: Under UCC Article 7, a common carrier is an insurer of the goods entrusted to it by a shipper. However, the common law recognizes five exceptions that may reduce or eliminate liability: (1) an Act of God, (2) an act of a public enemy, (3) an act of a public authority, (4) an act of the shipper, and (5) the inherent nature of the goods. However, a carrier is required to use reasonable care to prevent losses as a result of one of the exceptions. Article 7 provides that a common carrier may by contract limit its liability by trading a reduced rate in exchange for reduced liability.

12. Which of the following statements is correct concerning a bill of lading in the possession of Major Corp. that was issued by a common carrier and provides that the goods are to be delivered "to bearer"?

A. The carrier's lien for any unpaid shipping charges does not entitle it to sell the goods to enforce the lien.

B. The carrier will not be liable for delivering the goods to a person other than Major.

C. The carrier may require Major to endorse the bill of lading prior to delivering the goods.

D. The bill of lading can be negotiated by Major by delivery alone and without endorsement.

Answer (D) is correct. *(CPA, adapted)*

REQUIRED: The true statement about a bearer bill of lading.

DISCUSSION: A bill of lading is negotiable only if the written document contains order or bearer language. If the document provides that the bailed goods are to be delivered to bearer, the document is negotiated by delivery alone, and the carrier must deliver the goods to the holder.

Answer (A) is incorrect. A carrier has a lien on the goods that may be enforced by public or private sale (UCC 7-307 and 7-308). Answer (B) is incorrect. Major is the holder of the bearer bill of lading. Answer (C) is incorrect. The holder of a bearer bill of lading is entitled to delivery of the goods without endorsing the document.

13. Which of the following standards of liability best characterizes the obligation of a common carrier in a bailment relationship?

A. Reasonable care.

B. Gross negligence.

C. Shared liability.

D. Strict liability.

Answer (D) is correct. *(CPA, adapted)*

REQUIRED: The standard of liability that best characterizes the obligation of a common carrier in a bailment relationship.

DISCUSSION: Although most bailors must exercise reasonable care under the circumstances, a common carrier owes a higher standard of care. Thus, the common carrier is strictly liable without fault for damage to, or loss of, the goods being transported. However, the common law recognizes five exceptions that may reduce or eliminate liability: (1) an Act of God, (2) an act of a public enemy, (3) an act of a public authority, (4) an act of the shipper, and (5) the inherent nature of the goods.

17.2 Letters of Credit

14. A letter of credit is

A. A letter documenting a line of credit on which a customer may draw at its bank.

B. An engagement by a financial institution to pay drafts or other demands for payment for its customer.

C. A letter by a buyer or seller of goods that credit is due the other party for defective or returned goods.

D. A credit reference given by a bank.

Answer (B) is correct. *(Publisher, adapted)*

REQUIRED: The statement that correctly identifies a letter of credit.

DISCUSSION: A letter of credit is a definite undertaking by an issuer (such as a bank) to a beneficiary (such as a seller) at the request or for the account of an applicant (such as a buyer who is a customer of the bank) to honor a documentary presentation by payment or delivery of an item of value. The holder of a letter of credit merely needs to present the required drafts or other documents (usually documenting a sale of goods to the issuer's customer) and to receive payment from the bank or other issuer up to the limit specified.

Answer (A) is incorrect. It describes a credit on which a customer may borrow from a bank. Answer (C) is incorrect. It describes a credit memorandum. At the end of some agreed period, such memoranda are netted with invoices to determine what is due. Answer (D) is incorrect. A credit reference is a statement concerning the creditworthiness of a person.

15. A buyer is entitled to the goods purchased in a bill of lading and letter of credit transaction after the buyer's bank checks the

A. Goods purchased to verify that they conform to the contract of sale.

B. Contract for the purchased goods to verify that it conforms with the bill of lading.

C. Contract for the purchased goods to verify that it conforms with the letter of credit.

D. Bill of lading to verify that it conforms with the terms in the letter of credit.

Answer (D) is correct. *(Publisher, adapted)*

REQUIRED: The condition of a buyer's entitlement to goods purchased under a letter of credit.

DISCUSSION: In a bill of lading and letter of credit transaction, the seller is paid after the bill of lading is turned over to the confirming bank. The confirming bank sends the bill of lading to the buyer's bank that issued the letter of credit. The contract for the sale of goods is independent of the letter of credit and bill of lading. The buyer's bank checks the bill of lading to verify conformity with the letter of credit. If it conforms, the bank gives the bill of lading to the buyer, and (s)he takes the bill of lading to the transporting company's warehouse to retrieve the goods.

Answer (A) is incorrect. The buyer, not the confirming bank, should examine the goods. Answer (B) is incorrect. The buyer's bank does not check the contract for the sale of goods. It is independent of the bill of lading. Answer (C) is incorrect. The buyer's bank does not check the contract for the sale of goods. It is independent of the letter of credit.

16. Samantha Clothiers of Denver, Colorado, wants to buy men's suits from Altskool & Sons in Frankfurt, Germany. Samantha will send a buyer to Frankfurt carrying an irrevocable letter of credit issued by Big National Bank of Denver and naming Altskool as beneficiary. The letter of credit states that it is governed by UCC Article 5. It permits Altskool to draw a draft of up to $250,000 payable to Altskool through Big National. The bank is to honor the draft if it is accompanied by (1) a negotiable bill of lading issued by a carrier to which Altskool has delivered the suits for shipment and (2) a certificate of insurance covering the suits. In which of the following circumstances may Big National refuse to honor a draft drawn by Altskool?

A. The documents accompanying the draft do not on their face conform to the requirements of the letter of credit.

B. The suits as shipped contain hidden defects that constitute a breach of warranty.

C. Samantha has become insolvent and is unable to reimburse Big National for amounts Big National pays to Altskool.

D. All of the answers are correct.

Answer (A) is correct. *(D. Paas)*

REQUIRED: The circumstance(s) allowing dishonor of a letter of credit.

DISCUSSION: Under the 1995 amendments to Article 5, UCC 5-109 provides that an issuer (Big National) must honor a presentation that, as determined by standard practice, appear on its face strictly to comply with terms and conditions of the letter of credit. The issuer is not responsible for performance or nonperformance of the underlying contract, arrangement, or transaction. Thus, an issuer may dishonor a presentation if, as determined by the standard practice of financial institutions that regularly issue letters of credit, it does not on its face strictly comply with terms and conditions of the letter of credit (between Samantha and Altskool), but only if the documents conform on their face to the terms of the letter of credit.

Answer (B) is incorrect. The goods need not be conforming. Answer (C) is incorrect. An issuer must honor a letter of credit that is irrevocable once it is received by a party claiming rights under it. Because Altskool has received the letter of credit, Big National must honor its drafts if the documents conform on their face to the terms of the letter of credit. Answer (D) is incorrect. Big National may not dishonor a draft if the suits as shipped contain hidden defects that constitute a breach of warranty or if Samantha has become insolvent and is unable to reimburse Big National for amounts Big National pays to Altskool.

17. Which of the following is required for a valid letter of credit?

A. That consideration is given.

B. That it is in a form that is a record and is authenticated.

C. That it is irrevocable.

D. That consent by a beneficiary is given to amend or cancel it.

Answer (B) is correct. *(Publisher, adapted)*

REQUIRED: The characteristic of a valid letter of credit.

DISCUSSION: A letter of credit may be issued in any form that is a record and is authenticated (1) by a signature or (2) in accordance with the parties' agreement or the standard practice of financial institutions that regularly issue letters of credit (UCC 5-104).

Answer (A) is incorrect. Consideration is not necessary to establish a letter of credit under UCC 5-105. Answer (C) is incorrect. A letter of credit may be revocable, but only if it so provides (UCC 5-106). Answer (D) is incorrect. After its issuance, a letter of credit may be amended or canceled without consent of a beneficiary, applicant, confirmer, or issuer only if it is expressly revocable or states that the issuer may amend or cancel without consent.

18. A seller is paid in a bill of lading and letter of credit transaction when the bill of lading is given to the

A. Transport company.

B. Buyer.

C. Seller's bank.

D. Confirming bank.

Answer (D) is correct. *(Publisher, adapted)*

REQUIRED: The method by which a seller is paid in a bill of lading and letter of credit transaction.

DISCUSSION: The letter of credit and bill of lading transaction is used to assure that the seller will be paid. After the seller and buyer enter into an agreement for the sale of goods, the buyer arranges with a bank or other issuer to obtain a letter of credit. The buyer's bank arranges for a bank in the seller's city or country (the confirmer) to issue or confirm the letter of credit to the seller. The seller draws on the letter of credit by writing drafts. The seller is paid when the bill of lading is presented to the confirming bank.

Answer (A) is incorrect. The bill of lading is issued to the seller when (s)he delivers the purchased goods to the transporting company. Answer (B) is incorrect. The buyer receives the bill of lading after the seller is paid. The buyer does not pay the seller. Answer (C) is incorrect. The buyer's bank, not the seller's, receives the bill of lading.

19. Assume in the preceding question that Altskool delivers the suits to a carrier, but it cannot obtain insurance. Altskool forges a blank certificate of insurance so skillfully that the certificate appears to be genuine and complies with the letter of credit. Altskool then draws a draft for $200,000 payable to itself and attaches the bill of lading and the forged certificate. Which of the following statements is true?

A. If Altskool presents the draft to Big National, the bank must not pay it.

B. If Altskool presents the draft to Big National, the bank cannot pay if it knows of the forgery; but if it does not know, it may pay.

C. If Altskool negotiates the draft and other documents to a Frankfurt bank for value so that the bank becomes a holder in due course, Big National may choose to either pay or not pay the Frankfurt bank upon presentment of the draft.

D. If Altskool negotiates the draft and documents to a Frankfurt bank for value so that the bank becomes a holder in due course, Big National must pay the Frankfurt bank.

Answer (D) is correct. *(D. Paas)*

REQUIRED: The true statement about the negotiation of letters of credit when required documents are forged.

DISCUSSION: Under UCC 5-109, a distinction is drawn between (1) holders in due course (HDC) and certain other parties who have acted in good faith and (2) those who are not. An issuer (Big National) can refuse to honor a beneficiary's draft (such as one drawn and presented by Altskool, a party not a holder in due course) if required documents are forged or fraudulent. But even with respect to such a party, UCC 5-109 allows an issuer acting in good faith to honor a draft accompanied by forged documents if the presentation appears on its face strictly to comply with the letter of credit. If the party making a presentation that includes a forged document is an HDC or other protested party, however, the issuer must honor it if it complies with the letter of credit.

Answer (A) is incorrect. The forged insurance certificate is regular on its face and the bank can choose either to honor or dishonor Altskool's presentment. But under UCC 5-109, a holder in due course must always be paid if documents appear on their face to comply with the terms of the letter of credit. Answer (B) is incorrect. The forged insurance certificate is regular on its face and the bank can choose either to honor or dishonor Altskool's presentment. But under UCC 5-109, a holder in due course must always be paid if documents appear on their face to comply with the terms of the letter of credit. Answer (C) is incorrect. The documents are regular and Big National has no choice but to pay.

STUDY UNIT EIGHTEEN
SECURED TRANSACTIONS

To protect against the risk of nonpayment of a debt, a creditor may require the debtor to enter into a security agreement. A **security agreement** gives the creditor an interest in **specific personal property** owned by the debtor. A valid **security interest** allows the creditor, if the debtor defaults, to repossess the collateral, sell it at a reasonably conducted public or private sale, and apply the sale proceeds to the debt.

UCC Article 9, *Secured Transactions*, primarily covers any transaction that establishes by contract a security interest in personal property or fixtures, regardless of its form. A **security interest** is defined as "an interest in personal property or fixtures that secures payment or performance of an obligation." A **purchase money security interest** (PMSI) is important to creditors because of the priority it receives. A PMSI arises when (1) a person obtains credit (borrows money), (2) the credit is used to acquire (purchase) property, and (3) that property serves as collateral to secure the obligation to satisfy the debt (repay the money borrowed). The consignor's security interest in **consigned goods** is a PMSI in inventory.

EXAMPLE 1: John purchases an office copier from We-R-Copies. One week later, John borrows $10,000 from Bank, Inc. and gives Bank a security interest in all his office equipment. Bank's security interest in the copier is not a PMSI.

EXAMPLE 2: Jan starts her own business. Jan borrows $10,000 from Bank, Inc. to purchase office equipment. She gives Bank a security interest in the equipment she intends to purchase. The next day, Jan purchases a desk. Bank's security interest in the desk is a PMSI.

EXAMPLE 3: Caitlin purchased a computer on credit from Hardware Heaven. She also purchased in the same transaction additional software that she planned to install in the computer. Thus, Hardware Heaven (a seller that financed the purchase) has a PMSI in the computer and the software.

A **secured party** is a person in whose favor a security interest exists under a security agreement. A **lease of goods** may be a security interest if the parties objectively intend that the lease provide security. Whether a transaction is to be treated as a **true lease** or as establishing a security interest is determined by the facts of the case. **Lessors** do not file a financing statement in connection with a true lease. However, if the lease is for the **entire economic life of the goods**, the transaction will be treated as a **security interest**.

The application of Article 9 often depends on the **nature of collateral** involved. **Goods** are fixtures and all things movable at the time a security interest attaches. **Tangible personal property** includes four categories of goods. **Consumer goods** are used primarily for personal, family, or household purposes. **Inventory** encompasses goods to be held for sale or lease or to be furnished under a contract for service. Inventory includes raw materials, work in process, or supplies used or consumed in the business. **Farm products** are crops, born or unborn livestock, supplies used or produced in farming, and unprocessed products of crops or livestock. The goods must be in the possession of a debtor engaged in farming operations. **Equipment** includes goods not in another category. **Semi-intangible collateral** is represented by an indispensable writing. **Instruments** include negotiable instruments or any writing evidencing the right to receive money that is transferred by delivery with any necessary endorsement or assignment in the ordinary course of business, e.g., checks, other drafts, or promissory notes. **Documents** include documents of title and receipts, e.g., bills of lading and warehouse receipts. **Chattel paper** consists of writing(s) evidencing both a monetary obligation and a security interest in, or a lease of, specific goods, including goods with software or a license of software used in the goods. Chattel paper is often used in inventory financing. For example, if a seller retains a PMSI in goods sold on credit, it may sell (or borrow against) the security agreement and the note signed by the buyer (the chattel paper). The evidence of **electronic chattel paper** is stored on an electronic medium. **Investment property** includes securities whether or not certificated and whether held directly by the debtor (e.g., stock registered by a corporation) or indirectly (e.g., most publicly traded stock). If securities are held indirectly, the debtor has a **securities account**. A **security entitlement** consists of the rights and property interest of the **entitlement holder** (the debtor) in the account. These rights are assertable against the parties in the chain of **securities intermediaries**, such as brokers, banks, and depositories (e.g., the Depository Trust Company) that hold securities on behalf of brokers and banks. Investment property also includes **commodity contracts** and **commodity accounts**. Commodity contracts include commodity futures, options on commodity futures, and commodity options. **Deposit accounts** are time, savings, or demand accounts in a bank, S&L, credit union, or trust company. They are not evidenced by instruments, and they are not investment property. **Intangible collateral** consists of accounts and general intangibles. **Accounts** are rights to payment (1) for property disposed of, (2) for services rendered, (3) for an insurance policy, (4) for incurrence of secondary obligations (e.g, guarantees), (5) for energy, (6) resulting from credit card use, or (7) representing winnings in a state-approved game of chance. **General intangibles** include any personal property other than (1) the items listed above, (2) money, (3) commercial tort claims, (4) minerals before extraction, and (5) rights (other than the beneficiary's) under a letter of credit. Examples include goodwill, **payment intangibles** (general intangibles under which the primary obligation is monetary), software, or a patent. **Proceeds** constitute collateral that has changed in form. Proceeds include (1) what is obtained from the disposition of collateral (e.g., by sale, lease, license, or exchange), (2) collections on or distributions on account of collateral, (3) rights based on collateral, (4) claims arising from losses on collateral (e.g., from defects, damage, or nonconformity), and (5) insurance payable on the collateral.

Attachment of a security interest in collateral occurs when it becomes **enforceable** against the debtor, barring an explicit agreement otherwise. A security agreement is enforceable when the following events have occurred: (1) The debtor ordinarily must have **authenticated a security agreement** (e.g., by signing a writing or by electronic means) describing the collateral. The major exception is **possession** of the collateral by the secured party. (2) **Value** must have been given by the secured party. (3) The **debtor must have rights** in the collateral or the power to transfer such rights. Attachment of a security interest in collateral gives rights to **proceeds**.

A **security agreement** is a contract between the debtor and the secured party by which the secured party is granted a security interest in the collateral. The debtor and the secured party must intend that a security interest be conveyed. However, under federal law, a credit seller or lender may not obtain from a **consumer** a **nonpossessory, non PMSI** security interest in **household goods**. A security agreement may include optional items. An **after-acquired property clause** conveys an interest in debtor property to be acquired in the future (a floating lien). Such a clause is important to a lender that finances inventory. A security interest will attach to after-acquired **consumer goods** only if the debtor acquires rights in the goods not more than **10 days** after the secured party gives value. A **future advances clause** provides that the security agreement extends to future liabilities of the debtor to the secured party. An **acceleration of payment clause** provides for the full debt to mature immediately upon default or within a specified period if a default is not cured.

Perfection is the process by which the secured party gives notice of the security interest in the collateral to third parties (the debtor's other creditors). It gives the secured party **priority** over most of those third parties who may subsequently claim an interest. But it is not needed to enforce the secured party's rights against the debtor. **Perfection cannot occur prior to attachment**. Depending on the nature of the collateral, security interests are perfected by (1) filing a financing statement, (2) by possession or control of the collateral, (3) by delivery of a registered certificated security, or (4) automatically (but in certain cases for a brief period only). **Filing** is the typical means of perfection. It is required to perfect a security interest in the absence of a specific exception. Filing perfects security interests in instruments, negotiable documents, chattel paper, and investment property. The **financing statement** must contain (1) the names of the debtor and secured party and (2) an indication of the covered collateral. A financing statement may be filed before a security agreement is reached or a security interest attaches. Filing occurs when a record is communicated to a filing office and the fee is tendered or the filing office accepts the record. Errors or omissions do not make the financing statement ineffective unless they are seriously misleading (e.g., omitting the debtor's name). A duly filed financing statement is effective for 5 years from the filing date. A **continuation statement** extending perfection for 5 years may be filed during the last 6 months before expiration of this period. If it is not filed, the security interest becomes unperfected. Filing a **termination statement** causes the financing statement to lapse. If the collateral is consumer goods, a termination statement must be filed within 1 month of the debtor's fulfillment of its obligations. If the debtor makes an authenticated demand for a termination statement, the filing must be within 20 days. If the collateral is not consumer goods, the debtor must be provided a termination statement pursuant to an authenticated demand. Filing is not required.

A security interest may be perfected by **possession** of goods, negotiable documents, tangible chattel paper, instruments, and money. A security interest in a **registered certificated security** is perfected by **delivery**. If attachment occurs when the secured party takes possession of the collateral in accordance with the debtor's security agreement, perfection occurs **simultaneously** with attachment. Generally, if perfection is by possession, the security interest becomes unperfected when possession ceases unless the secured party files while in possession of the collateral.

Control perfects a security interest in investment property. Control of **investment property** depends on its form. If a **certificated security** is in **bearer form**, control is held by the secured party if delivery is made to it. If a **certificated security** is in **registered form**, control is held by the secured party if delivery is made to it, provided that (1) the certificate is endorsed in blank or to the secured party, or (2) the certificate is registered to the secured party. A secured party controls an **uncertificated security** if (1) it is delivered to the secured party, or (2) the issuer, with the consent of the owner, has agreed to follow the secured party's instructions.

Automatic perfection occurs when neither filing nor possession is required. A **PMSI in consumer goods** is automatically perfected. Exceptions are consumer goods subject to certain statutes, regulations, or treaties. For example, a **certificate-of-title statute** covering automobiles may require the security interest to be noted on the certificate. Compliance with the law in these circumstances is the equivalent of filing. Automatic perfection by attachment gives the secured party **priority over other creditors** of the debtor.

With respect to security interests in **instruments, certificated securities, or negotiable documents**, perfection is automatic for a **20-day period after attachment** to the extent that **new value** is given to obtain the security interest under an authenticated security agreement. Furthermore, a secured party having a perfected security interest may **relinquish possession for 20 days** without filing while retaining a perfected security interest. A similar rule applies to relinquishment of **goods in the possession of the bailee** who has not issued a negotiable document covering them. The purpose of this rule is to allow normal commercial activities, e.g., sale or exchange. During the period that goods are held by a bailee that has issued a **negotiable document** representing the goods, a security interest in the goods is perfected by perfecting a security interest in the document. Any other security interest in the goods is subject to that interest during that period. If goods are held by a bailee that has issued a **nonnegotiable document** representing them, a security interest in the goods is perfected by (1) issuance of a document in the secured party's name, (2) notice to the bailee of the secured party's interest, or (3) filing. Security interests in **assigned accounts or payment intangibles** are automatically perfected. But perfection is not automatic if the assignment, considered alone or with other assignments to the same assignee, transfers a significant part of the assignor's accounts or payment intangibles.

Typically, a security interest continues in collateral despite the disposition of the collateral, provided that the secured party did not consent to a disposition free of the security interest. Moreover, a security interest attaches to **identifiable proceeds**. This interest is **perfected** if the security interest in the collateral was perfected. A perfected security interest in proceeds becomes **unperfected at the end of 20 days after attachment**. Nevertheless, **perfection continues** if (1) the original collateral was covered by a **filed financing statement**, the proceeds are collateral in which a security interest may be perfected by filing in the place where the original financing statement was filed, and cash proceeds were not used to acquire the proceeds; (2) the proceeds are **identifiable amounts of cash**; or (3) perfection of the security interest in proceeds occurs at the time of **attachment or within 20 days** thereafter using a method other than that used with respect to the original collateral.

A **change in governing law** may occur because of removal of personal property from the state where the security interest was perfected or for other reasons. The **general rule** is that a security interest in collateral that is perfected in one state is treated as perfected in a state to which the collateral has been removed. However, perfection based on the **law of the debtor's location** lasts only until the earliest of (1) the time **perfection would lapse** in the original state; (2) **4 months** after the debtor moves to a new state; or (3) **1 year** after transfer to a person in another state who, as a result, has the status of a debtor. A **subsequent security interest** in the collateral that is perfected in the new state will prevail after the period described above. Moreover, the earlier security interest will thereafter be deemed to have been unperfected as against a person who became a **purchaser for value** after removal. However, if the **earlier security interest** is perfected in the new state before the end of the period described, it will prevail over any new security interest that attaches in the new state.

A **possessory interest** in collateral (other than goods covered by a certificate of title and as-extracted collateral) that is perfected in one state remains continuously perfected if the security interest is perfected upon entry into a second state. **Goods covered by a certificate of title** and subject to a security interest perfected under the law of one state may become covered by a certificate of title in a second state. **Perfection continues** until it would have lapsed under the law of the first state. However, this security interest becomes unperfected with regard to a **purchaser for value** and is considered never to have been perfected with regard to such a party. To avert this result, the requirements for perfection must be met before the earlier of (1) **lapse of perfection** under the law of the first state or (2) **4 months** after the goods become covered by a certificate of title in the second state.

The degree of protection provided by a security interest varies with its **priority** relative to other claims. One general rule is that, if **unperfected security interests** conflict, the **first to attach or become effective** has priority. A second general rule is that, if **perfected security interests** conflict, priority in the collateral or proceeds depends upon the **order of filing or perfection** with respect to the collateral. This rule applies as long as there was no period thereafter without filing or perfection.

An **unperfected security interest** is subordinate to, among others, (1) a perfected security interest in the same collateral; (2) the rights of a **lien creditor**, i.e., a creditor who acquires a lien by judicial process, an assignee for the benefit of creditors, a receiver in equity, or a trustee in bankruptcy; or (3) a **lessee of goods** who (a) gives value, (b) takes delivery, and (c) has no knowledge of the security interest.

An unperfected security interest has priority over claims of the debtor's **general creditors**.

Priority of perfected interests usually dates from the **time of filing or perfection**, whichever is first.

EXAMPLE 1: Bank agreed to lend Gran's Place, Inc. up to $50,000 during the next year. On January 2, Year 1, Gran's executed a financing statement covering all owned or after-acquired kitchen equipment. The statement included a future advances clause. Bank filed the financing statement on January 3. Finance, Inc. lent Gran's $10,000 on March 1. Gran's executed a financing statement covering all owned or after-acquired kitchen equipment. Finance perfected its security interest by filing the financing statement on March 9. On July 1, Bank lent Gran's $30,000. On July 31, Gran's declared bankruptcy. Bank's security interest has priority over Finance's security interest because Bank filed before Finance filed or perfected.

Bank's financing statement had been filed on July 1, Finance's security interest would have priority over Bank's security interest. Finance's priority would date from March 9 and Bank's from July 1.

If filing or perfection is not accomplished in a subsequent period, priority no longer dates from the time of filing or perfection. Thus, the filing or perfection must be **continuous** to maintain priority. If the security agreement contains a **future advances** clause, the perfected security interest ordinarily has the same priority for future advances as for the first advance. However, priority dates only from the **time of an advance** if the security interest was perfected by **attachment only or temporarily** when the advance was made, and the advance was **not under a commitment** existing before or during the time when the security interest was perfected by other means (e.g., filing, possession, or control).

Generally, a **duly perfected security interest** in goods is effective against **subsequent purchasers**. However, certain third parties may acquire the collateral (goods) free of the security interest, even though the interest has been perfected. A **buyer in the ordinary course of business** takes free of a perfected or unperfected security interest given by his/her seller to another. The buyer's knowledge of the security interest is irrelevant unless (s)he knows that the purchase violates that interest. Moreover, a **buyer of consumer goods from a consumer** takes free of a security interest if (s)he buys (1) without knowledge of the security interest, (2) for value, (3) for consumer purposes, and (4) before the secured party files.

Article 9 does not limit the rights of **a holder in due course** of a negotiable instrument, **a holder to whom a negotiable document of title has been duly negotiated**, or **a protected purchaser of securities**. These parties have priority over an earlier security interest whether or not perfected.

A **PMSI** in **consumer goods** usually is automatically perfected. Furthermore, a secured party with a PMSI who **files before or within 20 days after** the debtor receives delivery of the collateral ordinarily has priority over the rights of a **buyer, lessee, or lien creditor** that arose after the PMSI attached. A **perfected PMSI in goods** (other than inventory or livestock) has priority over a conflicting security interest in the goods if the PMSI is perfected **within 20 days after** the debtor takes possession. This priority ordinarily extends to a perfected security interest in the **identifiable proceeds** of goods.

EXAMPLE: On January 2, Bank lent Luke $50,000 and took a security interest in Luke's currently owned and after-acquired equipment. On June 2, Equip Corp. sold Luke equipment on credit and took a PMSI in the equipment. On June 19, Equip Corp. perfected the PMSI. Equip Corp. has priority over Bank.

A **perfected PMSI in inventory** has priority over a conflicting security interest if (1) the PMSI is perfected when the debtor takes possession, (2) an **authenticated notice** is sent to the other secured party, (3) this notice is received **within 5 years** before the debtor takes possession, and (4) the notice describes the collateral and states that the sender has or expects to have a PMSI in the debtor's inventory. **More than one generation of inventory** may be financed with the same money (loan or credit). The security interest must be **identifiable** to the inventory and should be able to float to subsequent generations of the same class of inventory. A perfected PMSI in inventory extends to (1) identifiable **cash proceeds** received no later than the time of delivery to a buyer and (2) proceeds in the form of instruments, chattel paper, and the proceeds of chattel paper.

Certain **liens arising by operation of law** have priority over perfected security interests if the lienholder furnishes services or materials with respect to the goods in the **ordinary course of business** and is **in possession**. If possession is relinquished, the lien becomes subordinate to a perfected security interest. Moreover, **knowledge of a security interest** by a lienholder has no effect on priority. However, a statute granting such a lien may expressly provide that it is subordinate to a perfected security interest (Study Unit 26).

Fixtures are goods (but not ordinary building materials) that have become so related to particular real property that an interest in them arises under real property law. One party may have a security interest in **personal property** that becomes a fixture, and another party may have a mortgage on or ownership interest in the **real property** itself. In the case of **non-PMSIs versus real estate interests**, the security interest has priority if (1) the debtor has a recorded interest in the real property or possession of it, (2) the security interest is perfected by filing a financing statement covering the goods **(a fixture filing)** before the competing real estate interest is recorded, and (3) the security interest has priority over an interest of a predecessor in title of the real estate interest. The real estate interest has priority if it is recorded first. In the case of **PMSIs versus real estate interests**, a PMSI has priority if (1) it is perfected by fixture filing, (2) the filing is before the goods become fixtures or within 20 days after, (3) the real estate interest arises before the goods become fixtures, and (4) the debtor has a recorded interest in the real property or is in possession of it. An exception to this rule is provided for **construction mortgages**, including a mortgage given to refinance a construction mortgage. This mortgage has priority over a security interest in fixtures if (1) the construction mortgage is recorded before the goods become fixtures, and (2) the goods become fixtures before construction is completed.

The secured party in **possession of collateral** is a **bailee**. (S)he must use **reasonable care** at all times to **preserve** the collateral, for example, in the case of instruments or chattel paper, by taking steps to preserve rights against prior parties. The secured party also must keep the collateral **identifiable**, although fungible collateral, such as grain, may be commingled. The bailee is **strictly liable** if it makes **unauthorized use** of the property or misdelivers it. However, the **debtor** bears the **cost of reasonable expenses** incurred for preservation, use, or custody of the collateral, e.g., insurance and taxes. A secured party with **possession or control** may (1) keep any **proceeds** from the collateral, other than money or funds, as additional security, and (2) create a **security interest** of the collateral. A secured party has a duty to surrender control if no secured obligation is outstanding, and no further commitment to give value exists. This action must be taken within 10 days after receipt of an authenticated demand by the debtor.

A secured party generally must comply with the **duty of confirming**, at the debtor's request, the unpaid amount of the debt. Thus, the debtor may make a "request regarding a statement of account." Compliance ordinarily should be within 14 days after receipt.

Generally, the **account debtor** may not restrict the **secured party's ability to assign** the property. Unless otherwise provided, the **assignee's rights** are subject to (1) the terms of the contract between the account debtor and the assignor, (2) claims or defenses arising from the contract, and (3) other claims or defenses of the account debtor arising before the account debtor is notified of the assignment.

The account debtor can waive rights to sue or defend against an **assignee** with a **waiver of defenses clause**. The clause is generally enforceable if the assignee takes the assignment (1) in good faith, (2) for value, and (3) without a notice of a claim or defense. The clause is generally ineffective to waive **real defenses** effective against a holder in due course of a negotiable instrument. A Federal Trade Commission rule has rendered ineffective waiver-of-defenses clauses in contracts for consumer goods. A **seller of goods on installment credit** (the assignor) who takes a security interest in the goods often assigns the security interest to a financing institution (secured party and assignee). The financing institution then lends the seller funds that are used in operations. The purchaser of the goods is commonly known as an **account debtor**.

Default occurs when the debtor fails to fulfill obligations under the security agreement. A security agreement may provide that an act or occurrence constitutes default. Typical **events constituting default** are (1) lack of current payments, (2) removal of or failure to insure the collateral, and (3) bankruptcy or insolvency of the debtor. If the debtor defaults, the secured party may (1) sue the debtor for the amount due, (2) peaceably take possession and dispose of the collateral, or (3) accept (retain) the collateral.

Upon the debtor's default, the secured party may resort to self-help repossession or repossession by judicial action. **Self-help repossession** is taking possession of the collateral without judicial action. Self-help repossession must be peaceable. **Peaceable** means not constituting a **breach of peace**. **Repossession by judicial action** generally requires obtaining a judicial order or judgment against the debtor. After repossession, the secured party may dispose of the collateral by **public or private proceedings**. **Reasonable authenticated notice** of the disposition must be given to the debtor and other appropriate parties, such as persons filing claims, other secured parties, and lienholders. A notice of **public disposition** must include the time and place. The notice of a **private disposition** must include only the time after which it may occur. In a **nonconsumer transaction**, notice is sent within a reasonable time if it is sent after default and at least 10 days before the earliest time of disposition. In other transactions, reasonableness is an issue of fact. A debtor may **waive notice**. The waiver generally must be authenticated. Notice to the debtor is not required if the collateral is of a type normally sold on a recognized market, perishable, or likely to decline quickly in value. All aspects of the disposition must be **commercially reasonable**, including the time, place, manner, method, and terms. A disposition is conclusively presumed to be commercially reasonable if it has been approved in any judicial proceeding or by any bona fide creditors' committee or representative of creditors. A **transferee for value in good-faith** (1) takes the collateral free of the security interest under which the disposition took place, (2) takes free of security interests in the collateral subordinate to that interest, and (3) receives all the debtor's rights in the collateral. The **secured party may buy** the collateral at any public disposition. If the collateral is of a type customarily sold in a recognized market or is the subject of widely distributed price quotations, the secured party may buy it at private disposition. The **proceeds of collection or enforcement** are applied in the following order: (1) **reasonable expenses** of collection or enforcement, (2) satisfaction of the debt owed to the **secured party**, (3) satisfaction of the debts owed to **subordinate secured parties**, and (4) payment of any surplus to the debtor. If the disposition is commercially reasonable but the **proceeds are insufficient**, the obligor is liable for any deficiency.

Acceptance of the collateral (also known as strict foreclosure) may be an alternative to disposition. The secured party keeps the collateral in satisfaction of the debt but must send an **authenticated notice** to other secured parties, lienholders, or claimants. Also, the debtor must **consent** to the acceptance. Acceptance of collateral is not allowed, and the collateral must be disposed of, if the **debtor or any party to whom notice is required to be sent** objects. The objection must be authenticated and, in most cases, received by the secured party within 20 days of sending the notice. Acceptance of collateral in **partial satisfaction** of the obligation is not allowed if the collateral is **consumer goods**. Moreover, disposition is required if the amount paid is at least (1) 60% of the cash price in the case of a **PMSI in consumer goods** or (2) 60% of the principal amount of the secured obligation in the case of a **non-PMSI in consumer goods**. The secured party must dispose of collateral within 90 days of taking possession of it. But the debtor and all secondary obligors may agree to a longer period in an authenticated agreement.

The **debtor's remedies** include **redemption** of his/her interest in the collateral at any time before (1) the debt is satisfied by acceptance of the collateral, (2) the collateral has been collected, (3) the collateral is disposed of, or (4) a contract for the disposition of the collateral is entered into. Failure by the secured party to comply with Article 9 provides the debtor with a **right to damages** for the resulting losses. In the case of **consumer goods**, the debtor may recover an amount not less than the greater of (1) the credit service charge plus 10% of the principal of the debt, or (2) the time-price differential plus 10% of the cash price.

EXAMPLE: The cash price of a chain saw is $800. If the chain saw is financed for 36 months, the payments total $1,200. The time-price differential is $400 ($1,200 – $800). Under (2), the debtor recovers not less than $400 plus 10% of $800, a total of $480. Under (1), the recovery is not less than $80 plus any credit service charges.

If a **deficiency or surplus** is put in issue in a legal proceeding and the secured party's compliance also is put in issue, the liability of a debtor or secondary obligor may be limited or eliminated. For example, this result may follow because the proceeds of a disposition were significantly less than the proceeds of a complying disposition.

QUESTIONS

18.1 Introduction and Definitions

1. Which of the following is included within the scope of the Secured Transactions Article of the UCC?

A. The outright sale of accounts receivable.

B. A landlord's lien.

C. The assignment of a claim for wages.

D. The sale of chattel paper as a part of the sale of a business out of which it arose.

Answer (A) is correct. *(CPA, adapted)*

REQUIRED: The transaction included within the scope of Article 9 of the UCC.

DISCUSSION: Article 9 of the UCC explicitly applies not only to transactions intended to create security interests in personal property or fixtures but also to agricultural liens; consignments; certain security interests arising under Articles 2, 2A, 4, and 5; and sales of accounts, payment intangibles, promissory notes, or chattel paper. However, Article 9 does not apply to a sale of accounts as part of the sale of a business out of which they arose, to an assignment of accounts for collection only, or to a transfer of one account to an assignee in satisfaction of a pre-existing debt.

Answer (B) is incorrect. A landlord's lien, other than an agricultural lien, is a transaction explicitly excluded from Article 9. Answer (C) is incorrect. The assignment of a claim for wages, salary, or other compensation of an employee is a transaction explicitly excluded from Article 9. Answer (D) is incorrect. The sale of accounts, chattel paper, payment intangibles, or promissory notes as part of the sale of a business out of which they arose is a transaction explicitly excluded from Article 9.

2. Which is the true classification of goods under UCC 9-102?

A. Consumer goods, instruments, and inventory.

B. Accounts, equipment, inventory, unextracted minerals.

C. Consumer goods, equipment, farm products, inventory.

D. Accounts, consumer goods, equipment, inventory.

Answer (C) is correct. *(Publisher, adapted)*

REQUIRED: The true classification of goods under UCC 9-102.

DISCUSSION: UCC 9-102 classifies goods into four categories. Consumer goods are those used or bought for use primarily for personal, family, or household purposes. Equipment means goods other than inventory, farm products, and consumer goods. Farm products are crops, livestock, supplies used or produced in farming operations, or products of crops or livestock in their unmanufactured states. They must be in the hands of one engaged in farming operations. If goods are farm products, they are not equipment or inventory. Inventory consists of goods (1) leased by a person as lessor; (2) held for sale or lease; (3) furnished under contracts of service; or (4) consisting of raw materials, work-in-process, or materials used or consumed in a business.

3. The Wu Wei Company manufactures abacuses. The Yin and Yang is the most complex model. The agreements with Wu Wei's customers take the form of leases. Wu Wei expressly retains title but grants the customer an option to purchase at the end of the lease period for an additional sum equal to 1% of the aggregate lease payments. Does Article 9 of the UCC on secured transactions govern the lease?

A. Yes. The inclusion of the option to purchase in itself makes the lease one intended for security.

B. Yes. The lease is one intended for security because the lessee has the option to become the owner of the property for a nominal consideration.

C. No. The express retention of title indicates that the transaction is a true lease and not a sale with retention of a security interest.

D. No. For the UCC to apply, Wu Wei would have to have filed a financing statement.

Answer (B) is correct. *(Publisher, adapted)*

REQUIRED: The applicability of Article 9 of the UCC to the lease.

DISCUSSION: Article 9 covers any transaction that establishes by contract a security interest in personal property or fixtures (UCC 9-109). The form of the transaction or the name by which the parties have called it is irrelevant if the parties have intended formation of a security interest. Under UCC 1-201, whether a lease is intended as security is to be determined by the facts of each case. A transaction gives rise to a security interest if the lessee has an option to buy the property for nominal consideration. Because the agreement states that, upon compliance with its terms, the lessee will become the owner of the property for nominal consideration, the lease is deemed to be one intended for security. The "lease" is therefore governed by Article 9.

Answer (A) is incorrect. UCC 1-201 states that the inclusion of an option to purchase does not by itself make the lease one intended for security. Answer (C) is incorrect. The general policy of the UCC is to ignore location of title in determining the rights and duties of the parties. Answer (D) is incorrect. Although Article 9 provides for financing statements, filing a financing statement is not necessary for the UCC to apply.

4. Case Corporation manufactures electric drills and sells them to retail hardware stores. Under the Uniform Commercial Code, it is likely that

A. The drills are inventory in Case's hands.

B. The drills are equipment in Case's hands.

C. The raw materials on hand to be used in the manufacturing of the drills are not inventory in Case's hands.

D. The drills are considered equipment in the hands of the hardware stores who purchased them.

Answer (A) is correct. *(CPA, adapted)*

REQUIRED: The true statement regarding the classification of property.

DISCUSSION: The classification of goods depends on who holds the property and the use to which it is put. Inventory consists of goods, other than farm products, that are held for sale or lease or to be provided under a contract for service; that are leased or provided under a contract for service; or that consist of materials used or consumed by a business, work-in-process, or raw materials. Electric drills are inventory in the hands of their manufacturer (or a retailer) because they are held for sale. The drills are consumer goods, however, in the hands of someone using them primarily for personal, family, or household purposes. They are equipment if they do not qualify as inventory, farm products, or consumer goods.

Answer (B) is incorrect. The drills are inventory in Case's hands. The UCC defines goods as equipment if they do not qualify as inventory, farm products, or consumer goods. Answer (C) is incorrect. Inventory includes raw materials, materials used or consumed by a business, and work-in-process. Answer (D) is incorrect. Drills are inventory in the hands of the hardware stores as long as they are held for sale to others.

18.2 Conveying a Security Interest

5. Lombard, Inc., manufactures exclusive designer apparel. It sells through franchised clothing stores on consignment, retaining a security interest in the goods. Gifford is one of Lombard's franchisees pursuant to a detailed contract signed by both Lombard and Gifford. For the security interest to be valid against Gifford with respect to the designer apparel in Gifford's possession, Lombard

A. Must retain title to the goods.

B. Does not have to do anything further.

C. Must file a financing statement.

D. Must perfect its security interest against Gifford's creditors.

Answer (B) is correct. *(CPA, adapted)*

REQUIRED: The action the secured party must take for the security interest to be effective against the debtor.

DISCUSSION: Attachment of a security interest is the process by which a security interest becomes enforceable against a debtor by a secured party. Attachment of a security interest in inventory collateral results as soon as the following three events occur (barring an explicit agreement otherwise): (1) The collateral is in the possession of the secured party pursuant to the debtor's security agreement or the debtor has authenticated a security agreement describing the collateral, (2) value has been given, and (3) the debtor has rights (or the ability to transfer rights) in the collateral. All these conditions have been satisfied. The detailed contract was a "security agreement" because it created or provided for a security interest. Value has been given because Lombard has effectively sold the goods on credit to Gifford. The debtor has rights in the goods because it has the power to sell the goods at a profit. Consequently, the security interest has attached, and Lombard need not do anything further to protect itself against Gifford.

Answer (A) is incorrect. As between the consignor and the consignee, the location of title to the goods is immaterial. Answer (C) is incorrect. Filing is a means of perfecting a security interest so as to gain priority over third parties. Answer (D) is incorrect. Attachment is sufficient against the debtor.

6. On January 1, Shemwell Co. signed a security agreement giving Jones a security interest in a crane Shemwell was planning to buy for its business. In exchange for the security agreement, Jones signed a contract to lend Shemwell $10,000 on request. On January 9, Shemwell purchased the crane. On January 15, Jones delivered $10,000 to Shemwell. On January 20, Jones filed the security agreement with the appropriate public officials. Under the UCC, when did Jones's security interest in the crane attach?

A. On January 1, when the security agreement was signed.

B. On January 9, when Shemwell purchased the crane for its business.

C. On January 15, when Jones delivered $10,000 to Shemwell.

D. On January 20, when Jones filed the security agreement.

Answer (B) is correct. *(J. Pittman)*

REQUIRED: The time of attachment of a security interest.

DISCUSSION: Attachment of a security interest in collateral occurs when the security interest is enforceable against the debtor. It is enforceable against the debtor and third parties when all of the following events have occurred unless the time is postponed by an explicit agreement: (1) value has been given; (2) the debtor has rights (or the ability to transfer rights) in the collateral; and (3) the collateral (other than a certificated security) is in the possession of the secured party pursuant to the debtor's security agreement, the debtor has authenticated a security agreement containing a description of the collateral, the secured party has control of investment property (or of deposit accounts, letter-of-credit rights, or electronic chattel paper) under the debtor's security agreement, or a registered certificated security has been delivered pursuant to the debtor's security agreement. The secured party gave value on January 1 when it entered into a contractual agreement to lend money to the debtor, the debtor had rights in the collateral on January 9, and the debtor authenticated a security agreement on January 1. Hence, the attachment requirements were met on January 9.

Answer (A) is incorrect. Shemwell did not have rights in the crane on January 1. Answer (C) is incorrect. Jones had given value before the loan proceeds were delivered. Value includes binding commitments to extend credit (UCC 1-201). Thus, Jones gave value on January 1. Answer (D) is incorrect. Filing is not necessary for attachment of a security interest.

7. Maxim Corporation, a wholesaler, was indebted to the Wilson Manufacturing Corporation in the amount of $50,000 arising out of the sale of goods delivered to Maxim on credit. Maxim authenticated a security agreement creating a security interest in certain collateral of Maxim. The collateral was described in the security agreement as "the inventory of Maxim Corporation, presently existing and thereafter acquired." In general, this description of the collateral

A. Applies only to inventory sold by Wilson to Maxim.

B. Is sufficient to cover all inventory.

C. Is insufficient because it attempts to cover after-acquired inventory.

D. Must be more specific for the security interest to be perfected against subsequent creditors.

Answer (B) is correct. *(CPA, adapted)*

REQUIRED: The true statement concerning the description of the collateral.

DISCUSSION: Unless the secured party takes possession of the inventory collateral, the security interest will not attach unless the debtor has authenticated a security agreement that adequately describes the collateral. Such a description is sufficient if it reasonably identifies what is described even though the language is not specific. For example, collateral may be reasonably identified by a type of collateral (other than a commercial tort claim or, in a consumer transaction, consumer goods, a security entitlement, a securities account, or a commodity account) defined in the UCC, such as inventory.

Answer (A) is incorrect. A security agreement may provide for a security interest in most forms of after-acquired collateral. Thus, the security interest attaches to inventory sold to the debtor by other parties as well as by the secured party. It covers all inventory owned by Maxim at any time while the security agreement is in effect, i.e., while Maxim owes Wilson money. Answer (C) is incorrect. A security interest (and the security agreement) may cover most forms of after-acquired property. Answer (D) is incorrect. A description is sufficient if it reasonably identifies what is described. The description in the security agreement signed by Maxim is adequate to allow interested parties to identify the collateral, i.e., all inventory.

8. Under the UCC Secured Transactions Article, which of the following after-acquired property may be covered by a debtor's security agreement with a secured lender?

	Inventory	Equipment
A.	Yes	Yes
B.	Yes	No
C.	No	Yes
D.	No	No

Answer (A) is correct. *(CPA, adapted)*

REQUIRED: The scope of an after-acquired property clause.

DISCUSSION: A security agreement may provide for a security interest in after-acquired property. The security interest does not attach to consumer goods, other than an accession (goods physically combined with other goods so that the character of the original goods is not lost) given as additional security, unless the debtor acquires rights in them within 10 days after the secured party gives value. The security interest in after-acquired property also does not attach to a commercial tort claim. An after-acquired property clause can apply to both inventory and equipment.

9. An add-on clause for a new installment purchase of goods is generally

A. Unethical because prior goods purchased from a vendor are subject to repossession.

B. Unethical because add-on clauses have been outlawed in many states.

C. Valid because it gives vendors in low-income areas additional security and thereby increases the availability of credit.

D. Valid because it allows finance companies to increase finance costs to poor credit risks.

Answer (C) is correct. *(Publisher, adapted)*

REQUIRED: The ethical issue that arises when an add-on clause is used in a sale of goods.

DISCUSSION: An add-on clause is an agreement that failure to make payment on the goods purchased permits not only the items purchased under the current contract to be repossessed, but also any prior items purchased from the same seller. Add-on clauses give vendors additional security. If add-on clauses are invalidated, vendors will be less likely to sell consumer goods on credit to low-income families. However, courts have sometimes invalidated such clauses because they offend notions of public policy.

Answer (A) is incorrect. An add-on clause is not per se unethical. One advantage of the arrangement for consumers is to give low-income families an opportunity to purchase goods on credit. Answer (B) is incorrect. States do not absolutely prohibit add-on clauses. Answer (D) is incorrect. Add-on clauses are used to provide vendors additional security, not to charge usurious rates.

difference in coverage - must pay.

10. When collateral covered under the Secured Transactions Article of the UCC is in the secured party's possession,

A. The risk of accidental loss is on the debtor to the extent of any deficiency in any effective insurance coverage.

B. The secured party will lose his/her security interest if (s)he commingles fungible collateral.

C. Reasonable expenses incurred to preserve the collateral are chargeable to the secured party.

D. The secured party may not operate the collateral.

Answer (A) is correct. *(CPA, adapted)*

REQUIRED: The parties' rights and duties when the secured party holds the collateral.

DISCUSSION: In most cases, a secured party in possession of the collateral must use reasonable care in its custody and preservation. However, Article 9 states that "the risk of accidental loss or damage is on the debtor to the extent of a deficiency in any effective insurance coverage."

Answer (B) is incorrect. The secured party must keep the collateral identifiable, but fungible collateral may be commingled. Answer (C) is incorrect. Reasonable expenses, including insurance and taxes, are chargeable to the debtor and are secured by the collateral. Answer (D) is incorrect. The secured party may use or operate the collateral (1) to preserve it or its value; (2) as permitted by a court; or, (3) except in the case of consumer goods, pursuant to an agreement with the debtor.

11. Retailer Corp. was in need of financing. To secure a loan, it made an oral assignment of its accounts receivable to J. Roe, a local investor, under which Roe lent Retailer, on a continuing basis, 90% of the face value of the assigned accounts receivable. Retailer collected from the account debtors and remitted to Roe at intervals. Before the debt was paid, Retailer filed a petition in bankruptcy. Which of the following is true?

A. As between the account debtors and Roe, the assignment is not an enforceable security interest.

B. Roe is a secured creditor to the extent of the unpaid debt.

C. Other unpaid creditors of Retailer Corp. who knew of the assignment are bound by its terms.

D. An assignment of accounts, to be valid, requires the debtors owing the accounts to be notified.

Answer (A) is correct. *(CPA, adapted)*

REQUIRED: The true statement concerning an oral assignment of accounts receivable.

DISCUSSION: Retailer's assignment does not constitute an enforceable security interest against either Retailer or third parties, such as the account debtors. When the collateral consists of accounts, a security interest does not become enforceable against the debtor and third parties (attach) until the debtor has authenticated a security agreement describing the collateral. Furthermore, the debtor must have received value, and the debtor must have rights (or the ability to transfer rights) in the collateral. Attachment of a security interest in accounts requires that the debtor authenticate a security agreement because the secured party cannot take possession, control, or delivery of accounts. However, an assignment that does not transfer a significant part of the assignor's receivables creates a security interest that is automatically perfected.

Answer (B) is incorrect. The security interest was not enforceable against the debtor. Retailer did not authenticate a security agreement describing the collateral. Answer (C) is incorrect. A security interest is not enforceable against third parties with respect to the collateral unless the requirements of attachment are met. Answer (D) is incorrect. An assignment of accounts receivable is valid even though the account debtors are not notified. However, their debts will be discharged if they pay the original creditor (the assignor) prior to receipt of a notice, authenticated by the assignor or assignee (the secured party), that payment is to be made to the assignee.

12. Shemwell Co. purchased a printing press from Jones Equipment, Inc. Shemwell signed a promissory note for the purchase price and signed a security agreement stating, "The buyer waives as against any assignee of the security interest any claim or defense that the buyer may have against the seller." Jones assigned the promissory note and security agreement to 1st Bank. The waiver-of-defenses clause is not enforceable against Shemwell if

A. Jones had issued a written warranty on the press.

B. 1st Bank did not give value for the assignment from Jones.

C. Jones knew the printing press could malfunction.

D. After the assignment, 1st Bank learned the printing press had malfunctioned.

Answer (B) is correct. *(J. Pittman)*

REQUIRED: The true statement about enforceability of a waiver-of-defenses clause.

DISCUSSION: A waiver-of-defenses clause contained in a security agreement is not always binding. For personal defenses in business transactions, the debtor is bound by the waiver only when the assignee has taken the assignment for value, in good faith, and without notice of a claim or defense. However, the clause will not be effective with respect to real defenses, i.e., those assertable against a holder in due course of a negotiable instrument.

Answer (A) is incorrect. A written warranty has no bearing on the enforceability of the waiver. Answer (C) is incorrect. Whether Jones knew the printing press could malfunction has no bearing on the enforceability of the waiver. Answer (D) is incorrect. Knowledge of possible defenses is immaterial if it is learned after the assignee has given value in good faith.

18.3 Perfection

13. Under UCC Article 9, what is the result of perfecting a security interest?

A. The secured party can enforce its security interest against the debtor.

B. The secured party has permanent priority in the collateral even if the collateral is removed to another state.

C. The debtor is protected against all other parties who subsequently acquire an interest in the collateral.

D. The secured party has priority in the collateral over most creditors who subsequently acquire a security interest in the same collateral.

Answer (D) is correct. *(CPA, adapted)*

REQUIRED: The result of perfecting a security interest by filing a financing statement.

DISCUSSION: Perfection of a security interest maximizes a secured party's rights with respect to the collateral. Although perfection will not give the secured party priority over all subsequent secured parties, it will give priority over all unperfected interests and over most subsequent secured interests.

Answer (A) is incorrect. Perfection is not required to enforce the secured party's rights against the debtor. Answer (B) is incorrect. Perfection will generally lapse within an appropriate period after the collateral is removed to another state. Answer (C) is incorrect. Perfection gives the secured party priority over all unperfected creditors and some, but not all, subsequent secured parties.

14. A secured creditor wants to file a financing statement to perfect its security interest. Under the UCC Secured Transactions Article, which of the following must be included in the financing statement?

A. An indication of the collateral.

B. An after-acquired property provision.

C. The creditor's signature.

D. The collateral's location.

Answer (A) is correct. *(CPA, adapted)*

REQUIRED: The item that must be included in the financing statement to perfect a security interest.

DISCUSSION: To be effective, the financing statement must (1) include the name of the debtor, (2) include the name of the secured party or representative, and (3) indicate the collateral covered. A financing statement that covers as-extracted collateral or timber to be cut or that covers goods that are to be fixtures must include additional information, for example, a description of the real property to which the collateral relates. If the collateral is growing crops, uncut timber, or unextracted minerals, the financing statement must also describe the pertinent real estate.

Answer (B) is incorrect. The inclusion of an after-acquired property provision is not required for the financing statement to be effective. Answer (C) is incorrect. The inclusion of the creditor's signature is not required for the financing statement to be effective. Answer (D) is incorrect. The inclusion of the collateral's location is not required for the financing statement to be effective.

15. On October 1, Winslow Corporation obtained a loan commitment of $250,000 from Liberty National Bank. Liberty filed a financing statement on October 2. On October 5, the $250,000 loan was consummated, and Winslow signed a security agreement granting the bank a security interest in inventory, accounts receivable, and proceeds from the sale of the inventory and collection of the accounts receivable. Liberty's security interest was perfected

A. On October 1.

B. On October 2.

C. On October 5.

D. By attachment.

Answer (C) is correct. *(CPA, adapted)*

REQUIRED: The time a security interest attached and was perfected.

DISCUSSION: A security interest is perfected when it has attached and when all of the necessary steps required for perfection have been taken. The security interest did not attach until October 5 when the security agreement was authenticated by the debtor. Because a financing statement had already been filed, October 5 was also the date when perfection occurred. NOTE: Priority among perfected security interests is determined by date of filing or perfection, whichever comes first. Thus, Liberty Bank has priority over a conflicting perfected security interest from the date of filing on October 2.

Answer (A) is incorrect. A security interest cannot be perfected prior to attachment. Answer (B) is incorrect. A security interest cannot be perfected prior to attachment. Answer (D) is incorrect. A security interest in inventory, accounts, and their proceeds must be perfected by filing rather than attachment alone.

16. The UCC provides for the filing of termination statements. Which of the following is true?

A. The requirements for filing termination statements are the same for all forms of property of the debtor.

B. In the case of inventory, the secured party must file a termination statement within one month after termination of any obligation.

C. When no further obligation exists, the secured party must cause the secured party of record upon authenticated demand to provide a termination statement within 20 days. The nature of the property determines whether it must be filed.

D. A termination statement need not be filed with respect to consumer goods.

Answer (C) is correct. *(Publisher, adapted)*

REQUIRED: The true statement concerning termination statements.

DISCUSSION: If the collateral consists of consumer goods, there is no obligation secured by the collateral, and there is no commitment to give value, the secured party must cause the secured party of record to file a termination statement within 1 month after there is no obligation or commitment. The filing must be within 20 days after receipt of an authenticated demand from the debtor, if earlier. If the property is not consumer goods, a termination statement must be filed or sent to the debtor within 20 days after the debtor makes an authenticated demand.

Answer (A) is incorrect. The UCC makes a distinction between consumer goods and other collateral as discussed above. Answer (B) is incorrect. The filing of a termination statement is required only with respect to consumer goods. Answer (D) is incorrect. The filing of a termination statement is required only with respect to consumer goods.

17. Wurke, Inc., manufactures and sells household appliances on credit directly to wholesalers, retailers, and consumers. Wurke can perfect its security interest in the appliances without having to file a financing statement or take possession of the appliances if the sale is made by Wurke to

A. Retailers.

B. Wholesalers that then sell to distributors for resale.

C. Consumers.

D. Wholesalers that then sell to buyers in the ordinary course of business.

Answer (C) is correct. *(CPA, adapted)*

REQUIRED: The true statement about perfection of security interest upon attachment.

DISCUSSION: A purchase money security interest (PMSI) is created when the security interest secures payment of the purchase price of the collateral. The appliances are consumer goods when they are purchased by consumers (for personal, family, or household purposes). A PMSI in consumer goods, other than those subject to certain statutes or treaties (e.g., a certificate-of-title statute), is perfected upon attachment.

Answer (A) is incorrect. Goods held by retailers are inventory. Inventory is not an exception to the filing requirement, and Wurke must file a financing statement to perfect a security interest in collateral held by retailers. Answer (B) is incorrect. Goods held by wholesalers are inventory. Inventory is not an exception to the filing requirement, and Wurke must file a financing statement to perfect a security interest in collateral held by wholesalers. Answer (D) is incorrect. Wurke must file regardless of the wholesalers' disposition of the inventory.

18. Which of the following transactions illustrates a secured party's perfection of its security interest by taking possession of the collateral?

A. A bank receives a mortgage on real property.

B. A wholesaler borrows to purchase inventory.

C. A consumer borrows to buy a car.

D. A pawnbroker lends money.

Answer (D) is correct. *(CPA, adapted)*

REQUIRED: The transaction in which a secured party perfects its security interest by possession.

DISCUSSION: A security interest in goods, instruments, money, negotiable documents, or tangible chattel paper (but not a security interest in electronic chattel paper, which is perfected by control) may be perfected by the secured party's taking possession of the collateral. Thus, a pawnbroker perfects a security interest when (s)he receives goods as collateral for a loan.

Answer (A) is incorrect. A bank's receiving a mortgage on real property is a transaction in which perfection is usually by filing. Possession in this case would defeat the purpose of the loan. Answer (B) is incorrect. A wholesaler's borrowing to purchase inventory is a transaction in which perfection is usually by filing. Possession in this case would defeat the purpose of the loan. Answer (C) is incorrect. A consumer borrowing to buy a car is a transaction in which perfection is usually by filing. Possession in this case would defeat the purpose of the loan.

19. A filing requirement for perfection applies to which of the following transactions under Article 9 (Secured Transactions) of the Uniform Commercial Code?

A. The factoring of a significant amount of the assignor's accounts receivable.

B. A collateralized bank loan, with certificated securities serving as the collateral.

C. The transfer of an interest in a life insurance policy to secure a loan.

D. The retention of title by a seller of land to secure payment under the terms of a land contract.

Answer (A) is correct. *(CPA, adapted)*

REQUIRED: The transaction with a filing requirement for perfection under Article 9.

DISCUSSION: The factoring of accounts receivable involves their outright sale and is governed by Article 9. In standard commercial practice, the distinction between transactions in accounts that are secured transactions and those that are sales is often obscure, so the UCC treats both as secured transactions. Perfection of a security interest in accounts ordinarily may only be achieved by filing because nothing exists to possess. An outright purchaser of accounts therefore must file a financing statement to perfect an ownership interest. Nevertheless, when an insignificant amount of the assignor's accounts is transferred, perfection is by attachment only, and a financing statement need not be filed.

Answer (B) is incorrect. No filing is required with respect to certificated securities (a form of investment property) when, for example, perfection is (1) by control achieved through delivery to the secured party, (2) automatic for 20 days after attachment to the extent new value is given under an authenticated security agreement, (3) temporary for 20 days when the secured party relinquishes possession for certain purposes, or (4) automatic as a result of a seller's delivery to another person also in the business of dealing with such assets. Answer (C) is incorrect. The transfer of an interest in an insurance policy to secure a loan is a transaction explicitly excluded from the coverage of Article 9. An exception is the assignment to a health-care provider of a health-care-insurance receivable and any subsequent assignment of the right to payment. Answer (D) is incorrect. The creation or transfer of an interest in or lien on real property is a transaction explicitly excluded from the coverage of Article 9.

20. The Town Bank makes collateralized loans to its customers at 1% above prime on securities owned by the customer, subject to existing margin requirements. In doing so, which of the following is true?

A. Notification of the issuer is necessary to perfect a security interest.

B. Filing is not a permissible method of perfecting a security interest in the securities.

C. Any dividend or interest distributions during the term of the loan belong to the bank.

D. Town Bank can obtain a perfected security interest in the securities by control.

Answer (D) is correct. *(CPA, adapted)*

REQUIRED: The true statement about loans using securities as collateral.

DISCUSSION: Investment property includes securities, whether certificated or not. A security interest in investment property may be perfected by control or by filing. Control of a certificated security in bearer form arises from delivery to the secured party. If the security is in registered form, control requires delivery and endorsement or delivery and registration. Control of an uncertificated security requires delivery or the issuer's agreement to comply with instructions without the further consent of the debtor-registered owner. Control of a security entitlement requires that the secured party become the holder or that the securities intermediary agree to comply with entitlement orders originated by the secured party without further consent by the debtor-entitlement holder. A secured party has control over a securities account if the secured party controls all security entitlements in the account.

Answer (A) is incorrect. Notification of the issuer (e.g., a corporation) is not necessary for the perfection of a security interest in securities. Answer (B) is incorrect. Filing is a permissible method of perfecting a security interest in investment property. Answer (C) is incorrect. A secured party having control of investment property must apply any money or funds received from the collateral to reduce the obligation, unless remitted to the debtor.

21. Tawney Manufacturing approached Worldwide Lenders for a loan of $50,000 to purchase vital components it used in its manufacturing process. Worldwide decided to grant the loan but only if Tawney would agree to a field warehousing arrangement. Pursuant to their understanding, Worldwide paid for the purchase of the components, took a negotiable bill of lading for them, and surrendered the bill of lading in exchange for negotiable warehouse receipts issued by the bonded warehouse company that had established a field warehouse in Tawney's storage facility. Worldwide did not file a financing statement. Under the circumstances, Worldwide

A. Has a security interest in the goods that has attached and is perfected.

B. Does not have a security interest that has attached because Tawney has not signed a security agreement.

C. Must file an executed financing statement in order to perfect its security interest.

D. Must not relinquish possession of any of the components to Tawney for whatever purpose, unless it is paid in cash for those released.

Answer (A) is correct. *(CPA, adapted)*

REQUIRED: The position of a creditor secured by goods held in a field warehouse.

DISCUSSION: The requirements of attachment have been satisfied. Value was given, the debtor had rights in the collateral, and the secured party had possession of the collateral. Whether the debtor authenticated a security agreement describing the collateral is irrelevant because the collateral is in the possession of the secured party pursuant to the debtor's security agreement. The warehouse company issued negotiable documents of title representing the goods. These negotiable documents are in the possession of the secured party. Also, value was given when Worldwide paid for the parts, and the debtor has rights in the collateral (use of the components in manufacturing). Perfection of a security interest in the goods has also occurred. Possession of the negotiable documents of title is a means of perfecting a security interest in them. Furthermore, perfecting a security interest in the negotiable documents is a means of perfecting a security interest in the goods they represent while the goods are held by the issuer of the documents.

Answer (B) is incorrect. Negotiable documents of title presenting the goods are in the possession of the secured party pursuant to the debtor's security agreement. Possession substitutes for the requirement of an authenticated security agreement. Answer (C) is incorrect. The security interest is perfected by possession of negotiable documents of title representing the goods. Answer (D) is incorrect. Worldwide's security interest in the goods will be perfected for a period of 20 days without filing after making them available to the debtor for processing or otherwise dealing with them in a way preliminary to their ultimate sale or exchange.

22. Mansfield Financial lends money on the strength of negotiable warehouse receipts. Its policy is always to obtain a perfected security interest in the receipts against the creditors of the borrowers and to maintain it until the loan has been satisfied. Insofar as this policy is concerned, which of the following is true?

A. Mansfield may transfer the warehouse receipts to another lending institution without the debtor's consent.

B. Relinquishment of the receipts is not permitted under any circumstances without the loss of the perfected security interest in them.

C. Mansfield has a perfected security interest in goods represented by the receipts.

D. If the receipts are somehow wrongfully duly negotiated to a holder, Mansfield's perfected security interest will not be prejudiced.

Answer (C) is correct. *(CPA, adapted)*

REQUIRED: The true statement about perfection of a security interest in negotiable warehouse receipts.

DISCUSSION: A warehouse receipt is a form of document of title issued by a person engaged in the business of storing goods. A warehouse receipt is negotiable if by its terms the goods that it represents are to be delivered to the bearer or to the order of a named person. During the period that goods represented by a document of title are in the possession of the issuer (bailee), a security interest in the goods may be perfected by perfecting a security interest in the document. Possession of the negotiable document is a means of perfecting a security interest in it.

Answer (A) is incorrect. A secured party may use or operate the collateral to preserve it, as permitted by a court, or (except for consumer goods) as agreed by the debtor. Repledging the collateral requires the debtor's consent. Answer (B) is incorrect. A security interest perfected by possession of negotiable documents will remain perfected for a 20-day period without filing when a secured party makes a temporary surrender of the documents to the debtor for purposes of dealing with them prior to ultimate sale or exchange. But a bona fide purchaser will take priority. Answer (D) is incorrect. The due negotiation to a holder (who takes in good faith, bar value, and without notice of a defense or claim) passes title to the document and the goods represented by it under Article 7.

23. Motor Sales, Inc., sells motor vehicles at retail. It borrowed money from Finance Company and gave a properly executed security agreement in its present and future inventory and in the proceeds therefrom to secure the loan. The security interest was duly perfected under the laws of the state where Motor does business and maintains its entire inventory. Thereafter, Motor sold a new pickup truck from its inventory to a consumer and received a certified check in payment of the full price. Which of the following is true?

A. Finance must file an amendment to the financing statement every time Motor receives a substantial number of additional vehicles from the manufacturer if Finance is to obtain a valid security interest in subsequently delivered inventory.

B. Finance's security interest in the certified check Motor received is perfected against Motor's other creditors.

C. Unless Finance specifically included proceeds in the financing statement it filed, it has no rights to them.

D. The term "proceeds" does not include used cars received by Motor because they will be resold.

Answer (B) is correct. *(CPA, adapted)*

REQUIRED: The true statement about the sale of inventory subject to a perfected security interest.

DISCUSSION: The certified check received by the debtor constitutes identifiable cash proceeds from the sale of the inventory. In general, a security interest attaches to identifiable proceeds of collateral. Moreover, this security interest is perfected if the security interest in the original collateral was also perfected. A perfected security interest in proceeds becomes unperfected on the 21st day after attachment unless (1) the proceeds are identifiable cash proceeds; (2) some other method is used to perfect the security interest at the time of attachment or within 20 days thereafter; or (3) a filed financing statement covers the original collateral, the proceeds are collateral in which a security interest could be perfected by filing in the same office as the original collateral, and the proceeds are not obtained using the cash proceeds. Because a certified check constitutes identifiable cash proceeds, Finance has a perfected security interest in it that will not lapse on the 21st day after attachment.

Answer (A) is incorrect. The after-acquired property (future inventory) clause in the perfected security agreement renders it unnecessary for Finance to file an amendment every time Motor receives additional vehicles from the manufacturer. Answer (C) is incorrect. A security interest continues in proceeds unless the security agreement provides otherwise, and the interest is perfected for a minimum of 20 days. Answer (D) is incorrect. The term "proceeds" includes whatever is received upon the sale, lease, license, exchange, collection, or other disposition of collateral. It includes insurance payments (except those made to nonparties to the security agreement), distributions with respect to investment property, cash proceeds (money, checks, deposit accounts, and the like), etc.

24. Mozart Manufacturers of Florida manufactured and sold three pianos to Virtuoso Piano School of Vandelay, Florida in a credit transaction. Mozart properly filed a 5-year financing statement with regard to the pianos in Florida on February 2, the day after the sale. Finding its business a trifle slow in Vandelay, Virtuoso packed up its pianos and moved to Atlanta, Georgia on May 2 of the same year. On September 1, Mozart properly filed a financing statement in Georgia. What is the status of Mozart's security interest?

A. Mozart's security interest was continuously perfected.

B. Mozart's security interest was unperfected during the interval of May 2 through September 1.

C. Mozart's filing on September 1 was retroactive to May 2.

D. Mozart's Georgia filing was unnecessary in order to continue perfection.

Answer (A) is correct. *(Publisher, adapted)*

REQUIRED: The status of the perfection of a security interest in goods moved from one state to another.

DISCUSSION: The perfection of the security interest in goods (the pianos) based on the law of the debtor's location (Florida) continues for the unexpired period in the original state, 4 months after the debtor moves to a new state, or 1 year after transfer to a person in another state who as a result has the status of a debtor, whichever period first expires. Here, the security interest was perfected from February 2 to May 2, the day of removal. It would have continued perfected from May 2 until September 2 without any action by Mozart. By taking the appropriate steps to perfect the security interest in the new state, Mozart ensured itself of a continuously perfected security interest.

Answer (B) is incorrect. Perfection continued for the 4-month period after the debtor moved to a new state. Answer (C) is incorrect. No provision in Article 9 creates retroactive perfection. Answer (D) is incorrect. If Mozart had failed to file in Georgia before the expiration of the 4-month period, its security interest would have been unperfected as of the end of that period.

18.4 Priorities

25. Cross has an unperfected security interest in the inventory of Safe, Inc. The unperfected security interest

A. Is superior to the interest of subsequent lenders who obtain a perfected security interest in the property.

B. Is subordinate to lien creditors of Safe who become such prior to any subsequent perfection by Cross.

C. Causes Cross to lose important rights against Safe as an entity.

D. May only be perfected by filing a financing statement.

Answer (B) is correct. *(CPA, adapted)*

REQUIRED: The true statement about the rights of an unperfected security interest in inventory.

DISCUSSION: Certain interests have priority over unperfected security interests. Included are the rights of a lien creditor, that is, a creditor who has acquired a lien on the property involved by judicial process, an assignee for the benefit of creditors, a receiver in equity, or a trustee in bankruptcy. The lien creditor takes the property subject to any security interest perfected before the lien attached, but its rights are superior to any security interest perfected after the lien attached.

Answer (A) is incorrect. A subsequent creditor who perfects its security interest will have priority over an unperfected security interest. Answer (C) is incorrect. Perfection has no effect on the relationship between debtor and creditor. Answer (D) is incorrect. Inventory is one type of collateral in which a security interest can be perfected by possession.

26. Larkin is a wholesaler of computers in the state of Whiteacre. Larkin sold 40 computers to Elk Appliance, which also does business in the state of Whiteacre, for $80,000. Elk paid $20,000 down and signed a promissory note for the balance. Elk also executed a security agreement giving Larkin a security interest in Elk's inventory, including the computers. Larkin perfected its security interest by properly filing a financing statement in the state of Whiteacre. Six months later, Elk moved its business to the state of Blackacre, taking the computers. On arriving in Blackacre, Elk secured a loan from Quarry Bank and signed a security agreement, putting up all inventory (including the computers) as collateral. Quarry perfected its security interest by properly filing a financing statement in the state of Blackacre. Two months after arriving in Blackacre, Elk went into default on both debts. Which of the following statements is true?

A. Quarry's security interest is superior because Larkin's time to file a financing statement in Blackacre had expired prior to Quarry's filing.

B. Quarry's security interest is superior because Quarry had no actual notice of Larkin's security interest.

C. Larkin's security interest is superior even though at the time of Elk's default Larkin had not perfected its security interest in the state of Blackacre.

D. Larkin's security interest is superior provided it repossesses the computers before Quarry does.

Answer (C) is correct. *(CPA, adapted)*

REQUIRED: The true statement concerning priority of the security agreements.

DISCUSSION: Larkin perfected its security interest in the state where the debtor and the collateral were located. The perfection of the security interest continues until the earlier of the time perfection would lapse in the original state, 4 months after a change of the debtor's location to another state, or 1 year after a transfer of the collateral to a new debtor located in another state. Here, the collateral was perfected until the day of removal. It would have continued perfected until 4 months later without any action by Larkin. Thus, 2 months after the debtor and the collateral arrived in Blackacre, Larkin's perfected security interest had priority over the subsequent security interest of Quarry Bank. The general rule is that conflicting perfected security interests rank according to time of filing or perfection.

Answer (A) is incorrect. Larkin had 4 months to file a financing statement in Blackacre after the debtor moved there. Answer (B) is incorrect. Larkin's perfection of the security interest in the state of Whiteacre provided constructive notice and priority over subsequently perfected security interests. Answer (D) is incorrect. Larkin need not repossess the collateral to maintain its priority over Quarry as long as its security interest is continuously perfected by other means.

27. Forward Motors, Inc., is a franchised automobile dealer for National Motors. National provides the financing of the purchase of its automobiles by Forward. It sells Forward 25 to 50 automobiles at a time and takes back promissory notes, a security agreement, and a financing statement on each sale. The agreement between Forward and National includes an after-acquired property clause. The financing statement covering this revolving inventory has been duly filed.

A. Each automobile sold to Forward must be described and the serial number listed on the financing statement.

B. Sales by Forward to buyers in the ordinary course of business will be subject to the rights of National.

C. No filing is required against the creditors of Forward because the automobiles are "consumer goods" in its hands.

D. As against the creditors of Forward, National has a valid "floating lien" against the automobiles and the proceeds from their sale.

Answer (D) is correct. *(CPA, adapted)*

REQUIRED: The true statement concerning the financing of an automobile dealer's inventory.

DISCUSSION: A "floating lien" is one that the secured party retains against the inventory of a debtor even though the individual items included in the inventory change over time. Such a lien arises pursuant to an after-acquired property clause in the security agreement. National Motors, as a purchase money secured creditor with a perfected "floating lien," has priority in the inventory against other creditors of Forward.

Answer (A) is incorrect. A financing statement covering property that is inventory in the hands of the debtor only needs to indicate the type of collateral. Answer (B) is incorrect. A sale by a dealer of an automobile in the ordinary course of business is not subject to the rights of the inventory financier. National will continue to have rights in the identifiable cash proceeds possessed by Forward but will not be able to proceed against the automobile in the hands of a buyer in the ordinary course of business, a party who takes free of a perfected security interest given by his/her seller. Answer (C) is incorrect. The automobiles are inventory in the hands of Forward, and National needs to file a financing statement to protect itself against Forward's creditors.

28. A party who filed a financing statement covering inventory on April 1 has an interest superior to that of which of the following parties?

A. A holder of a mechanic's lien whose lien was filed on March 15.

B. A holder of a purchase money security interest in after-acquired property perfected by filing on March 20.

C. A purchaser in the ordinary course of business who purchased on April 10.

D. A judgment lien creditor who filed its judgment on April 15.

Answer (D) is correct. *(CPA, adapted)*

REQUIRED: The party whose interest in inventory is inferior to that of a party who filed on April 1.

DISCUSSION: When two perfected security interests conflict, the first secured party to file or perfect ordinarily has priority. A secured party who filed on April 1 has priority over a judgment lien creditor (a person who acquired a lien by judicial process) who filed on April 15. However, the judgment lien creditor's interest is ordinarily superior to that of an unperfected security interest. An exception to the latter rule is made for an unperfected security interest if two criteria are satisfied before the person becomes a lien creditor: (1) a financing statement covering the collateral was filed, and (2) one of the conditions for attachment (other than the giving of value or the debtor's having rights in the collateral) was met.

Answer (A) is incorrect. A mechanic's lien is a statutory lien on real property securing payment for materials, services, or labor provided by the creditor with respect to the real property. A mechanic's lien filed before another secured party filed has priority. Answer (B) is incorrect. A PMSI in inventory collateral has priority over a conflicting security interest in the same collateral if (1) it is perfected at the time the debtor receives possession, (2) an authenticated notice is sent to the holder of the conflicting interest, (3) that interest is received within 5 years before the debtor takes possession, and (4) the notice describes the collateral and states that the sender has or expects to have a PMSI in the debtor's inventory. However, the notice requirements do not apply because the PMSI was perfected by filing before the other secured party filed. Accordingly, the PMSI has priority in any inventory of which the debtor took possession after the filing on March 20 that was covered by the after-acquired property clause. Answer (C) is incorrect. A buyer in the ordinary course of business takes the collateral free of a perfected security interest given by the seller even if the secured party did not authorize the sale.

29. Edie owned and operated a bowling alley. She obtained a loan from Bank secured by "the equipment and all other chattels and personal property used in the business." Bank properly filed a financing statement. Edie then borrowed funds from S & L, giving a first mortgage on "all real property used in the business." Edie became insolvent and filed a petition in bankruptcy. Which of the following is true?

A. Bank is entitled to resort to the personal property even against a trustee in bankruptcy.

B. Bank has a priority in bankruptcy and is entitled to defeat the claims of all creditors that are asserted against the personal property.

C. Bank has a security interest in Edie's central air conditioning system.

D. Edie's sale of all the business property to a bona fide purchaser will defeat Bank's security interest.

Answer (A) is correct. *(Publisher, adapted)*

REQUIRED: The true statement about the rights given by a perfected security interest.

DISCUSSION: Even in bankruptcy proceedings, a secured creditor with a perfected security interest may pursue its remedy against the particular property. The secured party has a property right in the property and the proceeds flowing from disposition of the collateral. However, the trustee in bankruptcy has the status of a hypothetical lien creditor and can defeat a nonperfected security interest in personal property.

Answer (B) is incorrect. Bank has a property right in the goods that it is entitled to assert before the goods become available to other creditors, whether they have a priority or not. Bank's interest is thus not a "priority." Answer (C) is incorrect. Bank's security interest covers only personal property. The central air conditioning system is a fixture and covered by the mortgage. With respect to real property, a trustee in bankruptcy has the rights of a good faith purchaser at the time the petition is filed. Answer (D) is incorrect. Bank's perfected security interest extends to the proceeds of the sale of the personal property and has priority.

18.5 Exceptions to the General Priority Rules

30. With regard to a prior perfected security interest in goods for which a financing statement has been filed, which of the following parties is most likely to have a superior interest in the same collateral?

A. A buyer in the ordinary course of business.

B. A subsequent buyer of consumer goods who purchased the goods from another consumer.

C. The trustee in bankruptcy of the debtor.

D. Lien creditors of the debtor.

Answer (A) is correct. *(CPA, adapted)*

REQUIRED: The party most likely to have a superior interest in collateral covered by a filed financing statement.

DISCUSSION: A buyer in the ordinary course of business, other than a person buying farm products from a farmer, takes the goods free of any security interest created by the seller. This right is extended to the buyer regardless of whether the security interest is perfected or the buyer has knowledge of its existence. A buyer of goods in the ordinary course of business buys in the ordinary course, from a person in the business of selling goods of that kind, in good faith, and without knowledge that the sale violates a third party's rights. This UCC rule does not extend to buyers of farm products from farmers. However, the federal Food Security Act of 1985 treats such parties as buyers in the ordinary course of business. A buyer of farm products from a farmer is not subject to a security interest created by the seller unless the buyer has received notice within 1 year before the purchase; the buyer has not registered with the secretary of state, and the secured party has perfected its interest centrally; or the secretary of state has notified the buyer that an effective financing statement (EFS) has been filed in addition to an Article 9 financing statement.

Answer (B) is incorrect. The subsequent bona fide purchaser will not have priority over a prior perfected security interest in consumer goods if the interest was perfected by filing a financing statement, but (s)he will have priority over any interest that was perfected automatically upon attachment. A buyer of consumer goods from a consumer takes free of a security interest if (s)he buys without knowledge of the security interest (but knowledge is imputed to the buyer if a financing statement has been filed), for value, for consumer purposes, and before the secured party files. Answer (C) is incorrect. A trustee in bankruptcy has priority over any unperfected security interests or any security interests perfected subsequent to the filing of the petition for relief. However, the trustee's rights are subordinate to those of a prior perfected security interest. Answer (D) is incorrect. A lien creditor has an interest superior to an unperfected security interest or to a security interest perfected after attachment of the lien.

31. On July 8, Ace, a refrigerator wholesaler, purchased 50 refrigerators that constituted its entire inventory. This purchase was financed under an agreement with Rome Bank that gave Rome a security interest in all refrigerators on Ace's premises, all future acquired refrigerators, and the proceeds of sales. On July 12, Rome filed a financing statement that sufficiently indicated the collateral covered. On August 15, Ace sold one refrigerator to Cray for personal use and four refrigerators to Zone Co. for its business. Which of the following statements is true?

A. The refrigerators sold to Zone will be subject to Rome's security interest.

B. The refrigerator sold to Cray will not be subject to Rome's security interest.

C. The security interest does not include the proceeds from the sale of the refrigerators to Zone.

D. The security interest may not cover after-acquired property even if the parties agree.

Answer (B) is correct. *(CPA, adapted)*

REQUIRED: The true statement concerning the scope and priority of a security interest in inventory.

DISCUSSION: The refrigerators held by Ace constitute inventory of the debtor. Accordingly, Rome must file a financing statement to perfect its purchase money security interest in the collateral. Filing would not have been necessary if the collateral had consisted of consumer goods. Thus, Rome Bank's PMSI was perfected on July 12. A buyer in the ordinary course of business (Cray), except one purchasing farm products from a person engaged in farming, takes the goods free of any security interest created by the seller. This right is extended to the buyer regardless of whether the security interest is perfected or the buyer has knowledge of its existence.

Answer (A) is incorrect. The purpose for which goods are purchased is irrelevant if the buyer purchases in the ordinary course of business. Answer (C) is incorrect. The security interest is perfected as to identifiable proceeds for at least 20 days. But Rome still does not have priority over the claim of the buyer in the ordinary course of business. Answer (D) is incorrect. The parties may agree that a security interest extends to after-acquired property.

32. Acorn Marina, Inc. sells and services boat motors. On April 1, Acorn financed the purchase of its entire inventory with GAC Finance Company. GAC required Acorn to execute a security agreement and financing statement covering the inventory and proceeds of sale. On April 14, GAC properly filed the financing statement pursuant to the UCC Secured Transactions Article. On April 27, Acorn sold one of the motors to Mary Wilks for use in her charter business. Wilks, who had once worked for Acorn, knew that Acorn regularly financed its inventory with GAC. Acorn has defaulted on its obligations to GAC. The motor purchased by Wilks is

A. Subject to the GAC security interest because Wilks should have known that GAC financed the inventory purchase by Acorn.

B. Subject to the GAC security interest because Wilks purchased the motor for a commercial use.

C. Not subject to the GAC security interest because Wilks is regarded as a buyer in the ordinary course of Acorn's business.

D. Not subject to the GAC security interest because GAC failed to file the financing statement until more than 10 days after April 1.

Answer (C) is correct. *(CPA, adapted)*

REQUIRED: The true statement about the rights of a buyer in the ordinary course of business.

DISCUSSION: A buyer in the ordinary course of business, other than a person buying farm products from a farmer, takes the goods free of any security interest created by the seller. This right is extended to the buyer regardless of whether the security interest is perfected or the buyer has knowledge of its existence. A buyer of goods in the ordinary course of business buys in the ordinary course, from a person in the business of selling goods of that kind, in good faith, and without knowledge that the sale violates a third party's rights. Because boat motors constitute the regular inventory of Acorn Marina, Inc., Wilks is a buyer in the ordinary course of business and takes the motor free of GAC's security interest.

Answer (A) is incorrect. Article 9 specifically states that the buyer will take the goods free of any security interest even though (s)he may have known of its existence (unless the buyer knew that the sale violated the security interest). Answer (B) is incorrect. The purpose for which a good is purchased is irrelevant if the buyer purchases in the ordinary course of business. Answer (D) is incorrect. Buyers in the ordinary course of business will prevail over perfected as well as unperfected security interests.

33. Jay Thrush, a wholesaler of television sets, contracted to sell 100 sets to Kara Kelly, a retailer. Kelly signed a security agreement with the 100 sets as collateral. The security agreement provided that Thrush's security interest extended to the inventory, to any proceeds therefrom, and to the after-acquired inventory of Kelly. Thrush filed his security interest. Later, Kelly sold one of the sets to Myra Haynes who purchased with knowledge of Thrush's perfected security interest. Haynes gave a note for the purchase price and signed a security agreement using the set as collateral. Kelly is now in default. Thrush can

A. Not repossess the set from Haynes but is entitled to any payments Haynes makes to Kelly on her note.

B. Repossess the set from Haynes because he has a purchase money security interest.

C. Repossess the set because his perfection is first, and first in time is first in right.

D. Repossess the set in Haynes's possession because Haynes knew of Thrush's perfected security interest at the time of purchase.

Answer (A) is correct. *(CPA, adapted)*

REQUIRED: The remedy available to a secured party after the defaulting debtor has sold the collateral.

DISCUSSION: Assuming Haynes bought in good faith, without knowledge that the sale was in violation of Thrush's security interest, in the ordinary course, and from a person in the business of selling television sets (not a pawnbroker), she qualifies as a buyer in the ordinary course of business. She therefore takes free of the purchase money security interest in inventory given by Kelly even though it was perfected and she knew of its existence (an exception to this UCC rule is made for a person buying farm products from a farmer). However, the security interest continues in the proceeds, so Thrush may recover payments made by Haynes to Kelly. A perfected PMSI in inventory extends to identifiable cash proceeds received no later than the time of delivery to a buyer and to proceeds in the form of instruments, chattel paper (e.g., the note and security agreement), and the proceeds of chattel paper.

Answer (B) is incorrect. A purchase money security interest confers certain special protections but not against a buyer in the ordinary course. Answer (C) is incorrect. The priority contest here is not between two parties with perfected security interests. Moreover, "first in time, first in right" is a principle with numerous exceptions. Answer (D) is incorrect. Mere knowledge of the interest does not prevent Haynes from qualifying as a buyer in the ordinary course of business.

34. On June 15, Harper purchased equipment for $100,000 from Imperial Corp. for use in its manufacturing process. Harper paid for the equipment with funds borrowed from Eastern Bank. Harper gave Eastern an authenticated security agreement covering Harper's existing and after-acquired equipment. On June 21, Harper was petitioned involuntarily into bankruptcy under Chapter 7 of the Federal Bankruptcy Code. A bankruptcy trustee was appointed. On June 23, Eastern duly filed a sufficient financing statement. Which of the parties will have a superior security interest in the equipment?

A. The trustee in bankruptcy, because the filing of the financing statement after the commencement of the bankruptcy case would be deemed a preferential transfer.

B. The trustee in bankruptcy, because the trustee became a lien creditor before Eastern perfected its security interest.

C. Eastern, because it had a perfected purchase money security interest without having to file a financing statement.

D. Eastern, because it perfected its security interest within the permissible time limits.

Answer (D) is correct. *(CPA, adapted)*

REQUIRED: The party with a superior security interest in equipment after bankruptcy.

DISCUSSION: The equipment is purchase money collateral that secures the purchase money obligation arising from the lender's giving value to permit the debtor to obtain rights in the collateral. Hence, Eastern Bank has a PMSI. A PMSI in goods other than inventory or livestock has priority over a perfected conflicting security interest in the same collateral if it is perfected at the time the debtor receives possession of the collateral or within 20 days thereafter. Even in bankruptcy proceedings, a secured creditor with a perfected security interest may pursue its remedy against the particular property. Thus, Eastern Bank's perfected PMSI in the equipment is superior (it is not inventory). However, the trustee in bankruptcy has the status of a hypothetical lien creditor and can defeat a nonperfected security interest in the equipment.

Answer (A) is incorrect. Filing is not a transfer. It perfects the PMSI. Answer (B) is incorrect. Eastern could perfect its PMSI and retain its priority in the equipment by filing for up to 20 days after the debtor received possession. Answer (C) is incorrect. Filing was required for perfection, even though it could be done up to 20 days after the debtor received possession of the collateral.

35. Milo Manufacturing Corp. sells baseball equipment to distributors, who in turn sell it to various retailers throughout the United States. The retailers then sell the equipment to consumers who use it for their own personal use. In all cases, the equipment is sold on credit with a security interest taken in the equipment by each of the respective sellers. Which of the following is true?

A. The security interests of all of the sellers remain valid and will take priority even against good faith purchasers for value, despite the expectation of resales.

B. The baseball equipment is inventory in the hands of all the parties concerned.

C. Milo's security interest is automatically perfected because Milo qualifies as a purchase money secured party.

D. Milo and the distributors must file a financing statement or take possession of the baseball equipment to perfect their security interests.

Answer (D) is correct. *(CPA, adapted)*

REQUIRED: The true statement about security interests held by sellers in the chain of distribution.

DISCUSSION: The equipment is inventory in the hands of Milo, the distributors, and the retailers. Milo and the distributors must therefore either take possession of the goods or file a financing statement to perfect their security interests.

Answer (A) is incorrect. Each buyer, whether a distributor, a retailer, or a consumer, is a buyer in the ordinary course of business and takes free of a security interest created by the seller even though the security interest is perfected and the buyer knows of its existence. Answer (B) is incorrect. The equipment is classified as consumer goods in the hands of buyers who purchase for personal, family, or household use. Answer (C) is incorrect. The only purchase money security interest that is automatically perfected is one in consumer goods.

36. Mozart Manufacturers has a perfected security interest in pianos owned by the Virtuoso Piano School. Virtuoso sends one of the pianos to Rachmaninoff Repair Service, which makes extensive repairs to the instrument. Virtuoso is unable to make payment for the repairs, and the piano remains in Rachmaninoff's possession. A state statute establishes an artisan's lien but is silent with regard to priority as against a perfected security interest.

A. Rachmaninoff will prevail in a priority contest because the statute did not expressly provide that the security interest took priority.

B. Mozart will prevail because its interest was perfected before Rachmaninoff gained possession.

C. Mozart will prevail because its interest was first in time.

D. Rachmaninoff will prevail because it has perfected by possession, which is superior to perfection by filing.

Answer (A) is correct. *(Publisher, adapted)*

REQUIRED: The priority between an artisan's lien and a prior perfected security interest.

DISCUSSION: Certain liens have priority over even a perfected security interest. If a state statute grants a lien in favor of a person who, in the ordinary course of business, furnishes services or materials with respect to goods subject to a security interest, and such person retains possession of the goods, the lien has priority over a perfected security interest unless the statute expressly provides otherwise.

Answer (B) is incorrect. Prior perfection of the security interest is not relevant against an artisan's lien unless the statute granting the lien expressly provides otherwise. Answer (C) is incorrect. Prior formation of the security interest is not relevant against an artisan's lien unless the statute granting the lien expressly provides otherwise. Answer (D) is incorrect. Perfection by filing is not necessarily inferior to perfection by possession. In any event, the contest here is not between two secured parties who have perfected but between an artisan's lien or and a secured party.

37. A fixture is a good that has become so related to particular real property that an interest in the fixture arises under real property law. Perfection of a security interest in a fixture usually requires

A. Filing of a financing statement in the office where a mortgage on the real estate would be recorded.

B. Filing in the office where financing statements covering other kinds of goods are recorded.

C. No filing if the secured party has a purchase money security interest.

D. Filing in both the personal property and real estate records.

Answer (A) is correct. *(Publisher, adapted)*

REQUIRED: The true statement about the requirements of a fixture filing.

DISCUSSION: A fixture filing is usually required to obtain priority over conflicting interests in fixtures. A fixture filing is not necessary for certain readily removable items. In addition to meeting the basic requirements for any financing statement, a fixture filing must (1) indicate that it covers fixtures and that it is to be filed in the real property records, (2) sufficiently describe the real property, and (3) provide the name of the record owner if the debtor has no recorded interest in the real property.

Answer (B) is incorrect. The filing must be in the real estate records. Answer (C) is incorrect. A purchase money security interest in a fixture is not perfected when it attaches unless it is a consumer good. Answer (D) is incorrect. A dual filing is unnecessary.

38. Winona Owner planned to add a wing to her house and to install central air conditioning. She obtained a loan from Bank to finance the construction and gave a mortgage on the realty as security. Bank recorded the mortgage on August 1. On July 29, Owner purchased on credit a central air conditioning unit from Seller. Seller took a security interest in the unit and made a proper fixture filing of a financing statement on August 2. The air conditioning unit was permanently installed on August 15 and construction of the house was completed on August 30.

A. Bank has priority over Seller because it has a recorded real estate mortgage against a perfected security interest in a fixture.

B. Bank has priority over Seller because the conditions for priority of a construction mortgage have been met.

C. Seller has priority over Bank because it recorded first.

D. Seller has priority over Bank because it has a perfected purchase money security interest in fixtures that was perfected by a fixture filing before the goods became fixtures.

Answer (B) is correct. *(Publisher, adapted)*

REQUIRED: The priority between a holder of a construction mortgage and a secured party with a perfected purchase money security interest.

DISCUSSION: Seller has a purchase money security interest in the air conditioning unit that was perfected by a proper fixture filing on August 2. The goods subsequently became fixtures on August 15. Nevertheless, the UCC gives Bank priority because the construction mortgage was recorded (August 1) before the goods became fixtures, and the goods became fixtures (August 15) before completion of construction (August 30).

Answer (A) is incorrect. A purchase money security interest in fixtures perfected by fixture filing before the goods become fixtures or within 20 days thereafter ordinarily has priority over any real estate interest arising before the goods become fixtures, provided that the debtor has a recorded interest in the real property or is in possession of it. Only construction mortgages meeting the conditions of the UCC are superior. Answer (C) is incorrect. Bank recorded first. Answer (D) is incorrect. A construction mortgage that meets the conditions of the UCC has priority over a purchase money security interest in fixtures.

18.6 Default and Remedies

39. Under the UCC Secured Transactions Article, if a debtor is in default under a payment obligation secured by goods, the secured party has the right to

	Reduce the Claim to a Judgment	Sell the Goods Secured and Apply the Proceeds toward the Obligations	Peacefully Repossess the Goods without Judicial Process
A.	Yes	Yes	No
B.	Yes	No	Yes
C.	No	Yes	Yes
D.	Yes	Yes	Yes

Answer (D) is correct. *(CPA, adapted)*

REQUIRED: The rights of a secured party when a debtor defaults on a payment obligation.

DISCUSSION: A secured party essentially may choose among three remedies. The secured party may (1) sue the debtor for the amount owed (reduce the claim to judgment); (2) peaceably take possession of (foreclose on) the collateral, with or without judicial process, and sell, lease, license, or otherwise dispose of it in a commercially reasonable manner that includes applying the proceeds to the costs of disposition and to the obligations secured; and (3) accept (retain) the collateral in full or partial satisfaction of the obligations secured if certain conditions, for example, consent of the debtor, are met. These remedies are cumulative and allow the creditor if unsuccessful by one method to pursue another remedy. They also may be exercised simultaneously.

Answer (A) is incorrect. The secured party has the right to repossess the collateral either privately or with judicial assistance. Answer (B) is incorrect. The secured party has the right to foreclose on the collateral and have the proceeds of a judicial sale applied to repayment of the obligations secured. Answer (C) is incorrect. The secured party has the right to sue the debtor for the amount paid.

40. Brian purchased an electric typewriter from Robert under a written contract. The contract provided that Robert retained title until the purchase price was fully paid and granted him the right to repossess the typewriter if Brian failed to make any of the required ten payments. Arthur, an employee of Robert, was instructed to repossess the machine on the grounds that Brian had defaulted in making the third payment. Arthur took possession of the typewriter and delivered it to Robert. It was then discovered that Brian was not in default. Which of the following conclusions is supported by the above facts?

A. Arthur is not liable to Brian.

B. Brian can sue either Arthur or Robert or both for damages, but can collect only once.

C. Neither party is liable because it was apparently an honest mistake.

D. If Arthur is sued and must pay the judgment obtained against him, he has no rights against Robert.

Answer (B) is correct. *(CPA, adapted)*

REQUIRED: The true statement concerning the legal effect of a wrongful repossession.

DISCUSSION: A secured party has the general right upon default to take possession of the collateral, which may be done without recourse to judicial process if this can be accomplished without breach of the peace. If such repossession is wrongful, however (e.g., if the debtor is not truly in default), the secured party and an agent employed by the secured party to effect the repossession will both be liable to the debtor in tort for damages. However, Brian is allowed only one recovery of his damages.

Answer (A) is incorrect. Agents are liable for their torts committed within the course and scope of their agency even though their principal is also liable. Answer (C) is incorrect. Brian is entitled to damages for the wrong of trespass or conversion caused by Robert and Arthur even if it was an honest mistake. Answer (D) is incorrect. An agent has the right to indemnification by his/her principal for any liability that the agent incurred as the result of doing an act, without knowledge of its unlawfulness, under the direction of the principal.

41. Pine has a security interest in certain goods purchased by Byron on an installment contract. Byron has defaulted on the payments resulting in Pine's taking possession of the collateral. Which of the following is true?

A. Byron may waive his right of redemption at the time he executes the security agreement.

B. Pine must sell the collateral if Byron has paid more than 60% of the cash price on a purchase money security interest in business equipment.

C. The collateral may be sold by Pine at a private proceeding and, if it is consumer goods, without notice to other secured parties.

D. Unless otherwise agreed, Pine must pay Byron for any increase in value of the collateral while it is in Pine's possession.

Answer (C) is correct. *(CPA, adapted)*

REQUIRED: The rights and duties of the parties after default and repossession.

DISCUSSION: The secured party may dispose of the collateral at a public or private proceeding provided that every aspect of the disposition is commercially reasonable. Unless the collateral is perishable, threatens to decline rapidly in value, or is of a type customarily sold on a recognized market, reasonable authenticated notice must be given to the debtor and any secondary obligor unless that right has been waived. In the case of consumer goods, no other notification need be sent to other secured parties because many PMSIs in consumer goods are perfected by attachment alone.

Answer (A) is incorrect. Except in an agreement entered into and authenticated after default, the right of redemption cannot be waived except in a consumer-goods transaction. Answer (B) is incorrect. Disposition is compulsory if the debtor has paid 60% in the case of a security interest in consumer goods, not equipment. Answer (D) is incorrect. The secured party in possession may hold as additional security any proceeds, except money or funds, received from the collateral. Money or funds so received, unless remitted to the debtor, is applied in reduction of the secured obligation.

42. In what order are the following obligations paid after a secured party rightfully sells the debtor's collateral after repossession?

I. Debt owed to any junior security holder
II. Secured party's reasonable sales expenses
III. Debt owed to the secured party

A. I, II, III.

B. II, I, III.

C. II, III, I.

D. III, II, I.

Answer (C) is correct. *(CPA, adapted)*

REQUIRED: The order for paying obligations after a secured creditor rightfully sells the debtor's collateral.

DISCUSSION: Proceeds of disposition are applied in the following order: (1) reasonable expenses of repossession, holding, preparation for disposition, processing and disposing, and, pursuant to agreement, reasonable attorneys' fees and legal expenses (if not barred by law), and repossession expenses; (2) the secured debt; and (3) subordinate security interests or other subordinate liens after receipt of authenticated demands for proceeds from the holders of such interests and liens.

Answer (A) is incorrect. The debt secured by the security interest under which the disposition is made is satisfied before subordinate secured debts. Answer (B) is incorrect. The debt secured by the security interest under which the disposition is made is satisfied before subordinate secured debts. Answer (D) is incorrect. Proceeds are first applied to reasonable costs of disposing of the collateral.

43. Bonn, a secured party, sells collateral at a private sale to a good faith purchaser for value after the debtor defaults. Which of the following statements is most likely true under the UCC Secured Transactions Article?

A. In all cases, the collateral will remain subject to the security interests of subordinate lien creditors.

B. The security interest under which the sale was made and security interests or liens subordinate to it will be discharged.

C. In all cases, Bonn may not buy the collateral at a private sale.

D. Bonn will be entitled to receive a first priority in the sale proceeds.

Answer (B) is correct. *(CPA, adapted)*

REQUIRED: The true statement about sale of collateral to a good faith purchaser for value.

DISCUSSION: A transferee for value will take property free of the security interest under which the disposition is made and free of any subordinate security interests and liens (other than those liens not dischargeable under specific statutes) when the secured party disposes of the collateral after default. Even if the secured party fails to comply with the requirements for the sale under Article 9, the transferee will take the property free of these interests if (s)he acts in good faith.

Answer (A) is incorrect. The transferee who acts in good faith will take the property free of any subordinate lien creditors' security interests (other than those liens not dischargeable under specific statutes). Answer (C) is incorrect. A secured party is permitted to buy the collateral at a private sale as long as the debtor is given reasonable authenticated notice, and the sale is conducted in a commercially reasonable manner. Answer (D) is incorrect. The secured party will take the sale proceeds subject to any superior interests that exist in the collateral.

44. Vega Manufacturing, Inc., manufactures and sells stereo systems and components to the trade and at retail. Repossession is frequently made from customers who are in default. Which of the following statements is true concerning the rights of the defaulting debtors who have had property repossessed by Vega?

A. Vega has the right to retain all the goods repossessed as long as it gives notice and cancels the debt.

B. It is unimportant whether the goods repossessed are defined as consumer goods, inventory, or something else in respect to the debtor's rights upon repossession.

C. If the defaulting debtor voluntarily authenticates a statement waiving rights in the collateral, the creditor must nevertheless resell them for the debtor's benefit.

D. If a debtor has paid 60% or more of the cash price of consumer goods in satisfaction of a purchase money security interest, the debtor has the right to have the creditor dispose of the goods.

Answer (D) is correct. *(CPA, adapted)*

REQUIRED: The true statement about the rights of debtors who have had property repossessed.

DISCUSSION: To protect the equity interest of debtors who have had property repossessed by secured parties, the UCC provides for compulsory disposition of the collateral in certain cases. In other cases, a secured party may retain the collateral if appropriate authenticated notice is given to the debtor and other parties to whom notice must be given, and no authenticated objection is received within 20 days of sending the notice. If the debtor has paid at least 60% of the cash price in the case of a PMSI in consumer goods, the secured party must dispose of the goods unless the debtor waives the right to require disposal by an agreement entered into and authenticated after default.

Answer (A) is incorrect. Vega may be compelled to dispose of the collateral in the case of consumer goods 60% paid for or if timely objection is made to Vega's retaining the collateral. Answer (B) is incorrect. The secured party is subject to compulsory disposition of certain consumer goods. Answer (C) is incorrect. A defaulting debtor may waive rights to disposition of the collateral, in which case the secured party may elect to sell or retain it. If the collateral is sold, the debtor receives any surplus and remains liable for any deficiency.

45. The Uniform Commercial Code contains numerous provisions relating to the rights and remedies of the parties upon default. With respect to a buyer, these provisions may

A. Not be varied even with the agreement of the buyer.

B. Only be varied if the buyer is apprised of the fact and initials the variances in the agreement.

C. Not be varied insofar as they require the secured party to account for any surplus realized on the disposition of collateral securing the obligation.

D. All be varied by agreement as long as the variances are not manifestly unreasonable.

Answer (C) is correct. *(CPA, adapted)*

REQUIRED: The circumstances in which the rights and remedies of the parties upon default may be varied.

DISCUSSION: If the security interest secures an indebtedness, the secured party must account to the debtor for any surplus on disposition of the collateral after default. This right of the buyer-debtor is absolute when the collateral is sold after default because the risk remains with the debtor (but it would not apply if the secured party is allowed to retain (accept) the collateral and later sells it at a profit).

Answer (A) is incorrect. Many provisions may be varied with the agreement of the buyer; e.g., under certain circumstances, a buyer in default has a right to a compulsory disposition of collateral, but it may be waived. Answer (B) is incorrect. Certain provisions for rights and remedies of the buyer upon default may not be waived. Answer (D) is incorrect. Certain rights and remedies of the buyer upon default may not be varied by agreement regardless of the reasonableness of the variance.

46. If a secured party does not comply with the UCC rules with respect to collateral after a debtor's default, the secured party will

A. Lose his/her security interest.

B. Be required to dispose of the collateral.

C. Be liable for any better price available by any other method of sale.

D. Be liable to another known secured party for losses resulting from not sending notification of sale.

Answer (D) is correct. *(Publisher, adapted)*

REQUIRED: The secured party's liability for not properly disposing of collateral.

DISCUSSION: In general, a secured party is liable for damages to the debtor or certain other parties as a result of losses they sustain when the secured party does not comply with UCC Article 9. For example, if another secured party ought to have been notified of a sale but was not, any losses resulting are recoverable.

Answer (A) is incorrect. It is not a penalty provided for by the UCC. Answer (B) is incorrect. The secured party also may be restrained from collection, enforcement, or disposition of collateral depending on the circumstances. Answer (C) is incorrect. A secured party need not dispose of collateral at the very best price, just in a commercially reasonable manner.

STUDY UNIT NINETEEN
SURETYSHIP

The suretyship relationship involves three parties: the **debtor**, the **creditor**, and the **surety**. A surety is contractually liable for the debt or default of another. The surety promises to answer for the payment of the debt or the performance of the duty if the debtor or obligor fails to pay or otherwise perform the obligation. Thus, suretyship provides security for the creditor by way of a third party's promise to be responsible for the obligation if the debtor defaults. When two or more persons are obligated to pay the same debt if the principal debtor defaults, they are **cosureties**. Sureties who are not paid are called gratuitous, voluntary, or **accommodation** sureties. **Compensated sureties** undertake the obligation for consideration. The promise of a compensated surety is often referred to as a **bond**. A **fidelity bond** provides for compensation to an employer for the costs of employee wrongdoing. A **bail bond** is security given for the due appearance of a prisoner in court. A **performance bond** secures contract performance. An **official bond** helps to minimize the loss from a public official's misconduct. A **judicial bond** compensates a party for the costs of delay or the inability to use property involved in a legal proceeding. A suretyship also arises from **assumption of a mortgage**. When a buyer of real estate assumes an existing mortgage, the seller remains liable because a novation has not occurred. Between the seller and buyer, the buyer has become the primary debtor, and the seller is a surety.

Some states still recognize a **technical distinction between a surety and a guarantor**. A surety is primarily liable for the debtor's obligation. Upon default, the creditor need not first proceed against the principal debtor to collect the debt but may proceed immediately and directly against the surety. A **guarantor** is secondarily liable. Upon default, the creditor must proceed against the principal debtor and obtain a judgment that is returned unsatisfied. Only then may the creditor proceed against the guarantor. The term **absolute surety** applies to a party who is a guarantor of payment and is liable to the creditor immediately upon the debt's maturity. The term **conditional guarantor of collection** applies to a party whose liability does not arise until the creditor has sued the debtor and is unable to collect the judgment.

The contract for suretyship or guaranty must ordinarily be in writing. The suretyship provision of the **statute of frauds** requires that a contract to answer for the debt of another be written and signed by the surety or guarantor. The purpose of this requirement is to provide reliable evidence of what was promised and to protect the surety from fraudulent claims. This section of the statute of frauds requires a writing to enforce a **collateral promise**, that is, a promise to pay a debt or perform a contract only if the principal debtor fails to pay. Collateral promises create **secondary liability**. They are conditional promises that are secondary or ancillary to the **primary contract** between a debtor and creditor. However, the statute of frauds is not applicable when the surety's promise is an original or primary undertaking that the contract will be performed. For example, if a buyer directs the seller to ship goods to a third person and agrees to pay $300 for them, the promise is original, and the promisor does not undertake to answer for the debt of another. Moreover, under the **main purpose doctrine**, if the main purpose of a surety's promise to answer for the debt of another is to secure some new economic benefit for him/herself, the promise is not within the statute of frauds and may be enforced even if it is oral.

A suretyship arrangement is usually formed by **express contract**. The agreement must contain the usual elements of a contract. Thus, it must be supported by legally sufficient consideration. Separate consideration is required unless the surety's promise is made at the same time that the creditor extends consideration to the debtor. In addition, a creditor must communicate to the surety, prior to formation of the contract, information concerning **significant risk to the surety**. Any facts that make the risk of default materially greater than the surety intends to assume must be disclosed. This duty exists only if the creditor has reason to believe that the surety does not know the facts. However, a surety cannot avoid liability on the surety contract because of **misconduct of the debtor** that induced the surety to enter into the contract. The surety contract is between the surety and the creditor, not the debtor.

An **absolute surety** becomes liable immediately after the debtor defaults. **Notice** of default is not required to hold the surety liable. A surety has **three types of defenses**: (1) the surety's personal contractual defenses, (2) some of the debtor's contractual defenses, and (3) special suretyship defenses. A person has no suretyship liability if a **valid contract of suretyship never arose**, for example, if an element of a contract is missing (capacity to contract legal purpose, mutual assent, or consideration), or the creditor procured the surety's promise by means of fraud or duress. Other personal contractual defenses of the surety include (1) the failure of an intended cosurety named in the contract to sign and (2) the absence of a writing if the surety's promise is collateral. It is collateral, not primary, if (1) the surety's promise is to answer for the debt of another, and (2) the main purpose of the promise is **not** to obtain an economic benefit or the surety. The surety also may assert against the creditor **defenses that the debtor could have asserted** had no suretyship agreement been reached. For example, a surety's valid defenses include (1) forgery of the debtor's signature, (2) fraudulent or material alteration of the contract by the creditor, (3) an invalid or unenforceable debtor-creditor contract, (4) performance by the debtor, (5) illegality or impossibility of performance, and (6) the creditor's refusal to accept tender or performance by the debtor or surety. Nevertheless, **personal defenses of the debtor** are available only to the debtor and not the surety. These defenses include (1) the debtor's incapacity due to infancy or mental incompetence, (2) the discharge of the debtor's obligation in bankruptcy, and (3) the debtor's claim against the creditor for set-off. **Special defenses** that only the surety may assert are (1) the creditor's release of the debtor (unless the creditor reserves his/her rights), (2) modification of the debtor-creditor contract, (3) the creditor's impairment of collateral, and (4) the surety's claim against the creditor for set-off.

A **surety's rights** against the principal debtor include reimbursement, subrogation, and exoneration. A **cosurety** also may have rights of exoneration, subrogation, and contribution against **other cosureties**. A surety, whether compensated or not, has a right to sue the debtor for **reimbursement** of amounts (s)he actually paid to the creditor. However, the surety is not entitled to reimbursement of amounts paid after receiving notice of a valid defense of the principal debtor to payment. The right of **subrogation** gives the surety all of the rights that the creditor had against the debtor, including the right to any security in the possession of the creditor. **Exoneration** is the right of a surety to request a court to compel a capable but reluctant debtor to pay the debt before the creditor collects the debt from the surety. The remedy of exoneration also is available against cosureties to the extent of their liability. Each cosurety who pays more than the share (s)he agreed to has a right to **contribution** by the other cosureties. Accordingly, the cosureties for the same debt and the same principal debtor are liable for the agreed-to proportionate part of the loss. A **cosurety's contributive share** equals the amount of the debt at default times the ratio of the maximum liability of the cosurety to the sum of maximum liabilities of the cosureties.

The **discharge** of a surety's liability to a creditor ordinarily occurs as a result of **performance** of the principal debtor's obligations, no matter by whom. However, discharge may occur through **rescission or revocation** of the principal contract (but not to the extent of any liability already incurred by the surety). Moreover, if the principal contract or the contract of suretyship is **materially altered, changed, or departed from** without the surety's knowledge or consent, the surety is likewise discharged from liability, although many courts will not discharge a compensated surety unless the unconsented-to material modification is also prejudicial to the surety's rights. Another basis for discharge is **release** by the creditor of a cosurety. In most states, if a cosurety is released, the **liability of the remaining cosureties** is the total liability of all cosureties prior to the release reduced by the portion for which the released cosurety would have been responsible. Nevertheless, other cosureties are not discharged if they **consented to the release** or the **creditor reserved rights** against them. A surety also is discharged to the extent of a creditor's **release of collateral**, because the release or impairment of collateral interferes with the surety's subrogation right. Still another basis for discharge of a surety is refusal by the creditor to accept a lawful **tender of payment** made by the surety or the principal debtor. **Extending time of payment** also may result in discharge. If a creditor grants a legally binding extension of time for payment of the debt to the principal debtor without actual or implied **consent by the surety**, an **uncompensated surety** will be absolutely released from liability. A **compensated surety** will be released by an unconsented-to extension given to the principal debtor, provided the surety can demonstrate that (s)he suffered an **actual injury** as a result of the extension. However, a surety will not be released from liability if the unconsented-to extension agreement provides for a **reservation of rights against the surety**. Furthermore, discharge does not occur if the extension agreement was not supported by consideration.

QUESTIONS

19.1 Basic Concepts of Suretyship

1. A surety is best defined as one who

A. Insures against a risk in return for compensation.

B. Holds an interest in collateral that secures payment or performance of an obligation.

C. Promises to answer to a third person for the debt or performance of another.

D. Signs an instrument in any capacity for the purpose of lending his/her name to it.

Answer (C) is correct. *(Publisher, adapted)*

REQUIRED: The best description of the nature of a surety.

DISCUSSION: A surety is contractually obligated to a creditor to pay a debt or to perform an obligation owed by the principal debtor to the creditor if the principal fails to pay or otherwise perform. Suretyship is therefore a security device.

Answer (A) is incorrect. It describes an indemnification agreement of an insuror. Answer (B) is incorrect. It is the definition of a secured party. Answer (D) is incorrect. It defines an accommodation party.

2. Which of the following is the most accurate statement of a reason for using a surety?

A. All work done for a governmental entity must be protected by a surety.

B. The costs of using a secured transaction may be excessive.

C. The contracts of a minor may be ratified when (s)he reaches his/her majority and certain other contracts are enforceable in spite of the party's infancy.

D. A building contractor for a commercial project may seek a performance bond to protect against failure of the owner to pay the contract price.

Answer (B) is correct. *(Publisher, adapted)*

REQUIRED: The most accurate statement of a reason for using a surety.

DISCUSSION: A surety may be used in addition to a secured transaction to provide further security. A surety may also be used instead of a secured transaction to avoid the trouble and expense of attaching, perfecting, and enforcing a security interest. Perfection by taking possession of the collateral, for example, may be especially costly and inconvenient.

Answer (A) is incorrect. Statutes require only certain kinds of work done for a governmental unit to have a surety. Answer (C) is incorrect. Minors may disaffirm many of their contracts. The advantage of a surety is to have someone with contractual capacity bound on the obligation. Answer (D) is incorrect. The performance bond is usually sought by the owner rather than the contractor.

3. To establish a cosurety relationship, two or more sureties must

A. Be aware of each other's existence at the time of their contract.

B. Sign the same contract creating the debt and the cosurety relationship.

C. Be bound to answer for the same debt or duty of the debtor.

D. Be bound for the same amount and share equally in the obligation to satisfy the creditor.

Answer (C) is correct. *(CPA, adapted)*

REQUIRED: The requirement to establish a cosurety relationship.

DISCUSSION: Cosureties exist when more than one surety is bound to answer for the same debt or duty of a debtor. Without an agreement to the contrary, cosureties equally share the loss caused by the debtor's default.

Answer (A) is incorrect. Cosureties are not required to know of each other at the time of their contract. They may also become sureties at different times. Answer (B) is incorrect. It is not necessary for a surety to sign the same contract signed by the debtor or the other cosurety. The surety must only contract to pay the debt if the debtor does not pay. Answer (D) is incorrect. Cosureties can guarantee unequal amounts of a debt. Each can guarantee any part of a debt.

4. Which of the following transactions does not establish Sam as a surety?

A. Says: "Ship goods to my son and I will pay for them."

B. Signs commercial paper as an accommodation endorser for one of his suppliers.

C. Guarantees a debt of a corporation he controls.

D. Sells an office building to Park and, as a part of the consideration, Park assumes a mortgage on the property.

Answer (A) is correct. *(CPA, adapted)*

REQUIRED: The transaction not establishing a person as a surety.

DISCUSSION: A surety makes a secondary promise (Sarah promises to pay if Doug does not), not a primary promise (Sarah promises to pay if Pete will send consideration to Doug). Sam's statement is of the latter variety because Sam is incurring his own debt and is not promising to answer for the debt or performance of another.

Answer (B) is incorrect. An accommodation endorser of commercial paper may be liable if another fails to pay (UCC 3-415), so an accommodation party is a surety. Answer (C) is incorrect. Sam qualifies as a surety if the corporation is the primary obligor on a debt. Answer (D) is incorrect. The party who assumes the mortgage becomes the primary debtor and the seller becomes a surety.

5. A party contracts to guarantee the collection of the debts of another. As a result of the guaranty, which of the following statements is true?

A. The creditor may proceed against the guarantor without attempting to collect from the debtor.

B. The guaranty must be in writing.

C. The guarantor may use any defenses available to the debtor.

D. The creditor must be notified of the debtor's default by the guarantor.

Answer (B) is correct. *(CPA, adapted)*

REQUIRED: The true statement about a guaranty of collection.

DISCUSSION: A person who guarantees the payment of a debt of another without qualification has primary liability; (s)he may be required to pay the debt upon default even though the creditor makes no effort to collect. In states that distinguish between sureties and guarantors, such a person is identified as a surety. The guarantor of collection is a person who guarantees the debt upon condition that the creditor first make use of ordinary legal means to collect from the debtor. Surety and guaranty arrangements that involve promises to answer for the debt of another are within the statute of frauds and are required to be in writing, assuming the main purpose of the promise is not to benefit the surety or guarantor.

Answer (A) is incorrect. A guarantor of collection is not liable until the creditor exercises due diligence in enforcing its remedies against the debtor. Answer (C) is incorrect. A guarantor may not use defenses that are personal to the debtor, e.g., infancy. Answer (D) is incorrect. The creditor should notify the guarantor of the debtor's default.

6. Sorus and Ace have agreed, in writing, to act as guarantors of collection on a debt owed by Pepper to Towns, Inc. The debt is evidenced by a promissory note. If Pepper defaults, Towns will be entitled to recover from Sorus and Ace unless

A. Sorus and Ace are in the process of exercising their rights against Pepper.

B. Sorus and Ace prove that Pepper was insolvent at the time the note was signed.

C. Pepper dies before the note is due.

D. Towns has not attempted to enforce the promissory note against Pepper.

Answer (D) is correct. *(CPA, adapted)*

REQUIRED: The guarantor's defense against the creditor.

DISCUSSION: An absolute surety is primarily liable for the debtor's obligation. A creditor may proceed directly against the surety immediately upon default by the debtor. A guarantor of collection has only secondary liability. The creditor must first proceed against the principal debtor. Only when a judgment is returned unsatisfied may (s)he proceed against the guarantor.

Answer (A) is incorrect. The creditor's rights do not depend on sureties' rights of exoneration and subrogation. Answer (B) is incorrect. Insolvency of the debtor is not a defense. However, if the debtor committed fraud in the inducement by misrepresenting his/her financial position, the guarantors will not be liable. Answer (C) is incorrect. The possibility of the debtor's death is a reason for a lender to enter into a surety contract.

7. Lester Dunbar sold to Walter Masters real property on which Charles Endicott held a first mortgage. Masters expressly assumed the mortgage debt. Subsequently, Masters defaulted in payment of the mortgage debt. Masters contends that Endicott must first proceed against Dunbar, the original mortgagor, because he is primarily liable for the mortgage debt. Based upon these facts,

A. Masters is correct in his assertion.

B. Endicott lost all rights against Dunbar upon learning of the sale to Masters and having made no objection thereto.

C. Dunbar is, in fact, a surety and must satisfy the mortgage if Masters does not.

D. Upon default, Endicott must elect to proceed against one of the parties involved.

Answer (C) is correct. *(CPA, adapted)*

REQUIRED: The true statement concerning a mortgage assumed by a buyer of real property.

DISCUSSION: When a buyer of real estate assumes an existing mortgage, the seller remains liable because a novation has not occurred. Between the seller and buyer, the buyer has become the primary debtor, and the seller is a surety. Because Dunbar is a surety of the assumed mortgage, he must pay if Masters does not.

Answer (A) is incorrect. Although Masters is primarily liable for the mortgage debt after assuming it, Dunbar is liable as a surety. Answer (B) is incorrect. The creditor, Endicott, lost no rights when the mortgage was assigned and assumed. In fact, he gained additional rights against the purchaser. Answer (D) is incorrect. The creditor need not elect to proceed against only one of the parties since they are jointly and severally liable. Endicott can sue either or both without making a binding election until a final judgment is obtained.

8. Which of the following contractual prerequisites is not usually necessary to establish a legally enforceable surety relationship?

A. A signed writing.

B. The solvency of the principal debtor.

C. Separate consideration for the surety's promise.

D. The legal capacity of the surety.

Answer (B) is correct. *(CPA, adapted)*

REQUIRED: The item not required for a creditor to recover from a surety.

DISCUSSION: A suretyship is a relationship in which one person agrees to answer for the debt or default of another person. Whether the principal debtor is solvent at the time the promise is made is immaterial. An insolvent person can incur debts and a surety can guarantee them. Separate consideration for the surety's promise is required unless the promise is made at the same time the creditor extends consideration to the debtor.

9. Which of the following best describes what is required of an uncompensated surety?

A. The uncompensated surety must have the legal capacity to make contracts generally.

B. The uncompensated surety cannot be a corporation.

C. The uncompensated surety benefits by a rule that requires a creditor to first proceed against the principal debtor before the surety can be held liable.

D. The uncompensated surety must not directly or indirectly benefit from the undertaking.

Answer (A) is correct. *(CPA, adapted)*

REQUIRED: The best description of a requirement of an uncompensated surety.

DISCUSSION: All parties to suretyship agreements (including both compensated and uncompensated sureties) are ordinarily required to have the legal capacity to make contracts. A suretyship agreement is a contract.

Answer (B) is incorrect. A corporation can be an uncompensated surety. Answer (C) is incorrect. A compensated and an uncompensated surety have the same liability. A creditor need not proceed first against the principal debtor before an uncompensated guarantor can be held liable. Answer (D) is incorrect. The uncompensated surety is permitted to benefit directly or indirectly from the undertaking (and frequently does so).

19.2 Liability and Defenses

10. Which of the following defenses by a surety will be effective to avoid liability?

A. Lack of consideration to support the surety undertaking.

B. Insolvency in the bankruptcy sense by the debtor.

C. Incompetency of the debtor to make the contract in question.

D. Fraudulent statements by the principal debtor which induced the surety to assume the obligation and which were unknown to the creditor.

Answer (A) is correct. *(CPA, adapted)*

REQUIRED: The defense by a surety that will be effective to avoid liability.

DISCUSSION: The contract of a surety must be supported by consideration or a legal substitute as must any other contract. If the surety enters into the agreement when the obligation is assumed by the debtor, the consideration given by the creditor to the debtor is extended to the surety. If the surety's promise is given later, separate consideration is required.

Answer (B) is incorrect. The possibility of the debtor's insolvency is one purpose for the creditor requiring a surety. Answer (C) is incorrect. The incompetency of the principal debtor has no effect on the surety's liability. Answer (D) is incorrect. While the fraud of the creditor would release the surety, fraud by the principal debtor upon the surety without the creditor's knowledge would not be a defense.

11. A surety will not be liable on an undertaking if

A. The principal is a minor.

B. The underlying obligation was illegal.

C. The principal was insolvent at the time of the surety's agreement to act as surety.

D. The surety was mistaken as to the legal implications of the surety agreement.

Answer (B) is correct. *(CPA, adapted)*

REQUIRED: The situation in which a surety will not be liable.

DISCUSSION: The obligation for which the surety assumes liability must be legal. A suretyship agreement is a contract, and one of the requirements for a valid contract is that the subject be legal.

Answer (A) is incorrect. The infancy of the principal debtor has no effect on a suretyship arrangement. Such incapacity is one of the reasons for use of the suretyship device. Answer (C) is incorrect. The insolvency of the principal debtor at the time the surety contract is formed has no effect on the surety's liability. Answer (D) is incorrect. A surety's mistake as to the legal implications of the surety agreement is a unilateral mistake that does not release him/her.

12. Ford was unable to repay a loan to City Bank when due. City refused to renew the loan unless an acceptable surety could be provided. Ford asked Owens to act as surety on the loan. To induce Owens to agree to become a surety, Ford made fraudulent representations about Ford's financial condition and promised Owens discounts on merchandise sold at Ford's store. Owens agreed to act as surety and the loan to Ford was renewed. Subsequently, Ford's obligation to City was discharged in Ford's bankruptcy and City wishes to hold Owens liable. Owens may avoid liability

A. Because the arrangement was void at the inception.

B. If Owens was an uncompensated surety.

C. If Owens can show that City Bank was aware of the fraudulent representations.

D. Because the discharge in bankruptcy will prevent Owens from having a right of reimbursement.

Answer (C) is correct. *(CPA, adapted)*

REQUIRED: The defense of a surety if the principal debtor has committed fraud.

DISCUSSION: A principal debtor's fraudulent misrepresentation is a material fact that the creditor has a duty to disclose to the surety. Because the surety arrangement is between the surety and the creditor, concealment or nondisclosure is a form of fraud against the surety by the creditor and is a personal defense of the surety. However, the principal debtor's fraud is not a defense against an innocent creditor.

Answer (A) is incorrect. The arrangement was voidable, not void. Answer (B) is incorrect. The loan renewal agreement and the suretyship contract were formed at the same time, so no separate consideration was required to bind the surety. Answer (D) is incorrect. A surety may not exercise certain defenses of the principal debtor, including discharge in bankruptcy, expiration of the statute of limitations, and the principal debtor's lack of capacity. Discharge in bankruptcy is not a permissible defense because protection from the debtor's nonperformance is the essence of suretyship.

13. Don loaned $10,000 to Jon, and Robert agreed to act as surety. Robert's agreement to act as surety was induced by (1) fraudulent misrepresentations made by Don concerning Jon's financial status and (2) a bogus unaudited financial statement of which Don had no knowledge, and that was independently submitted by Jon to Robert. Which of the following is true?

A. Don's fraudulent misrepresentations will not provide Robert with a valid defense unless they were contained in a signed writing.

B. Robert will be liable on his surety undertaking despite the facts because the defenses are personal defenses.

C. Robert's reliance upon Jon's financial statements makes Robert's surety undertaking voidable.

D. Don's fraudulent misrepresentations provide Robert with a defense that will prevent Don from enforcing the surety undertaking.

Answer (D) is correct. *(CPA, adapted)*

REQUIRED: The true statement about the legal effect of fraudulent misrepresentations made to the surety.

DISCUSSION: A surety may take advantage of all his/her available personal defenses on a contract, e.g., fraud or intentional misrepresentation. A creditor's fraudulent misrepresentations provide the surety with a defense that will prevent the creditor from enforcing the surety undertaking.

Answer (A) is incorrect. The law does not require that fraudulent misrepresentation be in writing in order to be assertable as a defense. Answer (B) is incorrect. While the surety may not exercise the debtor's personal defenses, (s)he may exercise his/her own personal defenses. Answer (C) is incorrect. The fraud committed by the debtor upon the surety has no effect on the surety's liability to the creditor unless the creditor had knowledge of it. The creditor is entitled to recover independently of the debtor's acts.

14. Ace, Inc., lent $10,000 to King, Inc., one of its best customers. The loan was for three years and was evidenced by a note. In addition, Walsh and Paxton, King's principal shareholders, had orally guaranteed the repayment of the loan. With respect to Walsh and Paxton, which of the following is a true statement?

A. Unless otherwise indicated, each guaranteed $5,000 of the loan.

B. They will be denied the usual surety defenses.

C. They are cosureties and, as such, their surety undertaking must be in a signed writing.

D. Some additional consideration, independent of the making of the loan by Ace, must pass directly to Walsh and Paxton.

Answer (C) is correct. *(CPA, adapted)*

REQUIRED: The true statement regarding an oral guaranty by two shareholders.

DISCUSSION: Walsh and Paxton each guaranteed the loan in full. This direct guaranty makes them sureties. Two or more persons who are sureties on the same obligation are known as cosureties. A valid defense of the shareholders in this situation is that the suretyship agreement was not in writing and signed as required.

Answer (A) is incorrect. Cosureties are jointly and severally liable. Each cosurety is liable to the creditor for the full amount of the debt. Answer (B) is incorrect. The facts do not indicate that they should be denied the usual surety defenses. Answer (D) is incorrect. These surety obligations arose at the time the loan was made, so the consideration given by the creditor to the debtor is considered extended to the cosureties.

15. Knott obtained a loan of $10,000 from Charles on January 1, payable on April 15. At the time of the loan, Beck became an uncompensated surety thereon by written agreement. On April 15, Knott was unable to pay and wrote to Charles requesting an extension of time. Charles made no reply, but did not take any immediate action to recover. On May 30, Charles demanded payment from Knott and, failing to collect from him, proceeded against Beck. Based upon the facts stated

A. Charles was obligated to obtain a judgment against Knott returned unsatisfied before he could collect from Beck.

B. Beck is released from his surety obligation because Charles granted Knott an extension of time.

C. Charles may recover against Beck although Beck was an uncompensated surety.

D. Beck is released because Charles delayed in proceeding against Knott.

Answer (C) is correct. *(CPA, adapted)*

REQUIRED: The liability of an uncompensated surety upon default.

DISCUSSION: If the promise of the surety is made at the same time as that of the principal debtor, the same consideration that supports the latter promise will support the former. That Beck was not compensated thus has no effect on his/her liability.

Answer (A) is incorrect. Only if the surety is a conditional guarantor of collection must the creditor exhaust legal remedies against the principal debtor before proceeding to collect from the surety. Answer (B) is incorrect. Although an extension of time without reservation of rights does release the surety, no such agreement was made by Charles, and a simple delay of 45 days in demanding payment has no effect on the creditor's rights against either the principal debtor or the surety. Answer (D) is incorrect. The delay was too brief to affect anyone's rights or duties.

19.3 Surety Rights

16. A surety paid the creditor upon default and then brought suit against the principal debtor for the amount paid. The surety exercised the right of

A. Subrogation.

B. Contribution.

C. Exoneration.

D. Reimbursement.

Answer (D) is correct. *(Publisher, adapted)*

REQUIRED: The right of a surety who has paid the creditor to receive payment from the principal debtor.

DISCUSSION: A surety who has paid the creditor has a right to be paid by the principal debtor. This right of reimbursement accrues only after actual payment and only for the amount paid.

Answer (A) is incorrect. Subrogation is the right of a surety who has paid the principal debtor's full obligation to exercise all the creditor's rights. Answer (B) is incorrect. Contribution is the right of a cosurety who has paid more than his/her proportionate or agreed share of the debt to proceed against the other cosureties for their share. Answer (C) is incorrect. Exoneration is the surety's right to compel performance by the principal debtor.

17. Burns borrowed $240,000 from Dollar Bank as additional working capital for his business. Dollar required that the loan be collateralized to the extent of 20%, and that an acceptable surety for the entire amount be obtained. Surety Co. agreed to act as surety on the loan and Burns pledged $48,000 of negotiable bearer bonds. Burns defaulted. Which of the following statements is true?

A. Dollar must first liquidate the collateral before it can proceed against Surety.

B. Surety is entitled to the collateral upon satisfaction of the debt.

C. Dollar must first proceed against Burns and obtain a judgment before it can proceed against the collateral.

D. Surety may proceed against Burns for the full amount of the loan even if Surety settles with Dollar for a lower amount.

Answer (B) is correct. *(CPA, adapted)*

REQUIRED: The right of a surety after default on a partially collateralized debt.

DISCUSSION: Subrogation is the right of a surety, after payment upon default of the debtor, to step into the creditor's shoes and recover from the debtor in the same manner as the creditor. This includes rights in the collateral provided by the principal debtor, a priority in bankruptcy, rights against other parties indebted on the same obligation, and rights against cosureties. Surety is therefore subrogated to Dollar's rights against the bonds.

Answer (A) is incorrect. Unless otherwise agreed, Dollar may proceed directly against Surety after default. Answer (C) is incorrect. The creditor must exhaust legal remedies against the principal debtor before proceeding to collect from the surety only if the surety is treated as a conditional guarantor of collection. Answer (D) is incorrect. The surety's right of reimbursement is limited to amounts paid to the creditor.

18. Susan is a surety on an obligation owed by Paul to Bank. Paul has transferred possession of 1,000 shares of common stock to Susan as collateral. Which of the following is true?

A. Susan is subrogated to Bank's rights against Paul, but Bank has no subrogation rights.

B. Bank may enforce Susan's rights against Paul.

C. If Susan returns the stock to Paul, the Bank's subrogation rights are voided.

D. Bank is powerless to prevent the return of the stock to Paul prior to the time the debt is due.

Answer (B) is correct. *(Publisher, adapted)*

REQUIRED: The creditor's right to collateral held by the surety.

DISCUSSION: A creditor as well as a surety has subrogation rights. Thus, a creditor may "step into the shoes" of the surety and enforce whatever rights the surety may have against the debtor. If the debtor places assets in the hands of the surety to provide against default, the creditor has the right to assert the surety's rights against those assets. Hence, Bank may enforce Susan's rights to the stock.

Answer (A) is incorrect. Both creditors and sureties have subrogation rights. Answer (C) is incorrect. If the stock is returned, the creditor may nevertheless obtain a lien against it. Answer (D) is incorrect. Bank can obtain an injunction to prevent the return. In effect, the stock can be held by the court until the due date and sold if the principal debt is not paid.

19. Prior to making payment, cosureties may seek the remedy of

A. Contribution.

B. Reimbursement.

C. Subrogation.

D. Exoneration.

Answer (D) is correct. *(CPA, adapted)*

REQUIRED: The remedy that may be sought by the cosureties prior to payment.

DISCUSSION: The principal debtor is expected to perform so that the surety will not be required to pay the creditor. The surety therefore has a right (exoneration) to compel performance by the principal debtor by obtaining a decree from a court exercising its equity powers.

Answer (A) is incorrect. Contribution is the right of a cosurety who has paid more than his/her proportionate or agreed share of the debt to proceed against the other cosureties for their proportionate or agreed share. Answer (B) is incorrect. Reimbursement is the right of a surety who has paid the creditor to be paid by the principal debtor. Answer (C) is incorrect. Subrogation is the right of a surety who has paid the principal debtor's full obligation to exercise all the rights that the creditor had against or through the principal debtor.

20. In relation to the principal debtor, the creditor, and a fellow cosurety, the cosurety is not entitled to

A. Exoneration against the debtor under any circumstances.

B. A pro rata contribution by fellow sureties if (s)he pays the full amount.

C. Be subrogated to the rights of the creditor upon satisfaction of the debt.

D. Avoid performance because the cosurety refuses to perform.

Answer (D) is correct. *(CPA, adapted)*

REQUIRED: The right not held by a cosurety against the other parties.

DISCUSSION: The obligation of a cosurety to perform under the suretyship agreement is not contingent upon the performance of another cosurety. Instead, a cosurety who pays is entitled to contribution from the other cosurety.

Answer (A) is incorrect. A cosurety is entitled to exoneration against the debtor (to bring a suit to compel the debtor to pay). Answer (B) is incorrect. A cosurety is entitled to contribution from another cosurety to the extent that (s)he has paid more than his/her pro rata share. Answer (C) is incorrect. A cosurety who has paid the creditor steps into the shoes of the creditor and may assert all rights that the creditor had.

21. Lane promised to lend Turner $240,000 if Turner obtained sureties to secure the loan. Turner agreed with Rivers, Clark, and Zane for them to act as compensated cosureties. The cosureties' agreement with Turner indicated that the maximum liability of each cosurety would be as follows: Rivers $240,000, Clark $80,000, and Zane $160,000. Lane made the loan to Turner. After paying 10 installments totaling $100,000, Turner defaulted. Clark's debts, including the surety obligation to Lane on the Turner loan, were discharged in bankruptcy. Later, Rivers properly paid the entire outstanding debt of $140,000. What amount may Rivers recover from Zane?

A. $0

B. $46,667

C. $56,000

D. $96,000

Answer (C) is correct. *(CPA, adapted)*

REQUIRED: The contribution recoverable from a cosurety when one cosurety's obligation was discharged in bankruptcy.

DISCUSSION: A cosurety who pays more than his/her share has a right of contribution, i.e., to proceed against the other cosureties to recover his/her proportionate or agreed-to share. A cosurety's contributive share is determined by dividing the maximum liability of each surety by the sum for all cosureties and multiplying the result by the amount of the default. But contribution cannot be obtained from the cosurety whose obligation was discharged in bankruptcy. Thus, Zane's contribution percentage is 40% [$160,000 ÷ ($160,000 + $240,000)], and Rivers may recover $56,000 ($140,000 × 40%) from Zane.

Answer (A) is incorrect. A cosurety who pays more than his/her share is entitled to contribution from the other cosureties. Answer (B) is incorrect. Clark's cosurety obligation was discharged in bankruptcy. Answer (D) is incorrect. Contribution is based on the amount of the default, not the original loan amount.

22. A distinction between a surety and a cosurety is that only a cosurety is entitled to

A. Reimbursement (indemnification).

B. Subrogation.

C. Contribution.

D. Exoneration.

Answer (C) is correct. *(CPA, adapted)*

REQUIRED: The right unique to a cosurety.

DISCUSSION: Contribution is the right of a cosurety who has paid more than a proportionate or agreed-to share to proceed against the other cosureties to recover the excess.

Answer (A) is incorrect. Reimbursement is the right of a surety who has paid the debt to be paid by the principal debtor. Indemnification arises from an agreement by one party to protect an obligor (debtor), not an obligee (creditor), from loss. Answer (B) is incorrect. Subrogation is the right of a surety who has paid the principal debtor's obligation to exercise rights the creditor had against or through the principal debtor. Answer (D) is incorrect. Exoneration is the right to request a decree from a court compelling performance by the principal debtor.

19.4 Discharge of a Surety

23. Which of the following events will release a noncompensated surety from liability to the creditor?

A. The principal debtor was involuntarily petitioned into bankruptcy.

B. The creditor failed to notify the surety of a partial surrender of the principal debtor's collateral.

C. The creditor was adjudicated incompetent after the debt arose.

D. The principal debtor exerted duress to obtain the surety agreement.

Answer (B) is correct. *(CPA, adapted)*

REQUIRED: The event that will release a noncompensated surety from liability to the creditor.

DISCUSSION: The creditor's impairment of collateral, for example, by returning it to the principal debtor or failing to maintain a perfected security interest in it, discharges the surety to the extent of the value of the lost collateral. The reason for permitting this defense is to protect a surety who assumed the obligation solely because the creditor held the security for the debt.

Answer (A) is incorrect. The manner in which the principal debtor entered into bankruptcy proceedings is irrelevant. It is one of the reasons a creditor enters into a surety contract. Answer (C) is incorrect. The mental capacity of the debtor, not the creditor, may raise an issue. Answer (D) is incorrect. The principle debtor is not a party to the surety agreement. Accordingly, the duress defense is not valid.

24. Dinsmore & Company was a compensated surety on the construction contract between Victor (the owner) and Gilmore Construction. Gilmore has defaulted and Victor has released Dinsmore for a partial payment and other consideration. The legal effect of the release of Dinsmore is

A. To release Gilmore as well.

B. Contingent on recovery from Gilmore.

C. Binding upon Victor.

D. To partially release Gilmore to the extent that Dinsmore's right of subrogation has been diminished.

Answer (C) is correct. *(CPA, adapted)*

REQUIRED: The legal effect of the release of the surety by the creditor.

DISCUSSION: Victor will be bound by the release of the surety. The contractual obligation of the surety to the creditor may be discharged by a release that meets the requirements of a contract (especially consideration). The partial payments and other consideration will thus support Victor's promise to release Dinsmore.

Answer (A) is incorrect. The release of a surety will not release the principal debtor. Answer (B) is incorrect. Unless otherwise stated, a release is not contingent upon any other factor. Answer (D) is incorrect. Gilmore has not been released from the obligation to any extent. Gilmore is the debtor in default and has no subrogation rights.

25. When approached by Bob Lanier regarding a $2,000 loan, Dina Dustin demanded a surety and collateral equal to 50% of the loan. Lanier obtained King Surety Company as his surety and pledged rare coins worth $1,000 with Dustin. Dustin was assured by Lanier one week before the due date of the loan that he would have no difficulty in making payment. He persuaded Dustin to return the coins because they had increased in value and he had a prospective buyer. What is the legal effect of the release of the collateral upon King Surety?

A. It totally releases King Surety.

B. It does not release King Surety if the collateral was obtained after its promise.

C. It releases King Surety to the extent of the value of the security.

D. It does not release King Surety unless the collateral was given to Dustin with the express understanding that it was for the benefit of King Surety as well as Dustin.

Answer (C) is correct. *(CPA, adapted)*

REQUIRED: The legal effect on the surety of the release of the collateral by the creditor.

DISCUSSION: When a debtor has put up security or collateral, the surety (after payment) succeeds to it if the creditor has not sold it to satisfy the debt. Hence, a creditor who releases collateral interferes with the subrogation rights of the surety to the collateral. This interference releases the surety. Thus, when Dustin released the $1,000 coin collection, she also released King Surety to that extent.

Answer (A) is incorrect. Release of security by the creditor only releases the surety to the extent of its value. Answer (B) is incorrect. A surety has subrogation rights to the collateral no matter when pledged. Thus, its release prejudices the surety, and (s)he is released. Answer (D) is incorrect. The surety has subrogation rights to the collateral automatically under law.

26. Mane Bank lent Eller $120,000 and received securities valued at $30,000 as collateral. At Mane's request, Salem and Rey agreed to act as uncompensated cosureties on the loan. The agreement provided that Salem's and Rey's maximum liability would be $120,000 each. Mane released Rey without Salem's consent. Eller later defaulted when the collateral held by Mane was worthless and the loan balance was $90,000. Salem's maximum liability is

A. $30,000

B. $45,000

C. $60,000

D. $90,000

Answer (B) is correct. *(CPA, adapted)*

REQUIRED: The effect of releasing a cosurety without the consent of the other cosurety.

DISCUSSION: When a creditor releases a cosurety without consent of, or reserving rights against, the other cosurety, the other cosurety is released to the extent (s)he cannot obtain contribution from the released cosurety. The share of each cosurety would have been half of the unpaid amount, or $45,000.

Answer (A) is incorrect. Collateral to the debtor-creditor loan does not affect surety liability unless it is impaired by the creditor. Answer (C) is incorrect. Collateral to the debtor-creditor loan does not affect surety liability unless it is impaired by the creditor. Answer (D) is incorrect. Salem is released to the extent Salem cannot obtain contribution from the released cosurety.

27. At the request of Pax, Somes and Tabor became cosureties on a loan from Cox to Pax. At the time they agreed to become sureties, Somes placed a limit of $30,000 on his liability and Tabor placed a limit of $20,000 on his; the loan was in the amount of $30,000. Somes and Tabor mutually intended to be cosureties and each promised to pay the loan to the extent of the limit placed should Pax default on payment at maturity. Based on these facts

A. A release of Tabor by Cox would result in a complete discharge of Somes.

B. A release of Somes by Cox, reserving Cox's rights against Tabor, would not reduce Tabor's obligations.

C. Insolvency of Somes would discharge Tabor.

D. Bankruptcy of Tabor before maturity of the note would limit Somes' potential liability to $18,000.

Answer (B) is correct. *(CPA, adapted)*

REQUIRED: The true statement regarding the liability of a cosurety.

DISCUSSION: If the creditor releases one cosurety, the others are released to the extent of the released cosurety's liability for contribution. The rule, however, is not applicable when the creditor reserves his/her rights against the remaining cosureties. The rationale of the exception is that the release with reservation of rights is a promise or covenant by the creditor not to sue the released cosurety and thus leaves the other cosureties' rights of reimbursement from the principal debtor and contribution from all the other cosureties intact. Thus, the release of Somes by Cox reserving Cox's rights against Tabor would not reduce Tabor's obligation because Tabor could still seek contribution from Somes and reimbursement from Pax.

Answer (A) is incorrect. A release of a cosurety does not result in a complete discharge of other cosureties but merely reduces their liability to the extent of the released cosurety's obligation of contribution. Answer (C) is incorrect. The insolvency of a cosurety would not discharge any other cosureties. Answer (D) is incorrect. Bankruptcy of a cosurety does not affect the liability of the remaining solvent cosureties.

28. Which of the following defenses will release a surety from liability?

A. Insanity of the principal debtor at the time the contract was entered into.

B. Failure by the creditor to promptly notify the surety of the principal debtor's default.

C. Refusal by the creditor, with knowledge of the surety relationship, to accept the principal debtor's unconditional tender of payment in full.

D. Release by the creditor of the principal debtor's obligation without the surety's consent but with the creditor's reservation of rights against the surety.

Answer (C) is correct. *(CPA, adapted)*

REQUIRED: The defense releasing a surety from liability.

DISCUSSION: The surety is released when the creditor refuses tender either by the debtor or by the surety. The debtor is not completely discharged by refusal of his/her tender, but accrual of interest on the obligation stops and the creditor will be unable to recover costs in a later suit on the debt.

Answer (A) is incorrect. Incapacity of the principal debtor is a personal defense only of the debtor since such incapacity may create a need for a suretyship arrangement. Answer (B) is incorrect. Lack of notice by the creditor is not a defense. Answer (D) is incorrect. The reservation of rights results in the release being treated merely as a covenant not to sue and thus not as a defense of the surety.

STUDY UNIT TWENTY
BANKRUPTCY

The governing federal statute is the **Bankruptcy Reform Act of 1978**, as amended by the **Bankruptcy Reform Act of 1994** and the **Bankruptcy Abuse Prevention and Consumer Protection Act of 2005**. Bankruptcy cases always are administered in federal bankruptcy courts, one for each federal judicial district. These courts provide a way of resolving the conflict between creditor rights and debtor relief. The objectives are to ensure that debtor assets are equitably distributed to creditors and that the debtor is given a fresh start.

This study unit addresses the following **chapters in the Bankruptcy Code**: Chapter 7, Liquidations; Chapter 11, Reorganization; and Chapter 13, Adjustment of Debts of an Individual with Regular Income. The **parties in interest** in a bankruptcy case are the debtor, the creditors, the trustee, and the creditor's committee. A **debtor** is an individual or organization that owes payment to a creditor. Under Chapter 7, a debtor may be an individual, partnership, or corporation. (But some entities may not file under Chapter 7, e.g., banks and insurers.) A **creditor** is an individual or an entity with a claim against the debtor that arose at the time of or before the order for relief. A **claim** is a right to payment.

The **trustee in bankruptcy** represents the debtor's estate. A trustee is required in cases under **Chapters 7 and 13**. A trustee is not required in a **Chapter 11** case. In the normal Chapter 11 case, a trustee is not appointed. Hence, the debtor-in-possession performs most of the trustee's functions. However, the court may, for cause, order the appointment of a trustee who may then be elected by the creditors as the permanent trustee. In Chapter 7 proceedings, the permanent trustee is usually elected by qualified creditors at their required meeting. Under all other chapters, the trustee, if any, is appointed by the **U.S. Trustee**, an official appointed by the U.S. Attorney General to perform administrative services for bankruptcy courts.

Creditor committees facilitate communication among the debtor, the trustee, and the creditors. The required **meeting of creditors** occurs within a reasonable time after the issuance of the order for relief. The bankruptcy judge is not permitted to appear at the meeting. However, the debtor must attend to be questioned under oath by the trustee and the creditors. Under **Chapter 7**, the creditors may choose a committee of unsecured creditors to represent them in dealings with the trustee and the judge. Under **Chapter 11**, the U.S. Trustee appoints a committee of unsecured creditors. Ordinarily, it consists of the largest creditors. Other committees also may be appointed to represent parties in interest, e.g., shareholders.

A bankruptcy court conducts **core proceedings**. They resolve issues directly affecting reorganization or discharge, such as (1) allowing creditor claims, (2) determining the relative priority of claims, (3) confirming a plan of reorganization, and (4) granting a discharge. **Noncore proceedings** are resolved in state or other federal courts. They may affect rights of the creditors or debtor relevant to the core proceedings, for example, rights to property.

A bankruptcy case begins with the **filing of a petition** specifying the chapter under which relief is requested. However, the filing results in an **estate** generally consisting of the property of the debtor (1) at the time of filing or (2) that becomes subject to the proceeding. The estate is a **legal entity** separate from the debtor. The filing of **any bankruptcy petition** operates as an **automatic stay** of most civil actions against the debtor or his/her property until the court takes further action. However, it does not terminate security interests or liens. The stay does not end until the debtor is discharged or the case is dismissed or closed. Furthermore, not all activity is stayed, e.g., (1) alimony and child support collection, (2) criminal proceedings, and (3) issuance of a notice of tax deficiency. **Insolvency** or a prior filing under another chapter is not a prerequisite to filing a petition.

Most petitions are filed voluntarily. Any person **eligible to be a debtor** under a specific chapter may file under that chapter. No minimum debt or number of creditors is required. A **voluntary petition** also results in an **automatic order for relief**. In the order, the court assumes exclusive authority over the case. The petition must include the following: (1) lists of all creditors (both secured and unsecured), all property owned by the debtor, and property claimed by the debtor to be exempt; (2) a statement of the debtor's affairs and a schedule of current income and expenditures; (3) a certificate indicating that the petitioner has received an informational notice; (4) evidence of payment within 60 days prior to filing by any employer of the debtor; (5) an itemized amount of monthly net income; and (6) a statement of reasonably expected increases in the next 12 months in income or expenses.

An **involuntary petition** is filed under **Chapter 7 or Chapter 11** (but not Chapter 13) against an eligible debtor. The law imposes no limit on the number or timing of involuntary petitions. An involuntary petition **cannot be filed** against (1) farmers, (2) banks, (3) insurance companies, (4) nonprofit corporations, (5) railroads, and (6) persons who owe less than $14,425. If the debtor has **12 or more different creditors**, any **three or more** who together hold **unsecured claims** of at least $14,425 can file an involuntary petition. If the debtor has **fewer than 12 creditors**, any **one or more** who alone or together have **unsecured claims** of at least $14,425 can file an involuntary petition. Any creditors who are the debtor's **employees or insiders**, e.g., officers or directors of a corporation, a corporation controlled by the debtor, relatives, or a partner, are not counted.

Filing an involuntary petition does **not** result in an **automatic order for relief**. However, if the debtor does not oppose the petition, the court will enter an order for relief. If the debtor opposes the petition, the court must hold a **hearing**, and the petitioner must post a **bond** to reimburse a debtor who successfully contests the petition. The court will order relief on behalf of the creditors if it finds that either of two **statutory grounds for involuntary bankruptcy** exists: (1) The debtor is not paying his/her undisputed debts as they become due; or, (2) within 120 days before the filing, a custodian, assignee, or general receiver took possession of all or most of the debtor's property to enforce a lien against the property. If neither ground for involuntary bankruptcy exists, the court will dismiss the case. It also may order the petitioning creditors to pay the debtor for costs, fees, and damages. A petitioner who acted in **bad faith** may be required to pay punitive damages for injury to the debtor's reputation.

Under Chapters 7 and 11, a case may be dismissed **for cause** after notice and a hearing. Under Chapter 13, the debtor always has a right to dismissal because the petition is voluntary. But an interested party may obtain a Chapter 13 dismissal only for cause.

Broad powers are granted to the trustee. They include the power or duty to (1) collect and account for property; (2) perform investigations; (3) set aside fraudulent conveyances and certain other property transfers; (4) accept or reject unperformed contracts or expired leases; (5) sell, use, or lease estate property; (6) operate the debtor's business; (7) invest estate money; (8) hire professionals; (9) file reports; (10) object to creditor claims; (11) object to a discharge in a proper case; and (12) distribute assets and close the estate. The trustee may perform professional services for **reasonable compensation** based on the fair value of the services. However, the trustee must be qualified and receive court approval. A CPA's service as a trustee impairs his/her **independence** regarding the debtor.

To be involved in the **distribution process**, a **creditor** must file a **proof of claim**. However, the debtor or the trustee also may file a proof of claim for a debt to avoid its becoming nondischargeable. Upon filing, the claim is deemed valid and allowable. But if an interested party, such as a creditor or the trustee, objects, the bankruptcy court must decide whether to allow the claim. If a debtor has a defense to an alleged debt (e.g., fraud or failure of consideration), the claim will not be allowed. Moreover, if the claim is (1) for unmatured interest, (2) subject to a right of offset, or (3) in excess of the reasonable value of services performed by an insider or attorney, it will be disallowed.

The creditors involved in the distribution of the debtor's estate are secured creditors, priority creditors (unsecured), and general creditors (other unsecured creditors). **Secured creditors** have property rights that are not affected by the trustee. They are paid in full if the collateral is sufficient. If the collateral is insufficient, the secured creditor is a general unsecured creditor as to the deficiency. After secured claims are paid to the extent of collateral, **priority creditors** (unsecured creditors who have a statutory preference because of the nature of their claims) are paid next. Members of a higher class of priority creditors are paid in full before members of a lower class receive anything. If the assets are insufficient to pay all claims in a given class, the claimants in the class share pro rata. The **classes of priority claims** listed in order of rank are as follows: (1) **domestic support obligations**; (2) claims for **administrative expenses** and expenses incurred in preserving and collecting the estate; (3) claims of tradespeople **(gap creditors)** who extend unsecured credit in the ordinary course of business after the filing of an involuntary petition but before the earlier of the appointment of a trustee or the entry of the order for relief; (4) **wages** (compensation) up to $11,725 per employee earned within the 180 days prior to the earlier of the filing or cessation of the debtor's business; (5) certain contributions owed to the debtor's **employee benefit plans** arising from employee services rendered within 180 days prior to the earlier of the filing or the cessation of the debtor's business; (6) claims of **grain or fish producers** for up to $5,775 each for grain or fish deposited with the debtor but not paid for or returned; (7) claims of **consumers** for the return of up to $2,600 each in prebankruptcy deposits paid to the debtor for services not rendered, or for the purchase or rental of property not delivered, if the services or property were for personal, family, or household use; (8) certain claims for unsecured federal, state, and local **taxes**; and (9) death and injury claims from operation of a motor vehicle or vessel by an intoxicated person. Finally, if any money remains, the **general creditors** are paid.

A bankruptcy judge may apply the doctrine of **subordination of claims** when equitable principles so dictate. Thus, if two claims have equal priority, the court may order that one be paid in full before the second receives anything. For example, the claim of a parent may be subordinated to the claims of other creditors of a subsidiary when the parent's wrongdoing contributed to the bankruptcy.

The **debtor** may continue to use, acquire, and dispose of his/her property until the bankruptcy court orders otherwise. Moreover, the debtor may incur new debts and operate a business. However, if necessary, the court may order the appointment of a **temporary trustee** to preserve the debtor's assets. With court approval, a debtor may file a bond and reacquire property under a trustee's control. **Additional duties of a debtor** include (1) attending and submitting to all court-scheduled examinations and testifying if called as a witness; (2) informing the trustee in writing of (a) the location of all real property in which the debtor has an interest and (b) the name and address of every person holding money or property subject to the debtor's withdrawal or order if a schedule of property has not yet been filed; (3) cooperating with the trustee in the preparation of an inventory, examination of proofs of claim, and administration of the estate; (4) informing the court of any change in the debtor's address; (5) attending hearings with respect to discharge; (6) providing (a) the most recent federal income tax return to the trustee or a requesting creditor and (b) tax returns or amendments filed during the case to a requesting party in interest or the court; (7), in a Chapter 7 or 13 case, completing an approved instructional **course on personal financial management** that is provided without regard to the debtor's ability to pay; and (8), within 180 days **prior to filing**, receiving (unless exempt) an individual or group briefing from an approved nonprofit **budget and credit counseling agency**. This agency must render services without regard to the debtor's ability to pay. The credit counseling requirement may be waived either by the court or because the U.S. Trustee or bankruptcy administrator determines the district has inadequate counseling resources.

Exempt assets of the debtor are considered basic necessities for a fresh start. Exempt assets are defined by either federal or state law. Only **individual debtors**, not corporations, are eligible for exemptions. **States** are permitted to require their citizens to accept the exemptions under state law. Otherwise, the debtor may choose the state or the federal list. However, the **state homestead exemption** is limited. The exemption may be decreased by the **value of an addition** to the homestead during the 10 years before filing. This rule applies if the added value resulted from a disposition by the debtor of nonexempt property that operated as a **fraud on creditors**. Moreover, any addition greater than $146,450 during the **1,215 days before filing** is not exempt unless it was carried over from a prior homestead in the same state. The maximum exemption is $146,450 if the debtor (1) has been convicted of a felony indicating bankruptcy abuse or (2) owes a debt arising from certain misconduct in the prior 5 years (e.g., securities fraud, an intentional tort or crime resulting in serious injury or death, or racketeering). Nevertheless, this provision does not apply if the property is reasonably necessary to support the debtor or a dependent. The following are the **federal exemptions**: (1) up to $21,625 in equity in the debtor's residence and burial plot; (2) an interest in a motor vehicle, up to a value of $3,450; (3) an interest, up to a value of $550, in any item of household goods and furnishings, clothing, appliances, books, animals, crops, or musical instruments, with an aggregate total limited to $11,525; (4) an interest in jewelry, up to a value of $1,450; (5) any other property worth up to $1,150, plus any unused part of the $21,625 equity in the debtor's residence, up to an amount of $10,125; (6) an interest in any tools of the debtor's trade, up to a value of $2,175 in the aggregate; (7) any unmatured life insurance owned by the debtor; (8) certain interests in accrued dividends or interest under life insurance owned by the debtor not exceeding $11,525; (9) professionally prescribed health aids; (10) the right to receive Social Security, certain welfare benefits, veterans' benefits, disability benefits, alimony and support, and certain pension benefits; (11) the right to receive certain personal injury and other awards up to $21,625; (12) unemployment compensation; (13) the ability to void certain judicial liens, e.g., on exempt property; and (14), regardless of which exemptions (federal or state) apply, amounts in tax exempt retirement accounts (but the amount in **IRAs** is capped at $1,171,650). However, exempt property is liable for nondischargeable domestic support obligations.

Upon commencement of a bankruptcy case, an **estate** is formed. The estate consists of all the debtor's nonexempt legal and equitable interests in property. **The estate excludes** (1) earnings of the debtor for services after a Chapter 7 proceeding began; (2) contributions to employee retirement plans; (3) contributions to educational accounts and state tuition programs made **more than 1 year before filing**; and (4) most property of the debtor acquired after the filing of the petition, including gifts. **The estate includes** (1) all property currently held (wherever located); (2) community property; (3) property the trustee recovers from third parties; (4) proceeds and profits from the property of **the estate**; (5) interests in property, such as inheritances received by will or intestate succession, rent, bond interest, insurance proceeds, property from divorce settlements, or life insurance proceeds, to which **the debtor** becomes entitled **within 180 days after filing**; and (6) interests in property acquired by **the estate** after the filing of the petition. The trustee is given several options regarding **leases**. All are subject to court approval. The options are to (1) assume and perform the unexpired lease, (2) assume and assign the unexpired lease to a third party, or (3) reject the unexpired lease.

The **trustee** stands in the shoes of the debtor. Thus, (s)he can assert **any defense of the debtor**. The trustee also can exercise the rights that would be held by an actual creditor who has obtained a judicial lien on the property of the debtor. Thus, the trustee is a **hypothetical (ideal) lien creditor**, one with the most favored status allowed under state law. Moreover, the trustee can obtain a **judicial lien** or a **writ of execution** to enforce the debtor's property rights. The trustee also has priority over a **secured creditor** whose security interest is unperfected. (But a secured creditor with a purchase-money security interest who perfects within 30 days after the debtor takes possession has priority over the trustee.) The trustee does not have the right to void **statutory liens** against the debtor's property that were effective before filing. But statutory liens on **real property** (e.g., mechanic's liens, including materialman's liens) that are not effective until the filing of the petition or until the time when the debtor becomes insolvent are voidable. In addition, the trustee may void liens that are not enforceable against a **good faith purchaser for value (GFP)** on the date of the filing. In general, a GFP of property with no notice of an adverse claim is not subject to that claim. (The claim is not enforceable against the GFP.) The trustee has, among others, the status of a GFP. However, even a GFP may have a subordinate claim. For example, a GFP's claim is subordinate to a mechanic's lien that was effective before filing.

EXAMPLE: Creditor lends money to Debtor and receives a mortgage on Debtor's real estate as security. Creditor does not record the mortgage in the county real property records. Debtor then sells the real estate to GFP, who had no notice, actual or constructive, of the mortgage because it was not recorded. GFP therefore would take the property free of the mortgage. Now assume that Debtor did not sell to GFP but instead filed for Chapter 7 bankruptcy. The trustee has the same right as a good faith purchaser to receive the real property free of the mortgage. It does not matter that no actual good faith purchaser exists. Accordingly, the trustee can void any transfer of property or debt incurred by the debtor that could be defeated by a (1) judicial lien creditor, (2) judgment creditor (one who has obtained a writ of execution), or (3) good faith purchaser for value without notice of an adverse claim. In other words, the trustee can exercise the same rights as the (1) debtor, (2) any actual creditors, and (3) the hypothetical creditors or purchasers listed. These rights allow the trustee to gather property for inclusion in the bankruptcy estate. The trustee can void any transfer of property or debt incurred by the debtor that could be voided by the hypothetical parties above. However, no such creditors or purchasers must actually exist.

The trustee can **void preferential transfers**. The transfer may be a voluntary property conveyance, a voluntary creation of a lien (a mortgage or a security interest), or the involuntary creation of a lien (e.g., a judgment lien obtained by a creditor). A **voidable preferential transfer** is one made (1) to or for the benefit of a creditor, (2) for or on account of an antecedent (pre-existing) debt, (3) during the debtor's insolvency, (4) within 90 days prior to filing the petition, and (5) for the purpose of entitling the creditor to receive a larger portion of its claim than otherwise would be received under a distribution in bankruptcy. The trustee may void preferential transfers and grants of security interests to **insiders** if made within **1 year before the filing** of the petition. The debtor must have been insolvent at the time of the transfer or grant. However, property purchased by an **innocent third party** from a preferential transferee cannot be recovered. That transfer is not voidable, but the preferential transferor may be liable for its value. **Other transfers not voidable** as preferences include (1) payments of accounts payable paid in the ordinary course of the debtor's and transferee's business or financial affairs; (2), if the debtor is an individual, payment of less than $600 on a **consumer debt** within 90 days preceding the filing of the petition; (3), if an individual's debts are primarily nonconsumer debts, any transfer worth less than $5,850; (4) asset transfers for current consideration (new value); (5) bona fide transfers for alimony, maintenance, or support to a spouse, former spouse, or child of the debtor; and (6) gifts that are not voidable preferences or fraudulent transfers because they are not on account of a debt. The trustee also can void **preferential liens**, including judgment liens and other liens obtained by any legal or equitable proceeding. These liens arise in the circumstances described for preferential transfers.

The trustee can void **fraudulent transfers**. Proof that a property transfer on or within **2 years prior to filing** was with actual intent to hinder, delay, or defraud creditors renders it voidable.

In a **Chapter 7 liquidation**, the **automatic stay** arising from filing the petition suspends most legal action and collection activity until the bankruptcy case is completed or the bankruptcy court vacates (terminates) the stay. Nevertheless, a **secured creditor** may petition the court to recognize the priority of the existing security interest and to grant relief from the automatic stay, thus permitting foreclosure. The stay also may be terminated (or not go into effect) because of **serial filings** suggestive of bad faith or abuse. However, the stay continues in effect if a party in interest shows that the new filing is in good faith. After a third filing within 1 year, the stay will not go into effect absent a showing of good faith. Furthermore, an **order of relief from the automatic stay** may be issued in appropriate circumstances involving (1) transfers of **real property** collateral without the creditor's consent or a court's approval or (2) multiple filings with respect to the same real property. **Eviction proceedings** also are not stayed in certain cases, for example, those involving endangerment of rented property, use of controlled substances, or the landlord's obtaining a judgment before the filing. However, provisions exist allowing the debtor to contest these exceptions.

Chapter 7 uses a liquidation approach by converting a debtor's nonexempt assets into cash. The cash is distributed and an **honest debtor** is discharged from most of the remaining debts. Proceedings under Chapter 7 apply to all debtors (persons), including individuals, partnerships, and corporations. Moreover, a married couple may file jointly. However, Chapter 7 is **not available** to (1) municipalities, (2) railroads, (3) insurance companies, (4) banks, (5) savings and loan associations, and (6) credit unions.

In addition, a Chapter 7 case may be dismissed or converted to a Chapter 13 case because of **abuse by an individual debtor with primarily consumer debts** (for example, credit card debt). Abuse is found when (1) the debtor does not pass the **means test** (if it results in an unrebutted presumption of abuse), or (2) **general grounds** exist for the finding (bad faith or that the totality of the circumstances indicates abuse). If the debtor's income exceeds the relevant **state median income**, any **party in interest** may seek dismissal for abuse on either basis. Otherwise, only the judge, U.S. Trustee, or bankruptcy administrator may move to dismiss (and then only on general grounds of abuse). The debtor's income for this purpose equals **current monthly income (CMI)** times 12. The means test determines the debtor's ability to repay general unsecured claims. CMI is a 6-month average of all income received by the debtor. However, Social Security and certain other items are excluded. **Presumed deductions** from CMI are allowed for support and payment of higher priority debt. They include (1) living expenses for which allowances are specified by the IRS, (2) actual expenses recognized by the IRS for which it provides no allowances, (3) secured debt coming due within 5 years divided by 60, (4) priority debt divided by 60, and (5) certain other deductions (e.g., continuing contributions to charity of up to 15% of gross income). The mandatory **trigger point** for presumed abuse is that the debtor has at least $195.42 of CMI after deductions. If CMI after deductions is **less than $117.08**, the presumption never arises. For other amounts, abuse is presumed if 5-year income [(CMI – allowed deductions) × 60] suffices to pay 25% or more of general unsecured debt. For example, if CMI after deductions is $150, abuse is presumed if general unsecured debt is no more than $36,000 [($150 × 60) ÷ 25]. The presumption of abuse may be rebutted by proof of **special circumstances** that justify increasing expenses or decreasing CMI.

Individual debtors under Chapter 7 may receive a **discharge from most debts** that remain unpaid after distribution of the debtor's estate. But corporations and partnerships are precluded from Chapter 7 discharge, and most other debtors are eligible for a discharge only **once every 8 years**. Grounds for **denial of a general discharge** include the debtor's (1) waiving discharge, (2) fraudulently transferring or concealing **property** within 1 year preceding the filing of the bankruptcy petition or the property of the estate after filing, (3) unjustifiably concealing or destroying **business records** or failing to keep adequate business records, and (4) other conduct that is wrongful or obstructive. **Nondischargeable debts** include the following: (1) federal **income tax** due within 3 years prior to bankruptcy; (2) debts incurred on the basis of materially false **financial statements** if (a) issued with the intent to deceive, and (b) the creditor reasonably relied on them; (3) debts not included in required filings in time to permit filing of a proof of claim; (4) debts resulting from fraud, misrepresentation, embezzlement, larceny, or violation of a fiduciary duty; (5) debts for alimony, maintenance, or child support awards; (6) debts arising from malicious injury to another person or illegal use or abuse of that person's property; (7) debts for certain **educational loans** made, funded, or guaranteed by a government; (8) governmental fines and penalties not related to dischargeable taxes; (9) debts arising from liability for operating a **motor vehicle while legally intoxicated**; (10) **credit card debts** greater than $600 owed to a single creditor by an individual debtor for luxury goods or services incurred on or within 90 days prior to filing; (11) cash advances aggregating more than $875 under an **open-end credit plan** obtained by an individual debtor within 70 days prior to filing; and (12) nondischarged debts from a prior bankruptcy.

If a Chapter 7 case is **dismissed**, the debtor will not be discharged. Dismissal for **cause** may result from, among other things, the debtor's (1) unreasonable delay; (2) failure to pay fees; (3) failure to furnish creditor's lists, financial statements, tax returns, other financial information, evidence of payment by an employer, and the certificate from a credit counselor; (4) lack of good faith; and (5) failure to complete a course in **personal financial management**. If the debtor is an individual whose debts are mostly consumer debts, the court may dismiss if a discharge would result in a **substantial abuse** of Chapter 7.

A debtor may enter into a **reaffirmation agreement** to perform an unsatisfied obligation to be discharged in bankruptcy if (s)he receives extensive disclosures and signs a statement disclosing financial information. The agreement must conspicuously state the debtor's right to rescind until the later of the discharge or 60 days after the agreement is filed with the court. If the debtor does not have an attorney, the court must conduct a hearing to approve the agreement.

A **discharge may be revoked** within 1 year if the trustee or a creditor proves that (1) the discharge was obtained fraudulently, (2) the debtor knowingly and fraudulently retained property of the estate, or (3) the debtor failed to obey a court order.

The primary purpose of a **Chapter 11 reorganization** is to allow a distressed business (partnerships, corporations, and railroads) or any person that may be a debtor under Chapter 7 to restructure its financial position. The restructuring allows the business to be continued and the creditors to be paid. Reorganization is primarily a process of negotiation allowing the debtor and its creditors to develop a plan for the adjustment and discharge of debts.

A case under Chapter 11 is begun by filing either a **voluntary or an involuntary petition**. Insolvency is not a condition precedent to a voluntary petition, and procedural rules similar to those for administering a liquidation case apply in a reorganization proceeding. Under Chapter 11, the debtor has the **exclusive right to file a plan of reorganization during 120 days after the order for relief**, unless a trustee has been appointed, and may file a plan at any time. A reorganization must divide creditor claims and shareholder interests into **classes**, and claims within each class must be treated equally. After a plan of reorganization has been prepared and filed, a court-approved disclosure statement is given to each claimant. After filing and before rejection of a **collective bargaining agreement (CBA)**, the trustee or debtor-in-possession must have set forth fair and equitable changes in the union contract. It also must have held good-faith negotiation with the union. If these actions have been taken, the court may order rejection of the CBA if (1) the union had no good cause to refuse the modifications, and (2) rejection reflects the balance of the equities. To become effective, the plan must be confirmed by the bankruptcy court. **Confirmation** makes the plan binding on the debtor, on creditors, on equity holders, and on others. Confirmation occurs by acceptance or by cramdown. **Acceptance** by a class of claims requires the holders of more than 50% of the claims representing at least two-thirds of the dollar totals to approve the plan. Approval is automatic if the class is unaffected. Rejection is automatic if the class will receive nothing. A class of **equity interests** accepts the plan if the holders of at least two-thirds of the voting interests in dollar amount approve. Subsequent to the vote, the court usually confirms the plan. To avoid a cramdown, the plan must be accepted by each class unless it is not adversely affected by the plan. The court may refuse confirmation of a plan that is not in the creditors' best interests. A spouse or child whose claims will not be paid in cash may block the plan. Confirmation over the objection of one or more classes is a **cramdown**. The requirements are (1) acceptance by at least one class, (2) a finding that the plan is fair, and (3) a finding that the plan does not discriminate unfairly against any creditors. An entity will be **discharged** from its debts and liabilities that occurred prior to the confirmation of the plan. However, exceptions may be provided for in the plan of reorganization, the order of confirmation, or the Bankruptcy Code. The effect of confirmation is to make the plan binding on all parties and to grant the debtor a discharge from claims not protected by the plan. In general, **consumer cases** under Chapter 11 are relatively similar to those under Chapter 13. Thus, (1) property of the estate includes after-acquired property, (2) discharge occurs only after plan completion, (3) plan funding is from future earnings, and (4) a 5-year minimum contribution of disposable income is required.

Chapter 13 provides for **adjustment of debts** of an **individual**. Its focus is on payment from future income. Thus, it may be preferable to liquidation because the debtor often is able to retain more assets. An adjustment is available to an individual with regular income who owes unsecured debts of less than $360,475 and secured debts of less than $1,081,400. **Sole proprietorships** also are eligible. The debts must be owing and unpaid at the time the debtor files the petition. If a debtor's income at least equals the relevant state median income, the **repayment plan** must have a minimum **5-year term** (unless it provides for earlier full payment). Otherwise, the plan's term is 3 years unless a longer term not greater than 5 years is approved for cause.

The plan requires the **approval of the bankruptcy judge** only. A confirmation hearing is held for this purpose. The plan must meet certain requirements to be confirmed: (1) The plan must be proposed in good faith and comply with the Code, (2) the debtor must be able to comply with the plan, (3) required amounts must have been paid (including adequate payments before confirmation of the plan made directly to secured creditors to protect against loss of value of collateral), and (4) the value of property to be distributed on each unsecured claim must at least equal the Chapter 7 amount. With regard to each **secured claim**, the plan must meet one of the following requirements: (1) The holder accepts the plan; (2) the holder retains the lien on the collateral, the value of the distributed property is not less than the claim, and the plan provides for adequate protection payments; or (3) the debtor surrenders the collateral to the holder. A plan may not **strip down** (reduce) a secured claim to the value of the collateral in the case of (1) a purchase money interest in a motor vehicle purchased within 90 days of the filing or (2) any other secured debt incurred within 1 year of bankruptcy. If the **trustee or an unsecured creditor** objects, the plan may be confirmed only if (1) the unsecured claim is paid in full with interest, or (2) all of the debtor's disposable income will be contributed to the plan for its minimum period. **Disposable income** is **current monthly income** not reasonably needed to support the debtor or a dependent. However, if the debtor's current monthly income exceeds the relevant state median, support needs are based on the **means test** for presumption of abuse.

Typically, the debtor will propose either a composition or an extension plan. A **composition plan** allows the debtor to pay less than 100% of claims on a pro rata basis for each class of claims. In an **extension plan**, the debtor pays the full amount but over a longer period than originally agreed to.

For the protection of creditors, the court may dismiss the proceeding or convert it into a Chapter 7 proceeding after a request by a party in interest, including the debtor. After a debtor completes all or substantially all payments under the plan, the court will grant a **discharge** of all debts, except for (1) alimony and child support; (2) student loans from any lender; (3) debts from unlawfully driving while impaired; (4) criminal restitution requirements and fines; (5) long-term debts requiring payment over a period longer than that of the plan; (6) taxes for unfiled, late-filed, or fraudulent returns; (7) debts for fraud (such as credit card misuse); (8) debts unscheduled because of failure to notify creditors; (9) debts arising from civil actions involving willful or malicious personal injury or wrongful death; (10) debts for embezzlement or breach of fiduciary duty; (11) **credit card debts** greater than $600 owed to a single creditor by an individual debtor for luxury goods or services incurred on or within 90 days prior to filing; and (12) cash advances aggregating more than $875 under an **open-end credit plan** obtained by an individual debtor within 70 days prior to filing. The Chapter 13 discharge upon completion of the plan bars another discharge in a Chapter 13 case for the **2-year period** preceding the entry of the order for relief in the subsequent case. If the prior discharge was in a Chapter 7, 11, or 12 case, **a 4-year period** applies. A **hardship discharge** is available if the debtor's failure is due to circumstances for which (s)he is not justly accountable, creditors have received what they would have been paid under Chapter 7, and modification of the plan is not feasible.

An **alternative to bankruptcy** is a **composition with creditors**. It is a contract in which the debtor agrees to pay the creditors some fraction of the amount owed in full satisfaction of their claims. The mutual promises made among the creditors provide **consideration**. A **nonconsenting creditor** is not bound. A nonparticipant may choose to pursue typical debt collection processes and proceed against the debtor's assets. Under general contract law, the original debts are not discharged until the debtor has performed the new obligations. One form of composition is an **extension agreement**. The debtor agrees to pay the full amount of all debts (with or without interest), and the creditors agree to allow the debtor to pay over a longer time than originally agreed to. Nonconsenting creditors are not bound by an extension agreement. They may pursue usual collection processes as to the amounts owed to them. In a composition, **liquidation** of an unliquidated claim means that a debtor and a creditor agree on the amount of a previously disputed claim. No **receiver** is appointed. Only a court may appoint a receiver.

Another alternative to bankruptcy is a **general assignment for the benefit of creditors**. It is a voluntary transfer by the debtor of title to all of his/her assets to a third party (the assignee or trustee). The trustee named by the debtor (1) receives the debtor's property, (2) converts it into cash, and (3) distributes the cash to the creditors in exchange for their promises to release the debtor from further liability. An assignment is similar to a composition. It usually allows creditors to receive more than they would in a bankruptcy proceeding. However, the consent of creditors is not required, and all creditors need not participate. An assignment for the benefit of creditors places the debtor's property out of the reach of creditors because **legal title passes to the assignee**. A basic requirement of a valid assignment is that the debtor act in **good faith**. An assignment that reserves to the assignor any interest in, or benefit of, the property conveyed to the detriment of creditors is probably a fraudulent conveyance. Thus, the assignment should be **general**. Some states treat a **partial assignment** as a fraudulent conveyance. The **creditors are presumed to have consented** to the assignment. If otherwise valid, the assignment will take effect unless the creditors decide to file an **involuntary bankruptcy petition**. The creditors have this right because the assignment satisfies one of the two statutory grounds for an involuntary filing. The **debtor cannot revoke** an assignment for the benefit of creditors. (S)he has no further interest in the assigned property. Thus, creditors cannot use judicial process to seize the property. An assignment for the benefit of creditors **discharges only debts paid in full by the trustee**. The debtor can emerge with some or all of his/her debts not fully paid. A third possibility is to transfer the debtor's business to a **creditor's committee** that has full management authority.

Not all transfers by a party facing bankruptcy are appropriate. A **fraudulent transfer** is any transfer of property that is made with the purpose and intent to delay, hinder, or defraud creditors. It is voidable by the transferor's creditors. Courts have developed various factors that will be considered indications of fraudulent conveyances. These factors are known as **badges of fraud**. They include (but are not limited to) (1) the debtor's retention of possession or a beneficial interest, (2) a transfer of substantially all assets, (3) a transfer in secret, (4) a transfer to a family member or insider, (5) a transfer for inadequate consideration, (6) a transfer in anticipation of legal action or financial problems, (7) removal or concealment of assets, and (8) insolvency at the time of or shortly after the transfer. The most recognized badges of fraud are currently listed in the **Uniform Fraudulent Transfer Act**.

QUESTIONS

20.1 Overview

1. Federal courts have jurisdiction over bankruptcy proceedings. Bankruptcy courts

A. Are Article III federal courts the judges of which have life tenure.

B. Are special administrative courts under the authority of the U.S. district courts.

C. Have full powers to decide collateral issues affecting the debtor, such as contract and tort claims.

D. Are presided over by trustees in bankruptcy who serve 14-year terms.

Answer (B) is correct. *(Publisher, adapted)*

REQUIRED: The true statement about bankruptcy courts in the federal system.

DISCUSSION: Bankruptcy courts are units of federal district courts and preside over specified core proceedings that concern the administration of the bankruptcy estate. Orders and judgments of the bankruptcy court are reviewed by the district court or a panel of three bankruptcy judges. Appeals may then be taken to a circuit court.

Answer (A) is incorrect. Bankruptcy judges do not have life tenure as do district and circuit judges and Supreme Court Justices. Answer (C) is incorrect. Bankruptcy courts have jurisdiction to issue final orders and judgments only with respect to core proceedings. Answer (D) is incorrect. Bankruptcy judges, who preside over the core proceedings, are appointed for 14-year terms.

2. The Bankruptcy Code allows for all but which of the following proceedings?

A. Equity receivership.

B. Reorganization.

C. Regular income adjustment plan.

D. Liquidation.

Answer (A) is correct. *(Publisher, adapted)*

REQUIRED: The proceeding not provided for in the Bankruptcy Code.

DISCUSSION: The Code does not allow for an equity receivership. This remedy may be given by a local court. A receiver is appointed as a fiduciary to collect and preserve the debtor's assets and may temporarily operate the debtor's business. Appointment of a receiver or custodian, whether by a state court or by the debtor, is a basis for an involuntary petition under the Code.

Answer (B) is incorrect. Chapter 11 provides for reorganization of debtor enterprises with a view to their continuation in business. Answer (C) is incorrect. Chapter 13 is a voluntary provision that allows individuals with regular incomes to obtain a discharge after complying with a court-approved repayment plan. Answer (D) is incorrect. Chapter 7 concerns straight bankruptcy that is the conversion of the debtor's assets into cash, its distribution to creditors, and a discharge of remaining debts.

3. Emma's creditors filed an involuntary petition in bankruptcy against her. An order for relief was entered and a trustee was elected by the creditors. The trustee wanted Emma to file a list of creditors, statement of her financial affairs, and other information. She was upset by being forced into bankruptcy and refused to cooperate. Which of the following is true?

A. Failure to provide the requested information may prevent her discharge.

B. Emma does not have to cooperate since the petition was involuntary.

C. The creditors must provide this information.

D. Because Emma is a citizen of a state, the federal court cannot issue sanctions against her.

Answer (A) is correct. *(Publisher, adapted)*

REQUIRED: The true statement regarding the debtor's refusal to provide financial information.

DISCUSSION: The Bankruptcy Code requires a debtor to file information about his/her debts, property, income, and other matters. The debtor has a duty to cooperate with the trustee and the court that includes surrendering the property of the estate and any pertinent records. The court can refuse to grant a discharge in bankruptcy if the debtor refuses to obey any lawful order.

Answer (B) is incorrect. The information listed is required whether the petition is voluntary or involuntary. Answer (C) is incorrect. Creditors must provide only information needed to verify their claims. Answer (D) is incorrect. Once an order for relief is entered, the debtor is subject to the jurisdiction of the bankruptcy court and can be held in contempt or denied a discharge.

4. In a bankruptcy proceeding, the trustee

A. Must be an attorney admitted to practice in the federal district in which the bankrupt is located.

B. Will receive a fee based upon the time and fair value of the services rendered, regardless of the size of the estate.

C. May not have had any dealings with the bankrupt within the past year.

D. Is the representative of the bankrupt's estate and as such has the capacity to sue and be sued on its behalf.

Answer (D) is correct. *(CPA, adapted)*

REQUIRED: The true statement about the trustee in bankruptcy.

DISCUSSION: The trustee in bankruptcy is the legal representative of the debtor's estate. In liquidation bankruptcy, the court will appoint an interim trustee when the order for relief is granted. The interim trustee serves until the creditors elect a permanent trustee. In other bankruptcy proceedings, the trustee is appointed by the court. The trustee has broad powers to administer the estate, including the right to sue and be sued on behalf of the estate.

Answer (A) is incorrect. A trustee is not required to be an attorney. Answer (B) is incorrect. Although the fee of the trustee is based on the criteria mentioned, the maximum limit is contingent upon the size of the estate. Answer (C) is incorrect. There is no such requirement.

5. In a bankruptcy case, the order for relief is a formal judicial declaration that the debtor is insolvent. After this order is issued,

A. An unsecured creditor may not obtain a judgment and execution against the debtor's property.

B. A creditor may not make a setoff of a debt owed to the debtor prior to the order.

C. The debtor retains his/her property in an involuntary liquidation proceeding until the permanent trustee is appointed.

D. A debtor who contests an involuntary petition nevertheless must surrender control of his/her property upon proper filing.

Answer (A) is correct. *(Publisher, adapted)*

REQUIRED: The effect of issuing an order for relief.

DISCUSSION: The order for relief results in an automatic stay of most legal proceedings or other collection efforts by creditors of the debtor. New and pending proceedings are stayed. Creditors, whether or not secured, also may not take action to gain possession of the debtor's property or to create, perfect, or enforce a lien on it. Thus, an unsecured creditor could not take advantage of a state "grab" law to obtain a judgment and execute it by seizing and selling property of the debtor without concern for the claims of other creditors.

Answer (B) is incorrect. The right of setoff is not stayed by the order for relief, although a setoff intended to prefer a creditor will be disallowed. For example, a creditor-bank may set off the debtor's deposit against a debt incurred before filing unless the deposit was intended to prefer the bank. Answer (C) is incorrect. An interim trustee is appointed promptly after the order is recorded. The trustee's duties include collecting the assets belonging to the bankruptcy estate. Answer (D) is incorrect. A debtor may usually continue in control until the order for relief is granted.

6. A federal bankruptcy judge

A. Decides all issues that affect the debtor's estate.

B. Has no authority to order the appointment of a permanent trustee.

C. Presides over core proceedings specified by statute.

D. Collects, preserves, and distributes the debtor's assets.

Answer (C) is correct. *(Publisher, adapted)*

REQUIRED: The function of a federal bankruptcy judge.

DISCUSSION: The bankruptcy judge may decide specified issues arising from "core" proceedings related to the administration of the debtor's estate, for example, decisions on claims and preferences, confirmation of plans, and discharge of debts. These decisions are reviewed by the district court of which the bankruptcy court is a unit or by a panel of three bankruptcy judges. Unless the parties agree otherwise, final orders or judgments on collateral issues affecting the debtor may not be made by the bankruptcy courts.

Answer (A) is incorrect. A bankruptcy court hears only certain matters specified by the Bankruptcy Act. Moreover, the district court of which the bankruptcy court is a unit must abstain with regard to state matters that are not independently cognizable by a federal court. Answer (B) is incorrect. The bankruptcy judge may order the appointment of a permanent trustee in a Chapter 13 case (adjustment of debts of an individual). Answer (D) is incorrect. A trustee collects, preserves, and distributes the debtor's assets.

7. Filing a voluntary petition in bankruptcy acts as an automatic stay of actions to

	Garnish the Debtor's Wages	Collect Alimony from the Debtor
A.	Yes	Yes
B.	Yes	No
C.	No	Yes
D.	No	No

Answer (B) is correct. *(CPA, adapted)*

REQUIRED: The actions affected by the automatic stay.

DISCUSSION: The filing of a voluntary petition in bankruptcy automatically postpones certain actions and proceedings that involve the debtor or his/her property. This automatic stay operates to give the debtor protection from creditors. Actions and proceedings not covered by the automatic stay include criminal prosecution of the debtor, collection of child support, and collection of alimony.

20.2 Bankruptcy Administration

8. To file for bankruptcy under Chapter 7 of the Federal Bankruptcy Code, an individual must

A. Have debts of any amount.

B. Be insolvent.

C. Be indebted to more than three creditors.

D. Have debts in excess of $13,475.

Answer (A) is correct. *(CPA, adapted)*

REQUIRED: The requirement to file for protection under the Bankruptcy Code.

DISCUSSION: Any person with a debt, if (s)he is a type of entity eligible under a particular Chapter of the Code, may file a voluntary petition.

Answer (B) is incorrect. Insolvency is not required to file a voluntary petition. It is only necessary that the person have a legal obligation. Answer (C) is incorrect. Number-of-creditors thresholds apply only to involuntary petitions filed by creditors. Answer (D) is incorrect. Amount-of-debt thresholds apply only to involuntary petitions.

9. A party involuntarily petitioned into bankruptcy under Chapter 7 of the Federal Bankruptcy Code who succeeds in having the petition dismissed could recover

	Court Costs and Attorney's Fees	Compensatory Damages	Punitive Damages
A.	Yes	Yes	Yes
B.	Yes	Yes	No
C.	No	Yes	Yes
D.	Yes	No	No

Answer (A) is correct. *(CPA, adapted)*

REQUIRED: The recovery allowed a debtor whose involuntary bankruptcy was dismissed.

DISCUSSION: A debtor who successfully opposes an involuntary bankruptcy petition could recover his/her costs, including reasonable attorney's fees. The court may require the petitioner to pay damages if (s)he is found to have acted in bad faith. A petitioner whose conduct is malicious or otherwise egregious also may be required to pay punitive damages.

10. A voluntary petition filed under the liquidation provisions of Chapter 7 of the Federal Bankruptcy Code

A. Is not available to a corporation unless it has previously filed a petition under the reorganization provisions of Chapter 11 of the Federal Bankruptcy Code.

B. Automatically stays collection actions against the debtor except by secured creditors.

C. Will be dismissed unless the debtor has 12 or more unsecured creditors whose claims total at least $14,425.

D. Does not require the debtor to show that the debtor's liabilities exceed the fair value of assets.

Answer (D) is correct. *(CPA, adapted)*

REQUIRED: The true statement concerning a voluntary petition under the Bankruptcy Code.

DISCUSSION: A debtor need not be insolvent to file for protection of the Bankruptcy Code. The debtor need merely state (s)he has a debt, and (s)he must be an eligible type of person.

Answer (A) is incorrect. A corporation is eligible to file a voluntary petition. It need not previously have filed under Chapter 11. Answer (B) is incorrect. The stay operates against a secured creditor. Only if the court grants a petition to vacate the stay might the secured party proceed to repossess the collateral or take other action. Answer (C) is incorrect. Number-of-creditors and amount-of-debt thresholds apply only to involuntary petitions.

11. Green owes the following amounts to unsecured creditors: Rice, $4,400; Vick, $5,525; Young, $13,000; and Zinc, $4,600. Green has not paid any creditor since January 1, 2012. On March 15, 2012, Green's sole asset, a cabin cruiser, was seized by Xeno Marine Co., the holder of a perfected security interest in the boat. On July 1, 2012, Rice, Vick, and Zinc involuntarily petitioned Green into bankruptcy under Chapter 7 of the Federal Bankruptcy Code. If Green opposes the involuntary petition, the petition will be

A. Upheld, because the three filing creditors are owed more than $14,425.

B. Upheld, because one creditor is owed more than $14,425.

C. Dismissed, because there are fewer than 12 creditors.

D. Dismissed, because the boat was seized more than 90 days before the filing.

Answer (A) is correct. *(CPA, adapted)*

REQUIRED: The status of an involuntary petition under Chapter 7.

DISCUSSION: If the debtor has fewer than 12 creditors, any one or more creditors who alone or together have unsecured claims of $14,425 or more can file an involuntary petition under Chapter 7 or 11. If there are 12 or more creditors, any three or more who together hold unsecured claims of at least $14,425 can file an involuntary petition.

Answer (B) is incorrect. Young did not join in filing the petition. Answer (C) is incorrect. A debtor with fewer than 12 creditors may be involuntarily petitioned into bankruptcy by one or more creditors who alone or together are owed more than $14,425. Answer (D) is incorrect. A challenged involuntary petition is not dismissed if the debtor is generally not paying his/her bills as they become due or, within 120 days before filing, a custodian or receiver took possession of all or most of the debtor's property to enforce a lien against the property.

12. Willa Wilk owes a total of $50,000 to eight unsecured creditors and one fully secured creditor. Rusk is one of the unsecured creditors and is owed $17,000. Rusk has filed a petition against Wilk under the liquidation provisions of the Bankruptcy Code. Wilk has been unable to pay her debts as they become due, and Wilk's liabilities exceed her assets. Wilk has filed the papers that are required to oppose the bankruptcy petition. Which of the following statements is true?

A. The petition will be granted because Wilk is unable to pay her debts as they become due.

B. The petition will be granted because Wilk's liabilities exceed her assets.

C. The petition will be dismissed because three unsecured creditors must join in the filing of the petition.

D. The petition will be dismissed because the secured creditor failed to join in the filing of the petition.

Answer (A) is correct. *(CPA, adapted)*

REQUIRED: The true statement about the entry of an order for relief in an involuntary bankruptcy case.

DISCUSSION: In an involuntary bankruptcy case, a single creditor may file a petition for relief if (s)he is owed $14,425 or more and there are fewer than 12 creditors. The petition will be granted, even if it is contested, if the creditor can prove either that the debtor is not paying his/her debts as they become due or that, during the 120 days preceding the filing of the petition, a custodian, assignee, or general receiver took possession of the debtor's property. In this case, Rusk has met the conditions to file the petition, and Wilk is unable to pay her debts as they become due. Thus, even though the petition was contested, it will still be granted.

Answer (B) is incorrect. Having liabilities in excess of assets is not a criterion for granting of an involuntary petition for relief. Answer (C) is incorrect. Three unsecured creditors must join in filing the petition only if there are 12 or more creditors. Answer (D) is incorrect. A secured creditor is not required to join in filing the petition.

13. Flax, a sole proprietor, has been petitioned involuntarily into bankruptcy under the Federal Bankruptcy Code's liquidation provisions. Simon & Co., CPAs, has been appointed trustee of the bankruptcy estate. If Simon also wishes to act as the tax return preparer for the estate, which of the following statements is true?

A. Simon is prohibited from serving as both trustee and preparer. Serving in a dual capacity is a conflict of interest.

B. Although Simon may serve as both trustee and preparer, it is entitled to receive a fee only for the services rendered as a preparer.

C. Simon may employ itself to prepare tax returns if authorized by the court and may receive a separate fee for services in each capacity.

D. Although Simon may serve as both trustee and preparer, its fee for services in each capacity is determined solely by the size of the estate.

Answer (C) is correct. *(CPA, adapted)*

REQUIRED: The authority and compensation of a trustee in bankruptcy.

DISCUSSION: The trustee in bankruptcy is either appointed by the U.S. Trustee or elected by the creditors to administer most of the bankruptcy proceeding. Primary duties include collecting estate property and liquidating it. The trustee has authority, with court approval, to employ professionals such as attorneys or accountants to perform services requiring expertise. If (s)he has appropriate qualifications, the trustee may employ him/herself to perform a professional service, with court approval. Professionals employed by the trustee are entitled to reasonable compensation for their services out of the bankruptcy estate.

Answer (A) is incorrect. The trustee also may provide services for hire in a professional capacity, but only with approval of the court. Answer (B) is incorrect. The trustee is also entitled to compensation for professional services rendered with court approval. Answer (D) is incorrect. Although the estate is the source of payment, the amount is based on the value of the services rendered.

14. The filing of an involuntary bankruptcy petition under the Federal Bankruptcy Code

A. Terminates liens on exempt property.

B. Terminates all security interests in property in the bankruptcy estate.

C. Stops the debtor from incurring new debts.

D. Stops the enforcement of judgment liens against property in the bankruptcy estate.

Answer (D) is correct. *(CPA, adapted)*

REQUIRED: The effect of filing an involuntary petition in bankruptcy.

DISCUSSION: The automatic stay resulting from filing the petition operates to postpone certain actions against the debtor and his/her property whether the filing is voluntary or involuntary. All acts, with certain exceptions, to establish, enforce, or perfect any lien against estate property are stayed when a petition in bankruptcy is filed. The stay also applies to judgment liens.

Answer (A) is incorrect. The automatic stay does not affect the existence of liens on exempt property but postpones efforts to foreclose the liens. Answer (B) is incorrect. The automatic stay does not affect the existence of all security interests in estate property. Answer (C) is incorrect. The debtor may incur new debts.

15. Which of the following requirements must be met for creditors to file an involuntary bankruptcy petition under Chapter 7 or Chapter 11 of the Federal Bankruptcy Code?

A. The debtor must owe at least $14,425.

B. The debtor has not been paying its bona fide debts as they become due.

C. There must not be more than 12 creditors.

D. At least one fully secured creditor must join in the petition.

Answer (A) is correct. *(CPA, adapted)*

REQUIRED: The requirement for creditors to file an involuntary bankruptcy petition.

DISCUSSION: An involuntary bankruptcy petition may be filed by one or more creditors who have unsecured claims of at least $14,425 if there are fewer than 12 creditors. If there are 12 creditors or more, three or more who have unsecured claims of at least $14,425 in the aggregate must sign the petition. The petition will be granted, even if it is contested, if the creditor can prove either that the debtor is not paying his/her undisputed debts as they become due or that, during the 120 days preceding the filing of the petition, a custodian took possession of the debtor's property.

Answer (B) is incorrect. The petition also may be filed if a custodian, assignee, or general receiver took possession of the debtor's property during the 120 days preceding the filing of the petition. Answer (C) is incorrect. Three unsecured creditors may join in filing the petition if there are 12 or more creditors. Answer (D) is incorrect. A secured creditor is not required to join in filing the petition.

16. A contested involuntary petition in bankruptcy will be dismissed if the debtor

A. Owes unsecured obligations exceeding $14,425 to fewer than three creditors.

B. Had all its property taken to enforce a lien within 120 days of filing.

C. Is failing to pay undisputed debts as they become due.

D. Is an individual engaged in the business of farming.

Answer (D) is correct. *(CPA, adapted)*

REQUIRED: The basis for dismissal of an involuntary petition in bankruptcy.

DISCUSSION: Creditors may petition a debtor involuntarily into bankruptcy proceedings under Chapters 7 and 11 of the Bankruptcy Code. The debtor must be a person eligible for protection under the particular chapter. But an individual engaged in the business of farming may not be involuntarily petitioned into bankruptcy.

Answer (A) is incorrect. If the debtor has fewer than 12 different creditors, any one creditor who has an unsecured claim of at least $14,425 may file an involuntary petition. Answer (B) is incorrect. An involuntary petition will not be dismissed if, within 120 days before filing, a custodian assigned or general receiver took possession of all or most of the debtor's property to enforce a lien against the property. Answer (C) is incorrect. An involuntary petition will not be dismissed if the debtor is generally not paying his/her undisputed debts as they become due in the ordinary course of business.

Questions 17 through 19 are based on the following information.

On May 1, Dart, Inc., a closely held corporation, was petitioned involuntarily into bankruptcy under the liquidation provisions of Chapter 7 of the Federal Bankruptcy Code. Dart contested the petition.

Dart has not been paying its business debts as they become due, has defaulted on its mortgage loan payments, and owes back taxes to the IRS. The total cash value of Dart's bankruptcy estate after the sale of all assets and payment of administration expenses is $100,000.

A listing of Dart's creditors is presented in the next column.

- Fracon Bank is owed $75,000 principal and accrued interest on a mortgage loan secured by Dart's real property. The property was valued at and sold, in bankruptcy, for $70,000.
- The IRS has a $12,000 recorded judgment for unpaid corporate income tax.
- JOG Office Supplies has an unsecured claim of $3,000 that was timely filed.
- Nanstar Electric Co. has an unsecured claim of $1,500 that was not timely filed.
- Decoy Publications has a claim of $14,000, of which $2,000 is secured by Dart's inventory that was valued and sold, in bankruptcy, for $2,000. The claim was timely filed.

17. Assuming the IRS does not join in the filing of the involuntary petition, which of the following must file?

I. JOG Office Supplies
II. Nanstar Electric Co.
III. Decoy Publications
IV. Fracon Bank

A. I, II, III, and IV.

B. II and III only.

C. I and II only.

D. III only.

Answer (D) is correct. *(CPA, adapted)*

REQUIRED: The creditor(s) required to join in the filing of an involuntary petition.

DISCUSSION: If a debtor has fewer than 12 creditors, an involuntary bankruptcy petition may be filed by any one or more creditors who alone or together have $14,425 or more of unsecured claims (in excess of security interests). Decoy must file to meet the statutory requirement because it has $12,000 of unsecured debt. JOG ($3,000) or Fracon ($75,000 – $70,000 = $5,000) must join in the petition to meet the $14,425 minimum requirement. Given that the IRS does not file, Decoy is an indispensable party.

18. Which of the following statements accurately describes the result of Dart's opposing the petition?

A. Dart will win because the petition should have been filed under Chapter 11.

B. Dart will win because there are not more than 12 creditors.

C. Dart will lose because it is not paying its debts as they become due.

D. Dart will lose because of its debt to the IRS.

Answer (C) is correct. *(CPA, adapted)*

REQUIRED: The result of the debtor's opposing the petition.

DISCUSSION: There are two grounds for filing an involuntary petition for bankruptcy. Either the debtor is not paying its bills on time or a receiver took possession of all or most of the debtor's property in order to enforce a lien against the property within 120 days of the filing of the petition. Because Dart was not paying its bills when they became due, Dart will lose.

Answer (A) is incorrect. The involuntary petition could have been filed under Chapters 7 or 11 because Dart is not paying its bills on time. Answer (B) is incorrect. A debtor having fewer than 12 creditors may be petitioned into bankruptcy by any one or more creditors having alone or together at least $14,425 unsecured claims. Answer (D) is incorrect. IRS claims will not allow the petitioner(s) to win even though the IRS claims against Dart cannot be discharged.

19. Which of the following events will follow the filing of an unopposed Chapter 7 involuntary petition?

	A Trustee Will Be Appointed	A Stay Against Creditor Collection Proceedings Will Go into Effect
A.	Yes	Yes
B.	Yes	No
C.	No	Yes
D.	No	No

Answer (A) is correct. *(CPA, adapted)*

REQUIRED: The event(s) following the filing of an involuntary petition.

DISCUSSION: When an involuntary petition in bankruptcy is filed, the court issues an order of relief if the petition is unopposed. Otherwise, a hearing is conducted. If the judge finds that one of the statutory criteria is satisfied, (s)he also will issue an order for relief. The effect of the filing is to suspend almost all legal action and collection activities against the debtor. An interim trustee is appointed by the U.S. Trustee to manage the bankruptcy estate assets. The interim trustee serves until replaced by a permanent trustee elected by the creditors.

20. An involuntary petition in bankruptcy

A. Will be denied if a majority of creditors in amount and in number have agreed to a common law composition agreement.

B. Can be filed by creditors only once in a 7-year period.

C. May be successfully opposed by the debtor by proof that the debtor is solvent in the bankruptcy sense.

D. If not contested will result in the entry of an order for relief by the bankruptcy judge.

Answer (D) is correct. *(CPA, adapted)*

REQUIRED: The true statement about an involuntary petition.

DISCUSSION: If the uncontested involuntary petition is in proper form, the court will issue an order for relief. The debtor will be required to furnish the court with the same information as would have been contained in a voluntary petition, an interim trustee will be appointed to take control of the estate, and a creditors' meeting will be called. In general, the procedure is the same whether the bankruptcy is voluntary or involuntary.

Answer (A) is incorrect. One creditor (three if there are 12 or more creditors) with unsecured, noncontingent claims of $14,425 or more may petition a debtor into bankruptcy. Answer (B) is incorrect. A discharge may be granted to a debtor only once every 8 years. Answer (C) is incorrect. Insolvency in the equity sense (not being able to pay debts as they fall due) is a ground for an involuntary petition.

21. Which of the following statements is true about the voluntary filing of a petition in bankruptcy?

A. The debtor must be insolvent.

B. The petition may be filed by a married couple jointly.

C. If the debtor has 12 or more creditors, the debtor's unsecured claims must total at least $14,425.

D. If the debtor has fewer than 12 creditors, the debtor's unsecured claims must total at least $14,425.

Answer (B) is correct. *(CPA, adapted)*

REQUIRED: The true statement about the voluntary filing of a petition in bankruptcy.

DISCUSSION: A bankruptcy case may be commenced voluntarily or involuntarily. In a voluntary case, the debtor files the petition with the bankruptcy court. Debtors can include individuals, partnerships, corporations, and couples, if the husband and wife file together.

Answer (A) is incorrect. Insolvency is not a prerequisite for filing a voluntary petition. Answer (C) is incorrect. The 12-creditor threshold and $14,425 minimum apply only to involuntary petitions. Answer (D) is incorrect. The 12-creditor threshold and $14,425 minimum apply only to involuntary petitions.

22. Which of the following statements is true with respect to a voluntary bankruptcy proceeding under the Bankruptcy Code?

A. The debtor must be insolvent.

B. The liabilities of the debtor must total $14,425 or more.

C. It may be properly commenced and maintained by any person who is insolvent.

D. The filing of the bankruptcy petition constitutes an order for relief.

Answer (D) is correct. *(CPA, adapted)*

REQUIRED: The true statement with respect to a voluntary bankruptcy proceeding.

DISCUSSION: The voluntary bankruptcy petition is a formal request by the debtor to the court for an order for relief. An order for relief is automatically given to the debtor upon the filing of the petition.

Answer (A) is incorrect. Insolvency is not required. A statement that the debtor has debts is all that is needed. Answer (B) is incorrect. In a voluntary bankruptcy proceeding, there is no minimum amount of debtor liabilities. Answer (C) is incorrect. The courts have discretion not to grant relief that would constitute a substantial abuse of the bankruptcy laws. Also, certain entities, e.g., banks, are not eligible for voluntary bankruptcy.

23. On June 5, Year 1, Green rented equipment under a 5-year lease. On March 8, Year 6, Green was involuntarily petitioned into bankruptcy under the liquidation provisions of the Bankruptcy Code, and a trustee was appointed. The fair value of the equipment exceeds the balance of the lease payments due. The trustee

A. Must assume the equipment lease because its term exceeds 1 year.

B. Must assume and subsequently assign the equipment lease.

C. May elect not to assume the equipment lease.

D. May not reject the equipment lease because the fair market value of the equipment exceeds the balance of the payments due.

Answer (C) is correct. *(CPA, adapted)*

REQUIRED: The true statement about the bankruptcy trustee's choices regarding a lease.

DISCUSSION: A trustee in bankruptcy has broad powers to administer the estate. (S)he can, for example, assign, assume, or reject the debtor's executory contracts or unexpired leases. The trustee is empowered to breach bad bargains but to retain those that are assumable or assignable under state law. Breach, however, creates a claim against the estate. In this case, the trustee has several options, all subject to court approval: to assume and perform the unexpired lease, to assume and assign the unexpired lease to a third party, or to reject the unexpired lease. The trustee must act to assume the lease within 60 days after the order for relief is entered or it is deemed to be rejected.

Answer (A) is incorrect. The trustee may, but is not required to, assume the lease. Answer (B) is incorrect. The trustee may, but is not required to, assume the lease. Answer (D) is incorrect. Regardless of the fair market value of the equipment, the trustee may reject the equipment lease.

24. Which of the following is a true statement regarding assets included in a debtor's bankruptcy estate?

A. Transfers voided by the trustee are not included because the assets were not the debtor's when the petition was filed in bankruptcy.

B. Property subject to a security interest is not included because the secured creditor has the right to it.

C. All of the debtor's property other than that exempt from claims of creditors is included.

D. Most legal or equitable property interests of the debtor are included.

Answer (D) is correct. *(Publisher, adapted)*

REQUIRED: The true statement regarding the assets included in a debtor's estate.

DISCUSSION: By definition, a debtor's estate includes most of his/her legal or equitable interests as of the commencement of the case. Most interests are included whether or not the property is exempt from creditor claims. However, such items as subsequent earnings, after-acquired property, and certain contributions (e.g., to retirement plans and educational accounts) are excluded.

Answer (A) is incorrect. Property reclaimed by a trustee because of preferential or fraudulent transfers is for the benefit of the creditors and is included in the debtor's estate. Answer (B) is incorrect. The debtor has a residual interest in property subject to a security interest. A secured party simply has first rights to the property to satisfy his/her debt. Answer (C) is incorrect. Property specified as exempt from creditor claims is part of the estate.

25. Under the federal Bankruptcy Code, certain property acquired by the debtor after the filing of the petition becomes part of the bankruptcy estate. An example of such property is

A. Municipal bond interest received by the debtor within 180 days after the filing of the petition.

B. Alimony received by the debtor within 1 year after the filing of the petition.

C. Social Security payments received by the debtor within 180 days after the filing of the petition.

D. Gifts received by the debtor within 1 year after the filing of the petition.

Answer (A) is correct. *(CPA, adapted)*

REQUIRED: The after-acquired property included in the bankruptcy estate.

DISCUSSION: Generally, property acquired after the filing of a petition in bankruptcy is not included in the bankruptcy estate and is not held by the trustee for distribution to the debtor's creditors. However, the Bankruptcy Code provides various exceptions for certain property to which the debtor becomes entitled within 180 days after filing becomes part of the estate. Included are (1) inheritances; (2) property settlements in a divorce; (3) life insurance proceeds; (4) proceeds, products, offspring, rents, or profits received from property in the estate such as interest on bonds, rent from a building, or property insurance proceeds; and (5) property acquired by the estate or by the trustee under the avoidance powers. Additionally, the Code exempts Social Security payments, welfare benefits, disability payments, alimony and support awards, and most pension proceeds.

26. The Bankruptcy Code provides that a debtor is entitled to claim as exempt property the right to receive

	Social Security Benefits	Disability Benefits
A.	No	No
B.	Yes	No
C.	Yes	Yes
D.	No	Yes

Answer (C) is correct. *(CPA, adapted)*

REQUIRED: The benefit a debtor is entitled to claim as exempt property.

DISCUSSION: The filing of a petition gives rise to an estate in property. The estate is a legal entity separate from the debtor. The estate consists of all the debtor's legal and equitable interests in property, wherever located, on the date of filing. Community property is included. Proceeds and profits from the property also are included, as is certain other property acquired after filing. Certain assets in the estate are exempt from claims of creditors, such as rights to receive Social Security, disability benefits, alimony, child support, and certain pension benefits.

27. Which of the following does not constitute a valid debt that may be proved and allowed against the bankrupt's estate even if objection is made?

A. A workers' compensation award if the injury occurred before the adjudication of bankruptcy.

B. An open account.

C. Unmatured interest.

D. Fixed liabilities evidenced by a written instrument absolutely owing but not due at the time of the filing of a petition.

Answer (C) is correct. *(CPA, adapted)*

REQUIRED: The debt that is not valid (not allowable) against the estate of a bankrupt.

DISCUSSION: Under the Bankruptcy Act, a claim is a "right to payment, whether or not such right is reduced to judgment, liquidated, unliquidated, fixed, contingent, matured, unmatured, disputed, undisputed, legal, equitable, secured, or unsecured." However, unmatured interest, that is, interest accruing after the petition was filed, is not allowable because it is not a debt at that time. The distinction is between an amount absolutely owing, but not due, and unmatured interest. Because of the possibility of prepayment, unmatured interest is not an obligation that is absolutely owing.

28. Peters Co. repairs computers. On February 9, Stark Electronics Corp. sold Peters a circuit tester. Peters executed an installment note for the purchase price, a security agreement, and a financing statement that Stark filed on February 11. On April 13, creditors other than Stark filed an involuntary petition in bankruptcy against Peters. What is Stark's status in Peters' bankruptcy?

A. Stark will be treated as an unsecured creditor because Stark did not join in the filing against Peters.

B. Stark's security interest constitutes a voidable preference because the financing statement was not filed until February 11.

C. Stark's security interest constitutes a voidable preference because the financing statement was filed within 90 days before the bankruptcy proceeding was filed.

D. Stark is a secured creditor and can assert a claim to the circuit tester that will be superior to the claims of Peters' other creditors.

Answer (D) is correct. *(CPA, adapted)*

REQUIRED: The status in bankruptcy of a seller with a perfected security interest.

DISCUSSION: An enabling security interest is not a voidable preference. It arises from a transaction in which the creditor gives new value that is used by the debtor to obtain property in which the creditor receives a security interest. This interest is not voidable if it is perfected within 30 days after the debtor obtains possession. Stark perfected its purchase-money security interest by filing 2 days after the debtor received possession of the equipment. Thus, Stark's security interest cannot be voided as a preference by the trustee in bankruptcy. As a secured party, Stark is therefore entitled to receive payment of its claim up to the value of the security.

Answer (A) is incorrect. A secured creditor does not forfeit priority by not joining in filing an involuntary petition in bankruptcy. Answer (B) is incorrect. The security interest is not voidable if it is perfected within 30 days after the debtor obtains possession. Stark perfected its purchase-money security interest by filing 2 days after the debtor received possession of the equipment. Answer (C) is incorrect. Stark's security interest is not a voidable preference even though the transaction occurred within 90 days of bankruptcy. The transaction constituted the giving of new value (the machine) for the debt and security interest, and it was not on account of an antecedent debt.

29. Which of the following unsecured debts of $500 each would have the highest relative priority in the distribution of a bankruptcy estate?

A. Tax claims of state and municipal governmental units.

B. Liabilities to employee benefit plans arising from services rendered during the month preceding the filing of the petition.

C. Claims owed to customers who gave deposits for the purchase of undelivered consumer goods.

D. Wages earned by employees during the month preceding the filing of the petition.

Answer (D) is correct. *(CPA, adapted)*

REQUIRED: The relative priorities of unsecured debts.

DISCUSSION: The Bankruptcy Code sets priorities for the claims of unsecured creditors. All of the claims at a higher priority level must be satisfied in full before any lower priority claims will be considered. After payment of secured claims, the priorities are as follows: (1) domestic support obligations, (2) administrative expenses, (3) unsecured claims arising in the ordinary course of business after the petition was filed but before the order for relief was granted, (4) unsecured claims up to $5,400 for wages earned by an individual within 90 days before filing, (5) unsecured claims for contributions to employee benefit plans, (6) unsecured claims of grain producers and fishermen, (7) unsecured claims of depositors of money for the purchase of undelivered consumer goods, and (8) unsecured tax claims of governmental units.

Answer (A) is incorrect. Tax claims of state and municipal governmental units have a lower relative priority in a bankruptcy case than wages. Answer (B) is incorrect. Liabilities to employee benefit plans have a lower relative priority in a bankruptcy case than wages. Answer (C) is incorrect. Claims owed to customers who gave deposits for the purchase of undelivered consumer goods have a lower relative priority in a bankruptcy case than wages.

30. Rick Clark is a surety on a $100,000 obligation owed by Thompson to Owens. The debt is also secured by a $50,000 mortgage to Owens on Thompson's factory. Thompson is in bankruptcy. Clark has satisfied the debt. Clark is

A. Only entitled to the standing of a general creditor in bankruptcy.

B. A secured creditor to the extent of the $50,000 mortgage and a general creditor for the balance.

C. Entitled to nothing in bankruptcy because he assumed the risk.

D. Not entitled to a priority in bankruptcy, even though Owens could validly claim it.

Answer (B) is correct. *(CPA, adapted)*

REQUIRED: The status of a surety on a partially secured obligation when the debtor is in bankruptcy.

DISCUSSION: Once a surety has satisfied the debt, (s)he becomes subrogated to (acquires) the rights of the creditor against the debtor. Thus, the surety will have the same standing and preferences in bankruptcy as the creditor except with respect to wages. Because Owens was a secured creditor to the extent of the $50,000 mortgage and a general creditor for the balance, Clark will have the same standing.

Answer (A) is incorrect. Clark is a secured creditor to the extent of the $50,000 mortgage. Answer (C) is incorrect. The surety is entitled to whatever the creditor could have recovered. Answer (D) is incorrect. If Owens could validly claim a priority in bankruptcy, the surety who has satisfied the debt also can.

31. On July 15, White, a sole proprietor, was involuntarily petitioned into bankruptcy under the liquidation provisions of the Bankruptcy Code. White's nonexempt property has been converted to $13,000 cash, which is available to satisfy the following claims:

Unsecured claim for a prior year's state income tax	$10,000
Fee owed to Best & Co., CPAs, for services rendered from April 1 to June 30	6,000
Unsecured claim by Stieb for wages earned as an employee of White during March	3,000

There are no other claims. What is the maximum amount that will be distributed for the payment of the prior year's state income tax?

A. $4,000

B. $5,000

C. $7,000

D. $10,000

Answer (D) is correct. *(CPA, adapted)*

REQUIRED: The maximum amount that will be distributed for the payment of the state income tax.

DISCUSSION: The Bankruptcy Code requires secured claims to be satisfied to the extent of the security before any unsecured claims can be paid. All higher-ranking unsecured claims must be paid in full before any lower-ranking claims can be paid. According to the system of priorities, the state taxes rank highest among the listed claims. Thus, they must be satisfied in full ($10,000) before any other claims can be satisfied. Next in order is the fee owed to the CPA, which is a claim of a general unsecured creditor. The wages owed to Stieb also will become a claim of a general unsecured creditor (they were earned more than 90 days before the petition was filed) and will therefore be prorated with the other claims at this level. Stieb will receive $1,000.

32. Burt Burton's business was faltering and the creditors were beginning to demand immediate payment. Burton's brother had recently set up a new corporation for real estate investments. With the intent to save some of his assets, Burton transferred them to the new corporation with an understanding that Burton would receive stock after resolution of his financial problems. Five months later, Burton filed for bankruptcy. Will a trustee who has discovered the transfer be able to recover the assets?

A. The trustee cannot recover the assets because the transfer was more than 90 days before the petition was filed in bankruptcy.

B. The assets can be recovered as a fraudulent conveyance.

C. The assets can be recovered as a preferential transfer.

D. The assets cannot be recovered because the corporation is a separate legal entity.

Answer (B) is correct. *(Publisher, adapted)*

REQUIRED: The true statement regarding recovery of assets transferred by a debtor prior to bankruptcy.

DISCUSSION: A fraudulent conveyance is one made with actual intent to hinder, delay, or defraud creditors. A conveyance is also fraudulent if it results in insolvency or if the debtor receives less than a reasonable value while (s)he is insolvent. Fraudulent conveyances are voidable if the transfers are made within 2 years before the petition is filed. Thus, without regard to whether the new corporation had knowledge of Burton's fraud or insolvency, the trustee can recover the assets because Burton transferred them with intent to defraud creditors within 2 years of bankruptcy.

Answer (A) is incorrect. The trustee can recover the assets. They were fraudulently transferred within 2 years prior to the bankruptcy. Answer (C) is incorrect. The transfer was not a preferential transfer, but a fraudulent conveyance. A preferential transfer is made when one creditor is preferred over another. Answer (D) is incorrect. A fraudulent conveyance is voidable no matter to whom the transfer was made.

33. The federal bankruptcy act contains several important terms. One such term is "insider." The term is used in connection with preferences and preferential transfers. Who is not an insider?

A. A secured creditor having a security interest in at least 25% or more of the debtor's property.

B. A partnership in which the debtor is a general partner.

C. A corporation of which the debtor is a director.

D. A close blood relative of the debtor.

Answer (A) is correct. *(CPA, adapted)*

REQUIRED: The statement that does not describe an insider.

DISCUSSION: An insider has a sufficiently close relationship with the debtor to benefit from early information about its troubled financial status by obtaining a preference. The 90-day period for avoiding preferences is extended to 1 year for insiders. A secured creditor who otherwise lacks a close relationship with the debtor would not be considered an insider regardless of the size of the interest in the debtor's property.

Questions 34 through 36 are based on the following information. On August 1, Hall filed a voluntary petition under Chapter 7 of the Federal Bankruptcy Code. Hall's assets are sufficient to pay general creditors 40% of their claims. The following transactions occurred before the filing:

- On May 15, Hall gave a mortgage on Hall's home to National Bank to secure payment of a loan National had given Hall 2 years earlier. When the loan was made, Hall's twin was a National employee.
- On June 1, Hall purchased a boat from Olsen for $10,000 cash.
- On July 1, Hall paid off an outstanding credit card balance of $500. The original debt had been $2,500.

34. The National mortgage was

A. Preferential, because National would be considered an insider.

B. Preferential, because the mortgage was given to secure an antecedent debt.

C. Not preferential, because Hall is presumed insolvent when the mortgage was given.

D. Not preferential, because the mortgage was a security interest.

Answer (B) is correct. *(CPA, adapted)*

REQUIRED: The reason for classifying a transfer as preferential or nonpreferential.

DISCUSSION: The trustee has legal authority to set aside a preferential transfer. A preferential transfer is one made for the benefit of a creditor, within 90 days prior to filing the petition, and on account of an antecedent debt. The transfer must have occurred when the debtor was insolvent, and it must result in the creditor's receiving a larger portion of its claim than it otherwise would have received as a distribution in bankruptcy.

Answer (A) is incorrect. An otherwise nonpreferential transfer is preferential if made to an insider between 1 year and 90 days prior to filing. However, National is not related to the debtor in such a way as to be classified as an insider. Answer (C) is incorrect. A debtor is presumed insolvent during the 90 days prior to filing for purposes of preferential transfers. The transfer is preferential because the insolvency and other definitional requirements were met. Answer (D) is incorrect. Transfer of a security interest can meet the requirements to be classified as preferential.

35. The payment to Olsen was

A. Preferential, because the payment was made within 90 days of the filing of the petition.

B. Preferential, because the payment enabled Olsen to receive more than the other general creditors.

C. Not preferential, because Hall is presumed insolvent when the payment was made.

D. Not preferential, because the payment was a contemporaneous exchange for new value.

Answer (D) is correct. *(CPA, adapted)*

REQUIRED: The reason for classifying a transfer as preferential or nonpreferential.

DISCUSSION: A preference voidable by the trustee is a transfer (1) of the debtor's property to or for the benefit of a creditor, (2) on an antecedent debt, (3) made within 90 days before filing (1 year if the creditor is an insider), (4) made while the debtor was insolvent, and (5) that enables the creditor to receive more than (s)he would have in the bankruptcy proceeding. One important exception is a contemporaneous exchange in which the debtor receives new value, even if from a creditor.

Answer (A) is incorrect. Although the payment was made within 90 days of the filing of the petition, the transfer was in a contemporaneous exchange between the debtor and another (even a creditor) for new value. Answer (B) is incorrect. Although the payment enabled Olsen to receive more than the other general creditors, the transfer was in a contemporaneous exchange between the debtor and another (even a creditor) for new value. Answer (C) is incorrect. Insolvency at the time of transfer is required for the transfer to be voidable.

36. The credit card payment made by Hall on July 1 was

A. Preferential, because the payment was made within 90 days of the filing of the petition.

B. Preferential, because the payment was on account of an antecedent debt.

C. Not preferential, because the payment was for a consumer debt of less than $600.

D. Not preferential, because the payment was less than 40% of the original debt.

Answer (C) is correct. *(CPA, adapted)*

REQUIRED: The reason for classifying a transfer as preferential or nonpreferential.

DISCUSSION: A preference voidable by a trustee is a transfer (1) of the debtor's property to or for the benefit of a creditor, (2) on an antecedent debt, (3) made within 90 days before filing, (4) made while the debtor was insolvent, and (5) that enables the creditor to receive more than (s)he would have in the bankruptcy proceeding. One exception is payment of less than $600 on a consumer debt within the 90-day period.

Answer (A) is incorrect. The transfer was a remittance of up to $600 on a consumer debt. Answer (B) is incorrect. The transfer was a remittance of up to $600 on a consumer debt. Answer (D) is incorrect. The percentage of the original debt remitted is not determinative of whether the exception to voidability of the preference applies. The otherwise voidable transfer may not be set aside by the trustee if it is less than $600 and made on a consumer debt.

37. A person who voluntarily filed for bankruptcy and received a discharge under Chapter 7 of the Federal Bankruptcy Code

A. May obtain another voluntary discharge in bankruptcy under Chapter 7 after 5 years have elapsed from the date of the prior filing.

B. Will receive a discharge of all debts owed.

C. Is precluded from owning or operating a similar business for 2 years.

D. Must surrender for distribution to the creditors any amount received as an inheritance within 180 days after filing the petition.

Answer (D) is correct. *(CPA, adapted)*

REQUIRED: The true statement about a discharge under Chapter 7.

DISCUSSION: The bankruptcy estate available for distribution to creditors includes all the debtor's nonexempt legal and equitable interests in property on the date of filing. It includes proceeds and profits from that estate. Certain property acquired after filing is also included: inheritances, property settlements (divorce), and life insurance proceeds to which the debtor becomes entitled within 180 days after filing.

Answer (A) is incorrect. Discharge is barred if there was a Chapter 7 discharge within the 8 years preceding filing the petition. Answer (B) is incorrect. Certain debts are nondischargeable. Answer (C) is incorrect. There is no such requirement.

Questions 38 and 39 are based on the following information. On February 28, Year 1, Master, Inc., had total assets with a fair value of $1.2 million and total liabilities of $990,000. On January 15, Year 1, Master made a monthly installment note payment to Acme Distributors Corp., a creditor holding a properly perfected security interest in equipment having a fair value greater than the balance due on the note. On June 15, Year 1, Master voluntarily filed a petition in bankruptcy under the liquidation provisions of Chapter 7 of the Federal Bankruptcy Code. One year later, the equipment was sold for less than the balance due on the note to Acme.

38. If Master's voluntary petition is filed properly,

A. Master will be entitled to conduct its business as a debtor-in-possession unless the U.S. Trustee appoints a trustee.

B. A trustee must be appointed by the creditors.

C. Lawsuits by Master's creditors will be stayed by the Federal Bankruptcy Code.

D. The unsecured creditors must elect a creditors' committee of three to 11 members to consult with the trustee.

Answer (C) is correct. *(CPA, adapted)*

REQUIRED: The effect of properly filing a voluntary petition.

DISCUSSION: If a voluntary petition has been properly completed, sworn to, and signed by the debtor, it functions as an automatic order for relief. One effect is to stay most legal proceedings and other activities of creditors seeking to collect from the debtor. Secured creditors' actions also are stayed. The court may decide a creditor is entitled to relief from the automatic stay on the grounds that it does afford the creditor adequate protection.

Answer (A) is incorrect. The U.S. Trustee appoints an interim trustee. But, with court approval, the debtor may file a bond and reacquire property under the trustee's control. Answer (B) is incorrect. Under Chapter 7, the U.S. Trustee appoints an interim trustee. The creditors may then elect a permanent trustee. Otherwise, the interim trustee continues as trustee. Answer (D) is incorrect. The creditors may, but do not have a legal duty to, elect such a committee.

39. Which of the following statements correctly describes Acme's distribution from Master's bankruptcy estate?

A. Acme will receive the total amount it is owed, even if the proceeds from the sale of the collateral were less than the balance owed by Master.

B. Acme will have the same priority as unsecured general creditors to the extent that the proceeds from the sale of its collateral are insufficient to satisfy the amount owed by Master.

C. The total proceeds from the sale of the collateral will be paid to Acme even if they are less than the balance owed by Master, provided there is sufficient cash to pay all administrative costs associated with the bankruptcy.

D. Acme will receive only the proceeds from the sale of the collateral in full satisfaction of the debt owed by Master.

Answer (B) is correct. *(CPA, adapted)*

REQUIRED: The portion of a bankruptcy estate distributable to a secured creditor.

DISCUSSION: Under the Bankruptcy Code, to the extent a creditor's claim is secured, it must be satisfied in full before distribution is made on any other claims. But the secured creditor is treated the same as a general unsecured creditor to the extent its claim exceeds the value of the collateral. Note that the collateral is part of the estate. The secured creditor is entitled to the security interest as opposed to the property itself.

Answer (A) is incorrect. Acme is treated as a general unsecured creditor with respect to any portion of its claim that exceeds the value of the collateral. Answer (C) is incorrect. The security interest must be satisfied to the extent of the security before priority claims are paid. Answer (D) is incorrect. Acme may receive an amount in addition to the proceeds of the collateral but only in its capacity as an unsecured creditor.

40. Under the federal Bankruptcy Code, which of the following rights or powers does a trustee in bankruptcy not have?

A. The power to prevail against a creditor with an unperfected security interest.

B. The power to require persons holding the debtor's property at the time the bankruptcy petition is filed to deliver the property to the trustee.

C. The right to use any grounds available to the debtor to obtain the return of the debtor's property.

D. The right to void any statutory liens against the debtor's property that were effective before the bankruptcy petition was filed.

Answer (D) is correct. *(CPA, adapted)*

REQUIRED: The right or power not held by a trustee in bankruptcy.

DISCUSSION: The trustee does not have the right to void statutory liens against the debtor's property that were effective before the petition was filed. But statutory liens on real property (e.g., mechanic's liens or materialman's liens) that are not effective until the filing of the petition or until the time when the debtor becomes insolvent are voidable. The trustee also may void liens that are not perfected against a good faith purchaser on the date of filing.

Answer (A) is incorrect. The trustee has rights in some circumstances that are equivalent to those of a judicial lien creditor. Such a creditor prevails against a creditor with an unperfected security interest. Answer (B) is incorrect. The trustee can marshal the assets of the debtor's estate. Answer (C) is incorrect. The trustee "stands in the shoes" of the debtor for some purposes.

41. Which asset is included in a debtor's bankruptcy estate?

A. Proceeds from a life insurance policy received 90 days after the petition was filed.

B. An inheritance received 270 days after the petition was filed.

C. Property from a divorce settlement received 365 days after the petition was filed.

D. Wages earned by the debtor after the petition was filed.

Answer (A) is correct. *(CPA, adapted)*

REQUIRED: The asset included in a debtor's bankruptcy estate.

DISCUSSION: Any asset in which the debtor has a legal or equitable interest at the date the proceedings began is included in the estate. Other property may be added to the estate. For example, it includes property acquired by the debtor within 180 days after filing the petition if the property was acquired (1) by inheritance by will or intestate succession, (2) as proceeds of a life insurance policy, or (3) from a property settlement in a divorce case.

Answer (B) is incorrect. An inheritance must be received within 180 days after filing to be included. Answer (C) is incorrect. The debtor must become entitled to property from a divorce settlement within 180 days after filing for it to be included. Answer (D) is incorrect. Wages earned by the debtor after the petition for relief was filed are not included in the estate.

42. Which of the following transfers by a debtor, within 90 days of filing for bankruptcy, could be set aside as a preferential payment?

A. Making a gift to charity.

B. Paying a business utility bill.

C. Borrowing money from a bank secured by giving a mortgage on business property.

D. Prepaying an installment loan on inventory.

Answer (D) is correct. *(CPA, adapted)*

REQUIRED: The reason for the status of a transfer as preferential or nonpreferential.

DISCUSSION: A preferential transfer is one made for the benefit of a creditor within 90 days prior to filing the petition and on account of an antecedent (preexisting) debt. The transfer must have been made when the debtor was insolvent, and it must have resulted in the creditor's receiving a larger portion of its claim than it otherwise would have received as a distribution in the bankruptcy proceeding. A prepayment is on account of an existing debt and is therefore a voidable preference.

Answer (A) is incorrect. A gift to a charity is not on account of an antecedent (preexisting) debt. Answer (B) is incorrect. Payment of accounts payable in the ordinary course of the debtor's business is not a voidable preference. Answer (C) is incorrect. A contemporaneous exchange between the debtor and another, even a creditor, for new value may not be set aside. The transfer of a security interest enables the debtor to acquire the new property.

43. In a voluntary bankruptcy proceeding under Chapter 7 of the Federal Bankruptcy Code, which of the following claims incurred within 180 days prior to filing will be paid first?

A. Unsecured federal taxes.

B. Utility bills up to $1,000.

C. Voluntary contributions to employee benefit plans.

D. Employee vacation and sick pay up to $11,725 per employee.

Answer (D) is correct. *(CPA, adapted)*

REQUIRED: The true statement about the relative priorities of claims in a bankruptcy case.

DISCUSSION: Secured claims must be satisfied in full before any unsecured claims may be paid. Unsecured claims with a higher priority are then paid in full before lower priority claims. Claims up to $11,725 for wages earned by an individual within 180 days before filing have a higher priority than all other unsecured claims except (1) domestic support obligations, (2) administrative expenses, and (3) claims arising in the ordinary course of business after the petition was filed but before the order for relief was granted (gap claims). Employee vacation pay and sick pay are forms of compensation (wages).

Answer (A) is incorrect. A claim for unsecured federal taxes has a lower priority than a claim for wages. Answer (B) is incorrect. A claim for utility bills up to $1,000 is not a priority claim. Answer (C) is incorrect. A claim for voluntary contributions to employee benefit plans has a lower priority than a claim for wages.

44. Molly Finn filed a voluntary petition in bankruptcy. She provided a list of creditors and debts to the courts as required. However, Ann Sawyer was unintentionally left out of the list of creditors and debts. The creditors held their first meeting on March 5. It is now May 31 and Sawyer has just learned of the bankruptcy of Finn. Will she be able to share in the distribution from the estate?

A. It is too late to file a claim in bankruptcy.

B. Sawyer is not entitled to share in the estate assets because (s)he was not listed by Finn.

C. Sawyer's claim will be given priority due to the mistake.

D. Sawyer can file a proof of claim, but it must be allowed by the court.

Answer (D) is correct. *(Publisher, adapted)*

REQUIRED: The true statement regarding a creditor who learns of the debtor's bankruptcy after being left out of the list of creditors.

DISCUSSION: To share in the distribution of the bankrupt's estate, a creditor must file a proof of claim with the court within 90 days after the first creditors' meeting. The proof of claim is simply a statement signed by the creditor explaining the nature and source of the claim and the date it is due. All claims not objected to are deemed allowed. If objected to, a claim may be allowed after a hearing to determine its validity.

Answer (A) is incorrect. A claim can still be filed because 90 days have not passed since the first creditors' meeting. Answer (B) is incorrect. Finn's failure to list Sawyer as a creditor does not prevent Sawyer from filing a timely proof of claim and sharing in the estate. Answer (C) is incorrect. No priority is allowed a creditor omitted from the list of creditors. However, if Sawyer had not learned of the bankruptcy, Finn would not be discharged as to that debt.

20.3 Bankruptcy Liquidations

45. Which of the following types of claims is paid first in the distribution of a bankruptcy estate under the liquidation provisions of Chapter 7 of the Federal Bankruptcy Code if the petition was filed on July 15?

A. A secured debt properly perfected on March 20.

B. Inventory purchased and delivered August 1.

C. Employee wages due April 30.

D. Federal tax lien filed June 30.

Answer (A) is correct. *(CPA, adapted)*

REQUIRED: The claim that will be paid first.

DISCUSSION: The Bankruptcy Act classifies creditors into several categories according to the priority of their claims against the debtor. It also states that secured creditors' claims will be satisfied in full up to the extent of the value of the security before unsecured creditors' claims will be considered. To the extent the security is insufficient, the secured creditor becomes an unsecured creditor. Even if it is a secured claim, the tax lien has a lower priority than the secured debt perfected earlier.

Answer (B) is incorrect. Secured claims are satisfied before unsecured claims are satisfied. Answer (C) is incorrect. Secured claims are satisfied before unsecured claims are satisfied. Answer (D) is incorrect. Even if the tax lien is a secured claim, the first perfected of two security interests has priority.

46. On June 9, Amy Aker transferred property she owned to her son. The property was collateral for Aker's obligation to Simon. Aker transferred the property with the intent to defraud Simon. On July 7, Aker filed a voluntary bankruptcy petition. Which of the following statements is true?

A. Only Simon's debt will be excepted from Aker's discharge in bankruptcy.

B. Aker will be denied a discharge in bankruptcy.

C. The transfer will be set aside because it constitutes a preference.

D. Aker will receive a discharge in bankruptcy of all debts.

Answer (B) is correct. *(CPA, adapted)*

REQUIRED: The true statement about transfers of property with the intent to defraud.

DISCUSSION: Under the Bankruptcy Code, the court will deny a general discharge of a debtor's liabilities if, within 2 years of filing the petition for relief, the debtor transfers property with the intent to hinder, delay, or defraud any creditor. Because Aker transferred the property with the intent to defraud Simon within 2 years of filing the petition for relief, she will be denied a general discharge.

Answer (A) is incorrect. The fraudulent act will lead to a denial of a general discharge of the debtor's liabilities. Answer (C) is incorrect. One of the elements of a preferential transfer is the transfer of property to a creditor. Aker's son was not a creditor. Answer (D) is incorrect. Aker will be denied a discharge in bankruptcy of all debts.

47. A claim will not be discharged in a bankruptcy proceeding if it

A. Is brought by a secured creditor and remains unsatisfied after receipt of the proceeds from the disposition of the collateral.

B. Is for unintentional torts that resulted in bodily injury to the claimant.

C. Arises from an extension of credit based upon false representations.

D. Arises out of the breach of a contract by the debtor.

Answer (C) is correct. *(CPA, adapted)*

REQUIRED: The grounds for a claim's not being discharged in bankruptcy.

DISCUSSION: A discharge terminates the dischargeable debts. It avoids existing judgments and operates as an injunction against further proceedings on the discharged obligations. But not all debts are dischargeable in bankruptcy. For example, debts incurred through false representations will not be discharged.

Answer (A) is incorrect. To the extent unsatisfied after receipt of proceeds of the collateral, a secured creditor is treated the same as a general unsecured creditor. Answer (B) is incorrect. Obligations arising from the debtor's negligence are dischargeable. Answer (D) is incorrect. Liability for breach of contract is dischargeable in bankruptcy.

48. Which of the following provable debts is not discharged by bankruptcy?

A. Hospital bills.

B. Wages earned more than 180 days prior to commencement of bankruptcy proceedings.

C. Liability for breach of a fiduciary duty resulting from a fraud committed by the debtor-fiduciary.

D. Rent payments due that have accrued within 3 months of the filing of the petition in bankruptcy.

Answer (C) is correct. *(CPA, adapted)*

REQUIRED: The provable debt not discharged by bankruptcy.

DISCUSSION: Generally, the debts of a qualified debtor are dischargeable in bankruptcy. Certain debts are excepted due to public policy. One such policy is that a fiduciary should not be able to escape the consequences of abusing his/her position. Liability for fraud committed by a fiduciary, therefore, is not dischargeable in bankruptcy.

Answer (A) is incorrect. Hospital bills may be discharged by bankruptcy. Answer (B) is incorrect. Wages earned more than 180 days prior to commencement of bankruptcy proceedings may be discharged by bankruptcy. Answer (D) is incorrect. Rent payments due that have accrued within 3 months of the filing of the petition in bankruptcy may be discharged by bankruptcy.

49. Larson, an unemployed carpenter, filed for voluntary bankruptcy on August 14. Larson's liabilities are listed below.

Credit card charges due 1 year ago	$3,000
Bank loans incurred 2 months ago	5,000
Medical expenses incurred 7 years ago	7,000
Alimony due 2 years ago	1,000

Under the provisions of Chapter 7 of the Federal Bankruptcy Code, Larson's discharge will not apply to the unpaid

A. Credit card charges.

B. Bank loans.

C. Medical expenses.

D. Alimony.

Answer (D) is correct. *(CPA, adapted)*

REQUIRED: The debt not discharged in Chapter 7 bankruptcy proceedings.

DISCUSSION: Under Chapter 7, assets of the debtor are liquidated and proceeds are applied to his/her debts. (S)he is then granted a general discharge from most obligations which remain unsatisfied. But certain obligations are not discharged, including unpaid alimony and child support, certain taxes, penalties imposed by governmental entities, and liabilities arising from false representations or actual fraud.

Answer (A) is incorrect. Credit card charges are subject to the general discharge under Chapter 7. Answer (B) is incorrect. Bank loans are subject to the general discharge under Chapter 7. Answer (C) is incorrect. Medical expenses are subject to the general discharge under Chapter 7.

50. Which of the following acts by a debtor could result in a bankruptcy court's revoking the debtor's discharge?

I. Failure to list one creditor.

II. Failure to answer correctly material questions on the bankruptcy petition.

A. I only.

B. II only.

C. Both I and II.

D. Neither I nor II.

Answer (B) is correct. *(CPA, adapted)*

REQUIRED: The basis, if any, for revoking a discharge in bankruptcy.

DISCUSSION: Fraud or dishonesty committed by the debtor during the bankruptcy proceedings is the basis for revocation of discharge by the Bankruptcy Court. Revocation may occur after a request by either the trustee or a creditor, notice, and a hearing. The time limit is 1 year. A debt to a creditor omitted from the list of creditors is not discharged, but proof of dishonesty or fraud is required to revoke the general discharge.

51. Danielle is a debtor with primarily consumer debts who has filed a voluntary petition under the Chapter 7 liquidation provisions of the Bankruptcy Code. Danielle's filing is presumed to be abusive under the means test if

A. Her current monthly income multiplied by 12 exceeds the applicable state median income.

B. Her current monthly income after deductions is $100, and her general unsecured debt is $25,000.

C. Her current monthly income after deductions is at least $195.42.

D. She filed the petition in bad faith.

Answer (C) is correct. *(Publisher, adapted)*

REQUIRED: The circumstance in which filing of a voluntary petition is presumed to be abusive under the means test.

DISCUSSION: Under the means test, the mandatory trigger point for presumed abuse is that the debtor has at least $195.42 of current monthly income after deductions. If CMI after deductions is less than $117.08, the presumption never arises. For other amounts, the presumption arises if 5-year income [(CMI – allowed deductions) × 60 months] suffices to pay 25% or more of general unsecured debt.

Answer (A) is incorrect. If the debtor's income (CMI × 12) exceeds the relevant state median income, any party in interest has standing to seek dismissal of the petition. But presumption of abuse is not automatic in this case. The means test is a function of the CMI after deductions and, possibly, general unsecured debt. Answer (B) is incorrect. General unsecured debt exceeds $24,000 [($100 × 60 months ÷ 25]. Answer (D) is incorrect. The presumption of abuse arises only under the means test. Bad faith is one of the general grounds for a finding of abuse.

52. Under the liquidation provisions of Chapter 7 of the Federal Bankruptcy Code, a debtor will be denied a discharge in bankruptcy if the debtor

A. Fails to list a creditor.

B. Owes alimony and support payments.

C. Cannot pay administration expenses.

D. Refuses to explain satisfactorily a loss of assets.

Answer (D) is correct. *(CPA, adapted)*

REQUIRED: The act resulting in a denial of discharge.

DISCUSSION: In a Chapter 7 proceeding, (1) the debtor's nonexempt assets are liquidated; (2) creditors are paid pro rata according to the priority of their claims; and (3) the debtor, if an individual, is discharged from unsatisfied obligations except certain nondischargeable debts listed in the Bankruptcy Act. The purpose of Chapter 7 is to assure a fair distribution of assets among the creditors and provide an honest individual with a fresh start. Failure of a debtor to explain satisfactorily the loss or disappearance of assets results in denial of discharge.

Answer (A) is incorrect. Not listing a creditor on a schedule required to be filed with the court will not result in denial of discharge, but the debtor will remain liable for the unlisted claim. Answer (B) is incorrect. Alimony and support payments are never discharged in bankruptcy. Answer (C) is incorrect. Individuals unable to pay administrative expenses are not denied discharge.

53. Eagle Corp. is a general creditor of Dodd. Dodd filed a petition in bankruptcy under the liquidation provisions of the Bankruptcy Code. Eagle wishes to have the bankruptcy court either deny Dodd a general discharge or not have its debt discharged. The discharge will be granted, and it will include Eagle's debt even if

A. Dodd filed and received a previous discharge in bankruptcy under the liquidation provisions within 5 years of the filing of the present petition.

B. Eagle's debt is unscheduled.

C. Eagle was a secured creditor not fully satisfied from the proceeds obtained on disposition of the collateral.

D. Dodd unjustifiably failed to preserve the records from which Dodd's financial condition might be ascertained.

Answer (C) is correct. *(CPA, adapted)*

REQUIRED: The circumstance that will allow discharge of a general creditor's debt.

DISCUSSION: Chapter 7 contains the liquidation provisions of the Bankruptcy Code. The nature of the debt or debtor or the debtor's conduct may prevent discharge of all or specific debts. However, secured creditor status does not guarantee full satisfaction of a debt. If the secured claim is not fully satisfied by the proceeds resulting from the sale of collateral, the unsatisfied portion of the debt may still be discharged.

Answer (A) is incorrect. Discharge will not be granted if an objection is made and the debtor was granted a discharge under Chapter 7 in a case commenced within 8 years of the petition in the current case. Answer (B) is incorrect. Unscheduled debts are not discharged. Answer (D) is incorrect. The debtor's unjustifiable failure to preserve the debtor's financial records is reason to deny discharge of all indebtedness.

54. Rolf Adenstedt, an individual, filed a voluntary petition in bankruptcy. A general discharge in bankruptcy will be denied if Rolf

A. Negligently made preferential transfers to certain creditors within 90 days of filing the petition.

B. Unjustifiably failed to preserve his books and records.

C. Filed a fraudulent federal income tax return 2 years prior to filing the petition.

D. Obtained a loan by using financial statements that he knew were false.

Answer (B) is correct. *(CPA, adapted)*

REQUIRED: The action that is grounds for denying a general discharge in bankruptcy.

DISCUSSION: Discharge will be denied if the debtor conceals or destroys property with the intent to hinder, delay, or defraud a creditor, or fails to adequately explain the loss of assets. Similarly, unjustifiable or fraudulent concealment or destruction of the debtor's financial records is a basis for denying discharge of indebtedness.

Answer (A) is incorrect. Preferential transfers resulting from the debtor's negligence will result only in avoidance of the transfers. Answer (C) is incorrect. Most tax debts are not dischargeable. Moreover, filing a fraudulent return will not affect the general discharge. Answer (D) is incorrect. The debtor's fraudulent use of financial statements may result in denial of discharge of the specific loan, but will not affect the general discharge.

55. In general, which of the following debts will be discharged under the voluntary liquidation provisions of the Bankruptcy Code?

A. A debt incurred more than 90 days before the filing of the bankruptcy petition and not disclosed in the petition.

B. Income taxes due as the result of filing a fraudulent return 7 years prior to the filing of the bankruptcy petition.

C. A debt arising before the filing of the bankruptcy petition caused by the debtor's negligence.

D. Alimony payments owed to the debtor's spouse under a separation agreement entered into prior to the filing of the bankruptcy petition.

Answer (C) is correct. *(CPA, adapted)*

REQUIRED: The debt that will be discharged under the voluntary liquidation provisions.

DISCUSSION: Discharge in a voluntary liquidation proceeding may be denied based on certain acts or circumstances of the debtor or the nature of particular debts if a trustee or creditor objects to the discharge. Examples of debts that will be statutorily denied a discharge include penalties imposed by government entities, unpaid taxes, and unpaid child support. A debt that was the result of negligence, e.g., from a malpractice claim, in contrast to willful or malicious activity, is dischargeable.

Answer (A) is incorrect. Debts not disclosed in the petition are not discharged unless the creditor had knowledge of the petition. Answer (B) is incorrect. Ordinarily, the only tax debts that will not be discharged are income taxes due from the filing of a tax return within the last 3 years. However, any debt that was incurred by fraudulent means will not be discharged regardless of the time the return was filed. Answer (D) is incorrect. The Code specifically denies a discharge for any unpaid alimony or child support.

Questions 56 through 58 are based on the following information.

On May 1, Dart Inc., a closely held corporation, was petitioned involuntarily into bankruptcy under the liquidation provisions of Chapter 7 of the Federal Bankruptcy Code. Dart contested the petition.

Dart has not been paying its business debts as they become due, has defaulted on its mortgage loan payments, and owes back taxes to the IRS. The total cash value of Dart's bankruptcy estate after the sale of all assets and payment of administration expenses is $100,000.

A listing of Dart's creditors is presented in the next column.

- Fracon Bank is owed $75,000 principal and accrued interest on a mortgage loan secured by Dart's real property. The property was valued at and sold, in bankruptcy, for $70,000.
- The IRS has a $12,000 recorded judgment for unpaid corporate income tax.
- JOG Office Supplies has an unsecured claim of $3,000 that was timely filed.
- Nanstar Electric Co. has an unsecured claim of $1,500 that was not timely filed.
- Decoy Publications has a claim of $14,000, of which $2,000 is secured by Dart's inventory that was valued and sold, in bankruptcy, for $2,000. The claim was timely filed.

56. Assuming the bankruptcy estate has been distributed, what dollar amount did Nanstar Electric receive?

A. $0

B. $800

C. $1,000

D. $1,200

Answer (A) is correct. *(CPA, adapted)*

REQUIRED: The amount distributed to an unsecured creditor who did not file a timely claim.

DISCUSSION: Nanstar will not receive any money when the bankruptcy estate is distributed because all the other parties either have claims secured by collateral or filed their claims in a timely manner. Because Nanstar did not properly file its claim in bankruptcy, all other creditors will be paid first. Nanstar will receive no payment because the other claims against the bankruptcy estate exceed the estate's cash value.

57. Assuming the bankruptcy estate has been distributed, what total dollar amount did Fracon Bank receive on its secured and unsecured claims?

A. $70,000

B. $72,000

C. $74,000

D. $75,000

Answer (C) is correct. *(CPA, adapted)*

REQUIRED: The amount distributed to a creditor with secured and unsecured claims.

DISCUSSION: Fracon will receive a total of $74,000 because $5,000 of its $75,000 claim against Dart was not recovered when the real estate was sold for $70,000. Hence, Fracon had a secured claim of $70,000, which will be fully paid, and an unsecured claim of $5,000. Because the bankruptcy estate was insufficient to pay the general unsecured claims in full, each creditor received a pro rata share of the remaining proceeds. Given that Fracon held one-fourth of the valid claims ($5,000 ÷ $20,000), it received one-fourth of the remaining proceeds of $16,000, or $4,000, to settle its unsecured claim.

58. Assuming the bankruptcy estate has been distributed, what dollar amount did the IRS receive?

A. $0

B. $8,000

C. $10,000

D. $12,000

Answer (D) is correct. *(CPA, adapted)*

REQUIRED: The amount distributed to the IRS by the bankruptcy estate.

DISCUSSION: The IRS should have received the full amount owed to it. Taxes are a priority claim that is paid in full before any general unsecured creditors are paid. Thus, the proceeds from the sale of Dart's assets would go to the IRS after satisfying the secured claims and any other unsecured claims having a higher priority than unpaid taxes.

Answer (A) is incorrect. Debts owed to the IRS for unpaid income taxes have priority over general unsecured creditors. Answer (B) is incorrect. The unpaid portion of the income taxes owed to the IRS is a priority unsecured claim. After secured claims, the taxes will be paid in full before payment on any general unsecured claims. Answer (C) is incorrect. The unpaid portion of the income taxes owed to the IRS is a priority unsecured claim. After secured claims, the taxes will be paid in full before payment on any general unsecured claims.

59. By signing a reaffirmation agreement on April 15, Year 1, a debtor agreed to pay certain debts that would be discharged in bankruptcy. On June 20, Year 1, the debtor's attorney filed the reaffirmation agreement and an affidavit with the court indicating that the debtor understood the consequences of the reaffirmation agreement. The debtor obtained a discharge on August 25, Year 1. The reaffirmation agreement would be enforceable only if it was

A. Made after discharge.

B. Approved by the bankruptcy court.

C. Not for a household purpose debt.

D. Not rescinded before discharge.

Answer (D) is correct. *(CPA, adapted)*

REQUIRED: The enforceable reaffirmation of debt.

DISCUSSION: To be enforceable, a reaffirmation agreement must conspicuously state the debtor's right of rescission. The debtor has the right to rescind the reaffirmation until the later of the discharge or 60 days after the agreement is filed with the court.

Answer (A) is incorrect. To be legally enforceable, the reaffirmation agreement must be entered into prior to the general discharge in bankruptcy. Answer (B) is incorrect. Court approval is required if the debtor has no attorney. In the alternative, the reaffirmation agreement may be accompanied by an affidavit filed by the debtor's attorney stating that (1) the debtor has been advised of the legal effect of reaffirmation, (2) the debtor voluntarily and knowingly entered into the agreement, and (3) payment will cause no undue hardship. Answer (C) is incorrect. Almost any debt, including one incurred for household purposes, may be reaffirmed.

60. On February 28, Year 1, Master, Inc., had total assets with a fair value of $1.2 million and total liabilities of $990,000. On June 15, Year 1, Master voluntarily filed a petition in bankruptcy under the liquidation provisions of Chapter 7 of the Federal Bankruptcy Code. If a creditor challenged Master's right to file, the petition would be dismissed

A. If Master had fewer than 12 creditors at the time of filing.

B. Unless Master can show that a reorganization under Chapter 11 of the Federal Bankruptcy Code would have been unsuccessful.

C. Unless Master can show that it is unable to pay its debts in the ordinary course of business or as they come due.

D. If Master is an insurance company.

Answer (D) is correct. *(CPA, adapted)*

REQUIRED: The prerequisite to filing a voluntary petition under Chapter 7's liquidation provisions.

DISCUSSION: A debtor may voluntarily file a petition for protection from creditors under Chapter 7's liquidation provisions. The debtor, if an eligible person, need only state that it has debts. Persons ineligible to file under Chapter 7 include insurance companies, banks, and others.

Answer (A) is incorrect. The number of creditors is relevant to creditor eligibility to file an involuntary petition. Answer (B) is incorrect. Liquidation and discharge under Chapter 7 is not restricted to cases in which Chapter 11 reorganization would not be successful. Answer (C) is incorrect. Insolvency is not a condition for Chapter 7 dismissal.

20.4 Reorganizations and Adjustments

61. A plan of reorganization under Chapter 11

A. May be filed by any party in interest for 120 days after entry of the order for relief.

B. Must be filed by the trustee and approved by the creditors within 180 days after entry of the order for relief.

C. Must treat all classes of claims and ownership interests equally.

D. Must treat all claims or interests in the same class equally.

Answer (D) is correct. *(Publisher, adapted)*

REQUIRED: The true statement about a plan of reorganization.

DISCUSSION: The plan must (1) designate classes of creditors' claims and owners' interests; (2) state the treatment to be given each class; (3) indicate which classes will or will not be impaired; (4) allow for equal treatment of the members within a class unless they agree otherwise; and (5) provide for an adequate method of payment. If the debtor is a corporation, the plan must also protect voting rights, state that no nonvoting stock will be issued, and require that selection of officers and directors be effected in a manner to protect the parties in interest.

Answer (A) is incorrect. Only the debtor may file a plan within 120 days after entry of the order for relief (unless a trustee has been appointed). If the debtor fails to file within 120 days after entry of the order for relief, any party in interest may file a plan. Answer (B) is incorrect. Only the debtor may file a plan within 120 days after entry of the order for relief (unless a trustee has been appointed). If the creditors do not approve of the plan within 180 days of the entry of the order for relief, any party in interest may file a plan. Answer (C) is incorrect. The plan must be fair and equitable but all classes need not be treated the same. However, no party may receive less than the amount that would have been distributed in a liquidation.

62. Englebert is a professor of business at a university. He expected a large raise this year and made a lot of expenditures, including a trip around the world, on credit. However, university funding has been reduced and the raise did not go through. Englebert cannot pay his debts as they become due. Englebert

A. Can request an adjustment of debts under Chapter 13.

B. Cannot request a reorganization under Chapter 11.

C. Can be required to go through a bankruptcy liquidation.

D. Can be required by creditors to go through an adjustment of debts under Chapter 13.

Answer (A) is correct. *(Publisher, adapted)*

REQUIRED: The true statement concerning an individual who cannot pay his/her debts.

DISCUSSION: Chapter 13 of the Bankruptcy Act provides a procedure for an individual with regular income to submit a plan for the payment of a portion of his/her debts while retaining a sufficient amount of income to live and support his/her family. The petitioner must be an individual who owes unsecured debts of less than $360,475 and secured debts of less than $1,081,400. The court grants a discharge of most remaining debts after the plan has been carried out.

Answer (B) is incorrect. Any person who may go through a liquidation bankruptcy (except stockbrokers and commodity brokers) may file for a reorganization under Chapter 11. Answer (C) is incorrect. An individual may request relief under Chapter 11 or Chapter 13 to avoid a bankruptcy liquidation if the requirements of those sections are met. Answer (D) is incorrect. Chapter 13 is a voluntary provision, and a creditor of the debtor cannot file an involuntary petition under Chapter 13.

63. Under Chapter 13 of the Bankruptcy Code, an individual debtor or sole proprietor may propose a composition plan to repay his/her debts. If the debtor's income at least equals the relevant state median income,

A. The debtor must repay all claims by creditors within 3 years.

B. The debtor is not entitled to injunctive relief against his/her creditors while the plan is being carried out.

C. The debtor pays creditors less than 100% of their claims.

D. No trustee may be appointed.

Answer (C) is correct. *(Publisher, adapted)*

REQUIRED: The true statement about a composition plan under Chapter 13.

DISCUSSION: A composition plan may be proposed by a debtor under Chapter 13 of the Bankruptcy Code. Under a composition plan, a debtor pays his/her creditors less than 100% of their claims on a pro rata basis for each class of claims. The repayment time for a Chapter 13 plan is 5 years if the debtor's income at least equals the relevant state median income. The debtor must give control of future income to a trustee who makes payments on the debtor's claims. Upon approval of the plan, the debtor is granted injunctive relief against creditors while the plan is being carried out, provided the unsecured creditors will receive amounts at least equal to those paid in straight liquidation. Approval of creditors is not required.

Answer (A) is incorrect. The plan must have a 5-year term barring earlier payment. Answer (B) is incorrect. While a composition plan is being carried out, a debtor is entitled to injunctive relief against his/her creditors. Answer (D) is incorrect. A trustee must be appointed in all Chapter 13 cases.

64. Under Chapter 13, unsecured creditors

A. Vote on Chapter 13 plans.

B. Receive less than they would receive in a Chapter 7 liquidation.

C. Receive at least the amounts they would receive in a Chapter 7 liquidation.

D. Rights are never unilaterally modified.

Answer (C) is correct. *(Publisher, adapted)*

REQUIRED: The true statement concerning unsecured creditors under Chapter 13.

DISCUSSION: A Chapter 13 plan is confirmed if, among other conditions, unsecured creditors would receive amounts equivalent to those that would be received under Chapter 7. Thus, the rights of unsecured creditors may unilaterally be modified, as long as all claims in a class receive the same treatment.

Answer (A) is incorrect. Unsecured creditors do not vote on Chapter 13 plans. Answer (B) is incorrect. Unsecured creditors must receive at least the same amounts as in a Chapter 7 liquidation. Answer (D) is incorrect. A Chapter 13 plan may modify an unsecured creditor's rights, as long as all unsecured creditor's rights are modified.

65. Under Chapter 11 of the Federal Bankruptcy Code, which of the following would not be eligible for reorganization?

A. Retail sole proprietorship.

B. Advertising partnership.

C. CPA professional corporation.

D. Savings and loan corporation.

Answer (D) is correct. *(CPA, adapted)*

REQUIRED: The entity ineligible for Chapter 11 reorganization.

DISCUSSION: Reorganization under Chapter 11 of the Bankruptcy Code is available only for eligible debtors. These include partnerships and corporations, railroads, and any person that may be a debtor under Chapter 7 (but not stock or commodity brokers). Ineligible debtors under Chapter 7 include municipalities, insurance companies, banks, credit unions, and savings and loan associations.

Answer (A) is incorrect. Individuals are generally eligible for Chapter 11 reorganization. Answer (B) is incorrect. Partnerships are generally eligible for Chapter 11 reorganization. Answer (C) is incorrect. Corporations are generally eligible for Chapter 11 reorganization.

66. A reorganization under Chapter 11 of the Federal Bankruptcy Code requires all of the following except the

A. Liquidation of the debtor.

B. The filing of a reorganization plan.

C. Confirmation of the reorganization plan by the court.

D. Opportunity for each class of claims to accept the reorganization plan.

Answer (A) is correct. *(CPA, adapted)*

REQUIRED: The item not required for reorganization under the Bankruptcy Code.

DISCUSSION: A reorganization proceeding under Chapter 11 of the Bankruptcy Code provides for payment of creditors and restructuring of the debtor's finances. It permits his/her business to be continued. Chapter 11 enables restructuring instead of liquidation.

Answer (B) is incorrect. A reorganization plan is required for a Chapter 11 restructuring. Answer (C) is incorrect. The plan must be confirmed by the bankruptcy court. Answer (D) is incorrect. A plan that the bankruptcy judge finds is fair and equitable may be confirmed without approval of all classes of creditors (a cramdown plan).

67. Terri Hall, CPA, is an unsecured creditor of Tree Co. for $15,000. Tree has a total of 10 creditors, all of whom are unsecured. Tree has not paid any of the creditors for three months. Under Chapter 11 of the federal Bankruptcy Code, which of the following statements is true?

A. Hall and two other unsecured creditors must join in the involuntary petition in bankruptcy.

B. Hall may file an involuntary petition in bankruptcy against Tree.

C. Tree may not be petitioned involuntarily into bankruptcy under the provisions of Chapter 11.

D. Tree may not be petitioned involuntarily into bankruptcy because it has fewer than 12 unsecured creditors.

Answer (B) is correct. *(CPA, adapted)*

REQUIRED: The true statement about an involuntary bankruptcy.

DISCUSSION: An involuntary bankruptcy proceeding can be commenced only under Chapter 7 and Chapter 11 against an eligible debtor. If the debtor has 12 or more different creditors, any 3 or more creditors who together hold unsecured claims of at least $14,425 can file an involuntary petition. If the debtor has fewer than 12 creditors, any 1 or more creditors who alone or together have unsecured claims of at least $14,425 can file an involuntary petition. Accordingly, Hall may file an involuntary petition in bankruptcy against Tree because she holds an unsecured claim of $15,000.

Answer (A) is incorrect. Hall has at least $14,425 in unsecured claims against Tree and can file the involuntary petition against Tree without the other creditors. Answer (C) is incorrect. Involuntary bankruptcy proceedings may be brought in Chapter 7 and 11 bankruptcy. Answer (D) is incorrect. Hall has at least $14,425 in unsecured claims against Tree and can file the involuntary petition even if she is the sole creditor.

68. Robin Corp. incurred substantial operating losses for the past 3 years. Unable to meet its current obligations, Robin filed a petition for reorganization under Chapter 11 of the Federal Bankruptcy Code. Which of the following statements is true?

A. The creditors' committee must select a trustee to manage Robin's affairs.

B. The reorganization plan may be filed only by Robin.

C. A creditors' committee, if appointed, will consist of unsecured creditors.

D. Robin may continue in business only with the approval of a trustee.

Answer (C) is correct. *(CPA, adapted)*

REQUIRED: The true statement about a Chapter 11 reorganization.

DISCUSSION: Under Chapter 11, the debtor may operate its own business as debtor-in-possession. A trustee would be appointed only for cause shown, such as dishonesty or mismanagement. Chapter 11 requires that, as soon as practicable after an order for relief has been granted, the U.S. Trustee appoint a committee of unsecured creditors. It may participate in formulating the plan of reorganization. Moreover, the court may order the U.S. Trustee to appoint additional committees to assure adequate representation.

Answer (A) is incorrect. A trustee is not required in a Chapter 11 case. Answer (B) is incorrect. The debtor has the exclusive right to file a plan during the 120 days after the order for relief. However, any party may file if a trustee has been appointed or if the debtor's plan is not accepted by the creditors or shareholders within 180 days. Answer (D) is incorrect. The debtor continues to operate the business unless, for good cause shown, the court orders appointment of a trustee.

69. Under Chapter 11 of the Federal Bankruptcy Code, which of the following actions is necessary before the court may confirm a reorganization plan?

A. Provision for full payment of administration expenses.

B. Acceptance of the plan by all classes of claimants.

C. Preparation of a contingent plan of liquidation.

D. Appointment of a trustee.

Answer (A) is correct. *(CPA, adapted)*

REQUIRED: The prerequisite to court confirmation of a reorganization plan.

DISCUSSION: The debtor generally has the exclusive right to file a reorganization plan during the 120 days after the order of relief. To be effective, the plan must be confirmed by the bankruptcy court. The plan must provide for full payment of administration expenses.

Answer (B) is incorrect. A plan that is fair and equitable may be confirmed without approval of all classes of creditors (a cramdown plan). Answer (C) is incorrect. Chapter 11 enables restructuring instead of liquidation. A contingent plan of liquidation is not required. Answer (D) is incorrect. The court has discretion to order appointment of a trustee when there is evidence of dishonesty or mismanagement or if such action is in the best interests of the parties. But normally the debtor remains in possession of his/her assets and continues to operate the business.

70. Under the reorganization provisions of Chapter 11 of the Federal Bankruptcy Code, after a reorganization plan is confirmed and a final decree closing the proceedings entered, which of the following events usually occurs?

A. A reorganized corporate debtor will be liquidated.

B. A reorganized corporate debtor will be discharged from all debts except as otherwise provided in the plan and applicable law.

C. A trustee will continue to operate the debtor's business.

D. A reorganized individual debtor will not be allowed to continue in the same business.

Answer (B) is correct. *(CPA, adapted)*

REQUIRED: The status of a debtor after completing a Chapter 11 reorganization.

DISCUSSION: At the conclusion of Chapter 11 proceedings, a corporate debtor is discharged from most debts of the business. Exceptions include debts that are provided for in the plan of reorganization approved by the creditors and certain nondischargeable debts.

Answer (A) is incorrect. A Chapter 11 reorganization allows the debtor's finances to be restructured, not liquidated. Answer (C) is incorrect. A trustee is usually not appointed to run the debtor's business. The court may, however, order the appointment of a trustee for cause or if such action is in the best interests of the parties. Answer (D) is incorrect. A reorganized individual debtor may continue in the same business without any restrictions.

Questions 71 and 72 are based on the following information. Strong Corp. filed a voluntary petition in bankruptcy under the reorganization provisions of Chapter 11 of the Federal Bankruptcy Code. A reorganization plan was filed and agreed to by all necessary parties. The court confirmed the plan and a final decree was entered.

71. Which of the following parties ordinarily must confirm the plan?

	One-half of the Secured Creditors	Two-thirds of the Shareholders
A.	Yes	Yes
B.	Yes	No
C.	No	Yes
D.	No	No

Answer (D) is correct. *(CPA, adapted)*

REQUIRED: The party(ies) that must confirm a reorganization plan.

DISCUSSION: Creditors and shareholders accept, but do not confirm, plans of reorganization under Chapter 11. Confirmation is performed by the bankruptcy court. The holders of more than 50% of the creditors' claims representing at least two-thirds of the dollar amount of the claims in a class must accept. A class of equity shareholders accepts the plan if holders of at least two-thirds in dollar amount of the interests approve the plan.

72. Which of the following statements best describes the effect of the entry of the court's final decree?

A. Strong Corp. will be discharged from all its debts and liabilities.

B. Strong Corp. will be discharged only from the debts owed creditors who agreed to the reorganization plan.

C. Strong Corp. will be discharged from all its debts and liabilities that arose before the date of confirmation of the plan.

D. Strong Corp. will be discharged from all its debts and liabilities that arose before the confirmation of the plan, except as otherwise provided in the plan, the order of confirmation, or the Code.

Answer (D) is correct. *(CPA, adapted)*

REQUIRED: The true statement about the bankruptcy court's final decree.

DISCUSSION: Under a Chapter 11 reorganization, generally, an entity that is granted Chapter 11 status will be discharged from its debts and liabilities that occurred prior to the confirmation of the plan, except as provided for in the plan of reorganization, the order of confirmation, or the Bankruptcy Code. The effect of confirmation is to make the plan binding on all parties and to grant the debtor a discharge from claims not protected by the plan.

Answer (A) is incorrect. The debtor will not be discharged from all its debts. A Chapter 11 bankruptcy proceeding allows a business to continue to operate after it has been reorganized and has restructured its debts and finances. Answer (B) is incorrect. The confirmation of a reorganization plan binds all parties in interest. Creditors may be forced to accept a reorganization plan approved by the court. Answer (C) is incorrect. Under a reorganization plan, the debtor may not be discharged from certain debts prior to the confirmation of the plan if the court finds it is inequitable to discharge those debts or if a discharge of debts is prohibited by the Code.

20.5 Alternatives to Bankruptcy

73. A client has joined other creditors of the Martin Construction Company in a composition agreement seeking to avoid the necessity of a bankruptcy proceeding against Martin. Which statement describes the composition agreement?

A. It provides a temporary delay, not to exceed 6 months, insofar as the debtor's obligation to repay the debts included in the composition.

B. It does not discharge any of the debts included until performance by the debtor has taken place.

C. It provides for the appointment of a receiver to take over and operate the debtor's business.

D. It must be approved by all creditors.

Answer (B) is correct. *(CPA, adapted)*

REQUIRED: The true statement describing a composition among creditors.

DISCUSSION: A composition with creditors is a common-law contractual undertaking between the debtor and the creditors. The participating creditors agree to extend time for payment, take lesser sums in satisfaction of the debts owed, or some other plan of financial adjustment. Under general contract law, the original debts will not be discharged until the debtor has performed the new obligations.

Answer (A) is incorrect. Although a composition may involve an extension of time, it is not limited to 6 months. Furthermore, the more common composition is to take lesser sums in satisfaction. Answer (C) is incorrect. It describes the appointment of a receiver. A composition agreement is a contractual agreement not involving judicial intervention. Answer (D) is incorrect. A composition agreement need not be approved by all creditors but is binding only upon those participating.

74. Brad Dexter had assets of $80,000 and liabilities of $100,000, all unsecured. He owed $25,000 to each of the following: Petrie, Dey, Mabley, and Norris. Petrie, Dey, and Mabley agreed with each other and with Dexter to accept 70 cents on the dollar in immediate satisfaction of their debts. Under these circumstances,

A. The agreement is void for lack of consideration.

B. The agreement is a composition with creditors.

C. Norris would be bound by the agreement.

D. The agreement described is an assignment for the benefit of creditors.

Answer (B) is correct. *(CPA, adapted)*

REQUIRED: The true statement concerning an agreement by a debtor with three of four creditors to accept reduced payment.

DISCUSSION: The agreement is a common-law composition with creditors. Under general contract law, Dexter's old debts of $25,000 to each of the three will not be discharged until he performs the new obligation of paying 70%. The problem with this arrangement is that Norris can still petition Dexter into involuntary bankruptcy and void the composition.

Answer (A) is incorrect. Consideration is found in the mutual promises made among the creditors to accept a lesser payment or is excused by the courts on the basis that public policy requires that informal settlement of debts should be encouraged. Answer (C) is incorrect. Norris is a nonparticipant and under general contract principles would not be bound. Answer (D) is incorrect. An assignment for the benefit of creditors occurs when the debtor places his/her assets in the hands of a trustee who distributes the property to the creditors on a proportional basis as the intended beneficiaries.

75. Herb Hance, doing business as Hance Fashions, is hopelessly insolvent. As a means of staving off his aggressive creditors and avoiding bankruptcy, Hance has decided to make a general assignment for the benefit of his creditors. Consequently, he transferred all his nonexempt property to a trustee for equitable distribution to his creditors. What are the legal consequences of Hance's actions?

A. A debtor may not make an assignment for the benefit of creditors if he has been adjudicated a bankrupt and discharged within the preceding 6 years.

B. All his creditors must participate in the assignment and distribution of property if a majority in number and amount participate.

C. Upon distribution of all his assigned property to the participating creditors, he is discharged from all liability.

D. He may be petitioned into bankruptcy by his creditors.

Answer (D) is correct. *(CPA, adapted)*

REQUIRED: The legal consequences of an assignment for the benefit of creditors.

DISCUSSION: An involuntary petition by the creditors will be upheld even if contested by the debtor if the debtor is not paying his/her debts as they come due, or if during the preceding 120 days before the filing of the petition, a custodian (trustee, receiver, etc.) was appointed or permitted to take possession of the debtor's property. For this reason, Hance may not be able to avoid bankruptcy.

Answer (A) is incorrect. An assignment for the benefit of creditors under state law is not an official proceeding and is not subject to federal bankruptcy rules. Answer (B) is incorrect. All creditors need not participate in the assignment, and distribution would not discharge any nonassenting creditors' claims. Answer (C) is incorrect. Distribution of assigned property to the participating creditors does not discharge the debtor from liability to the nonparticipants.

76. Assume that your client is in financial difficulty but does not want to go into bankruptcy. However, certain aggressive creditors are threatening to file an involuntary petition. Under the circumstances,

A. It would be proper to attempt, in every way possible, to prepare financial statements indicating the client is not insolvent in the bankruptcy sense even though this means not following generally accepted accounting principles.

B. Avoiding bankruptcy may be possible if your client and the creditors can agree to form a creditor's committee with the usual powers incidental to such an arrangement.

C. Your client cannot be forced into bankruptcy, even though (s)he owes more than $100,000 and a single creditor's claim is in excess of $50,000.

D. Your client can resist involuntary bankruptcy if a custodian has not taken control of his property.

Answer (B) is correct. *(CPA, adapted)*

REQUIRED: The true statement about a person threatened with involuntary bankruptcy.

DISCUSSION: One alternative to bankruptcy is to place the assets of the business in the hands of a committee of creditors. The committee would have full power to manage the business of the debtor. The advantages of such an arrangement are that it avoids the stigma of bankruptcy, the attendant formalities and legal expenses, and the losses incurred in a forced liquidation.

Answer (A) is incorrect. Preparing misleading financial statements is not only a violation of generally accepted accounting principles but also unethical and illegal. Answer (C) is incorrect. A debtor is subject to an involuntary petition for bankruptcy if the debtor has fewer than 12 creditors and a single creditor has unsecured claims aggregating $14,425 or more. If the debtor has 12 or more creditors, 3 creditors must have total unsecured claims of $14,425 or more. Answer (D) is incorrect. Not paying one's debts as they become due is sufficient to support a petition for involuntary bankruptcy.

STUDY UNIT TWENTY-ONE
PERSONAL PROPERTY AND BAILMENTS

The rules of law governing the ownership, possession, and use of things called property are among the most fundamental and significant in any legal system. Indeed, in the United States, the ownership of property is considered so important that both the **Fifth and Fourteenth Amendments to the U.S. Constitution** state that property may not be taken without due process of law. For legal purposes, the term **property** means the exclusive rights to possess, use, enjoy, and dispose of a thing. From a legal perspective, property refers not to a thing but to a bundle of rights in the thing. In the absence of law, things exist, but a civilized society identifies, defines, and enforces property rights. Thus, ownership of property is an incident of organized society.

The **bundle of rights** is not always held as a unit by one person. Sometimes, selected property rights to a thing are transferred by giving, lending, renting, or selling them, while others are retained or transferred to a different person. For example, a rental car company leases a car to a customer for one week. The lessee has exclusive right to possess, use, and enjoy the automobile for the lease period. The rental car company, as owner, has temporarily conveyed some of the "sticks" in the bundle of rights but retains the others, e.g., the right to sell the automobile.

Property may be classified as tangible or intangible. **Tangible property** has perceptible physical existence, e.g., land, buildings, automobiles, or jewelry. **Intangible property** has no necessary physical existence, e.g., patent rights, bonds, stocks, insurance policies, or leases. Intangible property has little if any value in itself. It merely represents value. However, the most significant classification of types of property is real and personal. **Real property** consists of land; things attached to the land, such as buildings or trees; whatever is beneath the land, such as minerals; and, to a limited degree, the area above the surface of the land. **Personal property** consists of all things movable that are not real property. The term **chattel** is sometimes used to describe personal property generally, but chattels also may be classified as chattels real and chattels personal. A **chattel real** is an interest in land, such as a lease. A **chattel personal** is movable personal property. When the term "chattel" is used in connection with intangible personal property, the property is referred to as **chattels personal in action**, or a chose in action. A **chose in action** is an intangible to which one has a right of possession; however, one may be required to take some legal action to enjoy possession. Examples of choses in action include corporate stock, negotiable instruments, contract rights, copyrights, and patents. **Intellectual property** is intangible personal property formed by intellectual, as opposed to physical, efforts. Among the types of intellectual property are patents, copyrights, trademarks, and trade secrets. A **patent** is the exclusive legal right to use or sell an invention or discovery. A **copyright** is a form of legal protection for the tangible expression of ideas. A **trademark** consists of words, names, symbols, or devices used to identify and distinguish goods. A **trade secret** is information protected by a business because it provides economic advantage (Study Units 7 and 22).

Title is a legal concept indicating **ownership**, not merely possession. Title confers upon the owner of property the exclusive right to possess, use, enjoy, and dispose of it. Persons acquire ownership of personal property in various ways. The most common method is by purchase. **Purchase** means that the rights of an owner of the property are transferred to another in exchange for something of value.

A **gift** is a voluntary transfer of property that is not for consideration. The requirements of a valid gift are donative intent, delivery, and acceptance. The intent must be a current intention to make a gift. If making physical delivery of an item is impracticable, the law permits a constructive or symbolic delivery, for example, by giving the donee a key or other means by which (s)he may acquire possession of the gift. Gifts are classified in three broad categories. An **inter vivos gift** is one made between living persons. The transfer occurs during the lifetime of the donor and the donee. A **testamentary gift** is intended to be effective at the death of the donor and must be made by a will. A gift **causa mortis** is a conditional transfer of personal property by a donor in the belief that (s)he will die imminently. If the donor recovers and lives, the gift is automatically revoked. Likewise, if the donee dies before the donor, the gift is revoked.

Ownership of personal property may also be acquired by **will or descent and distribution**, that is, by inheritance. When a person dies, either with or without leaving a will, the decedent's property passes to others called beneficiaries under a will or heirs under descent and distribution statutes.

Personal property may be lost, abandoned, or mislaid. A person who finds **lost property** does not acquire title merely by finding and possessing the property. The finder is entitled to possession against everyone in the entire world except the true owner. Finder's rights permit a finder to bring an action against any person who interferes with his/her possession of the property. **Abandonment** is the intentional relinquishment of all rights in an object without transferring ownership to another person. One may acquire ownership of abandoned property by taking possession of it with the intent to exclude others. The distinction between lost and abandoned property is in the intent of the owner. **Mislaid property** is property that the owner has voluntarily and intentionally placed in a particular location. Subsequently, (s)he forgets where (s)he has placed the property. Mislaid property is presumed to be left in custody of the owner or occupant of the premises on which it is found, and (s)he is generally entitled to possession of such property against all except the owner.

Development is another means of acquiring personal property. The developer of something of value is usually entitled to the fruits of that labor.

When property belonging to two or more persons becomes commingled to such an extent that separating the parts belonging to each is impossible, **confusion** has occurred. If the confusion is rightful, according to agreement, or innocent, each owner will share in the resulting property, or any losses, either according to their agreement or in proportion to their relative contributions to the whole mass. If the confusion is the result of one owner's **negligence**, the innocent owner is entitled to the return of his/her property, if possible. The negligent party is liable in **damages** for any injury to the innocent owner. When confusion results from **intentional wrongdoing** of one of the parties and the innocent party's property cannot be separated, the entire property belongs to the innocent party until or unless the wrongdoer proves his/her contribution to the value of the resulting mass.

Accession is a means of acquiring ownership of personal property through additions to property already in existence. Accession occurs when a person's property is changed into a new item by the addition of another's labor or property. It may occur by agreement or be unauthorized. When the article is created by the combination of goods of both parties, title is usually awarded to the owner of the principal good/chattel even if the owner willfully makes the changes. When the increase in value is caused by labor of an **innocent trespasser**, title is determined by evaluation of the relative contribution of the labor to the value of the finished product. With regard to **willful trespassers**, the general rule is that a willful trespasser cannot acquire title by accession even when a change of form or a substantial increase in value resulted.

A **bailment** is the legal relationship that results whenever one person, the **bailor**, transfers possession, but not title, of his/her personal property to another person, the **bailee**, who has the duty to return it or otherwise dispose of it, according to the bailor's instructions. To form a bailment, the owner must make **delivery of possession and control** of the personal property to the bailee, who must accept it. Whether or not a bailment exists is determined from all the facts and circumstances of a particular situation. A bailment differs from a **sale or gift** because (1) the bailee does not receive title, and (2) at the end of the term of bailment, the bailee must return or account for the property. A bailee has a duty to restore possession of the property to the bailor. Generally, the bailee is required to return the specific property unless the property is **fungible**. In cases of fungible goods, such as agricultural commodities, a bailee need only return goods of the same quality and quantity.

The legal rights and duties of bailor and bailee traditionally vary according to whether the bailment is involuntary, gratuitous, or ordinary, and according to whom it benefits. An **involuntary bailment** is one in which the bailee comes into possession of property without the consent of its true owner. In such situations, the law implies a bailment. For example, taking or having possession of lost or mislaid property may result in an involuntary bailment. The involuntary bailee owes the owner a slight duty of care and is only liable for gross negligence. A **gratuitous bailment** is one for which neither the bailor nor the bailee receives compensation. Thus, a contract bailment is not gratuitous.

Bailments are also classified according to which of the parties derives benefit from the bailment. A **bailment for the sole benefit of the bailee** exists when the owner of personal property permits another to use it without compensation or any other benefit. A bailment that is solely for the benefit of the bailee is often called a gratuitous bailment. A gratuitous bailee is liable for damages caused to bailed property by his/her slight negligence. The gratuitous bailee therefore has a duty to exercise **extraordinary or great care** with respect to the property. A **bailment for the sole benefit of the bailor** exists when a person stores or takes possession of personal property solely as an accommodation to the bailor. The bailee in such cases must exercise **slight care** and is not liable to the bailor in this situation absent proof that loss or injury occurred due to gross negligence or intentional misconduct. Most **mutual benefit bailments** involve a bailor or bailee who received direct compensation, and the bailee is liable only if the value of the personal property is reduced as a result of his/her fault. This liability encompasses loss or injury caused by failure to exercise ordinary care. Thus, the bailee is **liable for ordinary negligence**. The modern approach is for courts not to impose liability based upon different standards of care according to various categories of ordinary bailments. Rather, liability depends on whether the bailee exercised **reasonable care under all the circumstances**, e.g., type and value of goods, type of bailment, or type of business.

The **bailee's rights** under a bailment depend entirely on the express or implied terms of the parties' contract. If **the contract** provides that the bailee is to have possession for a specified period, and the bailor is to receive **compensation**, the bailee generally will have the right to retain possession for the entire period. Whether the bailee has the **right to use** the bailed property depends on the terms of the contract. When the purpose of the bailment is the use of the bailed article, the bailee has the right to use the article in a fair and reasonable manner. If the purpose of the bailment contract is **storage**, the bailor does not expect any use of his/her property, and the bailee has no right to such use. Thus, the bailee would be **strictly liable** for any use made of the property. Except when the parties have a clear understanding that the bailee is not to receive any payment, the bailee normally has the right to some form of compensation for services. If the amount is not expressly agreed to, the bailee is entitled to the reasonable value of his/her services. To secure payment, the bailee is ordinarily entitled to a **possessory lien**. Moreover, the bailee as well as the bailor has a property interest in the bailed goods and therefore a right of action against a third party who wrongfully interferes with the bailed property.

A **bailee's duties** include using and returning the bailed property in accordance with the bailment contract and exercising reasonable care when handling the property. If the bailee uses the property in any manner inconsistent with the bailor's rights, the bailee will be liable to the bailor for **misuse**. If property is lost or damaged while in the bailee's possession, most courts hold that the bailee is presumed to be negligent and require the bailee to prove that (s)he acted with due care under the circumstances. A bailee also is liable for any **unauthorized use or misdelivery** of the bailed property. Misdelivery is transfer of possession to anyone other than the bailor or a person designated in the bailor's express instructions. Thus, a bailee must be satisfied that the person to whom the property is delivered is the owner or has been authorized by the owner to take possession of the goods. Furthermore, the bailee's wrongful refusal to return the goods to the rightful owner is an act of **conversion**. The bailor may seek damages or to reacquire the property by means of an **action for replevin**. Damages are usually compensatory but may also be punitive.

An ordinary bailee may expand or limit his/her **liability for negligence or breach of contract** by a separate agreement or in the bailment contract. However, liability for willful misconduct may not be limited by provisions that are against public policy.

Special bailments involve professional bailees, such as innkeepers, common carriers, and warehouse companies. Special bailments are subject to the same rules as ordinary bailments and also to special rules and regulations.

QUESTIONS

21.1 Nature and Importance of Property

1. The exercise of the power of eminent domain

A. Must be by a governmental unit but the actual user of the condemned property may be private.

B. Is constitutionally limited to the taking of real property.

C. Must be by a governmental unit for its own direct use.

D. Is subject to a rational basis test of what constitutes a public use.

Answer (D) is correct. *(Publisher, adapted)*

REQUIRED: The true statement about the power of eminent domain.

DISCUSSION: Eminent domain is the right of the government to take privately owned property for "public use." In a 1984 decision, the Supreme Court stated a test that apparently defines "public use" very broadly. It held that, if "the exercise of the eminent domain power is rationally related to a conceivable public purpose," the court would not prohibit a compensated taking.

Answer (A) is incorrect. Governmental entities do authorize private entities to exercise the power (e.g., a utility to acquire property for utility lines). Answer (B) is incorrect. Eminent domain is the power to take "private property," not merely real property. The limitations are that it must be for a public use and compensated. Answer (C) is incorrect. In a recent controversial case, the Supreme Court upheld the use of eminent domain for private commercial purposes.

2. Which of the following would change if an asset were treated as personal property rather than as real property?

	Requirements for Transfer	Creditors' Rights
A.	Yes	No
B.	No	Yes
C.	Yes	Yes
D.	No	No

Answer (C) is correct. *(CPA, adapted)*

REQUIRED: The effect(s), if any, of classifying an asset as personal property rather than as real property.

DISCUSSION: Classification of property as real or personal has significant legal effect. Generally, personal property is movable, and real property consists of land and things attached to it. Delivery of a deed is an example of a requirement to transfer real but not personal property. Creditors' rights might also vary depending on property classification. For example, perfection affects the priority of creditors' rights in personal property, whereas recording provides constructive notice of interests in real property.

3. Which of the following statements concerning personal property is true?

A. A government subsidy is a personal property right that may not be discontinued.

B. Social Security benefits are not personal property rights and may be discontinued at any time.

C. A CPA's license to practice is a personal property right that may not be taken away without due process of law.

D. A license to operate a liquor store is a personal property right that is freely transferable.

Answer (C) is correct. *(CPA, adapted)*

REQUIRED: The true statement about personal property.

DISCUSSION: Property is created by the legal system of an organized society. Property is the bundle of legal rights which allows an owner to possess, use, enjoy, exclude, and dispose of something. Property has been broadly interpreted. The two major classifications are real and personal property. Personal property is anything capable of being owned that is not real property, and therefore includes many entitlements. The ownership of property is considered to be so important that the U.S. Constitution states that property cannot be taken without due process of law. Basically, due process requires notice, a fair hearing, and a statement of reasons for any taking. The courts have recognized a type of constitutional property rights in governmental benefits (welfare, licenses, employment, and education) that may not be deprived without due process. A CPA's license to practice is personal property and may not be taken without due process of law.

Answer (A) is incorrect. A government subsidy (even one that is property) can be discontinued in accordance with constitutional requirements. Answer (B) is incorrect. Social Security benefits are a form of personal property and can be denied or discontinued only on a showing of cause. Answer (D) is incorrect. A license to dispense liquor may not be transferred without the issuing agency's consent for reasons of public policy.

4. Property may be classified very generally as tangible or intangible or as real or personal. Which of the following is true?

A. Personal property is tangible but real estate may be either tangible or intangible.

B. The bundle of rights may not be held by more than one person at a time.

C. Personal property cannot exist independently of the evidence of its ownership.

D. Real property includes rights in the space above the surface.

Answer (D) is correct. *(Publisher, adapted)*

REQUIRED: The true statement about property.

DISCUSSION: Real property itself consists of the surface of land, the airspace above, things attached to the surface, such as buildings or trees, and the space below the land, including minerals. The law of real property involves legal rights in the property (e.g., mineral, air, and water rights) and, in general, the right to freely use, possess, enjoy, and transfer any interest in real estate.

Answer (A) is incorrect. Personal property may be intangible, which means that it has value and is transferable but has no physical form, e.g., goodwill and shares of a company. Answer (B) is incorrect. The "bundle of rights" concept includes different persons having rights in the same property. Answer (C) is incorrect. Intangible personal property exists even if its physical representation (e.g., a stock certificate) is destroyed.

5. Which of the following items generally will be considered personal property?

A. Crops sold as part of the sale of land.

B. Plumbing fixtures sold as part of the sale of a house.

C. Copyrights.

D. Air rights.

Answer (C) is correct. *(CPA, adapted)*

REQUIRED: The item that is personal property.

DISCUSSION: The legal definition of personal property is negative. Personal property is classified as anything capable of being owned that is not real property. Intellectual property is a type of intangible personal property that includes copyrights. Copyright law provides property rights to the author or originator of a literary or artistic production of a specified type. Works that are copyrightable include books, records, films, artwork, architectural plans, menus, music videos, product packaging, and computer software.

Answer (A) is incorrect. When crops are sold as part of the land on which they are growing, the entire sale is considered the sale of real property. Answer (B) is incorrect. Plumbing fixtures installed in a house are objectively intended to be permanently annexed, thus characterizing them as a form of real property. Answer (D) is incorrect. Air, light, view, mineral, water, and similar rights are real property.

6. Intellectual property is a type of intangible personal property interest that may take all of the following forms except a

A. Patent.

B. Trademark.

C. Copyright.

D. College degree.

Answer (D) is correct. *(Publisher, adapted)*

REQUIRED: The personal property that is not a form of intellectual property.

DISCUSSION: Intellectual property is intangible personal property. Patents, copyrights, and trademarks are major forms of intellectual property, but other forms, such as trade secrets and rights of publicity, also exist. A degree is a title conferred by an academic institution to signify completion of a course of study. It may have value, but it cannot be transferred and does not represent an exclusive right to use some specific, direct expression of intellect.

7. Under federal patent law,

A. An inventor granted a patent has unlimited monopoly power regarding the invention.

B. Patentable items include any new and useful process, machine, manufacture, composition of matter, or scientific principle.

C. A patent protects against an identical process developed independently.

D. Any patent resulting from an invention made by an employee on company time belongs to the employer.

Answer (C) is correct. *(Publisher, adapted)*

REQUIRED: The true statement about patents.

DISCUSSION: A patent is the exclusive legal right to use or sell an invention, such as a device or process. Patent law provides that a patent may be given to any new and useful process, machine, manufacture, or composition of matter, and any infringement upon a patent is valid ground for a lawsuit. An infringing item need not be identical to the device or process patented. But the patent holder has exclusive rights, even against a person who independently develops the patented item.

Answer (A) is incorrect. Most patents issued after June 1995 have a duration of 20 years. Answer (B) is incorrect. A scientific principle is not patentable. Answer (D) is incorrect. A person not hired to do inventive work will own patents (s)he obtains even if the work was done on company time and using company facilities. Under the shop rights doctrine, however, the employer has a nonexclusive, royalty-free license to use an invention developed in such circumstances.

8. Which of the following is subject to copyright protection?

A. Choreography.

B. Corporate symbols.

C. Trade secrets.

D. A new hybrid form of plant life.

Answer (A) is correct. *(Publisher, adapted)*

REQUIRED: The item subject to copyright protection.

DISCUSSION: A copyright is a form of legal protection for the tangible expression of ideas, but it does not protect the underlying ideas themselves. Thus, copyrights are used to protect literary works, music, recordings, art, films, and even choreography. The copyright covers the expression of the idea and gives the copyright holder exclusive rights to reproduce it, perform it, or display it.

Answer (B) is incorrect. Corporate symbols are subject to trademark, not copyright, protection. Answer (C) is incorrect. Trade secrets may only be ideas or information, not the tangible expression of an idea. Answer (D) is incorrect. A new hybrid plant is patentable, not copyrightable.

9. Barry Mason wrote to author Ella Street to convey an idea for Street's next novel. Mason suggested that it concern a lawyer who leaves her practice and moves to Australia. Street told Mason that the idea was ridiculous. Two years later, however, Street's novel, *Outback Lawyer*, was a best-seller. Does Mason have a legal claim against Street?

A. Yes, because the idea was so original that it was protected.

B. No, because Mason has no evidence that Street ever read his suggestion.

C. Yes, because the letter to Street is sufficient to show ownership of the idea.

D. No, because after voluntary communication to others, ideas become available for common use.

Answer (D) is correct. *(Publisher, adapted)*

REQUIRED: The likelihood of winning a lawsuit based on the use of an unsolicited idea.

DISCUSSION: The courts have ordinarily held that voluntary communication of ideas, conceptions, and truths to others results in their becoming freely available to others. An idea will only be protected if it is original, if it is expressed in some tangible form, and if the parties involved have a contractual or other relationship. An unsolicited idea is not protected.

Answer (A) is incorrect. The idea is not protected. It was unsolicited and not in finished form. Answer (B) is incorrect. The idea is not protected even if Street read the letter. Answer (C) is incorrect. An unsolicited idea is not protected.

10. The loss of trademark rights does not follow from

A. Failure to put the word “Trademark” or a similar term next to the mark itself.

B. Consistent failure to take enforcement action against known infringers.

C. The general usage of the mark as a generic term by the public.

D. Abandonment of the mark.

Answer (A) is correct. *(Publisher, adapted)*

REQUIRED: The act or event that does not cause the loss of trademark rights.

DISCUSSION: According to the Lanham Act of 1946, a trademark is a word, name, symbol, or device used by a manufacturer or merchant to identify its goods and distinguish them from the goods of others. Trademarks can be registered and protected from infringement, but rights to a trademark must first be established through use in commerce, providing that the mark does not infringe on a trademark already in use. A trademark holder should place the words “Trademark” or “Registered Trademark” next to the mark itself to protect it from becoming generic, but failure to do so does not automatically result in loss of trademark rights.

Answer (B) is incorrect. Consistent failure to take enforcement action against known infrigers results in the loss of trademark rights. Answer (C) is incorrect. The general usage of the mark as a generic term by the public results in the loss of trademark rights. Answer (D) is incorrect. Abandonment of the mark results in the loss of trademark rights.

21.2 Acquisition of Personal Property

11. Dave Doctor and a friend were nearby when Dana Donor told them she wanted to give her bank account to Dan Donee. Donor asked Doctor to give her savings bank book to Donee because it was locked in the cashier’s office, which would not be open until the next morning. Doctor, an agent of the hospital, informed Donor and Donee that he would comply with her request. Donee said that would be fine. Donor did not live through the night. Doctor gave Donee the bank book the next morning. What is the legal effect of these events?

A. If Donor died intestate, the money in the savings account will go to her heirs.

B. The gift was incomplete because no delivery occurred.

C. A gift causa mortis is irrevocable once it is made.

D. All the elements of a valid gift were present, so the attempted gift is valid.

Answer (D) is correct. *(Publisher, adapted)*

REQUIRED: The true statement regarding the validity of an attempted gift.

DISCUSSION: A valid gift requires intent of the donor, acceptance by the donee, and delivery. These requirements must occur during the lifetime of the donor. The depositing of the bank book with the hospital formed a bailment. Given that Doctor is an agent of the hospital (bailee), his agreement to hold the bank book for Donee constituted a delivery during the lifetime of the decedent. A delivery of a deposit book of a savings account is considered a constructive delivery of the balance of the funds in the account.

Answer (A) is incorrect. The inter vivos gift was valid, and the money in the savings account will not go to Donor’s heirs. Answer (B) is incorrect. The delivery of a deposit book of a savings account is considered a constructive delivery of the funds in the account, although the delivery of a book for a checking account would not have the same effect. Answer (C) is incorrect. A gift causa mortis is revocable, but an inter vivos gift is not.

12. Ada was hospitalized in critical condition. Just before going into surgery, she gave Bea, her sister, a check for $20,000, remarking that her chances of survival were not good and she wanted Bea to have the money in the event of her death. Ada survived the operation but died a month later from a cause unrelated to her original injury. She did not specifically revoke the gift. Which of the following is true?

A. Ada made a valid inter vivos gift.

B. The donee has no right to the money because the donor did not die from the contemplated cause.

C. A valid gift causa mortis was made because the gift was not revoked.

D. A valid gift causa mortis was not made because the gift was not properly delivered.

Answer (B) is correct. *(Publisher, adapted)*

REQUIRED: The requirements of gifts inter vivos and causa mortis.

DISCUSSION: A gift causa mortis (in contemplation of death) is a conditional gift. (1) It must be made in view of impending death from some specific illness or peril; (2) the donor must die from the illness or peril without having revoked the gift; (3) the donee must survive the donor; and (4) the subject matter must have been delivered to the donee. Given that Ada died from an unrelated cause, the gift was ineffective (automatically revoked) despite the lack of an express revocation.

Answer (A) is incorrect. A gift inter vivos is between the living and not conditional upon death. Answer (C) is incorrect. Failure to die from the specific cause automatically revoked the gift. The money must be returned to the estate. Answer (D) is incorrect. Revocation was by failure of a condition of the gift.

13. The Uniform Transfers to Minors Act (UTMA)

A. Provides that a gift is revocable if the donor fully complies.

B. Concerns only gifts of securities.

C. Requires that an account be established in a name other than that of the donor if an irrevocable gift is to be made.

D. Vests the custodial property in the custodian.

Answer (D) is correct. *(Publisher, adapted)*

REQUIRED: The true statement about operation of the UTMA.

DISCUSSION: The UTMA has been enacted in the majority of states to provide a means for making legal gifts or other transfers to minors, e.g., from estates, trusts, insurance companies, guardianships, and judgment debtors. The UTMA is a revision of the Uniform Gifts to Minors Act, which was adopted in all jurisdictions. One method is to deposit money in an account in a bank or other financial institution in the name of the custodian for the minor under the UTMA. The custodianship is not a separate legal entity or taxpayer, and the property is indefeasibly vested in the minor.

Answer (A) is incorrect. Compliance results in an irrevocable gift. Answer (B) is incorrect. The UTMA concerns gifts of any kind of property. Answer (C) is incorrect. The donor may be the custodian.

14. William knew he was fatally wounded, so he gave his valuable ring to a young man who had administered first aid, stating, “I am going fast. I’d like for you to have this.” William died a few minutes later in the emergency room of the hospital. As the young man was leaving the hospital, the ring slipped through a hole in his pocket and a nurse found the ring in the hallway just inside the hospital entrance. The young man has never been located. The hospital administrator, the executor of William’s estate, and the nurse all claim the ring. Who has the best claim?

A. The hospital, because the property was lost and found on its premises.

B. The nurse, because the property was lost in a public place.

C. William’s estate, because William lacked donative intent.

D. The young man, because he was the owner.

Answer (D) is correct. *(Publisher, adapted)*

REQUIRED: The ownership of a ring transferred by gift and lost.

DISCUSSION: At common law, an owner of personal property who loses or mislays it retains title against the finder and any other claimant. Title appears to have been vested in the young man by a valid gift from William. The three elements of a valid gift are intent, acceptance, and delivery.

Answer (A) is incorrect. The hospital’s claim is not as valid as the young man’s. One common law test gives the right to possession of lost property to the finder and mislaid property to the landowner. A newer test gives possession to the finder if in a public place and to the landowner if in a private place. The hospital entrance is probably a public-type place, so the nurse would prevail over the hospital. Answer (B) is incorrect. Her claim is secondary to the young man’s, but ahead of the hospital’s. Answer (C) is incorrect. It does not appear that William’s estate has any further claim to the ring.

15. Ann cut 1,000 logs belonging to Bob. Upon discovery that she had trespassed, Ann marked the logs as hers, mixed them with 100 of her own, and started them down river to market. The logs of Ann and Bob cannot be distinguished. Given these facts,

A. If Bob seizes the logs and sells them to Carol, Ann will be unable to recover any logs if Carol is a bona fide purchaser.

B. Ann and Bob are owners in common of the mass of logs.

C. Accession of personal property has occurred.

D. Ann should be entitled to half the logs because the trespass was not intended.

Answer (A) is correct. *(Publisher, adapted)*

REQUIRED: The true statement about the confusion of logs by a trespasser.

DISCUSSION: Confusion is a legal term describing the intermingling of property of different owners. If confusion of personal property results from an innocent act or accident and the goods are of the same kind, each person is an owner of a proportionate share of the confused mass. However, if the confusion results from wrongdoing or intentional trespass, most courts vest title to the entire mass in the innocent party until the wrongdoer proves a portion is his/hers. Thus, title is vested in Bob, and Carol has title free of any claim of Ann if Carol is a bona fide purchaser.

Answer (B) is incorrect. Ann and Bob are not owners in common of the mass. Ann was a willful confuser, and title vested in Bob. Answer (C) is incorrect. The problem concerns confusion, not accession. Answer (D) is incorrect. The confusion was intended.

16. Chewy Chukar owns 200 acres of Florida woodlands, most of which has the wild plant, Deer Tongue, growing on it. Bob White trespassed and picked 10,000 pounds of Deer Tongue, worth $8,000 after being picked and sacked. The value of the leaves standing in the woods was about 10 mills per pound or $100 for the amount picked. White sold the leaves to Don Deiler who dried and cured them, increasing their worth to about $16,000. Deiler used the Deer Tongue to flavor an inventory of Dawgweed worth about $250,000. What is the legal implication of these events?

A. Chukar can recover the Dawgweed only if Bob White was an innocent trespasser.

B. The type of trespass is not material because Chukar, the owner, can always recover property wrongfully taken from him.

C. Wildlife is ownerless, and title may be acquired by taking possession and control as Bob White did. Thus, Chukar cannot recover.

D. Chukar can recover the Dawgweed if Bob White was a willful trespasser.

Answer (D) is correct. *(Publisher, adapted)*

REQUIRED: The landowner's right to personal property taken by a trespasser and changed.

DISCUSSION: In accession by specification, new property results from the property of one person by the labor and materials of a wrongful taker so that the original property no longer exists. The prior owner is entitled to the value of his/her property at the time and place of taking. With respect to willful trespass, however, title to the finished product passes to the owner of the original materials. A bona fide purchaser takes no greater rights to the finished product than the trespasser. Thus, if White was a willful trespasser, Chukar should be entitled to recover the finished product.

Answer (A) is incorrect. The owner of property taken can recover damages but cannot recover the finished item if the taker is an innocent trespasser and has changed the property or enhanced its value sufficiently so that a court will determine that the original item no longer exists. Answer (B) is incorrect. Recovery of the property depends on the type of trespass. Answer (C) is incorrect. Plants are not wildlife, and a trespasser does not acquire title except when the trespass is innocent and the substantial change or enhancement of value test is met.

21.3 Ordinary Bailments

17. Mimi came into Palace Beauty Shop wearing an expensive fur coat. The shop had a waiting room in front. On a prior occasion, the proprietor had assured Mimi that "nothing has been stolen in our entire 20 years here." The coat was stolen from the waiting room while Mimi was in the beauty shop. With respect to the elements needed to establish a bailment, which of the following is true?

A. All elements of a valid bailment are present.

B. The element of consideration by the bailor, Mimi, is missing.

C. The element of delivery of possession and control to the shop is missing.

D. The shop could successfully defend Mimi's claim of bailment by showing that Mimi did not own the coat.

Answer (C) is correct. *(Publisher, adapted)*

REQUIRED: The true statement about whether a bailment existed.

DISCUSSION: A bailment is the legal relationship resulting from the transfer of possession of personal property from one person (the bailor) to another person (the bailee) under such circumstances that the bailee is under a duty to return the item to the bailor or dispose of it as directed by the bailor. No change of possession by delivery or acceptance occurred, so no bailment was formed.

Answer (A) is incorrect. The owner of the coat did not deliver possession and control to the beauty shop. Answer (B) is incorrect. Consideration is not required to establish a bailment. Furthermore, Mimi's promise to pay would be treated as made in exchange for the promise of the shop to render the services and to safeguard her coat. Answer (D) is incorrect. A possessor of personal property has a sufficient property interest (without ownership) to enter into a bailment contract and recover damages for its breach.

18. A bailment arises when possession of personal property is transferred and the transferee must return it or dispose of it at the owner's direction. Which of the following is false?

A. The property bailed might be returned in altered form to the owner.

B. The owner of the property is the bailee, and the party in possession is the bailor.

C. Strict liability is sometimes imposed in bailments.

D. A bailee who returns the bailed property damaged is presumed negligent.

Answer (B) is correct. *(Publisher, adapted)*

REQUIRED: The false statement about a bailment transaction.

DISCUSSION: A bailment is the legal relationship resulting from the transfer of possession of personal property from one person (the bailor) to another person (the bailee) under such circumstances that the bailee is under a duty to return the item to the bailor or dispose of it as directed by the bailor.

Answer (A) is incorrect. A bailment results when the identical property is to be returned in the same or in an altered form, e.g., repaired goods. Answer (C) is incorrect. Liability may be imposed in bailments of goods regardless of the bailor's fault if the goods prove to be unreasonably dangerous. Answer (D) is incorrect. Failure of the bailee to return the bailed property undamaged establishes a prima facie case of negligence.

19. Tom had a dairy products factory. He contracted with many dairymen to accept their surplus milk, which he agreed to manufacture into dairy products, such as butter, cottage cheese, and sour cream; market the products; deduct his commissions; and divide the remaining proceeds among the dairymen in proportion to the amount of milk each contributed. Tom's factory and its contents were completely destroyed in a fire. Which of the following is true?

A. The transaction is not a sale but a bailment with a power of sale granted to the bailee.

B. The transaction is a sale because the same item of property is not to be returned.

C. Until Tom sold the dairy products, title and risk of loss was on Tom.

D. Tom, as the party in possession of goods owned by another, is an insurer of the safety of the goods.

Answer (A) is correct. *(Publisher, adapted)*

REQUIRED: The true statement as to whether a bailment contract has been formed.

DISCUSSION: Title does not pass in a bailment. Here, a bailment resulted because the property is to be returned, even though in a changed form, as proceeds. The proceeds of sale were being divided among the milk suppliers in proportion to milk supplied. Tom was only providing services and receiving compensation for them. The transaction should thus be classified as a bailment (not a sale) with a power of sale granted to the bailee.

Answer (B) is incorrect. Tom was merely authorized to sell the property after processing it and was responsible to strictly account for the proceeds received from the sale. Answer (C) is incorrect. Tom never acquired title. The risk of loss remained on the dairymen at all times. A bailee has neither title nor risk of loss [provided (s)he acts in a nonnegligent manner]. Answer (D) is incorrect. A bailee is not an insurer of the goods, but must exercise reasonable care for their safety.

20. Marrieo and Dreddy built a custom roadster. They drove it through an automatic gate into a parking lot, received a ticket from a machine, parked, and took their keys with them. To leave, they are required to drive to the exit and present the ticket to an attendant who collects the parking fee. Which of the following statements is false?

A. If this arrangement were a bailment, the parking lot would be responsible for a spare tire, jack, and tools locked in the trunk.

B. Marrieo and Dreddy have rented a parking space because they retained control of their car.

C. The most important factor in deciding whether this arrangement is a bailment is that Marrieo and Dreddy received the ticket from a machine and not an attendant.

D. If a third person wrongfully damages personal property in the possession and control of a bailee, the bailee may bring suit for him/herself and for the bailor.

Answer (C) is correct. *(Publisher, adapted)*

REQUIRED: The false statement about parking a car in an automated lot.

DISCUSSION: In deciding whether a parking lot transaction is a bailment or lease of space, courts have determined that the most important factor is whether the keys are retained by the owner. Giving the keys to a parking attendant or leaving them in the car at the parking attendant's direction is a constructive delivery of possession and acceptance. However, a bailment of a parked vehicle can occur other than through delivery of keys (e.g., if the premises are locked up).

Answer (A) is incorrect. A bailee is responsible for the automobile and other items of personal property that (s)he knows, or could reasonably anticipate, are in the automobile, e.g., a spare tire, jack, and tools. Answer (B) is incorrect. Courts interpret retention of keys as retention of control of the car, resulting in a rental or lease of a parking space. Answer (D) is incorrect. The bailee's rights are generally held to be broad enough to permit him/her to bring an action against the third party for damages to the bailor's reversionary interest.

21. With respect to involuntary bailments, which of the following is true?

A. An involuntary bailee has no liability to the bailor-owner because (s)he is only a custodian.

B. The liability of an involuntary bailee will be the same as the liability of an ordinary bailee.

C. Common examples of involuntary bailments include a person's discovery of a lost wallet, a horse's straying onto a neighbor's property, or a storm's depositing property on another's land.

D. An involuntary bailee should not be entitled to recover for the value of his/her services in quantum meruit.

Answer (C) is correct. *(Publisher, adapted)*

REQUIRED: The true statement regarding an involuntary bailment.

DISCUSSION: Finding a lost wallet, an animal's straying onto a neighbor's property, or the deposit of property on another's land as a result of a storm may result in an involuntary bailment. The bailee has taken legal possession and control of the property of another due to the circumstances.

Answer (A) is incorrect. An involuntary bailee has a legal responsibility to the owner to exercise reasonable care under the circumstances. Answer (B) is incorrect. The courts do not impose the same liability on an involuntary bailee as on an ordinary one. Answer (D) is incorrect. An involuntary bailee is entitled to recover the value of his/her services. This equitable remedy is called quantum meruit.

22. The employees of Company must wear special clothing in the work area. Accordingly, Company provides a locker room with an attendant for storing personal items. Which of the following statements is true?

A. A gratuitous bailment has been formed because it is for the sole benefit of the bailee when a worker leaves his/her property in the storage room.

B. A mutual benefit bailment has been formed.

C. Company can avoid all liability for its workers' property by including an exculpatory clause in their contracts that states, "Not responsible for any property left in the locker room."

D. When a worker leaves his/her property in the locker room, (s)he is a mere lessee or licensee.

Answer (B) is correct. *(Publisher, adapted)*

REQUIRED: The true statement about storage of personal property by employees.

DISCUSSION: Mutual benefit bailments occur when both the bailor and bailee receive a benefit. The employees (bailors) benefit from the storage facilities. The employer (bailee) benefits from uncluttered work areas and a possible decrease in the chance of accidents.

Answer (A) is incorrect. The arrangement is a mutual benefit bailment. Answer (C) is incorrect. While exculpatory clauses are permitted in bailment agreements, they are unenforceable if, as here, they are so broad as to be unconscionable or in violation of public policy. Answer (D) is incorrect. A bailment has been formed. The worker has made a delivery to the owner of the premises (Company through its agent) so as temporarily to relinquish exclusive possession, control, and dominion over the property.

23. Gal lends Guy her car so that he may run errands for her. Subsequently, Gal lends Guy her lawn mower so that he may mow his own yard. Which is the correct statement concerning the traditional duties of care owed by the parties?

A. Guy is required to exercise ordinary care with respect to his use of the lawn mower.

B. If Guy had rented the lawn mower from Gal, she would have owed a duty to him to inform regarding defects that would have been discovered by the exercise of reasonable care.

C. Guy must exercise great care in the use of the car.

D. If Guy had been compensated by Gal for running the errands, he would have been required to exercise great care in the use of the automobile.

Answer (B) is correct. *(Publisher, adapted)*

REQUIRED: The duties of care traditionally imposed in bailments.

DISCUSSION: Under traditional tort principles, the duty of care owed by a party to a bailment depends upon the party benefited. When a bailment is for the mutual benefit of the bailor and the bailee, the bailor (Gal) has a duty of ordinary care. This duty includes an affirmative obligation to use reasonable care to discover dangerous defects. These duties have generally been replaced with the standard of reasonable care. Among other things, this standard requires informing the other party about known defects.

Answer (A) is incorrect. In a bailment for the bailee's sole benefit, (s)he is required to use great care. Answer (C) is incorrect. If the bailment is for the sole benefit of the bailor and the bailee is uncompensated, the bailee is required to exercise only slight care. Answer (D) is incorrect. If Guy had been compensated by Gal for running the errands, the bailment would have been mutually beneficial, and he would have only been required to use ordinary care.

24. In a bailment, the bailee

A. Has a right to a possessory lien if just compensation is not paid.

B. Has a right to a possessory lien but not to sell the goods at public auction.

C. Retains a lien on the bailed property only if (s)he retains the property.

D. Must bear the expenses of the bailment.

Answer (A) is correct. *(Publisher, adapted)*

REQUIRED: The rights of a bailee against a bailor.

DISCUSSION: If a bailment requires the bailee to perform services in regard to the bailed item, (s)he will be entitled to reasonable compensation. To secure payment, the bailee is ordinarily entitled to a possessory lien. Most states allow a bailee to foreclose the lien and sell the property at a public sale if the bailor does not pay.

Answer (B) is incorrect. The bailee may usually sell the property at auction if the bailor fails to pay. Answer (C) is incorrect. Many states also permit the bailee to retain the lien even if possession of the property has been returned to the bailor. Answer (D) is incorrect. An apportionment of expenses depends on whether the bailment is for the sole benefit of the bailor or the bailee or for their mutual benefit. Who pays also may depend on custom regarding the bailed goods, the intent of the parties, whether the expenses are ordinary or extraordinary, and whether they were caused by the fault of one or the other.

25. To recover when bailed property is damaged or lost while in the possession of the bailee, the plaintiff-bailor

A. Must prove fault.

B. Need not prove fault because the bailee is presumed to have been negligent.

C. Need not prove fault because the bailee is presumed to have been an insurer.

D. Must prove fault if the bailee explains the exact cause of the damage or loss.

Answer (B) is correct. *(Publisher, adapted)*

REQUIRED: The proof required in an action by a bailor against a bailee.

DISCUSSION: When the bailed item is damaged or lost, the presumption is that the bailee was at fault. Accordingly, (s)he has the burden of proving that (s)he exercised due care and of providing an explanation of the exact cause of the damage or loss. The burden is placed on the bailee because the item was in his/her possession, and the bailor would have difficulty obtaining proof of negligence. The legal principle involved is res ipsa loquitur (the thing speaks for itself).

Answer (A) is incorrect. The bailee's fault is rebuttably presumed. Answer (C) is incorrect. Absent an explicit agreement, the bailee is only liable for not acting with the care required in the circumstances. Answer (D) is incorrect. The bailee also has the burden of proving that (s)he was not negligent.

26. Bunny Bailee was instructed by the bailor to return the bailed property by means of Quickie Express. A man dressed similarly to the usual Quickie Express employee came into Bailee's office and called out, "Quickie Express." Bailee delivered the bailed property to him and signed an official Quickie Express receipt. Despite her exercise of reasonable care and good faith belief that she was dealing with a Quickie Express agent, the person taking the bailed property was an impostor. Which of the following is true?

A. Quickie Express is liable because Bailee acted in good faith in delivering to the impostor.

B. Bailee is liable, good faith or not.

C. The bailor must bear the loss because (s)he owns the property, and Bailee acted with reasonable care.

D. Bailee would have less liability if this bailment were for the sole benefit of the bailor.

Answer (B) is correct. *(Publisher, adapted)*

REQUIRED: The true legal conclusion regarding misdelivery of bailed property.

DISCUSSION: The usual standard of care imposed on bailees is reasonable care. However, the bailee owes a strict duty to return the bailed property to the bailor. Misdelivery of the bailed property to a third party who is not legally entitled to it results in strict liability of the bailee and cannot be justified by reasonable care and good faith.

Answer (A) is incorrect. Quickie Express is not liable for the actions of impostors unless it has been negligent in permitting uniforms to remain in the hands of ex-employees. The courts ask whom the impostor intended to deceive. Answer (C) is incorrect. Even though the bailor owns the property and the bailee may have acted with reasonable care, a bailee is strictly liable to the bailor for misdelivery. Answer (D) is incorrect. Strict liability for misdelivery applies to a gratuitous bailee also.

27. Thief steals goods from Owner. Thief then stores the goods with Bailee, who is unaware of the theft. Owner learns of the location of the goods and gives notice to Bailee. Which of the following is true?

A. If Owner demands the goods from Bailee and Bailee refuses to surrender them, Owner may seek the remedy of replevin.

B. If Bailee had no notice of the theft and returned the goods to Thief, Owner could bring an action for conversion against Bailee.

C. Owner should bring an action for trespass to chattels against Thief rather than an action for conversion.

D. If the goods are destroyed while in the possession of Bailee after (s)he has received notice from Owner, Bailee will be liable for conversion.

Answer (A) is correct. *(Publisher, adapted)*

REQUIRED: The legal consequence of storing stolen goods with an innocent bailee.

DISCUSSION: The tort of conversion is an intentional interference with the plaintiff's right to possess his/her property. The interference must be so serious that it would be appropriate for the defendant to pay the full value of the property to plaintiff in damages. Theft, destruction, or wrongful detention of property are acts of conversion. Bailee's refusal to return the goods to the rightful owner is also an act of conversion. Plaintiff may seek the actual damages or to reacquire the property by means of replevin (a civil action brought to regain possession of wrongfully detained property).

Answer (B) is incorrect. If Bailee acted in good faith and without notice that Thief had no right to the goods, Bailee will not be liable. Answer (C) is incorrect. The action for trespass to chattels is proper for a lesser interference with the plaintiff's right to possess, e.g., minor damage to the plaintiff's car. Answer (D) is incorrect. Bailee will not be liable for conversion if (s)he has not refused a request to return the goods to Owner.

28. Which of the following statements is true?

A. Don Bailor asked Neighbor to take care of his car while he was away on business. No compensation was involved. Neighbor is only required to exercise ordinary care under the traditional rule.

B. E is a bailee of R's goods. Thief steals the bailed property. Both E and R have an action against Thief.

C. Lessor leased a truck to Lessee who was injured due to mechanical failure of the truck. Lessee cannot recover on an implied warranty because no sale occurred.

D. A customer checks her coat with an attendant at a restaurant. In the pocket of the coat is a ring. A bailment exists for both the coat and ring.

Answer (B) is correct. *(Publisher, adapted)*

REQUIRED: The true statement about bailment transactions.

DISCUSSION: The bailor and bailee have a right of action against a third party who wrongfully interferes with the bailed property. The bailor and bailee both have a property interest in the bailed goods.

Answer (A) is incorrect. A gratuitous bailee is required to use only slight care to preserve or protect bailed property under the traditional rule. The modern rule requires reasonable care under the circumstances. Answer (C) is incorrect. In a bailment for hire, the bailor has an obligation to ensure that the bailed property is reasonably fit for its intended use. Lessor impliedly warranted the fitness of the vehicle. Answer (D) is incorrect. A party cannot be held to the obligations of a bailee unless (s)he has notice of his/her possession of the bailed property. No bailment of the ring exists, so the restaurant is not liable.

29. Hurts Corporation leases a car to Benny for 30 days. The lease can be terminated except by

A. Performance or the expiration of 30 days.

B. Mutual rescission of the parties.

C. The will of either party who gives notice of termination and agrees to pay damages to the other party.

D. Notification by Hurts to Benny that the lease is canceled because Benny has engaged in an unauthorized use (and abuse) of the vehicle.

Answer (C) is correct. *(Publisher, adapted)*

REQUIRED: The true statement about proper termination of a bailment.

DISCUSSION: A bailment for a definite time or purpose cannot, as a general rule, be terminated at the will of either party since a bailment of specific property gives the bailee a property interest that will be protected against everyone including the bailor. The bailment contract may be terminated at the will of the bailee if the bailee voluntarily surrenders his/her property interest in the bailed property.

Answer (A) is incorrect. It contains two proper methods of termination of a bailment. Answer (B) is incorrect. A bailment (like any other contract) may be terminated by mutual rescission. Answer (D) is incorrect. The bailor can notify the bailee that the bailment is canceled if the bailee has misused or abused the bailed property.

30. Molly Tiff visited Happy Landing Riding Stables and rented a horse. The stable was busy and Tiff was mistakenly given a spirited horse suitable only for excellent riders. However, Tiff was an inexperienced rider. Hondo, an employee of Riding Stables, in saddling the horse failed to tighten the saddle. Tiff fell when the saddle slipped. Based on these events,

A. Tiff cannot recover unless she clearly told the riding stable of her limited riding skills.

B. Tiff assumed those risks that are the natural dangers inherent in a particular activity and, because falling off a horse was the obvious danger, Tiff cannot collect.

C. The riding stable impliedly warranted the horse's suitability and the condition of its tack.

D. If Tiff ever returns to Happy Landing Stables, Happy Landing could avoid all liability by requiring Tiff to sign a disclaimer of liability.

Answer (C) is correct. *(Publisher, adapted)*

REQUIRED: The relationship between a riding stable and its customer.

DISCUSSION: The rental of the horse was a bailment. A bailor, absent a contrary agreement, impliedly warrants that the subject of the bailment is reasonably fit for its intended use or purpose. A spirited horse suitable only for an excellent rider is not reasonably fit for rental to the general public. The riding stable also impliedly warranted that the saddle and other equipment were in proper repair and correctly adjusted.

Answer (A) is incorrect. The burden is on the riding stable to furnish a horse that is suitable to the skills of the rider-customer. Answer (B) is incorrect. A customer of a riding stable does not assume the risk of being assigned a highly spirited horse or one whose saddle has not been properly attached. A rider only assumes the risks of natural dangers inherent in horseback riding. Answer (D) is incorrect. Such a disclaimer of liability is probably against public policy. It would not be upheld by the courts when the horse was known to be spirited and was improperly saddled.

31. Juan Solo enrolled as a student in Flight School. The plane Solo was flying went out of control and crashed, severely injuring him. A screwdriver apparently left by a mechanic had jammed some of the controls and caused the crash. The basis of School's liability will rest primarily on

A. The standard of care expressed by the parties in the contract.

B. Negligence in furnishing the plane with a screwdriver in the control panel that the court will presume was placed there by School's employees.

C. The legal doctrine of assumption of risk, since it is a known fact that small planes frequently crash without negligence on the part of anyone concerned.

D. The duty of Flight School to furnish its student with a plane reasonably fit for the use or purpose intended or one free of defects.

Answer (D) is correct. *(Publisher, adapted)*

REQUIRED: The basis of a bailor's liability for an airplane crash.

DISCUSSION: A bailor in a mutual benefit bailment is under a duty to inform a bailee of hidden defects in the bailed property. A gratuitous bailee would not have an affirmative duty to inspect to determine whether the property is free from defects. In a mutual benefit bailment for hire, the bailor has an obligation to ensure that the bailed property is reasonably fit for the purposes intended. This rule has been replaced in some jurisdictions by the doctrine of strict liability in tort, under which the bailor is liable for any defects.

Answer (A) is incorrect. In a majority of jurisdictions, the bailor may not limit his/her liability. Such agreements are opposed to public policy. Also, unless the bailor expressly informs the bailee of the limitation, it is not effective. Answer (B) is incorrect. Establishing negligence would be very difficult. When or how the screwdriver was left in the controls is not known. Answer (C) is incorrect. The airplane is required to be at least reasonably fit to fly, and assumption of the risk is not relevant.

21.4 Special Bailments

32. Ted and Alice are seeking to check in at the Zestful Night Hotel. Which is the true statement with respect to the Hotel's legal rights and obligations?

A. If Zestful Night has vacancies, the hotel still may turn away Ted, Alice, and any other unwanted guests by stating that all of its accommodations have been filled or reserved.

B. The hotel is not an insurer of the safety of guests on the hotel's premises and would not be liable for an injury to Alice caused by another guest.

C. If Ted and Alice run up a bill of $650 during their stay at Zestful Night, the hotel may take possession of their luggage and contents until they pay.

D. If the hotel sprinkler system malfunctions and damages Ted and Alice's property, they can recover but only by proving negligence by the hotel or its employees.

Answer (C) is correct. *(Publisher, adapted)*

REQUIRED: The true statement regarding a hotel's obligations to guests.

DISCUSSION: An innkeeper is given a lien on all goods brought onto the premises by guests to secure charges for the accommodations and services. At common law, this lien was only possessory but, under modern statutes, the innkeeper may ultimately sell such goods to enforce the lien.

Answer (A) is incorrect. A hotel owner or innkeeper is generally obligated to serve the public, and, while a hotel may turn away guests, it must not be as a result of discrimination. Answer (B) is incorrect. Unlike at common law, modern hotels or innkeepers are not insurers of the safety of guests on their premises, although they are held to a high standard of care and may be liable for an injury caused by another guest. Answer (D) is incorrect. The liability of hotels for damage to their guests' property has been amended by statute to relieve them of strict liability. However, a malfunctioning hotel fire sprinkler system may be a res ipsa loquitur situation that shifts the burden to the hotel to prove lack of negligence.

33. With respect to a carrier, which of the following is false?

A. Common carriers are strictly liable.

B. Common law provides that a common carrier is an insurer of the goods entrusted to it as a carrier without exception.

C. The liability of a carrier frequently changes to that of a warehouser.

D. A common carrier acquires a possessory lien on the goods to secure the shipping and storage charges.

Answer (B) is correct. *(Publisher, adapted)*

REQUIRED: The false statement regarding a carrier.

DISCUSSION: The common law imposes strict liability on a common carrier. A force majeure, acts of public enemy, acts of public authority, acts of the shipper, and damage due to the inherent nature of the goods themselves are excepted matters for which the common carrier is not liable. The carrier can also reduce its liability by contract.

Answer (A) is incorrect. A common carrier is subject to strict liability even if it exercises the utmost care. Answer (C) is incorrect. The liability of a common carrier changes to that of a warehouser after the carrier has fulfilled the carriage contract and is holding the goods for the consignee. Answer (D) is incorrect. Common carriers acquire a possessory lien on the goods they handle to secure shipping and storage charges.

34. Brenda McOwns took her property to Security Storage and Warehouse to be kept at 1220 South Main Street for storage. She paid a fee and was given a warehouse receipt in usual form. Later, the warehouser moved the goods from the original storage place to a different but equally safe building. The goods were destroyed by a fire set by an unknown arsonist. With respect to liability,

A. The warehouse has no liability to McOwns because title and risk of loss remained with the bailor.

B. The standard of care imposed on the warehouse is ordinary care under the circumstances.

C. A bailee cannot move goods from the agreed place of storage for any reason.

D. The warehouse is strictly liable for any harm to McOwns's goods.

Answer (D) is correct. *(Publisher, adapted)*

REQUIRED: The true statement about the liability of a warehouse.

DISCUSSION: A warehouser is subject to the general rules of bailment. When a bailee deviates from the terms of the contract, the law imposes strict liability for any harm to the bailor's goods instead of the usual standard of reasonable care. A contract apparently was made to store the goods at a particular location, and the bailee, without the bailor's consent, moved them to a different although equally safe place. Even though the goods were destroyed through no fault of the bailee, the bailee is liable for the value of the goods under the strict liability rule.

Answer (A) is incorrect. The warehouse is under an obligation to adhere to the contract and exercise reasonable care. Answer (B) is incorrect. The warehouse deviated from the terms of the contract, which results in strict liability. Answer (C) is incorrect. A bailee may move goods from the agreed place of storage, despite the contract, but only for reasons of safety.

Success stories!

The Gleim CIA Review materials are excellent. Not only do I recommend them to my students, but I used them myself when I studied for the CIA exam. As a result, I was able to pass the CIA exam on the first attempt and received one of the William S. Smith Certificate of Honor Awards. I attribute my exam results to the Gleim CIA Review materials.

- Professor Ed Etter, Ph.D., CPA, CIA, CFE, Associate Professor of Accounting, Eastern Michigan University

I found Gleim to be much more straight forward and efficient to use than other training materials. In fact, after reviewing my Gleim material with a few friends, they switched to Gleim. Gleim helped me pass with 4 up and 4 down.

- Mitch Tobias, CMA

I was very impressed with the quality of the materials and the effectiveness of the learning outlines. I particularly enjoyed the structure of each study unit since each had variety (visual presentation, multiple choice, true false, etc.). The support from my Personal Counselor was phenomenal.

- Nathan Alger

I found Gleim's Review System to be comprehensive, informative, and extremely easy to follow. The resources and tools provided by Gleim helped me pass each section of the CIA exam with ease, and confidence. I would strongly recommend Gleim's Review System to any aspiring CIA.

- Manoj Jonna, CIA, CPA

STUDY UNIT TWENTY-TWO
COMPUTERS AND THE LAW

Computer development and use, as well as the emergence of the Internet and other technologies, have resulted in an extension of existing legal principles by both statutory modification and judicial interpretation. New laws also have been enacted to address issues unique to a computerized society, such as the formation of contracts online.

Contract formation on the Internet is subject to common-law and UCC concepts of offer and acceptance. The online seller's offer should at the very least stipulate (1) what will constitute the buyer's acceptance, (2) policies for returns or refunds, (3) terms for payment of the price and taxes, (4) buyer's remedies and any limitations on them, (5) the statute of limitations, (6) disclaimers of liability for given uses of the product, (7) privacy policies, and (8) dispute resolution mechanisms (e.g., choice of the state or country with jurisdiction). The online seller should also provide a link to the entire contract and a means for the buyer to manifest acceptance. For example, a **click-on agreement** (click-on license or click-wrap agreement) results when the online buyer clicks on a box that includes words of acceptance. It is similar to the so-called **shrink-wrap agreement** (license) found in a software package. Agreement to the licensing, warranty, and other provisions "inside the shrink-wrap" is signified by retention of the product. This agreement is most often between the software developer (not the retailer) and the customer. The buyer's failure to object to the agreement combined with use of the product may be deemed an acceptance. However, if the parties are deemed to have entered into a contract before the buyer had notice of the terms in the shrink-wrap agreement, those terms may be treated only as proposals for addition to the contract. In a **browse-wrap** situation, terms and conditions need not be agreed to by the online customer before conducting a transaction, such as downloading software. Arguably, in the absence of a plain manifestation of assent to the terms (e.g., clicking on an "I agree" box) before being allowed to proceed, the customer is not bound.

Some contracts, for example, those involving sales of goods for a price of $500 or more, must be signed by the party to be bound. In electronic commerce, technologies have been developed to satisfy the signature requirement. One such technology is the **digital signature**, which uses public-key encryption to authenticate electronic documents. Another method employs **signature dynamics**. An actual signature is made and electronically measured, and the relevant information (time, date, identity, and measurements) is sent in encrypted form in a **biometric token** accompanying the electronic document. Still other possibilities are the use of a **smart card** inserted into a computer or the scanning of biometric traits (e.g., a fingerprint or retina) that could be matched with information held in the files of a security firm.

The **Uniform Electronic Transactions Act (UETA)** applies to the enforcement of electronic transactions (but not to wills, codicils to wills, trusts created by wills, and transactions governed by the UCC other than Articles 2 and 2A). However, it does not establish rules (such as requiring digital signatures) for them. Under this act, an electronic signature satisfies a requirement for a signature, an electronic record satisfies a requirement for a writing, and a contract is not denied legal effect solely because an electronic record was used in its formation. An **electronic signature** is an electronic symbol, sound, process, etc., logically related to a record and made by a person intending to sign the record. For example, it includes a name at the end of an email message intended to be a signature or a click on a website intended to identify a person. A **record** is information contained in a tangible medium or stored in some medium and retrievable in visual form. The federal law is the **Electronic Signatures in Global and National Commerce Act of 2000**, which applies to transactions in or affecting interstate or foreign commerce. It provides that signatures, contracts, or other records related to those transactions are not invalid solely because they are in electronic form. However, this act's scope excludes certain types of documents (court records, various notices to consumers, family law matters, etc.). Moreover, the agreements covered are mostly those involving sales or leases of goods.

A transaction involving computer equipment (including programs and supporting information bundled with the goods) is a sale of goods, and certain specific warranties arise pursuant to the UCC's Article 2. A **warranty** is an assurance or a guarantee that goods will conform to certain standards. If these standards are not met, the buyer may be able to recover from the seller based on the theory of breach of warranty. Sellers of computer products may attempt to limit their warranty liability by contractual means, such as by use of disclaimer clauses, limits on remedies, and integration clauses. These protective yet one-sided measures are counterbalanced by the buyer's right to seek remedies in tort, e.g., for fraud, negligence, and strict liability.

The seller of a computer may be liable in **tort** for fraud or negligence or may incur strict liability. A buyer who is fraudulently induced to purchase the computer may bring suit if (s)he can establish **fraud** on the part of the seller. A necessary element of fraud is the specific intent of the seller to misrepresent a material fact about the product. That is, the buyer must be injured as a result of fraudulent information supplied (or essential information not supplied) by the seller in the course of the sale, and the buyer must have reasonably relied on the information.

An injured buyer may also have a cause of action in **negligence** against the seller of a defective computer. The following are the traditional elements of negligence: a duty owed by defendant to plaintiff; breach of the duty; actual injury; and actual and proximate causation of the injury by the breach.

An injured buyer may have a cause of action based on **strict liability** concerning a defective computer. In a strict liability suit against a seller of a product, a plaintiff who has suffered physical harm or property damage must prove that the product was defective, the defect rendered it unreasonably dangerous, the unreasonably dangerous condition of the product caused the harm or damage, the seller was engaged in the business of selling the particular product, and the product reached the user or consumer without substantial change from the condition in which it was sold (Restatement of Torts, Second). Currently, most actions against computer manufacturers are for economic injuries as opposed to personal injury or property damage.

Traditional **tort law** concepts apply to online activities, but unique issues are also raised. For example, the **Communications Decency Act of 1996** absolves Internet service providers, that is, interactive computer service providers, of liability for defamatory materials placed online by another information content provider. Hence, an ISP is not deemed to be a publisher or speaker. Moreover, an ISP cannot disclose customer information without a court order. A defamed party may therefore need to sue the unknown person to obtain an order compelling disclosure. **Spam**, especially in its most abusive forms, may be deemed a trespass to property, and some states regulate its use.

Software is treated as **intellectual property**. Protection of intellectual property is provided for by copyright, trade secret, patent, and trademark laws. Copyright law protects the **expression** of an idea. The **Copyright Act of 1976** was amended in 1980 to cover software. The 1980 act states that a **computer program** is a "set of statements or instructions to be used directly or indirectly in a computer to bring about a certain result." Programs are included in one of the seven classifications under the heading "literary works." The structure, sequence, and organization of a computer program are most likely protected under the copyright laws. The courts disagree as to whether software menus, windows, commands, and other screen displays (the "look and feel") are protected. The amendments to the Copyright Act also permit a customer who purchases software to duplicate it solely for his/her own use. To avoid application of this amendment, software has been distributed under **licenses**, rather than **by direct sales**. A licensing agreement typically restricts the use of the software, including prohibitions on renting to others and on reverse engineering. However, a software licensing agreement usually allows one backup copy to be made. Installing the software on multiple computers and making additional copies are copyright violations. Extensive copying violates the **fair use** exception to copyright protection. The **No Electronic Theft Act of 1997** prohibits intentionally taking and distributing, e.g., over the Internet, copies of copyrighted works with a total retail value exceeding $1,000 during any 180-day period. In addition, unauthorized electronic copying of movies, music, etc., for personal use is prohibited. Copying may consist simply of loading a program into random access memory (RAM). Criminal penalties include a fine of up to $250,000 and 5 years imprisonment and may be imposed even if the defendant had no intent to profit from the theft. The **Digital Millennium Copyright Act of 1998** was a response to the U.S.'s adherence to the World Intellectual Property Organization (WIPO) treaty of 1996. The act and the treaty make the circumvention of antipiracy measures (such as encryption techniques) illegal. It is also illegal to produce, import, sell, etc., any circumvention devices or services, although the fair use of such devices or services by appropriate parties (scientists, libraries, etc.) is allowed. Furthermore, the act provides that an Internet service provider is not liable for copyright violations by a subscriber unless the ISP knew of them or did not take steps to stop them after notice. The Supreme Court in **MGM Studios, Inc. v. Grokster, Ltd. (2005)**, interpreted the DMCA as prohibiting the promotion of any service or device as a means of infringing copyrights. Thus, peer-to-peer services for sharing music files were held to be in violation of the act. Grokster was found to have actively attempted to profit from and induce direct infringement by its customers. Under the **Family Entertainment and Copyright Act of 2005**, it is a crime to infringe a copyright by distributing on a computer network a computer program, audiovisual work, music, or sound recording. This act is directed toward bootlegging of such materials or recording them from the audience. For a first offense, willful misconduct by a person who knew or should have known the work was intended for commercial use is punishable by up to 3 years in prison (5 years if the misconduct was for financial gain). Under the **Anti-Counterfeiting Amendments Act of 2004**, it is a crime to traffic knowingly in a counterfeit label or illicit authentication feature of (1) a phonorecord, (2) a copy of a computer program, (3) a copy of a motion picture or other audiovisual work, or (4) documentation or packaging. It is also illegal to traffic knowingly in counterfeit documentation or packaging. Moreover, this act provides for a civil suit by an injured copyright owner, potentially resulting in treble damages.

Trade secret law protects commercially valuable information not widely known in the owner's industry. Most states have adopted the Uniform Trade Secrets Act. Under this act, misappropriation gives rise to an action for damages. Moreover, many states and the federal government (in the **Economic Espionage Act of 1996**) make theft of trade secrets a crime. Trade secret law protects ideas, not just the expression of ideas. Consequently, the conceptual basis of a computer program may be protected by trade secret law. Unlike patent protection, trade secret protection is not predicated on registering the secret with the government. However, software ordinarily will not be protected as a trade secret if a competitor acquires knowledge of the idea by legal means. Thus, software manufacturers use various means to prevent discovery. Licensing agreements may include terms that prohibit disclosure and restrict program use to a single computer, e.g., by way of a site restriction; employees may be required to sign secrecy agreements; and access to software may be restricted to certain employees.

The Semiconductor Chip Protection Act (SCPA) of 1984 protects, for a 10-year period, mask works and semiconductor chip products. A **mask work** is a form of expression used on a chip design. It includes stencils used in the manufacturing of chips. **Semiconductor chip products** include analog chips, microprocessors, and RAM or ROM memory chips. The act requires mask work owners to register within 2 years of a work's first commercial exploitation. The SCPA does not grant the mask owner the right to prevent others from copying its product. Instead, some copying is permitted. For instance, the mask work can be **reverse-engineered** and used in other semiconductor chip products if the newly created products are the result of substantial study and not mere copying. Infringement of this protection can result in actual damages and loss of profits or statutory damages up to $250,000.

Federal **patent law** will protect software included in a process if the process is patentable. Whereas copyright law protects only expression, a patent protects the underlying idea behind the software. In defining the nature of a patentable process, the Supreme Court has stated, "A process is a mode of treatment of certain materials to produce a given result. It is an act, or a series of acts, performed upon the subject matter to be transferred and reduced to a different state or thing. If new and useful, it is just as patentable as is a piece of machinery. The machinery pointed out as suitable to perform the process may or may not be patentable; whilst the process itself may be altogether new and produce an entirely new result." Typically, the process must have utility, be novel, and not be obvious. Patent protection grants the software developer the exclusive right to use, make, and market the patented product for 20 years from the date of filing. Moreover, in the U.S., the first party to invent has priority, not, as in most countries, the first to file. Furthermore, court rulings narrowing the scope of what is nonpatentable have led to the patenting of **business processes**, especially those used in e-commerce, for example, online ordering or auction systems.

A **trademark** is a distinctive mark, word, letter, number, design, picture, or a combination thereof used by a manufacturer or merchant to identify its goods and distinguish them from the goods of others. **Service marks** have a similar function with regard to services. If a mark is inherently distinctive or has a secondary meaning, it may be registered for renewable 10-year periods with the U.S. Patent and Trademark Office provided that it has been used in commerce or the registrant has a bona fide intent to use it within 6 months. Formerly, the protection afforded to marks prohibited only use on competing or related goods or services. However, under the **Federal Trademark Dilution Act of 1995**, infringement is now prohibited when the same or a similar mark is used for an unrelated purpose. Internet **domain names** (e.g., gleim.com) are another source of trademark-related controversy. One approach to rights disputes was the establishment of the nonprofit **Internet Corporation for Assigned Names and Numbers (ICANN)** by the federal government. This entity not only helps resolve conflicts internationally but also has approved new top-level domains (.biz, .info, .name, .pro, .museums, .coop, and .aero).

A second approach was the enactment of the **Anticybersquatting Consumer Protection Act of 1999**, an amendment of the Lanham Trademark Act of 1946. The 1999 act prohibits registering, trafficking in, or using a domain name with a bad faith intent to profit if that name is the same as, or confusingly similar to, another party's trademark. Furthermore, the act has retroactive effect to any registration of a domain name. An aggrieved party may recover actual damages or the damages specified in the act. Another species of online trademark infringement is its appropriation in **meta tags** to improve a site's search engine results.

The computerized accumulation of information concerning private individuals poses a potential threat to an individual's **right of privacy**. Protection is provided by statutes and the common law. Both federal and state governments have enacted statutes to protect privacy rights. Federal statutes particularly relevant to computer use include the **Family Educational Rights and Privacy Act of 1974 (FERPA)**, which gives students over the age of 18 and parents of dependent students rights of inspection, correction, and disclosure of educational records at institutions of higher education. The **Right to Financial Privacy Act of 1978** restricts government access to customer records at financial institutions unless the customer authorizes disclosure or the government properly requests the records. The **Fair Credit Reporting Act** requires consumer credit reporting agencies to implement safeguards to ensure that only accurate information is included in consumer credit reports. The **Electronic Communications Privacy Act of 1986** prohibits intentional interception or disclosure of communications made by cell phone, email, etc. However, the act contains an exception to allow monitoring in the workplace if communications are in the ordinary course of business, and the devices used (e.g., email) are provided by the employer. A second exception is for monitoring consented to by employees. **The Computer Matching and Privacy Act of 1988** regulates computer programs that compare two or more automated systems of records. These types of matches are used to determine eligibility for, and compliance with, federal benefit programs, such as Social Security or student financial aid. The **Children's Online Privacy Protection Act of 1998** controls the information that is collected from children while they are online. Operators of commercial websites and online services directed to or knowingly collecting personal information from children under 13 must notify parents of their information practices, obtain verifiable parental consent, provide parental choice as to whether information is disclosed to third parties, provide parents access to their child's information, allow parents to prevent further use of collected information, not require that a child provide more information than is necessary, and maintain the confidentiality and security of the information. Under the **Children's Internet Protection Act of 2000**, public schools and libraries must install filtering software to prevent access to websites with specified URLs or meta tags (key words).

The widespread ability of individuals and businesses to use computers may have a significant potential impact on interests in, and rights to, the **privacy of persons acting in either a personal or business context**. The role of common law in recognizing and protecting privacy interests and rights may have become more crucial because of enhanced information-related capabilities. The conduct required to meet a **common-law duty of care affecting privacy** interests and rights may need to be effectively modified with respect to computerized environments. A professional, for example, might develop a computerized information file on a client that contains some confidential information. The professional may be subject to common-law liability for failure to adequately protect that information from unauthorized access by, or disclosure to, third parties. The steps a reasonable person or a reasonable professional person would be required to take to avoid liability to meet the required standard of care may be affected by the computer media in which the information is stored.

Computer crime is any illegal act that uses, involves, or is directed against computers. Computer crimes can be grouped into four categories: theft, financial crimes, damaging and destructive programming, and software piracy. Traditional criminal, tort, patent, copyright, trade secret laws, and new legislation are used to combat and prevent computer crime. **Theft** includes stealing computer equipment (hardware) and unauthorized use, for personal gain, of data stored in a computer system. **Financial crimes** include embezzlement, fraud, identity theft, and any other illegal act involving financial resources or transactions. **Damaging and destructive programming** includes physical abuse of hardware and computer programming that alters or destroys data. **Software piracy** involves unauthorized reproduction of software. Patent, copyright, and trade secret laws have recently been expanded to protect software against piracy.

Federal legislation forbids specific acts related to the use of computers. **The Counterfeit Access Device and Computer Fraud and Abuse Act** (as amended by the **National Infrastructure Protection Act of 1996**) prohibits unauthorized access to a **protected computer** online to obtain, alter, transmit, etc., protected government or private information. It is also a crime to traffic in passwords or other means of accessing a computer with intent to defraud. Furthermore, the act prohibits **hacking**. If the value of the taking (e.g., data or computer time) exceeds $5,000, the crime is a felony. Victims also may sue civilly. The **Controlling the Assault of Non-Solicited Pornography and Marketing Act of 2003** states that (1) senders of **spam** must not conceal its content or source, and (2) a recipient's decision not to receive it in the future from the same source must be respected. **The Electronic Funds Transfer Act** prohibits the sale, use, or interstate transportation of any lost, stolen, forged, counterfeit, altered, or fraudulently obtained device used to execute an electronic funds transfer.

QUESTIONS

22.1 Introduction

1. Which of the following is a true statement about the scope and origin of computer law?

A. Computer law developed as a distinct body of law solely from court cases involving computers.

B. Invasion of privacy involving computers is a constitutional issue rather than a computer law issue.

C. Copying of personal computer software is not a crime.

D. Computer law uses principles and precedents from other areas of law as well as court cases involving computers.

Answer (D) is correct. *(Publisher, adapted)*

REQUIRED: The true statement about computer law.

DISCUSSION: Computer law began to evolve with court cases involving the earliest computers, but the courts have usually relied on principles from other areas of law, such as contracts, warranty, torts, intellectual property, and statutory protection of privacy, in rendering decisions in cases involving computers.

Answer (A) is incorrect. Except for certain statutes, computer law is not a distinct body of law. Thus, it relies on principles and precedents from other areas of law. Answer (B) is incorrect. Invasion of privacy using a computer is both a constitutional and computer law issue. Answer (C) is incorrect. Introducing fraudulent data into a computer system and unauthorized duplication of copyrighted material could be criminal acts.

22.2 The UCC

2. Hacker Corporation sold Micro International its Hacker Operating System (HOS). Micro sold HOS bundled with its new computers to several thousand customers. On April 1, a Trojan horse program embedded in HOS's code was executed on all computers running HOS. The program rendered all of the programs, data, and files on these computers' hard disks unusable. If the transactions were transactions in goods, what is Hacker's potential liability to Micro and third parties?

	Economic Losses	Personal Injury	Punitive Damages
A.	Yes	Yes	Yes
B.	Yes	No	No
C.	No	Yes	No
D.	No	No	No

Answer (A) is correct. *(Publisher, adapted)*

REQUIRED: The liability by a software developer for damages resulting from the use of the software.

DISCUSSION: Hacker would be liable under the UCC for economic losses for breach of implied warranty of merchantability because the destruction of customers' data implies HOS was not fit for the ordinary purpose for which it was intended. If HOS were the proximate cause of the malfunction of computer operated equipment that injured employees, customers, or innocent bystanders, Hacker would be liable in tort for those personal injuries as well as any economic losses. If the Trojan horse program were intentionally embedded in HOS by Hacker's personnel, Hacker would be liable for punitive damages as well as economic loss and personal injury.

3. CPA Firm contracted to purchase 100 ISM Lap 10 personal computers. ISM's sales representative, Skip, claimed the computers would run an advanced operating system that ISM planned to market. The contract included a standard integration clause but was silent as to the advanced operating system. After the computers were delivered and paid for, ISM introduced the new system, which CPA Firm learned was incompatible with its Lap 10s. Is ISM liable to CPA Firm?

A. ISM is liable because the integration clause made Skip's claims part of the contract.

B. ISM is liable because Skip's action was fraudulent.

C. ISM is not liable because a salesperson's representations are excluded from sales contracts unless expressly included.

D. ISM is not liable because the parol evidence rule excludes the prior statements.

Answer (D) is correct. *(Publisher, adapted)*

REQUIRED: The liability of the seller of computer products for prior representations by its agent.

DISCUSSION: The integration clause indicates that the contract is meant to be complete, that is, to embody the entire understanding of the parties. Thus, the parol evidence rule will apply. It bars evidence of prior agreements or of contemporaneous oral agreements that would vary, alter, or contradict the terms of a written contract intended to be entire. Consequently, ISM will not be liable because evidence of Skip's representations is inadmissible.

Answer (A) is incorrect. An integration clause excludes rather than includes prior agreements. Answer (B) is incorrect. No evidence is given that the elements of fraud are present. Answer (C) is incorrect. In the absence of an integration clause, these representations may be included in sales contracts unless expressly excluded.

4. If a transaction involving computer products is considered a sale of goods, the UCC applies and

A. The seller may be liable for consequential damages even if the contract had an express exclusion of such damages.

B. The agreement of the parties to limit the buyer's remedies will be ineffective.

C. The seller is more likely to prevail because the UCC favors sellers rather than buyers.

D. The implied warranty of fitness for a particular purpose will protect the seller.

Answer (A) is correct. *(Publisher, adapted)*

REQUIRED: The seller's liability under the UCC for a transaction in computer products.

DISCUSSION: Under the UCC, a seller of goods is liable for economic losses resulting from breach of express and implied warranties. However, an exclusion of the seller's liability for consequential damages may be rendered invalid if it is unconscionable (UCC 2-719). Thus, a seller may be liable for consequential damages despite the terms of the contract.

Answer (B) is incorrect. A contractual modification or limitation of remedies is effective unless the circumstances cause an exclusive or limited remedy to fail of its essential purpose. Answer (C) is incorrect. Buyers are favored under the UCC, not sellers. Answer (D) is incorrect. An implied warranty of fitness for a particular purpose protects buyers, not sellers.

5. Which of the following result(s) in an express warranty with respect to a sale of a computer?

I. An advertisement for a personal computer system states that it includes a modem with a specified speed.

II. The seller states that its workstation has the hard disk capacity to function as the server for the buyer's local area network.

A. I only.

B. II only.

C. Both I and II.

D. Neither I nor II.

Answer (A) is correct. *(Publisher, adapted)*

REQUIRED: The factor(s), if any, resulting in an express warranty.

DISCUSSION: An express warranty results if any affirmation of fact or promise made by the seller to the buyer, e.g., the speed of the modem, that relates to the goods (by any description of the goods or by any sample or model) becomes part of the basis of the bargain (UCC 2-313). Reliance by the buyer need not be proven. An implied warranty of fitness for a particular purpose, not an express warranty, arises when the seller knows the particular purpose for which goods are required, and the buyer relies on the seller's expertise.

Questions 6 and 7 are based on the following information. Based on a model on display in the storefront of Cuenin's Computers, a retailer of personal computer systems and their components, Doug ordered 12 GTS computers for his small business. When the computers were delivered, he discovered that none had a DVD drive like those of the GTS computers on display.

6. Which of the following statements is true about a purchase made based on a model provided by the seller?

A. Cuenin's Computers violated an express warranty that the computers delivered will conform to the model.

B. Cuenin's Computers violated an implied warranty of fitness for a particular purpose because the purchase was based on the display model.

C. Doug has no warranty claim against Cuenin's because he did not specifically state his need for DVD drives.

D. Doug has no warranty claim against Cuenin's Computers because a warranty must be in writing to be enforceable.

Answer (A) is correct. *(Publisher, adapted)*

REQUIRED: The true statement about a purchase based on a display model.

DISCUSSION: Under UCC Article 2, any affirmation of fact or promise made by a seller to the buyer that (1) relates to the goods and (2) becomes part of the basis of the bargain creates an express warranty that the goods delivered will conform to the affirmation or promise. Such an affirmation may consist of an explicit verbal statement. However, express warranties may also be created by description, model, or sample. A bargain that is made based on a display model generates an express warranty that the goods will conform to the model.

Answer (B) is incorrect. The facts do not indicate that the seller knew the particular purpose for which the goods were to be used. Answer (C) is incorrect. An express warranty results if any affirmation of fact or promise made by the seller to the buyer that relates to the goods, i.e., a model, becomes part of the basis of the bargain. Answer (D) is incorrect. An express warranty need not be in writing.

7. Which of the following implied warranties would result from Doug's purchase from Cuenin's Computers?

I. Implied warranty of merchantability
II. Implied warranty of fitness for a particular purpose
III. Implied warranty of title

A. I only.
B. III only.
C. I and III only.
D. I, II, and III.

Answer (C) is correct. *(CPA, adapted)*

REQUIRED: The implied warranty or warranties.

DISCUSSION: A warranty of title is implied in every contract for the sale of goods, unless the parties agree otherwise. The warranty of merchantability is implied only when the seller is a merchant. Cuenin's Computers is a merchant because it deals in goods of the kind sold. The implied warranty of fitness for a particular purpose arises only when a seller has reason to know the particular purpose for which the goods are to be used and that the buyer is relying on the seller's skill and judgment to select the goods.

Answer (A) is incorrect. Absent contrary agreement, the warranty of title is implied in every contract for the sale of goods. Answer (B) is incorrect. The seller is a merchant. Thus, a warranty of merchantability is also implied. Answer (D) is incorrect. The seller did not know the particular purpose for which the goods were to be used.

8. Suzanne, the purchasing agent for a large medical research facility, tells a sales associate at Slaton's Computer World that she needs a computer with enough memory to store information regarding thousands of patients. This information is crucial to the facility's work. Which of the following is not express warranty with respect to the sale of the computer?

A. Slaton's Computer World advertises in the local newspaper that the computer has 1.5 GB of RAM.
B. The sales associate tells Suzanne that the computer is a perfect fit for her needs.
C. Slaton's Computer World distributes a brochure for the computer stating a promise to outperform all other Pentium IV computers.
D. A display of the computer is set up in the store.

Answer (B) is correct. *(Publisher, adapted)*

REQUIRED: The item that does not result in an express warranty.

DISCUSSION: Under UCC 2-315, a warranty of fitness for a particular purpose is implied (unless excluded or modified) when the seller has reason to know the particular purpose for which the goods will be used and that the buyer is relying on the seller's skill or judgment to choose the goods. Under UCC Article 2, any affirmation of fact or promise made by a seller to the buyer that (1) relates to the goods and (2) becomes part of the basis of the bargain creates an express warranty that the goods delivered will conform to the affirmation or promise. In addition to explicit verbal statements of fact or promises relating to the goods, express warranties also may be created by description, model, or sample.

Answer (A) is incorrect. Specifying memory capacity is an express warranty. Answer (C) is incorrect. Stating a promise to outperform other computers is an express warranty. Answer (D) is incorrect. A display of the computer set up in the store is an express warranty.

9. LDB Productions, Inc. entered into a contract with Ramsey Tech to purchase a used personal computer. LDB is in the business of selling new and used personal computers to the general public. Ramsey also stated in the contract that the personal computer had been used for only 3 months by its previous owner. The contract included the statement that the personal computer was being sold "as is," and this provision was in a larger and different type style than the remainder of the contract. With regard to the contract between LDB and Ramsey

A. An implied warranty of merchantability does not arise unless both LDB and Ramsey are merchants.
B. The "as is" provision effectively disclaims the implied warranty of title.
C. No express warranties are created by the contract.
D. The "as is" provision does not prevent Ramsey from being liable for a breach of any express warranties created by the contract.

Answer (D) is correct. *(Publisher, adapted)*

REQUIRED: The true statement about a contract with an "as is" provision.

DISCUSSION: The "as is" provision excludes only implied warranties. An express warranty is rarely effectively disclaimed. An express warranty and a disclaimer are construed as consistent with each other whenever reasonable. If such an interpretation is unreasonable, however, the disclaimer is ineffective and the express warranty prevails.

Answer (A) is incorrect. Only the seller need be a merchant. Answer (B) is incorrect. The warranty of title is not an implied warranty. Specific language or circumstances known by the buyer are necessary to disclaim the warranty of title. Answer (C) is incorrect. The contract expressly warrants the usage of the personal computer by the previous owner.

10. Jacqui bought a used laptop from JHS Computing, which disclaimed "any and all warranties" in connection with the sale. JHS Computing was unaware that the laptop had been stolen from Buffett. Jacqui surrendered it to Buffett when confronted with proof of the theft. Jacqui sued JHS Computing. Who is likely to prevail and why?

A. JHS Computing, because of the general disclaimer.

B. JHS Computing, because it was unaware of the theft.

C. Jacqui, because the warranty of title has been breached.

D. Jacqui, because JHS Computing is a merchant.

Answer (C) is correct. *(CPA, adapted)*

REQUIRED: The party likely to prevail upon sale of property not owned by the seller.

DISCUSSION: UCC 2-312 establishes a warranty of title by any seller that can only be excluded or modified by specific language or by the buyer's knowledge of circumstances relating to the title. A general disclaimer of warranty, such as a disclaimer of "any and all warranties," is ineffective regarding the warranty of title. JHS Computing therefore warranted the title by selling the laptop to Jacqui and will bear the loss. The loss is the fair market value of the property at the time it was taken from Jacqui plus consequential damages.

Answer (A) is incorrect. The language must be specific to disclaim the warranty of title. Answer (B) is incorrect. The warranty may be breached unintentionally. The loss is placed on the party (the seller) who is better able to avoid the loss. Answer (D) is incorrect. A nonmerchant seller also warrants the title unless (s)he makes a specific disclaimer.

22.3 Intellectual Property

11. Intellectual property embodied in computer software may be protected via

	Patent Law	Copyright Law	Trade Secret Protection
A.	No	No	No
B.	Yes	No	Yes
C.	Yes	Yes	Yes
D.	No	No	Yes

Answer (C) is correct. *(Publisher, adapted)*

REQUIRED: The area(s) of law applicable to intellectual property embodied in computer software.

DISCUSSION: To be patentable, the subject matter must be a process, a machine, or a composition of matter. Additionally, the subject matter of the patent must have utility, be a novelty, be nonobvious, and be adequately disclosed. Clearly, computer hardware is patentable. Moreover, the Supreme Court has stated that software may be patented if it is included in an invention. The courts have also given protection to software under the copyright laws as the expression of an idea, not the idea itself. Finally, hardware or software not patentable or copyrightable may be protected as a trade secret.

12. Under the Computer Software Copyright Act of 1980, a written program is

A. Protected only if it is written in source code.

B. Protected only if it is written in machine language.

C. Categorized under literary works.

D. Copyrightable as both an idea and the expression of an idea.

Answer (C) is correct. *(Publisher, adapted)*

REQUIRED: The true statement about the Computer Software Copyright Act of 1980.

DISCUSSION: The 1980 act states that a computer program is a "set of statements or instructions to be used directly or indirectly in a computer to bring about a certain result." Programs are included in one of the seven classifications under the heading "literary works."

Answer (A) is incorrect. A computer program is copyrightable if it is in machine language. Answer (B) is incorrect. A computer program is copyrightable if it is in source code. Answer (D) is incorrect. A computer program is copyrightable as an expression of an idea. An idea itself is not copyrightable.

13. Under U.S. patent law, software included in an invention will be protected for

A. 20 years from the time of filing, with the first party to invent having priority.

B. 17 years from the time of filing, with the first party to file having priority.

C. 14 years from the time of the invention, with the first party to file having priority.

D. 17 years from the time of the invention, with the first party to invent having priority.

Answer (A) is correct. *(Publisher, adapted)*

REQUIRED: The protection accorded to software by U.S. patent law.

DISCUSSION: Patent protection grants the software developer the exclusive right to use, make, and market the patented product for 20 years from the date of filing. Moreover, the first party to invent has priority, not the first party to file. In most nations, the first party to file has priority.

Answer (B) is incorrect. Prior to 1995, the duration of most patents was 17 years. Furthermore, in the U.S., the first to invent has priority. Answer (C) is incorrect. Only design patents have a life of 14 years from the date of filing, and the first to invent has priority. Answer (D) is incorrect. Under current law, most patents have a duration of 20 years from the date of filing.

14. Which of the following is a true statement about the protection offered by the law of patents, copyrights, or trade secrets?

A. Once granted, the patent is good for the life of the inventor plus 50 years.

B. Copyright law permits ideas to be protected, not expressions of those ideas.

C. Trade secrets must be registered.

D. Trade secrets have perpetual life until honestly discovered by others, and they require no public filings or disclosure.

Answer (D) is correct. *(Publisher, adapted)*

REQUIRED: The true statement about the protection of intellectual property.

DISCUSSION: Information is a trade secret if the information gives its owner an advantage, is a protected secret, has value, and is not easily discovered by others. A trade secret has a longer potential life than patents or copyrights, which are limited to 20 years (14 years for a design patent) or 70 years plus the author's life, respectively. A trade secret will be protected until honest discovery by another. Moreover, no public filings or disclosures are required for trade secrets.

Answer (A) is incorrect. A patent is good for 20 years. Answer (B) is incorrect. Copyrights protect the expression of ideas, not the ideas themselves. Answer (C) is incorrect. Trade secrets do not have to be registered.

15. Catfastic Company's signature product is Catfastic kitty litter. Accordingly, Catfastic Company has registered "Catfastic" as a trademark. However, an individual named Wilene Hackett applied for and received the Internet domain name, catfastic.com. Under current U.S. law and Internet domain dispute policy,

A. Hackett is entitled to the domain name on a first-come, first-served basis.

B. Hackett is entitled to the domain name if she uses it for commercial purposes unrelated to Catfastic's business.

C. Catfastic can enjoin Hackett's commercial use but cannot obtain the use of the domain name.

D. Catfastic can enjoin Hackett's commercial use and can obtain the use of the domain name.

Answer (D) is correct. *(Publisher, adapted)*

REQUIRED: The trademark holder's rights against an individual who has obtained a trademarked Internet domain name.

DISCUSSION: The Federal Trademark Dilution Act protects against infringement when the same or a similar mark is used for an unrelated purpose. Thus, the firm holding a registered trademark can obtain an injunction to prohibit another party's commercial use whether or not in a related business. Furthermore, Internet domain dispute policy allows for the issuance to the trademark holder of the corresponding domain name.

Answer (A) is incorrect. Domain names are customarily issued on a first-come, first-served basis, but current policy allows a trademark holder to challenge the prior issuance of a domain name that is identical or confusingly similar to its trademark. Answer (B) is incorrect. Prior law did not prohibit noncompeting uses of a trademark. Answer (C) is incorrect. Catfastic can reclaim the domain name.

16. During an audit to determine whether Hoyt, Inc. is in compliance with software copyright requirements, the auditor finds that a marketing manager purchased software from Meachem Technologies, Inc. The manager made a backup copy of the software for her own use and also provided a copy for each computer in the company. Which of the following is most likely true regarding compliance with copyright requirements?

A. The backup copy is a copyright infringement.

B. Making copies for each computer in the company is a copyright infringement.

C. The backup copy and making copies for each computer in the company are copyright infringements.

D. Hoyt, Inc. has not committed copyright infringement.

Answer (B) is correct. *(Publisher, adapted)*

REQUIRED: The true statement about compliance with software copyright requirements.

DISCUSSION: Copyright law protects the expression of an idea. The Copyright Act was amended in 1980 to cover computer software. These amendments permit a customer who purchases software to duplicate it solely for his/her own use. However, making additional copies for use on the other computers in the company most likely violates the fair use doctrine. Whether a use is fair and not a violation of copyright law depends on such factors as whether it is for commercial purposes, the extent of copying, and the possible impact on the copyright holder's sales.

Answer (A) is incorrect. Under the 1980 amendments to the Copyright Act, the purchaser of software may make a copy of the software, i.e., a backup copy, for his/her own use. Answer (C) is incorrect. The purchaser may make a backup copy. Answer (D) is incorrect. Software is customarily licensed to be used on a single computer.

17. An entrepreneur requires a copy of spreadsheet software for use on a single office personal computer. Which of the following actions will most likely not violate the software license agreement?

A. Making a backup copy.

B. Installing the spreadsheet software on a multi-user network.

C. Using the spreadsheet software at home for personal business.

D. Replacing the office computer and using the spreadsheet software on the new one.

Answer (A) is correct. *(CIA, adapted)*

REQUIRED: The action that most likely will not violate a software license agreement.

DISCUSSION: A licensing agreement typically restricts the use of the software, including prohibitions on renting to others and on reverse engineering. However, a software licensing agreement usually allows one backup copy to be made. Installing the software on multiple computers and making additional copies are copyright violations.

Answer (B) is incorrect. Installing the spreadsheet software on a multi-user network would make it available to multiple users. Answer (C) is incorrect. Not all vendors allow use on different machines. Answer (D) is incorrect. Some agreements require relicensing when a machine change occurs.

18. Redish Enterprises, Inc., developed software based on a particular algorithm, which it considers a trade secret. Its competitor, Smoove Corp., learned about this algorithm and used it to develop a version of the software. Under current law,

A. No matter how Smoove obtained the algorithm, Smoove is liable to Redish if it uses the trade secret information.

B. Redish is only protected under trade secret law if the algorithm was registered with the government.

C. If Smoove obtained the algorithm by legal means, Smoove is free to use the information without liability.

D. If Smoove obtained the algorithm by improper means, Smoove has committed a tort but not a crime.

Answer (C) is correct. *(Publisher, adapted)*

REQUIRED: The true statement about trade secret protection.

DISCUSSION: Trade secret law protects commercially valuable information not widely known in the industry. Trade secret law protects ideas, such as the conceptual basis of a computer program, not just the expression of ideas, such as the computer program itself. Under current law, the program, but not its conceptual basis, may be copyrighted or patented. Furthermore, protection as a trade secret is not available if a competitor acquires knowledge of the idea by legal means.

Answer (A) is incorrect. If a competitor acquires knowledge of a trade secret by legal means, it is no longer protected under trade secret law. Answer (B) is incorrect. Trade secrets are not required to be registered to be protected under trade secret law. Answer (D) is incorrect. Theft of trade secrets is a federal crime under the Economic Espionage Act of 1996.

19. Under the Semiconductor Chip Protection Act (SCPA) of 1984,

I. Semiconductor chip products protected under the SCPA include analog chips, microprocessors, and RAM or ROM memory chips

II. The SCPA protects the mask owner from reverse engineering of its product by others

III. The SCPA requires mask work owners to register within 2 years of a work's first commercial exploitation

A. II only.

B. I and III only.

C. II and III only.

D. I, II, and III.

Answer (B) is correct. *(Publisher, adapted)*

REQUIRED: The true statement(s) regarding the SCPA.

DISCUSSION: The Semiconductor Chip Protection Act (SCPA) of 1984 protects, for a 10-year period, mask works and the semiconductor chip products. A mask work is a form of expression used on a chip design. It includes stencils used in the manufacturing of chips. Semiconductor chip products include analog chips, microprocessors, and RAM or ROM memory chips. The act requires mask work owners to register within 2 years of a work's first commercial exploitation. The SCPA does not grant the mask owner the right to prevent others from copying its product. Instead, some copying is permitted. For instance, the mask work can be reverse-engineered and used in other semiconductor chip products if the newly created products are the result of substantial study and not mere copying.

22.4 Privacy

20. Which federal act gives a student rights with respect to his/her academic records stored on a university's computer?

A. The Family Educational Rights and Privacy Act of 1974.

B. The Freedom of Information Act.

C. The Privacy Act of 1974.

D. The Securities Act of 1933.

Answer (A) is correct. *(Publisher, adapted)*

REQUIRED: The federal act that protects the privacy of a student's academic records.

DISCUSSION: The Family Educational Rights and Privacy Act of 1974 gives students over 18 and parents of dependent students certain rights of inspection, correction, and disclosure of that information.

Answer (B) is incorrect. The Freedom of Information Act grants citizens access to federal government records. Answer (C) is incorrect. The Privacy Act of 1974 safeguards computerized data in federal agencies and the Federal Reserve Banks. Answer (D) is incorrect. The Securities Act of 1933 concerns the initial registration of publicly traded securities.

21. Hill frequently cashed checks of more than $10,000 (interest on municipal bonds) at First Bank. Hill deposited the money in her account at Second Bank. Second Bank notified the IRS of Hill's banking activity and allowed an IRS agent to search the bank's computer files for any information on Hill. Which of the following statements is true?

A. The bank had no authority to report the cash transactions.

B. The Freedom of Information Act specifically gives the IRS the right to examine banks' computer databases.

C. The Right to Financial Privacy Act of 1978 protects Hill's right to privacy from governmental intrusion.

D. The Privacy Act of 1974 protects Hill against governmental intrusion into her private banking records.

Answer (C) is correct. *(Publisher, adapted)*

REQUIRED: The true statement about computerized banking records.

DISCUSSION: In the absence of the customer's authorization, the IRS must prove that it followed the specific procedures outlined in the Right to Financial Privacy Act of 1978 when it accessed Hill's banking records.

Answer (A) is incorrect. The bank is required to report large cash deposits to federal banking authorities, not the IRS. Answer (B) is incorrect. The Freedom of Information Act concerns the public's right to access government records. Answer (D) is incorrect. The Privacy Act of 1974 relates to the privacy of government-held computerized databases.

22. To avoid possible liability for invasion of privacy, an organization's action plan covering privacy reasonably should include

I. Preparation of a plan to ensure that necessary privacy controls are integrated into the design of computer systems

II. Training of employees in the awareness of privacy and company policies

III. Preparation of a plan to inform customers of the organization's privacy policies

IV. Preparation of an analysis of the potential impact that privacy would have on the computer system

A. IV.

B. I and III.

C. II and IV.

D. I, II, III, and IV.

Answer (D) is correct. *(Publisher, adapted)*

REQUIRED: The step(s) that should be included in a privacy-related action plan.

DISCUSSION: Privacy considerations are among the many reasons for developing effective computer security. Failure to safeguard the privacy of confidential client information may result in both loss of business and litigation. Other information, such as trade secrets, must be shielded from disclosure to competitors. Moreover, some firms, e.g., defense contractors, may have access to information affecting national security. Accordingly, each of the listed steps is appropriate. Establishing a company code of ethics and a strong internal auditing function are among the other aspects of a control environment that stresses concern for privacy issues.

Answer (A) is incorrect. Steps I, II, and III should also be included. Answer (B) is incorrect. Steps II and IV should also be included. Answer (C) is incorrect. Steps I and III should also be included.

23. Defendant Co. published the false statement on its Internet website that its competitor, Plaintiff Corp., uses child labor in its factories. Defendant has committed

A. The tort of libel, not a crime.

B. A computer crime under the Counterfeit Access Device and Computer Fraud and Abuse Act of 1984.

C. Both a tort and a crime.

D. Neither a tort nor a crime.

Answer (A) is correct. *(Publisher, adapted)*

REQUIRED: The effect of publishing false statements on the Internet that may damage a company's reputation.

DISCUSSION: The use of a computer to publish intentionally damaging false statements about a business or individual constitutes a civil but not criminal wrong. Libel (defamation by written or other representational means) is a tort (a civil wrong not based on contract) that is actionable even though publication is on the Internet.

Answer (B) is incorrect. The Counterfeit Access Device and Computer Fraud and Abuse Act prohibits unauthorized use of a computer to obtain, alter, etc., restricted government information, information contained in the financial records of a financial institution, and information contained in a consumer reporting agency's files concerning a customer. Answer (C) is incorrect. Libel does not constitute a crime. Answer (D) is incorrect. The publishing of false information meant to damage the reputation of a business or individual constitutes a tort.

24. Which of the following is(are) true concerning the Fair Credit Reporting Act?

I. Consumers and businesses have the right to know what is reported about them by credit agencies

II. Consumers may file petitions to correct false information reported about them by a credit agency

III. Consumers have the right to know to whom information about them will be reported by a credit agency

A. I only.

B. I and II only.

C. II and III only.

D. I, II, and III.

Answer (C) is correct. *(Publisher, adapted)*

REQUIRED: The true statement(s) concerning the Fair Credit Reporting Act.

DISCUSSION: The Fair Credit Reporting Act requires consumer credit reporting agencies to implement safeguards to ensure that only accurate information is included in consumer credit reports. Consumers but not businesses have the right to know what information stored in computers is being reported about them by credit agencies and to whom this information is being disclosed. A credit reporting agency may not charge the consumer to receive his/her credit information and must correct any errors and notify recipients of the faulty information.

25. Herman used his modem and personal computer to breach the security of Ann's computer. Herman wrote a program that determined which of Ann's customers were the best traders by instantaneously calculating their returns. The program produced a list of securities to buy and sell. Herman gave the list to his neighbor, Mike, who used it to make large profits. Mike was bragging at the country club when one of Ann's successful traders learned that Mike was buying and selling exactly the same basket of stocks. Who is liable and for what?

A. Mike is liable under the Securities Exchange Act of 1934 for insider trading.

B. Ann cannot be liable for negligence for allowing Herman to breach her computer system.

C. Herman is liable under the Right to Financial Privacy Act of 1978.

D. Herman is liable for the tort of invasion of privacy.

Answer (D) is correct. *(Publisher, adapted)*

REQUIRED: The extent of liability for unauthorized access to private computerized data.

DISCUSSION: Under the tort theory of intrusion, a person is deemed to suffer damage from an invasion of his/her seclusion or solitude that a reasonable person would regard as offensive. Thus, one has a reasonable expectation of privacy for private records. Trading activities not required to be reported to the SEC are private information. Those who examine another's private records without authorization are liable in tort for invasion of privacy.

Answer (A) is incorrect. Mike is not an insider. Answer (B) is incorrect. Ann could be liable for negligence if her hardware or software did not reasonably control access to confidential customer data. Answer (C) is incorrect. The Right to Financial Privacy Act of 1978 addresses government access to private information held by financial institutions. Such access is permitted only if authorized by the customer or the government follows appropriate procedures.

26. Bill Galant purchased a car from Smith Motors that was financed by Smith's bank. Six months later, the bank contacted Galant by mail to give notice of default. Galant replied in writing that he had made the first six payments on time and had the check stubs to prove it. A week later, the bank physically repossessed the car. The bank later admitted that the repossession was a computer error made by an outside computer service bureau. The bank relied solely on the representations of the service bureau. The bank is potentially liable for

	Compensatory Damages	Punitive Damages
A.	No	Yes
B.	Yes	Yes
C.	Yes	No
D.	No	No

Answer (B) is correct. *(Publisher, adapted)*

REQUIRED: The creditor's liability for a computer error made by an outside computer service bureau.

DISCUSSION: The bank is certainly liable for compensatory damages because it was negligent for not ascertaining for itself whether Galant had made his payments according to the financing agreement. Because the bank relied solely on the report of the outside service bureau, it is probably liable for gross negligence, which would subject it to liability for punitive damages as well. Computer errors beyond the control of users do not excuse the users from liability for the damages caused.

22.5 Computer Crime

27. Criminal liability for the theft of computer time requires

A. A narrow interpretation of state and federal statutes.

B. The intent of the perpetrator to deprive the true owner of computer time.

C. Prosecution under the provisions of federal computer acts.

D. The true owners of the computer time to prove they were deprived by the perpetrator.

Answer (B) is correct. *(Publisher, adapted)*

REQUIRED: The requirement for criminal liability for theft of computer time.

DISCUSSION: Absent a specific statute, criminal liability for theft of computer time will often require a broad interpretation of traditional state or federal statutes that concern theft or larceny because not all courts regard computer time or data stored in a computer to be property. Also, intent by the perpetrator to deprive, and actual deprivation of, the true owner of his/her rights are necessary elements of the crime.

Answer (A) is incorrect. A broad interpretation of statutes is typically required in cases involving criminal liability for the theft of computer time. Answer (C) is incorrect. Criminal liability for theft of computer time may be prosecuted under state as well as federal statutes. Answer (D) is incorrect. The burden of proof in criminal cases rests on state or federal prosecutors, not victims.

28. Jon hacks into Victim Company's computer system and infects it with a virus that causes loss of data. Jon has committed a

A. Violation of the RICO Act.

B. Tort but not a crime.

C. Crime under the Electronic Funds Transfer Act.

D. Computer crime by damaging and destructive programming.

Answer (D) is correct. *(Publisher, adapted)*

REQUIRED: The violation resulting from infecting a system with a virus that causes loss of data.

DISCUSSION: Computer crime is any illegal act that uses, involves, or is directed against computers. Computer crimes can be grouped into four general categories: theft, damaging and destructive programming, software piracy, and financial crimes. Damaging and destructive programming includes physical abuse of hardware and computer programming that alters or automatically destroys data. Thus, infecting a system with a virus that destroys data is a crime.

Answer (A) is incorrect. The RICO Act (Racketeer Influenced and Corrupt Organizations Act) applies to the use of computers for illegal funds transfer, wire fraud, securities fraud, and money laundering. Answer (B) is incorrect. Shutting down an organization's computerized system is considered damaging and destructive programming and is therefore a computer crime. Answer (C) is incorrect. The EFT Act prohibits the sale, use, or interstate transportation of any lost, stolen, forged, counterfeit, altered, or fraudulently obtained device used to execute an electronics funds transfer.

29. Without the authorization or knowledge of their employer, Robb and Conn used the company computer to develop a set of programs to be marketed commercially for their personal gain. In furtherance of this scheme, they mailed promotional letters to potential clients. A state computer crime statute was enacted 6 months after these events. Robb and Conn are

A. Liable under the computer crime statute.

B. Liable under the federal mail fraud statute.

C. Not liable unless they appropriated property or money of the employer.

D. Not liable even if they appropriated computer programs and electronically stored information.

Answer (B) is correct. *(Publisher, adapted)*

REQUIRED: The liability of persons making unauthorized use of computer facilities.

DISCUSSION: In many cases, courts have had to extend existing law to apply to computers. In this case, the court found a scheme using the U.S. mails to defraud an employer for illicit personal gain. An activity otherwise fraudulent under state law becomes a federal crime when the mails are used to convey a writing furthering a scheme to solicit money under false pretenses.

Answer (A) is incorrect. Imposition of criminal sanctions retroactively (for actions before the statute existed) is unconstitutional. Answer (C) is incorrect. Various kinds of computer usage are illegal. For example, computers have been used to assist embezzlement or to steal intangibles, such as computer programs and electronically stored data. Answer (D) is incorrect. Various kinds of computer usage are illegal. For example, computers have been used to assist embezzlement or to steal intangibles, such as computer programs and electronically stored data.

30. Chuck Choppy was dismissed from his position as a management consultant for SNL, CPAs, when he failed to be promoted to partner. Choppy had advised SNL's financial institution clients about computer security of depositor records. After he was dismissed, he used his home computer to breach the security of several of SNL's clients' computers and transfer minuscule amounts from each depositor's account to his own account. Choppy is

A. Not criminally liable under state statutes because the amounts were immaterial.

B. Not criminally liable under the Counterfeit Access Device and Computer Fraud and Abuse Act of 1984 (as amended).

C. Criminally liable under both the Counterfeit Access Device and Computer Fraud and Abuse Act of 1984 as amended in 1986 and the Electronic Funds Act of 1978.

D. Criminally liable under a narrow interpretation of state and federal theft statutes.

Answer (C) is correct. *(Publisher, adapted)*

REQUIRED: The liability for theft of depositor funds using a computer.

DISCUSSION: The Counterfeit Access Device and Computer Fraud and Abuse Act of 1984 (as amended) prohibits, among other things, unauthorized access to financial institution computers. The Electronic Funds Transfer Act of 1978 prohibits unauthorized alteration of data in financial institution computers. Hence, Choppy is criminally liable under both acts.

Answer (A) is incorrect. Choppy is criminally liable regardless of materiality. Answer (B) is incorrect. Choppy is criminally liable regardless of materiality. Answer (D) is incorrect. Computer crimes ordinarily require a broad interpretation of state and federal theft statutes to subject an individual to criminal liability.

STUDY UNIT TWENTY-THREE
REAL PROPERTY: INTERESTS AND RIGHTS

Property is a set of legally recognized and enforceable rights in one or more things. **Personal property** consists of movable tangible (physical) and intangible things. **Real property** encompasses rights with respect to the surface of the land, items attached to the land, materials below the surface, and the airspace above. The legal rules pertaining to real property interests are governed by the common law and therefore vary from state to state.

An **estate in land** is **possessory** if it confers a right to exert control over specific land to the exclusion of the rights of others. A **freehold** estate in land gives possession through legal title. Nonfreehold estates merely grant possession.

A **fee simple** (or **fee simple absolute**) is the most extensive interest in land. It represents the totality of ownership rights recognized by law because it includes the rights of possession, exploitation, and full ownership for life or in perpetuity. A fee simple descends to the **owner's heirs upon death** and can be conveyed during his/her life. The modern trend is for every estate in land to be considered a fee simple unless a lesser or smaller estate is clearly indicated by the transferor.

A **fee simple determinable** is an estate that continues until automatically terminated by some limiting event. The transferor's interest is a **possibility of reverter**. An example is, "O to A and her heirs as long as the property is used as a school of accounting." A **fee simple subject to a condition subsequent** may be terminated at the option of the transferor upon the happening of a specified event. The transferor's interest is a **power of termination (right of entry for a condition broken)**. An example is, "O to A and her heirs, on condition that use of the property as an accounting school is commenced within 7 years. Otherwise, O may reenter the land." A **fee simple subject to an executory interest** passes to a **third party** upon the occurrence of a stated event. An example is, "O to A and his heirs as long as the property is used for an accounting school, then to C and her heirs." Some textbooks use the term **fee simple defeasible** (also qualified fee, base fee, conditional fee, etc.) for any fee simple estate that may end, whether or not automatically, upon the occurrence of some limiting event. Many jurisdictions have limited the duration of future interests or their transferability.

A **life estate** is a freehold estate measured by reference to the life or lives of one or more human beings. An example is, "O to A for life" or "O to A for life and then to B." A **life estate pur autre vie** is a life estate measured by the life of someone other than the life tenant. An example is "O to A for the life of C." A life tenant is entitled to all ordinary uses of and profits from the land but may not commit **waste** (impair the residual value of the land). A life tenant also has a duty to pay ordinary taxes as they accrue and must preserve the land and structures in a reasonable state of repair. A life estate may be sold or transferred. After transfer, it is a life estate pur autre vie.

A **future interest** is an estate in land that will not become possessory until a future date. Because a future interest is currently owned, it may be currently sold or otherwise transferred. The subject of future interests is quite complex, and the vocabulary is difficult. Thus, only a general introduction to future interests is presented here to facilitate recognition. A **reversion** is the estate that remains in a grantor/transferor who conveys a lesser estate than (s)he holds. A reversion is a future interest. It becomes possessory only after a limited or contingent estate has ended. For example, assume that Owen, the owner of a fee simple absolute, conveys an estate to "Able for life." Owen has retained a reversion in fee simple that will become possessory (returned to the grantor, Owen) only upon Able's death. Moreover, an owner of a freehold estate who grants a lease usually has a reversion. A reversion is transferable and inheritable. **A possibility of reverter** is the interest retained by the grantor of a fee simple determinable. The possibility of reverter ripens into a possessory estate upon occurrence of the stated event. A **power of termination** or **right of entry** for a condition broken is a future interest in the grantor who conveys a fee simple subject to a condition subsequent and expressly retains the power of termination. This power also may follow a lesser estate, for example, a life estate. The power retained by the grantor is a right to institute legal proceedings to regain title to the land. A **remainder** is a future interest conveyed to a third party that results in current possession only upon the natural termination of the prior possessory estate. A remainder must be formed by the same conveyance as the preceding estate, which must be less than a fee simple. An example is, "O to A for life and, on A's death, to B and her heirs." A has a current possessory life estate, and B has a remainder in fee simple. It is a remainder because, upon the expiration of A's life estate (a natural termination), B will be entitled to current possession and enjoyment of the property. A **vested remainder** is formed in an existing and ascertainable person and is not subject to any condition precedent except the natural termination of the preceding estate. In the preceding example, B has an indefeasible vested remainder that is certain to become possessory on the termination of A's life estate. [See Property OL, BAR/BRI, p. 10 et seq.] A **contingent remainder** is any remainder in favor of (1) an existing and ascertained person if the remainder is subject to a condition precedent, (2) an unborn person, or (3) an existing but unascertained person. An example is, "O to A for life and on A's death to B if B survives A." A has a life estate, and B has a contingent remainder in fee simple. B's remainder interest is contingent on the stated condition precedent that (s)he survive A. O, the transferor, has a reversion that will become a possessory estate only on the termination of A's life estate if B predeceases A.

To prevent unlimited restraints on the absolute and voluntary transfer of title and possession **(alienation)** or use of property, the common law developed the **rule against perpetuities**. The traditional statement of the rule is that a purported future interest is void unless with certainty it will vest, or fail to vest, no more than 21 years after the life of a person in being. Whether the interest could vest too remotely and therefore be void is determined when the deed is delivered or a trust becomes irrevocable, or on the death of a person leaving a will. For example, a deed is delivered and recorded that purports to grant the fee simple "to Joe until alcohol is consumed on the premises, then to Justy." Justy's apparent executory interest is subject to a condition that might not occur within the perpetuities period beginning with delivery of the deed. The contingent remainder is void.

Any interest in real property that can be owned by one party can also be owned jointly by two or more parties. The nature of a **concurrently owned estate** and the rights and obligations of the owners depend upon the form of concurrent ownership. **Joint tenancy** is a form of co-ownership in which each tenant owns an undivided interest in the entire estate. The distinctive characteristic of a joint tenancy is the **right of survivorship**. Upon the death of one joint tenant, the surviving co-tenants own the entire property. No interest in the property passes to the heirs of the decedent. Hence, a decedent's will has no effect on the property. A corporation, which has perpetual existence, usually cannot be a joint tenant.

At common law, **four unities** must exit to create a joint tenancy: (1) **time** (the interests must vest at the same time), (2) **title** (the interests must be acquired under the same instrument), (3) **interest** (the interests must be of the same type and duration), and (4) **possession** (the interests must represent identical rights of enjoyment). The modern view is that the conveyance to two or more parties must specifically express a clear intention to create a joint tenancy. Otherwise, a tenancy in common is presumed. Certain acts will terminate the joint tenancy. For example, a **conveyance** by a joint tenant severs the joint tenancy. The grantee or new tenant holds as a tenant in common with remaining joint tenants and has no right of survivorship. For example, if A, B, and C hold Whiteacre as joint tenants, and A conveys his/her undivided one-third interest to Z, B and C will subsequently hold their undivided two-thirds interest as joint tenants. Z holds a one-third interest as a tenant in common with B and C. A joint tenancy also may be severed by a **suit for partition**, an action that requests judicial separation of the interests in land of joint owners or tenants in common. If the partition is granted, each tenant takes control, possession, and enjoyment of his/her separate estate. Moreover, under the majority rule, a **contract for sale** terminates the joint tenancy, even in the absence of transfer of legal title. However, in the majority of states, **execution of a mortgage** does not terminate a joint tenancy. In a minority of states, a mortgage is regarded as a sufficient transfer of title to terminate the joint tenancy.

A **tenancy by the entirety** is an undivided estate held by **spouses with the right of survivorship**. Where it is recognized, it is formed by conveyance of an estate to both and, in most states, presumed from a joint conveyance to spouses. A tenancy by the entirety is terminated by (1) the death of either spouse, (2) mutual agreement, (3) divorce, or (4) a conveyance in which both join in the transfer. A tenancy by the entirety is essentially a joint tenancy between married persons. However, unlike a joint tenant, one tenant by the entirety cannot convey any interest without being joined by the other.

Community property is recognized by some western and southern states and Puerto Rico. It is property acquired during marriage and is equally owned by the spouses, regardless of which person's labor or skills produced the property. However, **separate property**, that is, property acquired before marriage or by gift or inheritance, is not community property. Moreover, property acquired in exchange for separate property is separately owned.

A **tenancy in common** is a concurrent estate with **no right of survivorship**. A transfer of an estate to two or more persons jointly (who are not spouses) is presumed to convey to each a tenancy in common. A tenant in common owns an undivided, separate, and distinct share of the underlying property but does not own the whole property as in a joint tenancy. Each tenant in common can dispose of his/her undivided fractional share by either a transfer during life **(inter vivos)** or a **testamentary transfer** by will. Concurrent ownership involves concurrent rights and obligations among and between the co-tenants. Each co-tenant has the right to possess all portions of the entire estate, and no co-tenant has the right to exclude a tenant from any one part. Courts carefully scrutinize the dealings between co-tenants. A confidential relationship exists between them, and one may not benefit from the property to the detriment of another.

Mere possession of land is a valuable right. Possession of land may result in legal recognition of specific rights. For example, the doctrine of **adverse possession** permits a person in possession of land for a statutorily determined period, such as 20 years, to have that possession ripen into title. To acquire title by adverse possession, certain requirements must usually be met. The possession must be (1) open and notorious, (2) continuous (without interruption), (3) adverse, (4) exclusive, and (5) peaceful. Periods of possession by successive adverse possessors can be added to reach the statutorily required number of years. Thus, continuous possession by the same person is not necessary if privity is maintained.

EXAMPLE: Whiteacre is owned by Orange, but Blue enters into adverse possession of the property and holds the land for 10 years. After Blue dies, Blue's son, Gator, holds Whiteacre for 11 years. The possession by Blue may be added to the possession by Gator to reach an applicable 20-year statutory period.

Sometimes, **parties not in possession of land** are legally permitted to enter and make limited use of land rightfully possessed by another. A **profit** (the name is from the French expression "profit à prendre") is a nonpossessory interest in land. Its holder is legally entitled to enter land in possession of another and take some part of the land itself or some product of the land, e.g., oil, gravel, sand, grass, or trees.

A **license** is a revocable personal privilege that permits one party to enter and make some use of land in possession of another without being considered a trespasser. A license is informal. It is personal to the licensee and therefore not assignable. A license is distinguished from a lease because the latter grants possession of the land but a license does not. Traditionally, tickets issued for sporting events or by theaters, race courses, golf courses, or other places of entertainment are licenses. Thus, the licensor, at will, may terminate the licensee's privilege to enter. When a license is revoked, the grantee may have an action at law for money damages on the contract.

An **easement** is the right of one person to legal entry onto, and limited use of, the land of another. An easement may arise from an **express grant** of the interest. The grant must be in writing and meet the formal requirements of a deed. In an **express reservation**, the grantor expressly reserves an easement. The transferor, in effect, conveys less than the full rights (s)he has in the property. An enforceable easement also can be acquired by **prescription** by meeting the same requirements with respect to use that are required to obtain title by adverse possession. Furthermore, easements may be **implied** by operation of law in the absence of an express grant or reservation and without regard to the statute of frauds. For example, an **easement by necessity** is implied when the owner of land conveys a part that has no access to a public road other than over the part retained by the seller. Moreover, an easement is implied by an existing use on the part of a tract of land conveyed. The use must be apparent, continuous, and reasonably necessary to the use and enjoyment of the part retained. For example, if a driveway is on the boundary of two lots under common ownership and the owner conveys one lot without mentioning the driveway, (s)he is assumed to have reserved an easement for use of the driveway and to have granted the transferee a similar easement. Easements also might arise from dedication of land to a governmental entity for public use or in a condemnation proceeding resulting from a government exercising the power of eminent domain.

An **easement appurtenant** benefits the owner of one tract of land by allowing the physical use or enjoyment of another tract of land. An easement appurtenant, by definition, relates to two tracts of land. One is the **dominant tenement** (which has the benefit of the easement) and the second is the **servient tenement** (which is burdened by, or subject to, the easement). For example, Bud owns lot 54 and Tom owns lot 55, adjoining tracts of land. By written agreement, Tom grants to Bud the right to cross Tom's lot, 55. Bud's use and enjoyment of lot 54 is benefited by the right to use lot 55 for this limited purpose. The right is an easement appurtenant. Tom remains the owner of lot 55. He has merely granted Bud the right to cross lot 55. There can be no conveyance of the easement apart from conveyance of the dominant tenement. However, all subsequent title holders of the dominant tenement are entitled to the benefit of the easement. An **easement in gross** benefits its owner personally. Thus, it relates directly only to one tract of land. That tract is owned by a party other than the holder of the easement in gross.

EXAMPLE: Doug conveys to Light and Power Corporation the right to install electrical transformers across his land. Light and Power Corporation, which does not own any land adjacent to Doug's land, has an easement in gross. An **affirmative easement** permits the owner of the dominant tenement to make affirmative use of the servient tenement, for example, to physically enter. A **negative easement** prevents the owner of the servient tenement from doing some act or making a particular use of his/her land, e.g., constructing any structure within 15 feet of the lot line obstructing an ocean view.

Land-use controls are classified according to whether they arise from private restrictions, tort law, or public regulation. **Covenants, conditions, and restrictions** based on contractual promises establish rules for owners in residential developments. The legal standing (right) to sue an owner or possessor of land in tort also can be viewed as a land-use control mechanism. **Relevant torts** are public nuisance, private nuisance, and trespass. The power of eminent domain, zoning laws, and other statutes and ordinances are included under public regulation. **Eminent domain** is the power of government to take land from private owners through condemnation proceedings for a **public use** and upon payment of **reasonable compensation**. When the power of eminent domain is exercised, all persons with vested interests must be paid but not those with mere contingent future interests. **Zoning** ordinarily consists of local ordinances enacted under the authority of a state statute for the purpose of planning and controlling development of real property. They must not violate public policy, and they must promote a valid purpose. Zoning codes ordinarily may not be retroactive, and they must provide for **variances**. An owner who cannot make a reasonable use of land as zoned may petition for a variance. Zoning ordinances are passed under the governmental **police power**. Regulations promulgated under the police power ensure the public health, safety, and welfare. Many other laws based on the inherent police power of government subunits affect land-use control. For example, a municipal ordinance may impose standards regarding roads, sewers, parks, and other infrastructure needs on new subdivision developments. Moreover, numerous federal, state, and local laws regulating the environment also may directly affect the possession, use, and enjoyment of private property.

QUESTIONS

23.1 Estates in Land

1. Interests in real property include certain subsurface rights. Which of the following is true?

A. Subsurface rights are not separately transferable.

B. Materials below the surface are not part of the realty.

C. Subsurface rights may have little value because the owner of the surface controls entry upon the land to remove materials below.

D. The usual rule regarding oil and gas is that the landowner does not have a specific right in any such materials beneath the surface.

Answer (D) is correct. *(Publisher, adapted)*

REQUIRED: The true statement about subsurface rights.

DISCUSSION: The basic principle is that the landowner has a right to the materials beneath the land unless subsurface rights have been separately conveyed. Because they flow from one location to another, oil and gas are exceptions. The majority rule is that the landowner does not own the oil and gas but simply has an exclusive right to drill on the property and extract what is found, regardless of the extent of the underground pool. Complex state and federal laws restrict the amounts that may be removed.

Answer (A) is incorrect. Subsurface rights are often transferred apart from those to the surface. Answer (B) is incorrect. Except for oil and gas, underground materials are clearly part of the realty unless separately conveyed. Answer (C) is incorrect. If subsurface rights are transferred separately, the grantee also acquires a right of entry.

2. Interests in real property include the airspace above the surface of the land. Which of the following is true?

A. The landowner owns all the airspace extending upward indefinitely from the surface of the land.

B. Airspace is not separately transferable.

C. No trespass occurs if an aircraft flies 1,000 feet above land in a populated area.

D. Because of the public interest in air transportation, no trespass is recognized for entry into a landowner's airspace.

Answer (C) is correct. *(Publisher, adapted)*

REQUIRED: The true statement about the rights of a landowner in airspace.

DISCUSSION: The modern rule is that a landowner owns the airspace necessary to the beneficial enjoyment of the land surface. Because airspace is regarded as a public resource, no trespass occurs as a result of an overflight if it is at a reasonable height and in accordance with governmental regulations. For example, the FAA does not ordinarily permit flight below 1,000 feet over populated areas or 500 feet over unpopulated areas.

Answer (A) is incorrect. The rule today greatly restricts the common law principle allowing unlimited rights in the airspace above the land. Answer (B) is incorrect. Airspace is often transferred separately, e.g., to one who wishes to build over an existing structure, such as over a railroad track. Answer (D) is incorrect. A landowner has a right to beneficial and convenient enjoyment of his/her property. If an intrusion into the airspace above the land is deemed to interfere with the right, an action for trespass may be brought.

3. Abrams owned a fee simple absolute interest in certain real property. Abrams conveyed it to Fox for Fox's lifetime with the remainder interest upon Fox's death to Charles. What are the rights of Fox and Charles in the real property?

A. Charles may not sell his interest in the property until the death of Fox.

B. Fox has a possessory interest in the land and Charles has a future interest.

C. Charles must outlive Fox to obtain any interest in the real property.

D. Any conveyance by either Fox or Charles must be joined in by the other party to be valid.

Answer (B) is correct. *(CPA, adapted)*

REQUIRED: The rights of the life tenant and the remainderman in the real property.

DISCUSSION: A fee simple absolute interest includes the full rights allowed by law. Abrams' conveyance split the ownership into two types: a life estate to Fox and a remainder interest to Charles. The life estate gives Fox the right to possess and enjoy the property for the duration of his life. The remainder interest gives Charles a future interest in the property, which will become a fee simple absolute upon termination of Fox's life estate.

Answer (A) is incorrect. Both a life estate and a remainder interest may be transferred at any time. Answer (C) is incorrect. Charles has a vested interest in the property that will become possessory upon the conclusion of the life estate. Charles' interest is both assignable and inheritable. Answer (D) is incorrect. Both Fox and Charles may separately convey their respective interests.

4. A life estate is the right of a person to use property for the rest of his/her life. This person is a life tenant. Certain duties and limitations are imposed on the life tenant to safeguard the remainderman's rights. The life tenant

A. Is entitled to the use of the land but must not take profits from it.

B. Is not responsible for taxes on the land because the remainderman is to receive the long-term benefits from the land.

C. May exploit natural resources of the land in reasonable amounts if the land was so used when the life estate was granted.

D. Must preserve the land in the same repair as when the life estate was granted.

Answer (C) is correct. *(Publisher, adapted)*

REQUIRED: The true statement concerning the rights and duties of a life tenant.

DISCUSSION: A life tenant is entitled to reasonable use of the land, including the profits. As a general rule, the life tenant is not entitled to exploit the natural resources of the land such as timber, minerals, and oil. But if the land was so used when the life estate was granted, the grantor is deemed to have intended continued reasonable use by the life tenant.

Answer (A) is incorrect. The life tenant is entitled to the profits from the land so long as waste is not committed. Answer (B) is incorrect. The life tenant is responsible to pay ordinary taxes on the land, but not those constituting assessments for permanent improvements. Answer (D) is incorrect. The life tenant is only responsible to maintain the land and structures on it in a reasonable state of repair, not necessarily the same as when the life estate was granted; reasonable depreciation is allowed.

23.2 Future Interests

Questions 5 through 9 are based on the following information. In Year 1, Rae Rogers, owner of both Blackacre and Whiteacre, executed and delivered two separate deeds by which she conveyed the two tracts of land as follows: Blackacre was conveyed "to Allan and his heirs as long as it is used exclusively for residential purposes, but, if it is ever used for other than residential purposes, then to the American Heart Association." Whiteacre was conveyed "to Bobbi and her heirs as long as it is used exclusively for residential purposes, but, if it is used for other than residential purposes prior to Year 21, then to the American Cancer Society." Rogers died in Year 6, leaving a valid will by which she devised all of her interests in real estate to her brother, John. The will had no residuary clause. Rogers was survived by John and her son, Tony, who received the balance of her estate.

5. In Year 7, the interest of John in Blackacre could best be described as

A. A possibility of reverter.

B. An executory interest.

C. An executory interest in a possibility of reverter.

D. A remainder.

Answer (A) is correct. *(Publisher, adapted)*

REQUIRED: The best description of John's interest in Year 7.

DISCUSSION: The conveyance by Rogers created a valid fee simple determinable and a void executory interest in the AHA. A future interest must comply with the rule against perpetuities. It must vest (or fail to vest) within some life in being plus 21 years. Because the time of vesting or failure may occur after this period, the AHA's interest is void. The failure of the executory interest left a possibility of reverter in Rogers that passed to John under the will. A possibility of reverter is a reversionary interest in the grantor that follows the termination of a fee simple determinable.

Answer (B) is incorrect. An executory interest is created in a transferee. John's interest was inherited from Rogers, a transferor. Answer (C) is incorrect. No valid executory interest was created. Answer (D) is incorrect. A remainder is a future interest conveyed to a third party that results in a fee simple possessory estate upon the natural termination of the prior estate. The prior estate must be less than a fee simple.

6. In Year 11, Allan and Tony entered into a contract with Mark in which they agreed to sell Blackacre to Mark in fee simple. After examining title, Mark refused to perform on the grounds that Allan and Tony could not give good title. Allan and Tony joined in an action against Mark for specific performance. Specific performance will be

A. Granted, because Allan and Tony together own a fee simple absolute in Blackacre.

B. Granted, because Allan alone owns the entire fee simple in Blackacre.

C. Denied, because John has a valid interest in Blackacre.

D. Denied, because the American Heart Association has a valid interest in Blackacre.

Answer (C) is correct. *(Publisher, adapted)*

REQUIRED: The result of a suit by Allan and Tony to sell Blackacre.

DISCUSSION: Allan and his heirs received a fee simple determinable subject to an executory interest. Because this interest might not vest (or fail to vest) in the AHA until well after the perpetuity period of a life in being plus 21 years, it was void under the rule against perpetuities. The result was that Allan had a valid fee simple determinable, and the grantor (Rogers) and her heirs had a possibility of reverter. Thus, given that the interest of the AHA was void, Blackacre would revert to Rogers or her heirs if it ceased to be used for residential purposes. This possibility of reverter was a future interest in real estate that would have been effectively devised to John in the Year 6 will, not to Tony. Mark will win the suit because Allan and Tony are unable to fulfill their contractual promise to sell the fee simple without John's joining in the sale.

Answer (A) is incorrect. Allan and John together own a fee simple absolute in Blackacre. Answer (B) is incorrect. Allan owns only the fee simple determinable, which may be divested whenever it is used for purposes other than residential. Answer (D) is incorrect. The AHA has no interest in Blackacre. The rule against perpetuities invalidated its executory interest that Rogers tried to convey.

7. Refer to the information on the preceding page(s). In Year 2, the interest of the American Heart Association (AHA) in Blackacre could be best described as a

A. Valid contingent remainder.

B. Void executory interest.

C. Valid executory interest.

D. Void contingent remainder.

Answer (B) is correct. *(Publisher, adapted)*

REQUIRED: The best description of the AHA's interest.

DISCUSSION: The conveyance by Rogers created a valid fee simple determinable in Allan and a void executory interest in the AHA. It was void because it violated the rule against perpetuities. This failed future interest was intended to be an executory interest. (1) It was in a transferee (as opposed to a reversionary interest in the transferor), and (2) it would arise by divesting the preceding estate (as opposed to taking effect upon the natural termination of the preceding estate as a remainder).

Answer (A) is incorrect. The interest of the AHA was invalid under the rule against perpetuities and was not a remainder. A remainder cannot follow an interest that may never terminate. Answer (C) is incorrect. The executory interest of the AHA is void under the rule against perpetuities. Answer (D) is incorrect. The interest is not a remainder.

8. Refer to the information on the preceding page(s). In Year 4, a contract was entered into in which Bobbi and the American Cancer Society agreed to sell Whiteacre to Fuller in fee simple. After examining title, Fuller refused to perform on the ground that Bobbi and the ACS could not convey marketable title. Bobbi and the ACS joined in an action for specific performance. Specific performance will be

A. Denied, because Bobbi and the ACS cannot convey marketable title unless Rogers joins in the deed.

B. Granted, because Bobbi and the ACS together own a fee simple absolute in Whiteacre.

C. Granted, because the attempted restrictions on the use of Whiteacre are void as a violation of the rule against perpetuities.

D. Granted, because the attempted restrictions on the use of Whiteacre are void as a violation of the rule against restraints on alienation.

Answer (A) is correct. *(Publisher, adapted)*

REQUIRED: The result of an action by Bobbi and the ACS to sell Whiteacre.

DISCUSSION: A marketable title is usually considered a fee simple title. Bobbi and the ACS together do not have a fee simple title in Whiteacre. Bobbi has a fee simple determinable subject to an executory interest, the ACS holds the executory interest, and Rogers has a possibility of reverter. Rogers (or an heir) has a possibility of reverter if the property is used for other than residential purposes after Year 21. If it is used for other than residential purposes before Year 21, the ACS will receive the fee simple absolute interest in Whiteacre.

Answer (B) is incorrect. Bobbi and the ACS own less than a fee simple absolute. Rogers retains a possibility of reverter. Answer (C) is incorrect. None of the interests is void under the rule against perpetuities. The executory interest will vest or fail to vest within some life in being plus 21 years (in this case, before Year 21), and interests retained by the grantor are not subject to the rule. Answer (D) is incorrect. The restrictions are upon use, not upon alienation (the power to transfer the interest).

9. Refer to the information on the preceding page(s). In Year 2, the interest of Bobbi in Whiteacre could best be described as a

A. Determinable fee.

B. Fee simple subject to a condition subsequent.

C. Fee simple subject to an executory interest.

D. Determinable fee subject to an executory interest.

Answer (D) is correct. *(Publisher, adapted)*

REQUIRED: The best description of Bobbi's interest in Whiteacre in Year 2.

DISCUSSION: Bobbi received a fee simple that would automatically terminate upon the subsequent occurrence of an event (failure to use the property for residential purposes). This estate is a determinable fee (or fee simple determinable). It is subject to an executory interest, that is, to a future interest in a transferee (the ACS) that divests the previous estate. This interest is valid because it complies with the rule against perpetuities. It will vest or fail to vest within some life in being plus 21 years.

Answer (A) is incorrect. Bobbi received an estate subject to an executory interest. Answer (B) is incorrect. A condition subsequent does not terminate the previous estate automatically. An example is, "If Whiteacre is not used for residential purposes, the ACS may enter and take title." Answer (C) is incorrect. Bobbi's interest in Year 2 was a determinable fee subject to an executory interest.

23.3 Concurrent Estates

10. Which of the following unities (elements) are required to establish a joint tenancy?

	Time	Title	Interest	Possession
A.	Yes	Yes	Yes	Yes
B.	Yes	Yes	No	No
C.	No	No	Yes	Yes
D.	Yes	No	Yes	No

Answer (A) is correct. *(CPA, adapted)*

REQUIRED: The unities required to establish a joint tenancy.

DISCUSSION: At common law, four unities must exist to create a joint tenancy: (1) time (the interests must vest at the same time); (2) title (the interests must be acquired under the same instrument); (3) interest (the interests must be of the same type and duration); and (4) possession (the interests must represent identical rights of enjoyment).

11. Green and Blue own a parcel of land as joint tenants with the right of survivorship. Blue wishes to sell the land to Ink. If Blue alone executes and delivers a deed to Ink, what will be the result?

A. Green will retain a 1/2 undivided interest in the 40-acre parcel, and will be unable to set aside Blue's conveyance to Ink.

B. Ink will obtain an interest in 1/2 of the parcel, or 20 acres.

C. Ink will share ownership of the 40 acres with Green as a joint tenant with a right of survivorship.

D. The conveyance will be invalid because Green did not sign the deed.

Answer (A) is correct. *(CPA, adapted)*

REQUIRED: The result of a purported conveyance of a joint tenancy with right of survivorship.

DISCUSSION: If joint tenants are married to each other, a presumption of tenancy by the entirety arises if both names are included on the deed or other title documents. If they hold as tenants by the entirety, the conveyance by one joint tenant is ineffective because a tenancy by the entirety may not be severed by a unilateral conveyance. However, Green and Blue held as joint tenants with the right of survivorship, so the conveyance would have severed the joint tenancy and resulted in a tenancy in common between Ink and Green.

Answer (B) is incorrect. A severed joint tenancy results in a tenancy in common. A tenant in common owns an undivided interest in the whole property. Answer (C) is incorrect. A severed joint tenancy results in a tenancy in common. Answer (D) is incorrect. A joint tenancy can be conveyed without consent of the other joint tenants. Only Blue's signature is required.

12. Abe, Bo, and Cy own a building as joint tenants with the right of survivorship. Abe gave his interest in the building to Zeb by executing and delivering a deed to Zeb. Neither Bo nor Cy consented to this transfer. Bo and Cy subsequently died. After their deaths, Zeb's interest in the building would consist of

A. A 1/3 interest as a tenant in common.

B. A 1/3 interest as a joint tenant.

C. Total ownership due to the deaths of Bo and Cy.

D. No interest because Bo and Cy did not consent to the transfer.

Answer (A) is correct. *(CPA, adapted)*

REQUIRED: The effect of a gift of a joint tenant's interest prior to the death of the other joint tenants.

DISCUSSION: The gift of the joint tenant's interest made during life severed the joint tenancy with respect to the interest transferred. It gave rise to a tenancy in common with a 1/3 interest held by the donee (Zeb) and a 2/3 interest held by Bo and Cy. The latter parties held their interest as joint tenants with rights of survivorship; that is, the gift did not sever the portion of the joint tenancy not transferred. Consequently, Bo's and Cy's deaths resulted in the passage to the heirs of the last to die of full ownership of the 2/3 interest.

Answer (B) is incorrect. The gift severed the joint tenancy with respect to the donor's interest. Answer (C) is incorrect. Abe's gift during life transferred a 1/3 interest to Zeb. The deaths of Bo and Cy had no effect on that interest. Answer (D) is incorrect. Their consent was unnecessary.

13. A person may own property as a joint tenant with the right of survivorship with any of the following except a(n)

A. Divorced spouse.

B. Related minor child.

C. Unaffiliated corporation.

D. Unrelated adult.

Answer (C) is correct. *(CPA, adapted)*

REQUIRED: The person who may not own property as a joint tenant with the right of survivorship.

DISCUSSION: Because a corporation is granted perpetual existence at law, it usually may not be a joint tenant of property. If a corporation were allowed to be a joint tenant, the right of survivorship would be meaningless to the other joint tenants.

Answer (A) is incorrect. A divorced spouse may hold property with a right of survivorship. Answer (B) is incorrect. A related minor child may hold property with a right of survivorship. Answer (D) is incorrect. An unrelated adult may hold property with a right of survivorship.

14. Paul Good's will left all of his commercial real property to his wife Dorothy for life and the remainder to his two daughters, Joan and Doris, as tenants in common. All beneficiaries are alive and over 21 years of age. Regarding the rights of the parties, which of the following is a true statement?

A. Dorothy may not elect to take against the will and receive a statutory share instead.

B. The daughters must survive Dorothy in order to receive any interest in the property.

C. Either of the daughters may sell her interest in the property without the consent of their mother or the other daughter.

D. If only one daughter is alive upon the death of Dorothy, she is entitled to the entire property.

Answer (C) is correct. *(CPA, adapted)*

REQUIRED: The true statement about the rights of the parties.

DISCUSSION: Even though their interests will not become possessory until the death of Dorothy, the daughters have vested future interests in the property that cannot be defeated by any subsequent event. Their interests (as tenants in common) may be transferred without the permission of the life tenant or of each other.

Answer (A) is incorrect. The surviving spouse of a testate decedent may choose to take under the will or under the state statute which provides for a minimum elective share. Answer (B) is incorrect. The daughters' remainder interests are not contingent upon surviving the life tenant. They vested in the daughters upon the death of the testator. Answer (D) is incorrect. The daughters took as tenants in common, not as joint tenants with rights of survivorship. The rights of a tenant in common are inheritable and the surviving daughter would have to share the property with her sister's heirs.

15. In 1990, Harold bought a house from Sydney. In 1992, Harold married Wilma, and they have lived continuously in the house together since then. Bart is now negotiating with Harold for the purchase of the house. Which of the following is true?

A. Bart should have Wilma sign the deed because she has acquired an interest by adverse possession.

B. Bart should have Wilma sign the deed because she may have rights in this property by virtue of her status as a spouse.

C. Because Harold owns the property in his name only, his signature will suffice to transfer the property.

D. If this house is in California, Bart should have Harold's children sign the deed because a house is community property.

Answer (B) is correct. *(M. Levin)*

REQUIRED: The spouse's right in real property.

DISCUSSION: At common law, a wife acquired a legal interest, typically a life estate, in land owned by her husband during their marriage. The interest was known as dower. In some states, a husband had a similar right (curtesy) in his wife's land. Today, many states recognize similar spousal rights by statute. Thus, if a husband conveys without his wife's joining in the deed, and his wife survives him, she may succeed to an interest in the land, even though a purchaser from the husband acted innocently.

Answer (A) is incorrect. The wife's interest is not one of adverse possession. Wilma's use of their residence is clearly permissive. Answer (C) is incorrect. A wife's interest may prevent conveyance solely by a husband. Answer (D) is incorrect. The community property system, which is followed in California and a minority of other states, recognizes that the husband and wife should share equally in property acquired by their joint efforts during marriage. It imparts no special interest to children, however.

16. Condominiums and cooperatives are two forms of common ownership of buildings. They have been traditionally used for residential purposes, although there is an increasing trend to use them for business purposes. Cooperatives and condominiums differ in that

A. Cooperative interests are freely transferable, whereas condominiums are not.

B. Condominium owners individually finance their units, whereas cooperatives finance through a blanket mortgage on the entire property.

C. Condominium owners pay their own taxes whereas the individuals have no liability for the taxes on a cooperative.

D. In a cooperative the residents own the common areas, whereas in a condominium they do not.

Answer (B) is correct. *(Publisher, adapted)*

REQUIRED: The manner in which cooperatives and condominiums differ.

DISCUSSION: Condominium owners individually own their units. They obtain whatever financing is necessary on the unit and are solely responsible for the payments. A cooperative is usually set up as a corporation that owns the building and rents to the shareholders. The corporation holding title to the building finances it with a blanket mortgage.

Answer (A) is incorrect. Condominiums are freely transferable, but cooperatives sometimes impose restrictions on the assignment or sublease of the apartments. Answer (C) is incorrect. The taxes are paid by the cooperative corporation, but the individuals are in turn liable to the corporation. Answer (D) is incorrect. In a cooperative, the corporation owns the common areas, whereas the individuals in a condominium own the common areas through the condominium association.

17. On July 1, Quick, Onyx, and Nash were deeded a piece of land as tenants in common. The deed provided that Quick owned 1/2 the property and Onyx and Nash owned 1/4 each. If Nash dies, the property will be owned

A. Quick 1/2, Onyx 1/2.

B. Quick 5/8, Onyx 3/8.

C. Quick 1/3, Onyx 1/3, Nash's heirs 1/3.

D. Quick 1/2, Onyx 1/4, Nash's heirs 1/4.

Answer (D) is correct. *(CPA, adapted)*

REQUIRED: The effect of the death of a tenant in common.

DISCUSSION: The essential aspect of a tenancy in common is that each of the co-tenants owns an undivided interest in the whole. Rather than owning a specific portion of the land, each co-tenant is considered to own a right to the entire property. But unlike a joint tenancy, the tenancy in common does not include a right of survivorship. The interest of a deceased co-tenant passes to his/her heirs.

Answer (A) is incorrect. Unlike a joint tenancy, the tenancy in common does not include a right of survivorship. Answer (B) is incorrect. Unlike a joint tenancy, the tenancy in common does not include a right of survivorship. Answer (C) is incorrect. The full interest of a deceased co-tenant passes to his/her heirs.

18. Community property is a form of property ownership in eight Western states. There are several ways in which community property law differs from the law determining ownership of property in the rest of the United States. Community property law

A. Is similar to the rules of a condominium association because each person owns a part of the property but is subject to the rules determined by the group.

B. Provides that a husband and wife each own a 1/2 interest in the property acquired during their marriage.

C. Has not been adopted in a majority of states because it is widely thought of as a step toward socialism.

D. Provides that people who move from a community property state to a noncommunity property state are relieved of the ownership sharing that had been imposed upon them.

Answer (B) is correct. *(Publisher, adapted)*

REQUIRED: The true statement concerning the community property form of ownership.

DISCUSSION: Community property law directly affects only the ownership of property between a husband and wife. Each owns a 1/2 interest in property acquired during their marriage. It applies to both real and personal property. It is similar to a tenancy in common, but the rights and duties of the husband and wife vary from state to state.

Answer (A) is incorrect. Community property law only exists between a husband and wife and is more similar to a tenancy in common than to condominium ownership. Answer (C) is incorrect. Community property is not considered a step toward socialism. It is, rather, a means of providing each party with equal benefits from his/her contributions to the marital family. Answer (D) is incorrect. The community property retains that status when people move from a community property state to a noncommunity property state.

23.4 Rights Incident to Possession and Ownership

19. Dunbar Dairy Farms, Inc., pursuant to an expansion of its operations in Tuberville, purchased from Moncrief a 140-acre farm strategically located in the general area in which Dunbar wishes to expand. Unknown to Dunbar, Lamont Cranston, an adjoining landowner, had fenced off approximately 5 acres of the land in question. Lamont Cranston installed a well, constructed a storage shed and garage on the fenced-off land, and continuously farmed and occupied the 5 acres for approximately 22 years prior to Dunbar's purchase. Cranston did this under the mistaken belief that the 5 acres of land belonged to him. Which of the following is a true statement?

A. Under the circumstances, Cranston has title to the 5 acres.

B. If Moncrief had properly recorded a deed that includes the 5 acres in dispute, Moncrief has good title to the five acres.

C. At best, the only right that Cranston could obtain is an easement.

D. If Dunbar is unaware of Cranston's presence and Cranston has failed to record, Dunbar can oust him as a trespasser.

Answer (A) is correct. *(CPA, adapted)*

REQUIRED: The true statement concerning land fenced by a neighbor.

DISCUSSION: Title to real property may be acquired by adverse possession if the following requirements are satisfied. First, actual and exclusive possession of land must be taken. Cranston's fencing, farming, etc., constituted actual and exclusive possession. Second, the possession must be open and notorious. Cranston met this requirement because the possession was in such a manner that the owner knew or should have known of the possession. Third, the possession must be adverse to the rights of the owner. Absent permission from Moncrief, the activities of Cranston would satisfy the requirement. Fourth, possession must continue uninterrupted for the full statutory term, which may be as long as 20 years. Finally, the possession must be peaceable.

Answer (B) is incorrect. Adverse possession will prevail against a properly recorded deed. Answer (C) is incorrect. Cranston can obtain title to the property by way of adverse possession. Answer (D) is incorrect. As a purchaser of real property, Dunbar is considered to have constructive notice of Cranston's presence. Cranston has acquired title by adverse possession, has nothing to record, and cannot be ousted as a trespasser.

20. Mark Moore has obtained title to land by adverse possession. He

A. Can convey good title to a subsequent purchaser.

B. Must record his interest in the property in order to perfect his interest against the holder of record.

C. Must have occupied the property initially with the permission of the owner of record.

D. Must personally have occupied the land for a period of time equal to or greater than the prescribed period.

Answer (A) is correct. *(CPA, adapted)*

REQUIRED: The true statement concerning title by adverse possession.

DISCUSSION: A person who has satisfied the requirements for obtaining title by adverse possession has a fee simple absolute interest in the land. (S)he can convey good title to a subsequent purchaser. However, such a title is not marketable because the records will not show the interest of the adverse possessor. A suit to quiet title is usually brought so that the court's judgment can be recorded to prove the adverse possession.

Answer (B) is incorrect. A person who has title by adverse possession can prevail over the holder of record, although a lawsuit may be required to quiet title. Furthermore, nothing exists to record until a judgment is obtained. Answer (C) is incorrect. A person who obtains title by adverse possession must have done so without the permission of the owner of record. Answer (D) is incorrect. Periods of possession by successive adverse possessors may be combined in some circumstances.

Questions 21 and 22 are based on the following information. Barry Jones began the erection of a two-story building on his land. In doing so he excavated to a depth of several feet up to but not over the property line. Barry did not provide Alexander (Alex) Taylor with any advance notice of the excavation. The excavation was performed in a careful manner except that no steps were taken to shore up Alex's building. As a result of the excavation, Alex's building settled, cracked, and was damaged.

---

21. Alex sued Barry for damages to Alex's building but was unable to show that no settling or falling of Alex's land would have occurred if it had been in its natural condition without the weight of the building upon it. Judgment for

A. Alex, because Alex is entitled as a matter of right to lateral support from adjoining lands.

B. Alex, if the failure to give Alex notice was negligent, and that negligence was the proximate cause of the injury suffered.

C. Barry, because a landowner has no obligation to provide support to artificial structures on his/her neighbor's land.

D. Barry, because his duty extends no further than to perform the excavation in a careful manner.

Answer (B) is correct. *(Publisher, adapted)*

REQUIRED: The party that prevails in a suit for damages caused by excavation of adjacent property.

DISCUSSION: A landowner has an absolute right to lateral support for his/her land from adjacent landowners. This absolute right extends only to the land in its natural condition. To allow the owner of the building to take any necessary steps, the excavator has the duty to give notice to the adjoining owner. A landowner also has a right that his/her buildings be free of damage from another's negligence. Thus, Alex can win by proving negligence and resulting damages.

Answer (A) is incorrect. Alex's right of lateral support is only for the land in its natural condition, not for the building. Answer (C) is incorrect. A landowner is obligated not to cause damage on adjacent land through negligent actions (e.g., excavations near another's building without notice). Answer (D) is incorrect. Barry also has a duty of reasonable care that given the circumstances might extend to giving notice of the excavation.

22. In an action brought by Alex against Barry for damage to Alex's building, proof was offered that, even if there had been no building on the land, Alex's land would have subsided as a result of Barry's excavation. The land had an especially pliable clay soil condition of which Barry was unaware prior to the excavation. Judgment for

A. Alex, because Alex is entitled to support for her land in its natural condition.

B. Alex, because Alex is entitled to support for her land in its improved condition.

C. Barry, because Barry is not liable for the peculiar condition of the soil.

D. Barry, because there was no showing of malice or ill will toward Alex.

Answer (A) is correct. *(Publisher, adapted)*

REQUIRED: The party that prevails if land would have subsided in its natural state as a result of excavation of adjacent property.

DISCUSSION: Barry has an absolute duty to provide lateral support for Alex's land in its natural state. The duty is imposed regardless of the standard of care observed. If this duty is violated, Alex can also recover for damages to the building.

Answer (B) is incorrect. Alex is only entitled to support for the land in the natural state. Answer (C) is incorrect. Barry must provide lateral support for Alex's land in its natural condition regardless of the conditions of the soil. Answer (D) is incorrect. The duty of lateral support for land in its natural condition is imposed regardless of the mental state of the defendant.

23. Real property may be transferred in many ways other than by private sale. Which of the following is not such a means of transfer?

A. Avulsion and accretion.

B. Eminent domain and escheat.

C. Testamentary disposition and descent.

D. Sale by public official and dedication.

Answer (A) is correct. *(Publisher, adapted)*

REQUIRED: The methods that do not result in a transfer of realty.

DISCUSSION: Accretion is the gradual increase in the land caused by the deposit of material by water. Avulsion is the sudden increase in the land by action of water, for example, by a flood. Accretion passes title to the riparian owner to whose land the addition has been made. Avulsion does not.

Answer (B) is incorrect. The government may condemn property under its eminent domain power for a public purpose if just compensation is awarded. Escheat is the transfer to the state of the property of one who dies intestate and without heirs. Answer (C) is incorrect. Real property may be transferred by will or under the intestacy statute. Answer (D) is incorrect. Real property is sometimes sold at a judicial sale to satisfy a judgment, mortgage, or unpaid taxes. Dedication is the gift to a governmental unit for a specified purpose, e.g., a park or street.

24. Ole McDonald owns a small farm located on the edge of a small creek that he uses for irrigation. Grubb, Inc. has purchased the land just upstream from McDonald and is building a 20-story condominium project. In the construction, the creek was blocked and detoured to another creekbed one mile away. The building will also cut off the sunlight needed to grow crops on McDonald's land. Which of the following rights does McDonald have?

A. The right to have the water continue to flow in its natural course.

B. The right to the sunlight in order to grow crops.

C. The right to be free from the construction dust and later from automobile exhaust.

D. The right to the magnificent mountain view that previously existed from McDonald's land.

Answer (A) is correct. *(Publisher, adapted)*

REQUIRED: The rights of a landowner when a new use is made of neighboring property.

DISCUSSION: A riparian landowner (one who owns land along a waterway) may make reasonable use of the water. However, a lower riparian owner has the right to the continued flow of the water without unreasonable diminution. The "natural flow" theory allows use of the water as long as the natural condition of the waterway is retained. The "reasonable use" theory allows use of the water as long as it does not interfere with other riparian owners. Under either theory, the blocking of the creek by Grubb is a violation of McDonald's right that may require the creek to be rediverted to its natural course.

Answer (B) is incorrect. There is no general right to have direct sunlight on one's property. Answer (C) is incorrect. There is no right to be free of air contaminants, although excessive air contamination could constitute a private nuisance. Answer (D) is incorrect. No general right to retain a view is recognized absent an express agreement.

25. Which of the following is a true statement about the classification of timber and growing crops?

A. Unless agreed otherwise, a sale of the real property on which they are growing includes timber and crops.

B. Timber to be cut and growing crops are personal property whether or not they are sold apart from the land and regardless of who does the severing.

C. Growing crops sold apart from the land are personal property only if severed by the seller.

D. Timber to be cut and sold apart from the land is classified as goods only if severed by the buyer.

Answer (A) is correct. *(Publisher, adapted)*

REQUIRED: The true statement about the status of timber and growing crops.

DISCUSSION: Whether or not cultivated, the vegetation on the land is transferred with the real property unless the seller expressly reserves rights to them. A seller who failed to do so could not harvest crops or timber growing on the land. If the timber has been felled or the crops have been harvested, however, they do not pass with the land. Furthermore, a contract for the separate sale of (1) growing crops or (2) timber to be cut is a contract for the sale of goods regardless of who is to do the severing (UCC 2-107). But minerals and a structure or its materials to be removed from the realty are goods (personal property) only if severance is to be by the seller.

Answer (B) is incorrect. Timber to be cut and growing crops are personal property only if they are sold apart from the land and are capable of severance without material harm. Answer (C) is incorrect. Timber to be cut and growing crops are personal property only if they are sold apart from the land and are capable of severance without material harm. Who does the severing is irrelevant. Answer (D) is incorrect. Who does the severing is irrelevant.

23.5 Nonpossessory Interests in Land

26. Which of the following is true with respect to an easement acquired by an express grant?

A. The easement is extinguished if the grantee dies.

B. The easement cannot be sold or transferred by the owner of the easement.

C. The easement gives the owner of the easement the right to physical possession of the property subject to the easement.

D. The easement must be in writing to be valid.

Answer (D) is correct. *(CPA, adapted)*

REQUIRED: The true statement regarding an easement acquired by express grant.

DISCUSSION: An easement is a nonpossessory interest in land that confers the right to use that land. The express grant of an easement is a transfer of an interest in land and therefore must be in writing and signed by the grantor to comply with the statute of frauds.

Answer (A) is incorrect. The typical easement acquired by express grant is not extinguished if the grantee dies. The easement could provide, however, for termination on the death of the grantee. Answer (B) is incorrect. Easements appurtenant are assignable as well as inheritable, but easements in gross are not. The typical easement appurtenant is transferred when the land to which it relates is sold or transferred. Answer (C) is incorrect. An easement is a nonpossessory right to use the land.

27. An easement cannot be

A. Acquired by reservation.

B. The mere right to the use of another's land but must be obtained for the benefit of the land owned by the party obtaining the easement.

C. Obtained by prescription if the claimant's use of the land has been interrupted by the prompt action of the landowner.

D. Conveyed by the easement owner to another party who purchases the land owned by the easement owner.

Answer (C) is correct. *(CPA, adapted)*

REQUIRED: The true statement regarding an easement.

DISCUSSION: Easements may be obtained by prescription if the use of the land proceeds continuously for the statutory period, is without the permission of the owner, and is open and notorious. If the use is interrupted before the statutory period has run, no easement by prescription exists because the continuity requirement is not met.

Answer (A) is incorrect. An easement may be retained, e.g., a sale of land by a grantor who reserves the right to use a road. Answer (B) is incorrect. An easement may be in gross as well as appurtenant. An easement is in gross if it is for the benefit of a particular person and does not relate to any specified parcel of real property. An easement is appurtenant if it benefits a particular parcel of land. Answer (D) is incorrect. If the easement is appurtenant, a conveyance of the land benefited by the easement also conveys the easement.

28. Glover Manufacturing, Inc. purchased a 4-acre tract of commercially zoned land. A survey prior to the closing revealed an unpaved road across the northeast corner of the land. The title search did not indicate any other defect in title. No recordation was made in connection with the unpaved road. Which of the following statements is true regarding Glover's title and rights to the land against adverse claims?

A. The road poses no potential problem if Glover promptly fences off the property and puts up "no trespassing" signs.

B. Glover does not have to be concerned with the unpaved road because nothing was recorded.

C. Use of the road as contrasted with occupancy of the land cannot result in any interest adverse.

D. The unpaved road may prove to be a valid easement.

Answer (D) is correct. *(CPA, adapted)*

REQUIRED: The buyer's rights to the land against adverse claims.

DISCUSSION: An easement is an interest in land in someone other than the landowner. It is a right to use the land that may be acquired either by conveyance, which is unlikely in this situation because no easement was recorded, or by prescription. An easement might be acquired by prescription if someone continuously used the road, without the permission of the owner, in an open and notorious manner for the statutory period. "Open and notorious" means that the land was used in such a manner that the owner should have known or at least had the means of knowing of the use.

Answer (A) is incorrect. Promptly fencing off the property and putting up signs is ineffective if a valid easement by prescription has already been acquired. Answer (B) is incorrect. A valid easement by prescription may be acquired without recordation. Answer (C) is incorrect. Use of the road could result in an easement by prescription.

29. An easement by necessity is recognized when

A. A parcel of realty is conveyed that is inaccessible or accessible only by a difficult route.

B. A grantee but not a grantor is left with a difficult access to realty as a result of a conveyance.

C. A landlocked parcel of realty is conveyed.

D. A grantor but not a grantee is left with a difficult access to realty as a result of a conveyance.

Answer (C) is correct. *(Publisher, adapted)*

REQUIRED: The condition necessary for recognition of an easement by necessity.

DISCUSSION: If the grantor conveys part of his/her realty without providing the grantee a means of access, a court will find that an easement across the grantor's remaining land was implied by necessity. This easement is recognized only if the parcel would otherwise be landlocked. Access by a difficult, circuitous, or otherwise inconvenient route defeats such an easement. Similarly, an easement by necessity may arise through an implied reservation when a conveyance leaves the grantor's property landlocked.

Answer (A) is incorrect. An easement by necessity arises only when a conveyance results in landlocked realty. Answer (B) is incorrect. Either a grantor or a grantee may be entitled to such an easement. Answer (D) is incorrect. Either a grantor or a grantee may be entitled to such an easement.

30. Abe Franklin and Teddy Jefferson own adjacent properties. There is a party wall down their property line that existed before each purchased his property. Jefferson wants the wall to be torn down, but Franklin does not. Which of the following is a true statement about their rights and duties?

A. Jefferson is entitled to have the wall torn down because it extends over his property line.

B. Franklin must compensate Jefferson if he does not agree to tear down the wall.

C. Each property owner has an undivided interest in the entire wall.

D. Franklin has an easement of support from Jefferson's side of the wall.

Answer (D) is correct. *(Publisher, adapted)*

REQUIRED: The rights and duties with respect to a party wall between adjacent landowners.

DISCUSSION: Each party is entitled to the use of a party wall and also has an easement of support from the other side. Without the easement, the right to retain an existing wall would be illusory.

Answer (A) is incorrect. Jefferson has no right to tear down the party wall unless such a right existed by agreement or has been acquired by adverse possession. Answer (B) is incorrect. Franklin is under no obligation to have the wall torn down or to agree to do so. Answer (C) is incorrect. They are not tenants in common. In most states, each is considered to own the part on his/her side and to have an easement of support from the other side.

31. Sandra, the owner and possessor of Largeacre, conveyed to Reliable Phone Company the right to construct and use an overhead phone line across Largeacre to serve other properties. The conveyance was in writing, but the writing made no provision concerning the responsibility for repair or maintenance of the line. Which of the following statements correctly describes duties of the owner of the easement and/or of the property?

A. The owner of an easement has a duty to maintain the easement.

B. The owner of an easement is absolutely liable for any damage caused by the easement.

C. The property owner has a duty to give the easement holder notice of defective conditions.

D. An easement holder's right to repair is a right for his/her own benefit only.

Answer (A) is correct. *(Publisher, adapted)*

REQUIRED: The duty of the owner of the easement or of the property.

DISCUSSION: An easement is a nonpossessory right to use the land of another. The owner of an easement is responsible for its maintenance. Thus, Reliable had an implied duty to take reasonable steps to keep the utility lines in good repair. Failure to do so results in liability for damages caused.

Answer (B) is incorrect. Reliable would not be liable for reasonable, nonnegligent use of the easement. However, an owner of an easement used for an inherently dangerous activity might be strictly liable. Answer (C) is incorrect. Reliable, as the user of the easement, has the duty to inspect and maintain the utility lines. Answer (D) is incorrect. The easement holder's duty to repair arises from the duty to prevent interference with the rights of the owner of the land.

32. An easement is terminated when

A. It is deeded back to the owner of the dominant tenement.

B. Its owner ceases to use it, although (s)he has no intent to abandon it.

C. The owner of the servient tenement merges his/her land with the adjacent property of a third party.

D. The requirements of adverse possession are met.

Answer (D) is correct. *(Publisher, adapted)*

REQUIRED: The true statement about one method of terminating an easement.

DISCUSSION: An easement may be terminated by adverse possession. The owner of the servient tenement must occupy the property openly and notoriously and in such a manner as to deny the rights of the owner of the easement. This conduct must continue for the statutory period.

Answer (A) is incorrect. A deed by the easement owner to the owner of the servient tenement (the realty subject to the easement) is the most usual means of termination. Answer (B) is incorrect. Abandonment results in termination only when nonuse is coupled with intent to abandon. Answer (C) is incorrect. Termination by merger occurs when the easement owner acquires the servient tenement.

33. Richard Rogers has a large lot on which he collected old cars. He gave permission to Tim Thomas to enter on his land and remove them. Thomas sells them, keeping all proceeds for himself. If after a month Rogers decides he wants Thomas to remove no more cars, his best legal argument is that Thomas

A. Is a trespasser.

B. Is a licensee.

C. Has a license coupled with an interest.

D. Has an easement.

Answer (B) is correct. *(Publisher, adapted)*

REQUIRED: The best legal argument to terminate another's right to use land.

DISCUSSION: A license is the mere right to be on the land of another without being a trespasser. It is revocable at any time. When the right is retracted, the licensee is required to leave the premises.

Answer (A) is incorrect. Rogers gave Thomas permission to enter his land, so Thomas cannot be a trespasser. Answer (C) is incorrect. A license coupled with an interest is not revocable. If Thomas had paid for the right to remove all the cars, he would have a license coupled with an interest to enter on Rogers' land. Answer (D) is incorrect. An easement is not terminable at will.

23.6 Land-Use Controls

34. Land-use controls may be public or private. They may be imposed by law or arise by agreement. Which of the following is a true statement about private means of control?

A. An equitable servitude is a promise that is enforceable only if the parties are in privity of estate.

B. An equitable servitude is enforceable although the promise is oral.

C. A covenant running with the land is enforceable by an action for damages brought by a successor of the covenantee against a successor of the covenantor.

D. A covenant running with the land must touch and concern the land but the original parties need not have intended that successors be bound.

Answer (C) is correct. *(Publisher, adapted)*

REQUIRED: The true statement about private methods of land-use control.

DISCUSSION: A covenant runs with the land if it touches and concerns the land, if the original parties intended it to bind their successors, if it is contained in a writing, and if the original parties were in privity of estate (e.g., grantor-grantee or testator-devisee). If X is a developer who sells a lot in a subdivision to Y, and the deed contains the restriction that Y and his/her successors, heirs, and assigns may use the property only for residential purposes, the restriction meets the criteria for a covenant that will run with the land. It will be enforceable by successors of X (other purchasers of lots in the subdivision) against a successor of Y (such as a person to whom Y sold the lot).

Answer (A) is incorrect. An equitable servitude is a restrictive covenant that is similar to a covenant running with the land except that no privity of estate is necessary. Answer (B) is incorrect. An equitable servitude will not be imposed absent a writing. Answer (D) is incorrect. Intent is a requirement.

35. The Civil Rights Act of 1968 is commonly known as the Federal Fair Housing Act. The act makes illegal the refusal to rent to someone because of

A. Marital status.

B. Disability.

C. Age.

D. Country of origin.

Answer (D) is correct. *(Publisher, adapted)*

REQUIRED: The illegal act under the Civil Rights Act of 1968.

DISCUSSION: The Federal Fair Housing Act was designed to end private discrimination in housing. The act is concerned with discrimination based on race, color, religion, national origin, and sex. Refusal to sell, rent, or negotiate because of any of these factors is illegal. Discrimination in housing based on marital status, disability, and age are not addressed by the act. Discrimination based on these factors is commonly addressed by state and local fair housing laws.

Answer (A) is incorrect. Discrimination based on marital status is commonly addressed by state and local law. Answer (B) is incorrect. Discrimination based on disability is commonly addressed by state and local law. Answer (C) is incorrect. Discrimination based on age is commonly addressed by state and local law.

36. The Civil Rights Act of 1968 contains exemptions from its housing provisions for certain persons and organizations. Which of the following may be exempt?

A. An owner who sells his/her home through a broker.

B. An owner who sells his/her home while owning an interest in a new home.

C. The owner of a rental property containing six units who resides in one of the units.

D. A religious organization that operates rental property and discriminates against a particular religion.

Answer (B) is correct. *(Publisher, adapted)*

REQUIRED: The person or organization exempt from the housing provisions of the Civil Rights Act of 1968.

DISCUSSION: Ordinarily, an owner who sells his/her home is not subject to the act, even if the owner has already acquired a new home or owns a second home prior to offering the residence for sale.

Answer (A) is incorrect. The exemption does not apply to an owner who uses a broker in the sales transaction. Answer (C) is incorrect. The rental property must contain four units or less to be exempt. Answer (D) is incorrect. A religious organization operating rental property may only discriminate in favor of a particular religion.

37. Cardosa purchased a ranch style house near the edge of town but within the city limits. She had a fee simple title and had paid the purchase price in full. Cardosa placed a sign by the road that read "Compadre Ranch." Cardosa had many friends living at the house in violation of local zoning. They partied until dawn making a lot of noise. The garbage in the yard also began to pile up. The city council tried to have Cardosa correct these problems, but Cardosa says she can do anything with the land because she owns it in fee simple. Which of the following can the city council or appropriate governmental body do?

A. Hold a sheriff's sale of Cardosa's land because she has not complied with the applicable zoning laws.

B. Prohibit the occupancy of the property if the garbage constitutes a health hazard.

C. Tear down the sign as a violation of the city sign ordinance.

D. Confiscate Cardosa's stereo equipment to reduce the noise level for the neighbors.

Answer (B) is correct. *(Publisher, adapted)*

REQUIRED: The action available to an appropriate governmental body to abate a nuisance.

DISCUSSION: Although a landowner ordinarily may use the land for any purpose, (s)he must not substantially and unreasonably interfere with neighboring landowners. Under the police power, a governmental body can take necessary steps to prevent a health hazard. If Cardosa does not clean up garbage that constitutes a health hazard, the city can prohibit occupancy of the property.

Answer (A) is incorrect. Noncompliance with the zoning laws is not a basis for a sheriff's sale; rather, it is a basis for a court order prohibiting the violations. Answer (C) is incorrect. The city first must obtain a court order to remove the sign. Answer (D) is incorrect. Cardosa's personal property cannot be confiscated without a court order. But a court would probably issue an injunction that, if ignored, could lead to a citation for contempt of court.

38. A person injured by an action prohibited by the Federal Fair Housing Act may file a complaint with the Secretary of Housing and Urban Development (HUD). If HUD refers the case to the U.S. Attorney General for prosecution, several remedies are available. Which of the following is not an available remedy?

A. Compensatory damages.

B. Punitive damages limited to $100,000.

C. Injunctive relief.

D. Attorney's fees and costs.

Answer (B) is correct. *(Publisher, adapted)*

REQUIRED: The remedy not available under the Federal Fair Housing Act.

DISCUSSION: Punitive damages are awarded to the injured party and assessed against the party who violated the act in order to punish the violator. The act limits punitive damages for first-time offenders. The limit does not affect the award of compensatory damages.

Answer (A) is incorrect. Compensatory damages may be awarded to the plaintiff by the court. Answer (C) is incorrect. Injunctive relief may be awarded to the plaintiff by the court. Answer (D) is incorrect. Attorney's fees and costs may be awarded to the plaintiff by the court.

39. Limitations, restrictions, and conditions on the ownership of real property are diverse. Which of the following statements is false?

A. Compensation for a taking of property under the power of eminent domain is paid only to possessory interests in property.

B. Property is taxed according to its highest and best use.

C. A mortgagee who has paid the real property taxes may recover them from the mortgagor.

D. Zoning ordinances may prohibit the most profitable use of the property.

Answer (A) is correct. *(Publisher, adapted)*

REQUIRED: The limitation not placed on real estate ownership.

DISCUSSION: Eminent domain is the power of a governmental unit to take private property for a public purpose for which the owners must be paid compensation. Those entitled to compensation include not only the persons in possession but also those with vested interests, e.g., one who has a remainder following a life estate. But contingent future interests are not compensable.

Answer (B) is incorrect. Real property taxes are usually based on an appraised value of land determined according to its highest and best use. Answer (C) is incorrect. A mortgagee who pays the taxes may add the amount paid to its claim against the debtor. Answer (D) is incorrect. Reasonable zoning ordinances have been upheld even though they prohibit the most profitable use of property.

40. Fifteen years ago, Mr. Xavier violated the zoning of his real estate in Allentown by erecting a gas station. The authorities have never proceeded against him because of the violation, and he operated his gas station without incident until he was ready to retire. Xavier tells the prospective buyer that he has a "pre-existing, nonconforming use," and that the buyer can continue to use the property for a gas station despite the violation of the zoning law. What is the status of the nonconforming use?

A. Pre-existing, nonconforming uses are those legal uses of property that preceded the enactment of a zoning law. The buyer therefore cannot continue the use.

B. The illegality of the use was cured by the passage of time.

C. Allentown is unable to use zoning laws to attack the current use of the property and curtail it.

D. Zoning laws can be defeated by showing that the illegal use of the property did not harm adjacent landowners.

Answer (A) is correct. *(E. O'Connor)*

REQUIRED: The status of a long-term use of property that has always been in violation of the zoning laws.

DISCUSSION: Zoning codes do not have retroactive effect. Hence, an existing legal use cannot be invalidated by enactment of a zoning ordinance or an amendment thereto. Such a nonconforming use may therefore continue, but it may not be expanded. Moreover, it runs with the land; that is, a subsequent buyer may continue the use. But if it terminates, for example, because of destruction of a building, it may not be resumed. Mr. Xavier's use, however, was simply illegal, not nonconforming, and neither Mr. Xavier nor a buyer has a right to continue the use.

Answer (B) is incorrect. No principle analogous to adverse possession applies to zoning violations. Answer (C) is incorrect. The municipality could immediately end an illegal use and require a nonconforming use to be stopped in a reasonable time. Answer (D) is incorrect. Absence of harm to owners of adjacent property does not validate an illegal use. A zoning ordinance will be defeated only if it is an invalid use of the police power, e.g., one that constitutes an uncompensated taking of the property.

41. Public control of the use of real property is achieved principally through zoning. Which of the following statements is true?

A. Zoning is an exercise of the police power of the state to take private property to promote public health, morals, safety, and welfare.

B. A zoning ordinance allows for nonconforming uses and variances.

C. Zoning is an inherent power of municipalities, and its use must have a rational relationship to its basis in public policy.

D. Floating zones have been held to be an unconstitutional use of the police power.

Answer (B) is correct. *(Publisher, adapted)*

REQUIRED: The true statement about zoning.

DISCUSSION: Zoning is used to plan and control the development of real property. The passage of a zoning ordinance, however, may not prohibit a lawful preexisting use. A nonconforming use must be allowed to continue for a reasonable time. The statute must also allow for variances. Zoning variances are granted upon the petition of a landowner if (s)he cannot make reasonable use of his/her land, if the adverse effect of the ordinance is unique to the petitioner, and if the character of the zone will not be substantially changed. Also, special use permits are used by local governments to control the location of some special types of development that may not be included in the regular zoning plan, such as churches and schools.

Answer (A) is incorrect. The police power may be used to regulate but not take property. Answer (C) is incorrect. Local governments ordinarily may not enact a zoning ordinance without an enabling statute (a state statute granting such authority to local governments). Answer (D) is incorrect. Floating zones are permissible. The amount of land to be designated for various uses is determined, but classifications are assigned to particular parcels only at a later time and upon the request of landowners.

42. A specialized type of zoning that has been found to be prima facie illegal by some states is

A. Regional zoning.

B. Limited-density zoning.

C. Performance standards zoning.

D. Large-lot zoning.

Answer (D) is correct. *(Publisher, adapted)*

REQUIRED: The type of zoning found by some courts to violate public policy.

DISCUSSION: Zoning and land-use regulations are intended to give communities some control over their growth and development. These regulations must promote a valid purpose and not violate public policy. Large-lot zoning sets excessively large minimum lot size standards for new construction. Whether intentionally or not, such standards discriminate against low and middle income housing. Some state courts, most notably in Pennsylvania, have ruled large-lot zoning to be prima facie illegal.

Answer (A) is incorrect. Regional zoning allows more comprehensive planning for regional needs and has been encouraged by various courts. Answer (B) is incorrect. Zoning is commonly used to control the density of development within reasonable limits. Limited-density zoning has also been used to provide a minimum of "green space" within a community. Answer (C) is incorrect. Performance standards zoning is a valid use of a community's police power to regulate public nuisances such as toxic wastes, noise, odors, and traffic. For example, a standard may specify the decibel level or the amount of vehicular traffic.

43. Wetlands are valuable natural resources. Which of the following statements concerning land-use controls instituted to protect wetlands is true?

A. Zoning is the control most widely used to protect wetlands.

B. Wetland protection controls are designed to stop all further destruction of wetlands as soon as possible.

C. Wetland protection controls are exempt from the prohibition against depriving property owners of all reasonable uses of their land.

D. Permitting is the control most widely used to protect wetlands.

Answer (D) is correct. *(Publisher, adapted)*

REQUIRED: The true statement about the protection of wetlands.

DISCUSSION: Preservation of certain special environments (such as wetlands and historic districts) has become more important as society's environmental awareness has grown. Wetlands in particular have been found to be vital for wildlife, flood control, and ground water maintenance. Various methods have been used to limit wetland destruction, but the most widely used control is permitting. For example, the Clean Water Act of 1972 requires a permit from the Corps of Engineers for dredging and filling operations.

Answer (A) is incorrect. Permitting, not zoning, predominates as a method to protect wetlands. Answer (B) is incorrect. The controls are designed to limit further destruction, not stop it entirely. Answer (C) is incorrect. There are no exemptions to the prohibition against "taking."

44. A court rules that city government regulations are overly restrictive of Mary's use of her land. The city government must

A. Condemn the land under its power of eminent domain and pay Mary reasonable compensation.

B. Condemn the land under its police power and provide Mary with an equivalent parcel of land elsewhere.

C. File a comprehensive plan with the court as a basis for seizing Mary's land.

D. Attempt to bargain with Mary to purchase the property because the court has ruled against the city.

Answer (A) is correct. *(Publisher, adapted)*

REQUIRED: The remedy available to a local government if its regulations are overly restrictive.

DISCUSSION: Public controls of land-use fall under two basic types: the power of eminent domain and police power. Eminent domain is the power of government to take land from private owners through condemnation when the taking is for a public purpose and the private owner is reasonably compensated. Police power is the broad power of state and local governments to promote the public health, safety, and welfare, for example, through land-use regulation. Under the police power, land is not appropriated by the government and compensation is not paid to the owner. Regulations that are so restrictive that the owner is deprived of all of the land, effect a "taking," and the government must pay reasonable compensation.

Answer (B) is incorrect. Condemnation is based on the power of eminent domain. Answer (C) is incorrect. A comprehensive plan is a set of standards that forms the basis of a zoning code. It is not necessarily a specific document and is not filed with a court, although a court may use it to evaluate the propriety of a zoning administration's actions. A comprehensive plan is not a basis for seizing property. Answer (D) is incorrect. The court's unfavorable ruling does not prevent the city from pursuing condemnation of the property.

STUDY UNIT TWENTY-FOUR
REAL PROPERTY: TRANSACTIONS

The purchase and sale of real property involves a **real estate contract** between two parties, the seller and the buyer. Under a typical contract, the seller transfers ownership of property to the buyer in exchange for the payment, or a promise to make payment, of a specified price in money or other consideration.

Real estate transactions are subject to **Title VIII of the Civil Rights Act of 1964** (as amended). It prohibits discrimination on the basis of race, color, religion, gender, national origin, disability, or family status. However, if the discrimination does not involve **race or color**, Title VIII exempts sales or rentals of (1) single-family housing when the owner is an (2) individual who (3) owns no more than three houses and (4) does not employ a broker or advertise in a discriminatory way.

A contract for the purchase and sale of land must be in writing. The typical **statute of frauds** provides: "No action shall be brought to charge any person upon any contract for the sale of lands, tenements, or any interest in or concerning them, for a longer term than one year, unless such contracts by some memorandum or note thereof shall be in writing and signed by the party to be charged." The statute is satisfied if the contract (1) is expressed in a writing, (2) identifies the parties, (3) describes the land, (4) recites the purchase price, (5) contains mutual promises to buy and sell land, and (6) is signed by the party to be held liable. Any alterations, amendments, or additions to the contract should be agreed to by both parties. Nevertheless, given **part performance**, a court, to prevent injustice, may grant **specific performance** of a real estate contract despite the absence of a writing. In a majority of jurisdictions, two of the following are required for a court to grant this equitable remedy: The buyer (1) is in actual possession of the land, (2) has made substantial improvements, or (3) has paid all or part of the purchase price.

In the absence of an agreement to the contrary, every contract for the sale of land includes an implied promise by the seller that (s)he will deliver to the buyer **marketable title** at the time of closing. The seller is obligated to deliver a title that is free from reasonable doubt as to its validity and that the buyer most likely will not need to defend in court. Title is marketable if a reasonably prudent buyer, who is ready, willing, and able to purchase, conducts a **title search** of the **public records**, concludes that the seller's title is valid, and accepts it. Thus, perfect title is not required, but a defect not specifically accepted by the buyer is a material breach of the contract. Common defects not recorded in the **chain of title** that may render title unmarketable include (1) an easement, (2) a restrictive covenant (an agreement to restrict land use), (3) an outstanding mortgage, or (4) any other encumbrance that the seller cannot or will not remove (for example, adverse possession or a mechanic's lien).

In most jurisdictions, a **builder-seller** of residences is deemed to make an **implied warranty of habitability**. This warranty extends to defects in a new building that would not be found in a reasonable inspection. Moreover, many jurisdictions require sellers to disclose latent defects.

The **seller's performance** includes tendering a **good and marketable title** on the date that the conveyance is to be completed. The buyer may not rescind a land contract before the time for that performance, i.e., before the closing date, without liability for breach of contract. Moreover, the **buyer's obligation to pay the purchase price** is typically deemed to be concurrent with the seller's obligation to convey title. If the buyer claims the seller's title is not marketable, (s)he must notify the seller and give reasonable time for the seller to cure the defect(s).

The primary **remedies** for breach of a real estate contract are damages and specific performance. **Damages** are usually measured by the difference between the contract price and the market value of the real estate on the day of the breach. A court may order **specific performance** when the remedy at law (damages) is inadequate. Because each parcel of land is deemed to be unique, monetary damages are rarely an adequate remedy.

In the absence of a contractual provision to the contrary, the majority rule is that the **risk of loss** is on the buyer once the **contract has been signed**. The buyer is regarded as the **equitable owner of the land**. The seller, although (s)he still holds legal title to the land, is regarded as the equitable owner of **personal property**, i.e., the right to the purchase price. This rule is the doctrine of **equitable conversion**. Thus, the buyer has the risk of loss for **casualty losses** that occur without the fault of either party after the contract has been signed. The buyer must pay the contract price despite loss of the property due to fire, storm, or other casualty. Some states have adopted the **Uniform Vendor and Purchaser Risk Act**, which provides that loss will be placed on the buyer, but only if (s)he has either legal title to, or possession of, the property at the time of the loss. Another consequence of the principle of equitable conversion is that, **if the seller dies** while a party to a specifically enforceable contract, the **beneficial interest** passes as personal property. Accordingly, the seller's heirs receive only bare legal title, which they must convey to the buyer when and if the buyer performs. **If the buyer dies** while a party to a specifically enforceable contract, the **right to receive the land** passes to his/her heirs, but the obligation to pay the purchase price falls on the personal representative of the buyer's estate.

Owners of rights in real estate frequently engage agents to market those rights and find purchasers. The contract between a property owner and a **real estate broker** is called a listing agreement. In an **exclusive listing agreement**, a seller typically promises to pay a percentage of the sale price if the broker (1) obtains a bona fide offer (2) from a willing and able buyer (3) to purchase the property rights (4) according to the terms stated in the listing agreement and (5) within a specified time. If, while the agreement is effective, the seller accepts an offer independently of the broker, the seller nevertheless is obligated to pay the agreed-to fee. Under an **open listing agreement**, however, the owner of property rights may agree to sell them to another, independently of the broker, without obligation to the broker. A property owner may generally bargain for and establish any contract with one or more brokers, provided the purpose is legal. Thus, the buyer may engage a broker as his/her agent for a flat or otherwise agreed-to fee, payable upon certain conditions.

The federal Real Estate Settlement Procedures Act (RESPA) is a consumer protection measure intended to promote disclosure of information, reduce settlement (closing) costs, and prohibit payment of unearned fees and kickbacks. The lender is required to make certain disclosures to the buyer and to permit the buyer an opportunity to obtain advance estimates of closing costs. The mandated use of the **Uniform Settlement Statement** helps to clarify what costs are to be paid by the buyer and seller.

Furthermore, the **National Affordable Housing Act of 1990** amended RESPA to require that a buyer be furnished an annual analysis of escrow accounts. Abusive practices, such as kickbacks, are generally prohibited. One may not receive payment for providing a referral to a given bank, insurer, or attorney. However, lenders may collect reasonable advance payments from borrowers for items such as insurance and taxes. Also, a seller may not specify a title insurer to be used by the buyer, but a lender may. Moreover, a lender is permitted to charge the seller a prepayment penalty if the new mortgage loan is not made with the same institution. The RESPA only applies when a federally related mortgage loan is made on a residential building other than a large apartment complex.

The statute of frauds requires the transfer of an interest in land to be in writing, but a writing that evidences **an intention to transfer an interest in land** will be sustained as a **conveyance** despite informal language. However, execution and delivery of a deed is the traditional method of transferring title. A **deed** is a written instrument expressing a grantor's intent to convey or pass an interest in real property to a grantee. Agreements in the contract of sale do not survive closing, unless the parties expressly agree otherwise, and any other agreements are merged into the deed. Thus, under the **merger concept**, the deed is treated as the entire agreement. Typically, the deed must contain (1) the name of the grantor, (2) the name of the grantee, (3) operative words of conveyance, (4) a legally sufficient description of the land, and (5) the signature of the grantor. Acknowledgment before a **notary** is not an essential element of making a deed operative, but it may be required by the state recording statute. Moreover, in a majority of states, a **seal** is not necessary to an effective conveyance of a possessory estate.

Delivery of the deed to the grantee by the grantor with an **intent to transfer title** is necessary to complete the transfer of real property. Absent delivery, the grantor retains legal title, and the grantee has no ownership interest in the land recognized at law. Once a deed has been delivered, **cancelation of the instrument** will not revest ownership of the property in the grantor. Ownership of real property does not pass to the grantee until (s)he **accepts delivery** of the deed. If the conveyance appears beneficial to the grantee, acceptance is presumed.

Generally, four **types of deeds** are used to convey interests in real property. A **quitclaim deed** purports to convey only the interest (not the land itself), if any, that the grantor has in a specified piece of property. The grantor, in a quitclaim deed, essentially states, "If I own an interest, and I may in fact own no interest, I am transferring whatever I do own to you." A **bargain and sale deed** purports to convey the land itself. The grantor may or may not have title to the real property, and (s)he makes no promise, express or implied, that (s)he has good title. Hence, the grantee is in no better position than the grantee of a quitclaim deed. A **general warranty deed** not only purports to transfer the land itself, but also contains warranties or assurances by the grantor of facts upon which the grantee may rely. Thus, the grantor warrants that (1) there are no undisclosed encumbrances, (2) (s)he owns the interest conveyed and has the right and power to do so, and (3) (s)he will **defend the grantee** from any and all claims that might arise from a defect in the grantor's purported ownership interest. This deed is the type most commonly used in real property transactions. The **special warranty (grant) deed** is typically used when the ownership of property changes frequently. It contains the same warranties as the general warranty deed. But the grantor warrants only that (s)he has not him/herself caused any defects in title. In a general warranty deed, the grantor warrants that no one else has caused any defects in title.

A **recording statute** assures a purchaser of real property that the grantor had title to convey, and it describes the state of such title. The rationale for recording statutes is that (1) ownership of real property should be determinable from **public records**, and (2) purchasers should be able to rely on these records. Recording is not essential to making a deed or other instrument valid as between **the grantor and the grantee**, but it does give **constructive notice** to the world of all transactions that affect title to specific real property. Although a transferee of title may **in fact** have no notice of legal claims to property, the law may imply such notice (knowledge). For example, a purchaser is presumed to have knowledge of interests recorded in the **chain of title** under the state recording statutes. The law also presumes the purchaser has inspected the property. Thus, the purchaser is deemed to know what inspection of the property would have disclosed (e.g., adverse possession). Moreover, a purchaser may have **actual notice** of an encumbrance on the property. (S)he does not take free of the encumbrance merely because (s)he is otherwise protected under the recording/notice statutes. Recording generally affords protection to a grantee against claims of all subsequent transferees (other than from the grantee) of the same property. A grantee who fails to record may lose his/her interest in the land to a subsequent purchaser under certain conditions. The three types of recording statutes are notice, race-notice, and race. A **notice recording statute** protects a **subsequent bona fide purchaser (BFP)** (a party who gives value in good faith and without actual or constructive notice of an adverse claim) regardless of who was the first to record. Priority is given to the purchaser qualifying as a BFP at the time the deed, mortgage, or other interest is acquired. A **race-notice recording statute** protects a subsequent BFP only if (s)he is the first to record. This common form of statute combines the features of both the notice and the race recording statutes. Priority is determined by which BFP records first. A **race recording statute** protects a subsequent purchaser, who need not be a BFP, only if (s)he is the first to record. Priority is determined by who wins the race to the recording office.

A purchaser of real property always should conduct a **title search** to determine whether the seller of real property has good title. Occasionally, the contract for sale will require the seller to furnish evidence of "good record title." A title search is an examination of public land records for all recorded interests **(the chain of title)** in a particular parcel of real property.

Title insurance repays the insured for a loss arising from defects in the title to real property. Thus, a title insurance policy, like other insurance, is a **contract of indemnification**. The title insurer conducts a title search prior to issuing the policy, which usually protects against loss if, among other things, (1) the title is nonmarketable, (2) title is actually in another person, (3) title is subject to an encumbrance, or (4) the insured has no access to the land. Title insurance ordinarily applies **only to recorded interests**. Other **common exceptions** listed in title insurance policies include (1) unpaid taxes, (2) mechanic's liens, (3) utility easements, and (4) defects caused by the purchaser.

A **fixture** is an article that was **once personal property** (a tangible, movable thing) but has become so closely connected to land or a building that **real property law** governs its transfer. Under the prevailing rule, whether a particular article is a fixture is primarily a question of the **intent of the annexor at the time of annexation**. This intent is determined by an **objective test** and may be inferred from factors such as the following: (1) the nature of the property being attached; (2) the manner of annexation; (3) injury to the land, if any, by its removal; (4) the integration of the item with the real property and how it is being used; (5) the relationship of the annexor to the real property, for example, as owner, tenant, invitee, licensee, or trespasser; and (6) the relationship of the annexor to the item, e.g., as owner, bailee, or thief. Given the requisite intent of the annexor, the item is deemed to be a fixture if it has been annexed either actually, e.g., a furnace bolted to the cement floor of a building, or constructively, e.g., a prefabricated house set on a preconstructed cement foundation. Because fixtures are real and not personal property, they are included in any **sale or transfer** of real property. Personal property is not included unless specifically provided for in the sale or transfer.

Trade fixtures are annexed to the land by a tenant for the tenant's own benefit during his/her tenancy. A **trade tenant** is permitted to remove trade fixtures within a reasonable time after expiration of a lease. Other important reasons exist for determining whether an article is real property by virtue of its classification as a fixture. For example, **tax rates** may vary between real and personal property. Also, distribution of real property **under a will** may go to one beneficiary and personal property to another. But the **Uniform Probate Code** does not make this distinction. In addition, a **mortgage on real property** will cover all fixtures, typically including those subsequently affixed.

QUESTIONS

24.1 The Real Estate Contract

1. Moss entered into a contract to purchase certain real property from Shinn. Which of the following statements is false?

A. If Shinn fails to perform the contract, Moss can obtain specific performance.

B. The contract is nonassignable as a matter of law.

C. The statute of frauds applies to the contract.

D. Any amendment to the contract must be agreed to by both Moss and Shinn.

Answer (B) is correct. *(CPA, adapted)*

REQUIRED: The false statement about a contract for the purchase of real property.

DISCUSSION: The general rule is that contracts of an impersonal nature (such as those for the purchase and sale of land) are assignable unless otherwise provided. Contracts for personal services, that involve a confidential relationship, or that have some other personal elements tend not to be assignable.

Answer (A) is incorrect. Specific performance is usually granted when the subject matter is unique, for example, real estate. Answer (C) is incorrect. The statute of frauds applies to the contract. The contract is for the sale of real estate. Answer (D) is incorrect. Modification of a real estate contract requires mutual assent.

2. Which of the following is a defect in marketable title to real property?

A. Recorded zoning restrictions.

B. Recorded easements referred to in the contract of sale.

C. An unrecorded lawsuit for negligence against the seller.

D. An unrecorded easement.

Answer (D) is correct. *(CPA, adapted)*

REQUIRED: The defect in marketable title.

DISCUSSION: Unless a contract for the sale of real property specifically states otherwise, the seller must deliver marketable title. A marketable title is clear of unrecorded restrictions, defects in the chain of title (e.g., a prior recorded conveyance by the seller), and other events preventing the buyer from obtaining a clear title (e.g., a taking by eminent domain). Unrecorded easements or restrictive covenants make a title unmarketable.

Answer (A) is incorrect. Recording provides constructive notice of the item recorded. Title is marketable notwithstanding recorded restrictions. Answer (B) is incorrect. Recorded easements referred to in the contract of sale do not prevent title from being marketable. Answer (C) is incorrect. An unrecorded lawsuit for negligence is not a defect in marketable title to real property. It does not inhibit transfer of the property.

3. A contract for the sale and purchase of real estate (the real estate binder)

A. Must satisfy the general requirements applicable to all contracts as well as the statute of frauds.

B. Does not transfer risk of loss to the buyer until the closing unless the parties expressly agree otherwise.

C. Transfers title but not possession.

D. Is not effective unless recorded.

Answer (A) is correct. *(Publisher, adapted)*

REQUIRED: The true statement about a contract to sell real estate.

DISCUSSION: A real estate binder is a contract, so the elements of a valid contract must be present: offer and acceptance, consideration, legality, and competent parties. The contract to sell also must be in writing and signed by the party to be bound. The contract should contain (1) a description of the property; (2) the time for conveyance; (3) the kind of deed; (4) the price; (5) the mode of financing; (6) the closing date; (7) the date of possession; (8) the date of prorating taxes, insurance, etc.; and (9) a provision for title insurance or an abstract of title.

Answer (B) is incorrect. The majority rule is that risk of loss passes to the buyer upon formation of the contract, but contracts for sale of real property frequently make other arrangements. Answer (C) is incorrect. Transfer of title by deed commonly occurs at the closing. Answer (D) is incorrect. The contract is effective between the parties when formed. Recording puts third parties on notice of the existence of the contract.

4. Fulcrum Enterprises, Inc. contracted to purchase a 4-acre tract of land from Devlin as a site for its proposed factory. The contract of sale is silent as to the type of deed to be received by Fulcrum and does not contain any title exceptions. The title search revealed that 15 zoning laws affect Fulcrum's use of the land and that back taxes are due. A survey revealed a stone wall encroaching upon a portion of the land Devlin is purporting to convey. A survey made 23 years ago also had revealed the wall. Regarding the rights and duties of Fulcrum, which of the following is correct?

A. The contract is invalid because it does not specify the type of deed.

B. The existence of the zoning laws will permit Fulcrum to avoid the contract.

C. Fulcrum must take the land subject to the back taxes.

D. The wall suggests a potential breach of the implied warranty of marketability.

Answer (D) is correct. *(CPA, adapted)*

REQUIRED: The rights and duties of a party contracting to purchase realty.

DISCUSSION: Absent an express provision to the contrary, every contract for the sale of real property contains an implied warranty of marketability. The seller warrants that the title is free from defects that would prevent a reasonable buyer from purchasing. The encroachment is a circumstance that would render the title unmarketable because it suggests that someone has acquired part of the property by adverse possession.

Answer (A) is incorrect. The contract is valid. When the contract is silent, the courts infer the intent is to provide the customary deed used in that community. This may be a full (general) warranty deed, special warranty deed, or quitclaim deed. Answer (B) is incorrect. Zoning laws are public restrictions assumed to be known by all parties and do not affect marketability of title. Answer (C) is incorrect. Unpaid back taxes would be a breach of the implied warranty of marketability and would relieve Fulcrum of performing if they are not paid before the closing.

5. A clause in a contract for the purchase of real estate providing that the seller shall be entitled to retain the purchaser's down payment as liquidated damages should the purchaser fail to close the transaction will usually be enforceable

A. In addition to the seller's right to recover compensatory damages.

B. As a penalty if the purchaser has intentionally defaulted.

C. If the amount of the down payment bears a reasonable relationship to the probable loss.

D. In all cases provided the parties have agreed in a signed writing.

Answer (C) is correct. *(CPA, adapted)*

REQUIRED: The enforceability of a liquidated damages clause in a real estate contract.

DISCUSSION: Liquidated damages are those provided for in the contract. A liquidated damages clause may save the trouble and expense of litigation, but the amount must have a reasonable relationship to the loss expected to result from breach.

Answer (A) is incorrect. The election of remedies doctrine provides that inconsistent remedies may not be sought. Both liquidated and compensatory damages cannot be obtained. Answer (B) is incorrect. A penalty is not a proper contract remedy. The purpose of contract remedies is not to punish the breacher but to put the nonbreacher in as good a position as (s)he would have occupied if the contract had been fully performed. Answer (D) is incorrect. A writing would not save an excessive liquidated damages clause.

6. Which of the following remedies is more likely to be available for a breach of a contract to sell real rather than personal property?

A. Rescission.

B. Specific performance.

C. Damages.

D. Replevin.

Answer (B) is correct. *(Publisher, adapted)*

REQUIRED: The remedy more likely to be available for a breach involving real rather than personal property.

DISCUSSION: The equitable remedy of specific performance will be granted when the legal remedy of damages is insufficient, for example, because the subject matter is unique. Each parcel of realty is considered unique, so contracts to sell real estate are specifically enforceable. While contracts for the sale of antiques, heirlooms, and other rare items are also specifically enforceable, most contracts concerning personal property are not.

Answer (A) is incorrect. The nonbreaching party may, if the breach is material, elect to rescind and not be bound by the contract. This remedy is customarily available for personal property. Answer (C) is incorrect. Damages is a typical remedy for breach of a contract involving personal property. Answer (D) is incorrect. Replevin is an action to recover personal property taken unlawfully.

7. Walt Fletcher entered into a contract to purchase a log cabin with an acre of land from Jeni Cook. Suppose that the log cabin was totally destroyed by fire before closing. In determining the rights of Jeni and Walt, the court would most likely consider the doctrine of

A. Marshaling.

B. Sequestration.

C. Subrogation.

D. Equitable conversion.

Answer (D) is correct. *(Publisher, adapted)*

REQUIRED: The doctrine most likely to be considered when real property is destroyed before closing.

DISCUSSION: Under the doctrine of equitable conversion, many states place the risk of loss by destruction on the buyer after the contract is entered into. This transfer of risk of loss prior to the conveyance of legal title is based on the theory that the buyer's contract right has been equitably converted to title because the contract is specifically enforceable. In equity, the equitable title holder will prevail over the legal title holder (seller). Thus, the equitable title holder (buyer) has the risk of loss.

Answer (A) is incorrect. Marshaling refers to the separation of assets into different categories so that they may be applied to claims according to an order of priority. Answer (B) is incorrect. Sequestration is the seizure and holding of property until claims are satisfied. Answer (C) is incorrect. Subrogation is the succession to the rights of another after paying the other's claim.

8. Jon Seller and Shannon Buyer enter into an agreement for the sale of real property. The state in which the property is located follows the principle of equitable conversion and has no statute to solve this problem. Seller dies before closing and leaves his personal property to Billy and his real property to Gwen. Which of the following is true?

A. Death, an event for which the parties could have provided, terminates the agreement if they did not so provide.

B. Gwen is entitled to the proceeds of the sale when it closes, because the doctrine of equitable conversion does not apply to these circumstances.

C. Billy is entitled to the proceeds of the sale when it closes.

D. Title was rendered unmarketable by Seller's death.

Answer (C) is correct. *(Publisher, adapted)*

REQUIRED: The true statement when a seller of real property dies before closing.

DISCUSSION: The doctrine of equitable conversion operates to transform the seller's interest into personal property. The underlying theory is that the buyer has acquired equitable title and the seller only has a contract right because the contract is specifically enforceable by the buyer. Billy, as the beneficiary of the personal property, would be entitled to the proceeds of the contract.

Answer (A) is incorrect. Death does not automatically terminate an agreement to sell real property. The contract is enforceable against the estate. Answer (B) is incorrect. The doctrine applies to such circumstances as well as to the situation in which the realty is destroyed after the execution of the contract. Answer (D) is incorrect. The personal representative of the seller's estate can convey a marketable title.

9. Buyer is a party to a valid contract to purchase real property but dies before the closing. Neither party was in breach of the agreement. Which of the following is appropriate in most jurisdictions?

A. Buyer's heirs may specifically enforce the agreement.

B. Seller has the right to return the down payment and cancel the contract.

C. Death terminates the agreement.

D. Any title acquired would be unmarketable by reason of Buyer's death.

Answer (A) is correct. *(Publisher, adapted)*

REQUIRED: The effect of the death of a buyer of real property before closing.

DISCUSSION: Buyers under a purchase agreement for real estate can obtain specific performance. In the event of death, their contract rights descend to their heirs. Thus, Buyer's heirs may specifically enforce the agreement.

Answer (B) is incorrect. Buyer's contractual right to purchase the real estate passes to his/her estate as both an obligation and an enforceable right. Answer (C) is incorrect. Death does not terminate an agreement to buy or sell. It only terminates personal service contracts. Answer (D) is incorrect. The marketability of the title is unrelated to Buyer's death.

10. A seller of real property may engage another person to locate a buyer. A real estate broker will generally serve as the seller's agent for this purpose. Which of the following is true?

A. Because the broker has no interest in the real estate, the brokerage contract need not be written.

B. The broker may not prepare the buyer's offer to purchase because of the prohibition against the unlicensed practice of law.

C. The broker's essential task is to find a buyer and enter into a binding contract on behalf of the seller.

D. The listing contract determines when the seller must compensate the broker.

Answer (D) is correct. *(Publisher, adapted)*

REQUIRED: The true statement about real estate brokers.

DISCUSSION: The listing agreement specifies the duration of the listing, the seller's terms of sale, and the compensation due the broker. In an open listing, an agent who produces a ready, willing, and able buyer will receive the commission. If the seller finds the buyer, no commission need be paid. However, under an exclusive-right-to-sell listing, the broker must be paid regardless of who produces the buyer.

Answer (A) is incorrect. Many states require that real estate broker commission arrangements be in writing. Answer (B) is incorrect. Many states allow the broker to perform this task, but an attorney must prepare the deed and other closing documents. Answer (C) is incorrect. The broker is generally authorized to find a ready, willing, and able buyer and to negotiate on behalf of the seller, but not to sign a contract binding the seller.

24.2 Conveyances

11. Park purchased Marshall's department store. At the closing, Park delivered a certified check for the balance due and Marshall gave Park a warranty deed with full covenants to the property. The deed

A. Must be recorded to be valid between the parties.

B. Must recite the actual consideration given by Park.

C. Must be in writing and contain the signature of both parties duly witnessed.

D. Usually represents an exclusive integration of the duties of the seller.

Answer (D) is correct. *(CPA, adapted)*

REQUIRED: The effect of a warranty deed with full covenants.

DISCUSSION: The usual effect of a deed is to represent the complete and exclusive agreement between the buyer and seller. A document intended to be complete and that contains all the elements of an agreement is called an exclusive integration. Thus, none of the provisions of the binder contract survive the delivery of the deed unless agreed to by the parties.

Answer (A) is incorrect. Recording a deed has no effect on the agreement between the parties. It only protects the buyer against third parties. Delivery of the deed is essential to its effectiveness. Answer (B) is incorrect. A deed is valid without consideration. Answer (C) is incorrect. A deed need only contain the signature of the grantor.

12. In the majority of states, a deed must be signed by

A. The grantor and grantee but not witnessed or acknowledged.

B. The grantor and grantee and acknowledged.

C. The grantor but not the grantee.

D. The grantor and the grantee and both witnessed and acknowledged.

Answer (C) is correct. *(Publisher, adapted)*

REQUIRED: The signor(s) of a deed.

DISCUSSION: Although the names of both appear on the deed, the grantor, not the grantee, is generally required to sign. Many states also require the deed to be witnessed and acknowledged before a notary. Notarization is useful in establishing the validity of any required signature.

13. A deed is used to convey real property. Which of the following statements is true with respect to deeds?

A. A deed purporting to convey real property, but that omits the day of the month, is invalid.

B. A deed that lacks the signature of the grantor is valid.

C. A quitclaim deed that purports to transfer to the grantee "whatever title the grantor has" is invalid.

D. A deed that purports to convey real property and recites a consideration of $1 and other valuable consideration is valid.

Answer (D) is correct. *(CPA, adapted)*

REQUIRED: The true statement concerning a deed to real property.

DISCUSSION: A deed may convey effective title to real property even though no consideration is involved in the transaction. Thus, a statement of "$1 and other valuable consideration" is sufficient. Furthermore, this common practice does not reveal (in the public records) the actual consideration. Binder contracts require consideration, and more care must be exercised to satisfy the requirements of consideration.

Answer (A) is incorrect. Omission of the day of the month of the conveyance from the deed does not invalidate the deed. Lack of a specific date simply means someone else may produce a deed with a specific date in that month and claim that his/her deed was earlier. Answer (B) is incorrect. A deed not signed by the grantor is invalid. Answer (C) is incorrect. All states recognize the validity of quitclaim deeds. In a quitclaim deed, the grantor simply conveys whatever title (s)he may have without making any warranties.

14. Ned executed a deed naming his son, John, as grantee. John paid no consideration. The deed described the property as follows: "All of my land and dwelling known as 72 Back Road, Crosstown, United States, being 1 acre." The property at 72 Back Road covered 7/8 of an acre of land. The description of 72 Back Road was

A. Sufficient, because the discrepancy in area is not fatal.

B. Not sufficient, because it contained no metes and bounds.

C. Not sufficient, because the acreage given was not correct.

D. Not sufficient, because a deed purporting to convey more than a grantor owns is void.

Answer (A) is correct. *(Publisher, adapted)*

REQUIRED: The sufficiency or insufficiency of the description of the property.

DISCUSSION: An effective conveyance of real property requires a legally sufficient description of the land. The description need not conform to any special requirements provided it is sufficient to reasonably locate the property. The 72 Back Road description is sufficient even with the discrepancy in area if Ned owned no other land with which to confuse it.

Answer (B) is incorrect. The description need not contain a surveyor's description by metes and boundaries. Answer (C) is incorrect. The discrepancy in acreage is not a fatal flaw. Answer (D) is incorrect. The deed is effective to convey the entire interest actually owned by the grantor.

15. For a deed to be effective between the purchaser and seller of real estate, one of the conditions is that the deed must

A. Contain the signatures of the seller and purchaser.

B. Contain the actual sales price.

C. Be delivered by the seller with an intent to transfer title.

D. Be recorded within the permissible statutory time limits.

Answer (C) is correct. *(CPA, adapted)*

REQUIRED: The condition for a deed to be effective between the purchaser and seller of real estate.

DISCUSSION: Real property cannot be conveyed unless a valid delivery and acceptance of the deed have occurred. The grantor must intend to transfer title and surrender control of the document. Subsequent return of the deed or destruction of the deed, even if intentional, is not sufficient to rescind the conveyance. A reconveyance is required.

Answer (A) is incorrect. Only the seller must sign. Answer (B) is incorrect. The deed must contain a recital of consideration but not the actual price; e.g., the phrase "$1 and other valuable consideration" is sufficient. Answer (D) is incorrect. Recording a deed protects against claims by third parties but has no effect on the grantor-grantee relationship.

16. Which of the following deeds gives the grantee the least amount of protection?

A. Bargain and sale deed.

B. Grant deed.

C. Quitclaim deed.

D. Warranty deed.

Answer (C) is correct. *(CPA, adapted)*

REQUIRED: The deed that gives the grantee the least amount of protection.

DISCUSSION: A quitclaim deed merely relinquishes to the grantee whatever interest the grantor may have. Such a deed contains no covenants (warranties). Thus, it does not warrant that the grantor has a clear title or any title at all. If an adverse claimant prevails, the grantee will have no recourse against the grantor.

Answer (A) is incorrect. A bargain and sale deed is essentially a contract, and the seller is considered to imply that (s)he has a right to convey the property. It may also contain a covenant that the seller has not impaired the title. Answer (B) is incorrect. A grant (special warranty) deed provides warranty protection, but only with respect to events occurring after the grantor acquired the property. Answer (D) is incorrect. A general warranty deed provides the best protection.

17. The special warranty deed

A. Makes no warranties but simply conveys whatever interest the grantor has.

B. Warrants that the grantor has not encumbered the property or transferred any interest in it to another person.

C. Includes a covenant that the owner has the right to transfer a fee simple title.

D. Warrants that the grantee will have quiet enjoyment of the property.

Answer (B) is correct. *(Publisher, adapted)*

REQUIRED: The characteristic of a special warranty deed.

DISCUSSION: A special warranty deed is one that contains some warranties but less than a full warranty deed (which warrants against all lawful claims). Such a deed transfers the grantor's interest and warrants that (s)he has not encumbered the property or transferred any interest in it to another person. It does not contain a warranty that the acts of others have not created a defect in the title.

Answer (A) is incorrect. A quitclaim deed makes no warranties but simply conveys whatever interest the grantor has. Answer (C) is incorrect. A general warranty deed includes a covenant that the owner has the right to transfer a fee simple title. Answer (D) is incorrect. A general warranty deed warrants that the grantee will have quiet enjoyment of the property.

18. Which of the following warranties is(are) contained in a general warranty deed?

I. The grantor has the right to convey the property.

II. The grantee will not be disturbed in possession of the property by the grantor or some third party's lawful claim of ownership.

A. I only.

B. II only.

C. I and II.

D. Neither I nor II.

Answer (C) is correct. *(CPA, adapted)*

REQUIRED: The warranty coverage given by a general warranty deed.

DISCUSSION: Of the deeds customarily used in modern conveyances, the warranty deed with full covenants (general warranty deed) provides the greatest protection for the buyer. The seller who gives such a deed warrants that (1) (s)he has the authority to convey the property, (2) there are no undisclosed encumbrances, and (3) (s)he will defend the rights of the buyer against the claims of any other person.

Answer (A) is incorrect. A general warranty deed provides that the grantee will not be disturbed in possession of the property by the grantor or some third party's lawful claim of ownership. Answer (B) is incorrect. A general warranty deed provides that the grantor has the right to convey the property. Answer (D) is incorrect. A general warranty deed provides that (1) the grantor has the right to convey the property, and (2) the grantee will not be disturbed in possession of the property by the grantor or some third party's lawful claim of ownership.

19. Pat conveyed land to Sam by a general warranty deed. Sam subsequently discovered that Pat had granted a right of way (unrecorded) to a neighbor, but had neither told Sam nor referred to it in the deed to Sam. Sam could recover substantial damages from Pat for breach of the covenant of

A. Right to convey.

B. Right to convey if the neighbor has commenced using the right of way.

C. Quiet enjoyment.

D. Quiet enjoyment if the neighbor has commenced using the right of way and Sam had given consideration for the deed.

Answer (D) is correct. *(Publisher, adapted)*

REQUIRED: The covenant for breach of which the grantee could recover damages because of the undisclosed easement.

DISCUSSION: The covenant of quiet enjoyment is a promise by the grantor that the grantee will not be disturbed in possession or enjoyment of the property by the lawful claim of a third party. Until the neighbor uses the easement, Sam's use of the land is not interfered with and the covenant is not violated. Furthermore, Sam suffered no damages unless he gave consideration for the deed.

Answer (A) is incorrect. The covenant of right to convey is simply a promise by the grantor that (s)he has a right to make the conveyance. Answer (B) is incorrect. The covenant of right to convey is simply a promise by the grantor that (s)he has a right to make the conveyance. Answer (C) is incorrect. A breach of the covenant of quiet enjoyment does not occur until such enjoyment is actually disturbed.

Questions 20 and 21 are based on the following information. Pam owned a 5-acre tract of land, 1 acre of which had previously been owned by Sally, but to which Pam had acquired title by adverse possession. Pam contracted to convey the full 5-acre tract to Alice, but the contract did not specify the quality of title Pam would convey.

20. Suppose Alice pays the purchase price and accepts the deed. Subsequently, Pam's title to the 1 acre proves inadequate and Sally ejects Alice from that acre. Alice sues Pam for damages. Which of the following statements applies most accurately to the determination of Alice's rights?

A. Pam's deed was fraudulent.

B. The terms of the deed control Pam's liability.

C. The only remedy available for breach of warranty of title is rescission.

D. Alice's rights are based on the implied covenant in the contract that the title conveyed shall be marketable.

Answer (B) is correct. *(Publisher, adapted)*

REQUIRED: The rights of a buyer when the seller's title has proven inadequate.

DISCUSSION: A seller's liability for inadequate title depends on the terms of the deed given. For example, a general warranty deed subjects the seller to full liability, but a quitclaim deed subjects the seller to no liability.

Answer (A) is incorrect. For the deed to have been fraudulent, Pam must have conveyed it with knowledge that she was making a false representation and with an intention to deceive. Answer (C) is incorrect. Damages are available for breach of warranty of title. Answer (D) is incorrect. The contract for sale does not survive closing unless expressly agreed; i.e., the deed merges the prior agreements, and a lawsuit can only be based on the deed. Merger means that the deed is intended to be the complete and final expression of the parties.

21. Suppose Pam's contract had called for the conveyance of a "good and marketable title." Pursuant to that contract, Alice paid the purchase price and accepted a deed from Pam containing no covenants of title. Pam's title to the 1 acre subsequently proved defective and Alice was ejected by Sally. Alice sued Pam. Which of the following results is most likely?

A. Alice will win because Pam's deed was fraudulent.

B. Alice will win because the terms of the deed control Pam's liability.

C. Pam will win because the terms of the deed control her liability.

D. Pam will win because the deed incorporates the terms of the contract.

Answer (C) is correct. *(Publisher, adapted)*

REQUIRED: The result of a suit against the grantor when the grantee's title is defective.

DISCUSSION: The agreements in the contract for sale do not survive closing unless expressly agreed by the parties. By accepting a deed containing no covenants of title, Alice lost her right to a marketable title. Pam will have no liability because she made no covenants of title in the deed.

Answer (A) is incorrect. The absence of covenants of title is not fraudulent. In fact, the absence of covenants of title is common in deeds. Answer (B) is incorrect. Although the terms of the deed control liability, Pam's deed continued no covenants of title. Answer (D) is incorrect. A deed does not incorporate the terms of the contract; instead, it merges any prior agreements.

22. Joe and Minnie Sixpack just purchased a new house from the contractor who built it. Under the law in their state, the seller of a new house is required to provide a warranty for at least one year against defects in workmanship. Under the typical statute, which of the following is covered by the warranty?

A. A serious crack in the foundation.

B. A mechanic's lien for work performed on the house by a subcontractor who was not paid by the contractor.

C. Installation of fixtures in the bathrooms different from those agreed upon.

D. Construction of a sidewalk by the city between the house and the road when the Sixpacks thought they had all rights to the land up to the road.

Answer (A) is correct. *(Publisher, adapted)*

REQUIRED: The legal protection given by a new home warranty against defects in workmanship.

DISCUSSION: New homes often come with warranties against defects in workmanship. Some state statutes impose these warranties. They generally cover such items as cracks in the foundation and any other flaws in the construction.

Answer (B) is incorrect. A mechanic's lien is not covered by a warranty against defects in workmanship but is included in the warranties given in a general warranty deed. Answer (C) is incorrect. Installing the wrong fixtures is a contractual breach rather than a breach of a new home warranty. Answer (D) is incorrect. The Sixpacks are deemed to have constructive notice of any right of way or easement held by the city (from the real property records). The warranty in question is not against encumbrances.

23. Which of the following is a true statement about the federal Real Estate Settlement Procedures Act (RESPA)?

A. It applies to all sales of residential real estate.

B. Advance payments from borrowers to lenders are prohibited.

C. Lenders cannot specify a title company or require a prepayment penalty.

D. It is intended to prevent abuses such as kickbacks.

Answer (D) is correct. *(Publisher, adapted)*

REQUIRED: The true statement about RESPA.

DISCUSSION: The act is a consumer protection measure intended to promote disclosure of information, reduce settlement (closing) costs, and prohibit payment of unearned fees and kickbacks. The lender is required to make certain disclosures to the buyer and to permit the buyer an opportunity to obtain advance estimates of closing costs. The mandated use of the Uniform Settlement Statement helps to clarify what costs are to be paid by the buyer and seller. Furthermore, the National Affordable Housing Act of 1990 amended RESPA to require that a buyer be furnished an annual analysis of escrow accounts. Abusive practices, such as kickbacks, are generally prohibited. One may not receive payment for providing a referral to a given bank, insurer, or attorney.

Answer (A) is incorrect. The act only applies when a federally related mortgage loan is made on a residential building other than a large apartment complex. Answer (B) is incorrect. Lenders may collect reasonable advance payments from borrowers for items such as insurance and taxes. Answer (C) is incorrect. A seller may not specify a title insurer to be used by the buyer, but a lender may. Also, a lender is permitted to charge the seller a prepayment penalty if the new mortgage loan is not made with the same institution.

24.3 Recording

24. Purdy purchased real property from Hart and received a warranty deed with full covenants. Recordation of this deed is

A. Not necessary if the deed provides that recordation is not required.

B. Necessary to vest the purchaser's legal title to the property conveyed.

C. Required primarily for the purpose of providing the local taxing authorities with the information necessary to assess taxes.

D. Irrelevant if the subsequent party claiming superior title had actual notice of the unrecorded deed.

Answer (D) is correct. *(CPA, adapted)*

REQUIRED: The true statement about recording a deed.

DISCUSSION: Recordation gives constructive notice to a subsequent purchaser who then cannot qualify as a bona fide purchaser and take superior title despite the earlier transfer. If the deed is not recorded, a purchaser without actual notice or another form of constructive notice may prevail over an earlier grantee of the same grantor. In most jurisdictions, however, grantee who has not recorded will prevail over a subsequent party with actual notice even if the latter records first.

Answer (A) is incorrect. The language of the deed does not determine the need to have it recorded. Answer (B) is incorrect. Recordation has no effect on the rights of the parties to the transaction against each other. It is a means of giving notice to third parties who lack actual notice. Answer (C) is incorrect. Notice is the primary purpose of recordation.

25. The failure to record a deed will

A. Not affect the rights between the parties to the deed.

B. Constitute a fraud upon the creditors of the seller.

C. Defeat the rights of the buyer if the seller subsequently conveys the property to a third party who has actual knowledge of the prior conveyance.

D. Be disregarded in respect to the rights of subsequent third parties if the deed is a mere quitclaim.

Answer (A) is correct. *(CPA, adapted)*

REQUIRED: The effect of failure to record a deed.

DISCUSSION: Failure to record a deed does not affect the rights between the grantor and grantee. The lawful delivery of a valid deed is sufficient to establish the rights between the parties to the transaction. The purpose of recording a deed is to protect against third parties.

Answer (B) is incorrect. Failure to record is not a fraud upon any parties unless it is accompanied by some fraudulent conduct. Answer (C) is incorrect. A subsequent purchaser with knowledge will not prevail over an unrecorded deed in most jurisdictions. Only a subsequent good faith purchaser without knowledge will usually prevail over an unrecorded deed. Answer (D) is incorrect. The type of deed is irrelevant to the recording requirement. A subsequent bona fide purchaser from the same grantor would, under most recording statutes, take free of the interests of a preceding grantee regardless of who may have received a quitclaim deed.

26. On February 2, Mazo deeded a warehouse to Parko for $450,000. Parko did not record the deed. On February 12, Mazo deeded the same warehouse to Nexis for $430,000. Nexis was aware of the prior conveyance to Parko. Nexis recorded its deed before Parko recorded. Who would prevail under the following recording statutes?

	Notice Statute	Race Statute	Race-Notice Statute
A.	Nexis	Parko	Parko
B.	Parko	Nexis	Parko
C.	Parko	Nexis	Nexis
D.	Parko	Parko	Nexis

Answer (B) is correct. *(CPA, adapted)*

REQUIRED: The interests having priority under different types of recording statutes.

DISCUSSION: Under a notice statute, an unrecorded deed is ineffective against a subsequent bona fide purchaser (for value and without notice). Under a race-notice statute, the subsequent bona fide purchaser must record before the prior grantee. Under a race statute, regardless of notice, the first to record prevails. Nexis is not a bona fide purchaser (Nexis had notice), so it has no priority over Parko under a notice or a race-notice statute. As the first to record, however, Nexis has priority over Parko in a race statute jurisdiction although it had actual notice.

Answer (A) is incorrect. Nexis was not a bona fide purchaser. Answer (C) is incorrect. Nexis was not a bona fide purchaser. Answer (D) is incorrect. Under a race statute, the first to record prevails without regard to notice.

27. Ms. Bean deeded her home to Park on July 1. The deed was never recorded. On July 5, Bean deeded the same home to Charles Noll. On July 9, Noll executed a deed, conveying his title to the same home to Baxter. On July 10, Noll and Baxter duly recorded their respective deeds. If Noll and Baxter are bona fide purchasers for value, which of the following statements is true?

A. Baxter's interest is superior to Park's.

B. Bean's deed to Park was void as between Bean and Park because it was not recorded.

C. Bean's deed to Noll was void because she had no interest to convey.

D. Baxter can recover the purchase price from Noll.

Answer (A) is correct. *(CPA, adapted)*

REQUIRED: The priority of interests.

DISCUSSION: Three kinds of recording statutes are in force. Under a notice statute, an unrecorded deed is ineffective against a subsequent bona fide purchaser (for value and without notice). Under a race-notice statute, the subsequent bona fide purchaser must record before the prior grantee. Under a race statute, regardless of notice, the first to record prevails. Because Noll and Baxter were bona fide purchasers who recorded before Park, they would prevail in every state.

Answer (B) is incorrect. Recording has no effect on the rights of the parties to the conveyance against each other. Answer (C) is incorrect. Before Park records, Bean has the power to make an effective conveyance to a subsequent bona fide purchaser who complies with the recording statute. Answer (D) is incorrect. Noll and Baxter are protected by recording. Baxter has a title superior to Park's and no basis for recovery against Noll.

28. Buyer purchased a rural lot from a person purporting to be Grantor 10 years ago and recorded the deed. Buyer paid the property taxes but had not seen the lot in years. On a vacation trip in the area, Buyer inspected the lot and found it to be occupied. Occupant stated that she had received the land 5 years ago in a testamentary transfer from Grantor. The signatures on the deed and the will by Grantor were dissimilar. Under these circumstances,

A. Buyer has a valid title insurance claim.

B. Occupant has a valid title insurance claim.

C. Buyer and Occupant are tenants in common.

D. Occupant would have priority even if Grantor had actually given Buyer a deed 10 years ago.

Answer (A) is correct. *(Publisher, adapted)*

REQUIRED: The outcome of a contest between an inter vivos transferee and a beneficiary under a will.

DISCUSSION: The deed received by Buyer was apparently a forgery. Accordingly, it conveyed no interest in the property, and recording it gave Buyer no rights against a subsequent transferee. This case should be distinguished from that in which an owner conveys the same property to more than one person. In that event, a subsequent bona fide purchaser for value who has no notice of the earlier conveyance will usually prevail. Thus, Buyer has incurred a loss of the kind that title insurance is meant to indemnify, that is, the loss resulting when title is actually in another person.

Answer (B) is incorrect. Occupant has a valid title obtained through Grantor's will. Answer (C) is incorrect. Buyer has no interest in the property. Answer (D) is incorrect. If Grantor had actually given Buyer a valid deed, Grantor could not have made an effective testamentary transfer, even if Buyer had not recorded. Occupant would not have been a bona fide purchaser.

29. Unless an exception to title is noted in the title insurance policy, a title insurance company will be liable to a land purchaser for

A. Closing costs.

B. Recorded easements.

C. Unrecorded assessments.

D. Zoning violations.

Answer (B) is correct. *(CPA, adapted)*

REQUIRED: The item for which the title insurance company will usually be liable.

DISCUSSION: The title insurer searches the public records. A title policy, like other insurance, is a contract of indemnification. The policy gives protection if title is actually in another person, if title is subject to an encumbrance or other kind of defect, if the insured has no access to his/her land, and possibly if (s)he suffers loss from nonmarketability of the title. A title insurer may be liable, even without having been negligent, for an unexcepted recorded easement.

Answer (A) is incorrect. Closing costs include such items as title insurance, and are not covered by title insurance. Answer (C) is incorrect. Although other risks may be insured, the policy usually only applies to recorded items. Answer (D) is incorrect. The title insurance company usually does not insure that the property has not been used in violation of a zoning ordinance.

30. A purchaser who obtains real estate title insurance will

A. Not have coverage greater than the amount of any first mortgage.

B. Be insured against all defects of record other than those excepted in the policy.

C. Have coverage for title defects that result from events that happen after the effective date of the policy.

D. Be entitled to transfer the policy to subsequent owners.

Answer (B) is correct. *(CPA, adapted)*

REQUIRED: The right obtained or the coverage not received by the buyer of title insurance.

DISCUSSION: Possible exceptions in a title policy include a taking under eminent domain, defects caused by the insured, or those known by the insured but not by the company. Mechanic's liens, unpaid taxes, and utility easements may also be excepted.

Answer (A) is incorrect. Title insurance for the benefit of an owner usually covers the purchase price. But a policy written to protect a mortgagee may be for the amount of the mortgage. Answer (C) is incorrect. Title insurance indemnifies from title defects that result from events that occur prior to the effective date of the policy. Answer (D) is incorrect. Title insurance is not assignable to a subsequent buyer. A new title examination is necessary before such a buyer can receive title insurance.

31. Taylor entered into an agreement to purchase a tract of land. The agreement specified that the seller was to provide title insurance, an attorney's opinion, or a title abstract at the purchaser's option. Which of the following is a true statement of the benefits of, and differences between, these three methods of title assurance?

A. An attorney's opinion is usually the safest assurance because (s)he will be liable for malpractice if the opinion is incorrect.

B. Title insurance from a licensed company usually provides the greatest protection against risk of loss.

C. An abstract of title is a guarantee that the title is held by the person named.

D. All of these methods are unnecessary because a seller warrants both title and the obligation of the seller to defend against claims of others in a general warranty deed.

Answer (B) is correct. *(Publisher, adapted)*

REQUIRED: The true statement concerning various methods of title assurance.

DISCUSSION: Title insurance obtained from a licensed company usually provides the greatest protection against risk of loss. These companies are licensed by the state and have certain requirements as to financial condition and maintenance of reserves. Title insurance companies indemnify against defects, whereas abstract companies and title examiners are required to not be negligent.

Answer (A) is incorrect. If an attorney does not maintain malpractice insurance, no source of funds may be available in the event (s)he becomes insolvent. Answer (C) is incorrect. An abstract of title is merely a collection of copies of all the recorded documents affecting a piece of property. An abstract is used to determine the status and quality of the title but is not a guaranty or assurance in itself. Answer (D) is incorrect. Although a seller does make such warranties in a warranty deed, (s)he may have left the jurisdiction or not be able to pay.

24.4 Fixtures

32. A tenant's personal property will become a fixture and belong to the landlord if its removal would

A. Increase the value of the personal property.

B. Cause a material change to the personal property.

C. Result in substantial harm to the landlord's property.

D. Change the use of the landlord's property back to its prior use.

Answer (C) is correct. *(CPA, adapted)*

REQUIRED: The consideration in determining whether personal property will become a fixture and belong to the landlord.

DISCUSSION: The intent of the parties controls whether a tenant's personal property will become a fixture and belong to the landlord. However, other factors may be considered to determine that intent in the absence of an explicit statement. The most important are the mode of annexation, the amount of damage to the realty and to the item if it is removed, and the degree to which the item is specifically adapted to the realty.

Answer (A) is incorrect. Whether removal will increase the value of the personal property, is not a significant consideration compared with damage to the real property. Answer (B) is incorrect. Whether removal will cause a material change to the personal property, is not a significant consideration compared with damage to the real property. Answer (D) is incorrect. Whether removal will change the use of the landlord's property back to its prior use, is not a significant consideration compared with damage to the real property.

33. Which of the following factors is least significant in determining whether an item of personal property has become a fixture?

A. The extent of injury that would be caused to the real property by the removal of the item.

B. The value of the item.

C. The manner of attachment.

D. The adaptability of the item to the real estate.

Answer (B) is correct. *(CPA, adapted)*

REQUIRED: The least significant factor in deciding whether personal property is a fixture.

DISCUSSION: If the intention of the party who attached the personal property to the realty is unclear, the court will examine other factors to deduce that intent. For example, the mode of annexation and the injury caused by removal are important factors in determining intent. Accordingly, a central heating system is usually deemed to be a fixture. If an item is beneficial or necessary (adapted) to the ordinary uses to which the realty is put, the court will usually infer an intent to make it a fixture even though it is easily removable. A hot water heater is an example. Intent may also be inferred from the parties' relationship. For instance, a lessee seldom intends to make a gift of a fixture to a lessor upon vacating the premises. Value, however, is not significant in determining whether personal property has become a fixture.

Answer (A) is incorrect. The extent of injury that would be caused to the real property by the removal of the item is a significant factor in determining intent as discussed above. Answer (C) is incorrect. The manner of attachment is a significant factor in determining intent as discussed above. Answer (D) is incorrect. The adaptability of the item to the real estate is a significant factor in determining intent as discussed above.

STUDY UNIT TWENTY-FIVE
MORTGAGES

The subject covered in this study unit overlaps with bankruptcy, contract, consumer, and credit law; suretyship; and secured transactions. It should be read with the study units on those topics.

Mortgages are flexible devices that increase the availability of credit. A **mortgage** is a security interest in real property (not subject to UCC Article 9), typically conveyed by a written instrument to guarantee the payment of a debt. It is a voluntary lien that **attaches** when the instrument is signed and delivered. The **mortgagor** conveys the mortgage and is the landowner and debtor. The **mortgagee** is the creditor or lender. For example, Mortgagor borrowed $250,000 from Mortgagee and signed two documents. The first, a promissory note, stated, "I promise to pay you $250,000 by Year 1." The other, the mortgage, stated, "If I do not pay you $250,000, you may sell my house to satisfy the debt." A mortgagor and mortgagee are free to negotiate most of the terms of the mortgage. However, the terms must conform to the law and public policy. Essentially, the mortgage is a **contractual device** that facilitates availability of credit. Without the security provided by mortgages, lenders would be more reluctant to lend substantial sums of money. Any obligation capable of being reduced to a monetary amount may be secured by a mortgage.

Generally, **every transfer of an interest in real property made as security for the performance of another act is considered to be a mortgage**. If the purpose of an instrument is to secure a debt, the form of the transaction is irrelevant. Thus, a deed intended as security is treated as a mortgage. For example, Husband and Wife need to borrow $25,000. They approach Third Party for a loan. Third Party declines, but states, "I will give you $25,000 and hold your deed until you pay $25,000 12 months from today. Then I will return your deed." The purpose of the deed in this example is to secure a debt, so it is treated as a mortgage.

A mortgage is drafted as either a conveyance to the mortgagee or a lien to secure the payment of debt. Under the **title theory**, a mortgage is a conveyance or transfer of property even though it is only for security purposes. However, although the mortgagee has title, (s)he acquires no right of possession unless the mortgagor defaults. Under the **lien theory**, the mortgage is not considered a conveyance of legal title but merely a lien on the property to secure payment of the debt. The mortgage serves merely to protect the mortgagee's interest and for no other purpose. Most states adhere to the lien theory.

The rights of the mortgagor include the right to (1) possess, use, and dispose of the property; (2) lease the property to another and collect rent; and (3) borrow additional sums of money from other creditors and convey subsequent mortgages to them (these mortgages are called second or junior mortgages). However, the mortgagor must preserve the value of the mortgaged property (not commit waste) and pay taxes and assessments levied on the underlying property.

The rights of the mortgagee include the right to (1) exercise such control over the mortgaged property as is granted by the mortgage document and the state mortgage statutes, with all remaining control exercised by the mortgagor; (2) protect his/her interest in the real property by obtaining insurance or paying off liens affecting that interest; (3) foreclose according to the terms of the mortgage; (4) assign or transfer the mortgage and underlying debt to a third person without the consent of the mortgagor; and (5) pass the mortgage to his/her heirs or beneficiaries as personal property. The mortgagee has a **duty to lend money** according to the terms of the mortgage instrument and the promissory note. Furthermore, if foreclosure is necessary, the mortgagee has a duty to act fairly and follow the statutory procedure of the state and the terms of the mortgage document.

A mortgage must meet the **common law and statutory requirements** of the state to be valid. Certain fundamental elements must be contained in every mortgage, and certain other elements vary. A mortgage relates to an interest in land and must be in writing as required by the **statute of frauds**. The **written instrument conveying the mortgage** must (1) clearly identify the parties, (2) adequately describe the real property, (3) be signed by the mortgagor, and (4) clearly identify and describe the debt that it secures. A mortgage extends to all improvements on the land, including structures and fixtures added after the mortgage is granted, unless the mortgage instrument specifically excludes them.

The **statutory requirements** of a mortgage vary from state to state. For example, some states require a seal. A corporate mortgage always should have the corporate seal affixed. Some states require that a valid mortgage contain the attestation of two witnesses to the authenticity of the mortgagor's signature. A mortgage also may have to be acknowledged before a **notary**. Failure to do so may render the mortgage void or ineligible for recording. Moreover, a **purchase money mortgage** or a **mortgage on a homestead** may require specific clauses for maximum effectiveness of the mortgage. However, a mortgage **need not be recorded**. In addition, the **mortgagor need not have personal liability** for repayment of the debt. The parties are free to agree that the mortgagee will rely solely on the real property as security for repayment of the debt.

A number of variations of the basic mortgage exist. For example, an **equitable mortgage** does not meet the technical requirements of a mortgage. However, a court will treat the agreement as a valid mortgage if one party expresses in writing a clear intent to make specific property security for a debt. A **purchase money mortgage (PMM)** is granted by a purchaser to secure payment of the purchase price. To be a PMM, a mortgage must be granted at the same time that the deed is delivered. However, a PMM need not necessarily be granted by the seller, and it may be granted to anyone, including a bank advancing the purchase money or credit. PMM mortgagees are usually entitled to preference over holders of other claims or liens. **Second mortgages** are common in real property sales, financing, and construction. An owner of property subject to an existing mortgage can grant a second mortgage on the same property to secure a debt. Although first mortgages take priority over second mortgages, all mortgages are often paid off simultaneously. Nevertheless, after default and foreclosure, the first mortgage has priority and is satisfied first out of the sale proceeds. An **open-end mortgage** is granted to secure not only current debt but **future advances**. The open-end mortgage permits the mortgagor to obtain advances of money upon request, subject to restrictions agreed to between the parties. They eliminate the need to reapply and thereby reduce transaction costs. A **wraparound mortgage** is a form of second mortgage. The face amount of the note is the sum of the existing first mortgage plus the amount of cash advanced or credit extended by the second mortgagee.

The wraparound mortgagor makes payments to the wraparound lender, who then makes payments on the first mortgage debt to the first mortgagee. The interest rate on a wraparound note is frequently higher than that on the underlying debt because a wraparound mortgage is used more often when interest rates are relatively high. The wraparound mortgagee receives interest on the full amount of the wraparound note, not only on the additional funds lent or credit extended. Under a **deed of trust (trust deed)**, the debtor transfers title in real property to a disinterested third party (the trustee) to be held in trust for the benefit of another as security for the performance of an obligation, usually the payment of a debt. The trustee has the power to sell the property if the debtor defaults. The proceeds are then applied toward payment of the debt. Thus, the deed of trust is functionally identical to the mortgage, although a mortgage has two parties and a trust deed three. The **trustee holds title** to the real property, but it is bare legal title, not a true ownership interest. The trust deed is generally **treated as a lien**. Upon satisfaction of the obligation, the trustee executes the necessary documents to reconvey legal title to the trustor-debtor. A **land sale contract** is an agreement for the conditional sale of land, subject to payment of the entire price by the purchaser. Upon execution of the land sale contract, the purchaser is entitled to possession and control of the land and any improvements. During the term of the land sale contract, the purchaser has the right to possess, control, use, and enjoy the land and improvements. However, (s)he may not materially change the real property without the permission of the seller, who retains ownership **(legal title)** of the real property until final payment is made. Accordingly, the purchaser does not acquire legal title to the land until the entire contract price has been paid. In some states, when the purchaser in a land sale contract defaults, the seller must follow the state statutory procedure used for foreclosing a mortgage.

The purpose of **recording** a mortgage is to give notice of it to transferees or subsequent mortgagees and others with interests in the underlying property. Recording involves presenting the necessary documents to a local government official who oversees the public real property records. Recording a mortgage is a purely statutory process that has a limited effect on the relationship between the **mortgagor and the mortgagee**. They have a contractual agreement that creates legal rights and duties between them **without recording** the mortgage. Recording does not change the amount of the debt, the description of the land subject to the mortgage, the terms of payment or default, or the interest rate. Nevertheless, recording has a profound effect on **third parties**. A **mortgagee's failure to record** his/her mortgage may result in its forfeiture or subordination. The rationale for recording statutes is to provide a method by which purchasers of interests in real property may obtain assurance that the grantor possesses valid legal title that (s)he can convey. By recording a mortgage, the mortgagee gives the public **constructive notice** (not actual notice) that a specific party claims a security interest in the real property. Importantly, the maxim "first in time, first in right" generally applies to mortgages. Any lien or encumbrance that attaches to mortgaged property or is recorded after proper recording of the first mortgage is **subject (subordinate) to** the first mortgage. Thus, a superior interest will be paid in full before any subordinate interest is paid anything. However, if an owner of real property mortgages a property twice, the first mortgage recorded will be given priority over all other mortgages or liens, unless the subsequent mortgagee knew of these other mortgages or liens at the time of execution. Failure to record also may invalidate the mortgage if the property is sold to a **bona fide purchaser**.

Upon full satisfaction of the debt, the mortgagee's security interest terminates automatically. The mortgagee's interest in land immediately reverts to the mortgagor by operation of law. A mortgagor who fails to satisfy the obligation when it matures is **in default**. Default by **nonperformance** may occur regarding any obligation in the contract, e.g., to (1) make a payment, (2) pay real property taxes, (3) maintain the property in reasonable repair, or (4) maintain fire and casualty insurance. An **acceleration clause** states that, upon failure of the mortgagor to pay any installment when due, the entire debt will become due and payable immediately. It permits foreclosure of the entire debt. A **due-on-sale clause** is an acceleration clause. It authorizes a mortgagee to accelerate the entire loan balance if the mortgagor sells or otherwise conveys the property without permission of the mortgagee. However, default on one mortgage is not default on another mortgage on the same property.

If the underlying debt is not satisfied, equitable action compelling payment of the obligation is taken by the mortgagee. This action is called **foreclosure**. The existence of both a mortgage and a promissory note provide the lender with alternative remedies in the event of default. Suit may be brought on the note and a personal judgment obtained against the debtor, or the real property may be sold and the proceeds applied against the debt.

Foreclosure by judicial sale is provided for in every state. The right to foreclose usually arises upon default. Foreclosure is an action by the **mortgagee** (or assignee) to (1) take the property from the **mortgagor**, (2) sell it to pay the debt, and (3) end the mortgagor's rights in the property. In the event of foreclosure, the mortgagee usually must initiate a **judicial proceeding** to secure an order of sale. The sheriff or other officer of the court then conducts a sale by auction as specified by state statute. Generally, the sale is confirmed by court order following a hearing. The debt is then satisfied with **proceeds** of the sale. If the sale proceeds are insufficient to cover the debt (plus costs and interest), the mortgagee may generally obtain a judgment against the mortgagor for the **deficiency**. A state may restrict a deficiency to the excess of the debt over the **fair value**. This rule recognizes that proceeds of a judicial sale usually are less than the fair value. In a state with an **antideficiency statute**, a **purchase-money mortgagor** is not liable for a deficiency. If the sale produces **surplus** proceeds (over mortgage debt and related costs), the surplus belongs to the mortgagor. Generally, the sale may be made to the mortgagee. However, the mortgagor has an **equitable right of redemption**. Prior to foreclosure, (s)he may regain rights by paying the mortgage debt plus interest and costs. The equity of redemption cannot be waived or relinquished by agreement. Any such attempt is considered void as against public policy. Redemption might be accomplished by refinancing. The mortgagor also may have a **statutory right of redemption**. The mortgagor may repurchase the property after the foreclosure sale, for the statutorily specified period (ordinarily not exceeding 1 year), by payment of the auction sale price. The **purchaser** at a judicial sale takes the property free of any claim. **Foreclosure by sale** is an alternative allowed in a majority of states. The **mortgagee** may sell the property at public auction without resort to the legal system. The mortgage agreement must permit this procedure, and the sale must comply with strict statutory requirements. **Strict foreclosure** is foreclosure without sale if the mortgagor does not pay within a time set by the court. The mortgagee automatically succeeds to the real property and need not sell it after the mortgagor defaults. Strict foreclosure is permitted in only a few states.

The mortgagor commonly may sell or otherwise **transfer** the property. However, apart from agreement to the contrary, the mortgagor may not **delegate performance** under the mortgage unless specifically released by the mortgagee (through a **novation**). A transfer of real property is **subject to the mortgage** when the buyer pays the seller his/her equity but is **not personally liable** on the existing mortgage loan to either the mortgagor or mortgagee. The **original mortgagor** remains liable. The mortgagee looks to the original mortgagor for payment if the buyer defaults. The land is still **security** for the debt. If the buyer does not pay the debt, the mortgagor is liable for any deficiency upon foreclosure. However, the buyer receives any surplus because the mortgagor has been paid for his/her equity. A **due-on-sale** or other acceleration clause may prevent the sale of property with an existing mortgage. If a buyer **assumes the mortgage**, the buyer pays the mortgagor the fair value of the land minus the amount of the debt secured by the mortgage. The buyer also **promises** that (s)he will pay the balance of the original debt. The buyer's promise may be made to the mortgagor or the mortgagee. If the promise is made to the mortgagor, it also is enforceable by the mortgagee as a **third-party beneficiary**. The mortgagor is a **surety**. If the buyer defaults, the mortgagor can be held liable. However, the mortgagor will have a right of **reimbursement** against the buyer. If the three parties agree to a **novation**, that is, if the mortgagee agrees to release the mortgagor and substitute the buyer, the mortgagor is no longer liable.

QUESTIONS

25.1 The Mortgage Device

1. Which of the following is a true statement about the real estate mortgage?

A. The mortgage is the debt owed by the mortgagor to the mortgagee.

B. The mortgage is security for the debt owed by the mortgagee to the mortgagor.

C. The substance of the transaction is that the mortgagee conveys ownership of the property to the mortgagor subject to nullification by payment of the debt.

D. The mortgagor executes a promissory note and a mortgage evidencing the debt and the conveyance of a security interest, respectively.

Answer (D) is correct. *(Publisher, adapted)*

REQUIRED: The true statement about a real estate mortgage.

DISCUSSION: Most states recognize the mortgage as a security interest. The mortgagor-debtor signs a promissory note for the sum borrowed from the mortgagee-creditor. (S)he also signs a mortgage document representing the right of the mortgagee to seek judicial foreclosure and sale of the property upon default. The mortgage is an interest in real property, so it should comply with the requirements of contract law, the statute of frauds, and the execution of deeds.

Answer (A) is incorrect. The mortgage is the interest in the realty that is security for the debt. Answer (B) is incorrect. The mortgagor-debtor conveys a security interest in the realty to the mortgagee-lender. Answer (C) is incorrect. Regardless of whether title is conveyed to the mortgagee-lender, almost all states treat the mortgagor-debtor as at the least the equitable owner of the realty.

2. Which of the following statements is true concerning a transfer of an interest in mortgaged property?

A. The mortgagee cannot transfer the note and mortgage because they represent a personal contract between the parties.

B. If the mortgagor transfers the property, (s)he will also be relieved of the mortgage.

C. The mortgagee can transfer the note and mortgage by an assignment in a lien theory state.

D. The mortgagor can transfer the property without paying off the mortgage if the agreement includes a due-on-sale clause.

Answer (C) is correct. *(Publisher, adapted)*

REQUIRED: The true statement concerning the assignment of a mortgage or the mortgaged property.

DISCUSSION: In a lien theory state, the mortgage is merely a security interest in the real property. Thus, it can be transferred by an assignment rather than by deed. In a title theory state, a deed must be given to transfer a mortgage.

Answer (A) is incorrect. A mortgagee is free to transfer the note and mortgage. They represent only a right to payment and security therefor. Answer (B) is incorrect. A mortgagor who transfers the mortgaged property remains liable on the debt unless the purchaser assumes the mortgage and the mortgagee releases the original mortgagor (e.g., by a novation). Answer (D) is incorrect. Due-on-sale clauses are usually upheld, and federally chartered lenders are permitted to require them. Indeed, under federal law, states may not prohibit due-on-sale clauses. Accordingly, the mortgagor must pay the mortgage if (s)he transfers the property.

25.2 Form and Elements of a Mortgage

3. Which of the following conditions must be met to have an enforceable mortgage?

A. An accurate description of the property must be included in the mortgage.

B. A negotiable promissory note must accompany the mortgage.

C. Present consideration must be given in exchange for the mortgage.

D. The amount of the debt and the interest rate must be stated in the mortgage.

Answer (A) is correct. *(CPA, adapted)*

REQUIRED: The condition that must be met to have an enforceable mortgage.

DISCUSSION: A mortgage relates to an interest in land and is within the statute of frauds. Because a mortgage is executed with the same formalities as a deed, it must contain a legally sufficient description of the property, that is, one precise enough to determine accurately the location of the land.

Answer (B) is incorrect. Although a mortgage secures an underlying obligation, enforceability of the mortgage does not depend on its being accompanied by a negotiable instrument. Answer (C) is incorrect. A mortgage represents the security interest for which value must be given. However, a mortgage may provide security for payment of an antecedent obligation. Answer (D) is incorrect. Although contained in most mortgages, the amount of debt and the interest rate are not required.

4. In general, which of the following statements is true with respect to a real estate mortgage?

A. The mortgage must be in writing and signed by both the mortgagor (borrower) and mortgagee (lender).

B. The mortgagee may assign the mortgage to a third party without the mortgagor's consent.

C. The mortgage need not contain a description of the real estate covered by the mortgage.

D. The mortgage must contain the actual amount of the underlying debt and the rate of interest.

Answer (B) is correct. *(CPA, adapted)*

REQUIRED: The true statement with respect to real estate mortgages.

DISCUSSION: The majority of states adhere to the lien theory, under which the mortgage is merely a security interest in the property. Consequently, the note and mortgage are freely assignable because they represent only a right to payment and security therefor.

Answer (A) is incorrect. The mortgage requires the signature of the mortgagor only. Answer (C) is incorrect. A legally sufficient description of the property must be included in the mortgage. Answer (D) is incorrect. Even though the amount of indebtedness and the rate of interest are usually included on most mortgages, they are not legally required.

25.3 Types of Mortgages

5. Cutter purchased a building and land from Murley. Cutter made a downpayment to Murley and gave a mortgage for the balance of the purchase price. The property was already subject to an existing mortgage that Murley agreed to continue to pay.

A. Murley's mortgage takes priority over a judgment that had been rendered against Cutter prior to the sale.

B. Murley has committed a fraud by taking a mortgage on the property without paying off the existing mortgage.

C. Murley's original mortgage became due immediately on the sale to Cutter.

D. In the event of a default on the mortgages, the mortgage from Cutter to Murley will take priority because it is a purchase-money mortgage.

Answer (A) is correct. *(Publisher, adapted)*

REQUIRED: The true statement concerning a wrap-around mortgage.

DISCUSSION: Murley obtained a purchase-money mortgage on the sale of the property. A purchase-money mortgage takes priority over pre-existing debts of the mortgagor. Accordingly, a prior judgment against Cutter might become a lien on the real property but would be junior to Murley's mortgage.

Answer (B) is incorrect. Selling property and taking a mortgage for part of the price while continuing to pay the old mortgage is not fraudulent. This arrangement is called a wrap-around mortgage. The new mortgage wraps around the old mortgage and the additional debt. Answer (C) is incorrect. A mortgage will only become due immediately on sale if specifically provided for. Answer (D) is incorrect. The original mortgage has priority. It was first in time and presumably first recorded. A purchase-money mortgage does not take priority over pre-existing liens on the property.

6. Sussex, Inc. had given a first mortgage when it purchased its plant and warehouse. Sussex needed additional working capital. It decided to obtain financing by giving a second mortgage on the plant and warehouse. Which of the following statements is true with respect to the mortgages?

A. Default on payment of the second mortgage will constitute default on the first mortgage.

B. The second mortgage may not be prepaid without the consent of the first mortgagee.

C. The second mortgagee may not pay off the first mortgage to protect its security.

D. If both mortgages are foreclosed, the first mortgage must be fully paid before paying the second mortgage.

Answer (D) is correct. *(CPA, adapted)*

REQUIRED: The true statement concerning the legal status of first and second mortgages.

DISCUSSION: The second mortgage is subordinate to the first mortgage. Upon foreclosure and judicial sale of the property, the proceeds would be distributed to all senior liens (the first mortgage) and to expenses of sale before the second mortgagee received anything. In some jurisdictions, foreclosure of a second mortgage leaves the first mortgage intact and unaffected by the foreclosure sale.

Answer (A) is incorrect. Default on one mortgage is not default on another mortgage. They are separate contractual undertakings. However, a provision can be placed in a mortgage agreeing that a breach of one mortgage is also breach of another. Answer (B) is incorrect. Prepayment does not require consent of the first mortgagee. Answer (C) is incorrect. The second mortgagee may pay off the first mortgage to protect its security.

7. Trudy purchased a tract of land giving a down payment and a promissory note for the balance. Trudy received a warranty deed for a fee simple title. Another document was filed in the real property records indicating that the seller had a security interest in the land which could be satisfied by foreclosure in the event the promissory note was not paid. This debt arrangement is called

A. A mortgage under the title theory.

B. A mortgage under the lien theory.

C. A deed of trust.

D. An installment land contract.

Answer (B) is correct. *(Publisher, adapted)*

REQUIRED: The debt arrangement in which a security interest is taken in land.

DISCUSSION: A mortgage is a security interest in real property. Under the lien theory, a mortgagor-debtor holds the title and has a right to possession. The mortgagee-lender has a security interest (lien) enforceable against the real property if the mortgagor-debtor defaults. Satisfaction of the debt is through a judicially ordered foreclosure and a sale.

Answer (A) is incorrect. Under the title theory, the mortgagee has a title that is voidable if the mortgagor makes the proper payments. Upon default, the mortgagee has an immediate right to possession, and the mortgagor has no right to a forced judicial sale or redemption. Today, very few states strictly observe that theory. Answer (C) is incorrect. A deed of trust creates a lien in favor of a third party (trustee) in trust to hold as the security for the debt owed to the seller. Answer (D) is incorrect. An installment land contract is an agreement between the buyer and the seller that the seller will retain title on default by the purchaser. Traditionally, the seller also was able to keep any payments received, but this rule has changed in most states.

8. Land contracts and trust deeds are alternatives to real estate mortgages that may be more beneficial to lenders. Which of the following is true?

A. The principal difference between a trust deed and a mortgage concerns foreclosure.

B. A trust deed permits the lender to hold the deed in trust until the buyer pays the obligation.

C. A land contract permits immediate forfeiture of the premises upon default although title is held by the buyer.

D. Under a land contract, the buyer holds the equitable but not legal title, and, in most states, the relation of lender and buyer is essentially that of landlord and tenant.

Answer (A) is correct. *(Publisher, adapted)*

REQUIRED: The true statement about land contracts and trust deeds.

DISCUSSION: Mortgage foreclosure is a costly and time-consuming procedure. Suit must be brought, the property must be sold at a public auction, and a redemption period is often allowed for. The trust deed's principal difference from the mortgage is the handling of this process. After the buyer receives the deed from the seller, (s)he gives a trust deed to a trustee who holds it on behalf of the lender. Upon default, the trustee sells the property and pays the lender the amount of the debt. The balance is paid to the debtor. This process involves no judicial foreclosure.

Answer (B) is incorrect. A third party acts as trustee. Answer (C) is incorrect. Under the traditional land sale contract (a conditional sale), the lender (who is frequently the seller) retains the deed and legal title until the last installment is paid. Answer (D) is incorrect. The buyer has the right of possession and equitable ownership. Upon default, some states permit the eviction of the debtor, forfeiture of his/her equity, and a resolution of the matter more rapidly than foreclosure of a mortgage or sale of a trust deed. However, the trend is to treat land sale contracts in much the same way as mortgages.

25.4 Recording a Mortgage

9. To be enforceable against the mortgagor, a mortgage must meet all the following requirements except

A. Be delivered to the mortgagee.

B. Be in writing and signed by the mortgagor.

C. Be recorded by the mortgagee.

D. Include a description of the debt and land involved.

Answer (C) is correct. *(CPA, adapted)*

REQUIRED: The false statement about a mortgage.

DISCUSSION: Recording the transfer of an interest in realty (whether a deed, mortgage, contract to sell, lien, or judgment) does not affect the rights of the parties to the transaction. Instead, it gives constructive notice of the interest to third parties. Thus, recording protects the rights of the mortgagee against third parties who do not have actual notice of the mortgage.

Answer (A) is incorrect. The mortgage must be delivered to the mortgagee. Answer (B) is incorrect. A mortgage is an interest in real property and is therefore within the statute of frauds. The mortgage must be in writing and signed by the party to be bound (the mortgagor). Answer (D) is incorrect. The mortgage must be executed with the same formalities as a deed. Hence, it must contain a legally sufficient description of the debt and of the property.

10. On April 6, Fiona Ford purchased a warehouse from Atwood for $150,000. Atwood had executed two mortgages on the property. The first was an unrecorded purchase-money mortgage given to Lang on March 2. The second mortgage was given to Young on March 9 and recorded the same day. Ford was unaware of the mortgage to Lang. Under the circumstances,

A. Ford will take title to the warehouse subject only to Lang's mortgage.

B. Ford will take title to the warehouse free of Lang's mortgage.

C. Lang's mortgage is superior to Young's mortgage because Lang's mortgage is a purchase-money mortgage.

D. Lang's mortgage is superior to Young's mortgage because Lang's mortgage was given first in time.

Answer (B) is correct. *(CPA, adapted)*

REQUIRED: The status of a purchaser of property subject to two mortgages.

DISCUSSION: If the mortgagee's interest is recorded, a subsequent purchaser has notice of the mortgage and will take subject to it. Recording also gives the mortgage priority over a subsequent mortgagee. However, Ford qualifies as a bona fide purchaser with respect to Lang's mortgage because she gave value and took title without notice of it. Ford will therefore take free of the unrecorded mortgage but not of the recorded mortgage.

Answer (A) is incorrect. A subsequent bona fide purchaser prevails over an unrecorded purchase-money mortgage. Thus, Ford takes subject only to Young's mortgage. Answer (C) is incorrect. If a subsequent mortgagee (Young) records his/her mortgage properly, (s)he will have priority over a first mortgagee who failed to record. Answer (D) is incorrect. The recorded mortgage prevails over the unrecorded mortgage.

11. Wyn bought real estate from Duke and gave Duke a purchase-money mortgage. Duke forgot to record the mortgage. Two months later, Wyn gave a mortgage on the same property to Goode to secure a property improvement loan. Goode recorded this mortgage 9 days later. Goode knew about the Duke mortgage. If these events took place in a state with a race-notice statute, which mortgage has priority?

A. Duke's, because it was the first mortgage given.

B. Duke's, because Goode knew of the Duke mortgage.

C. Goode's, because it was the first mortgage recorded.

D. Goode's, because it was recorded within 10 days.

Answer (B) is correct. *(CPA, adapted)*

REQUIRED: The effect of failure to record under a race-notice statute.

DISCUSSION: The effect of recording an interest in real property or failure to do so depends on the applicable type of recording statute. Under a race-notice statute, an unrecorded interest is ineffective against a subsequent bona fide (for value and without notice) acquirer of an interest who records before the prior grantee. But, because Goode knew of the Duke mortgage, Goode is not a bona fide acquirer of an interest in the property, and Duke's mortgage has priority.

Answer (A) is incorrect. Duke has priority. Goode had notice of the Duke mortgage and therefore was not a bona fide acquirer of an interest in the property. Answer (C) is incorrect. Duke has priority over a subsequent mortgagee who had notice of Duke's interest. Answer (D) is incorrect. A 10-day period is relevant to attachment or perfection of security interests under the UCC, which generally does not apply to security interests in real property.

12. On May 1, Year 1, Chance bought a piece of property by taking subject to an existing unrecorded mortgage held by Hay Bank. On April 1, Year 2, Chance borrowed money from Link Finance and gave Link a mortgage on the property. Link did not know about the Hay mortgage and did not record its mortgage until July 1, Year 2. On June 1, Year 2, Chance borrowed money from Zone Bank and gave Zone a mortgage on the same property. Zone knew about the Link mortgage but did not know about the Hay mortgage. Zone recorded its mortgage on June 15, Year 2. Which mortgage would have priority if these transactions took place in a race-notice state?

A. The Hay mortgage because it was first in time.

B. The Link mortgage because Zone had notice of the Link mortgage.

C. The Zone mortgage because it was the first recorded mortgage.

D. The Zone and Link mortgages share priority because neither had notice of the Hay mortgage.

Answer (B) is correct. *(CPA, adapted)*

REQUIRED: The mortgagee with priority in a race-notice state.

DISCUSSION: A race-notice statute gives priority to the first party to record unless (s)he had actual notice of a pre-existing interest. Zone had actual notice of the Link mortgage when it recorded, so its interest would be subordinate to Link's.

Answer (A) is incorrect. Link has priority over Hay. Link recorded and did not have actual notice of Hay's prior claim. Zone also has priority over Hay because Zone recorded and Hay did not. Answer (C) is incorrect. Only in one of the few states with a pure race statute (one that ignores a party's actual notice of an existing, unrecorded interest if (s)he is the first to record) would Zone have priority. Answer (D) is incorrect. The Link mortgage has priority in a race-notice state.

13. Ed Norton owned and operated a trucking business. He was financially hard pressed and obtained a loan from the First State Bank "secured by his equipment and including all other chattels and personal property used in his business." The loan security agreement was properly filed in the county records office. In addition, Norton obtained a loan from the Title Mortgage Company; the loan was secured by a first mortgage on all the real property used in the trucking business. Norton is now insolvent and a petition in bankruptcy has been filed. Which of the following is a true statement concerning the security interests in the properties?

A. If Title Mortgage failed to record its mortgage, the trustee in bankruptcy will be able to defeat Title's security interest.

B. Norton's central air conditioning and heating system is included in First State's security interest.

C. If Title Mortgage did not record its mortgage, First State is entitled to all fixtures, including those permanently annexed to the land.

D. A sale of all the personal and real business property by Norton to a bona fide purchaser will defeat First State's security interest unless First State recorded its security interest in both the appropriate real and personal property recordation offices.

Answer (A) is correct. *(CPA, adapted)*

REQUIRED: The true statement concerning the security interests in the properties.

DISCUSSION: A trustee in bankruptcy can assert the powers of a hypothetical lien creditor. A lien creditor would prevail over an unrecorded mortgage, so the trustee will also prevail.

Answer (B) is incorrect. First State's security interest covers only personal property. A central air conditioning and heating system is ordinarily deemed a fixture and therefore real property covered by the mortgage. Answer (C) is incorrect. Regardless of whether Title Mortgage recorded, First State is still entitled only to the collateral described in its security agreement, i.e., personal property. Fixtures are considered part of the real property. Answer (D) is incorrect. First State's security interest extends to the proceeds of the sale of the personal property.

14. The legal rights of a mortgagee may depend on the nature of the mortgage and of competing claims. Which of the following is false?

A. Jane wins a lawsuit and records a judgment against Dee. Dee subsequently finances the purchase of Redacre by giving a mortgage to Bank. Bank's interest in Redacre has priority over Jane's.

B. Buck mortgages Blueacre and its fixtures to pay a tort judgment. Buck then buys goods from Lindy and gives her a security interest in the goods and Blueacre's furnace. If Lindy properly files before Bank, she has priority in the furnace.

C. Bank finances the construction of White's new home. White then purchases a fixture from Green who immediately perfects a security interest in it by a proper filing. If the fixture is annexed to the realty before the completion of construction and Bank records its mortgage after Greene's filing but before annexation, Bank has priority in the fixture.

D. Nell raised business capital by giving a home mortgage to Bank, which it promptly recorded. Later, she purchased a fixture from Paul. He perfected a security interest in it by a proper fixture filing 15 days after its attachment. Paul has priority in the fixture.

Answer (D) is correct. *(Publisher, adapted)*

REQUIRED: The false statement about the rights of real estate mortgagees.

DISCUSSION: Under UCC 9-313, a perfected purchase money security interest in fixtures has priority over the conflicting interest of a mortgagee when the security interest is perfected by a fixture filing in the real estate records no later than 10 days after the goods become fixtures. The priority is given although the mortgagee filed first. Because Paul did not file within 10 days after annexation, Bank's earlier recorded real estate mortgage gives it priority in the fixture.

Answer (A) is incorrect. The general rule is that a recorded purchase money mortgage has priority over other liens that attach to the property. It will prevail even over a judgment entered against the mortgagor prior to the purchase. Answer (B) is incorrect. In a contest between a non-purchase money security interest in a fixture and a non-purchase money mortgagee of the realty, the first to make a proper filing has priority. Answer (C) is incorrect. A perfected purchase money security interest in fixtures is subordinate to a construction mortgage recorded before the goods become fixtures if the goods become fixtures before the construction is completed.

15. Emma Perkins was a real estate wheeler-dealer. She owned a tract of land on which she intended to build a shopping center. Perkins obtained a loan from Bill Brown, giving a mortgage in return. The mortgage provided that it was intended to secure the current loan and any future advances, and would also apply to any real property acquired by Perkins subsequent to the mortgage until the debt was repaid. Which of the following is true?

A. The after-acquired property clause is invalid.

B. A mortgage cannot secure future advances. Instead, an additional mortgage must be entered into when the subsequent loan is made.

C. If Perkins acquires additional property and then sells it, Brown will have a priority for his mortgage over any purchasers.

D. In many states, Brown can make an additional loan to Perkins, and retain priority over junior liens that have arisen after the mortgage was recorded.

Answer (D) is correct. *(Publisher, adapted)*

REQUIRED: The true statement concerning a mortgage with a future advance and after-acquired property clause.

DISCUSSION: In many states, a future advance clause permits the mortgagee to retain the same priority for a future advance as for the original mortgage. This rule is based on the theory that persons with subsequent liens have notice of the mortgage and the future advance clause.

Answer (A) is incorrect. An after-acquired property clause is valid. Answer (B) is incorrect. A real property mortgage can secure future advances just as readily as a personal property security interest. Answer (C) is incorrect. A subsequent purchaser would check title from Perkins back to her grantor and would not have notice of the after-acquired clause in a mortgage on the first property. The reason is that the first property is not in the chain of title of the after-acquired property. Such a clause is not effective because the creditor has no adequate protection against third persons unless a separate filing is made.

16. Joe Glenn borrowed $80,000 from City Bank. He executed a promissory note and secured the loan with a mortgage on business real estate he owned as a sole proprietor. Glenn neglected to advise City that he had previously mortgaged the property to Ball, who had failed to record the mortgage. City promptly recorded its mortgage. Subsequently, Glenn conveyed his business assets including the property to a newly-created corporation in exchange for all of its stock. Which of the following is true?

A. Ball's mortgage is prior in time and would take priority over City's mortgage.

B. Glenn's corporation will take the property subject to both mortgages.

C. The corporation will be deemed to have assumed both mortgages.

D. On foreclosure, Glenn could not be called upon to pay City any deficiency.

Answer (B) is correct. *(CPA, adapted)*

REQUIRED: The true statement about conveying mortgaged property after giving mortgages.

DISCUSSION: Glenn is the sole shareholder, so the corporation is deemed to have Glenn's knowledge of the transactions in question. Hence, the corporation cannot be a bona fide purchaser for value with respect to either Ball or City and will take the property subject to both mortgages. Absent the imputation of Glenn's knowledge to the corporation, it would be deemed to have constructive notice of City's recorded mortgage.

Answer (A) is incorrect. City's recorded mortgage has priority over Ball's unrecorded mortgage. Answer (C) is incorrect. The facts do not indicate that the corporation is genuinely separate from Glenn, so the courts would "pierce the corporate veil" and hold Glenn primarily liable. If an assumption of the mortgages had occurred, Glenn would still be liable but the corporation would be the primary obligor. Answer (D) is incorrect. Glenn is personally liable and must pay any deficiency.

25.5 Default and Foreclosure

17. If a borrower is in default under a purchase money mortgage loan, the

A. Lender can file suit to have the borrower declared insolvent.

B. Person who sold the real estate to the borrower can be forced to assume the mortgage debt.

C. Lender may file suit for foreclosure.

D. Lender may unilaterally obtain title without a foreclosure suit.

Answer (C) is correct. *(CPA, adapted)*

REQUIRED: The right when a borrower is in default under a purchase money mortgage loan.

DISCUSSION: In a lien theory state, the mortgage is a security interest in the real property. If the underlying loan agreement is not satisfied according to its terms, the lender is in default. The mortgagee institutes an action to compel payment. By this legal action, referred to as foreclosure, the mortgaged property (or proceeds from its sale) is applied in satisfaction of the debt.

Answer (A) is incorrect. The mortgagee's remedy is to institute a foreclosure action. Answer (B) is incorrect. The mortgagee's remedy is to institute a foreclosure action. Answer (D) is incorrect. Even in a state that provides for strict foreclosure, a court proceeding is required.

18. Default on a mortgage does not occur when the mortgagor

A. Fails to pay or makes delayed payments.

B. Transfers ownership or leases the premises.

C. Commits waste or maintains no insurance coverage.

D. Extracts minerals or cuts timber without express reservation in the agreement if such activities were not being carried out when the mortgage was created.

Answer (B) is correct. *(Publisher, adapted)*

REQUIRED: The actions not constituting a mortgage default.

DISCUSSION: The mortgagor has the right to use, possess, enjoy, and transfer the realty; to lease it and collect rent; to borrow money and use the property as security; and to pass the property to heirs or devisees. However, a mortgagor's rights may be limited by acceleration clauses for events that do not constitute a default. A due-on-sale clause requires full payment if the property is sold. A due-on-encumbrance clause accelerates payment when another lien is placed on the realty.

19. A mortgagor's right of redemption will be terminated by a judicial foreclosure sale unless

A. The proceeds from the sale are not sufficient to fully satisfy the mortgage debt.

B. The mortgage instrument does not provide for a default sale.

C. The mortgagee purchases the property for market value.

D. The jurisdiction has enacted a statutory right of redemption.

Answer (D) is correct. *(CPA, adapted)*

REQUIRED: The true statement concerning a mortgagor's right of redemption.

DISCUSSION: A foreclosure sale occurs when a mortgage is in default and the mortgagee elects to satisfy its debt by sale of the property rather than by obtaining a personal judgment against the mortgagor. It generally terminates the mortgagor's equitable right of redemption. A statutory right of redemption provides the mortgagor with the opportunity to repurchase the property after the foreclosure sale, for a certain statutorily specified period generally not exceeding 1 year, by payment of the auction sale price.

Answer (A) is incorrect. That proceeds are insufficient to satisfy the mortgage debt does not limit the statutory right of redemption. The mortgagee is entitled to the proceeds. Answer (B) is incorrect. Unless the statute so provides, failure to provide for a default sale in the mortgage instrument does not preclude the statutory right of redemption. Answer (C) is incorrect. The mortgagee is generally permitted to bid on and buy the property at a foreclosure sale. This action alone does not terminate a statutory right of redemption.

20. If a promissory note secured by a mortgage on real property is not paid, the creditor is entitled to sell the property to satisfy the debt. This proceeding is a foreclosure sale. Which statement is true concerning foreclosure in most states?

A. The mortgagee may sell the property at a public auction.

B. The mortgagee is limited to collection of the proceeds from the sale even if they do not satisfy the debt in its entirety.

C. The mortgagee is entitled to the entire proceeds of the foreclosure sale, regardless of the amount of the unpaid debt.

D. The mortgagor is entitled to repurchase the land within a statutory period.

Answer (D) is correct. *(Publisher, adapted)*

REQUIRED: The true statement concerning a foreclosure sale.

DISCUSSION: A foreclosure sale occurs when a mortgage is in default and the mortgagee elects to satisfy its debt by sale of the property rather than by obtaining a personal judgment against the mortgagor. After the sale, the mortgagor ordinarily has a right to redeem (to repurchase) the land for a statutory period.

Answer (A) is incorrect. The mortgagee does not sell the property; a trustee, sheriff, or other official sells the property at public auction. Answer (B) is incorrect. The mortgagee is entitled to seek payment from the mortgagor in the event that the foreclosure sale does not satisfy the debt in its entirety. Answer (C) is incorrect. The mortgagee is only entitled to payment of the debt and expenses, and any surplus must be turned over to the mortgagor.

21. If a mortgagor defaults in the payment of a purchase money mortgage, and the mortgagee forecloses, the mortgagor may do any of the following except

A. Obtain any excess monies resulting from a judicial sale after payment of the mortgagee.

B. Remain in possession of the property after a foreclosure sale if the equity in the property exceeds the balance due on the mortgage.

C. Refinance the mortgage with another lender and repay the original mortgage.

D. Assert the equitable right of redemption by paying the mortgage.

Answer (B) is correct. *(CPA, adapted)*

REQUIRED: The right not held by a defaulting mortgagor.

DISCUSSION: Most states recognize the mortgage as a security interest. The mortgagor-debtor signs a promissory note for the sum borrowed from the mortgagee-creditor. (S)he also signs a mortgage document representing the right of the mortgagee to seek judicial foreclosure of the mortgage and sale of the property upon default. The purchaser will receive a right to possession after the sale (or in some states after the redemption period elapses).

Answer (A) is incorrect. The mortgagor has an equity in the process equal to any amount left after payment of the debt, interest, and costs. Answer (C) is incorrect. Redemption might be accomplished by refinancing. Answer (D) is incorrect. A defaulting mortgagor has an equitable right to redeem the property before the foreclosure proceedings are complete by payment of the debt, interest, and costs. In many states, the mortgagor also has a statutory right of redemption after foreclosure.

22. Which of the following is true regarding foreclosure of a purchase money mortgage by judicial sale of the property?

A. The mortgagor has the right to any remaining sale proceeds after the mortgagee is paid.

B. The purchaser at the sale is liable for any deficiency owed the mortgagee.

C. The court must confirm any price received at the sale.

D. The mortgagor can never be liable for a deficiency owed the mortgagee.

Answer (A) is correct. *(CPA, adapted)*

REQUIRED: The true statement regarding foreclosure of a purchase money mortgage by judicial sale.

DISCUSSION: By a mortgage, the mortgagee acquires a right to initiate a foreclosure action. The court may order a sale of the property. The proceeds are applied to satisfy the mortgagor's obligation, interest, and costs. The mortgagor has the right to any remaining sale proceeds after the mortgagee is paid.

Answer (B) is incorrect. The mortgagor is generally liable for any deficiency owed the mortgagee. Answer (C) is incorrect. The court must confirm (approve) the sale (not the price), and will do so unless statutory procedure was not complied with or the price was so low as to be unconscionable. Answer (D) is incorrect. Unless otherwise agreed to, the mortgagor is generally liable for any deficiency owed the mortgagee.

23. The payment of a mortgage

A. Gives a mortgagee a right to a release enforceable by a court.

B. Imposes a duty on the mortgagee to give a satisfaction of the debt.

C. Ordinarily is not recorded.

D. Gives a mortgagor a right to a reversion of title.

Answer (B) is correct. *(Publisher, adapted)*

REQUIRED: The effect of payment of a mortgage.

DISCUSSION: Payment of the debt imposes a duty on the mortgagee to give a written release (satisfaction) to the mortgagor. When recorded, the release will remove the encumbrance from the title. Clearing the title obviously increases the property's marketability.

Answer (A) is incorrect. The mortgagor has made the payments and is entitled to a release so the title will be clear. Answer (C) is incorrect. The satisfaction must be recorded to remove the lien from the recorded title. Answer (D) is incorrect. The majority of states recognize the lien theory of mortgages, so the mortgagee has no title to be voided by payment.

24. Which of the following is a true statement about foreclosure of a mortgage?

A. A power of sale clause results in an agency coupled with an interest that may be revoked by the mortgagor.

B. Strict foreclosure is generally permitted in those states that adhere to the lien theory.

C. When the mortgagor gives a deed to the mortgagee in lieu of foreclosure, junior interests are extinguished.

D. Judicial foreclosure and sale is closely supervised by courts and by statute and may result in a deficiency decree.

Answer (D) is correct. *(Publisher, adapted)*

REQUIRED: The true statement about foreclosure.

DISCUSSION: The most common means of foreclosure is by action of a court. It will authorize sale at a public auction by the sheriff or other public official. The sale process is defined by statute. The proceeds are turned over to the court, which confirms the sale. Confirmation results in payment of the debt, interest, and costs, with the balance being given to the mortgagor. The purchaser receives a deed conveying the mortgagor's interest, subject to a statutory right of redemption. If the proceeds are insufficient, a deficiency decree may be issued against the mortgagor.

Answer (A) is incorrect. Such an agency cannot be revoked by the principal. The agent has a property interest in the subject matter. Answer (B) is incorrect. Strict foreclosure is allowed only in a few states that adhere to the title theory. Strict foreclosure conveys title to the mortgagee. Answer (C) is incorrect. This process does not extinguish the rights of third parties as in a strict foreclosure.

25. Sklar Corp. owns a factory that has a fair market value of $90,000. Dall Bank holds an $80,000 first mortgage and Rice Finance holds a $20,000 second mortgage on the factory. Sklar has discontinued payments to Dall and Rice, who have foreclosed on their mortgages. If the factory is properly sold to Bond at a judicial sale for $90,000, after expenses,

A. Rice will receive $10,000 out of the proceeds.

B. Dall will receive $77,500 out of the proceeds.

C. Bond will take the factory subject to the unsatisfied portion of any mortgage.

D. Rice has a right of redemption after the judicial sale.

Answer (A) is correct. *(CPA, adapted)*

REQUIRED: The true statement about the effects of a judicial sale.

DISCUSSION: A first mortgage holder has priority upon foreclosure and must be paid in full prior to payment of subsequent mortgage holder. Thus, Dall Bank will receive the first $80,000 of the proceeds, and Rice will receive the remaining $10,000. Rice will be an unsecured creditor for the remaining $10,000 of its debt.

Answer (B) is incorrect. Dall will receive payment in full before the second mortgage holder is paid anything. The proceeds are not prorated. Answer (C) is incorrect. The purchaser at the judicial sale will take the property free of any claim. Answer (D) is incorrect. The mortgagor (Sklar), not a mortgagee, has the right of redemption after the sale.

25.6 Transfer of Mortgaged Real Property

26. Miltown borrowed $60,000 from Strauss upon the security of a first mortgage on a business building owned by Miltown. The mortgage has been amortized down to $50,000. Sue Sanchez is buying the building from Miltown for $80,000. Sanchez is paying only the $30,000 excess over and above the mortgage. Sanchez may buy "subject to" the mortgage, or she may "assume" the mortgage. Which is a true statement under these circumstances?

A. The financing agreement ultimately decided upon must be recorded in order to be binding upon the parties.

B. The financing arrangement is covered by the Uniform Commercial Code if Sanchez takes "subject to" the existing first mortgage.

C. Sanchez will acquire no interest in the property if she takes "subject to" instead of "assuming" the mortgage.

D. Sanchez would be better advised to take "subject to" the mortgage rather than to "assume" the mortgage.

Answer (D) is correct. *(CPA, adapted)*

REQUIRED: The true statement concerning a purchase of mortgaged property.

DISCUSSION: By taking "subject to," Sanchez would avoid personal liability to both Strauss and Miltown. If Sanchez stopped making payments, the mortgagee could foreclose on the property and Sanchez would have no additional liability. On the other hand, by assuming the mortgage, Sanchez would be liable both to Miltown and to Strauss if foreclosure of the property yielded insufficient proceeds to satisfy the debt. If a mortgage is conveyed "without recourse," the creditor has no recourse against personal assets of a defaulting mortgagor. Thus, the mortgagor or one who assumes the mortgage is not liable for a deficiency after application of foreclosure sale proceeds.

Answer (A) is incorrect. Recording is necessary only to protect one's mortgage priority against subsequent mortgagees. Recording is not necessary between the parties to the arrangement. Answer (B) is incorrect. The UCC does not cover transactions in realty (except for certain transactions concerning fixtures). Answer (C) is incorrect. Sanchez would take precisely the same interest whether (s)he took "subject to" or "assumed" the mortgage.

27. Ritz owned a building on which there was a duly recorded first mortgage held by Lyn and a recorded second mortgage held by Jay. Ritz sold the building to Nunn. Nunn assumed the Jay mortgage and had no actual knowledge of the Lyn mortgage. Nunn defaulted on the payments to Jay. If both Lyn and Jay foreclosed and the proceeds of the sale were insufficient to pay both Lyn and Jay,

A. Jay would be paid after Lyn was fully paid.

B. Jay and Lyn would be paid proportionately.

C. Nunn would be personally liable to Lyn but not to Jay.

D. Nunn would be personally liable to Lyn and Jay.

Answer (A) is correct. *(CPA, adapted)*

REQUIRED: The result on foreclosure when the proceeds were insufficient to satisfy both mortgages.

DISCUSSION: When a buyer of real estate assumes an existing mortgage, the seller remains liable if there has been no novation. Between the seller and buyer, the buyer has become the primary debtor, and the seller is a surety. Because Nunn had constructive notice of both security interests, these interests are superior to Nunn's. Thus, both Lyn and Jay have a right to foreclose. When all mortgages on the same property are recorded, a first mortgage holder has priority upon foreclosure and must be paid in full prior to payment of a second mortgage holder.

Answer (B) is incorrect. The holder of a second mortgage is paid only any excess over a first mortgage holder's claim. Answer (C) is incorrect. Nunn agreed to assume personal liability to Jay, but not to Lyn. Answer (D) is incorrect. Nunn did not agree to assume personal liability to Lyn.

28. Ted Nix purchased 2 acres of land from Sally Pine. Nix paid 15% at the closing and gave his note for the balance secured by a 30-year mortgage. Five years later, Nix defaulted. Pine threatened to accelerate the loan and foreclose if Nix continued in default. Pine told Nix either to get the money or obtain an acceptable third party to assume the obligation. Nix offered the land to Quick Co. for $4,000 less than the equity Nix had in the property. This offer was acceptable to Pine, and at the closing Quick paid the arrearage, executed a new mortgage and note, and had title transferred to its name. Pine surrendered Nix's note and mortgage to him. The transaction is a(n)

A. Third party beneficiary contract.

B. Novation.

C. Purchase of land subject to a mortgage.

D. Assignment and delegation.

Answer (B) is correct. *(CPA, adapted)*

REQUIRED: The term for the transaction described.

DISCUSSION: A novation is a mutual agreement between concerned parties for the discharge of an existing agreement by substituting a new contract or new debtor. The three-way agreement among Nix, Quick, and Pine substitutes for the old agreement. The novation is the substitution of a new promisor (Quick) for the old (Nix).

Answer (A) is incorrect. A third party beneficiary contract intentionally benefits one who is not a party to the agreement. Answer (C) is incorrect. Quick accepted liability by executing a new mortgage, and Nix has been discharged from any liability. A purchaser who takes subject to a mortgage accepts no personal liability thereon. Answer (D) is incorrect. If Nix had assigned his rights and delegated his duties to Quick, he would not have been released from liability.

29. Pix borrowed $80,000 from Null Bank. Pix gave Null a promissory note and mortgage. Subsequently, Null assigned the note and mortgage to Reed. Reed failed to record the assignment or notify Pix of the assignment. If Pix pays Null pursuant to the note, Pix will

A. Be primarily liable to Reed for the payments made to Null.

B. Be secondarily liable to Reed for the payments made to Null.

C. Not be liable to Reed for the payments made to Null because Reed failed to record the assignment.

D. Not be liable to Reed for the payments made to Null because Reed failed to give Pix notice of the assignment.

Answer (D) is correct. *(CPA, adapted)*

REQUIRED: The consequences if the debtor pays the assignor.

DISCUSSION: The debtor (Pix) will not be held either primarily or secondarily liable to the assignee (Reed) for payments made to the assignor (Null). An assignee's failure to give notice to the debtor of the assignment permits discharge of the obligation by payment to the assignor rather than the assignee. However, the assignor will have a duty to account to the assignee.

Answer (A) is incorrect. The debtor (Pix) is not primarily liable to the assignee (Reed) for payments made to the assignor (Null) prior to receiving notice of the assignment. Answer (B) is incorrect. The debtor (Pix) is not secondarily liable to the assignee (Reed) for payments made to the assignor (Null) prior to receiving notice of the assignment. Answer (C) is incorrect. Recording gives constructive notice to parties who may have competing interests in the mortgage but is not sufficient against the debtor. An assignee must give some form of actual notice because expecting the mortgage debtor to search the property records before making each payment would be unfair.

STUDY UNIT TWENTY-SIX
CREDITOR LAW AND LIENS

A **lien** is a legal claim or charge on property, either real or personal, as security for payment or performance of a debt or obligation. **Personal property**, such as equipment, inventory, consumer goods, farm products, or securities, is anything movable. All other property is **real property**, such as land and buildings. A lien is classified as consensual, statutory, or judicial. It protects the interests of those who provide skills, materials, or services to property owners. **Consensual liens** are created by the contractual agreement of the parties. For example, a mortgage is a consensual lien on real property given by **contract** to secure a debt, e.g., the initial contract of purchase or a subsequent loan against equity. The authority for **statutory liens** is based on laws passed by state legislatures. Thus, they arise by operation of law, not by the consent of debtors. **Judicial liens** on debtor property arise from one party's use of the court system to collect a debt. They follow from actions taken by a judge who has ruled in favor of the creditor.

A **statutory lien** results when a party adds value to another party's **property** by agreement. Many such liens originated under the common law and were based on the right of one person to retain **possession** of the property of another until the owner paid for the goods or services. However, certain statutory liens are nonpossessory. Typical statutory liens are artisan's liens, mechanic's liens, bailee's liens, landlord's liens, hotelkeeper's liens, and tax liens.

An **artisan's lien** is held by a repairer or improver of **personal property**, such as an automobile or computer, who retains **possession** of the property until paid. The work or improvement must be performed subject to an express or implied agreement for **cash payment**. The lien does not attach unless the owner surrenders possession. The artisan's lien terminates when payment is tendered or when the repairer or improver surrenders possession of the property. If the lienholder **temporarily surrenders** the property subject to an agreement that it will be returned, the lien does not terminate. However, if a third party obtains rights to the property before it is returned, the lien terminates.

Mechanic's liens (including liens held by persons who provide materials) are liens against the **real property benefited**. Thus, they are not possessory. The liens secure unpaid debts from contracts for materials or services to improve specific real property. For example, a mechanic's lien may be held by the builder of a house or by someone who has merely remodeled a room in a house. The holder of a mechanic's lien normally must file a document (a **notice of lien**) that identifies the property subject to the lien. This document is filed with an official in the county office where real estate deeds are recorded. The filing gives notice to all third parties. **Perfection** is the result of a prescribed statutory scheme to ensure that a mechanic's lien is free from defect. The statute ordinarily provides for a **filing period** of 60 to 120 days after work is substantially complete. **Attachment** of the lien to the property ordinarily **dates back** to when the first work is done or materials are supplied. Thus, attachment may occur long before a notice of lien is filed. Because a title search may not detect the lien, the defect in the title may not be apparent to a potential holder of a competing interest.

Most states follow one of two statutory schemes **limiting the amount** of the mechanic's lien. Under one, the lien is not dependent upon the balance owed to the general contractor by the property owner. The lien may be enforced even if the general contractor has been paid in full. The other limits the lien to the **balance due to the general contractor** when the property owner receives notice of the lien or to the amount that may subsequently become due to the general contractor.

A **bailee's lien** is granted to a **common carrier** or **warehouser** to whom the debtor has entrusted goods. This possessory lien secures payment of shipment or storage charges. The goods must be covered by a **document of title**, a bill of lading issued by a carrier, or a warehouse receipt issued by a warehouser when the goods are received for transport or storage. A document of title is evidence that its possessor may receive, hold, and dispose of the document and the goods it covers. However, a **purchaser for value of a negotiable document of title** is liable only for charges stated in it or a reasonable charge. The lien is **terminated** by (1) receiving payment, (2) relinquishing possession of the goods, (3) unjustifiably refusing to deliver, or (4) selling the goods. A **landlord's lien** is a possessory lien placed on the personal property of a tenant who is located on the leased premises. It **secures payment of** rent. A **hotelkeeper's lien** arises when a guest fails to pay the agreed-upon hotel charges. The lien attaches to the guest's baggage. It **terminates** when payment is tendered, the hotelkeeper relinquishes possession, or the hotelkeeper converts the baggage. **Conversion** occurs when the hotelkeeper appropriates the property to his/her own beneficial use or enjoyment. A **tax lien** secures payment of taxes owed to a governmental entity. For example, it may be imposed on specific land on which the landowner has not paid the real property taxes. Moreover, a federal tax lien may be placed on all property of a delinquent tax payer. An **accountant** may acquire a lien upon a client's books and other documents and materials. But the AICPA's Code of Professional Conduct applies regardless of whether the state grants a member a lien on certain records. For example, client-provided records in the member's custody or control must be returned even if fees are due.

The **relative priority** of liens usually is in the **order of their acquisition**. The first in time is the first in right. Certain liens are based directly on **possession**. Such a lien arises only when possession is obtained and exists only as long as it is retained. **Concurrent liens** (simultaneously arising liens) have equal rank in distribution. However, a **government** has the power to fix the priorities of liens. It may give a statutory lien (e.g., a tax lien) priority over the other liens. A government also may exempt certain property from collection by creditors. For example, state **homestead exemption acts** may shield a debtor's equity in his/her home from most liens. But mortgage liens and tax liens are not exempted. Under UCC Article 9, **artisan's and mechanic's liens** have priority over all other security interests in property unless a statute expressly provides otherwise. For example, a mechanic's lien will have priority over a mortgage securing a loan made after the lien arose, even if the mortgage lender did not know of the lien, and the mortgage is recorded first. Likewise, in a sale of the real property, a deed may be recorded prior to the recording of an already existing mechanic's lien. In such instances, the lien has priority. But a **properly recorded real estate mortgage** has priority over a mechanic's lien that attaches after the mortgage is recorded.

A statutory lien is **enforceable** only as to items to which liens may legally attach. Statutes may allow the lienholder to **foreclose** the lien judicially and sell the property if the owner does not pay the debt. However, many statutes provide a specific, limited period, typically 1 year, within which suit may be filed to enforce the lien. The lienholder has this right only if a statute grants it and must give **notice** to the owner prior to foreclosure and sale. **Sale proceeds** are used to pay the costs of foreclosure and sale and to satisfy the debt. Any remaining proceeds are paid to the former owner. Moreover, a **good faith purchaser** of the goods takes free of the rights of persons against whom the lien was valid. The method for enforcing statutory liens is generally provided by the federal or state statutes that provide for the liens. The statutory remedy is **generally regarded as exclusive**. For example, federal law exempts Social Security benefits from garnishment. When statutes provide for a lien but not a method for its enforcement, an **ordinary action at law** may be maintained for the collection of the debt.

A **judicial lien** is a legally enforceable interest in property that secures performance of an obligation, such as payment of a debt. It is acquired by judgment, seizure (levy), or another judicial process. A court, after a civil proceeding, may issue a **monetary judgment** for one of the parties, e.g., the plaintiff. That party is a **judgment creditor**. If the other party fails to pay voluntarily (satisfy the judgment), the judgment creditor may, typically, petition the court to issue a **writ of execution** (a **postjudgment** remedy). It generally operates to authorize the sheriff to seize and sell specific nonexempt property of the judgment debtor to satisfy the judgment. The writ of execution may be **returned unsatisfied** to the court because the value of **personal property** seized and sold was less than the judgment amount. The judgment then becomes a **lien on any real property owned** by the judgment debtor that is located within the jurisdiction of the court. States generally require that the **judgment creditor file the judgment** with a specified county official to establish or perfect the judgment lien. Real property acquired in the jurisdiction by the judgment debtor after the judgment and prior to satisfaction becomes subject to it. A judgment creditor acquiring a lien on real property may be entitled to foreclose on the lien and have the judgment satisfied from proceeds of a judicial sale. In any event, the **judgment debtor** generally will not be able to transfer **marketable title** to the property prior to the satisfaction of the judgment. Nevertheless, a transferee might take the property subject to the lien.

Attachment, a prejudgment remedy, is the process of seizing a defendant's nonexempt property under judicial authorization and placing it in the custody of the court. Attachment is intended to secure satisfaction of a pending judgment. To obtain attachment, the creditor must strictly comply with state law requirements. The **usual procedures** require the creditor to (1) file an **affidavit** with the court describing the debt and providing evidence that the debtor is attempting to transfer the property, (2) post a bond, and (3) give the debtor notice and an opportunity to be heard. **Replevin** is similar to attachment. It is a prejudgment remedy intended to secure property already subject to a lien of, or a right of repossession by, the plaintiff. A typical example is the repossession of an automobile by a lender after the debtor's default. The creditor obtains a writ of replevin by filing an affidavit and posting a bond. The sheriff then seizes (replevies) the property and turns it over to the creditor pending resolution of legal proceedings. **Garnishment** is both a postjudgment and a prejudgment remedy involving property of the debtor that is in the hands of a third party. Examples of property subject to garnishment include wages and funds in bank accounts. In garnishment, the creditor requests a court to issue a **writ of garnishment** ordering the holder (the garnishee) to remit the property to the court on behalf of the judgment creditor. However, both federal and state law place limitations on garnishment of wages. In a **prejudgment garnishment**, the court orders the garnishee not to pay the debtor until the creditor's suit is resolved.

The right to retain an existing lien until the debt is paid is a substantive property right that may not be taken from a rightful lienholder. A lien is effective until it is **satisfied or otherwise terminated**. Generally, a lien dependent on possession is lost if the lienholder voluntarily and unconditionally **surrenders possession or control** of the underlying property. A lien also may be terminated by waiver or estoppel. A **waiver** is a voluntary surrender of a right, which may be expressed or implied from conduct that is inconsistent with the existence of the lien. The concept of **estoppel** prevents (estops) a lienholder that has engaged or not engaged in certain conduct, e.g., not registering a lien, from asserting the lien. Moreover, **destruction of property** subject to a lien terminates the lien. A lien is discharged by a proper and sufficient **payment or tender** of payment of the debt it secures. Tender (an offer to pay combined with a present ability to pay) also discharges liability for further interest or damages. It does not discharge the underlying debt. A lienholder has the duty to prepare, execute, and deliver to the debtor a valid **release** of the lien upon tender of the amount due. A debtor may owe **separate debts** to one creditor. If the debtor makes a partial payment, the creditor may apply the payments as (s)he chooses, absent instructions from the debtor.

QUESTIONS

26.1 Statutory Liens

1. Art owns a mobile automobile repair business. Ann's car would not start, so she called Art. Art went to Ann's home and replaced the distributor cap on Ann's car. Ann was unable to pay for the repair. Art is not entitled to an artisan's lien because

A. Ann did not relinquish possession of the car.

B. Artisan's liens attach only to improvements to real property.

C. Automobile repairers are essentially mechanics and therefore are entitled to mechanic's liens rather than artisan's liens.

D. The distributor cap did not appreciably increase the value of the car.

Answer (A) is correct. *(Publisher, adapted)*

REQUIRED: The reason the improver is not entitled to an artisan's lien.

DISCUSSION: An artisan's lien is a possessory lien. If possession of the personal property is not relinquished by the owner and retained by the improver, the lien cannot exist. Because Art repaired the car at Ann's home, Ann retained possession.

Answer (B) is incorrect. Artisan's liens attach to personal property. Answer (C) is incorrect. Mechanic's liens attach to real property. Answer (D) is incorrect. An increase in the value of the personal property is not a necessary condition of an artisan's lien. The lien arises for labor done or value added.

2. On April 14, Jack Jackson, CPA, watched as his copy machine malfunctioned. Jackson delivered the copier to Copy, Inc., for repair. Jackson agreed to pay $150 under terms of 2/10, n/30 for parts and labor if Copy would fix the copier by 8 a.m. on April 15. Jackson arrived at 8 a.m. on April 15 to pick up the copier but refused to pay for the repairs at that time. Copy is entitled to

A. An artisan's lien.

B. A mechanic's lien.

C. A materialman's lien.

D. Payment in 30 days.

Answer (D) is correct. *(Publisher, adapted)*

REQUIRED: The right to payment or a lien for services performed on personal property.

DISCUSSION: An artisan's lien is a possessory lien that arises in favor of a repairer or other improver of personal property as a result of a specific debt. The holder of an artisan's lien ordinarily must have agreed expressly or implicitly to perform the services on a cash basis. Payment terms of 2/10, n/30 are a common extension of credit. Because Copy agreed to bill Jackson for the repairs, the work was done on a credit basis, and Copy is not entitled to an artisan's lien. Copy must await performance under the contract.

Answer (A) is incorrect. Copy agreed to extend credit to Jackson. Answer (B) is incorrect. A mechanic's lien attaches to real property, and a copy machine is personal property. Answer (C) is incorrect. A materialman's lien attaches to real property, and a copy machine is personal property.

3. One night Chris Lee was driving to a client's office when her car collided with another vehicle. Both headlights on Lee's car were smashed in the collision. A police officer quickly arrived on the scene accompanied by a tow truck from XYZ Towing Co. As Lee signed a traffic citation, XYZ towed Lee's car to its lot at the direction of the police officer. The next day, Lee went to XYZ to get the car. XYZ charged Lee $100 for two new headlights that had been installed. Lee refused to pay for the headlights. Is XYZ entitled to a statutory lien for the value of the headlights?

A. Yes, XYZ is entitled to an artisan's lien for the value of the headlights.

B. No, XYZ is not entitled to a statutory possessory lien for the value of the headlights.

C. Yes, XYZ is entitled to a common carrier's lien for the value of the headlights.

D. No, but XYZ is entitled to a mechanic's lien for the value of the headlights.

Answer (B) is correct. *(Publisher, adapted)*

REQUIRED: The entitlement of a repairer to a statutory lien when the owner did not consent to the work.

DISCUSSION: Statutory possessory liens (e.g., artisan's, hotelkeeper's) require the owner's consent to performance of the work or service that benefited the property. Lee did not consent to XYZ's installation of new headlights, so XYZ is not entitled to a statutory possessory lien.

Answer (A) is incorrect. An artisan's lien is a statutory possessory lien and requires consent of the owner to the work. Answer (C) is incorrect. A common carrier's lien typically arises from freight charges for transportation of goods. Answer (D) is incorrect. Mechanic's liens attach to real property.

4. Tom planned to dump the excess cement from his cement truck. On the way to the dump, he noticed Ann's dirt driveway. Tom quickly drove onto Ann's lawn, dumped the cement, and paved the driveway. The next day, Tom sent Ann an invoice for paving. Ann refused to pay the invoice. Which of the following is true?

A. Tom is the holder of a materialman's lien.

B. Tom has an artisan's lien.

C. A mechanic's lien arose in favor of Tom by operation of law.

D. Tom does not have a mechanic's lien.

Answer (D) is correct. *(Publisher, adapted)*

REQUIRED: The true statement regarding Tom's right to a lien.

DISCUSSION: A mechanic's lien arises if the improver of real property performs work pursuant to a contract and is not paid. Some jurisdictions require the contract to be in writing. Because Tom paved the driveway without entering into a contract, a mechanic's lien did not arise.

Answer (A) is incorrect. The supplier of materials pursuant to a contract concerning specific real property has a materialman's lien, and the supplier of labor and materials has a mechanic's lien. Tom is not entitled to either lien because the parties had no contract. Answer (B) is incorrect. An artisan's lien is a possessory lien that attaches to personal property. Answer (C) is incorrect. A mechanic's lien must arise pursuant to statutory requirements. Mechanic's liens do not arise by operation of law. The lienholder must take affirmative action.

5. Contractor purchased shingles for inventory pursuant to a valid written contract with Supplier. Supplier delivered the shingles to Contractor's warehouse. Two weeks later, Contractor's crew used all of the shingles on Owner's new office building. Contractor refused to pay for the shingles because of financial difficulties. Supplier

A. Can obtain a mechanic's lien on Owner's office building because Contractor purchased the shingles pursuant to a valid contract.

B. Can obtain a materialman's lien on Owner's office building because Contractor purchased the shingles pursuant to a valid contract.

C. Cannot obtain a mechanic's lien on Owner's office building because the shingles were not purchased for use on specific property.

D. Cannot obtain a materialman's lien on Owner's office building because the shingles were not purchased for use on a specific property.

Answer (D) is correct. *(Publisher, adapted)*

REQUIRED: The rights of a supplier of materials used in construction of a building.

DISCUSSION: A supplier of materials may obtain a materialman's lien on real property improved by the materials only if (s)he sells the materials pursuant to a contract made with reference to a specific property. The shingles were sold for inventory and not for use on specific property. Hence, Supplier cannot assert a lien against Owner's office building even though it was improved by the shingles.

Answer (A) is incorrect. A supplier of materials cannot obtain a mechanic's lien unless services also are performed. Answer (B) is incorrect. The sale must be made in reference to a specific property, even if made pursuant to a valid contract, or the supplier cannot obtain a materialman's lien. Answer (C) is incorrect. A supplier of materials cannot obtain a mechanic's lien unless services also are performed.

6. Dolphin, Inc., began constructing a pool at the home of the Fin family, pursuant to an enforceable contract, on June 2. The pool was completed on June 30, and the Fins used it for the first time on July 13. Dolphin filed a notice of lien on July 10. Assume the applicable statute provides for a 60-day period in which a lienholder may perfect a mechanic's lien. On what date does the period for perfecting Dolphin's lien expire?

A. July 31.

B. August 1.

C. August 29.

D. September 8.

Answer (C) is correct. *(Publisher, adapted)*

REQUIRED: The date the period for perfecting a mechanic's lien ends.

DISCUSSION: The period for perfecting a lien begins when work is substantially completed. Because Dolphin completed the pool on June 30, the 60-day period ends on August 29.

Answer (A) is incorrect. July 31 is 60 days from the date of hire. Answer (B) is incorrect. August 1 is 60 days from the date work was commenced. Answer (D) is incorrect. September 8 is 60 days from the date the lien was filed.

7. The normal procedure for perfecting a mechanic's lien requires the lienholder to file a notice of

A. Attachment.

B. Garnishment.

C. Perfection.

D. Lien.

Answer (D) is correct. *(Publisher, adapted)*

REQUIRED: The document filed to perfect a mechanic's lien.

DISCUSSION: The holder of a mechanic's lien normally must file a document that identifies the property subject to the lien. This document is called a notice of lien and is filed with a county official in the county office where real estate deeds are recorded.

Answer (A) is incorrect. Attachment is a method of ensuring the collection of a judgment and is not pertinent to the perfection of a mechanic's lien. Answer (B) is incorrect. Garnishment is a procedure for collecting a judgment from a party owing money to the judgment debtor. Answer (C) is incorrect. Perfection is the result of a prescribed statutory scheme to ensure that a mechanic's lien is free from defect.

8. Fabs, Inc., supplied fabricated steel under a contract to ABC Co., which was erecting a building for Mr. Z on land he owns. ABC refused to pay for the delivered materials. Fabs filed its statutory lien on the property and then sued Z to foreclose. Fabs subsequently learned that Z had given an unrecorded deed to X&Y, a partnership, prior to the delivery of the steel. Which of the following is a true statement?

A. Under the recording acts, the true owner of the land is Mr. Z because the deed to X&Y was never recorded in the clerk's office where the land was located.

B. Delivery of an unrecorded but properly acknowledged deed has no legal validity, and the ownership remains in Mr. Z.

C. Recording acts are never intended to protect third-party purchasers from fraudulent conveyances by their grantor.

D. An unrecorded but delivered and acknowledged deed conveys title to the realty despite being unrecorded.

Answer (D) is correct. *(E. O'Connor)*

REQUIRED: The effect of failing to record a deed.

DISCUSSION: Recording protects the holder of an interest in real property by giving constructive notice to parties who subsequently acquire interests in the same property. But failure to record never affects the conveyance by the grantor to a grantee. Thus, the materialman (Fabs) must proceed against X&Y.

Answer (A) is incorrect. Failure to record does not destroy the conveyance to X&Y. The failure to record would only benefit a purchaser who recorded a deed from Z before X&Y. Answer (B) is incorrect. A duly acknowledged deed delivered by the grantor to the grantee is effective. Answer (C) is incorrect. Recording acts are in fact intended to prevent fraudulent conveyances prior to selling realty to an innocent purchaser for value.

9. Builder, Inc., contracts to sell Buyer a new house, with all work to be completed by June 1, the closing date. On June 1, the title search indicates no adverse interests of record; Buyer pays the $45,000 price and moves in. On June 25, Buyer receives a notice from Subcontractor that she claims a mechanic's lien in the amount of $30,000 on the house for work completed on May 25. Subcontractor has a valid direct lien pursuant to a state statute. Which of the following is false?

A. If Buyer does nothing and Subcontractor is not paid, Subcontractor can foreclose the lien, force the sale of Buyer's house, and receive the first $30,000 of proceeds.

B. The lawyer who prepared the title report is not liable for malpractice because the mechanic's lien was not of record on June 1.

C. If no recovery can be had from Builder and Buyer desires to keep the house, Buyer may have to pay an additional $30,000.

D. If Subcontractor does not file a foreclosure action within the specified statutory period, she will lose all of her rights.

Answer (D) is correct. *(Publisher, adapted)*

REQUIRED: The effect of a mechanic's lien as a hidden interest in property.

DISCUSSION: A mechanic's lien is statutory, and the specific rules vary from state to state. The notice periods under the various statutes range from 60 to 120 days after the last work is performed. A mechanic's lien filed within the allotted period attaches as of the time the first work is done. Consequently, the record may not reveal existence of the lien to third parties (in this case Buyer). Thus, Buyer should protect against a hidden lien by getting waivers or having funds retained in escrow. The foreclosure action must be filed within a limited period. However, failure to do so will not impair the lienholder's private contract rights against the party with whom (s)he contracted.

Answer (A) is incorrect. Subcontractor, as an unsatisfied lienholder, has typical foreclosure rights. Answer (B) is incorrect. A subcontractor, as an unsatisfied lienholder, has typical foreclosure rights. Answer (C) is incorrect. Subcontractor, as an unsatisfied lienholder, has typical foreclosure rights.

26.2 Priorities

10. Tricia took out a home equity loan from Friendly Finance Co. to add a pool to her home. She conveyed a second mortgage on the home to Friendly. She then engaged Chip to have the pool built. Chip also convinced her to have him build a changing room with a hot tub for an additional $10,000. When Tricia's car was stolen the next week, she discovered her insurance had lapsed. She used funds allocated for the construction to buy a new car. Thus, she could not timely pay Chip, who filed a mechanic's lien. Real property taxes on Tricia's home had become overdue. Which of the following liens has the highest priority?

A. The first mortgage.

B. The second mortgage.

C. The mechanic's lien.

D. The tax lien.

Answer (D) is correct. *(Publisher, adapted)*

REQUIRED: The lien with the highest priority.

DISCUSSION: The general rule of priority is that the first in time is the first in right. The perfected mechanic's lien has priority set by state statute. Its priority would generally be established as of the date the construction began, provided that recording was completed within the statutorily designated number of days after completing the work. However, statutes typically provide that liens for taxes have priority over otherwise superior liens.

Questions 11 and 12 are based on the following information. Bynow Mortgage Co. has held a properly recorded mortgage on Mr. Garcia's home since Year 1. On June 1, Year 3, Mr. Garcia hired Wetsun Pools, Inc., and Screenwall, Inc., to build a pool and a porch, respectively. Wetsun began construction of the pool on June 2, Year 3, and completed the pool on June 30, Year 3. Screenwall began and completed the porch on June 15, Year 3. Mr. Garcia was unable to pay Wetsun and Screenwall. On July 10, Year 3, both Wetsun and Screenwall filed a notice of lien.

11. Assume Wetsun properly forecloses on Mr. Garcia's property on September 1, Year 3. Among Bynow, Wetsun, and Screenwall, whose security interest has priority?

A. Bynow, because the mortgage was properly recorded in Year 1.

B. Wetsun, because construction of the pool began on June 2, Year 3, and mechanic's liens have priority over mortgages in foreclosure proceedings.

C. Screenwall, because porch construction was completed before pool construction, and mechanic's liens have priority over mortgages in foreclosure proceedings.

D. No one lien has priority. Proceeds from foreclosure will be allocated between Bynow, Wetsun, and Screenwall on a pro rata basis.

Answer (A) is correct. *(Publisher, adapted)*

REQUIRED: The lien that has priority in a foreclosure proceeding.

DISCUSSION: Properly recorded mortgages have priority over mechanic's liens that attach after the mortgage is recorded. Virtually all states have statutes providing that mortgages attach when properly recorded. The majority of states have statutes providing that mechanic's liens attach when work first begins. Priority is determined is according to when liens attach.

Answer (B) is incorrect. The mortgage was properly recorded before pool construction began. Answer (C) is incorrect. The mortgage was properly recorded before porch construction began. Answer (D) is incorrect. Bynow's mortgage was properly recorded and attached before the mechanic's liens. Foreclosure proceeds are only shared on a pro rata basis when several liens are considered equal in priority and funds are insufficient to fully satisfy all liens.

12. Assume only Wetsun and Screenwall have liens on Mr. Garcia's property. Which of the following is true?

A. Wetsun's lien has priority over Screenwall's lien.

B. Screenwall's lien has priority over Wetsun's lien.

C. Neither lien has priority because Mr. Garcia hired both companies on June 1.

D. Neither lien has priority because both are mechanic's liens.

Answer (A) is correct. *(Publisher, adapted)*

REQUIRED: The true statement concerning the priority of liens.

DISCUSSION: Mechanic's liens are entitled to priority based on when work is commenced by the lienholder. Thus, Wetsun's lien (June 2) has priority over Screenwall's (June 15).

Answer (B) is incorrect. Screenwall began work after Wetsun, and mechanic's liens are accorded priority based on when work is commenced. Answer (C) is incorrect. The date of hire is irrelevant for purposes of determining priority of mechanic's liens. Answer (D) is incorrect. All mechanic's liens do not have equivalent status. The date of attachment must be considered in determining priority between mechanic's liens.

26.3 Termination and Extinguishment

13. Dwight operates a fleet of limousines. Garage, Inc., repairs the limousines on a cash on delivery basis. Dwight delivered Limos No. 1 and No. 2 to Garage on Thursday. Dwight forgot his wallet when he went to get Limo No. 1 on Friday, but Garage allowed Dwight to take Limo No. 1 on condition that payment be made on Monday. Dwight failed to pay for the repairs on Monday. On Tuesday, Garage

A. Has an artisan's lien on Limo No. 1 because the repairs were requested by Dwight.

B. Has an artisan's lien on Limo No. 1 because Dwight delivered possession of Limo No. 1 to Garage.

C. Does not have a lien on Limo No. 1 because possession was relinquished to Dwight on Friday.

D. Has a lien against Limo No. 2 for the value of the repairs made to Limo No. 1.

Answer (C) is correct. *(Publisher, adapted)*

REQUIRED: The true statement about liens claimed by a repairer of personalty.

DISCUSSION: The repairer or other improver of property must retain possession of the property to assert a common law possessory lien. Once the improver (artisan) voluntarily surrenders possession of the property, (s)he loses the lien. Hence, Garage lost its lien on Limo No. 1 by relinquishing possession.

Answer (A) is incorrect. Possession of the property is required for an artisan's lien even if work is performed at the request of the owner. Answer (B) is incorrect. Possession of the property is required for an artisan's lien even if the owner delivers possession of the property to the improver. Answer (D) is incorrect. The lien is against the specific improved property only.

14. On Monday, April 1, Mr. Paint, in exchange for Kelly's promise to pay $250 cash on completion, agreed to paint Kelly's car at his shop. When the job was done on April 5, Kelly told Mr. Paint she was not yet able to pay. Kelly took her car, having assured Mr. Paint that she would return it on Monday, April 8. She consented to his stipulation that he would retain his lien until she paid in full. Mr. Paint perfected the lien by recording on April 9. Instead of returning the car, Kelly simply returned on foot Wednesday, April 10, and placed $250 cash in front of Mr. Paint as payment. As a fair equivalent to Kelly's not returning possession on Monday, Paint told her he would not accept her payment before Friday, April 12. The artisan's lien terminated on

A. April 8.

B. April 9.

C. April 10.

D. April 12.

Answer (C) is correct. *(Publisher, adapted)*

REQUIRED: The date the artisan's lien was terminated.

DISCUSSION: A proper and sufficient tender of payment discharges an artisan's lien. The tender also relieves the obligor from liability for further interest or damages (such as legal fees). But tender does not operate to discharge the underlying obligation, which, in this case, was to pay $250.

Answer (A) is incorrect. Mr. Paint's temporary surrender of possession was conditioned on an expressed intent to preserve the lien. Answer (B) is incorrect. The lien attached when the work was substantially completed and was not terminated by the conditional relinquishment of possession. Answer (D) is incorrect. The proper tender of the cash terminated the lien.

26.4 Enforcement and Remedies

15. Which of the following is a true statement about foreclosure by the holder of a lien?

A. The holder of an artisan's lien must foreclose within a prescribed period or lose the lien.

B. The sales proceeds resulting from statutorily permitted foreclosure and sale are awarded to the holder of an artisan's lien regardless of the size of the debt secured by the lien.

C. State statutes permitting a foreclosure and sale require a lienholder to give notice to the property owner.

D. The holder of an artisan's lien may foreclose on the real property subject to the lien.

Answer (C) is correct. *(Publisher, adapted)*

REQUIRED: The true statement concerning foreclosure by a lienholder.

DISCUSSION: An artisan's lien is a statutory possessory lien. The holder may retain possession of the secured property and may sue for payment of the debt. But unless a statute grants it, the artisan does not have the right to foreclose and sell the property. State statutes providing for foreclosure and sale also require prior notice to the property owner.

Answer (A) is incorrect. Unless a statute grants it, the artisan does not have the right to foreclose and sell the property. Answer (B) is incorrect. The lienholder is entitled only to satisfaction of the debt secured by the lien. Answer (D) is incorrect. An artisan's lien does not attach to real property.

16. Anna Park owed Bill Collins $1,000 and $2,000, respectively, on two separate unsecured obligations. Smythe Co. had become a surety on the $2,000 debt at the request of Park when Park became indebted to Collins. Both debts matured on June 1. Park was able to pay only $600 at that time, and she forwarded that amount to Collins without instructions. Under these circumstances,

A. Collins must apply the funds pro rata in proportion to the two debts.

B. Collins must apply the $600 to the $2,000 debt because there is a surety on it.

C. Smythe will be discharged to the extent of $400 if Collins on request of Smythe fails to apply $400 to the $2,000 debt.

D. Collins is free to apply the $600 to the debts as he sees fit.

Answer (D) is correct. *(CPA, adapted)*

REQUIRED: The manner in which a creditor may apply a partial payment to separate, unsecured obligations.

DISCUSSION: If a debtor gives instructions as to the application of partial payment, the creditor must comply. Without instructions, the creditor may apply the payment as (s)he chooses. In this case, Collins may apply the $600 wholly to either obligation or proportionately as he sees fit.

Answer (A) is incorrect. Collins may apply the funds however he chooses. Park gave no instructions. Answer (B) is incorrect. The presence of a surety for the $2,000 debt has no effect on the required application of the partial payment. Answer (C) is incorrect. Smythe has no authority to require application of any part of the partial payment to the debt on which it is a surety.

17. A debtor may attempt to conceal or transfer property to prevent a creditor from satisfying a judgment. Which of the following actions will be considered an indication of fraudulent conveyance?

	Debtor's Remaining in Possession after Conveyance	Secret Conveyance	Debtor's Retention of an Equitable Benefit in the Property Conveyed
A.	Yes	Yes	Yes
B.	No	Yes	Yes
C.	Yes	Yes	No
D.	Yes	No	Yes

Answer (A) is correct. *(CPA, adapted)*

REQUIRED: The actions that will be considered an indication of fraudulent conveyance.

DISCUSSION: Any transfer of property that is made with the purpose and intent to delay, hinder, or defraud creditors is voidable by the transferor's creditors. Various criteria are deemed to substitute for the intent needed to establish that a conveyance was fraudulent. These "badges of fraud" include the debtor's remaining in possession after conveyance, a transfer in secret, the debtor's retention of an equitable benefit in the property conveyed, a general transfer (one involving substantially all the debtor's assets), a transfer to a family member, a transfer for inadequate consideration, and a transfer in anticipation of litigation or financial difficulty. These criteria are currently embodied in the Uniform Fraudulent Transfer Act of 1984.

18. Low Point Distributors coerced Acme Manufacturing into withdrawing from distributorship negotiations with Jack. Jack intends to sue Low Point Distributors for intentional interference with potential contractual relations, but he fears Low Point will sell its assets and abandon its leased showroom before trial. Jack wants to protect against this potential problem. The most appropriate remedy for Jack to pursue is

A. Replevin.

B. Attachment.

C. Assignment for the benefit of creditors.

D. Garnishment.

Answer (B) is correct. *(Publisher, adapted)*

REQUIRED: The prejudgment remedy to ensure that the plaintiff will be able to reach the defendant's assets.

DISCUSSION: Attachment, a prejudgment remedy, is the process of seizing a defendant's property pursuant to judicial authorization and placing it in the custody of the court. Attachment is intended to secure satisfaction of a pending judgment.

Answer (A) is incorrect. Replevin is similar to attachment. It is a prejudgment remedy intended to secure property already subject to a lien of, or a right of repossession by, the plaintiff. Answer (C) is incorrect. An assignment for the benefit of creditors is a tool for debtor's relief. The debtor voluntarily transfers property to a trustee who liquidates it and uses the proceeds to pay the debtor's obligations. Answer (D) is incorrect. Garnishment is a prejudgment or postjudgment collection remedy directed against a third party (the garnishee) who holds property, or is a debtor, of the defendant.

19. Which of the following is a true statement about liens imposed on real property without the owner's consent?

A. An attachment lien is generally obtained by a secured creditor while an action is pending against the debtor.

B. A judgment lien is automatically imposed on behalf of the plaintiff when a judgment is rendered against the defendant.

C. An execution lien is directed to a specific parcel, not to all the realty of the debtor in the county where the lien is recorded.

D. A tax lien is automatically imposed when state or federal real property or income taxes are not paid.

Answer (C) is correct. *(Publisher, adapted)*

REQUIRED: The true statement about involuntary liens on realty.

DISCUSSION: When a judgment has been entered, the successful party becomes a judgment creditor. If the judgment is not paid, (s)he may then obtain a judgment lien on all real property of the judgment debtor in a given county by recording the judgment in that county. If further measures are necessary, the judgment creditor may then seek a writ of execution from a court directing the sheriff to seize and sell a specified parcel of property.

Answer (A) is incorrect. An unsecured creditor would seek an attachment lien. A secured creditor already has a legal interest in the specific property. An attachment lien is recorded in the real property records pending the conclusion of the suit. Answer (B) is incorrect. The lien must be recorded where the debtor has real property before it is effective to encumber the property. Answer (D) is incorrect. Real property tax liens are automatically effective without court action, but an income, sales, or other nonproperty tax lien generally arises only after filing of a notice in the county records.

20. A postjudgment remedy that permits the sheriff to seize and sell nonexempt property held by the debtor is

A. A writ of execution.

B. Attachment.

C. Garnishment.

D. Sequestration.

Answer (A) is correct. *(Publisher, adapted)*

REQUIRED: The postjudgment remedy that allows the seizure and sale of property held by the debtor.

DISCUSSION: The writ of execution is a remedy used for collection of judgments. It is issued by the clerk of the court and orders the sheriff to seize and sell any nonexempt property owned by the judgment debtor. The property may be realty or personalty. The debtor has the right to redeem the seized property prior to sale by satisfying the judgment. The judgment debtor's homestead and certain personal effects are examples of exempt property.

Answer (B) is incorrect. Attachment is a prejudgment remedy. Answer (C) is incorrect. Garnishment does not authorize seizure and sale of property held by the debtor. Garnishment is aimed at collecting a judgment from a third party who holds property of, or is indebted to, the judgment debtor. A writ of garnishment may be issued before or after judgment. If issued prejudgment, it orders the garnishee not to pay the defendant until a judgment has been rendered. Answer (D) is incorrect. Sequestration is a prejudgment remedy.

21. A homestead exemption ordinarily could exempt a debtor's equity in certain property from postjudgment collection by a creditor. To which of the following creditors will this exemption apply?

	Valid Home Mortgage Lien	Valid IRS Tax Lien
A.	Yes	Yes
B.	Yes	No
C.	No	Yes
D.	No	No

Answer (D) is correct. *(CPA, adapted)*

REQUIRED: The creditors that are affected by a homestead exemption.

DISCUSSION: State homestead exemption acts ordinarily exempt a debtor's equity in his/her home from postjudgment collections by a creditor. However, these acts generally do not apply to a holder of a valid mortgage against the home or a valid IRS tax lien.

22. Professor Tortmore teaches torts at the University of Nirvana. Ace Trustmenow of Trustmenow's Fine Automobiles sold Professor Tortmore a previously owned sedan. Ace financed the sale. Ace obtained a judgment against Tortmore after Tortmore defaulted on the last $500 installment. Tortmore failed to pay the judgment. Ace brought an action against Tortmore and the University of Nirvana seeking to collect the $500 from wages owed to Tortmore. Which remedy is the plaintiff most likely seeking?

A. A writ of execution.

B. Replevin.

C. Attachment.

D. Garnishment.

Answer (D) is correct. *(Publisher, adapted)*

REQUIRED: The action seeking collection of a debt from property of the debtor held by a third party.

DISCUSSION: After judgment, garnishment proceedings may be instituted to seize specific property of a judgment debtor that is held by a third party. Federal law limits the amount of wages that may be garnished. Any obligation owed to a debtor may be garnished, including wages owed by employers and bank accounts.

Answer (A) is incorrect. A writ of execution is a postjudgment collection remedy that orders the sheriff to seize and sell any of the debtor's property within the court's geographic jurisdiction. Answer (B) is incorrect. Replevin is a prejudgment remedy used to secure satisfaction of pending judgments. Answer (C) is incorrect. Attachment is a prejudgment remedy used to secure satisfaction of pending judgments.

STUDY UNIT TWENTY-SEVEN
LANDLORD AND TENANT

Rental of real property is based on a **lease** (rental agreement). The lessor-lessee (landlord-tenant) relationship is formed by the lease. A person who owns real property (the **lessor or landlord**) conveys the use and possession of (but not title to) the property to another (the **lessee or tenant**) for consideration called **rent**. By a lease, a tenant acquires an **estate in land**. This interest in real property is a **leasehold**. The lessor retains title to the property during the term of the lease and possesses a **reversionary interest** that is assignable (e.g., upon sale of an apartment building) and inheritable. The right of possession reverts upon termination of the lease. **Sale of the leased property** does not, of itself, affect the lease. But if it is purchased by the lessee, the lease is merged into the fee simple interest and is terminated. The lease also is a **contract**. The elements of offer, acceptance, consideration, capacity to contract, and lawful purpose must exist.

A lessor-lessee relationship can result from one of the following **four types of leaseholds**: tenancy for years, periodic tenancy, tenancy at will, and tenancy at sufferance. The **tenancy for years** (a term of years or a tenancy for a term) is an estate with the beginning and ending dates fixed in advance. The estate lasts for a fixed period. Its duration may be measured in days, weeks, months, or years. A tenancy for years terminates automatically without either party giving notice because the parties agreed when the tenancy would end. Death of a landlord or tenant does not terminate the tenancy. The rights and duties flow to the heirs or beneficiaries. The **periodic tenancy** (a tenancy from period to period) is a tenancy for successive periods of equal duration, e.g., year to year or month to month. Although the beginning date and duration of the periods are known, the lease does not specify how long the leasehold will last. The parties may **expressly contract** for periodic tenancy, or one may be implied from provision for periodic rental payments. For example, if the parties agree to weekly payment of rent, a periodic tenancy for successive periods of 1 week will be implied. In some states, a **holdover** by a tenant after the expiration of a tenancy for years with the landlord's approval creates a periodic tenancy. In other states, a holdover creates a tenancy at will. A periodic tenancy does **not automatically terminate** at the end of any period but renews for the next successive period, e.g., a week, month, or year. **Notice** required by an agreement or a statute must be given by either the landlord or the tenant to terminate a periodic tenancy. The **tenancy at will** exists for an indefinite period. It is terminable at the will of either landlord or tenant. A tenancy at will can arise from either of the following: (1) an **express agreement** between landlord and tenant (that either may terminate at will) or (2) the landlord's **permission** to the tenant to possess the premises without agreement on a specific period (single or renewable) of occupancy. A tenancy at will terminates by operation of law upon the (1) death of either party, (2) the tenant's commitment of waste or attempt to assign his/her interest, (3) the lessor's transfer of his/her interest, or (4) the lessor's grant of a term lease to a third party. A **tenancy at sufferance** arises when a tenant in lawful possession of property under one of the three leasehold estates remains in possession after expiration of the lease term without consent of the landlord (the tenant holds over). It results from unlawful possession by the tenant, not from agreement. **Eviction** ordinarily should be by a law enforcement official after **notice of termination**.

Under the **statute of frauds**, a lease for longer than 1 year must be in writing.

The foremost of the **lessor's rights** is **to collect rent**. Absent a specific agreement providing for payment of rent, a **reasonable amount** of rent is payable at the end of the term. In many states, the lessor has a **lien on personal property** of the tenant that is physically located on the premises. The landlord is entitled to hold personal property until the rent is paid. Otherwise, the property may be sold according to a court order. If a tenant vacates the premises early and refuses to pay any further rent, in many states the lessor has the burden of proof to show that (s)he attempted to mitigate damages. Thus, the lessor (1) must seek a new tenant to **mitigate damages** or the tenant's liability is reduced, or (2) may treat the tenant's actions as a **surrender of the premises** and reenter and take possession, terminating the tenancy. Also, security deposits may be kept only to the extent necessary to cover the actual loss it was intended to secure. The lessor's **right to inspect** the premises must be exercised in a reasonable manner so that the tenant's right to quiet enjoyment is not violated. Furthermore, the lessor may **transfer his/her interest** without terminating the leasehold and has a **right of possession** after lease termination.

The essence of the landlord-tenant relationship is that the tenant enjoys **exclusive possession** against all the world as though (s)he were the actual (title) owner. Thus, the lessor's duties include the **duty to deliver possession** of the premises. The majority rule requires the lessor in every lease to deliver actual possession to the tenant unless the lease has a contrary provision. Under the **covenant of quiet enjoyment**, the landlord may not interfere with the tenant's right to physical possession, use, and enjoyment of the premises. The tenant may be **constructively evicted** when (1) the landlord fails to fulfill a promise in the lease, (2) the result of that failure substantially interferes with the tenant's enjoyment of the premises, and (3) the tenant actually moves out.

EXAMPLE: Bill Landlord promised to make repairs. A tornado damaged the roof. When it rained, the den flooded. Bill refused to repair the damage, and the tenant moved out. A flooded den would be viewed as constructive eviction because it substantially interferes with the tenant's enjoyment of the premises. Bill breached the covenant of quiet enjoyment.

Most courts have implied a **warranty of habitability** in a lease of residential property. Landlords have an affirmative duty to furnish habitable premises during the period of the lease. The tenant's covenant to pay rent is dependent on the implied warranty of habitability. To make a claim for breach of this warranty, the tenant must (1) give notice to the lessor and (2) allow a reasonable time to make repairs. If a **landlord fails to correct the breach** of the implied warranty of habitability, a tenant can (1) vacate the premises, (2) rescind the lease, (3) offset repair costs against rent due, and (4) seek monetary damages. As a general rule, a landlord makes **no warranty that the premises are safe** for the use intended by the tenant. However, a landlord must give **notice of latent defects** (defects that are concealed, not readily apparent) that exist at the commencement of the lease. Notice is required if the landlord knew or should have known of such dangerous conditions. Moreover, certain duties imposed under **housing codes and local ordinances** may not be delegated to tenants. In some jurisdictions, a violation of a code or ordinance may be a breach of the warranty of habitability. Thus, without regard to the lease agreement, a lessor may be held liable for injury or loss caused by failure to comply with the code or ordinance. A lessor also may be liable for negligence for a **crime** that is reasonably foreseeable from a lessor's breach of duty. An example is a theft after the tenant notifies the landlord that a dead bolt lock is broken. Lessors have been held liable for failure to warn of or protect against crime after the lessor knew of repeated criminal acts against tenants and guests.

Tenant's rights generally include **exclusive possession and control** of the premises. The lessor has no right to go upon the premises except to collect rent and inspect for damage and must do so at a reasonable time after reasonable notice. A tenant has the **right to quiet enjoyment**. The tenant generally has the right to use the premises as if (s)he owns them. The key concept is **reasonable use**. The tenant may have a **right to repair** of the premises. In addition, tenants may be provided statutory protection against **retaliatory eviction**, i.e., for exercising rights such as a right to repair. A tenant generally has the **right to assign or sublease** the premises without the consent of the landlord. Covenants against subleasing or assignment are strictly construed against the lessor. The right may be restricted by the lease agreement. In many commercial leases, the tenant has the **right to remove trade fixtures** (s)he installed.

The **tenant's duties**, absent an express lease provision, include a statutory or contractual **duty to pay** a reasonable amount of rent on the last day of the lease term. Unless the landlord has a duty to repair, the tenant has a **duty to make ordinary repairs** to maintain the property in the same condition as at the inception of the lease. This duty does not include repairs for ordinary wear and tear or structural damage.

EXAMPLE: A tenant is not obligated to replace a leaking roof or a worn-out heating or air-conditioning system. However, a tenant is obligated to make minor repairs, such as replacing a broken window.

The tenant also has a duty not to commit **affirmative waste**. Failure to make minor repairs may result in affirmative waste. A tenant is responsible to use the property only for **legal purposes**. If the tenant has a duty to repair, (s)he may be liable for injuries suffered as a result of negligent failure to repair. A tenant, as occupier of the premises, may be liable in tort to third parties for dangerous conditions or activities on the leased property.

An **assignment** of a lease is the lessee's transfer of his/her interest in the leased premises for the **entire unexpired term** of the original lease. The assignee stands in the shoes of the original tenant (assignor) and is in privity of estate with the lessor. Unless prohibited by the terms of the lease, a tenant may assign the lease **without the consent** of the landlord. The assignee (new tenant) is **primarily liable** to the lessor for rent. The assignor remains **secondarily liable** to the lessor absent a novation or release. **Subleases** involve a **partial transfer** of the original tenant's rights under the lease. Unless prohibited by the terms of the lease, a lessee may sublet the rented premises **without the consent** of the lessor. A sublease is an agreement by which the tenant (sublessor) transfers part of his/her rights and interest in the leasehold to a sublessee. Unlike an assignor, the sublessor retains an interest in the leasehold. (S)he remains both in **privity of estate** and in **privity of contract** with the lessor. Thus, the sublessor remains **primarily liable** to the lessor. The sublessee is not liable to the lessor, but to the sublessor, for rent owing during the term of the sublease. A lease term that prohibits assignment alone does not operate to prohibit subleasing and vice versa.

QUESTIONS

27.1 Landlord and Tenant Concepts

1. Which of the following is false statement about a lease and its terms?

A. The lessee gives consideration in the form of rent.

B. The lease transfers exclusive possession to the lessee, and the lessor retains a reversionary interest.

C. The lease often contains an exculpatory clause relieving the lessor of tort liability.

D. The lease is real property.

Answer (D) is correct. *(Publisher, adapted)*

REQUIRED: The false statement about a lease.

DISCUSSION: The leasehold of a tenant is an interest in real property, but the lease itself is a bundle of mutual contract rights and duties. In that respect, the lease is personal property. Accordingly, if a lessee dies, his/her interest will pass under the will to the recipients of the personal property.

Answer (A) is incorrect. The lessee gives consideration in the form of rent. A lease is a type of contract for an interest in real property. The lessor gives the lessee the right to the use of land for a period of time in exchange for rent. Answer (B) is incorrect. The lease transfers exclusive possession to the lessee, and the lessor retains a reversionary interest. Although the lease need not be for a specified time, the lessor always retains a reversionary interest in the land. Answer (C) is incorrect. The lease often contains an exculpatory clause relieving the lessor of tort liability. However, courts do not favor exculpatory clauses. Some states have prohibited their use in leases because they are usually imposed when the parties lack equal bargaining power.

2. To be enforceable, a residential real estate lease must

A. Require the tenant to obtain liability insurance.

B. Entitle the tenant to exclusive possession of the leased property.

C. Specify a due date for rent.

D. Be in writing.

Answer (B) is correct. *(CPA, adapted)*

REQUIRED: The requirement for a residential lease to be enforceable.

DISCUSSION: A lease is a contract and conveys rights to use real property. A tenant also has an estate in land (through the lease) characterized by the right to possession. Thus, a lease can be described as a grant of an exclusive possessory right of finite duration.

Answer (A) is incorrect. Such a condition or covenant is not essential to a lease. Answer (C) is incorrect. Absent an express lease provision, the tenant generally has a duty to pay a reasonable amount of rent on the last day of the lease term. Answer (D) is incorrect. Generally, a lease for less than 1 year need not be in writing.

3. Which of the following is a true statement about applying the statute of frauds to leaseholds?

A. It does not apply.

B. If the lease contract cannot be performed within a specified period, it applies.

C. The majority of states apply it to all leases.

D. Partial performance has no effect on its application.

Answer (B) is correct. *(Publisher, adapted)*

REQUIRED: The true statement about applying the statute of frauds to leases.

DISCUSSION: Contracts that cannot be performed within the statutory time period (usually 1 year) are required to be in writing, be signed by the party to be bound, and state essential terms, such as an adequate description of the property to be leased.

Answer (A) is incorrect. If the lease is for the statutory period (e.g., 1 year), it must be in writing. Answer (C) is incorrect. Only in the minority of states that treat a lease as the sale of an interest in land must all leases be written. Answer (D) is incorrect. Partial performance (possession, payment of rent, improvement of the property) may permit a lessee to enforce an oral lease although the lease is required to be in writing.

4. A periodic tenancy is a lease

A. For a period of 1 year with a right to renew for another year.

B. For an indefinite period of time under which the rent is paid from period-to-period and the lease may be terminated upon notice after a notice period measured by the rent payment period.

C. For a 1-week period that is to recur each year.

D. Created when a tenant occupies the premises without permission.

Answer (B) is correct. *(Publisher, adapted)*

REQUIRED: The nature of a periodic tenancy.

DISCUSSION: A periodic tenancy continues from period to period until terminated. The period may be any period, e.g., a week, a month, or a year. If not expressly provided, it may be implied by the regular payment of rent and the requirement of a period's notice for termination. The measure of the notice period is subject to a statutory maximum.

Answer (A) is incorrect. A lease for 1 year is called a tenancy for years despite a right to renew. Answer (C) is incorrect. A lease for 1 week is also a tenancy for years or a definite time, even if only for a week or recurring each year. Answer (D) is incorrect. The occupation of premises without permission is a tenancy at sufferance.

5. Which of the following statements is true concerning the termination or duration of a periodic tenancy?

A. The tenancy is terminated by advance notice usually equivalent to one period of the tenancy.

B. The tenancy must last a minimum of 6 months.

C. A tenancy at sufferance is formed when the landlord allows the tenant to remain after terminating a periodic tenancy.

D. A tenant who remains after termination of a periodic tenancy without permission of the landlord is a tenant at will.

Answer (A) is correct. *(Publisher, adapted)*

REQUIRED: The true statement about termination of a periodic tenancy.

DISCUSSION: A periodic tenancy is terminated by advance notice that is usually equivalent to one period of the tenancy. If the tenancy is from month to month, the notice must be given 1 month prior to termination. If it is an annual tenancy, the notice must be given 1 year prior to termination. In some states, this advance notice has been shortened by statute.

Answer (B) is incorrect. A periodic tenancy has no minimum duration. Answer (C) is incorrect. A tenancy at will is formed (initially) if the landlord consents to the tenant's remaining after termination of a lease. Answer (D) is incorrect. A tenancy at sufferance exists when the tenant remains without permission. If the landlord subsequently recognizes the tenant as a tenant, e.g., accepts rent, then a periodic tenancy is established.

6. Termination of the landlord-tenant relationship may occur in many ways, some rightfully and some upon breach by one of the parties. Which of the following causes of termination must have been the result of a breach?

A. Forfeiture.

B. Destruction of the premises.

C. Expiration of the lease term.

D. Surrender.

Answer (A) is correct. *(Publisher, adapted)*

REQUIRED: The cause of termination that must have been the result of a breach.

DISCUSSION: A forfeiture is the surrendering of one's rights to the premises as a result of a breach of the lease. Frequently, the lease will require the tenant to forfeit the lease at the election of the landlord upon breach by the tenant.

Answer (B) is incorrect. Destruction of the premises may occur through no one's fault. If it occurs due to the negligence or wrongful act of the tenant, then there may have been a breach. Answer (C) is incorrect. Expiration of the lease term is a common termination of the landlord/tenant relationship without a breach. Answer (D) is incorrect. A surrender occurs when the tenant conveys his/her leasehold interest back to the landlord at any time. There may be a surrender with or without a breach of the lease.

7. Which of the following is a true statement about the kinds of leasehold estates?

A. Most states allow self-help dispossession by the lessor if the estate is at sufferance.

B. An estate at will terminates on the death of the lessor but not upon sale of the premises.

C. An estate from period to period does not terminate on the death of a party or sale of the premises, and notice of termination is not required.

D. An estate for years does not terminate on the death of a party or sale of the premises, and notice of termination is not required.

Answer (D) is correct. *(Publisher, adapted)*

REQUIRED: The true statement about the kinds of leasehold estates.

DISCUSSION: An estate for years is a lease for any definite time (1 week, 90 days, 10 years, etc.) with a definite beginning date and termination date. It arises only by agreement of the parties and requires no notice of termination. These leasehold estates may be inherited or pass by will and are not affected by the landlord's death or sale of his/her interest.

Answer (A) is incorrect. Most states require notice of termination. Eviction must usually be made by a law enforcement official. An estate at sufferance arises when a lessee holds over without consent. Answer (B) is incorrect. An estate at will is created when a lessee occupies the premises with consent. The landlord's death or sale of his/her interest terminates the estate. Answer (C) is incorrect. A periodic estate is for an indefinite time, although the other terms of the lease have been negotiated. The duration of the estate is for the payment period. It is automatically reserved for another period unless one party gives notice of termination.

27.2 Landlord's Rights and Duties

8. Rent is the consideration to be paid by a tenant to a landlord for the use and enjoyment of the premises. The tenant and the landlord have certain rights and obligations with regard to the rent. Which is a true statement of these rights and obligations in the absence of a statute?

A. Prepaid rent cannot be recovered if the tenancy is terminated prior to the end of a rent period.

B. The landlord has the right to terminate the lease if the tenant does not pay the rent.

C. The tenant may withhold the rent if the landlord does not perform his/her obligations.

D. If a lease is assigned, the landlord is under no obligation to accept rent from the assignee.

Answer (A) is correct. *(Publisher, adapted)*

REQUIRED: The true statement of the rights and obligations of the landlord and tenant.

DISCUSSION: Under common law, prepaid rent was not prorated on a daily or other basis less than the period of the lease. A lessee thus could not recover a portion of a rent prepayment.

Answer (B) is incorrect. Under common law, the landlord's obligation to provide the premises and the tenant's obligation to pay rent were separate. Breach by one party did not release the other from his/her obligation. Today, most statutes allow the landlord to terminate the lease if rent is not paid. Answer (C) is incorrect. Under common law, breach by one party did not release the other from his/her obligation. Thus, the tenant could not withhold rent. Answer (D) is incorrect. Unless the assignment is wrongful, the landlord must accept rent from the assignee.

9. Certain rights and duties of the landlord and tenant are implied in most leases. Which of the following is an implied right or duty at common law?

A. The tenant's right to possession will be enforced by the landlord.

B. The premises will be reasonably fit for the use for which they are rented.

C. The landlord will make all the necessary repairs to the premises.

D. The tenant must pay rent even if the landlord does not make repairs.

Answer (D) is correct. *(Publisher, adapted)*

REQUIRED: The right or duty implied in a lease at common law.

DISCUSSION: At common law, the obligations of a landlord to provide repairs and maintain the premises are separate from the obligation of the tenant to pay rent. Therefore, if repairs are not made by the landlord, a tenant who withholds rent would be in violation of the lease. The common law rights and duties, however, are often modified by statute.

Answer (A) is incorrect. A tenant does have the right to possession, but the landlord generally is not required to enforce it. Answer (B) is incorrect. The landlord does not warrant the condition of the premises. Answer (C) is incorrect. The tenant has traditionally been obligated to make all the necessary repairs to the premises.

10. Joe Davis, a tenant in an apartment, invited Sarah Bacon over as a guest. In the living room, Sarah stepped on a loose board that sprang up and hit her in the face. Davis was frightened and ran outside to seek help. On the way, Davis stepped in an old hole in the staircase and fell down the stairs, breaking his arm.

A. The landlord is liable to Sarah for the injury caused by the loose board.

B. The landlord is not liable to Davis for the injuries caused by the hole in the stairwell since Davis knew it was there from prior experience.

C. If the landlord had undertaken to repair the loose board in the living room, Sarah could recover from him.

D. If Sarah recovers from Davis, the landlord is liable to Davis.

Answer (C) is correct. *(Publisher, adapted)*

REQUIRED: The liability of a landlord for injuries to a tenant and a guest.

DISCUSSION: In the absence of an agreement otherwise or notice of a defect, a landlord is not responsible for making repairs to the interior of a residential apartment. But when a landlord does undertake to make a repair, (s)he is held liable for its sufficiency. Thus, Sarah could recover from the landlord for a faulty repair.

Answer (A) is incorrect. The landlord is generally not liable for making repairs inside a residential apartment. Answer (B) is incorrect. The landlord is responsible for making repairs in the common areas of an apartment building and would be liable to Davis for the hole in the stairwell regardless of Davis's prior knowledge. Answer (D) is incorrect. The tenant is usually responsible for repairs within the apartment, but the landlord is liable for hidden defects of which (s)he has knowledge that are undiscoverable by the tenant at the time the lease is made.

11. The Uniform Residential Landlord and Tenant Act (URLTA) has been enacted in many states. It substantially clarifies, modifies, and adds to the common law regarding residential leases. Which of the following is a true statement about the act's provisions?

A. In some instances, the lessee may make repairs and deduct their costs from the rent.

B. The lessor may generally enter the premises without the lessee's permission.

C. The lessee may use the premises for both residential and commercial purposes.

D. The lessor may hold the lessee's personal property until overdue rent is paid.

Answer (A) is correct. *(Publisher, adapted)*

REQUIRED: The true statement about the URLTA.

DISCUSSION: At common law, the landlord had no duty to repair, but the URLTA and similar statutes place the duty on the lessor to repair. If the lessor fails to do so, the tenant may make minor repairs (not more than the greater of $100 or half the periodic rent) and deduct the cost from the rent if (s)he gives the lessor 2 weeks' notice. An itemized expense statement must also be provided when the rent is paid.

Answer (B) is incorrect. Except in an emergency, the lessor has no right of entry without consent, but the lessee also may not unreasonably withhold consent when the lessor wishes to enter to effect repairs and inspect. Answer (C) is incorrect. The URLTA does not apply to a commercial lease. Answer (D) is incorrect. The URLTA abolishes this common law action. However, if a lessee holds over in bad faith, the lessor may sue for possession and for the greater of 3 months' rent or triple the lessor's damages.

12. In the majority of states, a landlord does not have a right to

A. Receive rent without apportionment and to recover possession of the premises.

B. Inspect and to sue for waste.

C. Have the tenant make repairs and insure the premises.

D. Sell the reversionary interest.

Answer (C) is correct. *(Publisher, adapted)*

REQUIRED: The item not stating a landlord's right in the majority of states.

DISCUSSION: Under the common law, the tenant has the duty to repair the premises, but the URLTA places the burden of repair on the landlord. Although the URLTA has been adopted in fewer than half of the states, many other states have statutes modernizing residential landlord-tenant law. Neither party is obligated to obtain insurance.

Answer (A) is incorrect. Collection of rent is the landlord's most basic right. Another right is the return of possession of the premises. Also, rent is not apportioned (prorated). A tenant who leaves prior to the end of the rental period cannot receive a partial refund unless (s)he was wrongfully evicted. Answer (B) is incorrect. The landlord may inspect pursuant to the lease. However, the URLTA provides that (s)he may not enter without the tenant's consent. Consent may not be unreasonably withheld. Answer (D) is incorrect. The landlord may sell, but the new owner will ordinarily be bound by existing leases.

13. Which of the following statements about the tort liability of a landlord is true?

A. The tenants as a group are liable for maintenance of common areas.

B. A landlord owes no duty to the tenant's guests.

C. A landlord generally is held to make an implied warranty that the premises are safe and suitable for the tenant's intended commercial use.

D. A landlord is liable for a third party's assault of a tenant if it is due to an inoperative security system, the existence of which was used to induce the tenant to rent.

Answer (D) is correct. *(Publisher, adapted)*

REQUIRED: The true statement about a landlord's tort liability.

DISCUSSION: Although landlords do not always have a duty to repair, it certainly exists if the inoperative item was promised to the tenant as an inducement to rent. The landlord can be held liable for injuries resulting when this duty is breached.

Answer (A) is incorrect. The landlord has control of, and should properly maintain, the common areas. Answer (B) is incorrect. The landlord owes the same duty to a guest that (s)he owes to the tenant. For example, (s)he must give notice of latent defects of which (s)he knows or should know. Moreover, if a landlord has a duty to repair or voluntarily undertakes to repair, (s)he has a duty to act nonnegligently. Answer (C) is incorrect. Although an implied warranty of habitability is found by many courts when the premises are residential, the warranty does not extend to commercial property (except as public health and safety codes may require).

14. Promises in a lease

A. Must be express, not implied.

B. Are construed as dependent.

C. Are often deemed to include an implied warranty of habitability.

D. Ordinarily are treated as conditions. Thus, breach by the lessee does not give the lessor right of eviction but only an action for damages.

Answer (C) is correct. *(Publisher, adapted)*

REQUIRED: The true statement about the promises in a lease.

DISCUSSION: In many states, courts have found a warranty of habitability to be implied in a residential lease. Whether a defect is a breach of the warranty depends on the circumstances. Factors considered are the existence of violations of building or housing codes and sanitary regulations, the effect on safety and sanitation, the fault of the tenant, and whether the defect is in a vital part of the premises. A breach may be grounds for rent reductions or termination of the lease.

Answer (A) is incorrect. Many leases contain only the most basic terms, so the law will find implied promises, for example, to make repairs, pay utilities, pay property taxes, etc. Answer (B) is incorrect. Under the common law, promises are generally independent. For example, the lessor's breach of a promise to repair does not justify the lessee's nonpayment of rent. The promise to pay rent is not dependent on the lessor's performance. Promises may be covenants or conditions. Answer (D) is incorrect. Promises may be covenants or conditions. Thus, if a lessee breaches a condition, the lessor may evict the tenant.

15. Which of the following is a true statement about the landlord's right to evict a tenant?

A. Most jurisdictions statutorily permit forcible entry to evict a wrongfully holding over tenant.

B. Self-help repossession is permitted in most states but only pursuant to a specific term in the lease.

C. In most states, the remedy for unlawful detainer is a suit pursuant to a summary procedure after proper notice has been given.

D. If a tenant's lease has been lawfully terminated, the landlord may sue to evict but may not resort to constructive eviction.

Answer (C) is correct. *(Publisher, adapted)*

REQUIRED: The true statement about eviction.

DISCUSSION: A tenant who wrongfully remains on the premises may be evicted by court action. Most states have a special summary procedure for the swift eviction of such a tenant. The defendant must be given adequate notice, and the plaintiff must prove a right to possession. If (s)he still remains on the premises, the tenant and his/her property will be forcibly removed by a law enforcement agent.

Answer (A) is incorrect. Most states do not allow forcible entry by the landlord (self-help) to evict a tenant. Answer (B) is incorrect. Most states do not allow forcible entry by the landlord (self-help) to evict a tenant. Answer (D) is incorrect. Constructive eviction, e.g., turning off utilities, is a permissible remedy.

16. Ralph owned 73 apartments that he rented on an annual basis. Ralph advertised one of the available apartments in the local paper. Tom saw the ad, contacted Ralph, and arranged to see the apartment. Upon meeting Tom, Ralph quickly explained that the apartment was unavailable. In reality, the apartment was available, but Ralph did not like Tom's race. Ralph's action is commonly known as

A. Steering.

B. Blockbusting.

C. Panic selling.

D. Gerrymandering.

Answer (A) is correct. *(Publisher, adapted)*

REQUIRED: The term for falsely representing that a dwelling is unavailable because of the potential occupant's race.

DISCUSSION: Falsely representing that a dwelling is unavailable because of race, color, national origin, religion, or sex is illegal under the Civil Rights Act of 1968. This practice is known as steering.

Answer (B) is incorrect. Blockbusting is a name for the practice of enticing a person to sell property because people of a certain race, sex, color, religion, or national origin are moving into the neighborhood. Answer (C) is incorrect. Panic selling is a name for the practice of enticing a person to sell property because people of a certain race, sex, color, religion, or national origin are moving into the neighborhood. Answer (D) is incorrect. Gerrymandering is the practice of drawing election or school district lines to benefit one group of people to the detriment of another.

27.3 Tenant's Rights and Duties

17. The rights of a tenant arising from the common law include

A. The landlord's covenant of quiet enjoyment.

B. Exclusive possession and control subject to a common law right of inspection.

C. Return of the security deposit plus interest but minus wear and tear.

D. The power to remove all except trade fixtures.

Answer (A) is correct. *(Publisher, adapted)*

REQUIRED: The common law right held by a tenant.

DISCUSSION: Every landlord impliedly promises that the tenant will have quiet enjoyment of the premises. The promise is breached when another party has paramount title to the premises such that the tenant will be dispossessed or at least prevented from making the intended use of the premises. Actual or constructive eviction is also a breach.

Answer (B) is incorrect. Under the common law, the landlord may enter only to collect rent, but leases commonly reserve a right to inspect for the lessor. Answer (C) is incorrect. A statute, not the common law, usually requires landlords to pay interest, to itemize charges against a deposit, to return deposits promptly, and not to charge for normal wear and tear. Answer (D) is incorrect. Tenants may remove trade fixtures but generally not other fixtures.

Questions 18 and 19 are based on the following information. Mini, Inc., has a 5-year lease with Rein Realtors. The lease was signed by both parties and immediately recorded. The leased building was to be used by Mini in connection with its business operations. To make it suitable for that purpose, Mini attached a piece of equipment to the wall of the building.

18. Which of the following statements is true regarding Mini's rights and liabilities?

A. Mini is prohibited from assigning the lease if it is silent in this regard.

B. Mini has a possessory interest in the building.

C. Mini is strictly liable for all injuries sustained by any person in the building during the term of the lease.

D. Mini's rights under the lease are automatically terminated by Rein's sale of the building to a third party.

Answer (B) is correct. *(CPA, adapted)*

REQUIRED: The true statement about a lessee's rights and duties.

DISCUSSION: Mini has a leasehold estate. It has a right to exclusive possession and control of the premises. But Mini must return possession to the owner of the freehold estate at the end of the lease term.

Answer (A) is incorrect. Barring a lease term specifically prohibiting such a transfer, the lessee may assign the lease. Answer (C) is incorrect. Mini will have a varying duty of care depending on the status of injured person (invitee, licensee, trespasser) but will not be strictly liable without fault. Answer (D) is incorrect. A lessor may transfer its reversionary interest subject to the rights of the lessee.

19. Which of the following is most important in determining whether the equipment became a fixture?

A. Whether the equipment can be removed without material damage to the building.

B. Whether the attachment is customary for the type of building.

C. The fair value of the equipment at the time the lease expires.

D. The fact that the equipment was subject to depreciation.

Answer (A) is correct. *(CPA, adapted)*

REQUIRED: The most important consideration in determining whether equipment is a fixture.

DISCUSSION: The intent of the parties controls. However, other factors may be considered to determine that intent in the absence of an explicit statement. The most important are the mode of annexation, the amount of damage to the realty and to the item if it is removed, and the degree to which the item is specifically adapted to the realty. Moreover, trade fixtures are presumed to belong to the lessee.

Answer (B) is incorrect. Whether the attachment is customary for the type of building is relatively insignificant. Answer (C) is incorrect. The fair value of the equipment at the time the lease expires is relatively insignificant. Answer (D) is incorrect. Whether the equipment was subject to depreciation is relatively insignificant.

20. Bessie is a tenant in an apartment building owned by Mel. She pays rent of $225 in advance each month and her lease contains no termination date. Bessie organized a tenants' association, which made demands concerning repairs. Mel notified Bessie that her rent for subsequent months would be $250. Bessie protested that all other tenants paid rent of $225 per month. Thereupon, Mel gave notice that the tenancy was being terminated. Bessie contests Mel's right to terminate. If Bessie succeeds, it will be because

A. This type of leasehold generally cannot be terminated by notice.

B. The doctrine prohibiting retaliatory eviction is part of the law of the jurisdiction.

C. The $250 rent demanded violates the agreement implied by the rate charged to other tenants.

D. The law implies a term of 1 year in the absence of any express agreement.

Answer (B) is correct. *(Publisher, adapted)*

REQUIRED: The true statement about a landlord's actions after a tenant asserted rights to repairs.

DISCUSSION: Under the URLTA, retaliation is forbidden. It consists of eviction, a decrease in services, or raising rent. The action is presumed to be illegal if it occurs within a year after a conflict between the lessor and the lessee. Activity in a tenants' union, complaints about maintenance, and reporting violations of building and housing codes to the authorities are defined as conflicts.

Answer (A) is incorrect. A month-to-month periodic tenancy may be terminated by giving appropriate notice. Answer (C) is incorrect. No rental rate is implied by the rate that other tenants pay. Answer (D) is incorrect. A periodic tenancy results if a tenancy is agreed to but no term is stated.

21. A tenant renting an apartment under a 3-year written lease that does not contain any specific restrictions may be evicted for

A. Counterfeiting money in the apartment.

B. Keeping a dog in the apartment.

C. Failing to maintain a liability insurance policy on the apartment.

D. Making structural repairs to the apartment.

Answer (A) is correct. *(CPA, adapted)*

REQUIRED: The circumstances under which the tenant may be evicted.

DISCUSSION: A tenant's basic responsibilities are to pay rent, avoid waste, return possession of the premises, perform the obligations agreed to in the lease, and not make illegal use of the property. A use of the property that constituted a nuisance (for example, raising hogs in a residential area) or a criminal activity (operating an illegal gambling establishment) would breach the obligation to make lawful use of the premises.

Answer (B) is incorrect. Eviction should not result unless keeping the dog breached an expressed dependent covenant or condition, resulted in waste, or constituted a nuisance. Answer (C) is incorrect. Eviction should not result unless maintaining the insurance was an express dependent covenant or a condition of the lease. Answer (D) is incorrect. A tenant who does not thereby cause waste to the premises may generally make structural repairs. In fact, under common law, the landlord had no duty to repair and maintain the premises.

27.4 Assignments and Subleases

Questions 22 through 24 are based on the following information. Landlord and Tenant signed a written lease of a store for a period of 5 years at $60,000, payable $1,000 monthly. One year later, Landlord sold the store to Owner subject to the lease. Tenant, unaware of Landlord's conveyance to Owner, continued paying the monthly rent payment to Landlord until she assigned the lease to Assignee without Owner's knowledge. Assignee has not made any payments but is occupying the premises.

22. In the absence of an applicable statute, the assignment of the lease by Tenant to Assignee was

A. Effective, whether or not it was in writing.

B. Effective, because the lease did not prohibit an assignment.

C. Not effective, because the lease contained no clause permitting assignment.

D. Not effective, because Tenant failed to give notice thereof to Owner.

Answer (B) is correct. *(Publisher, adapted)*

REQUIRED: The effectiveness of the assignment by Tenant to Assignee and the reason it is effective.

DISCUSSION: Leases are assignable unless expressly agreed otherwise. Prohibitions against assignment are narrowly construed against the lessor.

Answer (A) is incorrect. Both the original lease and its assignment exceed a year and are required to be in writing under the statute of frauds. Answer (C) is incorrect. Assignment is permitted unless expressly prohibited. Answer (D) is incorrect. Tenant had no duty to give notice to Owner absent an agreement to that effect.

23. If Owner sued Assignee for the rent due after the date of assignment, he would collect

A. Because equity requires that to be done which should be done and Assignee should have paid the rent.

B. If Assignee had notice of the conveyance to Owner.

C. Because they stood in privity of estate.

D. If the assignment were in writing.

Answer (C) is correct. *(Publisher, adapted)*

REQUIRED: The reason a lessor can collect from the assignee after the lessee assigns the lease.

DISCUSSION: An assignee is considered to stand in privity of estate with the landlord and is subject to all the terms of the lease. Privity of estate exists when both have taken their real property interests from a common grantor (or each other). Without privity, Assignee could only be held liable by Tenant.

Answer (A) is incorrect. Assignee has a legal (not equitable) obligation to pay the rent. Answer (B) is incorrect. Assignee is liable for rent without prior notice of the conveyance so long as (s)he did not pay rent to Landlord. Answer (D) is incorrect. A tenant is liable for rent after occupying the premises regardless of whether the assignment was in writing.

24. If Owner sued Tenant for the rent due for the period following the sale to Owner, he would

A. Collect because the conveyance made him the landlord and Tenant cannot dispute his landlord's title.

B. Collect if his conveyance had been recorded because recording is notice to the world.

C. Not collect because the assignment by Tenant was made before Owner commenced suit.

D. Not collect because Tenant did not receive notice of the conveyance.

Answer (D) is correct. *(Publisher, adapted)*

REQUIRED: The outcome of Owner's suit against Tenant for rent due after Owner purchased the leasehold.

DISCUSSION: Owner is an assignee of the lessor's interest in the leasehold and has the right to collect rent. But a debtor who pays the assignor without notice of the assignment will not be liable to the assignee. It was Owner's obligation to notify Tenant.

Answer (A) is incorrect. Tenant had no notice of the assignment (sale). Answer (B) is incorrect. Recording conveyances is deemed constructive notice to subsequent purchasers, not existing tenants. Answer (C) is incorrect. An assignment does not discharge the liability of the assignor.

25. Tell, Inc., leased a building from Lott Corp. Tell paid monthly rent of $500 and was also responsible for paying the building's real estate taxes. On January 1, Vorn Co. and Tell entered into an agreement by which Vorn was entitled to occupy the building for the remainder of the term of Tell's lease in exchange for monthly payments of $600 to Tell. For the year, neither Tell nor Vorn paid the building's real estate taxes, and the taxes are delinquent. Learning this, Lott demanded that either Tell or Vorn pay the delinquent taxes. Both refused, and Lott has commenced an action against them. Lott will most likely prevail against

A. Vorn but not Tell because the lease was assigned to it.

B. Tell and Vorn because they are jointly and severally liable for the delinquent taxes.

C. Tell without Vorn because their January 1 agreement constituted a sublease.

D. Vorn, but only to the extent of $100 for each month that it occupied the building.

Answer (B) is correct. *(CPA, adapted)*

REQUIRED: The obligations of a lessee and its transferee to the original lessor.

DISCUSSION: The legal relationship between an original lessee and a lessor is not altered by an assignment or a sublease. An assignment is a transfer of all of the lessee's rights, whereas a sublease is characterized by a retention of some right(s) by the lessee. If this agreement had constituted a sublease, Tell would remain liable to Lott for any breach of the terms of the original lease. But as sublessee, Vorn would not be in privity of contract or estate with Lott and could not be successfully sued by it for the delinquent taxes. However, the Tell-Vorn agreement apparently conveyed Tell's entire interest. Tell did not have a reversionary interest in possession, even for a few hours, and no mention is made of other rights retained by the lessee. Thus, the agreement is an assignment. Vorn is an assignee who stands in privity of estate with Lott, and both Tell and Vorn will be liable for the full amount of the taxes.

Answer (A) is incorrect. Whether the agreement constituted a sublease or an assignment, Tell remains liable. Answer (C) is incorrect. Vorn is liable as an assignee. Answer (D) is incorrect. Vorn is liable as an assignee for the full amount of the taxes.

STUDY UNIT TWENTY-EIGHT
WILLS, ESTATE ADMINISTRATION, AND TRUSTS

A **will** is a person's plan for the disposition of his/her estate after death. The discussion of wills requires familiarity with certain terms. In modern practice, the use of the word **testator** describes any person who makes a will, without regard to gender. Other terms, such as **executor** and **administrator**, also are used inclusively. A person who dies is a **decedent**. A decedent leaving a valid will is said to die **testate**. A decedent without a valid will is said to die **intestate**. A gift of **personal property** under a will is a **bequest** or **legacy**, and a gift of **real property** is a **devise**.

A **formal will** is one that has been prepared and executed in compliance with state law. Although the right to make a will may exist independently of statute, procedures for drafting, executing, and witnessing the formal document are governed by state statute. The applicable uniform act, the **Uniform Probate Code (UPC)**, has been adopted in many states.

A **holographic will** is one written entirely in the testator's handwriting and signed by the testator but not by attesting witnesses. A holographic will is statutory and must be made in accordance with appropriate state law. Most states allow a handwritten will that is signed by the decedent and witnessed by two attesting witnesses. This kind of handwritten will is technically formal and not a holographic will. **Noncupative wills** are oral wills and are permitted only under limited circumstances. Typically, they must have been recited during the decedent's last illness and are effective to dispose of personal property only. **Soldiers' and sailors' wills** are valid even if most of the formalities of execution are not observed, provided that the soldier is on active duty or the sailor is at sea. But they cannot convey title to real property. A **living will** states that life-sustaining or death-delaying treatment is not to be administered if its burdens outweigh the expected benefits.

Although requirements for a formal will vary from state to state, a person 18 years of age as of the date of execution ordinarily can make a will. For a will to be valid, the decedent must have had **testamentary capacity** at the time of its making. (S)he must have had the ability to understand (1) the nature and extent of his/her property, (2) the persons who are the natural objects of his/her bounty, and (3) in a general way the practical effect of the will as executed. Testamentary capacity is not the same as **contractual capacity**. Most courts presume a decedent had testamentary capacity, and the burden of producing evidence to the contrary is on the party alleging lack of capacity. **Other formal requisites** also must be satisfied to execute a valid formal will. It must be **written and signed** by the testator or by another person at the testator's direction and in his/her presence. In most states, a will is valid as long as the testator signs somewhere on the instrument. In other states, the testator must sign at the end of the will. In addition, the testator must sign or acknowledge a previous signature in the presence of the witnesses. Any mark made with the requisite intent suffices as a signature. Two or three disinterested **attesting witnesses** ordinarily are required, and they must sign in the testator's presence and in the presence of each other. Furthermore, some states require that the testator **publish the will**, i.e., communicate to the witnesses that they are signing a will as opposed to some other legal document.

Authentication of the will is facilitated if it is **self-proving**. Notarization of the signatures on the will itself or an affidavit sworn before a notary public attached to the will can render a will self-proving in some states. The signatures on the will are then presumed valid, and the will may be admitted to probate without testimony by one of the attesting witnesses or other evidence that it was validly executed by the testator(s).

A **codicil** is a testamentary instrument that alters, amends, or modifies a previously executed will. A codicil must be executed with the same formalities as a will. Moreover, in most states, an **extrinsic document** may be incorporated into the will **by reference** so that it is considered a part of the will. To incorporate a document by reference, three requirements must be met: (1) The document must be in existence at the time the will is executed, (2) it must be sufficiently described in the will so that its identification is certain, and (3) satisfactory proof must exist that the document presented for acceptance is the one described. Moreover, the independent significance doctrine allows the court to fill in the gaps of the will. For example, a bequest to "all the members of my bowling team" can be upheld because the act of belonging to the team has significance apart from directing testamentary conveyance of property.

Only property owned by the decedent at death can be disposed of by will. A will cannot dispose of **nonprobate assets**, that is, interests that pass at death other than by will or intestacy. The three primary categories of such property are (1) property passing by contract, such as life insurance proceeds; (2) property passing by right of survivorship, such as that held in a joint tenancy; and (3) property held in trust.

Testamentary dispositions may fail or be modified because of subsequent events. If a beneficiary under a will dies during the testator's lifetime, the gift lapses. A will cannot effect a gift to a dead person. Many states have enacted **anti-lapse statutes** that operate to save the gift if the predeceasing beneficiary was in a specified degree of relationship to the testator and left descendants who survive the testator. Anti-lapse statutes apply unless a contrary intention is expressed in the will. Under the doctrine of **ademption**, when specifically bequeathed property has been lost, destroyed, sold, or given away, it is adeemed (revoked) and the attempted gift fails. **Abatement** is the reduction of a bequest or devise. If the value of the estate is less than the total of debts plus all distributions directed to beneficiaries, all debts are paid and the gifts to beneficiaries are reduced according to state law. An **advancement** is an inter vivos gift by a parent to his/her child intended to represent all or part of the child's share of the parent's estate.

The decedent's family has historically enjoyed a variety of protections against intentional or unintentional disinheritance. The common law right of **dower** entitled a wife to a life estate in an undivided one-third of all lands that her husband owned during marriage. A surviving husband's right of **curtesy** granted him a life estate in all of his wife's lands if children were born of the marriage. Many states have abolished the common law rules of dower and curtesy and statutorily granted protection against disinheritance by providing an **elective share** to both husbands and wives. Typically, the amount of the elective share is 30% of the net estate, which ordinarily includes nonprobate property. If the elective share is claimed, the surviving spouse renounces the will's provisions in favor of the spouse. Generally, a surviving spouse must file notice of the election within a statutorily prescribed period and the election, once made, is irrevocable. A minority of states recognize **community property**, which is all property acquired with the earnings of either spouse during the marriage. Spouses are equal co-owners of such property.

The most common challenges to the validity of the will on grounds other than lack of capacity are based on fraud, mistake, and undue influence. When the execution of a will or the inclusion of a particular gift is the result of **fraud**, the will or the particular gift is void. An innocent misrepresentation does not constitute fraud. A **mistake** relating to the nature of the instrument affects whether the testator had the requisite testamentary intent. A mistake relating to the contents of the instrument is difficult to correct, especially an obvious ambiguity (the uncertainty appears on the face of the will). **Undue influence** such that a will or a term in a will is invalid is actual influence exerted on the testator that overpowered his/her judgment, resulting in a disposition of property that would not otherwise have been made. A presumption of undue influence arises if a person occupies a confidential relationship with the testator, is active in procuring the will, and is a substantial beneficiary under the will.

A will is ambulatory, that is, it is effective at death. Thus, a person who has testamentary capacity may completely or partially **revoke** his/her will at any time prior to death. A will or any part of it may be revoked or altered by a subsequent written will or codicil. In some states, revocation also may occur in a writing declaring such revocation even if it is not executed with the formalities required for a will. The common method of revoking a will is to execute a new will that states: "This is my last will and testament and I hereby revoke all previous wills and codicils thereto." A will or codicil can be revoked by a **physical act** of burning, tearing, canceling, defacing, obliterating, or destroying in any manner with the intent to revoke, but some states do not allow partial revocation by act. The **intention to revoke** must be present at the time of the physical act. Furthermore, dependent relative revocation is a doctrine that allows a court to give effect to a revoked will. It applies when the decedent apparently would not have revoked the will but for a mistaken belief that a subsequent instrument would effectively dispose of the estate. Consequently, the revocation of the first will may be ignored by the court given sufficient proof of the decedent's intent and of the terms of the original will. A valid will also may be partially or wholly revoked by **operation of law** in the event of certain events, such as subsequent marriage, divorce, or birth or adoption of a child or children. Under the UPC, marriage following the execution of a will has no effect on a preexisting will, even though it makes no provision for the new spouse. However, the new spouse in this case will receive, upon the testator's death, the share (s)he would have received if no will had been executed. Furthermore, a divorce following execution of a will revokes all gifts in favor of the former spouse. The balance of the will remains in force.

Every state has a **statute of descent and distribution** for the disposition of a decedent's estate when (s)he dies without leaving a valid will **(intestate)**. After paying the decedent's debts, the estate's administrator distributes the remaining assets in accordance with the statute. **Real property** descends according to the law of the state where the real property is located, and **personal property** is distributed according to the law of the state where the decedent was domiciled. Each statute also specifies the **surviving spouse's share**. Under the UPC, if the decedent is not survived by a parent or **lineal descendants** (children or grandchildren) but only by a spouse, the spouse takes the entire estate. The spouse also takes the entire estate if (1) the decedent's surviving descendants also are descendants of the spouse, and (2) the spouse has no other surviving descendant. If the decedent is not survived by a spouse or lineal descendants, the entire estate may pass to the **decedent's parents** in equal shares. If the decedent leaves no surviving lineal descendants or parents, the estate often goes to the decedent's brothers, sisters, nieces, and nephews. If a decedent is survived by none of the above, the estate may pass to the grandparents and their descendants (uncles, aunts, and cousins). Under the UPC, heirs are limited to kin no more remote than grandparents and their descendants. Within a class of heirs, a will or intestacy statute may provide for property to pass per stirpes or per capita. If the transfer is **per stirpes**, an heir of a given class succeeds only to a share of the interest of a deceased ancestor, i.e., by right of representation. If the transfer is **per capita**, the heirs share equally. In the absence of any heirs, the estate **escheats** (passes) to the state.

The **administration of an estate** involves the collection of the decedent's property, payment of his/her debts and taxes, and distribution of all remaining assets to those persons entitled to receive them. The estate is administered by the **personal representative** of the decedent in accordance with a statutory probate process. Probating a will involves proving to the probate court that the document was executed by a competent testator as his/her last will. The probate process is begun by filing the will with a court of competent jurisdiction, typically the probate court of the state and county where the decedent was domiciled. If there is a will, it may designate the decedent's choice of personal representative. If there is no will, or the will does not designate such a person, the probate court will appoint one in accordance with statutory procedure.

The appointment of the personal representative begins administration of the estate. (S)he publishes **notice** to creditors of the decedent in a newspaper of general circulation in the jurisdiction where the estate is probated. This notice informs creditors about where to file their claims and the applicable time limit. (S)he then develops an inventory of what is contained in the estate and pays the decedent's debts. If the estate is not sufficient to pay all debts, the priority of payment is determined by state statute. The usual statute mandates the following order of **priorities**: (1) a family allowance during the period of administration, a homestead exemption, and a personal property exemption; (2) administration expenses; (3) reasonable funeral expenses; (4) federal debts and taxes; (5) reasonable last illness expenses; (6) debts acquired after death; and (7) all other claims. The personal representative then submits a **final accounting** to the court. It discloses the assets accumulated and the debts paid. The probate court will hold a hearing to approve or reject the final accounting. Once the final accounting is approved, the remaining assets are distributed to the beneficiaries of the estate.

The personal representative is a **fiduciary** whose function is to administer the estate of the decedent in accordance with legally valid instructions expressed in the testator's will or the appropriate statutes governing intestate succession. To administer the estate properly, the personal representative may **exercise certain powers** and must **perform certain duties** prescribed by statute. Thus, as a fiduciary, a personal representative may be liable to beneficiaries for actions during administration of the estate. However, (s)he is not liable for any loss incurred due to reasonable reliance on the **advice of professionals**, such as accountants, attorneys, or investment advisors. Furthermore, a personal representative is entitled to **reasonable compensation** for the time, skill, and labor required to administer the estate. If (s)he is unable or unwilling to complete administration of the estate, a successor may be provided for by the terms of the will, or the probate court will appoint a replacement.

A **trust** is a legal device by which one person can hold **legal title** to property while another holds **equitable title**. In a trust, the property is held by a **trustee** for the benefit of a **beneficiary**. A trust need not be in writing unless an interest in land is involved, but the terms of the trust must comply with the law. A trust is formed when a **grantor or settlor** demonstrates intent to form a trust and transfers to it the trust property (the **res or corpus**). A trust established and effective during the life of the settlor is an **inter vivos**, or living, trust. If it is provided for in the settlor's will and is to become effective upon that person's death, it is a **testamentary trust**.

The trustee(s) is(are) appointed by the settlor. If the settlor fails to appoint a trustee, a court will appoint one. A trustee, who may be an individual or a corporation, is a **fiduciary** who holds **legal title** to the trust property for the benefit of the beneficiaries, who hold the **equitable title**. Moreover, the settlor may be a trustee or a beneficiary. However, if (s)he is both the sole trustee and the sole beneficiary, the legal and equitable title to the trust property will be merged, that is, held by one person. The effect of the **merger** is to terminate the trust.

The trustee owes a **duty of reasonable care and undivided loyalty** to the trust and its beneficiaries. A trustee also must (1) identify and segregate the trust property, (2) preserve and protect the trust property, (3) invest prudently, (4) be impartial toward the income beneficiaries and remaindermen (persons with a future interest in property), (5) maintain accurate records, and (6) not delegate trust powers.

Formation of a trust requires no special words. For example, the words "trust" and "trustee" need not be used. Nevertheless, **ambiguous language** may not clearly manifest intent to form the trust and is usually held not to give rise to an enforceable duty. State statutes also lack uniformity regarding trusts and their formation. However, certain basic types of trusts are allowed in most states. In addition to inter vivos and testamentary trusts, trusts may be **revocable** or irrevocable. Generally, a trust is **irrevocable** and cannot be amended by the settlor unless the power to revoke or amend is expressly retained in the trust instrument. An **express trust** is formed when a settlor clearly intends to, and does in fact, duly transfer property to a trustee for the benefit of beneficiaries. An **implied trust** arises by operation of law through inference fro the parties' actions. No intent to create a trust needs to exist. An implied trust may be resulting or constructive. A **resulting trust** is created by operation of law. It is generally implied when the beneficial interest has not passed to a beneficiary other than the trustee. A resulting trust may be implied by law when (1) an express or charitable trust fails, (2) the trust purpose has been performed but some trust property remains, or (3) a buyer makes installment payments to the seller while title to the purchased property is held by a third person. The law presumes that the settlor [(1) and (2)] or the buyer [(3)] has the remaining beneficial interest in the property. A **constructive trust** is implied by operation of law as a flexible remedy to prevent unjust enrichment. It arises when (1) a fiduciary violates his/her duty to deal fairly with the property of another person; (2) an embezzler converts proceeds and acquires other property; or (3) property is conveyed by fraud, duress, or misrepresentation. A **spendthrift trust** prohibits the beneficiaries from voluntarily assigning or transferring their trust assets or interests. Thus, creditors of beneficiaries of a spendthrift trust cannot reach the trust assets in the hands of the trustee. A **charitable trust** is established for charitable purposes only. The beneficiaries of a charitable trust must be indefinite, in contrast with the beneficiaries of a private express trust, who must be definite and ascertainable. Charitable trusts are usually categorized for relief of poverty, aid to education, advancement of religion, advancement of a governmental purpose, or the general benefit of the community. The doctrine of **cy pres** preserves a charitable trust by allowing the property to be used for a different charitable purpose. Cy pres will be applied by a court only if (1) a valid charitable trust existed; (2) the settlor possessed a general charitable intent; and (3) the trust purpose became impossible, impracticable, or illegal. Moreover, a charitable trust may last forever. Unlike other trusts, it is not subject to the **rule against perpetuities**. Under this rule, a purported future interest granted by the trust agreement ordinarily must vest or fail to vest within some life in being plus 21 years. A **Totten trust** is a savings account for which the depositor executes a document declaring that (s)he is a trustee of the account for the benefit of another. This trust, also known as a tentative trust, is entirely revocable during the depositor's life. A **real estate investment trust (REIT)** owns real estate or loans secured by real estate and managed for beneficiaries. A REIT must be taxable as a domestic corporation and meet requirements regarding assets, income, and distributions. (1) A REIT also must have at least 100 beneficiaries, (2) they must own transferable shares, and (3) an initial offering of interests in a REIT must be registered under the Securilies Act of 1933. An **honorary trust** has no private beneficiaries or charitable purposes. Examples of such trusts are those formed for maintenance of a cemetery plot or of pets.

If changes in circumstances not anticipated by the settlor occur, the trustee, settlor, or beneficiary may petition a court for **modification** of the terms of a trust. This action is plausible only when compliance with the trust's current administrative provisions would defeat or substantially impair a **material purpose of the trust**. A trust will **terminate automatically** when its duration is the life of a named person and that person dies, or upon expiration of a time specified in the trust. A settlor who reserves the **right or power of revocation** may terminate the trust at any time, and an irrevocable trust can be terminated by the settlor if all the beneficiaries consent. Furthermore, all the beneficiaries may join in a **suit to terminate a trust** if termination would not defeat a material purpose of the trust. However, **spendthrift trusts** cannot be terminated except by their terms, because to do so would defeat the material purpose of the trust. Still another basis for termination is the **merger of the legal and equitable titles** in one person.

Receipts and disbursements of a trust or estate must be **allocated between the principal and income accounts**. State law governs what is principal and income. Most states have adopted the **Uniform Principal and Income Act (UPIA)**. It provides that the trust instrument defines what is principal and income, but it also provides designations that control to the extent that the instrument is silent. **Trust income** is to be distributed in most cases to **income beneficiaries**, who have life estates. **Principal** includes property transferred gratuitously to the trust and any changes in that property's form. Principal is held to be delivered eventually to the **remaindermen**, who are defined as beneficiaries entitled to trust property after prior interests expire.

The UPIA generally allocates the following **receipts to principal:** (1) consideration for principal, including gain on sale; (2) replacement property acquired with principal; (3) insurance proceeds for loss of principal; (4) stock received in a stock split; (5) nontaxable stock dividends; (6) stock rights in a corporation distributing them; (7) liquidating dividends; and (8) gain attributable to acquiring bonded debt at a discount. The UPIA allocates only **extraordinary expenses** (not ordinary and current) **to principal**. The following are examples: (1) capital costs, such as major repairs, modifications, and local assessments; (2) payments on debt principal; (3) taxes on principal items, e.g., capital gains taxes; (4) fiduciary fees; (5) amortization of investments purchased at a premium; and (6) distributions to principal beneficiaries.

Income is the return in money or property on or for the use of principal. Income of a trust or estate is narrower than income for financial or individual income tax purposes. **Receipts credited to income** under the UPIA include (1) business income; (2) rents, including prepaid rent; (3) insurance proceeds for lost profits; (4) interest; (5) discount gain on redemption of treasury bills; (6) taxable cash or property dividends; (7) taxable stock dividends; (8) extraordinary dividends; and (9) royalties. Ordinary and current operating and administrative expenses are charged against income. The UPIA generally attributes the following **costs to income**: (1) ordinary and necessary business expenses, (2) costs of production of income, (3) insurance premiums, (4) maintenance and repair of trust property, (5) taxes on fiduciary income, (6) trustee insurance bond premiums, (7) ordinary loss passed through from a partnership, and (8) depreciation.

The act provides that **depreciation** is a required charge against income unless the trust instrument provides otherwise. Many state statutes grant the trustee discretion to determine whether to recognize it at all. Depreciation charged against income preserves principal.

QUESTIONS

28.1 Wills

1. One restriction on the power to convey one's property by will is the requirement of testamentary capacity. Gallagher's will is conclusively presumed to be invalid if

A. Gallagher was under legal guardianship when it was executed.

B. Gallagher was 17 when she properly executed it and was 77 when she died without having revoked it.

C. No proof of mental testamentary capacity is offered before the will is admitted to probate.

D. Gallagher had been adjudicated insane at the time of death but not at the time of execution.

Answer (B) is correct. *(Publisher, adapted)*

REQUIRED: The instance in which a will is conclusively presumed to be invalid.

DISCUSSION: A person cannot execute a valid will unless (s)he has attained the statutory age (usually 18 or 21) and has the requisite mental capacity. The age requirement applies at the time of execution. Age at the time of death is irrelevant. Accordingly, a will executed at age 17 cannot be admitted to probate.

Answer (A) is incorrect. A person under a legal guardianship may still be able to make a valid will. The mental capacity required for a will is less than that required to contract, but the maker must be aware that (s)he is making a will and able to understand the extent of his/her property and to whom it will pass. Answer (C) is incorrect. Proof of mental capacity is not required, unless an interested party objects. Answer (D) is incorrect. Mental capacity must exist when the will is executed, not at death.

2. Every state has detailed requirements for valid execution of a formal will. In general,

A. The will must be dated.

B. A mark may suffice as a signature.

C. The will must be notarized and filed in the public records.

D. The will is invalidated if witnessed by a beneficiary.

Answer (B) is correct. *(Publisher, adapted)*

REQUIRED: The true statement about execution of a formal will.

DISCUSSION: Any mark (even an "X") will suffice given proof that it was the mark of the testator and placed on the will with the intention of operating as his/her signature. In many states, a signature to a will must be placed at the end (subscribed).

Answer (A) is incorrect. A will should be, but is not required to be, dated. Answer (C) is incorrect. Wills are generally not filed in public records until probated, and they need not be notarized. However, a notarized affidavit by the witnesses is commonly used in admitting the will into court. Answer (D) is incorrect. This rule has been replaced in almost all states by statutes permitting beneficiaries to act as witnesses. In some states, however, the will may be purged of any provision in favor of such a person. Other states limit an essential witness to his/her intestate share.

3. Several months after executing their wills, Husband and Wife wanted to change a beneficiary. Which of the following is the true statement concerning an amendment to a will?

A. No additional documents are necessary since the changes can be made in the existing wills by crossing out the part to be changed, writing in the new change, and initialing the change in the margin.

B. An amendment to a will is called a codicil.

C. The amendment to the will does not have to be witnessed because it can refer to the original will that was witnessed.

D. An amendment to a will is called an ademption.

Answer (B) is correct. *(Publisher, adapted)*

REQUIRED: The true statement about an amendment to a will.

DISCUSSION: An amendment to a will is called a codicil. It must be executed with the same formalities as the original will. However, under case law in some jurisdictions, deletions in the original will can intentionally be made by physically striking out portions of the will.

Answer (A) is incorrect. Any physical crossing out in a will may revoke either that part of the will or (in some states) the entire will. Additions may never be made to the will without the same formalities as the original will. Answer (C) is incorrect. The amendment must be executed with the same formalities as the original will. A reference to the original will does not nullify this requirement. Answer (D) is incorrect. An ademption is the failure of a bequest or devise if specific property referred to in a will is not owned by the decedent at his/her death.

4. The elements constituting a will may not always be clear when the will is written on more than one piece of paper. When one document is treated as the will and another is referred to and included therein although it was not formally executed with the will,

A. The doctrine of integration is applied.

B. An act of independent significance has occurred.

C. The second document is incorporated by reference.

D. The second document is treated as a codicil.

Answer (C) is correct. *(Publisher, adapted)*

REQUIRED: The legal basis for including a document in a will although it was not formally executed with the will.

DISCUSSION: The usual requirements for applying the doctrine of incorporation by reference are the following: (1) The document existed when the will was executed; (2) the document was referred to in the will; (3) the document is clearly identified in the will; and (4) sufficient proof must be offered of the validity of the document. An example of incorporation by reference is the reference in a will to an already existing trust to hold a bequest for beneficiaries.

Answer (A) is incorrect. Under the doctrine of integration, separate papers are treated as one formally executed instrument. Answer (B) is incorrect. The independent significance doctrine allows the court to fill in the gaps of the will. For example, a bequest to "all the members of my bowling team" can be upheld because the act of belonging to the team has significance apart from directing testamentary conveyance of property. Answer (D) is incorrect. A codicil is an amendment to a will executed with the same formalities as a will.

5. Which of the following is a true statement with regard to ademption or abatement of testamentary gift?

A. Ademption prevents a bequest from lapsing if the beneficiary is no longer living.

B. Abatement is the failure of a bequest if the property is not owned by the decedent at the time of death.

C. Ademption establishes the order of payment of bequests and their valuation.

D. Abatement reduces a beneficiary's share under a will.

Answer (D) is correct. *(Publisher, adapted)*

REQUIRED: The true statement about ademptions and abatements.

DISCUSSION: Abatement is the reduction of testamentary gifts when the estate has insufficient assets to pay all creditors' claims, taxes, administrative expenses, bequests, and devises. An abatement statute determines how these gifts are to be reduced. Under the UPC, if the testator's intention in this regard cannot be determined, testamentary dispositions abate as follows: (1) intestate property, (2) residuary devises and bequests, (3) general devises and bequests, and (4) specific devises and bequests. If the assets cannot satisfy all gifts within a category, they are distributed proportionally.

Answer (A) is incorrect. An anti-lapse statute prevents a bequest from lapsing if the beneficiary is no longer living. Answer (B) is incorrect. Ademption is the failure of a bequest when the property is not owned by the decedent at the time of death. Answer (C) is incorrect. Ademption is the failure of a bequest when the property is not owned by the decedent at the time of death.

6. Which of the following is a gratuitous lifetime transfer made to a potential beneficiary under the donor's will with the intent that it will be applied against any share that the donee might receive?

A. Gift in contemplation of death.

B. Advancement.

C. Ademption.

D. Abatement.

Answer (B) is correct. *(Publisher, adapted)*

REQUIRED: The term for a transfer intended to be applied against the donee's share of the donor's estate.

DISCUSSION: Gifts are sometimes made to children or other relatives as an advance on their share of the donor's estate. Such a gift will only be considered an advancement if the donor clearly evidences the intent to reduce the beneficiary's share of his/her estate. Because the intent is a difficult matter to ascertain, most states provide that a gift will not be considered an advancement unless the donor clearly evidences his/her intent.

Answer (A) is incorrect. It describes a gift made with the intent that it will take effect only upon the donor's death. Answer (C) is incorrect. Ademption is the failure of a bequest or devise when the specific property is not in the decedent's estate at death. Answer (D) is incorrect. Abatement is the reduction of testamentary gifts when the estate has insufficient assets to pay all creditors' claims, taxes, administrative expenses, bequests, and devises.

7. Jean Bond's will left various specific property and sums of money to relatives and friends. She left the residue of her estate equally to her favorite niece and nephew. Which of the various properties described below will become a part of Bond's estate and be distributed in accordance with her last will and testament?

A. A joint savings account that listed her sister, who is still living, as the joint tenant.

B. The entire family homestead that she had owned in joint tenancy with her older brother who predeceased her and that was still recorded as jointly owned.

C. Several substantial gifts that she made in contemplation of death to various charities.

D. A life insurance policy that designated a former partner as the beneficiary.

Answer (B) is correct. *(CPA, adapted)*

REQUIRED: The property included in the decedent's estate.

DISCUSSION: If the homestead was owned in a joint tenancy with an older brother who had predeceased her, Bond would have become the sole owner of the property upon her death. Thus, the joint tenancy would have terminated regardless of how it is recorded. Joint tenancy is a form of property ownership in which surviving joint tenants succeed to the decedent's interests. As the sole owner, Bond could transfer the entire property as she wished, including by devise in her will.

Answer (A) is incorrect. An interest in a savings account held as a joint tenancy would pass to the surviving joint tenant under the right of survivorship in the property. Answer (C) is incorrect. Gifts made in contemplation of death are valid and would not be included in the donor's estate. Answer (D) is incorrect. The proceeds of a life insurance policy would pass to the designated beneficiary under the insurance contract.

8. Tessie executed a valid will bequeathing her personalty to Lock and devising her realty to Ness. She later physically canceled that will after executing a second instrument leaving a parcel of lakeshore property to Scott but otherwise not disturbing the original disposition of the estate. After Tessie's death, the second will was judicially declared to be invalid. Tessie would not have revoked the first document if she had known that the second would not be effective. What is the legal effect of her mistake?

A. A court may apply the doctrine of dependent relative revocation to revive the first will.

B. Courts can grant no relief for a mistake in the inducement to revoke a will.

C. Tessie is deemed to have died intestate.

D. If the second will was valid before her death, Tessie can revoke it to revive the first will.

Answer (A) is correct. *(Publisher, adapted)*

REQUIRED: The true statement about a revocation conditioned upon the validity of a second will.

DISCUSSION: Dependent relative revocation is a doctrine that allows a court to give effect to a revoked will. It applies when the decedent apparently would not have revoked the will but for a mistaken belief that a subsequent instrument would effectively dispose of the estate. Consequently, the revocation of the first will may be ignored by the court given sufficient proof of the decedent's intent and of the terms of the original will.

Answer (B) is incorrect. The theory of dependent relative revocation may be applied when a mistake was made in the inducement to revoke a will. Tessie's estate therefore can pass by testate succession. Answer (C) is incorrect. The court in this case may treat the first will as unrevoked. Answer (D) is incorrect. The revocation of a second will cannot revive a first will already revoked.

9. A will or any part of it is least likely to be revoked by the subsequent

A. Birth of an illegitimate child acknowledged by the decedent.

B. Adoption of a child.

C. Marriage or divorce of the testator.

D. Birth of a third child when the will left everything to the spouse.

Answer (D) is correct. *(Publisher, adapted)*

REQUIRED: The event least likely to revoke a will by operation of law.

DISCUSSION: Statutes often provide for a child born subsequent to the execution of a will to take an intestate share unless the will indicates a contrary intention. If the decedent had children at the date of executing a will but left the entire estate to the surviving spouse, such intention is shown.

Answer (A) is incorrect. Illegitimate children, or at least those legitimized under statutory procedures, have the same inheritance rights as legitimate children. Answer (B) is incorrect. An adopted child is treated as if (s)he were a biological child of his/her parents. Answer (C) is incorrect. Statutes often make provision for pretermitted spouses as well as children. Moreover, a subsequent divorce may result in statutory modification of a testamentary provision for the surviving ex-spouse.

28.2 Intestate Succession

10. If an individual dies without a valid will, what becomes of his/her property?

A. The property will be transferred under the applicable statute of descent and distribution.

B. All the real property escheats to the state where it is located and the rest to the state of domicile.

C. Real property descends to the heirs, but personal property is distributed according to the applicable state statute.

D. The principle of primogeniture applies.

Answer (A) is correct. *(Publisher, adapted)*

REQUIRED: The disposition of the property of one who dies intestate.

DISCUSSION: In effect, intestate disposition will be according to a statutory will drafted by the state legislature and called a statute of descent and distribution. This intestacy statute is based on a legislative presumption regarding the intent of the decedent to benefit his/her closest relatives. Accordingly, the real and personal property are generally divided between the surviving spouse and the children.

Answer (B) is incorrect. Only if the decedent had no heirs will the property be transferred (escheated) to the state. Answer (C) is incorrect. Both the real and personal property pass under the intestacy statute. Answer (D) is incorrect. Primogeniture is the archaic English common law rule by which real property automatically descended to the eldest son of the decedent.

11. A will provided that an estate was to be distributed "per stirpes" to the deceased's heirs. The only possible heirs are two daughters, who each have three children, and two children of a predeceased son. What fraction of the estate will each child of the predeceased son receive?

A. 0

B. 1/10

C. 1/6

D. 1/4

Answer (C) is correct. *(CPA, adapted)*

REQUIRED: The fraction of an estate distributed to certain heirs under per stirpes.

DISCUSSION: The distribution of the proceeds of a probate estate is according to the decedent's intent, if expressed. Otherwise, it is directed by statute. The general rule is that property not specifically distributed by will is divided equally among the children of the decedent living at the time of his/her death, with the share of any predeceased child divided equally among the children of such predeceased child. This type of distribution is taking by representation, or per stirpes. An alternative distribution is to give lineal descendants an equal share regardless of generation. This distribution is per capita. In this situation, the decedent died leaving two surviving children and two grandchildren of a predeceased child. Thus, under per stirpes, the estate will be distributed one-third to each surviving child and one-sixth each to the children of the predeceased child.

28.3 Estate Administration

12. After the will has been admitted to probate and the personal representative has been appointed, the actual administration of a decedent's estate can be undertaken. It does not include

A. An accounting made to the court by the recipients of estate property.

B. Filing of tax returns.

C. Notification of creditors.

D. Payment of an allowance to the surviving spouse during the period of administration.

Answer (A) is correct. *(Publisher, adapted)*

REQUIRED: The action not taken during administration of a decedent's estate.

DISCUSSION: The personal representative must collect, preserve, inventory, and appraise the assets of the estate. (S)he must give notice to creditors or other claimants against the estate. This notice allows the filing and proof of claims within some specified period. The family allowance also is paid. The personal representative must render an accounting to the probate court. Claimants and recipients of estate property are not required to make an accounting. Administration also includes payment of funeral and burial expenses, the decedent's medical bills, costs of administration, debts, and taxes. The responsibilities include filing federal estate tax and estate income tax returns. After all payments have been made, an accounting is made to the court (by the personal representative). When that is approved, the assets are distributed, the estate is closed, and the personal representative is discharged.

Answer (B) is incorrect. The personal representative files tax returns. Answer (C) is incorrect. The personal representative notifies creditors. Answer (D) is incorrect. The personal representative pays an allowance to the surviving spouse.

13. Generally, an estate is liable for which debts owed by the decedent at the time of death?

A. All of the decedent's debts.

B. Only debts secured by the decedent's property.

C. Only debts covered by the statute of frauds.

D. None of the decedent's debts.

Answer (A) is correct. *(CPA, adapted)*

REQUIRED: The scope of an estate's liability for decedent's debts.

DISCUSSION: An estate is an artificial legal entity that arises by operation of law when a person dies and immediately succeeds to his/her property. The estate is liable for all of the decedent's debts. The personal representative administering the estate has a duty to ascertain those liabilities and to cause them to be satisfied to the extent of probate assets.

Answer (B) is incorrect. Security interests affect the priority and rights of the creditor, not the estate's liability. Answer (C) is incorrect. The estate is also liable for debts not subject to the statute of frauds. Answer (D) is incorrect. By operation of law, the estate is liable for any and all debts of a person who dies.

14. A decedent's estate may include real property located other than where (s)he was domiciled. What type of probate administration may be necessary in the state where the property is located?

A. A summary administration.

B. An ancillary administration.

C. A family administration.

D. A nonintervention administration.

Answer (B) is correct. *(Publisher, adapted)*

REQUIRED: The term for probate in a state other than where the decedent was domiciled.

DISCUSSION: Ancillary administration is necessary if a nonresident dies leaving assets in a state other than the state of domicile. One may have more than one residence, but only one domicile. Ancillary administration applies only to assets located in the nondomiciliary state. Two of the objectives of ancillary administration are to prove title in the situs state (the state where the property is located) and to protect local creditors by subjecting the property to that state's probate process.

Answer (A) is incorrect. A summary administration is an expedited process available when the value of the entire estate does not exceed a relatively small amount, e.g., $25,000, or the decedent has been dead for more than 3 years. A will must be proved. A hearing is held. The court may enter an order of summary administration and permit distribution. Answer (C) is incorrect. A family administration is available if the estate is relatively small, e.g., less than $60,000, and the entire estate consists of personal property (or, if there is real property, formal administration has proceeded to the point that the estate is not indebted or all claims have been barred). Family administration typically permits collection of small bank accounts, wage claims, and transfer of title to automobiles. Answer (D) is incorrect. A nonintervention administration permits the personal representative to use the powers provided by the state statute without approval of each transaction by the court.

15. In his will, Vic named his son, Don, as the executor. Which of the following is a power or duty of Don as executor?

A. Don must post a surety bond even if a provision in the will exempts him.

B. Don has a duty to discover, collect, and distribute all the decedent's assets.

C. If the will is silent on the point, Don has complete discretion insofar as investing the estate's assets.

D. Don can sell real property without a court order, even though he has not been expressly authorized to do so.

Answer (B) is correct. *(CPA, adapted)*

REQUIRED: The true statement about the rights and duties of a personal representative.

DISCUSSION: The executor (personal representative) must be approved by the court. The executor then has the duty to discover, collect, preserve, and distribute the assets of the decedent to the beneficiaries.

Answer (A) is incorrect. The requirement in many states that the personal representative post a bond may frequently be waived on direction from the will or by court approval of a request. Answer (C) is incorrect. The personal representative must exercise reasonable care and is often subject to statutory limitations on investments. Answer (D) is incorrect. The sale of real property usually requires court approval unless the will directs otherwise.

16. A personal representative of an estate would breach fiduciary duties if (s)he

A. Combined personal funds with funds of the estate so that both could purchase treasury bills.

B. Represented the estate in a lawsuit brought against it by a disgruntled relative of the decedent.

C. Distributed property in satisfaction of the decedent's debts.

D. Engaged a non-CPA to prepare the records for the estate's final accounting.

Answer (A) is correct. *(CPA, adapted)*

REQUIRED: The breach of the personal representative's fiduciary duty.

DISCUSSION: The personal representative is responsible to administer the estate according to legal directions. (S)he is a fiduciary with respect to the estate, and must act primarily for the benefit of the estate. (S)he is accountable for the estate assets. One fiduciary duty is to keep the estate's property separate from his/her own.

Answer (B) is incorrect. Representing the estate in a lawsuit is a proper duty of a fiduciary. Answer (C) is incorrect. The estate is liable for all of the decedent's debts. Settling those debts is a duty of the personal representative. Answer (D) is incorrect. The final accounting of the estate need not be performed by an independent public accountant.

17. Which of the following is a true statement concerning the personal representative of an estate?

A. If the personal representative of an estate is unable to complete his/her administration, the court will appoint a successor.

B. An advantage of naming a corporate personal representative is that a successor need never be appointed.

C. An executor may resign but an administrator must complete the probate.

D. A court-appointed personal representative is called a testatrix.

Answer (A) is correct. *(Publisher, adapted)*

REQUIRED: The true statement concerning a personal representative.

DISCUSSION: When a personal representative resigns or is unable to complete the administration of the estate because of death, illness, or other incapacity, the probate court will appoint a successor. The original or the successor may be an individual, corporation, organization, or other legal entity. Moreover, any person appointed as a personal representative must have reached the statutory age and have contractual capacity.

Answer (B) is incorrect. A corporation can resign or become insolvent or bankrupt, which would require a successor to be appointed. Answer (C) is incorrect. An executor (executrix if female) is a personal representative named in a will. An administrator is one appointed by the court. Either can resign. Answer (D) is incorrect. A testatrix is a person (female) who executes a will (the masculine term is testator).

28.4 Trusts

18. To form a valid inter vivos trust to hold personal property, the trust must be

A. In writing and signed by the settlor (creator).

B. Specific concerning the property to be held in trust.

C. Irrevocable.

D. In writing and signed by the trustee.

Answer (B) is correct. *(CPA, adapted)*

REQUIRED: The characteristic of an inter vivos trust.

DISCUSSION: A trust is formed when one party transfers property to another to hold for the benefit of a third. All beneficiaries and trustees must be identified, the property must be sufficiently described so that legal title can pass to the trustee, and the settlor must deliver the property with intent to transfer title.

Answer (A) is incorrect. A trust may be established and funded orally if it involves only personal property. Answer (C) is incorrect. A trust is revocable in most states if the transferor reserves the right to revoke. It is generally presumed irrevocable unless the trust states it is not. Answer (D) is incorrect. The trust need not be written. Also, the trustee must be identified but need not sign a trust writing.

19. Abe transferred assets to the York Trust Company in trust for the benefit of his grandchildren irrevocably for a period of 21 years. In relation to the Abe Trust and the rights and duties of the parties in respect to it,

A. Such a trust is useful for skipping generations and securing ownership of property, because its duration can be potentially infinite.

B. The trust is not recognized as a legal entity for tax purposes, and Abe must include the trust income with his own.

C. York has legal title to the trust property, the grandchildren have equitable title, and Abe has a reversionary interest.

D. If the trust deed is silent on the point, York must not sell or otherwise dispose of the trust assets without Abe's permission.

Answer (C) is correct. *(CPA, adapted)*

REQUIRED: The rights and duties of the parties with respect to a trust created by a settlor for his grandchildren.

DISCUSSION: Abe, the settlor, has formed an inter vivos trust (one formed during the settlor's lifetime) to last for 21 years, at the end of which time the property will revert to him. During the term of the trust, the ownership of the trust property is separated. The trustee holds the legal title and the beneficiaries hold the equitable title.

Answer (A) is incorrect. The interests provided for by the trust agreement must conform to the rule against perpetuities, which provides that a future interest in the property is invalid unless it vests or fails to vest within some life in being plus 21 years. Answer (B) is incorrect. A trust is recognized as a separate legal entity, and the settlor does not include the income as his/her own if the trust lasts for more than 10 years and all other requirements are met. Answer (D) is incorrect. The trustee may not only sell or otherwise dispose of trust assets, but may be under an affirmative duty to do so. The trustee has a duty to invest the trust assets to make them productive.

20. If not expressly granted, which of the following implied powers would a trustee have?

I. Power to sell trust property
II. Power to borrow from the trust
III. Power to pay trust expenses

A. I and II.

B. I and III.

C. II and III.

D. I, II, and III.

Answer (B) is correct. *(CPA, adapted)*

REQUIRED: The trustee's implied powers.

DISCUSSION: A trustee is a fiduciary appointed by a settlor to hold, manage, and administer trust property for the sole benefit of the beneficiaries. To the extent not contrary to express provisions in the trust agreement or law, the trustee has implied power to do what is reasonably necessary to perform those functions. Provided that a trustee does so in accordance with any pertinent instructions expressed in the instrument and his/her duties of reasonable care and undivided loyalty, (s)he may sell trust property and pay trust expenses. However, a trustee's borrowing from the trust constitutes self-dealing that is a per se breach of the trustee's duty of undivided loyalty. The trustee must hold, manage, and administer trust property in the interests of the beneficiaries. However, engaging in a transaction with the trust in his/her individual capacity may be allowed if (1) a court approves the transaction, (2) the trust instrument provides for it, or (3) all beneficiaries consent to it.

21. K's will provided for a trust to take effect upon K's death. The will named K's spouse as both trustee and personal representative (executor). The will provided that all of K's securities were to be transferred to the trust and named K's child as the beneficiary of the trust. Which of the following statements is true in regard to the arrangement made by K's will?

A. K has provided for a testamentary trust.

B. K's spouse may not serve as both the trustee and personal representative because of the inherent conflict of interest.

C. K has formed an inter vivos trust.

D. The trust is invalid because it will not become effective until K's death.

Answer (A) is correct. *(CPA, adapted)*

REQUIRED: The true statement regarding a trust formed by a will.

DISCUSSION: An express trust formed by a will is a testamentary trust. The trust becomes effective upon the death of the testator (the person who made the will). It is only valid if the will was executed in accordance with the requirements of a valid will.

Answer (B) is incorrect. There is no inherent conflict of interest between a trustee of a testamentary trust and a personal representative of an estate. Answer (C) is incorrect. The settlor of an inter vivos trust must be alive when the trust takes effect. Answer (D) is incorrect. By definition, a testamentary trust becomes effective upon death of the settlor.

22. Resulting trusts and constructive trusts are implied. Which of the following is a true statement regarding resulting and constructive trusts?

A. A resulting trust arises only when an express trust fails and the settlor did not direct what should be done with the property in that event.

B. A resulting trust arises when someone embezzles property and converts the proceeds to acquire other property. The embezzler then holds the new property in a resulting trust for the benefit of the person embezzled.

C. A resulting trust and a constructive trust are one and the same.

D. A constructive trust will arise when a fiduciary violates his/her duty to deal fairly with the property of another person.

Answer (D) is correct. *(Publisher, adapted)*

REQUIRED: The true statement regarding resulting and constructive trusts.

DISCUSSION: Constructive trusts are implied to remedy unjust enrichment in many situations. They arise when a fiduciary violates his/her duty to deal fairly with the property of another person, when an embezzler converts proceeds and acquires other property, or when property is conveyed by fraud, duress, or misrepresentation.

Answer (A) is incorrect. Although a resulting trust will arise when an express trust fails, it will also arise when one person purchases property and leaves title in another's name. Answer (B) is incorrect. The embezzler is considered to hold the property in a constructive trust. Answer (C) is incorrect. Constructive trusts arise when the "trustee" has been unjustly enriched from a wrongful act, but a resulting trust arises in a purchase-money situation or upon the failure of an express trust.

23. A spendthrift clause is commonly used in trusts established for a testator's dependents to help provide a measure of security. A spendthrift clause performs which of the following functions?

A. Limits the trustee to using trust assets only for absolutely necessary expenditures.

B. Limits the trustee to making distributions to the beneficiaries only for their health, education, and support.

C. Restricts the beneficiaries from transferring their interests and limits availability of trust assets to creditors.

D. Prevents the settlor from modifying or revoking the trust.

Answer (C) is correct. *(Publisher, adapted)*

REQUIRED: The function of a spendthrift clause.

DISCUSSION: A spendthrift clause is a restraint on alienation to restrict the beneficiaries from transferring their interests in a trust. It also limits the ability of creditors to reach the assets of the trust for claims against the beneficiaries.

Answer (A) is incorrect. Limiting the trustee to using trust assets only for absolutely necessary expenditures is not a restraint on transfer of a beneficiary's interest. Answer (B) is incorrect. A trust that limits distributions to those for health, education, and support is commonly known as a support trust. Answer (D) is incorrect. The settlor is prevented from modifying or revoking the trust (1) if the trust agreement so specifies and (2), in most states, unless it is specifically revocable.

24. Trusts set up for charitable purposes are usually subject to liberal rules concerning their creation, duration, and management. Which of the following is not a requirement for a trust to qualify as charitable?

A. The settlor's motive must have been charitable.

B. The effect of the trust must be to benefit the public or the community.

C. The beneficiaries must be indefinite.

D. Any profits received by the beneficiary must be applied to the charitable activity.

Answer (A) is correct. *(Publisher, adapted)*

REQUIRED: The statement not a requirement for a trust to qualify as charitable.

DISCUSSION: The motive of the settlor is generally not important in determining whether a valid charitable trust has been formed. If the effect of the trust is to benefit the public, the community, or some indefinite segment of it, the trust is charitable regardless of the settlor's motive.

Answer (B) is incorrect. The effect must be charitable in that the trust benefits the public, e.g., the furtherance of art, education, science, recreation, religion, or public health and welfare. Answer (C) is incorrect. The beneficiaries may consist of a small or even a fixed class if the membership is indefinite. For instance, a trust to assist victims of a specific flood could qualify as charitable. Answer (D) is incorrect. If the beneficiary receives profits from the trust, they must not be paid to owners.

25. The cy pres doctrine

A. Allows a trustee to make distributions at his/her discretion among a class of beneficiaries.

B. May allow a court to change the beneficiary named by the settlor of a trust.

C. Applies to noncharitable as well as charitable trusts.

D. Is subject to the rule against perpetuities.

Answer (B) is correct. *(Publisher, adapted)*

REQUIRED: The true statement about the cy pres doctrine.

DISCUSSION: Cy pres is a doctrine that allows a court to substitute a new charitable beneficiary when a named charitable beneficiary either ceases to exist or ceases to qualify as charitable, or when the bequest is or becomes impracticable. The doctrine permits a court to carry out as nearly as possible the settlor's purpose. To apply this doctrine, an equity court must find that the settlor had a broad or general intent to aid charity or a specific type of charity. Absent a showing of such intent, the trust will fail.

Answer (A) is incorrect. Cy pres permits a court to follow a settlor's charitable intent but does not otherwise give the trustee discretion in distributions. Answer (C) is incorrect. Cy pres applies to charitable trusts only. Answer (D) is incorrect. The legal title of a charitable trust must vest in the trustee within the period of the rule, but otherwise cy pres has nothing to do with the rule against perpetuities.

26. A group of real estate dealers has decided to form a Real Estate Investment Trust (REIT) to invest in diversified real estate holdings. A public offering of $10,000,000 of trust certificates is contemplated. Which of the following is a false statement?

A. Those investing in the venture will not be insulated from personal liability.

B. The entity will be considered an "association" for tax purposes.

C. The offering must be registered under the Securities Act of 1933.

D. If the trust qualifies as a REIT and distributes all its income to the investors, it will not be subject to federal income tax.

Answer (A) is correct. *(CPA, adapted)*

REQUIRED: The false statement about a real estate investment trust.

DISCUSSION: A real estate investment trust is a business trust similar in structure to an ordinary trust, but its purpose is to act as an investment vehicle (like a limited partnership) for real estate ventures. Limited partnerships are now more commonly used. However, the REIT began under common law before statutes were enacted authorizing limited partnerships. The REIT legally is similar to ordinary trusts and provides limited liability for the beneficiaries (investors).

Answer (B) is incorrect. The entity will be considered an "association" for tax purposes. Answer (C) is incorrect. The offering must be registered under the Securities Act of 1933. Answer (D) is incorrect. If the trust qualifies as a REIT and distributes all its income to the investors, it will not be subject to federal income tax.

27. Dart created an irrevocable trust naming Larson as trustee. The trust provided that the trust income would be paid to Frost for 15 years, with the principal then reverting to Dart. Larson died after 10 years, Frost died after 20 years, and Dart died after 22 years. When does the trust terminate?

A. After 10 years.

B. After 15 years.

C. After 20 years.

D. After 22 years.

Answer (B) is correct. *(CPA, adapted)*

REQUIRED: The date of termination of an irrevocable trust.

DISCUSSION: A trust is formed by a settlor or grantor delivering property (called trust res or corpus) to a trustee to be administered for the benefit of designated beneficiaries. A settlor who reserves the power of revocation may terminate the trust at any time, but an irrevocable trust is difficult to modify or terminate because such action requires court approval. Furthermore, any trust terminates upon expiration of the time specified in the declaration of trust. The trust created by Dart specified a duration of 15 years. In the absence of a valid modification or termination, the trust will terminate automatically after 15 years.

Answer (A) is incorrect. The death of the trustee does not terminate a trust. Answer (C) is incorrect. Frost's rights as a beneficiary terminated after 15 years and his later death has no relevance to the duration of the trust. Answer (D) is incorrect. By its terms, the trust terminated and the property reverted to Dart after 15 years, and his date of death has no effect on the earlier trust.

28. An irrevocable trust that contains no provision for change or termination can be changed or terminated only by the

A. Trustee.

B. Grantor.

C. Courts.

D. Consent of the majority of the beneficiaries.

Answer (C) is correct. *(CPA, adapted)*

REQUIRED: The ability to modify or terminate an irrevocable trust with no provision for change or termination.

DISCUSSION: Most states follow the rule that a trust is irrevocable unless expressly made revocable. An irrevocable trust cannot be changed unless the trustee, grantor, or beneficiary petitions a court to do so.

Answer (A) is incorrect. The trustee may not change or terminate the trust. Answer (B) is incorrect. A grantor may not revoke or amend a trust unless the power to revoke or amend is expressly reserved in the trust instrument. Answer (D) is incorrect. Beneficiaries cannot change or terminate the trust. An irrevocable trust may be terminated by the grantor, however, if all beneficiaries consent.

28.5 Allocation Between Principal and Income

29. Jay properly established an inter vivos trust. The trust's sole asset is a fully rented office building. Rental receipts exceed expenditures. The trust instrument is silent about allocation of items between principal and income. Among items to be allocated during the year are insurance proceeds received as a result of fire damage to the building and mortgage interest payments made during the year. Properly allocable to principal is/are

	Insurance Proceeds on Building	Current Mortgage Interest Payments
A.	No	No
B.	No	Yes
C.	Yes	No
D.	Yes	Yes

Answer (C) is correct. *(CPA, adapted)*

REQUIRED: The allocation of insurance proceeds for damage to trust property and of mortgage interest payments between principal and income of a trust.

DISCUSSION: Generally, receipts representing change in form or return of principal and extraordinary disbursements are allocated to trust principal. The trust instrument may designate an item as chargeable to trust principal or income. Otherwise, designations provided in the Uniform Principal and Income Act control. Insurance proceeds upon damage to, or loss of, trust property are principal. Interest paid on a debt owed by the trust is charged against income.

30. Cox transferred assets into a trust under which Smart is entitled to receive the income for life. After Smart's death, the remaining assets are to be given to Mix. In 2003, the trust received rent of $1,000, stock dividends of $6,000, interest on certificates of deposit of $3,000, municipal bond interest of $4,000, and proceeds of $7,000 from the sale of bonds. Both Smart and Mix are still alive. What amount of the 2003 receipts should be allocated to trust principal?

A. $7,000

B. $8,000

C. $13,000

D. $15,000

Answer (C) is correct. *(CPA, adapted)*

REQUIRED: The allocation between trust principal and income.

DISCUSSION: Trust principal is property gratuitously acquired and any changes in its form. It is held for eventual delivery to remaindermen. Trust income is return for use of principal and is held for or distributed to the income beneficiary. Unless the trust instrument specifically otherwise allocates a receipt or expense to principal or income, default designations in the Uniform Principal and Income Act control. Rent and interest (even if tax-exempt) are allocated to income. Nontaxable stock dividends are allocated to principal, as are proceeds from the sale of principal ($6,000 + $7,000 = $13,000). Gain on the sale of property that constitutes principal, even if partially attributable to an interest feature, is generally principal.

Answer (A) is incorrect. Nontaxable dividends of stock issued by the distributee are allocated to principal. Answer (B) is incorrect. Rent is income (return on principal), but nontaxable dividends of stock issued by the distributee are principal. Answer (D) is incorrect. Interest and rent are allocated to income. A stock dividend and consideration received for trust principal are allocated to principal.

31. Farrel's will provided for a testamentary trust naming Gordon as life income beneficiary, with the principal going to Hall on Gordon's death. The trust's sole asset was a commercial office building valued at $200,000. The trustee sold the building for $250,000. To what amount of the sale price is Gordon entitled?

A. $0

B. $50,000

C. $200,000

D. $250,000

Answer (A) is correct. *(CPA, adapted)*

REQUIRED: The allocation of the gain on the sale of real estate held in trust to the income beneficiary.

DISCUSSION: The Uniform Principal and Income Act provides that the trust instrument may designate receipt and disbursement items as allocated to principal or income, and the act provides default allocations for items on which the instrument is silent. Change in the form of the principal is principal, as is the consideration or proceeds received for the principal, including gain on its sale. The remainderman (Hall) is entitled to all principal amounts.

32. An enforceable spendthrift trust was formed with a life income beneficiary and a residuary beneficiary. The trust's sole asset was an office building. Which of the following will be allocated to trust principal?

	Annual Property Tax	Monthly Mortgage Principal Payment
A.	Yes	Yes
B.	Yes	No
C.	No	Yes
D.	No	No

Answer (C) is correct. *(CPA, adapted)*

REQUIRED: The proper allocation of property tax and monthly mortgage principal payments between principal and income.

DISCUSSION: Generally, ordinary operating expenses are chargeable to trust income, but extraordinary expenses and principal payments on indebtedness are chargeable to trust principal. Thus, regularly recurring property taxes are not allocated to trust principal, but monthly mortgage principal payments are.

33. Which of the following expenditures resulting from a trust's ownership of commercial real estate would be allocated to the trust's principal?

A. Building management fees.

B. Real estate taxes.

C. Sidewalk assessments.

D. Depreciation

Answer (C) is correct. *(CPA, adapted)*

REQUIRED: The expenditure allocated to trust principal.

DISCUSSION: Costs not necessary to current and ordinary trust administration and operation are generally allocable to principal. Unless the trust instrument specifically allocates an item to principal or income, the default designations in the Uniform Principal and Income Act apply. Extraordinary costs (e.g., to set up a trust, to buy or sell investments, or to make capital improvements in trust assets) are charges against principal. A local assessment for roads, sidewalks, etc., is a capital improvement that materially enhances the value of property. It is charged against principal.

Answer (A) is incorrect. It is an ordinary expense of producing income, chargeable to income. Answer (B) is incorrect. Although tax on capital gains is allocated to principal, real property tax is treated as an expense of income production and is charged against income. Answer (D) is incorrect. Under the rules of the UPIA, depreciation would be allocated to income.

STUDY UNIT TWENTY-NINE
AGENCY

Agency is an express or implied consensual relationship not necessarily based on contract that is formed when two parties agree that one, the **agent**, will represent the other, the **principal**, in dealing with third parties. The agent is subject to the principal's control and can affect the principal's legal relationships with third parties. Absent special circumstances, the principal ordinarily has **contractual liability to third parties** for contracts entered into by the agent on behalf of the principal. Because the relationship is representative, the agent has derivative authority to act for, and in place of, the principal. Thus, the intended result of a valid agency relationship is to **bind the principal** and to insulate the agent from personal liability to third parties.

The principal must represent that the agent may act on the principal's behalf. The test for the existence of an authorized agency is objective. However, an agency may be **implied in law** in the absence of intent. For example, an **agency by estoppel** may arise if a person holds him/herself out as an agent, the alleged principal knows or should know of the representation and fails to deny it adequately, and a third party detrimentally relies on the existence of an agency.

Formation of an agency also requires that the agent agree to act on the principal's behalf and that the agency have a legal purpose. However, if the agency arises by contract, all elements of a contract must be present. Indeed, most agencies are created by contract. Furthermore, formalities are not required to form an agency. Thus, oral agreement is sufficient to form an agency even if the agent is to enter into contracts that must be in writing under the **statute of frauds**. But if the contract to be negotiated by the agent is subject to the statute of frauds, e.g., the sale of land or a promise to answer for the debt of another, state law may require a writing (the **equal dignity** rule). Some states require a writing only if the contract involves a sale of land. Others apply the rule to any contract within the statute of frauds.

A **power of attorney** is a formal appointment of an agent that must be signed by the principal. It is often used to authorize an agent to enter into a transaction or execute documents. Despite the name, the agent need not be an attorney at law. A **general power of attorney** authorizes the agent to do anything that may be necessary to transact the principal's legal affairs. A **special power of attorney** grants authority for only specifically enumerated acts. Under the common law, a power of attorney ends upon the **death or incapacity** of the principal. A **durable power of attorney** is effective during the period of incapacity of the principal if the agency power was conferred in a writing that expressly provides for the agency to exist after the principal becomes incompetent. In some states, a durable power of attorney can also function as a **living will**.

If the principal does not have the **legal capacity** to perform the act authorized by the agency, the act of the agent on behalf of the principal may not be enforceable at law. However, an **incompetent agent** can bind a competent principal. The agent's capacity is irrelevant because an agent's act is deemed to be the act of a principal. However, incapacity of the agent to perform the act authorized by the principal may suspend or terminate the agency.

The common types of agency relationships and agents include special, general, and universal agents. **Special agents** are engaged for a particular transaction and are authorized to perform specific activities subject to specific instructions. **General agents** are authorized to perform all acts relevant to the purpose for which they are engaged. **Universal agents** are unlimited general agents who are authorized to conduct all of the principal's business that the principal may legally delegate. Uncompensated agents are known as **gratuitous agents**. A **del credere agent** is a surety. (S)he guarantees the obligations of the third party to the principal. The obligation of the del credere agent is based on a promise to answer for the debt of another. However, because its main purpose is to benefit the agent, not the debtor, it is not subject to the **statute of frauds**. Thus, the agreement may be oral. An **employee** is not necessarily an agent. Employment may be for the purpose of performing services that do not include acting as a business representative of the employer with third parties. The term **servant** has often been used for an agent whose physical efforts are subject to the control of the principal.

Principals may be disclosed, partially disclosed, or nondisclosed. Whether the principal is disclosed does not affect the duties of the principal and agent to each other. Also, the third party has no right to disclosure. A **disclosed principal** is known to exist by the third party. The third party knows the agent is acting for the principal and knows who the principal is. A **partially disclosed principal** is known to exist by the third party. The third party knows the agent is acting for a principal but does not know the principal's identity. A **nondisclosed principal** is not known to the third party. The third party believes that (s)he is dealing with a principal and not an agent. Thus, the third party believes the agent is acting on his/her own behalf. Under general contract law principles, the third party can sue the **agent of the nondisclosed principal** personally, and vice versa. The third party intended to deal only with the agent. When an agent contracts for a **partially disclosed or a nondisclosed principal**, the **principal and the agent** are liable to the third party. The liability of the agent and a **partially disclosed** principal is **joint and several**. The third party may sue either or both and collect any amount from either until the judgment is satisfied. The **nondisclosed principal** can generally **sue on the contract** made on his/her behalf, except when it would be unfair or unjust to the other party. Under traditional common law rules, once the nondisclosed principal is **discovered**, the third party must **elect** whether to hold the principal or the agent liable for performance. Moreover, the discovered principal also may have tort liability. If the agent acts **outside the scope of actual authority**, the nondisclosed principal is generally not liable to the third party. The nondisclosed principal may **ratify** a contract formed beyond the scope of the agent's actual authority by accepting the benefits of the contract or other affirmative conduct. However, the third party has no **right to ratification**.

Except in the case of a gratuitous or noncontractual relationship, agents are either **employees or independent contractors**. The distinction depends on the quantity of control retained or exercised by the principal over the agent. The distinction is significant for many reasons. For example, an employer pays Social Security and unemployment taxes on the wages of employees but not independent contractors. Also, an employer owns the copyright of a **work for hire**, i.e., one generated by an employee under instructions from the employer within the course and scope of employment. However, absent a written agreement between the parties or if the work is not within one of the specific categories defined in the Copyright Act, an independent contractor (e.g., a computer programmer) will own the copyright. A principal-employer has **actual control** over the physical efforts of an **employee**.

In contrast, a principal does not have control over the physical efforts of an **independent contractor**. The latter is responsible only for the finished product of his/her labor. The **degree of control** a principal exerts may not be clear. The status of the agent is a factual determination based on such considerations as (1) the agreement of the parties as to the control to be exercised by the principal, (2) the extent of supervision (but a right of inspection is consistent with independent contractor status), (3) whether the agent provides services exclusively for the principal, (4) the relationship between the nature of the principal's business and the occupation and work of the agent, (5) the specialization required for the task, (6) how the agent is paid, and (7) the duration of the relationship. Still another consideration is which party provides the agent's place of work, tools, and supplies, or otherwise pays the agent's overhead expenses. (NOTE: The degree-of-control criterion is the only one used by the IRS.)

The employee-independent contractor distinction is crucial to determining the principal's liability when the agent commits a **tort**. To the extent that a person has the right to control another, (s)he may be liable for the results of the other's conduct. Under the doctrine of **respondeat superior**, an employer is liable for employees' intentional or unintentional torts that are committed **within the scope and during the course of employment**. Hence, the employer has **vicarious liability**. This liability arises **without fault** by the employer. However, a principal is usually not liable for the **torts of an independent contractor**, although exceptions exist. For example, some duties may not be delegated as a matter of law or public policy, such as a duty of an employer to provide employees with a **safe workplace**. An employer therefore cannot escape liability by engaging an independent contractor to ensure a safe workplace. **Ultrahazardous activity** is another example. A principal may not avoid liability by contracting out ultrahazardous activities or a project that includes them. Furthermore, a principal who commits negligence in the hiring, direction, or training of any agent is directly liable.

The law of agency establishes certain fundamental duties owed by the agent and the principal to each other in addition to their contractual obligations. Ordinarily, parties may modify or eliminate, by agreement, one or all of these fundamental duties. The **agent owes five basic duties** to the principal. They arise by operation of law regardless of whether they are expressed in the agency agreement. The **duty of obedience** requires the agent to follow all lawful and explicit instructions of the principal. If an emergency arises and the agent cannot reach the principal, the agent may deviate from the principal's instructions to the extent the deviation is reasonable. The **duty of care and diligence** requires the agent to use the care and skill of a reasonable person in like circumstances. The agent must use any special skills or knowledge that (s)he has. The **duty of notification** requires the agent to use reasonable efforts to notify the principal of all information (s)he possesses that is relevant to the subject matter of the agency and that (s)he knows will be imputed to the principal. The **duty to account** requires the agent to account for money or other property received or expended on behalf of the principal. An agent must not commingle his/her own money or property with money or property received from or for the principal. The **fiduciary duty** requires the agent to act with utmost loyalty and good faith solely for his/her principal's interest. Thus, the agent must not compete with the principal and must not represent the principal if (s)he has a conflict of interest unless the principal consents to representation by the agent after receiving full knowledge of all material facts. The agent also may not buy from him/herself for the principal without permission or make secret profits on transactions entered into for the principal.

The agent is customarily liable to the principal for losses resulting from the agent's breach of a duty. A **constructive trust** in favor of the principal will be imposed on any profits obtained by the agent as a result of breach of his/her fiduciary duty. If the principal is sued for the agent's negligence or the agent violates the principal's instructions, the principal has the right to indemnification from the agent.

The **principal's duties to the agent** include the duties to compensate, reimburse, and indemnify. They do not include a fiduciary duty. Unless an agent has agreed to act gratuitously, the principal has a **duty to compensate** the agent for his/her services. The duty to compensate is implied if not expressed. If the rate or amount of compensation is not expressed, compensation is an amount equal to the reasonable value of the agent's services. The **duty to reimburse** requires payment to the agent for authorized payments made or expenses occurred on behalf of the principal. The principal has a **duty to indemnify** the agent for losses suffered or expenses incurred while the agent acted as instructed in a legal transaction or in a transaction the agent did not know to be wrongful. The principal's duties to the agent also include a **duty not to impair the agent's performance** and to exercise reasonable care for the safety of the agent. Moreover, the principal has a duty to **disclose known risks** involved in the task for which the agent was engaged if (s)he knows or should know of the risk and knows or should know the agent is unaware of the risk. The **agent's remedies** for a principal's breach of a duty include (1) terminating the agency relationship, (2) counterclaiming if the principal sues, (3) demanding an accounting, and (4) filing a civil action seeking normal tort and contract remedies.

The agent can legally bind the principal only when the agent has authority. The **Restatement (Second) of Agency** defines **authority** as the agent's ability to affect the principal's relations with third parties. **Actual authority** results from consent by the principal manifested to the agent. Actual authority grants the agent the right and power to bind the principal to third parties. Actual authority may be implied by the principal's words or conduct. It is authority necessary to carry out the purposes for which the agency was established. Implied actual authority may also be indicated by the custom and usage of the business or by the agent's position relative to the purposes for which the agency is formed. Actual authority is unaffected by nondisclosure of the principal. **Apparent authority** (or **authority by estoppel**) is granted by language or conduct of the principal manifested to a third party that reasonably induces the third party to rely on the agent's authority. Apparent authority gives the agent the **power but not the right** to bind the principal to third parties, but actual authority confers both the right and power. Because apparent authority requires a manifestation from the principal to the third party, it cannot be based on the words or actions of the agent, and it cannot exist if the **principal is undisclosed**. The basis of apparent authority is **justifiable reliance** on the conduct of the principal. Thus, the third party must not have knowledge of the agent's lack of actual authority.

Ordinarily, an agent does not have the **power to delegate authority** or to appoint a **subagent**. However, the principal may intend that the agent be permitted to delegate authority. Evidence of such intent may be found in (1) an express authorization, (2) the character of the business, (3) usage of trade, and (4) prior conduct of the principal and agent. If the agent lacks authority to appoint a subagent but does so anyway, the subagent cannot bind the principal.

Ratification by the principal is a voluntary election to adopt an act purportedly done on the principal's behalf and to treat the act as if it were originally authorized. Effective ratification requires the principal to be aware of all material facts when agreeing to be bound by the agent's act and to ratify all of the transaction. Ratification may be either **express or implied**. It may be indicated by the principal's language or conduct that reasonably indicates intent to ratify. It is also **irrevocable**. An important consequence of ratification is that **an agent has no liability to the third party after ratification**. But if the principal does not ratify, the agent is liable to the third party for breach of the implied warranty of authority.

The agent is **liable on contracts** unless (s)he has authority and the principal's identity is disclosed or known to the third party. An agent may assume liability on any contract by making the contract in his/her own name, co-making the contract with the principal, or guaranteeing the principal's performance. An agent, by purporting to represent a principal, **implicitly warrants** that (s)he has actual authority for his/her conduct and also warrants that the principal is legally competent. Thus, the agent can be liable to a third party for breach of the implied warranty of authority. Moreover, the agent is always liable for his/her own torts.

Because an agency is based on mutual consent of the parties, **termination of the relationship** may be by either the principal or the agent, even if termination breaches a contract. A principal may revoke the grant of authority and terminate the agency relationship. The agent may renounce the grant of authority by giving notice to the principal. Other acts of the parties that terminate an agency relationship include mutual agreement, fulfillment of the purpose of the agency, and lapse of the agency's specified duration. An agency also may be terminated automatically by **operation of law**. Examples include (1) bankruptcy of the principal, (2) a judicial declaration of incompetence (e.g., because of the insanity of the principal or agent), (3) death of either the principal or the agent, (4) destruction of the subject matter of the agency, (5) a change of law that makes a formerly authorized agency illegal, and (6) the agent's serious violation of his/her fiduciary duty.

In **an agency coupled with an interest**, the agent has a specific, current, **beneficial interest** in property that is the subject matter of the agency. The interest is in the item over which the agent's authority is to be exercised. Accordingly, this kind of agency is **irrevocable**. For example, Dan borrowed $100,000 from Bank, giving Bank security in the form of a grant of authority to sell Dan's farm in case of default. An agency coupled with an interest is an agency in form but not in theory. The relationship is created primarily to benefit the agent rather than the principal.

Actual authority ceases to exist upon **termination** of an agency relationship, whether by act of the parties or by operation of law. **Apparent authority** ceases to exist upon termination of the agency by operation of law. Notice to third parties is not required. However, apparent authority continues to exist until the third party receives notice of the termination, if the termination is by an act of the parties. **Actual notice** to the third party is required if the third party previously dealt with the agent, the agent was specially credited to the third party, and the agent and third party had begun to deal. **Constructive notice**, such as in a trade journal or in a paper of general circulation in the area where the agent operated, is sufficient for other third parties. Because of the equal dignity rule, when the authorization of the agent was written, the revocation of authorization must also be written.

An **electronic agent** is a program or other automated means that independently initiates actions or responds to electronic messages without review by a human (defined in the **Uniform Computer Information Transactions Act**). An electronic agent may be programmed to search for and copy information on the Internet, to compare prices, and even to buy products online. Hence, issues may arise as to whether the electronic agent had authority to enter into agreements or whether certain terms are part of an agreement. For example, a program serving as an agent may ignore the terms of a **click-on agreement** for licensing of software. The UCITA provides that a person using an electronic agent for "authentication, performance, or agreement, including manifestation of assent," is bound even if no human reviewed the agent's operations.

QUESTIONS

29.1 Nature

1. A principal and agent relationship requires a

A. Meeting of the minds and consent to act.

B. Specified consideration.

C. Written agreement.

D. Power of attorney.

Answer (A) is correct. *(CPA, adapted)*

REQUIRED: The requirement of a principal-agent relationship.

DISCUSSION: The requirements to form an agency relationship are an agreement between principal and agent on the relationship and subject matter, legality of the subject matter, and capacity of the principal.

Answer (B) is incorrect. Formation of the agency relationship does not require consideration. Answer (C) is incorrect. Most agency relationships do not require a written agreement. Answer (D) is incorrect. A power of attorney is a specific type of agency.

2. Which of the following acts can a principal employ an agent to perform?

A. Sell real property.

B. Vote for a political candidate with a power of attorney.

C. Commit a crime.

D. Sign a will with a power of attorney.

Answer (A) is correct. *(Publisher, adapted)*

REQUIRED: The act that a principal can employ an agent to perform.

DISCUSSION: An agent can perform most acts the principal could lawfully perform. Selling real property is an ordinary business transaction that can be performed by an agent. However, many states require that such an agency be in writing.

Answer (B) is incorrect. Voting is a personal act that cannot be delegated to an agent even with a power of attorney. Answer (C) is incorrect. An act must be lawful to be delegable to an agent. Answer (D) is incorrect. Signing a will is a personal act that cannot be delegated to an agent even with a power of attorney.

3. Simpson, Ogden Corp.'s agent, needs a written agency agreement to

A. Enter into a series of sales contracts on Ogden's behalf.

B. Hire an attorney to collect a business debt owed Ogden.

C. Purchase an interest in undeveloped land for Ogden.

D. Retain an independent general contractor to renovate Ogden's office building.

Answer (C) is correct. *(CPA, adapted)*

REQUIRED: The agency agreement that must be in writing.

DISCUSSION: Formalities, such as a writing, are not required to form an agency relationship. But the equal dignity rule requires a writing when the principal would not be bound if (s)he entered into the agreement on his/her behalf without a writing. A principal's contract to buy real property is unenforceable absent a writing signed by the principal. Thus, authorization for an agent to do so must be in writing if the contract is to be enforceable against the principal.

Answer (A) is incorrect. The agreement to enter into a series of sales contracts on Ogden's behalf would be binding if the principal made it orally. Answer (B) is incorrect. The agreement to hire an attorney to collect a business debt owed Ogden would be binding if the principal made it orally. Answer (D) is incorrect. The agreement to retain an independent general contractor to renovate Ogden's office building would be binding if the principal made it orally.

4. Noll gives Carr a written power of attorney. Which of the following statements is true regarding this power of attorney?

A. It must be signed by both Noll and Carr.

B. It must be for a definite period of time.

C. It may continue in existence after Noll's death.

D. It may limit Carr's authority to specific transactions.

Answer (D) is correct. *(CPA, adapted)*

REQUIRED: The true statement regarding a power of attorney.

DISCUSSION: A power of attorney is a written authorization for the agent to act on behalf of the principal. It can be general or it can grant the agent restricted authority.

Answer (A) is incorrect. A power of attorney is a delegation of authority and need only be signed by the principal. Answer (B) is incorrect. To be effective, a written power of attorney need not be for a definite period of time. However, the statute of frauds may render an oral power of attorney unenforceable. Answer (C) is incorrect. In the absence of a special statute, the death of a principal terminates an agency relationship.

5. Hill is an agent for Newman. On behalf of Newman, Hill contracts to purchase furniture from A&M Wholesalers. Hill has previously purchased furniture on behalf of Newman from A&M Wholesalers. This contract is voidable by Newman if

A. It was not in writing.

B. Newman is a minor.

C. A&M Wholesalers is owned 50% by Newman.

D. Hill is a minor.

Answer (B) is correct. *(Publisher, adapted)*

REQUIRED: The circumstances in which a contract entered into by the agent is voidable.

DISCUSSION: Any person may act through an agent to the same extent the person may act on his/her own, but a principal cannot gain greater contractual capacity through an agent. Thus, if Newman is a minor, a contract made by his/her agent is voidable to the same extent it would be if made by Newman.

Answer (A) is incorrect. An agency relationship is not normally required to be written. Answer (C) is incorrect. A contract is valid between a shareholder and a substantially owned corporation. An agent of the shareholder would have the capacity to contract with such a corporation. Answer (D) is incorrect. An agent does not need the capacity to contract if the principal has that capacity.

6. Jenni Jones, a clerk in a lumber yard, decided to take a lunch break. Bob Smith came in to buy some nails. Not seeing anyone around, Smith sat down on the counter to wait. Walter Proctor came in to buy some lumber. Thinking Smith worked there, Proctor asked Smith if the lumber could be delivered that afternoon. Smith assured Proctor that it would be done. Proctor paid Smith and left. Smith kept the money and also left. Which statement is false?

A. Smith had apparent authority to sell the lumber or agree to deliver it.

B. Jones was in violation of her fiduciary duty to the principal for neglecting her duty.

C. Proctor cannot hold the lumber company liable for not delivering the lumber.

D. Proctor can hold Smith liable.

Answer (A) is correct. *(Publisher, adapted)*

REQUIRED: The false statement about liability resulting from an impostor's acting as an agent.

DISCUSSION: Because Smith was not the lumber yard's agent, he did not have express or implied authority to sell the lumber. Smith did not have apparent authority because no conduct of the principal induced Proctor to rely on Smith's authority. Because the principal did nothing to make Proctor rely on Smith's authority, no agency by estoppel exists.

Answer (B) is incorrect. Jones was in violation of her fiduciary duty by leaving the lumber yard unattended. Answer (C) is incorrect. The lumber company cannot be held liable for not delivering the lumber as promised because no apparent authority existed. Answer (D) is incorrect. Proctor can hold Smith liable directly for his promise.

7. Paul employed Terry as his agent to purchase a tract of real property, to sell some bonds owned by Paul, and to investigate a potential investment in a city 1,000 miles away. Terry is a

A. Universal agent.

B. Servant.

C. General agent.

D. Special agent.

Answer (D) is correct. *(Publisher, adapted)*

REQUIRED: The type of agent.

DISCUSSION: A special agent is one authorized to conduct a certain transaction. A person may be a special agent with regard to several specific transactions. As long as the authorization is not to perform all transactions, it is still a special agency.

Answer (A) is incorrect. A universal agent is one authorized to perform all acts and transactions which a principal may delegate. Answer (B) is incorrect. A servant is not authorized to contract on behalf of the principal. Answer (C) is incorrect. A general agent is one authorized to perform all transactions in a certain area. A general agent's authority is broader than a special agent's but narrower than a universal agent's.

8. Which of the following rights will a third party be entitled to after validly contracting with an agent representing an undisclosed principal?

A. Disclosure of the principal by the agent.

B. Ratification of the contract by the principal.

C. Performance of the contract by the agent.

D. Election to void the contract after disclosure of the principal.

Answer (C) is correct. *(CPA, adapted)*

REQUIRED: The right of a third party contracting with an agent representing an undisclosed principal.

DISCUSSION: The third party is entitled to enforce a contract against the agent of an undisclosed principal and against the undisclosed principal when the third party discovers the principal and elects to hold him/her liable.

Answer (A) is incorrect. Business may be conducted by a principal without disclosing the agency relationship. The third party does not have a legal right to disclosure of the relationship. Answer (B) is incorrect. An undisclosed principal may ratify a contract beyond the scope of the agent's actual authority. The third party does not, however, have a legal right to it. Answer (D) is incorrect. There is no right to void a contract based on disclosure of an undisclosed principal.

9. Which of the following statements is(are) correct regarding the relationship between an agent and a nondisclosed principal?

I. The principal is required to indemnify the agent for any contract entered into by the agent within the scope of the agency agreement.

II. The agent has the same actual authority as if the principal had been disclosed.

A. I only.

B. II only.

C. Both I and II.

D. Neither I nor II.

Answer (C) is correct. *(CPA, adapted)*

REQUIRED: The relationship of a nondisclosed principal to his/her agent.

DISCUSSION: An agent can legally bind the principal only when the agent has authority. An agent's authority is either actual (express or implied) or apparent. Actual authority is the principal's manifestation of consent for the agent to bind the principal to third parties and is not affected by nondisclosure of the principal's identity. An agent acting for an undisclosed principal cannot have apparent authority because apparent authority derives from the principal's action or inaction or from the agent's position. An agent who contracts within the scope of the agency relationship for a nondisclosed principal binds both the agent and the undisclosed principal. Furthermore, one of the principal's fundamental duties is to indemnify (reimburse) the agent for any payments or expenses incurred in any contract entered into by the agent within the scope of the agency agreement.

10. Lee repairs high-speed looms for Sew Corp., a clothing manufacturer. Which of the following circumstances best indicates that Lee is an employee of Sew and not an independent contractor?

A. Lee's work is not supervised by Sew personnel.

B. Lee's tools are owned by Lee.

C. Lee is paid weekly by Sew.

D. Lee's work requires a high degree of technical skill.

Answer (C) is correct. *(CPA, adapted)*

REQUIRED: The factor supporting the view that a person is an employee.

DISCUSSION: An employee is any person who is hired by another person or business for a wage or fixed payment in exchange for personal services and who does not provide these services as part of an independent business. Additional characteristics of employment are determined on a case-by-case basis. The answer choice "Lee is paid weekly by Sew" best fits the description of an employee.

Answer (A) is incorrect. That Lee's work is not supervised by Sew personnel suggests that an employee- employer relationship does not exist. Answer (B) is incorrect. That Lee owns the tools used to provide the service indicates that Lee is an independent contractor. Answer (D) is incorrect. A high degree of technical skill required for a job suggests that Lee is an independent contractor.

29.2 Rights and Duties

11. The duty of an agent to a principal

A. Includes communicating notice given to the agent, but a principal has no liability to a third party if the duty is breached.

B. Does not include communicating pertinent information if the parties have no agreement to do so.

C. May sometimes involve refusing to obey reasonable instructions.

D. To use due care and skill does not apply to an uncompensated agency.

Answer (C) is correct. *(Publisher, adapted)*

REQUIRED: The true statement about an agent's duty to the principal.

DISCUSSION: An agent is under the control of the principal and must therefore obey reasonable instructions and refrain from unauthorized actions. An exception is that the agent may deviate from the instructions in an emergency. For example, an agent instructed not to make expenditures above a certain amount might (in good faith) do so to protect the principal from loss in an emergency.

Answer (A) is incorrect. An agent is impliedly expected to communicate information relevant to the agency to the principal. A principal may incur liability when an agent fails to communicate because the law assumes that notice given to the agent is also given to the principal. Answer (B) is incorrect. An agent is impliedly expected to communicate information relevant to the agency to the principal. Answer (D) is incorrect. All agents undertake to use the care and skill required for the agency.

12. What fiduciary duty, if any, exists in an agency relationship?

A. The agent owes a fiduciary duty to third parties he deals for and on behalf of the principal.

B. The principal owes a fiduciary duty to the agent.

C. The agent owes a fiduciary duty to the principal.

D. There is no fiduciary duty in an agency relationship.

Answer (C) is correct. *(CPA, adapted)*

REQUIRED: The fiduciary duty in an agency relationship.

DISCUSSION: The agent owes a fiduciary duty to the principal. An agent may not profit at the expense of or compete with the principal and must also disclose material facts and obey reasonable instructions.

Answer (A) is incorrect. The agent owes no duty to third parties. The agent should seek the utmost benefit for the principal in his/her relations with third parties. Answer (B) is incorrect. The principal owes only a contractual duty to the agent to comply with their arrangement, to compensate and indemnify the agent, and not to put the agent in unreasonable danger of harm. Answer (D) is incorrect. The agent is a fiduciary of the principal.

13. Jill Jackson engaged Tod Taylor to purchase 1,000 shares of XYZ stock on her behalf. Jackson did not know Taylor owned 1,000 shares of XYZ stock that he wished to sell. Taylor sold these 1,000 shares of XYZ stock to Jackson at the current market price. Taylor's purchase of his stock on behalf of Jackson was

A. Unethical only if Taylor made a profit.

B. A breach of a fiduciary duty.

C. Not unethical unless Taylor could have found a better deal elsewhere.

D. An act that terminated the agency relationship.

Answer (B) is correct. *(Publisher, adapted)*

REQUIRED: The true statement about the agent's sale of the agent's own property to the principal.

DISCUSSION: An agent is a fiduciary with respect to the principal and owes the duty of utmost loyalty. An agent may not sell his/her own property to the principal without the knowledge and consent of the principal, whether or not the agent makes a profit or the principal benefits. The principal may bring an action to recover secret profits.

Answer (A) is incorrect. Self-dealing is a violation of the agent's duty whether or not profit is made. Answer (C) is incorrect. Self-dealing is a violation of the agent's duty even if the deal is the best available. Answer (D) is incorrect. An agent's violation of his/her duty does not terminate the agency automatically. However, it would give the principal the right to terminate.

14. The principal has a variety of available remedies when the agent breaches his/her duties. Which of the following best states a remedy for the given breach?

A. Representation of parties on both sides of a transaction without full disclosure and consent. Remedy is damages but not rescission.

B. Misappropriation of trade secrets. Remedy is recovery of profits made by the agent or by knowing third-party users.

C. Taking advantage of a business opportunity that should have been offered to the principal. Remedy is an injunction, recovery of profits, and punitive damages.

D. Failure to maintain accounts and render an accounting. No remedy because only a principal has a duty to account.

Answer (B) is correct. *(Publisher, adapted)*

REQUIRED: The principal's remedies for an agent's breach.

DISCUSSION: The principal may (1) terminate the agency, (2) withhold the agent's compensation, (3) recover secret profits, (4) impose a constructive trust on resources in the agent's possession, (5) seek an injunction against breach, (6) obtain damages for breach of the agency contract, (7) seek reimbursement for liability to third persons caused by the agent's misconduct, and (8) rescind certain contracts. When an agent has misappropriated confidential information, the principal also may recover profits made by the agent or by third parties aware of the misappropriation. An injunction against use of the information may also be obtained.

Answer (A) is incorrect. The contract may also be rescinded. Answer (C) is incorrect. Punitive damages are seldom allowed in contract cases. Answer (D) is incorrect. The duty to account may be imposed on both principals and agents with regard to monies held by one for the other.

15. Smith has been engaged as a general sales agent for the Victory Medical Supply Company. Victory, as Smith's principal, owes Smith several duties that are implied as a matter of law. Which of the following duties is owed by Victory to Smith?

A. Not to compete.

B. To reimburse Smith for all expenditures as long as they are remotely related to Smith's employment and not specifically prohibited.

C. Not to dismiss Smith without cause for one year from the making of the contract if the duration of the contract is indefinite.

D. To indemnify Smith for liability for acts done in good faith upon Victory's orders.

Answer (D) is correct. *(CPA, adapted)*

REQUIRED: The duty owed by a principal to an agent.

DISCUSSION: A principal is under a duty to indemnify his/her agent for liabilities and to reimburse him/her for expenses incurred while acting in good faith upon the principal's orders. An agent should not suffer loss through his/her actions for the principal. The principal is also under a duty to compensate the agent.

Answer (A) is incorrect. It is the agent (Smith) who owes a duty not to compete with the principal (Victory). Answer (B) is incorrect. Victory has the duty to reimburse Smith only for those expenditures which are directly related to Smith's employment and are authorized. Answer (C) is incorrect. The agency relationship may be terminated at will by either party if the duration of the relationship is not stated.

29.3 Authority of Agent

16. Alice Able, on behalf of Pix Corp., entered into a contract with Sky Corp. by which Sky agreed to sell computer equipment to Pix. Able disclosed to Sky that she was acting on behalf of Pix. However, Able had exceeded her actual authority by entering into the contract with Sky. If Pix does not want to honor the contract, it will nonetheless be held liable if Sky can prove that

A. Able had apparent authority to bind Pix.

B. Able believed she was acting within the scope of her authority.

C. Able was an employee of Pix and not an independent contractor.

D. The agency relationship between Pix and Able was formalized in a signed writing.

Answer (A) is correct. *(CPA, adapted)*

REQUIRED: The important factor in determining whether a principal is liable for unauthorized acts of an agent.

DISCUSSION: Apparent authority is what third parties believe an agent possesses because of the actions of the principal or the outward appearances of the agency relationship. It is a form of estoppel. Express limitations do limit an agent's actual authority. But if they are not known by third parties, they do not affect apparent authority.

Answer (B) is incorrect. What Sky reasonably believed is important, not what Able believed. An objective standard is applied. Answer (C) is incorrect. Employees and independent contractors can both be agents. Answer (D) is incorrect. The signed writing does not affect apparent authority with respect to third parties. The signed writing primarily affects the parties involved.

17. Bill Gladstone has been engaged as a sales agent for the Doremus Corporation. Under which of the following circumstances may Gladstone delegate his duties to another?

A. When an emergency arises and the delegation is necessary to protect the principal's interests.

B. When it is convenient for Gladstone to do so.

C. Only with the express consent of Doremus.

D. If Doremus sells its business to another.

Answer (A) is correct. *(CPA, adapted)*

REQUIRED: The circumstances in which an agent may delegate duties.

DISCUSSION: As a general rule, an agent may not delegate his/her duties without the consent of the principal. However, an agent may delegate his/her duties when the delegation is necessary to meet an emergency.

Answer (B) is incorrect. Gladstone may not delegate merely when convenient. Answer (C) is incorrect. Although Gladstone may delegate his duties with the consent of Doremus, the delegation may also be allowed in other situations, such as an emergency. Answer (D) is incorrect. The sale of the business does not give Gladstone the right to delegate his duties. Depending on the agency agreement, the sale may terminate the agency, or Gladstone will continue as agent for the purchaser.

18. Blue, a used car dealer, appointed Gage as an agent to sell Blue's cars. Gage was authorized by Blue to appoint subagents to assist in the sale of the cars. Vond was appointed as a subagent. To whom does Vond owe a fiduciary duty?

A. Gage only.

B. Blue only.

C. Both Blue and Gage.

D. Neither Blue nor Gage.

Answer (C) is correct. *(CPA, adapted)*

REQUIRED: The fiduciary duty in an agency relationship.

DISCUSSION: If the agent is authorized to appoint a subagent, the subagent (1) is an agent of both the principal and the agent, (2) binds the principal as if (s)he is the agent, and (3) owes a fiduciary duty to both the principal and the agent.

19. Able exceeded her actual authority when she concluded an agreement with Sky Corp. on behalf of Pix Corp. If Pix wishes to ratify the contract with Sky, which of the following statements is correct?

A. Pix must notify Sky that Pix intends to ratify the contract.

B. Able must have acted reasonably and in Pix's best interest.

C. Able must be a general agent of Pix.

D. Pix must have knowledge of all material facts relating to the contract at the time it is ratified.

Answer (D) is correct. *(CPA, adapted)*

REQUIRED: The requirement to ratify an unauthorized act.

DISCUSSION: The person who ratifies becomes legally bound on a contract that was entered into by another who, without authority, purported to act as the principal's agent. To ratify a contract, the principal must have full knowledge of the material facts.

Answer (A) is incorrect. A principal does not need to notify a third party to make a ratification effective. Answer (B) is incorrect. Whether the agent acted reasonably and in the principal's best interest is irrelevant if the principal has the power to ratify and knows all material facts. Answer (C) is incorrect. Whether the agency was general does not affect the power to ratify.

20. Ratification

A. Is not applicable to situations in which the party claiming to act as the agent for another has no express or implied authority to do so.

B. Is designed to apply to situations in which the principal was originally incompetent to have made the contract himself but who, upon becoming competent, ratifies.

C. Requires the principal to ratify the entire act of the agent, and the ratification is retroactive.

D. Applies only if the principal expressly ratifies the contract made on his/her behalf within a reasonable time in writing.

Answer (C) is correct. *(CPA, adapted)*

REQUIRED: The true statement regarding the ratification doctrine.

DISCUSSION: For a principal to ratify an unauthorized act of an "agent," the entire act must be ratified. Otherwise, a principal could pick and choose from unauthorized acts by "agents," which would be unfair to the third parties with whom the "agent" is dealing. Ratification is also retroactive (relates back) to the time the "agent" entered into the contract.

Answer (A) is incorrect. The ratification doctrine specifically applies to situations in which a purported agent has no authority to act. Answer (B) is incorrect. The principal must be competent when the purported agent entered into the contract. The ratification relates back. Answer (D) is incorrect. Ratification may be oral or implied by conduct, and it may occur at any time before the third party withdraws from the contract.

29.4 Liability to Third Parties

21. North, Inc. hired Sutter as a purchasing agent. North gave Sutter written authorization to purchase, without limit, electronic appliances. Later, Sutter was told not to purchase more than 300 of each appliance. Sutter contracted with Orr Corp. to purchase 500 tape recorders. Orr had been shown Sutter's written authorization. Which of the following statements is true?

A. Sutter will be liable to Orr because Sutter's actual authority was exceeded.

B. Sutter will not be liable to reimburse North if North is liable to Orr.

C. North will be liable to Orr because of Sutter's actual and apparent authority.

D. North will not be liable to Orr because Sutter's actual authority was exceeded.

Answer (C) is correct. *(CPA, adapted)*

REQUIRED: The true statement regarding liability for a contract beyond the agent's actual authority.

DISCUSSION: A principal is liable on contracts made by the agent with actual or apparent authority. Sutter had apparent authority to make the contract because of the principal's communication (letter) manifested to the third party. The third party's rights are not limited by the secret limits placed on actual authority. Sutter had actual authority for up to 300 units and apparent authority for the balance.

Answer (A) is incorrect. The agent is not liable to the third party for acting as an agent with apparent authority. Answer (B) is incorrect. The agent is liable to the principal for acting beyond actual authority. Answer (D) is incorrect. The principal is liable for acts of the agent within actual or apparent authority.

22. Farley Farms, Inc. shipped 100 bales of hops to Burton Brewing Corporation. Burton asserted that the hops did not conform to the contract. Farley's general sales agent agreed to relieve Burton of liability and to have the hops shipped elsewhere. This was done, and the hops were sold at a price less than Burton was to have paid. Farley sued Burton for the amount of its loss. Under these circumstances,

A. Farley will prevail only if the action by its agent was expressly authorized.

B. Even if Farley's agent had authority to make the adjustment, it would not be enforceable unless ratified in writing by Farley.

C. Because the hops were sold for less than Burton had agreed to pay, Burton would be liable for the loss.

D. Farley is bound because its agent expressly, impliedly, or apparently had the authority to make the adjustment.

Answer (D) is correct. *(CPA, adapted)*

REQUIRED: The party liable on a contract when an agent releases a third party.

DISCUSSION: A principal is bound when its agent releases a third party from a contract as long as the agent has authority. At a minimum, the general sales agent had apparent authority because it is reasonable to expect a general sales agent to be able to enter into and release parties from such contracts.

Answer (A) is incorrect. Farley could win only if the agent lacked any authority to give a release and if Burton's rejection of the goods was wrongful. Answer (B) is incorrect. An adjustment in a contract by a sales agent need not be ratified in writing by the principal. Under UCC 2-209, a modification or waiver of a contractual obligation need not be in writing. Answer (C) is incorrect. Burton would be liable if the release was ineffective, and its rejection of the goods was wrongful.

23. Delta sent its agent, Otto Bismark, to purchase some equipment. Bismark was instructed to charge the purchase to Delta's account. However, Bismark charged it to a personal account and did not indicate it was for Delta. Upon returning to Delta, Bismark showed Delta the personal charge and Delta reimbursed Bismark. Later Bismark disappeared and the store seeks to hold Delta liable.

A. Delta is not liable because Bismark charged the goods to his personal account.

B. Delta is not liable because it already paid the price to Bismark.

C. Delta is liable as a partially disclosed principal.

D. Delta is liable because Bismark was instructed to make the purchase.

Answer (D) is correct. *(Publisher, adapted)*

REQUIRED: The liability of a principal for purchases by an agent using his/her own credit.

DISCUSSION: Bismark had express authority to make the purchase and did so on behalf of Delta. Thus, Delta is liable for the purchase price. This is similar to the situation in which an undisclosed principal is held liable for contracts entered into by its agent. A few cases take the view that, because the agent's credit was originally trusted, the principal should not be required to pay twice. In jurisdictions following this view, the store could not recover from Delta.

Answer (A) is incorrect. The fact that Bismark charged the goods to his personal account does not affect the liability of the principal. Answer (B) is incorrect. The third party has not been paid. In most jurisdictions, this liability of the principal is not discharged by payment to an agent. Answer (C) is incorrect. Delta is an undisclosed principal, not a partially disclosed principal.

24. Kent works as a welder for Mighty Manufacturing, Inc. He was specially trained in safety precautions applicable to installing replacement mufflers on automobiles, including a rule against installing a muffler on any auto that had heavily congealed oil or grease or that had any leaks. Kent disregarded this rule, and, as a result, a customer's auto caught fire, causing extensive property damage and injury to Kent. Which of the following is true?

A. Mighty is not liable to Kent under the worker's compensation laws.

B. Mighty is not liable to the customer because Mighty's rule prohibited Kent from installing the muffler in question.

C. Kent has no personal liability to the customer for the loss because he was acting for and on behalf of his employer.

D. Mighty is liable to the customer irrespective of its efforts to prevent such an occurrence and its exercise of reasonable care.

Answer (D) is correct. *(CPA, adapted)*

REQUIRED: The liability when an employee disregards an employer's instructions and damage results.

DISCUSSION: A principal is liable to third parties for all acts of its agents and employees committed within the course and scope of their employment. Mighty is therefore vicariously liable to the customer for the damage caused by Kent, even though Mighty made reasonable efforts to prevent such an occurrence and was not negligent.

Answer (A) is incorrect. The workers' compensation laws provide that a worker injured on the job is entitled to compensation regardless of fault or negligence. Answer (B) is incorrect. A principal is liable to a third party for an agent's act even though the agent was instructed not to perform the act. Answer (C) is incorrect. An agent is always liable for his/her wrongful acts, even when committed in the course of employment. The fact that Kent was acting for and on behalf of Mighty merely makes Mighty liable in addition to Kent.

25. Generally, a disclosed principal will be liable to third parties for its agent's unauthorized misrepresentations if the agent is an

	Employee	Independent Contractor
A.	Yes	Yes
B.	Yes	No
C.	No	Yes
D.	No	No

Answer (B) is correct. *(CPA, adapted)*

REQUIRED: The type(s) of agent for whose unauthorized misrepresentations the principal is liable.

DISCUSSION: A principal is liable to third parties for all acts of its employees committed within the course and scope of their employment (even if the employee was instructed not to do the act). A principal is generally not liable for the acts of an independent contractor because an independent contractor is not subject to the control of the employer. There are exceptions, e.g., if the principal authorizes fraud.

Answer (A) is incorrect. A principal is generally not liable for the acts of an independent contractor because an independent contractor is not subject to the control of the employer. Answer (C) is incorrect. A principal is liable to third parties for all acts of its employees committed within the course and scope of their employment. Answer (D) is incorrect. A principal is generally not liable for the acts of an independent contractor because an independent contractor is not subject to the control of the employer.

26. For which of the following is a principal liable for damages caused by an independent contractor acting on behalf of the principal?

A. An automobile accident.

B. A dynamite explosion.

C. Fraud.

D. Injury to an independent contractor's workmen when a large beam fell on them.

Answer (B) is correct. *(Publisher, adapted)*

REQUIRED: The activity in which a principal is liable for damages caused by an independent contractor.

DISCUSSION: A principal is generally not liable for the acts of an independent contractor because an independent contractor is not subject to the control of the employer. However, strict liability is imposed when the activity is ultrahazardous. The use of dynamite has traditionally been considered an ultrahazardous activity for which a principal can be held liable for damages caused by an independent contractor.

Answer (A) is incorrect. Automobile use is generally not considered an ultrahazardous activity. Answer (C) is incorrect. A principal is generally not liable for the torts committed by an independent contractor unless the act is authorized by the principal. The activity is not under the control of the principal. Answer (D) is incorrect. A principal does not control an independent contractor's workers and is not liable for damages to them.

27. Wanamaker, Inc. engaged Adolph Anderson as its agent to purchase original oil paintings for resale by Wanamaker. Anderson's express authority was specifically limited to a maximum purchase price of $25,000 for any collection provided it contained a minimum of five oil paintings. Anderson purchased a seven-picture collection on Wanamaker's behalf for $30,000. Based upon these facts, which of the following is a correct legal conclusion?

A. The express limitation on Anderson's authority negates any apparent authority.

B. Wanamaker cannot ratify the contract because Anderson's actions were clearly in violation of his contract.

C. If Wanamaker rightfully disaffirms the unauthorized contract, Anderson is personally liable to the seller.

D. Neither Wanamaker nor Anderson is liable on the contract because the seller was obligated to ascertain Anderson's authority.

Answer (C) is correct. *(CPA, adapted)*

REQUIRED: The correct legal conclusion when an agent exceeds his/her authority.

DISCUSSION: An agent who enters into a contract without authority can be held personally liable by the third party on the theory of breach of warranty of authority. If Wanamaker does not disaffirm the contract, however, Anderson's act will be ratified and Anderson will not be liable.

Answer (A) is incorrect. Apparent authority arises from conduct of the principal that leads third parties to believe the agent has authority in excess of that actually given. If a third party is not aware of a limitation, apparent authority can still exist. Answer (B) is incorrect. The purpose of ratification is to validate a contract when a purported agent did not have authority. Answer (D) is incorrect. The seller is not obligated to ascertain Anderson's authority and should be able to rely on the agent's representation and apparent authority.

28. Ann Agent is acting on behalf of a disclosed principal. She will not be liable to a third party if she

A. Signs a negotiable instrument in her own name and does not indicate her agency capacity.

B. Commits a tort in the course of discharging her duties.

C. Is acting for a nonexistent principal that subsequently comes into existence after the time of the agent's actions on the principal's behalf.

D. Lacks specific express authority but is acting within the scope of her implied authority.

Answer (D) is correct. *(CPA, adapted)*

REQUIRED: The circumstances in which an agent of a disclosed principal will not be liable to third parties.

DISCUSSION: An agent of a disclosed principal who signs any written agreements in a representative capacity is not liable to third parties when (s)he has actual authority. Implied authority is a type of actual authority that is inferred from the circumstances or is needed to carry out acts within the agent's express authority.

Answer (A) is incorrect. An agent who signs negotiable instruments in his/her own name without indicating the agency capacity is personally liable. However, the agent can seek indemnification from the principal if the action was proper. Answer (B) is incorrect. An agent is always personally liable for any torts (s)he commits. Answer (C) is incorrect. An agent is personally liable if there is no principal, e.g., a corporation yet to be formed.

29.5 Termination

29. Buck Dent is an agent for George Wein pursuant to a written agreement with a 3-year term. After 2 years of the term, Wein decides that he would like to terminate the relationship with Dent. Wein may terminate the relationship

A. Without cause but may be held liable for breach of contract.

B. Even if Dent is an agent coupled with an interest.

C. Without cause but may be held liable for the intentional interference with an existing contract.

D. Only if Dent breaches the fiduciary duties owed to Wein.

Answer (A) is correct. *(CPA, adapted)*

REQUIRED: The true statement about early termination of an agency.

DISCUSSION: Either the principal or the agent has a power of termination that (s)he may exercise at will (without cause). Because the termination would occur prior to the end of the contracted-for term, however, the principal does not have the right to terminate and would be liable in damages for breach of contract.

Answer (B) is incorrect. An agency coupled with an interest cannot be terminated at will. The agent generally has a legal interest in the property of the agency. Answer (C) is incorrect. The principal is a party to the agreement and may be held liable for breach. Only a third party could be liable for the tort of intentional interference with the contract. Answer (D) is incorrect. An agency not coupled with an interest may be terminated by the parties at any time for any reason.

30. Young was a purchasing agent for Wilson, a sole proprietor. Young had the express authority to place purchase orders with Wilson's suppliers. Young conducted business through the mail and had little contact with Wilson. Young placed an order with Vanguard, Inc. on Wilson's behalf after Wilson was declared incompetent in a judicial proceeding. Young was aware of Wilson's incapacity. With regard to the contract with Vanguard, Wilson (or Wilson's legal representative) will

A. Not be liable because Vanguard dealt only with Young.

B. Not be liable because Young did not have authority to enter into the contract.

C. Be liable because Vanguard was unaware of Wilson's incapacity.

D. Be liable because Young acted with express authority.

Answer (B) is correct. *(CPA, adapted)*

REQUIRED: The effect of the principal's legal incompetence on an agent's authority.

DISCUSSION: An agency relationship is terminated by operation of law if the principal becomes legally incompetent. (Some exceptions apply.) Apparent authority ceases upon termination that occurs by operation of law.

Answer (A) is incorrect. Notice to third parties is not required for apparent authority to cease when an agency terminates by operation of law. Answer (C) is incorrect. Notice to third parties is not required for apparent authority to cease when an agency terminates by operation of law. Answer (D) is incorrect. Actual authority ceases when an agency terminates, whether by act of the parties or by operation of law.

31. Which of the following remedies is available to a principal when an agent fraudulently breaches a fiduciary duty?

	Termination of the Agency	Constructive Trust
A.	Yes	Yes
B.	Yes	No
C.	No	Yes
D.	No	No

Answer (A) is correct. *(CPA, adapted)*

REQUIRED: The remedy(ies), if any, of a principal when an agent fraudulently breaches a fiduciary duty.

DISCUSSION: Most agency relationships are contractual, and the parties must perform according to the terms of the agreement. In addition, various duties of the agent to the principal arise by operation of law. They include the fiduciary duty, which requires an agent (1) to act with utmost loyalty and good faith solely in the principal's interest, (2) not to compete with the principal, (3) not to buy from him/herself for the principal without permission, (4) not to make a secret profit in transactions made for the principal, and (5) not to represent the principal if (s)he has a conflict of interest without permission. When an agent fails to perform a duty, the principal may (1) terminate the agency, (2) withhold the agent's compensation, (3) recover secret profits, (4) impose a constructive trust on resources in the agent's possession, (5) seek an injunction against breach, (6) obtain damages for breach of the agency contract, (7) seek reimbursement for liability to third persons caused by the agent's misconduct, and (8) rescind certain contracts.

Answer (B) is incorrect. Both termination of the agency relationship and imposition of a constructive trust are appropriate when an agent breaches a fiduciary duty. Answer (C) is incorrect. Both termination of the agency relationship and imposition of a constructive trust are appropriate when an agent breaches a fiduciary duty. Answer (D) is incorrect. Both termination of the agency relationship and imposition of a constructive trust are appropriate when an agent breaches a fiduciary duty.

32. Pell is the principal and Astor is the agent in an agency coupled with an interest. In the absence of a contractual provision relating to the duration of the agency, who has the right to terminate the agency before the interest has expired?

	Pell	Astor
A.	Yes	Yes
B.	No	Yes
C.	No	No
D.	No	No

Answer (B) is correct. *(CPA, adapted)*

REQUIRED: The person with the right to terminate an agency coupled with an interest.

DISCUSSION: An agency coupled with an interest is one in which the agent has a specific, present, beneficial interest in property that is the subject matter of the agency. A principal does not have the right or power to terminate an agency coupled with an interest. In any agency relationship, the agent may terminate at any time without liability if no specific period for the agency has been established.

STUDY UNIT THIRTY
PARTNERSHIPS AND OTHER ENTITIES

The partnership is the most common form of business organization involving more than one person. In the U.S., partnership law has been codified in the **Revised Uniform Partnership Act (RUPA)**. The RUPA recognizes the supremacy of the **partnership agreement** in most situations. Nevertheless, it cannot (1) unreasonably restrict access to books and records, (2) eliminate the duty of loyalty or the obligation of good faith and fair dealing, (3) unreasonably reduce the duty of care, (4) vary the power to dissociate, (5) waive or vary the right to seek court expulsion of another partner, (6) vary the law applying to a limited liability partnership (LLP), (7) vary the right to dissolution and winding up, or (8) restrict third-party rights. The act is therefore a series of default rules that govern the relations among partners in situations not addressed in their partnership agreement.

Partnerships can be formed **without any formality**. Consequently, parties may disagree as to whether their business is a legal partnership, particularly absent a writing. According to the RUPA, a **partnership** is "an association of two or more persons to carry on as co-owners a business for profit." A **business** is any trade, occupation, or profession. An arrangement outside this definition is not a partnership even if the parties intend to form one. A problem arises when evidence is insufficient to establish any of the definitional elements. Thus, the RUPA provides that **sharing profits of a business creates a presumption that a partnership exists**. However, sharing profits as payment of or for any of the following does not result in a presumption that a partnership exists: (1) interest or other charge on debt; (2) debt; (3) compensation to an employee or independent contractor; (4) rent; (5) an annuity or other health or retirement benefit to a beneficiary, designee, or representative of a deceased or retired partner; or (6) sale of goodwill or other property.

Partnerships are either general or limited. In a **general partnership**, all partners have unlimited liability for partnership debts and activities. It is the most common form of partnership. A **limited partnership** consists of one or more general partners with unlimited liability and one or more limited partners each with liability only for the amount (s)he invested in the firm. In a **limited liability partnership (LLP)**, all partners have limited liability, and no partner is personally liable for partnership obligations. Recovery by creditors is limited to the assets of the LLP. Partnerships also are classified as "for a term" or "at will." In a **partnership for a definite term or a particular undertaking**, the partners specify the duration of the partnership for a specific term or until the completion of a specific project. A **partnership at will** has no fixed duration and can be dissolved at any time by any partner.

A partnership is treated as an **entity** distinct from its members in several ways: (1) The **partnership assets** are deemed to be those of the business unit and not individual assets of its members, (2) title to **real property** may be acquired in the partnership name, (3) each partner is considered a **fiduciary** and an **agent** of the partnership, and (4) the partnership can sue or be sued in the partnership name rather than in the partners' names. Moreover, a **judgment against the partnership** is not a judgment against a partner. When a partnership is not regarded as a separate legal entity, it is treated as an aggregate of the individual partners. As an **aggregate**, a partnership's debts are ultimately the debts of the individual partners, and it lacks continuity of existence. Furthermore, when a partner's interest is transferred, the transferee does not become a partner without the consent of all the partners. In addition, the partnership is not required to pay the usual federal income tax, although it must file an **information return** stating the names of the partners and the income or loss allocated to each.

Formation of a partnership may be written, oral, or implied by conduct. Any legal person who has the **capacity to enter into a contract** may enter into a partnership agreement. For an association to be a partnership, each of the parties must be a co-owner. **Co-ownership** means they share profits and losses in the venture and management authority, unless agreed otherwise. To form a partnership, the co-owners also must **intend that their business make a profit** even if no profit is earned. Thus, organizations that are not for profit are not partnerships. The legal existence of a partnership depends on the **parties' explicit or implicit agreement** and their association in a business for profit as co-owners. However, whether the parties do or do not intend to be partners is immaterial. Furthermore, a **partnership by estoppel** may be recognized when an actual partnership does not exist. The duties and liabilities of a partner may be imposed on a nonpartner (a **purported partner**) who has represented him/herself as a partner or has consented to such representation. A third party who has reasonably relied on the representation may assert the existence of a partnership, and the defendant will be prevented (estopped) from denying it.

Partnership property is "property acquired by a partnership." It is "property of the partnership and not of the partners individually." Thus, it is acquired in the name of (1) the partnership or (2) a partner(s) with an indication in the instrument transferring title of (a) partnership capacity or (b) the existence of a partnership. Furthermore, **property purchased with partnership assets** is presumed to be partnership property. Partners do not own any specific partnership property directly or individually. It is owned by the **partnership as a legal entity**. Likewise, the **creditors and heirs** of an individual partner have no right to specific partnership property, only a lien on the partner's interest. A partner's interest in specific partnership property is a **joint right to possess partnership property for partnership purposes only**. The partner's interest in a specific item of property is not transferable and cannot be attached by personal creditors or pass through a deceased partner's estate.

A **partnership interest** is transferable to the extent it consists of a partner's share of partnership profits and losses and the right to receive distributions. **Partners may sell or otherwise transfer their interests** to the partnership, another partner, or a third party without loss of the rights and duties of a partner (except the interest transferred). Moreover, unless all the other partners agree to accept the assignee as a new partner, **the assignee does not become a partner**. When a partner dies, his/her partnership interest becomes part of the estate. The interest is **personal property** and may be inherited according to the decedent's will. Heirs of the partnership interest are assignees, not partners.

The **rights, duties, and powers of partners** are based on the rules of law applicable to **agents**. Partners may agree to limit certain rights to which individual partners may otherwise be entitled, but they may not modify legal obligations to third parties. Partners' specific rights with respect to the business include the **right to participate in management**. Each partner is entitled to equal participation, and ordinary business problems are settled by a decision of the majority. Extraordinary decisions and amendments of the partnership agreement require unanimity. A partner also has the **right to distributions** of partnership property from the partnership to a partner. A distribution may be (1) a share of profits or return of capital, (2) compensation for services (but see below), (3) reimbursement for payments made and liabilities incurred in the ordinary course of business or to preserve the business or its property, and (4) reimbursement for advances to the partnership in excess of agreed contributions. The items in (3) and (4) are **loans** that accrue interest. A partner's **right of access to partnership information** is the right to inspect and copy the partnership books and records. The **right to share in profits**, unless otherwise agreed, allows each partner an equal share in partnership profits even if contributions are unequal. Also, unless agreed otherwise, each partner must contribute in proportion to his/her share of the profits toward any **losses**. The **right to compensation for services** is in essence the right to receive a share of the profits. A partner is not entitled to be paid for services rendered for the partnership except winding up its business. However, a partnership agreement often does provide for additional compensation. The **right to use or possess partnership property** may be exercised only on behalf of the partnership. The **right to choose associates** means that no partner may be forced to accept any person as a partner. "A person may become a partner only with the consent of all of the partners." When a partner transfers his/her interest to another, the transferee is entitled only to the distributions allocated to the interest (s)he has acquired. A partner also has a broad **right to sue** the partnership or other partners for legal or equitable relief. Suit may be brought to enforce rights under the partnership agreement or the RUPA or to protect interests arising independently of the partnership.

Legal duties of partners are the **fiduciary duties** of loyalty and care. The **duty of loyalty** is limited to (1) not competing with the partnership; (2) not dealing with the partnership in its business as (or for) a party with an adverse interest; and (3) accounting to the partnership and holding for it in trust any benefit from the partnership business or use of partnership property, including appropriation of a partnership opportunity. The **duty of care** is not to engage in knowing violations of the law, intentional wrongdoing, gross negligence, or reckless conduct. A partner also has an obligation of **good faith and fair dealing**. However, no duty or obligation is violated solely because a partner acts in his/her own interest. Furthermore, a partner may lend money to, or otherwise do business with, the partnership on the same basis as a nonpartner.

The **powers** of each partner are governed by law and the partnership agreement. A partner's status grants **apparent authority** to act as an agent of the partnership in any legal transaction that is apparently for "carrying on in the ordinary course the partnership business or business of the kind carried on by the partnership." The partnership is bound even if the partner had no actual authority unless the third party knew or had received notice of lack of authority. However, if a partner acts without **actual authority** on a matter not within the apparent scope of partnership business, neither the partnership nor the other partners are bound by the act unless the other partners ratify the transaction. The filing of a **statement of partnership authority** gives notice of **limitations** on the authority of a partner. A **statement of denial** also may be filed. The statement of authority may be relied upon by a person dealing with a partner who gives value without contrary knowledge (assuming no other filing cancels the authority). If the filing limits a partner's authority to transfer **real estate** and filing is in the real property records, knowledge of the filing is imputed to a person who is not a partner. However, except for these filings and filings of **statements of dissociation or dissolution**, a person who is not a partner is not deemed to know of a limitation solely because of a filing.

A partner acts concurrently as a **principal** and an **agent** for the partnership and also acts as an agent for co-partners. When an actual partner appears to a third party to be carrying on the business of a partnership in the usual manner, or when a partner is authorized by the other partners to take an unusual action, (s)he can obligate the partnership and co-partners. Accordingly, a **partnership is liable** for loss or injury caused by the **actionable conduct** (wrongful acts or omissions) of any partner while the partner is acting within the ordinary course of the partnership business or with its authority. Each **general partner** normally has **joint and several liability** for **any partnership obligation**. Thus, partners are individually liable for the full partnership obligation and also liable as a group. Joint and several liability allows either joint suits or separate actions (and separate judgments) at the plaintiff's option. If a creditor obtains a **judgment against a partner based on a claim against the partnership**, the partner will be liable if (1) the partnership is in bankruptcy; (2) attempts to use judicial process to collect from the partnership are unsuccessful; (3) the court rules that (a) partnership assets are clearly insufficient, (b) exhaustion of its assets is unduly burdensome, or (c) equity will be served by permitting suit against the partner; (4) the partner agrees that the creditor need not exhaust partnership assets; or (5) the partner is independently liable. A partner may obligate the partnership and partners **by contract** when (1) specifically authorized by the partnership agreement, (2) apparently carrying on the business of a partnership in the usual manner, or (3) acting with the actual or implicit consent of the other partners. Furthermore, when partners agree to limit the authority of a partner to act for the partnership, a third party who has **no notice** of the limitation is not bound by it.

Admission into an existing partnership results in liability for partnership obligations. A newly admitted partner is liable for **antecedent debts** and other obligations of the partnership only to the extent of his/her investment. An incoming partner may expressly or implicitly assume personal liability for existing debt, and (s)he has unlimited liability for partnership obligations arising after admission. A judgment creditor may reach a partner's **transferable interest in the partnership** only by securing from a proper court a **charging order**, i.e., a lien on the transferable interest. The court may order foreclosure of the interest at any time. After such order, the debtor's interest is sold at judicial sale. Before the sale, the debtor, the other partners, or the partnership itself may redeem the interest by paying the debt.

The process to end a partnership consists of dissociation, dissolution, winding up, and termination. **Dissociation** is the legal effect of a partner's ceasing to be associated in carrying on the business. Thus, management rights (except winding up) terminate. After dissociation, the business either continues after purchase of the dissociated partner's interest, or dissolution begins. Dissociation terminates the duty not to compete, and the other aspects of the duty of loyalty and the duty of care continue only with regard to predissociation matters and events unless the partner participates in winding up. Dissociation results from, for example, (1) notice of an express will to withdraw, (2) an event stipulated in the agreement, (3) expulsion of the partner, (4) death, (5) incapacity, or (6) insolvency. The partnership is **not necessarily dissolved** by dissociation unless it occurs by **express will** of the partner. A **statement of dissociation** may be filed by the partnership or a dissociated partner. It provides notice of dissociation 90 days after filing. Such notice terminates the partner's apparent authority and liability for the partnership's post-dissociation obligations. If the business is not wound up, the partnership must **purchase the dissociated partner's interest**. The price is the amount distributable to the partner if the partnership were sold on the dissociation date at the greater of (1) liquidation value or (2) the sales value of the going concern without the dissociated partner. The buyout price is offset by damages for wrongful dissociation and other amounts owed to the partnership.

Dissolution ends the normal working relationships of the partners. Dissolution results, for example, from (1) notice of a partner's express will to withdraw; (2) expiration of the definite term of the partnership or completion of the undertaking for which it was formed; (3) an event stated in the partnership agreement; (4) illegality of the business; or (5) a judicial determination of (a) frustration of the partnership's economic purpose, (b) impracticability of doing business with a particular partner given his/her/its conduct, (c) impracticability of doing business under the partnership agreement, or (d) a showing by a transferee of a partner's interest that winding up is equitable. However, a partnership continues until the **winding up** of partnership affairs is complete. All partners are entitled to participate in the liquidation process except a partner who has wrongfully dissociated. The **actual authority** of a partner to act on behalf of the partnership terminates upon dissolution except as necessary to wind up partnership affairs. **Apparent authority** of a partner may continue to exist throughout the winding up process unless notice of the dissolution has been communicated to the other party to the transaction. The fiduciary duties of the partners also continue, but a duty not to compete ceases after dissolution. A **statement of dissolution** may be filed by any partner who has not wrongfully dissociated. It provides notice to nonpartners 90 days after the filing of dissolution and the limitation of the partners' authority.

Winding up is the administrative process of settling partnership affairs, including the use of partnership assets and any required contributions by partners to pay creditors. The person winding up may (1) continue the business as a going concern for a reasonable time, (2) prosecute and defend actions and proceedings, (3) settle and close the business, (4) dispose of and transfer property, (5) discharge liabilities, (6) distribute assets, (7) settle disputes by mediation or arbitration, and (8) perform other necessary acts. **Partners who are creditors** share equally with nonpartner creditors. After payment of creditors, any surplus is paid **in cash** to the partners. (A partner has no right to, and is not required to accept, a **distribution in kind**.) To settle **partnership accounts**, each partner receives a **distribution** equal to the excess of credits over debits to his/her account. Thus, no distinction is made between distributions of capital and of profits.

Profits and losses from liquidation of assets are credits and debits, respectively. **Prior credits** to an account include contributions made and the partner's share of profits. **Prior debits** include distributions received and the partner's share of losses. If the account has a debit balance, the partner is liable to **contribute** the amount of the balance. If a partner does not make a required contribution, the other partners must make up the difference **in the same proportion in which they share losses**. A partner making an excess contribution may recover the excess from the other partners. Moreover, the representative of creditors of the partnership or of a partner (e.g., a trustee in bankruptcy) may enforce the obligation to contribute to the partnership. One effect of these rules is that, consistent with the **Bankruptcy Code**, partnership creditors (1) have priority in partnership assets and (2) share pro rata with creditors of partners in the partners' separate assets.

A **limited partnership** has characteristics of a general partnership and a corporation. It facilitates investments by those who want a financial interest in the operation of a commercial venture but do not want a management interest or unlimited liability. A limited partnership is formed under a state statute by two or more persons, including one or more general partners and one or more limited partners. A **general partner** assumes the management of the partnership and has full personal liability for debts. A **limited partner** makes a contribution of cash or other property in exchange for an interest and a liability for partnership debts that is restricted to the contribution. However, a limited partner may not manage the partnership. Nevertheless, a person may be both a general partner and a limited partner in the same partnership at the same time.

To form a limited partnership, a **certificate of limited partnership** must be filed as a public record of the state where it is organized. The certificate must be signed by all the firm's general partners and contain (1) the name of the limited partnership, (2) the address of its office, (3) the name and address of its agent for service of process, (4) the name and address of each general partner, (5) the latest date upon which the partnership is to dissolve, and (6) any other matters that the general partners include. If the limited partnership desires to do business in any other state, it must register as a foreign limited partnership with that state. If the certificate is not filed, a limited partnership is not formed, and the organization is treated as an ordinary partnership with all partners subject to unlimited liability.

A **limited partnership agreement**, although not legally required, is commonly executed by the partners. The agreement sets forth the rights and duties of the general and limited partners, and the terms and conditions of operation, dissolution, and termination. Absent a separate agreement, the certificate of limited partnership serves as the articles of limited partnership, and state law (the **Revised Uniform Limited Partnership Act** in most states) fills in omissions in the agreement. A **general partner** in a limited partnership has the same powers and is subject to the same restrictions and liabilities as a partner in an ordinary general partnership. A **limited partner** has the right to share in profits and losses, distributions, and surplus on termination in proportion to the relative value of his/her contributions to capital or as otherwise agreed. A limited partner may assign his/her interest, but the assignee does not become a partner unless all of the partners agree or the partnership agreement permits. Typically, a limited partner risks losing only his/her investment. A **limited partner's liability** is extended when (1) no limited partnership certificate is filed, (2) (s)he knowingly permits his/her surname to be used as part of the name of the limited partnership, or (3) (s)he takes part in control of the partnership business beyond the boundaries permitted by the RULPA or the partnership agreement. **Control** means participation in day-to-day management decisions. A limited partner whose participation is substantially the same as that of a general partner is liable to the same extent to persons who reasonably believe the limited partner to be a general partner. However, the RULPA provides a safe harbor for limited partners, and it provides guidelines for avoiding personal liability.

Like a general partnership, a limited partnership goes through the process of **dissolution** and **winding up** before it is terminated. A limited partnership is dissolved when (1) the time or the event specified in writing in the certificate of limited partnership occurs; (2) all the partners agree, in writing, to the dissolution; or (3) a court so orders. Dissolution also results when a **general partner** dies or withdraws from the partnership, unless the written terms of the agreement provide that the business may be carried on by the remaining partners. If there is no remaining general partner, the limited partners must agree in writing to continue the business and appoint a new general partner.

Winding up a limited partnership is conducted by a general partner who has not caused the dissolution. Absent a general partner, it may be performed by the limited partners or by a person designated by the court. At the conclusion of winding up, assets, if any, are distributed to (1) creditors, including partners; (2) current and former partners for distributions previously due and unpaid, except as otherwise provided in the agreement; (3) the partners with respect to return of their contributions, except as otherwise provided in the agreement; and (4) to the partners according to the terms of the agreement (to the extent of any remaining assets). The distribution of the assets terminates the limited partnership.

Certain hybrid business associations of two or more persons are similar to general and limited partnerships. One hybrid, common in international business, is the joint venture. In a **joint venture**, individuals or businesses associate to accomplish a specific business purpose or objective. A joint venture is commonly organized solely for a single transaction. Although a joint venture has many similarities to a partnership, it does not meet the strict definition in the RUPA, which requires carrying on a business, not an isolated transaction. In all other respects, joint ventures are formed in the same manner as a partnership and are governed by the RUPA. Furthermore, they are partnerships for federal income tax purposes. A **cooperative** is an incorporated or unincorporated entity that provides a service to its shareholders or members, such as consumer purchasing or seller marketing, through combining their resources. An incorporated cooperative provides limited liability and usually makes distributions relative to shareholders' transactions with the entity. An unincorporated cooperative is normally regarded as essentially a partnership. A **joint stock company** is, for most legal purposes, classified as a partnership, but owners receive transferable shares of stock and are not agents of the entity. Moreover, a joint stock company has perpetual existence and has directors and managers. A **business trust** provides limited liability to investor-beneficiaries who exchange assets for trust certificates. The trustees manage the assets, which are owned by the trust. A **private franchise** is a contractual agreement by a **franchisor** to license business rights, including use of trade names, trademarks, copyrights, goodwill, processes, and equipment, to a **franchisee** to operate a franchised business, ordinarily as a full-time activity of the franchisee with support by the franchisor. The objective is to deliver products and services, or an entire business concept, within a defined market. The franchisee usually provides operational resources and management. The written agreement prescribes marketing practices, each party's contribution to operations, and operating procedures. Furthermore, the franchisor and franchisee have a common public identity, although they are usually independent legal entities.

Typical franchise arrangements are for chains (e.g., fast-food), distributorships (e.g., motor vehicles or beer), and manufacturing or processing (e.g., soft drinks). Federal law protects certain types of franchisees from a franchisor's wrongful termination of the agreement: the **Automobile Dealers' Franchise Act of 1965** and the **Petroleum Marketing Practices Act of 1979** (gas station franchisees). Antitrust law also may be relevant to franchise agreements. Moreover, the FTC's **Franchise Rule** mandates disclosure by franchisors of material facts to potential franchisees regarding the purchase (for example, operating costs, other expenses, profits, and evidence to support these amounts). State laws also protect franchisees from unjust termination and require franchisor disclosures. In general, statutes and courts emphasize good faith and fair dealing. In addition, general contract law and, if goods are sold, UCC Article 2 apply to franchising arrangements. Among the issues are whether the franchisee (1) is actually an employee, (2) has exclusive rights in a given territory, (3) will purchase products at established prices from the franchisor, (4) pays a percentage of sales to the franchisor, (5) pays some advertising costs, (6) leases or purchases a business location, and (7) maintains the quality of goods or services sold. An emerging issue is **electronic encroachment** on a franchisee's rights via sale of competing products online, by phone, or by mail order.

Most states have statutes providing for organization of a **limited liability company (LLC)**. The uniform act is the **Uniform Limited Liability Company Act (ULLCA)**, which has not been adopted in a majority of jurisdictions. An LLC is an entity that may enter into contracts, sue, be sued, and own property. Moreover, the owner-investors (known as **members**) may file **derivative suits** on behalf of the LLC. The members, who may include foreign investors, and managers of the LLC have limited liability. That is, they have **no personal liability** for the obligations of the LLC solely as a result of their status. However, members may agree in writing to be liable for the LLC's obligations if a provision to that effect is included in the articles of organization. Members also are **taxed as partners** because, under an IRS ruling that treats unincorporated businesses as partnerships, the LLC is a flow-through entity unless it elects otherwise. (Taxation as a corporation may be advantageous if reinvestment is desired and corporate rates are lower than personal rates.) An LLC is **formed** by one or more persons who file **articles of organization** with the appropriate secretary of state (or equivalent). Under the ULLCA, the articles (1) state the entity's name, which must indicate by words or abbreviations that it is an LLC; (2) include certain basic information (such as the names and addresses of organizers, the initial agent for service of process, and initial managers); (3) provide for existence (a) for a specified **term** or (b) **at-will**; (4) indicate whether management will be by owners or managers; and (5) state whether one or more members will be liable for the LLC's obligations. The members' **operating agreement**, which is not legally required and may be oral, may address such matters as (1) management arrangements, (2) voting rights (absent a contrary agreement, statutes often apportion votes by capital contributions), (3) member meetings, (4) sharing of profit or loss or distributions (NOTE: The ULLCA provides for equal sharing absent a contrary agreement, but many statutes provide for sharing based on capital contributions.), (5) transfer of members' interests, and (6) the circumstances causing dissolution. Under the ULLCA, in a **member-managed LLC**, all members have a right to participate, and most business matters are decided by the majority. In a **manager-managed LLC**, each manager has equal rights, and most business matters are decided by the manager or by a majority of the managers. Managers are selected or removed by a majority vote of the members and are fiduciaries regarding the LLC and the members. The ULLCA further provides that, in any LLC, members must **unanimously agree** about some matters, for example, amending the operating agreement or the articles, dissolution, waiver of the right to have the business wound up, merger, and admission of new members.

The RUPA provides for a **limited liability partnership (LLP)**. The **shield from personal liability** is for any **partnership obligation** (for contribution or otherwise) incurred while the partnership was an LLP. It exists even if the partnership agreement contained an inconsistent provision prior to the vote to become an LLP. But a partner who personally and directly incurs an obligation in the conduct of partnership business is fully liable. **Changing to LLP status** is equivalent to **amending the partnership agreement**. Moreover, partners must register by filing a **statement of qualification** to become an LLP. An LLP, or a **foreign LLP** authorized to transact business in the state, also must file an **annual report** containing updated information (name, state where formed, and facts sufficient for service of process). Errors or later changes in the information have no effect on LLP status or the liability of partners. But failure to file may result in revocation of LLP status. The result may be a gap in the liability shield. Nevertheless, a corrective filing within 2 years will close the gap. In addition, the end of an LLP's **name** (e.g., Registered Limited Liability Partnership) and the other requirements give notice of the liability shield to those who do business with an LLP.

The most basic and common form of business organization is the **sole proprietorship**. It consists of one individual who may be engaged in any kind of business. A sole proprietorship is ordinarily a small enterprise. Because it is not distinct from its owner, it is **not a separate legal entity**. **Formation** is easy and inexpensive. Most filing, registration, and attorney's fees are avoided. It is formed (or terminated) at the will of the proprietor. However, a proprietor doing business under a **fictitious name** usually must make a **"doing business as"** filing under state law. The proprietor has the advantage of receiving all profits. (S)he has the disadvantage of **unlimited personal liability** for all losses and debts. The personal assets of the proprietor are therefore at risk. The proprietor and the proprietorship are not distinct entities, so the deductions and income or loss of the business are reported on the proprietor's tax return.

QUESTIONS

30.1 Nature and Formation

1. Which of the following statements about the form of a general partnership agreement is true?

A. It must be in writing if the partnership is to last for longer than 1 year.

B. It must be in writing if partnership profits would not be equally divided.

C. It must be in writing if any partner contributes more than $500 in capital.

D. It could not be oral if the partnership would deal in real estate.

Answer (A) is correct. *(CPA, adapted)*

REQUIRED: The true statement regarding whether a general partnership agreement must be in writing.

DISCUSSION: Most oral agreements to enter into a partnership are valid. If the partnership agreement is for a definite period in excess of 1 year, however, the majority of states require that the partnership agreement be in writing to be enforceable. If the statute of frauds is not complied with, a partnership at will results.

Answer (B) is incorrect. A choice by the partners to divide profits unequally has no impact on whether the partnership agreement must be written. Answer (C) is incorrect. There is no threshold on contributions beyond which a written agreement is required. Answer (D) is incorrect. A partnership agreement to enter into the real estate business does not involve the transfer of real estate and therefore does not need to be in writing.

2. Bonnie was a very bright and mature 16-year-old who invented a new wangle. She persuaded the following persons to meet one afternoon: her rich aunt (on furlough from a mental hospital), to contribute money; her uncle, who was a very good salesman when sober; and the president of Ultra Corporation, which had the capability to manufacture the wangles. These four decided to form a partnership to manufacture and sell the wangles. They all signed a partnership agreement, although the uncle was extremely intoxicated at the time, and the president signed on behalf of Ultra Corporation. Which of the following could become a partner?

A. Bonnie, only with the consent of her legal guardian.

B. The aunt.

C. The uncle.

D. Ultra Corporation.

Answer (D) is correct. *(Publisher, adapted)*

REQUIRED: The person with the capacity to become a partner.

DISCUSSION: The general rule is that anyone who has the capacity to contract can become a partner. A corporation has the capacity to become a partner unless its articles of incorporation (or by-laws) provide otherwise.

Answer (A) is incorrect. Minors have the capacity to contract. But contracts with minors are voidable at the election of the minor. If a minor disaffirms a partnership agreement, (s)he may be required to leave his/her capital in the business if withdrawal imperils the creditors. Answer (B) is incorrect. The aunt may have been adjudicated legally incompetent when committed to the mental hospital. If not, the facts suggest she is without contractual capacity. Answer (C) is incorrect. The uncle was probably unable to understand and appreciate the consequences of the agreement.

3. Many states require partnerships to file the partnership name under laws known as fictitious name statutes. These statutes

A. Require a proper filing as a condition precedent to formation.

B. Are designed primarily to provide registration for tax purposes.

C. Are designed to clarify the rights and duties of the members of the partnership.

D. Have little effect on formation or operation other than imposition of a fine or other minor penalty for noncompliance.

Answer (D) is correct. *(CPA, adapted)*

REQUIRED: The true statement about fictitious name statutes.

DISCUSSION: Fictitious name statutes have been enacted in most states for the protection of creditors. Registration permits creditors to discover the persons liable for the debts of the enterprise. However, a partnership need not adopt a name, although use of a name may help to distinguish a partnership action from that of a partner. Use of a name does not necessarily indicate the existence of a partnership or that a named person is a member of the firm.

Answer (A) is incorrect. A general partnership may be formed with no legal formalities. Answer (B) is incorrect. The fictitious name statutes are designed to protect creditors. Answer (C) is incorrect. The fictitious name statutes are designed to protect creditors.

4. B approached L and proposed they form a partnership to exploit a profitable idea of B's. L declined, citing the risk of unlimited liability. B then proposed that L lend B $50,000 and that B go into the business as a sole proprietor. L would receive half the profits and the right to veto any of B's decisions. The debt would have a long-term maturity date to facilitate operation of the business during its development stage. If L accepts the above proposition, the likely result is that

A. A debtor-creditor relationship exists between B and L.

B. B and L are not partners as to each other, or third parties.

C. B and L have formed a partnership even if they did not intend to.

D. If L promises orally to become a partner of B and to transfer real property to the business, the statute of frauds would prohibit enforcement of the promise.

Answer (C) is correct. *(Publisher, adapted)*

REQUIRED: The relationship of a sole proprietor with a lender who receives a share of the profits and has a veto over business decisions.

DISCUSSION: A partnership can be formed without actual intent if there is an association of two or more persons to carry on a business as co-owners for profit. In addition to sharing in profits, L funded the venture and has the right to participate in management. Hence, B and L's arrangement constitutes co-ownership, and a partnership was thereby formed.

Answer (A) is incorrect. B and L have formed a partnership. The "loan" is really a capital contribution. Answer (B) is incorrect. B and L are partners as to each other; however, even if they were not partners as to each other, they could be held liable as partners by estoppel to third parties. Answer (D) is incorrect. Even though the statute of frauds denies enforcement of an oral agreement for the sale or transfer of real property, most courts do not appear to apply it to an oral agreement concerning contribution of land to a partnership.

5. The distinction between specific partnership property and a partner's property is important not only to the partners and the partnership but also to creditors, heirs, and others. Which of the following is true?

A. Real property held in the name of a partner is conclusively presumed to be the partner's.

B. Property held in the partnership name is presumed to be partnership property.

C. The form of title to property controls over the partners' intent.

D. A personal creditor of a partner may proceed against partnership property held by the partners together.

Answer (B) is correct. *(Publisher, adapted)*

REQUIRED: The true statement about partnership property.

DISCUSSION: The RUPA states that property is partnership property if acquired in the name of the partnership or of one or more partners if that status or the existence of the partnership is noted on the instrument transferring title. Property is presumed to belong to the partnership if acquired with partnership assets. Thus, when title is held by the partnership, the presumption is that the property is partnership property.

Answer (A) is incorrect. Partnership property may be held in the name of a partner. Answer (C) is incorrect. The partners' intent controls over the form of title. Answer (D) is incorrect. A personal creditor of a partner cannot reach the specific partnership property (but can attach the partner's interest in the partnership).

6. James Quick was a partner in the Fast, Sure, and Quick Factors partnership. He subsequently died. His will left everything to his wife, including a one-third interest in the land and building owned by Fast, Sure, and Quick.

A. Mrs. Quick is a one-third owner of Fast, Sure, and Quick's land and building.

B. The real property in question was held by the partnership as a tenancy in common.

C. Mrs. Quick automatically becomes the partner of Fast and Sure upon her husband's death.

D. Mrs. Quick has the right to receive a settlement for her husband's interest in the partnership.

Answer (D) is correct. *(CPA, adapted)*

REQUIRED: The true statement regarding the partnership interest of a deceased partner.

DISCUSSION: A partner's transferable interest is the partner's share of profits and losses and the right to distributions. Upon a partner's death and dissolution of the partnership, his/her estate (or beneficiaries) is entitled to the value of the decedent's transferable interest but not to any specific partnership property.

Answer (A) is incorrect. The surviving partners have survivorship rights to the partnership property. Answer (B) is incorrect. The partnership owned the entire interest in the property, and there was no tenancy in common. Answer (C) is incorrect. All partners must agree to accept a new partner.

7. Unless the partnership agreement prohibits it, a partner in a general partnership may validly assign rights to

	Partnership Property	Partnership Distributions
A.	Yes	Yes
B.	Yes	No
C.	No	Yes
D.	No	No

Answer (C) is correct. *(CPA, adapted)*

REQUIRED: The assignability of a partner's right to specific partnership property or distributions.

DISCUSSION: A partner may assign his/her interest in the partnership but is not allowed to assign rights in specific partnership property. Thus, although a partner engaging in a legal transaction within the ordinary course and scope of partnership business has apparent authority to transfer partnership property, such transfer is wrongful against the other partners without their consent. However, unless the partnership agreement prohibits it, a partner in a general partnership may validly assign rights to his/her share of partnership distributions.

8. Allen, Burton, and Carter were equal partners for the purpose of buying and selling real estate for profit. For convenience, title to all property purchased was taken in the name of Allen. Allen died with partnership real estate and partnership personal property valued at $250,000 and $5,000, respectively, standing in his name. The partnership had no debts. Allen had bequeathed all his personal property to his children. In this situation,

A. Allen's wife has a valid dower right to all the real property held in her deceased husband's name.

B. Allen's wife is entitled only to his share of undistributed partnership profits.

C. Allen's children are entitled to one-third of all partnership personal property.

D. Allen's estate is entitled to settlement for the value of his partnership interest.

Answer (D) is correct. *(CPA, adapted)*

REQUIRED: The true statement regarding partnership property standing in the name of the decedent.

DISCUSSION: No partner has a right to use the partnership property for him/herself even if title is in his/her name. Upon the death of a partner, the decedent's estate is only entitled to the value of the deceased partner's interest in the partnership, not any of the specific partnership real or personal property.

Answer (A) is incorrect. A partner's right in specific partnership property is not subject to dower, courtesy, or allowances to widows, heirs, or next-of-kin. Answer (B) is incorrect. The value of the partnership interest, not just the undistributed profits, becomes part of the decedent's estate. Answer (C) is incorrect. Heirs of a deceased partner have no rights in specific partnership real or personal property.

30.2 Rights and Authority of Partners

9. Skip & Trip decide to start a boutique selling preppy clothing. They sign a partnership agreement providing that Skip will contribute $6,000 toward the necessary $10,000 in start-up capital, and Trip will contribute $4,000. If the agreement is silent as to management and profits, Skip should receive

A. 60% of the profits and share management equally with Trip.

B. 60% of the profits and control 60% of the management functions.

C. 50% of the profits and share management equally with Trip.

D. 50% of the profits and control 60% of the management functions.

Answer (C) is correct. *(I. Schwartz)*

REQUIRED: The partners' rights respecting profits and the management of the partnership business.

DISCUSSION: Absent a contrary agreement, partners have equal rights in the management and conduct of the partnership business. In addition, absent an agreement to the contrary, each partner has the right to share equally in partnership profits even if their contributions are unequal. Skip and Trip had no such contrary agreement.

Answer (A) is incorrect. Trip is entitled to an equal share of the profits and equal rights in the management of the business. Answer (B) is incorrect. Trip is entitled to an equal share of the profits and equal rights in the management of the business. Answer (D) is incorrect. Trip is also entitled to equal rights in the management of the business.

10. Gillie, Taft, and Dall are partners in an architectural firm. The partnership agreement is silent about the payment of salaries and the division of profits and losses. Gillie works full-time in the firm, and Taft and Dall each work half-time. Taft invested $120,000 in the firm, and Gillie and Dall invested $60,000 each. Dall is responsible for bringing in 50% of the business, and Gillie and Taft 25% each. How should profits of $120,000 for the year be divided?

	Gillie	Taft	Dall
A.	$60,000	$30,000	$30,000
B.	$40,000	$40,000	$40,000
C.	$30,000	$60,000	$30,000
D.	$30,000	$30,000	$60,000

Answer (B) is correct. *(CPA, adapted)*

REQUIRED: The division of partnership profits when the partnership agreement is silent about salaries and the division of profits and losses.

DISCUSSION: Partners are not entitled to compensation for their services performed for the partnership, except reasonable compensation for winding up the business, unless such an arrangement is explicitly provided for in the partnership agreement. The partnership agreement is silent on this point, so salaries are not paid to the partners. Profits and losses may be divided among the partners according to any formula stipulated in the partnership agreement. In the absence of such a stipulation, partners share equally in the profits. Partners share losses in proportion to their shares of profits. Thus, each partner will receive $40,000.

11. Woody Wilson and Garret Levy entered into a partnership for a 5-year period to repair appliances. Wilson did the work in the store and Levy made the service calls. Wilson discovered that Levy has been pocketing some of the payments for the service calls and not turning them all in to the partnership. Wilson

A. Cannot sue Levy for breach of the partnership contract.

B. May bring suit to demand a formal accounting and dissolution of the partnership.

C. Cannot sue Levy in tort for fraud.

D. May take all of the funds (to make up for Levy's dishonesty) and walk away from the partnership.

Answer (B) is correct. *(Publisher, adapted)*

REQUIRED: The remedies of a partner against another partner.

DISCUSSION: A partner may sue the partnership or another partner for legal or equitable relief, with or without an accounting as to partnership business, to enforce rights under the partnership agreement or the RUPA, or to enforce rights and interests that are independent of the partnership relationship. One of the enforceable rights of a partner is to recover for another partner's breach of the duty of loyalty. This duty includes accounting to the partnership and holding as trustee for it any benefits obtained by the partner in the conduct of the partnership business. Another right upon which suit may be brought is the right to compel a dissolution and winding up of the partnership.

Answer (A) is incorrect. A partner may sue another partner to enforce rights under the partnership contract. Answer (C) is incorrect. A partner may sue another partner for a tort committed in connection with the partnership business. Such an action is based on a right that is independent of the partnership relationship. Answer (D) is incorrect. Wilson would be in breach of the partnership agreement if he takes all of the funds and leaves the partnership. This action is a wrongful dissociation.

12. Cobb, Inc., a partner in TLC Partnership, assigns its partnership interest to Bean, who is not made a partner. After the assignment, Bean asserts the rights to

I. Participate in the management of TLC.
II. Cobb's share of TLC's partnership profits.

Bean is correct as to which of these rights?

A. I only.

B. II only.

C. I and II.

D. Neither I nor II.

Answer (B) is correct. *(CPA, adapted)*

REQUIRED: The rights of a transferee of a partnership interest.

DISCUSSION: The transfer of partnership rights is allowed without the dissolution of the partnership. The transferee is only entitled to receive those profits the partner would normally receive. The transferee does not automatically become a partner and would not have the right to participate in managing the business or to inspect the books and records of the partnership.

13. Partners have a fiduciary relationship with each other. Accordingly, a partner

A. May engage in a business that competes with the partnership if it is operated with his/her own resources.

B. May take advantage of a business opportunity within the scope of the partnership enterprise if the partnership agreement will terminate before the benefit will be received.

C. Must exercise a degree of care and skill as a professional.

D. May not earn a secret profit in dealings with the partnership or partners.

Answer (D) is correct. *(Publisher, adapted)*

REQUIRED: The true statement about the duties owed by partners to each other.

DISCUSSION: A partner is an agent of the partnership and the other partners and thus owes fiduciary duties of loyalty and due care. A partner also has an obligation of good faith and fair dealing. In dealings with the partnership or other partners, a partner may not earn a secret profit. (S)he must account to the partnership and hold as trustee for it any benefit derived in the conduct or winding up of the partnership business or from use of partnership property (including appropriation of a partnership opportunity).

Answer (A) is incorrect. A partner's duty of loyalty precludes competition with the partnership. Answer (B) is incorrect. A partner's duty of loyalty precludes competition with the partnership. Answer (C) is incorrect. A partner's duty of care to the partnership and other partners is limited to refraining from gross negligence, reckless conduct, intentional misconduct, or knowing violation of the law. (S)he is not liable for ordinary negligence to fellow partners if his/her honest errors of judgment are not intended and do not result in personal benefit.

14. The apparent authority of a partner to bind the partnership in dealing with third parties

A. Will be effectively limited by a formal resolution of the partners of which third parties are aware.

B. Will be effectively limited by a formal resolution of the partners of which third parties are unaware.

C. Does not permit a partner to execute an instrument in the partnership name.

D. Must be derived from the express powers and purposes contained in the partnership agreement.

Answer (A) is correct. *(CPA, adapted)*

REQUIRED: The true statement concerning apparent authority of a partner.

DISCUSSION: Each partner in a general partnership is an agent of the partnership. The partners may not limit partnership liability to third parties by agreement between the partners alone. But apparent authority is effectively limited to the extent a third party knows of limitations imposed on a partner's authority. For example, a statement of authority filed in the real estate records provides constructive notice of a limitation of the authority of a partner to transfer real estate held in the partnership name. Moreover, a statement of dissociation or dissolution gives constructive notice 90 days after the filing. However, a person, not a partner, is otherwise not deemed to know of a limitation solely because it is contained in a filing.

Answer (B) is incorrect. The scope of apparent authority is limited by communications by the principal (the partnership) of which the third party is deemed to be aware. Answer (C) is incorrect. A partner's act, such as execution of an instrument in the partnership name, for apparently carrying on in the ordinary course the partnership business, or business of the kind carried on by the partnership, is binding unless the partner lacked actual authority and the other party knew or had notice of such lack. Answer (D) is incorrect. Apparent authority is the authority to bind the partnership that a third party reasonably believes the partner has.

15. In a general partnership, which of the following acts must be approved by all the partners?

A. Dissolution of the partnership.

B. Admission of a partner.

C. Authorization of a partnership capital expenditure.

D. Conveyance of real property owned by the partnership.

Answer (B) is correct. *(CPA, adapted)*

REQUIRED: The partnership act that requires partner approval.

DISCUSSION: The rights, duties, and powers between and among partners are largely defined by the rules of law applicable to agents. Additionally, no person can become a member of a general partnership without the consent of all existing partners.

16. Buster and Rover formed a partnership to invest in real estate. However, Buster also decided to sell TVs on the side. Buster went to Harold, a wholesaler, and purchased 20 TVs on credit in the name of the partnership. Harold knew the partnership was formed for the purpose of investing in real estate because he had been solicited to be one of the partners. If Buster does not pay for the TVs,

A. The partnership is liable because Buster had apparent authority to sign for the TVs as a partner.

B. As a partner, Rover is personally liable to Harold.

C. Harold can seize Buster's partnership interest and collect his/her profits.

D. The partnership is not liable because it is not a trading partnership.

Answer (D) is correct. *(Publisher, adapted)*

REQUIRED: The true statement regarding liability on a debt incurred by a partner of a nontrading partnership.

DISCUSSION: The partner of a trading partnership (one that normally buys and sells goods) has apparent authority to contract in the name of the partnership for the purchase of goods. However, a partner of a nontrading partnership does not have such apparent authority if the third party specifically knows the nature of the partnership. Harold has no reason to believe the goods are being purchased for partnership business, i.e., for resale.

Answer (A) is incorrect. Harold knew that the partnership was not a trading partnership. Answer (B) is incorrect. The partnership is not liable to Harold. Thus, Rover is not liable as a partner. Answer (C) is incorrect. A creditor must obtain a charging order from a court to seize a partnership interest.

30.3 Partner's Liability to Third Parties

17. Harry, Harriet, and Horance operate the Triple H used car lot as a general partnership. Pursuant to their agreement, each drives a Triple H vehicle to and from work, makes various business trips about the city either from home or the lot, and keeps a "for sale" sign displayed in the vehicle's windshield. Each car is for sale at all times of the day and night and at any location. One afternoon, Harriet was driving on a business trip when her car collided with one driven by Paine, who was seriously injured. Harriet's conduct was found to be criminally negligent. In a tort action by Paine against Harry, Harriet, and Horance, both as individuals and as the Triple H partnership, who is liable?

A. All defendants because Harriet was acting within the ordinary course of the partnership business.

B. Only Harriet because her tort was not authorized by the other partners.

C. Only Harriet because a crime cannot be imputed to the partnership.

D. Only Harriet and Triple H.

Answer (A) is correct. *(Publisher, adapted)*

REQUIRED: The liability in a tort action against a partnership and its partners for an act of one partner.

DISCUSSION: Loss or injury caused to any person not a partner by the wrongful act or omission or other actionable conduct of a partner acting in the ordinary course of the partnership business or with authority of the partnership results in liability to the partnership. If the partnership is liable, each partner has joint and several liability for the partnership obligation. Because the Triple H partnership business was not transacted solely at the lot but was carried on wherever the partners and their cars happened to be, Harriet was acting within the ordinary course of the partnership business, and the partnership and the partners are therefore liable in tort.

Answer (B) is incorrect. Partners are jointly and severally liable for the torts of each other committed when acting within the ordinary course of the partnership business or with authority of the partnership. Answer (C) is incorrect. The wrong also constituted a tort. Moreover, the partnership and the partners can be criminally liable for illegal partnership activities, although not for other crimes by partners. Answer (D) is incorrect. Torts may be imputed to the partnership, and the partners are jointly and severally liable.

18. Stanley and Martin formed a partnership to engage in the trucking business. Stanley contributed the capital and Martin was to contribute the labor. However, Stanley did not want his name associated with the partnership due to interests in other trucking businesses. Martin was involved in an accident while carrying goods on behalf of the partnership. Which of the following would Stanley not be liable for as a result of the accident?

A. Damages caused by the accident.

B. Illegal drug activities when the police discovered their business was transporting illegal drugs.

C. Rental of the truck when the lessor thought it was dealing with Martin individually.

D. Illegal drug activities when Martin was also carrying illegal drugs in the truck unknown to Stanley.

Answer (D) is correct. *(Publisher, adapted)*

REQUIRED: The activity for which a silent partner is not liable.

DISCUSSION: Stanley is an undisclosed and dormant partner. An undisclosed partner is one who is not held out as a partner; a dormant partner is one who does not take an active part in the business. A partner, whether or not (s)he is undisclosed or dormant, is jointly and severally liable for the obligations of the partnership unless otherwise agreed by the claimant or provided by law. However, a partner is not liable for the crimes of another partner that are committed outside the ordinary course of the partnership business and that (s)he did not participate in, assent to, or authorize.

Answer (A) is incorrect. Stanley is liable for the damages caused by the accident given that it occurred during the course of the partnership business. Answer (B) is incorrect. A partner is liable for crimes (illegal drug activities) that are the business of the partnership. Answer (C) is incorrect. A partner is liable for contractual obligations of the partnership even if the contract was entered into by another partner in his/her own name.

19. Amanda Blake, a partner in QVM, a general partnership, wishes to withdraw from the partnership and sell her interest to Kathleen Nolan. All of the other partners in QVM have agreed to admit Nolan as a partner and to hold Blake harmless for the past, present, and future liabilities of QVM. As a result of Blake's withdrawal and Nolan's admission to the partnership, Nolan

A. Must contribute cash or property to QVM to be admitted with the same rights as the other partners.

B. Is personally liable for partnership debts arising before and after being admitted as a partner.

C. Has the right to participate in QVM's management.

D. Acquired only Blake's share of QVM's profits.

Answer (C) is correct. *(CPA, adapted)*

REQUIRED: The rights and obligations of a newly admitted partner.

DISCUSSION: A transferee of a partnership interest is admitted as a partner only by consent of all partners at the time. However, if a transferee is admitted by all the other partners, (s)he becomes a partner and has all rights of a partner, including the right to participate in management, and is not personally liable for partnership obligations incurred before admission. Furthermore, the hold-harmless agreement is effective among the partners who agreed to it but does not limit Blake's liability for partnership obligations to third parties.

Answer (A) is incorrect. Consent of all the partners is all that is required. Answer (B) is incorrect. The newly admitted partner's liability for partnership debts arising before admission is limited to his/her capital contribution. Thus, (s)he is not personally liable. Answer (D) is incorrect. A transferee acquires only the transferable interest (share of profits and losses and the right to receive distribution) if the partners have not consented to his/her admission as a partner.

20. Bill Daniels, Jess Beal, and Sydney Wade formed the DBW Partnership. Daniels contributed $20,000, Beal $15,000, and Wade $5,000. They also agreed that all losses exceeding capital contributed would be assumed by Daniels, and he would hold his fellow partners harmless from any additional amounts lost. If the partnership becomes insolvent and the partnership debts exceed assets by $15,000, which of the following is true?

A. Daniels is a surety insofar as partnership debts in excess of $40,000 are concerned.

B. Those creditors who were aware of the oral agreement among the partners regarding partnership liability are bound by it.

C. Partnership creditors must first proceed against Daniels and have a judgment returned unsatisfied before proceeding against Beal or Wade.

D. Each partner is jointly and severally liable to firm creditors.

Answer (D) is correct. *(CPA, adapted)*

REQUIRED: The rights of creditors of an insolvent partnership.

DISCUSSION: Each member of the partnership is jointly and severally liable for the obligations of the partnership unless otherwise agreed by the claimant or provided by law. Even though Daniels has agreed to hold his fellow partners harmless with respect to losses in excess of their capital contributions, that agreement does not bind the creditors of the partnership, who may hold Beal and Wade as well as Daniels jointly and severally liable for the partnership debts. Joint and several liability means the plaintiff may sue all or some of the partners together or any partner individually and may collect equal or unequal damages from each. However, the total collected may not exceed the amount of the judgment. Moreover, the other partners may seek indemnification from Daniels.

Answer (A) is incorrect. Daniels is not a surety. Rather, he is a principal debtor. A surety is a person who binds him/herself to a creditor for the payment of an obligation of another. Answer (B) is incorrect. Partners cannot limit their liability to creditors by an agreement among themselves. Answer (C) is incorrect. The partnership creditors may proceed against the partners jointly or severally.

21. A general partner will not be personally liable for which of the following acts or transactions?

A. The gross negligence of one of the partnership's employees while carrying out the partnership business.

B. A contract entered into by the majority of the other partners but to which the general partner objects.

C. A personal mortgage loan obtained by one of the other partners on his residence to which that partner, without authority, signed the partnership name on the note.

D. A contract entered into by the partnership in which the other partners agree among themselves to hold the general partner harmless.

Answer (C) is correct. *(CPA, adapted)*

REQUIRED: The act or transaction for which a general partner will not be personally liable.

DISCUSSION: Reasonable third parties should realize that a partner lacks apparent authority to bind the partnership for personal benefit and therefore should require proof of express authority. A partner who signs the partnership name to a note securing a mortgage on his/her personal residence is not doing so for apparently carrying on in the ordinary course of (1) the business of the partnership or (2) business of the kind carried on by the partnership.

Answer (A) is incorrect. The partnership and the partners are liable for the tortious conduct of an employee acting within the course and scope of his/her employment. Answer (B) is incorrect. In the absence of an agreement to the contrary, ordinary management decisions are by a majority of the partners. Answer (D) is incorrect. A contract entered into among the partners is not binding on creditors.

22. When a partner in a general partnership lacks actual or apparent authority to contract on behalf of the partnership, and the party contracted with is aware of this fact, the partnership will be bound by the contract if the other partners

	Ratify the Contract	Amend the Partnership Agreement
A.	Yes	Yes
B.	Yes	No
C.	No	Yes
D.	No	No

Answer (B) is correct. *(CPA, adapted)*

REQUIRED: The act that binds a partnership to an unauthorized contract.

DISCUSSION: A general partnership is bound on a contract made by a partner acting within the scope of his/her actual authority (either express or implied) or by the apparent authority a third party reasonably believes an agent has. A partnership may also be liable on an unauthorized contract by ratification. Ratification is approval after the fact of an unauthorized act and binds the partnership as if the partner had been initially authorized. Ratification may be express or implied from conduct of the principal. However, amending the partnership agreement alone would not imply ratification.

23. Joe Perone was a member of Caddy, Shack, & Perone, a general trading partnership. He died and the partnership is being liquidated in a bankruptcy proceeding, but Perone's estate is substantial. The creditors of the partnership are seeking to collect on their claims from Perone's estate. Which of the following statements is true insofar as their claims are concerned?

A. The death of Perone caused a dissolution of the firm, thereby freeing his estate from personal liability.

B. Partnership creditors and Perone's personal creditors are on an equal footing regarding the assets of Perone's estate.

C. The creditors must first proceed against the remaining partners before Perone's estate can be held liable for the partnership's debts.

D. The liability of Perone's estate cannot exceed his capital contribution plus that percentage of the deficit attributable to his capital contribution.

Answer (B) is correct. *(CPA, adapted)*

REQUIRED: The true statement regarding the claims of partnership creditors against the estate of a deceased partner.

DISCUSSION: The partnership creditors have first claim to the assets of a bankrupt partnership. To the extent their claims are not satisfied, they are entitled to share pro rata with the general unsecured creditors of individual partners in the partners' personal assets.

Answer (A) is incorrect. The death of a partner does not automatically dissolve a partnership at will or extinguish the liability of the estate. Answer (C) is incorrect. Perone's estate has the same liability as the surviving partners with respect to the firm's debts. Answer (D) is incorrect. The estate may be held liable for the entire amount of the firm's debts. However, the estate would have a right of contribution against the surviving partners.

24. The partnership of Josephine Baker, Al Green, and Jim Madison is insolvent. The partnership's liabilities exceed its assets by $123,000. The liabilities include a $25,000 loan from Madison. Green's personal liabilities exceed his personal assets by $13,500. Green has filed a voluntary petition in bankruptcy. Under the RUPA, the partnership creditors

A. Must proceed jointly against the partnership and all the general partners so that losses may be shared equitably among the partners.

B. Rank first in payment and all (excluding Madison) will share proportionately in the partnership assets to be distributed.

C. Will have the first claim to partnership property to the exclusion of the personal creditors of Green.

D. Do not have the right to share pro rata with Green's personal creditors in Green's personal assets.

Answer (C) is correct. *(CPA, adapted)*

REQUIRED: The status of partnership creditors when the partnership and one partner are insolvent.

DISCUSSION: The creditors of the partnership will have first priority in the distribution of the assets of the partnership. The personal creditors of Green can only reach Green's transferable interest (not specific partnership assets) through a charging order.

Answer (A) is incorrect. An action may be brought against the partnership and any or all partners, but a judgment against the partnership is not sufficient to recover from a partner. A judgment must be obtained against any partner from whom recovery is sought. However, all partners need not be sued because partner liability is joint and several. Answer (B) is incorrect. A partner who is a creditor of the partnership has a claim that has the same priority as that of the other creditors of the partnership. Answer (D) is incorrect. Partnership creditors have the right to share pro rata with Green's personal creditors.

30.4 Dissolution and Winding Up

25. A partnership may be dissolved by a judicial determination sought by a partner. Which of the following is least likely to be a reason for such a dissolution?

A. Insanity of a partner if the partnership is for a definite term.

B. A partner's continual and serious breaches of the partnership agreement.

C. Insolvency of a partner if the partnership is at will.

D. The failure of a business with no reasonable prospect of profits in the future.

Answer (C) is correct. *(Publisher, adapted)*

REQUIRED: The event for which a court is least likely to dissolve a partnership.

DISCUSSION: Insolvency of a partner dissolves a partnership for a definite term or undertaking, with or without a judicial determination. However, if the partnership is at will, insolvency results only in dissociation. Dissolution on the application of a partner follows from a judicial determination of (1) unreasonable frustration of the economic purpose of the partnership, (2) impracticability of carrying on the business with a partner because of that partner's conduct regarding the business, or (3) impracticability of carrying on the business under the partnership agreement.

Answer (A) is incorrect. Insanity of a partner is a reason for dissociation of a partner. In a partnership for a definite term or undertaking, it is also grounds for dissolution. Answer (B) is incorrect. Serious and continual breaches of the partnership agreement by a partner is a basis for the court to dissolve a partnership. Answer (D) is incorrect. A court may dissolve a partnership that can be carried on only at a loss.

26. Which of the following will not result in a dissolution of a partnership?

A. An event making continuation of the partnership business illegal.

B. In a partnership for a definite undertaking, wrongful dissociation.

C. In a partnership for a definite term, a partner's death.

D. The transfer by a partner of his/her entire partnership interest.

Answer (D) is correct. *(CPA, adapted)*

REQUIRED: The circumstance that will not result in a dissolution of a partnership.

DISCUSSION: A transfer by a partner of his/her/its interest in the partnership does not by itself dissolve the partnership or even cause the partner's dissociation. The partnership continues, and the transferee is entitled to the transferor partner's share of profits and losses and right to receive distributions. However, a partner is dissociated if the partner is expelled by unanimous vote of the other partners after a transfer of substantially all of the partner's transferable interest, other than a transfer for security purposes.

Answer (A) is incorrect. An event making continuation of substantially all of the partnership business illegal causes dissolution unless the illegality is cured within 90 days after notice of the event to the partnership. Answer (B) is incorrect. In a partnership for a definite term or undertaking, dissolution occurs 90 days after a partner's (1) wrongful dissociation or (2) dissociation by death, bankruptcy, incapacity, or certain other causes. Answer (C) is incorrect. In a partnership for a definite term or undertaking, dissolution occurs 90 days after a partner's (1) wrongful dissociation or (2) dissociation by death, bankruptcy, incapacity, or certain other causes.

27. A partner has the power to dissociate from a partnership but may not have the right. In some circumstances, the dissociation may be wrongful. One consequence that does not follow from a wrongful dissociation from a partnership at will is the loss of the

A. Payment for the partnership interest.

B. Right to wind up.

C. Right to continue the business.

D. Right to receive the full value of the partnership interest.

Answer (A) is correct. *(Publisher, adapted)*

REQUIRED: The consequence not accruing to a wrongfully dissociating partner.

DISCUSSION: Dissociation is wrongful if it breaches an express provision of the partnership agreement. Dissociation is also wrongful if the partnership is for a definite term or undertaking, and, prior to completion of the term or undertaking, the partner (1) expressly withdraws (unless withdrawal is within 90 days after another partner has dissociated in certain cases or has wrongfully dissociated); (2) is expelled by judicial determination; (3) becomes a debtor in bankruptcy; or (4) is not an individual, nonbusiness trust, or estate, and it willfully dissolved or terminated and as a result is expelled or dissociated. The dissociating partner is nevertheless entitled to the buyout price of his/her partnership interest, minus damages for breach and all other amounts owing to the partnership.

Answer (B) is incorrect. A wrongfully dissociating partner may not participate in winding up the business. Answer (C) is incorrect. A partner's dissociation, whether or not wrongful, terminates the right to participate in the management and conduct of the business. Answer (D) is incorrect. A partner's dissociation without dissolution, whether or not wrongful, requires the partnership to purchase the partner's interest. The price equals the amount that would be distributable in a dissolution if, on the dissociation date, the partnership assets were sold for the greater of (1) liquidation value or (2) going-concern value without the dissociated partner. However, damages for wrongful dissociation and all other amounts owing are subtracted.

28. Gia Grande, a general partner, retired. The partnership held a testimonial dinner for her and invited 10 of its largest customers. A week later a notice was placed in various trade journals indicating that Grande had retired and was no longer associated with the partnership in any capacity. Which of the following best describes Grande's status?

A. Release by the remaining partners and assumption of all past and future debts of the partnership via a "hold harmless" clause is a novation.

B. Grande has apparent authority to bind the partnership in contracts with persons unaware of her retirement who have previously dealt with the partnership.

C. Grande has no liability to past creditors who have been informed of her withdrawal and her release from liability, if they do not object within 60 days.

D. Grande is a limited partner for the 3 years required to pay her the balance of the buyout price of her partnership interest.

Answer (B) is correct. *(CPA, adapted)*

REQUIRED: The best description of the legal status of a retired partner.

DISCUSSION: A retired partner has dissociated and therefore has no actual authority, but (s)he continues to have the apparent authority to bind the partnership with respect to parties who have no notice or knowledge of the retirement and who have extended credit to the partnership prior to the partner's retirement. This concept of continuing apparent authority is based on agency law. A filed statement of dissociation eliminates apparent authority. It is effective as notice to nonpartners 90 days after the filing.

Answer (A) is incorrect. The release or indemnification of Grande by the remaining partners does not constitute a novation. A novation requires the creditors to agree to release Grande and accept the others in her place. Answer (C) is incorrect. A dissociating partner is still liable on existing (past) debts unless the creditors agree to release her. Answer (D) is incorrect. Grande has the legal status of creditor (and no status as a partner) during the time required to pay the balance of the buyout price of her partnership interest.

29. After dissolution, the only actual authority of a partner who is winding up is that needed to liquidate the partnership's affairs. The apparent authority of a winding-up partner continues with regard to which of the following persons?

A. Prior creditors of the partnership who had knowledge of the dissolution but did not receive notice of the dissolution from the partnership.

B. Persons who had not previously extended credit, knew of the partnership, and had no knowledge or notice of dissolution.

C. Any person for 120 days after filing of a statement of dissolution.

D. Persons who had not previously dealt with the partnership but knew of its existence and had only constructive notice of dissolution.

Answer (B) is correct. *(Publisher, adapted)*

REQUIRED: The apparent authority of a partner after dissolution.

DISCUSSION: A winding up partner has apparent authority for apparently carrying on in the ordinary course of the business of the partnership or business of the kind carried on by the partnership, provided that other parties to the transactions have no knowledge or notice of dissolution or other limitations on authority. A partner also has apparent authority to bind the partnership by a postdissolution act that is appropriate for winding up the business. However, a nonpartner is deemed to have notice of dissolution and the consequent limitation on authority 90 days after filing of a statement of dissolution.

Answer (A) is incorrect. Knowledge defeats apparent authority. Answer (C) is incorrect. A statement of dissolution is effective 90 days after filing. Answer (D) is incorrect. Constructive notice, for example, the notice given by a statement of dissolution 90 days after filing, defeats apparent authority.

30. During the winding up of a general partnership, what is the order of distributions in satisfaction of the following claims?

I. Amounts owed to nonpartner creditors

II. Amounts owed partners for the excess of credits over debits in their accounts

III. Amounts owed partners for loans to the partnership

A. III, I, II.

B. I, II, III.

C. II has first priority, and I and III share second priority.

D. I and III share first priority.

Answer (D) is correct. *(Publisher, adapted)*

REQUIRED: The priority of distributions in winding up a partnership.

DISCUSSION: Assets of the partnership and any required partner contributions are first used to pay creditors, including creditors who are partners. Any surplus is then used to pay partners for the excess of credits over debits in their accounts. A partner account is credited for contributions and the share of profits and debited for distributions received and the share of losses. Profits and losses include those from liquidation of assets. If a partner's account has an excess of debits over credits, the partner must contribute that amount to the partnership.

31. Dee, Edie, Faye, and Gina formed a general partnership. Their written partnership agreement provided that the profits would be divided so that Dee would receive 40%; Edie, 30%; Faye, 20%; and Gina, 10%. There was no provision for allocating losses. At the end of its first year, the partnership had losses of $200,000. Before allocating losses, the partners' capital account balances were: Dee, $120,000; Edie, $100,000; Faye, $75,000; and Gina, $11,000. Gina has no assets and can make no contributions to the partnership. Ignore the effects of federal partnership tax law. After losses were allocated to the partners' accounts and all liabilities were paid, the partnership's sole asset was $106,000 in cash. How much would Edie receive on dissolution of the partnership?

A. $33,000
B. $36,000
C. $37,000
D. $40,000

Answer (C) is correct. *(CPA, adapted)*
REQUIRED: The share of assets received by a partner on dissolution.
DISCUSSION: Absent agreement, the loss is allocated in the same proportion as profits (Dee, $80,000; Edie, $60,000; Faye, $40,000; Gina, $20,000). Gina's excess over her account balance ($9,000) is her liability for contributions. Because she has no assets, this amount must be allocated to the other partners in the remaining ratio for sharing losses (4:3:2). Hence, $4,000 is allocated to Dee; $3,000 to Edie; and $2,000 to Faye. The $106,000 in cash is distributed in full based on the balances of partnership accounts (Dee, $36,000; Edie, $37,000; Faye, $33,000).
Answer (A) is incorrect. The amount of $33,000 equals the distribution to Faye. Answer (B) is incorrect. The amount of $36,000 equals the distribution to Dee. Answer (D) is incorrect. The amount of $40,000 equals Dee's balance without regard to her share of the loss from Gina's failure to contribute.

32. A partnership agreement provides that upon death or dissociation, a partner is entitled to the carrying amount of his/her partnership interest and the partnership shall continue. This provision

A. Is unconscionable on its face.
B. Prevents dissolution upon death or dissociation of a partner.
C. Eliminates the need to wind up upon dissociation of a partner by express will.
D. Is not binding upon the spouse of a deceased partner if the carrying amount is less than the fair value.

Answer (C) is correct. *(CPA, adapted)*
REQUIRED: The effect of a partnership agreement providing for continuation of the business.
DISCUSSION: In a partnership at will, the partnership's notice of a partner's express will to withdraw serves not only to dissociate the partner but also to dissolve the partnership and cause the winding up of its business. Dissolution in these circumstances may be avoided by unanimous agreement of the partners (other than a wrongfully dissociating partner). Dissolution also may be forestalled by a provision in the partnership agreement.
Answer (A) is incorrect. Such contracts are common. Moreover, a dissociating partner's or his/her estate's interest is purchased if the partnership is not dissolved. Answer (B) is incorrect. Death or other dissociation of a partner does not automatically dissolve the partnership. Answer (D) is incorrect. The estate (or spouse as beneficiary) can have no greater interest in the partnership than the partner had. If the partner was only entitled to the carrying amount, the estate is entitled to that and no more.

30.5 Limited Partnerships

33. A valid limited partnership

A. Cannot be treated as an "association" for federal income tax purposes.
B. May have an unlimited number of partners.
C. Is exempt from all Securities and Exchange Commission regulations.
D. Must designate in its certificate the name, address, and capital contribution of each general partner and each limited partner.

Answer (B) is correct. *(CPA, adapted)*
REQUIRED: The true statement regarding a valid limited partnership.
DISCUSSION: A valid limited partnership has no maximum limit on the number of partners (limited or general). The only requirement is that it have at least one limited and one general partner. In contrast, S corporations currently have a limit of 100 shareholders.
Answer (A) is incorrect. A partnership will be treated as an association (and taxed as a corporation) if it has more corporate than partnership attributes. Answer (C) is incorrect. A limited partnership interest is considered a security and generally subject to SEC regulations. Answer (D) is incorrect. The name and business address of each general partner (but not the other information) must be included in the certificate.

34. Which of the following statements is true?

A. Directors owe fiduciary duties to the corporation, and limited partners owe such duties to the partnership.

B. Corporations and limited partnerships must be formed pursuant to a state statute. A copy of the organizational document must be filed with the proper state agency.

C. Shareholders may be entitled to vote on corporate matters, whereas limited partners are prohibited from voting on partnership matters.

D. Stock of a corporation may be subject to registration under federal securities laws, but limited partnership interests are automatically exempt from such requirements.

Answer (B) is correct. *(CPA, adapted)*

REQUIRED: The true statement comparing corporations and limited partnerships.

DISCUSSION: Both corporations and limited partnerships are recognized only under the authority of statutes. Common law cannot be a basis for their formation. Both require the filing with appropriate state authorities of organizational documents (articles of incorporation or certificates of limited partnership).

Answer (A) is incorrect. Limited partners are not fiduciaries and owe no such duty to the partnership. Answer (C) is incorrect. Although not allowed to participate in management, limited partners may still vote on such partnership matters as dissolution of the partnership or the removal of a general partner. Answer (D) is incorrect. Limited partnership interests are subject to registration requirements.

35. Marshall formed a limited partnership for the purpose of engaging in the export-import business. Marshall obtained additional working capital from Franklin and Lee by selling them each a limited partnership interest. Under these circumstances, the limited partnership

A. Will usually be treated as a taxable entity for federal income tax purposes.

B. Will lose its status as a limited partnership if it has more than one general partner.

C. Can limit the liability of all partners.

D. Can exist as such only if it is formed in a state that has adopted the original or revised Uniform Limited Partnership Act or a similar statute.

Answer (D) is correct. *(CPA, adapted)*

REQUIRED: The true statement regarding a limited partnership.

DISCUSSION: The limited partnership is not available as a form of business organization under the common law. An organization purporting to be a limited partnership but formed in a state with no statutory authority for such a form of business organization will very likely be treated as a general partnership.

Answer (A) is incorrect. A partnership is not a taxable entity for federal income tax purposes. Partnerships are required to file informational returns only. Answer (B) is incorrect. A limited partnership may have more than one general partner. The minimum is at least one limited and one general partner. Answer (C) is incorrect. At least one general partner must have unlimited personal liability.

36. Which of the following rights would a limited partner not be entitled to assert?

A. To have a formal accounting of partnership affairs whenever the circumstances render it just and reasonable.

B. To have the same rights as a general partner to a dissolution and winding up of the partnership.

C. To have reasonable access to the partnership books and to inspect and copy them.

D. To be elected as a general partner by a majority vote of the limited partners in number and amount.

Answer (D) is correct. *(CPA, adapted)*

REQUIRED: The right that a limited partner is not entitled to assert.

DISCUSSION: A new general partner may be admitted to a limited partnership only with the specific written consent of each and every partner (both limited and general). The limited partners therefore do not have the power to admit new general partners, and unanimous consent is needed unless the partnership agreement provides otherwise. A limited partner has such rights as are reasonably necessary to protect his/her investment, but not those giving him/her the power to manage or control the enterprise.

37. A limited partner's capital contribution to the limited partnership

A. Results in the limited partner's having an intangible personal property right.

B. Can be withdrawn at the limited partner's option at any time prior to the filing of a petition in bankruptcy against the limited partnership.

C. Can only consist of cash or marketable securities.

D. Must be indicated in the limited partnership's certificate.

Answer (A) is correct. *(CPA, adapted)*

REQUIRED: The true statement regarding a limited partner's capital contribution.

DISCUSSION: The limited partner's interest is an investment in the entity as a whole. The interest is personal property. It constitutes an intangible because the limited partner has no right to specific partnership property.

Answer (B) is incorrect. A limited partner's right of withdrawal of his/her capital contribution is restricted. It may be withdrawn upon the dissolution of the partnership, at the date specified in the certificate, upon 6 months' notice in writing to all the members, or with the consent of all the members but only if all creditors are paid or sufficient assets are available for creditors. Answer (C) is incorrect. A limited partner's capital contribution may consist of cash, other property, or services. Answer (D) is incorrect. A limited partner's contribution need not be described in the certificate.

38. A limited partner

A. May not withdraw his/her capital contribution absent sufficient limited-partnership property to pay all general creditors.

B. Must not own limited-partnership interests in other competing limited partnerships.

C. Is automatically an agent for the partnership with apparent authority to bind the limited partnership in contract.

D. Has no liability to creditors even if (s)he takes part in the control of the business as long as (s)he is held out as being a limited partner.

Answer (A) is correct. *(CPA, adapted)*

REQUIRED: The true statement concerning a limited partner.

DISCUSSION: Outside creditors have priority over liabilities to limited partners for the return of their capital contributions. Thus, a limited partner may not withdraw his/her capital contribution if the effect is to impair the creditors' rights.

Answer (B) is incorrect. The reason that a limited partner may own an interest in competing partnerships or compete in other ways is that (s)he does not engage in the management of the partnership. Answer (C) is incorrect. Limited partners are not agents of the partnership and have no apparent or other authority to bind the partnership. Answer (D) is incorrect. A limited partner who takes part in the control of the business will become personally liable to creditors, even if held out as a limited partner.

39. The XYZ Limited Partnership has two general partners, Smith and Jones. A provision in the partnership agreement allows the removal of a general partner by a majority vote of the limited partners. The limited partners vote to remove Jones as a general partner. Which of the following statements is true?

A. The limited partners are now liable to third parties for partnership obligations.

B. Limited partners may vote to remove a general partner without losing their status as limited partners.

C. By voting to remove a general partner, the limited partners are presumed to exercise control of the business.

D. Limited partners may participate in management decisions without limitation if this right is provided for in the limited partnership agreement.

Answer (B) is correct. *(D.B. MacDonald)*

REQUIRED: The effect on the status of limited partners of voting for removal of a general partner.

DISCUSSION: A limited partner is not liable to third parties for partnership obligations as long as the limited partner does not take part in the control of the business. Voting on the removal of a general partner does not constitute taking part in the control of the business.

Answer (A) is incorrect. Voting on the removal of a general partner is allowed. Answer (C) is incorrect. Voting on the removal of a general partner is allowed. Answer (D) is incorrect. Excessive involvement in the management of the business may constitute taking part "in the control of the business." The result would be liability to those parties who have knowledge of the limited partner's participation in control or, if the limited partner is exercising the powers of a general partner, to all third parties.

40. Stanley Kawalski is a well-known retired movie personality who purchased a limited partnership interest in Terrific Movie Productions upon its initial syndication. Which of the following is true?

A. If Stanley permits his name to be used in connection with the business and is held out as a participant in the management of the venture, he will be liable as a general partner.

B. The sale of these limited partnership interests is not subject to SEC registration.

C. This limited partnership may be formed with the same informality as a general partnership.

D. The general partners are prohibited from also owning limited partnership interests.

Answer (A) is correct. *(CPA, adapted)*

REQUIRED: The true statement concerning a limited partnership.

DISCUSSION: A limited partner who permits his/her name to be used in the name of the partnership or in connection with the business will be liable to creditors who give credit without actual knowledge that (s)he is not a general partner. Such a limited partner will forfeit his/her limited liability because the use of his/her name may have led unsuspecting creditors to believe that (s)he was a general partner with unlimited liability.

Answer (B) is incorrect. Limited partnership interests are considered to be securities and must be registered with the SEC unless an exemption applies. Answer (C) is incorrect. A limited partnership can only be formed pursuant to a statute permitting the formation and existence of limited partnerships, and such statutes require many formalities. Answer (D) is incorrect. A general partner may also be a limited partner.

41. Ms. Wall is a limited partner of the Amalgamated Limited Partnership. She is insolvent and her debts exceed her assets by $28,000. Goldsmith, one of Wall's largest creditors, is resorting to legal process to obtain the payment of Wall's debt to him. Goldsmith has obtained a charging order against Wall's limited partnership interest for the unsatisfied amount of the debt. As a result of Goldsmith's action, which of the following will happen?

A. The partnership will be dissolved.

B. Wall's partnership interest must be redeemed with partnership property.

C. Goldsmith automatically becomes a substituted limited partner.

D. Goldsmith becomes in effect an assignee of Wall's partnership interest.

Answer (D) is correct. *(CPA, adapted)*

REQUIRED: The result of a creditor's obtaining a charging order against an insolvent limited partner's interest.

DISCUSSION: A charging order is a court order that has the effect of an involuntary assignment of the limited partner's interest to the judgment-creditor (or an independent third party called a receiver). The limited partner's interest may be temporarily assigned until the profits distributed pay off the debt, or it may be permanently assigned using its fair market value to pay off the debt.

Answer (A) is incorrect. A limited partnership is not dissolved by the bankruptcy of a limited partner or by assignment of his/her interest. Answer (B) is incorrect. Wall's partnership interest is not required to be redeemed. Answer (C) is incorrect. An assignee of a limited partnership interest does not become a substituted limited partner unless the assignor gives the assignee that right pursuant to the limited partnership agreement, or all the members of the partnership agree.

42. Unless otherwise provided in the certificate of limited partnership, which of the following is true if Grey, one of the limited partners, dies?

A. Grey's personal representative will automatically become a substituted limited partner.

B. Grey's personal representative will have all the rights of a limited partner for the purpose of settling the estate.

C. The partnership will automatically be dissolved.

D. Grey's estate will be free from any liabilities incurred by Grey as a limited partner.

Answer (B) is correct. *(CPA, adapted)*

REQUIRED: The effect of the death of a limited partner.

DISCUSSION: The death of a limited partner does not result in dissolution of the partnership. The limited partner's estate will retain all of Grey's rights and liabilities as a limited partner, and Grey's personal representative will act as limited partner for the purpose of settling the estate.

Answer (A) is incorrect. A limited partner's personal representative is not actually made a limited partner but is only entitled to act in that capacity for purposes of settling the estate. Answer (C) is incorrect. A partnership is not automatically dissolved upon the death of a limited partner. Answer (D) is incorrect. The estate retains both the rights and liabilities that would accrue to Grey as a limited partner.

43. Absent any contrary provisions in the agreement, under which of the following circumstances will a limited partnership be dissolved?

A. A limited partner dies and his/her estate is insolvent.

B. A personal creditor of a general partner obtains a judgment against the general partner's interest in the limited partnership.

C. A general partner retires and all the remaining general partners do not consent to continue.

D. A limited partner assigns his/her partnership interest to an outsider and the purchaser becomes a substituted limited partner.

Answer (C) is correct. *(CPA, adapted)*

REQUIRED: The circumstance in which a limited partnership will be dissolved.

DISCUSSION: Retirement of a general partner will generally dissolve a limited partnership just as it would dissolve a general partnership. However, dissolution can be avoided if the business is continued by the remaining general partners either with the consent of all partners or pursuant to a stipulation in the partnership agreement.

Answer (A) is incorrect. The death of a limited partner, regardless of the solvency of the estate, does not dissolve the partnership. Answer (B) is incorrect. A judgment against the interest of a general partner is similar to an assignment of that interest, which does not dissolve the partnership. Answer (D) is incorrect. The assignment of a limited partnership interest does not dissolve the partnership. It makes no difference whether the assignee becomes a substituted limited partner.

44. Wichita Properties is a limited partnership created in accordance with the provisions of the Uniform Limited Partnership Act. The partners have voted to dissolve and settle the partnership's accounts. Which of the following will be the last to be paid?

A. General partners for unpaid distributions.

B. Limited partners in respect to capital.

C. Limited and general partners in respect to their undistributed profits.

D. General partners in respect to capital.

Answer (C) is correct. *(CPA, adapted)*

REQUIRED: The lowest priority of distribution upon liquidation of a limited partnership.

DISCUSSION: Under the RULPA, limited and general partners are treated equally. Unless the partnership agreement provides otherwise, assets are distributed as follows:

1) Creditors (including all partners)
2) Partners for unpaid distributions (i.e., declared but not paid)
3) Partners for capital
4) Partners for remaining assets (i.e., undistributed profits) in proportions for sharing distributions

30.6 Other Entities

45. A joint venture is

A. An association limited to no more than two persons in business for profit.

B. An enterprise of numerous co-owners in a nonprofit undertaking.

C. A corporate enterprise for a single undertaking of limited duration.

D. An association of persons engaged as co-owners in a single undertaking for profit.

Answer (D) is correct. *(CPA, adapted)*

REQUIRED: The definition of a joint venture.

DISCUSSION: A joint venture is similar to a partnership, but it does not carry on a business. The joint venture is an association of persons to undertake a specific business project for profit.

Answer (A) is incorrect. The association is not limited to two persons, and the venture involves only a specific project, not a business. Answer (B) is incorrect. A joint venture is undertaken for profit. Answer (C) is incorrect. A corporation formed for a single undertaking is governed by corporate, not partnership, law.

46. Under the Uniform Limited Liability Company Act, the members of an LLC may determine in their operating agreement how their business will be conducted. In the absence of a provision in the operating agreement, the act provides that

A. Failure of the LLC to follow the usual formalities in the exercise of its powers results in personal liability for the members.

B. The managers have personal liability for obligations of the LLC.

C. A majority of the managers may exclusively decide most business matters.

D. In a member-managed LLC, voting rights with respect to most business matters are in proportion to capital contributions.

Answer (C) is correct. *(Publisher, adapted)*

REQUIRED: The provision of the ULLCA regarding operation of an LLC.

DISCUSSION: The articles of organization must state whether the LLC is manager-managed. If the operating agreement is silent about the powers of the manager(s) in a manager-managed LLC, the ULLCA provides that each manager has equal rights in the management and conduct of the business, the majority of managers may exclusively decide matters relating to the business of the LLC (except for certain specified matters requiring unanimous consent of the members), a manager must be chosen or removed by a majority of the members, and a manager holds office (barring removal or resignation) until a successor is elected and qualified.

Answer (A) is incorrect. Failure of the LLC to observe the usual formalities in the exercise of its powers or management of the business is not a basis for holding members or managers personally liable for obligations of the LLC. Answer (B) is incorrect. The obligations of an LLC, however arising, are solely those of the LLC. A manager is not personally liable for those obligations solely by reason of being a manager. Answer (D) is incorrect. In a member-managed LLC, members have equal rights in the management and conduct of the business. Furthermore, most business matters are decided by a majority of members.

47. The Revised Uniform Partnership Act (RUPA) provides for a limited liability partnership (LLP). Under the act,

A. A partner of an LLP is not personally liable for any partnership obligation.

B. A partnership must file a statement of qualification to become an LLP, but errors in the information filed prevent achievement of LLP status.

C. An LLP's failure to file an annual report may result in revocation of LLP status, but, if an application for reinstatement is granted, the reinstatement relates back to the revocation date.

D. A foreign LLP must file a statement of qualification in a state to transact business there.

Answer (C) is correct. *(Publisher, adapted)*

REQUIRED: The true statement about an LLP.

DISCUSSION: An LLP must file an annual report containing substantially the same types of information (but updated) required in the statement of qualification. One difference is that a foreign LLP must disclose the state of its formation. An LLP that fails to file an annual report is subject to revocation of the statement of qualification, and a nonfiling foreign LLP may not maintain an action or proceeding in the state. However, a partnership whose statement of qualification has been revoked may within 2 years apply for reinstatement. If granted, LLP status continues as if revocation had not occurred.

Answer (A) is incorrect. The shield from personal liability is only for partnership obligations incurred while the partnership was an LLP. Answer (B) is incorrect. LLP status and the personal liability of partners are unaffected by errors or later changes in the information. Answer (D) is incorrect. A foreign LLP that is authorized to do business in the state must file a statement of foreign qualification. This statement does not contain the election to become an LLP.

48. The formation of a sole proprietorship

A. Requires registration with the federal government's Small Business Administration.

B. Requires a formal "doing business as" filing under state law if the proprietor will be conducting business under a fictitious name.

C. Requires formal registration in each state the proprietor plans to do business in.

D. Is not as easy and inexpensive to form as an S corporation.

Answer (B) is correct. *(Publisher, adapted)*

REQUIRED: The true statement about forming a sole proprietorship.

DISCUSSION: A proprietor doing business under a fictitious name is usually required to make a d/b/a or "doing business as" filing under state law. Otherwise, the formation of a sole proprietorship is subject to few legal requirements, such as local zoning and licensing. In this respect, the sole proprietorship is the easiest and least expensive to create of all business organizations.

Answer (A) is incorrect. The Small Business Administration (SBA) is a source of loans for sole proprietor- ships. No formal registration is required with the SBA. Answer (C) is incorrect. A sole proprietorship may conduct business in any state without having to file, register, or otherwise qualify to do business in that state. Answer (D) is incorrect. Of all business organizations, the sole proprietorship is the easiest and least expensive to create.

49. Which of the following is not a characteristic of both a sole proprietorship and a general partnership?

A. Equity capital may not be raised by selling shares of the business.

B. The business's profits and losses are passed through to the owner(s).

C. The death of an owner causes the termination of the business.

D. A "doing business as" filing is usually required if the owner(s) will conduct business under a fictitious name.

Answer (C) is correct. *(Publisher, adapted)*

REQUIRED: The characteristic not common to a sole proprietorship and a general partnership.

DISCUSSION: In a sole proprietorship, the death of the proprietor causes the automatic termination of the business. However, the death of a general partner results in dissociation, not the termination of the partnership.

Answer (A) is incorrect. Neither the proprietors nor general partners may sell shares of the business to raise additional equity capital. Answer (B) is incorrect. Both a sole proprietorship and a general partnership act as pass-through entities for the taxation of the business income. Answer (D) is incorrect. Similar statutes exist requiring both proprietors and partners to make "doing business as" filings if conducting business under a fictitious name.

STUDY UNIT THIRTY-ONE
CORPORATIONS: NATURE, FORMATION, AND FINANCING

The **corporation** is the dominant form of business organization in the United States. The fundamental characteristic that distinguishes a corporation from partnerships and sole proprietorships is its status as a **separate legal entity** with rights and liabilities that are separate from those of its shareholders/owners. It is able to enter into contracts; sue or be sued in the corporate name; and acquire, hold, and convey real and personal property. A corporation exists as an artificial person solely by virtue of an applicable state incorporation statute. Furthermore, a corporation is a person for most purposes under the **U.S. Constitution**. Thus, it has the right to equal protection, due process, freedom from unreasonable searches and seizures, and freedom of speech. However, commercial speech, e.g., advertising, and political speech, e.g., political contributions, are given less protection than that afforded to the same speech by natural persons.

Corporations can be classified in a variety of ways. **Public corporations** are formed for public purposes related to the administration of government. **Private corporations** are organized to earn profits for their owners or for charitable, educational, social, religious, or philanthropic purposes. The two most common types of private corporations are close corporations and publicly held corporations. A **close corporation** is often distinguished by the following features: (1) It is owned by a relatively small number of shareholders; (2) it does not sell its stock to the public; (3) generally, the officers and directors own all of the stock in the corporation; (4) the shareholders are active in its management and control; (5) transfer of shares is often restricted; and (6) a supermajority (or unanimity) of owners may be required for many decisions. A **publicly held corporation** sells its stock to the public at large, and the stock is usually traded on a national recognized stock exchange. Stock or shares in a corporation represent units of property interest in the net assets of the entity, including an interest in its profits. A corporation is classified as a **domestic corporation** in the state in which it is organized. It is a **foreign corporation** in all other states or jurisdictions. A corporation organized in another country is classified as an **alien corporation**. Other types of corporations are formed for specific advantages or benefits. The **S corporation** is a close corporation that has made an election under the Internal Revenue Code that allows it to be taxed as a partnership if it meets stated criteria. **Professional corporations** permit accountants, lawyers, dentists, physicians, architects, and other professionals to incorporate under special state incorporation statutes. The **advantages of a corporation** are (1) the limited liability of the shareholders/owners, (2) separation of ownership from management, (3) free transferability of interests, (4) perpetual life of the entity, (5) the relative ease of raising capital, and (6) status as a **person** for most purposes under the U.S. Constitution. **Disadvantages of a corporation** are (1) reduced individual control of the business, (2) payment of taxes on corporate income and payment by the shareholders of taxes on distributions received from the corporation (unless the entity qualifies for and elects S corporation status), (3) substantial costs of meeting the requirements of corporate formation and operation, (4) hostile takeover of a publicly traded corporation, (5) transfer of unrestricted shares in a close corporation to unknown parties, (6) an inability of a minority shareholder in a close corporation to liquidate his/her interest or to influence the conduct of the business, and (7) becoming subject to state and federal regulation of securities transactions through reporting and registration requirements.

The **Revised Model Business Corporation Act (RMBCA)** applies to both publicly held and closely held corporations and is followed in most recent textbooks. Its purpose is to provide legislators, lawyers, and legal commissions with a basis for drafting and amending state incorporation laws. It also provides judges with a guide for resolving disputes. One of the notable features of the RMBCA is that it permits the shareholders to change by unanimous agreement the provisions otherwise applicable to corporate governance. This flexibility may allow a close corporation to function more nearly as a partnership without loss of corporate status. Thus, **RMBCA 7.32** provides for a shareholder agreement set forth in the articles of incorporation, bylaws, or a separate signed agreement and approved by all shareholders that "governs the exercise of the corporate powers or the management of the business and affairs of the corporation or the relationship among the shareholders, the directors, and the corporation, or among any of them, and is not contrary to public policy." For example, the **shareholder agreement** may (1) eliminate the board or restrict its powers; (2) permit dividends not in proportion to ownership; (3) determine who will be officers and directors, their terms of office, and how they are chosen or removed; (4) set voting requirements (in general or for specific issues) for actions by shareholders or directors; (5) establish the terms of any agreement for transfer of property or provision of services between (a) the corporation and (b) a shareholder, officer, director, or employee, or among any of them; (6) transfer authority to (a) exercise corporate powers, (b) manage the business or other affairs, or (c) resolve a deadlock among shareholders or directors; and (7) require corporate dissolution upon (a) request of a shareholder(s) or (b) occurrence of a given event.

Under the **state incorporation statute**, the **articles of incorporation** (also called a charter), and **the common law**, a corporation has **broad but limited powers**. The RMBCA states that, barring contrary language in the articles, a corporation has perpetual existence and "the same powers as an individual to do all things necessary or convenient to carry out its business and affairs." Accordingly, a corporation has the power to (1) sue and be sued; (2) have a corporate seal; (3) make and amend bylaws; (4) acquire, own, and dispose of interests in real or personal property; (5) hold, acquire, and dispose of shares of stock; (6) lend money and guarantee obligations of others; (7) participate in other entities, for example, as a partner in a partnership; (8) conduct business within or without the state; (9) make donations for the public welfare or for charitable, scientific, or educational purposes; (10) pay pensions and establish profit sharing and other incentive plans for corporate officers, directors, and employees; (11) elect directors and appoint officers, employees, and agents; (12) fix the compensation of these individuals and lend them money; (13) transact any lawful business that will aid governmental policy; (14) acquire its own shares; and (15) do any other lawful act "that furthers the business and affairs of the corporation."

Corporations have inherent powers, statutory powers, express powers, and implied powers. Powers derived from the corporation's status as a legal entity are **inherent powers**. Together with others specifically stated in the state incorporation statute, they are referred to as **statutory powers**. **Express powers** are specifically granted to a particular corporation by its articles of incorporation. **Implied powers** are necessary and appropriate to carry out express powers. There will be little, if any, likelihood of a successful court challenge to the propriety or exercise of the powers described if the articles authorize the corporation to "enter into any lawful business transaction." Acts that are outside the corporation's express or implied powers are **ultra vires**. The RMBCA eliminates the availability of the doctrine of ultra vires as a **corporate defense** to liability and shifts responsibility for improper or unauthorized conduct to the corporation's officers and directors.

The process of organizing a corporation begins with the promotion of the proposed entity by its organizers. The **promoters** arrange for the capital structure and financing of the corporation. They also may procure the necessary personnel, licenses, equipment, leases, etc. Promoters cause the articles of incorporation to be prepared, in which process they select the state of incorporation and a corporate name and plan special provisions to be included. Upon incorporation, the promoters' task is complete.

Prior to incorporation, the promoters usually enter into ordinary and necessary contracts required for initial operation of the business. Thus, they are liable unless they have effectively disclaimed liability. A **preincorporation contract** made by promoters in the name of a corporation and on its behalf does not bind the corporation, except if so provided by statute. Prior to formation, a corporation has no capacity to enter into contracts or to employ agents or representatives. Thus, the corporation, once formed, is **unable to ratify contracts entered into by promoters**. To avoid this dilemma, the courts have created a legal substitute called **adoption**, which essentially is acceptance of the assignment of rights and the delegation of duties by the promoters to the corporation. If the corporation **accepts the benefits** of a promoter's contract, adoption may be implied. Promoters owe a **fiduciary duty** to each other, to the corporation, to subscribers who agree to purchase the initial offerings of stock, and shareholders. If an independent board of directors has not been elected, full disclosure of all dealings with respect to the corporation must be made by the promoters to all shareholders. Typically, the duty of disclosure arises when a promoter transfers his/her own property to the corporation.

Part of a promoter's duty is recruitment of investors in the soon-to-be formed corporation. The promoter secures potential investors using stock subscription agreements. The person agreeing to invest in the corporation is a subscriber. A **stock subscription agreement** obliges a subscriber to purchase a certain amount of stock of the soon-to-be formed corporation at a specified price payable at an agreed future date. The RMBCA provides that a subscription agreement is **irrevocable for a period of 6 months** unless otherwise provided for in the subscription agreement or unless all the subscribers consent to the revocation of the subscription. State law may provide that a subscriber is a shareholder when the corporation is formed or it adopts the agreement. A **public corporation** cannot use subscriptions.

Although the procedures for organizing a corporation may vary in some detail, generally, each state requires the articles of incorporation to be **filed with the secretary of state**. The persons who sign the articles are **incorporators**. The RMBCA requires that the articles include the (1) corporation's name, (2) number of shares the corporation is authorized to issue, (3) street address of the corporation's initial registered office, (4) name of the corporation's registered agent at that office (for service of process purpose), and (5) name and address of each incorporator. Most states provide standardized forms for corporate organization. When the articles have been received and processed by the appropriate state official, they are considered officially filed. Under the RMBCA, a corporation is first recognized as a **legal entity when the articles are filed** with the secretary of state. However, some states require additional filings in designated counties. Incorporation may be in any state and may be done by mail or online.

After the articles have been filed, the incorporators elect the members of the **board of directors** if they have not been named in the articles. The incorporators then resign, and the board holds an **organizational meeting** to take all the steps needed to complete the organizational structure. At this meeting, the board adopts **bylaws** that will govern the internal management of the corporation and elects **officers**, typically consisting of a president, treasurer, and secretary. Other activities of the board at its organizational meeting may include (1) adopting or rejecting preincorporation contracts of the promoters, (2) adopting the form of certificate representing shares of the company's stock, (3) accepting or rejecting stock subscriptions, (4) complying with requirements for doing business in other states, and (5) considering all other transactions necessary or appropriate for furthering the business purposes of the corporation.

A corporation organized in strict compliance with statutory requirements is a **de jure corporation**. A **de facto** corporation is formed when a **good faith effort** was made to comply with the statutory provisions but some statutory provisions were not complied with. The RMBCA treats the filing of the articles (an official act done by the secretary of state) as **conclusive proof** that all conditions have been satisfied. The effect is to treat a corporation as de jure even though a mandatory provision was not complied with.

If a corporation exists, either de jure or de facto, the general rule is that the law recognizes the corporation as a separate legal entity. If the entity is **so defectively formed that it does not even qualify as a de facto corporation**, the RMBCA imposes liability on "all persons purporting to act on or behalf of a corporation, knowing that there was no incorporation under this act." The RMBCA therefore excuses inactive parties and those not knowing of the defective incorporation. An organization that is neither a de jure nor a de facto corporation may be treated as a **corporation by estoppel** in a suit by a third party. Thus, the organization will be prevented (estopped) from denying corporate status if (1) the organization has represented itself as a corporation, (2) the representation is followed by reasonable reliance and material alteration of position by a third party based on that representation, (3) the third party demonstrates fair and equitable conduct, and (4) injustice can be avoided only by treating the business as a corporation.

In certain instances, courts will **pierce the corporate veil**, that is, disregard the corporate entity when it is formed to commit wrongdoing, protect shareholders from liability for fraud, or otherwise circumvent the law. When courts pierce the corporate veil, **shareholders may be personally liable** for corporate acts. The shareholders in this case may include a **parent** corporation, one owning more than 50% of the voting shares and exercising control. Typically, the corporate veil is pierced when a court finds that the corporation is merely the alter ego of a shareholder, for example, when (1) it is undercapitalized, (2) the assets of the corporation and the shareholders are commingled, (3) corporate formalities are ignored, or (4) the corporation is established for a sham purpose.

Subject to federal and state constitutional limits, states have enacted statutes to exert personal **(in personam) jurisdiction** (authority) over corporations and to effect **personal service of process** (a means of giving proper notice to the defendant). Generally, a state may exercise in personam jurisdiction over a corporation based on a **specific event or set of events**, for example, when a corporation's agent commits a tort in the course of performance of a contract within the state. Furthermore, **domestic and registered foreign corporations** are subject to in personam jurisdiction of the state for all purposes. Thus, a court may validly exercise jurisdiction over a corporation regarding a transaction or a matter that has no relationship to the state other than that it concerns the corporation subject to its jurisdiction. Process may be served personally on officers of the corporation or the agent for service of process. A foreign corporation may have contacts with a state or its citizens yet not be required to register in the state. State **long-arm statutes** authorize jurisdiction over such corporations to the degree permitted by constitutional due process constraints.

The two basic ways to acquire capital to finance a corporation are to issue equity securities or debt securities. **Debt securities** generally represent the corporation's promise to repay principal and interest while the debt is outstanding. Debt securities can be classified as **secured**, in which case a lien is granted upon specific corporate property, or **unsecured**, in which case the debt is backed only by the general credit of the corporation. **Equity securities** represent ownership interests in the corporation. They include both common and preferred stock. Shareholders, as owners, have a significantly different relationship to the issuing corporation than do its debtholders.

Typically, shares of stock are sold by a corporation for **cash**, but they may be issued for **property or services**. Some states do not permit a corporation to issue stock in exchange for an unsecured promissory note or future services. The RMBCA provides that **consideration** may consist "of any tangible or intangible property or benefit to the corporation, including cash, promissory notes, services performed, contracts for services to be performed, or other securities of the corporation." However, the RMBCA also provides for placing shares in escrow or making other restrictive arrangements until "the services are performed, the note is paid, or the benefits are received."

Corporations are authorized to issue two or more classes of stock. The most widely used are common and preferred. **Common stock** is an ownership interest in the corporation with the right to participate in the voting control of the corporation. **Preferred stock** generally confers the right to receive dividends at a specified rate stated on the face of the shares before common dividends are paid. It also confers the right to receive distributions in the event of a corporate liquidation or bankruptcy after creditors but before the holders of common stock. Preferred stock is a nonvoting interest in the corporation that may be cumulative, participating, convertible, or redeemable.

The articles may authorize a corporation to issue shares with or without a par value. **Par value** is an arbitrary price set by the promoters or by the corporation's board of directors. It is a dollar amount below which the shares may not be sold by the issuer without possible future assessments. The RMBCA permits a corporation **to elect to establish a par value**. Anything in excess of par is surplus.

Treasury stock is stock that was issued and later reacquired by the issuing corporation. But reacquisition is subject to the equity insolvency and net assets tests (see below). Treasury stock may be held, resold, retired, or used for a stock dividend. Treasury stock is not voted and does not receive dividends. The RMBCA does not use the term "treasury stock," and it treats reacquired shares as authorized but unissued. These shares may not be voted, and dividends may not be paid on them.

Persons who invest in corporate stock are motivated in part by the expectation of receiving **dividends**. Two general prerequisites to the declaration of a dividend are **corporate profits and a resolution by the directors** to declare a dividend. To ensure the corporation's financial health and growth, profits or some portion can be reinvested in the corporation. The corporation's directors determine the time and amount of dividends, if any. However, if the directors **refuse to declare a dividend** and they have clearly abused their discretion, a court may require payment of a dividend. The vote to declare a dividend is irrevocable. Once declared, payment of the dividend is a **legal obligation** of the corporation. When dividends are declared, they are usually paid in cash, but they may be paid in other property, such as stock or stock rights. All states impose the **equity insolvency test**, which prohibits any distribution when the effect is that the corporation will not be able to pay its debts as they become due in the usual course of business. Also, under the RMBCA's **net assets test**, a distribution is improper if total assets would be less than the sum of total liabilities and amounts payable to holders of preferential rights upon dissolution.

UCC Article 8, *Investment Securities*, applies to transfers of certificated or uncertificated securities and the ways in which rights in those securities are acquired against the issuer or third parties. Most securities are required to be **registered**. For example, under the RMBCA, a corporation (or its agent) must maintain a written record of its shareholders (or a record convertible to writing in a reasonable time) that includes the number and classes of shares held by each. Thus, UCC 8-207 permits an issuer to treat the registered owner as exclusively entitled to exercise the rights (e.g., to receive dividends or interest) and powers (e.g., to vote) of an owner. Securities may be **certificated** or **uncertificated**. A certificated security may be in **registered form** (transfer may be registered on books maintained for that purpose by or for the issuer, and the certificate specifies a person entitled to it) or in **bearer form** (the security is payable to its bearer according to its terms but not by way of an endorsement). A security in registered form (bearer form) is transferred by **delivery** and an **effective** endorsement (delivery only). An **endorsement** may be **in blank** (the holder's signature only) or **special** (specifying the transferee). As a result of a blank (special) endorsement, a security is subsequently transferable by delivery alone (by delivery and the special endorsee's endorsement). However, a **transfer restriction** may be imposed by the issuer, such as a close corporation. Under UCC 8-204, such a restriction is ineffective against a person without knowledge of it unless the security is certificated (uncertificated) and the restriction is noted conspicuously (the registered owner is notified). If a security is uncertificated, an **instruction**, i.e., a notification, is communicated to the issuer to direct the registration of the transfer. Article 8 provides **warranty protection** to purchasers for value and certain other parties. For example, a transferor of a certificated security and an endorser in a transfer by endorsement make the following warranties to a purchaser for value or any subsequent purchaser, respectively: (1) The certificate is genuine and has not been materially altered, (2) the warrantor knows of no fact impairing the validity of the security, (3) no adverse claim exists, (4) no transfer restriction is violated, (5) an endorsement is by an **appropriate person**, and (6) the transfer is otherwise effective and rightful. The originator of an instruction to register transfer of an uncertificated security makes substantially the same warranties. A **purchaser** of a security obtains whatever rights the transferor had power to transfer. A **protected purchaser**, which is one who (1) gives value, (2) has no notice of an adverse claim, and (3) has **control** of the security, acquires its interest free of any adverse claim (UCC 8-303). Delivery confers control of a certificated security in bearer form. When it is in registered form, the purchaser has control if, in addition to delivery, the certificate is (1) effectively endorsed to the purchaser or in blank, or (2) it is registered in the purchaser's name upon original issue or registration of transfer by the issuer. If a certificate is **lost, stolen, or wrongfully taken**, UCC 8-405 and 8-406 apply. If the owner claims loss, destruction, or theft, the issuer is obligated to issue a new certificate if the owner (1) makes the request before the issuer has notice of the certificate's acquisition by a protected purchaser, (2) files a sufficient bond with the issuer, and (3) satisfies the issuer's other reasonable requirements. An owner who does not notify the issuer within a reasonable time after the owner has notice of loss, destruction, or theft may not assert a claim for (1) a new certificate or (2) improper registration of a transfer of the security to a person not entitled to it. When a protected purchaser presents the original for registration after issuance of a new certificate, the issuer must register the transfer, but may assert rights under the bond and recover the new certificate unless it was transferred to a protected purchaser.

Investment securities include securities, whether or not certificated. The beneficial owner may hold them directly (e.g., registered on the books of an issuer) or indirectly (e.g., held by securities intermediaries). If they are **held indirectly**, the beneficial owner has a **securities account**, which is an arrangement under which the party administering the account agrees to recognize the person for whom the account is administered as entitled to exercise the rights embodied by the financial assets. A **security entitlement** consists of the rights and property interest of the **entitlement holder** (the beneficial owner) in the specified financial assets. These rights, such as the right to vote and receive dividends, are assertable against the parties in the chain of securities intermediaries, such as brokers, banks, and depositories (e.g., the Depository Trust Company) that hold securities on behalf of brokers and banks. Active investors, whether individuals or institutions, almost invariably hold their securities indirectly. Consequently, Article 8 prescribes the rights and duties of entitlement holders and securities intermediaries and addresses such issues as (1) the requirements for control of a security entitlement, (2) the effectiveness of an **entitlement order** (a notification to a securities intermediary directing transfer or redemption of a financial asset to which the entitlement holder has a security entitlement), and (3) the warranties made by the parties involved in an indirect holding.

QUESTIONS

31.1 Basic Characteristics of a Corporation

1. Which of the following statements is true concerning similarities between a limited partnership and a corporation?

A. Each is formed under a statute and must file a copy of its certificate with the proper state authorities.

B. All corporate shareholders and all partners in a limited partnership have limited liability.

C. Both are recognized for federal income tax purposes as taxable entities.

D. Both are allowed statutorily to have perpetual existence.

Answer (A) is correct. *(CPA, adapted)*

REQUIRED: The true statement of a similarity between a corporation and a limited partnership.

DISCUSSION: Corporations and limited partnerships are artificial legal entities, recognized only if they are formed under the authority of a state statute. Filing organizational documents with applicable state authorities is a requirement for legal entity status for each.

Answer (B) is incorrect. A limited partnership has at least one general partner with unlimited personal liability. Answer (C) is incorrect. A limited partnership is not usually subject to federal tax on its income. Answer (D) is incorrect. The statutes authorizing corporations permit perpetual existence. Those for limited partnerships do not.

2. Unless prohibited by the documents creating the organization, a shareholder in a publicly held corporation or the owner of a limited partnership interest has the right to

A. Ownership of the business's assets.

B. Control management of the business.

C. Assign his/her interest in the business.

D. An investment that has perpetual life.

Answer (C) is correct. *(CPA, adapted)*

REQUIRED: The right common to owners of a corporation and a limited partnership.

DISCUSSION: Either a limited partner or a shareholder in a corporation may assign his/her ownership interest. The assignee of the partnership interest is only admitted as a partner by consent of all other partners.

Answer (A) is incorrect. Neither owns the business assets. Each owns an intangible property right in an undivided share of all the assets of the business. Answer (B) is incorrect. Neither has the right to manage the business. Each participates by voting on fundamental matters, such as selection of directors or removal of a general partner. Answer (D) is incorrect. Statutes authorizing corporations provide for their perpetual existence, whereas those providing for limited partnerships do not.

3. A corporation is a separate legal entity for most purposes. A significant issue is whether it is also separate from its owners for tax purposes. Which of the following is true?

A. Certain for-profit corporations may elect to avoid federal income taxation.

B. Corporations file information returns but are not taxpayers.

C. All for-profit corporations pay federal taxes on their income.

D. If the corporation pays tax on its income, dividends distributed out of that income are not taxable.

Answer (A) is correct. *(Publisher, adapted)*

REQUIRED: The true statement about taxation of corporations.

DISCUSSION: Unlike partnerships, corporations are usually subject to taxation at the local, state, federal, and international levels. However, an entity that meets the criteria of an S corporation may avoid U.S. federal income taxation. An S corporation is incorporated in the U.S., is closely held, and has elected to be taxed similarly to a partnership, that is, to be treated essentially as a pass-through entity. The shareholders are taxed on current earnings and may personally benefit from corporate losses. An S corporation is limited to a single class of stock, may have no more than 100 shareholders, cannot be a financial institution or a member of an affiliated group, and should not have excessive net passive investment income. Shareholders are limited to individuals, estates, and qualified trusts, and nonresident aliens may not own shares.

Answer (B) is incorrect. Ordinarily, partnerships file information returns but are not taxpayers. Corporations are usually taxpaying entities. Answer (C) is incorrect. An S corporation is taxed similarly to a partnership. Answer (D) is incorrect. The corporate tax is levied on corporate income before dividends, and most dividends are taxable to the recipients. However, a special corporate deduction is allowed for certain dividends received from domestic taxable corporations.

4. A corporation formed by a political unit to effectuate a governmental purpose is best described as

A. Quasi-public.

B. Public.

C. Nonprofit.

D. Publicly held.

Answer (B) is correct. *(Publisher, adapted)*

REQUIRED: The best term for a corporation formed by a government to achieve its purposes.

DISCUSSION: A public corporation is formed and funded by a local, state, or federal political unit to achieve some governmental purpose. Examples are incorporated cities, school and water districts, and state universities.

Answer (A) is incorrect. A quasi-public corporation is formed privately and is for-profit. However, it is often heavily regulated because of its substantial effect on the public interest and its special privileges. Examples are banking institutions, railroads, and utilities. Answer (C) is incorrect. Nonprofit corporations are formed to achieve a charitable, educational, social, religious, or philanthropic purpose. Answer (D) is incorrect. A company is publicly held if its ownership is widely distributed and management is distinct from the shareholders.

5. JBR Corporation was organized in the United States and incorporated in State Q. It wishes to do business in State R. The shareholders all reside in State X. From State R's perspective, the corporation is best described as

A. Alien.

B. Domestic.

C. Foreign.

D. Multinational.

Answer (C) is correct. *(Publisher, adapted)*

REQUIRED: The best term for a corporation organized in another state.

DISCUSSION: A corporation is a domestic corporation in the state of incorporation. Hence, JBR is a domestic corporation in State Q. In every other state it is deemed a foreign corporation.

Answer (A) is incorrect. An alien corporation is one formed in another country. Answer (B) is incorrect. With respect to a given state, a domestic corporation is one incorporated in that state. Answer (D) is incorrect. A multinational corporation is one with widespread foreign operations.

6. Traditional concepts applicable to large publicly held corporations often do not meet the needs of closely held ones. Accordingly, the RMBCA addresses these needs. Under the RMBCA,

A. A qualifying entity is automatically treated as a close corporation if it has fewer than 50 shareholders.

B. A shareholder may have power to dissolve a close corporation that is similar to a partner's.

C. Transfer of shares of a close corporation is restricted by means of a statutory buy-and-sell arrangement.

D. A board of directors is required for a close corporation but shareholders have absolute power to restrict its discretion.

Answer (B) is correct. *(Publisher, adapted)*
REQUIRED: The true statement about the RMBCA's provisions regarding the needs of close corporations.
DISCUSSION: Many close corporations are like partnerships in which all of the shareholders are active in management or are friends and relatives of those who are. In a partnership, a partner's interest is protected by his/her power to dissolve the association at any time and receive the value of his/her interest. Traditional corporate law did not provide that option for minority shareholders. The RMBCA allows a shareholder agreement (1) set forth in the articles of incorporation, the bylaws, or a separate signed writing and (2) approved by all shareholders at the time of the agreement to include a provision enabling any shareholder to dissolve the corporation either at will or upon the happening of a certain event.

Answer (A) is incorrect. The RMBCA establishes no limit on the number of shareholders that may, by unanimous agreement, dispense with many corporate formalities. Answer (C) is incorrect. The RMBCA permits the shareholders to restrict the transfer of shares, such as by obligating the corporation or other persons to acquire the restricted shares. However, the restriction itself is not statutory. Answer (D) is incorrect. No board is required if the shareholders unanimously agree to operate without one.

7. Hobson, Jones, Carter, and Wolff are medical doctors who have worked together for several years. Their attorney formed a typical professional corporation for them. Which of the following is true?

A. Such a corporation will not be recognized for federal tax purposes.

B. The state in which they incorporated must have enacted professional corporation statutes.

C. Upon incorporation, the doctor-shareholder is insulated from personal liability beyond his capital contribution.

D. The majority of states prohibit the formation of professional corporations by physicians.

Answer (B) is correct. *(CPA, adapted)*
REQUIRED: The true statement regarding the formation of a professional corporation.
DISCUSSION: Professionals were not permitted to incorporate under general incorporation statutes. Now most states have enacted special statutes permitting members of professions such as law, medicine, and public accounting to use the corporate form.

Answer (A) is incorrect. One reason for allowing professionals to incorporate is to provide them equal tax treatment. Answer (C) is incorrect. Ordinary corporate insulation from personal liability extends only to the nonprofessional activities of the shareholder-practitioners. Answer (D) is incorrect. The majority of states now permit formation of professional corporations by physicians and other professionals.

8. Limited liability of shareholders is one of the advantages of incorporation. Generally, a shareholder is personally liable

A. For torts of the corporation although (s)he did not participate in them.

B. For crimes of the corporation although (s)he did not participate in them.

C. Only for his/her investment in the corporation.

D. For the corporation's debts.

Answer (C) is correct. *(Publisher, adapted)*
REQUIRED: The true statement about a shareholder's personal liability.
DISCUSSION: One of the principal advantages of incorporation is limited liability. If the corporation is properly formed and operated as an entity distinct from its owners, the shareholders will ordinarily have no personal liability beyond the amount of their investment. The corporation is a separate legal person capable of being held liable for its independent actions. Thus, a corporation can be held liable for torts and crimes, but a shareholder who did not participate in the wrongful conduct or to whom the actions are not otherwise attributable is insulated from liability.

Answer (A) is incorrect. A shareholder is not personally liable for corporate torts if (s)he did not participate in them. Answer (B) is incorrect. A shareholder is not personally liable for corporate crimes if (s)he did not participate in them. Answer (D) is incorrect. Shareholders are not answerable for corporate debts or vice versa.

9. A shareholder of a professional corporation has committed malpractice. Which of the following is the rule least likely to be adopted by a state regarding personal liability?

A. Only the corporation will be liable.

B. Only the corporation and the wrongdoer are liable.

C. All the shareholders are liable as if they were partners.

D. The other shareholders are liable but only in the amount of the required insurance.

Answer (A) is correct. *(Publisher, adapted)*

REQUIRED: The least likely rule of liability applied to professional corporation shareholders.

DISCUSSION: Incorporation does not limit the liability that a professional would otherwise have incurred for malpractice as a sole practitioner. Whether the professional-shareholder-employee is protected from personal liability for the malpractice of others in which (s)he did not participate is an issue yet to be clarified. The shareholder will usually not be personally liable for the torts of others that are not related to malpractice.

Answer (B) is incorrect. Incorporation does not limit the liability that a professional would otherwise have incurred for malpractice as a sole practitioner. Answer (C) is incorrect. Treating all shareholders as partners is unlikely. However, it is more likely than shielding a shareholder who has committed malpractice. Answer (D) is incorrect. Limiting the liability of other shareholders to the amount of the required insurance is a likely option.

10. Modern corporations wield a wide variety of powers. A corporation

A. Can do anything permitted by the incorporation statute.

B. Can exercise any power as long as it is expressly conferred by statute or the articles.

C. Has the powers expressly or impliedly conferred by the bylaws.

D. Has the powers expressly or impliedly conferred by resolutions of the board.

Answer (A) is correct. *(Publisher, adapted)*

REQUIRED: The true statement about the source of corporate powers.

DISCUSSION: Subject to the limitations imposed by the federal or state constitution, a state incorporation statute is the primary source of a corporation's powers. The articles of incorporation may narrow the grant of authority but cannot broaden it. The powers include not only those expressed in the statute or articles but also those implied as reasonably necessary to carry out the expressed powers and purposes.

Answer (B) is incorrect. The RMBCA grants to the corporation all powers necessary or convenient to effect its purposes. Answer (C) is incorrect. Bylaws are the rules adopted by a corporation to regulate its internal affairs. Answer (D) is incorrect. The board must act within limits set by the state incorporation statute, the articles, and the bylaws.

11. Corporations generally may

A. Make political contributions to candidates for federal office.

B. Make contributions for charitable, scientific, or educational purposes.

C. Not lend money.

D. Not act as a surety.

Answer (B) is correct. *(Publisher, adapted)*

REQUIRED: The true statement about specific corporate powers.

DISCUSSION: The RMBCA states that a corporation "has the same powers as an individual to do all things necessary or convenient to carry out its business and affairs." One specific power formerly denied but now generally permitted to a corporation is the right "to make donations for the public welfare or for charitable, scientific, or educational purposes."

Answer (A) is incorrect. Contributions to federal election campaigns are prohibited (but, in some states, corporations can make contributions to state and local political campaigns). Answer (C) is incorrect. The MBCA permits a corporation to lend money for its corporate purposes. Answer (D) is incorrect. The MBCA specifically grants the power to make contracts and guarantees, and also to incur liabilities.

12. Which one of the following statements is a true characterization of federal policy toward political action committees (PACs)?

A. Corporations may use company funds to organize and administer a PAC.

B. Corporations may make corporate contributions to PACs.

C. Unions may help organize PACs, but corporations may not.

D. Individuals may only make political contributions through PACs.

Answer (A) is correct. *(CMA, adapted)*

REQUIRED: The true statement about political action committees (PACs).

DISCUSSION: Federal law prohibits business corporations from donating to political election campaigns at the federal level. But this law does not prohibit donations to state election campaigns, although some states have such laws. Political action committees (PACs) have grown in importance as a means of circumventing this prohibition.

Answer (B) is incorrect. Direct corporate contributions are not allowed. Answer (C) is incorrect. Corporations, trade associations, and unions may form PACs and encourage employees to participate. Their funds may be used to organize and administer the PAC. Answer (D) is incorrect. Individuals may give funds either directly to candidates or to PACs.

13. Golden Enterprises, Inc., entered into a contract with Hidalgo Corporation for the sale of its mineral holdings. The transaction proved to be ultra vires. Which of the following parties may properly assert the ultra vires doctrine and why?

A. Golden Enterprises to avoid performance.

B. A shareholder of Golden Enterprises to enjoin the sale.

C. Hidalgo Corporation to avoid performance.

D. Golden Enterprises to rescind the consummated sale.

Answer (B) is correct. *(CPA, adapted)*

REQUIRED: The party that may properly assert that the transaction was ultra vires.

DISCUSSION: The doctrine of ultra vires states that a corporation may not act beyond the powers inherent in the corporate existence or provided in the articles of incorporation and the incorporation statutes. Ultra vires has been eliminated as a defense. The RMBCA states that, with certain exceptions, "the validity of corporate action may not be challenged on the ground that the corporation lacks or lacked power to act." Those exceptions provide a cause of action in three instances in which the power to act may be questioned: (1) A shareholder can seek an injunction, (2) corporations can proceed against directors or officers, and (3) the state attorney general can proceed against the corporation.

Answer (A) is incorrect. The ultra vires doctrine is not allowed as a defense. Answer (C) is incorrect. The ultra vires doctrine is not allowed as a defense. Answer (D) is incorrect. Courts will not use the ultra vires doctrine to rescind a fully executed contract.

14. Blanche was vice president of the Jupiter Corporation, a major weapons dealer. She used corporate funds to bribe a government official of a small European country. Blanche also caused advertisements to be published in the U.S. press that defamed Jupiter's chief competitor. What is the legal effect of Blanche's actions?

A. Jupiter cannot be found guilty of a crime because a corporation cannot form the requisite intent.

B. Jupiter will prevail on a defense of ultra vires.

C. Both Jupiter and Blanche are liable in tort and guilty of a crime.

D. Blanche is guilty of a crime but is not liable in tort.

Answer (C) is correct. *(Publisher, adapted)*

REQUIRED: The liability of a corporation for torts and crimes.

DISCUSSION: The facts indicate that Blanche, acting as an agent for Jupiter, committed the tort of defamation and the crime of bribing a foreign governmental official. An agent is personally liable for his/her crimes and torts. Under agency law, Jupiter is liable for the torts of its agents acting within the scope of their employment.

Answer (A) is incorrect. Criminal intent may be imputed to the corporation from the agent who actually committed the crime. Answer (B) is incorrect. A corporation is liable for actions beyond its powers (ultra vires). The officers might be liable for acting beyond their powers. Answer (D) is incorrect. An agent is individually liable for his/her torts even though the principal may also be liable.

31.2 Formation of a Corporation

15. Rice, as a promoter of Dex Corp., signed a 9-month contract with Roe, a CPA. Prior to the incorporation, Roe rendered accounting services pursuant to the contract. After rendering accounting services for an additional period of 6 months pursuant to the contract, Roe was discharged without cause by the board of directors of Dex. Absent agreements to the contrary, who will be liable to Roe for breach of contract?

A. Both Rice and Dex.

B. Rice only.

C. Dex only.

D. Neither Rice nor Dex.

Answer (A) is correct. *(CPA, adapted)*

REQUIRED: The liability of a corporation and a promoter on a preincorporation agreement.

DISCUSSION: A promoter who contracts for a nonexistent corporation is personally liable on such contracts. Dex is also liable because it impliedly adopted the contract by accepting Roe's performance.

Answer (B) is incorrect. The corporation impliedly ratified the contract by accepting its benefits. An alternative theory is that an assignment and delegation was made to Dex. Answer (C) is incorrect. A promoter is generally liable on preincorporation contracts. Answer (D) is incorrect. Rice was not released, and no novation occurred. Dex ratified the contract by implication.

16. Tiffany Grandiose secured an option to purchase a tract of land for $100,000. She then organized the Dunbar Company and subscribed to 51% of the stock of the corporation. It was issued for her 3-month promissory note for $100,000. As the controlling director, she had the corporation authorize the purchase of the land for $200,000. She then promptly redeemed the promissory note. A disgruntled shareholder subsequently brought suit against Grandiose on the corporation's behalf. Which of the following is a true statement?

A. Grandiose breached a fiduciary duty to the corporation.

B. The judgment of the board of directors was conclusive.

C. Grandiose is entitled to retain the profit because she controlled the corporation.

D. The giving of the promissory note was not payment for the shares.

Answer (A) is correct. *(CPA, adapted)*

REQUIRED: The true statement concerning a profit made by a promoter, director, and majority shareholder.

DISCUSSION: Grandiose is a fiduciary with respect to the newly organized corporation, but breached this fiduciary obligation as a promoter. She had a duty to act in good faith, to make full disclosure, and to not make a secret profit at the expense of the corporation. The corporation can recover the profits for violation of this duty.

Answer (B) is incorrect. The board of directors acted without full knowledge and subject to Grandiose's control. Answer (C) is incorrect. Grandiose is accountable to the corporation for the secret profit. Answer (D) is incorrect. Under the RMBCA, a promissory note is considered proper consideration for the issuance of stock.

17. John Watson entered into an agreement to purchase 1,000 shares of the Marvel Corporation, a corporation to be organized. Watson has since had second thoughts. Applying the RMBCA, which of the following is true?

A. A written notice of withdrawal prior to incorporation will be valid.

B. A transfer of the agreement to another party will eliminate his liability.

C. Watson may not revoke the agreement for a period of 6 months.

D. Watson may avoid liability if a majority of the other subscribers release him.

Answer (C) is correct. *(CPA, adapted)*

REQUIRED: The true statement regarding a pre-incorporation stock subscription agreement.

DISCUSSION: Under the RMBCA, such an agreement may not be revoked for 6 months unless otherwise provided by the terms of the subscription agreement or unless all other subscribers agree. The rationale is that the subscription agreement represents an irrevocable continuing offer for the administrative convenience of the promoter.

Answer (A) is incorrect. Even a written notice of withdrawal of the agreement will not be valid until the expiration of 6 months. Answer (B) is incorrect. An assignment of the agreement to a third party will not eliminate the liability of the assignor if the assignee fails to perform. Answer (D) is incorrect. Watson can avoid liability only by obtaining the consent of all the other subscribers to release him.

18. In general, which of the following must be contained in articles of incorporation?

A. Names of states in which the corporation will be doing business.

B. Name of the state in which the corporation will maintain its principal place of business.

C. Names of the initial officers and their terms of office.

D. Number of shares of stock authorized to be issued by the corporation.

Answer (D) is correct. *(CPA, adapted)*

REQUIRED: The information required in articles of incorporation.

DISCUSSION: Articles of incorporation must contain the name of the corporation, the number of authorized shares, the address of the initial registered office of the corporation, the name of its first registered agent at that address, and the names and addresses of the incorporators. The articles may also include names and addresses of the initial directors; purpose and duration of the corporation; par value of shares; provisions for managing the corporation and regulating its internal affairs; powers of the corporation, its board, and its shareholders; liability of shareholders for corporate debts; a provision limiting directors' liability (except for certain intentional wrongs); and any provision that may be set forth in the bylaws.

19. State incorporation statutes prescribe certain formalities as conditions precedent to the forming of a corporation. Which of the following statements best describes the effect of defective formation?

A. A de jure corporation is formed when all statutory provisions are not complied with, but a good faith effort was made to do so.

B. The significance of the de facto incorporation doctrine has been reduced.

C. A corporation by estoppel will be found when a good faith effort has been made to comply with the incorporation law.

D. A de facto corporation is formed if the mandatory provisions of the statute have been complied with.

Answer (B) is correct. *(Publisher, adapted)*

REQUIRED: The true statement about defective corporate formation.

DISCUSSION: A de facto corporation is formed when a good faith effort was made to comply with the statutory provisions but some statutory provisions were not complied with. The RMBCA treats the filing of the articles (an official act done by the secretary of state) as conclusive proof that all conditions have been satisfied. The effect is to treat a corporation as de jure even though a mandatory provision was not complied with.

Answer (A) is incorrect. A de facto corporation is formed when all statutory provisions are not complied with, but a good faith effort was made to do so. Answer (C) is incorrect. The estoppel doctrine applies when a corporation is neither de jure nor de facto. It allows a person who has dealt with a business association in reliance on its (false) representation of corporate status to hold the association liable. Answer (D) is incorrect. A de jure corporation is formed.

20. Portavoy and Bredstock are the major shareholders of and active participants in the management of Port-a-Stock Corporation. Mann is an investor who owns 10% of the shares but is otherwise uninvolved. Kalik is a promoter and 5% shareholder who has no voice in management. Unfortunately, Port-a-Stock was defectively formed and does not even qualify as a de facto corporation. The RMBCA would impose personal liability

A. On all the shareholders.

B. Only on Portavoy, Bredstock, and Kalik.

C. On no one.

D. Only on those purporting to act on behalf of Port-a-Stock.

Answer (D) is correct. *(Publisher, adapted)*

REQUIRED: The liability of shareholders of a defectively formed corporation.

DISCUSSION: The RMBCA imposes liability on "all persons purporting to act as or on behalf of a corporation, knowing that there was no incorporation under this Act." The RMBCA therefore excuses inactive parties and those not knowing of the defective incorporation.

Answer (A) is incorrect. The MBCA imposes joint and several liability on "all persons who assume to act as a corporation without authority so to do." The liability is that imposed on the partners of a general partnership. No distinction is made between the active and inactive participants. Answer (B) is incorrect. Kalik is not liable under the RMBCA. Answer (C) is incorrect. Portavoy and Bredstock are liable under the RMBCA.

21. A major characteristic of the corporation is its recognition as a separate legal entity. As such, it is capable of withstanding attempts to "pierce the corporate veil." The corporation that is least likely to resist such attempts successfully is one that

A. Was formed for tax savings.

B. Was formed to insulate its owners from personal liability.

C. Is a wholly owned subsidiary.

D. Only holds assets to defraud creditors.

Answer (D) is correct. *(CPA, adapted)*

REQUIRED: The situation in which "piercing the corporate veil" is possible.

DISCUSSION: A corporation is a separate legal entity that may be organized and used for a variety of purposes. The corporate form may be disregarded, however, if it is used in a manner contrary to public policy, e.g., to defraud creditors.

Answer (A) is incorrect. Tax minimization is a valid reason for incorporation. Answer (B) is incorrect. Liability avoidance is a valid reason for incorporation. Answer (C) is incorrect. If the wholly owned subsidiary maintains a reasonably separate existence from its parent corporation, it will be recognized as a separate legal entity.

22. Case Corp. is incorporated in State A. Under the Revised Model Business Corporation Act, which of the following activities engaged in by Case requires that Case obtain a certificate of authority to do business in State B?

A. Maintaining bank accounts in State B.

B. Collecting corporate debts in State B.

C. Hiring employees who are residents of State B.

D. Maintaining an office in State B to conduct intrastate business.

Answer (D) is correct. *(CPA, adapted)*

REQUIRED: The interstate business activity that requires a certificate of authority.

DISCUSSION: A state may exercise authority over a foreign corporation if the corporation has at least minimum contacts with the state. The minimum contacts might consist of activity that is not isolated and that is purposefully directed towards the state, or places a product in the stream of interstate commerce.

Answer (A) is incorrect. Maintaining bank accounts in State B is not sufficient to meet the minimum contacts test. Answer (B) is incorrect. Collecting corporate debts in State B is not sufficient to meet the minimum contacts test. Answer (C) is incorrect. Hiring employees who are residents of State B is not sufficient to meet the minimum contacts test.

23. Dexter, Inc., incorporated in its home state, does 20% of its business in a neighboring state in which it maintains a permanent facility. It has not filed any papers in the neighboring state. Which of the following statements is false?

A. Dexter has automatically appointed the secretary of state of the neighboring state as its agent for service of process.

B. Dexter will be able to bring suit in the neighboring state if it subsequently obtains a certificate of authority.

C. Dexter cannot defend against a suit brought against it in the neighboring state's courts.

D. The attorney general of the neighboring state can recover all back fees and franchise taxes that would have been imposed.

Answer (C) is correct. *(CPA, adapted)*

REQUIRED: The false statement about doing business outside the state of incorporation.

DISCUSSION: Because of the constitutional provision of due process, a corporation cannot be prevented from defending a lawsuit regardless of its failure to comply with local laws. Consequently, Dexter is permitted to defend against a lawsuit, even though it did not comply with the statute governing operations of foreign corporations and is not allowed to bring an action regarding its intrastate business.

Answer (A) is incorrect. Dexter has automatically appointed the secretary of state of the neighboring state as its agent for service of process. Answer (B) is incorrect. Dexter will be able to bring suit in the neighboring state if it subsequently obtains a certificate of authority. Answer (D) is incorrect. The attorney general of the neighboring state can recover all back fees and franchise taxes that would have been imposed.

24. Acme Corp. is incorporated in Delaware. Its principal place of business is in Miami, Florida, and it does business in all 50 states. For purposes of diversity of citizenship, Acme Corp. is considered to be a citizen of

A. Delaware only.

B. Florida only.

C. Delaware and Florida.

D. All 50 states.

Answer (C) is correct. *(K.J. Elwell)*

REQUIRED: The citizenship of a corporation.

DISCUSSION: For the purpose of federal court jurisdiction in cases involving parties with diverse citizenship, a corporation is a citizen of the state in which it is incorporated and of the state in which it has its principal place of business. If these are different states, the corporation is a citizen of both states.

Answer (A) is incorrect. The corporation is a citizen of both states. Answer (B) is incorrect. The corporation can be a citizen of both states. Answer (D) is incorrect. The corporation cannot be a citizen of more than two states.

25. Business activity in interstate commerce often presents the question of when a corporation will be subject to suit in a state court. The in personam jurisdiction of a state court will extend to a corporation only when

A. The corporation maintains an office or registered agent within the state.

B. The corporation is incorporated in the state.

C. The corporation has sufficient minimum contacts with the state that suits would not be unfair to the defendant.

D. The corporation is subject to taxation by the state.

Answer (C) is correct. *(Publisher, adapted)*

REQUIRED: The circumstances in which a corporation may be sued in a court of a given state.

DISCUSSION: The U.S. Supreme Court has held that due process is not violated when a corporation is compelled to be a defendant in a state court if the corporation has sufficient minimum contacts with that state that it would not be unfair for the courts of that state to exercise power over it.

Answer (A) is incorrect. Although maintaining an office or an agent within the state would result in personal jurisdiction, lesser contacts could be sufficient, e.g., committing a tortious act within the state. Answer (B) is incorrect. Although incorporation in the state would permit a corporation to be sued there, it is not necessary for a finding of jurisdiction. Answer (D) is incorrect. A state's personal (in personam) jurisdiction may extend to entities not subject to its taxation.

31.3 Financing Structure and Dividends

26. Which of the following statements about financing a for-profit corporation is true?

A. Stocks and bonds are the exclusive means of financing used by corporations.

B. Some corporations rely entirely on debt financing.

C. Large corporations usually have a blend of debt and equity financing.

D. Small corporations and governmental units rely on the issuance of bonds.

Answer (C) is correct. *(Publisher, adapted)*

REQUIRED: The true statement about financing a corporation.

DISCUSSION: A for-profit corporation can raise capital by issuing equity securities (stock) or by incurring debt. The advantage of equity is that it does not have to be repaid and it does not result in periodic fixed charges. The advantage of debt is that it does not give voting control to the creditor and may permit trading on leverage (borrowing is favorable if the cost of capital is less than the company's return). Corporations generally prefer a combination of these financing methods.

Answer (A) is incorrect. Accounts and notes payable, leases, and retained earnings are also used. Answer (B) is incorrect. All for-profit corporations must issue stock. Answer (D) is incorrect. Large corporations are far more likely than small ones to issue bonds, which are long-term debt securities paying a fixed amount of interest at specified periods and having a fixed maturity date for repayment of principal. Bonds are a means of dividing large-scale borrowing into small units to facilitate marketing.

27. If a corporation wishes to issue securities to the public, it must comply with the applicable securities laws. Which of the following statements is true?

A. The enactment of federal securities laws preempted state regulation.

B. Few states have adopted the Uniform Securities Act.

C. A sale of securities may not be concurrently subject to both state and federal regulation.

D. Some states have statutes permitting regulators to pass on the merits of securities.

Answer (D) is correct. *(Publisher, adapted)*

REQUIRED: The true statement about state securities laws.

DISCUSSION: Most state "blue-sky" laws require registration of nonexempt securities, provide for licensing or registration of brokers and dealers, prohibit fraud in the issuance and subsequent trading of securities, and impose full disclosure standards. These provisions are similar in many ways to federal law. However, some states have also established merit or fairness standards for the issuance of securities; that is, securities may not qualify for registration until a state regulator has evaluated them to determine whether they are unduly risky. By contrast, federal law assumes that full disclosure is sufficient to protect investors.

Answer (A) is incorrect. The federal securities law recognizes concurrent state power over securities issues and trading. Answer (B) is incorrect. The majority of states have passed the Uniform Securities Act to provide consistent legal standards. Answer (C) is incorrect. A sale of securities in interstate commerce usually is subject to both federal law and the laws of various states.

28. Which of the following securities are corporate debt securities?

	Convertible Bonds	Debenture Bonds	Warrants
A.	Yes	Yes	Yes
B.	Yes	No	Yes
C.	Yes	Yes	No
D.	No	Yes	Yes

Answer (C) is correct. *(CPA, adapted)*

REQUIRED: The securities classified as corporate debt securities.

DISCUSSION: A corporation may be financed by issuing equity and debt securities. Debt securities represent a debtor-creditor relationship between the corporation and the security holder. Equity securities represent an ownership interest. A bond is a negotiable security expressing the corporation's promise to pay the amount of the bond at a future date (and interest). A convertible bond is convertible into a share or shares of stock. A debenture is an unsecured bond, backed only by the general obligation of the corporation to pay. A stock warrant is a right to purchase shares of stock at a specified price and within a specified time period. Thus, it is an equity security.

29. The shares actually held by shareholders are best described as

A. Authorized shares.

B. Issued shares.

C. Treasury shares.

D. Outstanding shares.

Answer (D) is correct. *(Publisher, adapted)*

REQUIRED: The term best describing shares actually held by shareholders.

DISCUSSION: Shares are outstanding if they are authorized and issued to shareholders but have not been reacquired by the corporation.

Answer (A) is incorrect. Authorized shares are those permitted by the articles of incorporation to be issued. Answer (B) is incorrect. Issued shares are those actually issued, including shares reacquired by the corporation. Answer (C) is incorrect. Treasury shares are authorized and issued, but not outstanding. The RMBCA, however, abolishes treasury shares. It treats reacquired shares as authorized but unissued.

30. In general, which of the following statements concerning treasury stock is true?

A. A corporation may not reacquire its own stock unless specifically authorized by its articles of incorporation.

B. On issuance of new stock, a corporation has preemptive rights with regard to its treasury stock.

C. Treasury stock may be distributed as a stock dividend.

D. A corporation is entitled to receive cash dividends on its treasury stock.

Answer (C) is correct. *(CPA, adapted)*

REQUIRED: The characteristic of treasury stock.

DISCUSSION: Shares may be issued pro rata and without consideration to the shareholders by an action of the directors. Treasury shares have the status of authorized but unissued shares that may be used for stock dividends. The RMBCA, however, abolishes treasury shares. It treats reacquired shares as authorized but unissued.

Answer (A) is incorrect. A corporation may acquire its own shares, provided it remains solvent. Answer (B) is incorrect. A corporation has no dividend rights regarding treasury stock. Answer (D) is incorrect. A corporation has no preemptive rights regarding treasury stock.

31. Which of the following most accurately states an advantage or disadvantage of preferred shareholders?

A. They incur more risk than common shareholders.

B. They incur less risk than bondholders.

C. They have less opportunity for benefiting from the growth of the corporation than common shareholders.

D. They have a stronger position upon dissolution than bondholders or common shareholders.

Answer (C) is correct. *(Publisher, adapted)*

REQUIRED: The advantage or disadvantage of preferred stock.

DISCUSSION: Preferred stock offers a fixed return, whereas common stock dividends may grow as the firm prospers. Preferred stock is also frequently redeemable for a fixed price at the corporation's option. Thus, common shareholders are more likely to benefit from appreciation of the value of their shares. Preferred shareholders, however, may have participation or conversion rights that offset these disadvantages. NOTE: The RMBCA does not use the terms "preferred" and "common," but it provides for classes of stock with varying rights and limitations.

Answer (A) is incorrect. Preferred stock has preferences regarding both dividends and dissolution. Answer (B) is incorrect. Bonds pay a return regardless of dividends. Bondholders are creditors with priority of payment over all shareholders in dissolution. Answer (D) is incorrect. Creditors, including bondholders, are paid before shareholders when the corporation is liquidated.

32. An owner of common stock will not have any liability beyond actual investment if the owner

A. Paid less than par value for stock purchased in connection with an original issue of shares.

B. Agreed but failed to perform future services for the corporation in exchange for original issue par value shares.

C. Purchased treasury shares for less than par value.

D. Failed to pay the full amount owed on a subscription contract for no-par shares.

Answer (C) is correct. *(CPA, adapted)*

REQUIRED: The liability of a shareholder for the shares.

DISCUSSION: Under traditional rules, if stated par value exceeds the amount a shareholder paid for shares at issuance, the shareholder remains liable to creditors for the difference. A purchaser of treasury shares is not liable for any such excess. Moreover, under the RMBCA, any shareholder is liable only for the authorized consideration agreed to be paid.

Answer (A) is incorrect. A shareholder who paid less than par value for stock remains liable for the difference between the amount paid and the authorized consideration. Answer (B) is incorrect. Future services may be valid consideration for the issuance of shares, but not if they are not performed. Answer (D) is incorrect. A subscriber who has failed to perform the subscription contract is liable for the unpaid balance.

33. Johns owns 400 shares of Abco Corp. cumulative preferred stock. In the absence of any specific contrary provisions in Abco's articles of incorporation, which of the following statements is true?

A. Johns is entitled to convert the 400 shares of preferred stock to a like number of shares of common stock.

B. If Abco declares a cash dividend on its preferred stock, Johns becomes an unsecured creditor of Abco.

C. If Abco declares a dividend on its common stock, Johns will be entitled to participate with the common shareholders in any dividend distribution made after preferred dividends are paid.

D. Johns will be entitled to vote if dividend payments are in arrears.

Answer (B) is correct. *(CPA, adapted)*

REQUIRED: The rights of a holder of cumulative preferred stock.

DISCUSSION: The holder of preferred stock must be paid the stated dividend before a common shareholder may receive any dividends. If payment of the stated dividend is not made to a cumulative preferred shareholder in any year(s), the dividends accumulate and must be paid in full prior to payment of any dividends to common shareholders. But a dividend on any stock does not become a payment obligation (debt) of the corporation until it has been declared.

Answer (A) is incorrect. Cumulative preferred stock is not necessarily convertible. Answer (C) is incorrect. Cumulative preferred stock is not necessarily participating. Answer (D) is incorrect. Cumulative preferred stock is not necessarily endowed with voting rights.

34. Shares of stock without par value may be issued for such consideration (in dollars) as may be fixed by a corporation's

A. Creditors.

B. Officers.

C. Board of directors.

D. Minority shareholders.

Answer (C) is correct. *(CPA, adapted)*

REQUIRED: The parties who may fix consideration for issuance of no-par stock.

DISCUSSION: The board of directors has authority to fix the amount of consideration to be received for the issuance of no-par stock, as well as all other stock. The board is obligated to act in good faith (without fraud) and to exercise reasonable business judgment. Capital surplus (additional paid-in capital) arises not only from receipt of amounts in excess of any par value but also from an allocation of amounts received for no-par shares or from a reappraisal of certain assets. NOTE: The RMBCA and many states have abolished the concepts of par value, stated capital, and capital surplus. However, the RMBCA allows a company to elect to establish a par value.

Answer (A) is incorrect. Creditors have no management rights. Answer (B) is incorrect. Officers only manage day-to-day business. Answer (D) is incorrect. Minority shareholders only vote to elect directors, approve fundamental corporate changes, etc.

35. Rocco Pierre was an 80% shareholder of La Bos Company, which was formed with his contribution of $2,000 of assets. His sister, Petra, provided $500 worth of assets and held the remaining stock. As the need for operating capital arose, Rocco and Petra advanced funds to the company. These advances eventually totaled $250,000. Annual sales averaged $300,000. When La Bos went into receivership, Rocco and Petra asserted their position as creditors of equal dignity with the other general creditors for the purpose of distribution of assets. They cited the existence of promissory notes signed by the corporate officers as evidence of their standing. The most likely result is that Rocco and Petra

A. Have the status of creditors.

B. Have no standing as creditors because loans by controlling shareholders are per se capital contributions.

C. Will be liable for all the debts of the corporation.

D. Have no standing as creditors under the Deep Rock doctrine.

Answer (D) is correct. *(Publisher, adapted)*

REQUIRED: The effect of too-thin capitalization.

DISCUSSION: If the debt to equity ratio is unreasonably high given its needs, nature, and size, a corporation is thinly capitalized. The potential tax advantages are that the corporation can deduct interest expense and repayments are not taxed to the lender as dividends. A further advantage is that, in bankruptcy proceedings, the claims of creditors are superior to those of owners. Under the Deep Rock doctrine (established in a Supreme Court decision), loans made by insiders to a too thinly capitalized corporation are treated as contributions of capital. The lenders, Rocco and Petra, controlled the corporation based on a nominal capital investment grossly disproportionate to its need for funds. Hence, they should not have standing as creditors.

Answer (A) is incorrect. They are owners. The loans were effectively capital contributions. Answer (B) is incorrect. Controlling shareholder loans are not capital contributions per se, but they are strictly scrutinized by courts to determine their real substance. Answer (C) is incorrect. The corporate veil might be pierced and the shareholders held liable as if they were partners given thin capitalization, commingling of personal and company assets, and failure to observe corporate formalities.

36. Surplus of a corporation means

A. Net assets in excess of stated capital.

B. Liquid assets in excess of current needs.

C. Total assets in excess of total liabilities.

D. Contributed capital.

Answer (A) is correct. *(CPA, adapted)*

REQUIRED: The definition of the surplus of a corporation.

DISCUSSION: Surplus of a corporation is traditionally defined as the excess of net assets over stated capital (par value or stated value of no par stock). This amount is also equivalent to the total of capital surplus (excess of selling price over par or stated value) and earned surplus (retained earnings). Net assets equal total assets minus total liabilities.

Answer (B) is incorrect. The excess of liquid assets over current liabilities is the accounting definition of net quick assets. Answer (C) is incorrect. Total assets in excess of total liabilities is the total capital of the corporation. Answer (D) is incorrect. Contributed capital includes both stated capital and capital surplus.

37. When no-par shares are issued by a corporation in a state that requires it to maintain a stated capital, the amount that must be allocated to capital surplus as distinct from stated capital is

A. The carrying amount of the shares.

B. The fair value of the shares.

C. The entire amount of the consideration received.

D. Any portion of the proceeds so directed by the board of directors.

Answer (D) is correct. *(Publisher, adapted)*

REQUIRED: The amount that must be allocated to capital surplus for no-par shares.

DISCUSSION: If the state statute requires that the corporation maintain a stated or legal capital account, and if no-par shares are issued, the entire consideration received for the shares must be allocated to the stated capital of the corporation except to the extent that the directors in their discretion allocate (within 60 days) any part of the proceeds to capital surplus (additional paid-in capital).

38. Assuming no agreement on the matter between the buyer and seller of stock, who is entitled to a declared dividend?

A. If the stock is listed on a stock exchange, the buyer if the purchase was 6 days before the record date.

B. If the stock is not listed on a stock exchange, the seller if the purchase was between the ex dividend and record dates.

C. If the stock is listed on a stock exchange, the buyer if the purchase was after the record date.

D. If the stock is not listed on a stock exchange, the shareholder of record at the ex dividend date.

Answer (A) is correct. *(Publisher, adapted)*

REQUIRED: The party entitled to a declared dividend.

DISCUSSION: When the dividend is declared, the board sets a date of record. The corporation will have no liability to third parties if it pays the dividend to the recorded shareholders at that date. Between the transferor and transferee of shares, their contractual agreement controls disposition of the dividend. In the absence of an agreement, the transferor receives the dividend if the transfer occurred after the record date. But if the stock is listed on a stock exchange, the transferor is entitled to the dividend if the transfer occurred after the ex dividend date (4 business days before the record date). Accordingly, a buyer 6 days prior to the record date has a right to the dividend.

Answer (B) is incorrect. If the stock is not listed, the ex dividend date is not relevant. A transferee before the record date is entitled to the dividend. Answer (C) is incorrect. Whether or not the stock is listed, the transferor has a right to the dividend if the transfer is after the record date. Answer (D) is incorrect. If the stock is not listed, the ex dividend date is not relevant. A transferee before the record date is entitled to the dividend.

39. The articles of incorporation of Divy Company prohibit dividends in any year in which the corporation has not earned an after-tax profit. For the year just ended, Divy had a net loss. Nevertheless, the board declared a dividend because it has a substantial surplus from prior years. Which of the following statements is true?

A. The directors are personally liable only if the dividend was statutorily prohibited.

B. Shareholders who knew that the dividend was improper will be liable.

C. All shareholders who received a dividend will be liable.

D. The directors are personally liable only if the dividend rendered the corporation insolvent.

Answer (B) is correct. *(Publisher, adapted)*

REQUIRED: The true statement about liability for an unlawful dividend.

DISCUSSION: Dividends may be restricted both contractually and statutorily. Agreements with lenders, bondholders, and preferred shareholders as well as the articles, stock exchange rules, and statutes affect dividends. The directors have joint and several personal liability to the corporation or its creditors for illegal or improper dividends unless they acted in good faith, with due care, and in a manner reasonably expected to be in the corporation's interests. Moreover, shareholders who knew of the impropriety can also be held liable.

Answer (A) is incorrect. The directors are liable for any improper distribution. Answer (C) is incorrect. Innocent shareholders are generally not liable unless the corporation is insolvent. Answer (D) is incorrect. The directors are liable for any improper distribution.

40. The board of directors of Wilcox, Inc., has noted a 7% drop in the market price of its preferred stock and decides to purchase 100,000 shares of the stock for an amount below the redemption price of the stock. Under these circumstances, which of the following is a true statement?

A. The corporation will realize a taxable gain as a result of the transaction.

B. The preferred stock so acquired must be retired and may not be held as treasury stock.

C. The corporation may not acquire its own shares unless the articles of incorporation so provide.

D. Such shares may be purchased by the corporation to the extent of unreserved and unrestricted retained earnings.

Answer (D) is correct. *(CPA, adapted)*

REQUIRED: The true statement regarding the reacquisition of a corporation's own stock.

DISCUSSION: A corporation may reacquire its own stock (called a redemption), provided certain conditions are met. Under the RMBCA, the redemption of stock must not render the corporation insolvent, and the total assets after the distribution may not be less than the sum of total liabilities and liquidation preferences. Thus, redemptions may be made out of retained earnings that is not restricted.

Answer (A) is incorrect. The redemption of stock is a taxable event to the corporation only if appreciated property is used to purchase the stock. Answer (B) is incorrect. Either common or preferred stock may be held as treasury shares. Answer (C) is incorrect. A corporation may acquire its own shares even if the articles of incorporation do not specifically address the matter.

41. All of the following distributions to shareholders are considered asset or capital distributions except

A. Liquidating dividends.

B. Stock splits.

C. Property distributions.

D. Cash dividends.

Answer (B) is correct. *(CPA, adapted)*

REQUIRED: The distribution not from corporate capital or other assets.

DISCUSSION: A stock split is not a distribution from assets or capital. The amount of earned or capital surplus or stated capital does not change. Each share of a class of stock is merely divided into a multiple of one share. The value of each share changes, but not the shareholder's proportionate ownership interest. Under the RMBCA, a distribution is "a direct or indirect transfer of money or other property (except its own shares) or incurrence of indebtedness by a corporation to or for the benefit of its shareholders in respect of any of its shares."

Answer (A) is incorrect. A dividend distributed on liquidation of the corporation is from asset surplus. Answer (C) is incorrect. A distribution to shareholders of noncash property might constitute a dividend or a return of capital. Answer (D) is incorrect. Dividends are usually distributed in the form of money or property from corporate assets.

42. Opal Corp. declared a 9% stock dividend on its common stock. The dividend

A. Requires a vote of Opal's shareholders.

B. Has no effect on Opal's earnings and profits for federal income tax purposes.

C. Is includible in the gross income of the recipient taxpayers in the year of receipt.

D. Must be registered with the SEC pursuant to the Securities Act of 1933.

Answer (B) is correct. *(CPA, adapted)*

REQUIRED: The nature and effect of a stock dividend.

DISCUSSION: A stock dividend is a distribution of additional shares of the corporation's stock in proportion to current holdings. Total equity is not changed. The value is transferred from earned or capital surplus to stated capital or the equivalent. Earnings and profits is a tax account that is unchanged by a stock dividend.

Answer (A) is incorrect. Dividend policy is within the discretion of the board. Answer (C) is incorrect. Stock dividends normally are not treated as gross income for federal income tax purposes. Stock dividends do not affect equity. Answer (D) is incorrect. Stock issued to shareholders of previously issued stock need not be registered.

43. The essential difference between a stock dividend and a stock split is that a

A. Stock split will increase the amount of equity.

B. Stock split will increase a shareholder's percentage of ownership.

C. Stock dividend must be paid in the same class of stock as held by the shareholder.

D. Stock dividend of newly issued shares will result in a decrease in retained earnings.

Answer (D) is correct. *(CPA, adapted)*

REQUIRED: The difference between a stock dividend and a stock split.

DISCUSSION: A stock dividend is an issuance of additional shares of the company's stock proportionate to current holdings. Total equity is unaffected because it is merely represented by a greater number of shares. Generally accepted accounting principles require a transfer from retained earnings to contributed capital of the fair value of the shares distributed as a stock dividend.

A stock split differs in that par value rather than retained earnings is reduced and the number of authorized shares is increased.

Answer (A) is incorrect. A stock dividend requires a transfer between capital accounts; a split results in a reduction of par value. Answer (B) is incorrect. The distribution is proportionate to existing holdings. Answer (C) is incorrect. A preferred shareholder may, for example, receive a dividend of common stock.

44. The Larkin Corporation is contemplating a two-for-one stock split of its common stock. Its $4 par value common stock will be reduced to $2 after the split. It has two million shares issued and outstanding out of a total of three million authorized. The distribution of the additional shares to the shareholders requires

A. Both authorization by the board of directors and approval by the shareholders.

B. The recipients to recognize a taxable dividend.

C. That surplus equal to the par value of the existing number of shares issued and outstanding be transferred to the stated capital account.

D. The trustees of trust recipients of the additional shares to allocate them ratably between income and corpus.

Answer (A) is correct. *(CPA, adapted)*

REQUIRED: The true statement regarding the legal or tax consequences of a two-for-one stock split of common stock.

DISCUSSION: The effect of the stock split will be to increase the number of shares issued and outstanding from two million to four million, which will exceed the number of authorized shares. Such a transaction is a fundamental change in the corporate financial structure and therefore must be approved by the shareholders as well as by the board of directors.

Answer (B) is incorrect. Stock splits are normally nontaxable. The proportional ownership of the corporation remains the same. Answer (C) is incorrect. No retained earnings need be transferred to the stated capital account. The stock split does not change the aggregate par value, if any, of the shares issued and outstanding. Answer (D) is incorrect. Stock dividends and splits are allocated solely to the principal (corpus) of the trust.

31.4 Investment Security Rules

45. Under Article 8 of the Uniform Commercial Code, *Investment Securities*, a security is

A. Issued in registered form and not bearer form.

B. Of a long-term nature not intended to be disposed of within one year.

C. Only an equity security or debenture security, not a secured obligation.

D. An obligation of an issuer or a share, participation, or other interest in an issuer or in property or an enterprise of an issuer.

Answer (D) is correct. *(CPA, adapted)*

REQUIRED: The characteristic of a security.

DISCUSSION: A security is defined in UCC 8-102 as "an obligation of an issuer or a share, participation, or other interest in an issuer or in property or an enterprise of an issuer" that is (1) represented by a certificate in bearer or registered form or whose transfer may be registered by or for the issuer, (2) one of a class or series or is divisible into a class or series, and (3) dealt in or traded on securities exchanges or markets or is a medium for investment and expressly provides that it is a security under Article 8.

Answer (A) is incorrect. A security may be in registered or bearer form. Answer (B) is incorrect. A security may be short-term. Answer (C) is incorrect. A security may be an obligation of the issuer secured by specific collateral as opposed to an unsecured obligation, such as debenture bonds.

46. Wilberforce & Company has in its possession certificated securities that it purchased in good faith and for value from Dunlop. An adverse claim has been asserted against the securities. Which of the following warranties may Wilberforce validly assert against Dunlop, its prior transferor?

A. The prior chain of title contains no defect.

B. The securities are genuine and have not been materially altered.

C. No defect exists that might impair the validity of the securities.

D. Dunlop will defend the purchaser's title from adverse claims or defects that would impair the validity of the securities.

Answer (B) is correct. *(CPA, adapted)*

REQUIRED: The warranty made by a person transferring securities for value.

DISCUSSION: Under UCC 8-108, a person who transfers a certificated security to a purchaser for value makes certain warranties to the purchaser. An endorser (assuming the transfer is by endorsement) makes the same warranties to a subsequent purchaser. These parties warrant that (1) the certificate is genuine and has not been materially altered, (2) the transferor (endorser) knows no fact that might impair its validity, (3) no adverse claim exists, (4) the transfer violates no transfer restriction, (5) an endorsement made to effect the transfer was by an appropriate person (or by an agent with actual authority to act for the appropriate person), and (6) the transfer is otherwise effective and rightful. However, a transferor is not an absolute guarantor of the validity of a security. The holder of a security that circulates freely in commercial channels cannot feasibly be aware of all aspects of prior transactions involving the security. Thus, the transferor is held only to warranties of those aspects of transactions within his/her control or knowledge.

47. Glenn Corporation is closely held by two shareholders, Jenny and Garp, who entered an agreement giving each other a right of first refusal if either wished to sell the stock. The restriction on transfer of shares was conspicuously noted in their written contract. In violation of the agreement, Garp sold his shares to Fields. The stock transfer restriction is most likely to be disregarded by a court

A. If neither the bylaws nor the articles of incorporation mentioned it.

B. If it was not conspicuously noted on the certificates.

C. Because it was unreasonable.

D. Even though the transferee knew of it.

Answer (B) is correct. *(Publisher, adapted)*

REQUIRED: The best reason for disregarding a stock transfer restriction.

DISCUSSION: Under UCC 8-204, a transfer restriction on a security imposed by the issuer is ineffective against any person without knowledge of it unless (1) the security is certificated and the restriction is noted conspicuously on it, or (2) the security is uncertificated and the registered owner has been notified of the restriction. Under the RMBCA, a restriction contained in the articles of incorporation, the bylaws, a shareholder agreement, or an agreement between the shareholders and the corporation is enforceable if (1) its existence is noted conspicuously on the certificate, or (2), when shares are issued without certificates, it is contained in a written statement of information required to be included on the certificate and sent to the shareholder within a reasonable time.

Answer (A) is incorrect. The restriction may be included in an agreement among the shareholders in addition to the articles or bylaws. Answer (C) is incorrect. A restriction must not be manifestly unreasonable. The desire to maintain control of a close corporation is a reasonable purpose, and the provision for a right of first refusal is reasonable. Answer (D) is incorrect. Knowledge by the transferee makes a reasonable restriction valid even if not noted on the certificates.

48. Assuming all other requirements have been met, which of the following terms ordinarily must be included in a writing or an authenticated record to satisfy the UCC statute of frauds regarding the sale or purchase of securities?

	Price	Quantity	Time of Payment
A.	Yes	Yes	Yes
B.	No	No	No
C.	Yes	No	Yes
D.	Yes	Yes	No

Answer (B) is correct. *(CPA, adapted)*

REQUIRED: The term(s), if any, ordinarily required in a writing or an authenticated record evidencing a sale or purchase of securities.

DISCUSSION: No statute of frauds applies to sale or purchase of securities (UCC 8-113). Contracts or modifications of contracts for the sale or purchase of securities are enforceable without a signed writing or a record authenticated by the party sought to be bound, even if the agreements cannot be performed within 1 year.

49. Mike Hargrove lost some stock certificates of Apex Corporation that were in registered form but that he had endorsed in blank. Flagg found the securities and sold them through a brokerage house to Lauren Waldorf, who had no notice of the adverse claim. Apex, unaware of Hargrove's problem, registered their transfer to Waldorf. Hargrove is seeking to recover the securities or damages for their value. Which of the following is true?

A. The stock in question is transferable but Waldorf takes subject to Hargrove's claim of title.

B. Waldorf is a holder in due course of a negotiable instrument and therefore will prevail.

C. Apex is liable for wrongfully transferring Hargrove's stock to Waldorf.

D. Waldorf qualifies as a protected purchaser and acquires the stock free of Hargrove's adverse claim.

Answer (D) is correct. *(CPA, adapted)*

REQUIRED: The legal effect of the transfer of lost securities in registered form that had been endorsed in blank.

DISCUSSION: Waldorf is a protected purchaser because she (1) gave value, (2) had no notice of an adverse claim, and (3) obtained control of the certificated securities. A purchaser has control of a certificated security in registered form if it is delivered to the purchaser, and (1) the certificate is endorsed to the purchaser or in blank by an effective endorsement, or (2) the certificate is registered in the name of the purchaser upon either original issue or registration of transfer by the issuer. An endorsement is effective if made by the appropriate person, that is, the person specified either by the certificate or by an effective special endorsement to be entitled to the security. Hence, the blank endorsement was effective because it was made by Hargrove, the person specified by the certificates as entitled to the securities. Moreover, after the effective endorsement in blank, the securities could be controlled by a subsequent party without further endorsement (by delivery alone). Accordingly, Waldorf meets the control criterion for protected-purchaser status on both grounds stated above (in addition to delivery). As a protected purchaser, Waldorf acquired her interest in the securities free of any adverse claim.

Answer (A) is incorrect. Waldorf, as a protected purchaser, takes free of any adverse claims. Answer (B) is incorrect. UCC Article 3, which applies to negotiable instruments and defines the rights of a holder in due course, does not apply to securities governed by Article 8. Under Article 8, Waldorf is a protected purchaser rather than a holder in due course (the concepts are similar). Answer (C) is incorrect. When a security certificate has been lost and the owner fails to notify the issuer, the issuer may register a transfer of the security. The owner is precluded from asserting any claim for (1) wrongful registration or (2) replacement (UCC 8-406).

STUDY UNIT THIRTY-TWO
CORPORATIONS: OPERATIONS AND MANAGEMENT

The **powers of a corporation** are exercised by or under the authority of its **board of directors**, who are elected by the shareholders. The board is the source of **overall corporate policy**, which is implemented by the officers and other employees of the corporation. The board directs the corporate business; the officers implement the board's directives by conducting day-to-day transactions. Each state has a specific requirement with respect to the **number of directors** elected to sit on the board. Many states require a minimum of three. Under the RMBCA, a minimum of one director is usually required. However, the RMBCA permits a corporation to dispense with a board of directors under a **unanimous shareholder agreement**. The **initial board of directors** is usually appointed by the incorporators or named in the articles of incorporation, and this board serves until the first meeting of the shareholders. **Subsequent directors** are elected by a vote of the shareholders at the annual meeting. Most publicly held corporations have two types of directors. **Inside directors** are officers of the corporation and full-time employees, and **outside directors** may be unaffiliated with the corporation except for stock ownership.

Normally, each shareholder has one vote for each share owned, and directors are elected by a plurality of votes. In many states, shareholders have the right of **cumulative voting** for the election of directors. Cumulative voting allows **minority shareholders** to obtain representation on the board if they own a certain minimum number of shares. If cumulative voting is allowed, the number of votes each shareholder may cast equals the **shares held times the number of directors to be elected**. For example, if a shareholder has 25,000 shares out of a total outstanding of 100,000 and four directors are to be elected, the shareholder can cast all 100,000 votes (25,000 × 4) for one director and be assured of representation no matter how the other 300,000 votes (75,000 × 4) are allocated. In most states, shareholders also may, **by a majority vote**, remove, with or without cause, any director or the entire board of directors. If a **vacancy** occurs on the board, including one arising from an increase in the number of directors, the remaining directors may elect a director to fill the vacancy until the next shareholders' meeting. Moreover, the RMBCA authorizes a court to issue an order to **remove a director** in a proceeding brought by the corporation or by shareholders who own at least 10% of the outstanding shares of any class of stock. The court must find that removal of the director is in the **best interests of the corporation** and that the director either engaged in fraudulent or dishonest conduct or grossly abused his/her authority or discretion.

The board of directors establishes and implements overall corporate policy by (1) selection and removal of officers, (2) decisions about capital structure, (3) initiation of fundamental changes, (4) determining the timing and amounts of dividends, and (5) setting management compensation. In addition, either the incorporators or the board may adopt the initial **bylaws** governing the internal structure and operation of the corporation. Bylaws ordinarily may be amended or repealed by the board or the shareholders.

Although the directors determine overall corporate policy, a director is **not an agent** of the corporation. (S)he cannot act individually to bind the corporation. Nevertheless, directors are **fiduciaries** who must perform their duties in good faith, with due care, and in the best interests of the corporation. Action by the board is usually taken at **meetings**, but the trend is to permit boards to act by telephone conference call, by videoconference, or by unanimous written consent of each director. Regular meetings are held at fixed intervals established in the bylaws. **Special meetings** can be held after proper notice has been given to all directors. Unless provided otherwise, a **quorum** consists of a majority of board members. However, directors are **not allowed to vote by proxy**. The director must attend the meeting to be counted for purposes of attaining a quorum.

Directors must adhere to very high **standards of conduct** with respect to the corporation and the shareholders. They must be diligent and careful in managing the corporation's business. They can be held personally liable for **failure to be informed** of matters internal to, and external but relevant to, the corporation. A director's conduct is **tested objectively**. The RMBCA provides that a director shall discharge his/her duties (1) in **good faith**, (2) with the care an **ordinarily prudent person** in a similar position would exercise under similar circumstances, and (3) in a manner (s)he reasonably believes to be in the **best interests of the corporation**. In exercising reasonable care, a director may **rely on information or opinions** presented by officers, employees, professionals (e.g., CPAs or attorneys), or committees of the board whom the director **reasonably believes** to be reliable and competent.

Directors also owe a **duty of loyalty** to the corporation and its shareholders. In accordance with this fiduciary duty, a director is required to make **full disclosure** to the corporation of any financial interests (s)he may have in any transaction to which both the director and the corporation may be a party. However, if it is fair to the corporation, a **conflicting interest transaction** will not result in sanctions (e.g., damages), be enjoined, or be set aside even if the director is counted for the quorum and votes to approve the transaction. Furthermore, a conflicting interest transaction will not result in sanctions, etc., if it is approved after the required disclosure either by a majority of disinterested directors or by a majority of shares voted by disinterested parties. **Loans to directors** also are subject to the foregoing conflict-of-interest principles. Moreover, under the **Sarbanes-Oxley Act of 2002**, a public company generally may not make **personal loans** to its directors and officers.

Directors may not usurp any **corporate opportunity**. A director must give the corporation the right of first refusal. A corporate opportunity is one in which the corporation has a right, property interest, or expectancy. A corporate opportunity arises when (1) a director becomes aware of the opportunity in his/her corporate capacity; (2) the opportunity is within the scope of corporate activity; or (3) corporate capital, equipment, personnel, or facilities were used to develop the opportunity. Generally, a corporate opportunity does not exist if (1) action by the corporation would be beyond its powers, (2) the corporation cannot obtain necessary financing or capital to take advantage of the opportunity, or (3) the opportunity is rejected by a majority vote of disinterested directors.

Directors who approve **unlawful distributions** are personally liable to the corporation for excess distributions if they failed to comply with their duty of care.

Controlling or majority shareholders owe duties similar to those of directors. For example, courts will often protect the interests of minority shareholders by ordering the payment of dividends that were withheld in bad faith or by compelling a seller of a controlling block of shares to distribute ratably among all shareholders any "control premium" paid in excess of the fair value of the stock.

Directors make decisions that require the balancing of potential benefits and costs to the corporation. The **business judgment rule** protects directors and officers from liability related to their decisions if the directors adhered to the standards of conduct described above (good faith, due care, and action in the corporation's best interests). This rule permits directors to make **honest mistakes of judgment**. Thus, when the board complies with the business judgment rule, its action is conclusive.

The **officers** of a corporation are elected or appointed **by the board of directors**. Officers are **agents of the corporation** and have actual and apparent authority to conduct the day-to-day operations of the business. Typically, the officers are the president, vice president, secretary, and treasurer, but the RMBCA states that the corporation has only those officers described by the bylaws and appointed by the board. Generally, corporate officers serve at the will of the board of directors, which may remove any officer at any time. However, the board may not remove without cause an officer who was elected or employed by shareholders. As agents of the corporation, officers possess **express authority** conferred on them by either the bylaws or the board of directors. Officers also possess implied authority to do things that are reasonably necessary to accomplish their expressed duties. Officers who exceed their corporate authority may be personally liable. Officers are in positions of trust and owe **fiduciary duties** to the corporation that are the same as those of directors.

The **Sarbanes-Oxley Act of 2002**, a response to numerous financial reporting scandals involving large public companies, contains provisions relating to corporate governance. The act applies to issuers of publicly traded securities subject to federal securities laws. It requires that each member of the **audit committee**, including at least one who is a **financial expert**, be an **independent** member of the issuer's **board of directors**. An independent director is not affiliated with, and receives no compensation (other than for service on the board) from, the issuer. The audit committee must be directly responsible for **appointing, compensating, and overseeing** the work of the public accounting firm employed by the issuer. In addition, this audit firm must **report directly** to the audit committee, not to management. Another function of the audit committee is to implement procedures for the receipt, retention, and treatment of **complaints about accounting and auditing matters**. The audit committee also must be appropriately funded by the issuer and may hire independent counsel or other advisors. The **chief executive officer** and **chief financial officer** of the issuer must **certify** that the issuer's **financial statements and disclosures** "fairly present, in all material respects, the operation and financial condition of the issuer." This statement must accompany the audit report. A CEO or CFO will be liable only if (s)he **knowingly and intentionally** violates this part of the act. The maximum penalty is a fine of $1,000,000 and imprisonment for 10 years. It is also illegal for an officer or director to exert **improper influence on the conduct of an audit** with the intent to make financial statements materially misleading. Moreover, if an issuer materially **restates its financial statements** as a result of material noncompliance with reporting requirements, the CEO and CFO must return to the issuer any amounts received within 12 months after the issuance or filing in the form of (1) incentive- or equity-based compensation and (2) profits from sale of the issuer's securities. The SEC also may **freeze extraordinary payments** to directors, officers, and others during an investigation of securities law violations, and it may prohibit anyone convicted of **securities fraud** from serving as an officer or director of a publicly traded firm. Sarbanes-Oxley created a new **25-year felony for defrauding shareholders of publicly traded companies**. This measure is a broad, generalized provision. It criminalizes the knowing or attempted execution of any scheme to defraud persons in connection with securities of issuers or to obtain their money or property in connection with the purchase or sale of securities. It gives prosecutors flexibility to protect current and future shareholders against any frauds that inventive criminals may devise. The maximum prison term for **mail or wire fraud** was increased from 5 to 25 years. Moreover, the maximum term for violating the Securities Exchange Act of 1934 was increased from 10 to 20 years. Furthermore, management must establish and document internal control and include in the annual report an assessment of **internal control over financial reporting**.

The SEC requires issuers to provide detailed disclosures about **executive compensation** paid to the CEO, CFO, and the next three highest paid officers: (1) base pay, (2) share options and grants, and (3) other benefits. The reporting of equity awards should conform to that in the financial statements. These awards are expensed over the required service period.

An acquisition of a share of stock makes a person an owner of the corporation issuing the stock. However, a shareholder has no right to manage the corporation directly. The **shareholders'** primary participation in corporate policy and management is by **meeting annually and electing directors** by majority vote. By their power to remove any and all directors, shareholders indirectly control the actions of the corporation. In addition to electing directors, shareholders must **approve amendments to the articles of incorporation and fundamental corporate changes**, such as (1) all actions of merger or consolidation, (2) proposals to sell or lease not in the ordinary course of business all or substantially all of the corporation's assets, (3) compulsory exchanges of the corporation's shares, and (4) dissolution. Unless a class of stock is established with no voting rights, each shareholder is entitled to one vote for each outstanding share owned. Shareholders may exercise their voting rights at either annual or special meetings. The most significant shareholder voting right is the right to elect directors through straight or cumulative voting. Another alternative is **class voting**. The RMBCA permits a corporation to designate the voting rights of each class of shares. Thus, even a closely held corporation may have two or more classes of common shares with different voting rights.

Some additional shareholder control devices include shareholder voting agreements, voting trusts, and proxies. These devices are permitted because shareholders are free to agree contractually how they will vote their shares. A written **voting agreement** may provide for the manner in which the signatory shareholders will vote their shares. This agreement is specifically enforceable under the RMBCA. The RMBCA also specifically allows shareholders to transfer their shares to one or more trustees in exchange for **voting trust** certificates. The trustees elect directors based on instructions from the shareholders. Because shareholders are frequently unable to attend meetings, they sometimes delegate authority to vote their shares by issuing **proxies**. Typically, a valid proxy authorizing someone else to vote on behalf of the shareholder must be in writing, is revocable at any time, and is effective for a period of no more than 11 months unless otherwise permitted by statute and specifically included in the writing.

Other important rights of the shareholder of a corporation are the preemptive right and the right to inspect the corporate records. A **preemptive right** gives a shareholder an option to subscribe to a new issuance of shares in proportion to his/her current interest in the corporation. It prevents dilution of existing shareholder equity in the corporation when new shares are issued. Under the RMBCA, a preemptive right does not exist unless granted in the articles, and, unless specifically provided for, it does not apply to (1) shares issued for compensation, (2) issues within 6 months of incorporation, (3) shares that have been issued but reacquired by the corporation **(treasury stock)** if reissued, or (4) stock issued for something other than money (e.g., shares issued to effect a merger). **Warrants (also called rights)** are issued to shareholders pursuant to their preemptive rights. They are options to purchase a certain number of shares at a given price that may be publicly traded. Shareholders also possess the fundamental **right to inspect** the corporation's books and records. To exercise the right of inspection, a shareholder must present a written demand to the corporation. Inspection must be made in good faith and for a proper purpose.

Shareholders exercise their rights at annual or special meetings. **Annual meetings** are required and must be held at a time fixed in the bylaws. The primary purpose of the annual shareholder meeting is to elect new directors and conduct other necessary business. Notice of an annual meeting need not include a detailed agenda unless shareholders will be asked to approve fundamental corporate changes. **Special meetings** may be called whenever an issue arises that requires shareholder action. Special meetings may be called by the board of directors, the holders of at least 10% of all votes entitled to be cast at the meeting, and any other persons authorized in the articles. A **quorum** of the outstanding shares must be represented in person or by proxy to conduct business at a shareholders' meeting. Unless the law or the articles provide otherwise, the RMBCA defines a quorum as a majority of the votes entitled to be cast by a voting group on the matter at issue. Generally, shareholders can act only at a duly called meeting. However, the RMBCA permits **action without a meeting** if all the shareholders entitled to vote consent in writing to the action. All annual and special meetings require written **notice** setting forth the date, time, and place. Moreover, notice of a special meeting must describe the purpose(s). Lack of notice or defective notice voids any action taken at the shareholders' meeting.

Shareholders have certain rights to litigate either against or on behalf of the corporation. An individual shareholder has standing to bring a **direct suit** on his/her own behalf to enforce shareholder rights, for example, to compel payment of declared dividends, to inspect books and records, to exercise the preemptive right, or to vote. Shareholders may also bring a **class suit** (representative suit or class action) to recover from the corporation for a wrong done to the class of shareholders. A shareholder may also file suit in a proceeding in which the corporation itself would normally be expected to file. A shareholder **derivative suit** is a legal action to recover for wrongs done to the corporation. The action is for the benefit of the corporation, and any recovery belongs to it and not to the shareholder. Thus, a derivative suit may be brought because of an ultra vires act, to recover improper dividends, to obtain a remedy for management's breach of duty, etc. For a shareholder to file a derivative suit, the RMBCA requires that the plaintiff prove that (1) (s)he was a shareholder at the time of the alleged wrongdoing, (2) a written demand was made on the directors, and (3) 90 days have expired since the demand (unless notice of rejection has been given or irreparable harm will be done to the corporation). A derivative suit will be dismissed if independent directors or a court-appointed panel determines in good faith after reasonable inquiry that the action is not in the best interests of the corporation.

Shareholders ordinarily **do not have liability for corporate obligations beyond their capital contributions**. However, shareholders may be held personally liable in certain cases, for example, when the corporation is defectively formed, or when the **corporate veil has been pierced**. Shareholders also may be liable for knowing receipt of an improper dividend, failure to pay in accordance with the stock subscription agreement, or, in some states, receipt of stock at less than the stated par value. Receipt of **watered stock** may also result in liability. When a corporation issues stock as fully paid but full payment has not been made, the stock is said to be "watered." This situation can arise when stock is issued in exchange for property or services that are held out to have value equivalent to the stock but that actually are substantially overvalued.

Some changes affect a corporation in such a fundamental manner that they are beyond the authority of the board and require shareholder approval. Shareholder approval of **fundamental changes** does not usually require unanimity. In some instances, minority shareholders have the **right to dissent** and recover the fair value of their shares after appraisal. The fundamental changes requiring approval of shareholders include **amendments to the articles**. Generally, the board adopts a resolution setting forth, in writing, the proposed amendment. The resolution must then be approved by a majority of the shareholders entitled to vote. After the amendment is approved by the shareholders, articles of amendment are filed with the secretary of state. The amendment becomes effective upon issuance of the certificate of amendment. **Sale or lease of all or substantially all corporate assets** requires shareholder approval only if such a sale or lease is not in the ordinary or usual course of business. However, when the selling or leasing corporation has significantly changed its position and ability to carry on the type of business originally operated, such a sale or lease must be approved by the shareholders. However, a mortgage or pledge of all the property and assets of a corporation, whether or not in the ordinary course of business, requires director but not shareholder approval. The most fundamental change is **dissolution**. A corporation that issued stock and commenced business dissolves upon board approval of a dissolution resolution, shareholder vote of approval, and filing of articles of dissolution with the secretary of state petitioning the state to dissolve the corporation. **Voluntary dissolution** without a board resolution is permitted upon the unanimous vote of the shareholders. A court may enjoin an otherwise proper dissolution on the grounds that public policy requires the corporation's continuation. **Administrative dissolution** in a proceeding commenced by the secretary of state may be effected on grounds of failure to (1) pay any franchise tax or penalty, (2) deliver an annual report, or (3) maintain a registered office or agent in the state. **Expiration of the period of duration** stated in the articles is also grounds for such action. Under the RMBCA, shareholders may seek a **court-ordered dissolution** if (1) a corporate deadlock develops; (2) those in control have acted, are acting, or will act illegally, oppressively, or fraudulently; or (3) assets are being misapplied or wasted.

A **merger** is a combination of all the assets of two or more corporations. In a merger, one corporation is absorbed by another corporation and ceases to exist. A merger requires the approval of **each board and a majority of shareholders entitled to vote** for each corporation. State statutes often set forth specific procedures for mergers, including filing of **articles of merger**. The surviving corporation succeeds to the rights, duties, liabilities, and assets of the merged corporation. The shareholders of a merged corporation may receive stock or other securities issued by the surviving corporation as provided for in the merger agreement. In a **short-form merger** under the RMBCA, a parent that owns 90% or more of a subsidiary may effect a merger without approval of the subsidiary's shareholders or directors, provided that the subsidiary's shareholders are given notice within 10 days.

A **consolidation** of two or more corporations requires that a new corporation be formed and all of the original entities cease operating separately. Consolidations require the affirmative vote of the boards as well as the majority vote of approval by shareholders in each of the involved corporations. In a **compulsory share exchange**, one corporation acquires all the outstanding shares of one or more classes of stock of another corporation through an exchange that is mandatory for all holders of the acquired shares. Each board and the shareholders of the **corporation whose shares are to be acquired** must approve. A compulsory share exchange has the advantage of maintaining the separate corporate existence of both entities.

A business combination is sometimes undertaken to **take a public corporation private** for the purpose of avoiding federal regulation or eliminating minority shareholders. One possibility for a corporate acquirer that owns at least 90% of the target's shares is a short-form merger. Another is the purchase of the corporation's shares in the market or by tender offer (see below). A third possibility is a **cashout combination**. After obtaining a controlling stake in the target entity, e.g, by a tender offer, the acquirer may seek a forced buyout of the minority shareholders. One method is to create a new corporation, which would be wholly owned by the acquirer. In a subsequent cashout merger of the target and the new corporation, all the shareholders of the target (except the acquirer) would receive cash for their shares. If the acquirer is a corporation, it could merge the target with itself. An alternative to a cashout merger is a purchase for cash of all the assets of the target. This approach leaves the minority shareholders with an interest in the cash paid, not in a business. Under state law, a cashout combination must be fair to all parties. Moreover, some states require it to have a **valid business purpose**. A fourth means of taking a public corporation private is a **management buyout**, also known as a **leveraged buyout**. Management and institutional investors create a new corporation in which management's stake is greater than that in the original entity. The new entity then issues debt to the institutional investors to obtain the funds needed to acquire the shares or assets of the original entity. The assets of this entity serve as security for the debt. An important implication of a management buyout is management's **conflict of interest**. Furthermore, the transaction is disadvantageous for the acquired business because of the new debt burden.

Not all shareholder votes on fundamental changes are unanimous. Shareholders who disagree with fundamental corporate changes may receive **appraisal rights** (dissenter's rights). Appraisal rights require the corporation to pay dissenting shareholders the fair value of their stock in cash. Most state statutes exclude from appraisal shares traded on a nationally recognized exchange.

Management of a corporation that is the subject of a proposed acquisition may dissuade the board from approving the combination to protect their own interests or those of other current employees or shareholders. An acquiring corporation may bypass approval by the board of the target corporation by extending a **tender offer** directly to its shareholders to purchase a certain number of the outstanding shares. After obtaining control of the target corporation, the tender offeror can effect a merger or consolidation. Managements of target corporations have implemented diverse strategies to counter hostile tender offers. Courts apply the **business judgment rule** when such strategies are challenged. Generally, courts have upheld the strategies. Tender offers are regulated by the federal **Securities Exchange Act of 1934**.

QUESTIONS

32.1 Directors

1. Which of the following statements about the directors of a corporation is true?

A. Under the Revised Model Business Corporation Act, a corporation may dispense with a board of directors in certain circumstances.

B. Directors may serve only from one annual meeting to the next.

C. Directors may be elected by the shareholders only.

D. The number of directors may not exceed the number of shareholders.

Answer (A) is correct. *(Publisher, adapted)*

REQUIRED: The true statement about corporate directors.

DISCUSSION: In the absence of a shareholder agreement meeting the requirements of the RMBCA, a corporation must have a board of directors consisting of at least one individual. Some states require a minimum of three directors but permit the number of directors to equal the number of shareholders if less than three. Other states require at least three directors. Given a unanimous agreement, however, the RMBCA permits the shareholders to dispense with directors.

Answer (B) is incorrect. Under the RMBCA, staggered multi-year terms are also allowed if the corporation has at least nine directors. Answer (C) is incorrect. The remaining directors may fill vacancies resulting from the death, removal, or resignation of directors until the next shareholders' meeting. They may also fill new positions established by amendment of the bylaws or articles. Answer (D) is incorrect. No requirement to limit the maximum number of directors to the number of shareholders is stated in the RMBCA.

2. A director of a corporation

A. Must usually be a resident of the state of incorporation.

B. Is often removable for cause by the other directors.

C. Must ordinarily be a shareholder.

D. Must usually be at least 21 years old.

Answer (B) is correct. *(Publisher, adapted)*

REQUIRED: The true statement about a corporate director.

DISCUSSION: The RMBCA allows the shareholders to remove a director with or without cause at a meeting called for that purpose. Many states permit the board to remove a director for cause, e.g., insanity or conviction of a felony, subject to shareholder review.

Answer (A) is incorrect. Residency requirements are imposed by statute in only a few states. Answer (C) is incorrect. Directors ordinarily need not be shareholders. Answer (D) is incorrect. Age requirements are imposed by statute in only a few states.

3. Absent a specific provision in its articles of incorporation, a corporation's board of directors most likely has the power to do all of the following, except

A. Repeal the bylaws.

B. Declare dividends.

C. Fix compensation of directors.

D. Amend the articles of incorporation without shareholder approval.

Answer (D) is correct. *(CPA, adapted)*

REQUIRED: The limit on the board's authority.

DISCUSSION: Authority to formulate and implement corporate policy is vested in the board, including selection of officers, determining capital structure, proposing fundamental changes, declaring dividends, and setting management compensation. Amending the articles, however, is a power reserved to the shareholders except in limited circumstances.

Answer (A) is incorrect. The board has authority to add, amend, or repeal bylaws to govern the corporation's internal structure and operation. Answer (B) is incorrect. The board has discretion to formulate and implement dividend policy. Answer (C) is incorrect. Director compensation is fixed by the board.

4. Iago and Des are the sole directors, officers, and shareholders of the ID Corporation, a theatrical group incorporated in Florida. They regularly hold board meetings outside of Florida or by videoconferencing. Recently, without a meeting, Des increased compensation of the directors and declared the regular dividend. Iago later filed in the minutes a signed, written consent to the actions taken. If the articles and by-laws are silent on these matters,

A. Board meetings must be held in the state of incorporation or where the corporation has its principal business and must be conducted in person.

B. The board may declare dividends but may not fix its own compensation.

C. ID is in violation of the Revised Model Business Corporation Act because it has fewer than three directors.

D. Unanimous written consent of all directors may substitute for a meeting.

Answer (D) is correct. *(Publisher, adapted)*

REQUIRED: The true statement concerning the formalities required of a close corporation.

DISCUSSION: Traditionally, the board of directors could act only after a formal meeting at which a quorum was present. Under modern statutes, unanimous written consent filed in the minutes is a sufficient basis for action by the board.

Answer (A) is incorrect. Board meetings may be conducted anywhere and are not required to be in person; e.g., the meetings may be held by videoconference. Answer (B) is incorrect. The board of directors may routinely declare dividends and may also fix its own compensation unless the articles provide otherwise. Answer (C) is incorrect. The RMBCA provides for a minimum of one director. Furthermore, the shareholders may unanimously agree to dispense with the board.

5. Delegation of the powers of the board of directors is generally

A. Prohibited.

B. Allowed with regard to any matter upon which the board may act.

C. Prohibited except when required by an outside agency, for example, a stock exchange that requires members to have audit committees.

D. Allowed except with regard to specified important transactions.

Answer (D) is correct. *(Publisher, adapted)*

REQUIRED: The true statement about delegation of directors' authority.

DISCUSSION: If the articles or bylaws permit, the directors may by majority vote of the full board delegate authority to specified directors constituting an executive or other committee. The committee may exercise all the powers of the board except with regard to significant or extraordinary transactions such as declaring dividends, issuing stock, or amending bylaws. The committee must consist only of directors.

Answer (A) is incorrect. Executive, audit, finance, and other committees are normally allowed. Answer (B) is incorrect. Certain powers may not be delegated. Answer (C) is incorrect. Committees are not established solely to meet requirements, such as the New York Stock Exchange's rule requiring members to establish audit committees of outside directors.

6. Seymore was recently invited to become a director of Buckley Industries, Inc. If Seymore accepts and becomes a director, he along with the other directors will not be personally liable for

A. Lack of reasonable care.

B. Honest errors of judgment.

C. Declaration of a dividend that the directors know will impair legal capital.

D. Diversion of corporate opportunities to themselves.

Answer (B) is correct. *(CPA, adapted)*

REQUIRED: The situation in which a director will not be held personally liable.

DISCUSSION: The directors of a corporation owe a fiduciary duty to the corporation and the shareholders. They are also expected to exercise reasonable business judgment. The law does recognize human fallibility and allows for directors to be safe from liability for honest mistakes of judgment.

Answer (A) is incorrect. Directors are personally liable for failure to exercise reasonable care. Answer (C) is incorrect. Directors are prohibited from declaring dividends that would violate a state statute establishing a minimum legal capital. Answer (D) is incorrect. A director may not exploit opportunities presented to him/her in his/her capacity as a director for his/her own benefit without first offering them to the corporation.

7. Laser Corporation lent $5,000 to Mr. Jackson, a member of its board of directors. Mr. Jackson was also vice-president of operations. The board of directors, but not the shareholders, of Laser authorized the loan on the basis that the loan would benefit the corporation. The loan made to Mr. Jackson is

A. Improper because Mr. Jackson is both a director and an employee.

B. Improper because Mr. Jackson is an employee.

C. Improper because Mr. Jackson is a director.

D. Proper.

Answer (D) is correct. *(CPA, adapted)*

REQUIRED: The propriety of a loan made by a corporation to a director-officer.

DISCUSSION: Approval of a loan to a fellow director is not a per se violation of the director's fiduciary obligation to the corporation. Subject to that obligation and the duty to act with reasonable care, the directors may approve a loan that in their judgment would benefit the corporation. It would be inappropriate for Jackson to vote on the loan resolution, but his vote would not necessarily make it voidable. The shareholders need not authorize the loan. A conflicting interest transaction will not result in sanctions (e.g., damages), be enjoined, or be set aside if it is fair to the corporation or if it is approved after required disclosure by a majority of disinterested directors or of shares voted by disinterested parties.

8. A corporate director commits a breach of duty if

A. The director's exercise of care and skill is minimal.

B. A contract is awarded by the company to an organization owned by the director.

C. An interest in property is acquired by the director without prior approval of the board.

D. The director's action, prompted by confidential information, results in an abuse of corporate opportunity.

Answer (D) is correct. *(CIA, adapted)*

REQUIRED: The breach of a corporate director's duty.

DISCUSSION: Corporate directors have a fiduciary duty to provide the corporation with business opportunities that come to them in their positions as directors of the corporation. A director who personally takes such a business opportunity has breached his/her duty.

Answer (A) is incorrect. A director is under a duty to use good business judgment, but (s)he is not responsible for the highest standard of care and skill. Answer (B) is incorrect. A director is not prohibited from entering into a conflicting interest transaction if it is fair to the corporation or if it is approved after required disclosure by a majority of disinterested directors or of shares voted by disinterested parties. Answer (C) is incorrect. A director is under no duty to report personal property investments unless they relate to corporate business.

9. Davis, a director of Active Corp., is entitled to

A. Serve on the board of a competing business.

B. Take sole advantage of a business opportunity that would benefit Active.

C. Rely on information provided by a corporate officer.

D. Unilaterally grant a corporate loan to one of Active's shareholders.

Answer (C) is correct. *(CPA, adapted)*

REQUIRED: The action not a breach of a director's duties.

DISCUSSION: A director is a fiduciary of the corporation and its shareholders. (S)he has duties of care and loyalty. Thus, a director must perform, without conflict or usurping an opportunity in which the corporation has an interest, with the care an ordinarily prudent person in a similar position would exercise under similar circumstances. But in exercising good business judgment or reasonable care, a director is entitled to rely on information provided by an officer (or professional specialist) if the director reasonably believes the officer has competence in the relevant area.

Answer (A) is incorrect. Serving as a director of a competing business is a conflict of interest. Answer (B) is incorrect. Usurping a business opportunity of the corporation is a breach of the director's fiduciary duty of loyalty. Answer (D) is incorrect. A director is not an agent of the corporation, and directors authorize corporate transactions by approving resolutions as a board.

10. Which of the following actions is required to ensure the validity of a contract between a corporation and a director of the corporation?

A. An independent appraiser must render to the board of directors a fairness opinion on the contract.

B. The director must disclose the interest to the independent members of the board and refrain from voting.

C. The shareholders must review and ratify the contract.

D. The director must resign from the board of directors.

Answer (B) is correct. *(CPA, adapted)*

REQUIRED: The action to ensure the validity of a contract between a corporation and a director.

DISCUSSION: To protect the corporation against self-dealing, a director is required to make full disclosure of any financial interest (s)he may have in any transaction to which both the director and the corporation may be a party. Under the RMBCA, a transaction is not voidable merely on the grounds of a director's conflict of interest if the transaction is fair to the corporation or has been approved by a majority of (1) informed, disinterested qualified directors or (2) holders of qualified shares. This rule applies even if the director was counted for the quorum and voted to approve the transaction. A qualified director does not have (1) a conflict of interest regarding the transaction or (2) a special relationship (familial, professional, financial, etc.) with another director who has a conflict of interest. Shares are qualified if they are not controlled by a person with (1) a conflict of interest or (2) a close relationship with someone who has a conflict. Thus, the director who contracts with the corporation cannot provide the vote that approves the contract.

Answer (A) is incorrect. The RMBCA states no such requirement. However, shareholders who disagree with fundamental corporate changes have appraisal rights to receive the fair value of their shares. Answer (C) is incorrect. Shareholder ratification is unnecessary. However, if the transaction is fair, approval by shareholders prevents it from being voided. Furthermore, unanimous shareholder approval may release the director from liability even if the transaction is unfair. Answer (D) is incorrect. Resignation is not required. Self-dealing transactions are permissible in many cases.

32.2 Officers

11. Generally, officers of a corporation

A. Are elected by the shareholders.

B. Are agents and fiduciaries of the corporation, having actual and apparent authority to manage the business.

C. May be removed by the board of directors without cause only if the removal is approved by a majority vote of the shareholders.

D. May declare dividends or other distributions to shareholders as they deem appropriate.

Answer (B) is correct. *(CPA, adapted)*

REQUIRED: The true statement about corporate officers.

DISCUSSION: Officers are agents of a corporate principal, and agency law prescribes their real and apparent authority to bind the corporation. The bylaws and board resolutions may specifically limit that authority. Usual duties of an officer also define the officer's apparent authority. Any principal, including a corporation, may be estopped from asserting a lack of actual authority on the part of its officers and other employees. Officers are also fiduciaries. Like directors, they owe a duty of loyalty, good faith, and fair dealing when transacting business with or on behalf of the corporation.

Answer (A) is incorrect. Officers customarily are elected by the directors. Answer (C) is incorrect. Officers are removable at any time without cause by the board of directors. Answer (D) is incorrect. The directors declare dividends.

12. Jeri Fairwell is executive vice-president and treasurer of Wonder Corporation. She was named as a party in a shareholder derivative action in connection with certain activities she engaged in as a corporate officer. In the lawsuit, she was held liable for negligence in performance of her duties. Fairwell seeks indemnity from the corporation. The board of directors would like to indemnify her, but the articles of incorporation do not contain any provisions regarding indemnification of officers and directors. Indemnification

A. Is not permitted because the articles of incorporation do not so provide.

B. Is permitted only if Fairwell is found not to have been grossly negligent.

C. Cannot include attorney's fees because Fairwell was found to have been negligent.

D. May be permitted by court order although Fairwell was found to be negligent.

Answer (D) is correct. *(CPA, adapted)*

REQUIRED: The true statement about indemnification of a negligent officer of a corporation.

DISCUSSION: Usually, an officer or director who is liable to the corporation because of negligence in the performance of his/her duties is not entitled to indemnification. However, a court may order indemnification of an officer or director of a corporation (even though found negligent) if the court determines (s)he is fairly and reasonably entitled to it in view of all the relevant circumstances.

Answer (A) is incorrect. Indemnification is permitted unless the articles expressly prohibit it. Answer (B) is incorrect. A court may order indemnification if it determines that the officer is reasonably entitled to it in view of all the relevant circumstances, even if the officer was negligent. Answer (C) is incorrect. An officer who is entitled to indemnification may receive attorney's fees.

13. An officer-shareholder of a corporation could be held personally liable for which one of the following debts?

A. Unpaid U.S. corporate income taxes.

B. A bank note signed by a shareholder in his/her capacity as president of the corporation.

C. Federal payroll taxes that were withheld from the employees' wages but never remitted to the IRS.

D. A judgment against the corporation stemming from a tort committed by a former employee.

Answer (C) is correct. *(Publisher, adapted)*

REQUIRED: The debts for which an officer-shareholder can be held personally liable.

DISCUSSION: An employer is required to withhold from an employee's salary income taxes and Social Security taxes (FICA). If an officer-shareholder is deemed to be a "responsible party" by the IRS, (s)he can be held personally liable for these taxes because they are considered to be held "in trust" for the benefit of the employee until remitted to the IRS.

Answer (A) is incorrect. Personal liability is not extended to unpaid U.S. corporate income taxes. Answer (B) is incorrect. The officer-shareholder is not personally liable on the bank note if (s)he signed as an agent of the corporation. In closely held corporations, two signatures are often required, one as an agent of the corporation and one in an individual capacity. Answer (D) is incorrect. The corporation insulates owners from liability for torts of their employees.

32.3 Shareholders

14. A corporate shareholder is entitled to which of the following rights?

A. Elect officers.

B. Receive annual dividends.

C. Approve dissolution.

D. Prevent corporate borrowing.

Answer (C) is correct. *(CPA, adapted)*

REQUIRED: The right of a shareholder.

DISCUSSION: Shareholders do not have the right to manage the corporation or its business. Shareholder participation in policy and management is through electing directors. Shareholders also have the right to approve fundamental corporate changes, such as amendments of the articles, disposition of all or substantially all of the corporation's assets, mergers and consolidations, and dissolutions.

Answer (A) is incorrect. The board usually elects officers. Answer (B) is incorrect. A shareholder does not have a general right to receive dividends. The board determines dividend policy. Answer (D) is incorrect. Determining capital structure and whether the corporation should borrow are policy and management determinations to be made according to the board's business judgment.

15. All of the following are legal rights of shareholders in U.S. publicly traded companies except the right to

A. Vote on major mergers and acquisitions.

B. Receive dividends if declared.

C. Vote on charter and bylaw changes.

D. Vote on major management changes.

Answer (D) is correct. *(CMA, adapted)*

REQUIRED: The item that is not a basic legal right of shareholders in publicly traded corporations.

DISCUSSION: A corporation is owned by shareholders who elect a board of directors to manage the company. The board of directors then hires managers to supervise operations. Shareholders do not vote on major management changes because the powers of the board include selection and removal of officers and the setting of management compensation. Shareholders in publicly traded U.S. corporations have the right to (1) vote on fundamental corporate changes (such as mergers and consolidations), (2) receive declared dividends and annual reports, (3) vote on other matters, (4) exercise any preemptive right that may have been granted, (5) attend meetings, (6) inspect corporate records, and (7) bring shareholder suits.

Answer (A) is incorrect. Shareholders may vote on major mergers and acquisitions. Answer (B) is incorrect. Shareholders may receive dividends if declared. Answer (C) is incorrect. Shareholders may vote on charter and bylaw changes.

16. Shareholder voting

A. Is required to be cumulative in most states.

B. May usually be accomplished by oral or written proxy.

C. May usually be by proxy, but the agency thus created is generally limited to a specific issue.

D. May be by proxy, but a proxy may be revoked if the shareholder signs a later proxy.

Answer (D) is correct. *(Publisher, adapted)*

REQUIRED: The true statement about shareholder voting.

DISCUSSION: A proxy is a written authorization to vote another person's shares. The rule that the last proxy signed by a shareholder revokes prior proxies is a significant issue in proxy battles. A proxy is also revoked when the shareholder actually attends the meeting and votes his/her shares or when (s)he dies.

Answer (A) is incorrect. Cumulative voting, which facilitates minority representation, is allowed but not required in most states. For example, if three directors are to be elected and a shareholder has 40 of the 100 outstanding shares, (s)he has 120 votes, which can all be cast for one director. Answer (B) is incorrect. A proxy must usually be written. Answer (C) is incorrect. Proxies commonly authorize action regarding all matters presented at the shareholders' meeting.

17. Shareholders representing a majority of the voting shares of Nadier, Inc. have transferred their shares to Thomasina Trusty to hold and vote irrevocably for 10 years. Trusty has issued certificates to the shareholders and pays over to them the dividends received. The agreement

A. Is an illegal voting trust and is void because it is against public policy.

B. Is valid if entered into pursuant to a written voting trust agreement.

C. Need not be filed with the corporation.

D. May be revoked because it is in essence a proxy.

Answer (B) is correct. *(Publisher, adapted)*

REQUIRED: The legal status of a voting trust agreement.

DISCUSSION: The RMBCA provides that an irrevocable voting trust agreement authorizing a trustee to hold and vote shares for a period of up to 10 years (unless extended by a new agreement) is valid if written and filed with the corporation where it will be available for inspection by shareholders.

Answer (A) is incorrect. The voting trust is a legal arrangement that has a statutory or case law basis in most states. Answer (C) is incorrect. One of the statutory requirements for a valid voting trust is that the agreement be filed with the corporation and be available for inspection. Answer (D) is incorrect. The voting trust differs substantially from a proxy. It is irrevocable for the agreed period.

18. A shareholder of a corporation

A. Has no right to a stock certificate because ownership rights are intangible.

B. Generally has a preemptive right to the extent permitted by the articles.

C. Has an absolute right to dividends in any year when the corporation is profitable.

D. Has no right to have his/her name recorded in the corporation's stock record book.

Answer (B) is correct. *(Publisher, adapted)*

REQUIRED: The true statement about the specific rights of a shareholder.

DISCUSSION: A preemptive right is a shareholder's right to purchase a proportionate share of a new stock issue so that his/her percentage interest in the entity can be maintained. Some statutes grant the preemptive right but allow it to be denied in the articles, while other statutes, including the RMBCA, deny the right but allow it to be granted in the articles. The articles are therefore generally determinative.

Answer (A) is incorrect. Shareholders generally have the right to evidence of their ownership. However, the trend is toward uncertificated shares. Answer (C) is incorrect. The directors have broad discretion to withhold declaration of dividends even if ample funds are available. Answer (D) is incorrect. Recordation of shareholders' names in the corporate books is the basis for voting rights, notice of meetings, payment of dividends, and distribution of reports.

19. A shareholder's right to inspect books and records of a corporation will be properly denied if the shareholder

A. Wants to use corporate shareholder records for a personal business.

B. Employs an agent to inspect the books and records.

C. Intends to commence a shareholder's derivative suit.

D. Is investigating management misconduct.

Answer (A) is correct. *(CPA, adapted)*

REQUIRED: The basis for denying shareholder inspection of books and records.

DISCUSSION: Every shareholder has a right to inspect specified corporate books and records. But the right must be exercised for a proper purpose, in good faith, upon prior written notice, and during regular business hours. Use of corporate shareholder records for a personal business is not a proper purpose.

Answer (B) is incorrect. An agent may exercise the right on the shareholder's behalf. Answer (C) is incorrect. A shareholder's derivative suit is a proper purpose, unless it is instituted in bad faith. Answer (D) is incorrect. Investigating management misconduct is a proper purpose. It concerns the shareholder's ownership interest in the corporation.

20. If the directors of the Garrett Co. wish to call a special meeting of shareholders to consider a proposed merger,

A. The shareholders must be given specific notice of the meeting and the issues on the agenda.

B. At least 1 week's notice must be given.

C. If notice is not given to shareholders entitled to vote at the record date, action taken at the meeting will be invalid even if all the shareholders attend and participate in the meeting.

D. A majority of shareholders entitled to vote must be represented in person at the meeting to constitute a quorum, unless otherwise provided in the articles.

Answer (A) is correct. *(Publisher, adapted)*

REQUIRED: The legal requirements for special shareholders' meetings.

DISCUSSION: Notice is not usually required for regular meetings because the time and place of such meetings are normally specified in the bylaws. The ordinary business of the corporation may be transacted at regular meetings without specific notice being given to shareholders. Special meetings must be the subject of a timely notice specifying the time, place, and issues on the agenda.

Answer (B) is incorrect. Under the RMBCA, at least 10 days' notice must be given. Answer (C) is incorrect. Attendance and participation in the meeting by shareholders who did not receive notice is generally a waiver of the right to notice. Answer (D) is incorrect. A majority of the shares entitled to vote must be represented to constitute a quorum, but they may be represented in person or by proxy.

21. Shareholder action on fundamental changes in a large publicly held corporation generally requires that a meeting be convened. Under the RMBCA, and unless the articles or bylaws stipulate otherwise,

A. Holders of not less than 10% of the voting shares may call a special meeting.

B. Action on extraordinary transactions may only be taken at the annual meeting.

C. Notice of a special but not an annual meeting must include an agenda if extraordinary transactions are to be approved.

D. Action on extraordinary transactions taken at special but not annual meetings is void absent notice, waiver of notice, or attendance without objection.

Answer (A) is correct. *(Publisher, adapted)*

REQUIRED: The true statement about shareholder meetings.

DISCUSSION: When shareholder action is required concerning a fundamental corporate change, a meeting must be held. If the issue must be resolved before the annual meeting, a special meeting may be called by the board, by a person authorized by the bylaws (e.g., the president), or by holders of not less than 10% of the shares entitled to be voted at the meeting.

Answer (B) is incorrect. Action also may be taken at special meetings. Answer (C) is incorrect. Notice or the equivalent must be given prior to any meeting or the action taken is void. If extraordinary changes are to be voted on, the purposes must be stated in the notice, including that for an annual meeting. Answer (D) is incorrect. Notice or the equivalent must be given prior to any meeting.

22. Basil Hardheart is the majority shareholder and chairman of the board of Close Corporation. Carrie Carter and Gina Kelly are respectively a minority common shareholder and a holder of nonvoting preferred stock. Basil has diverted corporate assets to personal use. Basil has also caused the board to declare and pay common stock dividends without paying preferred dividends. Under these circumstances,

A. Carter may bring a representative action against Close Corporation based on Hardheart's diversion of assets.

B. Kelly may bring a representative action against Close Corporation based on Hardheart's diversion of assets.

C. Carter may bring a derivative action against the corporation for withholding the preferred dividends.

D. Kelly may bring a representative action against the corporation for withholding the preferred dividends.

Answer (D) is correct. *(Publisher, adapted)*

REQUIRED: The appropriate legal action given certain causes of action.

DISCUSSION: Both representative and derivative suits are shareholder suits in which the plaintiff represents a class of (or all) shareholders. The representative suit (class action) is brought directly against the corporation for a wrong done by the corporation itself. The derivative action is brought on behalf of the corporation for a wrong done to the corporation. The withholding of the preferred dividends is a right of action by the preferred shareholders against the corporation. Thus, Kelly could bring a representative action as a preferred shareholder.

Answer (A) is incorrect. Carter may bring a derivative suit against Hardheart. Answer (B) is incorrect. Kelly may bring a derivative suit against Hardheart. Answer (C) is incorrect. The suit for withholding the preferred dividend would be a representative suit. It could not be brought by Carter because she is not a preferred shareholder.

23. Fundamental corporate changes require shareholder approval. Under the RMBCA, which of the following is false?

A. Notice must be given to shareholders whether or not entitled to vote.

B. The articles may require a supermajority vote.

C. The board of directors usually gives prior approval to the change.

D. At least a majority of each class must approve even though the rights of a class may not be affected.

Answer (D) is correct. *(Publisher, adapted)*

REQUIRED: The false statement about procedures for making fundamental changes.

DISCUSSION: Under the RMBCA, the first step is approval of the change by the board. All shareholders must then be notified, including those without voting rights regarding the matter. A majority vote of the shareholders taken at an annual or special meeting is sufficient to pass the proposal unless the articles require a greater percentage. Voting by class is required by the RMBCA for share exchanges and mergers if the interests of a class are significantly affected. The articles may provide that class voting is required on other transactions.

Answer (A) is incorrect. All shareholders must be notified. Answer (B) is incorrect. A greater-than-majority vote may be required by the articles. Answer (C) is incorrect. Approval by the directors is the initial step.

24. For what purpose will a shareholder of a publicly held corporation be permitted to file a shareholders' derivative suit in the name of the corporation?

A. To compel payment of a properly declared dividend.

B. To enforce a right to inspect corporate records.

C. To compel dissolution of the corporation.

D. To recover damages from corporate management for an ultra vires management act.

Answer (D) is correct. *(CPA, adapted)*

REQUIRED: The basis for a shareholder's derivative suit.

DISCUSSION: A derivative suit is a cause of action brought by one or more shareholders on behalf of the corporation to enforce a right belonging to the corporation. Shareholders may bring such an action when the board of directors refuses to act on the corporation's behalf. Under the RMBCA, the shareholder must show (1) (s)he owned stock at the time of the wrongdoing, (2) (s)he made a demand to the corporation to bring suit or take other appropriate action, and (3) 90 days have elapsed since the demand was made (unless notice of rejection has been received or irreparable harm will be done to the corporation). The recovery, if any, belongs to the corporation. An action to recover damages from corporate management for an ultra vires act is an example of a derivative suit. An ultra vires act is one beyond the limits of the corporate purposes defined in the articles of incorporation.

Answer (A) is incorrect. Shareholders must sue directly on their own behalf to compel payment of a properly declared dividend. Answer (B) is incorrect. Shareholders must sue directly on their own behalf to enforce a right to inspect corporate records. Answer (C) is incorrect. Shareholders must sue directly on their own behalf to compel dissolution of the corporation.

25. The term "watered stock" typically refers to

A. The decline in value of a share of stock following a stock split.

B. The issuance of stock as fully paid in exchange for overvalued property or services.

C. The issuance of stock at less than the proportionate carrying amount of the corporation's net assets.

D. The difference between the amount received by the corporation and the amount subscribed.

Answer (B) is correct. *(Publisher, adapted)*

REQUIRED: The statement describing watered stock.

DISCUSSION: When a corporation issues stock as fully paid but full payment has not been made, the stock is said to be "watered." This situation can arise when stock is issued in exchange for property or services that are held out to have value equivalent to the stock but that actually are substantially overvalued.

Answer (A) is incorrect. Stock splits have no effect on the capitalization of the corporation. A stock split increases the number of shares without altering the proportionate ownership. Answer (C) is incorrect. The directors may fix the price at which stock will be sold; there is no "water" as long as the price is fully paid. The carrying amount of net assets is not relevant to the issue of stock. Answer (D) is incorrect. It describes the unpaid portion of a stock subscription, which is an enforceable debt.

26. Which of the following statements is true regarding the fiduciary duty?

A. A director's fiduciary duty to the corporation may be discharged by merely disclosing his/her self-interest.

B. A director owes a fiduciary duty to the shareholders but not to the corporation.

C. A promoter of a corporation to be formed owes no fiduciary duty to anyone, unless the contract engaging the promoter so provides.

D. A majority shareholder as such may owe a fiduciary duty to fellow shareholders.

Answer (D) is correct. *(CPA, adapted)*

REQUIRED: The fiduciary duty of directors, promoters, and shareholders.

DISCUSSION: Directors and officers owe a fiduciary duty to the corporation to act in its best interests, to be loyal, to use due diligence in carrying out their responsibilities, and to disclose conflicts of interest. Controlling as well as majority shareholders owe a similar duty. Courts will often protect the interests of minority shareholders by ordering the payment of dividends that were withheld in bad faith or by compelling a seller of a controlling block of shares to distribute ratably among all shareholders any "control premium" paid in excess of the fair value of the stock.

Answer (A) is incorrect. The fiduciary duty is far more extensive. Answer (B) is incorrect. The duty is owed to the corporation, not the shareholders. Answer (C) is incorrect. A promoter owes a fiduciary duty of fair dealing, good faith, and full disclosure to subscribers, shareholders, and the corporation.

32.4 Fundamental Corporate Changes

27. Acorn Corp. wants to acquire the entire business of Trend Corp. Which of the following methods of business combination will best satisfy Acorn's objectives without requiring the approval of the shareholders of either corporation?

A. A merger of Trend into Acorn, whereby Trend shareholders receive cash or Acorn shares.

B. A sale of all the assets of Trend, outside the regular course of business, to Acorn, for cash.

C. An acquisition of all the shares of Trend through a compulsory share exchange for Acorn shares.

D. A cash tender offer, by which Acorn acquires at least 90% of Trend's shares, followed by a short-form merger of Trend into Acorn.

Answer (D) is correct. *(CPA, adapted)*

REQUIRED: The acquisition method that does not require shareholder approval.

DISCUSSION: A merger, consolidation, or purchase of substantially all of a corporation's assets requires approval of the board of directors of the corporation whose shares or assets are acquired. An acquiring corporation may bypass board approval by extending a cash tender offer directly to shareholders to purchase a certain number of the outstanding shares. After obtaining control of the target corporation, the tender offeror may effect a merger or consolidation.

28. Which of the following statements, if any, is(are) true regarding the methods a target corporation may use to ward off a takeover attempt?

I. The target corporation may make an offer ("self-tender") to acquire stock from its own shareholders.

II. The target corporation may seek an injunction against the acquiring corporation on the grounds that the attempted takeover violates federal antitrust law.

A. I only.

B. II only.

C. Both I and II.

D. Neither I nor II.

Answer (C) is correct. *(CPA, adapted)*

REQUIRED: The true statement regarding methods a corporation may use to ward off a takeover attempt.

DISCUSSION: Managers of target corporations have implemented diverse strategies to counter hostile tender offers. Examples of anti-takeover strategies include self-tender and legal action as well as persuasion, creation of poison pills, reverse tenders, crown-jewel transfers, and white knight mergers.

29. Which of the following must take place before a corporation may be voluntarily dissolved?

A. Passage by the board of directors of a resolution to dissolve.

B. Approval by the officers of a resolution to dissolve.

C. Amendment of the certificate of incorporation.

D. Unanimous vote of the shareholders.

Answer (A) is correct. *(CPA, adapted)*

REQUIRED: The act usually a precondition to voluntary dissolution.

DISCUSSION: A corporation that issued stock and commenced business dissolves upon board approval of a dissolution resolution, shareholder vote of approval, and filing of articles of dissolution with the secretary of state petitioning the state to dissolve the corporation. Voluntary dissolution without a board resolution is permitted upon the unanimous vote of the shareholders. A court may enjoin an otherwise proper dissolution on the grounds that public policy required the corporation's continuation.

Answer (B) is incorrect. A corporation may voluntarily dissolve without approval by its officers. Answer (C) is incorrect. Filing articles of dissolution, not an amendment of the charter, is required. Answer (D) is incorrect. A majority of shares is usually sufficient to approve a board-approved dissolution resolution. If voting is by classes of stock, each class of stock with voting rights must approve the dissolution by at least a majority vote.

30. Under the RMBCA, which of the following statements about involuntary dissolution of a corporation is true?

A. The attorney general, shareholders, or the directors may dissolve a corporation through court action. Creditors may not.

B. Administrative dissolution by the secretary of state may result from failure to pay franchise taxes or to deliver an annual report.

C. If otherwise properly formed, the corporation cannot be dissolved on the grounds that its articles were obtained by fraud.

D. A creditor may seek dissolution only if (s)he has reduced a claim to judgment.

Answer (B) is correct. *(Publisher, adapted)*

REQUIRED: The true statement about involuntary dissolution.

DISCUSSION: Administrative dissolution in a proceeding commenced by the secretary of state may be effected on grounds of failure to pay any franchise tax or penalty, to deliver an annual report, or to maintain a registered office or agent in the state. Expiration of the period of duration stated in the articles is also grounds for such action.

Answer (A) is incorrect. Creditors of an insolvent corporation may sue for its dissolution if a judgment has been returned unsatisfied or the corporate debt has been admitted in writing.
Answer (C) is incorrect. The attorney general may sue for dissolution if the articles were obtained by fraud or if the corporation is exceeding or abusing its authority or is corrupt.
Answer (D) is incorrect. Creditors may sue for dissolution if corporate debt has been admitted in writing.

31. Under the Revised Model Business Corporation Act, a dissenting shareholder's appraisal right generally applies to which of the following corporate actions?

	Consolidations	Short-Form Mergers
A.	Yes	Yes
B.	Yes	No
C.	No	Yes
D.	No	No

Answer (A) is correct. *(CPA, adapted)*

REQUIRED: The corporate action warranting a right of appraisal by a dissenting shareholder.

DISCUSSION: Shareholders participate indirectly in corporate policy and management by (1) electing directors and (2) voting on formal resolutions of the board of directors to approve fundamental corporate changes, including all mergers or consolidations. Shareholders who disagree with the fundamental corporate changes may have appraisal (dissenter's) rights. A shareholder demanding appraisal must (1) have the right to vote on the action to which (s)he objects, (2) not vote in favor of the proposed action, and (3) make written demand before the vote that the corporation purchase his/her stock if the petition is approved. If the conditions are met, the corporation must pay dissenters the fair value of their stock within 60 days. Generally, shares traded on a stock exchange are excluded from appraisal rights.

STUDY UNIT THIRTY-THREE
FEDERAL SECURITIES REGULATION

The two major federal securities acts are the **Securities Act of 1933** and the **Securities Exchange Act of 1934**. State securities laws also apply. The purpose of the 1933 act is to regulate the initial offering of securities by requiring the filing of a registration statement with the SEC prior to sale or an offer to sell. The 1934 act governs dealings in securities subsequent to their initial issue. A student's emphasis should be on (1) the purposes of the securities laws, (2) the registration process, (3) the securities and transactions that are exempt from registration, (4) the antifraud provisions, and (5) the accountant's role and liability in securities transactions. The 1933 act has two **objectives**. Both pertain to the **initial offering** of securities for sale to the public: (1) disclosure to potential investors of all material information and (2) prevention of fraud. The 1934 act primarily addresses **secondary distribution** (resale) of securities. One of its primary elements is registration of all regulated public companies with the **Securities and Exchange Commission (SEC)**. The SEC is an administrative agency created by the 1934 act to enforce the federal securities laws. It has the power to (1) issue rules, (2) investigate violations, (3) conduct hearings to decide whether violations have occurred (adjudication), and (4) impose penalties. The SEC may deny, suspend, or revoke registration, or it may order a suspension of trading of the securities. These sanctions are in addition to civil and criminal liability imposed by the federal securities laws. Moreover, the SEC may prohibit an individual who has committed **securities fraud** from serving as an officer or director of a public company. It also may freeze extraordinary payments during an investigation of securities law violations. Another function of the SEC is oversight of the auditing profession through the **Public Company Accounting Oversight Board**. In addition, as part of its responsibility for accounting standards, the SEC has recognized the **FASB** as the standard setter for GAAP. Other primary elements of the 1934 act are (1) periodic reporting, which requires providing up-to-date statements about all business operations and matters potentially affecting the value of securities; (2) antifraud provisions; and (3) insider liability for short-swing profits. **Each state** has adopted its own securities laws **(blue-sky laws)**. Generally, an issuer must comply with both federal and state securities laws. However, federal securities laws **partially preempt** blue-sky laws.

The 1933 act **defines a security** to include almost any offering that constitutes an investment:

> *Any note; stock; treasury stock; bond; debenture; evidence of indebtedness; certificate of interest or participation in any profit-sharing agreement; collateral-trust certificate; preorganization certificate or subscription; transferable share; investment contract; voting-trust certificate; certificate of deposit for a security; fractional undivided interest in oil, gas, or other mineral rights; any put, call, straddle, option, or privilege on any security or, in general, any interest or instrument commonly known as a "security," or any certificate of interest or participation in, temporary or interim certificate for receipt for, guarantee of, or warrant or right to subscribe to or purchase any of the foregoing.*

The test of whether something is a security requires analysis of whether (1) a person invests in a common enterprise (2) with a reasonable expectation of profits (3) to be derived solely from the efforts of a promoter or third party but not the investors themselves. Courts have held an investment to be a security even though the investor provided some of his/her own effort. **Securities markets** may have a physical location, such as the New York Stock Exchange (NYSE), or no physical location, such as the over-the-counter (OTC) market. The 1934 act defines **exchange** as "any organization, association, or group of persons, whether incorporated or unincorporated, which constitutes, maintains, or provides a marketplace or facilities for bringing together purchasers and sellers of securities." The **parties to an issuance** under the 1933 act include every person involved in the **initial offering and sale** of securities. These persons may be classified as issuers, underwriters, or dealers. An **issuer** is the individual or the business organization initially offering a security for sale to the public (generally, to raise money). An issuer includes a controlling person, one who owns more than 10% of the company's stock. An **underwriter** is any person who participates in the original offering of securities from the issuer with the intention of distributing them. A **dealer** is any person who is engaged in the business of offering, selling, dealing, or otherwise trading in securities issued by another. A dealer also may be a **broker**, a person who executes securities transactions for others.

Securities registration is required by the 1933 act for any offer or sale to the public unless a specific exemption applies. Thus, an issuer must prepare and file a registration statement and a prospectus. Under the SEC's **integrated disclosure** system, four categories of issuers are recognized. A **nonreporting issuer** (one who need not file reports under the 1934 act) must use detailed **Form S-1**. An **unseasoned issuer** has reported for at least 3 consecutive years under the 1934 act. It must use **Form S-1** but provides less detailed information and may include some information by reference to other 1934 act reports. A **seasoned issuer** has filed for at least 1 year and has a market capitalization of at least $75 million. It may use **Form S-3** to report even less detail and may include even more information by reference. A **well-known seasoned issuer** has filed for at least 1 year and (a) has a worldwide market capitalization of at least $700 million or (b) has issued for cash in a registered offering at least $1 billion of debt or preferred stock in the past 3 years. Such an issuer also may use **Form S-3**. A **registration statement** is a complete disclosure to the SEC of all material information with respect to the issuance of the specific securities. It includes the **prospectus** that will be provided to each potential investor. The **purpose of registration** is to provide adequate and accurate **disclosure** of financial and other pertinent information that potential investors may use to evaluate the merits of the securities. Generally, registration calls for a description of (1) the registrant's **business, property, and competition**; (2) the significant **provisions of the security** to be offered for sale, its relationship to the registrant's other capital securities, the plan for its distribution, and the uses of the proceeds; (3) management, compensation of **directors and officers**, their holdings of the registrant's securities, and material transactions with these individuals; and (4) material **legal proceedings**. The following also must be disclosed: (1) the most recent **audited financial statements** (comparative balance sheets for 2 years and comparative income statements, statements of cash flows, and statements of changes in equity for 3 years); (2) management's discussion and analysis (MD&A); and (3) whether the registrant's **independent public accountant** has changed within the past 2 fiscal years. The issuer, a majority of the directors, the CEO, the CFO, and the chief accounting officer must sign the registration statement. The SEC does not judge the merits of an investment or guarantee the accuracy of the information. Thus, registration does not insure investors against loss. SEC rules protect investors in low-cost, high-risk **penny stocks**. Brokers who sell penny stocks must provide potential investors with documents that explain the (high) risks of the investments and the related commission structure. The registration statement is effective on the **20th day after filing** unless the SEC accelerates the effective date or requires an amendment.

A new 20-day period begins after an amendment. After the effective date, the issuer may make sales if the purchaser has received a final prospectus. A **prospectus** must be furnished to any interested investor. Its purpose is to supply sufficient facts to make an informed investment decision. However, **access is equated with delivery**. Thus, actual delivery of a hard copy is not required if the prospectus was timely filed with the SEC. The cover page, summary, and risk factors sections must be in **plain English**, be inviting to users, and not obscure important information.

SEC regulations regarding communications prior to and during registered offerings define a **free-writing prospectus** as a written offer, including one in an electronic format, that is not a statutory prospectus. Any issuer, under certain conditions, may use a free-writing prospectus after the registration statement is filed. **Well-known seasoned issuers**, under certain conditions, may at any time make any communications, including a free-writing prospectus. Any **reporting issuer** may at any time publish regularly released factual business information and forecasts. **Nonreporting issuers** may at any time publish regularly released factual business information intended for use by noninvestors. Issuer communications **more than 30 days prior to a filing** must not refer to a filing subject to registration.

Generally, the entire allotment of securities is made available for purchase on the effective date of the registration statement. An exception is a **shelf registration**. After the registration statement is filed, the securities are held for up to 3 years until the best time for an offering is determined. A shelf registration is available only to **seasoned issuers** and **well-known seasoned issuers**. Well-known seasoned issuers are eligible for automatic effectiveness of shelf registration statements and a simplified procedure. The information in the original registration (shelf registration) must be continually updated in quarterly and annual filings to be accurate and current.

Exemptions under the 1933 act apply to specific transactions or securities. Most **secondary trading** is exempt. **Section 4(1)** of the act generally exempts transactions by any person other than an issuer, an underwriter, or a dealer. **Section 4(3)** exempts transactions by **dealers** that do not involve original distributions or resales within a limited period after the effective date of a registration. **Section 4(4)** exempts **unsolicited brokers' transactions** that execute customer orders on an exchange or over the counter. Furthermore, the 1933 act exempts from registration **securities** of (1) domestic governments used for a governmental purpose, (2) not-for-profit organizations, (3) domestic banks and savings and loan associations, and (4) issuers that are federally regulated common carriers. It also exempts securities issued (1) by a receiver or trustee in bankruptcy with prior court approval, (2) with respect to a corporate reorganization approved by a court or other governmental body, and (3) solely for exchange with the issuer's existing security holders if no commission or other consideration is paid. (Thus, stock dividends and stock splits are generally exempt.) Insurance policies and annuity contracts issued by state-regulated insurers (but not other securities issued by insurers) are likewise exempt. **Short-term commercial paper** is exempt if it consists of any note, draft, or banker's acceptance issued to acquire working capital that has a maturity of **not more than 9 months** when issued. But an investment vehicle (e.g., a money market fund) that holds short-term commercial paper is not exempt.

The **safe harbor** provisions of **Rule 147** define when the **intrastate offerings exemption** cannot be challenged: (1) The issuer is organized or incorporated in the state in which the issue is made, (2) 80% of the proceeds are to be used in that state, (3) 80% of its assets are located there, (4) the issuer does at least 80% of its business (gross revenues) within that state, (5) all the purchasers and offerees are **residents of the state**, (6) no resales to nonresidents occur for at least 9 months after the initial sale by the issuer is completed, and (7) steps are taken to prevent interstate distribution.

Regulation A permits **issuers** to offer up to **$5 million** of securities in any 12-month period without full registration. It imposes no limitations on the number and nature of investors, and resale is not restricted. The SEC **integrates** all registrations and exempted offerings. Thus, three registrations of $2 million each would not qualify for exemption under Regulation A if issued within one 12-month period. The SEC does not integrate an offering unless it is made within 6 months before or after another offering. Regulation A filings are less detailed, time consuming, and costly than full registration statements. A formal registration statement and prospectus are not required. An offering statement containing a notification and an **offering circular** must be filed with the SEC's regional office, and the 20-day waiting period must be observed. The offering circular also must be provided to offerees and purchasers of the underlying securities. Sales may be made after the SEC has approved the filing. The issuer may "test the waters" by use of broadcast or written advertisements. However, no **oral communications with buyers** are allowed until the SEC receives the advertisements. **No sales** are allowed until the offering statement is approved by the SEC.

Regulation D establishes three exemptions (Rules 504, 505, and 506) related to small issues and small issuers. **Certain procedural rules** generally must be complied with to qualify for the exemption. However, except for the notice to the SEC, the following rules **do not apply to Rule 504** transactions: (1) No **general solicitation or advertising** is permitted; (2) the issuer must exercise reasonable care to ensure that purchasers are not underwriters and are purchasing strictly for their own **investment purposes**; (3) the SEC must be notified by filing **Form D** within 15 days of the first offering; (4) the exemption is only **for transactions** in which securities are offered or sold by the issuer; (5) the securities are **restricted**, and resale must be after registration or under some exemption; (6) immediate rollover of the securities is precluded; and (7), if the offering is to any **nonaccredited investors**, prior to the sale, they must be furnished with material information about the issuer, its business, and the securities being offered. Under **Rule 504**, qualified issuers may sell up to **$1 million** of securities during a 12-month period to any number or type of purchasers without registration and without providing specific financial information. General solicitation is allowed, and the securities issued are **not restricted** and can be freely traded if the offering is (1) registered in a state that requires a publicly filed registration statement, and disclosure documents are delivered to investors, or (2) sold exclusively according to state law exemptions that permit general solicitation and advertising, as long as sale is only to **accredited investors**. **Rule 505** provides exemption from registration to all issuers other than investment companies for a **limited offering** of securities up to **$5 million** in any 12-month period. The issue may be purchased by an unlimited number of accredited investors. Under Regulation D, **accredited investors** include most institutional investors and individuals that meet income or net worth thresholds. The issuer must reasonably believe that there are no more than **35 nonaccredited investors/offerees**. **Section 4(2)** provides a **private placement** exemption from registration for "transactions by an issuer not involving any public offering." **Rule 506** under Regulation D implements this exemption. Rule 506, unlike Rules 504 and 505, has **no ceiling amount**. It provides a safe harbor for a private placement, but noncompliance does not necessarily mean that the exemption cannot be claimed. The offering may be purchased by **an unlimited number of accredited investors**. The issuer must reasonably believe that there are no more than **35 nonaccredited investors/offerees**.

Each nonaccredited purchaser must have the knowledge and experience in financial and business matters needed to evaluate the merits and risks of the investment, or the issuer must reasonably believe that such purchasers meet this requirement. Generally, the issuer requires the purchaser to sign an **investment letter** stating that (s)he is purchasing for investment only and not for resale. For this reason, shares issued under Rule 506 are called **lettered stock**. **Section 4(6)** exempts up to **$5 million** of offers and sales if made **only to accredited investors**. The number of such investors may be unlimited, and no information is required to be given to them, but general advertising and solicitation are not permitted. Moreover, the SEC must be informed of sales under the exemption, resale is restricted, and precautions must be taken to prevent nonexempt or unregistered resales.

An exemption may not apply to a public resale of **restricted securities**, for example, securities exempted under Rules 505 and 506 and Section 4(6). Generally, resale must be made by registration or under another exemption. **Rule 144** provides an exception to the registration requirement. It permits the resale of restricted securities provided that (1) adequate public information is available about the issuer; (2) the reseller has owned and fully paid for the securities for a period not less than 1 year prior to resale; (3) the amount of securities sold during any subsequent 3-month period generally does not exceed (a) 1% of the stock outstanding, (b) the average weekly reported volume of trading in the securities on all national securities exchanges for the preceding 4 weeks, or (c) the average weekly volume of trading of the securities reported through the consolidated transactions reporting system (NASDAQ); (4) sales are through brokers' transactions or in transactions with a market maker; and (5) notice of resale is provided to the SEC if the amount of securities sold in reliance on Rule 144 in any 3-month period exceeds 500 shares, or if they have an aggregate sales price in excess of $10,000. Persons who are not **affiliates** (entities that control the issuer, are controlled by it, or are under common control) and have owned the securities for at least 2 years are not subject to the foregoing requirements. However, state securities laws may impose different requirements and must be complied with before a purchase. **Rule 144A** allows **qualified institutional investors** (those owning and investing at least $100 million of securities) to purchase unregistered securities without regard to the holding periods specified in Rule 144. The securities must not belong to a class listed on an exchange or traded through an automated quotation system. **Regulation A** also provides an exemption for sales by **nonissuers** of up to $1.5 million in any 12-month period. Use of this exemption requires compliance with all the conditions imposed under Regulation A on **issuers**.

The 1933 act imposes **civil liability** for noncompliance with the act's requirements with respect to submission of a registration statement. Under **Section 11, any person** who acquires a security issued in connection with a **misstatement or omission of a material fact** may sue (1) the issuer; (2) every person who signed the registration statement; (3) every director of the corporation or partner in the partnership issuing the security; (4) experts who participated in preparation of the registration statement, e.g., accountants, engineers, and lawyers; and (5) every underwriter. To recover under Section 11, a **plaintiff must prove** (1) (s)he acquired a security subject to registration, (2) the registration statement contained a material misstatement or omission, and (3) (s)he incurred a loss. The **plaintiff need not prove** an intent to deceive, negligence (lack of due care), reliance, privity of contract, or that (s)he gave value. The term **material** for purposes of the securities acts has been interpreted by the courts to mean "a fact which if it had been correctly stated or disclosed would have deterred or tended to deter the average prudent investor from purchasing the securities in question."

Exercising **due diligence** with respect to material information in the registration statement is a **defense to liability** for all defendants except the issuer. **Other defenses** to liability under Section 11 include (1) no misstatement or omission occurred; (2) the misstatements or omissions did not concern material facts; (3) the plaintiff knew of the misstatements or omissions; (4) the plaintiff's loss was not caused by the omission or misstatements; or (5) the statute of limitations has expired. Liability under Section 11 is for the amount paid for the security minus either its value at the time of suit or the price for which it was sold. The 1933 act also imposes civil liability if (1) the required registration was not made; (2) a registered security was sold, but a prospectus was not delivered or was not current; or (3) an offer to sell was made before a required registration. Under **Section 12**, the plaintiff must prove (1) reliance, (2) privity of contract, and (3) that the transaction involved interstate commerce or the mails. **Section 12(a)(1)** imposes strict civil liability for sales or offers that violate the registration requirements of the 1933 act. Suit may be in state or federal court for damages or rescission of the contract. Moreover, the purchaser may only sue his/her seller.

Antifraud provisions under the **1933 act** apply to **all securities**, registered and exempt. Under **Section 12(a)(2)**, liability is imposed on any person who offers or sells a security by means of a prospectus or oral communication that contains a material misstatement or omission. The seller's liability extends only to the **immediate purchaser**. The offeror or seller may avoid liability by proving that (1) (s)he did not know and should not have known of the misstatement or omission, or (2) the loss was caused by something other than a false statement or omission by the seller. Under **Section 17(a)**, a general antifraud provision, liability is imposed on an offeror or seller for fraud, material misrepresentations, and omissions in securities sales. However, these broad provisions do **not allow for a private remedy** for the purchaser. **Criminal sanctions** are imposed on any person who willfully violates any of the provisions of the 1933 act or its rules and regulations. Conviction carries a penalty of a fine of up to $10,000 and up to 5 years of imprisonment.

Reporting requirements under the **1934 act** govern dealings in securities after their initial issue (resales). All regulated publicly-held companies must register with the SEC. However, merely **doing business in interstate commerce** is not a sufficient condition for requiring registration. **Registration** is required of all companies (covered corporations) that (1) list securities on a national securities exchange or (2) have at least 500 shareholders of equity securities and total gross assets exceeding $10 million. An **over-the-counter issuer** may terminate its registration if (1) the holders of its registered equity securities are fewer than 300, or (2) the issuer has had fewer than 500 shareholders and less than $10 million in assets on closing day in each of the last 3 years. Also required to report under the 1934 act are (1) an issuer that has **registered securities under the 1933 act** and (2) national securities exchanges. Registration and reporting requirements under the 1934 act are in addition to, not a substitute for, those under the 1933 act. These one-time registrations apply to an entire class of securities. Registration requires **disclosure** of (1) corporate organization; (2) financial structure; (3) a description of all securities; (4) names of officers, directors, underwriters, and holders of more than 10% of a nonexempt equity security; (5) description of the nature of the business; (6) financial statements; and (7) details about executive compensation.

Following registration, an **issuer** must file **reports** with the SEC. **Annual reports** certified by the CEO and CFO are filed on **Form 10-K**. The report must be filed within 60 days of the last day of the fiscal year for **large accelerated filers** ($700 million or more in public float, that is, shares held by the public and not insiders), 75 days for **accelerated filers** ($75 million to $700 million), and 90 days for **nonaccelerated filers** (less than $75 million). In addition to audited financial statements, the 10-K report contains information about (1) business activities, (2) securities, (3) stock prices [but not all price changes], (4) management-related persons [e.g., officers], (5) disagreements about accounting and disclosure, (6) audited financial statements, and (7) other matters. **Quarterly reports** certified by the CEO and CFO are filed on **Form 10-Q**. They need not contain audited financial statements. But the quarterly financial information must be reviewed by an independent auditor. Form 10-Q must be filed within 40 days of the last day of the first three fiscal quarters for both large accelerated filers and accelerated filers, and within 45 days for nonaccelerated filers. In addition to financial information, Form 10-Q reports changes during the quarter, for example, (1) legal proceedings, (2) changes in nature or amount of securities or indebtedness, (3) matters submitted to shareholders for a vote, (4) exhibits and reports on Form 8-K, (5) other material events not reported on Form 8-K, and (6) the anticipated effect of recently issued accounting standards on financial statements when they are adopted in a future period. **Current reports** must be promptly filed on **Form 8-K**. It describes the following **material events** that must be disclosed within **4 business days**: (1) changes in control of the registrant, (2) the acquisition or disposition of a significant amount of assets other than in the ordinary course of business, and (3) bankruptcy or receivership, (4) resignation of a director, and (5) a change in the registrant's certifying accountant. Reporting of material **other events** involving changes in financial condition or operations is optional. Thus, no mandatory time for filing is established. Nevertheless, registrants are encouraged to file promptly and with due regard for the accuracy, completeness, and currency of the information. Also, Form 8-K is a means of making **Regulation FD** disclosures. This regulation requires prompt public disclosure of material nonpublic information that the issuer discloses to certain **market professionals** or to **shareholders likely to trade** on the information. If selective disclosure is intentional, public disclosure must be simultaneous. Any person or group of persons who acquire beneficial ownership of **more than 5%** of a class of registered equity securities of certain issuers must file **Schedule 13D** within 10 days after the acquisition. **Proxy solicitation** is unlawful with respect to any registered security in contravention of SEC rules and regulations. A **proxy** is a power of attorney given by a shareholder to a third party authorizing the party to exercise the voting rights of the shares. Solicitation includes any request for a proxy or any request to revoke a proxy. Ten days prior to mailing a **proxy statement** to shareholders, the issuing company must **file a copy** with the SEC. A **tender offer** is a general invitation by an individual or a corporation to all shareholders of another corporation to tender their shares for a specified price. It usually must be kept open for 20 business days, and **discrimination among offerees** by the offeror is illegal. The following must **file a statement** (within 10 days in the case of a post-acquisition tender offer) with the SEC, the issuing company, and the securities exchanges: (1) any person or group that acquires beneficial ownership of more than 5% of a class of registered securities, (2) a person or group that makes a tender offer for more than 5% of such securities, (3) an issuer offering to repurchase its registered securities, and (4) the target of a hostile tender offer.

Under Section 16 of the 1934 act, **insiders** required to report to the SEC are directors, officers, and any person beneficially owning more than 10% of the stock of a corporation listed on a national stock exchange or registered with the SEC. Insiders must report on **Form 3** (the initial filing), **Form 4** (changes), and **Form 5** (an annual statement) the following: (1) an ownership statement within 10 days of becoming an insider, (2) a statement by the end of the second business day following the day on which the insider engaged in a transaction in the company's equity securities, and (3) an annual statement within 45 days after the company's fiscal year-end. Such reports must be filed electronically with the SEC and posted on the filer's website. Under **Section 16(b)**, insiders may be sued by the issuer (or a shareholder suing derivatively) for **short-swing profits**. These are from sale and purchase (purchase and sale) of the issuer's stock within a 6-month period. **Profit** is based on the highest sales price and lowest purchase price during the period. Furthermore, liability is strict. The insider need not have had inside information.

The **1934 act** imposes **civil liability** under **Section 18(a)** on a person, including a corporation, responsible for any false or misleading statement in an application, document, or report filed with the SEC. To avoid liability, the defendant must prove that the action was in good faith and without knowledge that the statement was false or misleading. **Section 32(a)** imposes **criminal liability** for willfully and knowingly making materially false and misleading statements in a document filed with the SEC.

Section 10(b) of the 1934 act and **SEC Rule 10b-5** are **antifraud provisions**. They apply to certain wrongful acts done through the mail, any other use of interstate commerce, or through a national securities exchange. They make it unlawful for **any person** in connection with the **purchase or sale of any security** to (1) employ any device, scheme, or artifice to defraud; (2) make any untrue statement of a material fact or omit a material fact necessary to make the statements not misleading in the light of the circumstances under which they were made; or (3) engage in any act, practice, or course of business that operates, or would operate, as a fraud or deceit upon any person. The difference between Rule 10b-5 fraud and common law fraud is that Rule 10b-5 requires **disclosure of material facts**. Rule 10b-5 is most frequently applied to **insider trading** and **corporate misstatements**. Rule 10b-5 applies to the purchase or sale of any security, whether or not required to be registered. **There are no exemptions.** Any **actual** buyer or seller of any security who suffers a monetary loss may bring a civil suit to rescind the transaction or to receive monetary damages. Punitive damages are not recoverable. The SEC or a private party may sue. A **plaintiff must prove** each of the following: (1) an oral or written misstatement or omission of a material fact or other fraud; (2) its connection with any purchase or sale of securities; (3) the defendant's intent to deceive, manipulate, or defraud (the **scienter** element of fraud); (4) reliance on the misstatement; and (5) loss caused by the reliance. If the plaintiff is the SEC, reliance is not required. A private plaintiff ordinarily is not required to prove reliance in omission cases. Indirect reliance is presumed based on the **fraud-on-the-market theory**. The plaintiff might never have seen the misstated information, but material misrepresentations to the public affect market price, which is usually assumed to reflect available information. This presumption may be rebutted by proof that the investor did not rely indirectly on the misstatement. For example, "market makers" may have known of the misstatement and not have included it in their pricing decisions.

Any person who violates Rule 10b-5, whether or not (s)he actively participated in the purchase or sale of the security, may be sued. The rule has been applied to hold underwriters, dealers, accountants, and lawyers accountable. All that is required is that the party's activity be connected with the purchase or sale of the security. For Rule 10b-5 purposes, **insider trading** is the purchase or sale of securities by individuals who have access to **material nonpublic information** and have a **fiduciary obligation** to shareholders and potential investors. Insiders are defined much more broadly than under Section 16(b). Thus, they include (1) officers, (2) directors, (3) consultants, (4) lawyers, (5) engineers, (6) auditors, (7) bankers, (8) reporters, (9) public relations advisors, (10) tippees, and (11) personnel in government agencies entrusted with confidential corporate information for corporate purposes.

The SEC may bring a **civil action** against anyone violating the 1934 act by "purchasing or selling a security while in possession of material nonpublic information." Liability is imposed not only on violators but also on those who control them (e.g., employers). **Controlling persons** are liable for knowledge or reckless disregard of the likelihood of a violation and not taking preventive action. Furthermore, mere possession of inside information does not result in liability for trading stocks, e.g., when transactions were arranged before the inside information was obtained. A **private suit** for damages may be brought by a contemporaneous purchaser or seller of shares of the same class. The SEC may award **bounties** to those who provide information leading to prosecution. **Corporate misstatement** is a basis for claims by buyers or sellers of securities claiming reliance and damages under Section 10(b). These claims often arise in connection with releases of information by corporations through reports, speeches, public announcements, or press releases about mergers, research developments, rumors, or other matters of material importance. The **Private Securities Litigation Reform Act of 1995** provides a **safe harbor** from liability for companies that make such statements if they are accompanied by **meaningful cautionary statements** that identify risk factors that could cause actual results to differ from those in the statement.

Criminal liability under the 1934 act is imposed for **willful** violations. False material statements in applications, reports, documents, registration statements, and press releases result in penalties. For **an individual**, the penalty is a fine not to exceed $5 million or 20 years in prison, or both. An individual who proves (s)he had no knowledge of the rule or regulation will not be imprisoned. If the person is **not a natural person** (e.g., a corporation), the maximum fine is $25 million. **Reckless disregard** for the truth or falsity of a statement is sometimes deemed to be the equivalent of a willful violation.

The Sarbanes-Oxley Act created a **25-year felony for defrauding shareholders of publicly traded companies**. This measure is a broad, generalized provision. It criminalizes the knowing execution or attempted execution of any scheme or artifice to defraud persons in connection with securities of publicly traded companies or to obtain their money or property in connection with the purchase or sale of such securities. It is intended to give prosecutors flexibility to protect shareholders and prospective shareholders against any frauds that inventive criminals may devise. This act also prohibits stock transactions by insiders during **pension fund blackout periods** (periods during which stock of the issuer held in a fund may not be disposed of by the beneficiaries). Profits are recoverable by the issuer. If the issuer fails to pursue recovery diligently, suit may be brought by any owner of any security of the issuer.

The **Foreign Corrupt Practices Act (FCPA)** of 1977 was enacted as an amendment to the 1934 act. The FCPA is designed to prevent secret payments using corporate funds for purposes determined by Congress to be contrary to public policy. The FCPA applies to all domestic concerns, whether or not doing business overseas and whether or not registered with the SEC. It imposes **accounting record keeping** and **internal control** requirements and prohibits bribery. Thus, a firm must keep accurate and fair records and maintain an accounting system that provides reasonable assurance that all transactions are recorded and are not illegal. The anti-bribery provisions of the act prohibit all domestic concerns from offering or authorizing **corrupt payments** to a (1) foreign official, (2) foreign political party, or (3) candidate for political office in a foreign country. These payments exclude those for expediting routine government actions or that are legal in the foreign nation. A firm may be fined up to $2 million and an individual up to $100,000. The employer may not pay the fine of an individual. In 1997, 34 nations, including the U.S., signed the **Organization for Economic Cooperation and Development's Convention on Combating Bribery of Foreign Public Officials in International Business Transactions**. In 1998, Congress extended the FCPA to (1) payments to secure any "improper advantage" from public officials, (2) any foreigner who furthers a foreign bribe while in the U.S., and (3) officials of public international organizations.

The **online environment** raises new issues for securities regulation. For example, the SEC has stated that any information (e.g., a prospectus) deliverable by traditional means may be transmitted electronically as long as SEC rules are followed. However, an online offeror must be careful not to provide **links to information** not appropriate for inclusion in the offering materials, such as a securities analyst's recommendations. Furthermore, placing information on a website may prevent an offeror from qualifying for an exemption that requires no **general solicitation or advertising**. The Internet also permits offerings of stock to be made by **foreign companies** without registration with the SEC, a circumstance that raises unique enforcement issues for U.S. regulators. Moreover, the availability of the Internet makes enforcement of the antifraud provisions of the securities laws more difficult. For example, a purchaser of a stock may promote it by posting favorable messages in numerous chat rooms. If this strategy succeeds in creating demand for the stock and increasing its price, it can be sold at a profit. The process is called **pumping and dumping**.

QUESTIONS

33.1 Securities Regulation: Introduction

1. A basic purpose of the securities laws in the United States is to regulate the issuance of investment securities by

A. Requiring disclosure of all relevant information so that investors can make informed decisions.

B. Prohibiting the issuance of non-investment grade securities.

C. Ensuring that all shareholders have an equal vote in the election of a board of directors.

D. Providing a regulatory framework for those states that do not have their own securities laws.

Answer (A) is correct. *(CMA, adapted)*

REQUIRED: The means by which the issuance of investment securities are regulated in the United States.

DISCUSSION: The basic purpose of the federal securities laws in the United States, primarily the Securities Act of 1933 and the Securities Exchange Act of 1934, is to provide complete and fair disclosure to potential investors. The emphasis is on disclosure that allows informed investors to make intelligent decisions.

Answer (B) is incorrect. The SEC does not evaluate the merits of investments or define an investment-grade security. Answer (C) is incorrect. A corporation's by-laws provide for voting rights. For example, preferred stock rarely has a vote. Answer (D) is incorrect. The federal laws apply in all states regardless of the existence of applicable state laws.

2. A main provision of the Securities Act of 1933, as amended in 1934, is the requirement that

A. Bonds be issued only under a trust indenture approved by the Securities and Exchange Commission (SEC).

B. Public utility holding companies register with the SEC.

C. New securities offered for sale in interstate commerce be registered with the SEC.

D. All security brokers be licensed by the SEC.

Answer (C) is correct. *(CMA, adapted)*

REQUIRED: The true statement about the provisions of the Securities Act of 1933, as amended in 1934.

DISCUSSION: The Securities Act of 1933 was designed to provide complete and fair disclosure to potential investors. The 1933 act applies only to the initial issuance of securities. Disclosure is accomplished through the requirement that a registration statement be filed with the SEC. Given complete disclosure, the assumption is that potential investors can make reasonable decisions.

Answer (A) is incorrect. The SEC does not have to approve a trust indenture. Answer (B) is incorrect. The 1933 act requires disclosure of nonexempted new issuances of securities, including those of public utility holding companies, not registration of particular entities. Answer (D) is incorrect. The Securities Exchange Act of 1934 requires registration of brokers.

3. Which of the following is least likely to be considered a security under the Securities Act of 1933?

A. General partnership interests.

B. Limited partnership interests.

C. Stock options.

D. Warrants.

Answer (A) is correct. *(CPA, adapted)*

REQUIRED: The investment least likely to be considered a security under the Securities Act of 1933.

DISCUSSION: The term "security" is defined very broadly by the Securities Act of 1933, as interpreted by the Supreme Court. In general, a security is an investment in a common enterprise with an expectation of profits based solely on the efforts of others. A general partner is entitled to participate directly in the management of the business. Thus, return on the investment in the partnership might be attributed to his/her own efforts.

Answer (B) is incorrect. The owner of limited partnership interests might reasonably anticipate a return on the investment solely through the efforts of others. Answer (C) is incorrect. The owner of stock options might reasonably anticipate a return on the investment solely through the efforts of others. Answer (D) is incorrect. The owner of warrants might reasonably anticipate a return on the investment solely through the efforts of others.

4. All of the following are functions of the Securities and Exchange Commission except the

A. Review of stock trades by corporate insiders.

B. Regulation of interstate offerings of new securities to the public.

C. Setting of rules concerning the proxy process of large public companies.

D. Determination of fair trading prices for the common stock of large public companies.

Answer (D) is correct. *(CMA, adapted)*

REQUIRED: The item that is not a function of the SEC.

DISCUSSION: The SEC is charged with enforcement of federal securities laws. Under the Securities Act of 1933, the offer or sale of a security to the public requires registration with the SEC absent a specific exemption. However, the 1933 act is essentially a disclosure statute. The SEC does not evaluate the merits of securities. Its role is to enforce the laws ensuring the public availability of information to potential investors.

Answer (A) is incorrect. Insider trading is prohibited by Section 10(b) of the Securities Exchange Act of 1934 and by the SEC's Rule 10b-5. Answer (B) is incorrect. An issuer that wishes to make an interstate offering of new securities to the public must file a registration statement with the SEC. Answer (C) is incorrect. The Securities Exchange Act of 1934 provides rules with regard to proxy solicitations and tender offers.

5. The Securities and Exchange Commission is not empowered to

A. Seek an injunction that will suspend trading in a given security.

B. Sue for treble damages.

C. Recommend criminal proceedings against accountants.

D. Suspend a broker-dealer.

Answer (B) is correct. *(CPA, adapted)*

REQUIRED: The true statement regarding the SEC's powers.

DISCUSSION: The SEC is not empowered to sue for damages at all. A lawsuit for treble damages is a civil remedy provided for violations of the antitrust laws, and the SEC has no jurisdiction over antitrust violations. However, the SEC can bring an action in a federal district court to impose civil penalties, for example, for insider trading. Moreover, in an action for violation of the securities laws, the SEC may seek any equitable relief that may be appropriate to benefit investors (Sarbanes-Oxley Act of 2002).

Answer (A) is incorrect. The SEC has authority to seek an injunction in federal court to suspend trading. Answer (C) is incorrect. The SEC may make referrals to the Justice Department for criminal proceedings against accountants who willfully make an untrue statement or omit a material fact in the registration statement. Answer (D) is incorrect. The SEC has supervisory and disciplinary powers over brokers, dealers, attorneys, accountants, stock exchanges, investment advisors, investment companies, etc.

6. Given evidence of a violation of the federal securities laws, the SEC lacks the power to

A. Subpoena witnesses.

B. Compel the production of books and records anywhere in the United States.

C. Determine responsibility for a violation in an administrative hearing and impose certain sanctions.

D. Prosecute criminal cases.

Answer (D) is correct. *(CPA, adapted)*

REQUIRED: The power that is not exercisable by the SEC.

DISCUSSION: The SEC is a federal administrative agency with both quasi-legislative and quasi-judicial authority. It issues rules and regulations under the securities laws, but it is also empowered to enforce these laws. Its powers include the ability to subpoena witnesses, books, and records and to conduct administrative hearings to adjudicate cases involving alleged breaches of the rules and regulations. It can also issue cease-and-desist orders directed against potential as well as actual violations. Because administrative agencies cannot impose criminal sanctions, the Justice Department must prosecute criminal cases involving violations of the securities laws.

Answer (A) is incorrect. The SEC subpoena witnesses. Answer (B) is incorrect. The SEC may compel the production of books and records anywhere in the United States. Answer (C) is incorrect. The SEC may determine responsibility for a violation in an administrative hearing and impose certain sanctions.

7. Blue sky laws are

A. Federal laws that make it unlawful to use deceptive practices in the sale of securities.

B. Federal laws that limit the amount of air pollution in a specific geographic area.

C. State laws that regulate the sale of securities.

D. State laws that regulate the environment.

Answer (C) is correct. *(CMA, adapted)*

REQUIRED: The definition of blue sky laws.

DISCUSSION: Blue sky laws are state laws designed to prevent fraudulent or misleading security issues. The name came from the fact that some of the earliest laws prohibited "everything under the blue skies which is fraudulent."

Answer (A) is incorrect. Blue sky laws are state laws. Answer (B) is incorrect. Blue sky laws are state laws. Answer (D) is incorrect. Blue sky laws do not regulate the environment; they regulate sales of investment securities.

33.2 Securities Act of 1933

8. Which of the following facts will result in an offering of securities being exempt from registration under the Securities Act of 1933?

A. The sale or offer to sell the securities is made by a person other than an issuer, underwriter, or dealer.

B. The securities are nonvoting preferred stock.

C. The issuing corporation was closely held prior to the offering.

D. The securities are AAA-rated debentures that are collateralized by first mortgages on property that has a fair value of 200% of the offering price.

Answer (A) is correct. *(CPA, adapted)*

REQUIRED: The basis for an exemption of an offering of securities from registration.

DISCUSSION: The Securities Act of 1933 requires registration unless the security or transaction is exempt. The act provides an exemption for transactions by any person other than an issuer, underwriter, or dealer. Moreover, transactions by dealers that do not involve original distributions or resales within a limited time after the effective date of a registration are exempt. Unsolicited brokers' transactions executed according to customer orders on an exchange or over the counter are likewise exempt. These rules apply to the great majority of securities transactions conducted by ordinary investors.

9. Dee is the owner of 12% of the shares of common stock of D&M Corporation that she acquired in Year 1. She is the treasurer and a director of D&M and is a controlling person. The corporation registered its securities in Year 2 and made a public offering pursuant to the Securities Act of 1933. If Dee decides to sell part of her holdings in Year 8, the shares

A. Will be exempt from registration because the corporation previously registered them within 3 years.

B. Must be registered regardless of the amount sold or manner in which they are sold.

C. Will be exempt from registration because she is not an issuer.

D. Must be registered if Dee sells 50% of her shares through her broker to the public.

Answer (D) is correct. *(CPA, adapted)*

REQUIRED: The true statement as to whether a controlling person's stock sale must be registered.

DISCUSSION: Dee is considered an issuer because she is a controlling person, that is, one who owns more than 10% of the company's stock and who has the direct or indirect ability to control the company. A sale of 6% of D&M's common stock to the public in the ordinary course of business (e.g., through a broker) does not qualify for an exemption under the Securities Act of 1933 and is subject to SEC registration.

Answer (A) is incorrect. The previous registration is irrelevant. Answer (B) is incorrect. Under Rule 144, an affiliate of the issuer, such as a controlling person, who has held restricted securities for at least 1 year may resell without registration, in any 3-month period, the greater of 1% of the total shares of that class outstanding or the average weekly volume traded. Rule 144 also requires that notice be given to the SEC and that adequate information about the issuer be publicly available. Also, the sale might be exempt if no public offer is made or if certain other requirements are met. Answer (C) is incorrect. A controlling person is an issuer.

10. Which of the following disclosures must be contained in a securities registration statement filed under the Securities Act of 1933?

A. A list of all existing shareholders.

B. The principal purposes for which the offering proceeds will be used.

C. A copy of the corporation's latest proxy solicitation statement.

D. The names of all prospective accredited investors.

Answer (B) is correct. *(CPA, adapted)*

REQUIRED: The disclosure required in a registration statement filed under the 1933 act.

DISCUSSION: The purpose of registration is to provide adequate and accurate disclosure of financial and other pertinent information with which potential investors may evaluate the merits of the securities. Generally, registration calls for disclosure of a description of the registrant's business and property; a description of management; a description of the significant provisions of the security to be offered for sale, its relationship to registrant's other capital securities, and the use of the proceeds of the issuance; and the most recent certified financial statements. Disclosures must also be made about the compensation of officers and directors, their holdings of the registrant's securities, and their business dealings with the registrant.

Answer (A) is incorrect. Disclosure of a list of all existing shareholders is not required in a registration statement filed under the 1933 act. Answer (C) is incorrect. Disclosure of a copy of the corporation's latest proxy solicitation statement is not required in a registration statement filed under the 1933 act. Answer (D) is incorrect. Disclosure of the names of all prospective accredited investors is not required in a registration statement filed under the 1933 act.

11. Which of the following statements concerning the prospectus required by the Securities Act of 1933 is true?

A. The prospectus is a part of the registration statement.

B. The prospectus should enable the SEC to pass on the merits of the securities.

C. The prospectus must be filed after an offer to sell.

D. The prospectus is prohibited from being distributed to the public until the SEC approves the accuracy of the facts stated.

Answer (A) is correct. *(CPA, adapted)*

REQUIRED: The true statement about the prospectus required by the Securities Act of 1933.

DISCUSSION: A prospectus is prepared as part of the registration statement. It is a written document proposing a sale of securities to potential investors. The prospectus contains most of the information in the registration statement. It must be furnished to each potential investor prior to the time of delivery of the securities.

Answer (B) is incorrect. The SEC does not pass on the merits of any security. Answer (C) is incorrect. As part of the registration statement, it must be filed prior to the time that offers to sell are made. Answer (D) is incorrect. The SEC does not determine the accuracy of facts stated in the prospectus.

12. An offering made under the provisions of Regulation A of the Securities Act of 1933 requires that the issuer

A. File an offering circular with the SEC.

B. Sell only to accredited investors.

C. Provide investors with the prior 4 years' audited financial statements.

D. Provide investors with a proxy registration statement.

Answer (A) is correct. *(CPA, adapted)*

REQUIRED: The requirement for a stock offering made under Regulation A.

DISCUSSION: Under Regulation A, a small public issue of securities is exempt from full registration with the SEC if certain requirements are met. Regulation A applies to issuances not exceeding $5 million if the issuer (1) files an offering statement with the SEC, which includes a notification and an offering circular; (2) provides the circular to each offeree and purchaser; and (3) observes the 20-day waiting period. However, investment companies and issuers that must report under the 1934 act may not claim the exemption.

Answer (B) is incorrect. Regulation A does not restrict resale, have an investor sophistication requirement, or limit the number of buyers. Answer (C) is incorrect. Regulation A provides an exemption from the otherwise required filing of a registration statement and prospectus. Answer (D) is incorrect. Filing proxy statements is required under the 1934 act. Regulation A provides exemption from filing requirements of the 1933 act.

13. Maco Limited Partnership intends to sell $6 million of its limited partnership interests. The state in which Maco was organized is also the state in which it carries on all of its business activities. If Maco intends to offer the limited partnership interests in reliance on Rule 147, the intrastate registration exception under the Securities Act of 1933, which one of the following statements is true?

A. Maco may make up to five offers to nonresidents without the offering being ineligible for the Rule 147 exemption.

B. The offering is not exempt under Rule 147 because it exceeds $5 million.

C. Under Rule 147, certain restrictions apply to resales of the limited partnership interests by purchasers.

D. Rule 147 limits to 100 the number of purchasers of the limited partnership interests.

Answer (C) is correct. *(CPA, adapted)*

REQUIRED: The true statement about the intrastate offering exemption.

DISCUSSION: One exemption from registration under the Securities Act of 1933 is an intrastate issue of securities. Under the safe harbor provision of SEC Rule 147, an issue qualifies as intrastate if the issuer is organized or incorporated in the state in which the issue is made, 80% of the proceeds are to be used in that state, 80% of its assets are located there, the issuer does at least 80% of its business (gross revenues) within that state, all the purchasers and offerees are residents of the state, no resales to nonresidents occur for at least 9 months after the last sale, and steps are taken to prevent interstate distribution.

Answer (A) is incorrect. No nonresident may purchase if the Rule 147 exemption is to apply. Answer (B) is incorrect. Rule 147 states no dollar limit on the amount of the offering. Answer (D) is incorrect. Rule 147 states no limit on the number of intrastate purchasers.

14. Which of the following securities is exempt from registration under the Securities Act of 1933?

A. A class of stock given in exchange for another class by the issuer to its existing shareholders without the issuer's paying a commission.

B. Limited partnership interests sold for the purpose of acquiring funds to invest in bonds issued by the United States.

C. Corporate debentures that were previously subject to an effective registration statement, provided they are convertible into shares of common stock.

D. Shares of nonvoting common stock, provided their par value is less than $1.00.

Answer (A) is correct. *(CPA, adapted)*

REQUIRED: The securities exempt from registration under the Securities Act of 1933.

DISCUSSION: If securities are transferred between the issuer and its existing shareholders without payment of commissions or other consideration, the transaction is exempt from registration. Hence, stock dividends and stock splits are exempt. Securities issued in mergers and reorganizations are also exempt if no cash is involved and the securities are given solely for other securities.

Answer (B) is incorrect. The purpose for which funds will be used is irrelevant to whether an exemption is available. Answer (C) is incorrect. Any offer or sale to the public must be registered in the absence of a specific exemption. Prior registration for a different offer or sale is not a specific basis for exemption. Answer (D) is incorrect. Par value is not a basis for exemption.

15. Bird Corp. made a $5 million exempt common stock offering under Rule 505 of Regulation D of the Securities Act of 1933, Thus, the shares were restricted securities. As the issuer of restricted securities, Bird must

A. Make a reasonable effort to determine that purchasers are buying for themselves and not for others.

B. Publicly advertise that the shares are not registered.

C. Provide information to all purchasers as to how they can register their shares so that resale will be permitted.

D. Apply to the SEC for contingent exemptions so that purchasers may resell their shares as exempt.

Answer (A) is correct. *(CPA, adapted)*

REQUIRED: The requirement of an issuer of restricted securities under Rule 505 of Regulation D.

DISCUSSION: Exemption from the 1933 act requirements under Rules 505 and 506 of Regulation D applies to particular transactions, not the securities offered and sold. Securities sold under one of these exemptions are restricted. An issuer of restricted securities is therefore required to make a reasonable effort to determine that purchasers are not underwriters and that they are purchasing strictly for their own investment purposes.

16. Frey, Inc., intends to make a $2 million common stock offering under Rule 505 of Regulation D of the Securities Act of 1933. Frey

A. May sell the stock to an unlimited number of accredited investors.

B. May make the offering through a general advertising.

C. Must notify the SEC within 15 days after the first sale of the offering.

D. Must provide all investors with a prospectus.

Answer (A) is correct. *(CPA, adapted)*

REQUIRED: The true statement concerning a securities offering under Rule 505.

DISCUSSION: Rule 505 provides an exemption from the requirements of the 1933 act to all issuers other than investment companies for sales of securities up to $5 million in any 12-month period. Under Rule 505, securities may be sold to no more than 35 nonaccredited investors and to an unlimited number of accredited investors.

Answer (B) is incorrect. General advertising and solicitation are not allowed under Rules 505 and 506. Answer (C) is incorrect. Under Regulation D, the issuer must notify the SEC within 15 days after the first offering. Answer (D) is incorrect. A prospectus need not be provided. However, nonaccredited investors must be furnished with material information about the issuer, its business, and the securities being offered.

17. Under Regulation D of the Securities Act of 1933, which one of the following conditions applies to private placement offerings? The securities

A. Cannot be sold for longer than a 6-month period.

B. Cannot be the subject of an immediate unregistered reoffering to the public.

C. Must be sold only to accredited institutional investors.

D. Must be sold to fewer than 20 nonaccredited investors.

Answer (B) is correct. *(CPA, adapted)*

REQUIRED: The condition that applies to private placement offerings under Regulation D.

DISCUSSION: Rule 506 under Regulation D provides for sale of securities under the private placement exemption. Securities sold under Rules 505 and 506 are restricted securities and may be resold only by registration or in a transaction exempt from registration. Hence, the certificates bear a legend that the shares are restricted and purchased for personal investment.

Answer (A) is incorrect. Under Rules 504 and 505, the sales period is 12 months. However, no such limit is specified under Rule 506. Answer (C) is incorrect. Under Rule 506, sales are not limited to accredited institutional investors. Accredited investors are persons or entities that are considered to be sufficiently sophisticated to assume risk and obtain information without the aid of the securities acts. Answer (D) is incorrect. Securities may be sold to not more than 35 nonaccredited investors.

18. Taso Limited Partnership intends to offer $400,000 of its limited partnership interests under Rule 504 of Regulation D of the Securities Act of 1933. These interests are registered under state law. Which of the following statements is true?

A. The exemption under Rule 504 is not available to an issuer of limited partnership interests.

B. The limited partnership interests may be sold only to accredited investors.

C. The total number of nonaccredited investors who purchase the limited partnership interests may not exceed 35.

D. The resale of the limited partnership interests by a purchaser generally will not be restricted.

Answer (D) is correct. *(CPA, adapted)*

REQUIRED: The true statement about exemption under Regulation D.

DISCUSSION: A purchaser of securities under Rules 505 and 506 of Regulation D may not immediately resell without being considered an underwriter. Thus, the exemption from registration for transactions by a person not an issuer, underwriter, or dealer is inapplicable. Moreover, the issuer must take steps to prevent nonexempt, unregistered resale and must notify the SEC of the sale. After the securities have been held for 1 year, limited resales are allowed under SEC Rule 144 without registration. Unlimited resales by a nonaffiliate purchaser are allowed after 2 years. However, these limits on resale do not apply to the exemption under Rule 504. Securities issued under Rule 504 are unrestricted and may be resold without federal registration if they are registered under a state law that requires delivery of a substantive disclosure document.

Answer (A) is incorrect. Rule 504 applies to issuers of securities, even when the security is a limited partnership interest. Answer (B) is incorrect. Rule 504 allows qualified issuers to sell up to $1 million of securities during a 12-month period to any number or kind of purchasers without registration. Answer (C) is incorrect. Rule 504 allows sales to an unlimited number of investors, without regard to whether they are accredited or unaccredited.

19. Pursuant to Regulation D of the Securities Act of 1933, Pate Corp. is offering $3 million of its securities solely to accredited investors. Under Regulation D, Pate is

A. Not required to provide any specified information to the accredited investors.

B. Required to provide the accredited investors with audited financial statements for the 2 most recent fiscal years.

C. Permitted to make a general solicitation.

D. Not eligible for an exemption if the securities are debentures.

Answer (A) is correct. *(CPA, adapted)*

REQUIRED: The true statement about an offering made solely to accredited investors.

DISCUSSION: Rule 504 of Regulation D does not apply to this offering because it exceeds $1 million. But Rules 505 ($5 million limit) and 506 (no dollar limit) may be relevant. Under Rules 505 and 506 of Regulation D, no financial disclosure is necessary if all investors are accredited. But, if some are nonaccredited, they must receive certain material information.

Answer (B) is incorrect. Disclosure is not necessary if all investors are accredited. Answer (C) is incorrect. Rules 505 and 506 prohibit general advertising and solicitation. Answer (D) is incorrect. Debentures are within the broad definition of securities stated in the 1933 act.

20. To be successful in a civil action under Section 11 of the Securities Act of 1933 concerning liability for a misleading registration statement, the plaintiff must prove the

	Defendant's Intent to Deceive	Plaintiff's Reliance on the Registration Statement
A.	Yes	Yes
B.	Yes	No
C.	No	Yes
D.	No	No

Answer (D) is correct. *(CPA, adapted)*

REQUIRED: The element(s) of a plaintiff's case under Section 11.

DISCUSSION: Under the 1933 act, the issuer, its chief executive and directors, its chief finance and accounting officers, other signers, the underwriters, and experts who prepared or attested to the statement are liable for misstatements or omissions of material fact. In a private action, a plaintiff establishes a prima facie case under Section 11 by proving damages and that (s)he was an acquirer of a security issued under a registration statement that misstated or omitted a material fact. Intent to deceive, negligence, reliance, privity, or that the plaintiff gave value need not be proven. Exercise of due diligence in determining the accuracy of the statement is a defense. An issuer, however, cannot assert the due diligence defense, but any defendant may show that the plaintiff knew of the misstatement or omission at the time of acquisition.

Answer (A) is incorrect. Intent to deceive, negligence, reliance, privity, or that the plaintiff gave value need not be proven. Answer (B) is incorrect. Intent to deceive need not be proven. Answer (C) is incorrect. Reliance need not be proven.

21. A requirement of a private action to recover damages for violation of the registration requirements of the Securities Act of 1933 is that

A. The plaintiff acquired the securities in question.

B. The issuer or other defendants committed either negligence or fraud in the sale of the securities.

C. A registration statement was filed.

D. The securities were purchased from an underwriter.

Answer (A) is correct. *(CPA, adapted)*

REQUIRED: The requirement of a private action for registration violations.

DISCUSSION: The Securities Act of 1933 permits a civil action by an acquirer of securities if (1) the required registration was not made; (2) a registered security was sold, but a prospectus was not delivered; (3) a security was sold using a prospectus that was not current; or (4) an offer to sell was made before a required registration. Section 11 allows an acquirer to sue on the basis of misstatements or omissions of material facts in the registration statement.

Answer (B) is incorrect. Liability for failure to register is absolute. Neither fraud nor negligence need be shown. Answer (C) is incorrect. The failure to file may be the basis for liability. Answer (D) is incorrect. Liability is imposed on anyone who violates the rules regarding the time, manner, or content of sales and offers to sell.

22. Spiffy Manufacturing plans to offer a new issue of voting stock to the investing public. Assuming that it properly takes advantage of an exemption from registration under the 1933 act, Spiffy

A. Is also exempt from the antifraud rules of the federal securities laws.

B. Need not supply any offerees and purchasers with any material information about itself or the stock being sold.

C. Need not register with any state securities regulators.

D. Must adhere to both federal antifraud rules and state law.

Answer (D) is correct. *(Publisher, adapted)*

REQUIRED: The true statement about legal requirements regarding an exempt offering of stock.

DISCUSSION: An exemption from federal registration will almost never have any effect on the need to register with states where a security is to be sold. Neither will an exemption from registration excuse a seller from obeying antifraud rules.

Answer (A) is incorrect. The Securities Act of 1933 and the Securities Exchange Act of 1934 specifically apply the antifraud rules in the absence of registration. Answer (B) is incorrect. The amount of the offering and the nature of the offerees will determine whether disclosure is needed. Also, state law may require disclosure even if federal law does not. Answer (C) is incorrect. The federal securities laws specifically preserve the right of the states to regulate securities transactions concurrently with the federal government.

33.3 Securities Exchange Act of 1934

23. Integral Corp., with assets in excess of $4 million, has issued common and preferred stock and has 350 shareholders. Its stock is sold on the New York Stock Exchange. Under the Securities Exchange Act of 1934, Integral must be registered with the SEC because

A. It issues both common and preferred stock.

B. Its shares are listed on a national stock exchange.

C. It has more than 300 shareholders.

D. Its shares are traded in interstate commerce.

Answer (B) is correct. *(CPA, adapted)*
REQUIRED: The basis for required registration under the Securities Exchange Act of 1934.
DISCUSSION: The Securities Exchange Act of 1934 requires all regulated publicly held corporations to register with the SEC. Covered corporations either (1) list shares on a national securities exchange or (2) have at least 500 shareholders of equity securities and total gross assets exceeding $10 million.
Answer (A) is incorrect. Issuing preferred stock is not a sufficient condition for registering or reporting under the 1934 act. Answer (C) is incorrect. The threshold is 500 shareholders and total gross assets exceeding $10 million. Answer (D) is incorrect. That shares trade in interstate commerce is insufficient to trigger registration requirements under the 1934 act.

24. Which of the following events must be reported to the SEC under the reporting provisions of the Securities Exchange Act of 1934?

	Tender Offers	Insider Trading	Solicitation of Proxies
A.	Yes	Yes	Yes
B.	Yes	Yes	No
C.	Yes	No	Yes
D.	No	Yes	Yes

Answer (A) is correct. *(CPA, adapted)*
REQUIRED: The events that must be reported to the SEC under the Securities Exchange Act of 1934.
DISCUSSION: The Securities Exchange Act of 1934 governs dealings in securities subsequent to their initial issuance. It requires all regulated publicly held companies to register with the SEC. The act requires disclosure of matters concerning tender offers, insider trading, and the solicitation of proxies.

25. Under the Securities Exchange Act of 1934, which of the following conditions generally will allow an issuer of securities to terminate the registration of a class of securities and suspend the duty to file periodic reports?

	The Corporation has Fewer than 300 Shareholders	The Securities are Listed on a National Securities Exchange
A.	Yes	Yes
B.	Yes	No
C.	No	Yes
D.	No	No

Answer (B) is correct. *(CPA, adapted)*
REQUIRED: The condition allowing an issuer to terminate registration and reporting under the 1934 act.
DISCUSSION: The 1934 act requires all publicly held companies to register with the SEC. Registration is required of all companies that (1) list shares on a national securities exchange or (2) have at least 500 shareholders of its equity securities and total gross assets of at least $10 million. Following registration, an issuer must file specific up-to-date and accurate reports with the SEC to ensure fair trading practices for investors. An over-the-counter issuer may terminate its registration if the holders of its registered equity securities number fewer than 300 or if the issuer has had fewer than 500 shareholders and less than $10 million in assets on closing day in each of the last 3 years.

26. The registration provisions of the Securities Exchange Act of 1934 require disclosure of all of the following information except the

A. Names of owners of at least 5% of any class of nonexempt equity security.

B. Bonus and profit-sharing arrangements.

C. Financial structure and nature of the business.

D. Names of officers and directors.

Answer (A) is correct. *(CPA, adapted)*
REQUIRED: The information that need not be disclosed under the registration provisions of the 1934 act.
DISCUSSION: Registration under the 1934 act requires disclosure of (1) corporate organization; (2) financial structure; (3) description of all securities; (4) names of officers, directors, and underwriters; (5) names of all owners of more than 10% of any class of nonexempt equity security; (6) description of the nature of the business; (7) financial statements; and (8) bonus and profit-sharing arrangements.
Answer (B) is incorrect. Bonus and profit-sharing arrangements must be disclosed. Answer (C) is incorrect. Financial structure and nature of the business must be disclosed. Answer (D) is incorrect. Names of officers and directors must be disclosed.

27. Which of the following statements is true concerning corporations subject to the reporting requirements of the Securities Exchange Act of 1934?

A. The annual report (Form 10-K) need not include audited financial statements.

B. The annual report (Form 10-K) must be filed with the SEC within 20 days of the end of the corporation's fiscal year.

C. A quarterly report (Form 10-Q) need only be filed with the SEC by those corporations that are also subject to the registration requirements of the Securities Act of 1933.

D. A report (Form 8-K) must be filed with the SEC after a material important event occurs.

Answer (D) is correct. *(CPA, adapted)*
REQUIRED: The reporting required under the Securities Exchange Act of 1934.
DISCUSSION: Current reports must be filed on Form 8-K describing specified material events: (1) changes in control of the registrant, (2) the acquisition or disposition of a significant amount of assets other than in the ordinary course of business, (3) bankruptcy or receivership, (4) resignation of a director, and (5) a change in the firm's certifying accountant. Also, Form 8-K is a means of making Regulation FD disclosures. This regulation requires prompt public disclosure of material nonpublic information that the issuer discloses to certain market professionals or to shareholders likely to trade on the information. If selective disclosure is intentional, public disclosure must be simultaneous.
Answer (A) is incorrect. Form 10-K must include audited financial statements: comparative balance sheets and statements of income, cash flows, and changes in equity. Answer (B) is incorrect. Form 10-K is due 60 days after the entity's fiscal year-end. Answer (C) is incorrect. An entity required to file Form 10-K must also file Form 10-Q for each of the first three quarters.

28. Under the Securities Exchange Act of 1934, a corporation whose common stock is listed on a national stock exchange

A. Is prohibited from making private placement offerings.

B. Must submit Form 10-K to the SEC except in those years in which the corporation has made a public offering.

C. Must distribute copies of Form 10-K to its shareholders.

D. Is subject to having the registration of its securities suspended or revoked.

Answer (D) is correct. *(CPA, adapted)*
REQUIRED: The effect of the 1934 act on a corporation whose common stock is listed on a national stock exchange.
DISCUSSION: The SEC is authorized by the 1934 act to impose sanctions to enforce its provisions. The SEC may deny, suspend, or revoke registration, or it may suspend trading of the securities. These sanctions are in addition to civil and criminal liability imposed by the federal securities laws.
Answer (A) is incorrect. An exemption from registration under the 1933 act is independent of the 1934 act. The 1934 act contains no such prohibition. Answer (B) is incorrect. Reporting requirements under the 1934 act do not substitute for those under the 1933 act. Answer (C) is incorrect. A covered corporation under the 1934 act is not required to provide copies of Forms 10-K, 10-Q, or 8-K to its shareholders. But the annual report required to be sent to shareholders is comparable to the Form 10-K.

29. Corporations that are exempt from registration under the Securities Exchange Act of 1934 are subject to the act's

A. Provisions dealing with the filing of annual reports.

B. Provisions imposing periodic audits.

C. Antifraud provisions.

D. Proxy solicitation provisions.

Answer (C) is correct. *(CPA, adapted)*
REQUIRED: The provisions of the 1934 act to which a corporation not required to register under the act is subject.
DISCUSSION: A corporation required to register under the 1934 act must comply with its reporting requirements. The antifraud provisions of the act apply to any person who performs a prohibited act in connection with the purchase or sale of any security, whether or not the security is registered.
Answer (A) is incorrect. Only a corporation required to register (a covered corporation) by the 1934 act is subject to provisions dealing with the filing of annual reports. Answer (B) is incorrect. Only a corporation required to register (a covered corporation) by the 1934 act is subject to provisions imposing periodic audits. Answer (D) is incorrect. Only a corporation required to register (a covered corporation) by the 1934 act is subject to proxy solicitation provisions.

30. The SEC's antifraud Rule 10b-5 prohibits trading on the basis of inside information of a business corporation's stock by

A. Officers and directors only.

B. All officers, directors, and shareholders only.

C. Officers, directors, and beneficial holders of 10% of the corporation's stock only.

D. Anyone who bases his/her trading activities on the inside information.

Answer (D) is correct. *(CMA, adapted)*

REQUIRED: The person(s) prohibited from trading securities based on inside information.

DISCUSSION: Rule 10b-5 is the SEC rule under the Securities Exchange Act of 1934 that prohibits any person from engaging in manipulative or deceptive acts in the purchase or sale of any security. It prohibits trading on the basis of material inside information and applies to anyone who has not made a full disclosure of the inside information. However, mere possession of inside information about stock to be traded is not always a basis for liability. For example, transactions may have been arranged prior to the insider's obtaining the information.

31. The antifraud provisions of Rule 10b-5 of the Securities Exchange Act of 1934

A. Apply only if the securities involved were registered under the Securities Act of 1933 or the Securities Exchange Act of 1934.

B. Require that the plaintiff show negligence on the part of the defendant in misstating facts.

C. Require that the wrongful act be accomplished through the mail, any other use of interstate commerce, or through a national securities exchange.

D. Apply only if the defendant acted with intent to defraud.

Answer (C) is correct. *(CPA, adapted)*

REQUIRED: The element of a violation of the antifraud provisions of Rule 10b-5.

DISCUSSION: The scope of Rule 10b-5 is broad but not absolute. Rule 10b-5 prohibits any person from directly or indirectly performing fraudulent (deceptive) acts by use of any means or instrumentality of interstate commerce, the mails, or any facility of any national securities exchange, in connection with the purchase or sale of any security.

Answer (A) is incorrect. Rule 10b-5 also applies to unregistered securities. Answer (B) is incorrect. Plaintiff must prove a material misstatement or omission with an intent to deceive, not mere negligence. Also, intent must be proved. Answer (D) is incorrect. Any act that would operate as a deceit is sufficient.

32. Which of the following is the true statement with regard to materiality under the antifraud provisions of federal securities law?

A. Material information does not concern future earnings that cannot be estimated with accuracy.

B. Materiality is a function of whether a reasonable person would attach importance to the information and includes the balancing of both the probability that the event may occur and its potential impact relative to the total company activities.

C. The SEC has ruled for administrative convenience that any event involving less than $100,000 is not material.

D. The courts have ruled that any event or information that the buyer or seller of securities took into account is material.

Answer (B) is correct. *(Publisher, adapted)*

REQUIRED: The true statement about materiality under the antifraud provisions.

DISCUSSION: Materiality is not specifically defined under the securities acts or the SEC regulations. Several courts have attempted to define materiality in connection with the case before the court. It generally depends on whether a reasonable person would attach importance to the information in deciding on a course of action. It also involves the balancing of the probability that the event may occur and its potential impact relative to total company activities.

Answer (A) is incorrect. Those facts that may affect the future of the company are relevant to investors trading in the company's securities. Answer (C) is incorrect. The SEC has not ruled any specific dollar amount to be the limit of materiality. Answer (D) is incorrect. The courts generally have held that materiality depends upon the importance a reasonable person would attach to it.

33. Which one of the following laws addresses the issue of insider trading?

A. Federal Trade Commission Act.

B. Securities Exchange Act.

C. Clayton Act.

D. North American Free Trade Agreement.

Answer (B) is correct. *(CMA, adapted)*

REQUIRED: The law that addresses insider trading.

DISCUSSION: The Securities Exchange Act of 1934 addresses the issue of insider trading. Specifically, insiders must turn over to the corporation any profits earned on purchases and sales of their company's stock that fall within six months of each other. They are also prohibited from buying or selling stock based on inside information not available to the public.

Answer (A) is incorrect. The Federal Trade Commission Act of 1914 prohibits unfair methods of competition in or affecting interstate commerce. Moreover, it created the Federal Trade Commission to enforce the Clayton and Robinson-Patman Acts. The FTC is authorized to proceed against unfair or deceptive acts or practices. Answer (C) is incorrect. The Clayton Act of 1914 was intended to prevent monopolies. A probability of a significant anticompetitive effect is a basis for most violations of the act. It specifically addresses price discrimination, tying contracts, exclusive dealing arrangements, mergers, and interlocking directorates. Answer (D) is incorrect. The North American Free Trade Agreement is an agreement providing for free trade among the USA, Canada, and Mexico.

34. Which of the following persons is not an insider of a corporation subject to the Securities Exchange Act of 1934 registration and reporting requirements?

A. The president.

B. A member of the board of directors.

C. A shareholder who owns 8% of the outstanding common stock and whose spouse owns 4% of the outstanding common stock.

D. An owner of 15% of the total face value of the corporation's outstanding debentures.

Answer (D) is correct. *(CPA, adapted)*

REQUIRED: The individual not deemed an insider.

DISCUSSION: For the purposes of Section 16(b), an insider is an officer, a director, or a beneficial owner of 10% or more of any class of equity securities registered under the 1934 act. The holder of debentures is not an insider because a debenture is a debt security, not an equity security.

Answer (A) is incorrect. An officer is an insider. Answer (B) is incorrect. A director is an insider. Answer (C) is incorrect. A 12% owner is considered an insider even though 4% of the ownership is beneficial. A shareholder is a beneficial owner if shares are owned by his/her spouse, minor children, a relative with the same residence, or a trust of which (s)he is a beneficiary.

35. Which of the following statements is true regarding the proxy solicitation requirements of Section 14(a) of the Securities Exchange Act of 1934?

A. A corporation does not have to file proxy revocation solicitations with the SEC if it is a reporting company under the Securities Exchange Act of 1934.

B. Current unaudited financial statements must be sent to each shareholder with every proxy solicitation.

C. A corporation must file its proxy statements with the SEC if it is a reporting company under the Securities Exchange Act of 1934.

D. In a proxy solicitation by management relating to election of officers, all shareholder proposals must be included in the proxy statement.

Answer (C) is correct. *(CPA, adapted)*

REQUIRED: The true statement regarding proxy solicitation requirements of Section 14(a) of the 1934 act.

DISCUSSION: Ten days prior to mailing a proxy statement to shareholders, a company reporting under the Securities Exchange Act of 1934 must file its proxy statements with the SEC.

Answer (A) is incorrect. A proxy revocation solicitation is treated as a proxy solicitation and must be filed. Answer (B) is incorrect. Financial statements need not accompany every proxy solicitation sent to shareholders. However, all information material to the matter subject to vote must be sent. If directors are to be elected, or if a merger or issuing of new shares is to be voted on, an annual report must be furnished (including audited financial statements). Answer (D) is incorrect. A shareholder proposal may be excluded for any one of several reasons, e.g., that the issue relates to ordinary business operations.

36. Rey Corp.'s management intends to solicit proxies relating to its annual meeting at which directors will be elected. Rey is subject to the registration and reporting requirements of the Securities Exchange Act of 1934. As a result, Rey must furnish its shareholders with

A. A copy of its registration statement and bylaws.

B. A preliminary copy of its proxy statement at the same time it is filed with the SEC.

C. An annual report containing its audited statements of income for the 5 most recent years.

D. An annual report containing its audited balance sheets for the 2 most recent years.

Answer (D) is correct. *(CPA, adapted)*

REQUIRED: The true statement about proxy solicitation requirements.

DISCUSSION: Financial statements of the company must be provided only for annual meetings at which directors are to be elected (in the annual report) or if a merger or authorization to issue new shares is at issue. Audited balance sheets for the last 2 years and audited statements of income, cash flows, and changes in equity for the last 3 years should be included. Furthermore, even when no solicitation is made, management must still furnish an information statement similar to a proxy statement to all shareholders who have the right to vote at the meeting.

Answer (A) is incorrect. There is no such requirement. Answer (B) is incorrect. Section 14 seeks to ensure that proxy solicitations are accompanied by adequate disclosure of information about the agenda items for which authority to vote is being sought. One requirement is that the proxy statement be filed with the SEC at least 10 days prior to mailing proxy materials to shareholders. The proxy statement must identify the party making the solicitation and details about the matters to be voted on, such as mergers, authorizations to issue new stock, or election of directors. Answer (C) is incorrect. Audited statements of income for the last 3 years must be included.

37. Integral Corp. is subject to the reporting provisions of the Securities Exchange Act of 1934. For its 1999 fiscal year, Integral filed the following with the SEC: quarterly reports, an annual report, and a periodic report listing newly appointed officers of the corporation. Integral did not notify the SEC of shareholder "short-swing" profits; did not report that a competitor made a tender offer to Integral's shareholders; and did not report changes in the price of its stock as sold on the New York Stock Exchange. Under the SEC reporting requirements, which of the following was Integral required to do?

A. Report the tender offer to the SEC.

B. Notify the SEC of shareholder "short-swing" profits.

C. File the periodic report listing newly appointed officers.

D. Report the changes in the market price of its stock.

Answer (C) is correct. *(CPA, adapted)*

REQUIRED: The reporting required of a covered corporation under the 1934 act.

DISCUSSION: A covered corporation is required to file annual (10-K), quarterly (10-Q), and current events (8-K) reports with the SEC. Similar reports are sent to shareholders. The 10-K report contains information about the entity's business activities, securities, management, related parties, disagreements about accounting principles and disclosure, audited financial statements, etc. It is intended to bring the information in the registration statement up to date. Thus, newly appointed officers will be listed.

Answer (A) is incorrect. The target need only file a statement with the SEC if the tender offer is hostile (unsolicited). Answer (B) is incorrect. Insiders are liable to the corporation for short-swing profits. Insiders include directors, officers, and persons owning more than 10% of the corporation's stock. Answer (D) is incorrect. Although the annual report (Form 10-K) requires disclosure of the market price of the common stock of the registrant (including the high and low sales prices) for each quarter of the last 2 fiscal years and any subsequent interim periods, not every change in the market price of its stock need be reported.

38. On May 1, Apel purchased 7% of Stork Corp.'s preferred stock traded on a national securities exchange. After the purchase, Apel owned 9% of the outstanding preferred stock. Stork is registered under the Securities Exchange Act of 1934. With respect to the purchase, Apel

A. Is not required to file any report or information with the SEC because Apel owns less than 10% of the preferred stock.

B. Is not required to file any report or information with the SEC because the security purchased was preferred stock.

C. Must file with the SEC, the issuer, and the national securities exchange information about the purpose of the acquisition.

D. Must file only with the SEC information about the source of the funds used to purchase the preferred stock.

Answer (C) is correct. *(CPA, adapted)*

REQUIRED: The effect of purchasing more than 5% of the outstanding preferred shares of a company.

DISCUSSION: As part of its regulation of tender offers, the Securities Exchange Act of 1934 requires any person who has acquired more than 5% of any registered equity security to file reports with the issuer, the exchange on which the security is traded, and the SEC. The information reported includes (1) the identity of the purchaser, (2) the source of funding, (3) the purpose of the acquisition, and (4) the number of shares owned.

Answer (A) is incorrect. Notification is required if more than 5% (not 10%) of a registered equity security is acquired. Answer (B) is incorrect. The preferred stock was required to be registered, so reports must be filed. Answer (D) is incorrect. Reports also must be sent to the issuer and the exchange.

39. James Fisk recently acquired Valiant Corporation by purchasing all of its outstanding stock pursuant to a tender offer. Fisk demanded and obtained the resignation of the existing board of directors and replaced it with his own slate of nominees. Under these circumstances,

A. Fisk had no right to demand the resignation of the existing board members; their resignations are legally ineffective, and they remain as directors.

B. If Valiant is listed on a national stock exchange, Fisk must file his tender offer with the SEC.

C. The former shareholders of Valiant are parties to a tax-free reorganization. Hence, they are not subject to federal income tax on their gain, if any, on transferring their stock to Fisk.

D. If Valiant is engaged in interstate commerce, the acquisition is exempt under the antitrust laws because the SEC has jurisdiction.

Answer (B) is correct. *(CPA, adapted)*

REQUIRED: The true statement about the acquisition of a corporation's stock by a tender offer.

DISCUSSION: A tender offer is an offer to shareholders to buy their stock in order to gain control of a corporation. Under the Securities Exchange Act of 1934, anyone who makes a tender offer that would result in the purchase of more than 5% of a class of registered equity securities must file his/her tender offer with the SEC. Because Valiant is listed on a national stock exchange, its shares must be registered, and Fisk's tender offer must be filed prior to acquisition.

Answer (A) is incorrect. Although in some states a director of a corporation may be removed only for cause prior to the expiration of his/her term, a director may resign at any time. Answer (C) is incorrect. Fisk's acquisition of Valiant was a purchase, not a tax-free reorganization. The former shareholders of Valiant are subject to tax on their gains. Answer (D) is incorrect. SEC jurisdiction does not exempt the transaction from antitrust laws.

40. Which of the following statements is true with respect to criminal prosecution under the securities acts?

A. Reckless disregard for the truth may be a sufficient basis for a criminal conviction.

B. Personal monetary gain from the alleged criminal conduct is required in order to be convicted.

C. The antifraud provisions of the Securities Acts are the only basis upon which a person can be indicted and convicted.

D. Corporations are not subject to criminal prosecution.

Answer (A) is correct. *(CPA, adapted)*

REQUIRED: The true statement about criminal prosecution under the securities laws.

DISCUSSION: Criminal liability under the federal securities laws is based on willful violation. A reckless disregard for the truth or falsity of a statement is sometimes deemed a willful or intentional act.

Answer (B) is incorrect. Personal gain is not an element of the prosecution's case. For example, an intentional falsification of a registration statement need not result in actual personal gain to be subject to a criminal sanction. Answer (C) is incorrect. Uniform criminal penalties may be imposed on any person for willful violation of federal securities statutes, rules, or regulations, or for willful falsification or omission of a material fact needed for an accurate representation in any document required to be filed with the SEC. For example, the Sarbanes-Oxley Act of 2002 created a new 25-year felony for defrauding shareholders of a publicly traded corporation. Answer (D) is incorrect. A corporation is a person for the purpose of criminal prosecution under the securities acts.

NOTE: See Subunit 40.4 for additional questions on federal securities law and on Rule 10b-5 in particular.

33.4 Foreign Corrupt Practices Act (FCPA)

41. A major impact of the Foreign Corrupt Practices Act of 1977 is that registrants subject to the Securities Exchange Act of 1934 are now required to

A. Keep records that reflect the transactions and dispositions of assets and to maintain a system of internal accounting controls.

B. Provide access to records by authorized agencies of the federal government.

C. Prepare financial statements in accord with international accounting standards.

D. Produce full, fair, and accurate periodic reports on foreign commerce and/or foreign political party affiliations.

Answer (A) is correct. *(CMA, adapted)*

REQUIRED: The major impact of the Foreign Corrupt Practices Act of 1977.

DISCUSSION: The main purpose of the Foreign Corrupt Practices Act of 1977 is to prevent bribery by firms that do business in foreign countries. A major ramification is that it requires all companies that must register with the SEC under the Securities Exchange Act of 1934 to maintain adequate accounting records and a system of internal accounting control.

Answer (B) is incorrect. Authorized agents of the federal government already have access to records of SEC registrants. Answer (C) is incorrect. Although some international accounting standards have been promulgated, they are incomplete and have not gained widespread acceptance. Answer (D) is incorrect. There are no requirements for providing periodic reports on foreign commerce or foreign political party affiliations.

42. Which of the following corporations are subject to the accounting requirements of the Foreign Corrupt Practices Act (FCPA)?

A. All corporations engaged in interstate commerce.

B. All domestic corporations engaged in international trade.

C. All corporations that have made a public offering under the Securities Act of 1933.

D. All corporations whose securities are registered pursuant to the Securities Exchange Act of 1934.

Answer (D) is correct. *(CPA, adapted)*

REQUIRED: The corporations subject to the accounting requirements of the FCPA.

DISCUSSION: The accounting requirements of the FCPA apply to all companies required to register and report under the Securities Exchange Act of 1934. These companies must maintain books, records, and accounts in reasonable detail that accurately and fairly reflect transactions. The FCPA also requires these companies to maintain a system of internal accounting control that provides certain reasonable assurances, including that corporate assets are not used for bribes.

43. Under the Foreign Corrupt Practices Act (FCPA), an action may be brought that seeks

A. Treble damages by a private party.

B. Injunctive relief by a private party.

C. Criminal sanctions against both the corporation and its officers by the Department of Justice.

D. Damages and injunctive relief by the Securities and Exchange Commission.

Answer (C) is correct. *(CPA, adapted)*

REQUIRED: The possible result of an action under the FCPA.

DISCUSSION: The SEC may investigate violations of the FCPA, bring civil actions for its enforcement, and recommend that the Justice Department prosecute criminal violations. A director, officer, shareholder, or other agent who acts on behalf of the corporation in willful violation of the FCPA is subject to a fine of up to $100,000 and a prison term of up to 5 years or both. A corporation is subject to a fine of up to $2 million.

Answer (A) is incorrect. Private parties may not bring an action under the FCPA. Answer (B) is incorrect. Private parties may not bring an action under the FCPA. Answer (D) is incorrect. Although the SEC is empowered to seek injunctions, the Justice Department must seek penalties. Damages are sought by private parties who cannot sue under this statute.

STUDY UNIT THIRTY-FOUR
INSURANCE

The **primary function of insurance** is the transfer of risk exposure due to a particular danger or peril by spreading losses among many parties subject to it. This transfer is accomplished by entering into a two-party contract called an **insurance policy**. Under a typical insurance policy, in exchange for a payment called a **premium**, an insurance company **(the insurer)** agrees with **the insured** to assume a specified risk. Because the insurance relationship is **contractual**, the elements of an enforceable agreement are relevant: (1) offer and acceptance, (2) mutual assent, (3) consideration, (4) capacity, and (5) legality of purpose.

The purchaser of insurance is one of a large number of persons, some of whom are likely to incur loss. In effect, **each insured accepts a relatively small loss (payment of premiums) to avoid a larger loss**. The premiums paid and the **insurer's investment returns** provide the resources to pay the claims of the insured parties who actually suffer the loss insured against. Thus, the members of the class of insured parties share the losses incurred by a few. For this arrangement to be effective, **accurate actuarial determinations** must be made about the incidence and amount of losses during a given period.

If the insured suffers a loss that is covered by the policy, the insurer makes payment in accordance with the terms of the policy. Payment for the actual loss is called **indemnity**. Under the principle of indemnity, insurance is a system for distributing losses, but **not for generating a profit for the insured**. Thus, in the event of a casualty or injury, a person is limited to **reimbursement for loss actually suffered**. By limiting insurance recovery to losses actually incurred, indemnification limits the incentive to cause or permit damage to the property insured or the occurrence of the event purportedly insured against.

An important **general requirement** is that a person who procures insurance must have an insurable interest in the property or the life that is being insured. A person has an **insurable interest** in the subject matter insured if (s)he will derive monetary benefit or advantage from its preservation or will suffer monetary loss or damage from its destruction. Ownership or a possessory interest is not necessary. Indeed, for a business, the nature of the insurable interest is broadly defined because insurance may protect a business from virtually any type of liability. **Persons with an insurable interest** in property include (1) a lessee (tenant) in leased premises; (2) a partner in partnership property; (3) a person with contract rights in the subject matter of the contract; (4) a secured creditor in the collateral, e.g., a mortgagee; (5) a bailee; (6) a grantor liable for a mortgage; (7) the buyer of goods under the Sales Article of the UCC when goods are identified to the contract, i.e., when specific goods are designated as the subject matter of the contract; (8) a majority shareholder of a corporation that owns the insured property; (9) a beneficiary of a trust that holds legal title to the insured property; and (10) a corporation in its property. An insurable interest must exist for **life insurance at the time the policy is issued** and for **property insurance at the time of loss**.

Although insurance is based on contract, **the industry is heavily regulated**. This regulation is initiated, implemented, and enforced directly and primarily at the state level. **State insurance commissions** have been delegated authority to use specialized expertise to protect both the public and the private interest in ensuring that insurers, and policies issued by them, conform to prescribed standards. The **McCarran Ferguson Act of 1945** expressly delegated regulation of the insurance industry to states. Under its police power, each state regulates domestic and foreign insurers to provide for the health, safety, and welfare of its citizens. If state regulation of the insurance industry is inadequate or contrary to the interests of the public, Congress is able to impose direct regulation on the industry under the **Commerce Clause**.

Insurance is deemed to affect **the public interest**. Purchasers of insurance reasonably expect that insurers will not seek to avoid or delay payment of bona fide claims. Because of the fiduciary-like aspect of the insurer-insured relationship, state regulation of the industry seeks to prevent the insolvency of insurers and to protect the public if insolvency occurs. Thus, states have enacted **insolvency laws** that, in effect, require solvent insurers to pay valid unpaid claims made against insolvent insurers. Moreover, **competition among insurers is regulated** to address perceived public concerns. Marginal insurers might engage in practices that destabilize the industry to the detriment of the public. For example, a marginal insurer might offer insurance at low rates to attract business and obtain rapid cash flow and short-term profits. Stable insurers, to retain market share, might respond with rate reductions. Insolvent insurers, unpaid claims, and public burdens would follow. Other reasons for the higher degree of regulation of the state insurance industry include the needs for **adequate availability of insurance** and **equity** (that is, reasonableness, impartiality, and fairness).

Because of the great public interest in the **financial stability of insurers**, numerous aspects of their business are regulated by **state insurance commissions**, such as (1) licensing of insurers and their agents, (2) rates and rate changes, (3) required reserves, and (4) asset investments. Furthermore, **standard policy forms** are required for particular coverages, e.g., workers' compensation. Certain **provisions or clauses** also must be included in policies covering certain risks, e.g., life and health. These provisions are supplied by law, even if omitted from a policy by an insurer. Some examples required in life insurance policies are clauses covering incontestability, nonforfeiture, a grace period, reinstatement, and suicide.

The state insurance commissions are authorized by enabling legislation to perform quasi-legislative, quasi-judicial, and quasi-executive functions. They include (1) issuing regulations, (2) investigating compliance, (3) enforcing rules, (4) setting rates, (5) issuing licenses, (6) holding hearings, and (7) conducting judicial proceedings. As in other administrative agencies, rules, orders, and decisions of state insurance commissions are subject to **judicial review**.

Insurance is marketed primarily by agents and brokers. An **insurance agent** is a person who enters into contracts on behalf of the insurer. An **insurance broker** does not represent an insurer. (S)he places an order for insurance on behalf of the buyer and acts as the **buyer's agent**. Agents and brokers must exercise **good faith and reasonable diligence** in respect to matters of insurance.

An **insurance policy** is a contract, and the basic principles of contract law apply to it. The first step in the process of entering into an insurance contract is **the application**. It is an offer or a proposal for a contract that must be accepted by the insurer before a contract of insurance is issued. **Acceptance** of the application **(offer)** makes the policy binding and effective. An insurer's liability under a policy attaches at the time agreed to by the parties. The **statute of frauds** does not apply, but an insurer generally must deliver a written policy to the insured. Accordingly, an **oral contract for property or liability insurance** is enforceable if the parties have agreed to the essential terms. Moreover, **payment of the premium and delivery of the policy** are **not conditions precedent** to the insurer's liability unless provided for in the application. In the case of **life insurance**, an application typically will state that coverage will not take effect until it is delivered and while the insured is in good health. Delivery may be **actual or constructive** (by mailing the policy or giving it to an agent for delivery to the policyholder). Pending formal acceptance of an application, an insurance company may issue a binder. A **binder** is temporary insurance that is itself a contract, providing coverage subject to the same terms and conditions as the formal policy. As previously mentioned, a fundamental requirement of an insurance policy is that an insured have an **insurable interest** in the subject matter of the insurance. Without an insurable interest, a policyholder is merely wagering on the occurrence of an event. Gambling contracts are unenforceable, and insurance contracts issued to a party without an insurable interest are likewise unenforceable. Thus, lack of an insurable interest results in a **void contract**, and no benefits are payable, but a purchaser of the purported insurance may be entitled to a refund of all premiums paid. Some types of insurance policies are **assignable**. Generally, contracts involving property or liability are not assignable without the consent of the insurer. The reason is that the law treats most property and liability insurance policies as **personal contracts**. However, **marine insurance** procured on a ship and its cargo while at sea generally may be assigned, and **life insurance** is more freely assignable than most other types of insurance. **Premiums** are the consideration paid by an insured to an insurer for indemnification. A **statement of the rates and the basis upon which the premium is to be determined and paid** is a required part of an insurance policy. Nearly all insurance policies also contain provisions requiring that the insurer be given timely **notice** of a loss or occurrence. The notice provision gives the insurer the opportunity to review its rights and liabilities and to investigate the claim and settle if possible. An insurer has an obligation of **good faith and fair dealing** in every insurance policy to protect the insured from unwarranted liability. In entering into contracts, insurers can impose any conditions that are clearly expressed and not contrary to law or public policy. However, courts **interpret ambiguous clauses** in insurance policies in accordance with the reasonable expectations of the insured party and against the insurer that drafted the contract.

A **representation** is an oral or written statement given by the insured before the contract is made. A representation is made during the formation of a contract and is **not necessarily incorporated into the policy**. However, a false representation that is material will generally be incorporated and void the policy. A **warranty** is a statement, description, or undertaking by an insured in the insurance policy that relates to the risk insured against. Generally, a warranty is **part of the completed contract**. The traditional view is that a breach of warranty voids the insurance policy. However, because of the harsh results of this rule and the public interest in compensating insured parties, the trend is to treat all **statements by the insured** as representations rather than warranties or, as an alternative, to require that a breach of warranty be material. The test of **materiality** is whether a fact, if stated, might reasonably have influenced the insurer either to reject the claim or to accept it and charge a higher premium. A concealment by the applicant of matters that are material to the risk invalidates a policy.

EXAMPLE: Owner states, as a condition of coverage, that (s)he will not store petrochemicals on the property. The property is shown to have been damaged more by a fire than it would have been had gasoline not been stored on the premises. Recovery under the policy might be precluded because the owner's statement was material and relied on by the insurer.

Cancelation is commonly defined as the exercise of a right to rescind, abandon, or nullify a contract of insurance. The **form and notice** of proper cancelation are determined by provisions in the policy. Both the insurer and the insured can cancel or rescind an insurance policy on the basis of **fraud or misrepresentation**, but statutes and administrative rules or regulations may restrict cancelation.

Life insurance is a contract to pay a specified sum to a named beneficiary or the decedent's estate when the insured dies. Thus, it **transfers the mortality risk** to the insurer. Life insurance can be procured for a number of purposes, the primary one being to insure against the loss of future income by the **beneficiaries named** in the policy. Insurers offer several **methods for payment** of life insurance proceeds. **Settlement options** include (1) lump sum, (2) interest only, (3) payments for a stated term, (4) payments of a stated amount, and (5) income for life. A growing variety of life insurance products also include an **investment element**.

Whole life insurance remains in force for the entire life of the insured. Whole life is considered a form of **forced savings** or investment because the insured has a right to borrow from the insurer an amount not to exceed the **cash surrender value** of the policy. The cash surrender value is the amount the insurer will pay on a given life insurance policy if the policy is canceled prior to the death of the insured. Variations of the whole life insurance policy include **ordinary or straight life** (equal periodic premiums paid until the insured reaches an advanced age), **limited-payment life** (payments made for a given number of years or up to a given age), and **single-premium life**.

Term life insurance is a contract that furnishes protection for a fixed term but does not build cash surrender or loan value. Thus, term insurance is the **least expensive form of insurance**. Under **level term** policies, the benefits payable on the insured's death remain level during the term of the policy. Under a **decreasing term** policy, the benefits payable gradually decline during the terms of the policy. An example of decreasing term is credit life insurance. The initial insured amount is the amount of the debt. It is reduced as the debt is paid off.

An **endowment insurance** policy pays a stated amount if the insured dies during a specified period, or pays the same amount if the insured is living at the end of the period. Endowment policies build up cash value that gradually increases until, at the end of the endowment period, it equals the **face amount of the policy**. Endowment insurance also is a form of **forced savings** protected by life insurance. Insureds who live until their policies mature reach their savings goals by means of their premium payments. Moreover, the **protection aspect** of the policy assures them that their savings goals will be reached even if they die prematurely..

Because life insurance cash values build up **income tax free**, a number of insurers offer **hybrid financial products** that combine basic insurance protection with an increased return on tax-free buildup of cash value. For example, **universal life insurance** has two parts. The first part is **term insurance**, which is renewed regularly until the end of life. The second part is **an investment element** funded by the portion of the premium payment that exceeds the cost of the term insurance. The **excess premiums** are invested and accumulate over the insured's life. Thus, the **accumulation value** will depend on the insurer's returns (subject to a guaranteed minimum). Universal life policies also provide flexibility. For example, a holder may vary premium amounts, temporarily discontinue payments, and change the death benefit. Moreover, such policies provide transparency by clearly separating their insurance, investment, and expense components.

A life insurance policy contains an **incontestability clause** under which the insurer is barred from contesting the policy after a stated period (often specified by state law) following its effective date. The most common period is 2 years. If the clause is omitted, it is usually **implied by law** to be part of the insurance contract. Nevertheless, the insurer may be able to contest enforcement of a policy on certain grounds, such as (1) lack of an insurable interest by the policyholder; (2) failure to pay premiums when due; (3) impersonation, for example, when a physical examination required for issuance of a policy was conducted on a person other than the insured; and (4) misrepresentation of age. If the insured's age was misstated, the amount of benefits the insurer is obligated to pay is recomputed to the amount of insurance entitlement an identical person of the insured's age could have purchased for the premium amounts paid. Another common provision is a **suicide clause**, which provides that, after 2 years, the policy covers death by suicide in the same way as death from other causes. However, when the insured commits suicide within the first 2 years of the policy, recovery by the beneficiary is limited to the premiums paid.

Rights of the owner/holder of a life insurance policy generally may be **assigned**. Such rights may include **redesignating the beneficiaries** or **obtaining credit** against the policy's value. The initial owner/holder must have an insurable interest in the life insured, but assignment, if otherwise effective, generally may be to one without such an insurable interest. Moreover, the general rule is that a **life insurance policy may be assigned without the consent of the insurer**. However, consent of an irrevocably designated beneficiary is required before an assignment may effectively designate another to receive proceeds.

Property insurance protects the owner of, or another person with an insurable interest in, real or personal property against loss resulting from damage to, or destruction of, the property by fire or other specified perils. A **loss** is defined as an unexpected destruction, reduction, or disappearance of economic value. Losses do not include damage that is intentionally inflicted on property by the insured. A **peril** is the cause of a loss. A single peril can cause more than one type of loss. Commonly insured perils to property include fire, theft, explosion, lightning, hail, water damage from faulty plumbing, smoke damage, and windstorms. Property insurance may be distinguished from **casualty insurance**, which typically covers loss due to damage or destruction of personal property by various causes other than fire or the elements. Property insurance may be in the form of a specified perils contract or an all-risk contract. Under a **specified perils contract**, the insurer indemnifies the insured only for losses resulting from one or more perils specifically included by the contract. Under an **all-risk contract**, the insurer indemnifies the insured for loss resulting from any perils except those specifically excluded by the contract.

Fire insurance is the most standardized kind of insurance. Following the lead of New York, almost all states enacted a **standard fire policy (SFP)** either by legislative or administrative action. However, the SFP has been replaced by **homeowner's policies** for residential property and the **commercial package policy (CPP)** for commercial property. Both the homeowner's policy and the CPP are packages of different types of insurance. The **advantages of packaging** include reduced costs and elimination of gaps in coverage compared with buying separate policies for different purposes. Nevertheless, many of the provisions of the SFP are contained in current policies. For example, fire insurance coverage is usually limited to losses from hostile fires, not friendly fires. A **friendly fire** is one that is contained where it is intended, for example, a fire in a fireplace. A **hostile fire** is any other fire that is unintended or not in its usual place.

A **coinsurance clause** is used by many property and casualty insurers. It encourages policyholders to insure property, especially commercial property, for an amount near its full value. A coinsurance clause typically requires the property to be insured for at least a stated percentage (usually 80%) of its full value. If so, any loss will be paid in full up to the face amount of the policy. However, the coinsurance requirement may be for a stated percentage of replacement cost or an agreed value. The **coinsurance requirement** is the stated percentage times the value of the insured property **at the time of the loss.**

$$\textit{Coinsurance requirement} = \textit{Stated \%} \times \textit{Value at time of loss}$$

The amount of insurance coverage may be less than the required coinsurance amount. In that case, the insurer pays only a fraction of the repair or replacement cost:

$$\frac{\textit{Amount of insurance}}{\textit{Coinsurance requirement}} \times \textit{Loss} = \textit{Recovery amount}$$

The coinsurance requirement applies only to **partial losses**. Accordingly, **total losses** result in recovery of the face amount of the policy. The insurer is liable to pay no more than the **face amount**, even if the formula yields a recovery amount greater than the face amount.

A risk of property loss may be covered under more than one policy. An **other insurance** or **pro rata** clause is common. A typical **pro rata clause** specifies that, if an insured obtains insurance on the same property from multiple insurers, each is responsible for only a proportionate share of the loss.

EXAMPLE: Store, Inc. has two fire insurance policies on its building: X Insurance Co. for $40,000 and Y Insurance Co. for $20,000. Each policy includes an 80% coinsurance clause and a pro rata clause. A fire caused $80,000 damage when the building was worth $100,000. The coinsurance requirement was $80,000 ($100,000 × 80%). The liability of the insurers was 75% ($60,000 ÷ $80,000) of the actual loss, or $60,000. X's liability was 66-2/3% of that loss ($40,000 ÷ $60,000). Y's was 33-1/3% ($20,000 ÷ $60,000).

A property insurance policy may be valued or open. A **valued policy** insures the full value of the property, an amount agreed upon when the contract was formed. In case of a complete loss, this amount, not the value at the time of the loss, is paid. Under an **open policy**, the amount paid will be the value just before the loss. EXAMPLE: A house is insured for $500,000 and, at the time of the loss, its value is $400,000. They payment for a total loss is $500,000 under a valued policy and $400,000 under an open policy. Marine insurance of ships and cargo is normally valued. Other property insurance is deemed to be open.

Most **property insurance policies** reinforce the tort principle that, to the extent an insurer has paid a loss, the insurer succeeds to the rights of its policyholder against third parties. This right of **subrogation** is **not available to an insurer against its own policy holder**. For example, an insurer that pays a malpractice claim against a CPA is not subrogated to any rights against the CPA. Subrogation also is **never applicable to life insurance** and rarely to health insurance. Subrogation precludes double recovery for the same loss, which is viewed as a form of unjust enrichment. Thus, the beneficiary or insured may not recover from both the insurer and a third party.

Liability insurance provides the insured with money to cover losses suffered by others for personal injury or property damage if the insured is held liable. Liability insurance **protects against tort liability**, not criminal liability. **Personal liability protection** typically insures the policyholder against the financial risk of injuries to, or damages to the property of, others that might occur in the course of a policyholder's personal activities. Personal liability protection is usually part of a **homeowner's or renter's insurance policy**, but it can be purchased as a separate personal liability policy. Liability coverage under a homeowner's policy usually applies only to personal, not business or professional, activities. Businesses also may insure against their own negligence by obtaining either **comprehensive general liability insurance** or **specific insurance coverage**. For example, a manufacturer may obtain insurance for **products liability**, and sellers of alcoholic beverages may obtain coverage for liability under **dramshop laws**. These laws impose potential liability on the seller or possibly the owner of the premises, when third parties incur damages because the defendant served an intoxicated person or a minor. Another form of liability insurance is available to professionals. **Malpractice insurance** shifts risk of loss due to negligence to the insurance carrier. These professional liability policies are written on either a claims-made or an occurrence basis. On a **claims-made basis**, the insurer is responsible only for claims filed during the policy period. On an **occurrence basis**, the insurer is responsible for all events occurring during the policy period regardless of when claims are filed.

QUESTIONS

34.1 Nature of Insurance and Contract Formation

1. Insurance may best be defined as

A. A system for transferring risk through risk avoidance or loss control.

B. Any contract that conveys an insurable interest.

C. A form of pure risk called gambling.

D. A means of combining many loss exposures so that losses are shared by all participants.

Answer (D) is correct. *(Publisher, adapted)*

REQUIRED: The best definition of insurance.

DISCUSSION: Insurance is a method of spreading losses that arise from risks to which many persons are subject. Loss is an unanticipated diminution in economic value as opposed to normal depreciation. Risk is uncertainty about the occurrence or the amount of loss. For example, buildings are subject to the risk of loss by fire. If the owners all pay small fees (premiums) for insurance coverage, every participant bears part of the loss instead of a few bearing all the loss.

Answer (A) is incorrect. Risk avoidance and loss control do not transfer risk of loss. Answer (B) is incorrect. An insurable interest is merely a potential for economic loss if an event occurs. Answer (C) is incorrect. An insurable interest is a requirement to enter into an insurance contract. Its presence prevents the contract from being a mere wager.

2. That an individual who takes out a large insurance policy on a building has less motivation to protect the building from potential fire than a person without insurance is an example of

A. Moral hazard.

B. Fraud.

C. Innocent misrepresentation.

D. Defamation.

Answer (A) is correct. *(Publisher, adapted)*

REQUIRED: The term used when a person has less incentive to exercise reasonable care.

DISCUSSION: Moral hazard is a term used in the insurance industry when people take out large insurance policies with low deductibles. They are less likely to take precautions because they may be indifferent to the consequences.

Answer (B) is incorrect. Fraud is an intentionally or recklessly false representation of a material fact. Answer (C) is incorrect. Innocent misrepresentation is an unintended false representation. Answer (D) is incorrect. Defamation is publication that causes injury to a person's reputation.

3. An insurance contract is not enforceable if the person insuring lacks an insurable interest in the subject matter of the policy. The insurable interest requirement

A. Is inconsistent with the indemnity principle.

B. Provides no safeguard against moral hazards.

C. Reflects a public policy that permits wagering agreements.

D. Need not be met when a person insures his/her own life.

Answer (D) is correct. *(Publisher, adapted)*

REQUIRED: The characteristic of an insurable interest.

DISCUSSION: The person who takes out an insurance policy must have the potential to sustain financial loss when the risk insured against occurs. If there is no insurable interest, the insurance contract is mere speculation for gain. The exception is insurance of one's own life. One who insures his/her life is presumed to be motivated to avoid death.

Answer (A) is incorrect. Absent an insurable interest, a person would improve his/her position if the event insured against occurred. A person with an insurable interest would merely be indemnified. Answer (B) is incorrect. The moral hazard of indifference to, or an active desire to cause, the loss insured against is limited by the requirement of an insured interest. Answer (C) is incorrect. Lacking a prospect of loss from the event insured against, the insuring person would in effect be wagering.

4. Booth applied to Ace Insurance Company for a life insurance policy on Abe's life. Because Abe already carried a policy on his own life with Ace, Ace had all the requisite medical and other information concerning Abe. Booth falsely represented that he had an insurable interest. If Booth kills Abe,

A. Booth is entitled to recover on the insurance policy because Ace did collect the premiums and issue the policy.

B. Ace may be liable to Abe's estate for wrongfully issuing the insurance policy to Booth.

C. Ace is not liable on the policy.

D. Booth has no liability to Abe's estate.

Answer (B) is correct. *(Publisher, adapted)*

REQUIRED: The liability when a life insurance policy is issued to a person who kills the insured.

DISCUSSION: Any person who is issued an insurance policy on a life other than his/her own must have an insurable interest in the person whose life is insured. At least one case has held that a murdered person's estate could recover from insurance companies that wrongfully issued life insurance policies to the murderer.

Answer (A) is incorrect. Booth is not entitled to recover on the insurance policy. Booth did not have an insurable interest, and it is a violation of public policy for a murderer to collect. Answer (C) is incorrect. Ace may have to pay someone. It issued the policy and collected the premiums. The law is not clear with respect to who will collect. Answer (D) is incorrect. Booth is liable to Abe's estate for wrongful death and fraud.

5. Insurance companies are usually either stock or mutual companies. Which of the following is a true statement?

A. Mutual companies are for-profit corporations.

B. Mutual companies are strongest in the property insurance field.

C. Stock and mutual companies have similar operational characteristics.

D. Stock and mutual companies write all the insurance issued in the U.S.

Answer (C) is correct. *(Publisher, adapted)*

REQUIRED: The true statement about stock and mutual insurance companies.

DISCUSSION: Stock insurance companies are for-profit corporations. Shareholders are not necessarily policyholders. Mutual companies are in principle cooperatives. Policyholders pay a fee for membership, and any profit earned is returned as a rebate on premiums. The everyday business activities of these kinds of companies vary little. They cover the same risks and provide the same services.

Answer (A) is incorrect. Mutual companies are a type of nonprofit organization that returns all "profits" to policyholders. Answer (B) is incorrect. Stock companies dominate the insurance field except with regard to life insurance. Answer (D) is incorrect. Federal governmental agencies provide Social Security benefits, life insurance for members of the military, insurance for deposits in financial institutions, and real estate mortgages on residences. State agencies and fraternal organizations are also insurers.

6. In which way does an insurance contract differ from any other contract?

A. The insurance contract requires that the insured have an insurable interest.

B. The insurance contract is not valid unless written.

C. Consideration is not needed for the formation of an insurance contract.

D. Only the insured can breach an insurance contract.

Answer (A) is correct. *(Publisher, adapted)*

REQUIRED: The manner in which an insurance contract differs from other contracts.

DISCUSSION: An insurance contract is very similar to any other. An additional requirement is that the insured must have an insurable interest.

Answer (B) is incorrect. There is no general requirement that an insurance contract be written. Oral binders are given every day in the insurance business. Answer (C) is incorrect. Consideration is needed for the initial formation of an insurance contract. If the premium is not paid immediately, the promise to pay is consideration. Answer (D) is incorrect. The insurance company can also commit a breach by refusing to pay the proceeds of the policy upon the occurrence of the event.

7. Which of the following is not a reason generally given to justify insurance regulation by the government?

A. To protect the purchaser of insurance because most insurance contracts are not subject to bargaining and negotiation.

B. To protect the purchaser of insurance in view of the technical and complicated nature of the insurance contract.

C. To prevent the use of insurance for gambling and illegal purposes.

D. To provide protection for the insurer against competition from other unregulated companies.

Answer (C) is correct. *(Publisher, adapted)*

REQUIRED: The statement not a reason for governmental regulation of insurance.

DISCUSSION: Insurance regulation protects consumers. Regulation is intended to prevent insolvency of, and fraud by, insurers so that beneficiaries will receive payment. Regulation also seeks to make insurance available at a fair and affordable price, but preventing the use of insurance for gambling and illegal purposes is not generally a reason for regulation. Requirements such as the need for an insurable interest are presumed to protect against such abuses.

Answer (A) is incorrect. Insurance contracts are generally considered contracts of adhesion. The greater bargaining power of the insurer gives the insured no choice as to terms of the contract. Answer (B) is incorrect. The complexity of insurance contracts requires regulation to protect the consumer. Answer (D) is incorrect. A responsible insurer needs protection from companies that have lower costs when not regulated.

8. Which of the following is the best functional definition of insurance?

A. A legal contract by which the insurer, in return for consideration, agrees to pay another person if a stated loss or injury occurs.

B. A legal contract by which an insurance company, in return for premiums, agrees to pay the policyholder if a certain event occurs.

C. A written promise by the insurer to pay the beneficiary if loss occurs from the occurrence of a contingent event.

D. A writing issued by an insurance company, for a consideration, that promises to indemnify a beneficiary for a loss from an existing risk or one that arises later.

Answer (A) is correct. *(Publisher, adapted)*

REQUIRED: The best functional definition of insurance.

DISCUSSION: An insurance contract (a policy) must satisfy the usual requirements: offer and acceptance, consideration, legality, and capacity of the parties. The insured must have an insurable interest in the subject matter of the contract. Also, the subject matter generally must exist at the time of contracting. In the contract, the insurer makes a promise to pay a stated amount for loss or injury incurred as a result of a contingent event.

Answer (B) is incorrect. The payee may be a stranger to the contract. A person who insures his/her own life names a third party as a beneficiary. Moreover, not every insurer is an insurance company, and the contingent event insured against must involve a risk. Answer (C) is incorrect. The statute of frauds will not apply when performance may occur within 1 year. Answer (D) is incorrect. The contract may often be oral, and, if the risk is not already in existence, the transaction is in essence a wager, not insurance.

9. Hugh Long purchased a life insurance policy with Tempo Life Insurance Co. The policy named Long's daughter as beneficiary. Six months after the policy was issued, Long died of a heart attack. Long had failed to disclose in response to a question on the insurance application a known preexisting heart condition that caused the heart attack. Tempo refused to pay the death benefit to Long's daughter. If Long's daughter sues, Tempo will

A. Win, because Long's daughter is an incidental beneficiary.

B. Win, because of Long's failure to disclose the preexisting heart condition.

C. Lose, because Long's death was from natural causes.

D. Lose, because Long's daughter is a third-party donee beneficiary.

Answer (B) is correct. *(CPA, adapted)*

REQUIRED: The legal effect of a health misrepresentation on a life insurance application.

DISCUSSION: Statements made in an application for life insurance are required by statute to be interpreted as representations and not warranties in most states. For an insurance company to avoid liability on a policy because of a misrepresentation, it must prove the misrepresentation was material and would have prevented issuance of the policy. Failure of Long to disclose he had a known preexisting heart condition would be considered material to the risk of the insurance company and would probably have prevented issuance of the policy.

Answer (A) is incorrect. Although a beneficiary's interest in life insurance proceeds is fixed by contract when the insured dies, Long's daughter was a beneficiary of a policy that was invalid due to Long's misrepresentation. Answer (C) is incorrect. Long's death was caused by the known, undisclosed, preexisting heart condition. Answer (D) is incorrect. Long's daughter loses as a result of the invalidity of the policy.

10. Jewelry, Inc. took out an insurance policy with Insurance Company covering its stock of jewelry. Insurance agreed to indemnify for losses due to theft of the jewels displayed. The application contained the following provision: "It is hereby warranted that the maximum value of the jewelry displayed shall not exceed $10,000." The insurance policy's coverage was for $8,000. Subsequently, thieves smashed the store window and stole $4,000 worth of jewels when the total value of the display was $12,000. Which of the following is true?

A. Jewelry, Inc. will recover nothing.

B. Jewelry, Inc. will recover $2,000, the loss minus the amount in excess of the $10,000 display limitation.

C. Jewelry, Inc. will recover the full $4,000 because the warranty will be construed as a mere representation.

D. Jewelry, Inc. will recover the full $4,000 because attaching the application to the policy is insufficient to make it a part thereof.

Answer (A) is correct. *(CPA, adapted)*

REQUIRED: The amount the insured will recover when a warranty is breached.

DISCUSSION: Conditions precedent, called warranties, are part of the property insurance policy. Breach of a warranty precludes recovery and results in a forfeiture. Because the law disfavors forfeitures, courts construe questions of interpretation favorably to the insured and against the insurer that drafted the policy. However, if the parties expressly agree that certain statements are warranties, a court would recognize them as such. Given that Jewelry warranted never to display more than $10,000 of jewelry, the breach of warranty prevents recovery.

Answer (B) is incorrect. Jewelry will recover nothing; it is not entitled to $2,000. Answer (C) is incorrect. The warranty will not be construed as a mere representation; the intention of the parties clearly was to make a warranty. Answer (D) is incorrect. Attachment of the application to the policy is usually sufficient to make it a part thereof. It may also be incorporated into the policy by reference to it.

11. Which of the following is a true statement about a legal doctrine that assists the insured in pressing a claim against an insurer?

A. A general equitable principle is that the law abhors a forfeiture.

B. The insurer acts through agents but is not bound when they go beyond their actual authority.

C. Insurance policies are strictly construed against insured persons.

D. Contract concepts such as estoppel, waiver, or election may not be asserted by the insured who breaches a condition.

Answer (A) is correct. *(Publisher, adapted)*

REQUIRED: The true statement about a legal doctrine assisting the insured to recover.

DISCUSSION: The typical contract of insurance is a complex document drafted by the insurer that contains many restrictions on the insured's right of recovery. These could defeat the insured's reasonable expectations for recovery. Consistent with the equitable maxim that the law abhors a forfeiture (in this case, of premiums paid by an insured who has acted in substantial good faith), courts have shown a tendency to favor the insured so as to avoid unfair results.

Answer (B) is incorrect. An agent binds the insurer by acts within his/her apparent as well as actual authority. Answer (C) is incorrect. Insurance contracts are construed in favor of the insured. The insurer drafted the agreement and imposed its terms on the insured. Answer (D) is incorrect. These concepts can be asserted by the insured. For example, an insurer who accepts a premium after breach of a condition by the insured may have elected to choose its right to further performance rather than to treat the contract as rescinded.

34.2 Life Insurance

12. A life insurance policy

A. Is a contract of indemnity.

B. Is usually short-term.

C. Covers only the mortality risk.

D. Generally has no cash value.

Answer (A) is correct. *(Publisher, adapted)*

REQUIRED: The true statement about the characteristics of life insurance.

DISCUSSION: Life insurance is usually purchased to protect against the cessation of income needed for support of the family and to shield them from the decedent's debts.

Answer (B) is incorrect. Life insurance is customarily long-term if not for life. Answer (C) is incorrect. Unlike other forms of insurance, life insurance does not attempt to reimburse for the actual amount of a loss. Loss of life is not measurable. Life insurance is intended to replace economic benefits lost by a person's death. Answer (D) is incorrect. Except for term policies, life insurance differs from other kinds of coverage in providing cash value.

13. A typical term life insurance policy

A. Builds up a cash value during its duration against which the policyholder can borrow.

B. Is assignable.

C. Grants a vested interest in the named beneficiary.

D. Does not require an insurable interest in the person taking out the policy as do other types of life insurance policies.

Answer (B) is correct. *(CPA, adapted)*

REQUIRED: The true statement with respect to a typical term life insurance policy.

DISCUSSION: A life insurance policy, including a term policy, is generally assignable. Consent of the insurance company is frequently not required; the effect is to give the assignee the first claim against the proceeds of the policy.

Answer (A) is incorrect. Term life insurance policies do not build up cash value. Answer (C) is incorrect. The general rule is that a beneficiary has a contingent expectancy only and can be replaced prior to the death of the insured. Answer (D) is incorrect. A person insuring the life of another must have an insurable interest.

14. Jack financed the purchase of a new truck with Acme Financing Co. The financing arrangement requires Jack to make 48 monthly payments of principal and interest. Acme wants to be sure that Jack's obligation will be paid in full if Jack dies before satisfying the obligation. Acme will most likely require Jack to purchase

A. Ordinary life insurance.

B. Whole life insurance.

C. Credit life insurance.

D. Universal life insurance.

Answer (C) is correct. *(Publisher, adapted)*

REQUIRED: The type of policy normally used to protect creditors in consumer financing transactions.

DISCUSSION: Credit life policies are a type of decreasing term insurance. Credit life insurance is carried by a debtor in connection with a specific credit transaction. The debtor names his/her creditor as the beneficiary of the policy, and the benefit decreases as the debtor's obligation decreases. The policy expires when the obligation is satisfied.

Answer (A) is incorrect. Ordinary (straight) life is whole life insurance with level premiums payable for life. Acme has no interest in insurance of the debtor's entire life. Answer (B) is incorrect. Whole life insurance is designed to remain in effect for the entire life of the insured. Neither a creditor nor a debtor has a legitimate interest in providing insurance for the protection of the creditor once an obligation is satisfied. Answer (D) is incorrect. Universal life is a flexible variation of ordinary life that includes an investment feature.

15. Lincoln lent Carly Osgood $20,000 and obtained an unsecured negotiable promissory note for that amount. Lincoln wishes to obtain a life insurance policy on Osgood's life as added protection of the loan. With respect to this policy, which of the following is true?

A. Lincoln has an insurable interest in Osgood's life and may legally assign the insurance policy to a transferee of the note.

B. If Osgood consented to Lincoln's insuring her for an amount in excess of the loan, Lincoln would be able to recover the face amount of the policy.

C. Lincoln does not have an insurable interest because the note is negotiable.

D. The only policy that Lincoln may legally obtain is a term policy.

Answer (A) is correct. *(CPA, adapted)*

REQUIRED: The true statement regarding a creditor's interest in a debtor's life.

DISCUSSION: An unsecured creditor ordinarily may insure the life of the debtor to the extent of the unpaid debt. Because Lincoln has an insurable interest due to the debtor-creditor relationship, the policy is valid. Furthermore, a validly issued policy may be assigned.

Answer (B) is incorrect. An unsecured creditor has an insurable interest only to the extent of the unpaid debt at the inception of the policy. Answer (C) is incorrect. Lincoln, the creditor, has an insurable interest, and the form of the note is immaterial. Answer (D) is incorrect. A creditor may legally obtain any type of life insurance policy.

16. Tom wants to purchase insurance that includes both ordinary life insurance protection and an investment feature. Tom should probably purchase

A. Universal life insurance.

B. An endowment contract.

C. Term insurance.

D. Whole life insurance.

Answer (A) is correct. *(Publisher, adapted)*

REQUIRED: The insurance contract that provides life insurance protection and a savings feature.

DISCUSSION: Universal life insurance has two parts. The first part is term insurance, which is renewed regularly until the end of life. The second part is an investment feature funded by the portion of the premium payment that exceeds the cost of the term insurance. The excess premiums are invested and accumulate over the insured's life. Thus, the accumulation value will depend on the insurer's returns (subject to a guaranteed minimum). Universal life policies also provide flexibility. For example, a holder may vary premium amounts, temporarily discontinue payments, and change the death benefit. Moreover, such policies provide transparency by clearly separating their insurance, investment, and expense components.

Answer (B) is incorrect. An endowment contract provides term life insurance protection as well as an agreement by the insurer to pay a lump sum of money to the insured when (s)he reaches a certain age. Answer (C) is incorrect. Term insurance pays a benefit only if the insured dies within a specified period; it does not provide a savings feature. Answer (D) is incorrect. Whole life does not provide an investment feature, although the insured has the right to borrow an amount up to the cash surrender value of the policy from the insurer. The loan is secured by an assignment to the insurer of the policy's proceeds up to the amount of the loan.

17. Orr is an employee of Vick Corp. Vick relies heavily on Orr's ability to market Vick's products and, for that reason, has acquired a $50,000 insurance policy on Orr's life. Half of the face value of the policy is payable to Vick, and the other half is payable to Orr's spouse. Orr dies shortly after the policy is taken out but after leaving Vick's employ. Which of the following statements is true?

A. Orr's spouse does not have an insurable interest because the policy is owned by Vick.

B. Orr's spouse will be entitled to all of the proceeds of the policy.

C. Vick will not be entitled to any of the proceeds of the policy because Vick is not a creditor or relative of Orr.

D. Vick will be entitled to its share of the proceeds of the policy regardless of whether Orr is employed by Vick at the time of death.

Answer (D) is correct. *(CPA, adapted)*

REQUIRED: The true statement regarding effectiveness of a life insurance policy.

DISCUSSION: For an insurance policy to be valid, the insured must satisfy the insurable interest requirement. An insurable interest is not found only when the insured has a legally or equitably recognized current, or vested future, interest. The insured need have only a potential for economic loss if the risk insured against occurs. In the case of life insurance, the potential for loss must exist at the time the policy is issued.

Answer (A) is incorrect. Having an insurable interest is independent of policy ownership. It relates to who may receive proceeds. Answer (B) is incorrect. Vick has an insurable interest, so it is entitled to half the proceeds. Answer (C) is incorrect. Other parties may have an insurable interest in another's life if, at the time of issuance, the party may suffer economic loss if the insured dies.

18. The incontestable clause in a life insurance policy usually provides that

A. The insured is covered on delivery of the policy regardless of any misstatement in the application.

B. If death occurs after a specified period, a misstatement in the application will not constitute a defense by the insurer.

C. Suicide of the named insured will not constitute a defense by the insurer.

D. Only the estate of the insured may contest the named beneficiary's rights to proceeds of the policy.

Answer (B) is correct. *(CPA, adapted)*

REQUIRED: The usual provisions of an incontestable clause.

DISCUSSION: The standard life insurance policy provides in an incontestable clause that, after the passage of a specified time (usually 2 years), misstatements in the application will not constitute a defense by the insurance company. In other words, the insurer will not contest a policy after a 2-year period.

Answer (A) is incorrect. The policy is clearly contestable until the incontestable period has expired. Answer (C) is incorrect. Suicide is not regulated by the incontestable clause. Answer (D) is incorrect. The standard incontestable clause does not determine who may contest the named beneficiary's rights to a policy. However, the insurance company and any party with a contingent interest could contest the beneficiary's right to proceeds.

19. The Devon Insurance Company issued a $50,000 whole life insurance policy to Erin Finn. Finn's age was incorrectly stated in the application. As a result, she paid a smaller premium than that applicable to her age. How much will Finn's beneficiary collect?

A. The entire amount of the policy if the incontestable clause applies.

B. Nothing, unless the beneficiary can establish that Finn was unaware of her correct age.

C. The amount of insurance that the premium would have purchased if the correct age had been stated.

D. The amount of premium Finn paid during her lifetime with interest at the legal rate.

Answer (C) is correct. *(CPA, adapted)*

REQUIRED: The result when the age of the insured has been misstated on the application.

DISCUSSION: A standard clause required by most states provides that, if the insured's age is misstated, the life insurance policy will not be invalidated. However, the benefits will be adjusted down based on the amount of insurance that the premium would have purchased if the correct age had been stated.

Answer (A) is incorrect. The incontestable clause does not override the misstatement of age. The policy can be adjusted any time after its discovery. Answer (B) is incorrect. Misstatement of age, though material, does not invalidate a standard life insurance policy regardless of whether the misstatement is intentional or accidental. Answer (D) is incorrect. The beneficiary will receive the face amount of the policy adjusted for the age discrepancy. Refund of premiums occurs only when the policy is invalid.

20. A person is treated as having an insurable interest in his/her own life. The obvious desire of most human beings to continue their existence provides protection for the insurer that is otherwise afforded by the pecuniary insurable interest requirement. The standard life insurance contract furnishes an additional safeguard by incorporating a suicide clause. If the insured dies by suicide,

A. Payment consists only of a refund of premiums paid up to the date of death.

B. The beneficiary will receive nothing.

C. The policy will be fully enforceable if death occurs more than two years after its effective date.

D. The incontestable clause will override the suicide clause.

Answer (C) is correct. *(Publisher, adapted)*

REQUIRED: The effect of a suicide clause.

DISCUSSION: A standard suicide clause operates like a statute of limitations. The typical clause provides that, after two years, the policy applies to suicide the same as to death from other causes. However, if the insured commits suicide within the first two years of the policy, the beneficiary will receive only the premiums paid.

Answer (A) is incorrect. If death by suicide occurs within two years of issuance of the policy, the beneficiary will receive only the premiums paid up to the date of death. After two years, death by suicide is not treated differently from death by any other cause. Answer (B) is incorrect. The beneficiary will receive, at a minimum, the premiums paid to date. Answer (D) is incorrect. The incontestable clause generally applies to misstatements in the application, not to suicide.

21. Dilbert Dobbins insured his life for $100,000, naming his wife as beneficiary. After the policy had been in effect for 10 years and had a cash surrender value in excess of $15,000, Dobbins assigned the policy to Suburban National Bank to secure a $20,000 loan. A copy of the assignment was filed with Suburban at its home office. Dobbins has died, and his widow and Suburban are seeking to recover on the $100,000 life insurance policy. Which of the following is true?

A. Suburban's recovery is limited to the loan outstanding plus interest.

B. The assignment to Suburban was void without the beneficiary's consent.

C. Suburban will be denied recovery due to a lack of an insurable interest.

D. The widow had a vested interest in the insurance policy.

Answer (A) is correct. *(CPA, adapted)*

REQUIRED: The assignee's rights to the proceeds of a life insurance policy.

DISCUSSION: A life insurance policy is generally assignable. The assignee will prevail over a previously named beneficiary. However, an assignment for security (as in the case of Suburban National Bank) will entitle the assignee to only the amount of the loan outstanding plus accrued interest.

Answer (B) is incorrect. The assignment to the Suburban Bank was valid without the beneficiary's consent. It had the effect of subordinating the beneficiary's contingent rights to as much of the policy as needed to secure the loan. Answer (C) is incorrect. A creditor has an insurable interest in the life of the debtor, and an assignee does not need an insurable interest. Answer (D) is incorrect. A beneficiary has a contingent right, not a vested right, unless the designation is irrevocable.

22. Fargo Corp. provides its employees with free group life insurance. Marsha Maxwell is an executive vice-president of Fargo. Consistent with state laws, Maxwell has assigned the group policy to her spouse, John. Which of the following is true?

A. The assignee of a group policy must have an insurable interest in the life of the insured.

B. The assignment of the policy to John transferred all the legal incidents of ownership to him.

C. Maxwell cannot have income for income tax purposes as a result of Fargo's payment of the insurance premiums.

D. The proceeds from the group policy will be an asset of Maxwell's estate.

Answer (B) is correct. *(CPA, adapted)*

REQUIRED: The true statement about the assignment of a group life policy.

DISCUSSION: The assignment of the policy from one spouse to another transferred all the legal incidents of ownership of the policy. This arrangement is unlike the designation of a beneficiary, which gives the beneficiary only a contingent right to proceeds. To make the assignment effective against the insurer, a copy of the assignment or other notice must be furnished.

Answer (A) is incorrect. An assignee of a life insurance policy need not have an insurable interest in the life of the insured. Answer (C) is incorrect. Only the cost of the first $50,000 of group term life insurance provided by an employer is a tax-exempt benefit. Answer (D) is incorrect. Maxwell assigned the policy; if she retains no incidents of ownership, it will not be included in her estate.

23. At his death, Millard Filmore owned a $100,000 life insurance policy on his life in which he designated his wife as the beneficiary. The insurer paid the proceeds of the policy directly to Mrs. Filmore after his death. Which of the following is true?

A. Filmore could not by will designate a person other than his wife to receive the proceeds of the insurance policy.

B. Upon receipt of the proceeds, Mrs. Filmore will have received $100,000 of taxable income, but income averaging is permitted.

C. The insurance proceeds are not includible in Filmore's estate for federal estate tax purposes.

D. Filmore's designation of his wife as the beneficiary of the policy was irrevocable unless she died or they were divorced.

Answer (A) is correct. *(CPA, adapted)*

REQUIRED: The true statement about the disposition of proceeds of a life insurance policy.

DISCUSSION: A person has an insurable interest in his/her own life and may name anyone as beneficiary. Whether the insured can replace the initial beneficiary depends on the terms of the policy. In any event, the beneficiary's interest in the proceeds is fixed by contract at the moment of death of the insured. Hence, Filmore could not change the beneficiary of the policy by a testamentary provision because a will is "ambulatory;" it is revocable at any time and is therefore not effective until the death of the testator.

Answer (B) is incorrect. The proceeds of an insurance policy are not taxable income to the beneficiary provided the policy was not transferred for valuable consideration. Answer (C) is incorrect. Whenever a decedent owns a policy or retains any incident of ownership, the proceeds are included in the estate for federal estate tax purposes. Answer (D) is incorrect. The standard life insurance policy reserves the right of the insured to change the designated beneficiary.

24. Under a buy-sell agreement to be funded by life insurance, each of three partners took out a $50,000 policy on the life of each of the other two partners. The agreement provided that each of the survivors of the first to die would collect the proceeds of the policy (s)he owned on the life of the decedent. Each would then purchase one-half of the decedent's estate for that amount. Each partner paid premiums from nonpartnership funds. In this situation,

A. Prior to the death of any partner, the policies are partnership assets.

B. On the death of a partner, a surviving partner has the right to purchase from the decedent's estate the policy of insurance (on the survivor's life) owned by the decedent.

C. Continued ownership and payment of premiums by the estate of a deceased partner on a policy the decedent had owned covering a former partner would probably give rise to a defense of lack of insurable interest if the insured partner later died.

D. On the death of a partner, the estate of the decedent could transfer the policy it held on the life of one surviving partner to the other.

Answer (D) is correct. *(CPA, adapted)*

REQUIRED: The true statement regarding a buy-sell agreement among partners funded by life insurance.

DISCUSSION: A life insurance policy is assignable. Approval of the insurance company is usually not required. Upon a partner's death, the policies (s)he owned on the surviving partners' lives are owned by the estate. The estate could validly transfer one or more policies to any person.

Answer (A) is incorrect. Policies purchased by partners with their individual funds are the property of the partners and not partnership assets. Answer (B) is incorrect. After the death of a partner, the policies on the lives of the surviving partners are owned by the estate, and the surviving partners have no rights in them. The surviving partners had no rights in them even while their partner was living. Answer (C) is incorrect. An insurable interest is required only at the time the policy is issued, not at the time of death.

34.3 Property Insurance

25. A property insurance policy ordinarily indemnifies for losses arising from

A. Friendly but not hostile fires.

B. Hostile but not friendly fires.

C. Both hostile and friendly fires.

D. Smoke produced by friendly or hostile fires.

Answer (B) is correct. *(Publisher, adapted)*

REQUIRED: The losses caused by fire that will be indemnified.

DISCUSSION: Ordinarily, smoke, water, or other damage caused by hostile but not friendly fires will be indemnified under an insurance policy. Hostile fires are those ignited in places where they are not meant to be. A friendly fire is one that burns where it is intended to burn, such as a fireplace or furnace. For example, if a friendly fire is kept within its usual container, damage caused by smoke from it will not be reimbursed.

26. The typical property insurance policy

A. Covers all damages caused by fire, whatever the source.

B. Does not cover water damage resulting from the fire department's extinguishing a fire.

C. Will not permit recovery for business interruption unless a special endorsement is attached.

D. Prohibits the assignment of the policy both before and after a loss.

Answer (C) is correct. *(CPA, adapted)*

REQUIRED: The true statement regarding the typical property insurance policy.

DISCUSSION: The typical property insurance policy insures only damage to physical property. It does not permit recovery for business interruption, lost profits, or other special matters. However, a special endorsement may be attached to a property-liability policy to change the contract's coverage.

Answer (A) is incorrect. The typical property insurance policy does not cover damages caused by intentional acts of the insured or by "friendly" fires, e.g., damage to the insured's chair because the chair is too close to the fireplace. Answer (B) is incorrect. The typical property insurance policy covers water damage resulting from attempts to extinguish a fire. Answer (D) is incorrect. The typical property insurance policy does not and cannot prohibit the assignment of the policy (right to proceeds) after a loss.

27. Which of the following wrongful acts prevents recovery under a policy of property insurance?

A. Arson by the insured's employees or agents.

B. Arson by third persons unrelated to the insured.

C. An act by the insured intended to cause the damage.

D. Gross negligence but not amounting to recklessness and willful misconduct.

Answer (C) is correct. *(Publisher, adapted)*

REQUIRED: The wrongful act preventing an insurance recovery.

DISCUSSION: Arson, fraud, or another intentional act of the insured calculated to cause the damage insured against will preclude recovery. The parties to an insurance contract have an implied duty not to bring about the very event that is the subject matter of the policy.

Answer (A) is incorrect. Agency rules do not apply; i.e., the intentional act of an agent will not be imputed to the insured under the doctrine of respondeat superior. Arson by an agent without the actual knowledge or conspiracy of the insured will not preclude recovery. Answer (B) is incorrect. Arson is compensable unless intended by the insured. Answer (D) is incorrect. Negligence without fraud will not prevent recovery by an insured who has acted in good faith.

28. The usual homeowner's insurance policy does not

A. Have to meet the insurable interest test if this requirement is waived by the parties.

B. Provide for subrogation of the insurer to the insured's rights upon payment of the amount of the loss covered by the policy.

C. Cover losses caused by the negligence of the insured's agent.

D. Permit assignment of the policy prior to loss without the consent of the insurer.

Answer (D) is correct. *(CPA, adapted)*

REQUIRED: The true statement concerning the usual homeowner's insurance policy.

DISCUSSION: The standard homeowner's insurance policy may not be assigned prior to loss without consent of the insurer because of the personal nature of property insurance and inherent risks in the activities of the insured. If not expressed, this restraint is implied. However, proceeds from policies may be assigned after loss without the consent of the insurer.

Answer (A) is incorrect. The parties cannot waive the insurable interest requirement. Answer (B) is incorrect. The insurance company is entitled to subrogation to the insured's rights after payment. Answer (C) is incorrect. The usual homeowner's policy covers losses caused by negligence of the insured and his/her agents.

29. The insurable interest requirement with regard to property insurance

A. May be waived by a writing signed by the insured and insurer.

B. May be satisfied by a person other than the legal owner of the property.

C. Must be satisfied at the time the policy is issued.

D. Must be satisfied by the insured's legal title to the property at the time of loss.

Answer (B) is correct. *(CPA, adapted)*

REQUIRED: The true statement about the insurable interest requirement with regard to property.

DISCUSSION: An insurable interest is found not only when the insured has a legally or equitably recognized current, or vested future, interest but also in many other situations in which the insured could incur economic loss. For example, if the insured has a contract with a supplier whose productive property is vital to performance, and damage to the property would cause loss to the insured through breach of the contract, an insurable interest exists.

Answer (A) is incorrect. The rule is not waivable. It is based on a public policy designed to prevent wagering contracts and to reduce moral hazards. Answer (C) is incorrect. The requirement is satisfied if the interest exists when loss occurs. Answer (D) is incorrect. Anyone who would suffer an economic loss from destruction of the property has an insurable interest.

30. Rebecca West is seeking to collect on a property insurance policy covering certain described property that was destroyed. The insurer has denied recovery based upon West's alleged lack of an insurable interest in the property. In which of the situations described below will the insurance company prevail?

A. West is not the owner of the insured property but a mere long-term lessee.

B. The insured property belongs to a general trade debtor of West, and the debt is unsecured.

C. The insured property belongs not to West but to a corporation that she controls.

D. The property has been willed to West's father for life and, upon her father's death, to West as the remainderman.

Answer (B) is correct. *(CPA, adapted)*

REQUIRED: The instance in which no insurable interest will be found.

DISCUSSION: A general creditor has no insurable interest in specific property of the debtor if damage to, or destruction of, the property will not cause an economic loss to the creditor. Because the debt was unsecured, no collateral has been impaired. Also, the facts do not suggest that any contract rights of the creditor were dependent upon the welfare of the property.

Answer (A) is incorrect. One who has a legal or equitable interest in the property has an insurable interest. A leasehold is a legally recognized interest. Answer (C) is incorrect. A dominant or controlling shareholder has an equitable interest in property owned by the corporation, the legal owner. Answer (D) is incorrect. A vested future interest of a remainderman suffices for an insurable interest.

31. The earliest time a purchaser of existing goods will acquire an insurable interest in those goods is when

A. The purchaser obtains possession.

B. Title passes to the purchaser.

C. Performance of the contract has been completed or substantially completed.

D. The goods are identified to the contract.

Answer (D) is correct. *(CPA, adapted)*

REQUIRED: The earliest time a purchaser will have an insurable interest in the goods.

DISCUSSION: Under UCC 2-501, a buyer of goods has an insurable interest in them when they are identified to the contract. This identification can occur when the seller selects goods that correspond to the description in the contract and marks or otherwise designates them as belonging to the contract.

Answer (A) is incorrect. A purchaser can acquire an insurable interest as soon as the goods are identified and need not wait until delivery. Answer (B) is incorrect. Passage of title is irrelevant to acquiring an insurable interest. Answer (C) is incorrect. Whether performance of the contract has been completed or substantially completed is irrelevant to acquiring an insurable interest.

32. The partnership of Cox & Hayes, CPAs, is a medium-sized accounting firm. The senior staff member, Jake Walton, is the office manager. The office building is owned by the partnership, and title is duly recorded in the partnership name. With regard to life and property insurance, which of the following is a true statement?

A. A partner has no insurable interest in the lives of the other partners.

B. The partnership does not have an insurable interest in the life of Walton because he is not a partner.

C. Each individual partner has an insurable interest in the partnership property even though title to the property is in the partnership name.

D. Only the partnership can insure the firm's building against property damage.

Answer (C) is correct. *(CPA, adapted)*

REQUIRED: The true statement of the rights of a partnership and partners with respect to insurance.

DISCUSSION: An office building owned by a partnership with title in the partnership name can be insured by the partnership. Also, each individual partner has an insurable interest in the partnership property because (s)he has an obvious potential for pecuniary loss should the partnership property be destroyed.

Answer (A) is incorrect. Both the partnership and the partners have insurable interests in the lives of each partner. Answer (B) is incorrect. The partnership has an insurable interest in the life of its office manager (a key employee). His death would cause pecuniary damage to the firm. Answer (D) is incorrect. Both the partnership and the partners can insure the firm's office building against property damage.

33. One of the primary purposes of including a coinsurance clause in a property insurance policy is to

A. Encourage the policyholder to insure the property for an amount close to its full value.

B. Make the policyholder responsible for the entire loss caused by some covered perils.

C. Cause the policyholder to maintain a minimum amount of liability insurance that will increase with inflation.

D. Require the policyholder to insure the property with only one insurance company.

Answer (A) is correct. *(CPA, adapted)*

REQUIRED: The purpose of the coinsurance clause.

DISCUSSION: A coinsurance clause requires the insured to maintain insurance equal to or greater than a specified percentage (usually 80%) of the value of the insured property. The purpose is to prevent the insured from insuring for a minimal amount (and minimal premium) and recovering in full for a partial loss.

Answer (B) is incorrect. This issue is addressed by an exclusion clause. Answer (C) is incorrect. Liability insurance protects against tort liability. Answer (D) is incorrect. A coinsurance clause is intended to prevent underinsuring, not multiple insurance.

34. A building was purchased for $350,000 and insured under a $300,000 fire insurance policy containing an 80% coinsurance clause. Several years later, the building, having a fair market value of $500,000, sustained fire damage of $40,000. What is the amount recoverable from the insurance company?

A. $28,000

B. $30,000

C. $32,000

D. $40,000

Answer (B) is correct. *(CPA, adapted)*

REQUIRED: The amount recoverable under a fire insurance policy with an 80% coinsurance clause.

DISCUSSION: Coinsurance is a provision under which the insured agrees to keep the property insured for a stated percentage (usually 80%) of its full value. The purpose of a coinsurance clause is to reduce the insurance company's liability and make the insured party proportionately liable for any partial losses to the insured property if the minimum coverage is not obtained. In this problem, the coinsurance requirement of $400,000 was not met.

$$80\% \times \$500,000 \textit{ (Full value at time of loss)} = \$400,000$$

$$\frac{\textit{Amount of insurance}}{\textit{Coinsurance requirement}} \times \textit{Loss} = \textit{Recovery}$$

$$\frac{\$300,000}{\$400,000} \times \$40,000 = \$30,000$$

Thus, the insurance company is liable for $30,000 of the partial loss, and the insured's proportionate share of the partial loss is $10,000.

35. In Year 1, King bought a building for $250,000. At that time, King took out a $200,000 fire insurance policy with Omni Insurance Co. and a $50,000 fire insurance policy with Safe Insurance Corp. Each policy contained a standard 80% coinsurance clause. In Year 5, when the building had a fair value of $300,000, a fire caused $200,000 in damage. What dollar amount would King recover from Omni?

A. $100,000

B. $150,000

C. $160,000

D. $200,000

Answer (C) is correct. *(CPA, adapted)*

REQUIRED: The pro rata share of a person who is insured under multiple policies with coinsurance clauses.

DISCUSSION: A coinsurance clause requires the insured to maintain insurance equal to or greater than a specified percentage (usually 80%) of the full value of the insured property. If the insured has not carried the specified percentage and a partial loss occurs, the insurance company is liable for only a proportionate part of the loss. A pro rata clause generally provides that a person who is insured with multiple policies can collect from each insurance company only a proportionate amount of the loss based on the amount of insurance carried with each insurer. King was in compliance with the coinsurance clause (80% × $300,000 = $240,000). King's total coverage was $250,000 and therefore King would recover in full. The pro rata share King would recover from Omni Insurance Co. is $160,000 [($200,000 ÷ $250,000) × $200,000].

36. Bernard Manufacturing, Inc., recently purchased a three-story building. The purchase price was $200,000, of which $160,000 was financed by the proceeds of a mortgage loan from the Cattleman Savings and Loan Association. Bernard immediately procured a standard fire insurance policy on the premises for $200,000 from the Magnificent Insurance Company. Cattleman also took out fire insurance of $160,000 on the property from the Reliable Insurance Company of America. The property was subsequently totally destroyed as a result of a fire that started in an adjacent loft and spread to Bernard's building. Insofar as the rights and duties of Bernard, Cattleman, and the insurers are concerned, which of the following is a true statement?

A. Cattleman lacks the requisite insurable interest to collect on its policy.

B. Bernard can collect only $40,000.

C. Reliable is subrogated to Cattleman's rights against Bernard upon payment of Cattleman's insurance claim.

D. The maximum amount that Bernard can collect from Magnificent is $40,000, the value of its insurable interest.

Answer (C) is correct. *(CPA, adapted)*

REQUIRED: The true statement describing the rights of the parties.

DISCUSSION: An insurance company that issues a policy on a building in favor of a mortgagee and pays the mortgagee's insurance claim is subrogated to the mortgagee's rights against the insured. Thus, if Cattleman had acquired no insurance, and the building had been destroyed, Cattleman would have had the legal right to collect the balance of the $160,000 mortgage from Bernard. This is the right to which Reliable is subrogated by having paid Cattleman's claim.

Answer (A) is incorrect. Cattleman had an insurable interest by virtue of holding a $160,000 mortgage on Bernard's building. Answer (B) is incorrect. Bernard can collect $200,000, the face amount of the policy. Answer (D) is incorrect. Bernard had an insurable interest of $200,000 composed of $40,000 equity and $160,000 of debt.

34.4 Liability Insurance

37. Which of the following is not a type of insurance policy that provides liability insurance?

A. Malpractice insurance.

B. Homeowner's insurance.

C. Automobile insurance.

D. Fire insurance.

Answer (D) is correct. *(Publisher, adapted)*

REQUIRED: The type of insurance policy not providing liability coverage.

DISCUSSION: Fire insurance generally protects the insured from damage to the insured property as a result of fire. It does not cover the insured for causing a fire on someone else's property.

Answer (A) is incorrect. Malpractice insurance is a special form of liability insurance protecting professionals from lawsuits by third parties for negligence. Answer (B) is incorrect. Homeowner's insurance generally contains a liability section in the event guests are injured on the premises. Answer (C) is incorrect. A primary purpose of automobile insurance is to protect the owner or driver from liability in the event (s)he is responsible for damage to another person or property.

38. Alicia Andrews was home on Saturday mowing the lawn and doing general yard work. She was hot and tired from the exertion. A particularly obnoxious salesman stopped by. Andrews punched the salesman in the face and broke his nose. The salesman has sued Andrews. What insurance coverage, if any, does Andrews have?

A. Andrews should notify her homeowner's insurance company because such accidents are covered by the liability section.

B. Neither liability nor any other insurance will cover an intentional tort.

C. If Andrews has an umbrella policy, her liability will be covered up to the maximum amount.

D. Andrews will be covered only if she has a specific liability insurance policy.

Answer (B) is correct. *(Publisher, adapted)*

REQUIRED: The true statement concerning liability coverage for an intentional tort.

DISCUSSION: Andrews committed battery by punching the salesman in the face. This act was an intentional tort and is excluded from insurance coverage. Insurance will cover negligence and damage from intentional torts by others, but it generally does not cover the insured for his/her intentional wrongs. To cover such acts would be against public policy.

39. Ralph and Ted live in one of approximately 25 states that have some form of no-fault automobile insurance. Ralph drove his car into the rear of Ted's car. Ralph and Ted each received minor injuries, as did Ted's passenger, John. Sue, a pedestrian, was also injured when the impact drove Ted's car into the crosswalk, knocking Sue to the ground. Sue was treated at the emergency room for minor scrapes and bruises and released. Which of the following is most likely true concerning recovery for personal injuries?

A. Sue cannot recover from either Ralph or Ted because no-fault systems require pedestrians to provide coverage for minor injuries they suffer.

B. Ted can recover from Ralph's insurer because Ted is clearly without fault.

C. John can recover from Ralph's insurer because Ralph is clearly at fault.

D. Ted can recover from his own insurer regardless of who is at fault.

Answer (D) is correct. *(Publisher, adapted)*

REQUIRED: The true statement regarding recovery for minor personal injuries in a no-fault automobile insurance state.

DISCUSSION: No-fault automobile insurance systems compensate persons injured in automobile accidents without regard to fault. Up to a tort immunity threshold, the typical no-fault insurance policy covers personal injury sustained by the named insured, members of his/her household, passengers, pedestrians, and authorized operators of the vehicle.

Answer (A) is incorrect. No-fault systems do not require pedestrians to insure against injuries caused by another's negligence. Answer (B) is incorrect. Under a no-fault system, fault is irrelevant in determining which insurer compensates for minor personal injuries. Answer (C) is incorrect. Under a no-fault system, fault is irrelevant in determining which insurer compensates for minor personal injuries.

40. Alphonse, a sole CPA practitioner, obtained a malpractice insurance policy from the Friendly Casualty Company. In regard to this coverage,

A. Expression of an unqualified opinion by Alphonse when he knows that financial statements are materially misstated does not give Friendly a defense.

B. The policy would automatically cover the work of a new partnership formed by Alphonse and Borne.

C. Friendly will not be subrogated to rights against Alphonse for his negligent conduct of an audit.

D. Coverage includes injury to a client resulting from a slip on a rug negligently left loose in Alphonse's office

Answer (C) is correct. *(CPA, adapted)*

REQUIRED: The true statement regarding coverage on a malpractice insurance policy.

DISCUSSION: Subrogation is the insurer's right after paying a claim to succeed to whatever rights the insured may have had against third parties. It applies to fire, automobile collision, accident, and most property policies. However, subrogation rights are not created by malpractice or life insurance. An insurance company that pays a claim for the malpractice of a CPA would not be subrogated to any rights against the CPA. Subrogation never confers rights on an insurer against its own insured, only against third parties.

Answer (A) is incorrect. Expression of an unqualified opinion in these circumstances is intentional misconduct and would not be covered by malpractice insurance. Answer (B) is incorrect. A new malpractice policy would be necessary to cover Borne. Answer (D) is incorrect. Malpractice insurance covers negligence only in providing professional services, not personal injury liability.

41. Marcross Corporation owns a fleet of taxicabs it has insured with the Countrywide Insurance Company against loss from liability and collision. Nabor, one of its drivers, deliberately backed one of the cabs into two other parked cabs in the corporation's garage after a heated dispute with the garage manager. While waiting for a traffic signal, another Marcross cab was hit in the rear by a negligently driven truck. Each cab involved had damages in excess of the minimum deductible.

A. Marcross can recover against Countrywide for damages to all the cabs minus the minimum deductible.

B. Countrywide has no rights against Nabor.

C. General creditors of Marcross could insure Marcross's cabs against collision and other types of loss because in the event of bankruptcy the creditors would have to resort to the corporation's property to satisfy their claims.

D. Marcross must first sue the negligent truck driver, or the driver's principal, for damages to its cab before it can collect against Countrywide.

Answer (A) is correct. *(CPA, adapted)*

REQUIRED: The true statement of the rights and liabilities of the parties under an automobile liability and collision policy.

DISCUSSION: An insured under an automobile collision policy can recover against the insurance company for damages to the insured's vehicles so long as the damage is not directed by the insured. This recovery is not denied because the damage was caused by the negligent or even intentional conduct of the insured's employee.

Answer (B) is incorrect. The insurance company under an automobile collision policy is subrogated to the rights of the insured after payment. Thus, the insurance company would have Marcross's rights against the driver who deliberately damaged the three vehicles. Answer (C) is incorrect. General creditors of a business lack the requisite insurable interest to obtain insurance on the property of the debtor. Answer (D) is incorrect. The insured need not sue negligent third parties who cause damage to its property. This is the risk insured against. After Countrywide pays under the policy, it will be subrogated to the rights of Marcross against the negligent third party (the driver of the truck).

STUDY UNIT THIRTY-FIVE
ENVIRONMENTAL LAW

Environmental law reflects policy choices about preservation of the environment, balanced with its use and enjoyment. It consists of federal and state constitutions and statutes; local ordinances; regulations of federal, state, and local agencies; and decisions interpreting those laws and regulations. Environmental litigation usually involves disputes between private parties and governmental agencies.

The federal **Environmental Protection Agency (EPA)** ensures compliance with environmental laws. The EPA holds formal and informal hearings and renders decisions involving environmental law. Enforcement actions in the courts are normally referred to the Department of Justice. Also, states are delegated powers to enforce federal environmental programs. **Citizen suits** typically grant citizens the right to participate in or initiate civil enforcement actions. **Private enforcement actions** seek damages for personal injuries allegedly caused by violation of environmental laws. Nevertheless, the greatest responsibility is borne by the EPA through civil enforcement actions. The EPA's administrative actions and assessment of penalties avoids litigation. In evaluating the appropriate **civil or criminal penalty** for an environmental law violation, courts and the EPA consider certain factors that may justify extending leniency to a violator. These include conducting periodic audits to determine compliance, self-reporting of possible violations to the EPA or other government agencies, and the violator's compliance history.

The **National Environmental Policy Act (NEPA)** declares a national environmental policy and promotes consideration of environmental issues by all federal agencies. However, environmental issues need not have greater weight than other concerns. Thus, the act requires that an **environmental impact statement (EIS)** be included in every recommendation or report on proposals for legislation and other major federal action significantly affecting the quality of the environment. Before preparing the EIS, an agency must consult with any other agency having expertise relevant to the impact. **Federal action** includes not only action undertaken directly but also decisions to grant permits or issue licenses for major activities that may be potentially subject to federal control and responsibility. An EIS must contain the impact of the proposed action, any adverse environmental effects that cannot be avoided, alternatives to the proposed action, the effects on the long-term productivity of the environment affected by the proposal, and the irreparable commitment of resources as a result of the action. If a federal agency determines that an EIS is not necessary, it must prepare a finding of no significant impact (FONSI) setting forth the reasons why the proposed action does not require an EIS.

The most common regulatory approach is to set standards, including those for pollution control technology, and to impose penalties for violations. The **Pollution Prevention Act** shifts some pollution regulation away from dictated standards and mandated technology. The act encourages industry to prevent the initial creation of pollution. It establishes a new EPA office, provides grant funds to promote source reduction, and creates a clearinghouse for source reduction technology transfer. However, the primary mode of preventing pollution of the environment remains traditional regulatory enforcement.

The goal of the **Clean Water Act (CWA)** is to restore and maintain the chemical, physical, and biological integrity of the nation's navigable waters. It broadly prohibits discharges not compliant with the act. It also creates a national effluent standard for each industry, water quality standards, and a discharge permit program. Moreover, it (1) has special provisions for unique situations, such as oil spills; (2) provides for a construction grant program for publicly owned treatment plants; (3) prohibits the dredging or filling of protected wetlands; and (4) imposes criminal as well as civil liability. Industrial point sources must install equipment to control the discharge of pollutants into waterways. **Point sources** are distinct places from which pollutants are discharged into water, such as paper mills, electric utility plants, sewage treatment facilities, and factories. Existing industrial sources must install pollution control equipment meeting the **best practical technology (BPT)** standard. This standard considers cost, severity of pollution, and time required to install. The EPA has also established certain time periods within which existing point sources must meet the **best available technology (BAT)** standard. BAT consists of the best control and treatment measures that have been or are capable of being achieved. Any new industrial point source must install the most effective water pollution control equipment under the BAT standard. The **Safe Drinking Water Act** provides national primary drinking water regulations (NPDWRs) for public water systems that establish maximum contaminant levels (MCLs) or specific treatment techniques. Private persons may sue public water systems in federal court for failure to meet the standards. The EPA must, every 5 years, publish a new **list of substances** that contaminate or are expected to contaminate public systems. In addition, the EPA must decide every 5 years whether to regulate a minimum of five of the listed items. If state standards are at least as restrictive as those at the federal level, and state procedures (monitoring, inspection, etc.) are sufficient, the state will have primary enforcement authority.

The **Clean Air Act (CAA)** made health protection a priority and forced heavy industry to meet specific emission standards. The EPA is required to publish and revise periodically a list of pollutants that may reasonably be anticipated to endanger public health or welfare and that are emitted from stationary or mobile sources. The act requires **national ambient air quality standards (NAAQSs)** for each pollutant. They cover six categories: (1) hydrocarbons, (2) carbon monoxide, (3) sulphur dioxide, (4) nitrogen oxides, (5) photochemical oxidants, and (6) particulates. These standards are based on public health benefits and are revised to reflect new scientific data but need not consider economic costs. Standards may be **primary and health-oriented** (to be attained within 3 years) or **secondary** (to be attained within a reasonable time). Standards also vary depending on whether (1) an area is already polluted or (2) the source is an existing one or a major new source. The standards for major sources are based on **maximum achievable control technology (MACT)**. Thus, (1) acid rain has been reduced by requiring coal-burning power plants to lower emissions, (2) utilities receive **pollution credits** (unused credits can be sold to other polluters), (3) steps have been taken to lower ozone levels at ground level, (4) chemicals (e.g., chlorofluorocarbons) that damage the ozone layer have been banned, and (5) landfills must install gas collection and control systems for hazardous air pollutants (e.g., asbestos, benzene, and mercury). Uniform national emissions standards are set for new stationary sources (factories, refineries, service stations, mines, power plants, and agriculture) and mobile sources (airplanes and automobiles). A **stationary source** is a major source if it has the potential to emit at least 100 tons of air pollutants. A **state implementation plan (SIP)** is the mechanism through which emission controls are imposed by the states on stationary sources. The SIP must (1) contain a plan for attaining primary NAAQSs as expeditiously a practicable; (2) contain a plan for attaining secondary NAAQSs within a reasonable time; and (3) include an enforcement program regarding emission limitations for modifying, constructing, or operating any stationary source.

The EPA has divided each state into **air quality control regions (AQCRs)**, and an SIP must include a description of the air quality in each AQCR. If a state submits an inadequate plan, the EPA must issue regulations. If an AQCR does not meet the NAAQSs, the EPA can designate the area as a nonattainment area, and the state must develop a revised SIP. It must provide for the implementation of all **reasonably available control measures (RACM)** as expeditiously as practicable. In the interim, the CAA requires reasonably available control technology to be used. **Mobile sources of pollution** are regulated via a certification and registration program. The EPA develops standards to reflect the greatest emission reduction achievable through technology that the EPA determines will be obtainable for the model year to which the standards apply. The EPA also may regulate the manufacture and sale of motor vehicle fuel and fuel additives. Manufacturers of new motor vehicles, engines, and components must (1) establish and maintain records; (2) perform tests; (3) permit EPA access to the records and the results of the tests; and (4) authorize the EPA to inspect all files, papers, and processes.

The **Toxic Substances Control Act (TSCA)** requires notice to the EPA before production of a new chemical or a new use of one in production. If the data provided in the premanufacturing notice are insufficient, the EPA may prohibit its production or distribution, but this remedy is rarely used. The TSCA also may require testing of such chemicals. However, the EPA considers the relative costs of various methods of conducting any required tests and must impose the least burdensome restrictions on manufacturers. The act also requires that the EPA compile a list of toxic substances. An item not on this list is subject to the preproduction review. Furthermore, the EPA maintains a priority list of not more than 50 chemicals to be tested at a given time. Another provision of the TSCA allows the regulation of imminent hazards, that is, chemicals presenting an unreasonable risk of widespread injury.

The **Resource Conservation and Recovery Act (RCRA)** provides cradle-to-grave control of **hazardous waste** (newly generated solid waste that may pose a threat to health or the environment). It imposes management requirements on generators, transporters, and owners of waste, as well as on operators of treatment, storage, and disposal facilities. The policy is reduction or elimination of hazardous waste as soon as possible. All waste must be handled so as to minimize any threat to the environment. EPA regulations identify **specific hazardous wastes**, either by listing them or identifying the characteristics that render them hazardous. All handlers must notify the EPA of their activities. Any representative of the EPA or an appropriate state official may inspect the premises and records of any person who generates, treats, stores, transports, disposes of, or otherwise handles hazardous or solid waste. A **generator** is “any person, by site, whose act or process produces hazardous waste or whose act first causes hazardous waste to become subject to regulation.” All generators must prepare a uniform **hazardous waste manifest** that identifies and accompanies the waste. Parties handling the waste receive copies. When hazardous materials are transported to a **treatment, storage, and disposal facility (TSD)**, a final copy of the manifest must be returned to the generator or retained for at least 3 years. Periodic reports must describe the cradle-to-grave handling of all hazardous and solid waste. However, small generators are conditionally exempt from RCRA. Any person engaged in the off-site transportation of hazardous waste by air, rail, highway, or water is a **transporter**. Transporters are subject to strict regulation of the movement of hazardous or solid waste. Each transporter must obtain an EPA identification number and strictly comply with labeling, packaging, handling, and transportation regulations. If a spill or other discharge occurs, the transporter is liable for cleanup. The EPA sets specific design, construction, and operating standards **for each type of TSD facility**, including containers, tanks, storage compounds, landfills, incinerators, and solid waste piles. Every owner or operator must obtain a permit.

The **Comprehensive Environmental Response, Compensation, and Liability Act (CERCLA)** addresses abandoned hazardous waste sites and sites that the owners were financially incapable of cleaning up. It is intended to deal with sites that were established without negligence. In these circumstances, no one was aware that a cleanup would be required in the future, so the cleanup costs were not built into pricing structures. The CERCLA establishes what is known as the **Superfund**. Taxes on the petroleum and chemical industries are allocated for cleanup of hazardous waste. The act covers all environmental media, including air, surface water, ground water, and soil. It also applies to any commercial, industrial, or noncommercial facility. The act requires anyone who releases unauthorized amounts of hazardous substances to notify the government, which can order those responsible to clean up such releases. The CERCLA imposes liability for site remediation costs. These costs may be allocated to any one or all of the following **potentially responsible parties (PRPs)**: (1) current and past owners, including trustees and operators of the site, but not necessarily including a corporate parent of a PRP; (2) parties who transported waste to the site; (3) parties who arranged for waste to be disposed of or treated, either directly with an owner/operator or indirectly with a transporter; and (4) lenders who participate in a borrower's management or can influence hazardous waste policy. Moreover, corporate officers who were responsible for disposal of hazardous waste and secured creditors who participate in management of a waste site have been held to be PRPs. Furthermore, the act imposes **liability on those responsible for unauthorized discharges of hazardous waste** without proof of negligence. The liability is retroactive, strict, and joint and several. Liability can be imposed for damage to natural resources as well as for cleanup costs. A hazardous substance is any substance that the EPA has designated for special consideration under the CAA, the CWA, the RCRA, or the Toxic Substances Control Act. Moreover, the EPA must designate additional substances as hazardous that may present substantial danger to health and the environment. For example, asbestos is a hazardous substance subject to the provisions of CERCLA. The **innocent landowner's defense** is available. The owner must have purchased the land after the placement of the hazardous substances occurred. Moreover, the owner must prove that (s)he did not know or have any reason to know that such substances were on the land. Finally, the owner must show that someone else (or a *force majeure*) caused the release or threat of release of the substances and that (s)he exercised reasonable care and took reasonable precautions in preventing the release of such substances. The **Small Business Liability Relief and Brownfields Revitalization Act** promotes the cleanup and use of property not sufficiently polluted to receive a high priority for remediation. It offers an exemption from CERCLA liability for purchasers, developers who participate in a voluntary cleanup program, or owners of land subject to migrating pollutants.

The common law of torts also addresses environmental issues. See Study Unit 7 for coverage of such issues as trespass to land, nuisance, and inherently dangerous activities.

QUESTIONS

35.1 Environmental Law: Introduction

1. The most widely used regulatory approach to pollution control in the United States is

A. Pollution charges and fees.

B. Private markets in which pollution rights can be bought and sold.

C. Environmental standards and penalties for noncompliance.

D. Total deregulation of pollution control resulting in state regulation with no federal involvement.

Answer (C) is correct. *(CMA, adapted)*

REQUIRED: The most widely used regulatory approach to pollution control in the United States.

DISCUSSION: Congress passed the National Environmental Policy Act and formed the Environmental Protection Agency to control the pollution of air, water, and land in the United States. Other legislation, such as the Clean Air Act, Water Pollution Control Act, Noise Control Act, and Solid Waste Disposal Act, has been passed by Congress. Many states have enacted environmental laws that in some instances are more stringent than the federal standards. Violation of federal and state environmental regulations are subject to civil and criminal penalties stated in the written legislation.

Answer (A) is incorrect. Charges and fees are imposed when environmental regulations are violated. Answer (B) is incorrect. The government regulates how much pollution can be in the environment. Answer (D) is incorrect. The environment is subject to federal, state, and municipal regulations.

2. Which of the following remedies is available against a real property owner to enforce the provisions of federal acts regulating air and water pollution?

	Citizen Suits against the Environmental Protection Agency to Enforce Compliance with the Laws	State Suits Against Violators	Citizen Suits Against Violators
A.	Yes	Yes	Yes
B.	Yes	Yes	No
C.	No	Yes	Yes
D.	Yes	No	Yes

Answer (A) is correct. *(CPA, adapted)*

REQUIRED: The remedy available against a real property owner to enforce provisions of federal acts regulating air and water pollution.

DISCUSSION: Most environmental statutes permit some form of citizen suit. These statutes grant citizens the right to participate in or initiate civil enforcement actions. The citizens must, however, notify the EPA and Department of Justice. The primary responsibility for enforcing air quality standards lies with the states, but the federal government has the right to step in and enforce the standards when the states fail to.

3. Which of the following actions should a business take to qualify for leniency if an environmental violation has been committed?

	Conduct Environmental Audits	Report Environmental Violations to the Government
A.	Yes	Yes
B.	Yes	No
C.	No	Yes
D.	No	No

Answer (A) is correct. *(CPA, adapted)*

REQUIRED: The actions to qualify a business for leniency for environmental law violations.

DISCUSSION: Congress has enacted a wide variety of laws to protect and improve the nation's environment. The EPA has the primary responsibility for administering these laws. The emphasis of national environmental policy is to prevent harm through education as well as regulation and enforcement. In evaluating the appropriate civil or criminal penalty for an environmental law violation, courts and the EPA consider certain factors that may justify leniency. These include a business conducting periodic audits to determine compliance, self-reporting of possible violations to the EPA or other government agencies, and the violator's compliance history.

35.2 National Environmental Policy Act

4. Which of the following statements about the National Environmental Policy Act (NEPA) is most likely to be false?

A. The NEPA requires federal agencies to consider environmental consequences in their decision-making process.

B. The NEPA allows the federal government to bring suit against any private person who violates NEPA's provisions.

C. Under the NEPA, federal agencies do not have to give environmental considerations priority over other concerns in their decision-making processes.

D. The NEPA augments the power of existing agencies with respect to considering environmental consequences of proposed actions.

Answer (B) is correct. *(Publisher, adapted)*

REQUIRED: The false statement about the NEPA.

DISCUSSION: The provisions of NEPA focus on federal governmental actions. Federal agencies are specifically directed to incorporate an analysis of environment consequences in their decision-making processes. Actions of private persons are affected by the NEPA only when federal involvement (approval, funding, etc.) is necessary before such persons may act (e.g., federal approval before drilling for oil in ocean waters within U.S. jurisdiction). Otherwise, NEPA does not directly concern activities of private persons.

Answer (A) is incorrect. Under the NEPA, federal agencies must consider environmental consequences. Answer (C) is incorrect. Under the NEPA, federal agencies must give environmental considerations a weight equal to but not greater than that afforded nonenvironmental concerns. Answer (D) is incorrect. The NEPA augments the existing powers of federal agencies to deal with these environmental matters.

5. The environmental impact statement (EIS) lies at the heart of the NEPA. Which of the following states a condition that must be present before a federal agency is required to prepare an EIS?

A. There must be a recommendation or report on a proposal for legislation or certain other "major" federal action.

B. If a "major" federal action is involved, all that is needed is a slight chance that a small amount of irreparable environmental damage may result.

C. An embryonic discussion of a legislative proposal is all that is necessary to trigger the requirement for an EIS.

D. Congress must specifically direct a federal agency to begin preparing an EIS.

Answer (A) is correct. *(Publisher, adapted)*

REQUIRED: The condition necessary for the preparation of an EIS.

DISCUSSION: The NEPA directs federal agencies to prepare an EIS for inclusion in every recommendation or report on proposals for legislation and other major federal actions significantly affecting the quality of the human environment.

Answer (B) is incorrect. More than a small amount of environmental damage is needed. The term "significantly affecting" implies more harm (or potential harm) is necessary. Answer (C) is incorrect. The legislation must at least have been prepared, not be in its earliest stage. Answer (D) is incorrect. If a federal agency already is empowered to act in a manner that constitutes "major" federal action, the agency is not allowed to wait until it receives a congressional directive to prepare an EIS.

6. Before actually preparing an EIS, a federal agency is required under the NEPA to

A. Obtain local approval for its proposed actions through an official referendum presented to the people of the locality that will be affected by the agency's actions.

B. Consult with any federal agency that has special expertise with respect to any environmental impact involved.

C. Disregard any comments made by any federal agency with special expertise because, in effect, the NEPA requires that each federal agency become its own expert in any environmental area.

D. Obtain approval for its proposed actions from the highest official in each affected locality.

Answer (B) is correct. *(Publisher, adapted)*

REQUIRED: The requirement before a federal agency prepares an EIS.

DISCUSSION: Prior to preparing an EIS, the federal agency preparing the action must consult with any federal agency that has jurisdiction over the proposal or special expertise with respect to any environmental impact involved. This is consistent with another broad NEPA requirement of a systematic, interdisciplinary approach to decision making.

Answer (A) is incorrect. The NEPA does not require any formal local approval for an agency's proposed actions. However, the EIS, once prepared, must be open to public comment. Answer (C) is incorrect. Agencies with special expertise must be consulted. Answer (D) is incorrect. The NEPA does not require any formal local approval for an agency's proposed actions.

7. An EIS need not contain

A. The environmental impact of the proposed action.

B. Alternatives to the proposed action.

C. Any adverse environmental effects that cannot be avoided.

D. An independent opinion on the proposed action prepared by the Council on Environmental Quality.

Answer (D) is correct. *(Publisher, adapted)*

REQUIRED: The item that an EIS need not contain.

DISCUSSION: An EIS must contain, in detail, the environmental impact of the proposed action, any adverse environmental effects that cannot be avoided should the proposal be implemented, alternatives to the proposed action, the effects on maintaining the long-term productivity of the environment affected by the proposal, and the irreparable commitment of resources as a result of the action. The NEPA established the Council on Environmental Quality in the Executive Office of the President. It has an advisory function but has also promulgated regulations. It does not render opinions.

8. Under the NEPA, if a federal agency determines that an EIS is not necessary, it must nonetheless

A. Inform the governor of each state that will be affected by its actions of the decision not to prepare an EIS.

B. Prepare and circulate for public comment a statement of nonassessment of environmental consequences (NEC).

C. Prepare a finding of no significant impact (FONSI) setting forth the reasons why the proposed action does not require an EIS.

D. Inform the Director of the EPA, via certified mail, why an EIS is not required.

Answer (C) is correct. *(Publisher, adapted)*

REQUIRED: The appropriate course of action when an agency determines that an EIS is unnecessary.

DISCUSSION: An agency must consider environmental issues at the earliest stage of planning. The threshold decision is whether to prepare an EIS. If the proposed action is on an agency list of actions that do or do not require an EIS, the appropriate step is taken automatically. Otherwise, an environmental assessment is prepared. If the decision is that an EIS is not needed, regulations promulgated by the Council on Environmental Quality that interpret the NEPA require the federal agency to prepare a FONSI setting forth the reasons.

35.3 Clean Water Act (CWA)

9. Which of the following statements regarding the Clean Water Act (CWA) is true?

A. It allows persons to discharge pollutants into waters subject to its jurisdiction as long as navigation thereon will not be permanently obstructed.

B. The CWA subjects all bodies of water located in the United States, whether flowing or not, to its protection.

C. The notion of protecting waters within the jurisdiction of the United States began with the CWA.

D. The CWA seeks to restore and maintain the physical and biological integrity of the waters of the United States.

Answer (D) is correct. *(Publisher, adapted)*

REQUIRED: The true statement about the CWA.

DISCUSSION: The CWA (1972) substantially amended the Federal Water Pollution Control Act of 1948. It seeks to restore and maintain the physical and biological integrity of the waters of the United States. Its objectives are to render water suitable for recreation and propagation of fish and other wildlife and to eliminate discharges of pollutants.

Answer (A) is incorrect. The CWA broadly prohibits any discharges of pollutants into waters, except if in compliance with the act. Impairment of navigation is irrelevant. Answer (B) is incorrect. To be subject to the CWA, the waters must be "navigable waters." Answer (C) is incorrect. The Rivers and Harbors Act of the late 1800s was used to combat pollutive discharges, although its original purpose was to keep waterways clear from obstructions to navigation.

10. Which of the following is most likely not covered by the Clean Water Act?

A. Boston Harbor.

B. The Mississippi River.

C. A tributary of the Mississippi capable of sustaining barge traffic through several states.

D. Sawyer's Ditch, a small creek feeding into a farm pond, both of which are located wholly within the same parcel of land in South Carolina and never achieve a depth of more than 1 ft.

Answer (D) is correct. *(Publisher, adapted)*

REQUIRED: The body of water not likely to be considered a navigable water of the United States.

DISCUSSION: The concept of a sovereign's ownership of its navigable waterways can be traced to early common law in England. This concept, in much the same form, is carried forward and permeates the CWA's definition of navigable waters, the jurisdictional basis of the act. In its most general sense, waters subject to the federal jurisdiction of the United States must be capable of providing navigation in the aid of interstate commerce and be located within 3 miles of the U.S. shoreline.

11. Under the federal statutes governing water pollution, which of the following areas is regulated?

	Dredging of Coastal or Freshwater Wetlands	Drinking Water Standards
A.	Yes	Yes
B.	Yes	No
C.	No	Yes
D.	No	No

Answer (A) is correct. *(CPA, adapted)*

REQUIRED: The activities, if any, regulated by federal water pollution statutes.

DISCUSSION: Under the Federal Water Pollution Control Act, commonly referred to as the Clean Water Act, standards have been established regulating discharges of pollutants into navigable waters. The term "navigable waters" is interpreted to include wetlands. Thus, dredging of coastal or freshwater wetlands falls within the statute. The Safe Drinking Water Act provides national standards for public water systems. Private wells are not regulated.

Answer (B) is incorrect. Drinking water standards are also within the federal statutes covering water pollution. Answer (C) is incorrect. Dredging of wetlands is also within the federal statutes covering water pollution. Answer (D) is incorrect. Dredging of wetlands and drinking water standards are within the federal statutes covering water pollution.

12. Portions of the requirements under the Clean Water Act (CWA) can be viewed as technology forcing, i.e., requirements that force industry to implement or design new or innovative techniques for reducing pollutant discharges. This concept is best reflected in the CWA's requirement that certain point sources use the best

A. Practicable control technology currently available (BPT).

B. Available technology economically achievable (BAT).

C. Conventional pollutant control technology (BCT).

D. Generic technology overall achievable (BGT).

Answer (B) is correct. *(Publisher, adapted)*

REQUIRED: The most stringent pollution control technology required under the CWA.

DISCUSSION: As the name suggests, BAT is the most stringent of the technology requirements under the CWA. Unlike BPT and BCT, BAT does not require the EPA to take into account prevailing industry practices or cost-benefit analyses when establishing BAT requirements. Thus, BAT best reflects the concept of technology-forcing requirements.

Answer (A) is incorrect. BPT is technology based. Answer (C) is incorrect. BCT is technology based. Answer (D) is incorrect. The acronym BGT does not appear anywhere in the CWA.

13. A person who violates the Clean Water Act may be subject to

A. Civil liability, but only for the actual harm caused by the violations.

B. Criminal liability, but only if the person knowingly violated the CWA.

C. Civil and criminal liability.

D. No liability because the CWA, like the NEPA, pertains only to the actions of federal governmental agencies.

Answer (C) is correct. *(Publisher, adapted)*

REQUIRED: The liability to which violators of the Clean Water Act (CWA) may be subjected.

DISCUSSION: Persons who violate the CWA are subject to civil and criminal liability, e.g., damages, civil penalties and cleanup costs. Fines of as much as $50,000 a day and prison terms of up to 3 years are possible sanctions for "knowing violations."

Answer (A) is incorrect. A civil action may be brought for any appropriate relief, including a permanent or temporary injunction. Answer (B) is incorrect. Criminal liability may also be imposed on violators who were negligent, a mental state not involving actual knowledge of a violation. Answer (D) is incorrect. The CWA applies to the actions of persons other than federal agencies.

35.4 Clean Air Act (CAA)

14. Under the Clean Air Act, a state must submit a state implementation plan (SIP) after the promulgation of a national ambient air quality standard (NAAQS). The Environmental Protection Agency must approve the SIP if all the statutorily prescribed SIP requirements are contained therein. Which of the following is not a general SIP requirement?

A. The SIP must contain a plan for attaining primary NAAQSs as expeditiously as practicable.

B. The SIP must contain a plan for attaining secondary NAAQSs within a reasonable time.

C. The SIP must include an enforcement program regarding emission limitations for modifying, constructing, or operating any stationary source.

D. The SIP must provide for a so-called pollution tax, which the CAA stipulates must be no less than $500 per stationary source.

Answer (D) is correct. *(Publisher, adapted)*

REQUIRED: The alternative that is not a general SIP requirement.

DISCUSSION: Nowhere in the CAA is a SIP required to contain a pollution tax. However, the CAA does provide for civil and criminal sanctions. The primary NAAQSs are public health oriented, and the secondary standards are directed toward protection of vegetation, climate, economic values, etc. Also, point sources are defined as stationary (e.g., power plants and factories) and moving (automobiles, etc.), and standards have been issued for each category.

Answer (A) is incorrect. The SIP must contain a plan for attaining primary NAAQSs as expeditiously as practicable. Answer (B) is incorrect. The SIP must contain a plan for attaining secondary NAAQSs within a reasonable time. Answer (C) is incorrect. The SIP must include an enforcement program regarding emission limitations for modifying, constructing, or operating any stationary source.

15. Under the Clean Air Act, a major stationary source is

A. A facility whose emissions will cause an air quality control region of a state to exceed the primary NAAQS.

B. A source that directly emits 10 tons per year or more of sulphur dioxide.

C. Any stationary facility or source of air pollutants that emits 2 tons per year or more of any air pollutant.

D. Any source of air pollutants that indirectly emits 10 tons per year or more of an air pollutant for which an NAAQS has been promulgated.

Answer (B) is correct. *(Publisher, adapted)*

REQUIRED: The definition of a major stationary source under the CAA.

DISCUSSION: A major stationary source is any stationary facility or source of air pollutants that directly emits, or has the potential to emit, 10 tons per year or more of any hazardous air pollutant or 25 tons per year of any combination of hazardous pollutants. The NAAQSs cover six pollutant categories: hydrocarbons, carbon monoxide, sulphur dioxide, nitrogen oxides, photochemical oxidants, and particulates.

Answer (A) is incorrect. A major stationary source is any stationary facility or source of air pollutants that directly emits, or has the potential to emit, 10 tons per year or more of any air pollutant. Answer (C) is incorrect. The statutory threshold amount is 10 tons, not 2 tons. Answer (D) is incorrect. Ten tons, not 2 tons, of any air pollutant satisfies the definition, and the pollutant need not be one for which an NAAQS has been promulgated.

16. Part D of a state implementation plan (SIP) is required to be submitted by a state that has not attained the NAAQS for any listed pollutant in one or more air quality control regions located within its borders. Which of the following is a provision that a Part D SIP must contain?

A. A system for issuing permits to allow new or modified major stationary sources to emit air pollutants.

B. A mechanism for closing highways located in residential areas where the actual levels of pollution exceed primary and secondary NAAQSs.

C. Provision for the implementation of all reasonably available control measures (RACM) as expeditiously as possible.

D. Before full implementation of RACM, a requirement to use the best available control technology (BACT).

Answer (A) is correct. *(Publisher, adapted)*

REQUIRED: The content of Part D of a SIP.

DISCUSSION: The CAA prescribes many requirements for Part D. One is the permit requirement for new or modified major stationary sources.

Answer (B) is incorrect. The CAA does not specifically require that heavily traveled highways be closed. Answer (C) is incorrect. A Part D SIP must provide for the implementation of all reasonably available control measures (RACM) as expeditiously as practicable, not as possible. Answer (D) is incorrect. In the interim, the CAA requires reasonably available control technology to be used.

17. A person who desires to build a new major stationary source must first obtain a permit. Which of the following will not be a condition of obtaining such a permit in a state that must submit Part D of a state implementation plan?

A. The proposed new source must comply with the lowest achievable emission rate.

B. The owner or operator of the proposed new source must demonstrate that all other major stationary sources owned or operated by the person in the state are in compliance (or on schedule for compliance) with all applicable emissions limitations.

C. The new source will not impede the attainment of reasonable further progress toward NAAQS compliance otherwise required of a state under a Part D SIP.

D. The new source cannot be constructed in a "dirty air area."

Answer (D) is correct. *(Publisher, adapted)*
REQUIRED: The item not a condition for obtaining a permit to construct a new major stationary source.
DISCUSSION: The Part D SIP requirements established by the 1977 amendments to the CAA departed from the path taken by Congress in the original CAA's SIP requirements. Originally, states were given significant leeway in deciding how to achieve the NAAQSs. Part D of the CAA now imposes specific restrictions on persons who desire to construct new, or modify old, major stationary sources. Under Part D, states are required to impose certain uniform restrictions. One restriction is on construction in "dirty air areas." New sources are permitted if they have the lowest achievable emission rates and if other sources under the operator's control are in compliance with applicable standards.
Answer (A) is incorrect. Compliance with the lowest achievable emission rate is an important restriction on a person who wishes to build or modify a major stationary source in a state subject to the Part D SIP provisions. Answer (B) is incorrect. The owner or operator of the proposed new source must demonstrate that all other major stationary sources owned or operated by the person in the state are in compliance (or on schedule for compliance) with all applicable emissions limitations. Answer (C) is incorrect. The new source will not impede the attainment of reasonable further progress toward NAAQS compliance otherwise required of a state under a Part D SIP.

35.5 Resource Conservation and Recovery Act

18. The Resource Conservation and Recovery Act (RCRA) defines hazardous waste broadly. The act generally applies to which of the following?

A. Solid waste.

B. Liquid waste.

C. Corrosive ash buried in an inactive waste site.

D. Airborne particulate matter.

Answer (A) is correct. *(Publisher, adapted)*
REQUIRED: The substance(s) to which the RCRA applies.
DISCUSSION: The policy of RCRA is reduction or elimination of hazardous waste as soon as possible. The act defines hazardous waste as solid waste that may cause or significantly contribute to an increase in mortality or serious illness or pose a hazard to human health or the environment if improperly managed. RCRA applies primarily to operating facilities and to new waste, rather than to abandoned or inactive sites.

19. The Resource Conservation and Recovery Act of 1976 (RCRA) imposes requirements on generators, transporters, and owners of waste. A generator may include

A. A person the law recognizes as holding title to waste with high uranium content.

B. A person engaged in off-site transportation by water of hazardous waste.

C. A person whose process produces hazardous waste.

D. All of the answers are correct.

Answer (D) is correct. *(Publisher, adapted)*
REQUIRED: The generators of waste under the RCRA.
DISCUSSION: The RCRA is designed to provide comprehensive control of hazardous waste. A generator must, for example, prepare a Uniform Hazardous Waste Manifest to identify and accompany the hazardous waste at all times. A generator is any person whose act or process produces hazardous waste. A transporter may be a generator as well if (s)he also fits the above definition. For example, a transporter might generate hazardous waste by allowing two wastes to mix in transit.

35.6 CERCLA

20. Under the Comprehensive Environmental Response, Compensation, and Liability Act (CERCLA), if land is found to be contaminated, which of the following parties would be least likely to be liable for cleanup costs?

A. A bank that foreclosed a mortgage on the land and purchased the land at the foreclosure sale.

B. A parent corporation of the corporation that owned the land.

C. A minority shareholder of the public corporation that owned the land.

D. A trustee appointed by the owner of the land to manage the land.

Answer (C) is correct. *(Publisher, adapted)*

REQUIRED: The party least likely to be liable for cleanup costs under CERCLA.

DISCUSSION: The CERCLA imposes liability for site remediation costs. These costs may be allocated to any one or all of the following potentially responsible parties (PRPs): (1) current and past owners, including trustees and operators of the site; (2) parties who transported wastes to the site; (3) parties who arranged for wastes to be disposed of or treated, either directly with an owner/operator, or indirectly with a transporter; and (4) lenders that participate in a borrower's management or can influence hazardous waste policy. Moreover, corporate officers who were responsible for disposing of hazardous waste and secured creditors who participate in management of a waste site have been held to be PRPs. However a minority shareholder of a public company is not a PRP. Such a party has at risk only the investment in the entity.

Answer (A) is incorrect. A bank that purchased the land at the foreclosure sale is an owner and therefore a PRP. Answer (B) is incorrect. A parent of the corporation that owned the land is a PRP if it is an operator of the waste site. However, it is not a PRP solely by reason of the parent-subsidiary relationship. Answer (D) is incorrect. A trustee appointed by the owner of the land to manage the land presumably arranged for disposal of wastes and is therefore a PRP.

21. Dan bought a vacation home in the mountains of North Carolina. One day as he was sitting on the porch of his vacation home, Dan saw a stream of gray liquid bubbling up from an opening in his front yard. Dan immediately notified the EPA, which, after extensive examination, informed him that hazardous substances (within the meaning of CERCLA) had been previously buried deep beneath his house and a shift in the rock formation underlying his house caused a barrel to rupture, releasing its contents. Under CERCLA, Dan

A. Will be liable for the actions of the previous owner since CERCLA will not provide him with any defense to CERCLA liability.

B. Is released from all liability simply because he immediately notified the EPA of the release.

C. Will not be liable because he did not own the land at the time when the substances were buried.

D. Will not be liable, despite the act's broad liability, if he is able to avail himself of the so-called innocent landowner's defense.

Answer (D) is correct. *(Publisher, adapted)*

REQUIRED: The potential liability of a homeowner under CERCLA.

DISCUSSION: Liability under CERCLA is broadly applied to all owners or operators of "facilities" where releases of hazardous substances occur. Thus, all owners of land where such releases occur are subject to liability under CERCLA. However, the so-called innocent landowner's defense is available under CERCLA. For the exception to apply, the owner must have purchased the land after the placement of the hazardous substances occurred. Moreover, the owner must prove that (s)he did not know or have any reason to know that such substances were on the land. Finally, the owner must show that someone else, or a force majeure, caused the release or threat of release of the substances and that (s)he exercised reasonable care and took reasonable precautions in preventing the release of such substances. If Dan proves the foregoing, he will not be subject to CERCLA liability.

Answer (A) is incorrect. CERCLA does provide for defenses, albeit very limited ones. Answer (B) is incorrect. By itself, immediate notification of a release by an owner or operator of an onshore facility will not absolve such person of CERCLA liability. Answer (C) is incorrect. CERCLA liability applies to both past and current owners of property.

22. Under CERCLA, proof by a preponderance of the evidence of which of the following is not a defense to liability?

A. Release of hazardous substances was caused solely by a force majeure.

B. Release of hazardous substances was caused solely by an act of war.

C. Payment of cleanup costs will result in personal or business financial ruin.

D. The release was caused by an act or omission of an unrelated third party, and the owner or operator exercised reasonable care and took reasonable precautions.

Answer (C) is correct. *(Publisher, adapted)*

REQUIRED: The defense to liability not available under CERCLA.

DISCUSSION: Liability under CERCLA is retroactive, strict, and joint and several. Thus, exercise of due care or the inability to pay damages is not an absolute bar to liability under CERCLA.

Answer (A) is incorrect. Causation by an event or effect that cannot be reasonably anticipated or controlled (a force majeure) is a defense. Answer (B) is incorrect. Causation by an act of war is a defense. Answer (D) is incorrect. The facts that the release was caused by an act or omission of an unrelated third party, and the owner or operator exercised reasonable care and took reasonable precautions is a defense. A fourth exception, the so-called innocent landowner's defense, is indirectly available through this exception.

STUDY UNIT THIRTY-SIX
ANTITRUST

The primary purpose of antitrust law is to foster **competition**. It seeks to ensure a system in which prices and output are determined in a free and competitive market as a result of consumer demand. Many scholars believe that efficient allocation of scarce resources, lower prices, higher-quality products, greater output, and increased innovation are by-products of competition. The major federal antitrust statutes include the Sherman Antitrust Act, the Clayton Act, the Federal Trade Commission Act, and the Robinson-Patman Act. The antitrust laws apply to activity in **interstate commerce** or activity with a substantial effect on interstate commerce. Thus, they also apply to wholly intrastate activity that affects interstate commerce.

The **Justice Department** and the **Federal Trade Commission (FTC)** are the primary government enforcers of the antitrust laws. However, the FTC does not have authority to impose criminal sanctions on violators but must refer possible criminal activities to the Justice Department. **Fines** for corporate violators and individuals may be imposed. An individual also may be imprisoned. These criminal penalties are imposed by the Sherman Act. Furthermore, the Justice Department may seek **injunctive relief** in the federal courts, for example, to prohibit certain acts, to order divestiture of a subsidiary, to create a new company, or to cancel a contract. The FTC also is empowered to issue **cease and desist orders** prohibiting unfair methods of competition and unfair or deceptive acts or practices. A rarely used remedy is **forfeiture** of property subject to a contract, combination, or conspiracy in restraint of trade. Still another remedy is **private action** for damages by a party (an individual or a corporation) whose property or business is injured as a direct result of a violation of antitrust law. The private person can recover **treble damages** under most statutes. However, a consumer may sue for violation of antitrust law only if (s)he purchased a product or service directly from the person who violated the law. The connection must be direct. Otherwise, the plaintiff's case will be dismissed for lack of standing. An additional avenue for redress is an action for treble damages by a state attorney general on behalf of the people of a state. The foregoing enforcement structure does not apply only to actions in the U.S. market or in trade between U.S. and foreign firms, but also, under a policy adopted by the Justice Department, to actions by foreign firms that injure U.S. exports of goods and services.

The **Sherman Act** was passed to regulate interstate commerce by prohibiting anticompetitive practices. The jurisdictional reach of the act extends to activities substantially affecting interstate commerce, including those of parties in foreign countries. It consists of two main sections. **Section 1** states, "Every contract, combination in the form of trust or otherwise, or conspiracy, in restraint of trade or commerce among the several states, or with foreign nations, is declared to be illegal." Literally, this statutory language proscribes every contract. To avoid such an extreme interpretation, the courts have construed this section to invalidate only **unreasonable restraints of trade**.

The Supreme Court has developed two fundamentally different approaches in analyzing proscribed behavior. It has concluded that some forms of behavior always have a negative effect on competition. Such behavior is classified as **per se unreasonable**. Behavior that is not classified as per se unreasonable is judged under the **rule of reason**. Under this test, a court determines whether the anticompetitive effect of a restraint is outweighed by its benefits, such as greater economic efficiency. Thus, a **covenant not to compete** is enforceable as long as it is for a reasonable time and area. Also, **vertical territorial limitations** between a seller and its distributors and retailers are acceptable if they do not have an unreasonable effect on competition. Section 1 of the Sherman Act prohibits concerted action, not unilateral conduct. The essence of the illegal activity is the agreement or the act of joining together unreasonably to restrain trade. Restraints may be horizontal or vertical. A restraint is **horizontal** if it involves collaboration among competitors at the same functional level in the chain of distribution. Examples are price fixing, division of markets, and group boycotts. A restraint is **vertical** if it is made by parties who are not in direct competition at the same functional level of distribution. Examples are (1) resale price maintenance; (2) tying arrangements; (3) exclusive dealing agreements; and (4) customer, territorial, and location restrictions.

The Supreme Court, in developing its definition of per se unreasonableness, has stated that certain types of restrictive activities are so inherently anticompetitive that as a matter of law, they unreasonably restrain trade. If an activity is illegal per se, mere proof of the activity is sufficient to establish its anticompetitive nature. **Horizontal price fixing** is the primary example of a per se violation of the Sherman Act. Price fixing includes any agreement among sellers to establish either minimum or maximum prices or to restrict output. The aim and result of every price-fixing agreement, if effective, is the elimination of a form of competition. **Market allocations** among competitors also have been declared illegal per se. A market allocation exists when competitors agree not to compete with each other in specific markets, that is, markets defined by geographical area, type of product or service, or type of customer. **Group boycotts**, or **concerted refusals to deal**, are other per se violations. For example, a manufacturer violates Section 1 of the Sherman Act if it induces other manufacturers to refuse to deal with wholesalers or retailers who do not adhere to suggested price guidelines. However, a unilateral refusal to deal announced in advance by a seller, for example, a refusal to sell to parties who will not observe a resale price maintenance policy, has been held not to violate Section 1 because of the absence of a contract, combination, or conspiracy. Still another type of per se violation is a tying arrangement. In a **tying arrangement**, a seller of a product or service conditions its sale upon the buyer's purchasing a second item from the seller. Tying arrangements limit the freedom of choice of buyers and may exclude competitors. A tying arrangement exists when a seller exploits its economic power in a market (tying product) to expand its market share of sales of another product (tied product). Tying arrangements are evaluated under the Sherman Act (Section 1) and the Clayton Act (Section 3). They are considered illegal per se when (1) the seller has considerable economic power in the tying product and (2) a "not insubstantial" amount of interstate commerce in the tied product is affected. **Resale price maintenance** is a vertical price fixing arrangement in which a seller agrees with a buyer to limit the price at which the buyer may resell. This practice is no longer a per se violation of the Sherman Act. The Supreme Court has ruled that such agreements must be evaluated under the rule of reason. In recent years, the federal courts have applied a **quick look** variation of the rule of reason. It is used when the per se standard is not appropriate but the action in question clearly is anticompetitive. Nevertheless, the extent of the "quick look" may vary substantially with the facts of the case.

Section 2 of the Sherman Act prohibits any person's monopolizing, attempting to monopolize, or conspiring with others to monopolize any part of interstate or foreign commerce. **Monopoly power** is the ability to control prices or exclude competitors from the marketplace. Accordingly, Section 2 is primarily concerned with actions by a single firm to obtain monopoly power rather than the concerted action prohibited by Section 1. Courts have taken different approaches as to what must be proved to demonstrate a violation of Section 2. Generally, an objective intent to monopolize must be proved. Monopoly power maybe obtained lawfully if a superior product or business acumen, or simply the nature of the local market, positions the defendant as a monopolist. Thus, an **act of monopolization** requires a combination of (1) possession of monopoly power in the relevant market and (2) either the unfair attainment of such power or the intent to unlawfully exercise such power once lawfully obtained. The separate felonies of **attempt to monopolize** and **conspiracy to monopolize** do not require proof of monopoly power.

Courts use a **structural analysis** that considers many factors in determining whether a firm can control prices or exclude competitors in a **relevant market**. Some of these factors include (1) the size of the market share, (2) whether the size of the firm was achieved through internal natural growth or by acquisition of competitor's assets, (3) the number of competitors, (4) their financial strength, (5) barriers to entry, (6) product differentiation, (7) the degree of vertical integration, (8) industry cost structure, and (9) the degree of concentration in the market. Other factors include whether the defendant engaged in unlawful exclusionary practices to prevent entry into the market by potential competitors and the extent to which the defendant used unduly coercive tactics to suppress competition. Although no precise statutory or judicial formulas exist, a **market share** (share of the relevant product and geographic markets) of 75% or greater usually indicates that a monopoly exists, but a share of less than 50% does not. If a defendant has between 50% and 75% of the market share, courts will examine other factors. A relevant market consists of the product market and the geographic market. The relevant **product market** consists of products that can be closely substituted for the firm's product on the basis of price, quality, and demand. The relevant **geographic market** is that territory in which the firm makes sales of its products or services.

Section 2 also prohibits attempts and conspiracies to monopolize. An **attempt to monopolize** requires **specific intent** to injure competitors or obtain a monopoly. This intent should be contrasted with that required to prove monopolization, which is a **general intent** to do acts that, however legal and "honestly industrial" they may be in themselves, are ultimately determined to create or maintain a monopoly. Thus, an attempt to monopolize includes (1) a **specific intent** to obtain monopoly power, (2) anticompetitive or predatory actions directed toward that end, and (3) a "dangerous probability of success" in achieving monopoly power. Specific intent to monopolize is proved if it is shown that the single firm engaged in predatory activities, such as unlawfully (1) injuring actual competitors, (2) excluding potential competitors, (3) erecting barriers to market entry, and (4) deliberately lowering the price of products to below marginal cost (predatory pricing) until competitors are driven out of the market. However, the mere size of a firm is not itself a violation of Section 2 of the Sherman Act. **Conspiracy to monopolize** (an offense under Sections 1 and 2) consists of (1) an agreement by two or more entities or people with (2) specific intent to eradicate competition or create a monopoly. However, the existence of a monopoly need not be proved.

The **Clayton Act** was designed to strengthen the Sherman Act by prohibiting specified anticompetitive practices and by attacking them in their incipiency. **Mergers or acquisitions of assets or stock** are prohibited if the effect may be to **lessen competition substantially** or **tend to create a monopoly**. Thus, the justice department may prevent mergers before they occur, and **prior notice of a merger** must be given **(Antitrust Improvements Act of 1976)**. The substantive provisions of the Clayton Act concern price discrimination, tying arrangements, exclusive dealing contracts, mergers, and interlocking directorates. **Section 2** of the Clayton Act (as amended by the **Robinson-Patman Act of 1936**) prohibits **price discrimination**. Thus, it bars a person (1) engaged in commerce, (2) in the course of such commerce, (3) either directly or indirectly (4) from discriminating in price (5) between different purchasers of commodities of like grade and quality, (6) if the purchases are in commerce and (7) the effect "may be substantially to lessen competition or tend to create a monopoly in any line of commerce," or to injure competition with anyone who grants or knowingly receives the benefit of that discrimination, or with customers of either of them. As amended, the act reaches not only discrimination by a seller that injures other sellers on the same functional level **(primary line)** but also discrimination in favor of buyers on levels below that of the discriminating seller **(secondary line and tertiary line)**. It makes illegal **predatory pricing** by a seller to drive a competitor out of a market while continuing to charge higher prices elsewhere. The act also is intended to eliminate the advantage a buyer might demand over a smaller buyer (secondary line) merely because of the larger buyer's mass purchasing ability. Moreover, if the favored buyer passes the benefits on to its buyers (e.g., a wholesaler-retailer relationship), the injury also may exist at a tertiary line. Among the practices outlawed are payments of brokerage commissions to the buyer or its agents (effectively, rebates) and the granting of preferences regarding promotional allowances or services (e.g., for advertising, counter displays, and samples). However, **price differentials** are permitted when justified by proof of (1) a cost savings to the seller, (2) a good-faith price reduction to meet the lawful price of a competitor, or (3) changing conditions. **Section 3** of the Clayton Act relates to tying arrangements and exclusive dealing contracts. **Tying arrangements**, as previously discussed, are per se violations in specified circumstances. An **exclusive dealing contract** is an agreement to buy only from a given seller or not to deal with the seller's competitors. It is not a per se violation, but it violates Section 3 if a court believes it probable that performance of the contract will foreclose competition in a substantial share of the line of commerce affected. However, a reciprocal dealing is a per se violation. It occurs when a buyer uses its purchasing power to require the seller to purchase its products.

Section 7 is the primary authority concerning **mergers**. As amended, it provides that no person engaged in commerce or in any activity affecting commerce shall acquire any of the **stock or assets** of another person, if it will tend to lessen competition substantially or produce a monopoly in any line of commerce in any area of the country. In determining whether a merger or an acquisition is illegal under Section 7, courts examine the relevant markets or lines of commerce. The analysis is similar to that used for a monopolization case under Section 2 of the Sherman Act. The relevant markets or lines of commerce are the relevant product markets and relevant geographic markets or areas of effective competition. After determining the relevant product and geographic markets, the plaintiff must prove that the effect of the merger may be to lessen competition substantially or tend to produce a monopoly. The act allows the Justice Department to prevent mergers before they occur. A lessening of competition occurs when, for example, reciprocal buying will reduce the probability that other firms will enter the market. A **horizontal merger** (between competitors) is most closely scrutinized by the Justice Department because it usually has the greatest tendency to lessen competition. The Federal Trade Commission and the Justice Department have jointly issued **Horizontal Merger Guidelines**.

These guidelines describe the analytical process used to determine whether a horizontal merger will be challenged. The five factors traditionally considered are whether (1) the merger will significantly increase market concentration, (2) the merger will result in adverse competitive effects, (3) market entry would deter or counteract any adverse competitive effects, (4) any efficiency gained could be reasonably achieved by other means, and (5) but for the merger either party to the merger would be likely to fail. The **Herfindahl-Hirschman Index (HHI)** is a measure of market concentration used to evaluate whether to challenge a merger. The HHI is the sum of the squares of the market shares of the firms in the market. For example, if each of the 20 firms in a market has a 5% share, the HHI is 500 (20 firms × 5^2). If the HHI after the merger is **below 1,500**, the market is deemed to be unconcentrated. If it is from **1,500 to 2,500**, the market is deemed to be moderately concentrated. If the HHI is **above 2,500**, the market is deemed to be highly concentrated. However, the thresholds are not a "rigid screen," and numerous other factors are considered before a merger is challenged.

In addition, **Section 7A** requires that notice of large mergers be given to the Justice Department and the FTC. A **horizontal merger** is presumed to violate Section 7 if it (1) produces a firm controlling an undue percentage share of the relevant market and (2) results in a significant increase in the concentration of firms in that market. However, the presumption is overcome by evidence clearly showing that the merger is not likely to have such anticompetitive effects. A **vertical merger** involves firms in the supplier-customer chain. The major issue is **foreclosure** of the opportunity of competitors of the merger partners to sell to, or buy from, those entities. The lower the proportion of the supplier or customer market foreclosed, the less likely the merger will be challenged. A **conglomerate merger** is a merger that is not a horizontal or vertical merger. A **diversification** or pure conglomerate merger combines firms whose products are entirely unrelated. A **market-extension** merger is a combination of firms selling the same products in different geographic areas. A **product-extension** merger combines firms with distinct but related products. These two types may be challenged under Section 7 on the grounds of interference with **potential competition**, especially when the acquiree is dominant in the market, if (1) the market is concentrated, (2) the acquirer was a potential new entrant by internal expansion, and (3) the acquirer's potential entry premerger lessened the possibility of oligopolistic behavior by the current market participants. Conglomerate mergers also create greater potential for **reciprocal dealing**. Thus, if a diversified conglomerate has both buyer-seller and seller-buyer relationships in different markets with another firm, the effect is anticompetitive if those relationships are contingent on each other. **Entrenchment** is still another negative effect. A large conglomerate's resources may allow an already dominant firm in a market to become unassailable.

The most important defense available under Section 7 of the Clayton Act is the **failing company** doctrine. It applies when (1) the acquiree is in failing condition, (2) the possibility of reorganization is extremely low, and (3) no other acquirer would have a less anticompetitive effect.

Section 8 of the Clayton Act prohibits **interlocking directorates**. Consequently, a person may not be a member of the board of directors of two or more competing corporations if (1) the firms are engaged in interstate or foreign commerce; (2) each corporation's combined capital, surplus, and undivided profits exceeds the annually adjusted statutory threshold (currently $26,867,000); (3) the elimination of competition by agreement between the firms would amount to a violation of any of the antitrust laws; and (4) no grace period or *de minimis* exception applies. However, simultaneous service is not illegal if competitive sales are below one of several thresholds. **Competitive sales** are of one firm in competition with another. Competitive sales of (1) either firm must be less than the annually adjusted statutory threshold (currently $2,686,700), (2) either firm must be less than 2% of its total sales, or (3) each firm must be less than 4% of its total sales.

Exemptions from antitrust regulation include the following: (1) intrastate commerce; (2) labor unions (not exempt if the union primarily intends to restrain trade or conspires with nonlabor groups to monopolize); (3) regulated utilities; (4) reasonable noncompetition clauses between buyers and sellers of businesses, partners in a partnership, and purchasers of technology or equipment; (5) patents and copyrights; (6) agricultural and fishing organizations; (7) financial institutions; (8) transport industries; (9) major league baseball; and (10) companies qualifying for certificates of antitrust immunity issued by the Commerce Department (after concurrence by the Justice Department) under the Export Trading Company Act.

The **Federal Trade Commission** was created as an independent agency by the Federal Trade Commission Act of 1914. The FTC enforces that act and the Clayton Act by means of administrative proceedings that may lead to cease and desist orders. The FTC's primary functions are the maintenance of economic competition and consumer protection. When performing its antitrust enforcement function, the FTC is permitted to halt acts or practices in their incipiency that, if continued, would violate the other antitrust laws. It may also halt acts or practices that violate the spirit of those laws or that are unfair. Thus, the FTC investigates not only possible violations of antitrust laws, that is, "unfair methods of competition in or affecting commerce," but also "unfair or deceptive acts or practices in or affecting commerce," such as false or misleading advertisements, inadequate labeling, and discriminatory rebates and discounts. The FTC has stated that, to justify a finding of **unfairness**, the injury must (1) be substantial, (2) be an injury that consumers themselves could not reasonably have avoided, and (3) not be outweighed by any countervailing benefits to consumers or competition produced by the practice. The FTC will find an act or practice to be **deceptive** if (1) there is a misrepresentation, omission, or practice that is likely to mislead the consumer; (2) the act or practice is unreasonable from the perspective of the consumer; and (3) the act or practice is material.

Individual states have enacted laws, known as **Little FTC Acts**, that may provide more extensive protection and remedies to consumers for deceptive and unfair trade practices.

QUESTIONS

36.1 Basic Concepts

1. Which of the following is the best statement about the policy in the United States behind legislation and enforcement of antitrust laws?

A. The legal theory is that large concentration of economic power or market dominance is illegal.

B. The economic theory is that large size alone without abusing market power is not illegal.

C. The economic theory is that competition is best protected by letting the market take care of itself without government interference.

D. Both the economic theory and the legal theory are applied but not consistently.

Answer (D) is correct. *(Publisher, adapted)*

REQUIRED: The best statement about the policy in the U.S. with respect to antitrust.

DISCUSSION: There are two major theories with respect to antitrust and anticompetitive behavior. The legal theory is that large size alone is not illegal. Illegality occurs through abuse of market power. The economic theory is that heavy concentration of economic power or market dominance is bad and therefore should be illegal. Both theories have been applied but not consistently.

Answer (A) is incorrect. The economic theory is that large concentration of economic power or market dominance is illegal. Answer (B) is incorrect. The legal theory is that large size alone without abusing market power is not illegal. Answer (C) is incorrect. The doctrine of laissez-faire is that competition is best protected by letting the market take care of itself without government interference. It is inconsistent with the antitrust laws enacted beginning in the late 1800s.

2. The intent of antitrust laws is to

A. Establish a range of allowable profit rates for firms in oligopolistic industries.

B. Prohibit firms from engaging in joint ventures with foreign firms.

C. Require firms with high earnings to relinquish any exclusive patent rights they own.

D. Prohibit agreements that limit individual firm output.

Answer (D) is correct. *(CMA, adapted)*

REQUIRED: The intent of antitrust laws.

DISCUSSION: Antitrust laws are designed to promote more efficient allocation of resources, greater choice for consumers, greater business opportunities, fairness in economic behavior, and avoidance of concentrated political power resulting from economic power. Competition results in greater output and lower prices than other market structures.

Answer (A) is incorrect. Profits and prices are not set by antitrust laws other than to the extent that price discrimination is prohibited. Answer (B) is incorrect. Firms may enter into joint ventures with foreign firms. Answer (C) is incorrect. Patents are available to all inventors, regardless of size.

3. For the federal antitrust laws to apply, the illegal activity must affect goods moving in interstate commerce or

A. Be committed by a business engaged in interstate commerce.

B. Affect a business engaged in interstate commerce.

C. Adversely affect the price of goods sold in interstate commerce.

D. Have a significant effect on interstate commerce.

Answer (D) is correct. *(Publisher, adapted)*

REQUIRED: The interstate commerce requirement for jurisdiction.

DISCUSSION: Congress has the power to regulate interstate commerce. The antitrust laws apply to activity that either restrains commerce interstate in character itself or has a substantial effect on interstate commerce. In the latter case, it is enough if interstate commerce is indirectly affected by solely intrastate activity.

Answer (A) is incorrect. Trade restrictions can have a significant effect on interstate commerce regardless of whether the business committing the violation is in interstate commerce. Answer (B) is incorrect. Trade restrictions can have a significant effect on interstate commerce regardless of whether the business directly affected is in interstate commerce. Answer (C) is incorrect. If interstate commerce is significantly affected, a trade restriction is illegal regardless of whether it has an adverse or beneficial impact.

4. Wanton Corporation, its president, and several other officers of the corporation have been found guilty of conspiring with its major competitor to fix prices. Which of the following sanctions would not be applicable under federal antitrust laws?

A. Suspension of the corporate right to engage in interstate commerce for not more than 1 year.

B. Treble damages.

C. Seizure of Wanton's property illegally shipped in interstate commerce.

D. Fines against Wanton and fines and imprisonment of its president and officers.

Answer (A) is correct. *(CPA, adapted)*

REQUIRED: The sanction not applicable under federal antitrust laws for price fixing.

DISCUSSION: The Justice Department and the FTC are the primary but not sole enforcers of antitrust laws. Some remedies and sanctions for antitrust violations include the following: (1) court injunctions, forfeitures (seizures of property transported in interstate commerce), and forced divestitures that may result from actions by either the public or the government; (2) cease and desist orders issued by the FTC; (3) treble (triple) damages recovered by private parties; and (4) criminal penalties, including fines and prison sentences, assessed by the government. The sanctions available to the Justice Department and individuals for violation of antitrust laws do not include suspension of a corporation's right to engage in interstate commerce.

Answer (B) is incorrect. It is a current sanction applicable under federal antitrust laws for price fixing. A corporate defendant is subject to a maximum fine of $10 million per violation. Any other defendant is subject to a maximum fine of $350,000, imprisonment for as much as 3 years, or both, for each offense, and injunctions against further wrongful acts. Answer (C) is incorrect. The sanctions available to the Justice Department and individuals for violation of antitrust laws do not include suspension of a corporation's right to engage in interstate commerce. Answer (D) is incorrect. The sanctions available to the Justice Department and individuals for violation of antitrust laws do not include suspension of a corporation's right to engage in interstate commerce.

5. With respect to federal antitrust laws, regulated industries are

A. Completely exempt.

B. Covered as determined by statute and the courts.

C. Covered as determined by the Department of Justice.

D. Covered to the same extent as any other industry.

Answer (B) is correct. *(CMA, adapted)*

REQUIRED: The true statement about regulated industries.

DISCUSSION: With respect to antitrust laws, regulated industries are covered unless specifically exempted by statute or the courts. For example, regulated public utilities are specifically exempted because they are viewed as natural monopolies.

Answer (A) is incorrect. Some regulated industries are subject to antitrust laws. Answer (C) is incorrect. The Justice Department must look to statute or the courts to enforce antitrust laws. Answer (D) is incorrect. Some regulated industries, such as utilities, are exempt from antitrust laws.

6. Which of the following is a true statement regarding enforcement of the antitrust laws?

A. Any person whose business or property is injured as a direct result of violation of antitrust laws may sue.

B. A consumer may sue for a violation of the antitrust laws regardless of whether (s)he purchased directly from the person violating the antitrust laws.

C. The U.S. Justice Department may enforce all federal antitrust laws except the Federal Trade Commission Act.

D. The Federal Trade Commission may enforce only the Federal Trade Commission Act.

Answer (A) is correct. *(Publisher, adapted)*

REQUIRED: The true statement about who enforces the antitrust laws.

DISCUSSION: The Justice Department and the Federal Trade Commission are the primary government enforcers of the antitrust laws. But any private person (including individuals, corporations, etc.) whose business or property is injured as a direct result of a violation of antitrust laws may sue the violator. The private person also can recover treble damages under most statutes.

Answer (B) is incorrect. The consumer may sue for a violation of the antitrust laws only if (s)he purchased a product or service directly from the person who violated the antitrust laws. There must be a direct connection. Answer (C) is incorrect. The U.S. Justice Department may enforce all the antitrust laws. Answer (D) is incorrect. The Federal Trade Commission may enforce all antitrust laws except the Sherman Act.

36.2 Sherman Act, Section One – Restraints of Trade

7. Resale price maintenance is an example of

A. Horizontal price fixing.

B. Vertical price fixing.

C. Preemptive buying.

D. Tying arrangements.

Answer (B) is correct. *(CMA, adapted)*

REQUIRED: The true statement about resale price maintenance.

DISCUSSION: Resale price maintenance agreements are a form of vertical price fixing because a manufacturer or wholesaler restricts the price that may be charged by a retailer. Such agreements are analyzed under the rule of reason.

Answer (A) is incorrect. Horizontal price fixing occurs between two competitors at the same level in the distribution process (e.g., between two retailers in the same industry). Answer (C) is incorrect. Preemptive buying is not associated with resale price maintenance. Answer (D) is incorrect. Tying arrangements require a buyer to purchase other products in addition to the one that is desired.

8. The term "illegal per se" as it is frequently used in antitrust law

A. Applies exclusively to illegal price fixing and other related activities by competitors.

B. Must be established by the Justice Department to impose criminal sanctions under the Federal Trade Commission Act.

C. Represents anticompetitive conduct or agreements that are inherently illegal and without legal justification.

D. Applies exclusively to illegal anticompetitive activities by competitors.

Answer (C) is correct. *(CPA, adapted)*

REQUIRED: The meaning of the term "illegal per se."

DISCUSSION: "Illegal per se" means an action is conclusively presumed to be unreasonable and illegal without inquiry as to the harm caused or any business excuse. Agreements that are determined to be illegal per se are those that are so harmful to competition as to be deemed illegal without further inquiry.

Answer (A) is incorrect. Many types of agreements besides price fixing are illegal per se. Answer (B) is incorrect. Certain activities have already been determined to be illegal per se without action by the Justice Department. They are illegal under various acts, especially the Sherman Act. Answer (D) is incorrect. Certain anticompetitive activities between buyers and sellers (vertical) are also per se illegal.

9. The Sherman Antitrust Act

A. Established the Federal Trade Commission.

B. Prohibits collective boycotts.

C. Prohibits price discrimination.

D. Established the concept of a patent.

Answer (B) is correct. *(CMA, adapted)*

REQUIRED: The true statement about the Sherman Antitrust Act.

DISCUSSION: The Sherman Act of 1890 makes illegal every contract, combination, or conspiracy in restraint of trade in interstate or foreign commerce. Some types of arrangements between competitors are to be considered unreasonable without inquiry. These are known as per se violations. Price fixing, division of markets, group boycotts, and resale price maintenance are per se violations.

Answer (A) is incorrect. The FTC was established by the Federal Trade Commission Act of 1914. Answer (C) is incorrect. Price discrimination is prohibited by the Robinson-Patman Act of 1936, which was an amendment to the Clayton Act of 1914. Answer (D) is incorrect. Patent laws were in effect long before the Sherman Act of 1890. Thus, the U.S. Constitution (Article I, Section 8) grants to Congress the power "to promote the progress of science and useful arts, by securing for limited times to authors and investors the exclusive right to their respective writings and discoveries."

10. What pricing agreement among competitors is legal?

A. An agreement aimed at lowering prices.

B. An agreement aimed at eliminating cutthroat competition by stabilizing prices.

C. An agreement that seeks to fix prices reasonably and fairly for the consumers' benefit.

D. None. Competitors are forbidden to enter into agreements that determine the price of the product they sell.

Answer (D) is correct. *(CPA, adapted)*

REQUIRED: The pricing agreement among competitors that is legal.

DISCUSSION: No pricing agreements among competitors are legal because the antitrust laws forbid competitors to agree on the price of the products they sell.

Answer (A) is incorrect. A pricing agreement among competitors, even if aimed at lowering prices, is illegal per se. It is assumed that such an agreement over the long run will substantially lessen competition. Answer (B) is incorrect. Pricing agreements aimed at eliminating cutthroat competition and stabilizing prices are also illegal. Answer (C) is incorrect. It is presumed that even reasonable and fair agreements that fix prices will lessen competition.

11. Which one of the following examples of corporate behavior most clearly represents a violation of the Sherman Act?

A. A retailer offers quantity discounts to large institutional buyers.

B. The members of a labor union meet and agree not to work for a specific firm unless the starting wage is at least $10 per hour.

C. Two firms that are in different, unrelated industries merge.

D. Two firms in the same industry agree in a telephone conversation to submit identical bids on a government contract.

Answer (D) is correct. *(CMA, adapted)*

REQUIRED: The item that most clearly represents a violation of the Sherman Act.

DISCUSSION: The Sherman Act of 1890 makes illegal every contract, combination, or conspiracy in restraint of trade in interstate or foreign commerce. Some types of arrangements, called per se violations, are considered unreasonable without inquiry. These violations include price fixing, division of markets, group boycotts, and resale price maintenance. Agreeing to submit identical bids on a government contract is a form of price fixing, a per se violation.

Answer (A) is incorrect. Quantity discounts are not prohibited by the Sherman Act. Answer (B) is incorrect. The Sherman Act does not apply to labor unions. Answer (C) is incorrect. The Sherman Act does not prohibit mergers; only those that could lead to restraint of trade are outlawed.

12. Which one of the following statements regarding the application of antitrust rules to professional fees is true?

A. Most professionals, including physicians, lawyers, engineers, and accountants, are exempt from the antitrust laws.

B. Agreements to increase fees are legal if the quality of services provided improves.

C. Fee discrimination in any form is illegal.

D. Agreements to set either minimum or maximum fees are illegal.

Answer (D) is correct. *(CMA, adapted)*

REQUIRED: The true statement about the application of antitrust laws to professional fees.

DISCUSSION: In general, professionals (such as lawyers and public accountants) cannot make agreements that provide for either minimum or maximum fees because price fixing by collusion among competitors is a per se violation of the Sherman Act.

Answer (A) is incorrect. Professionals and their organizations are not exempt from the antitrust laws. Answer (B) is incorrect. Agreements among competitors to increase fees are illegal per se. Answer (C) is incorrect. Fee discrimination is not illegal per se. For example, a professional might properly charge a lower price if a service is to be performed during a normally slow period.

13. Dick Grubar's appliance sales constitute less than .001% of the market. The marketplace has an abundance of retailers, and competition is vigorous. The manufacturers and the retailers dislike Grubar's price cutting. They jointly decided to boycott Grubar to limit his access to appliances and to drive him out of business. Grubar has commenced legal action against the various parties based upon a violation of the Sherman Act. He is seeking injunctive relief and damages. Under the circumstances,

A. Grubar is entitled to the relief requested because the facts indicate a per se violation.

B. Grubar's complaint should be dismissed because it alleges only a private wrong as opposed to a public wrong.

C. Grubar is entitled to the relief requested against the interstate commerce manufacturers, but not the intrastate retailers.

D. Grubar is not entitled to injunctive relief. Only the Department of Justice is entitled to such relief.

Answer (A) is correct. *(CPA, adapted)*

REQUIRED: The result of the legal action by someone who has been subject to a group boycott.

DISCUSSION: The manufacturers and retailers jointly boycotted Grubar, which is per se illegal under the Sherman Act. Thus, Grubar will be entitled to the relief requested. That Grubar's sales constitute less than .001% of the market makes no difference.

Answer (B) is incorrect. The antitrust laws are public laws, not private laws. Also, injunctive relief under the circumstances should be available regardless of whether it was a private or a public wrong. Answer (C) is incorrect. The intrastate retailers are also subject to antitrust laws if, as a group, they affect interstate commerce. Answer (D) is incorrect. The Sherman Act may be enforced by individuals as well as the Department of Justice. Either can obtain an injunction. Individuals are also entitled to treble damages.

14. The Flick Corp. manufactured almost exclusively a gizmo that was sold throughout the United States. Flick required all purchasers to take at least two other Flick products to obtain the gizmo over which it has almost complete market control. As a result of this plan, gross sales of the other items increased by an amount that was a substantial portion of the total market for those items. Which of the following best describes the legality of the above situation?

A. It is illegal only if the products are patented products.

B. It is an illegal tying arrangement.

C. It is legal as long as the price charged to retailers for the other products is competitive.

D. It is legal if the retailers do not complain about purchasing the other products.

Answer (B) is correct. *(CPA, adapted)*

REQUIRED: The legality of requiring customers to purchase two other products in addition to the product they wish to order.

DISCUSSION: A seller's requiring a buyer to take one or more other products to receive the desired product is a tying arrangement. It is illegal if the seller has sufficient economic power in the market for the tying product, and a substantial amount of commerce in the tied product is affected. Because the results of this plan increased gross sales by an amount that was a substantial portion of the total market for the tied products, and the seller controls the market for the tying product, Flick's requirement is an illegal tying arrangement.

Answer (A) is incorrect. The described activity is illegal no matter what products are involved due to the substantial amount involved. Answer (C) is incorrect. A tying arrangement is illegal due to the substantial amount involved, even if the prices charged to retailers for the other products are competitive. Answer (D) is incorrect. Tying arrangements are illegal if they have a substantial impact on commerce, regardless of whether complaints are filed by the retailers.

36.3 Sherman Act, Section Two – Monopolies

15. The Duplex Corporation has been charged by the U.S. Justice Department with an "attempt to monopolize" the duplex industry. In defending itself against such a charge, Duplex will prevail if it can establish that

A. It had no intent to monopolize the duplex industry.

B. Its percentage share of the relevant market was less than 50%.

C. Its activities do not constitute an unreasonable restraint of trade.

D. It does not have monopoly power.

Answer (A) is correct. *(CPA, adapted)*

REQUIRED: The valid defense to "an attempt to monopolize" charge.

DISCUSSION: The Sherman Act prohibits contracts, combinations, or conspiracies in restraint of trade in addition to the formation of monopolies and attempts to monopolize. Because the Sherman Act provides for criminal sanctions, the Justice Department must prove that the defendant specifically intended the illegal act of an "attempt to monopolize." If a defendant can show no intent to monopolize, the government will not prevail.

Answer (B) is incorrect. No set percentage of the relevant market need be proven as an element of an attempt to monopolize. Answer (C) is incorrect. The rule-of-reason defense does not apply to a charge of an attempt to monopolize. Answer (D) is incorrect. Actual monopoly power is not an element of an attempt to monopolize.

16. The U.S. Department of Justice has alleged that Variable Resources, Inc., the largest manufacturer and seller of variable-speed drive motors, is a monopolist. It is seeking an injunction ordering divestiture by Variable of a significant portion of its manufacturing facilities. Variable denies it has monopolized the variable-speed drive motor market. Which of the following is true?

A. The government must prove that Variable is the sole source of a significant portion of the market.

B. To establish monopolization, the government must prove that Variable has at least 70% of the market.

C. If Variable has the power to control prices or exclude competition, it has a monopoly.

D. Unless Variable has been a party to a contract, combination, or conspiracy in restraint of trade, it is not guilty of monopolization.

Answer (C) is correct. *(CPA, adapted)*

REQUIRED: The true statement about whether a monopoly has been established.

DISCUSSION: The purpose of antitrust laws is to preserve and promote competition. The working definition of monopoly in antitrust law is that the defendant has the power to control prices or exclude competition. Under the Sherman Act, formation of, or the attempt to form, a monopoly is illegal.

Answer (A) is incorrect. Many cases have held that 60% or less of the market constitutes monopolistic power. Answer (B) is incorrect. The government need not prove a particular percentage of the market to establish that an illegal monopoly or attempt to monopolize has occurred. However, a percentage share of the market is an important determining factor in monopoly cases. Answer (D) is incorrect. The Sherman Act prohibits monopolies and attempts to monopolize, that is, actions by a single firm, in addition to contracts, combinations, and conspiracies that restrain trade.

17. Gritney, Inc., manufactures and sells foibles in competition with about four other firms in the United States. It sells about 90% of the foibles sold in the Midwest, but only about 10% nationally. Gritney will probably be found

A. To have monopoly power, if the relevant market is determined to be the Midwest.

B. Guilty of monopolization regardless of the relevant market.

C. Guilty of monopolization if it has not evidenced an intent to monopolize even if it has engaged in predatory practices.

D. Guilty of monopolization if the only reason for its market share is that competitors left due to lack of sales.

Answer (A) is correct. *(Publisher, adapted)*

REQUIRED: The result of an action against a firm for monopolization.

DISCUSSION: In determining monopoly power, an important determinant is the relevant market, consisting of the relevant product market and the relevant geographic market. If the relevant market is determined to be the Midwest, Gritney has 90% of the market, which is usually considered to be monopoly power. Monopoly power alone does not make a firm guilty of violating antitrust laws. Therefore, this is the best answer choice.

Answer (B) is incorrect. If the relevant market is the entire United States, Gritney has only 10% of the market. Even if there are few competitors, 10% is not usually considered monopoly power even in an oligopoly. Answer (C) is incorrect. The courts have found a business liable regardless of intent to monopolize if monopoly power exists and if predatory practices accompany the firm's growth to monopoly power. Predatory pricing is proof of intent to monopolize. Answer (D) is incorrect. No intent to monopolize can be found if a monopoly is thrust upon a firm, with no intent to monopolize and no predatory practices by the firm.

36.4 Clayton Act

18. The Clayton Act, as amended, prohibits all of the following except

A. Price discrimination by sellers.

B. Interlocking directorates in large competing organizations.

C. Unfair and deceptive business practices, such as misleading advertising.

D. A merger of companies that substantially lessens competition.

Answer (C) is correct. *(CMA, adapted)*

REQUIRED: The item not prohibited by the Clayton Act.

DISCUSSION: The Clayton Act of 1914 prohibits (1) mergers that may lessen competition or tend to create a monopoly, (2) sales that prevent the buyer from dealing with the seller's competitors, (3) tie-in sales (requiring a buyer to take other products in order to buy the first product), (4) price discrimination, and (5) interlocking directorates. The Federal Trade Commission Act addresses unfair and deceptive business practices such as false advertising.

Answer (A) is incorrect. The Clayton Act prohibits price discrimination by sellers. Answer (B) is incorrect. The Clayton Act prohibits interlocking directorates in large competing organizations. Answer (D) is incorrect. The Clayton Act prohibits a merger of companies that substantially lessens competition.

19. Government Business Machines (GBM) has greater than an 80% share of the sales of computers to local and state governments. GBM requires all purchasers of its computers also to purchase its proprietary operating system, called GOS. Furthermore, GBM government contracts require all application software and peripherals to be purchased from GBM. Which of the following is a true statement about this tying arrangement?

A. The test of whether a tying arrangement is illegal is essentially the same as for exclusive dealing.

B. The test of whether a tying arrangement is illegal is essentially the same under the Sherman Act and the Clayton Act.

C. It is not illegal under the Clayton Act because it is an agreement to restrain trade, which is not covered by the Clayton Act.

D. It is not illegal if the tied goods are not sold by the offeror of the desired goods.

Answer (B) is correct. *(Publisher, adapted)*

REQUIRED: The true statement about a tying arrangement.

DISCUSSION: A tying arrangement is a form of exclusive dealing and therefore is subject to the Clayton Act. It occurs when a supplier requires a buyer to purchase one or more additional goods to obtain the desired good. It will be found illegal under the Clayton Act if its effect may be substantially to lessen competition or tend to create a monopoly. It will be found illegal under the Sherman Act if it constitutes a contract, combination, or conspiracy in restraint of trade whose character or effect is unreasonably anticompetitive. Under both acts, the arrangement must affect more than an insubstantial amount of commerce in the tied product, and the supplier must have sufficient economic power in the market for the tying product. A limitation of the Clayton Act's provision regarding exclusive dealing (and therefore tying arrangements) is that it applies only to goods (tangible personal property). However, a sale of hardware and mass-produced software (e.g., the GOS operating system) is usually treated as a sale of goods. The sale of custom-designed software is deemed to be a sale of services.

Answer (A) is incorrect. Tying arrangements are generally described by courts as per se violations once the required tests are met. Exclusive dealing arrangements are judged more under the rule of reason, i.e., using both qualitative and quantitative tests. Answer (C) is incorrect. The Clayton Act prohibits activity that tends substantially to lessen competition. Answer (D) is incorrect. The arrangement may still be illegal. For example, the supplier may manufacture the tied goods to be sold by someone else.

20. A franchisor's requirement that its franchisees buy inputs from a particular supplier is

A. Illegal according to the provisions of the Robinson-Patman Act.

B. Illegal according to the principles of common law.

C. Legal, but the franchisor must receive approval from the Federal Trade Commission.

D. Legal as long as such a requirement is necessary to assure product quality.

Answer (D) is correct. *(CMA, adapted)*

REQUIRED: The true statement about a franchisor's requirement that franchisees buy inputs from a particular supplier.

DISCUSSION: The Clayton Act of 1914 prohibits exclusive-dealing requirements. However, a franchise relationship is contractual, and the agreement is in force for a specified period. Because the franchisee and the franchisor have a common public identity, an exclusive-dealing contract is allowable if it is necessary to assure product quality. Without the exclusive-dealing requirement, a low-quality product sold by the franchisee could reflect badly on the reputation of the franchisor. Under the act, this type of intrabrand restriction is considered to promote interbrand competition, thus having a net positive effect on competition.

Answer (A) is incorrect. The Robinson-Patman Act concerns price discrimination, not exclusive-dealing contracts. Answer (B) is incorrect. Exclusive-dealing contracts are the subject of federal antitrust law. They are not illegal under common law. Answer (C) is incorrect. There is no requirement to seek approval from the FTC.

21. The Clayton Act of 1914 prohibits

A. Closed-shop labor unions.

B. Sellers' price discrimination.

C. Group boycotts.

D. Oligopolies.

Answer (B) is correct. *(CMA, adapted)*

REQUIRED: The prohibition by the Clayton Act.

DISCUSSION: The Clayton Act of 1914 prohibits price discrimination if it directly or indirectly lessens competition such that it tends to create a monopoly. The Robinson-Patman Act amended the Clayton Act to prohibit sellers of goods from granting, and buyers from inducing, unfair discounts and other preferences. However, price differentials are justified by a cost savings to the seller or a good faith effort to meet, but not undercut, the lawful price of a competitor.

Answer (A) is incorrect. The closed shop was prohibited by the Taft-Hartley Act of 1947. Answer (C) is incorrect. Group boycotts were prohibited by the Sherman Act of 1890. Answer (D) is incorrect. Oligopolies are not prohibited by the Clayton Act.

22. The difference between exclusive dealing arrangements and reciprocal dealing arrangements is that

A. Exclusive dealing and reciprocal dealing are per se illegal.

B. Exclusive dealing is per se illegal, and reciprocal dealing is judged under the rule of reason.

C. Reciprocal dealing is only a violation of the Sherman Act, and exclusive dealing is only a violation of the Clayton Act.

D. In reciprocal dealing, a purchaser requires the seller to buy its product also; in exclusive dealing, a seller requires that a buyer not carry products of the seller's competitors.

Answer (D) is correct. *(Publisher, adapted)*

REQUIRED: The difference between exclusive and reciprocal dealing arrangements.

DISCUSSION: Reciprocal dealing occurs when one company uses its purchasing power to require the company from whom it purchases to buy its products. Opportunities for such reciprocity often arise in conglomerate mergers. Exclusive dealing occurs when a supplier conditions its sales such that the buyer will not use or deal in goods of the seller's competitors. As vertical restraints of trade, exclusive dealing arrangements are analyzed under the rule of reason. Reciprocal dealing arrangements are analyzed under per se analysis.

Answer (A) is incorrect. Exclusive dealing is analyzed under the rule of reason. Answer (B) is incorrect. Reciprocal dealing is illegal per se. Answer (C) is incorrect. Both violate the Sherman Act and the Clayton Act. The Sherman Act requires that a substantial volume be affected and applies to a broad range of commercial activity. The Clayton Act applies only to the lease or sale of goods, merchandise, machinery, supplies, and other commodities, but it also requires proof of only a tendency to lessen competition.

23. Section 7 of the Clayton Act is the primary statutory provision used by the Department of Justice in controlling anticompetitive mergers and acquisitions. In general, the Clayton Act is invoked because

A. It provides for harsher criminal penalties than does the Sherman Act.

B. It enables the Department of Justice to proscribe mergers and acquisitions in their incipiency.

C. It provides for exclusive jurisdiction over such activities.

D. The Sherman Act applies to asset mergers or acquisitions only, not to stock mergers or acquisitions.

Answer (B) is correct. *(CPA, adapted)*

REQUIRED: The reason the Clayton Act is used in controlling mergers and acquisitions.

DISCUSSION: The Clayton Act prohibits acquisition of stock or assets of another corporation if the effect may be to lessen competition substantially or tend to produce a monopoly. The Department of Justice may attack mergers and acquisitions in their incipiency rather than waiting for the merger or acquisition to occur and then having to prove that it has had the harmful effect.

Answer (A) is incorrect. Criminal penalties are provided for under the Sherman Act, not the Clayton Act. Answer (C) is incorrect. The Sherman Act, the Federal Trade Commission Act and the Clayton Act may all be applicable with respect to mergers and acquisitions. Answer (D) is incorrect. The Sherman Act applies to any situation in which a monopoly exists or there is an attempt to monopolize, regardless of the method of acquisition.

24. Expansion Corp. is seeking to obtain control of Resistance Corp. Expansion does not currently buy from, sell to, or compete with Resistance. Which of the following statements applies?

A. Given that Expansion does not buy from, sell to, or compete with Resistance, antitrust laws do not apply.

B. If Expansion can consummate the acquisition before there is objection to it, the acquisition cannot be set aside.

C. The acquisition is likely to be declared illegal if there will be reciprocal buying and there is a likelihood that other entrants into the market would be precluded.

D. The acquisition is legal on its face if cost efficiency will result from combined marketing and advertising.

Answer (C) is correct. *(CPA, adapted)*

REQUIRED: The statement applicable to a proposed takeover of a corporation.

DISCUSSION: The Clayton Act of 1914, as amended, supplemented the Sherman Act to prohibit a corporation from acquiring the stock or assets of another corporation (merger) if the effect might be to lessen competition substantially or tend to create a monopoly. If, after the acquisition, there is to be reciprocal buying that produces a likelihood that entry of other firms into the market would be precluded, the acquisition is likely to be declared illegal as a lessening of competition.

Answer (A) is incorrect. Conglomerate mergers are prohibited if they will substantially lessen competition. Answer (B) is incorrect. Both the government and private individuals can take action subsequent to a merger. Answer (D) is incorrect. Cost efficiencies resulting from combined marketing and advertising do not justify a merger if there is a substantial lessening of competition.

25. In contesting the validity of a previously consummated vertical merger,

A. The Justice Department must proceed within 5 years of the consummation of the merger.

B. That the acquiring corporation deliberately failed to apply for a ruling is presumptive evidence of bad faith.

C. The Justice Department must show the likelihood that competition may be foreclosed in a substantial share of that market.

D. Only a showing of actual substantial lessening of competition will be sufficient to establish illegality.

Answer (C) is correct. *(CPA, adapted)*

REQUIRED: The requirements to contest a vertical merger that has already occurred.

DISCUSSION: A vertical merger is between buyers and sellers, as opposed to competitors (called horizontal mergers). It will be attacked if entry of other firms into the market thereby becomes more difficult, or if it would make the company disproportionately large compared with competitors. A horizontal merger is presumed illegal if it results in a high level of market power for the merged firm.

Answer (A) is incorrect. No time limit has been set to contest the validity of a vertical merger. The Sherman Act makes monopolization (at any time) illegal. Answer (B) is incorrect. No application for rulings is required for mergers. The merging corporations must notify the Justice Department and the FTC. Answer (D) is incorrect. Increased barriers to market entry as well as actual substantial lessening of the competition will make the merger illegal.

26. In a pure conglomerate merger,

A. The government must establish an actual restraint on competition in the marketplace in order to prevent the merger.

B. The acquiring corporation neither competes with, nor sells to/buys from, the acquired corporation.

C. The merger is prima facie valid unless the government can prove the acquiring corporation had an intent to monopolize.

D. Some form of additional anticompetitive behavior must be established (e.g., price fixing) to provide the basis for the government's obtaining of injunctive relief.

Answer (B) is correct. *(CPA, adapted)*

REQUIRED: The true statement about a pure conglomerate merger.

DISCUSSION: A conglomerate merger is neither a horizontal nor a vertical merger. The corporations neither compete with each other nor sell to/buy from each other. This usually means they are in different industries.

Answer (A) is incorrect. An actual restraint on competition need not be proven. If one of the firms might have been a likely entrant to the marketplace, the merger might be prevented based on a substantial lessening of competition. Answer (C) is incorrect. The Clayton Act requires only a substantial lessening of competition, not an intent to monopolize. Answer (D) is incorrect. Additional anticompetitive behavior such as price fixing is sometimes needed under the Sherman Act. Under the Clayton Act, substantial lessening of competition alone suffices.

27. Which of the following actions, if potentially anticompetitive, is least likely to be a violation of the antitrust laws?

A. The merger of a financially sound corporation with a competitor in a failing condition.

B. The acquisition of substantially all of the assets of a competing corporation.

C. The acquisition of a controlling stock interest in a directly competing corporation.

D. A horizontal merger of competing corporations.

Answer (A) is correct. *(Publisher, adapted)*

REQUIRED: The fundamental corporate change least likely involving an antitrust violation.

DISCUSSION: The Clayton Act, as amended, prohibits the acquisition of a controlling stock interest, the acquisition of a controlling stock interest, the acquisition of substantially all the assets, and the merger of competing corporations if the effect may be to lessen competition substantially. However, an exception has been provided by the courts for mergers and acquisitions to save a failing corporation. The most important defense available under Section 7 of the Clayton Act is the failing company doctrine. It applies when (1) the acquiree is in failing condition, (2) the possibility of reorganization is extremely low, and (3) no other acquirer would have a less anticompetitive effect.

Answer (B) is incorrect. The acquisition of substantially all of the assets of a competing corporation is a potential violation. Answer (C) is incorrect. The acquisition of a controlling stock interest in a directly competing corporation is a potential violation. Answer (D) is incorrect. A horizontal merger of competing corporations is a potential violation.

28. Gould Machinery builds bulldozers. Prior to this year, it sold a substantial amount of equipment to Mace Contractors on credit. Mace recently went into bankruptcy. To protect its investment, Gould took over Mace. Erhart Contractors now complains that the acquisition harms its business, alleging that its business would have improved had Gould not entered the market as a competitor. Erhart can

A. Not recover damages under the antitrust laws.

B. Recover treble damages.

C. Recover only its actual damages.

D. Obtain injunctive relief ordering divestiture.

Answer (A) is correct. *(CPA, adapted)*

REQUIRED: The true statement about a creditor's acquisition of a debtor's business.

DISCUSSION: Acquisition of a contractor by a machinery manufacturer could result in a substantial lessening of competition. However, the failing company doctrine provides that a merger that may reduce competition is allowable if the company acquired is failing and there is no other purchaser whose acquisition of the company would reduce competition less. Gould might also defend under the rule of reason by showing the acquisition was for the purpose of furthering a legitimate business interest (protecting its investment and assuring the continuation of a valuable outlet for its equipment) rather than to reduce competition.

Answer (B) is incorrect. A private claimant under the antitrust laws can recover treble damages, but only if it is able to show that antitrust violations have occurred. Answer (C) is incorrect. The plaintiff cannot recover any damages if no violation occurred. Answer (D) is incorrect. A private person may obtain only preliminary injunctive relief. Divestiture is a Justice Department remedy.

29. The U.S. Justice Department and the FTC have jointly promulgated the Horizontal Merger Guidelines to inform the public of their views on the factors and considerations to be taken into account in ascertaining whether a merger is potentially illegal. The guidelines are

A. Strongly influenced by the factor of size, that is, of percentage shares of the market of the parties to the proposed merger.

B. Based exclusively upon the decisions of the U.S. Supreme Court.

C. Binding on all parties affected by them subsequent to the date of their promulgation.

D. Not of great importance because they are too indefinite and uncertain to have any meaning in respect to an actual merger.

Answer (A) is correct. *(CPA, adapted)*

REQUIRED: The true statement about the Horizontal Merger Guidelines.

DISCUSSION: The Horizontal Merger Guidelines are strongly influenced by the factor of size as reflected in the existing market shares of the merging firms and the relative concentration in the market after the merger as determined by an index. However, nonmarket share factors are also considered, such as barriers to entry, whether one of the firms is a leader in the market, the nature of the product, market performance, and other factors.

Answer (B) is incorrect. The guidelines are based on decisions of the Supreme Court as well as on policy formulated within the Justice Department's Antitrust Division, and the FTC. Answer (C) is incorrect. They are not binding law but merely guidelines to forewarn the public of the current views of the Justice Department and the FTC with respect to mergers. Answer (D) is incorrect. The guidelines provide definite standards for an actual merger.

30. Glick, Inc. and Yeats Corp. are large manufacturers of goods that are in substantial competition throughout the United States. Each has capital, surplus, and undivided profits aggregating more than $26,867,000. Over a 6-year period, Yeats acquired 46% of the outstanding stock of Glick. Yeats's current directors own stock in both corporations and are on the board of directors of each. Which of the following statements applies to the above situation?

A. Nothing in these facts would constitute a violation of the federal antitrust laws.

B. The interlocking directorate is not illegal because less than 50% of the Glick stock is owned by Yeats.

C. The interlocking directorate is a clear violation of federal antitrust laws.

D. No violation of the federal antitrust laws exists unless there is improvement in the competitive position of Yeats or Glick.

Answer (C) is correct. *(CPA, adapted)*

REQUIRED: The true statement about stock ownership and interlocking directorates of competitors.

DISCUSSION: Section 8 of the Clayton Act prohibits interlocking directorates. Consequently, a person may not be a member of the board of directors of two or more competing corporations. Section 8 is applicable under the following conditions: (1) the firms are engaged in interstate or foreign commerce; (2) each has combined capital, surplus, and undivided profits totaling more than $26,867,000; (3) the elimination of competition by agreement between the firms would amount to a violation of any of the antitrust laws; and (4) no grace period or de minimis exception applies. However, simultaneous service is not illegal if (1) competitive sales of either firm are less than $2,686,200, (2) competitive sales are less than 2% of either firm's total sales, or (3) competitive sales of each firm are less than 4% of that firm's total sales.

Answer (A) is incorrect. The interlocking directorates violate the antitrust laws if the firms compete significantly in a line of business that is important to overall operations. Answer (B) is incorrect. Interlocking directorates are illegal regardless of stock ownership. Answer (D) is incorrect. An interlocking directorate violates antitrust laws even if there has been no marked improvement in the competitive position.

31. The Justice Department and the FTC use the Herfindahl-Hirschman Index to calculate market concentration data. They are most likely to challenge a merger if the postmerger HHI is

A. 800

B. 1,500

C. 1,800

D. 2,600

Answer (D) is correct. *(Publisher, adapted)*

REQUIRED: The HHI data most likely to result in challenge to a merger.

DISCUSSION: The HHI is found by summing the squares of the market shares of the firms in a market. For example, if each of five firms has a market share of 20%, the HHI is 2,000 ($20^2 + 20^2 + 20^2 + 20^2 + 20^2$). The Justice Department and the FTC are most likely to challenge a merger if the postmerger HHI is over 2,500.

Answer (A) is incorrect. A postmerger HHI of less than 1,500 is unlikely to result in a challenge. Answer (B) is incorrect. If the postmerger HHI is between 1,500 and 2,500, a challenge is more likely than if the HHI is below 1,500, but less likely than if it exceeds 2,500. Answer (C) is incorrect. If the HHI is between 1,500 and 2,500, the market is deemed to be moderately concentrated.

36.5 Robinson-Patman Act

32. Which one of the following laws prohibits price discrimination and other exclusionary practices that may give certain firms a competitive advantage over other firms in the same market?

A. Celler-Kefauver Act.

B. Federal Trade Commission Act.

C. Sherman Act.

D. Robinson-Patman Act.

Answer (D) is correct. *(CMA, adapted)*

REQUIRED: The law that prohibits price discrimination.

DISCUSSION: The Robinson-Patman Act of 1936 amended the Clayton Act with respect to price discrimination. Price discrimination by both buyers and sellers is prohibited in interstate commerce of goods of like grade and quality. The purpose of the act is to protect competition. However, price differentials are allowed if justified by a cost savings to the seller or a good-faith effort to meet a competitor's lawful price.

Answer (A) is incorrect. The Celler-Kefauver Act of 1950 prohibits the acquisition of the stock or assets of another business if the effect may be to lessen competition substantially or to create a monopoly. Answer (B) is incorrect. The Federal Trade Commission Act of 1914 prohibits unfair methods of competition in or affecting interstate commerce. It also created the Federal Trade Commission, which has authority to enforce the Clayton and Robinson-Patman Acts. The FTC also is authorized to proceed against unfair or deceptive acts or practices. Answer (C) is incorrect. The Sherman Act of 1890 makes illegal every contract, combination, or conspiracy that unreasonably restrains trade in interstate or foreign commerce. It also prohibits monopolization and attempts and conspiracies to monopolize.

33. Pratt Co. manufactures and sells clocks. Its best-selling item is a grandfather clock. Taylor Co. purchased 100 of the clocks from Pratt at $99 each. Taylor discovered that Stewart, one of its competitors, had purchased the same clock from Pratt at $94 per clock. In the event the issue is litigated,

A. Taylor has a presumption in its favor that it has been harmed by price discrimination.

B. Pratt will prevail if it can show it did not intend to harm Taylor.

C. Pratt will prevail if it can show that it sold the clocks at the lower price to all customers who had been doing business with it for 10 years or more.

D. Pratt will prevail if it can establish that Taylor could have dealt with several other clock companies.

Answer (A) is correct. *(CPA, adapted)*

REQUIRED: The probable outcome of litigation concerning price discrimination.

DISCUSSION: When a person files a complaint alleging price discrimination, the courts presume that competition has been harmed when the price discrimination involves competing purchasers from the same seller. Taylor has this presumption in its favor.

Answer (B) is incorrect. Intent is not an essential element of discriminatory pricing policies under the Robinson-Patman Act. Answer (C) is incorrect. Price differentials are allowed only if the defendant proves they are directly related to lower costs, are offered to meet lawful competition, or are responses to changing conditions. Answer (D) is incorrect. The availability of other companies with which the plaintiff could have dealt is not a defense.

34. Which one of the following transactions would be considered a violation of the Robinson-Patman Act?

A. The sale of goods of like quality at different prices to two different wholesalers, both of whom are located outside the United States.

B. The sale of goods of like quality within the United States at different prices based on cost differences related to the method of delivery.

C. The sale of goods of like quality within the United States at different prices to two different wholesalers; all parties are located within the same state.

D. The sale of goods of like quality within the United States but across state lines at different prices to two different wholesalers in the same geographic area.

Answer (D) is correct. *(CMA, adapted)*

REQUIRED: The transaction that would be in violation of the Robinson-Patman Act of 1936.

DISCUSSION: The Robinson-Patman Act of 1936, an amendment to the Clayton Act, outlaws price discrimination that would lead to restraint of trade. Both buyer and seller can be found guilty of price discrimination under the provisions of the Robinson-Patman Act. Price differentiation between customers is allowed if there is a difference in costs. For instance, quantity discounts are permitted if it can be shown that larger quantities can be shipped with a cost savings. Charging competing wholesalers different prices for similar goods would be a violation of the act.

Answer (A) is incorrect. The act does not apply to export sales. Answer (B) is incorrect. Cost differences related to delivery are a justification for charging different prices. Answer (C) is incorrect. The act applies only to sales in interstate commerce.

35. Super Sports, Inc., sells branded sporting goods and equipment throughout the United States. It sells to wholesalers, jobbers, and retailers who in turn sell the goods to their respective customers. The wholesalers and jobbers, who do not sell at retail, are charged lower prices than retailers but are required to purchase in larger quantities than retailers with the cost savings inherent in such purchases accounting for the lower prices. The retailers are all charged the same prices but receive discounts for quantity purchases based exclusively upon the cost savings resulting from such quantity purchases. Girard sues Super alleging an illegal price discrimination. Which defense will be most likely to prevail?

A. Girard does not have the right to sue under the Robinson-Patman Act.

B. The discounts are functional.

C. Super does not have the requisite intent to discriminate among its purchasers.

D. The prices Super charges are reasonable, and its profit margins are low.

Answer (B) is correct. *(CPA, adapted)*

REQUIRED: The best defense to a price discrimination charge.

DISCUSSION: The Robinson-Patman Act makes it unlawful for any seller engaged in interstate commerce to discriminate in price between purchasers of commodities of like grade and quality if the effect of such discrimination may be to lessen competition substantially or tend to produce a monopoly in any line of commerce. Price differentials are allowed if directly related to lower cost caused by production and sales in quantity, or if the buyers are in different markets so there is no injury to competition. These are called functional discounts because the buyers are differentiated by function, such as the wholesalers and jobbers who do not compete with the retailers in this question.

Answer (A) is incorrect. The retailer does have the right to have the price differential examined under the provisions of the Robinson-Patman Act. Answer (C) is incorrect. Intent is not a prerequisite to a price discrimination charge, so absence of intent is not a defense. Answer (D) is incorrect. The legislative purpose of the Robinson-Patman Act is to eliminate discriminatory pricing policies even if the prices charged are reasonable under the circumstances.

36. The Antitrust Improvements Act of 1976

A. Requires pre-approval from the Federal Trade Commission for interlocking directorates.

B. Prohibits price discrimination.

C. Requires notification prior to a merger.

D. Prohibits restraints of trade and monopoly.

Answer (C) is correct. *(CMA, adapted)*

REQUIRED: The provisions of the Antitrust Improvements Act of 1976.

DISCUSSION: The Antitrust Improvements Act of 1976 requires corporations with annual net revenues or total assets exceeding $131,900,000 for one corporation and $13,200,000 for the other to give advance notice to the Justice Department and the FTC of any acquisition.

Answer (A) is incorrect. The Clayton Act of 1914 prohibits interlocking directorates in competing companies. Answer (B) is incorrect. The Robinson-Patman Act of 1936 prohibits price discrimination. Answer (D) is incorrect. The Sherman Act of 1890 prohibits restraint of trade and monopoly.

37. Over the years, various groups and activities have been exempted from coverage by the U.S. antitrust laws. Which one of the following statements regarding such exemptions is true?

A. All sales and purchases of products by American firms outside of the U.S. are automatically exempt from coverage by the antitrust laws.

B. All resale price maintenance agreements between manufacturers and retailers selling the manufacturers' product brands are exempt from the federal antitrust laws.

C. Under certain conditions, a person who wishes to form an export trading company may obtain a certificate of antitrust immunity from the Commerce Department after concurrence by the Justice Department.

D. Water common carriers in foreign trade may enter into price fixing and market sharing treaties or agreements provided the agreements are ratified by the U.S. Senate before being put into effect.

Answer (C) is correct. *(CMA, adapted)*

REQUIRED: The true statement regarding exemption from U.S. antitrust laws.

DISCUSSION: The various exemptions from antitrust laws include intrastate commerce, labor unions, regulated utilities, patents, copyrights, and reasonable noncompetition clauses between buyers and sellers of businesses, partners in a partnership, and purchasers of technology or equipment. Agricultural and fishing organizations, financial institutions, broadcasting, transportation industries, and professional baseball also have varying levels of exemption. Moreover, in 1982, Congress enacted the Export Trading Company Act. The purpose of the ETCA is to encourage export of U.S. produced goods and services. Persons who wish to form an export trading company may obtain from the Commerce Department a certificate of antitrust immunity (called a certificate of review) after concurrence by the Justice Department. This certificate is issued if certain conditions are met. These prohibit unfair export competition, substantial lessening of competition or restraint of trade in the U.S., unreasonable effects on U.S. prices, and sale or resale of the goods or services in the U.S.

Answer (A) is incorrect. The Sherman Act makes illegal every restraint of trade in interstate or foreign commerce. Answer (B) is incorrect. The Sherman Act prohibits resale price maintenance if it fails to pass a rule of reason analysis. Answer (D) is incorrect. The Sherman Act makes illegal every restraint of trade in interstate or foreign commerce.

36.6 Federal Trade Commission Act

38. The two major functions of the Federal Trade Commission are

A. Antitrust actions and the regulation of foreign trade.

B. Import quality inspections and anti-dumping measures.

C. Antitrust actions and consumer protection.

D. Price discrimination and unfair trade practices.

Answer (C) is correct. *(CMA, adapted)*

REQUIRED: The two major functions of the Federal Trade Commission (FTC).

DISCUSSION: The FTC Act of 1914 prohibits unfair methods of competition and unfair or deceptive acts in commerce. The basic objectives are to initiate antitrust actions and protect consumers.

Answer (A) is incorrect. The regulation of foreign trade is not within the jurisdiction of the FTC. Answer (B) is incorrect. The regulation of foreign trade is not within the jurisdiction of the FTC. Answer (D) is incorrect. Price discrimination and unfair trade practices are merely elements of the overall mission of the FTC.

39. Which one of the following is not exempted from federal antitrust regulation?

A. Labor unions.

B. Intrastate commerce.

C. Telecommunications companies.

D. Major league baseball.

Answer (C) is correct. *(CMA, adapted)*

REQUIRED: The entity that is not exempted from federal antitrust regulation.

DISCUSSION: Several types of entities and contracts are exempt from antitrust regulation. These include firms not operating in interstate commerce, labor unions, regulated public utilities, patents and copyrights, agricultural and fishing organizations, financial institutions, transport industries, professional baseball, and companies qualifying under the Export Trading Company Act. The telecommunications industry is not exempt.

Answer (A) is incorrect. Labor unions are specifically exempted. Answer (B) is incorrect. Intrastate commerce is specifically exempted. Answer (D) is incorrect. Major league baseball is specifically exempted.

STUDY UNIT THIRTY-SEVEN
CONSUMER PROTECTION

Through the enactment of statutes and regulations, legislative bodies and administrative agencies at the federal and state levels actively seek to shield consumers from a broad range of harm. The most common abuses involving consumer transactions occur in the extension of credit, deceptive trade practices, unsafe products, and unfair pricing. A **consumer transaction** is generally defined as involving goods, credit, services, or land acquired for personal, household, or family purposes.

The **Magnuson-Moss Warranty Act of 1975** applies only when the seller gives a written warranty. It attempts to improve the quality of warranties given by manufacturers to consumers. The act does **not regulate the safety or quality of consumer goods** but does seek to (1) make consumer warranties easier to understand, (2) prevent deceptive warranty practices, and (3) provide a relatively effective method of enforcing warranty obligations. Its main provisions require certain **disclosures** about written warranties and place **limits on disclaimers** of written warranties and of implied warranties. **Enforcement** may be through informal dispute resolution involving independent entities provided for in the warranty, consumer suits in state or federal court (including class actions), and suits in federal court by the **Federal Trade Commission (FTC)** or Attorney General. The act specifically applies to **any written affirmation of fact** by a supplier to a purchaser relating to the quality or performance of a consumer product, affirming that it is free from defect or that it will meet a specified level of performance over a period of time. It also applies to **any written undertaking** to refund, repair, replace, or take other action if a consumer product fails to meet written specifications. However, the act applies only to the purchase and sale of **consumer products**, and it does **not require** a warranty on consumer goods. The seller must voluntarily choose to make a written affirmation of fact concerning a consumer product to come within the statute. Furthermore, although the act creates no implied warranties, it prohibits a **disclaimer of implied warranties** (e.g., those under UCC Article 2) whenever an express written warranty is given or a service contract is made with a consumer.

When a written warranty is provided for a product actually costing more than $10 (exclusive of taxes), it must be labeled as either **full or limited**. Under a **full warranty**, the seller must assume certain minimum obligations and duties. (S)he must agree to fix within a reasonable time and without charge a product that is defective, that malfunctions, or that does not conform to the warranty. If the warrantor makes a reasonable number of attempts to remedy one of the aforementioned problems and is unable to do so, the consumer can choose to receive a cash refund or replacement of the product without charge. The warrantor may not limit the duration of any **implied warranty** covering the product. The warrantor also may not exclude or limit **consequential or special damages** for breach of any written or implied warranty unless such exclusion or limitation is conspicuously apparent on the face of the warranty. In addition, a warrantor who gives a full written warranty may not impose any conditions precedent on repair, replacement, or refund, e.g., return of a warranty registration card.

A written warranty that does not meet any one of the foregoing minimum requirements must be designated conspicuously as a **limited warranty**. If a consumer product costs more than $5, it must contain certain **full and conspicuous disclosures** in readily understood language, including step-by-step procedures for the consumer-owner to obtain the benefit of the warranty. Moreover, a limited warranty may **limit the duration of implied warranties** to the duration of the written warranty if reasonable, not unconscionable, and clearly and unmistakably displayed. However, it must state that some states do not allow limitation of the duration of implied warranties or the exclusion or limitation of incidental or consequential damages, "so the above limitation or exclusion may not apply to you."

The **Consumer Credit Protection Act (CCPA)** regulates extensions of credit for personal, family, household, or agricultural purposes. The CCPA includes, among other things, (1) the Truth-in-Lending Act, (2) the Fair Credit Reporting Act, (3) the Equal Credit Opportunity Act, (4) the Fair Debt Collection Practices Act, and (5) the Fair Credit Billing Act. Consumer credit protection laws provide for (1) access to the consumer credit market by creditors and consumers, (2) full disclosure of information to the consumer, (3) regulation of contract terms, (4) fair reporting of credit information about consumers, and (5) creditor's remedies.

The **Truth-in-Lending Act (TILA)**, implemented through **Regulation Z** issued by the Federal Reserve Board, requires disclosure by creditors of the terms and conditions of consumer credit before they extend credit to consumer-debtors. The act applies to all transactions in which (1) the lender is in the business of extending credit in connection with a loan of money, a sale of property, or the furnishing of services; (2) the debtor is a natural person, not a corporation or other business association; (3) a finance charge may be imposed; (4) the credit is obtained primarily for personal, family, household, or agricultural purposes; and (5) the amount financed is $25,000 or less. The **Consumer Leasing Act** (implemented by Regulation M) amended the TILA to cover consumer leases of goods (e.g., motor vehicles) in the ordinary course of business if the lease is for more than 4 months and the price is $25,000 or less. This act requires written disclosure of all material lease terms.

The **disclosure** provisions of the TILA are complex. In general, they require disclosure of the costs of credit (sales finance and interest charges). These costs must be quoted in terms of an annual percentage rate calculated uniformly. Precisely what must be disclosed depends on whether the transaction is for closed-end credit or open-end credit. **Closed-end credit** is extended for a specific period, and the total amount financed, number of payments, and due dates are all agreed on at the time of the transaction. The disclosure required before the completion of a closed-end transaction is full and specific: (1) total amount financed; (2) total number of payments; (3) amount and due date of each payment; (4) annual interest rate; (5) total finance charge; (6) total dollar value of all payments; (7) all late charges assessable for past-due payments; (8) any security interest taken by the creditor and the collateral; and (9) information about an **adjustable rate mortgage (ARM)** for a loan period of more than 1 year and secured by a principal residence. **Open-end credit** arrangements, such as those under a credit card (e.g., VISA or MasterCard), involve a plan that permits the consumer to enter into a series of transactions with the option of paying in variable installments or in full. Under open-end credit arrangements, it is not always possible to disclose the total amount financed, the total number of payments, etc. But the creditor must disclose (1) how finance charges are calculated, (2) when they are incurred, and (3) whether the creditor has a security interest. The creditor also must make certain disclosures in billing statements, such as the effects of making only minimum payments.

They also must be uniformly calculated. The Federal Reserve requires marketing information to include a table displaying the APR and other disclosures (e.g., the annual fee). The **Bankruptcy Abuse Prevention and Consumer Protection Act of 2005** requires disclosures about introductory rates (e.g., how long they will be effective and the successor rates). Furthermore, this act governs disclosures in billing statements (late payment charges, payment due date, and the effects of making only the minimum payment). The TILA provisions also prohibit a creditor from **baiting** customers by advertising credit terms that it does not generally make available.

The TILA was amended by the **Credit Card Fraud Act**. It limits a **credit cardholder's liability** for unauthorized use of the card to a maximum of $50. It imposes criminal penalties for (1) unauthorized possession of credit cards, (2) altering or counterfeiting them, (3) use of account numbers alone, and (4) use of cards obtained from a third party with consent (e.g., when a cardholder fraudulently reports a card stolen). Federal law also states that a charge may be added to the purchase price for the use of a credit card rather than payment with cash or check. Moreover, credit cards may not be distributed to persons who have not applied for them, and a credit card issuer must place a notice on the consumer contract that any holder is subject to the consumer's defenses against the seller. A person who has **a problem with property or services** purchased with a credit card has the right not to pay the amount due. However, the purchaser must first attempt in good faith to return the goods or give the merchant a chance to correct the problem. This right to refuse to pay applies if (1) the goods are purchased in the consumer's home state or within 100 miles from home, and (2) the purchase price of the goods was more than $50. A credit cardholder who **loses his/her card** will avoid all liability for any unauthorized charges if **notice is given to the issuer** before any charges are made. Furthermore, under the act, an addressee who is sent an **unsolicited credit card** has no liability to the issuer for charges made prior to receipt and acceptance of the card.

The **Home Equity Loan Consumer Protection Act** applies to open-end credit arrangements. It requires disclosures when an application is made for a customer loan **secured by a principal residence** (including a second home or a vacation home). If the arrangement involves an **ARM**, the consumer has a minimum 3-day period during which (s)he may rescind the agreement. If the loan amount exceeds the fair value of the home, the lender must tell the debtor that the excess is not tax deductible.

Civil and criminal penalties are imposed for violation of the TILA. The civil liability provisions make creditors liable to debtors for an amount equal to twice the finance charge, but not less than $100 or more than $1,000. The costs of filing suit plus attorney's fees also are recoverable. The Department of Justice may institute criminal action against those who willfully and knowingly violate the act.

In addition to the TILA, other federal and state laws and regulations protect consumers in **sales transactions**. See, for example, the warranty provisions of UCC Article 2 (Study Unit 14) and the adoption by some states of the **Uniform Consumer Credit Code's (UCCC's)** provisions concerning contract terms and disclosures, interest rates, credit insurance, referral sales, home solicitation, and garnishment and other creditors' remedies. Furthermore, some states have enacted **cooling-off laws** with respect to sales made by door-to-door sellers. Such a law permits a buyer to cancel a contract within a short period after the sale. A similar FTC rule states that a seller must allow a 3-day grace period and notify the buyer in Spanish of this right if the oral discussions were in Spanish.

An FTC rule also addresses **mail-order and telephone sales**. For example, it requires mail-order sellers to ship goods within the period promised by their advertisements, to give notice of shipping delays, and to provide a refund within a stipulated period after a customer's cancelation. The **Postal Reorganization Act of 1970** concerns the related problem of unsolicited shipments of goods. Under the act, the recipient has no obligation to the sender. The goods may be retained and used or disposed of at the discretion of the recipient. Other federal laws applicable to consumer sales protection are the criminal statutes prohibiting **mail fraud and wire fraud**. The elements of the crime of mail fraud are (1) causing the mailing of a writing for the purpose of carrying out a scheme to defraud and (2) a contemplated or organized scheme to defraud. (NOTE: The scheme itself need not violate federal law.) The wire fraud statute applies to fraudulent uses of telephone, radio, or television transmissions. It also applies to the use of the Internet.

The **Fair Credit Reporting Act (FCRA)** was enacted to require consumer credit reporting agencies to adopt reasonable procedures to maintain the confidentiality, accuracy, and relevancy of their records while meeting the needs of lenders. An **investigative report** (on character, reputation, etc.) is not to be prepared on a consumer until (s)he is notified and given the right to request information about the investigation. **Consent** to request the report is commonly required when an individual makes an application for which the report is needed, e.g., employment or insurance. The information kept in the credit file will include employment history, judgments, and arrest records. The FCRA imposes a duty on **users of credit reports** to disclose to the individual affected that (1) the report has been requested; (2) (s)he has the right to obtain further disclosure with respect to the request; and (3) the report may contain information on the individual's character, reputation, personal traits, and mode of living. The user of a credit report incurs a **duty to disclose** whenever such user rejects an application for consumer credit, insurance, or employment or charges a higher rate for credit or insurance. The user must maintain reasonable procedures for advising the affected individual that it relied on the credit report in making its decision. The user also must supply the individual with the name and address of the consumer reporting agency that supplied the report. Typically, the consumer credit reporting agency must, if contacted, disclose to the affected individual (1) the nature and substance of all of its information about the individual, (2) the source of all information, and (3) the names of any users of the report who have received the consumer's file in the last 6 months (in the last 2 years if employment was involved). A consumer has a right to have **correct information in his/her file**, so the reporting agency must investigate any alleged error and must assume that the correction is not frivolous or irrelevant. Upon request, the reporting agency must notify any users of the report of the disputed information, and if a requested change is refused, the consumer may file an additional report that must be kept in the file.

The FCRA was amended in 1997 to provide greater protections when **credit reports** are used to make **employment decisions**. An individual is entitled to **written notice and must give consent** before an employer may request his/her credit report from a credit bureau. The employer also must make a **pre-adverse action disclosure** (copy of the report and the FTC's summary of rights under the FCRA) before relying on the report to deny a job application, terminate employment, etc. After adverse action, the employer **must give notice** (written, oral, or electronic) about the action, including information about the credit bureau and a notice of the individual's right to dispute items in the credit report. An employer that does not comply with these requirements may be sued for damages and be subject to civil penalties imposed by the FTC.

The **Financial Services Modernization Act of 1999 (Gramm-Leach-Bliley)** addresses the protection of the privacy of consumer financial information. It prohibits a **financial institution** (any entity engaged in a financial activity or one incidental or complementary to a financial activity) from transmitting **private personal information** to unaffiliated parties **without notice** to the customer and without a customer choice to prevent such transmission. (CPAs are not subject to the notice requirement. They are already covered by state laws prohibiting disclosure without consent of clients' personal information.) It also prohibits transmission of access numbers or codes to unaffiliated parties who want to use them for marketing. A financial institution must notify its consumer customers about these policies at the outset and annually thereafter. However, the act does not affect sharing among affiliates or allow a private right of action against violators. Moreover, it does not affect an FCRA provision allowing consumers to opt out of the sharing of nontransaction information (e.g., a credit report) with affiliates.

The **Equal Credit Opportunity Act (ECOA)** prohibits discrimination in any aspect of a consumer credit transaction. **Protected categories** include sex, marital status, race, color, age, religion, national origin, receipt of welfare, or good-faith exercise of rights under the CCPA. A **commercial lender** may not ask for information about race, color, religion, or national origin. Questions about marital status, age, or sex may be asked only for limited purposes (e.g., statistical monitoring by the government). Inquiries about birth control practices, childbearing plans, and former spouses are prohibited. The ECOA applies to all businesses and individuals that regularly extend credit, including financial institutions, retail stores, and credit card services. The ECOA also affects automobile dealers, real estate brokers, and others who steer consumers to lenders. The **FTC**, as well as individuals, may sue to enforce the ECOA, and an injured person may recover actual and punitive damages and attorney's fees. The credit extender must consider all income disclosed by an applicant, but the sources of income generally are not to be considered. Nevertheless, the credit extender may consider the likelihood of receiving income, such as alimony and child support. For example, the prior job history of a former spouse is relevant in determining whether an applicant will be able to pay the charges. The credit extender is required to tell the applicant that (s)he does not need to disclose these sources of income unless (s)he relies on them for credit. The credit extender has 30 days from the application date to give notice of the action taken and the reasons for denial of credit. Lack of assets or income is an allowable reason for denying credit. A **married woman** may not be prevented from obtaining credit separately from her husband. Indeed, asking about marital status is prohibited. Credit should be reported in the names of both spouses while they are married.

The **Fair Debt Collection Practices Act (FDCPA)** was enacted to prevent abusive, deceptive, and unfair debt collection practices of debt collectors. The act is directed at agencies that collect debts for others, not businesses that are trying to collect their own accounts. The debts in question must involve money, property, insurance, or services obtained by a consumer and used for personal, family, or household purposes. Under FDCPA, a collector generally may not use (1) harassing or intimidating practices, (2) abusive language, or (3) false or misleading tactics. A collector also **may not contact the consumer** (1) at work if the employer objects, (2) at unusual or inconvenient times, or (3) at all if the debtor is represented by an attorney. Moreover, unless specifically authorized by a court, a collector **may not contact third parties** other than a spouse, parent, or financial advisor expressly about the account. Finally, the collector may not contact the consumer-debtor about the account after receiving a **written refusal to pay**, except to notify the consumer of possible ramifications of nonpayment. If payment is made with a **postdated check**, a debt collector must not deposit it until the effective date. The FTC is the principal enforcement agency for the FDCPA, which also permits civil actions, including class actions, by the affected debtor or debtors.

The **Fair Credit Billing Act** gives the consumer a method of **correcting errors** on bills and bringing **disputed charges** to the attention of the creditor. The creditor is required to inform the customer of his/her rights with each billing statement. This need only be a short-form disclosure. However, a long-form disclosure is required twice a year. A creditor is not obligated to investigate the records until the customer makes an inquiry about a bill. The correction must be made within 90 days after the consumer's inquiry. The creditor cannot take action (e.g., act to collect the questioned amount, report a delinquency, or restrict use of an open-end account) until it responds to the inquiry. A customer has 60 days after receiving a bill to make an inquiry or objection. A creditor will forfeit the charge in dispute only up to $50 if (s)he fails to comply with the act.

The **Federal Trade Commission Act of 1914** established the FTC as an independent administrative agency charged with preventing "unfair methods of competition" in interstate commerce (Study Unit 36). In 1938, Congress passed the **Wheeler-Lea Act** to give the FTC power to protect consumers from "unfair or deceptive acts or practices." In 1975, Congress broadened the reach of the statute to include methods and acts or practices "affecting" interstate commerce. The FTC has actively used its powers to protect consumers primarily against **false or deceptive advertising**. The FTC may regulate two fundamental aspects of advertising by businesses: business activities that are deceptive and those that are unfair. The **deceptiveness** of a business activity is a question of fact that the FTC decides on a case-by-case basis. The FTC has issued policy statements on deception. To be considered deceptive, advertising must involve a misrepresentation, omission, or practice that would likely mislead a consumer acting reasonably under the circumstances. In addition, the representation, omission, or practice must be **material**, that is, likely to affect the choice of a product or service. For example, the FTC considers express statements to be material. If the FTC finds a business practice to be deceptive or unfair, it can issue a cease-and-desist order. In certain cases, the FTC also may go to court to seek civil penalties or injunctive relief. The FTC's concerns about deceptive advertising also extend to the Internet. For example, it has issued guidelines (not new rules) regarding **online advertising**. For example, any information that limits the claims made must be clearly and conspicuously disclosed near the claim on the website if not within the claim itself. Use of links to disclosures is discouraged. Another regulatory concern is **telemarketing** abuse. Under the **Telephone Consumer Protection Act of 1991**, advertising may not be sent via fax without the consent of the recipient. It also proscribes use of automatic dialing systems and prerecorded voices. The FCC enforces this legislation, but consumers may also bring suit for the greater of actual loss or $500 per violation, with treble damages possible for willful or knowing misconduct. Under the **Telemarketing and Consumer Fraud and Abuse Act of 1994**, FTC rules require telemarketers to state that the call is for sales purposes, give the seller's name, identify the product, state its total cost, describe any restrictions on receipt or use of the product, and indicate whether the sale is final and the price not refundable. Furthermore, it is illegal to misrepresent information (e.g., risk of an investment or the nature of a prize to be awarded), and a telemarketer must comply with a consumer's directive to remove his/her name from the list of prospects.

The FTC may address **unfair acts or practices** that injure consumers independently from those that are deceptive. Hence, it may promulgate rules defining unfair acts or practices that are **prevalent**. To exercise this authority, the FTC must prove that a widespread pattern of the acts or practices defined exists or that it has previously issued cease and desist orders regarding them. Furthermore, an act or practice is deemed to be unfair only if it "causes or is likely to cause substantial injury to consumers that is not readily avoidable by consumers themselves and not outweighed by countervailing benefits to consumers or to competition" (1994 amendment to Section 5 of the FTC Act).

Although the Supreme Court has given **commercial speech**, such as advertising, a significant degree of First Amendment protection, the constitutional safeguards do not extend to unfair or deceptive advertising acts or practices. One common type of advertising traditionally attacked by the FTC concerns deceptive price and savings claims. The FTC has issued a series of guidelines regarding deceptive pricing that set forth certain principles by which the FTC will judge the merit of price claims. Another common deceptive retail trade practice is **bait-and-switch**. Bait (or bait-and-switch) advertising is an attractive but insincere offer to sell a product or service that the advertiser does not intend or desire to sell. Its purpose is to switch customers from the advertised merchandise to the purchase of something else, usually at a higher price or on a basis more advantageous to the advertiser. This practice is prohibited by the FTC. The FTC guidelines list several unfair trade practices with respect to such advertising, for example, deliberately discouraging the potential buyer from purchasing the advertised product, refusing to demonstrate the advertised product or demonstrating a defective product, disparaging the product, failing to stock enough of the advertised product to meet anticipated demand, and stating that delivery of the advertised product will take an inordinate amount of time.

The **Fair Packaging and Labeling Act of 1966** enables consumers to obtain accurate information with respect to the quantity of the contents of products and to make meaningful comparisons with similar products. Under the act, the Department of Health and Human Services and the FTC developed rules that require a packaged or labeled consumer product to contain specific information, including the name and address of the manufacturer, packer, or distributor of a product; the net quantity, e.g., weight, volume, etc., which must appear conspicuously on the front of the package; and an accurate description of the contents.

A comprehensive statute, the **Federal Food, Drug, and Cosmetic Act (FFDCA)**, provides the basis for regulations concerning the manufacture, testing, distribution, and sale of food, drugs, cosmetics, and other medical devices or products. The objective of the regulation is to ensure wholesomeness and safety. Approval by the **Food and Drug Administration (FDA)** is required for these products to be advertised or distributed to the public.

The **Consumer Product Safety Act (CPSA) of 1972** established the Consumer Product Safety Commission (CPSC), an independent agency, and a Product Safety Advisory Council. **Consumer products** include any article customarily produced or distributed for a consumer's use, consumption, or enjoyment in or around a permanent or temporary household or residence or a school, in recreation, or otherwise. There is no requirement that the goods be sold. Thus, the law covers free samples and products sold to others but used by consumers. However, it excludes tobacco products, motor vehicles, drugs, cosmetics, and various other items covered by specific statutes. The purposes of the CPSC, as stated in the CPSA, are to (1) protect the public against unreasonable risk of injury associated with consumer products, (2) assist consumers in evaluating the comparative safety of consumer products, and (3) develop uniform safety standards for consumer products. The CPSC also minimizes conflicting federal and state regulations with respect to consumer products safety and expands and promotes research with respect to the causes and prevention of consumer product-related death, illness, and injury.

The CPSC sets **product safety standards** regarding performance of, and the provision of adequate warnings and instructions for, consumer products. A standard must be reasonably necessary to prevent or reduce an unreasonable risk associated with a consumer product. Moreover, the CPSA requires that **voluntary private standards** be relied upon if they will adequately reduce the risk and substantial compliance is likely. The CPSC also may (1) ban unsafe products; (2) issue recall orders requiring repair, replacement, or refunds for substantially hazardous products; and (3) bring suit in federal court to eliminate dangers presented by imminently hazardous consumer products. The CPSA provides for injunctive relief, seizure of products, and both civil and criminal penalties. Furthermore, the CPSC has authority to administer other laws relating to product safety, such as the Flammable Fabrics Act and the Federal Hazardous Substances Act (which includes the Child Protection and Toy Safety Act, the Child Protection Act, and the Hazardous Substances Labeling Act).

American law provides consumers with a diverse array of protective provisions. For example, a broad spectrum of protection devices may be raised under **general contract law** or the **Uniform Commercial Code**. In addition, numerous FTC rules protect against specific practices that tend to place consumers at a disadvantage. The FTC rule that protects consumers from a **holder in due course** of a negotiable instrument is an example. Another example is the rule that allows a buyer, who was subjected to solicitation at his/her home, 3 days in which to cancel a contract for goods or services for $25 or more. Furthermore, unsolicited goods sent by mail may be treated as a gift by the recipient. Finally, almost every general area of law can be a source for protection of consumers.

QUESTIONS

37.1 The Magnuson-Moss Act (Warranty Protection)

1. Tina Timely purchased a watch for which the written information contained an explanation that it was a "full" warranty. Shortly thereafter, the watch stopped working. Timely went back to the store where she purchased the watch and requested that it be exchanged for a new one. The store explained it could not be exchanged, but the manufacturer would repair it under the warranty for a $3.00 service charge. What are Timely's rights?

A. Under a full warranty, Timely is entitled to have the watch replaced with a new one.

B. Under a full warranty, Timely may not be assessed a service charge.

C. If the warranty had stated "limited," the warranty of merchantability could have been disclaimed.

D. Timely can either have the watch repaired or obtain a new one if she can prove that she did not cause the damage.

Answer (B) is correct. *(Publisher, adapted)*

REQUIRED: The purchaser's rights under a "full" warranty for a defective product.

DISCUSSION: Under the Magnuson-Moss Warranty Act, written warranties must use the words "full" or "limited." Under a full warranty, the purchaser is entitled to have a defective product repaired or replaced by the seller (manufacturer) without charge and within a reasonable time. Because Timely received a full warranty, the manufacturer must repair or replace the watch and cannot require a $3.00 service charge. There are many other stringent requirements when a full warranty is given, and for this reason almost all warranties today are limited.

Answer (A) is incorrect. The manufacturer may choose to have the watch repaired instead of replaced. Answer (C) is incorrect. The warranty of merchantability is an implied warranty. Implied warranties cannot be disclaimed when a written warranty is given. Answer (D) is incorrect. Timely is not required to prove that she did not cause the damage. Unless there is evidence that she did damage the watch, the manufacturer is required to repair or replace it.

2. The warranty rules of the UCC must be read in light of the federal Magnuson-Moss Warranty Act, which

A. Implies warranties in addition to those provided by the UCC.

B. Requires that the seller of consumer goods give a "full warranty" in writing.

C. Requires that the seller of consumer goods give either a "full warranty" or a "limited warranty" in writing.

D. Limits the ability of sellers to disclaim implied warranties.

Answer (D) is correct. *(Publisher, adapted)*

REQUIRED: The true statement about the Magnuson-Moss Warranty Act.

DISCUSSION: The Magnuson-Moss Act supplements and modifies rather than displaces the UCC's warranty rules. The act does not require a seller of consumer goods to give any warranty. If (s)he gives a written warranty, however, it must be either full or limited. A full warranty must meet the federal minimum standards (refund, repair, or replace without cost in a reasonable time). A limited warranty is one that fails to meet full warranty criteria but fairly puts the buyer on notice that the warranty is not full and may not meet certain standards. Whether a warranty is full or limited must be conspicuously designated in writing, and its duration must be stated. When a seller has given a written warranty in a sales contract (or in a sales contract combined with a contract for service that is entered into within 90 days of the original agreement), the seller may not modify or disclaim the implied warranties of fitness for a particular purpose or merchantability.

Answer (A) is incorrect. The act grants no implied warranties. Answer (B) is incorrect. A seller of consumer goods need not give a warranty. Answer (C) is incorrect. A seller of consumer goods need not give a warranty.

37.2 Credit Protection

3. The Consumer Credit Protection Act was enacted due to unfair and predatory practices by creditors in their extension of credit to consumers. Which of the following was not enacted as a part of, or as an amendment to, the Consumer Credit Protection Act?

A. Truth in lending.

B. Fair credit reporting.

C. Uniform Consumer Credit Code.

D. Fair credit billing.

Answer (C) is correct. *(Publisher, adapted)*

REQUIRED: The provisions not enacted as part of the Consumer Credit Protection Act.

DISCUSSION: The Uniform Consumer Credit Code is a model act similar to the Uniform Commercial Code, Model Business Corporation Act, and Uniform Partnership Act. It contains many provisions similar to the Consumer Protection Act; however, it has been enacted by only a few states and is not expected to be a significant uniform statute.

4. Due to the widespread use of credit cards, federal regulation was needed to control extension and use of this credit. Which of the following statements is not a requirement of those who issue or accept credit cards?

A. A charge cannot be added to the purchase price for the use of a credit card rather than payment with cash or check.

B. Credit cards may not be distributed to persons who have not applied for them.

C. A credit card issuer must place a notice on the consumer contract that any holder is subject to the consumer's defenses against the seller.

D. A credit cardholder cannot be liable for more than $50 if the card is stolen or lost.

Answer (A) is correct. *(Publisher, adapted)*

REQUIRED: The statement not a requirement for the issuance or acceptance of credit cards.

DISCUSSION: There is no longer a prohibition against adding a charge to the purchase price for the use of a credit card. Prior federal law did prohibit this practice, but the law no longer exists. The Truth-in-Lending Act states that a credit card issuer may not prohibit a merchant from offering a discount for payment by cash, checks, etc.

Answer (B) is incorrect. The issuance of credit cards is prohibited except in response to those who apply for them. Answer (C) is incorrect. The credit card issuer must include the anti-holder-in-due-course statement. Answer (D) is incorrect. A credit cardholder is not liable for more than $50 when the card is stolen or lost.

5. Pico Mirandola purchased a stereo for $400 with his credit card. At home, Pico discovered the stereo did not work properly. Pico

A. Can refuse to pay the credit card bill if he attempted in good faith to return the stereo or give the store an opportunity to correct the problem.

B. Can refuse to pay the credit card bill if the purchase was made more than 100 miles from home.

C. Cannot refuse to pay the credit card bill because it was for a purchase of more than $50.

D. Must pay the credit card bill but has a right to damages and attorney's fees against the store under the Uniform Consumer Credit Code.

Answer (A) is correct. *(Publisher, adapted)*

REQUIRED: The rights of a credit card user when merchandise is defective.

DISCUSSION: A person who has a problem with property or services purchased with a credit card has the right not to pay the amount due. However, the purchaser must first attempt in good faith to return the goods or give the merchant a chance to correct the problem.

Answer (B) is incorrect. This right to refuse to pay applies if the goods are purchased in Pico's home state or within 100 miles from home. Answer (C) is incorrect. The right to refuse to pay applies if the purchase price of the goods was more than $50. Answer (D) is incorrect. Pico does have the right to refuse to pay for the goods, and damages and attorney's fees are not available for this problem under the Uniform Consumer Credit Code.

6. Mabel has a long history of using credit. She repaid most debts, but at other times she defaulted on loans. With regard to credit information about Mabel that may have been collected by credit reporting agencies, which of the following statements is true?

A. The credit files on Mabel kept by credit reporting agencies may contain only information about the existence of prior debts and repayment.

B. Mabel is entitled to notification and the right to request information before an investigative report is prepared on her.

C. Employers are entitled to receive a credit report on Mabel without her approval.

D. Mabel is entitled to see her report file and adjust it.

Answer (B) is correct. *(Publisher, adapted)*

REQUIRED: The true statement about credit reporting.

DISCUSSION: Under the Fair Credit Reporting Act, an investigative report (concerning character, reputation, etc.) is not to be prepared on a consumer until (s)he is notified and given the right to request information about the investigation. Consent to request the report is commonly required by institutions when an individual makes an application for which the report is needed, e.g., employment or insurance.

Answer (A) is incorrect. The information kept in the file will include employment history, judgments, and arrest records. Answer (C) is incorrect. Under the 1997 amendments to the FCRA, an employer must obtain consent before obtaining a credit report on an individual from a credit reporting agency. Answer (D) is incorrect. Although an individual is entitled to see his/her report file, (s)he has no right to make an adjustment to the file. (S)he is entitled to request that items be changed, but if the request is refused, (s)he may only file an additional memorandum that must be kept in the file.

7. The Fair Credit Billing Act places the burden on the creditor to correct billing errors. Under this act,

A. The creditor has 90 days after sending out a bill to make corrections to it.

B. The creditor must inform the customer of his/her rights with each billing statement.

C. The customer has 90 days in which to make an objection about a bill.

D. The creditor is subject to forfeiting the disputed charge up to $100 for failure to comply with the act.

Answer (B) is correct. *(Publisher, adapted)*

REQUIRED: The true statement about the Fair Credit Billing Act.

DISCUSSION: The Fair Credit Billing Act gives the consumer a method of correcting errors on bills and bringing disputed charges to the attention of the creditor. The creditor is required to inform the customer of his/her rights with each billing statement. This need only be a short-form disclosure. However, a long-form disclosure is required twice a year.

Answer (A) is incorrect. A creditor is not obligated to investigate the records until the customer makes an inquiry about a bill. The correction must be made within 90 days after the consumer's inquiry. Answer (C) is incorrect. A customer has 60 days after receiving a bill to make an inquiry or objection. Answer (D) is incorrect. A creditor will forfeit the charge in dispute only up to $50 if (s)he fails to comply with the act.

8. The Equal Credit Opportunity Act was enacted to prevent discrimination in credit extension. Which of the following is not prohibited by the act?

A. Discriminating based on receipt of welfare.

B. Preventing a married woman from opening a credit account separate from her husband's.

C. Asking whether the credit applicant is married.

D. Denying credit based on lack of assets.

Answer (D) is correct. *(Publisher, adapted)*

REQUIRED: The item not prohibited by the Equal Credit Opportunity Act.

DISCUSSION: The act prohibits discrimination based on race, sex, marital status, etc. However, it does not prevent a denial of credit based on a lack of assets. Lack of assets and lack of income are allowable and logical reasons for denying credit.

Answer (A) is incorrect. A lender may not discriminate based on receipt of welfare. The source of a person's income is generally not to be considered. Answer (B) is incorrect. A married woman may not be prevented from opening a credit account separate from her husband's. Answer (C) is incorrect. Asking whether a credit applicant is married is prohibited. Marital status is not to be considered.

9. Gertrude was receiving both alimony and child support, but her former husband had never held a job for a long period of time. Which of the following statements is true regarding Gertrude's application for credit with Dacy Department Store?

A. Gertrude must disclose her alimony and child support.

B. Dacy may consider the likelihood of Gertrude's receiving these payments based on her former husband's work record.

C. Dacy need not consider former credit extended to Gertrude and her husband in his name only.

D. Dacy may consider the alimony and child support but not public assistance Gertrude may be receiving.

Answer (B) is correct. *(Publisher, adapted)*

REQUIRED: The true statement about an application for credit.

DISCUSSION: A credit extender may consider the likelihood of receiving income such as alimony and child support. The prior job history of Gertrude's former husband is relevant for Dacy to use as a factor in determining whether Gertrude will be able to pay the charges.

Answer (A) is incorrect. Although Dacy must consider Gertrude's alimony and child support if disclosed, Dacy is also required to tell Gertrude that she does not need to disclose these sources of income unless she relies on them for the credit. Answer (C) is incorrect. A woman is entitled to establish a credit history, which requires credit to be reported in the name of both spouses while married. Answer (D) is incorrect. Dacy must consider all income that Gertrude receives and discloses, including public assistance.

10. Tom Debtor incurred substantial debts. Much of this debt was turned over to a collection agency. Employees of this agency called Debtor repeatedly at home during the middle of the night. They also made collect telephone calls to Debtor from distant places and confronted him in the presence of his neighbors and coworkers. In these circumstances,

A. Debtor can prevent this harassment with a written note to the collection agency.

B. Debtor can end this harassment only by filing a lawsuit against the collection agency.

C. Debtor can prevent the disparaging remarks in front of neighbors and coworkers, but telephone calls are not subject to restrictions.

D. To have any recourse against the collection agency, Debtor must be able to prove damages.

Answer (A) is correct. *(Publisher, adapted)*

REQUIRED: The true statement about a debtor who is harassed by a collection agency.

DISCUSSION: A debtor need only notify the collection agency in writing of his/her wish that the agency refrain from contacting him/her or informing the neighbors and coworkers of the debts. The collection agency is then required to stop all further contact, and its sole remedy is to sue the debtor.

Answer (B) is incorrect. Debtor can write a letter. He does not have to file a lawsuit. Answer (C) is incorrect. Telephone calls by debt collectors are prohibited before 8 a.m. and after 9 p.m., and all collect calls are prohibited. Answer (D) is incorrect. A debt collector can be liable for up to $1,000 without proof of damages for violation of the Fair Debt Collection Practices Act.

37.3 Deceptive Trade Practices

11. Gardener ordered an exotic plant by mail from an advertisement in a magazine. Seller received Gardener's check and order, but the plant was out of season. If the plant will not be available for shipment for 3 months but the seller deposited Gardener's check in its bank anyway,

A. Seller can send Gardener a letter explaining that the plant will not be available for delivery for 3 months.

B. Seller must promptly refund Gardener's check.

C. Seller can wait until it has the plants for shipment because Gardener did not pay with a charge card.

D. Gardener's only recourse is to file a suit if Seller refuses to refund the payment.

Answer (B) is correct. *(Publisher, adapted)*

REQUIRED: The true statement about the requirement imposed on a mail-order seller who cannot ship an order.

DISCUSSION: When a purchaser orders merchandise by mail, the seller must either ship within a reasonable time (not to exceed 30 days) or promptly refund the purchase price. This rule applies if payment was by check or a credit card.

Answer (A) is incorrect. Seller is required to refund the payment if it cannot ship within 30 days. Answer (C) is incorrect. The 30-day shipment rule applies to both checks and credit card purchases. Answer (D) is incorrect. Gardener can file a complaint with the Federal Trade Commission for an unfair trade practice and also can request the state attorney general of the state where Seller does business to act on the problem.

12. The Federal Trade Commission (FTC) was given its authority under the Federal Trade Commission Act. A major power of the FTC is to regulate unfair or deceptive acts or practices in trade. Which of the following is not a power held by the FTC?

A. The issuance of a consent order or a cease-and-desist order.

B. The imposition of criminal sentences.

C. Rule making in the area of advertising.

D. The investigation of misleading advertising and deceptive practices.

Answer (B) is correct. *(Publisher, adapted)*

REQUIRED: The power not held by the FTC.

DISCUSSION: Although the FTC has the power to enforce many of the antitrust laws, it is engaged mostly in preventing deceptive trade practices. But the FTC is a regulatory agency with no power to impose criminal sentences. These are pursued by the United States Justice Department and handed down by a court of law.

Answer (A) is incorrect. The FTC does have the power to issue a consent order or a cease-and-desist order. These remedies are commonly used by the FTC. Answer (C) is incorrect. The FTC does have broad rule-making power in the area of advertising. One of its functions is to prevent unfair or deceptive acts or practices against consumers. Answer (D) is incorrect. The FTC is empowered to and does investigate misleading advertising and deceptive practices.

13. A television commercial depicts a set of false teeth dunked in a glass of bubbly water and then pulled out shining clean and white. In reality, the set of false teeth is not the same stained set that was put into the bubbly water. Is this commercial deceptive?

A. No, because there is not enough time during the commercial for the entire cleaning process to occur.

B. No, as long as the product actually works.

C. Yes, unless it is first cleared with the FTC.

D. Yes, because the public is being misled as to the seller's objective proof of a product claim.

Answer (D) is correct. *(Publisher, adapted)*

REQUIRED: The true statement about the deceptiveness of the television commercial.

DISCUSSION: The Supreme Court has ruled that when an experiment or demonstration is depicted, the advertiser must inform the viewing public if it is not an actual test or demonstration or if a use of props is undisclosed. In this case, the use of different false teeth is deceptive or misleading unless the public is informed.

Answer (A) is incorrect. Lack of time is not an excuse for deceptive advertising. According to the Supreme Court, such an argument indicates only that television may not be a suitable medium for that type of commercial. Answer (B) is incorrect. The actual efficacy of the product does not prevent the advertising from being deceptive or misleading. Answer (C) is incorrect. There is no exception for deceptive advertising cleared with the FTC.

14. Corrective advertising is sometimes an appropriate remedy after a seller has made false or deceptive advertising statements. Which statement about such corrective advertising is true?

A. The FTC can order such corrective advertising.

B. The FTC must apply to a court for an order for corrective advertising.

C. Corrective advertising must be agreed to by a seller to avoid a lawsuit for damages on behalf of the consumers.

D. The seller must indicate that it is corrective advertising.

Answer (A) is correct. *(Publisher, adapted)*

REQUIRED: The true statement about corrective advertising.

DISCUSSION: The FTC is empowered to order corrective advertising if companies have previously created false impressions or have been guilty of wrongdoing in their advertising. An example of this occurred when the Listerine commercials were required to disclose that Listerine would not help prevent colds or sore throats.

Answer (B) is incorrect. The Listerine case determined that the FTC has the power to issue such an order. Answer (C) is incorrect. Corrective advertising may be required by an FTC order and not just as an agreement by the seller. Answer (D) is incorrect. In the Listerine case, the court did not require Listerine to indicate that its advertising was corrective. However, the court did not specify that it would never be required.

15. ABC Co. manufactures popular skin care products. It has used the term "baby oil" with its products for so long that much of the public associates the term "baby oil" with ABC products. SLZ Co. comes out with a new skin care product and uses the term "baby oil" on it. Which of the following is true?

A. SLZ can be stopped only if "baby oil" is a trademark of ABC.

B. ABC has a cause of action against SLZ, but consumers do not.

C. SLZ must be sued under common-law principles of business torts, e.g., palming off.

D. SLZ can be held liable even without intent to deceive and without a showing of damages.

Answer (D) is correct. *(Publisher, adapted)*

REQUIRED: The legal position of a company using a description on its products similar to that of a well-known product.

DISCUSSION: Under the Lanham Act, any person who uses a false designation or false description in connection with goods or services, including words or symbols falsely describing or representing the origin of the product, is liable to any person who believes (s)he is likely to be damaged by the false description or representation. This act can be used to hold a company such as SLZ liable without any intent to deceive and without a showing of actual damages. However, it is primarily designed to provide competitors with a statutory remedy. Consumers might use it if they fit within its terms, but they also have such recourses as the Federal Trade Commission, a local attorney general, and the common law of torts.

Answer (A) is incorrect. An injunction can be had against SLZ if a court decides that it has falsely described or represented its product leading buyers to think it is another's. An injunction is possible even without violation of statutory trademark or trade name laws. Answer (B) is incorrect. Consumers also have a cause of action against SLZ if they are being misled into believing that the product is actually that of ABC Co. This is deceptive advertising. Answer (C) is incorrect. The Lanham Act is a statutory remedy for this type of problem in addition to the common-law principles of business torts.

16. The Federal Trade Commission has issued a rule called "Guides on Bait Advertising." Which of the following statements about this rule is true?

A. Its purpose is to prevent abuses in the sporting goods industry.

B. It is primarily directed at used-car dealers.

C. Its purpose is to prohibit discouraging customers from purchasing advertised merchandise as part of a bait scheme to sell other merchandise.

D. The FTC can take action only if the seller refuses to show the item that was advertised.

Answer (C) is correct. *(Publisher, adapted)*

REQUIRED: The true statement about bait advertising.

DISCUSSION: Bait (or bait-and-switch) advertising is an attractive but insincere offer to sell a product or service that the advertiser does not intend or desire to sell. Its purpose is to switch customers from the advertised merchandise to the purchase of something else, usually at a higher price or on a basis more advantageous to the advertiser. This practice is prohibited by the FTC.

Answer (A) is incorrect. The rule against bait advertising is not directed at a specific industry, although it would apply to it also. Answer (B) is incorrect. The rule against bait advertising is not directed at a specific industry. Answer (D) is incorrect. The FTC can also take action if the seller discourages employees from selling such an item, fails to have adequate stock on hand, or does not deliver the goods within a reasonable period of time.

17. Basil read an advertisement in the newspaper for a sale of "Major" stereos (a very well-known and reputable brand) by Hoodwink Discounters, a large chain distributor of electronics. Basil bought a stereo, but when he got home, he discovered it was a "Magor" brand, which looked just like the "Major" brand. Basil returned to Hoodwink but was told that the store had no more "Majors" and that "Magor" was essentially the same. It turned out that "Magor" was manufactured by Hoodwink. Basil could not obtain a refund. Which of the following is not a remedy available to Basil?

A. File a civil lawsuit for damages on the basis of deceptive advertising and possibly fraud.

B. File a civil lawsuit seeking an injunction against Hoodwink on behalf of Basil and all others similarly situated.

C. File a lawsuit seeking criminal penalties against Hoodwink.

D. File a complaint with state authorities and request them to prosecute Hoodwink.

Answer (C) is correct. *(Publisher, adapted)*

REQUIRED: The remedy not available to a consumer who has been duped by deceptive advertising.

DISCUSSION: A consumer who has been duped by deceptive advertising can sue for his/her damages and can seek an injunction against the deceptive advertiser to prohibit the continuation of such conduct. To obtain an injunction, the individual must belong to a class harmed by the deceptive advertising. An individual also can seek assistance from governmental authorities. A local district or state attorney, the attorney general of the state, or the Federal Trade Commission are examples of governmental authorities who can act on complaints from consumers and assist in recovering damages and criminally prosecuting the offender. However, an individual has no authority to seek criminal penalties. Criminal prosecution can be undertaken only by the government (federal, state, or local).

37.4 Products and Safety

NOTE: See product liability and warranties subunits in Study Units 7 and 14 for additional questions on these topics.

18. If a product is believed to pose an imminent hazard to consumers, the Consumer Product Safety Commission (CPSC) may

A. Seek a court order to have the product banned or seized.

B. Ban or seize the product upon a majority vote by the commissioners of the CPSC.

C. Ban or seize the product, but only after a notice has been published in the Federal Register for 30 days.

D. Ban or seize the product based on the decision of an administrative law judge of the CPSC.

Answer (A) is correct. *(CMA, adapted)*

REQUIRED: The true statement about the activities of the Consumer Product Safety Commission (CPSC).

DISCUSSION: The CPSC (1) publishes product safety standards; (2) issues rules banning certain hazardous products; (3) brings federal suits to eliminate dangers presented by imminently hazardous consumer products; and (4) requires manufacturers, distributors, and retailers to give notice if they have reason to know that their products present a substantial hazard. Remedies include injunctive relief, seizure of products, and civil and criminal penalties. The CPSC must file suit in federal court to have a product banned or seized. It cannot ban or seize a product without a court order.

19. The National Traffic and Motor Vehicle Safety Act of 1996 was enacted to reduce accidents and the deaths and injuries occurring in such accidents. In addition to design and construction, the Secretary of Transportation is directed to set safety standards for automobiles and related equipment. What has hindered the Secretary of Transportation from establishing more thorough standards than now exist?

A. The costs to, and dissatisfaction of, the public.

B. The refusal of the automobile industry to cooperate.

C. The National Motor Vehicle Safety Advisory Council.

D. The lack of authority given to the Secretary of Transportation in the act.

Answer (A) is correct. *(Publisher, adapted)*

REQUIRED: The item hindering the Secretary of Transportation from establishing more thorough vehicle safety standards.

DISCUSSION: In setting automotive safety standards, there is a necessary balancing between the cost involved and the desired degree of safety. These costs and public dissatisfaction have hindered development of safety standards for motor vehicles by the Secretary of Transportation.

Answer (B) is incorrect. The automobile industry has generally cooperated with the Secretary of Transportation, although it has lobbied hard in Congress and the media against these required standards. Answer (C) is incorrect. The National Motor Vehicle Safety Advisory Council is established by, and works with, the Secretary of Transportation. Answer (D) is incorrect. The Secretary of Transportation has broad authority under the act to establish safety standards.

20. Goop Foods, a maker of baby foods, was warned by the Food and Drug Administration (FDA) through written reprimands after an inspection of unsanitary conditions in its warehouses. The president of Goop was specifically provided with these letters. One year later, the FDA made another inspection of Goop's warehouses and discovered the problems had not been resolved at all. The FDA filed charges against Goop and the president under the Federal Food, Drug, and Cosmetic Act. Who can be held criminally liable under the act?

A. Only Goop because the president would not have been personally involved in the violations.

B. Only the president because a corporation cannot be criminally liable.

C. Both Goop and the president.

D. Neither Goop nor the president because the FDA does not have the power to charge violators with criminal conduct.

Answer (C) is correct. *(Publisher, adapted)*

REQUIRED: The parties that can be held liable by the FDA for food product violations.

DISCUSSION: The FDA has the authority to make investigations and issue sanctions for violations of the FDA's sanitary standards. A corporation that violates these standards can be held criminally liable by means of fines. In addition, an officer in a managerial position, such as a president, can be held criminally liable if (s)he had notice of the violations and was in a position to correct them. Proof of intent to commit the wrongful acts is not required.

Answer (A) is incorrect. The president was provided with notice of the violations and would have the ability to correct them. Answer (B) is incorrect. A corporation can be held criminally liable, although it would be fined rather than imprisoned. Answer (D) is incorrect. The FDA does have the power to charge violators with criminal conduct.

37.5 Other Protective Provisions

21. Naive met Slick at a party in Ohio. Slick said she was involved in real estate in Florida where the hot deals were available. Naive had extra cash to invest, so he invited Slick to come by the next day. Slick showed Naive pictures of beautiful ocean-front property, assured Naive that she had personally visited the property, and told him that it was a "steal." Relying on this information, Naive gave Slick money and received a properly executed warranty deed with a legal description of land in Florida. Naive took a trip to Florida a few weeks later to look at the land and discovered that the property described in the deed was located in the middle of a swamp. What is Naive's best remedy?

A. Nothing because the contract was completed, and a valid deed cannot be returned.

B. Damages based on the warranties given in the deed.

C. Rescission based on fraud.

D. Nothing because the parol evidence rule will prevent introduction of the oral statements made by Slick.

Answer (C) is correct. *(Publisher, adapted)*

REQUIRED: The best remedy for a buyer who has received a deed to property that was misrepresented by the seller.

DISCUSSION: Fraud is present when a misstatement of a material fact has been made with the intent to deceive, and the plaintiff justifiably relied on the misstatement to his/her detriment. Rescission of a contract is a proper remedy for fraud because there was not a meeting of the minds on the "agreement." The purchaser clearly had different expectations (this would also be true in the case of innocent misrepresentation, which is similar to fraud without the intent to deceive). Naive may also seek damages under tort law for the fraud.

Answer (A) is incorrect. A deed can be rescinded, reformed, or returned if it was accepted on the basis of fraud. Answer (B) is incorrect. The warranties would provide only that Slick owned and had the right to transfer the land described. If Slick owned the swampland prior to Naive's purchase, the warranties will not provide Naive any remedies. Answer (D) is incorrect. There are many exceptions to the parol evidence rule, one of which always allows evidence of fraud to be admitted.

22. Judy entered into an agreement with Ralph to buy diamonds from him for $100,000. Which of the following will not prevent Ralph from enforcing the agreement?

A. Ralph said they were worth $100,000, but an appraisal obtained by Judy revealed the fair value to be $85,000.

B. Ralph threatened to break Judy's husband's leg if she did not buy them.

C. Judy knows nothing about financial transactions, and Ralph is a trustee and financial adviser for all her assets.

D. The agreement is not in writing.

Answer (A) is correct. *(Publisher, adapted)*

REQUIRED: The defense to a contract.

DISCUSSION: Although fraud and innocent misrepresentation are grounds for preventing a seller from enforcing a contract, there is no indication that either is present in these facts. Fraud and innocent misrepresentation require a misrepresentation of fact. An opinion of value is not considered fact. Also, contract law does not require that a person obtain equal economic value.

Answer (B) is incorrect. A threat to break Judy's husband's leg is duress. Generally, a contract entered into under duress is not void but is voidable by the innocent party. Answer (C) is incorrect. When a trustee sells to a client, the contract is voidable by the purchaser if undue influence is exerted. Answer (D) is incorrect. A sale of goods for $500 or more must be in writing and signed by the person against whom enforcement is sought.

23. Alice entered into a contract with Kool-it, Inc., to purchase and have installed central air-conditioning in her home. Kool-it required her to sign its standard form contract. Alice is paying for the air conditioner and installation in three monthly payments. Installation is to take place in the month after the second payment. Which of the following will not be upheld by a court?

A. A clause relieving Kool-it from installation until the second payment is made.

B. A clause relieving Kool-it of any liability (in contract or in tort) if a claim is not made within 10 days of installation.

C. A clause allowing additional charges for difficult installation even if the contract is determined to be one of adhesion.

D. A clause providing for an additional fee if Alice's payments are late or her checks bounce.

Answer (B) is correct. *(Publisher, adapted)*

REQUIRED: The clause of a contract that will not be upheld by a court.

DISCUSSION: An exculpatory clause is one that excuses a party from a duty or liability. It can be upheld provided it is reasonable. A clause that tries to limit liability in an unreasonable manner will not be upheld. A clause relieving Kool-it of any liability in contract or tort is much too broad. It would attempt to eliminate even product liability.

Answer (A) is incorrect. There is no reason a seller of a product cannot limit its obligations until proper payment. Answer (C) is incorrect. A contract of adhesion is a standard form contract required to be used by one of the parties. Such contracts are often upheld based on the efficiencies of using them. A person can contract to allow additional charges when an installation proves more difficult than expected. Answer (D) is incorrect. Late payment charges or returned check charges are proper, provided they are fully disclosed in advance to the customer.

24. Danny Driver was going on a summer vacation with his family and leased a motor home from Nogo Enterprises. A provision in the form lease disclaimed all liability and warranties for the condition of the motor home, damages resulting from use of the motor home, and any repairs needed on the motor home. Driver was required to initial this provision on the contract in addition to signing the entire agreement. One hundred miles out of town, the transmission broke. A repair shop estimated it would take 1 week to fix and cost $500. Driver left the motor home at the shop and made the trip by airplane. Nogo Enterprises now seeks to hold Driver liable for both the cost of the repairs and the rental of the motor home. Driver is

A. Liable for the rent but not the repair because repairs are always a responsibility of the lessor.

B. Liable for the repair but not the rent because he did obtain the use of the motor vehicle.

C. Liable for both the rent and the repair because he initialed the clause in the contract indicating agreement to it.

D. Not liable at all because the contract is unconscionable.

Answer (D) is correct. *(Publisher, adapted)*

REQUIRED: The extent of Driver's liability for the repairs and rental of the motor home.

DISCUSSION: Courts tend to find consumer contracts (or clauses therein) not enforceable if they are unconscionable (so one-sided or oppressive that it would be against public policy to enforce them). Under UCC 2-302, courts are specifically allowed to refuse to enforce a contract for the sale of goods to avoid an unconscionable result, and courts may refer to this section as an analogy in contracts not for the sale of goods. Furthermore, this rental was a bailment under which the bailor was responsible to provide goods that were reasonably fit for the purpose intended. Obviously, the motor home was not reasonably fit because it broke down after 100 miles.

Answer (A) is incorrect. A court would probably not hold Driver liable for the rent. He used the motor home for only the first 100 miles of the trip and then had to switch modes of transportation. Answer (B) is incorrect. Although the parties can shift liability for repairs by contract, this repair was so major that requiring the lessee to pay for it would be unfair and oppressive. Answer (C) is incorrect. The initialing of a clause in a form contract will not bind the party if the court finds that the contract is unconscionable.

25. Leah Rubin purchased a set of encyclopedias from a salesperson who called upon her at home. Rubin was a schoolteacher who needed the encyclopedias, which were of good quality and were reasonably priced. However, the next day Rubin discovered that she could obtain a competitor's encyclopedias at a lower price. Rubin wishes to rescind the purchase of the encyclopedias from the home salesperson. Which of the following is true?

A. The Federal Trade Commission allows a purchaser 3 days to cancel a contract or sale entered into with a salesperson who called at home.

B. Although a contract to purchase the encyclopedias could have been rescinded, the completed sale cannot be rescinded.

C. Rubin's purchase cannot be rescinded because the sale was reasonable and Rubin's only reason for rescinding is to obtain a lower price.

D. Rubin cannot rescind the sale because home sales are treated the same as any other sales.

Answer (A) is correct. *(Publisher, adapted)*

REQUIRED: The true statement about a consumer's ability to rescind a home solicitation sale.

DISCUSSION: The Federal Trade Commission (FTC) allows a consumer who is a party to a house solicitation sale, lease, or rental a grace period of 3 days in which to rescind the contract if it was for goods or services costing $25 or more. This rule applies whether the transaction was for cash or on credit. This cooling-off period allows in-home buyers to reconsider an agreement that they may have been pressured into entering. Many states have also adopted similar laws.

Answer (B) is incorrect. The right under the FTC regulation to cancel a sale applies whether it is a contract that has been entered into or a completed sale. Answer (C) is incorrect. The 3-day cooling-off period is available regardless of the reason for canceling the sale. Answer (D) is incorrect. Home sales are specially treated due to the pressure used by door-to-door salespeople.

26. Just before Christmas, Willy received an unordered silk scarf in the mail from a manufacturer. Several days later, the scarf was followed by a bill and letter explaining that it was sent for Willy's convenience to use as a Christmas gift. Which of the following statements is correct concerning Willy's liability for payment?

A. Willy has an obligation to pay for the goods or return them.

B. Willy is obligated for the scarf only if he uses it.

C. Willy has 10 days to decide whether to keep the scarf and pay for it or to return it at the manufacturer's expense.

D. Willy may keep and use the scarf without an obligation to pay for it.

Answer (D) is correct. *(Publisher, adapted)*

REQUIRED: The liability of a person for unordered merchandise received in the mail.

DISCUSSION: Under both federal law and many state laws, unsolicited goods sent by mail may be treated as a gift by the recipient, who may retain, use, or dispose of them as (s)he sees fit. Willy may therefore keep and use the scarf without paying for it.

Answer (A) is incorrect. Federal law relieves a mail recipient of unordered merchandise from liability. Answer (B) is incorrect. It is a statement of common law under which use of an unordered good constituted acceptance. Federal and many state laws have exempted mailed merchandise from this rule. Answer (C) is incorrect. Willy may return the scarf at the manufacturer's expense, but he is not required to, and there is no 10-day limit.

27. The Real Estate Settlement Procedures Act (RESPA) is a federal statute enacted to protect buyers of residential property from certain abuses. Which of the following is a true statement about the requirements of the act?

A. The lender must disclose all costs that the buyer will incur at the closing in addition to the down payment.

B. The act applies to all sales of residential property to consumers.

C. Violation of the act can result only in rescission of the sale.

D. The act applies only to a real estate closing.

Answer (A) is correct. *(Publisher, adapted)*

REQUIRED: The true statement about the Real Estate Settlement Procedures Act (RESPA).

DISCUSSION: Under RESPA, a lender must inform the purchaser of a residential home of all costs that will be incurred at closing. These costs include attorney's fees, appraisal fees, credit reports, taxes, and any other items for which a buyer will be responsible.

Answer (B) is incorrect. RESPA applies only to federally related mortgage lenders and would not apply to a sale by an owner who takes back the mortgage him/herself. Answer (C) is incorrect. A violation of the act can result in the greater of actual damages or $500. Answer (D) is incorrect. In addition to a real estate closing, the act covers secured loans on a residential home even if the loan was not incurred for the purchase of the home.

STUDY UNIT THIRTY-EIGHT
EMPLOYMENT REGULATION

By tradition, employment relations were governed by the common law of contracts, agency, and tort law. Beginning in the late 1920s, state and federal governments began to enact laws regulating employment. The major areas of employment regulation are reviewed in this study unit.

The terms **master** and **servant** were once used to describe the relationship when one person employed another. Today, the terms **employer** and **employee** are used, and much has changed in the relationship. That relationship is contractual and can be written or oral, formal or informal. At common law, unless the contract is for a fixed and definite period, it is for an indefinite period and terminable at the will of either party for any reason without notice. However, the modern trend is to erode or greatly modify the employment at will principle. Courts today generally recognize an underlying principle of **good faith and fair dealing** implicit in all employment contracts. For example, employers must constantly balance the right to conduct business with the employee's individual rights. Nevertheless, current employment law also benefits the employer. An employee must exercise reasonable skill in managing or controlling any aspects of the employer's business for which (s)he is hired. An employee has a duty to further an employer's interest and must not engage in conduct detrimental to the employer's interest or in a business that competes with that of the employer. An employee also may be required to account for any secret profit, gift, gratuity, or benefit (s)he receives in his/her capacity as an employee. Thus, property acquired by the employee in connection with employment ordinarily belongs to the employer.

Collective bargaining between employers and employees was established when Congress passed the **Railway Labor Act** of 1926. This act regulated labor relations in the railroad industry, a dominant industry at the time. Later, it was amended to include airlines. The Railway Labor Act was followed by the **Norris-LaGuardia Act of 1932**, which limited the circumstances in which federal courts could enjoin strikes and picketing in labor disputes. This act also made **yellow-dog contracts** illegal. They are agreements by which an employer requires employees to agree not to join a union. In 1935, Congress passed the **National Labor Relations Act (NLRA)**. Principally, the act extends legal protection to the unionizing efforts of employees and encourages their collective, as opposed to individual, bargaining. It authorized and established the **National Labor Relations Board (NLRB)**, an independent administrative agency. The NLRB's main functions are to oversee union representation elections and to investigate (and prosecute) charges of unfair labor practices. Many employees are exempt from the NLRA, for example, employees of government, nonprofit hospital workers, those subject to the Railway Labor Act, supervisors who are managerial employees, independent contractors, agricultural employees, and domestic workers. The jurisdiction granted the NLRB by Congress encompasses all businesses that affect interstate commerce. The NLRB, however, has limited exercise of that jurisdiction to industries and businesses that have a substantial impact on commerce. Substantial impact is measured largely by annual gross volume of sales or services. Nevertheless, businesses not meeting the NLRB criteria may be subject to state labor laws.

Section 8 of the NLRA is its most important provision. This section declared it an **unfair labor practice** for an employer to (1) interfere with employees in the exercise of their rights to form, join, and assist labor unions and other concerted activities for mutual aid or protection; (2) interfere with formation or administration of a union; (3) discriminate against employees (a term that includes applicants in hiring or granting of tenure) because of union membership; (4) discriminate against employees because they have filed charges or given testimony under the NLRA; and (5) refuse to bargain collectively with any duly designated representative of the employees.

Elections supervised by the NLRB determine, generally, whether a union will be selected and certified as the **collective bargaining representative** of a group of employees called the bargaining unit. An election is held if at least 30% of workers agree. During an election campaign, an employer may prohibit electioneering on company property if (1) it has a legitimate business reason and (2) the ban is nondiscriminatory. However, election activity may not be prohibited during nonwork hours, and, although management may campaign against union certification, it must not coerce employees. Upon a vote favoring representative bargaining in a valid election, the union is **certified** by the NLRB as the agent representing the employees. The representation is exclusive and the employer may no longer negotiate contracts with individual employees. The employer and the certified union must bargain in good faith with regard to "wages, hours, and other terms and conditions of employment." Refusal by either party to bargain in good faith is an unfair labor practice. Successful collective bargaining results in a contract. The **collective bargaining contract** then governs hours, wages, working conditions, and other matters of employment consistent with statutory and regulatory requirements.

Employees generally have a right to **strike**, but a court may enjoin a strike by employees or a lockout by an employer if the parties have agreed to a no-strike clause in the collective bargaining agreement. An employer may not permanently replace employees who strike on the basis of any **unfair labor practice**. If employees go on strike regarding any collective bargaining issue (an **economic strike**), the employer may not permanently discharge them. The employer may hire replacements. After the strike, the employer must recall the (previously striking) employees if and when positions open. If the collective bargaining agreement requires arbitration of disputes, a court may enjoin the strike. Strikes other than unfair labor practice or economic strikes are either illegal (e.g., in violation of a valid executive order) or otherwise unprotected. For example, if one side notifies the other of its intent to terminate the agreement, the law mandates a **60-day cooling-off-period**. The employer may, generally, permanently discharge employees who participate in an illegal or unprotected strike. A **lockout** is the employer analogue to a strike. If undertaken for appropriate economic or business purposes, and not to retaliate against workers for union activities, to eliminate the union, or to avoid collective bargaining obligations, a lockout is ordinarily legal.

The National Labor Relations Act was amended in 1947 by the **Labor Management Relations Act (LMRA)**, also called the **Taft-Hartley Act**. It proscribed practices that would constitute **unfair labor practices** if engaged in by unions and employees. Under the NLRA, the balance of power between management and labor had shifted in favor of unions. The Taft-Hartley Act was enacted to curtail the power of the unions as exhibited by crippling nationwide strikes. It was aimed at equalizing the bargaining power of management and labor. In addition to establishing unfair labor practices by unions, the Taft-Hartley Act established an **80-day cooling off period**. Under this provision, the President may request a federal court to issue an injunction to stop a strike or lockout that may imperil national safety or health. Such an injunction may last for a period of 80 days. The act also established the **Federal Mediation and Conciliation Service** to assist in settlement of labor disputes. Another provision outlaws the closed shop.

A **closed shop** is one in which a person must be a union member as a condition of employment, but Taft-Hartley permits union shop agreements. In a **union shop**, an employee must become a union member on or during a specified time after employment. However, a state may enact a **right-to-work law**. Such a law renders union-shop agreements ineffective in that state.

The National Labor Relations Act was further amended in 1959 by the **Labor Management Reporting and Disclosure (Landrum-Griffin) Act**, which sought to eliminate corruption in labor unions. This act established a **bill of rights** for union members and imposed financial reporting and disclosure requirements upon unions and union officials. To eliminate internal corruption and to guarantee that rank-and-file union members control the union, the Landrum-Griffin bill of rights provides that union members can sue and testify against the union, can vote on an increase in dues or fees, and can express themselves freely at union meetings. Union members also may nominate candidates, vote in regularly scheduled union elections using secret ballots, attend membership meetings, and have a voice in business transactions. Furthermore, they must be given a copy of the collective bargaining agreement and be accorded a full and fair hearing before any disciplinary action is taken by the union against them. Thus, the theory of Landrum-Griffin is to allow rank-and-file members to use the ballot box to eliminate corruption by union officers. In addition, the act prohibits **secondary boycotts**, i.e., union tactics directed toward secondary parties to exert pressure on the primary party (the employer with which the union has a dispute). For example, a union may not ask the employees of suppliers or customers of the primary party to refuse to handle the primary party's products. Moreover, the union may not picket secondary parties. Another practice proscribed by the act is the **hot-cargo agreement**, which is an employer's agreement to engage in a voluntary secondary boycott of a nonunion entity or one involved in a dispute with the union.

Job discrimination may be defined as an employer behavior that penalizes certain individuals because of personal traits that bear no relation to job performance. The most far reaching federal statute prohibiting job discrimination is **Title VII of the Civil Rights Act of 1964**. Title VII applies to all employers or labor unions that have 15 or more employees or members. It also applies to state, federal, and local employees because of an amendment included in the **Equal Employment Opportunity Act of 1972**. Title VII forbids discrimination in employment on the basis of race, color, religion, sex, or national origin. Title VII is enforced through lawsuits by private individuals and by the **Equal Employment Opportunity Commission**, a federal administrative agency. A successful plaintiff suing under Title VII may obtain back pay, lost wages, and attorney fees.

Job discrimination encompasses more than hiring. Title VII bars employers from discriminating with respect to any term, condition, or privilege of employment, including, but not limited to, compensation, job assignment, promotion, transfer, or discharge. Illegal discrimination occurs when a plaintiff shows that (s)he has been the victim of **disparate treatment**. A prima facie case of discrimination exists if the plaintiff shows that (s)he has been treated differently from a person not of his/her race, color, religion, sex, or national origin. Once the plaintiff establishes a prima facie case (a case that suffices for the plaintiff to prevail absent presentation of a defense), the burden shifts to the defendant-employer to articulate legitimate and nondiscriminatory reasons for the plaintiff's treatment. A second theory of illegal discrimination is based on **disparate impact**, which results from an employer's adoption of neutral rules that have an adverse impact on a protected class and that are not both job-related for the position in question and consistent with business necessity. Examples of such neutral rules include testing, high school diploma requirements, and height, weight, or strength standards. However, if the employer successfully argues the business necessity defense, the employee still prevails by proof of the existence of an alternative practice that is less discriminatory.

If a plaintiff proves a violation of Title VII, the employer may still assert **defenses** based on the recognition that certain discriminatory actions are justified, for example, (1) a bona fide seniority or merit system, (2) production based on quality or quantity of output, (3) a professionally developed test of ability, (4) business necessity in a disparate impact case, (5) a bona fide occupational qualification **(BFOQ)** in a disparate treatment case (a BFOQ is not available in a **race discrimination** case), and (6) national security reasons. To facilitate evidence-gathering by plaintiffs in job discrimination suits, equal opportunity records concerning job applications, hiring and firing, promotions and demotions, compensation, or protected groups must be retained for 6 months, and they may not be destroyed while a charge of discrimination is pending. In cases involving **religious discrimination**, the foregoing approach is applied under Title VII. However, a religious group that is an employer is allowed to treat religious affiliation as a BFOQ even for a secular job. Furthermore, an employer must **reasonably accommodate** an employee's religious beliefs. In cases involving **sex discrimination**, the general Title VII approach is likewise applied. The plaintiff must prove that the applicant's sex was determinative in the employer's wrongful act when all the circumstances are considered. The **Pregnancy Discrimination Act of 1978** extended Title VII protections to require that pregnant women be treated the same as other persons with a similar ability to work. **Sexual harassment** cases also are within the scope of Title VII if they include the element of sex discrimination. Such cases involve unwelcome sexual advances, requests for sexual favors, and other verbal or physical conduct of a sexual nature. **Quid pro quo sexual harassment** entails an employer's making job benefits (hiring, salary raises, promotions, etc.) dependent upon the employee's giving sexual favors or submitting to unwelcome advances. **Hostile-environment sexual harassment** has been defined by the Supreme Court as occurring when "the workplace is permeated with discriminatory intimidation, ridicule, and insult, that is sufficiently severe or pervasive to alter the conditions of the victim's employment and create an abusive working environment." If sexual harassment is by a supervisor, another employee, or even a nonemployee (e.g., a customer), the employer may nevertheless be held vicariously liable even though the employee suffered no adverse job consequences and the employer did not know of the harassment. However, the Supreme Court has held that an employer may raise an affirmative defense. This defense requires proof "(a) that the employer exercised reasonable care to prevent and correct promptly any sexually harassing behavior, and (b) that the plaintiff employee unreasonably failed to take advantage of any preventive or corrective opportunities provided by the employer or to avoid harm otherwise." The Supreme Court has also held that same-sex harassment is prohibited by Title VII.

Neither Title VII nor the EEOC Act forbids discrimination based on age. The **Age Discrimination in Employment Act (ADEA) of 1967** is intended to prohibit age discrimination and requires job applicants and employees to be evaluated on the basis of ability rather than age. The act protects individuals at least 40 years of age, but it states no maximum age. Those who must comply with the ADEA include individuals, partnerships, corporations, labor unions (with 25 or more members), and state and local governments. Each of the foregoing parties must be engaged in an industry affecting interstate commerce and employ at least 20 people. Employment agencies that make referrals to any covered employers are within the act's scope regardless of the agency's size. Remedies include unpaid back wages and other benefits related to the discrimination, attorney's fees, equitable relief, and, perhaps, promotions.

Certain rules pertaining to discrimination against people with disabilities are provided by the **Rehabilitation Act**, which requires employers with federal contracts to take affirmative action to employ and advance qualified individuals. The **Americans with Disabilities Act (ADA) of 1990** expands the Civil Rights Act of 1964 and the Vocational Rehabilitation Act to include protection from employment discrimination for persons with disabilities with respect to hiring, promotion, and termination. The employment provisions of the act are administered by the EEOC, and private enforcement actions by a claimant are allowed. Employers are required by the ADA to make reasonable accommodation for applicants or employees with disabilities. The **Vietnam-Era Veterans Readjustment Assistance Act** requires those employers who are recipients of federal contracts to take affirmative action to hire and promote qualified veterans with disabilities and qualified veterans of the Vietnam era.

The purpose of the **Occupational Safety and Health Act of 1970** is to develop safety standards, prevent injuries, and promote job safety. The act applies to all employees engaged in a business affecting interstate commerce. It also applies to virtually all employers unless specifically exempted. The act is administered by the **Occupational Safety and Health Administration (OSHA)** in the Department of Labor. OSHA is authorized to develop detailed health and safety standards and to enforce them. It investigates complaints and conducts inspections, and it has developed procedures to encourage compliance.

Employers are required to provide employees with a workplace free from recognized hazards that are likely to cause death or serious physical harm. They must keep detailed records of job-related injuries, post annual summaries of the records, and report serious accidents to OSHA. However, employers can insist that OSHA obtain a search warrant prior to inspection. If an employer is found to be in violation of the act, OSHA inspectors will direct immediate correction of the unsafe condition. For conditions that are not immediately correctable, OSHA will issue a citation that states the nature of the violation and fixes a date by which it must be corrected. Contested citations are reviewed by the **Occupational Safety and Health Review Commission**, a three-member board composed of Presidential appointees. Further review by OSHA in federal courts is possible. OSHA may assess civil penalties of up to $7,000 for each serious violation, and fines of up to $7,000 are also possible even for nonserious violations. Willful violations result in fines of at least $5,000 and as much as $70,000. Moreover, repeat offenders (within 3 years) may be assessed fines as high as $70,000 per violation. These fines are in addition to potential criminal liability. However, an injured employee may not use the act as a basis for recovery of civil damages. The act also imposes responsibility on employees to comply with OSHA standards. Employees who fail to comply can be discharged.

The **Fair Labor Standards Act of 1938 (FLSA)** establishes a federal **minimum wage**, mandates extra pay for **overtime** work, and regulates the employment of children. The FLSA is also known as the wage and hour law. It applies to all employers whose business affects interstate commerce. Certain employees are exempt from some or all of the FLSA minimum wage and overtime provisions. Others are exempt from the overtime but not the minimum wage provisions of the FLSA. The FLSA's key provisions entitle an employee covered by the act to at least the minimum wage per hour for up to the first 40 hours in a week and one and one-half times his/her regular rate of pay for hours worked in excess of 40 per week. In calculating hours worked, employers must include all hours at work, not merely those formally scheduled. The wages and hours requirements apply to salaried employees, unless they are otherwise exempt. An hourly rate is determined for such employees by dividing the salary by the hours normally worked during the period.

The FLSA also prohibits certain kinds of **child labor**. Persons under 18 are not permitted to be employed in occupations that are declared hazardous by the Secretary of Labor. The basic minimum age for employment is 16. Employment of 14- and 15-year-olds is limited to certain occupations, such as sales and clerical work. The act is enforced by the Department of Labor.

The **Equal Pay Act of 1963** amended the FLSA. It prohibits an employer from discriminating among employees on the basis of sex by paying unequal wages for the same work. The act permits wage differences based on seniority, merit, or quality or quantity of work. Unlike the FLSA, it covers executive, administrative, professional, and state and local government employees.

The **Family and Medical Leave Act** was enacted by Congress in 1993 to balance the demands of the workplace with the needs of families. It entitles an eligible employee to 12 work weeks of leave without pay and without losing his/her job. Leave is provided for birth of a child; a serious health condition; or the care of a spouse, son, daughter, or parent who has a serious health condition. A health condition is defined as one needing continued treatment and an absence of more than 3 days. However, persons with chronic conditions may take leave for shorter periods over an extended time. Eligibility requires employment by the employer for at least 12 months and 1,250 hours during the preceding 12 months. Only employers with 50 or more employees and the federal, state, and local governments must comply with the act.

The **Worker Adjustment and Retraining Notification Act of 1988 (WARN)** requires certain employers to provide 60 days' notice of a plant closing or mass layoff. The period is shorter in emergency situations or if the company is failing. The act applies to employers with at least 100 employees who work in the aggregate at least 2,000 hours per week.

The **Employee Retirement Income Security Act of 1974 (ERISA)** applies to employers that choose to provide benefit plans for their employees. Plans may be **contributory** (employers and employees contribute) or **noncontributory** (only employers contribute). The **fund manager** who need not be an employee, owes a fiduciary duty to the fund. However, employees generally may not make investment decisions. A **plan** is not allowed to lend money to the employer or its insiders or invest more than 10% of its assets in the employer's securities. **Contributions by employees** must vest immediately. **Contributions by employers** must be completely nonvested for up to 5 years and then fully vested thereafter, or gradually vested over a maximum of 7 years. The act also establishes **record keeping and disclosure** requirements. Participation in the **Pension Benefit Guaranty Corporation** is mandatory and provides for payment of some benefits when underfunded plans default.

The **Consolidated Omnibus Budget Reconciliation Act of 1985 (COBRA)** amended ERISA. An employee, spouse, and other beneficiaries must be notified and offered the opportunity to continue their **group health insurance**, including dental and visual benefits, for 18 months after termination (or loss of coverage due to certain events) at the employee's expense. **Employers** of 20 or more workers are required to comply with COBRA. Federal government agencies and religious entities are exempt from COBRA. **Employees** with disabilities are eligible to continue coverage for 29 months. Coverage may be discontinued if (1) the employee was terminated for gross misconduct, (2) the employer ceases to provide group coverage, (3) the premium is not paid, or (4) the employee obtains group coverage from a new (or spouse's) employer or becomes eligible for Medicare.

The **Health Insurance Portability and Accountability Act of 1996** also amended ERISA. This act requires a group health plan to cover **new employees** previously covered for at least 12 months by a prior employer's plan. Such employees cannot be excluded because of a preexisting condition. Health insurers and health maintenance organizations (HMOs) must cover **small employers** (fewer than 50 employees).

The **Pension Protection Act of 2006** requires an employer with a defined-benefit pension plan to eliminate underfunding within 7 years. However, an employer with an at-risk plan must make accelerated contributions. Moreover, if a plan is **more than 20% underfunded**, benefits may not be increased unless paid for immediately. If a plan is more than 20% overfunded, the employer may use plan assets to fund retiree health benefits. The following are other notable provisions: (1) An employer may not force employees to invest their contributions in the employer's shares; (2) the increases in IRA contribution limits enacted in 2001 were made permanent; (3) an employer with a defined benefit plan may offer automatic enrollment in a defined-contribution plan, e.g., a 401(k) plan; and (4) **executive deferred compensation** is restricted if a plan is severely underfunded.

Several statutes address **privacy issues** in the workplace. For example, the **Employee Polygraph Protection Act of 1988** prohibits private employers from requiring or using lie detector tests as a basis for employment decisions or inquiring about the results of such tests. A private employer may use a lie detector test as part of an investigation of economic loss or injury to its business if the employer reasonably suspects the employee was involved in a workplace incident of theft or embezzlement. However, employment decisions, such as termination, may not be based solely on the test. Drug and alcohol testing in the employment setting is permitted but is subject to many restrictions. The **Drug-Free Workplace Act of 1988** requires all firms with more than $100,000 of business with the federal government to certify that they will provide a drug-free workplace. The **Rehabilitation Act** and the **Americans with Disabilities Act** both prohibit an employer from making employment decisions on the basis of past drug or alcohol abuse. Current use may be an acceptable basis for not hiring or promoting or for termination. Generally, a government employer may use random or universal testing if the public health or safety or national security is involved. It may use selective testing if there is sufficient cause to believe an employee has a substance abuse problem. Employer testing for AIDS is another potential invasion of employee privacy. Under the ADA, a disease such as AIDS is treated as a disability, and employers must reasonably accommodate employees with disabilities. Hence, whereas testing may be allowed, dismissal for a positive result may not be. **Electronic monitoring** of workers, such as reading email and tracking activities on the Internet, raises questions about the extent to which employers may use electronic means to (1) safeguard against illegal employee use of the online environment and (2) evaluate employee performance. Beyond appropriate measures undertaken for these purposes, employees enjoy a zone of privacy at work. Under the **Electronic Communications Privacy Act of 1986**, an employer and others may not intercept wire or electronic communications or disclose or otherwise use the information acquired. Nevertheless, the act provides an exception for monitoring in the **ordinary course of business**, for example, monitoring of employee Internet activity using employer-provided systems. The act prohibits the monitoring of personal communications but not if employees have consented to such oversight. Furthermore, courts usually hold that employees have no reasonable expectation of privacy regarding email.

Workers' compensation laws have been passed by all 50 states to pay compensation to employees for losses sustained because of work-related injury or disease, regardless of who, if anyone, was at fault. **Negligence**, including disobeying an employer safety rule, does not prevent recovery of workers' compensation benefits. The key requirement is that the employee be injured and the injury **arise out of and in the course of** his/her employment. Exempt employers are usually businesses that employ less than a stated number of employees, e.g., three. Independent contractors are not covered, nor are casual, agricultural, or domestic employees. Workers' compensation **funding** is through various methods. Private insurance may be purchased or payments may be made to a state fund, and some states allow self-insurance. However, no federal insurance fund is available for this purpose. Workers' compensation statutes establish administrative commissions or boards to determine whether an injured employee is entitled to receive compensation and, if so, how much. Workers' compensation statutes allow the injured employee to recover on the basis of **strict liability**, thereby eliminating the need to prove the employer's negligence. After an injury occurs, the worker must give **notice** of the injury within a statutory period, and a **statute of limitations** also applies to filing the claim. Generally, the amounts recoverable are fixed by statute according to the type of injury and are less than a court or jury would typically award. **Recoveries** include reasonable medical expenses; wages loss benefits; specified recoveries for loss of body members, e.g., finger, hand, arm, etc.; and survivors' death benefit. Recovery of benefits under the statute for applicable injuries is the employee's exclusive remedy against the employer. However, if a third party causes the injury, the employee is not limited to a recovery based on workers' compensation. (S)he may bring suit in tort against the third party. A portion of any such recovery is used to reimburse the employer for workers' compensation payments. However, no recovery is permitted for an injury resulting from intentional self-infliction, willful intoxication, fighting, and pre-existing physical conditions.

The **Social Security Act of 1935** was enacted to provide limited retirement and death benefits to certain employees. Subsequent legislation established programs for employees with disabilities and their families and for families of retired and deceased workers. The current Social Security system contains four major benefit programs: old age and survivor's insurance, disability insurance, hospitalization insurance, and supplemental security income. Both employers and employees contribute under this program to compensate for loss of income on retirement or disability.

Under the **Federal Insurance Contributions Act (FICA)**, employers are required to contribute based on the employee's pay. The **employer** must pay the following (for 2011): (1) 6.2% of the first $106,800 of wages paid for old age, survivor's, and disability insurance (OASDI), plus (2) 1.45% of all wages for hospital insurance (HI). The employer must withhold (for 2011) 4.2% from the first $106,800 of **employee wages** and 1.45% of all employee wages. It is the employer's responsibility to withhold the employee's contribution and to forward the full amount of tax to the IRS. **Self-employed persons** are required to report their own taxable income and pay Social Security tax. The FICA tax liability of a self-employed individual is equal to the combined employer-employee contribution. In 2011, it equals 13.3% (10.4% OASDI rate applied to the net earnings base for 2011 of $106,800 + 2.9% applied to all net earnings).

Benefits under the FICA vary greatly depending on the status of the beneficiary. A fully insured worker is entitled to the maximum monthly benefit. To be fully insured, an employee must be credited with 40 quarters of coverage, or 10 years. A quarter of coverage is received for each $1,120 of earnings in a year up to a maximum of 4 quarters per year. A **currently insured worker** is one who has been credited with at least 6 quarters of coverage in the last 3 years. The benefits are somewhat less than those paid to a **fully insured worker**. Retirement benefits are payable to retired workers who are at least 62 years old, their spouses and divorced spouses who are 62, and dependent children or grandchildren. Employees who are unable to engage in gainful employment are eligible for disability benefits if they have been disabled for 5 months and the disability is likely to continue for 12 months.

The FICA also funds **Medicare**. For persons over the full retirement age, Medicare provides insurance for hospitalization costs and for supplementary medical costs, such as doctor's office visits. The Social Security Act of 1935 also authorized a system to provide temporary financial assistance for unemployed workers.

Under the **Federal Unemployment Tax Act (FUTA)**, a tax is imposed on employers of one or more individuals for some portion of a day in each of 20 weeks in the current or preceding calendar year. The act also applies to employers who pay $1,500 or more in wages in any calendar quarter of a current or preceding calendar year. The tax is 6.0% of the first $7,000 wages paid to each employee. However, an employer may take a credit of up to 5.4% of the first $7,000 of wages paid to an employee for state unemployment taxes. The employee does not pay any part of the FUTA tax. Generally, unemployed workers can receive payments for a maximum of 26 weeks. Ordinarily, the requirements to collect unemployment compensation are that the worker (1) was employed and laid off through no fault of the worker; (2) filed a claim for benefits; and (3) is able, available, and willing to work but cannot find employment.

Federal immigration law prohibits hiring of illegal immigrants and requires employers to verify that employees have a right to work in the U.S. **(Immigration Reform and Control Act of 1986)**. Moreover, employers who wish to hire employees from foreign countries must undergo a certification process and demonstrate (1) a shortage of qualified American workers in the relevant field and (2) that hiring from abroad will not have a negative impact on the labor market **(Immigration Reform Act of 1990)**. These requirements are most likely to be met with regard to very skilled workers, e.g., those in information technology.

Whistleblower statutes at the state and federal levels protect employees when they report employer misconduct. An example is the federal **Whistleblower Protection Act of 1989**. Another law, the **False Claims Reform Act of 1986**, provides that a whistleblower in a case of fraud against the federal government will receive 15-25% of the recovery in a suit against the guilty party.

QUESTIONS

38.1 Collective Bargaining

1. What are yellow-dog contracts?

A. Agreements that everyone must belong to the union.

B. Agreements between employers to identify union organizers.

C. Agreements with certain employees to spy on coworkers for union activities.

D. Agreements that employees would not join unions.

Answer (D) is correct. *(Publisher, adapted)*

REQUIRED: The definition of yellow-dog contracts.

DISCUSSION: Employers saw unions as a threat to their right to manage and were very much against the organization of unions in the beginning of the 20th century. "Yellow-dog" contracts were common. They were agreements prohibiting employees from joining a union, providing for liquidated damages, and allowing the employee to be fired if the agreement was not kept. These contracts were later outlawed by legislation.

Answer (A) is incorrect. Agreements between a union and an employer that all employees must belong to a union are called "closed-shop" or "union shop" agreements. Answer (B) is incorrect. There is no term associated with such agreements. Answer (C) is incorrect. There is no term associated with such agreements.

2. The National Labor Relations Act (also known as the Wagner Act) was enacted in 1935 to regulate labor activities in which way?

A. Prohibit unfair labor practices.

B. Outlaw "closed shops."

C. Require all union contracts to be reviewed by the National Labor Relations Board.

D. Exempt child labor from union agreements to discourage its use in the labor market.

Answer (A) is correct. *(Publisher, adapted)*

REQUIRED: The way in which the National Labor Relations Act regulates labor activities.

DISCUSSION: The NLRA establishes the right of labor to organize and to bargain collectively with management. The act requires employers to recognize unions and bargain with them in good faith. It also prohibits unfair labor practices, such as discrimination against union members, refusal to bargain with unions, and interference with the rights of employees to organize. The act also established the National Labor Relations Board to settle labor disputes and take action against unfair labor practices.

Answer (B) is incorrect. Closed shops (required union membership to be hired) were outlawed by the Taft-Hartley Act of 1947. Answer (C) is incorrect. The NLRB has never been required to review all union contracts. Answer (D) is incorrect. Child labor is not exempted from union contracts.

3. The National Labor Relations Board (NLRB) was formed under the National Labor Relations Act in 1935. The NLRB

A. Determines which unions will represent a group of employees.

B. Has become weak and ineffective.

C. Serves in an advisory capacity to the courts.

D. Is responsible for the conduct of representative elections.

Answer (D) is correct. *(Publisher, adapted)*

REQUIRED: The true statement concerning the National Labor Relations Board.

DISCUSSION: The NLRB, an administrative agency, has jurisdiction over labor-management relations affecting interstate commerce. It supervises union representation elections, ensures that elections are fairly conducted, and certifies the results. It also has jurisdiction over unfair labor practices by both unions and employers.

Answer (A) is incorrect. The employees of a business largely determine by election which union will represent them. Answer (B) is incorrect. The NLRB has power over both employers and unions in the collective bargaining process. Answer (C) is incorrect. The NLRB adjudicates controversies itself, subject to court review. Decisions of the NLRB are final unless properly appealed and overturned by a U.S. Court of Appeals or the Supreme Court.

4. Morning, Inc., refused to recognize a union that had not been elected by the employees. The union had lost in a representation election 8 months previously but now claimed that it had the support of the majority of employees. The union began picketing Morning to try to force recognition.

A. Morning has committed an unfair labor practice by refusing to recognize the union.

B. An election must be held.

C. The employees cannot cross the picket line.

D. The union has committed an unfair labor practice.

Answer (D) is correct. *(Publisher, adapted)*

REQUIRED: The true statement about picketing by a nonelected union that is not recognized by the employer.

DISCUSSION: Unions, as well as employers, may not commit unfair labor practices. It is often legal for a union to picket an employer for recognition purposes. However, it is an unfair labor practice for a union to picket an employer to try to force recognition when the union has not been certified by the NLRB and a valid representation election has been conducted within the past year.

Answer (A) is incorrect. It would be an unfair labor practice for Morning to recognize a union that has lost an election and is not certified by the NLRB. Answer (B) is incorrect. An election need only be held if a substantial number of employees (30%) want the election. Answer (C) is incorrect. Attempting to prevent employees from crossing a picket line is illegal for the union and the individual picketers.

5. Atlas, Inc., did not believe that the union representing its employees was supported by the employees any longer. Who can be assured of getting a representation election held?

A. 30% of the employees.

B. Atlas, Inc.

C. Another union.

D. The attorney general of the state.

Answer (A) is correct. *(Publisher, adapted)*

REQUIRED: The party or group who may demand that a representation election be held.

DISCUSSION: A representation election to decertify a union requires almost the same petition as an original representation election. A substantial number of employees must assert that the current bargaining representative is no longer their choice. To be substantial, 30% of the employees must support such a petition.

Answer (B) is incorrect. Although the employer can file a petition for an election if it in good faith believes the union is no longer representative of the employees, the NLRB investigates the petition and decides if an election should be held. Answer (C) is incorrect. Another union would have to prove the same facts as an employer, and would also be subject to review by the NLRB. Answer (D) is incorrect. The attorney general of a state has no authority in the collective bargaining process regulated by the federal government.

6. A factory moves from a non-right-to-work state to a right-to-work state, and the union continues to represent the employees. In the right-to-work state,

A. The employees can be forced to join the union before they start to work.

B. The employees can be forced to join the union after thirty days on the job.

C. The employees can decide not to be involved with the union.

D. The employees can be forced to make payments to the union.

Answer (C) is correct. *(CMA, adapted)*

REQUIRED: The true statement about union representation in a right-to-work state.

DISCUSSION: Some states have right-to-work laws that allow employees to work at any job without union membership. Thus, employees can decide not to be involved with a union even though the union represents the workers in the shop.

Answer (A) is incorrect. A closed shop requires an employee to be a member of the union in order to get a job. Answer (B) is incorrect. A union shop requires an employee to join the union after employment. Answer (D) is incorrect. Paying dues is equivalent to the requirements of a union shop.

7. Hanson Tire Company did not want to bargain with the union elected by the majority of its employees. Hanson does not have to bargain in good faith with the union about

A. Overtime pay.

B. Cleanliness of the plant.

C. Time that the plant is open.

D. A no-strike clause.

Answer (D) is correct. *(Publisher, adapted)*

REQUIRED: The item about which an employer does not have to bargain in good faith with a union.

DISCUSSION: Once a union is selected (certified) as the collective bargaining representative, the employer must bargain in good faith with that union (although it may not result in an agreement). However, the employer need only bargain in good faith over wages, hours, and other conditions of employment. A no-strike clause is not a mandatory condition of employment over which an employer is required to bargain in good faith, but most employers are interested in doing so.

Answer (A) is incorrect. Overtime pay is an element of wages. Answer (B) is incorrect. Cleanliness of a plant is a condition of employment. Answer (C) is incorrect. The time the plant is open affects hours worked.

8. Employer fired Employee who was a member of Union. Union and Employer had a collective bargaining agreement under which a grievance concerning discharge of a worker would be sent to binding arbitration if the parties could not agree to resolve the matter. Employee filed a grievance and Union and Employer could not reach an agreement. The arbitrator found for Employee. Review by

A. A federal court is the usual appellate procedure in arbitration.

B. A court is unlikely.

C. The NLRB is mandatory if the grievance also involved an unfair labor practice.

D. A state court is the usual appellate procedure in arbitration.

Answer (B) is correct. *(Publisher, adapted)*

REQUIRED: The true statement about a grievance procedure providing for binding arbitration.

DISCUSSION: The majority of states and the federal government have passed statutes that establish standards for arbitration and make arbitration agreements irrevocable. The parties must therefore abide by the arbitrator's decision and cannot seek judicial review of the result except in very limited circumstances. These include a dispute that is not arbitrable, that is, one outside the scope of the collective bargaining agreement and not involving interpretation or application of the agreement; conduct in bad faith by the arbitrator; a decision or award beyond the power granted to the arbitrator; or a decision that violates the law, such as upholding an illegal provision in the agreement.

Answer (A) is incorrect. The purpose of arbitration is to avoid the cost and delay of litigation. Answer (C) is incorrect. The policy of both the courts and the NLRB is to defer to the arbitrator. Answer (D) is incorrect. The purpose of arbitration is to avoid the cost and delay of litigation.

9. Workers have the right to strike but certain kinds of strikes are illegal. Which of the following statements is true?

A. If the collective bargaining agreement is for a definite period, no strike may be called until it expires.

B. If the collective bargaining agreement is for an indefinite period, 30 days' notice must be given to the employer.

C. If the collective bargaining agreement is for a definite period, 60 days' notice must be given if the union wishes to strike to seek modification of the agreement.

D. If the strike concerns an employer's unfair labor practice, 60 days' notice must be given.

Answer (C) is correct. *(Publisher, adapted)*

REQUIRED: The true statement about strikes by workers.

DISCUSSION: The general principle is that the employer and the Federal Mediation and Conciliation Service must be given 60 days' notice of a strike. This cooling-off period gives the parties an opportunity to negotiate their differences without the necessity of a strike. The 60-day requirement applies whether the collective bargaining agreement is for a fixed or indefinite term and whether the union plans to strike upon the agreement's expiration or while it is still in force.

Answer (A) is incorrect. Absent a "no strike" clause, a strike to terminate or modify the agreement is not illegal per se. Answer (B) is incorrect. A total of 60 days' notice must be given. Answer (D) is incorrect. The notice requirement is inapplicable if the strike is to protest an employer's unfair labor practice.

10. Which of the following statements about the status of strikers is true?

A. Even an illegal striker may not be discharged during a strike.

B. An economic striker may not be discharged during a strike and must be rehired at its conclusion.

C. A striker over an unfair labor practice by the employer may not be discharged during a strike and must be rehired unless a permanent replacement must be discharged as a result.

D. A striker over an unfair labor practice by the employer but not an illegal or economic striker is entitled to reinstatement.

Answer (D) is correct. *(Publisher, adapted)*

REQUIRED: The true statement about the status of strikers.

DISCUSSION: If workers have engaged in a legal strike to protest their employer's unfair labor practice, they are entitled to reinstatement. This rule applies even if permanent replacements hired during the strike must be discharged.

Answer (A) is incorrect. An illegal striker (when the strike is illegal) has no right to reinstatement. Answer (B) is incorrect. An economic striker (when the strike is legal and over economic benefits) has a right to a nondiscriminating review of his/her application for reinstatement but not to displace a permanent employee hired during the strike. Answer (C) is incorrect. An employee who strikes over an employer's unfair labor practice is entitled to have his/her job back even if it displaces a permanent replacement.

11. The Taft-Hartley Act of 1947 shifted the balance between the rights and obligations of employees and those of employers by

A. Permitting strikes in cases of health and safety violations.

B. Outlawing the union shop.

C. Designating a list of unfair labor practices on the part of unions.

D. Providing for compulsory binding arbitration in case of a national emergency.

Answer (C) is correct. *(CMA, adapted)*

REQUIRED: The provision of the Taft-Hartley Act of 1947.

DISCUSSION: The 1947 act prohibited certain unfair labor practices by unions: coercion of employees to join unions, discrimination against nonunion employees except when a valid union shop agreement is in place, refusal to bargain in good faith, secondary strikes, featherbedding (payment by employers for work not performed), and charging new members excessive initiation fees.

Answer (A) is incorrect. The 1947 act does not authorize strikes in particular circumstances. Its intent was to equalize the power of unions and management. Answer (B) is incorrect. It outlawed the closed shop (union membership a condition of employment) but allowed the union shop (membership may be required after employment). Answer (D) is incorrect. The 1947 act gives the President power to seek an injunction imposing an 80-day cooling-off period, but not binding arbitration.

12. Several states in the United States now have "right-to-work laws." In these states,

A. The closed shop is legal.

B. The checkoff, i.e., the deduction of union dues from employee paychecks, is required in all labor contracts.

C. Compulsory union membership is illegal.

D. The nonunion shop is illegal.

Answer (C) is correct. *(CMA, adapted)*

REQUIRED: The true statement about right-to-work laws.

DISCUSSION: The Taft-Hartley Act of 1947 outlawed the closed shop, one in which union membership is a condition of employment. It did allow the union shop, in which the employee is required to join the union after employment. But the 1947 act also authorized states to enact right-to-work laws. These prohibit union shops, thereby making compulsory union membership illegal.

Answer (A) is incorrect. The closed shop is illegal. Answer (B) is incorrect. A checkoff is not required in right-to-work states. Answer (D) is incorrect. No state makes the nonunion shop illegal.

13. If a strike produces a national emergency, the Taft-Hartley Act provides for an 80-day cooling-off period. This provision

A. Is invoked after appointment of a board of inquiry and the Attorney General's petition for a federal court injunction.

B. Results in binding arbitration by the Federal Mediation Service.

C. Does not apply to lockouts.

D. Allows the rank-and-file to vote only on a contract agreed to by the employer and the union bargaining agent.

Answer (A) is correct. *(Publisher, adapted)*

REQUIRED: The true statement about the cooling-off provision of the Taft-Hartley Act.

DISCUSSION: If a strike or lockout would have a substantial effect on the national economy, impair the national defense, or affect key industries, the President may appoint a board to investigate. If the board finds a national emergency will result, the President may instruct the Attorney General to petition a federal court for an injunction ordering the cessation of the strike or lockout for 80 days. During this period, the Federal Mediation Service works with the parties. If they do not agree, the board conducts new hearings and the company submits the final offer. The members of the union vote on this proposal. If they reject it, the strike or lockout may then resume for an indefinite period.

Answer (B) is incorrect. The mediators have no authority to bind the parties. Answer (C) is incorrect. Lockouts are also within the statute. Answer (D) is incorrect. The union members may vote directly on management's final offer if no agreement is reached.

14. Which one of the following federal acts requires unions to retain financial records and submit financial reports to federal authorities?

A. Taft-Hartley Act of 1947.

B. Wagner Act of 1935.

C. Securities Exchange Act of 1934.

D. Landrum-Griffin Act of 1959.

Answer (D) is correct. *(CMA, adapted)*

REQUIRED: The act requiring unions to retain financial records and submit financial reports to federal authorities.

DISCUSSION: The Landrum-Griffin Act of 1959 (the Labor Management Reporting and Disclosure Act) requires unions to maintain financial records and submit reports to the federal government. The intent of the act was to extend the provisions of the National Labor Relations Act to the internal affairs of unions to make the organizations more democratic and give members more rights.

Answer (A) is incorrect. The Taft Hartley Act did not address internal affairs such as financial records and reports. Answer (B) is incorrect. The Wagner Act of 1935 gave more power to unions. Answer (C) is incorrect. The Securities Exchange Act of 1934 did not address reports by labor unions.

38.2 Discrimination

15. Which of the following statements about Title VII of the Civil Rights Act of 1964 (as amended in 1972) is true?

A. Bona fide occupational qualification, merit, and seniority, but not mere business judgment, are defenses to an employment discrimination charge.

B. Covered entities must keep records related to employment opportunities for 6 months and also file annual reports.

C. State and local governments are excluded from coverage.

D. The federal government is excluded from coverage.

Answer (B) is correct. *(Publisher, adapted)*

REQUIRED: The true statement about Title VII of the CRA of 1964, as amended.

DISCUSSION: Title VII essentially covers all employers (e.g., individuals, corporations, partnerships, unions, state and local governments, and the federal government) with 20 or more employees if engaged in an industry affecting interstate commerce. Covered entities must maintain records concerning job applications, hiring and firing, promotions and demotions, compensation, etc. of protected groups. These must be retained for 6 months and may not be destroyed while a charge of discrimination is pending. Annual reports about employment of protected classes must also be filed.

Answer (A) is incorrect. A plaintiff must show discrimination to prevail in a suit, but an act affecting the plaintiff that is motivated by reasonable business judgment is not discrimination. An example of this is firing an employee for incompetence. Answer (C) is incorrect. State and local governments are covered. Answer (D) is incorrect. The federal government is covered.

16. The Americans with Disabilities Act (ADA) of 1990

A. Permits employers to inquire about a job applicant's prior health insurance claims.

B. Bans discrimination against employees with physical disabilities but not those with mental disabilities.

C. Requires organizations with 15 or more employees to provide reasonable accommodation for employees with disabilities.

D. Provides federal funds to employers who implement its provisions.

Answer (C) is correct. *(CMA, adapted)*

REQUIRED: The true statement about the Americans with Disabilities Act (ADA) of 1990.

DISCUSSION: The ADA requires organizations with 15 or more employees to provide reasonable accommodation for employees and job applicants with disabilities. The ADA bans employment discrimination against people with mental or physical disabilities, provides tax incentives for compliance costs, and requires remodeling of facilities to provide access by individuals with disabilities. Another provision of the ADA is that employers are prohibited from inquiring into a job applicant's disability with questions concerning medical history, prior workers' compensation or health insurance claims, work absenteeism due to illness, past treatment for alcoholism, or mental illness.

Answer (A) is incorrect. The ADA prohibits employers from inquiring about a job applicant's prior health insurance claims. Answer (B) is incorrect. The ADA applies to both physical and mental impairments. Answer (D) is incorrect. The ADA provides no federal funds for implementation of its provisions.

17. Jane Adams applied for a job driving a forklift truck in a factory. The job requirements included weighing at least 160 pounds to have sufficient strength to pick up the 100-pound boxes the forklift carried and which frequently fell off. Jane only weighs 150 pounds and was refused the job on this basis. Under these facts,

A. The weight requirement is invalid under the Civil Rights Act.

B. The weight requirement can be justified by the work required.

C. The factory must hire Jane.

D. The weight requirement discriminates against women under the Fair Labor Standards Act.

Answer (A) is correct. *(Publisher, adapted)*

REQUIRED: The true statement regarding a minimum weight requirement for a job.

DISCUSSION: The Civil Rights Act prohibits discrimination on the basis of race, color, national origin, religion, or sex. Height and weight requirements are discriminatory if they have the effect of screening out employees on the basis of race, sex, national origin, etc. The employer has the burden of proving that the requirement has a valid business purpose and that no alternate method of selection is less discriminatory.

Answer (B) is incorrect. The weight requirement cannot be justified since a strength test would be less discriminatory. Answer (C) is incorrect. The factory need not hire Jane, but it must give her an opportunity to apply for the job in a nondiscriminatory manner. Answer (D) is incorrect. Discrimination in wages, not discrimination in hiring, is covered by the Fair Labor Standards Act.

18. Under Title VII of the 1964 Civil Rights Act, which of the following forms of discrimination is not prohibited?

A. Sex.

B. Age.

C. Race.

D. Religion.

Answer (B) is correct. *(CPA, adapted)*
REQUIRED: The type of discrimination not prohibited under Title VII of the 1964 Civil Rights Act.
DISCUSSION: The Civil Rights Act prohibits discrimination on the basis of race, color, national origin, religion, or sex. Title VII does not prohibit discrimination based on age.

19. Which of the following statements about the treatment of sex discrimination in employment under Title VII of the Civil Rights Act of 1964 (as amended) is true?

A. Title VII prohibits discrimination based on an employee's or applicant's sexual preference.

B. Employer health insurance plans need not treat pregnancy in a manner similar to other ailments affecting the ability to work.

C. Title VII's prohibition against sex discrimination applies only to women.

D. Sexual harassment is a basis for suit even though it is not used in exchange for employment opportunities.

Answer (D) is correct. *(Publisher, adapted)*
REQUIRED: The true statement about employment discrimination based on sex.
DISCUSSION: Sexual harassment is a basis for a Title VII recovery when sexual advances, requests for sexual favors, and other sexual misconduct occur, and (1) submission thereto is at least implicitly a term or condition of employment, (2) employment decisions affecting the person are based on response to such behavior, or (3) the conduct creates an offensive environment or condition of work.
Answer (A) is incorrect. Discrimination based on sexual preference, e.g., homosexuality, is not barred by Title VII. Answer (B) is incorrect. The Pregnancy Discrimination Act of 1978 amended Title VII to bar discrimination based on pregnancy, childbirth, and related conditions. Hiring, firing, sick leave, and health and disability insurance are included. Answer (C) is incorrect. Men are also protected.

20. The Age Discrimination in Employment Act of 1967

A. Applies generally to employers that engage in interstate commerce and have 20 or more employees.

B. Does not apply to governmental entities.

C. Applies to individuals between the ages of 21 and 65.

D. Is limited to discrimination in hiring and discharging employees.

Answer (A) is correct. *(Publisher, adapted)*
REQUIRED: The true statement about the ADEA.
DISCUSSION: The ADEA covers most employers (individuals, partnerships, unions, corporations) engaged in interstate commerce that have 20 or more employees. It also applies to referrals by an employment agency to a covered employer regardless of the agency's size.
Answer (B) is incorrect. State and local governmental units are covered. A separate section of the act sets standards for some parts of the federal government. Answer (C) is incorrect. The ADEA applies to age discrimination against individuals who are at least 40 years old. Answer (D) is incorrect. The act applies to nearly all terms, conditions, and benefits of employment.

38.3 Safety

21. Which of the following statements is true regarding the scope and provisions of the Occupational Safety and Health Act (OSHA)?

A. OSHA requires employers to provide employees a workplace free from risk.

B. OSHA prohibits an employer from discharging an employee for revealing OSHA violations.

C. OSHA may inspect a workplace at any time regardless of employer objection.

D. OSHA preempts state regulation of workplace safety.

Answer (B) is correct. *(CPA, adapted)*
REQUIRED: The true statement about OSHA.
DISCUSSION: The Occupational Safety and Health Act (OSHA) prohibits an employer from discharging or discriminating against any employee who exercises a right under the act and, in particular, if an employee reveals OSHA violations.
Answer (A) is incorrect. The purpose of OSHA is to assure safe and healthy working conditions in the place of employment and to prevent injuries. The act does not ensure a workplace free from risk. Answer (C) is incorrect. An OSHA inspection is a search within the meaning of the Fourth Amendment and, when an employer objects to such an inspection, the OSHA representatives are required to obtain a search warrant. Answer (D) is incorrect. OSHA does not preempt state regulation of workplace safety. However, state regulation must not conflict with the provisions of OSHA.

22. Which of the following statements about a duty of an employer to protect employees from cigarette smoke of coworkers is true?

A. Any duty must rest upon federal law since the federal government has preempted the field of occupational safety.

B. Any right of the employee must be vindicated through workers' compensation proceedings.

C. Any such duty would have to be based upon enactment of a federal or state statute.

D. Employees could reasonably argue that they have a right to a smoke-free working environment based upon both common law and federal and state statutes.

Answer (D) is correct. *(Publisher, adapted)*

REQUIRED: The true statement about an employer's duty to protect employees from cigarette smoke.

DISCUSSION: Employers have a common law duty to maintain reasonable, safe working conditions. Employers are also subject to federal (OSHA) and state legislation regulating occupational hazards. Under OSHA, an employer is liable for failing to render the work place free of hazards that are recognized as likely to cause death or serious physical harm. Secondary smoke is recognized as a health hazard that is both foreseeable and preventable by the employer.

Answer (A) is incorrect. OSHA recognizes a concurrent state power to regulate occupational safety. Answer (B) is incorrect. Workers' compensation laws relate to monetary recoveries for work-related injuries and do not prohibit administrative action against occupational hazards. Answer (C) is incorrect. The common law duty of employers is also a basis for an action.

23. Which of the following statements about OSHA inspections is true?

A. The employer must be given at least 24 hours' notice.

B. An employee may request an inspection of his/her employer.

C. If an employer refuses to permit an inspection, OSHA may obtain a search warrant upon a showing of probable cause.

D. OSHA gives priority to random inspections of businesses.

Answer (B) is correct. *(Publisher, adapted)*

REQUIRED: The true statement about OSHA inspections.

DISCUSSION: An employee may file a written request for an inspection when violation of a standard results in a threat of physical harm or there is an imminent danger. An employee who has no reasonable alternative may in good faith refuse to work and as a result be exposed to the dangerous condition. But the Supreme Court has ruled that an employer need not pay an employee who refuses to work because of a dangerous condition.

Answer (A) is incorrect. An advance notice of no more than 24 hours is permitted in a few situations, but surprise inspections are the rule. Answer (C) is incorrect. The search warrant may be issued under a lesser standard than probable cause, for example, upon a showing that the inspection is at random. Answer (D) is incorrect. OSHA gives highest priority to inspections of imminently dangerous hazards. Next in order are investigations of fatalities and catastrophes, of complaints, and of certain high-risk industries.

24. Which of the following is a true statement about penalties provided by OSHA?

A. The act grants workers a private right of action.

B. No criminal penalties may be sought for OSHA violations.

C. The Secretary of Labor cannot issue an injunction to prevent future violations.

D. Penalties are in lieu of workers' compensation awards.

Answer (C) is correct. *(Publisher, adapted)*

REQUIRED: The true statement about penalties provided by OSHA.

DISCUSSION: The Secretary of Labor can assess penalties for violations of the Act and of rules and orders issued under it. The extent of the penalties depends upon whether violations are serious, willful, or repeated. Criminal and civil sanctions are available, including jail terms. The Secretary may also seek injunctions against future violations but may not issue them. Only a court can issue an injunction.

Answer (A) is incorrect. OSHA does not recognize a cause of action for workers against employers, third parties, or against the federal government for violations or not enforcing the act. Answer (B) is incorrect. OSHA provides for criminal penalties when serious, willful violations are found. Answer (D) is incorrect. OSHA does not affect workers' compensation laws.

38.4 Other Federal Statutes

25. The Fair Labor Standards Act (FLSA) as amended

A. Applies to all employers whether or not engaged in interstate commerce.

B. Requires that double time be paid to any employee working in excess of 8 hours in a given day.

C. Prohibits discrimination based upon the sex of the employee.

D. Requires all employees doing the same job to receive an equal rate of pay.

Answer (C) is correct. *(CPA, adapted)*

REQUIRED: The true statement about the FLSA.

DISCUSSION: The Fair Labor Standards Act regulates the relationship between an employer and employees by providing for minimum wages, overtime, and prohibition of child labor. Also, the equal pay provision prohibits discrimination on the basis of sex. It requires equal pay for equal work.

Answer (A) is incorrect. The FLSA applies only to employers engaged in interstate commerce. That is the limit on federal jurisdiction over commerce. Answer (B) is incorrect. The general overtime requirement is to pay at least time-and-one-half the regular rate for all hours worked over 40 per week. Answer (D) is incorrect. The FLSA permits pay differentials on the basis of seniority, merit, quality, or quantity.

26. Darren Stephens is an employee of the Jensen Manufacturing Company, a multi-state manufacturer of rollerskates. The plant in which he works is unionized and Stephens is a dues-paying union member. Which statement about the federal Fair Labor Standards Act (FLSA) is true?

A. The act allows a piece-rate method to be employed in lieu of the hourly-rate method when appropriate.

B. Jensen is permitted to pay less than the minimum wage to employees because they are represented by a bona fide union.

C. The act sets the maximum number of hours that an employee can work in a given day or week.

D. The act excludes from its coverage the employees of a labor union.

Answer (A) is correct. *(CPA, adapted)*

REQUIRED: The true statement about the FLSA.

DISCUSSION: The federal Fair Labor Standards Act (FLSA) provides for equal pay, minimum wages, and overtime, and prohibits child labor. Under the minimum pay and equal pay provisions, compensation need not be paid on an hourly basis if another method equals the minimum standard. Under the equal pay standard, an employer may differentiate among the employees on the basis of quality or quantity produced. The piece-rate method generally satisfies these requirements.

Answer (B) is incorrect. The act does not exempt members of a labor union. It also does exempt executive, administrative, and professional employees. Answer (C) is incorrect. The act does not set the maximum number of hours an employee can work in a given day or week. Answer (D) is incorrect. The act does not exempt employees of a union.

27. Which of the following classes of employees is exempt from both the minimum wage and maximum hours provisions of the federal Fair Labor Standards Act (FLSA)?

A. Members of a labor union.

B. Administrative personnel.

C. Hospital workers.

D. No class of employees is exempt.

Answer (B) is correct. *(CPA, adapted)*

REQUIRED: The class of employees exempt from the minimum wage and maximum hour provisions.

DISCUSSION: Certain employees are partially excluded from coverage of the FLSA, including administrative personnel (managers, not general office workers) who usually receive some minimum guaranteed annual wage and are required by conditions of their employment to work as long as necessary to accomplish their task.

Answer (A) is incorrect. Employees who belong to a labor union are not exempt. Answer (C) is incorrect. Although hospital workers are not exempt from minimum wages, they are partially exempt from the overtime provision if they so agree. Hospitals must pay overtime for more than 8 hours daily and for more than 80 hours in 14 days, but not for more than 40 hours in a week. Answer (D) is incorrect. Certain classes of employees are excluded, including executives, professionals, administrators, and outside salespersons. Partial exemptions exist for certain others.

28. Which of the following employees are exempt from the overtime provisions of the Fair Labor Standards Act (FLSA)?

A. Independent contractors.

B. Railroad and airline employees.

C. Members of a union recognized as the bargaining agent by the National Labor Relations Board.

D. Office workers.

Answer (B) is correct. *(CPA, adapted)*

REQUIRED: The employees not covered by the overtime provisions of the FLSA.

DISCUSSION: Certain workers are excluded from the overtime but not minimum wage provisions. Railroad and air carrier employees, taxi drivers, certain employees of motor carriers, sailors on American vessels, and certain local delivery employees are in this category.

Answer (A) is incorrect. An employer cannot escape coverage under the FLSA by designating a person as an independent contractor if the circumstances of the employment relation suggest that (s)he is an employee. Answer (C) is incorrect. This group is covered. Answer (D) is incorrect. This group is covered.

29. Under the Fair Labor Standards Act (FLSA), certain employment of children is considered oppressive and is prohibited. Which of the following is not a legal exception to the FLSA?

A. Employment in agriculture outside of school hours.

B. Employment of children under 16 by a parent.

C. Newspaper delivery.

D. After school part-time work in the fast-food industry.

Answer (D) is correct. *(CPA, adapted)*

REQUIRED: The activity not an exception to the prohibition against child labor.

DISCUSSION: Under the child labor section of the FLSA, most employment of children is considered oppressive and is prohibited. Children ages 14 and 15, in a light work occupation, outside school hours, and for a limited number of hours are exempted from the age 16 requirement. Legal exceptions also permit employment of children in agriculture outside of school hours, employment of children under age 16 by their parents and employment of children for newspaper delivery. However, there is no general exemption for children to work part-time after school in the fast-food industry.

30. The federal Fair Labor Standards Act

A. Prohibits any employment of a person under 16 years of age.

B. Requires payment of time-and-one-half for overtime to actors engaged in making television productions.

C. Contains an exemption from the minimum wage provisions for manufacturing plants located in areas of high unemployment.

D. Prohibits the delivery by a wholesaler to a dealer in another state of any goods if the wholesaler knew that oppressive child labor was used in their manufacture.

Answer (D) is correct. *(CPA, adapted)*

REQUIRED: The true statement regarding the federal Fair Labor Standards Act (FLSA).

DISCUSSION: The FLSA makes it illegal for any person knowing goods were produced in violation of the Act to ship or sell them in interstate commerce. One objective of the FLSA is to prohibit child labor, generally defined as employment of children under 16 but subject to some exceptions.

Answer (A) is incorrect. The FLSA does permit employment of children 14 or 15 in light work outside school hours for a limited number of hours, in agriculture, as actors, by their parents, or for newspaper delivery. Answer (B) is incorrect. Actors are professionals exempt from the FLSA. Answer (C) is incorrect. There are no exemptions from minimum wage provisions for manufacturers located in areas of high unemployment.

31. Under the Fair Labor Standards Act (FLSA) the Secretary of Labor does not have the power to

A. Issue subpoenas compelling attendance by a witness and the production of records by an employer.

B. Conduct investigations regarding practices subject to the act.

C. Issue a wage order that requires an employer to pay wages found to be due and owing under the act.

D. Issue injunctions to restrain obvious violations of the act.

Answer (D) is correct. *(CPA, adapted)*

REQUIRED: The power not given to the Secretary of Labor by the FLSA.

DISCUSSION: The department has power to order an employer to comply with the act. With regard to back wages, the department may supervise payment, the Secretary of Labor may file suit on behalf of employees (and obtain an equal amount as liquidated damages), or the employees themselves may sue. The Secretary of Labor has no authority under the FLSA to issue an injunction. (S)he may, however, seek an injunction from a court to prohibit violations of the act.

Answer (A) is incorrect. The Secretary may issue subpoenas compelling attendance by a witness and the production of records by an employer. Answer (B) is incorrect. The Secretary may conduct investigations regarding practices subject to the act. Answer (C) is incorrect. The Secretary may issue a wage order that requires an employer to pay wages found to be due and owing under the act.

32. The Equal Pay Act of 1963

A. Adopts the comparable worth principle of equal pay for comparable work.

B. Is an amendment of the Fair Labor Standards Act and covers the same employees.

C. Does not apply to pay differentials based on seniority, merit, quality or quantity of production, or any factor other than sex.

D. Applies only to women.

Answer (C) is correct. *(Publisher, adapted)*

REQUIRED: The true statement about the Equal Pay Act.

DISCUSSION: The Equal Pay Act requires equal pay for equal work. Equal work means that substantially equal effort, skill, and responsibility are required and that the work is performed under similar but not necessarily equal working conditions. Nevertheless, pay differentials between men and women performing equal work may be lawfully based on certain factors. Length of time on the job (seniority); an objective means of merit determination communicated and applied to all employees (merit); and piecework, commission, or quality-control payment methods (quality or quantity of production) are such factors.

Answer (A) is incorrect. The Equal Pay Act did not accept the comparable worth principle. While the act would apply to male and female flight attendants, it would not operate to equalize pay between, for example, male secretaries and female park rangers. Answer (B) is incorrect. The Equal Pay Act also applies to executives, administrators, professionals, outside salespersons, and employees of state and local governments. Answer (D) is incorrect. The act applies to men and women.

33. Under the Federal Consolidated Budget Reconciliation Act of 1985 (COBRA), when an employee voluntarily resigns from a job, the former employee's group health insurance coverage that was in effect during the period of employment with the company

A. Automatically ceases for the former employee and spouse if the resignation occurred before normal retirement age.

B. Automatically ceases for the former employee's spouse but continues for the former employee for an 18-month period at the former employer's expense.

C. May be retained by the former employee at the former employee's expense for at least 18 months after leaving the company but must be terminated for the former employee's spouse.

D. May be retained for the former employee and spouse at the former employee's expense for at least 18 months after leaving the company.

Answer (D) is correct. *(CPA, adapted)*

REQUIRED: The status of a former employee's group health insurance coverage after the employee voluntarily resigns from a job.

DISCUSSION: The Consolidated Budget Reconciliation Act of 1985 (COBRA) provides that an employee of a private employer or the employee's beneficiaries must be offered the opportunity to continue their group health insurance for 18 months after termination or the loss of coverage due to certain qualifying events. The employer must notify the employee and his/her beneficiaries of their rights under the act.

Answer (A) is incorrect. Continued coverage must be offered if resignation occurs before normal retirement age. Answer (B) is incorrect. The former employee must pay the premium, and coverage may continue for the spouse. Answer (C) is incorrect. Coverage may continue for the spouse.

34. A U.S. employer sponsors a defined-benefit pension plan. Under the Pension Protection Act of 2006,

A. The employer may require employees to invest their contributions in the employer's shares.

B. Underfunding must be eliminated within 7 years if the plan is not at risk.

C. The employer may not offer a contributory plan.

D. Plan assets may never be used to fund employee health benefits.

Answer (B) is correct. *(Publisher, adapted)*

REQUIRED: The provision of the Pension Protection Act of 2006.

DISCUSSION: The Pension Protection Act of 2006 requires an employer with a defined-benefit pension plan to eliminate underfunding within 7 years. However, an employer with an at-risk plan must make accelerated contributions. Moreover, if a plan is more than 20% underfunded, benefits may not be increased unless paid for immediately. If a plan is more than 20% overfunded, the employer may use plan assets to fund retiree health benefits.

Answer (A) is incorrect. The plan is not contributory. Moreover, in a contributory plan, an employer may not force employees to invest their contributions in the employer's shares. Answer (C) is incorrect. An employer with a defined-benefit plan may offer automatic enrollment in a defined-contribution plan, e.g., a 401(k) plan. Answer (D) is incorrect. If a plan is more than 20% overfunded, the employer may use plan assets to fund retiree health benefits.

38.5 Workers' Compensation and Employer Liability

35. The primary purpose for enacting workers' compensation statutes was to

A. Eliminate all employer-employee negligence lawsuits.

B. Enable employees to recover for injuries regardless of negligence.

C. Prevent employee negligence suits against third parties.

D. Allow employees to recover additional compensation for employer negligence.

Answer (B) is correct. *(CPA, adapted)*

REQUIRED: The primary purpose for enacting workers' compensation statutes.

DISCUSSION: Workers' compensation laws were enacted to provide a sure remedy for injured employees. Under common law, they had to sue the employer, prove negligence, and be subject to various defenses. Workers' compensation is usually the exclusive remedy for an injured employee against the employer.

Answer (A) is incorrect. Certain employers are exempt, such as employers with fewer than a certain number of employees. Answer (C) is incorrect. An injured employee may, in addition to recovering workers' compensation benefits, pursue legal action against a third party. Answer (D) is incorrect. Workers' compensation is usually the exclusive remedy for an injured employee against the employer.

36. Which of the following parties generally is ineligible to collect workers' compensation benefits?

A. Minors.

B. Truck drivers.

C. Union employees.

D. Temporary office workers.

Answer (D) is correct. *(CPA, adapted)*

REQUIRED: The parties not eligible to collect workers' compensation benefits.

DISCUSSION: Workers' compensation laws were passed by all 50 states to reimburse employees for losses sustained because of work-related injury or disease regardless of who, if anyone, was at fault. Independent contractors and casual (e.g., temporary), agricultural, or domestic employees are not covered.

Answer (A) is incorrect. Minors are eligible to collect workers' compensation benefits. Answer (B) is incorrect. Truck drivers are eligible to collect workers' compensation benefits. Answer (C) is incorrect. Union employees are eligible to collect workers' compensation benefits.

37. Which one of the following statements about workers' compensation laws is generally true?

A. Employers are strictly liable without regard to whether or not they are at fault.

B. Workers' compensation benefits are not available if the employee is negligent.

C. Workers' compensation awards are not reviewable by the courts.

D. The amount of damages recoverable is based on comparative negligence.

Answer (A) is correct. *(CPA, adapted)*

REQUIRED: The true statement about workers' compensation laws.

DISCUSSION: Workers' compensation is a form of strict liability. The employer is liable (even if (s)he is not negligent) to an employee for injuries or diseases sustained by the employee that arise out of and in the course of employment. The employee is generally entitled to workers' compensation benefits without regard to fault.

Answer (B) is incorrect. The employee will receive workers' compensation despite his/her negligence. Answer (C) is incorrect. The outcome of an administrative hearing may be appealed to the courts. Answer (D) is incorrect. The amount of damages the employee will be allowed is not based on comparative fault but on a scheme prescribed by state statute, usually a percentage of the injured employee's wages.

38. Which of the following would be the employer's best defense to a claim for workers' compensation by an injured route salesman?

A. A route salesman is automatically deemed to be an independent contractor, and therefore excluded from workers' compensation coverage.

B. The salesman was grossly negligent in carrying out the employment.

C. The salesman's injury was caused primarily by the negligence of an employee.

D. The salesman's injury did not arise out of and in the course of employment.

Answer (D) is correct. *(CPA, adapted)*

REQUIRED: The employer's best workers' compensation defense to a route salesman's claim.

DISCUSSION: The injury must be work-related. It must arise out of the employment in that it must be typical of the kind of employment involved. It must occur in the course of the employment in the sense that the worker must have been actively at work or away from the job location performing employment-related duties. In general, the requirement is liberally construed in favor of workers.

Answer (A) is incorrect. A route salesman is under the control of the employer as to the means of accomplishing the work and is thus not an independent contractor. Independent contractors must furnish their own insurance. Answer (B) is incorrect. Under workers' compensation law, the defense of contributory negligence is unavailable. Answer (C) is incorrect. Under workers' compensation law, the defense that the injury was caused by a fellow servant is not allowed.

39. Workers' compensation laws provide for all of the following benefits except

A. Burial expenses.

B. Full pay during disability.

C. The cost of prosthetic devices.

D. Monthly payments to surviving dependent children.

Answer (B) is correct. *(CPA, adapted)*

REQUIRED: The benefit not provided for by workers' compensation laws.

DISCUSSION: Amounts awarded under typical workers' compensation laws may be for (1) wage loss, (2) medical costs and devices, (3) loss of body members, and (4) death. Only a portion of wage-earning capacity is usually awarded.

Answer (A) is incorrect. Death benefits under workers' compensation include burial expenses. Answer (C) is incorrect. Medical expenses covered include the cost of prosthetic devices. Answer (D) is incorrect. Death benefits under workers' compensation include payments to surviving dependents.

40. Musgrove Manufacturing Enterprises is subject to compulsory workers' compensation laws in the state in which it does business. It has complied with the state's workers' compensation provisions. State law provides that when there has been compliance, workers' compensation is normally an exclusive remedy against the employer. However, the remedy will not be exclusive if

A. The employee has been intentionally injured by the employer personally.

B. The employee dies as a result of his injuries.

C. The accident was entirely the fault of a fellow-servant of the employee.

D. The employer was only slightly negligent and the employee's conduct was grossly negligent.

Answer (A) is correct. *(CPA, adapted)*

REQUIRED: The circumstance in which workers' compensation is not the exclusive remedy.

DISCUSSION: An injury covered by a typical workers' compensation statute is accidental and arises out of and in the course of employment. Thus, an employer is not permitted to use the workers' compensation statutes to insulate him/herself from intentional or egregious wrongdoing.

Answer (B) is incorrect. Normally the exclusive remedy for an injury (including death) is that the employee or his/her estate must accept the scheduled benefit under state workers' compensation acts. Answer (C) is incorrect. Even though an accident is entirely the fault of a fellow employee, workers' compensation will still be the exclusive remedy against the employer. (Under the common-law fellow-servant doctrine, the negligence of a fellow employee is not attributed to the employer. However, the injured employee could sue the third party). Answer (D) is incorrect. Workers' compensation acts are the exclusive remedy for an injured employee without regard to whether the employee or the employer was negligent or grossly negligent.

41. Kroll, an employee of Acorn, Inc., was injured in the course of employment while operating a forklift manufactured and sold to Acorn by Trell Corp. The forklift was defectively designed by Trell. Under the state's mandatory workers' compensation statute, Kroll will be successful in

	Obtaining Workers' Compensation Benefits	A Negligence Action against Acorn
A.	Yes	Yes
B.	Yes	No
C.	No	Yes
D.	No	No

Answer (B) is correct. *(CPA, adapted)*

REQUIRED: The true statement about the rights of an injured employee.

DISCUSSION: The law of workers' compensation permits recovery for a work-related injury (arising out of and in the course of employment), but a negligence suit against the employer is barred. However, when an employee's injuries are caused by a third party, the injured employee may, in addition to recovering workers' compensation benefits, pursue a legal action against the third party. Thus, a strict liability suit against the manufacturer of defective equipment is not barred.

42. If an employee is injured, full workers' compensation benefits are not payable if the employee

A. Was injured because of failing to abide by written safety procedures.

B. Was injured because of the acts of fellow employees.

C. Intentionally caused self-inflicted injury.

D. Brought a civil suit against a third party who caused the injury.

Answer (C) is correct. *(CPA, adapted)*

REQUIRED: The circumstances under which full workers' compensation benefits are not payable.

DISCUSSION: Workers' compensation is usually awarded an employee for injury that arises out of and occurs during the course of employment. But benefits are unavailable for injury resulting from intentional self-infliction, willful intoxication, fighting not induced by the employer, or pre-existing physical conditions.

Answer (A) is incorrect. An employee's failure to abide by safety procedures is not a defense to a workers' compensation claim. Answer (B) is incorrect. Such a claim is compensable provided it arose out of and in the course of employment. Answer (D) is incorrect. If a third party causes the injury, the employee may receive workers' compensation and sue the third party.

43. Which of the following statements about workers' compensation claim procedures is true?

A. No statute of limitations applies to claims.

B. A notice of injury must be given within the statutory period.

C. In the majority of states, courts decide contested claims.

D. Appeals from the decision of the trier of fact are not permitted.

Answer (B) is correct. *(Publisher, adapted)*

REQUIRED: The true statement about workers' compensation claim procedures.

DISCUSSION: After the injury occurs, the worker must give notice of the injury within the statutory limit. A statute of limitations also applies to the filing of the claim. In the majority of states, claims are heard by an administrative agency. In some states, courts decide these cases (but most claims are uncontested). When a claim is heard by an agency, the proceeding is judicial but with a more simplified and informal procedure. After hearing testimony and receiving evidence, a decision is made that may be appealed to the court system.

Answer (A) is incorrect. Both notice of injury and filing of a claim are subject to time limits. Answer (C) is incorrect. Most states have administrative agencies for this purpose. Answer (D) is incorrect. Whether the trier of fact is an administrative agency or a court, the decision is appealable.

38.6 Social Security and Unemployment Benefits

44. Hexter Manufacturing is a small business as defined by the Small Business Administration. Regarding Hexter's relationship to requirements of the Social Security Act, which of the following is true?

A. Because Hexter is a small business, it is exempt from the Social Security Act.

B. Social Security payments made by Hexter's employees are tax deductible for federal income tax purposes.

C. Hexter has the option to be covered or excluded from the provisions of the Social Security Act.

D. The Social Security Act applies to both Hexter and its employees.

Answer (D) is correct. *(CPA, adapted)*

REQUIRED: The relationship of a small business to the Social Security Act.

DISCUSSION: The Social Security Act covers most workers or employees in the United States today. Persons employed in industry and commerce, the self-employed, household employees, farm employees, clergy, and members of the armed forces are included. The act makes no distinction between small and large businesses; all employees are covered.

Answer (A) is incorrect. No employer is exempt from the Social Security Act. Answer (B) is incorrect. Payments made by employees to the Social Security system are not deductible for federal income tax purposes. Answer (C) is incorrect. No employee or employer has the option to be excluded from Social Security; coverage is mandatory.

45. An employer who fails to withhold Federal Insurance Contributions Act (FICA) taxes from covered employees' wages, but who pays both the employer and employee shares,

A. Is entitled to a refund from the IRS for the employees' share.

B. Is allowed no federal tax deduction for any payments.

C. Has a right to be reimbursed by the employees for the employees' share.

D. Owes penalties and interest for failure to collect the tax.

Answer (C) is correct. *(CPA, adapted)*

REQUIRED: The effect of an employer's payment of an employee's share of FICA taxes after failing to withhold it.

DISCUSSION: An employer is primarily liable to pay an employee's share of FICA tax if the employer fails to pay and remit it. The employer then has a right to reimbursement by the employee of the amount paid.

Answer (A) is incorrect. The employer's right is to reimbursement from the employee. No IRS refund is payable for satisfying a liability. Answer (B) is incorrect. The employer's share of FICA tax paid is deductible by the employer. Answer (D) is incorrect. Failure to collect the employee shares of FICA tax is not subject to penalty and interest.

46. Which of the following types of income is subject to taxation under the provisions of the Federal Insurance Contributions Act (FICA)?

A. Interest earned on municipal bonds.

B. Capital gains of $3,000.

C. Car received as a productivity award.

D. Dividends of $2,500.

Answer (C) is correct. *(CPA, adapted)*

REQUIRED: The type of income to which Social Security tax applies.

DISCUSSION: The Social Security tax imposed by the Federal Insurance Contributions Act (FICA) applies to virtually all compensation received for employment, including money or other forms of wages, bonuses, commissions, vacation pay, severance allowances, and tips. A car received as a productivity award is a form of compensation for employment which is not excepted from application of FICA tax. Income derived from an investment, as opposed to compensation for employment, is not subject to FICA tax.

47. Under the Federal Insurance Contributions Act (FICA), all of the following are considered wages except

A. Contingent fees.

B. Reimbursed travel expenses.

C. Bonuses.

D. Commissions.

Answer (B) is correct. *(CPA, adapted)*

REQUIRED: The type of payment not treated as wages for purposes of the Social Security FICA tax.

DISCUSSION: The Social Security tax imposed by the Federal Insurance Contributions Act (FICA) applies to virtually all compensation received for employment, including money or other forms of wages, bonuses, commissions, vacation pay, severance allowances, and tips. Reimbursed travel expenses are not included as wages to the extent a corresponding deduction is allowable.

Answer (A) is incorrect. Contingent fees are treated as a form of compensation from employment for purposes of FICA. Answer (C) is incorrect. Bonuses are treated as a form of compensation from employment for purposes of FICA. Answer (D) is incorrect. Commissions are treated as a form of compensation from employment for purposes of FICA.

48. Which of the following statements is true with respect to Social Security taxes and benefits?

A. A self-employed individual with net earnings of $35,000 will pay more tax than an employee with wages of $35,000.

B. Both employees and self-employed individuals are subject to Social Security taxes based on their respective gross wages or gross earnings from self-employment.

C. To the extent the amount received as retirement benefits is less than the amount contributed to the Social Security fund by the individual, it will never be included in the individual's adjusted gross income for federal income tax purposes.

D. An individual whose gross income exceeds certain maximum limitations is required to include the entire amount received as disability benefits in the computation of the individual's adjusted gross income for federal income tax purposes.

Answer (A) is correct. *(CPA, adapted)*

REQUIRED: The true statement about Social Security taxes and benefits.

DISCUSSION: The employer must pay the following (for 2011): (1) 6.2% of the first $106,800 of wages paid for old age, survivor's, and disability insurance (OASDI), plus (2) 1.45% of all wages for hospital insurance (HI). The employer must withhold (for 2011) 4.2% from the first $106,800 of employee wages and 1.45% of all employee wages. Self-employed persons are required to report their own taxable income and pay Social Security tax. The FICA tax liability of a self-employed individual is equal to the combined employer-employee contribution. In 2011, it equals 13.3% (10.4% OASDI rate applied to the net earnings base for 2011 of $106,800 + 2.9% applied to all net earnings).

Answer (B) is incorrect. Net earnings from self-employment, not gross earnings, is the Social Security tax base for a self-employed individual. Answer (C) is incorrect. A portion of Social Security benefits received by an individual may be included in the individual's adjusted gross income. Answer (D) is incorrect. Only a portion of an individual's disability benefits is included in his/her gross income if certain limitations on gross income are exceeded. The exact amount is computed on the basis of a formula set forth in the Internal Revenue Code.

49. After serving as an active director of Lee Corp. for 20 years, Ryan was appointed an honorary director with the obligation to attend directors' meetings with no voting power. In the most recent tax year, Ryan received an honorary director's fee of $5,000. This fee is

A. Reportable by Lee as employee compensation subject to Social Security tax.

B. Reportable by Ryan as self-employment income subject to Social Security self-employment tax.

C. Taxable as "Other income" by Ryan, not subject to any Social Security tax.

D. Considered to be a gift not subject to Social Security self-employment or income tax.

Answer (B) is correct. *(CPA, adapted)*

REQUIRED: The tax treatment of honorary director's fees.

DISCUSSION: A person is not an employee of a corporation when acting as a director. However, fees for acting as a director are treated as earnings from self-employment, subject to both income tax and Social Security self-employment tax.

50. Under the Federal Insurance Contributions Act (FICA) and the Social Security Act (SSA),

A. Persons who are self-employed are not required to make FICA contributions.

B. Employees who participate in private retirement plans are not required to make FICA contributions.

C. Death benefits are payable to an employee's survivors only if the employee dies before reaching the age of retirement.

D. The receipt of earned income by a person who is also receiving Social Security retirement benefits may result in a reduction of such benefits.

Answer (D) is correct. *(CPA, adapted)*

REQUIRED: The true statement about FICA and the Social Security Act (SSA).

DISCUSSION: Retired employees under full retirement age are subject to an annual earnings limitation (which changes periodically) that reduces the amount of Social Security benefits when exceeded. A limitation is no longer effective when the retiree reaches full retirement age (65 currently but rising to 67).

Answer (A) is incorrect. Self-employed persons are subject to FICA tax on net earnings from self-employment. Answer (B) is incorrect. Participation by an employee in a private retirement plan affects deductibility of contributions to IRAs, but not liability for FICA tax. Answer (C) is incorrect. There is no such condition upon entitlement to the benefits.

51. Social Security benefits may be obtained by

A. Qualifying individuals who are also receiving benefits from a private pension plan.

B. Qualifying individuals or their families only upon such individual's disability or retirement.

C. Children of a deceased worker who was entitled to benefits until such children reach age 25 or complete their education, whichever occurs first.

D. Only those individuals who have made payments while employed.

Answer (A) is correct. *(CPA, adapted)*

REQUIRED: The availability of Social Security benefits.

DISCUSSION: The federal Social Security Act permits qualifying individuals to receive benefits even if they currently receive benefits from a private pension plan as long as the individual has worked for the statutory period of time and/or earned the specified amount of wages.

Answer (B) is incorrect. Qualifying individuals or their families are eligible for benefits upon death of the individual in addition to retirement or disability. Answer (C) is incorrect. Benefits may be received by dependents of a qualifying deceased worker until the dependents reach age 18 or complete their education, whichever comes first. Answer (D) is incorrect. Benefits are not limited to individuals who have made payments while employed. Survivors' benefits are paid to certain members of a deceased worker's family. Also, certain dependents of a disabled worker may receive payments. None of these recipients is required to have made contributions.

52. Social Security benefits may include all of the following except

A. Payments to divorced spouses.

B. Payments to disabled children.

C. Medicare payments.

D. Medicaid payments.

Answer (D) is correct. *(CPA, adapted)*

REQUIRED: The payment that is not a Social Security benefit.

DISCUSSION: Benefits provided by the Social Security Act as amended are paid to retired workers over a certain age, to the surviving spouse and children of deceased workers, and to disabled workers and certain of their dependents. Also, health and medical insurance are provided for the elderly under Medicare. Medicaid payments are not funded as a Social Security benefit.

Answer (A) is incorrect. Payments to divorced spouses may be made as a Social Security benefit. Answer (B) is incorrect. Payments to disabled children may be made as a Social Security benefit. Answer (C) is incorrect. Medicare payments may be made as a Social Security benefit.

53. Eligibility to receive Social Security benefits

A. Is limited to retired and disabled workers.

B. Depends on achieving fully insured status.

C. Depends on having earnings from employment for a specified number of calendar quarters.

D. Is limited to those with fully insured or disability status.

Answer (C) is correct. *(Publisher, adapted)*

REQUIRED: The true statement about eligibility to receive Social Security benefits.

DISCUSSION: Benefits provided by the Social Security Act are paid to retired workers over a certain age, to a surviving spouse and children of deceased workers, and to disabled workers and certain of their dependents. Also, health and medical insurance are provided for the elderly. Fully insured status is attained by earning nominal amounts (as low as $50) per calendar quarter as an employee or a self-employed person for a certain number of quarters. This number of quarters must be at least 6. A person who falls in between 6 and 40 quarters is eligible if the number is equal to the lesser of the excess of one's age over 21 or the number of years since 1950. This entitles a person to full old age and survivors' benefits. Currently insured (not fully insured) status is based on receipt of credit for at least 6 quarters in the preceding 13. Persons in this status are entitled to only part of the benefits provided to those who have fully insured status. Disability status is based on receipt of credit for 20 of the 40 quarters preceding disablement.

Answer (A) is incorrect. Dependents also may receive benefits. Answer (B) is incorrect. Those on currently insured status qualify but receive lower benefits. Answer (D) is incorrect. Those on disability status qualify but receive lower benefits.

54. Taxes payable under the Federal Unemployment Tax Act (FUTA) are

A. Deductible by the employer as a business expense for federal income tax purposes.

B. Payable by employers for all employees.

C. Withheld from the wages of all covered employees.

D. Calculated as a fixed percentage of all compensation paid to an employee.

Answer (A) is correct. *(CPA, adapted)*

REQUIRED: The true statement about the federal unemployment tax.

DISCUSSION: Federal unemployment tax must be paid by an employer who employs one or more persons covered under the federal Social Security Act for at least some part of a day in any of 20 or more different weeks, or who pays wages of $1,500 or more during any calendar quarter. The tax is calculated as a fixed percentage of each covered employee's salary up to a stated maximum. The employer is permitted to deduct these payments as a business expense for federal income tax purposes. Moreover, the employer is allowed a credit against FUTA tax for unemployment tax paid to a state.

Answer (B) is incorrect. They are only payable for covered employees. Also, an employer who pays less than $1,500 to all employees during the calendar quarter may not be liable to pay FUTA tax. Answer (C) is incorrect. Federal unemployment taxes are only imposed on the employer, not the employee. Thus, the employer does not withhold them. Answer (D) is incorrect. The tax is a fixed percentage of each covered employee's salary up to a stated maximum.

55. An employer who experiences an unemployment tax rate of 3.2% in a state having a standard unemployment tax rate of 5.4% may take a credit against federal unemployment tax of

A. 3.0%

B. 3.2%

C. 5.4%

D. 6.0%

Answer (C) is correct. *(CPA, adapted)*

REQUIRED: The credit against federal unemployment tax allowable to an employer who pays state unemployment tax.

DISCUSSION: An employer is allowed a credit against FUTA tax for unemployment tax paid to a state. The credit is the tax paid to the state, but is limited to 5.4% of the first $7,000 of wages paid. Because the state in the question taxes 5.4% of wages, that is the amount of the credit.

Answer (A) is incorrect. Although the amount paid to the state usually depends upon the employer's prior experience regarding the frequency and amount of unemployment claims, the state in question has a standard rate of 5.4%. Answer (B) is incorrect. Although the amount paid to the state usually depends upon the employer's prior experience regarding the frequency and amount of unemployment claims, the state in question has a standard rate of 5.4%. Answer (D) is incorrect. The credit is limited to 5.4% of the first $7,000 of wages paid each employee.

56. In general, which of the following statements is true with respect to unemployment compensation?

A. An employee who is unable to work because of a disability is entitled to unemployment compensation.

B. An individual who has been discharged from employment because of work-connected misconduct is ineligible for unemployment compensation.

C. The maximum period during which unemployment compensation may be collected is uniform throughout the United States.

D. The maximum amount of weekly unemployment compensation payments made by a state is determined by federal law.

Answer (B) is correct. *(CPA, adapted)*

REQUIRED: The true statement with respect to unemployment compensation under FUTA.

DISCUSSION: A worker ordinarily must meet three conditions to collect unemployment compensation: (1) The worker was employed and laid off through no fault of the worker; (2) the worker filed a claim for the benefits; and (3) the worker is able, available, and willing to work but cannot find employment.

Answer (A) is incorrect. To collect unemployment compensation, an individual must be able, available, and willing to work. Answer (C) is incorrect. Although federal law provides general guidelines, standards, and requirements for the program, the states administer the benefit payments under the program. A state may determine the maximum amount of and period for unemployment compensation. Answer (D) is incorrect. A state determines maximum weekly payments.

57. An unemployed CPA generally will receive unemployment compensation benefits if the CPA

A. Was fired as a result of the employer's business reversals.

B. Refused to accept a job as an accountant while receiving extended benefits.

C. Was fired for embezzling from a client.

D. Left work voluntarily without good cause.

Answer (A) is correct. *(CPA, adapted)*

REQUIRED: The circumstances in which a person will generally qualify to receive unemployment compensation benefits.

DISCUSSION: There are ordinarily three conditions to collect unemployment compensation: (1) The worker was employed and laid off through no fault of the worker; (2) the worker filed a claim for the benefits; and (3) the worker is able, available, and willing to work but cannot find employment. A worker is disqualified if (s)he refuses other suitable work, was discharged for good cause, or quit voluntarily.

Answer (B) is incorrect. The CPA is not required to accept the other job but is not entitled to the unemployment compensation if (s)he refuses the job. Answer (C) is incorrect. A worker is disqualified if (s)he was discharged for good cause. Answer (D) is incorrect. A worker is disqualified if (s)he left work voluntarily without good cause.

STUDY UNIT THIRTY-NINE
INTERNATIONAL BUSINESS LAW

Virtually every major business considers foreign countries to be potential markets for its products or services and as sources of products, materials, and labor. For this reason, otherwise independent nations voluntarily agree to be governed by **international business law** to facilitate commerce. It governs the actions of individuals and business associations and is drawn from a variety of sources. However, no single body of law binds all nations and no system of courts has compulsory process or jurisdiction to render decisions valid and binding across all national boundaries. Nevertheless, international law does exist. The **sources of international law** include (1) the customary norms recognized by all civilized societies, (2) general principles of law common to all civilized states, (3) international treaties or agreements, (4) judicial precedent, (5) scholarly writings and pronouncements of international political organizations, and (6) trade communities.

Customs regarding trade between nations are developed over a period of time, based on nations' business and political dealings. **Treaties** are formalized agreements between or among independent nations. **Conventions** are a functional equivalent of treaties. They are agreements signed by two or more countries but sponsored by international organizations, as opposed to a particular country or countries. For example, the United States has joined many other countries in adopting the United Nations Convention on **Contracts for the International Sale of Goods (CISG)**, which is equivalent to UCC Article 2 (Chapters 13 and 14). The CISG establishes substantive law governing the formation of international sales contracts and the rights and obligations of both the buyer and the seller. The CISG does not apply to consumer or service transactions. **Precedent**, established by a series of judicial decisions, can be used as guidelines for commercial activity. **Scholarly writings** have contributed greatly to the body of international law by influencing policy makers in the development of new law. **International political organizations** also contribute significantly to international business law. An example is the UN's judicial branch (the **International Court of Justice**, or World Court), which sits at The Hague in the Netherlands. It has 15 judges representing the major legal systems of the world and only hears cases involving countries. The International Court of Justice may issue advisory opinions on international business law. Other UN organizations also play important roles. The **UN Commission on International Trade Law (UNCITRAL)** was formed in an effort to standardize commercial practices and agreements. The **UN Conference on Trade and Development (UNCTAD)** is a permanent organization of the UN General Assembly. It was formed to address international trade reform and redistribution of income through trade.

International trade communities are groups of member nations that adopt and adhere to common trade policies and rules. The most developed and powerful international trade community is the **European Union (EU)**. The EU is important to American business because, as an economic unit, it is the largest importer of American products in the world. Other such communities include (1) the Andean Common Market, (2) the Asian Pacific Economic Cooperation, (3) the Association of Southeastern Nations, (4) the Caribbean Community Market, (5) the Central American Common Market, (6) the Common Market for Eastern and Southern Africa, (7) the Economic Community of West African States, (8) the Gulf Cooperation Council, and (9) the Latin American Trading Group.

International trade agreements provide regulatory authority for businesses in international trade. Until recently, the broadest and most important of these agreements was the **General Agreement on Tariffs and Trade (GATT)**. Under GATT, the signatory countries agreed to equal treatment of all member nations, multilateral negotiations to reduce tariffs, and the abolition of import quotas. However, GATT was replaced by the **World Trade Organization (WTO)**. The WTO, which was established on January 1, 1995, is the product of the Uruguay Round of international trade negotiations. It is a permanent body with a secretariat based in Geneva, Switzerland. The **WTO Agreement** is a permanent set of commitments by more than 153 member nations designed to prohibit trade discrimination among member nations and between imported and domestic products. Most of the rules of GATT are still applicable with respect to trade in goods. The WTO Agreement applies to trade in services and intellectual property as well as goods. The **General Agreement on Trade in Services (GATS)** applies GATT's principles to reduce trade barriers regarding services. The TRIPS agreement applies to intellectual property. In addition to market access, the WTO's mandate also extends to (1) antidumping rules, (2) subsidies and countervailing measures, (3) import licensing, (4) rules of origin, (5) technical barriers to trade, (6) sanitary measures, (7) emergency protection from imports ("safeguards"), and (8) preshipment inspection. The WTO provides for a **multilateral dispute settlement** apparatus. If bilateral consultations and mediation efforts fail, a panel is established to examine the case and make recommendations. If a violation is found, trade retaliation by the complainant against an offending country may be approved if that country does not comply with the recommendations. The **North American Free Trade Agreement (NAFTA)** encompasses the U.S., Canada, and Mexico, the largest trading block in the world. Like the EU, NAFTA's sovereign members allow certain aspects of their national law to become secondary to regional international law. This process includes relinquishing some government functions to a regional government. NAFTA eliminates barriers to the flow of goods, services, and investment within the trade area. Like the EU, NAFTA incorporates labor, environmental, and consumer protection law in addition to the trade and tariff law. International agreements on intellectual property include the **Paris Convention of 1883** (patents and trademarks). It permits nationals of one signatory country to file in any other signatory country. The **Berne Convention of 1886** applies to copyrights. Publication in a signatory country requires all other signatories to honor the copyright even if the author is not from a country that has ratified the convention. However, the 1994 **Agreement on Trade-Related Aspects of Intellectual Property Rights (TRIPS)** is the most important in this area. Members must enact laws to protect intellectual property rights and provide adequate remedies for violation of these rights. Moreover, members cannot discriminate against the citizens of other member countries. Thus, adequate procedures must be available to such parties to enforce their rights. TRIPS also contains a dispute resolution procedure. Specific sections of TRIPS apply to copyrights, patents, and trademarks. Software is specifically recognized as copyrightable.

Various methods to conduct trade with entities in a foreign country are available to American business. A firm seeking to enter into or increase business transactions that bridge international borders must consider various means of entering such markets. For example, the simplest and perhaps least risky approach is for a domestic manufacturer to sell directly to a foreign buyer. An American business also may sell property rights, intellectual copyrights in particular, to selected buyers in another country. This sale is typically accomplished by a licensing agreement. A **license** permits the licensee to exploit the subject matter of the license for a specified purpose and for a specified time.

For example, if an American business owns certain unique product technology or patent rights to an innovative product or manufacturing technique, it may sell a right to use that technology or patent to a business in another country. The foreign business usually agrees to pay royalties in exchange for the license to use the technology or patent. Unless agreed otherwise, however, all other rights are retained by the owner of the intellectual property. Another possibility in conducting international business is to create **distributorships**. A domestic business entity may enter into an arrangement where it agrees to market its products through the sales effort of a foreign-based distributor. Typically, a distributor is free to develop the target market in any manner it sees fit. It is free to buy and sell for its own account, maintain inventories, and sell at prices it sets. **Direct foreign investment** is a method of conducting foreign trade in which a domestic corporation may do business through a **subsidiary** located in the foreign country. Typically, a parent corporation owns shares representing a controlling interest in the subsidiary. A **branch** is in principle a hybrid of direct foreign sales and investment. The branch is not a separate entity but is an extension of the domestic enterprise in a host country. The enterprise might establish an international site in the host country that requires direct investment. Some possibilities include research and experimental facilities, a manufacturing plant for local sales or export, and an operation that sells both its own products and those of other enterprises. Still another vehicle for international trade is the **joint venture**. The only legally or politically accepted means of directly investing in a foreign country may be a joint venture with a foreign entity located within the foreign country. Although a joint venture is usually thought of as a partnership, it may be a corporation or other organizational form. Joint ventures for export purposes are encouraged by the **Export Trading Company Act of 1982**. This act provides an exemption from the antitrust laws for an export trade association or export trading company that is issued a Certificate of Review. An applicant qualifies if its operations will (1) not substantially lessen competition or restrain trade in the U.S. or substantially restrain a competitor's export trade, (2) not unreasonably affect U.S. prices, (3) not constitute unfair competition, and (4) not result in sale or resale of products or services in the U.S. The **U.S. Export-Import Bank** provides loan guarantees to U.S. banks that lead to U.S. export trading companies. Another statute that promotes U.S. economic activity abroad is the **National Cooperative Research and Production Act of 1993**. Under this act, joint research and production of products, processes, or services are subject to rule of reason antitrust standard, not the harsher per se standard. Also, a joint venturer that notifies the FTC and the Justice Department will not be liable for more than actual damages in a private antitrust suit. Still another means is the granting of tax advantages to exporters who sell abroad using certain foreign sales corporations (see the **Revenue Act of 1971**). Perhaps the most important means of promoting U.S. foreign trade was the creation of the **Overseas Private Investment Corporation**. It protects foreign investment by insuring against (1) expropriation of assets [a taking consistent with the foreign country's law that is for (a) a public purpose and (b) just compensation]; (2) confiscation (an illegal taking); (3) war, revolution, or other civil strife; and (4) a prohibition of (a) repatriation of investment capital or (b) conversion of earnings into dollars. However, exports also may be restricted. The Constitution states, "No Tax or Duty shall be laid on Articles exported from any State." Nevertheless, exports may be limited by imposition of quotas or by prohibition of the transfer of sensitive technology (see the **Export Administration Act of 1979**).

U.S. **antitrust laws** have sweeping application in the international setting, and Congress has clarified the extraterritorial scope of American antitrust law. The extraterritorial application of antitrust laws is limited to situations in which conduct has a direct, substantial, and reasonably foreseeable effect on the domestic, import, or export activities of the United States. However, certain types of restrictive activities are inherently anticompetitive as a matter of law. Such a **per se violation** may consist of an agreement between a U.S. and a foreign firm with respect to restraints on the distribution of goods, price fixing, or production control. The injured party, even a foreign citizen, business entity, or government, has a right to file an action for treble damages in a U.S. court against the party or parties who have engaged in trade practices in violation of U.S. antitrust law.

U.S. **federal securities laws** (see Study Unit 33) apply when foreign entities issue securities in the U.S. However, some nonexempt foreign issuers may avoid registration under the 1934 act by making all the disclosures publicized in their home nation. Moreover, a few large issuers are allowed to file financial statements with the SEC that are based on **International Financial Reporting Standards (IFRSs)**. This development is part of a process that is expected to result in convergence of U.S. GAAP and IFRSs within a few years. The worldwide association of securities regulators is the **International Organization of Securities Commissions**. Its objectives are to promote (1) the creation and integrity of markets, (2) standard setting, (3) cooperation, (4) information gathering and exchange, and (5) effective enforcement.

The risk of disputes is inherent in any business transaction, whether foreign or domestic. However, the nature of international transactions as well as political and economic circumstances can subject an enterprise to greater loss in this context. For example, the simple geographic separation of buyers and sellers creates uncertainties about contractual performance. Sellers need assurance that they will be paid, and buyers need assurance of delivery before they pay. For this reason, **letters of credit** are often employed to provide assurance to the parties (see Study Unit 17). Some other matters that may be considered in anticipation of possible disputes are discussed below.

Each party to a dispute, whether foreign or domestic, seeks to have the dispute resolved as quickly, predictably, and inexpensively as possible. Many factors affect the outcome of a dispute, but one factor that the parties may control at the outset is the **choice of law** that will be applied. To ensure that a dispute is resolved in a manner consistent with the intent of the parties, they can expressly stipulate in their written agreement which specific body of law is to be applied in the event of a dispute. If parties fail expressly or implicitly to choose a governing body of law, the court adjudicating the dispute will refer to its own choice-of-law principles to determine what law it will apply. Choice of law is sometimes referred to as **conflict of laws**. Another factor that the parties may control at the outset is the **choice of forum**. Thus, a forum selection clause in an agreement is intended to provide certainty in the dispute resolution process. It represents the parties' agreement as to where they will litigate any unresolved dispute arising from the contract. In selecting the forum, parties should evaluate a variety of issues, including which forum has a reputation for fairness, litigates many similar issues, or has expertise in international matters. For example, the forum best able to apply the law of a given country or state is a court located in that country or state. Hence, a U.S. court's application of U.S. law theoretically provides the most rapid, consistent, predictable, and cost-efficient results compared with the application of U.S. law by a foreign court. Still another means of avoiding disputes is a **choice of language** clause. Because complex or technical terminology used by one party may not translate readily into the other party's language, stipulating the official language of an international contract may avert subsequent difficulties.

The overall environment within which international business is proposed and transacted provides limited predictability. Resolution of disputes by litigation in courts can be costly and may not produce a result consistent with the reasonable expectations of the parties. Enforcing legal judgments also may be hindered. An **arbitration** clause is a means for parties to improve their chances of receiving the benefits of their bargains and to reduce overall transaction costs. Upon contracting to engage in international transactions, parties frequently also agree to subject any disputes to arbitration and to be bound by that outcome. Organizations have developed sets of rules for conducting arbitration. Parties to an agreement to arbitrate may incorporate by reference such a set of rules. UNCITRAL's rules are an example of arbitration rules. However, the domestic law of the country where enforcement of an arbitration award is sought must provide procedures for enforcement. The **United Nations Convention on the Recognition and Enforcement of Foreign Arbitral Awards** has been adopted by most countries, including the U.S., and signatory countries agree to enforce arbitration agreements and awards pursuant to their terms. However, the convention does not require enforcement of an award contrary to the public policy of the country.

In the international environment, various doctrines, principles, and laws sometimes serve as barriers to legal remedies available to parties in international transactions. **Comity** is the recognition by one country of the executive, legislative, and judicial acts of another if those acts are consistent with the public policy of the recognizing country. Comity arises from mutual courtesy and friendship. Two defenses commonly invoked by both private foreign litigants and foreign governments are the act of state doctrine and sovereign immunity. The **act of state doctrine** is an international law principle that precludes the courts of one country from adjudicating politically sensitive disputes that would require the courts to examine the validity of public acts engaged in by a recognized foreign government within its own territory. Under the **doctrine of sovereign immunity**, domestic courts of some countries refrain from asserting jurisdiction over acts of another country's government. A foreign sovereign is generally immune from most kinds of suits in the United States. This doctrine demonstrates a policy of U.S. courts to respect the autonomy of foreign states. However, it does not extend to strictly commercial acts. This view of sovereign immunity is codified in the **Foreign Sovereign Immunities Act of 1976**. Under the act, the foreign sovereign is not immune from civil suits in U.S. courts if (1) it has waived its immunity, (2) the suit is based on the foreign sovereign's commercial acts in the U.S., or (3) the suit is based on its commercial acts outside the U.S. that have a direct effect in the U.S.

To control potential liability of parties to international commercial transactions in an environment that might produce unpredictable results due to differing and changing political, regulatory, and other variables, **contractual limitations** may have a more significant role than in a domestic setting. For example, **liquidated damages** clauses may limit liability between parties as to specified foreseeable impediments to full contract performance or other losses arising from the contract. **Force majeure** clauses allocate potential liability and risk of loss for events beyond the control of the parties, generally unforeseen at the time of the contract formation, that might materially impede full performance of a contract. Such a clause might be more expansive in coverage than an analogous one in a domestic setting. It might address such events as fire, flood, or storm; interruption of transportation; war or embargo; nationalization (either expropriation or confiscation) by a government; or governmental action, such as regulation or restriction of exports or imports.

One of the primary concerns in an international business transaction is assurance that compensation will be received in the currency acceptable in a given country or in a medium that is readily convertible to that currency. Thus, foreign exchange markets exist to facilitate conversion of currencies based on rates set by supply and demand. No central authority controls a world monetary system. However, since 1944, many of the most commercially active nations have formulated agreements on relationships between and among currencies and international monetary institutions. Both the **International Monetary Fund (IMF)** and the **International Bank for Reconstruction and Development (World Bank)** were formed to encourage postwar reconstruction and provide a new exchange stability in the world monetary system. The IMF was intended, among other things, to stabilize currency exchange rates and to assist countries with their balance of payments. Member countries contribute to a pool to acquire necessary reserves. Reserves permit a country to borrow money from other IMF members or the IMF itself for the purpose of stabilizing the relationship of its currency to other world currencies. The World Bank was specifically intended to facilitate loans by capital surplus countries to those countries needing foreign investment for economic development after World War II. Among other things, it has created the **Multilateral Investment Guarantee Agency (MIGA)** to provide investment risk insurance covering losses from expropriation, war, revolution, etc. The aggregation of the IMF, the World Bank, and the regional development banks is loosely termed the **international monetary system**. The primary purpose of the international monetary system is stability of money values worldwide.

Also see the summary of the **Foreign Corrupt Practices Act of 1977 (FCPA)** in Study Unit 33.

QUESTIONS

39.1 Nature and Scope of International Business Law

1. The European Union (EU)

A. Provides insurance to American citizens and businesses against certain risks associated with doing business in Europe.

B. Meets 1 month per year to draft uniform international trade laws.

C. Was formed to reduce trade restrictions and tariffs among all nations.

D. Promotes tariff-free trade among its members and has common tariffs for nonmembers.

Answer (D) is correct. *(Publisher, adapted)*

REQUIRED: The purpose of the European Union.

DISCUSSION: The EU is an economic and political entity that was formed under the treaty of Rome in 1957 to promote the free movement of workers, goods, and capital. It has also phased in a single monetary unit (the Euro) used by those members who belong to the European Monetary Union (17 of 27 members). The EU is governed by the European Commission (the executive branch, headed by a president), the Council of the European Union and the European Parliament (the legislative branch, consisting of a representative from each country), and the Court of Justice of the European Union (the judicial branch). Disputes among members are taken to the Court of Justice, which establishes binding precedents. Nonmembers of the EU are subject to tariffs.

Answer (A) is incorrect. Providing insurance to businesses with transactions overseas is the purpose of the Overseas Private Investor Corporation, an organization created by the U.S. Congress. Answer (B) is incorrect. The purpose of the United Nations Commission on International Trade Law is to draft uniform trade laws for all countries. An example of a model act is the U.N. Convention on Contracts for the International Sale of Goods. Answer (C) is incorrect. The purpose of the World Trade Organization (WTO) and its predecessors (e.g., GATT) is to reduce trade restrictions and tariffs among its many signatories.

2. The sources of international law do not include

A. Treaties.

B. Common law.

C. Customs.

D. Conventions.

Answer (B) is correct. *(Publisher, adapted)*

REQUIRED: The sources of international law.

DISCUSSION: International law is a broad area. It is the law that nations recognize when dealing with one another. International law consists of treaties, conventions, and customs. A treaty is a formal agreement between nations, which usually must be ratified by their lawmaking bodies, e.g., the U.S. Congress. A convention is another term for a treaty. It is often used to describe an agreement among many nations, e.g., the Geneva Convention on the treatment of prisoners of war. Customs are long-established practices serving as unwritten law. Common law is not a source of international law because it relates to law made within a country founded upon judicial decisions.

3. The Foreign Corrupt Practices Act prohibits

A. Bribes to all foreigners.

B. Small bribes to foreign officials that serve as facilitating or grease payments.

C. Bribery only by corporations and their representatives.

D. Bribes to foreign officials to influence official acts.

Answer (D) is correct. *(Publisher, adapted)*

REQUIRED: The action prohibited by the Foreign Corrupt Practices Act.

DISCUSSION: The Foreign Corrupt Practices Act (FCPA) prohibits any U.S. firm from making bribes to foreign officials to influence official acts. The businesses subject to the FCPA include corporations, partnerships, limited partnerships, business trusts, and unincorporated organizations. Violations of the FCPA are federal felonies. The penalties are up to 5 years in prison or up to a $250,000 fine or both for an officer, director, or shareholder who helps make the bribe.

Answer (A) is incorrect. The Foreign Corrupt Practices Act (FCPA) prohibits any U.S. firm from making bribes to foreign officials to influence official acts. Answer (B) is incorrect. The prohibited payments exclude those for expediting routine government actions or that are legal in the foreign country. Answer (C) is incorrect. All U.S. firms are subject to the anti-bribery provisions.

4. The Foreign Corrupt Practices Act of 1977 has enormous significance for U.S. corporations doing business abroad. The act

A. Only applies to bribery of foreign officials.

B. Imposes heavy civil but not criminal sanctions upon violators.

C. Does not apply to U.S. firms doing business solely in the United States if they are subject to the Securities Exchange Act of 1934.

D. Applies to all U.S. firms.

NOTE: For further questions on the FCPA, refer to Study Unit 33.

Answer (D) is correct. *(Publisher, adapted)*

REQUIRED: The true statement about the Foreign Corrupt Practices Act of 1977.

DISCUSSION: The Foreign Corrupt Practices Act of 1977 attempted to put an end to bribery of foreign officials by U.S. corporations and their subsidiaries. It also imposes stringent accounting requirements on firms subject to the Securities Exchange Act of 1934 to promote accountability for assets. The bribery provisions of the act apply to all U.S. firms.

Answer (A) is incorrect. In addition to prohibiting bribery of foreign officials, the act requires an adequate system of internal control to maintain accountability for assets. Answer (B) is incorrect. Individual violators may be liable for criminal penalties of up to $250,000 in fines and 5 years in prison. A corporation may be fined up to $2,000,000. Answer (C) is incorrect. The accounting provisions of the act apply to all U.S. firms subject to the Securities Exchange Act of 1934.

5. The sale of militarily sensitive equipment from a U.S. company to Iran is subject to the restrictions of

A. Sovereign immunity.

B. COCOM.

C. U.S. antitrust laws.

D. Foreign Corrupt Practices Act.

Answer (B) is correct. *(Publisher, adapted)*

REQUIRED: The restrictions placed on militarily sensitive equipment.

DISCUSSION: The Coordinating Committee for Multilateral Export (COCOM) is a group of western countries that impose export controls on certain goods for political purposes. Agreement must be unanimous, and the restrictions are then enforced through laws passed in each country. A seller's failure to abide by the restrictions will lead to administrative penalties. The sale of militarily sensitive equipment will be restricted by COCOM because Iran currently is an unfriendly government.

Answer (A) is incorrect. Sovereign immunity immunizes a government and not persons or corporations. Answer (C) is incorrect. Antitrust laws apply when a restraint on trade may occur and the U.S. company could otherwise sell the equipment without being subject to COCOM restrictions. Answer (D) is incorrect. The Foreign Corrupt Practices Act prohibits U.S. companies from giving bribes to foreign officials.

6. Ethical issues arise when U.S. companies build plants in third world countries because

A. U.S. citizens are being deprived of employment.

B. U.S. corporations are avoiding paying income taxes.

C. U.S. companies are escaping many U.S. safety and environmental regulations.

D. U.S. companies are not acting in the best interests of their shareholders.

Answer (C) is correct. *(Publisher, adapted)*

REQUIRED: The ethical considerations that arise when a corporation builds plants in third world countries.

DISCUSSION: U.S. companies build factories in foreign countries for economic reasons, such as a lower cost of labor. Ethical issues are involved if the reason is to take advantage of lax safety regulations. An example is the Union Carbide factory that leaked 25 tons of methyl isocyanate that caused 2,000 deaths and 100,000 injuries in Bhopal, India. The plant in India did not have a computerized safety system, a requirement in the United States.

Answer (A) is incorrect. A U.S. company is not under an ethical duty to give U.S. citizens employment. Answer (B) is incorrect. U.S. companies operating outside the United States are still subject to income tax. Answer (D) is incorrect. Increasing business productivity overseas may be in the best interests of the corporation.

7. The return to the home country of income earned by a domestic firm in a foreign country is

A. Expropriation.

B. Bankruptcy.

C. Repatriation.

D. Reinvestment.

Answer (C) is correct. *(Publisher, adapted)*

REQUIRED: The return to the home country of income earned in a foreign country.

DISCUSSION: Many firms have business operations abroad. Repatriation is conversion of funds held in a foreign country into another currency and remittance of these funds to another nation. A firm must often obtain permission from the currency exchange authorities to repatriate earnings and investments. Regulations in many nations encourage a reinvestment of earnings in the country.

Answer (A) is incorrect. Expropriation is a foreign government's seizure (nationalization) of the assets of a business for a public purpose and for just compensation. Answer (B) is incorrect. Bankruptcy occurs when a person's liabilities exceed assets or (s)he cannot meet obligations when they are due. Answer (D) is incorrect. Reinvestment in the foreign country is a purpose of restricting repatriation.

8. The World Trade Organization

A. Introduced fixed exchange rates among the United States, Canada, and members of the European Union.

B. Created the International Monetary Fund.

C. Encourages reductions in trade barriers between countries.

D. Introduced exchange rates that adjust in response to changes in trade deficits and surpluses.

Answer (C) is correct. *(CMA, adapted)*

REQUIRED: The true statement about the World Trade Organization.

DISCUSSION: International trade agreements provide regulatory authority for businesses in international trade. The WTO, which was established on January 1, 1995, is the product of the Uruguay Round of international trade negotiations. It is a permanent body with a secretariat based in Geneva, Switzerland. The WTO Agreement is a permanent set of commitments by more than 120 nations designed to prohibit trade discrimination among member nations and between imported and domestic products.

Answer (A) is incorrect. The WTO is a worldwide agreement concerning trade barriers, not exchange rates. Today, moreover, exchange rates are not pegged (fixed) but are allowed to float. Answer (B) is incorrect. The IMF was founded in 1944 to stabilize exchange rates. Answer (D) is incorrect. The WTO is a worldwide agreement concerning trade barriers, not exchange rates. Today, moreover, exchange rates are not pegged (fixed) but are allowed to float.

9. The creation of a regional economic bloc of trading nations, such as the European Union (EU),

A. Discourages foreign investment by nonmember multinational companies.

B. Encourages trade between the member nations and nonmember nations.

C. Requires the adoption of a common monetary unit.

D. Discriminates economically against nonmember nations.

Answer (D) is correct. *(CMA, adapted)*

REQUIRED: The effect of the creation of a regional economic bloc of trading nations.

DISCUSSION: A trading bloc provides trading incentives to member nations and discriminates against nonmember nations. For example, the European Union calls for abolition of internal tariffs and import quotas, free movement of capital and labor within the market, and implementation of common policies for the member nations. However, the EU also imposed a common system of tariffs on goods of nonmember nations.

Answer (A) is incorrect. Foreign investment may be welcomed under the appropriate conditions. Answer (B) is incorrect. The EU provides incentives to trade with other members, not nonmembers. Answer (C) is incorrect. Currencies are not affected by bloc membership.

10. A permanent set of commitments by more than 153 nations designed to prohibit trade discrimination is known as the

A. General Agreement on Tariffs and Trade.

B. World Trade Organization.

C. Export-Import Bank.

D. European Union.

Answer (B) is correct. *(Publisher, adapted)*

REQUIRED: The name of a permanent set of free-trade commitments.

DISCUSSION: The World Trade Organization is a permanent set of commitments by more than 153 nations designed to prohibit trade discrimination among member nations and between imported and domestic products.

Answer (A) is incorrect. The General Agreement on Tariffs and Trade was replaced by the World Trade Organization on January 1, 1995. Answer (C) is incorrect. The Export-Import Bank is the U.S. federal government's official export credit agency. Answer (D) is incorrect. The European Union is an economic and political association of European countries that currently consists of 27 members.

11. Which of the following is a false statement about the North American Free Trade Agreement (NAFTA)?

A. Mexico's economy has benefited greatly as a result of the agreement.

B. NAFTA arranged for the gradual phasing-out over a period of 15 years of tariffs on almost all products sold between the three member nations.

C. NAFTA did not create a new set of administrative bodies to oversee the trading activities of the three member nations.

D. The agreement ended all substantial trade disputes between the three member nations.

Answer (D) is correct. *(Publisher, adapted)*

REQUIRED: The false statement about NAFTA.

DISCUSSION: Disputes still arise. Disagreements have long existed over the importation of softwood lumber products from Canada to the U.S. The dispute-resolution bodies of NAFTA have repeatedly found in favor of Canada, leading the U.S. to impose anti-dumping rules and countervailing duties.

Answer (A) is incorrect. Mexico's economy has benefited greatly as a result of NAFTA. Answer (B) is incorrect. NAFTA arranged for the gradual phasing-out over a period of 15 years of tariffs on almost all products sold between the three member nations. Answer (C) is incorrect. In contrast with the European Union, NAFTA did not create a new set of administrative bodies to oversee the trading activities of the three member nations.

39.2 Business Transactions in the International Marketplace

12. XCo is an American company that wants to sell widgets to DCo, a Danish Corporation. XCo is unsure about DCo's ability to pay. XCo should

A. Not transact business with DCo.

B. Transact business with DCo because American law requires DCo to pay.

C. Transact business with DCo because Danish law requires DCo to pay.

D. Require DCo to obtain a letter of credit.

Answer (D) is correct. *(Publisher, adapted)*

REQUIRED: The method to prevent a foreign corporation from not paying an American corporation for goods purchased.

DISCUSSION: If a U.S. company sells goods to a foreign company, the U.S. company may not know whether the foreign company will pay the contract price, is solvent, or whether it will reject a delivery of the goods. Requiring a letter of credit addresses the problem. A letter of credit is an engagement by the issuing bank (DCo's bank in Denmark) to pay on behalf of its customer when the requirements of the letter of credit are complied with. When the beneficiary (XCo) is in another country, the letter of credit is often sent to a confirming bank (in the U.S. in this case), which will pay the beneficiary directly upon presentation of a document of title. The confirming bank will then be paid by the issuing bank.

Answer (A) is incorrect. XCo may find it profitable to transact business with DCo if it can obtain assurance through a letter of credit. Answer (B) is incorrect. Requiring a letter of credit may be preferable to relying on litigation in the event of a breach. Answer (C) is incorrect. Requiring a letter of credit may be preferable to relying on litigation in the event of a breach.

13. Which of the following is a false statement about a bill of lading?

A. It is a receipt showing that a seller transferred possession of goods to a shipper.

B. It is a contract under which the shipper agrees to transport goods to the buyer.

C. It is an engagement by a bank or other person made at the customer's request to pay drafts or other demands for its customer.

D. It is a document of title.

Answer (C) is correct. *(Publisher, adapted)*

REQUIRED: The false statement about a bill of lading.

DISCUSSION: A problem in an international sale is whether the seller will be paid. The problem is solved by using a letter of credit and a bill of lading. A bill of lading is a document of title evidencing receipt of goods by the carrier for shipment. A bill of lading is not an agreement with a bank to pay drafts or other demands for its customer. Such an agreement is a letter of credit (UCC 5-103). A seller is paid when (s)he presents the bill of lading to the buyer's bank.

Answer (A) is incorrect. A bill of lading is a receipt showing that a seller transferred possession of goods to a shipper. Answer (B) is incorrect. A bill of lading is a contract under which the shipper agrees to transport goods to the buyer. Answer (D) is incorrect. A bill of lading is a document of title.

14. A distribution agreement is

A. An association of two or more persons who as co-owners engage in a limited business transaction.

B. The supplying of manufacturing equipment and other items necessary to operate a foreign business.

C. A contract between a seller and independent contractor in which the independent contractor will sell the goods on his/her own behalf.

D. A contract between a seller and a foreign corporation in which the foreign corporation is paid a commission on the goods it sells.

Answer (C) is correct. *(Publisher, adapted)*

REQUIRED: The definition of a distribution agreement.

DISCUSSION: A distributor purchases goods, resells them, and retains the profits earned. By setting up a distributorship, the U.S. firm will not have to make a large investment to establish a subsidiary, and it will be able to avoid foreign labor laws applicable to commercial agents in foreign countries. The U.S. firm is not subject to any contracts the distributorship enters into and rids itself of title to the goods, the need to establish business relationships in the foreign country, and the pressure to resell goods at a profit.

Answer (A) is incorrect. An association of two or more persons who as co-owners engage in a limited business transaction is a joint business venture in a foreign country. Answer (B) is incorrect. A turnkey operation is formed when a firm provides the necessaries for starting a foreign business and turns the operation over to a foreign firm. Answer (D) is incorrect. An agency agreement is formed. In contrast with a distributor, an agent does not have title to the goods and does not buy the goods.

15. With respect to foreign commerce, the antitrust laws

A. Apply only if U.S. commerce is affected.

B. Apply only to activity occurring in the United States.

C. Do not apply.

D. Do not apply to an activity that completely takes place in foreign countries.

Answer (A) is correct. *(Publisher, adapted)*

REQUIRED: The application of the antitrust laws to foreign commerce.

DISCUSSION: The commerce clause of the U.S. Constitution also allows Congress to regulate foreign commerce. Therefore, the antitrust laws apply to foreign commerce, but only to the extent there is an effect on U.S. commerce. Without an effect on U.S. commerce, the courts have ruled that the antitrust laws do not apply. These court decisions were codified in a statute passed in 1982.

Answer (B) is incorrect. U.S. commerce can be affected by activity occurring in foreign countries. For example, a U.S. firm could conspire with a foreign country to manufacture goods in a foreign country which may later be shipped to the United States. Answer (C) is incorrect. Antitrust laws do apply to foreign commerce provided there is an effect by U.S. commerce. Answer (D) is incorrect. Activities of U.S. citizens completely taking place in a foreign country are covered by the U.S. antitrust laws if such activities would have an effect on U.S. commerce.

16. With regard to activity outside the U.S., U.S. antitrust laws

A. May never be enforced against foreign corporations.

B. May always be enforced against U.S. and foreign corporations.

C. May be enforced against foreign but not U.S. corporations if the activity outside the United States has some substantial effect within the U.S.

D. May be enforced against U.S. and foreign corporations if the activity outside the U.S. has some substantial effect on commerce within the United States.

Answer (D) is correct. *(Publisher, adapted)*

REQUIRED: The applicability of the U.S. antitrust rules.

DISCUSSION: The Sherman Act states that "every contract, combination, or conspiracy in restraint of trade or commerce among the several states or with foreign nations is declared illegal." A considerable amount of litigation has involved determining how the U.S. can control activities outside its borders. The Foreign Trade Antitrust Improvements Act of 1982 states that the U.S. can control activities that have a direct, substantial, and reasonably foreseeable effect on U.S. commerce or exports. However, a foreign country's laws will be deferred to if the U.S. interest is outweighed by the foreign country's interest in regulating the activity.

Answer (A) is incorrect. U.S. antitrust laws can be enforced against U.S. or foreign corporations but only when the activity outside the U.S. has some substantial effect on commerce within the U.S. Answer (B) is incorrect. The activity outside the U.S. must have some substantial effect within the U.S. Moreover, some U.S. activities are exempt. Answer (C) is incorrect. Antitrust laws are enforced against U.S. corporations engaged in foreign activity with some substantial effect within the U.S.

17. Articles 101 and 102 of the Treaty on the Functioning of the EO (TFEO) that founded what is now called the European Union established a body of law to

A. Impose tariffs on goods imported into Europe.

B. Forbid anticompetitive acts among members.

C. Establish a single monetary unit within Europe.

D. Establish the proper forum for a dispute to be resolved between two European corporations.

Answer (B) is correct. *(Publisher, adapted)*

REQUIRED: The content of Articles 101 and 102.

DISCUSSION: Articles 101 and 102 serve the same purpose as antitrust law. Those laws decide whether prohibited business conduct has occurred and whether a dominant enterprise has exploited its position in a geographic area. Articles 101 and 102 are enforced by the European Commission. When the Commission receives a complaint about a violation, it investigates and can take enforcement action against firms that have violated EU antitrust laws.

39.3 International Dispute Resolution

18. Which clause in an international contract states that the laws of a certain country are to apply?

A. Choice of forum.

B. Force majeure.

C. Choice of law.

D. Arbitration.

Answer (C) is correct. *(Publisher, adapted)*

REQUIRED: The clause in a contract stating that the laws of a certain country are to be applied.

DISCUSSION: When a court must decide which country's law will apply to an international business transaction, a conflict of law arises. A choice of law clause will be enforced by the court hearing the case unless it is contrary to the policies of the forum nation.

Answer (A) is incorrect. A choice of forum clause is an agreement as to where a dispute will be litigated. Answer (B) is incorrect. A force majeure ("superior power") clause provides for certain contingencies, e.g., fire, war, or embargo. The clause usually excuses performances when the listed natural disasters or other events occur. Answer (D) is incorrect. An arbitration clause is an agreement by the parties to be bound by a decision of a third party who will resolve the dispute.

19. A clause in a contract between a Florida corporation and a Jamaican corporation that states all disputes will be resolved by a Florida court is an example of a(n)

A. Choice of law clause.

B. Choice of forum clause.

C. Arbitration clause.

D. Force majeure clause.

Answer (B) is correct. *(Publisher, adapted)*

REQUIRED: The contract clause that determines where a dispute is to be resolved.

DISCUSSION: A choice of forum clause is an agreement by parties to a contract as to where a dispute will be resolved. If the effect of the agreement would be unfair or unreasonable, it will not be valid. The question of whether the clause is unreasonable must be decided by ascertaining whether it was negotiated in good faith.

Answer (A) is incorrect. A choice of law clause defines what law will apply to the transaction. Answer (C) is incorrect. An arbitration clause is an agreement among the parties that a neutral third party will resolve their dispute. Answer (D) is incorrect. A force majeure clause in a contract states the parties' responsibilities if a natural disaster or other calamity occurs.

20. The government of a foreign country owns all the country's silver mines. No company can mine the silver unless it has government approval. If the foreign country gives Walker Co. a permit to mine, the doctrine that prevents a U.S. court from declaring the permit illegal is

A. Sherman Antitrust Act.

B. Sovereign compulsion.

C. Act of State doctrine.

D. Repatriation.

Answer (C) is correct. *(Publisher, adapted)*

REQUIRED: The doctrine that prevents a U.S. court from declaring a foreign government's action illegal.

DISCUSSION: The Act of State doctrine prevents U.S. courts from interfering in foreign affairs. Foreign countries are immune from a lawsuit in U.S. courts with regard to their actions in their own territory. Thus, a U.S. court cannot invalidate the permit given to Walker Co. by the foreign government because that government is immune to suit in the U.S. for actions in its own country.

Answer (A) is incorrect. Antitrust law is concerned only with restraints on U.S. commerce. Answer (B) is incorrect. The sovereign compulsion doctrine provides a defense to private parties that have been compelled by a non-U.S. government to commit acts within that country's territory that would violate U.S. antitrust laws. Answer (D) is incorrect. Repatriation is the conversion of funds held in a foreign country to another currency and their transfer out of that country.

21. If a U.S. company brings an action against a foreign country in a U.S. court, the issue raised is

A. Repatriation.

B. Expropriation.

C. Sovereign immunity.

D. Dumping.

Answer (C) is correct. *(Publisher, adapted)*

REQUIRED: The problem that arises when an action is brought in an American court against a foreign country.

DISCUSSION: The Foreign Sovereign Immunities Act (FSIA) was enacted in 1976 to exempt foreign governments and their agents from liability. A foreign government can be sued if it waives the defense of sovereign immunity or carries on a commercial activity within the United States. A commercial activity is defined as one typically carried on by nongovernmental entities for profit.

Answer (A) is incorrect. Repatriation is the conversion of funds held in a foreign country to another currency and their transfer out of that country. Answer (B) is incorrect. Expropriation is a foreign government's seizure (nationalization) of the assets of a business for a public purpose and usually for just compensation. Answer (D) is incorrect. Dumping is the sale by a foreign business of goods at very low prices to gain market share in a domestic market. Dumping is prevented by imposing tariffs.

22. Goodman Co., a U.S. corporation, manufactures paper clips in the Philippines. During 1992, a political revolution occurs and all industries in the Philippines are nationalized. The Philippine government pays Goodman 40% of the value of the assets it seized. The seizure of Goodman's assets and payment of less than just compensation is

A. Expropriation.

B. Repatriation.

C. Confiscation.

D. Bribery.

Answer (C) is correct. *(Publisher, adapted)*

REQUIRED: The term for seizure of assets by a foreign government without just compensation.

DISCUSSION: Many companies have manufacturing facilities and property in foreign countries. Some of these countries are unstable and subject to political change. Under a standard espoused by western nations, expropriation is a domestic government's seizure (nationalization) of a foreign firm's assets in accordance with national law, for a public purpose, and for just compensation (prompt, adequate, and effective compensation for the loss). Confiscation is an unlawful taking that does not meet this standard. U.S. citizens and firms may insure against losses from expropriation, confiscation, war, or other adverse events through the Overseas Private Investment Corporation (OPIC), a federal governmental agency, or private insurers.

Answer (A) is incorrect. Expropriation is a foreign government's seizure (nationalization) of the assets of a business for a public purpose and for just compensation. Answer (B) is incorrect. Repatriation involves transfer of funds out of a foreign country. Answer (D) is incorrect. Bribery in an international business environment entails payments to foreign officials to obtain favorable treatment in that country.

23. Which of the following should not be included in an international contract?

A. A force majeure clause.

B. An open price term clause.

C. A choice of law and forum clause.

D. A commercial arbitration clause.

Answer (B) is correct. *(Publisher, adapted)*

REQUIRED: The clause that should not be included in an international contract.

DISCUSSION: A contract between foreign parties should be as simple, precise, and complete as possible. The contract should define all essential terms. In a domestic setting, when parties state that the price term is left open, UCC 2-305 provides that the price will be determined at a later time. In an international setting, UCC 2-305 and other gap-filler provisions are not applicable.

39.4 Money and International Business Law

24. Which one of the following groups would be the primary beneficiary of a tariff?

A. Domestic producers of export goods.

B. Domestic producers of goods protected by the tariff.

C. Domestic consumers of goods protected by the tariff.

D. Foreign producers of goods protected by the tariff.

Answer (B) is correct. *(CMA, adapted)*

REQUIRED: The primary beneficiaries of a tariff.

DISCUSSION: Despite the advantages of free trade, nations often levy tariffs to discourage the importation of certain products. A tariff is a tax on imports intended to protect a domestic producer from foreign competition. For instance, a tariff on imported autos benefits U.S. auto manufacturers because it is an additional cost imposed on U.S. consumers of such products, which makes domestic autos relatively cheaper. The disadvantages of the tariff are that it may protect an inefficient domestic producer and increase prices paid by domestic consumers.

Answer (A) is incorrect. Domestic producers of export goods are not benefited. Indeed, they may be harmed by retaliatory tariffs. Answer (C) is incorrect. Domestic consumers must pay higher prices for imported goods. Answer (D) is incorrect. The foreign producers will be forced to bear an additional cost.

25. Which of the following statements is false with respect to the international monetary system?

A. Its primary purpose has been the stability of monetary values worldwide.

B. One aspect is to facilitate funding of development projects by establishing a reserve for loans.

C. It refers to an informal aggregate of the International Monetary Fund, the World Bank, and the regional development banks.

D. It superseded the Federal Reserve Board as an independent central authority controlling the world monetary system.

Answer (D) is correct. *(Publisher, adapted)*

REQUIRED: The false statement about the international monetary system.

DISCUSSION: The governments of all of the nations have not forfeited their sovereignty with respect to exchange media to a single central authority. That is, the nations do not recognize a single central authority as controlling a unitary world monetary system.

Answer (A) is incorrect. The system's primary purpose has been the stability of monetary values worldwide. Answer (B) is incorrect. One aspect is to facilitate funding of development projects by establishing a reserve for loans. Answer (C) is incorrect. The system is an informal aggregate of the International Monetary Fund, the World Bank, and the regional development banks.

STUDY UNIT FORTY
ACCOUNTANTS' LEGAL RESPONSIBILITIES

This study unit describes an accountant's responsibility to clients and third parties under state law and federal statutes. Thus, CPAs may be liable to clients and third parties based on the doctrines of breach of contract, negligence, or fraud. Especially significant is an accountant's exposure to liability under the federal securities laws, which are discussed in Study Unit 33. The focus is to whom and for what accountants have responsibility (liability). Also covered are ownership and confidentiality of working papers, tax return preparation responsibility, and accountants' privileged communications.

The accountant-client contract is a **personal service contract**. All of the **elements of a contract** must exist: offer, acceptance, consideration, competent parties, and legal purpose. The contract must be in writing if it cannot be completed **within 1 year**. The accountant is implicitly bound by the contract to perform the engagement with **due care** (nonnegligently) and in compliance with **professional standards**. Moreover, an accountant must comply with the law and is responsible for exercising independent professional judgment. The accountant should establish an understanding with the client about the services to be performed. For an audit of financial statements, the understanding should be communicated in an **engagement letter**. The letter sets forth the contract between the accountant and the client. However, the letter is not necessary to the formation of a contract. An engagement letter may provide for services or procedures beyond those required by generally accepted auditing standards **(GAAS)**, standards of the Public Company Accounting Oversight Board **(PCAOB)** applicable to performance of services for public companies, or generally accepted accounting principles **(GAAP)**. For example, a provision for positive confirmation of all accounts receivable might be made. The accountant is usually an **independent contractor**, not an agent or employee of the client. (S)he (1) may not delegate responsibility for the engagement to another without the client's permission, (2) may hire another as an employee to assist in performing the engagement, or (3) may perform services for the client's competitors. Accountants are liable for **breach of contract** both to clients and to those third parties who are intended beneficiaries of the contract. Intended beneficiaries and clients are in privity of contract with the accountant. **Privity** means a direct contractual relationship. It confers the right to sue. **Damages** for breach of contract depend on the nature of the breach. Recovery for breach of contract is ordinarily limited to **compensatory damages**. Punitive damages are rarely allowed. If the breach is material, expectancy damages may be recovered. **Expectancy damages** are the value of the benefit expected from the contract. If the breach is minor, i.e., if the accountant **substantially performs** all contractual duties, (s)he is entitled to the agreed-upon fee minus losses suffered.

An accountant may be liable in tort to a client for losses caused by **negligence**. A **tort** is a private wrong for which relief may be granted in a civil lawsuit. The plaintiff must prove that (1) the defendant breached a legal duty to the plaintiff, and (2) the breach proximately caused the plaintiff's damages. The duty is one imposed by society, not created by contract or other private relationship. The accountant's duty is to exercise **reasonable care and diligence**. (S)he should have the degree of skill commonly possessed by other accountants. Thus, (s)he should have the judgment, competence, and knowledge of an ordinarily prudent accountant in the same or similar circumstances. Ordinary negligence (failure to exercise reasonable care and diligence) may be an **act or an omission**. An omission is a failure to act given a duty to act, e.g., not observing inventory during an audit. **Gross negligence** is failure to use even slight care. An accountant is not liable for **punitive damages** if (s)he is ordinarily negligent. Extreme or aggravated circumstances must exist for punitive damages to be awarded. Courts have held that auditor-accountants are not guarantors and therefore have **no general duty to discover fraud**. Nevertheless, an auditor is held liable for failure to discover fraud when the auditor's negligence prevented discovery. An auditor, regardless of whether (s)he is an AICPA member, who fails to follow GAAS or PCAOB standards and does not discover fraud will probably be liable if compliance would have detected the fraud. GAAS and PCAOB standards require an auditor to plan and perform the audit to provide **reasonable assurance** about whether the financial statements are free of material misstatement, whether caused by error or fraud. An auditor must (1) identify risks of material misstatement due to fraud; (2) identify and assess those risks; and (3) respond by changing the nature, timing, and extent of procedures. Accountants may be liable for **failure to communicate** to the client findings or circumstances that indicate misstatements in the accounting records or fraud. They also must communicate all significant deficiencies and material weaknesses in internal control to the client's management and the governance body. The accountant's duty extends to **correcting the report** if (s)he subsequently discovers it is erroneous. The accountant should ordinarily disclose the new information to any user relying on the previous report. An attorney should be consulted. A lesser standard applies to an engagement to prepare (compile) **unaudited financial statements**. The accountant must adhere to standards of loyalty and honesty. A client may recover for losses resulting from negligence. Information supplied by the entity may come to the accountant's attention that is incorrect, incomplete, or otherwise unsatisfactory. If **fraud or an illegal act** is indicated, the accountant should communicate with management and consider the effect on his/her report. If management does not provide additional or revised information, **withdrawal** from the engagement is indicated.

Liability for fraud (intentional misrepresentation) may result in punitive as well as compensatory damages. A finding of fraud requires proof of the following: (1) The accountant made a **misrepresentation**; (2) the misrepresentation was made with **scienter**, that is, with actual or implied knowledge of fraud; (3) the misrepresentation was of a **material fact**; (4) the misrepresentation induced **reliance**; (5) another person **justifiably relied** on the misstatement; and (6) the other person suffered a **loss**. The element of **intent** may be satisfied by proof of a reckless disregard for the truth, which is synonymous with **gross negligence**. The result is **constructive fraud**, that is, fraud with the scienter requirement satisfied by constructive knowledge. Liability is to **all reasonably foreseeable users** of the work product. A foreseeable user is any person that the accountant should have reasonably foreseen would be injured by justifiable reliance on the misrepresentation. **Privity** is not required. (Privity, in this context, means that the accountant and the plaintiff were parties to the contract that resulted in the loss.) The status of a foreseeable user provides the standing to sue. **Negligent misrepresentation** includes all elements of fraud except scienter.

Compliance with professional standards is a defense to malpractice. **GAAS** and **PCAOB** standards prescribe rules and procedures for conducting audits. **Audits** are examinations made to determine whether recorded financial information fairly reflects the economic events for a given period. **GAAP** prescribe rules for presentation of financial information. Failure to comply with GAAS, PCAOB standards, or GAAP is evidence of malpractice (professional negligence). Such failure is sufficient in itself to establish malpractice absent contradictory evidence. The AICPA's **Conduct Rule 203** recognizes that, due to unusual circumstances, adherence to GAAP may cause the financial statements to be misleading. Thus, despite a material departure from GAAP, a CPA may in unusual circumstances express an opinion or state affirmatively that the financial statements or other financial data of any entity are presented in accordance with GAAP. However, the CPA must demonstrate why the departure was justified. Courts occasionally insist on standards higher than the professional standards. An accountant's effort to **disclaim liability** by including an **exculpatory clause** in a contract is usually not favored by the courts. A court will consider the relative bargaining positions of the parties, but properly worded disclaimers might succeed. Unclear disclaimers are interpreted against the accountant. Also, disclaimers often are invalidated because they violate public policy.

Contractual defenses include the following: (1) failure of consideration, (2) alleged obligation not within scope of contract, (3) full or substantial performance rendered, (4) illegal purpose, (5) suspension or termination of performance justified because of client's breach, and (6) failure of a condition precedent.

Defenses to negligence include the following: (1) The alleged duty was not owed; (2) the accountant did not breach the duty because (s)he exercised reasonable care; (3) the plaintiff did not suffer a loss; (4) the accountant's behavior was not the cause of the party's loss, for example because it was caused by the party's own negligence or fault or by a third party; (5) the plaintiff is not within a class of parties to whom an accountant is potentially liable under the applicable state law; (6) the person alleging harm assumed the risk, e.g., by accepting a contract containing an effective disclaimer; and (7) the statute of limitations has expired.

A plaintiff has the burden to prove **each element of fraud**. Credible evidence that the accountant can introduce to disprove one of those elements tends to negate liability. Negligence of a client is not a defense, but expiration of the statute of limitations is a defense.

The traditional view is that an accountant is liable for **negligence** only to a plaintiff that was in **privity of contract** with the accountant or a primary beneficiary of the engagement. Typically, a third party is considered to be a **primary beneficiary** if the following apply: (1) The accountant is retained principally to benefit the third party; (2) the third party is identified; and (3) the benefit pertains to a specific transaction, so the accountant knows the particular purpose for which the third party will use and rely upon the work.

EXAMPLE: Smith, CPA, was engaged by Client, Inc. to audit Client's annual financial statements. Client told Smith that the audited financial statements were required by Bank in connection with a loan application. Bank is a primary beneficiary and may recover damages caused by the CPA's negligence.

A primary beneficiary is the same as an intended third-party beneficiary in general contract law. The primary beneficiary test for negligence liability has been abandoned by the majority of states. For example, the *Restatement (Second) of Torts* extends the accountant's liability to foreseen (but not necessarily individually identified) third parties (foreseen users and users within a foreseen class of users). This approach appears to be the majority rule. **Foreseen third parties** are those to whom the accountant intends to supply the information or knows the client intends to supply the information. They also include persons who use the information in a way the accountant knows it will be used. They do not include all persons who might reasonably be expected ultimately to have access to the information and take some action as a result. The accountant's liability is limited to losses that foreseeably result from his/her negligence.

EXAMPLE: Smith, CPA, was engaged by Client, Inc. to audit its annual financial statements. Client's president told Smith that the financial statements would be distributed to South Bank in connection with a loan application. Smith was negligent in performing the audit. Subsequently, the financial statements were given to West Bank as well. West Bank lent Client $50,000 in reliance on the financial statements. West Bank suffered a loss on the loan. Smith is liable to West Bank because West Bank is within a foreseen class of users, and the loan is a transaction similar to that for which the financial statements were audited.

Some (not most) courts adopt a broader approach based on ordinary principles of negligence law. The accountant is liable to all **reasonably foreseeable third parties**. They are all members of the class of persons whose reliance on the financial statements the accountant may reasonably anticipate.

EXAMPLE: Smith, CPA, is engaged to audit the annual financial statements of Client. Smith is not informed of the intended use of the statements. However, Smith knows that they are routinely distributed to lessors, suppliers, trade creditors, and lending institutions. Client uses the statements, which were negligently prepared, to obtain a lease from XYZ, Inc., a foreseeable party. Smith will be liable to XYZ because it is a member of a class of reasonably foreseeable third parties. Reasonable foreseeability is the standard followed in **fraud** cases involving accountant-defendants. Strict liability in tort, that is, strict liability without fault, is not a basis for recovery from an accountant.

The Private Securities Litigation Reform Act of 1995 amends the 1933 and 1934 acts. Among its provisions are (1) a prohibition on solicitation or acceptance of **referral fees** from an attorney by brokers, dealers, and associated persons for obtaining the representation of a customer in any implied private action; (2) a prohibition on the payment of legal fees to private parties seeking funds paid solely as the result of an action brought by the SEC; (3) modification of class action guidelines; (4) a statute of limitations for private rights of action; and (5) the safe harbor rules for forward-looking statements mentioned on the previous page. Of special interest to accountants are the act's provisions concerning audit requirements for fraud detection and disclosure and proportionate liability. Audits should (1) provide reasonable assurance of detecting **illegal acts** having a **direct and material effect** on financial statement amounts, (2) be designed to identify material **related-party transactions**, and (3) include an evaluation as to whether there is a substantial doubt about the issuer's ability to continue as a **going concern**. Accountants **must report** illegal acts to the appropriate level of management and the audit committee unless they are clearly inconsequential. Senior management and the board may **fail to take action** on reported material illegal acts. If this failure will result in a departure from a standard report or resignation from the audit, the accountants should report their conclusions to the board immediately. The board must then, within 1 business day, notify the SEC. If the accountants do not receive a copy of the notice within the 1-day period, they must give the SEC a copy of their report within 1 business day. **Joint and several liability** is imposed only for a knowing violation of the securities laws.

Otherwise, liability is proportionate to the defendant's percentage of responsibility for the total damages. If a share of the judgment is uncollectible, each defendant is jointly and severally liable to an individual plaintiff who suffered damages exceeding 10% of his/her net worth. Such a plaintiff must have a net worth less than $200,000. With respect to other plaintiffs, the defendant is liable for the uncollectible share in proportion to his/her percentage of responsibility. However, the defendant's liability in this regard is limited to 50% of his/her proportionate share of the total damages.

Tax return preparer liability is based on the Internal Revenue Code (IRC or tax code). A **tax return preparer** is a person who prepares for compensation, or who hires a person to prepare for compensation, a substantial portion of any tax return, amended return, or claim for a refund. Taking an **undisclosed** position **without a reasonable belief that it is more likely than not to be sustained on its merits** results in a penalty equal to the greater of $1,000 or 50% of the income derived. If the position is **disclosed,** its tax treatment must have a **reasonable basis**. The penalty does not apply if the preparer proves both of the following: (1) (S)he acted in good faith, and (2) there is reasonable cause for the understatement. Consequently, an accountant may not be liable to a client for not signing a return in which the client insists on taking a position contrary to established law. **Understatement of liability** that is willful or is caused by intentional disregard of IRS rules and regulations is subject to a penalty equal to the greater of $5,000 or 50% of the income derived. **Aiding or abetting** in preparation of any document is subject to a $1,000 penalty ($10,000 for a corporation) if using the document would result in an **understatement of tax liability**. Any act that constitutes a **willful attempt to evade federal tax liability**, even that of another person, is subject to criminal penalties, including imprisonment. Furthermore, any person who willfully aids or assists in preparation or presentation of a materially false or fraudulent return is guilty of a felony. Any income tax return preparer who endorses or otherwise **negotiates any income tax refund check** issued to a taxpayer is liable for a $500 penalty (for each check), unless the check is deposited into the taxpayer's account. Violations of tax preparer rules may result in disciplinary action by the Director of Practice of the IRS. Also, the ability to represent clients in matters with the IRS may be jeopardized. **Other provisions** of the tax code and general laws impose liability on CPAs. A preparer will be subject to a $50 penalty (up to a maximum of $25,000 per person) for not signing a return or for failing to do any of the following: (1) provide the taxpayer with a copy of the tax return, (2) include an identifying number on the return, (3) keep names and ID numbers of taxpayers or copies of returns prepared, and (4) make available a list of preparers employed. A person who promotes an **abusive tax shelter** is subject to a penalty equal to 50% of the gross income derived or to be derived from the plan or arrangement activities. The **penalty** for promotion of activities involving gross valuation overstatements is an amount equal to the lesser of $1,000 or 100% of the gross income derived or to be derived by the promoter from the activity. In applying the penalty, promotion of each entity or activity is a separate activity and each sale of an interest in the shelter is a separate activity. The IRS also may seek to enjoin the promoter from engaging in further acts subject to the penalty. Preparers are subject to penalties for **using or disclosing information** other than for return preparation ($250 up to a maximum of $10,000 per disclosure). This penalty will not be imposed if the disclosure is for peer review, under administrative order by a state agency, or under a court order.

A court may prohibit the following: (1) reckless or intentional disregard of rules or regulations, or willful understatement of tax liability; (2) misrepresentation of eligibility to practice before the IRS; (3) guaranteeing tax refunds or allowance of credits; and (4) other fraudulent or deceptive conduct. A preparer also must make appropriate inquiries to determine the existence of facts required by a tax code section or regulation as a condition to claiming a deduction. A preparer may generally rely in good faith without verification on **information furnished by the taxpayer**, although the preparer may not ignore the implications of information furnished to the preparer or actually known to the preparer. A preparer may use estimates provided by the taxpayer if they are reasonable under the circumstances. However, some deductions are disallowed for a taxpayer who has not retained substantiating records (e.g., for travel, meals, and entertainment expense). **Diligence** must be exercised in preparing, approving, and filing (1) returns, (2) documents, (3) claims for the **earned income credit**, and (4) other papers relating to IRS matters. This requirement also extends to, for example, supervising assistants, engaging specialists, and advising clients about matters administered by the IRS.

The **Sarbanes-Oxley Act of 2002** is comprehensive legislation that was a response to numerous accounting scandals. It applies to issuers of publicly traded securities subject to federal securities laws. Among other things, it regulates the public accounting profession. For this purpose, it established a body called the **Public Company Accounting Oversight Board (PCAOB)**. Violations of the Board's rules are deemed to be violations of the **Securities Exchange Act of 1934** and are subject to the same penalties. The PCAOB (1) registers public accounting firms; (2) establishes or adopts by rule standards for audit reports; (3) inspects and investigates accounting firms; (4) conducts disciplinary proceedings; (5) imposes sanctions; and (6) enforces compliance with its rules, the act, professional standards, and securities laws relevant to audit reports and the obligations of accountants. The audit committee must be directly responsible for **appointing, compensating, and overseeing** the work of the public accounting firm employed by the issuer. In addition, this audit firm must **report directly** to the audit committee, not to management. The act requires that each member of the **audit committee**, including at least one who is a **financial expert**, be an **independent** member of the issuer's **board of directors**. An independent director is not affiliated with, and receives no compensation (other than for service on the board) from, the issuer. Under **Section 404** of the act, management must establish and document internal control procedures and include in the annual report a report on the company's **internal control over financial reporting**. This report is to include (1) a statement of management's responsibility for internal control; (2) management's assessment of the effectiveness of internal control as of the end of the most recent fiscal year; (3) identification of the framework used to evaluate the effectiveness of internal control (such as the report of the Committee of Sponsoring Organizations); (4) a statement about whether significant changes in controls were made after their evaluation, including any corrective actions; and (5) a statement that the external auditor has issued an attestation report on management's assessment. Because of Section 404, **two audit opinions** are expressed: one on internal control and one on the financial statements. The auditor must evaluate whether the structure and procedures (1) include **records** accurately and fairly reflecting the firm's transactions and (2) provide **reasonable assurance** that transactions are recorded so as to permit statements to be prepared in accordance with GAAP. The auditor's report also must describe any material weaknesses in the controls. The evaluation is not to be the subject of a separate engagement. It must be in conjunction with the audit of the financial statements.

SEC regulations issued under the act prohibit auditors of public companies from performing certain **nonaudit services** absent a specific exemption from the PCAOB. Audit firms may continue to provide conventional **tax planning** and other nonaudit services not specifically prohibited to audit clients if **preapproved by the audit committee**. Moreover, the Board may grant exemptions from these prohibitions on a case-by-case basis, subject to approval by the SEC. Still another provision of the act prohibits the **conflict of interest** that arises when the CEO, CFO, controller, chief accounting officer, or the equivalent was employed by the company's public accounting firm within one year preceding the audit. Auditors must retain their audit **working papers** for at least 7 years. Under Title VIII of the act (also known as the Corporate and Criminal Fraud Accountability Act of 2002), it is a **crime** for auditors to fail to maintain all audit or review working papers for 5 years. **Second-partner review** and approval of audit reports is required. Furthermore, the **lead audit partner** and the **reviewing partner** must rotate off the audit every 5 years. Public accounting firms must register with the PCAOB and be subject to inspection every 3 years (1 year for large firms). Moreover, they must adopt **quality-control standards** and **reasonably supervise any associated person** with regard to auditing and quality control standards. Registrants must file an **annual report** with the PCAOB that contains basic information about firm activities. They also must file a **special report** within 30 days of a reportable event, e.g., initiation of legal action against the firm. **Audit reports** to **audit committees** must include (1) all critical accounting policies and practices to be used, (2) all material alternative treatments of financial information within GAAP discussed with management, (3) ramifications of the use of alternative disclosures and treatments, and (4) the treatment preferred by the external auditors. **Correcting adjustments** identified by the public accountants must be disclosed in an issuer's required periodic GAAP-based reports. **Tampering with records**, for example, altering, destroying, or concealing audit **working papers** for the purpose of impairing their integrity or availability for use in an official proceeding or to obstruct such a proceeding, is a crime punishable by up to 20 years in prison. The act created a new **25-year felony for defrauding shareholders** of publicly traded companies. This measure is a broad, generalized provision that criminalizes the knowing execution or attempted execution of any fraud upon persons in connection with securities of publicly traded companies or the purchase or sale of such securities. It is intended to give prosecutors flexibility to protect shareholders and prospective shareholders against any frauds that inventive criminals may devise.

Federal law does not recognize a broad **privilege for accountant-client** communications. However, the **Internal Revenue Service Restructuring and Reform Act of 1998** extends a confidentiality privilege to most tax advice provided to a current or prospective client by any individual (CPA, attorney, enrolled agent, or enrolled actuary) qualified under federal law to practice before the IRS. The federal law does not apply to criminal tax matters, private civil matters, disclosures to other federal regulatory bodies, or state and local tax matters. The privilege is available only in matters brought before the IRS or in proceedings in federal court in which the U.S. is a party. The privilege applies only to advice on legal issues. A majority of the states do not recognize a privilege for accountant-client communications. A **minority of the states** have statutes that grant the privilege. It is applicable in criminal and civil matters and is not limited to the subject matter of the audit.

EXAMPLE: State law provides for an accountant-client privilege. The IRS, in conducting a proper investigation, requests Accounting Firm to provide it with records on Client. Firm complies. Client sues Firm in state court. Firm asserts that federal law does not recognize the privilege and preempts state law. State court determines that, because the disclosure was without notice to the client and was made in the absence of service of legal process compelling disclosure, it is not inconsistent with federal law to hold Firm liable for the voluntary disclosure.

If the privilege exists, it belongs to the **client**. If any part of the privileged communication is **disclosed** by either the client or the accountant, the privilege is lost completely.

EXAMPLE: Continuing the previous example, disclosure by Firm to a third party (the IRS) negates the privilege with respect to the information. The information is no longer recognized as protected confidential communication(s) under the law of the state. Client communications with accountants retained by attorneys to aid in litigation are protected by the **attorney-client privilege**. This privilege is recognized in both federal and state courts. The accountant is considered the attorney's agent.

Working papers are confidential records made by an accountant while performing an engagement. Working papers may include each of the following: (1) plans for the engagement, (2) documentation of the client's accounting system, (3) results of tests performed, (4) written representations from the client or the client's legal counsel, (5) explanations, and (6) reconciliations. Working papers are deemed to be the **property of the accountant**. They are prepared by the accountant and provide the best evidence of the accountant's efforts in the event of a lawsuit. However, working papers ordinarily may be subpoenaed by a third party for use in litigation because only a few states recognize a privilege for accountant-client communications. Absent a court order or client consent, third parties are **not allowed access** to working papers. The accountant may be liable for malpractice if (s)he allows a third party, including a purchaser of his/her practice, unauthorized access to working papers. The AICPA *Code of Professional Conduct* (Rule 301) states that a member shall not disclose any confidential client information except with the specific **consent of the client**. If confidential accountant-client communications are privileged under state law, disclosure is not permitted except in limited circumstances, for example, when the statute allows disclosure to a state peer review board or federal law preempts the state law. At a minimum, an accountant that does not audit public companies should **retain working papers** until the state statute of limitations on litigation that might arise has lapsed. The limitations period varies by state and according to the type of claim. Retention of working papers ensures that the accountant will have the evidence necessary to defend against claims in a lawsuit.

QUESTIONS

<u>40.1 General Standards of Care</u>

1. Which of the following statements best explains why the CPA profession has found it essential to promulgate ethical standards and to establish means for ensuring their observance?

A. Vigorous enforcement of an established code of ethics is the best way to prevent unscrupulous acts.

B. Ethical standards that emphasize excellence in performance over material rewards establish a reputation for competence and character.

C. A distinguishing mark of a profession is its acceptance of responsibility to the public.

D. A requirement for a profession is to establish ethical standards that stress primarily a responsibility to clients and colleagues.

Answer (C) is correct. *(CPA, adapted)*

REQUIRED: The reason for promulgation of ethical standards.

DISCUSSION: Article II of the AICPA Code of Professional Conduct states, "Members should accept the obligation to act in a way that will serve the public interest, honor the public trust, and demonstrate commitment to professionalism." According to the accompanying explanation, "A distinguishing mark of a profession is acceptance of its responsibility to the public."

Answer (A) is incorrect. Vigorous enforcement is significant but secondary to fostering a professional environment of voluntary adherence to ethical principles. Answer (B) is incorrect. Excellence in performance is but one of the effects of accepting responsibility to the public. Answer (D) is incorrect. The responsibility of CPAs is to a public that is not limited to clients and colleagues but includes all those who rely on their objectivity and integrity.

2. When CPAs fail in their duty to carry out their contracts for services, liability to clients may be based on

	Breach of Contract	Strict Liability
A.	Yes	Yes
B.	Yes	No
C.	No	No
D.	No	Yes

Answer (B) is correct. *(CPA, adapted)*

REQUIRED: The basis(es), if any, for a CPA's liability to a client for failure to perform the contract.

DISCUSSION: The courts and legislatures have decided that one party in certain circumstances without regard to fault is better able to bear a loss than the injured party. Thus, strict liability in tort is imposed even in the absence of negligence or intentional misconduct. For example, manufacturers may be liable for injuries caused by defective products. However, liability to clients for breach of contract is not strict.

Answer (A) is incorrect. A CPA's liability for breach of contract is not strict. Answer (C) is incorrect. CPAs are liable for breach of contract. Answer (D) is incorrect. CPAs are liable for breach of contract, but it is not strict liability.

3. Ford & Co., CPAs, expressed an unqualified opinion on Owens Corp.'s financial statements. Relying on these financial statements, Century Bank lent Owens $750,000. Ford was unaware that Century would receive a copy of the financial statements or that Owens would use them to obtain a loan. Owens defaulted on the loan. To succeed in a common-law fraud action against Ford, Century must prove, in addition to other elements, that Century was

A. Free from contributory negligence.

B. In privity of contract with Ford.

C. Justified in relying on the financial statements.

D. In privity of contract with Owens.

Answer (C) is correct. *(CPA, adapted)*

REQUIRED: The element of a prima facie case of common-law fraud.

DISCUSSION: The tort of intentional misrepresentation (fraud, deceit) consists of a material misrepresentation made with scienter and an intent to induce reliance. The misstatement must also have proximately caused damage to a defendant who justifiably relied upon it. Scienter exists when the defendant makes a false representation with knowledge of its falsity or with reckless disregard as to its truth.

Answer (A) is incorrect. Contributory negligence is a defense to negligence, not fraud. Answer (B) is incorrect. As a foreseeable third party, Century will have standing to bring an action based on fraud. Answer (D) is incorrect. In a fraud action, a plaintiff need not be in privity with the defendant.

4. A CPA will be liable to a tax client for damages resulting from all of the following actions except

A. Failing to timely file a client's return.

B. Failing to advise a client of certain tax elections.

C. Refusing to sign a client's request for a filing extension.

D. Neglecting to evaluate the option of preparing joint or separate returns that would have resulted in a substantial tax savings for a married client.

Answer (C) is correct. *(CPA, adapted)*

REQUIRED: The action that will not result in a CPA being liable to a tax client.

DISCUSSION: An accountant owes a general duty to exercise the skill and care of an ordinarily prudent accountant in the same circumstances. Moreover, the accountant is responsible to exercise independent professional judgment and to comply with law. If the CPA does not agree the client has a valid reason for obtaining an extension, (s)he will not be liable for refusing to sign the client's request.

5. Which of the following statements best describes whether a CPA has met the required standard of care in conducting an audit of a client's financial statements?

A. The client's expectations with regard to the accuracy of audited financial statements.

B. The accuracy of the financial statements and whether the statements conform to generally accepted accounting principles.

C. Whether the CPA conducted the audit with the same skill and care expected of an ordinarily prudent CPA under the circumstances.

D. Whether the audit was conducted to investigate and discover all acts of fraud.

Answer (C) is correct. *(CPA, adapted)*

REQUIRED: The statement that best describes whether a CPA has met the required standard of care.

DISCUSSION: An accountant owes a general duty to exercise the skill and care of the ordinarily prudent accountant in the same circumstances. The purpose of an independent external audit of financial statements is the expression of an opinion on whether they are fairly presented in conformity with GAAP. To achieve this objective, the CPA must follow GAAS. However, GAAS contemplate planning and performing the audit to obtain only reasonable assurance that the statements are free of material misstatements, whether caused by errors or fraud.

Answer (A) is incorrect. The standard is the conduct of an ordinarily prudent accountant under the circumstances. Answer (B) is incorrect. An ordinarily prudent accountant may, under certain circumstances, do more than is required by GAAP. Answer (D) is incorrect. An accountant does not guarantee detection of all material errors or acts of fraud.

6. If a shareholder sues a CPA for common-law fraud based on false statements contained in the financial statements audited by the CPA, which of the following, if present, would be the CPA's best defense?

A. The shareholder lacks privity to sue.

B. The false statements were immaterial.

C. The CPA did not financially benefit from the alleged fraud.

D. The client was contributorily negligent.

Answer (B) is correct. *(CPA, adapted)*

REQUIRED: The best defense of a CPA sued for common-law fraud by a third party.

DISCUSSION: To recover for the tort of fraud, a plaintiff must prove that (1) the defendant made a misrepresentation, (2) with knowledge that it was false or with a reckless disregard for the truth, (3) with intent that it should be relied upon, and (4) regarding a material fact that was justifiably relied upon by the third party to his/her detriment. The CPA's best defense is that the false statements were immaterial.

Answer (A) is incorrect. Privity with the injured party is not an element of common-law fraud. Answer (C) is incorrect. A detriment to the plaintiff, not a benefit to the defendant, must be proven. Answer (D) is incorrect. The negligence of a client does not excuse a CPA from liability for intentional misconduct.

7. Mix & Associates, CPAs, expressed an unqualified opinion on the financial statements of Glass Corp. for the year ended December 31. It was determined later that Glass's treasurer had embezzled $300,000 from Glass during the year. Glass sued Mix because of Mix's failure to discover the embezzlement. Mix was unaware of the embezzlement. Which of the following is Mix's best defense?

A. The audit was performed in accordance with GAAS.

B. The treasurer was Glass's agent and, therefore, Glass was responsible for preventing the embezzlement.

C. The financial statements were presented in conformity with GAAP.

D. Mix had no actual knowledge of the embezzlement.

Answer (A) is correct. *(CPA, adapted)*

REQUIRED: The best defense of CPAs who failed to discover embezzlement.

DISCUSSION: To determine whether financial statements are in conformity with GAAP, the CPA must follow GAAS. The auditors do not guarantee that all material errors or fraud will be detected. Following GAAS does not eliminate the possibility of negligence, but it is strong evidence of adherence to the due care standard, which would be the CPA's best defense.

Answer (B) is incorrect. Contributory negligence of the client in engaging another agent reduces the amount of damages recoverable, but does not excuse the CPA's negligence. Answer (C) is incorrect. The accountant's defense would be based on his/her performance of the implied duty to perform the audit in accordance with GAAS. Answer (D) is incorrect. Negligence can be based on failure to discover knowledge that would have been acquired if the accountant had exercised reasonable care.

40.2 Liability to Clients under Common Law

8. Ritz Corp. wished to acquire the stock of Stale, Inc. In conjunction with its plan of acquisition, Ritz hired Fein, CPA, to audit the financial statements of Stale. Based on the audited financial statements and Fein's unqualified opinion, Ritz acquired Stale. Within 6 months, it was discovered that the inventory of Stale had been overstated by $500,000. Ritz commenced an action against Fein. Ritz believes that Fein failed to exercise the knowledge, skill, and judgment commonly possessed by CPAs in the locality, but is not able to prove that Fein either intentionally deceived it or showed a reckless disregard for the truth. Ritz also is unable to prove that Fein had any knowledge that the inventory was overstated. Which of the following two causes of action would provide Ritz with proper bases upon which Ritz would most likely prevail?

A. Negligence and breach of contract.

B. Negligence and gross negligence.

C. Negligence and fraud.

D. Gross negligence and breach of contract.

Answer (A) is correct. *(CPA, adapted)*

REQUIRED: The bases upon which a client will most likely prevail when an auditor fails to exercise due care.

DISCUSSION: An accountant's common-law liability to a client can be based upon breach of contract, negligence, or fraud. A breach of contract occurs when an accountant fails to perform duties required under a contract. These duties can either be express or implied. All contracts carry the implied duty to perform in a nonnegligent manner. To prevail in an action for negligence, the client must prove that the accountant did not act with the same degree of skill and judgment possessed by accountants in the locality. In an action for fraud, the client must prove scienter (intent to deceive or a reckless disregard for the truth). Ritz will most likely prevail in an action brought for negligence or breach of contract if Fein failed to perform with the knowledge, skill, and judgment commonly possessed by CPAs in the area.

9. Which of the following may a CPA do only with permission of the client?

A. Hire other CPAs as employees to help complete the engagement.

B. Hire non-CPAs as employees to help complete the engagement.

C. Delegate the engagement to another CPA.

D. Receive a commission for referring the engagement to another CPA.

Answer (C) is correct. *(Publisher, adapted)*
REQUIRED: The action a CPA may not take without permission of the client.
DISCUSSION: The engagement to perform professional services is a personal service contract. It may not be delegated without permission of the other contracting party (client).
Answer (A) is incorrect. A CPA may hire others (CPAs or non-CPAs) to assist in performing the engagement as long as the CPA hired by the client supervises the job and is responsible for it. Answer (B) is incorrect. A CPA may use the work of suitable assistants even if they are not CPAs. Answer (D) is incorrect. In no event may a CPA receive a commission for referring an engagement.

10. Which of the following can a CPA firm legally do?

A. Accept a competing company in the same industry as another of its clients.

B. Establish an association of CPAs for the purpose of determining minimum fee schedules.

C. Effectively disclaim liability to third parties for any and all torts.

D. Effectively establish an absolute dollar limitation on its liability for a given engagement.

Answer (A) is correct. *(CPA, adapted)*
REQUIRED: The action of a CPA firm that is legally permissible.
DISCUSSION: Although a CPA contracts with a client to perform services, (s)he is an independent contractor and may also work for others. A CPA firm can legally accept a competing company in the same industry as another client. This practice is advantageous because it permits CPAs to "specialize" and become more knowledgeable and efficient, as well as to be of more assistance to clients.
Answer (B) is incorrect. Minimum fee schedules are considered a restraint of trade. Answer (C) is incorrect. Liability for fraud cannot be disclaimed. Answer (D) is incorrect. A CPA firm cannot establish a dollar limit on its liability for any engagement (partly because the CPA cannot know all the parties who may rely upon his/her work).

11. Sun Corp. approved a merger plan with Cord Corp. One of the determining factors in approving the merger was the financial statements of Cord that were audited by Frank & Co., CPAs. Sun had engaged Frank to audit Cord's financial statements. While performing the audit, Frank failed to discover certain irregularities that later caused Sun to suffer substantial losses. For Frank to be liable under common-law negligence, Sun at a minimum must prove that Frank

A. Knew of the irregularities.

B. Failed to exercise due care.

C. Was grossly negligent.

D. Acted with scienter.

Answer (B) is correct. *(CPA, adapted)*
REQUIRED: The element of an action for common-law negligence.
DISCUSSION: An accountant has a duty to exercise the skill and care that an ordinarily prudent accountant would in the same circumstances. An accountant who fails to exercise due care is negligent.
Answer (A) is incorrect. If the accountant knew of the irregularities, (s)he would be negligent for failure to investigate further or to notify Sun of the irregularities. Answer (C) is incorrect. Failure to exercise due care, not failure to exercise slight care, is required to establish common-law negligence. Answer (D) is incorrect. Proving scienter is necessary to establish fraud but not negligence.

12. The firm Meek & Co., CPAs, was engaged by Reed, the president of Sulk Corp., to issue by June 15 an opinion on Sulk's financial statements for the fiscal year ended March 31. Meek's engagement and its fee of $20,000 were approved by Sulk's board of directors. Meek did not issue its opinion until June 30 because of Sulk's failure to supply Meek with the necessary information to complete the audit. Sulk refuses to pay Meek. If Meek sues Sulk, Meek will

A. Prevail based on the contract.

B. Prevail based on quasi-contract.

C. Lose, because it breached the contract.

D. Lose, because the June 15 deadline was a condition precedent to Sulk's performance.

Answer (A) is correct. *(CPA, adapted)*
REQUIRED: The probable outcome of an action by CPAs to recover fees.
DISCUSSION: Meek's failure to meet the deadline did not result in a breach of contract. Rather, the failure of performance was caused by Sulk's failure to supply Meek with the necessary information to complete the audit. Every contract contains an implied promise that each party will not interfere with the other party's performance. Consequently, Meek can enforce the contract because Meek was not in breach.
Answer (B) is incorrect. A quasi-contract is an equitable remedy applied when one party has been unjustly enriched at the expense of the other. It is not necessary in this case because the parties formed an express contract. Answer (C) is incorrect. Sulk's supplying the necessary information was a condition precedent to Meek's duty to perform. Answer (D) is incorrect. The condition would have been effective only if Sulk had not interfered with Meek's ability to perform.

13. A CPA will most likely be negligent when the CPA fails to

A. Correct errors discovered in the CPA's previously issued audit reports.

B. Detect all of a client's fraudulent activities.

C. Include a negligence disclaimer in the CPA's engagement letter.

D. Warn a client's customers of embezzlement by the client's employees.

Answer (A) is correct. *(CPA, adapted)*

REQUIRED: The omission by a CPA that most likely constitutes negligence.

DISCUSSION: A CPA has a duty to correct his/her audit report if (s)he subsequently discovers the report is erroneous. The CPA should disclose the new information to any user relying on the previous report. But an attorney should be consulted.

Answer (B) is incorrect. A CPA has a duty to exercise due care, but not to discover all acts of fraud or embezzlement. (S)he is not an insurer or guarantor. Answer (C) is incorrect. A disclaimer of negligence by a CPA is generally ineffective. Answer (D) is incorrect. A CPA is not responsible to notify a client's customers of employee embezzlement. The CPA must, however, notify the client.

14. You are a CPA retained by the manager of a cooperative retirement village to do "write-up work." You are expected to prepare unaudited financial statements with each page marked "unaudited" and accompanied by a disclaimer of opinion stating no audit was made. In performing the work, you discover that there are no invoices to support $25,000 of the manager's claimed disbursements. The manager informs you that all the disbursements are proper. What should you do?

A. Submit the expected statements but omit the $25,000 of unsupported disbursements.

B. Include the unsupported disbursements in the statements because you are not expected to make an audit.

C. Obtain from the manager a written statement that you informed him/her of the missing invoices and his/her assurance that the disbursements are proper.

D. Notify the owners that some of the claimed disbursements are unsupported and withdraw if the situation is not satisfactorily resolved.

Answer (D) is correct. *(CPA, adapted)*

REQUIRED: The appropriate action by a CPA who discovers a material irregularity while doing compilation work.

DISCUSSION: This situation describes the 1136 Tenants' Corporation case. A CPA doing compilation work was held liable for not pursuing an investigation of a situation that appeared questionable on its face. Although the CPA need not audit the information, (s)he is responsible to take further action on information that is incorrect, incomplete, or otherwise unsatisfactory. Such action includes communication with the owners.

Answer (A) is incorrect. To exclude the unsupported disbursements subjects the CPA to liability for not following up on a questionable item. Answer (B) is incorrect. To include the unsupported disbursements subjects the CPA to liability for not following up on a questionable item. Answer (C) is incorrect. The owners must be notified and the situation resolved before the CPA continues.

15. Krim, president and CEO of United Co., engaged Smith, CPA, to audit United's financial statements so that United could secure a loan from First Bank. Smith issued an unqualified opinion on May 20, but the loan was delayed. On August 5, on inquiry to Smith by First Bank, Smith, relying on Krim's representation, made assurances that there was no material change in United's financial status. Krim's representation was untrue because of a material change that took place after May 20. First relied on Smith's assurances of no change. Shortly thereafter, United became insolvent. If First sues Smith for negligent misrepresentation, Smith will be found

A. Not liable, because Krim misled Smith, and a CPA is not responsible for a client's untrue representations.

B. Liable, because Smith should have undertaken sufficient auditing procedures to verify the status of United.

C. Not liable, because Smith's opinion only covers the period up to May 20.

D. Liable, because Smith should have contacted the chief financial officer rather than the chief executive officer.

Answer (B) is correct. *(CPA, adapted)*

REQUIRED: The auditor's liability for assurances given about events subsequent to the report.

DISCUSSION: Under GAAS, written representations corroborate information received orally from management, but they do not substitute for the procedures necessary to afford a reasonable basis for the assurances given. Moreover, the auditor ordinarily has no responsibility for events after the end of field work. If the auditor decides to assume such responsibility, (s)he must comply with GAAS. Accordingly, the auditor will be liable for failure to exercise due care.

Answer (A) is incorrect. A CPA should make an independent investigation. Answer (C) is incorrect. Smith made assurances to the bank that covered the period subsequent to May 20 and therefore assumed responsibility for the additional period. Answer (D) is incorrect. Smith should have performed additional audit procedures and not have relied solely on management's representations, including those of the chief financial officer.

16. Which of the following elements, if present, would support a finding of constructive fraud on the part of a CPA?

A. Gross negligence in applying generally accepted auditing standards.

B. Ordinary negligence in applying generally accepted accounting principles.

C. Identified third party users.

D. Scienter.

Answer (A) is correct. *(CPA, adapted)*

REQUIRED: The element supporting a finding of constructive fraud on the part of a CPA.

DISCUSSION: Scienter is a prerequisite to liability for fraud. Scienter generally means that the person knowingly made a representation. For constructive fraud, the scienter requirement is shown by gross negligence (reckless disregard for the truth).

Answer (B) is incorrect. Failure to apply GAAP and GAAS in good faith is evidence of negligence. To prove fraud, more is required. Answer (C) is incorrect. For fraud, a CPA may be liable to all foreseeable users of his/her work. Answer (D) is incorrect. Scienter is a necessary element of fraud. For constructive fraud, the scienter element is proved by evidence of gross negligence.

17. Walters & Whitlow, CPAs, failed to discover a fraudulent scheme used by Davis Corporation's head cashier to embezzle corporate funds during the past 5 years. Walters & Whitlow would have discovered the embezzlements promptly if they had not been negligent in their annual audits. Under the circumstances, Walters & Whitlow will normally not be liable for

A. Punitive damages.

B. The fees charged for the years in question.

C. Losses occurring after the time the fraudulent scheme should have been detected.

D. Losses occurring prior to the time the fraudulent scheme should have been detected that could have been recovered had it been so detected.

Answer (A) is correct. *(CPA, adapted)*

REQUIRED: The damages not payable by CPAs for negligent failure to discover fraud.

DISCUSSION: If the CPAs have merely been negligent, they will not be liable for punitive damages. Punitive damages are awarded only when the situation presents a case of extreme or aggravated circumstances.

Answer (B) is incorrect. The fees charged would be a proper element of the plaintiff's damages. The defendant violated both its contractual and tort duties to perform in a competent manner. Answer (C) is incorrect. A loss occurring after a scheme should have been discovered is properly recoverable in damages. It flows directly from the defendant's misconduct. Answer (D) is incorrect. Although an accountant is not normally liable for losses occurring before a scheme should have been discovered, the accountant is liable when the losses could have been recovered.

40.3 Liability to Third Parties

18. A CPA who fraudulently performs an audit of a corporation's financial statements will

A. Probably be liable to any person who suffered a loss as a result of the fraud.

B. Be liable only to the corporation and to third parties who are members of a class of intended users of the financial statements.

C. Probably be liable to the corporation even though its management was aware of the fraud and did not rely on the financial statements.

D. Be liable only to third parties in privity of contract with the CPA.

Answer (A) is correct. *(CPA, adapted)*

REQUIRED: The persons to whom a CPA who fraudulently performs an audit is liable.

DISCUSSION: Because fraud entails moral turpitude, the courts permit all reasonably foreseeable users of an accountant's work product to bring suit. The distinctive feature of fraud is scienter, that is, intentional misrepresentation or reckless disregard for the truth (sometimes found in gross negligence).

Answer (B) is incorrect. Accountant liability can extend to all reasonably foreseeable users of an accountant's work product who incur loss resulting from the accountant's fraud. Answer (C) is incorrect. An element of a fraud action is that the plaintiff relied justifiably on the material misstatement. Answer (D) is incorrect. Accountant liability can extend to all reasonably foreseeable users of an accountant's work product who incur loss resulting from the accountant's fraud.

19. While conducting an audit, a CPA failed to detect material misstatements included in his/her client's financial statements. The CPA's unqualified opinion was included with the financial statements in a registration statement and prospectus for a public offering of securities made by the client. In a suit by a purchaser against the CPA for common-law fraud, the CPA's best defense would be that

A. The CPA did not have actual or constructive knowledge of the misstatements.

B. The CPA's client knew or should have known of the misstatements.

C. The CPA did not have actual knowledge that the purchaser was an intended beneficiary of the audit.

D. The CPA was not in privity of contract with his/her client.

Answer (A) is correct. *(CPA, adapted)*

REQUIRED: The best defense of a CPA sued for common-law fraud by a third party.

DISCUSSION: To recover for the tort of fraud, a plaintiff must prove that the defendant made a misrepresentation, with knowledge that it was false or with a reckless disregard for the truth, with intent that it should be relied upon, and regarding a material fact that was actually relied upon by the third party to his/her detriment. The CPA's reckless disregard for the truth can satisfy the scienter element even when the CPA was without knowledge of a misstatement.

Answer (B) is incorrect. The negligence of a client does not exculpate a CPA from liability to a third party. Answer (C) is incorrect. Liability for fraud is to all foreseeable users of the CPA's work. Answer (D) is incorrect. Privity with the injured party is not an element of fraud.

20. Which of the following statements is(are) correct regarding the common law elements that must be proven to support a finding of constructive fraud against a CPA?

I. The plaintiff has justifiably relied on the CPA's misrepresentation.

II. The CPA has acted in a grossly negligent manner.

A. I only.

B. II only.

C. Both I and II.

D. Neither I nor II.

Answer (C) is correct. *(CPA, adapted)*

REQUIRED: The statement(s), if any, of the common law elements that must be proven to support a finding of constructive fraud.

DISCUSSION: The tort of intentional misrepresentation (fraud, deceit) consists of a material misrepresentation made with scienter and an intent to induce reliance. The misstatement must also have proximately caused damage to a plaintiff who justifiably relied upon it. Scienter exists when the defendant makes a false representation with knowledge of its falsity or with reckless disregard as to its truth. For constructive fraud, the scienter requirement is met by proof of gross negligence (reckless disregard for the truth).

21. Hark, CPA, failed to follow generally accepted auditing standards in auditing Long Corp.'s financial statements. Long's management had told Hark that the audited statements would be submitted to several banks to obtain financing. Relying on the statements, Third Bank gave Long a loan. Long defaulted on the loan. In a jurisdiction applying the *Ultramares* decision, if Third sues Hark, Hark will

A. Win because there was no privity of contract between Hark and Third.

B. Lose because Hark knew that banks would be relying on the financial statements.

C. Win because Third was contributorily negligent in granting the loan.

D. Lose because Hark was negligent in performing the audit.

Answer (A) is correct. *(CPA, adapted)*

REQUIRED: The liability of a CPA to a third party under the *Ultramares* decision.

DISCUSSION: An accountant is not liable to all persons who are damaged by his/her negligence. Lack of privity is still a defense in some states. For example, in the *Ultramares* case, an accountant was only liable for negligence if the plaintiff was in privity of contract with the accountant or a primary beneficiary of the engagement. Under the primary benefit test, the accountant must have been aware that (s)he was hired to produce a work product to be used and relied upon by a particular third party.

Answer (B) is incorrect. *Ultramares* required that the accountant be engaged principally to benefit the third party and that the third party be identified. Answer (C) is incorrect. Although contributory negligence is a complete or partial limit on liability in certain circumstances, under *Ultramares*, Hark is not liable to Third. Answer (D) is incorrect. Hark had not contracted to perform for Third, and Third was not a primary beneficiary of Hark's contract with Long.

22. One traditional test of whether a third party can recover from an accountant for negligence is the primary benefit test. Which of the following has standing under the primary benefit test?

A. A bank that is considering a loan to the accountant's client and is waiting for the financial statements on which to base its decision.

B. A bank when the accountant was aware financial statements would be sent to many banks as part of loan applications by the client.

C. A shareholder of the client.

D. A general trade creditor of the client.

Answer (A) is correct. *(Publisher, adapted)*

REQUIRED: The third party who has standing under the primary benefit test.

DISCUSSION: Under the primary benefit test, the accountant must have been aware that (s)he was hired to produce a work product to be used and relied upon by a particular third party. This is the narrowest test, and most courts allow such a third party to sue the accountant for ordinary negligence.

Answer (B) is incorrect. This bank is only a member of a foreseen class of third parties, not a primary beneficiary. Answer (C) is incorrect. Shareholders are merely foreseeable users. Answer (D) is incorrect. General trade creditors are merely foreseeable users.

23. Beckler & Associates, CPAs, audited and expressed an unqualified opinion on the financial statements of Queen Co. The financial statements contained misstatements that resulted in a material overstatement of Queen's net worth. Queen provided the audited financial statements to Mac Bank in connection with a loan made by Mac to Queen. Beckler knew that the financial statements would be provided to Mac. Queen defaulted on the loan. Mac sued Beckler to recover for its losses associated with Queen's default. Which of the following must Mac prove in order to recover?

I. Beckler was negligent in conducting the audit.
II. Mac relied on the financial statements.

A. I only.

B. II only.

C. Both I and II.

D. Neither I nor II.

Answer (C) is correct. *(CPA, adapted)*

REQUIRED: The proof to recover from a CPA when the financial statements contain material misstatements.

DISCUSSION: An accountant has a duty to exercise the skill and care that an ordinarily prudent accountant would in the same circumstances. An accountant who fails to exercise due care is negligent. Assuming the foreseen user test is applied, liability for breach of the duty is to any person whom the accountant knows will be given the work product and will rely on it.

24. Brown & Co., CPAs, expressed an unqualified opinion on the financial statements of its client, King Corp. Based on the strength of King's financial statements, Safe Bank loaned King $500,000. Brown was unaware that Safe would receive a copy of the financial statements or that they would be used in obtaining a loan by King. King defaulted on the loan. If Safe commences an action for negligence against Brown and Brown is able to prove that it conducted the audit in conformity with GAAS, Brown will

A. Be liable to Safe because Safe relied on the financial statements.

B. Be liable to Safe because the statute of frauds has been satisfied.

C. Not be liable to Safe because there is a conclusive presumption that following GAAS is the equivalent of acting reasonably and with due care.

D. Not be liable to Safe because of a lack of privity of contract.

Answer (D) is correct. *(CPA, adapted)*

REQUIRED: The outcome of a negligence suit by a third party who the auditors did not know would use the financial statements.

DISCUSSION: The auditors could not be held liable for fraud or gross negligence because they followed GAAS. Gross negligence or fraud involves an intentional or reckless failure to exercise due care, but adherence to GAAS indicates at least a good faith effort to apply professional standards. Thus, the auditors are liable at most for ordinary negligence. In most jurisdictions, however, a party who is merely a foreseeable user and not (1) a foreseen user, (2) a member of a class of foreseen users, or (3) in privity of contract will have no standing to bring suit for ordinary negligence.

Answer (A) is incorrect. Safe's reliance is irrelevant. It was not within the class of parties to whom Brown owed a duty. Answer (B) is incorrect. The statute of frauds is not relevant to this case. Answer (C) is incorrect. Depending on the facts, adherence to GAAS may not be a complete defense.

40.4 Liability under Federal Securities Law

25. Which of the following best describes a trend in litigation involving CPAs?

A. Common law is being used more due to the difficulty of suing under securities laws.

B. There are substantially more lawsuits filed against CPAs and larger judgment amounts.

C. They are being held criminally liable less frequently.

D. State laws are rarely used anymore because of the existence of the SEC.

Answer (B) is correct. *(Publisher, adapted)*

REQUIRED: The trend in litigation involving CPAs.

DISCUSSION: The number of lawsuits filed against CPAs has substantially increased, in part because of a general awareness of an auditor's exposure to liability. The judgments against CPAs have also been much larger, making it even more important for a CPA to exercise due diligence in his/her work.

Answer (A) is incorrect. Securities laws rather than common law have been used more frequently in recent years. Answer (C) is incorrect. Criminal sentences are now being applied more frequently. Answer (D) is incorrect. State laws also are being used more frequently to hold CPAs liable.

26. How does the Securities Act of 1933, which imposes civil liability on auditors for misrepresentations or omissions of material facts in a registration statement, expand auditors' liability to purchasers of securities beyond that of common law?

A. Purchasers only have to prove loss caused by reliance on audited financial statements.

B. Privity with purchasers is not a necessary element of proof.

C. Purchasers have to prove either fraud or gross negligence as a basis for recovery.

D. Auditors are held to a standard of care described as "professional skepticism."

Answer (B) is correct. *(CPA, adapted)*

REQUIRED: The factor that results in expanded liability of a CPA under the Securities Act of 1933.

DISCUSSION: Under the Securities Act of 1933, a purchaser need only prove damages resulting from the purchase of securities covered by a registration statement containing a false statement or omission of a material fact in a section audited or prepared by the auditor. The auditor must then prove that (s)he was not negligent (or fraudulent), usually by showing that (s)he acted with "due diligence."

To recover damages at common law based on contract or negligence, privity between the plaintiff and accountant may be required. To recover under the Securities Act of 1933, however, a purchaser of securities need not prove privity of contract with a CPA.

Answer (A) is incorrect. More must be proved under the 1933 act, e.g., material misstatement or omission. Answer (C) is incorrect. Purchasers need not even prove negligence under the 1933 act. Answer (D) is incorrect. Such a standard does not apply at common law or under the 1933 act.

27. Gold, CPA, rendered an unqualified opinion on the financial statements of Eastern Power Co. Silver purchased Eastern bonds in a public offering subject to the Securities Act of 1933. The registration statement filed with the SEC included the financial statements. Gold is being sued by Silver under Section 11 of the Securities Act of 1933 for the misstatements contained in the financial statements. To prevail, Silver must prove

	Scienter	Reliance
A.	No	No
B.	No	Yes
C.	Yes	No
D.	Yes	Yes

Answer (A) is correct. *(CPA, adapted)*

REQUIRED: The element(s) of the plaintiff's case under Section 11.

DISCUSSION: The plaintiff's case has the following elements: The plaintiff purchased securities subject to a registration statement, the plaintiff suffered a loss, and a part of the registration statement for which the defendant was responsible contained a misstatement or omission of a material fact. Plaintiff and defendant need not have been in privity of contract; plaintiff need not have relied on the misstatement or omission; and the defendant need not have intended to deceive, manipulate, or defraud anyone.

Answer (B) is incorrect. Reliance is not an element of the case. Answer (C) is incorrect. Scienter is not an element of the case. Answer (D) is incorrect. Neither scienter nor reliance must be shown.

28. Under the liability provisions of Section 11 of the Securities Act of 1933, an auditor may help to establish the defense of due diligence if

I. The auditor performed an additional review of the audited statements to ensure that the statements were accurate as of the effective date of a registration statement.

II. The auditor complied with GAAS.

A. I only.

B. II only.

C. Both I and II.

D. Neither I nor II.

Answer (C) is correct. *(CPA, adapted)*

REQUIRED: The basis(es), if any, for the defense of due diligence.

DISCUSSION: A CPA is strictly liable to investors under Section 11 but will not be liable if (s)he can prove due diligence. This defense requires proof that a reasonable investigation was conducted and that the CPA reasonably believed that the financial statements were accurate on the effective date of the registration statement. Proof of adherence to GAAP and GAAS is the usual basis for such a due diligence defense. For example, GAAS require that subsequent events procedures be performed. The auditor should extend his/her procedures from the date of the report up to the effective date of a 1933 act filing or as close to it as is reasonable and practicable (AU 711).

29. Petty Corp. made a public offering subject to the Securities Act of 1933. In connection with the offering, Ward & Co., CPAs, rendered an unqualified opinion on Petty's financial statements included in the SEC registration statement. Huff purchased 500 of the offered shares. Huff has brought an action against Ward under Section 11 of the Securities Act of 1933 for losses resulting from misstatements of facts in the financial statements included in the registration statement. Ward's weakest defense would be that

A. Huff knew of the misstatements when Huff purchased the stock.

B. Huff's losses were not caused by the misstatements.

C. Ward was not in privity of contract with Huff.

D. Ward conducted the audit in accordance with GAAS.

Answer (C) is correct. *(CPA, adapted)*

REQUIRED: The defense least helpful to an accountant sued under the Securities Act of 1933.

DISCUSSION: Under Section 11, the plaintiff-purchaser of securities issued under a registration statement containing a misstatement or omission of a material fact need not prove either reliance or privity.

Answer (A) is incorrect. The plaintiff's knowledge of the material misstatement or omission at the time of purchase will defeat the claim. Answer (B) is incorrect. Other possible defenses are that the plaintiff's losses were the result of another's misstatements or omissions or of a widespread stock market decline. Answer (D) is incorrect. Proof of adherence to GAAS and GAAP is the usual basis for a due diligence defense, i.e., that the accountant was not negligent.

30. Dart Corp. engaged CPA Firm to assist in a public stock offering. CPA Firm audited Dart's financial statements and gave an unqualified opinion, despite knowing that the financial statements contained misstatements. Firm's opinion was included in Dart's registration statement. Kelly purchased shares in the offering and suffered a loss when the stock declined in value after the misstatements became known. If Kelly succeeds in a Section 11 suit against Dart and the CPA firm, Kelly would be entitled to

A. Damages of three times the original public offering price.

B. Rescind the transaction.

C. Monetary damages only.

D. Damages, but only if the shares were resold before the suit was started.

Answer (C) is correct. *(CPA, adapted)*

REQUIRED: The remedies of an investor under Section 11 of the Securities Act of 1933.

DISCUSSION: In a civil suit under Section 11 of the 1933 act, a purchaser's remedy is a suit for monetary damages. The damages are measured as the difference between the price paid for the securities and (1) the sales price, if the security was sold before suit; (2) the market value of the security at the time of the suit, if the security was not sold; or (3) the sales price, if the security was disposed of after suit and the sales price exceeded the market value of the security at the time the suit was brought.

Answer (A) is incorrect. The damages generally are a measure of the investor's loss. Answer (B) is incorrect. Section 11 does not provide for rescission as a remedy. Answer (D) is incorrect. Resale before suit is not prerequisite to recovery under Section 11.

31. Holly Corp. engaged Yost & Co., CPAs, to audit the financial statements to be included in a registration statement required to be filed under the Securities Act of 1933. Yost failed to exercise due diligence and did not discover the omission of a fact material to the statements. A purchaser of Holly's securities may recover from Yost under Section 11 of the Securities Act of 1933 only if the purchaser

A. Brings a civil action within two years of the discovery of the omission and within five years of the offering date.

B. Proves that the registration statement was relied on to make the purchase.

C. Proves that Yost was negligent.

D. Establishes privity of contract with Yost.

Answer (A) is correct. *(CPA, adapted)*

REQUIRED: The requirement to recover, under the Securities Act of 1933, for a CPA's failure to discover a material fact.

DISCUSSION: The statute of limitations on an action by a purchaser of securities relying on the Securities Act of 1933 is 2 years after the false statements or omissions of material fact were discovered or should have been discovered. The latest the suit may be brought is within 5 years after the security was first offered to the public.

Answer (B) is incorrect. The plaintiff need not prove reliance, but the defendant can plead the plaintiff's knowledge of the misstatement or omission as a defense. Answer (C) is incorrect. The plaintiff need not show negligence. Answer (D) is incorrect. Privity of contract is not required under Section 11 of the Securities Act of 1933.

32. CPA prepared a Form 10-K for X Corporation. The report made a misleading statement with respect to a material fact. Which of the following statements is false?

A. Unlike the Securities Act of 1933, the Securities Exchange Act of 1934 placed the burden of proof on the investor to prove that (s)he relied on the statement.

B. The Securities Exchange Act of 1934 requires proof that the CPA made the misleading statement with the intent to deceive or defraud. Thus, good faith is a valid defense.

C. The statute of limitations for the Securities Exchange Act of 1934 is the same as for the Securities Act of 1933.

D. Mere negligence results in liability under the Securities Act of 1933 and the Securities Exchange Act of 1934.

Answer (D) is correct. *(W. Schuster)*

REQUIRED: The false statement about a CPA's liability under the securities acts.

DISCUSSION: Section 18(a) of the 1934 act applies to misleading or false statements in reports to the SEC. To hold the CPA civilly liable, proof of scienter (intent to deceive, manipulate, or defraud) is required. Thus, mere negligence is not sufficient for recovery under Section 18(a) of the 1934 act. Under Section 11 of the 1933 act, the plaintiff need not show reliance, privity, negligence, or scienter if a registration statement misstated or omitted a material fact.

Answer (A) is incorrect. The liability provisions of the 1934 act do place a greater burden of proof on the plaintiff. Answer (B) is incorrect. The 1934 act does require proof of scienter. Answer (C) is incorrect. Each has a 2-year/5-year statute of limitations. Suit must be brought within 2 years of discovery of the violation but no later than 5 years after the violation occurred (Section 18 of the 1934 act) or the securities were offered to the public (Section 11 of the 1933 act) or sold (Section 12 of the 1933 act).

33. Dean, Inc., a publicly traded corporation, paid a $10,000 bribe to a local zoning official. The bribe was recorded in Dean's financial statements as a consulting fee. Dean's unaudited financial statements were submitted to the SEC as part of a quarterly filing. Which of the following federal statutes did Dean violate?

A. Federal Trade Commission Act.

B. Securities Act of 1933.

C. Securities Exchange Act of 1934.

D. North American Free Trade Act.

Answer (C) is correct. *(CPA, adapted)*

REQUIRED: The statute violated.

DISCUSSION: Quarterly filings under the Securities Exchange Act of 1934 are made on Form 10-Q. Under Section 18(a) of this act, a person, including a corporation, responsible for any false or misleading statement in an application, document, or report filed with the SEC is civilly liable unless the defendant proves that the action was in good faith and without knowledge that the statement was false or misleading. Under Section 32(a), criminal liability is imposed for willfully and knowingly making materially false and misleading statements in a document filed with the SEC.

Answer (A) is incorrect. The Federal Trade Commission Act does not require quarterly filings with the SEC. Answer (B) is incorrect. The Securities Act of 1933 does not require quarterly filings with the SEC. Answer (D) is incorrect. The North American Free Trade Act does not require quarterly filings with the SEC.

34. Dart Corp. engaged CPA Firm to assist in a public stock offering. CPA Firm audited Dart's financial statements and gave an unqualified opinion, despite knowing that the financial statements contained misstatements. Firm's opinion was included in Dart's registration statement. Kelly purchased shares in the offering and suffered a loss when the stock declined in value after the misstatements became known. In a suit against CPA Firm under the antifraud provisions of Section 10(b) and Rule 10b-5 of the Securities Exchange Act of 1934, Kelly must prove all of the following except that

A. Kelly was an intended user of the false registration statement.

B. Kelly relied on the false registration statement.

C. The transaction involved some form of interstate commerce.

D. CPA Firm acted with intentional disregard of the truth.

Answer (A) is correct. *(CPA, adapted)*

REQUIRED: The element an investor need not prove under Rule 10b-5 to recover damages from a CPA.

DISCUSSION: A CPA can be held liable for a misstatement or omission of a material fact relied upon by a purchaser or seller of a security, provided the misconduct involves interstate commerce, the mails, or a national securities exchange. The intent to deceive, manipulate, or defraud (called scienter) must be shown in a private action under Rule 10b-5, and the wrongful act must have caused the plaintiff's damages. Liability runs to any actual purchaser or seller who incurs a loss that results from the reliance.

Answer (B) is incorrect. The purchaser or seller must prove that Kelly relied on the false registration statement to recover. Answer (C) is incorrect. The purchaser or seller must prove that the transaction involved some form of interstate commerce. Answer (D) is incorrect. Although more than gross negligence is required under Section 10(b), intentional disregard of the truth would satisfy the scienter element.

35. West & Co., CPAs, was engaged by Sand Corp. to audit its financial statements. West issued an unqualified opinion on Sand's financial statements. Sand has been accused of making negligent misrepresentations in the financial statements that Reed relied upon when purchasing Sand stock. West was not aware of the misrepresentations and was not negligent in performing the audit. If Reed sues West for damages based upon Section 10(b) and Rule 10b-5 of the Securities Exchange Act of 1934, West will

A. Lose, because the statements contained negligent misrepresentations.

B. Lose, because Reed relied upon the financial statements.

C. Prevail, because some element of scienter must be proved.

D. Prevail, because Reed was not in privity of contract with West.

Answer (C) is correct. *(CPA, adapted)*

REQUIRED: The outcome of a suit under Rule 10b-5 against nonnegligent accountants who were unaware of misrepresentations.

DISCUSSION: Rule 10b-5 is an antifraud provision that requires proof of scienter, that is, of an intent to deceive, manipulate, or defraud. In this context, even gross negligence probably does not satisfy the scienter requirement, although some courts have held that it does if the accountants had a fiduciary duty (such as that owed to a client) to the plaintiff. Thus, Reed cannot prove scienter, and West will prevail.

Answer (A) is incorrect. West was not negligent. Moreover, mere negligence is not a basis for recovery under Rule 10b-5. Answer (B) is incorrect. Reed must prove scienter as well as reliance. Answer (D) is incorrect. The class of plaintiffs is much broader than those in privity of contract.

36. If a purchaser of shares of an issue for which the registration statement included financial statements certified by a CPA succeeds in a Section 10(b) and Rule 10b-5 suit, the purchaser would be entitled to

A. Only recover the original public offering price.

B. Only rescind the transaction.

C. The amount of any loss caused by the fraud.

D. Punitive damages.

Answer (C) is correct. *(CPA, adapted)*

REQUIRED: The remedy or remedies available to a private plaintiff under Section 10(b) of the 1934 Act.

DISCUSSION: Section 10(b) and Rule 10b-5 do not expressly provide for a private right of action. But courts have implied such a right. Remedies for violations include rescission of the securities contract, damages, and injunctions. Courts are divided over the measure of damages recoverable from a CPA. The amount of loss caused by the fraud, however, is recoverable.

Answer (A) is incorrect. Other remedies are available under Section 10(b). Answer (B) is incorrect. Other remedies are available under Section 10(b). Answer (D) is incorrect. Section 10(b) does not provide for punitive damages.

37. Jay and Co., CPAs, audited the financial statements of Maco Corp. Jay intentionally expressed an unqualified opinion on the financial statements even though material misstatements were discovered. The financial statements and Jay's unqualified opinion were included in a registration statement and prospectus for an original public offering of Maco stock. Which of the following statements is true regarding Jay's liability to a purchaser of the offering under Section 10(b) and Rule 10b-5 of the Securities Exchange Act of 1934?

A. Jay will be liable if the purchaser relied on Jay's unqualified opinion on the financial statements.

B. Jay will be liable if Jay was negligent in conducting the audit.

C. Jay will not be liable if the purchaser's loss was under $500.

D. Jay will not be liable if the misstatement resulted from an omission of a material fact by Jay.

Answer (A) is correct. *(CPA, adapted)*

REQUIRED: The true statement regarding liability to a purchaser of the offering under Section 10(b).

DISCUSSION: A CPA can be held liable for a misstatement or omission of a material fact relied upon by a purchaser or seller of a security. The intent to deceive, manipulate, or defraud (called scienter) must be shown in a private action under Rule 10b-5, and the wrongful act must have caused the plaintiff's damages. Scienter requires at least reckless disregard for the truth or gross negligence. Note that, under Section 10(b), it is sufficient that the purchaser or seller would not have invested given correct or additional information and that (s)he was damaged in some way by investing.

Answer (B) is incorrect. More than negligence is required for liability under Rule 10b-5. Answer (C) is incorrect. There is no minimum amount to the loss requirement for liability under Rule 10b-5. Answer (D) is incorrect. Liability can result from an omission that makes the work product misleading.

38. Ivor and Associates, CPAs, audited the financial statements of Jaymo Corporation. As a result of Ivor's negligence in conducting the audit, the financial statements included material misstatements. Ivor was unaware of this fact. The financial statements and Ivor's unqualified opinion were included in a registration statement and prospectus for an original public offering of stock by Jaymo. Thorp purchased shares in the offering. Thorp received a copy of the prospectus prior to the purchase but did not read it. The shares declined in value as a result of the misstatements in Jaymo's financial statements becoming known. Under which of the following Acts is Thorp most likely to prevail in a lawsuit against Ivor?

	Securities Act of 1933, Section 11	Securities Exchange Act of 1934, Section 10(b), Rule 10b-5
A.	Yes	Yes
B.	Yes	No
C.	No	Yes
D.	No	No

Answer (B) is correct. *(CPA, adapted)*

REQUIRED: The most likely statutory basis for recovery from the CPAs.

DISCUSSION: Under Section 11, the investor need only prove that (s)he suffered losses in a transaction involving the particular securities covered by the registration statement, and that the registration statement contained a false statement or an omission of a material fact for which the CPAs were responsible, e.g., in the audited financial statements. The investor need not show (s)he relied on the financial statements. Rule 10b-5 liability is for fraud. Scienter must be proved. Scienter (intent) is more than mere negligence.

39. A CPA is subject to criminal liability

A. Under the Securities Act of 1933 but not the Securities Exchange Act of 1934.

B. For performing an audit in a negligent manner.

C. For willfully omitting a material fact required to be stated in a registration statement.

D. For willfully breaching the contract with the client.

Answer (C) is correct. *(CPA, adapted)*

REQUIRED: The basis for a CPA's criminal liability.

DISCUSSION: Under the Securities Act of 1933, any person who willfully makes a false statement or omits a material fact required in a registration statement is subject to criminal liability with a maximum fine of $10,000 and/or up to 5 years of imprisonment.

Answer (A) is incorrect. A CPA can be criminally liable under either the 1933 or the 1934 act. The 1934 act is frequently used to impose criminal liability on a CPA. A CPA can be subject to a maximum fine of $100,000 or up to 5 years of imprisonment under the 1934 act. Answer (B) is incorrect. This is not a criminal act. A tort, such as negligence, is the violation of a civil duty imposed by the law. Answer (D) is incorrect. This is not a criminal act. A breach of contract is a violation of a civil duty created by agreement.

40. When Congress passed the Sarbanes-Oxley Act of 2002, it imposed greater regulation on public companies and their auditors and required increased accountability. Which of the following is not a provision of the act?

A. Executives must certify the appropriateness of the financial statements.

B. The act provides criminal penalties for fraud.

C. Auditors may not provide specific nonaudit services for their audit clients.

D. Audit firms must be rotated on a periodic basis.

Answer (D) is correct. *(Publisher, adapted)*

REQUIRED: The provision not included in the Sarbanes-Oxley Act.

DISCUSSION: The act requires rotation of the lead audit or coordinating partner and the reviewing partner on audits of public clients every 5 years. However, the act does not require the rotation of audit firms.

Answer (A) is incorrect. The CEO and CFO of a public company must provide a statement to accompany the audit report. This statement certifies the appropriateness of the financial statements and disclosures. However, a violation of this requirement must be knowing and intentional. Answer (B) is incorrect. Title VIII, *Corporate and Criminal Fraud Accountability Act of 2002*, creates a new crime for securities fraud with penalties of fines and imprisonment, extends the statute of limitations on securities fraud claims, and makes it a felony to create or destroy documents to impede a federal investigation. Answer (C) is incorrect. The act makes it unlawful for a registered public accounting firm to perform certain nonaudit services for audit clients, for example, bookkeeping, systems design, management functions, or any other service the Public Company Accounting Oversight Board (PCAOB) determines by regulation to be impermissible.

41. Firms subject to the reporting requirements of the Securities Exchange Act of 1934 are required by the Foreign Corrupt Practices Act of 1977 to maintain satisfactory internal control. Moreover, the Sarbanes-Oxley Act of 2002 requires that annual reports include (1) a statement of management's responsibility for establishing and maintaining adequate internal control and procedures for financial reporting, and (2) management's assessment of their effectiveness. The role of the registered auditor relative to the assessment made by management is to

A. Disclaim an opinion on the assessment and controls.

B. Report clients with unsatisfactory internal control to the SEC.

C. Express an opinion on whether the client is subject to the Securities Exchange Act of 1934.

D. Attest to, and report on, the assessment made by management.

Answer (D) is correct. *(Publisher, adapted)*

REQUIRED: The role of the auditor relative to reporting on the assessment by the management of a public client of internal control and procedures for financial reporting.

DISCUSSION: The registered auditor that issues the audit report for a public client must attest to, and report on, the assessment made by management in the internal control report. The attestation must be made in accordance with standards for attestation engagements issued or adopted by the Public Company Accounting Oversight Board (PCAOB). However, the auditor's evaluation must be in conjunction with an audit of the financial statements. It must not be the subject of a separate engagement. The auditor must determine whether the entity's transactional records are (1) accurate and fair and (2) provide reasonable assurance that financial statements may be prepared in conformity with GAAP. The auditor also must describe material weaknesses in internal control.

Answer (A) is incorrect. The auditor is required to attest to internal control of a public client. Answer (B) is incorrect. The auditor's report on internal control is issued in conjunction with the audit report on the financial statements. Answer (C) is incorrect. Public clients must report to the SEC, but the auditor need not express an opinion on whether the client is subject to the Securities Exchange Act of 1934.

42. The Sarbanes-Oxley Act of 2002 (SOX) has strengthened auditor independence by requiring that management of a public company

A. Engage auditors to report in accordance with the Foreign Corrupt Practices Act.

B. Report the nature of disagreements with former auditors.

C. Select auditors through audit committees.

D. Hire a different CPA firm from the one that performs the audit to perform the company's tax work.

Answer (C) is correct. *(CPA, adapted)*

REQUIRED: The Sarbanes-Oxley requirement that strengthened auditor independence.

DISCUSSION: The audit committee must hire and pay the external auditors. Such affiliation inhibits management from changing auditors to gain acceptance of a questionable accounting method. Also, a successor auditor must inquire of the predecessor before accepting an engagement.

Answer (A) is incorrect. No report under the FCPA is required. Answer (B) is incorrect. Reporting disagreements with auditors is a long-time SEC requirement. Answer (D) is incorrect. The SOX does not restrict who may perform tax work. Other engagements, such as outsourcing internal auditing or certain consulting services, are limited.

43. Which of the following most likely is an allowable service that an auditor may provide to a public client?

A. Internal audit outsourcing.

B. Legal services.

C. Management consulting services.

D. Tax compliance services.

Answer (D) is correct. *(Publisher, adapted)*

REQUIRED: The type of service that an audit firm most likely may provide to an audit client.

DISCUSSION: The Sarbanes-Oxley Act prohibits audit firms from providing consulting, legal, and internal auditing services to public audit clients. However, the PCAOB may, on a case-by-case basis, create exemptions from the prohibition against providing certain nonaudit services at the time of the audit. Audit firms may provide conventional tax planning and compliance services to public audit clients.

Answer (A) is incorrect. Internal audit outsourcing is a service that may not be provided to public audit clients. Answer (B) is incorrect. Legal services are services that may not be provided to public audit clients. Answer (C) is incorrect. Management consulting services are services that may not be provided to public audit clients.

44. Inspections performed by the PCAOB focus on quality control of registered CPA firms that perform audits of public companies (issuers). As required by the Sarbanes-Oxley Act, inspections determine all of the following except that

A. The lead partner of a client is rotated every 5 years.

B. A second partner review is performed.

C. Independence is maintained by audit staff.

D. Only staff with prior experience work on audits.

Answer (D) is correct. *(Publisher, adapted)*

REQUIRED: The issue not considered in a PCAOB inspection.

DISCUSSION: Staff members are required to be trained and supervised in accordance with auditing standards. However, there is no requirement that they have prior experience.

Answer (A) is incorrect. The lead partner must be rotated at least every 5 years. Answer (B) is incorrect. A second partner review is required for each audit engagement of an issuer. Answer (C) is incorrect. Registered firms must have "policies and procedures in place to comply" with applicable independence requirements.

45. An auditor has withdrawn from an audit engagement of a publicly held company after finding fraud that may materially affect the financial statements. The auditor should set forth the reasons and findings in correspondence to the

A. Securities and Exchange Commission.

B. Client's legal counsel.

C. Stock exchanges on which the company's stock is traded.

D. Audit committee.

Answer (D) is correct. *(CPA, adapted)*

REQUIRED: The party or parties to be notified when an auditor withdraws after finding fraud.

DISCUSSION: When an audit indicates the presence of errors or fraud that require a modification of the opinion and the client refuses to accept the auditor's report as modified, the auditor should withdraw and communicate the reasons for withdrawal to the audit committee of the board of directors. Withdrawal may or may not be appropriate in other circumstances, depending on the diligence and cooperation of management and the board in investigating the matter and taking action. Moreover, the Private Securities Litigation Reform Act of 1995, which applies to public companies, requires the auditor to report directly to the board these conclusions regarding lack of remedial action: (1) An illegal act materially affects the financial statements, (2) senior management has not taken appropriate remedial action, and (3) this failure will result in a modified report or the auditor's withdrawal. The company then has one business day to notify the SEC.

Answer (A) is incorrect. The auditor is usually under no obligation to report fraud to outside parties. The firm, however, is required to disclose the reason for a change in auditors on SEC Form 8-K. Answer (B) is incorrect. The auditor may wish to consult his/her legal counsel but not the client's counsel. Answer (C) is incorrect. The auditor is usually under no obligation to report fraud to outside parties. The firm, however, is required to disclose the reason for a change in auditors on SEC Form 8-K.

40.5 Tax Return Preparer Liability

46. Tax preparers who aid and abet federal tax evasion are subject to

	Injunction to Be Prohibited from Acting as Tax Preparers	General Federal Criminal Prosecution
A.	No	No
B.	Yes	No
C.	No	Yes
D.	Yes	Yes

Answer (D) is correct. *(CPA, adapted)*

REQUIRED: The sanction(s) imposed on tax preparers who aid and abet federal tax evasion.

DISCUSSION: Any act that constitutes a willful attempt to evade federal tax liability (even of another) is subject to criminal penalty, even imprisonment (26 USC Sec. 7201). Furthermore, any person who willfully aids or assists in preparation or presentation of a materially false or fraudulent return is guilty of a felony [26 USC Sec. 7206(2)]. Violations of tax preparer rules may result in disciplinary action by the director of the IRS. The IRS may seek an injunction to prohibit the violator from acting as a tax return preparer.

47. Starr, CPA, prepared and signed Cox's Year 1 federal income tax return. Cox informed Starr that Cox had paid doctors' bills of $20,000, although Cox actually had paid only $7,000 in doctors' bills during Year 1. Based on Cox's representations, Starr computed the medical expense deduction that resulted in an understatement of tax liability. Starr had no reason to doubt the accuracy of Cox's figures, and Starr did not ask Cox to submit documentation of the expenses claimed. Cox orally assured Starr that sufficient evidence of the expenses existed. In connection with the preparation of Cox's Year 1 return, Starr is

A. Liable to Cox for interest on the underpayment of tax.

B. Liable to the IRS for negligently preparing the return.

C. Not liable to the IRS for any penalty or interest.

D. Not liable to the IRS for any penalty, but is liable to the IRS for interest on the underpayment of tax.

Answer (C) is correct. *(CPA, adapted)*

REQUIRED: The CPA's liability for preparing a return understating tax liability.

DISCUSSION: An income tax return preparer is any person who prepares for compensation any return of tax or any claim for refund of tax imposed by Subtitle A of the IRC. The Code imposes penalties on preparers for understatement of a taxpayer's liability. A tax return preparer can in good faith rely upon information provided by the taxpayer without having to obtain third-party verification. But the preparer may not ignore implications of information furnished by the taxpayer.

Answer (A) is incorrect. Liability to the client might be based on negligence of the CPA. An ordinarily prudent CPA in these circumstances might reasonably rely on the client's representations and assurances. Answer (B) is incorrect. Tax return preparer liability to the federal government is statutory. The liability is not based on negligence, as the word is generally used. Answer (D) is incorrect. Tax return preparer penalties do not include interest on underpayments by the taxpayer. Liability for interest is imposed on the taxpayer.

48. A CPA who prepares clients' federal income tax returns for a fee must

A. File certain required notices and powers of attorney with the IRS before preparing any returns.

B. Keep a completed copy of each return for a specified period of time.

C. Receive client documentation supporting all travel and entertainment expenses deducted on the return.

D. Indicate the CPA's federal identification number on a tax return only if the return reflects tax due from the taxpayer.

Answer (B) is correct. *(CPA, adapted)*

REQUIRED: The duty of a tax return preparer.

DISCUSSION: A CPA who prepares clients' federal income tax returns for a fee meets the definition in the federal tax code of an income tax return preparer. An income tax return preparer is subject to penalties for certain types of failures. For example, for each failure to retain a copy of a prepared return, the penalty is $50. The copy must be retained for 3 years.

Answer (A) is incorrect. The IRC does not require such filing. Answer (C) is incorrect. The preparer is not required to examine documents to independently verify information provided by the taxpayer. But (s)he must make reasonable inquiry if the information appears to be incorrect or incomplete or to determine the existence of required facts and circumstances incident to a deduction. Answer (D) is incorrect. The preparer is required to indicate his/her federal identification number on each return filed.

Questions 49 through 55 are based on the following information. The AICPA's Tax Executive Committee in Statements on Standards for Tax Services (SSTSs) has issued enforceable rules. Statements 1-8 have been issued (codification prefix TS). The AICPA's Code of Professional Conduct requires that members comply with SSTSs.

49. According to the accounting profession's standards, which of the following statements is true regarding the standards a member of the AICPA should follow when recommending tax return positions and preparing tax returns?

A. A member may recommend a position that (s)he concludes is frivolous as long as the position is adequately disclosed on the return.

B. A member may recommend a position if (s)he has a good faith belief that the position has a realistic possibility of being sustained if challenged.

C. A member will usually not advise the client of the potential penalty consequences of the recommended tax return position.

D. A member may sign a tax return as preparer if the return takes a position that is frivolous, provided that the taxpayer wishes to take that position.

Answer (B) is correct. *(CPA, adapted)*

REQUIRED: The true statement about the standards followed in recommending tax return positions and preparing returns.

DISCUSSION: A member has the right and responsibility to be an advocate for the client. However, a member should not recommend a tax return position without "a good faith belief that the position has a realistic possibility of being sustained administratively or judicially on its merits if challenged." Nevertheless, a member may recommend a position that is not frivolous if (s)he advises the client to make appropriate disclosures (TS 100).

Answer (A) is incorrect. A member may not recommend a frivolous position, regardless of disclosure. Answer (C) is incorrect. A member should advise the taxpayer of the potential penalty consequences of an unrealistic position and the opportunity to avoid penalties through disclosure. Answer (D) is incorrect. A member should not prepare or sign a tax return if (s)he believes that a tax position taken is frivolous, that is, knowingly advanced in bad faith and patently improper.

50. A member of the AICPA who is engaged to prepare an income tax return has a duty to prepare it in such a manner that the tax is

A. The legal minimum.

B. Computed in conformity with generally accepted accounting principles.

C. Supported by the taxpayer's audited financial statements.

D. Not subject to change upon audit.

Answer (A) is correct. *(CPA, adapted)*

REQUIRED: The member's duty in preparing a client's income tax return.

DISCUSSION: A member should serve to the best of his/her ability and with professional concern for the taxpayer's best interests, consistent with responsibilities to the public. According to TS 100, "... it is well established that the taxpayer has no obligation to pay more taxes than are legally owed, and a member has a duty to the taxpayer to assist in achieving that result." Within the limits of the law and ethical practice, a member should strive for the legal minimum tax, not for tax evasion.

Answer (B) is incorrect. The tax according to the tax return is computed based on statutes and pronouncements of the taxing authority. Answer (C) is incorrect. The tax expense according to the statements is based on GAAP, which will likely differ from the legal tax due computed on the tax return. Moreover, the tax preparer need not audit the taxpayer's statements. Answer (D) is incorrect. Discovery of errors may necessitate a change.

51. Must a member of the AICPA in public practice be independent in fact and appearance when providing the following services?

	Compilation of Personal Financial Statements	Preparation of a Tax Return	Compilation of a Financial Forecast
A.	Yes	No	No
B.	No	Yes	No
C.	No	No	Yes
D.	No	No	No

Answer (D) is correct. *(CPA, adapted)*

REQUIRED: The service(s), if any, requiring a member to be independent in fact and appearance.

DISCUSSION: TS 100, *Tax Return Positions*, states that a member has the right and the responsibility to be an advocate for the taxpayer regarding tax return positions that meet the standards described in TS 100. An advocate cannot also be independent. Furthermore, independence standards apply only to attestation services. Hence, an accountant may prepare a tax return or issue a compilation report when (s)he lacks independence. Neither service requires attestation by the accountant.

52. In accordance with the AICPA's Statements on Standards for Tax Services, when a reasonable basis exists for omission of an answer to an applicable question on a tax return,

A. The preparer need not provide an explanation for the omission on the return.

B. A brief explanation of the reason for the omission must be provided on the return.

C. The question should be marked as nonapplicable.

D. A note on the return should state that the answer will be provided if the information is requested.

Answer (A) is correct. *(CPA, adapted)*

REQUIRED: The proper action when a reasonable basis exists for omission of an answer on a tax return.

DISCUSSION: According to TS 200, the member should sign the preparer's declaration when a question has not been answered only if (s)he has made "a reasonable effort to obtain from the taxpayer the information necessary to provide appropriate answers to all questions on a tax return." Given reasonable grounds for the omission, the member is not required to provide an explanation on the return, although (s)he must consider whether the omission may cause the return to be incomplete.

Answer (B) is incorrect. Given reasonable grounds for omissions, the member is not required to provide an explanation. Answer (C) is incorrect. Omissions may be reasonable on grounds other than inapplicability. Answer (D) is incorrect. Given reasonable grounds for omissions, the member is not required to provide an explanation.

53. According to the standards of the accounting profession, which of the following sources of information should a member of the AICPA consider before signing a client's tax return?

I. Information actually known to the member from the tax return of another taxpayer

II. Information provided by the taxpayer that appears to be correct based on the taxpayer's returns from prior years

A. I only.

B. II only.

C. Both I and II.

D. Neither I nor II.

Answer (C) is correct. *(CPA, adapted)*

REQUIRED: The source(s) of information, if any, considered before signing a client's tax return.

DISCUSSION: TS 300 states that members who prepare tax returns are not required to examine or verify supporting data. In preparing the return, the member ordinarily may rely on information furnished by the taxpayer (including tax returns from prior years) unless it appears to be incorrect, incomplete, or inconsistent. The member also should consider relevant information actually known to that member from the tax return of another taxpayer.

54. Which of the following statements is true concerning the responsibility of a member of the AICPA when (s)he uses taxpayer estimates in preparing a tax return?

A. Tax preparation requires the member to exercise judgment but prohibits the use of estimates and approximations.

B. Use of taxpayer estimates in a tax return is prohibited unless they are specifically disclosed by the member.

C. When all facts relating to a transaction are not accurately known because records are missing, reasonable estimates made by the taxpayer of the missing data may be used by the member.

D. The member may prepare tax returns involving the use of taxpayer estimates even if it is practicable to obtain exact data.

Answer (C) is correct. *(CPA, adapted)*

REQUIRED: The member's responsibility when using taxpayer estimates in preparing a tax return.

DISCUSSION: TS 400 permits the member to prepare tax returns involving the use of estimates if it is impracticable to obtain exact data and the amounts are reasonable. Estimates must not be presented so as to imply greater accuracy than exists. The taxpayer is responsible for the estimated amounts.

Answer (A) is incorrect. The use of estimates is permitted under TS 400. Answer (B) is incorrect. Estimates are allowed in a tax return, and specific disclosures are not required except in unusual circumstances. Answer (D) is incorrect. Estimates are only permissible when it is impracticable to obtain exact data.

55. Refer to the information on the preceding page(s). Jones, CPA, prepared Smith's federal income tax return and appropriately signed the preparer's declaration. Several months later, Jones learned that Smith improperly altered several figures before mailing the tax return to the IRS. Jones should communicate disapproval of this action to Smith and

A. Take no further action with respect to the current year's tax return but consider the implications of Smith's actions for any future relationship.

B. Inform the IRS of the unauthorized alteration.

C. File an amended tax return.

D. Refund any fee collected, return all relevant documents, and refuse any further association with Smith.

Answer (A) is correct. *(CPA, adapted)*

REQUIRED: The proper action of a tax preparer after the taxpayer improperly altered the return.

DISCUSSION: When the member discovers an error, (s)he must inform the taxpayer and recommend the measures to be taken. It is then the taxpayer's responsibility to correct the error. If the IRS is likely to bring criminal charges, the taxpayer should be advised to seek legal counsel. If the error is not corrected, "The member should consider whether to continue a professional or employment relationship with the taxpayer" (TS 600).

Answer (B) is incorrect. The member may not inform the IRS, except if required by law. Answer (C) is incorrect. The member may not file an amended return without the taxpayer's permission. Answer (D) is incorrect. TS 600 does not mention refunding fees and returning documents.

56. Which of the following acts by a CPA will not result in incurring an IRS penalty?

A. Failing, without reasonable cause, to provide the client with a copy of an income tax return.

B. Failing, without reasonable cause, to sign a client's tax return as preparer.

C. Understating a client's tax liability as a result of an error in calculation.

D. Negotiating a client's tax refund check when the CPA prepared the tax return.

Answer (C) is correct. *(CPA, adapted)*

REQUIRED: The act that will not result in incurring an IRS penalty.

DISCUSSION: Understating a client's tax liability as a result of an error in calculation will not result in an IRS penalty unless it is the result of gross negligence or a willful attempt to avoid tax liability.

Answer (A) is incorrect. A CPA is required to provide his/her client with a copy of the tax return. Answer (B) is incorrect. A tax preparer is required to sign the return. Answer (D) is incorrect. Any tax return preparer who endorses or otherwise negotiates a refund check issued to a taxpayer is liable for a $500 penalty.

57. Clark, a professional tax return preparer, prepared and signed a client's Year 1 federal income tax return that resulted in a $600 refund. Which one of the following statements is correct with regard to an Internal Revenue Code penalty Clark may be subject to for endorsing and cashing the client's refund check?

A. Clark will be subject to the penalty if Clark endorses and cashes the check.

B. Clark may endorse and cash the check, without penalty, if Clark is enrolled to practice before the Internal Revenue Service.

C. Clark may not endorse and cash the check, without penalty, because the check is for more than $500.

D. Clark may endorse and cash the check, without penalty, if the amount does not exceed Clark's fee for preparation of the return.

Answer (A) is correct. *(CPA, adapted)*

REQUIRED: The correct statement regarding a penalty for endorsing and cashing the client's tax refund check.

DISCUSSION: Sec. 6695(f) of the Internal Revenue Code provides that any income tax return preparer who endorses or otherwise negotiates any check made in respect of income taxes that is issued to a taxpayer will be subject to a penalty of $500 with respect to each such check. This does not apply to the deposit by a bank in the taxpayer's account.

Answer (B) is incorrect. No exception is provided for persons enrolled to practice before the IRS. Answer (C) is incorrect. The penalty is imposed without regard to the amount of the refund check. Answer (D) is incorrect. No exception is provided with regard to a preparer's fee.

58. Brown, CPA, helped Cook organize a partnership that was actually an abusive tax shelter. Brown induced clients to participate by making false statements concerning the allowability of deductions and tax credits. As a result of these activities, Cook derived $100,000 gross income, and Brown derived $50,000 gross income. What is Brown's federal statutory liability under the provision of the Internal Revenue Code specifically relating to promoting abusive tax shelters?

A. $1,000
B. $10,000
C. $50,000
D. $100,000

Answer (A) is correct. *(CPA, adapted)*
REQUIRED: The statutory liability of a CPA under IRC Sec. 6700.
DISCUSSION: A person who promotes an abusive tax shelter is subject to a penalty equal to the lesser of $1,000 or 100% of the gross income derived or to be derived from the activity (IRC Sec. 6700). The IRS may also seek to enjoin the promoter from engaging in further acts subject to the penalty [IRC Sec. 7408(a)].
Answer (B) is incorrect. The penalty is the greater amount of $1,000 or 100% of the gross income derived. Answer (C) is incorrect. The penalty is measured by the promoter's gross income. Answer (D) is incorrect. The penalty is limited to $1,000 per promoting activity.

40.6 Working Papers and Accountant-Client Privilege

59. To which of the following parties may a CPA partnership provide its working papers without either the client's consent or a lawful subpoena?

	The IRS	The FASB
A.	Yes	Yes
B.	Yes	No
C.	No	Yes
D.	No	No

Answer (D) is correct. *(CPA, adapted)*
REQUIRED: The permitted disclosure of working papers by a CPA without the client's consent.
DISCUSSION: The AICPA Code of Professional Conduct (Conduct Rule 301) states that a member in public practice shall not disclose any confidential client information except with the specific consent of the client. However, Conduct Rule 301 does not prohibit a CPA from disclosing confidential client information

1. In compliance with a validly issued and enforceable subpoena or summons,
2. In the proper discharge of his/her professional obligations under Conduct Rules 202, *Compliance with Standards*, and 203, *Accounting Principles*,
3. In a review of the CPA's professional practice under AICPA or state CPA society or board of accountancy authorization, or
4. During the initiation of a complaint with, or in response to any inquiry made by, the professional ethics division, trial board of the AICPA, or an investigative or disciplinary body of a state society or board of accountancy.

Consequently, a CPA partnership may not provide its working papers to the IRS or the FASB without client consent or a lawful subpoena because the activities of those organizations do not fall within one of the exceptions listed in 2. through 4. above.

60. An external auditor is not permitted to discuss confidential client information except with the specific consent of the client. This ethical proscription

A. Is unenforceable.

B. Will prevent the auditor from engaging another auditing firm to conduct a peer review.

C. Will not preclude the auditor from complying with a validly issued court subpoena.

D. Is often used by a client to blunt the auditor's efforts to modify the standard auditor's report.

Answer (C) is correct. *(CMA, adapted)*

REQUIRED: The effect of prohibiting disclosure of confidential client information.

DISCUSSION: Conduct Rule 301 does not prohibit a CPA from disclosing confidential client information

1. In compliance with a validly issued and enforceable subpoena or summons,
2. In the proper discharge of his/her professional obligations under Conduct Rules 202, *Compliance with Standards*, and 203, *Accounting Principles*,
3. In a review of the CPA's professional practice under AICPA or state CPA society or board of accountancy authorization, or
4. During the initiation of a complaint with, or in response to any inquiry made by, the professional ethics division, trial board of the AICPA, or an investigative or disciplinary body of a state society or board of accountancy.

Answer (A) is incorrect. Conduct rules are enforceable through the AICPA, state CPA societies, etc. Answer (B) is incorrect. An exception is made for peer reviews. Answer (D) is incorrect. The CPA is not independent if the client can dictate the content of the report. However, the auditor cannot ordinarily disclose, without the client's specific consent, information not required to be disclosed in financial statements to comply with GAAP.

61. A CPA partnership may, without being lawfully subpoenaed or without the client's consent, make client working papers available to

A. An individual purchasing the entire partnership.

B. The IRS.

C. The SEC.

D. Any surviving partner(s) on the death of a partner.

Answer (D) is correct. *(CPA, adapted)*

REQUIRED: The accountant's permitted disclosure without the client's consent.

DISCUSSION: A CPA may respond to an inquiry made by an investigative body of a state CPA society, the trial board of the AICPA, or an AICPA or state peer review body, or pursuant to a validly issued and enforceable subpoena. Also, making client working papers available to any surviving partner(s) on the death of a partner generally does not constitute disclosure.

Answer (A) is incorrect. No exception to Rule 301 permits disclosure to another CPA. Answer (B) is incorrect. Although federal law does not recognize a broad accountant-client privilege, unconsented-to disclosure is not allowed unless an exception applies. Answer (C) is incorrect. Although federal law does not recognize a broad accountant-client privilege, unconsented-to disclosure is not allowed unless an exception applies.

62. Which of the following statements is true with respect to ownership, possession, or access to a CPA firm's audit working papers?

A. Working papers may never be obtained by third parties unless the client consents.

B. Working papers are not transferable to a purchaser of a CPA practice unless the client consents.

C. Working papers are subject to the privileged communication rule, which, in most jurisdictions, prevents any third-party access to the working papers.

D. Working papers are the client's exclusive property.

Answer (B) is correct. *(CPA, adapted)*

REQUIRED: The true statement about a CPA firm's working papers.

DISCUSSION: Transferring working papers to a purchaser of a practice constitutes communication of the information they contain and violates the AICPA's Conduct Rule 301, *Confidential Client Information*. However, this rule does not prohibit review of the CPA's practice, including a review in conjunction with the purchase, sale, or merger of the practice.

Answer (A) is incorrect. A third party may obtain working papers without client consent when they are lawfully subpoenaed. Answer (C) is incorrect. The privileged communication rule does not exist at common law but has been provided for by statute in a minority of states. Answer (D) is incorrect. The working papers are the property of the CPA unless agreed otherwise. However, a CPA must not only return client records upon request but also make available information in the working papers not reflected in the client's books and records, without which the client's financial information would be incomplete.

63. In a state jurisdiction having an accountant-client privilege statute, to whom may a CPA turn over working papers without a client's permission?

A. Purchaser of the CPA's practice.

B. State tax authorities.

C. State court.

D. State CPA society quality control panel.

Answer (D) is correct. *(CPA, adapted)*

REQUIRED: The accountant's permitted disclosure(s) without the client's consent.

DISCUSSION: The AICPA Code of Professional Conduct (Rule 301) states that a member shall not disclose any confidential client information except with the specific consent of the client. But this rule does not preclude a CPA from responding to an investigative body of a state CPA society, the trial board of the AICPA, or an AICPA or state quality review body, or pursuant to a valid subpoena. In the minority of states that protect confidential accountant-client communications by statute, disclosure to a state CPA quality control panel would not be prohibited.

Answer (A) is incorrect. No exception to Rule 301 permits disclosure to a successor CPA. Answer (B) is incorrect. The privilege statute protects working papers from disclosure to the extent the information was confidential. Answer (C) is incorrect. The privilege statute protects working papers from disclosure to the extent the information was confidential.

64. Pym, CPA, was engaged to audit Silo Co.'s financial statements. During the audit, Pym discovered that Silo's inventory contained stolen goods. Silo was indicted, and Pym was subpoenaed to testify at the criminal trial. Silo claimed accountant-client privilege to prevent Pym from testifying. Silo will be able to prevent Pym from testifying

A. If the action is brought in a federal court.

B. About the nature of the work performed in the audit.

C. Due to the common law in the majority of the states.

D. Where a state statute has been enacted creating a client-accountant privilege of confidentiality.

Answer (D) is correct. *(CPA, adapted)*

REQUIRED: The true statement about accountant-client privilege.

DISCUSSION: Although communication between lawyers and clients is privileged, no common-law concept extends this privilege to the accountant-client relationship. A minority of states have enacted statutes recognizing as privilege confidential communication between an accountant and client.

Answer (A) is incorrect. Federal law recognizes a privilege for accountant-client communications only in limited circumstances. The legislation that restructured the IRS created a limited privilege in civil tax cases in matters brought before the IRS or in proceedings in federal court in which the U.S. is a party. Answer (B) is incorrect. Federal law does not recognize the nature of the work as privileged from disclosure. Answer (C) is incorrect. No general common-law concept provides for an accountant-client privilege. But a minority of states have statutes that grant the privilege.

65. If a CPA is engaged by an attorney to assist in the defense of a criminal tax fraud case involving the attorney's client, information obtained by the CPA from the client after being engaged

A. Is not privileged because the matter involves a federal issue.

B. Is not privileged in jurisdictions that do not recognize an accountant-client privilege.

C. Will be deemed privileged communications under certain circumstances.

D. Will be deemed privileged communications provided that the CPA prepared the client's tax return.

Answer (C) is correct. *(CPA, adapted)*

REQUIRED: The status of information obtained from an attorney's client by a CPA retained to assist in a tax fraud case.

DISCUSSION: The attorney-client privilege would protect the information. The defendant is the client of the attorney, and the CPA is the agent of the attorney. Hence, communications between the CPA and the defendant are, in effect, between the attorney and the defendant. However, if the defendant is the CPA's client, their communications will not be privileged in a criminal case unless the case involves a state tax matter in a jurisdiction that has enacted a statute protecting accountant-client communications.

Answer (A) is incorrect. Federal courts recognize the attorney-client privilege even if a federal question is at issue. Answer (B) is incorrect. The attorney-client privilege protects this information. Answer (D) is incorrect. No accountant-client privilege is recognized in federal criminal tax cases. However, the legislation that restructured the IRS created a limited privilege in civil tax cases.

66. With respect to privileged communications of accountants, which of the following is true?

A. A state statutory privilege will be recognized in a case being tried in a federal court involving a federal question.

B. Most courts recognize a common-law privilege between an accountant and the client.

C. As a result of legislative enactment and court adoption, the client-accountant privilege is recognized in the majority of jurisdictions.

D. The privilege will be lost if the party asserting the privilege voluntarily submits part of the privileged communications into evidence.

Answer (D) is correct. *(CPA, adapted)*

REQUIRED: The true statement about privileged accountant-client communications.

DISCUSSION: When the accountant-client privileged communication rule exists (if a state's statutes so provide), it is lost if any part of the privileged communication is voluntarily submitted. The privileged communication rule is technical and must be adhered to strictly.

Answer (A) is incorrect. The federal courts do not recognize it if the issue involves a federal question except in limited circumstances. The legislation that restructured the IRS created a limited privilege in civil tax cases. Answer (B) is incorrect. There is no common law privilege of communication between an accountant and a client. Answer (C) is incorrect. Only in a minority of jurisdictions have statutes been enacted recognizing the privilege.

67. Which of the following statements is true regarding an accountant's working papers?

A. The accountant owns the working papers and generally may disclose them as the accountant sees fit.

B. The client owns the working papers but the accountant has custody of them until the accountant's bill is paid in full.

C. The accountant owns the working papers but generally may not disclose them without the client's consent or a court order.

D. The client owns the working papers but, in the absence of the accountant's consent, may not disclose them without a court order.

Answer (C) is correct. *(CPA, adapted)*

REQUIRED: The true statement regarding an accountant's working papers.

DISCUSSION: Conduct Rule 501 states that a member's working papers, including any analyses and schedules prepared by the client at the request of the member, are the member's property, not the client's. However, the accountant may have produced supporting records, such as entries and related calculations. These records contain information not in the client's records and without which they are not complete. If supporting records are not otherwise available, they should be given to the client upon request unless fees are due. Members have an obligation to their clients not to disclose any information to the public without the client's consent or a court order.

Answer (A) is incorrect. The accountant may not disclose client information without the client's consent or a court order. Answer (B) is incorrect. The client does not own the accountant's working papers. Answer (D) is incorrect. The client does not own the accountant's working papers.

68. With respect to records in a CPA's possession, the *Code of Professional Conduct* provides that

A. An auditor may retain client-provided records after a demand is made for them if fees due with respect to a completed engagement have not been paid.

B. Supporting records that contain journal entries not reflected in the client's records need not be furnished to the client upon request.

C. Extensive analytical review schedules prepared by the client at the auditor's request are working papers that belong to the auditor and need not be furnished to the client upon request.

D. The auditor who returns client records must comply with any subsequent requests to again provide such information.

Answer (C) is correct. *(Publisher, adapted)*

REQUIRED: The true statement regarding records in the CPA's possession.

DISCUSSION: According to an Interpretation of Conduct Rule 501, a member's working papers are the member's property, not client records, and need not be made available. However, the PCAOB's Auditing Standard No. 3, *Audit Documentation*, relating to public clients is silent on property rights in working papers. Moreover, a statute, regulation, or contract may state otherwise.

Answer (A) is incorrect. After a demand is made for them, client-provided records must be returned even if fees have not been paid. Answer (B) is incorrect. Supporting records containing client financial information not reflected in the client's books must be returned to the client upon request if the engagement is complete. Answer (D) is incorrect. Once the member has complied with the requirements for the return of client records, (s)he has no further obligation to provide such information except in the case of a natural disaster or act of war.

69. A CPA's retention of client-provided records after a demand has been made for them is an action that is

A. Not addressed by the AICPA *Code of Professional Conduct*.

B. Acceptable if sanctioned by state law.

C. Prohibited under the AICPA *Code of Professional Conduct*.

D. A violation of GAAS.

Answer (C) is correct. *(CPA, adapted)*

REQUIRED: The profession's policy concerning a CPA's retention of client-provided records.

DISCUSSION: An Interpretation of Conduct Rule 501, *Acts Discreditable*, defines client-provided records as "accounting or other records belonging to the client that were provided to the member by or on behalf of the client." This interpretation prohibits the retention (after a demand is made for them) of client-provided records to enforce payment or for any other purpose. Such an act is deemed to be discreditable to the profession.

Answer (A) is incorrect. Conduct Rule 501 prohibits retention of client-provided records after a demand has been made for them. Answer (B) is incorrect. A state's grant of a lien on records in the CPA's possession does not change his/her duty under the Code. Answer (D) is incorrect. Retention of client-provided records after a demand has been made for them is prohibited by the *Code of Professional Conduct*, not by GAAS.

70. Which of the following statements is(are) correct regarding a CPA employee of a CPA firm taking copies of information contained in client files when the CPA leaves the firm?

I. A CPA leaving a firm may take copies of information contained in client files to assist another firm in serving that client.

II. A CPA leaving a firm may take copies of information contained in client files as a method of gaining technical expertise.

A. I only.

B. II only.

C. Both I and II.

D. Neither I nor II.

Answer (D) is correct. *(CPA, adapted)*

REQUIRED: The act(s), if any, considered discreditable to the profession.

DISCUSSION: Conduct Rule 501 states that a member shall not commit an act discreditable to the profession. Under an Ethics Ruling, after the relationship of a member who is not an owner of the firm is terminated, the member may not take or retain copies or originals from the firm's client files or proprietary information without permission.

APPENDIX A
CROSS-REFERENCES TO BUSINESS LAW AND LEGAL STUDIES TEXTBOOKS

This section contains the tables of contents of current textbooks with cross-references to the corresponding study units and subunits in this study manual. The texts are listed in alphabetical order by the first author. As you study a particular chapter in your textbook, you can easily determine which subunit(s) to study in this manual.

Professors and students should note that, even though new editions of the texts listed below may be published as you use this book, the new tables of contents usually will be very similar, if not the same. Thus, this edition of *Business Law and Legal Studies Exam Questions and Explanations* will remain current and useful.

If you are using a textbook that is not included in this list or if you have any suggestions on how we can improve these cross-references to make them more relevant/useful, please submit your request/feedback at www.gleim.com/crossreferences/LAW or email them to LAWcrossreferences@gleim.com.

BUSINESS LAW TEXTBOOKS

Anderson, Twomey, and Jennings, *Anderson's Business Law and the Legal Environment*, Twenty-first Edition, South-Western College Publishing, 2011.

Ashcroft and Ashcroft, *Law for Business*, Seventeenth Edition, South-Western College Publishing, 2010.

Bagley and Savage, *Managers and the Legal Environment: Strategies for the 21st Century*, Sixth Edition, South-Western College Publishing, 2010.

Barnes, Dworkin, and Richards, *Law for Business*, Eleventh Edition, McGraw-Hill/Irwin, 2012.

Bohlman and Dundas, *The Legal, Ethical, and International Environment of Business*, Sixth Edition, South-Western College Publishing Co., 2005.

Cheeseman, *Business Law: Legal Environment, Online Commerce, Business Ethics, and International Issues*, Sixth Edition, Prentice Hall, Inc., 2010.

Cheeseman, *Contemporary Business Law and Online Commerce Law*, Seventh Edition, Prentice Hall, Inc., 2012.

Clarkson, Miller, Jentz, and Cross, *West's Business Law Text and Cases: Legal, Ethical, Regulatory, International and E-Commerce Environment*, Eleventh Edition, South-Western College Publishing, 2009.

Cross and Miller, *The Legal Environment Today: Business in its Ethical, Regulatory, E-Commerce, and Global Setting*, Sixth Edition, South-Western College Publishing, 2010.

Cross and Miller, *The Legal Environment of Business: Text, Cases, Ethical, Regulatory, Global and Corporate Issues*, Eighth Edition, South-Western College Publishing, 2010.

Davidson, Knowles, and Forsythe, *Business Law: Principles and Cases in the Legal Environment*, Eighth Edition, South-Western College Publishing, 2004.

Fisher and Phillips, *The Legal, Ethical, and Regulatory Environment of Business*, Ninth Edition, South-Western College Publishing, 2007.

Hollowell and Miller, *Business Law, Text and Exercises*, Sixth Edition, South-Western College Publishing, 2010.

Jentz, Miller, and Cross, *West's Business Law*, Alternate Edition, Eleventh Edition, South-Western College Publishing, 2010.

Kubasek, Brennan, and Browne, *The Legal Environment of Business: A Critical Thinking Approach*, Sixth Edition, Prentice Hall Business Publishing, 2012.

Mann and Roberts, *Business Law and the Regulation of Business*, Tenth Edition, South-Western College Publishing, 2010.

Mann and Roberts, *Smith and Roberson's Business Law*, Fifteenth Edition, South-Western College Publishing, 2011.

McAdams, *Law, Business, and Society*, Ninth Edition, McGraw-Hill/Irwin, 2009.

Miller and Jentz, *Business Law Today, Standard Edition*, Ninth Edition, South-Western College Publishing, 2010.

Miller and Jentz, *Fundamentals of Business Law: Summarized Cases*, Eighth Edition, South-Western College Publishing, 2010.

Reed, Shedd, Morehead, and Pagnattaro, *The Legal and Regulatory Environment of Business*, Fifteenth Edition, McGraw-Hill, Inc., 2010.

BUSINESS LAW TEXTBOOKS

Anderson, Twomey, and Jennings, *Anderson's Business Law and the Legal Environment*, Twenty-first Edition, South-Western College Publishing, 2011.

Part I - The Legal and Social Environment of Business
- Chapter 1 - The Nature and Sources of Law - SU 1
- Chapter 2 - The Court System and Dispute Resolution - SU 2, SU 3
- Chapter 3 - Business Ethics, Social Forces, and the Law - SU 1, 40.1
- Chapter 4 - The Constitution as the Foundation of the Legal Environment - SU 4
- Chapter 5 - Government Regulation of Competition and Prices - SU 36
- Chapter 6 - Administrative Agencies - 5.1-5.4
- Chapter 7 - The Legal Environment of International Trade - SU 39
- Chapter 8 - Crimes - SU 6, 22.5
- Chapter 9 - Torts - SU 7
- Chapter 10 - Intellectual Property Rights and the Internet - 21.1, 22.3
- Chapter 11 - Cyberlaw - SU 22

Part II - Contracts
- Chapter 12 - Nature and Classes of Contracts: Contracting on the Internet - 8.1, SU 22
- Chapter 13 - Formation of Contracts: Offer and Acceptance - 8.2-8.3
- Chapter 14 - Capacity and Genuine Assent - 10.1, 10.3
- Chapter 15 - Consideration - SU 9
- Chapter 16 - Legality and Public Policy - 10.2
- Chapter 17 - Writing, Electronic Forms, and Interpretation of Contracts - 10.4, 11.1, 22.1
- Chapter 18 - Third Persons and Contracts - SU 12
- Chapter 19 - Discharge of Contracts - 11.3
- Chapter 20 - Breach of Contract and Remedies - 11.4

Part III - Sales and Leases of Goods
- Chapter 21 - Personal Property and Bailments - SU 21
- Chapter 22 - Legal Aspects of Supply Chain Management - N/A
- Chapter 23 - Nature and Form of Sales - 13.1-13.3
- Chapter 24 - Title and Risk of Loss - 13.4-13.5
- Chapter 25 - Product Liability: Warranties and Torts - 14.6
- Chapter 26 - Obligations and Performance - 14.1-14.2
- Chapter 27 - Remedies for Breach of Sales Contracts - 14.3-14.5

Part IV - Negotiable Instruments
- Chapter 28 - Kinds of Instruments, Parties, and Negotiability - 15.1-15.3
- Chapter 29 - Transfer of Negotiable Instruments and Warranties of Parties - 15.4-15.5
- Chapter 30 - Liability of the Parties under Negotiable Instruments - 16.1
- Chapter 31 - Checks and Funds Transfers - 16.3-16.4

Part V - Debtor-Creditor Relations
- Chapter 32 - Nature of the Debtor/Creditor Relationship - SU 19, SU 26
- Chapter 33 - Consumer Protection - SU 37
- Chapter 34 - Secured Transactions in Personal Property - SU 18
- Chapter 35 - Bankruptcy - SU 20
- Chapter 36 - Insurance - SU 34

Part VI - Agency and Employment
- Chapter 37 - Agency - SU 29
- Chapter 38 - Third Persons in Agency - 29.4
- Chapter 39 - Regulation of Employment - SU 38
- Chapter 40 - Equal Employment Opportunity Law - 38.2

Ashcroft and Ashcroft, *Law for Business*, Seventeenth Edition, South-Western College Publishing, 2010.

Part I - The Legal System and the Legal Environment of Business
- Chapter 1 - Introduction to Law - SU 1, SU 4
- Chapter 2 - Courts and Court Procedure - SU 2, SU 3
- Chapter 3 - Business Torts and Crimes - SU 6, SU 7, 22.5
- Chapter 4 - Government Regulation of Business - SU 33, SUs 35-38

Part II - Contracts
- Chapter 5 - Nature and Classes of Contracts - 8.1
- Chapter 6 - Offer and Acceptance - 8.2-8.3
- Chapter 7 - Capacity to Contract - 10.1
- Chapter 8 - Consideration - SU 9
- Chapter 9 - Defective Agreements - 10.3
- Chapter 10 - Illegal Agreements - 10.2
- Chapter 11 - Written Contracts - 10.4
- Chapter 12 - Third Parties and Contracts - SU 12
- Chapter 13 - Termination of Contracts - SU 11

Part III - Personal Property
- Chapter 14 - Nature of Personal Property - 21.1-21.2
- Chapter 15 - Special Bailments - 21.3-21.4

Part IV - Sales
- Chapter 16 - Sales of Personal Property - 13.1-13.3
- Chapter 17 - Formalities of a Sale - 14.1-14.5
- Chapter 18 - Transfer of Title and Risk in Sales Contracts - 13.4-13.5
- Chapter 19 - Warranties, Product Liability, and Consumer Protection - 14.6, SU 37

Part V - Negotiable Instruments
- Chapter 20 - Nature of Negotiable Instruments - 15.1
- Chapter 21 - Essentials of Negotiability - 15.3
- Chapter 22 - Promissory Notes and Drafts - 15.2
- Chapter 23 - Negotiation and Discharge - 15.4, 16.2
- Chapter 24 - Liabilities of Parties and Holders in Due Course - 15.5, 16.1
- Chapter 25 - Defenses - 15.5

Part VI - Agency and Employment
- Chapter 26 - Nature and Creation of an Agency - 29.1
- Chapter 27 - Operation and Termination of an Agency - 29.2-29.5
- Chapter 28 - Employer and Employee Relations - 29.1, SU 38
- Chapter 29 - Employees' Rights - 38.1-38.6
- Chapter 30 - Labor Legislation - 38.1

Part VII - Business Organization
- Chapter 31 - Introduction to Business Organization - 30.1, 30.5-30.6, 31.1
- Chapter 32 - Creation and Operation of a Partnership - 30.1-30.3
- Chapter 33 - Dissolution of a Partnership - 30.4
- Chapter 34 - Nature of a Corporation - 31.1-31.2
- Chapter 35 - Ownership of a Corporation - 31.3-31.4
- Chapter 36 - Management and Dissolution of a Corporation - SU 32

Part VIII - Risk-Bearing Devices
- Chapter 37 - Principles of Insurance - 34.1
- Chapter 38 - Types of Insurance - 34.2-34.4
- Chapter 39 - Security Devices - SU 18, SU 19, SU 25, SU 26
- Chapter 40 - Bankruptcy - SU 20

Part IX - Real Property
- Chapter 41 - Nature of Real Property - SU 23
- Chapter 42 - Transfer of Real Property - SU 24
- Chapter 43 - Real Estate Mortgages - SU 25
- Chapter 44 - Landlord and Tenant - SU 27
- Chapter 45 - Wills, Inheritances, and Trusts - SU 28

Bagley and Savage, *Managers and the Legal Environment: Strategies for the 21st Century*, Sixth Edition, South-Western College Publishing, 2010.

Unit I: Foundations of the Legal and Regulatory Environment
Chapter 1 - Law, Value Creation, and Risk Management - 1.1, 40.1
Chapter 2 - Ethics and the Law - 1.1, 40.1
Chapter 3 - Courts, Sources of Law, and Dispute Resolution - 1.2-1.4, SU 2, 3.1-3.5
Chapter 4 - Constitutional Bases for Business Regulation - SU 4
Chapter 5 - Agency - SU 29
Chapter 6 - Administrative Law - SU 5
Unit II: The Legal Environment
Chapter 7 - Contracts - SUs 8-12
Chapter 8 - Sales, Licensing, and E-Commerce - SUs 13-14, SU 22
Chapter 9 - Torts and Privacy Protection - 7.1-7.6
Chapter 10 - Product Liability - 7.7
Chapter 11 - Intellectual Property - 21.1, SU 22
Unit III: Human Resources in the Legal and Regulatory Environment
Chapter 12 - The Employment Agreement - 38.1
Chapter 13 - Civil Rights and Employment Discrimination - 38.2
Chapter 14 - Executive Compensation and Employee Benefits - SU 38
Unit IV: The Regulatory Environment
Chapter 15 - Criminal Law - SU 6
Chapter 16 - Environmental Law - SU 35
Chapter 17 - Antitrust - SU 36, 39.2
Chapter 18 - Consumer Protection - SU 37
Chapter 19 - Real Property and Land Use - SUs 23-25
Unit V: Corporate Governance, Ownership, and Control
Chapter 20 - Forms of Business Organizations - SUs 30-32
Chapter 21 - Directors, Officers, and Controlling Shareholders - 32.1-32.3
Unit VI: Securities and Financial Transactions
Chapter 22 - Public and Private Offerings of Securities - SU 33
Chapter 23 - Securities Fraud and Insider Trading - SU 33
Chapter 24 - Debtor-Creditor Relations and Bankruptcy - SU 19, SU 20
Unit VII: International Business
Chapter 25 - International Law and Transactions - SU 39

Barnes, Dworkin, and Richards, *Law for Business*, Eleventh Edition, McGraw-Hill/Irwin, 2012.

Part I - Introduction to Law
Chapter 1 - Law, Legal Reasoning, and the Legal Profession - SU 1
Chapter 2 - Dispute Settlement - SU 2, SU 3, SU 5
Chapter 3 - Business Ethics and Corporate Social Responsibility - SU 1
Chapter 4 - Business and the Constitution - SU 4
Chapter 5 - Crimes - SU 6, 22.5
Chapter 6 - Intentional Torts - 7.1-7.3
Chapter 7 - Negligence and Strict Liability - 7.4-7.7
Part II - Contracts
Chapter 8 - The Nature and Origins of Contracts - 8.1
Chapter 9 - Creating a Contract: Offers - 8.2
Chapter 10 - Creating a Contract: Acceptances - 8.3
Chapter 11 - Consideration - SU 9
Chapter 12 - Capacity to Contract - 10.1
Chapter 13 - Voluntary Consent - 10.3
Chapter 14 - Illegality - 10.2
Chapter 15 - The Form and Meaning of Contracts - 10.4, 11.1
Chapter 16 - Third Parties' Contract Rights - SU 12
Chapter 17 - Performance and Remedies - 11.2-11.4
Part III - Sales
Chapter 18 - Formation and Terms of Sales Contracts - SU 13
Chapter 19 - Warranties and Product Liability - 14.6
Chapter 20 - Performance of Sales Contracts - 14.1-14.2
Chapter 21 - Remedies for Breach of Sales Contracts - 14.3-14.5
Part IV - Agency and Employment
Chapter 22 - The Agency Relationship – – Creation, Duties, and Termination - SU 29
Chapter 23 - Liability of Principals and Agents to Third Parties - 29.4
Chapter 24 - Employment Laws - SU 38

Part V - Business Organizations
- Chapter 25 - Which Form of Business Organization? - SUs 30-32
- Chapter 26 - Partnerships - SU 30
- Chapter 27 - Formation and Termination of Corporations - 31.1-31.2
- Chapter 28 - Management of the Corporate Business - 32.1-32.2
- Chapter 29 - Financing the Corporation and the Role of the Shareholders - 31.3
- Chapter 30 - Securities Regulation - SU 33
- Chapter 31 - Legal Liability of Accountants - SU 40

Part VI - Property
- Chapter 32 - Personal Property and Bailments - SU 21
- Chapter 33 - Real Property - SUs 23-25
- Chapter 34 - Landlord and Tenant - SU 27
- Chapter 35 - Estates and Trusts - SU 28
- Chapter 36 - Insurance - SU 34

Part VII - Commercial Paper
- Chapter 37 - Negotiable Instruments - 15.1-15.2
- Chapter 38 - Negotiation and Holder in Due Course - 15.3-15.5
- Chapter 39 - Liability of Parties - 16.1-16.2
- Chapter 40 - Checks and Electronic Funds Transfers - 16.3-16.4

Part VIII - Credit Transactions
- Chapter 41 - Introduction to Security - SUs 18-19
- Chapter 42 - Security Interest in Personal Property - SUs 18-19
- Chapter 43 - Bankruptcy - SU 20

Part IX - Government Regulation
- Chapter 44 - The Antitrust Laws - SU 36, 39.2
- Chapter 45 - Consumer Protection Laws - SU 37
- Chapter 46 - Environmental Regulation - SU 35

Bohlman and Dundas, *The Legal, Ethical, and International Environment of Business*, Sixth Edition, South-Western College Publishing Co., 2005.

Part I - Introduction to Law
- Chapter 1 - Basics of the Law - 1.1, 1.4
- Chapter 2 - Ethics and Corporate Social Responsibility - 1.1, 40.1
- Chapter 3 - The Judicial System and Litigation - SU 2, SU 3
- Chapter 4 - Alternative Dispute Resolution Procedures - 3.6
- Chapter 5 - The Constitution and the Regulation of Business - SU 4
- Chapter 6 - Administrative Agencies and the Regulation of Business - SU 5
- Chapter 7 - Regulation of Business through Criminal Law - SU 6, 22.5

Part II - Business and Private Law
- Chapter 8 - Torts - SU 7
- Chapter 9 - Contract Formation - SUs 8-10
- Chapter 10 - Contract Defenses and Remedies - SU 11, SU 12
- Chapter 11 - Sales Law and Product Liability - 7.7, SU 13, SU 14
- Chapter 12 - Negotiable Instruments and Secured Transactions - SUs 15-18
- Chapter 13 - International Business Law - SU 39
- Chapter 14 - Rights of Consumers, Debtors, and Creditors - SU 19, SU 20, SU 26
- Chapter 15 - Consumer Protection - SU 37
- Chapter 16 - Property Law, Intellectual Property Law, and Computer Law - SUs 21-25

Part III - Business Formation
- Chapter 17 - Agency Law and Private Employment Law - SU 29
- Chapter 18 - Business Enterprises: Noncorporate Business Entities - SU 30
- Chapter 19 - Corporate Law and Franchising Law - SU 31, SU 32

Part IV - Business and Government Regulation
- Chapter 20 - Securities Law - SU 33
- Chapter 21 - Antitrust Law - SU 36, 39.2
- Chapter 22 - Legislative Control over Labor and Labor Relations - 38.1
- Chapter 23 - Employment Law and Equal Opportunity - 38.2-38.6
- Chapter 24 - Environmental Law - SU 35

Cheeseman, *Business Law: Legal Environment, Online Commerce, Business Ethics, and International Issues*, Sixth Edition, Prentice Hall, Inc., 2010.

Part I - Legal Environment of Business and E-Commerce
- Chapter 1 - Legal Heritage and Critical Legal Thinking - SU 1
- Chapter 2 - Court Systems and Jurisdiction - SU 2
- Chapter 3 - Litigation and Alternative Dispute Resolution - SU 3
- Chapter 4 - Constitutional Law for Business and Online Commerce - SU 4

Part II - Torts, Crimes, and Internet Law
- Chapter 5 - Torts and Cyber Privacy - 7.1-7.5, 22.4
- Chapter 6 - Strict Liability and Product Liability - 7.6-7.7
- Chapter 7 - Intellectual Property and Internet Law - 21.1, 22.3
- Chapter 8 - Business and Online Crimes - SU 6, 22.5

Part III - Traditional and E-Commerce Contracts
- Chapter 9 - Nature of Traditional and Online Contracts - 8.1
- Chapter 10 - Agreement - 8.2-8.3
- Chapter 11 - Consideration and Equity - SU 9
- Chapter 12 - Capacity and Legality - 10.1-10.2
- Chapter 13 - Genuineness of Assent - 10.3
- Chapter 14 - Writing and Formality - 10.4, 11.1
- Chapter 15 - Third Party Rights and Discharge - 11.3, SU 12
- Chapter 16 - Remedies for Breach of Traditional and Online Contracts - 11.4
- Chapter 17 - E-Contracts - 22.1-22.2

Part IV - Domestic and International Sales and Lease Contracts
- Chapter 18 - Formation of Sales and Lease Contracts - 13.1-13.3
- Chapter 19 - Performance of Sales and Lease Contracts - 13.4-13.5, 14.1-14.2
- Chapter 20 - Remedies for Breach of Sales and Lease Contracts - 14.3-14.5
- Chapter 21 - Sales and Lease Warranties - 14.6

Part V - Negotiable Instruments and Electronic Banking
- Chapter 22 - Creation and Transfer of Negotiable Instruments - 15.1-15.2
- Chapter 23 - Transferability and Holder in Due Course - 15.3-15.5
- Chapter 24 - Liability, Defenses, and Discharge - 16.1-16.2
- Chapter 25 - Checks, Banking, and Wire Transfers - 16.3-16.4

Part VI - Credit and Bankruptcy
- Chapter 26 - Credit and Security Interests in Real Property - SU 25, 26.2-26.4
- Chapter 27 - Secured Transactions and Security Interests in Personal Property - SU 18
- Chapter 28 - Bankruptcy Law and Consumer Debt Adjustment - SU 20

Part VII - Agency and Employment
- Chapter 29 - Agency Formation and Termination - 29.1-29.3, 29.5
- Chapter 30 - Liability of Principals and Agents - 29.4
- Chapter 31 - Employment and Worker Protection Laws - 38.3-38.6
- Chapter 32 - Labor Law - 38.1
- Chapter 33 - Equal Opportunity in Employment - 38.2

Part VIII - Business Organizations and Ethics
- Chapter 34 - Entrepreneurship, Sole Proprietorships, and General Partnerships - 30.1-30.4
- Chapter 35 - Limited Partnerships - 30.5
- Chapter 36 - Domestic and Multinational Corporations - 31.1-31.3
- Chapter 37 - Corporate Directors, Officers, and Shareholders - 32.1-32.3
- Chapter 38 - Corporate Mergers, Tender Offers, and Shareholder Resolutions - 32.4
- Chapter 39 - Limited Liability Companies and Limited Liability Partnerships - 30.6
- Chapter 40 - Franchises and Special Business Forms - 30.6
- Chapter 41 - Investor Protection and Online Securities Transactions - 31.4, 32.4, SU 33
- Chapter 42 - Ethics and Social Responsibility of Business - 1.1

Part IX - Government Regulation
- Chapter 43 - Administrative Law - SU 5
- Chapter 44 - Consumer Protection - SU 37
- Chapter 45 - Environmental Protection - SU 35
- Chapter 46 - Antitrust Law - SU 36, 39.2

Part X - Property
- Chapter 47 - Personal Property and Bailments - SU 21
- Chapter 48 - Real Property - SUs 23-24
- Chapter 49 - Landlord-Tenant Relationship and Land Use Regulation - SU 27, 23.6

Part XI - Special Topics
- Chapter 50 - Insurance - SU 34
- Chapter 51 - Liability of Accountants - SU 40
- Chapter 53 - Wills, Trusts, and Living Wills - SU 28
- Chapter 53 - Family Law - N/A

Part XII - Global Environment
- Chapter 54 - International and World Trade Law - SU 39

Cheeseman, *Contemporary Business Law and Online Commerce Law*, Seventh Edition, Prentice Hall, Inc., 2012.

Part I: The Legal, Ethical, and Digital Environment
- Chapter 1 - Legal Heritage and the Information Age - SU 1
- Chapter 2 - Constitutional Law for Business and E-Commerce - SU 4
- Chapter 3 - Courts and Jurisdiction - SU 2
- Chapter 4 - Judicial, Alternative, Administrative, and E-Dispute Resolution - SU 3
- Chapter 5 - Torts and Strict Liability - SU 7
- Chapter 6 - Criminal Law and Cyber Crimes - SU 6, 22.5
- Chapter 7 - Intellectual Property and Cyber Piracy - 21.1, 22.3
- Chapter 8 - Ethics and Social Responsibility of Business - 1.1, 40.1

Part II: Contracts and E-Commerce
- Chapter 9 - Nature of Traditional and E-Contracts - 8.1
- Chapter 10 - Agreement and Consideration - 8.2-8.3, SU 9
- Chapter 11 - Capacity and Legality - 10.1-10.2
- Chapter 12 - Genuineness of Assent and Statute of Frauds - 10.3-10.4, 11.1
- Chapter 13 - Third-Party Rights and Discharge - 11.3, SU 12
- Chapter 14 - Breach of Contract and Remedies - 11.4
- Chapter 15 - Digital Law and E-Commerce - SU 22

Part III: Sales and Lease Contracts and Product Liability
- Chapter 16 - Formation of Sales and Lease Contracts - 13.1-13.3
- Chapter 17 - Performance of Sales and Lease Contracts - 13.4-13.5, 14.1-14.2
- Chapter 18 - Remedies for Breach of Sales and Lease Contracts - 14.3-14.5
- Chapter 19 - Warranties and Product Liability - 7.7, 14.6

Part IV: Negotiable Instruments, Banking, and E-Money
- Chapter 20 - Creation and Transfer of Negotiable Instruments - 15.1-15.2
- Chapter 21 - Holder in Due Course and Liability of Parties - 15.3-15.5, 16.1-16.2
- Chapter 22 - Banking System, E-Money, and Financial Reform - 16.3-16.4

Part V: Credit, Secured Transactions, and Bankruptcy
- Chapter 23 - Credit and Secured Transactions - SU 18, SU 19, SU 25, SU 26
- Chapter 24 - Bankruptcy and Reorganization - SU 20

Part VI: Business Organizations and Investor Protection
- Chapter 25 - Agency Law - SU 29
- Chapter 26 - Small Business, Entrepreneurship, and Partnerships - 30.1-30.5
- Chapter 27 - Corporate Formation and Financing - 31.1-31.3
- Chapter 28 - Corporate Governance and Sarbanes-Oxley Act - 31.1, SU 33
- Chapter 29 - Corporate Acquisitions and Multinational Corporations - 32.4
- Chapter 30 - Limited Liability Company and Limited Liability Partnership - 30.6
- Chapter 31 - Franchise and Special Forms of Business - 30.6
- Chapter 32 - Investor Protection, E-Securities Transactions, and Wall Street Reform - 31.4, SU 33

Part VII: Government Regulation and Employment Law
- Chapter 33 - Antitrust Law and Unfair Trade Practices - SU 36, 39.2
- Chapter 34 - Consumer Safety, Consumer Financial Protection, and Environmental Protection - SU 35, SU 37
- Chapter 35 - Labor, Worker Protection, Employment, and Immigration Law - 38.1, 38.3-38.6
- Chapter 36 - Equal Opportunity in Employment - 38.2

Part VIII: Property, Insurance, and Estates
- Chapter 37 - Personal Property, Bailment, and Insurance - SU 21, SU 34
- Chapter 38 - Real Property, Landlord-Tenant Law, and Land Use Regulation - SU 23, SU 24, SU 27
- Chapter 39 - Family Law, Wills, and Trusts - SU 28

Part IX: Accounting Profession
- Chapter 40 - Accountants' Liability - SU 40

Part X: Global Environment
- Chapter 41 - International and World Trade Law - SU 39

Clarkson, Miller, Jentz, and Cross, *West's Business Law Text and Cases: Legal, Ethical, Regulatory, International and E-Commerce Environment*, Eleventh Edition, South-Western College Publishing, 2009.

Unit I - The Legal Environment of Business
- Chapter 1 - Introduction to Law and Legal Reasoning - SU 1
- Chapter 2 - Courts and Alternative Dispute Resolution - SU 2, 3.6
- Chapter 3 - Court Procedures - 3.1-3.5
- Chapter 4 - Constitutional Authority to Regulate Business - SU 4
- Chapter 5 - Ethics and Business Decision Making - 1.1

Unit II - Torts and Crimes
- Chapter 6 - Intentional Torts - 7.1-7.4
- Chapter 7 - Negligence and Strict Liability - 7.5-7.7
- Chapter 8 - Intellectual Property and Internet Law - 21.1, 22.3
- Chapter 9 - Criminal Law and Cyber Crimes - SU 6, 22.5

Unit III - Contracts and E-Contracts
- Chapter 10 - Nature and Terminology - 8.1
- Chapter 11 - Agreement - 8.2-8.3
- Chapter 12 - Consideration - SU 9
- Chapter 13 - Capacity and Legality - 10.1-10.2
- Chapter 14 - Mistakes, Fraud, and Voluntary Consent - 10.3
- Chapter 15 - The Statute of Frauds - Writing Requirement - 10.4
- Chapter 16 - Third Party Rights - SU 12
- Chapter 17 - Performance and Discharge - 11.1-11.3
- Chapter 18 - Breach of Contract and Remedies - SU 11
- Chapter 19 - E-Contracts and E-Signatures - 22.1-22.2

Unit IV - Domestic and International Sales and Lease Contracts
- Chapter 20 - The Formation of Sales and Lease Contracts - 13.1-13.3
- Chapter 21 - Title, Risk, and Insurable Interest - 13.4-13.5
- Chapter 22 - Performance and Breach of Sales and Lease Contracts - 14.1-14.5
- Chapter 23 - Warranties and Product Liability - 7.7, 14.6

Unit V - Negotiable Instruments
- Chapter 24 - The Function and Creation of Negotiable Instruments - 15.1-15.3
- Chapter 25 - Transferability and Holder in Due Course - 15.4-15.5
- Chapter 26 - Liability, Defenses, and Discharge - 16.1-16.2
- Chapter 27 - Checks and Banking in the Digital Age - 16.3-16.4

Unit VI - Creditors' Rights and Bankruptcy
- Chapter 28 - Creditors' Rights and Remedies - SU 19, 20.5, SU 26
- Chapter 29 - Secured Transactions - SU 18
- Chapter 30 - Bankruptcy Law - SU 20

Unit VII - Agency and Employment
- Chapter 31 - Agency Formation and Duties - 29.1-29.3
- Chapter 32 - Liability to Third Parties and Termination - 29.4-29.5
- Chapter 33 - Employment and Labor Law - 38.1, 38.3-38.6
- Chapter 34 - Employment Discrimination - 38.2

Unit VIII - Business Organizations
- Chapter 35 - Sole Proprietorships and Franchises - 30.6
- Chapter 36 - Partnerships and Limited Liability Partnerships - 30.1-30.5
- Chapter 37 - Limited Liability Companies and Special Business Forms - 30.6
- Chapter 38 - Corporations – Formation and Financing - 31.1-31.3
- Chapter 39 - Corporations – Directors, Officers, and Shareholders - 32.1-32.3
- Chapter 40 - Corporations – Merger, Consolidation, and Termination - 32.4
- Chapter 41 - Corporations – Securities Law and Corporate Governance - 31.1, SU 33
- Chapter 42 - Law for Small Business - SU 30

Unit IX - Government Regulation
- Chapter 43 - Administrative Law - SU 5
- Chapter 44 - Consumer Law - SU 37
- Chapter 45 - Environmental Law - SU 35
- Chapter 46 - Antitrust Law - SU 36, 39.2

Unit X - Property
- Chapter 47 - Personal Property and Bailments - SU 21
- Chapter 48 - Real Property and Landlord-Tenant Relationships - SUs 23-25, SU 27

Unit XI - Special Topics
- Chapter 49 - Insurance - SU 34
- Chapter 50 - Wills and Trusts - SU 28
- Chapter 51 - Professional Liability and Accountability - SU 40
- Chapter 52 - International Law in a Global Economy - SU 39

Cross and Miller, *The Legal Environment Today: Business in its Ethical, Regulatory, E-Commerce, and Global Setting*, Sixth Edition, South-Western College Publishing, 2010.

Unit I - The Foundations
- Chapter 1 - Business and its Legal Environment - SU 1
- Appendix - Finding and Analyzing the Law - SU 1
- Chapter 2 - Ethics and Business Decision Making - 1.1, 40.1
- Chapter 3 - Courts and Alternative Dispute Resolution - SU 2, SU 3
- Chapter 4 - Constitutional Authority to Regulate Business - SU 4
- Chapter 5 - Torts and Cyber Torts - SU 7, 22.1-22.4
- Chapter 6 - Criminal Law and Cyber Crime - SU 6, 22.5
- Chapter 7 - International Law in a Global Economy - SU 39

Unit II - The Commercial Environment
- Chapter 8 - Intellectual Property and Internet Law - 7.4, 21.1, SU 22
- Chapter 9 - Contract Formation - SU 8, SU 9, SU 10, SU 13
- Chapter 10 - Contract Performance, Breach, and Remedies - SU 11, SU 12, SU 14
- Chapter 11 - Sales, Leases, and E-Contracts - 22.1, 22.2
- Chapter 12 - Strict Liability and Product Liability - 7.6-7.7
- Chapter 13 - Creditor-Debtor Relations and Bankruptcy - SUs 18-20, SUs 25-26

Unit III - Business and Employment
- Chapter 14 - Small Business Organizations - SUs 30-32
- Chapter 15 - Corporations - SU 31, SU 32
- Chapter 16 - Agency - SU 29
- Chapter 17 - Employment, Immigration, and Labor Law - SU 38
- Chapter 18 - Employment Discrimination - 38.2

Unit IV - The Regulatory Environment
- Chapter 19 - Powers and Functions of Administrative Agencies - SU 5
- Chapter 20 - Consumer Protection - 7.4, SU 37
- Chapter 21 - Protecting the Environment - SU 35
- Chapter 22 - Land-Use Control and Real Property - SU 23
- Chapter 23 - Antitrust Law and Promoting Competition - SU 36
- Chapter 24 - Investor Protection and Corporate Governance - 31.4, SU 32, SU 33

Cross and Miller, *The Legal Environment of Business: Text, Cases, Ethical, Regulatory, Global and Corporate Issues*, Eighth Edition, South-Western College Publishing, 2010.

Unit I - The Foundations
- Chapter 1 - Business and its Legal Environment - SU 1
- Chapter 2 - The Court System - SU 2
- Chapter 3 - Alternative and Online Dispute Resolution - 3.6
- Chapter 4 - Ethics and Business Decision Making - 1.1, 40.1

Unit II - The Public and International Environment
- Chapter 5 - Constitutional Law - SU 4
- Chapter 6 - Administrative Law - SU 5
- Chapter 7 - Criminal Law and Cyber Crimes - SU 6, 22.5
- Chapter 8 - International Law in a Global Economy - SU 39

Unit III - The Commercial Environment
- Chapter 9 - Contract Formation - 8.1-8.3, SU 9, SU 10, SU 13
- Chapter 10 - Contract Performance, Breach, and Remedies - SU 11, SU 12, SU 14
- Chapter 11 - Sales, Leases, and E-Contracts - SU 13, SU 14, 22.1-22.4
- Chapter 12 - Torts and Cyber Torts - SU 7, 22.1-22.4
- Chapter 13 - Strict Liability and Product Liability - 7.6-7.7
- Chapter 14 - Intellectual Property and Internet Law - 7.4, 21.1, SU 22
- Chapter 15 - Creditor-Debtor Relations and Bankruptcy - SUs 18-20, SU 25, SU 26
- Chapter 16 - Mortgages and Foreclosures after the Recession - N/A

Unit IV - The Business Environment
- Chapter 17 - Sole Proprietorships, Franchises, and Partnerships - SU 30
- Chapter 18 - Limited Liability Companies and Limited Partnerships - 30.5-30.6
- Chapter 19 - Corporations - SU 31, SU 32

Unit V - The Employment Environment
- Chapter 20 - Agency - SU 29
- Chapter 21 - Employment Relationships - 38.3-38.6
- Chapter 22 - Employment Discrimination - 38.2
- Chapter 23 - Immigration and Labor Law - 38.1

Davidson, Knowles, and Forsythe, *Business Law: Principles and Cases in the Legal Environment*, Eighth Edition, South-Western College Publishing, 2004.

Fisher and Phillips, *The Legal, Ethical, and Regulatory Environment of Business*, Ninth Edition, South-Western College Publishing, 2007.

Module One - Legal and Business Ethics, Overview, and Finding the Law
Chapter 1 - The Law: Legal and Business Ethics - 1.1, 40.1
Chapter 2 - Overview and Finding the Law - SU 1
Module Two - Business and Legal Systems: Courts, Legislatures, Administrative Agencies, Constitutional and International Law Affecting Regulation
Chapter 3 - Sources of Law: Political and Institutional - SU 2
Chapter 4 - Settling Legal Disputes: Alternative Dispute Resolution and Civil Lawsuits - SU 3
Chapter 5 - Business and the Constitution - SU 4
Chapter 6 - Government Regulation: Overview - 5.1-5.2
Chapter 7 - Government Regulation: Anatomy and Enforcement of a Regulation - 5.3-5.5
Chapter 8 - Public Law in International Business - SU 39
Chapter 9 - Private Business Dealings in International Contexts - SU 39
Module Three - Private Law Affecting Entrepreneurs
Chapter 10 - Torts: Negligence, Strict Liability, and Intentional - SU 7
Chapter 11 - Nature, Definition, and Classification of Contracts - SUs 8-14
Chapter 12 - Property - SU 21, SUs 23-25, SU 28
Chapter 13 - Intellectual Property and Technology - 21.1, 22.3
Module Four - Law Affecting the Human Resources Department
Chapter 14 - Employer-Employee Relations: Common Law Rules - SU 29
Chapter 15 - Important Statutes in Employer-Employee Relations - 38.3-38.6
Chapter 16 - Employment Discrimination - 38.2
Chapter 17 - Federal Labor Law: Unionization and Collective Bargaining - 38.1
Module Five - Law Affecting Business Financing
Chapter 18 - Business Organizations - 30.1, 30.5-30.6, 31.1-31.3
Chapter 19 - Securities Regulation - SU 33
Module Six - Law Affecting the Marketing Department
Chapter 20 - Antitrust Law - 36.1-36.5, 39.2
Chapter 21 - The Federal Trade Commission Act, Franchising, and Unfair Competition - 36.6
Chapter 22 - Consumer Protection - SU 37
Module Seven - Law Affecting the Manufacturing Department
Chapter 23 - Product Liability - 7.7, 14.6
Chapter 24 - Environmental Law - SU 35

Hollowell and Miller, *Business Law, Text and Exercises*, Sixth Edition, South-Western College Publishing, 2010.

Part I - The Law and Our Legal System
Chapter 1 - Introduction to the Law and Our Legal System - SU 1
Chapter 2 - Ethics - 1.1, 40.1
Chapter 3 - The Role of Courts in Our Legal System - SU 2, SU 3
Chapter 4 - Constitutional Law - SU 4
Chapter 5 - Torts and Cyber Torts - SU 7, 22.1-22.4
Chapter 6 - Intellectual Property - 21.1, 22.3
Chapter 7 - Criminal Law - SU 6, 22.5
Part II - Contracts
Chapter 8 - Introduction to Contracts - 8.1
Chapter 9 - Offer and Acceptance - 8.2-8.3
Chapter 10 - Consideration - SU 9
Chapter 11 - Capacity - 10.1
Chapter 12 - The Legality of Agreements - 10.2
Chapter 13 - Mistakes and Other Contract Defects - 10.3
Chapter 14 - Written Contracts - 10.4
Chapter 15 - Third Party Rights - SU 12
Chapter 16 - Contract Discharge and Remedies - 11.3-11.4
Chapter 17 - E-Contracts - SU 22
Part III - Sales and Leases
Chapter 18 - Introduction to Sales and Lease Contracts - 13.1-13.3
Chapter 19 - Title and Risk of Loss - 13.4-13.5
Chapter 20 - Performance and Breach - 14.1-14.5
Chapter 21 - Warranties and Product Liability - 7.7, 14.6
Chapter 22 - Consumer Protection - SU 37
Part IV - Negotiable Instruments
Chapter 23 - The Essentials of Negotiability - 15.1-15.3
Chapter 24 - Transferability and Liability - 15.4-15.5, 16.1-16.2
Chapter 25 - Checks, the Banking System, and E-Money - 16.3-16.4

Part V - Agency and Employment
- Chapter 26 - Agency - SU 29
- Chapter 27 - Employment Law - 38.3-38.6
- Chapter 28 - Discrimination and Labor Law - 38.1-38.2

Part VI - Business Organizations
- Chapter 29 - Sole Proprietorships, Partnerships, and Limited Liability Companies - SU 30
- Chapter 30 - Formation and Termination of a Corporation - 31.1-31.3, 32.4
- Chapter 31 - Ownership and Management of a Corporation - 32.1-32.3

Part VII - Credit and Risk
- Chapter 32 - Secured Transactions - SU 18
- Chapter 33 - Creditors' Rights and Remedies - SU 19, SU 26
- Chapter 34 - Bankruptcy - SU 20
- Chapter 35 - Insurance - SU 34

Part VIII - Property
- Chapter 36 - Personal Property and Bailments - SU 21
- Chapter 37 - Real Property - SUs 23-25
- Chapter 38 - Landlord and Tenant - SU 27
- Chapter 39 - Wills and Trusts - SU 28

Part IX - Special Topics
- Chapter 40 - Administrative Law - SU 5
- Chapter 41 - Antitrust - SU 36, 39.2
- Chapter 42 - International Law - SU 39

Jentz, Miller, and Cross, *West's Business Law*, Alternate Edition, Eleventh Edition, South-Western College Publishing, 2010.

Unit I - The Legal Environment of Business
- Chapter 1 - Introduction to the Law and Legal Reasoning - SU 1
- Chapter 2 - Courts and Alternative Dispute Resolution - SU 2, 3.6
- Chapter 3 - Court Procedures - 3.1-3.5
- Chapter 4 - Constitutional Authority to Regulate Business - SU 4
- Chapter 5 - Ethics and Business Decision Making - 1.1, 40.1

Unit II - Torts and Crimes
- Chapter 6 - Intentional Torts - 7.1-7.4
- Chapter 7 - Negligence and Strict Liability - 7.5-7.7
- Chapter 8 - Intellectual Property and Internet Law - 21.1, 22.3
- Chapter 9 - Criminal Law and Cyber Crime - SU 6, 22.5

Unit III - Contracts and E-Contracts
- Chapter 10 - Nature and Terminology - 8.1
- Chapter 11 - Agreement - 8.2-8.3
- Chapter 12 - Consideration - SU 9
- Chapter 13 - Capacity and Legality - 10.1-10.2
- Chapter 14 - Mistakes, Fraud, and Voluntary Consent - 10.3
- Chapter 15 - The Statute of Frauds - Writing Requirement - 10.4
- Chapter 16 - Third Party Rights - SU 12
- Chapter 17 - Performance and Discharge - 11.1-11.3
- Chapter 18 - Breach of Contract and Remedies - 11.4
- Chapter 19 - E-Contracts and E-Signatures - SU 22

Unit IV - Domestic and International Sales and Lease Contracts
- Chapter 20 - The Formation of Sales and Lease Contract - 13.1-13.3
- Chapter 21 - Title, Risk, and Insurable Interest - 13.4-13.5, SU 34
- Chapter 22 - Performance and Breach of Sales and Lease Contracts - 14.1-14.5
- Chapter 23 - Warranties and Product Liability - 7.7, 14.6

Unit V - Negotiable Instruments
- Chapter 24 - The Function and Creation of Negotiable Instruments - 15.1-15.3
- Chapter 25 - Transferability and Holder in Due Course - 15.4-15.5
- Chapter 26 - Liability, Defenses, and Discharge - 16.1-16.2
- Chapter 27 - Checks and Banking in the Digital Age - 16.3-16.4

Unit VI - Creditor's Rights and Bankruptcy
- Chapter 28 - Creditors' Rights and Remedies - SU 19, SU 26
- Chapter 29 - Secured Transactions - SU 18
- Chapter 30 - Bankruptcy Law - SU 20

Unit VII - Agency and Employment
Chapter 31 - Agency Formation and Duties - 29.1-29.3
Chapter 32 - Liability to Third Parties and Termination - 29.4-29.5
Chapter 33 - Employment and Labor Law - 38.1, 38.3-38.6
Chapter 34 - Employment Discrimination - 38.2
Unit VIII - Business Organizations
Chapter 35 - Sole Proprietorships and Franchises - 30.6
Chapter 36 - Partnerships and Limited Liability Partnerships - SU 30
Chapter 37 - Limited Liability Companies and Special Business Forms - 30.6
Chapter 38 - Corporations – Formation and Financing - 31.1-31.3
Chapter 39 - Corporations – Directors, Officers, and Shareholders - 32.1-32.3
Chapter 40 - Corporations – Merger, Consolidation, and Termination - 32.4
Chapter 41 - Corporations – Securities Law and Corporate Governance - SU 33
Chapter 42 - Law for Small Business - 30.6
Unit IX - Government Regulation
Chapter 43 - Administrative Law - SU 5
Chapter 44 - Consumer Law - SU 37
Chapter 45 - Environmental Law - SU 35
Chapter 46 - Antitrust Law - SU 36, 39.2
Unit X - Property
Chapter 47 - Personal Property and Bailments - SU 21
Chapter 48 - Real Property and Landlord-Tenant Relationships - SUs 23-25, SU 27
Unit XI - Special Topics
Chapter 49 - Insurance - SU 34
Chapter 50 - Wills and Trusts - SU 28
Chapter 51 - Professional Liability and Accountability - SU 40
Chapter 52 - International Law in a Global Economy - SU 39

Kubasek, Brennan, and Browne, *The Legal Environment of Business: A Critical Thinking Approach*, Sixth Edition, Prentice Hall Business Publishing, 2012.

Part I - An Introduction to the Law and the Legal Environment of Business
Chapter 1 - Critical Thinking and Legal Reasoning - SU 1
Chapter 2 - Introduction to Law and the Legal Environment of Business - SU 1
Chapter 3 - The American Legal System - SU 1, SU 2
Chapter 4 - Alternative Tools of Dispute Resolution - 3.6
Chapter 5 - Constitutional Principles - SU 4
Chapter 6 - Cyberlaw and Business - SU 22
Chapter 7 - White-Collar Crime and the Business Community - 6.6
Chapter 8 - Ethics, Social Responsibility, and the Business Manager - 1.1
Chapter 9 - The International Legal Environment of Business - SU 39
Part II - Private Law and the Legal Environment of Business
Chapter 10 - The Law of Contracts and Sales – I - SUs 8-14
Chapter 11 - The Law of Contracts and Sales – II - SUs 8-14
Chapter 12 - The Law of Torts - SU 7
Chapter 13 - Product and Service Liability Law - 7.7, 14.6
Chapter 14 - Law of Property: Real and Personal - SU 21, 22.3, SUs 23-25
Chapter 15 - Law of Intellectual Property - 21.1, SU 22
Chapter 16 - Agency Law - SU 29
Chapter 17 - Business Organizations I - SUs 30-33
Chapter 18 - Business Organizations II - SUs 30-33
Part III - Public Law and the Legal Environment of Business
Chapter 19 - The Law of Administrative Agencies - SU 5
Chapter 20 - The Employment Relationship - 38.3-38.6
Chapter 21 - Laws Governing Labor-Management Relations - 38.1
Chapter 22 - Employment Discrimination - 38.2
Chapter 23 - Environmental Law - SU 35
Chapter 24 - Rules Governing the Issuance of Securities - SU 33
Chapter 25 - Antitrust Law - SU 36, 39.2
Chapter 26 - Laws of Debtor-Creditor Relations and Consumer Protection - SUs 18-20, SU 26, SU 37

Mann and Roberts, *Business Law and the Regulation of Business*, Tenth Edition, South-Western College Publishing, 2010.

Part I - Introduction to Law and Ethics
- Chapter 1 - Introduction to Law - SU 1
- Chapter 2 - Business Ethics - 1.1, 40.1

Part II - The Legal Environment of Business
- Chapter 3 - Civil Dispute Resolution - SU 2, SU 3
- Chapter 4 - Constitutional Law - SU 4
- Chapter 5 - Administrative Law - SU 5
- Chapter 6 - Criminal Law - SU 6
- Chapter 7 - Intentional Torts - 7.1-7.4
- Chapter 8 - Negligence and Strict Liability - 7.5-7.7

Part III - Contracts
- Chapter 9 - Introduction to Contracts - 8.1
- Chapter 10 - Mutual Assent - 8.1-8.2
- Chapter 11 - Conduct Invalidating Assent - 10.3
- Chapter 12 - Consideration - SU 9
- Chapter 13 - Illegal Bargains - 10.2
- Chapter 14 - Contractual Capacity - 10.1
- Chapter 15 - Contracts in Writing - 10.4
- Chapter 16 - Third Parties to Contracts - SU 12
- Chapter 17 - Performance, Breach, and Discharge - 11.1-11.3
- Chapter 18 - Contract Remedies - 11.4

Part IV - Sales
- Chapter 19 - Introduction to Sales and Leases - 13.1-13.3
- Chapter 20 - Performance - 14.1-14.2
- Chapter 21 - Transfer of Title and Risk of Loss - 13.4-13.5
- Chapter 22 - Product Liability: Warranties and Strict Liability - 7.7, 14.6
- Chapter 23 - Sales Remedies - 14.3-14.5

Part V - Negotiable Instruments
- Chapter 24 - Form and Content - 15.1-15.3
- Chapter 25 - Transfer - 15.4
- Chapter 26 - Holder in Due Course - 15.5
- Chapter 27 - Liability of Parties - 16.1-16.2
- Chapter 28 - Bank Deposits, Collections, and Funds Transfers - 16.3-16.4

Part VI - Agency
- Chapter 29 - Relationship of Principal and Agent - 29.1-29.3, 29.5
- Chapter 30 - Relationship with Third Parties - 29.4

Part VII - Business Associations
- Chapter 31 - Formation and Internal Relations of General Partnerships - 30.1, 30.4
- Chapter 32 - Operation and Dissolution of General Partnerships - 30.2-30.4
- Chapter 33 - Limited Partnerships and Limited Liability Companies - 30.5-30.6
- Chapter 34 - Nature and Formation of Corporations - 31.1-31.2
- Chapter 35 - Financial Structure of Corporations - 31.3-31.4
- Chapter 36 - Management Structure of Corporations - 32.1-32.3
- Chapter 37 - Fundamental Changes of Corporations - 32.4

Part VIII - Debtor and Creditor Relations
- Chapter 38 - Secured Transactions and Suretyship - SU 18, SU 19
- Chapter 39 - Bankruptcy - SU 20

Part IX - Regulation of Business
- Chapter 40 - Securities Regulation - SU 33
- Chapter 41 - Intellectual Property - 21.1, 22.3
- Chapter 42 - Employment Law - SU 38
- Chapter 43 - Antitrust - SU 36
- Chapter 44 - Accountants' Legal Liability - SU 40
- Chapter 45 - Consumer Protection - SU 37
- Chapter 46 - Environmental Law - SU 35
- Chapter 47 - International Business Law - SU 39

Part X - Property
- Chapter 48 - Introduction to Property, Property Insurance, Bailments, and Documents of Title - 17.1, SU 21, SU 34
- Chapter 49 - Interests in Real Property - SU 23
- Chapter 50 - Transfer and Control of Real Property - SU 24
- Chapter 51 - Trusts and Wills - SU 28

Mann and Roberts, *Smith and Roberson's Business Law*, Fifteenth Edition, South-Western College Publishing, 2011.

Part I - The Legal Environment of Business
- Chapter 1 - Introduction to Law - SU 1
- Chapter 2 - Business Ethics and the Social Responsibility of Business - 1.1, 40.1
- Chapter 3 - Civil Dispute Resolution - SU 2, SU 3
- Chapter 4 - Constitutional Law - SU 4
- Chapter 5 - Administrative Law - SU 5
- Chapter 6 - Criminal Law - SU 6
- Chapter 7 - Intentional Torts - 7.1-7.4
- Chapter 8 - Negligence and Strict Liability - 7.5-7.7

Part II - Contracts
- Chapter 9 - Introduction to Contracts - 8.1
- Chapter 10 - Mutual Assent - 8.2-8.3
- Chapter 11 - Conduct Invalidating Assent - 10.3
- Chapter 12 - Consideration - SU 9
- Chapter 13 - Illegal Bargains - 10.2
- Chapter 14 - Contractual Capacity - 10.1
- Chapter 15 - Contracts in Writing - 10.4
- Chapter 16 - Third Parties to Contracts - SU 12
- Chapter 17 - Performance, Breach, and Discharge - 11.1-11.3
- Chapter 18 - Contract Remedies - 11.4, 14.3-14.5

Part III - Agency
- Chapter 19 - Relationship of Principal and Agent - 29.1-29.3, 29.5
- Chapter 20 - Relationship with Third Parties - 29.4

Part IV - Sales
- Chapter 21 - Introduction to Sales and Leases - 13.1-13.3
- Chapter 22 - Performance - 14.1-14.2
- Chapter 23 - Transfer of Title and Risk of Loss - 13.4-13.5
- Chapter 24 - Products Liability: Warranties and Strict Liability in Tort - 7.7, 14.6
- Chapter 25 - Sales Remedies - 14.3-14.5

Part V - Negotiable Instruments
- Chapter 26 - Form and Content - 15.1-15.3
- Chapter 27 - Transfer - 15.4
- Chapter 28 - Holder in Due Course - 15.5
- Chapter 29 - Liability of Parties - 16.1-16.2
- Chapter 30 - Bank Deposits, Collections, and Funds Transfers - 16.3-16.4

Part VI - Unincorporated Business Associations
- Chapter 31 - Formation and Internal Relations of General Partnerships - 30.1
- Chapter 32 - Operation and Dissolution of General Partnerships - 30.2-30.4
- Chapter 33 - Limited Partnerships and Limited Liability Companies - 30.5-30.6

Part VII - Corporations
- Chapter 34 - Nature, Formation, and Powers - 31.1-31.2
- Chapter 35 - Financial Structure - 31.3-31.4
- Chapter 36 - Management Structure - 32.1-32.3
- Chapter 37 - Fundamental Changes - 32.4

Part VIII - Debtor and Creditor Relations
- Chapter 38 - Secured Transactions and Suretyship - SU 18, SU 19
- Chapter 39 - Bankruptcy - SU 20

Part IX - Regulation of Business
- Chapter 40 - Protection of Intellectual Property - 21.1, 22.3
- Chapter 41 - Antitrust - SU 36
- Chapter 42 - Consumer Protection - SU 37
- Chapter 43 - Employment Law - SU 38
- Chapter 44 - Securities Regulation - SU 33
- Chapter 45 - Accountants' Legal Liability - SU 40
- Chapter 46 - Environmental Law - SU 35
- Chapter 47 - International Business Law - SU 39

Part X - Property
- Chapter 48 - Introduction to Property, Property Insurance, Bailments, and Documents of Title - 17.1, SU 21, SU 34
- Chapter 49 - Interests in Real Property - SU 23
- Chapter 50 - Transfer and Control of Real Property - SU 24
- Chapter 51 - Trusts and Decedents' Estates - SU 28

McAdams, *Law, Business, and Society*, Ninth Edition, McGraw-Hill/Irwin, 2009.

Unit I - Business and Society
- Chapter 1 - Capitalism and the Role of Government - N/A
- Chapter 2 - Business Ethics - 1.1, 40.1
- Chapter 3 - The Corporation and Public Policy: Expanding Responsibilities - SU 31, SU 32

Unit II - Introduction to Law
- Chapter 4 - The American Legal System - SUs 1-3
- Chapter 5 - Constitutional Law and the Bill of Rights - SU 4
- Chapter 6 - Contracts - SUs 8-14
- Chapter 7 - Torts and Product Liability - 7.6-7.7, 14.6

Unit III - Trade Regulation and Antitrust
- Chapter 8 - Government Regulation of Business - 5.1
- Chapter 9 - Business Organizations and Securities Regulation - SU 33
- Chapter 10 - Antitrust Law – Restraints of Trade - SU 36
- Chapter 11 - Antitrust Law – Monopolies and Mergers - SU 36

Unit IV - Employer-Employee Relations
- Chapter 12 - Employment Law I: Employee Rights - 38.3-38.6
- Chapter 13 - Employment Law II: Discrimination - 38.2
- Chapter 14 - Employment Law III: Labor–Management Relations - 38.1

Unit V - Business and Selected Social Issues
- Chapter 15 - Consumer Protection - SU 37
- Chapter 16 - Product Liability - 7.7
- Chapter 17 - Environmental Protection - SU 35
- Chapter 18 - Internet Law and Ethics - 1.1, SU 22

Miller and Jentz, *Business Law Today, Standard Edition*, Ninth Edition, South-Western College Publishing, 2010.

Unit I - The Legal Environment of Business
- Chapter 1 - The Legal Environment - SU 1
- Chapter 2 - Constitutional Law - SU 4
- Chapter 3 - Courts and Alternative Dispute Resolution - SU 2, SU 3
- Chapter 4 - Torts and Cyber Torts - SU 7, 22.5
- Chapter 5 - Intellectual Property and Internet Law - 21.1, 22.3
- Chapter 6 - Criminal Law - SU 6, 22.5
- Chapter 7 - Cyber Crime - N/A
- Chapter 8 - Ethics and Business Decision Making - 1.1, SU 40

Unit II - Contracts
- Chapter 9 - Nature and Classification - 8.1
- Chapter 10 - Agreement in Traditional and E-Contracts - 8.2-8.3
- Chapter 11 - Consideration, Capacity, and Legality - SU 9, 10.1-10.2
- Chapter 12 - Defenses to Contract Enforceability - 10.3-10.4
- Chapter 13 - Third Party Rights and Discharge - 11.1-11.3, SU 12
- Chapter 14 - Breach and Remedies - 11.4

Unit III - Commercial Transactions
- Chapter 15 - The Formation of Sales and Lease Contracts - 13.1-13.3
- Chapter 16 - Performance and Breach of Sales and Lease Contracts - 14.1-14.5
- Chapter 17 - Warranties and Product Liability - 7.7, 14.6
- Chapter 18 - Negotiable Instruments: Negotiability and Transferability - SU 15
- Chapter 19 - Checks and Banking in the Digital Age - 16.3-16.4, SU 22
- Chapter 20 - Security Interests in Personal Property - SU 18
- Chapter 21 - Creditors' Rights and Bankruptcy - SU 19, SU 20, SU 26
- Chapter 22 - International Law in a Global Economy - SU 39

Unit IV - Agency and Employment Law
- Chapter 23 - Agency Relationships in Business - SU 29
- Chapter 24 - Employment, Immigration, and Labor Law - SU 38
- Chapter 25 - Employment Discrimination - 38.2

Unit V - Business Organizations
- Chapter 26 - Sole Proprietorships and Private Franchises - 30.6
- Chapter 27 - All Forms of Partnerships - 30.1-30.5
- Chapter 28 - Limited Liability Companies and Special Business Forms - 30.6
- Chapter 29 - Corporate Formation, Merger, and Termination - SU 31
- Chapter 30 - Corporate Directors, Officers, and Shareholders - 32.1-32.3
- Chapter 31 - Investor Protection, Insider Trading, and Corporate Governance - 31.4, SU 33

Miller and Jentz, *Fundamentals of Business Law: Summarized Cases*, Eighth Edition, South-Western College Publishing, 2010.

Reed, Shedd, Morehead, and Pagnattaro, *The Legal and Regulatory Environment of Business*, Fifteenth Edition, McGraw-Hill, Inc., 2010.

Chapter 1 - Law as the Foundation of Business - SU 1
Chapter 2 - The Ethical Basis of Law and Business Management - SU 1
Chapter 3 - The Court System - SU 2
Chapter 4 - Litigation - 3.1-3.5
Chapter 5 - Negotiation and Alternative Dispute Resolution Systems - 3.6
Chapter 6 - The Constitution and Regulation of Business - SU 4
Chapter 7 - The Property-Based Legal System - SU 21, SUs 23-25
Chapter 8 - Introduction to Contracts -- Classifications, Terminology, and Formation - SUs 8-14
Chapter 9 - Contractual Issues -- Form, Interpretation, Performance, and Discharge - SUs 8-14
Chapter 10 - Torts in the Business Environment - SU 7
Chapter 11 - Intellectual Property in the Property System - 21.1
Chapter 12 - Criminal Law and Business - SU 6, 22.5
Chapter 13 - International Law - SU 39
Chapter 14 - Formation and Operation of Business Organizations - SUs 30-32
Chapter 15 - Sarbanes-Oxley and Securities Regulations - SU 5, SUs 31-33
Chapter 16 - Antitrust Laws -- Regulating Competition - SU 36
Chapter 17 - Consumer Protection - SU 37
Chapter 18 - Environmental Laws and Pollution Control - SU 35
Chapter 19 - Agency & Employment Laws - 38.1, 38.3-38.6
Chapter 20 - Discrimination in Employment - 38.2
Chapter 21 - Labor-Management Relationship - 38.1, 38.3-38.6

INDEX

Pass the CIA Exam
with less time and effort
GLEIM® - The #1 CIA REVIEW provider
for over 30 years.
GLEIM CIA REVIEW SYSTEM:
• A Personal Counselor to help you develop a personalized study plan
• Study almost anywhere - including while commuting
• Review material guaranteed to be current for 18 months
• Emulates the look and feel of the Exam
SUCCESS GUARANTEED!
GLEIM
KNOWLEDGE
TRANSFER
SYSTEMS®
gleim.com/cia
800.874.5346

GLEIM®
Professor-Led Review
• LIVE study sessions
• Leadership of a Professor
• Interactive Online Community
• Proven self-study materials
Contact GLEIM
for the location
nearest you.
GLEIM
KNOWLEDGE
TRANSFER
SYSTEMS®
gleim.com • 800.874.5346

CPA

GLEIM CPA REVIEW SYSTEM

All 4 sections, including Gleim Online, Review Books, *Test Prep Software Download*, *Simulation Wizard*, Audio Review, *CPA Review: A System for Success* Booklet, plus bonus Book Bag. $989.95 x ____ = $________

Also available by exam section (does not include Book Bag).

CMA

GLEIM CMA REVIEW SYSTEM

Includes: Gleim Online, Review Books, *Test Prep Software Download*, Audio Review, *Essay Wizard*, *CMA Review: A System for Success* Booklet, plus bonus Book Bag. $739.95 x ____ = $________

Also available by exam part (does not include Book Bag).

CIA

GLEIM CIA REVIEW SYSTEM

Includes: Gleim Online, Review Books, *Test Prep Software Download*, Audio Review, *CIA Review: A System for Success* Booklet, plus bonus Book Bag. $824.95 x ____ = $________

Also available by exam part (does not include Book Bag).

EA

GLEIM EA REVIEW SYSTEM

Includes: Gleim Online, Review Books, *Test Prep Software Download*, Audio Review, *EA Review: A System for Success* Booklet, plus bonus Book Bag. $629.95 x ____ = $________

Also available by exam part (does not include Book Bag).

EQE

"THE GLEIM REVIEW SERIES" EXAM QUESTIONS AND EXPLANATIONS

Includes: 5 Books and *Test Prep Software Download.* $112.25 x ____ = $________

Also available by part.

CPE

GLEIM ONLINE CPE

Try a FREE 4-hour course at gleim.com/cpe

- Easy-to-Complete
- Informative
- Effective

Contact
GLEIM® PUBLICATIONS
for further assistance:

gleim.com
800.874.5346
sales@gleim.com

SUBTOTAL $________

Complete your order on the next page

GLEIM® PUBLICATIONS, INC.

P. O. Box 12848 Gainesville, FL 32604

TOLL FREE: 800.874.5346
LOCAL: 352.375.0772
FAX: 352.375.6940
INTERNET: gleim.com
E-MAIL: sales@gleim.com

Customer service is available (Eastern Time):
8:00 a.m. - 7:00 p.m., Mon. - Fri.
9:00 a.m. - 2:00 p.m., Saturday
Please have your credit card ready, or save time by ordering online!

SUBTOTAL (from previous page) $______
Add applicable sales tax for shipments within Florida. ______
Shipping (nonrefundable) 24.00

TOTAL $______

Fax or write for prices/instructions on shipments outside the 48 contiguous states, or simply order online.

NAME (please print) ______________________

ADDRESS ______________________ Apt. ______
(street address required for UPS/Federal Express)

CITY ______________ STATE ____ ZIP ______

____ MC/VISA/DISC ____ Check/M.O. Daytime Telephone ( )________

Credit Card No. ______ - ______ - ______ - ______

Exp. ____/____ Signature ______________________
Month / Year

Email address ______________________

1. We process and ship orders daily, within one business day over 98.8% of the time. Call by 3:00 pm for same day service.
2. Gleim Publications, Inc. guarantees the immediate refund of all resalable texts, unopened and un-downloaded Test Prep Software, and unopened and un-downloaded audios returned within 30 days. Online courses may be canceled within 30 days if no more than the first study unit or lesson has been accessed. In addition, Online CPE courses may be canceled within 30 days if no more than the Introductory Study Questions have been accessed. This policy applies only to products that are purchased directly from Gleim Publications, Inc. No refunds will be provided on opened or downloaded Test Prep Software or audios, partial returns of package sets, or shipping and handling charges. Any freight charges incurred for returned or refused packages will be the purchaser's responsibility.
3. Please PHOTOCOPY this order form for others.
4. No CODs. Orders from individuals must be prepaid.

Subject to change without notice.
08/11

For updates and other important information, visit our website.

GLEIM KNOWLEDGE TRANSFER SYSTEMS®

gleim.com